Fodor's 96
Caribbean

"When it comes to information on regional history, what to see and do, and shopping, these guides are exhaustive."
—*USAir Magazine*

"Usable, sophisticated restaurant coverage, with an emphasis on good value."
—Andy Birsh, *Gourmet Magazine* columnist

"Valuable because of their comprehensiveness."
—*Minneapolis Star-Tribune*

"Fodor's always delivers high quality...thoughtfully presented...thorough."
—*Houston Post*

"An excellent choice for those who want everything under one cover."
—*Washington Post*

Fodor's Travel Publications,
New York • Toronto • Lond

D0281282

Copyright

Fodor's Caribbean

Editor: Melanie A. Sponholz
Contributors: Pamela Acheson, Robert Andrews, Robert Blake, Hannah Borgeson, Gail Gillen de Haas, Barbara Hults, Dawn Lawson, Bevin McLaughlin, Kristen Perrault, Marcy Pritchard, Melissa Rivers, Mary Ellen Schultz, M.T. Schwartzman, Kate Sekules, Jordan Simon, Dinah Spritzer, Jane E. Zarem
Creative Director: Fabrizio La Rocca
Cartographer: David Lindroth
Cover Photograph: Catherine Karnow/Woodfin Camp
Text Design: Between the Covers

Special Sales

Fodor's Travel Publications are available at special discounts for bulk purchases for sales promotions or premiums. Special editions, including personalized covers, excerpts of existing guides, and corporate imprints, can be created in large quantities for special needs. For more information, contact your local bookseller or write to Special Markets, Fodor's Travel Publications, 201 East 50th Street, New York, NY 10022. Inquiries from Canada should be directed to your local Canadian bookseller or sent to Random House of Canada, Ltd., Marketing Department, 1265 Aerowood Drive, Mississauga, Ontario L4W 1B9. Inquiries from the United Kingdom should be sent to Fodor's Travel Publications, 20 Vauxhall Bridge Road, London, England SW1V 2SA.

MANUFACTURED IN THE UNITED STATES OF AMERICA

10 9 8 7 6 5 4 3 2 1

CONTENTS

Maps and Plans

ON THE ROAD WITH FODOR'S

A GOOD TRAVEL GUIDE is like a wonderful traveling companion. It's charming, it's savvy on how-tos, it's brimming with sound recommendations and solid ideas, it pulls no punches in describing lodging and dining establishments, and it's consistently full of fascinating facts that make you view what you've traveled to see in a rich new light. In creating *Caribbean 96*, we at Fodor's have gone to great lengths to provide you with the very best of all possible traveling companions—and to make your trip the best of all possible vacations.

About Our Writers

The information in these pages is the result of a collaboration of extraordinary writers.

Pamela Acheson spent 18 years in New York City as a publishing executive before heading south to divide her time between Florida and the Caribbean. She writes extensively about both areas and is a regular contributor to *Travel & Leisure*, *Caribbean Travel and Life*, *Florida Travel and Life*, *Fodor's Florida*, *Fodor's Caribbean*, and *Fodor's Virgin Islands*. She is the author of *The Best of the British Virgin Islands* and is currently working on *The Best of St. Thomas* and a guide to cruising the Caribbean.

Marcy Pritchard lives in New York and plans to buy a villa in St. Barts as soon as travel writing pays off.

Melissa Rivers was married barefoot on a sugary beach in Montego Bay. If she had to plan a honeymoon there today, she'd be hard pressed to choose a place to stay. She also covered the Caymans, and as an avid snorkeler and diver, could not recommend the islands more highly. Melissa travels extensively and has also contributed to *Fodor's Mexico*, *Fodor's Canada*, *Fodor's USA*, *Fodor's Great American Learning Vacations*, and *Fodor's Great American Sports and Adventure Vacations*.

Kate Sekules has covered Trinidad, Tobago, Grenada, St. Vincent, the Grenadines, and St. Lucia, and says she's working her way.

She has contributed to *Fodor's London*, *Fodor's Great Britain*, and *Fodor's New York City* and hopes to eventually live on the islands.

Jordan Simon has visited nearly every speck of land in the Caribbean for Fodor's, *Caribbean Travel & Life*, *Modern Bride*, *Physicians Travel & Meeting Guide*, *Travel & Leisure*, and *Travelage*. He is the author of *Fodor's Colorado*, *Fodor's Branson*, and the *USA Today Ski Atlas*.

Jane Zarem is a freelance writer from Connecticut who travels frequently to the Caribbean. Among the score of islands she has explored, she finds it difficult to pick a favorite—she loves them all. She is a member of the New York Travel Writers Association and has contributed to *Fodor's New England*.

What's New

Big things are happening at Fodor's—and in the Caribbean.

A New Design

If this is not the first Fodor's guide you've purchased, you'll immediately notice our new look. More readable and easier-to-use than ever? We think so—and we hope you do, too.

Travel Updates

Just before your trip, you may want to order a Fodor's Worldview Travel Update. From local publications all over the Caribbean, the lively, cosmopolitan editors at Worldview gather information on concerts, plays, opera, dance performances, gallery and museum shows, sports competitions, and other special events that coincide with your visit. See the order blank at the back of this book, call 800/799-9609, or fax 800/799-9619.

And in the Caribbean

A decade ago some Caribbean islands put more emphasis on tourism than others did. St. Maarten and the Virgin Islands actively sought tourists, while St. Lucia relied on its banana crop and Guadeloupe on sugarcane for revenue. Now, however, the scramble for tourists and the dollars they bring is fast becoming the primary focus of all the Caribbean islands.

Although the competition for tourists hasn't led to lower prices—in fact, some governments have been increasing tourist taxes to pay for advertising—it has created more travel options. New hotels open all the time, old hotels are renovated, and ways to get to and from the islands are multiplying.

Airline service to and from the Caribbean is expanding. **American Airlines** now covers most of the islands with either direct flights from the mainland or with connecting flights through San Juan on its subsidiary, American Eagle. American also has plans to build its own wing at the **Donald Sangster International Airport** in Montego Bay, Jamaica, although construction had not begun by press time. **ALM,** the Antillean airline, is also becoming a major carrier to many of the islands, with departures from Atlanta and Miami as well as interisland flights. **Turks & Caicos Islands Airways** began nonstop service from Miami to both Provo and Grand Turk in late 1993. Renovations of Trinidad's **Piarco Airport,** although not complete at press time, have created a modern island airport; and changes in the customs area of the **Las Américas International Airport** in the Dominican Republic may succeed in reducing baggage problems and keeping taxi hustlers at bay.

Hotel and resort development continues with megaresorts in the ABC's, including Aruba's big new **Hilton** and Bonaire's **Harbour Village Beach Resort,** with a new spa opening and a golf course and casino on the horizon. In Puerto Rico, the **San Juan Marriott** opened its doors in January 1995, at a prime location on Condado Beach. The **Grand Cayman Westin Resort** was under construction at press time, scheduled for completion in November 1995. The Puerto Rican government recently announced the sale of the **Gran Hotel El Convento** in Old San Juan. The 17th-century property is now in the hands of the Hostal El Convento Group and is slated for restoration and renovation. Meanwhile, on Jamaica, two more resorts are in the works, the all-inclusive, adults-only **Braco Village Resort** in Rio Bueno, just west of Runaway Bay, and the **Comfort Suites Resort,** set on a beautifully landscaped hillside in Ocho Rios, overlooking

the bay. Both of these were scheduled to open before press time.

Golfers will be pleased to hear that **The Links at Safehaven,** the Cayman Islands' first 18-hole championship golf course, is now complete. The Roy Case–designed, par 71, 6,519-yard course caters to golfers of all skill levels by offering five placements at each tee. Aruba also has its first 18-hole course at the **Tierra del Sol** recreation complex. It was designed by Robert Trent Jones to emphasize the island's arid, desertlike terrain, where cactus grows by the sea. The new **Negril Hills Golf Club** in Negril, Jamaica, was scheduled for completion by mid-1995, but only nine holes were up and running by press time.

How to Use This Book

Organization

Up front is **The Gold Guide,** two sections that are chock-full of information about traveling in general and in the Caribbean. Both are in alphabetical order by topic. **Important Contacts A to Z** gives you addresses and telephone numbers of organizations and companies that offer detailed information and publications. Here's where you'll find information about traveling to the Caribbean from wherever you are. **Smart Travel Tips A to Z** gives you specific tips on how to enhance the way you travel and get the most out of your travels as well as information on how to accomplish what you need to in your destination. In both Contacts and Tips, individual sports are grouped in one section and listed alphabetically within that section.

Stars

Stars in the margin are used to denote the most highly recommended hotels and restaurants.

Restaurant and Hotel Criteria and Price Categories

Restaurants and lodging places are chosen with a view to giving you the cream of the crop in each location at every price range.

Hotel Facilities

Note that in general, you incur charges when you use many hotel facilities; we wanted to let you know what facilities the hotel has to offer, but we don't always specify whether or not there's a charge, so when planning a resort vacation that entails a stay of several days, it's wise to ask about what's included in your rates.

Hotel Meal Plans

Hotels in the Caribbean often have a range of rates based on the following meal plans: **European Plan** (EP, with no meals), **Full American Plan** (FAP, with all meals), **Modified American Plan** (MAP, with breakfast and dinner daily), **Continental Plan** (CP, with a Continental breakfast daily), and **All-inclusive** (all meals and most activities). At the end of each review, we have listed the meal plans the hotel offers.

A Full American Plan may be ideal for travelers on a budget who don't want to worry about additional expenses, but travelers who enjoy a different dining experience each night will prefer to book rooms on the European Plan. Since some hotels insist on the Modified American Plan, particularly during the high season, you might want to find out whether you can exchange dinner for lunch or for meals at neighboring hotels.

Dress Code in Restaurants

The **What to Wear** section at the beginning of the individual chapters' dining sections tells you what's most common in that area. In general, we note dress code only when men are required to wear a jacket or a jacket and tie.

Credit Cards

The following abbreviations are used: **AE,** American Express; **D,** Discover; **DC,** Diners Club; **MC,** MasterCard; and **V,** Visa.

Please Write to Us

Everyone who has worked on *Fodor's Caribbean* has worked hard to make the text accurate. All prices and opening times are based on information supplied to us at press time, and the publisher cannot accept responsibility for any errors that may have occurred. The passage of time will bring changes, so it's always a good idea to call ahead and confirm information when it matters—particularly if you're making a detour to visit specific sights or attractions. When making reservations at a hotel or inn, be sure to mention if you have a disability or are traveling with children, if you prefer a private bath or a certain type of bed, or if you have specific dietary needs or any other concerns.

Did the restaurants we recommended fit the description? Did our hotel picks exceed your expectations? Did you find a museum we recommended a waste of time? Positive or negative, we would love your feedback. If you have complaints, we'll look into them and revise our entries when the facts warrant it. If you've happened upon a special place that we haven't included, we'll pass the information along to the writers so they can check it out. So please send us a letter or post card (we're at 201 East 50th Street, New York, New York 10022.) We'll look forward to hearing from you. And in the meantime, have a wonderful trip!

Karen Cure
Editorial Director

The Caribbean

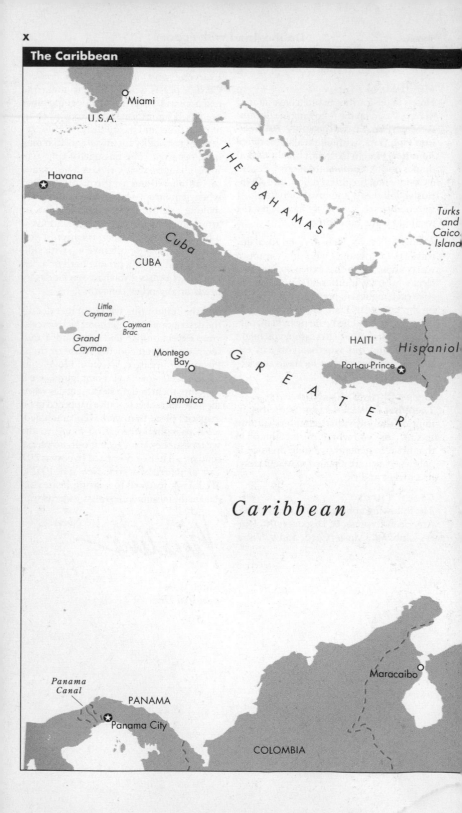

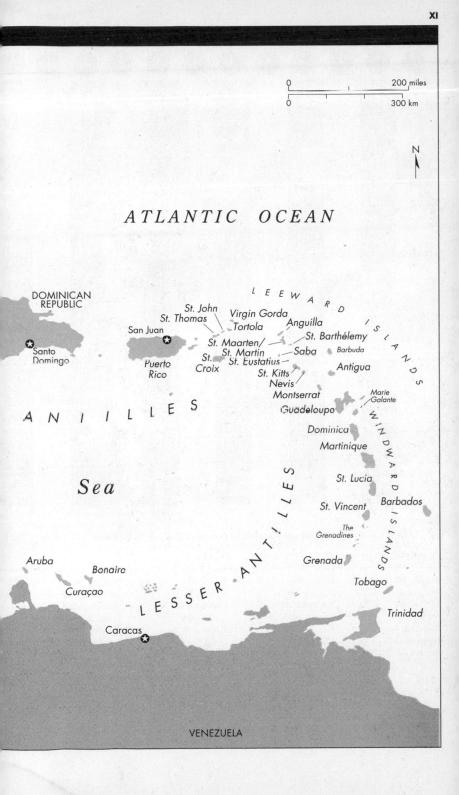

0 ____ 200 miles

0 ____ 300 km

N

ATLANTIC OCEAN

DOMINICAN
REPUBLIC

LEEWARD ISLANDS

St. John
St. Thomas
Virgin Gorda
Tortola
Anguilla
San Juan
St. Maarten/
St. Barthélemy
Santo
Domingo
St. Martin
Saba
Barbuda
St.
Croix
Puerto
Rico
St. Eustatius
Antigua
St. Kitts
Nevis
Montserrat
Guadeloupe
Marie
Galante
A N I I L L E S
Dominica
Martinique
WINDWARD ISLANDS
Sea
St. Lucia
St. Vincent
Barbados
The
Grenadines
Aruba
Bonaire
Grenada
Curaçao
Tobago
LESSER ANTILLES
Trinidad
Caracas

VENEZUELA

World Time Zones

Numbers below vertical bands relate each zone to Greenwich Mean Time (0 hrs.).
Local times frequently differ from these general indications,
as indicated by light-face numbers on map.

Algiers, **29**
Anchorage, **3**
Athens, **41**
Auckland, **1**
Baghdad, **46**
Bangkok, **50**
Beijing, **54**

Berlin, **34**
Bogotá, **19**
Budapest, **37**
Buenos Aires, **24**
Caracas, **22**
Chicago, **9**
Copenhagen, **33**
Dallas, **10**

Delhi, **48**
Denver, **8**
Djakarta, **53**
Dublin, **26**
Edmonton, **7**
Hong Kong, **56**
Honolulu, **2**

Istanbul, **40**
Jerusalem, **42**
Johannesburg, **44**
Lima, **20**
Lisbon, **28**
London
(Greenwich), **27**
Los Angeles, **6**
Madrid, **38**
Manila, **57**

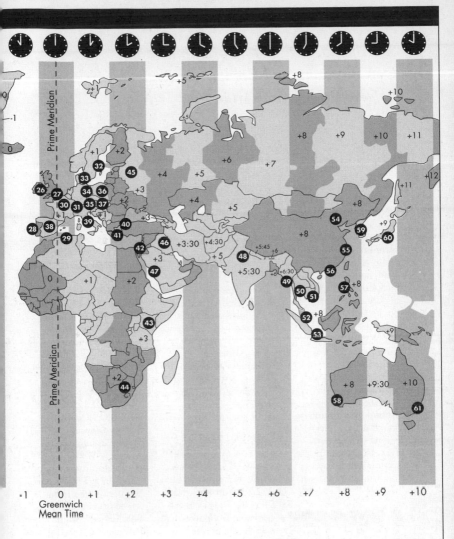

IMPORTANT CONTACTS A TO Z

An Alphabetical Listing of Publications, Organizations, and Companies That Will Help You Before, During, and After Your Trip

No single travel resource can give you every detail about every topic that might interest or concern you at the various stages of your journey—when you're planning your trip, while you're on the road, and after you get back home. The following organizations, books, and brochures will supplement the information in Fodor's *Caribbean '96.* For related information, including both basic tips on visiting the Caribbean and background information on many of the topics below, study Smart Travel Tips A to Z, the section that follows Important Contacts A to Z.

A
AIR TRAVEL

For information on airports and major airlines serving the Caribbean from the United States, see individual island chapters.

For inexpensive, no-frills flights, contact **Carnival Air Lines** (☎ 800/824–7386), which serves the Caicos and Puerto Rico, and **Kiwi International** (☎ 800/538–5494), based in Newark and New York, serving San Juan.

FROM THE U.K.

British Airways (☎ 0345/222–111), and **British West Indian Airways** (☎ 017/839–9333) offer direct flights from London to the Caribbean.

COMPLAINTS

To register complaints about charter and scheduled airlines, contact the U.S. Department of Transportation's **Office of Consumer Affairs** (400 7th St. NW, Washington, DC 20590, ☎ 202/366–2220 or 800/322–7873).

CONSOLIDATORS

TFI Tours International (34 W. 32nd St., New York, NY 10001, ☎ 212/736–1140 or 800/745–8000) is an established consolidator that sells to the public.

PUBLICATIONS

For general information about charter carriers, ask for the Office of Consumer Affairs' brochure **"Plane Talk: Public Charter Flights."** The Department of Transportation also publishes a 58-page booklet, **"Fly Rights"** ($1.75; Consumer Information Center, Dept. 133-B, Pueblo, CO 81009).

For other tips and hints, consult Consumers Union's monthly **"Consumer Reports Travel Letter"** ($39 a year; Box 53629, Boulder CO 80322, ☎ 800/234–1970) and the newsletter **"Travel Smart"** ($37 a year; 40 Beechdale Rd., Dobbs Ferry, NY 10522, ☎ 800/327–3633); *The Official Frequent Flyer Guidebook*, by Randy Petersen ($14.99 plus $3 shipping; 4715-C Town Center Dr., Colorado Springs, CO 80916, ☎ 719/597–8899 or 800/487–8893); *Airfare Secrets Exposed*, by Sharon Tyler and Matthew Wonder (Universal Information Publishing; $16.95 plus $3.75 shipping from Sandcastle Publishing, Box 3070-A, South Pasadena, CA 91031, ☎ 213/255–3616 or 800/655–0053); and *202 Tips Even the Best Business Travelers May Not Know*, by Christopher McGinnis ($10 plus $3.00 shipping; Irwin Professional Publishing, Box 52927, Atlanta, GA 30355, ☎ 708/789–4000 or 800/634–3966).

B
BETTER BUSINESS BUREAU

For local contacts in the hometown of a tour

operator you may be considering, consult the **Council of Better Business Bureaus** (4200 Wilson Blvd., Arlington, VA 22203, ☎ 703/276–0100).

C
CAR RENTAL

For information on car-rental agencies and costs in the Caribbean, see individual island chapters.

RENTAL WHOLESALERS

Contact the **Kemwel Group** (106 Calvert St., Harrison, NY 10528, ☎ 914/835–5555 or 800/678–0678).

CHILDREN AND TRAVEL
FLYING

Look into **"Flying with Baby"** ($5.95 plus $1 shipping; Third Street Press, Box 261250, Littleton, CO 80126, ☎ 303/595–5959), cowritten by a flight attendant. **"Kids and Teens in Flight,"** free from the U.S. Department of Transportation's Office of Consumer Affairs, offers tips for children flying alone. Every two years the February issue of *Family Travel Times* (*see* Know-How, *below*) details children's services on three dozen airlines.

KNOW-HOW

Family Travel Times, published 10 times a year by Travel with Your Children (TWYCH; 45 W. 18th St., New York, NY 10011, ☎ 212/206–0688; annual subscription $55), covers

destinations, types of vacations, and modes of travel.

The *Family Travel Guides* catalogue ($1 postage; ☎ 510/527–5849) lists about 200 books and articles on family travel. *Traveling with Children—And Enjoying It,* by Arlene K. Butler ($11.95 plus $3 shipping; Globe Pequot Press, Box 833, 6 Business Park Rd., Old Saybrook, CT 06475, ☎ 203/395–0440 or 800/243–0495, 800/962–0973 in CT) helps you plan your trip with children, from toddlers to teens. Also check *Take Your Baby and Go! A Guide for Traveling with Babies, Toddlers and Young Children,* by Sheri Andrews, Judy Bordeaux, and Vivian Vasquez ($5.95 plus $1.50 shipping; Bear Creek Publications, 2507 Minor Ave., Seattle, WA 98102, ☎ 206/322–7604 or 800/326–6566). Also from Globe Pequot are *Recommended Family Resorts in the United States, Canada, and the Caribbean,* by Jane Wilford with Janet Tice ($12.95), and *Recommended Family Inns of America* ($12.95). Travel with Your Children (*see above*) also publishes *Cruising with Children* ($22).

LODGING

Hotels and resorts that offer special programs for children include:

In Aruba, the **Sonesta Resorts at Seaport Village** (☎ 800/766–3782); in Puerto Rico, the **Hyatt Regency Cerromar Beach** and the **Hyatt Dorado Beach** (☎

800/233–1234), and the **El San Juan Hotel and Casino** (☎ 800/468–2818); in Jamaica, **Boscobel Beach** (☎ 800/859–7873); and in St. Thomas in the U.S. Virgin Islands, the **Stouffer Grand Beach Resort** (☎ 800/468–3571); in Nevis, **Four Seasons** (☎ 800/332–3442).

TOUR OPERATORS

Contact **Rascals in Paradise** (650 5th St., Suite 505, San Francisco, CA 94107, ☎ 415/978–9800 or 800/872–7225).

If you're outdoorsy, look into **Ecology Tours** (c/o the Audubon Center of the North Woods, Box 530, Sandstone, MN 55072, ☎ 612/245–2648), which combines travel and nature study; and the **American Museum of Natural History** (79th St. and Central Park W, New York, NY 10024, ☎ 212/769–5700 or 800/462–8687).

CRUISING

To find out which ships are sailing where and when they depart, contact the **Caribbean Tourism Organization** (20 E. 46th St., 4th Floor, New York, NY 10017, ☎ 212/682–0435). The **Cruise Lines International Association** (CLIA) publishes a useful pamphlet entitled "Cruising Answers to Your Questions"; to order a copy send a self-addressed business-size envelope with 52¢ postage to CLIA (500 5th Ave., Suite 1407, New York, NY 10110).

Cruise lines that operate in the Caribbean in-

THE GOLD GUIDE / IMPORTANT CONTACTS

clude **American Canadian Caribbean Line** (Box 368, Warren, RI 02885, ☎ 401/247–0955 or 800/556–7450), **Carnival Cruise Lines** (Carnival Pl., 3655 N.W. 87th Ave., Miami, FL 33178, ☎ 305/599–2600), **Celebrity Cruises** (5200 Blue Lagoon Dr., Miami, FL 33126, ☎ 800/437–3111), **Clipper Cruise Line** (7711 Bonhomme Ave., St. Louis, MO 63105, ☎ 800/325–0010), **Club Med** (40 W. 57th St., New York, NY 10019, ☎ 800/258–2633), **Commodore Cruise Line** (800 Douglas Rd., Coral Gables, FL 33134, ☎ 305/529–3000), **Costa Cruise Lines** (World Trade Center, 80 S.W. 8th St., Miami, FL 33130, ☎ 800/462–6782), **Crystal Cruises** (2121 Ave. of the Stars, Los Angeles, CA 90067, ☎ 800/446–6620), **Cunard Line** (555 5th Ave., New York, NY 10017, ☎ 800/221–4770), **Diamond Cruise Inc.** (600 Corporate Dr., Suite 410, Fort Lauderdale, FL 33334, ☎ 800/333–3333), **Dolphin/Majesty Cruise Lines** (901 South American Way, Miami, FL 33132, ☎ 800/532–7788), **Fantasy Cruise** (5200 Blue Lagoon Dr., Miami, FL 33126, ☎ 800/437–3111), **Holland America Line** (300 Elliott Ave. W, Seattle, WA 98119, ☎ 800/426–0327), **Norwegian Cruise Line** (95 Merrick Way, Coral Gables, FL 33134, ☎ 800/327–7030), **Premier Cruise Line** (Box 517, Cape Canaveral, FL 32920, ☎ 800/473–3262), **Princess Cruises** (10100 Santa Monica Blvd., Los Angeles, CA 90067, ☎ 310/553–1770), **Regency Cruises** (260 Madison Ave., New York, NY 10016, ☎ 212/972–4499), **Renaissance Cruises** (1800 Eller Dr., Suite 300, Box 350307, Fort Lauderdale, FL 33335, ☎ 800/525–2450), **Royal Caribbean Cruise Line** (1050 Caribbean Way, Miami, FL 33132, ☎ 800/327–6700), **Royal Cruise Line** (1 Maritime Plaza, San Francisco, CA 94111, ☎ 415/956–7200), **Royal Viking Line** (Kloster Cruise Limited, 95 Merrick Way, Coral Gables, FL 33134, ☎ 800/422–8000), **Seabourn Cruise Line** (55 Francisco St., San Francisco, CA 94133, ☎ 800/351–9595), **Seawind Cruise Line** (1750 Coral Way, Miami, FL 33145, ☎ 800/258–8006), **Silversea Cruises** (110 E. Broward Blvd., Fort Lauderdale, FL 33301, ☎ 305/522–4477 or 800/722–6655), **Special Expeditions** (720 5th Ave., New York, NY 10019, ☎ 800/762–0003), **Star Clippers** (4101 Salzedo Ave., Coral Gables, FL 33146, ☎ 800/442–0551), **Sun Line Cruises** (1 Rockefeller Plaza, Suite 315, New York, NY 10020, ☎ 800/872–6400), and **Windstar Cruises** (300 Elliott Ave. W, Seattle, WA 98119, ☎ 800/258–7245).

CUSTOMS

U.S. CITIZENS

The **U.S. Customs Service** (Box 7407, Washington, DC 20044, ☎ 202/927–6724) can answer questions on duty-free limits and publishes a helpful brochure, "Know Before You Go." For information on registering foreign-made articles, call 202/927–0540.

CANADIANS

Contact **Revenue Canada** (2265 St. Laurent Blvd. S, Ottawa, Ontario, K1G 4K3, ☎ 613/993–0534) for a copy of the free brochure **"I Declare/Je Déclare"** and for details on duties that exceed the standard duty-free limit.

U.K. CITIZENS

HM Customs and Excise (Dorset House, Stamford St., London SE1 9NG, ☎ 0171/202–4227) can answer questions about U.K. customs regulations and publishes **"A Guide for Travellers,"** detailing standard procedures and import rules.

D

FOR TRAVELERS WITH DISABILITIES

COMPLAINTS

To register complaints under the provisions of the Americans with Disabilities Act, contact the U.S. Department of Justice's **Public Access Section** (Box 66738, Washington, DC 20035, ☎ 202/514–0301, TDD 202/514–0383, FAX 202/307–1198).

LODGING

Divi Hotels (☎ 800/367–3484), which has six properties in the Caribbean, runs one of the best dive programs for people with disabilities at its resort in **Bonaire.**

ORGANIZATIONS

FOR TRAVELERS WITH HEARING IMPAIRMENTS➤ Contact the **American Academy of Otolaryngology** (1 Prince St., Alexandria, VA 22314, ☎ 703/836–4444, FAX 703/683–5100, TTY 703/519–1585).

FOR TRAVELERS WITH MOBILITY PROBLEMS➤ Contact the **Information Center for Individuals with Disabilities** (Fort Point Pl., 27–43 Wormwood St., Boston, MA 02210, ☎ 617/727–5540, 800/462–5015 in MA, TTY 617/345–9743), **Mobility International USA** (Box 10767, Eugene, OR 97440, ☎ and TTY 503/343–1284, FAX 503/343–6812), the U.S. branch of an international organization based in Britain (*see below*) that has affiliates in 30 countries; **MossRehab Hospital Travel Information Service** (1200 W. Tabor Rd., Philadelphia, PA 19141, ☎ 215/456–9603, TTY 215/456–9602); the **Society for the Advancement of Travel for the Handicapped** (347 5th Ave., Suite 610, New York, NY 10016, ☎ 212/447–7284, FAX 212/725–8253); the **Travel Industry and Disabled Exchange** (TIDE; 5435 Donna Ave., Tarzana, CA 91356, ☎ 818/344–3640, FAX 818/344–0078); and **Travelin' Talk** (Box 3534, Clarksville, TN 37043, ☎ 615/552–6670, FAX 615/552–1182).

FOR TRAVELERS WITH VISION IMPAIRMENTS➤ Contact the **American Council of the Blind** (1155 15th St. NW, Suite 720, Washington, DC 20005, ☎ 202/467–5081, FAX 202/467–5085) or the **American Foundation for the Blind** (15 W. 16th St., New York, NY 10011, ☎ 212/620–2000, TTY 212/620–2158).

IN THE UNITED KINGDOM➤ Contact the **Royal Association for Disability and Rehabilitation** (RADAR; 12 City Forum, 250 City Rd., London EC1V 8AF, ☎ 0171/250–3222) or **Mobility International** (Rue de Manchester 25, B1070 Brussels, Belgium, ☎ 00–322–410–6297), an international clearinghouse of travel information for people with disabilities.

PUBLICATIONS

Several free publications are available from the U.S. Information Center (Box 100, Pueblo, CO 81009, ☎ 719/948–3334): **"New Horizons for the Air Traveler with a Disability"** (address to Dept. 355A), describing legally mandated changes; the pocket-size **"Fly Smart"** (Dept. 575B), good on flight safety; and the Airport Operators Council's worldwide **"Access Travel: Airports"** (Dept. 575A).

The 500-page **Travelin' Talk Directory** ($35; ☎ 615/552–6670) lists people and organizations who help travelers with disabilities. For specialist travel agents worldwide, consult the

Directory of Travel Agencies for the Disabled ($19.95 plus $2 shipping; Twin Peaks Press, Box 129, Vancouver, WA 98666, ☎ 206/694–2462 or 800/637–2256) and the **Directory of Travel Agencies for the Disabled,** by Helen Hecker ($19.95 plus $3.50 handling; Disability Bookshop, Box 129, Vancouver, WA 98666; ☎ 206/694–2462).

TRAVEL AGENCIES AND TOUR OPERATORS

The Americans with Disabilities Act requires that travel firms serve the needs of all travelers. However, some agencies and operators specialize in making group and individual arrangements for travelers with disabilities, among them **Access Adventures** (206 Chestnut Ridge Rd., Rochester, NY 14624, ☎ 716/889–9096), run by a former physical-rehab counselor; **Travel Trends** (2 Allan Plaza, 4922–51 Ave., Box 3581, Leduc, Alberta, T9E 6X2, ☎ 403/986–9000), which has group tours and is especially good for cruises; and **Tomorrow's Level of Care** (Box 470299, Brooklyn, NY 11247, ☎ 718/756–0794 or 800/932–2012), which offers nursing services and medical equipment. In addition, many of the operators and agencies listed below (*see* Tour Operators, *above*) can also arrange vacations for travelers with disabilities.

FOR TRAVELERS WITH HEARING IMPAIRMENTS➤ **International Express** (7319-B Baltimore Ave.,

College Park, MD 20740, ☎ TDD 301/699–8836, FAX 301/699–8836) arranges group and independent trips.

FOR TRAVELERS WITH MOBILITY IMPAIRMENTS➤ A number of operators specialize in working with travelers with mobility impairments: **Accessible Journeys** (35 W. Sellers Ave., Ridley Park, PA 19078, ☎ 610/521–0339 or 800/846–4537, FAX 610/521–6959), a registered nursing service that arranges vacations; **Hinsdale Travel Service** (201 E. Ogden Ave., Suite 100, Hinsdale, IL 60521, ☎ 708/325–1335 or 800/303–5521), a travel agency that will give you access to the services of wheelchair traveler Janice Perkins; and **Wheelchair Journeys** (16979 Redmond Way, Redmond, WA 98052, ☎ 206/885–2210), which can handle arrangements worldwide.

FOR TRAVELERS WITH DEVELOPMENTAL DISABILITIES➤ Contact the nonprofit **New Directions** (5276 Hollister Ave., Suite 207, Santa Barbara, CA 93111, ☎ 805/967–2841) for travelers with developmental disabilities and their families, as well as the general-interest operations above.

DISCOUNTS

Options include **Entertainment Travel Editions** (fee $25–$48, depending on destination; Box 1068, Trumbull, CT 06611, ☎ 800/445–4137), **Great American Traveler** ($49.95 annually; Box 27965, Salt Lake City, UT 84127, ☎ 800/548–2812), **Moment's Notice Discount Travel Club** ($25 annually, single or family; 425 Madison Ave., New York, NY 10017, ☎ 212/486–0503), **Privilege Card** ($74.95 annually; 3391 Peachtree Rd. NE, Suite 110, Atlanta GA 30326, ☎ 404/262–0222 or 800/236–9732), **Travelers Advantage** ($49 annually, single or family; CUC Travel Service, 49 Music Sq. W, Nashville, TN 37203, ☎ 800/548–1116 or 800/648–4037), and **Worldwide Discount Travel Club** ($50 annually for family, $40 single; 1674 Meridian Ave., Miami Beach, FL 33139, ☎ 305/534–2082).

DIVING

The Caribbean offers some of the best scuba diving in the world. For a list of training facilities where you can earn your diving certification card, write to **PADI** (Professional Association of Diving Instructors, 1251 E. Dyer Rd., #100, Santa Ana, CA 92705). For more information, *see* Diving *under* What's Where, *below.*

E

ELECTRICITY

Send a self-addressed, stamped envelope to the **Franzus Company** (Customer Service, Dept. B50, Murtha Industrial Park, Box 142, Beacon Falls, CT 06403, ☎ 203/723–6664) for a copy of the free brochure "Foreign Electricity Is No Deep Dark Secret."

F

FURTHER READING

Caribbean Style (Crown Publishers) is a coffee-table book with magnificent photographs of the interiors and exteriors of homes and buildings in the Caribbean. Short stories—some dark, some full of laughs—about life in the southern Caribbean made *Easy in the Islands* by Bob Schacochis a National Book Award winner. Schacochis has an ear for local patois and an eye for the absurd. To familiarize yourself with the sights, smells, and sounds of the West Indies, pick up Jamaica Kincaid's *Annie John,* a richly textured coming-of-age novel about a girl growing up on Antigua. The short stories in *At the Bottom of the River,* also by Kincaid, depict island mysteries and manners. *Omeros* is Nobel Prize–winning Trinidadian poet Derek Walcott's imaginative Caribbean retelling of the *Odyssey.* Anthony C. Winkler's novels, *The Great Yacht Race, The Lunatic,* and *The Painted Canoe,* provide scathingly witty glimpses into Jamaica's class structure. Another notable chronicle of Caribbean life and customs is the provocative, imaginative novel *Wide Sargasso Sea,* by Jean Rhys. James Michener depicted the islands' diversity in his novel *Caribbean.* To probe island cultures more deeply, read V. S.

Naipaul, particularly his *Guerrillas, The Loss of El Dorado* and *The Enigma of Arrival*; Eric William's *From Columbus to Castro*; and Michael Paiewonsky's *Conquest of Eden*.

GAY AND LESBIAN TRAVEL

ORGANIZATION

The **International Gay Travel Association** (Box 4974, Key West, FL 33041, ☎ 800/448–8550), a consortium of 800 businesses, can supply names of travel agents and tour operators.

PUBLICATIONS

The premier international travel magazine for gays and lesbians is **Our World** ($35 for 10 issues; 1104 N. Nova Rd., Suite 251, Daytona Beach, FL 32117, ☎ 904/441–5367). The 16-page monthly "Out & About" ($49 for 10 issues; ☎ 203/789–8518 or 800/929–2268) covers gay-friendly resorts, hotels, cruise lines, and airlines.

TOUR OPERATORS

Cruises and resort vacations are handled by **R.S.V.P. Travel Productions** (2800 University Ave. SE, Minneapolis, MN 55414, ☎ 800/328–RSVP) for gay travelers and **Olivia** (4400 Market St., Oakland, CA 94608, ☎ 800/631–6277) for lesbian travelers. For mixed gay and lesbian travel, contact **Atlantis Events** (8335 Sunset Blvd., West Hollywood, CA 90069, ☎ 800/628–5268) and **Toto Tours** (1326 W. Albion Suite 3W,

Chicago, IL 60626, ☎ 312/274–8686 or 800/565–1241); both have group tours worldwide.

TRAVEL AGENCIES

The largest agencies serving gay travelers are **Advance Travel** (10700 Northwest Freeway, Suite 160, Houston, TX 77092, ☎ 713/682–2002 or 800/695–0880), **Islanders/Kennedy Travel** (183 W. 10th St., New York, NY 10014, ☎ 212/242–3222 or 800/988–1181), **Now Voyager** (4406 18th St., San Francisco, CA 94114, ☎ 415/626–1169 or 800/255–6951), and **Yellowbrick Road** (1500 W Balmoral Ave., Chicago, IL 60640, ☎ 312/561–1800 or 800/642–2488). **Skylink Women's Travel** (746 Ashland Ave., Santa Monica, CA 90405, ☎ 310/452–0506 or 800/225–5759) works with lesbians.

H
HEALTH ISSUES

FINDING A DOCTOR

For members, the **International Association for Medical Assistance to Travellers** (IAMAT, 417 Center St., Lewiston, NY 14092, ☎ 716/754–4883; 40 Regal Rd., Guelph, Ontario N1K 1B5, ☎ 519/836–0102; 1287 St. Clair Ave., Toronto, Ontario M6E 1B8, ☎ 416/652–0137; 57 Voirets, 1212 Grand-Lancy, Geneva, Switzerland; membership free) publishes a worldwide directory of English-speaking physi-

cians meeting IAMAT standards.

MEDICAL-ASSISTANCE COMPANIES

Contact **International SOS Assistance** (Box 11568, Philadelphia, PA 19116, ☎ 215/244–1500 or 800/523–8930; Box 466, Pl. Bonaventure, Montréal, Québec H5A 1C1, ☎ 514/874–7674 or 800/363–0263), **Medex Assistance Corporation** (Box 10623, Baltimore, MD 21285, ☎ 410/296–2530 or 800/573–2029), **Near Services** (Box 1339, Calumet City, IL 60409, ☎ 708/868–6700 or 800/654–6700), and **Travel Assistance International** (1133 15th St. NW, Suite 400, Washington, DC 20005, ☎ 202/331–1609 or 800/821–2828). Because these companies also sell death-and-dismemberment, trip-cancellation, and other insurance coverage, there is some overlap with the travel-insurance policies sold by the companies listed under Insurance, *below*.

I
INSURANCE

Travel insurance covering baggage, health, and trip cancellation or interruptions is available from **Access America** (Box 90315, Richmond, VA 23286, ☎ 804/285–3300 or 800/284–8300), **Carefree Travel Insurance** (Box 9366, 100 Garden City Plaza, Garden City, NY 11530, ☎ 516/294–0220 or 800/323–3149), **Near** (Box 1339, Calumet

THE GOLD GUIDE / IMPORTANT CONTACTS

City, IL 60409, ☎ 708/868–6700 or 800/654–6700), **Tele-Trip** (Mutual of Omaha Plaza, Box 31716, Omaha, NE 68131, ☎ 800/228–9792), **Travel Insured International** (Box 280568, East Hartford, CT 06128-0568, ☎ 203/528–7663 or 800/243–3174), **Travel Guard International** (1145 Clark St., Stevens Point, WI 54481, ☎ 715/345–0505 or 800/826–1300), and **Wallach & Company** (107 W. Federal St., Box 480, Middleburg, VA 22117, ☎ 703/687–3166 or 800/237–6615).

IN THE U.K.

The **Association of British Insurers** (51 Gresham St., London EC2V 7HQ, ☎ 0171/600–3333; 30 Gordon St., Glasgow G1 3PU, ☎ 0141/226–3905; Scottish Provident Bldg., Donegall Sq. W, Belfast BT1 6JE, ☎ 01232/249176; call for other locations) gives advice by phone and publishes the free **"Holiday Insurance,"** which sets out typical policy provisions and costs.

L
LODGING

APARTMENT AND VILLA RENTAL

Among the companies to contact are **At Home Abroad** (405 E. 56th St., Suite 6H, New York, NY 10022, ☎ 212/421–9165), **Europa-Let** (92 N. Main St., Ashland, OR 97520, ☎ 503/482–5806 or 800/462–4486), **Heart of the Caribbean** (Box 550,

New York, NY 11018, ☎ 718/855–8737 or 800/231–5303), **Property Rentals International** (1008 Mansfield Crossing Rd., Richmond, VA 23236, ☎ 804/378–6054 or 800/220–3332), **Rent-a-Home International** (7200 34th Ave. NW, Seattle, WA 98117, ☎ 206/789–9377 or 800/488–7368), **Vacation Home Rentals Worldwide** (235 Kensington Ave., Norwood, NJ 07648, ☎ 201/767–9393 or 800/633–3284), **Villas and Apartments Abroad** (420 Madison Ave., Suite 1105, New York, NY 10017, ☎ 212/759–1025 or 800/433–3020), and **Villas International** (605 Market St., Suite 510, San Francisco, CA 94105, ☎ 415/281–0910 or 800/221–2260). Members of the travel club **Hideaways International** ($99 annually; 767 Islington St., Portsmouth, NH 03801, ☎ 603/430–4433 or 800/843–4433) receive two annual guides plus quarterly newsletters, and arrange rentals among themselves.

HOME EXCHANGE

Principal clearinghouses include **HomeLink International/Vacation Exchange Club** ($60 annually; Box 650, Key West, FL 33041, ☎ 305/294–1448 or 800/638–3841), which gives members four annual directories, with a listing in one, plus updates; and **Loan-a-Home** ($35–$45 annually; 2 Park La., Apt. 6E, Mount Vernon, NY 10552-3443, ☎ 914/

664–7640), which specializes in long-term exchanges.

M
MONEY MATTERS

ATMS

For specific foreign **Cirrus** locations, call 800/424–7787; for foreign Plus locations, consult the **Plus** directory at your local bank.

CURRENCY EXCHANGE

If your bank doesn't exchange currency, contact **Thomas Cook Currency Services** (41 E. 42nd St., New York, NY 10017, or 511 Madison Ave., New York, NY 10022, ☎ 212/757–6915 or 800/223–7373 for locations) or **Ruesch International** (☎ 800/424–2923 for locations).

WIRING FUNDS

Funds can be wired via **American Express MoneyGram** (☎ 800/926–9400 from the United States and Canada for locations and information) or **Western Union** (☎ 800/325–6000 for agent locations or to send using Mastercard or Visa, 800/321–2923 in Canada).

P
PASSPORTS AND VISAS

U.S. CITIZENS

For fees, documentation requirements, and other information, call the **Office of Passport Services** information line (☎ 202/647–0518).

CANADIANS

For fees, documentation requirements, and other information, call the Ministry of Foreign Affairs and International Trade's **Passport Office** (☎ 819/994–3500 or 800/567–6868).

U.K. CITIZENS

For fees, documentation requirements, and to get an emergency passport, call the **London passport office** (☎ 0171/271–3000).

For local access numbers abroad, contact **AT&T** USA Direct (☎ 800/874–4000), **MCI** Call USA (☎ 800/444–4444), or **Sprint** Express (☎ 800/793–1153).

The **Kodak Information Center** (☎ 800/242–2424) answers consumer questions about film and photography.

S

EDUCATIONAL TRAVEL

The nonprofit **Elderhostel** (75 Federal St., 3rd Floor, Boston, MA 02110, ☎ 617/426–7788), for people 60 and older, has offered inexpensive study programs since 1975. The nearly 2,000 courses cover everything from marine science to Greek myths and cowboy poetry. Fees for two- to three-week international trips—including room, board, and transportation from the United States—range from $1,800 to $4,500.

ORGANIZATIONS

Contact the **American Association of Retired Persons** (AARP, 601 E St. NW, Washington, DC 20049, ☎ 202/434–2277; $8 per person or couple annually). Its Purchase Privilege Program gets members discounts on lodging, car rentals, and sightseeing. AARP also arranges group tours and cruises through AARP Travel Experience from American Express (400 Pinnacle Way, Suite 450, Norcross, GA 30071, ☎ 800/927–0111 or 800/745–4567).

For other discounts on lodgings, car rentals, and other travel products, along with magazines and newsletters, contact the **National Council of Senior Citizens** (membership $12 annually; 1331 F St. NW, Washington, DC 20004, ☎ 202/347–8800) and **Mature Outlook** (subscription $9.95 annually; 6001 N. Clark St., Chicago, IL 60660, ☎ 312/465–6466 or 800/336–6330).

PUBLICATIONS

The 50+ Traveler's Guidebook: Where to Go, Where to Stay, What to Do, by Anita Williams and Merrimac Dillon ($12.95; St. Martin's Press, 175 5th Ave., New York, NY 10010, ☎ 212/674–5151 or 800/288–2131) offers many useful tips. **"The Mature Traveler"** ($29.95; Box 50820, Reno, NV 89513), a monthly newsletter, covers travel deals.

HOSTELING

Contact **Hostelling International–American Youth Hostels** (733 15th St. NW, Suite 840, Washington, DC 20005, ☎ 202/783–6161) in the United States, **Hostelling International–Canada** (205 Catherine St., Suite 400, Ottawa, Ontario K2P 1C3, ☎ 613/748–5638) in Canada, and the **Youth Hostel Association of England and Wales** (Trevelyan House, 8 St. Stephen's Hill, St. Albans, Hertfordshire AL1 2DY, ☎ 01727/855215 and 01727/845047) in the United Kingdom. Membership ($25 in the United States, C$26.75 in Canada, and £9 in the United Kingdom) gives you access to 5,000 hostels worldwide that charge $7–$20 nightly per person.

I.D. CARDS

For discounts on transportation and admissions, get the **International Student Identity Card** (ISIC) if you're a bona fide student, or the **International Youth Card** (IYC) if you're under 26. In the United States, the ISIC and IYC cards cost $16 each and include basic travel-accident and illness coverage, plus a toll-free travel hot line. Apply through CIEE (*see* Organizations, *below*). Cards are available for $15 each in Canada from Travel Cuts (187 College St., Toronto, Ontario M5T 1P7, ☎ 416/979–2406 or 800/667–2887) and in the United Kingdom for £5 each at student unions and student travel companies.

ORGANIZATIONS

A major contact is the **Council on International Educational Exchange** (CIEE, 205 E. 42nd St., 16th Floor, New York, NY 10017, ☎ 212/661–1450), with locations in Boston (729 Boylston St., Boston, MA 02116, ☎ 617/266–1926), Miami (9100 S. Dadeland Blvd., Miami, FL 33156, ☎ 305/670–9261), Los Angeles (1093 Broxton Ave., Los Angeles, CA 90024, ☎ 310/208–3551), 43 college towns nationwide, and the United Kingdom (28A Poland St., London W1V 3DB, ☎ 0171/437–7767). Twice a year, it publishes *Student Travels* magazine. The CIEE's Council Travel Service is the exclusive U.S. agent for several student-discount cards.

Campus Connections (325 Chestnut St., Suite 1101, Philadelphia, PA 19106, ☎ 215/625–8585 or 800/428–3235) specializes in discounted accommodations and airfares for students. The **Educational Travel Centre** (438 N. Frances St., Madison, WI 53703, ☎ 608/256–5551) offers rail passes and low-cost airline tickets, mostly for flights departing from Chicago.

In Canada, also contact **Travel Cuts** (*see* above).

TOUR OPERATORS

Among the companies selling tours and packages to the Caribbean, the following have a proven reputation, are nationally known, and offer plenty of options.

PACKAGES

For independent vacation packages throughout the Caribbean, contact **American Airlines Fly AAway Vacations** (☎ 800/321–2121), **Delta Dream Vacations** (☎ 800/872–7786), **Domenico Tours** (750 Broadway, Bayonne, NJ 07002, ☎ 201/823–8687 or 800/554–8687), and **Globetrotters** (139 Main St., Cambridge, MA 02142, ☎ 617/621–9911 or 800/999–9696). **Gogo Tours,** based in Ramsey, New Jersey, sells packages only through travel agents. **Club Med** (☎ 800/258–2633) sells packages that include charter airfare and accommodations at its family, couples and singles resorts throughout the Caribbean.

For packages in Jamaica, Antigua, or the U.S. Virgin Islands, try **Continental Airlines' Grand Destinations** (☎ 800/634–5555). For packages in Puerto Rico or Grand Cayman, call **United Vacations** (☎ 800/328–6877). For a greater selection of properties in the Cayman Islands, try **Cayman Airtours** (☎ 800/247–2966).

Regional operators specialize in putting together packages for travelers from their local area. Arrangements may include charter or scheduled air. Contact **Apple Vacations** (25 Northwest Point Blvd., Elk Grove Village, IL 60007, ☎ 708/640–1150 or 800/365–2775), **Friendly Holidays** (1983 Marcus Ave., Lake Success, NY 11042, ☎ 516/338–1200 or 800/221–9748), **Travel Impressions** (465 Smith St., Farmingdale, NY 11735, ☎ 516/845–7000 or 800/224–0022), and **Trans National Travel** (2 Charlesgate W, Boston, MA 02215, ☎ 617/262–0123 or 800/262–0123).

FROM THE U.K.

Packages to the Caribbean are available from **Caribbean Connection** (Concorde House, Forest St., Chester CH1 1QR, ☎ 01244/341131), which publishes a 100-page catalogue devoted to Caribbean holidays; **Caribtours** (161 Fulham Rd., London SW3 6SN, ☎ 0171/581–3517), another Caribbean specialist; **Kuoni Travel** (Kuoni House, Dorking, Surrey RH5 4AZ, ☎ 01306/742222); and **Tradewinds** (Wavell House, Holcombe Rd., Helmshore, Rossendale, Lancs., BE4 4NB, ☎ 01706/219111).

THEME TRIPS

ADVENTURE➢ **All Adventure Travel** (5589 Arapahoe #208, Boulder, CO 80303, ☎ 800/537–4025) can book biking, hiking, kayaking, diving, rafting, and many adventures throughout the Caribbean. **American Wilderness Experience** (Box 1486, Boulder, CO 80306, ☎ 303/444–0099 or 800/444–0099) and **Ocean Voyages** (1709 Bridgeway, Sausalito, CA 94965,

☎ 415/332–4681) offer adventure cruises.

DIVING➤ Leading dive packagers to the Caribbean include **Tropical Adventures** (111 2nd Ave., North Seattle, WA 98109, ☎ 206/441–3483 or 800/247–3483) and **Go Diving** (5610 Rowland Rd. #100, Minnetonka, MN 55343, ☎ 800/328–5285). For a dive vacation aboard a live-aboard boat, try **Sea & Sea Travel Service** (50 Francisco St. #205, San Francisco, CA 94133, ☎ 415/434–3400 or 800/348–9778).

GOLF➤ Try **GolfTrips** (Box 2314, Winter Haven, FL 33883-2314, ☎ 813/324–1300 or 800/428–1940).

HEALTH➤ Look into **Spa-Finders** (91 5th Ave., New York, NY 10003, ☎ 800/255–7727).

HORSEBACK RIDING➤ For Jamaica custom packages, call **FITS Equestrian** (685 Lateen Rd., Solvang, CA 93463, ☎ 805/688–9494 or 800/600–3487).

LEARNING VACATIONS➤ **Earthwatch** (680 Mount Auburn St., Watertown, MA 02272, ☎ 617/926–8200) recruits volunteers to assist scientists on research expeditions. The **Smithsonian Institution's Study Tours and Seminars** (1100 Jefferson Dr. SW, Room 3045, Washington, DC 20560, ☎ 202/357–4700) runs natural-history cruises and diving programs. Natural-history cruises are also available from the **National Audubon**

Society (700 Broadway, New York, NY 10003, ☎ 212/979–3066).

SINGLES➤ SingleWorld (401 Theodore Fremd Ave., Rye, NY 10580, ☎ 914/967–3334 or 800/223–6490) has cruises to the Caribbean on dozens of major cruise ships.

YACHT CHARTERS➤ For crewed or uncrewed charters, try **Lynn Jachney Charters** (Box 302, Marblehead, MA 01945, 617/639–0787 or 800/223–2050), **Huntley Yacht Vacations** (210 Preston Rd., Wernersville, PA 19565, ☎ 610/678–2628 or 800/322–9224), **Sail Away** (15605 Southwest 92nd Ave., Miami, FL 33157, ☎ 305/253–SAIL or 800/724–5292), **The Moorings** (19345 U.S. Hwy. 19 N, 4th Floor, Clearwater, FL 34624, ☎ 813/538–8760 or 800/437–7880), and **Russell Yacht Charters** (404 Hulls Hwy., Suite 175, Southport, CT 06490, ☎ 203/255–2783 or 800/635–8895).

ORGANIZATIONS

The **National Tour Operators Association** (546 E. Main St., Lexington, KY 40508, ☎ 606/226–4444 or 800/682–8886) and **United States Tour Operators Association** (USTOA, 211 E. 51st St., Suite 12B, New York, NY 10022, ☎ 212/750–7371) can provide lists of member operators and information on booking tours.

PUBLICATIONS

Consult the brochure **"Worldwide Tour & Vacation Package**

Finder" from the National Tour Operators Association (*see above*) and the Better Business Bureau's **"Tips on Travel Packages"** (publication No. 24-195, $2; 4200 Wilson Blvd., Arlington, VA 22203.

TRAVEL AGENCIES

For names of reputable agencies in your area, contact the **American Society of Travel Agents** (1101 King St., Suite 200, Alexandria, VA 22314, ☎ 703/739–2782).

V

VISITOR INFO

Almost all islands have a U.S.–based tourist board, listed with its name and address under Important Addresses in the individual island chapters that follow. The **Caribbean Tourism Organization** (20 E. 46th St., New York, NY 10017-2452, ☎ 212/682–0435, FAX 212/697–4258) is another resource, especially for smaller islands. There is no overall tourist organization in the United Kingdom for the Caribbean; check the phone book for individual island tourist offices.

W

WEATHER

For current conditions and forecasts, plus the local time and helpful travel tips, call the **Weather Channel Connection** (☎ 900/932–8437; 95¢ per minute) from a touch-tone phone.

SMART TRAVEL TIPS A TO Z

Basic Information on Traveling in the Caribbean and Savvy Tips to Make Your Trip a Breeze

The more you travel, the more you learn about how to make trips run like clockwork. To help make your travels hassle-free, Fodor's editors have rounded up dozens of tips from our contributors and travel experts all over the world, as well as basic information on visiting the Caribbean. For names of organizations to contact and publications that can give you more information, *see* Important Contacts A to Z, *above*.

A

AIR TRAVEL

If time is an issue, **always look for nonstop flights,** which require no change of plane and makes no stops. If possible, **avoid connecting flights,** which stop at least once and can involve a change of plane, although the flight number remains the same; if the first leg is late, the second waits.

CUTTING COSTS

The Sunday travel section of most newspapers is a good source of deals.

MAJOR AIRLINES➣ The least-expensive airfares from the major airlines are priced for round-trip travel and are subject to restrictions.

You must usually **book in advance and buy the ticket within 24 hours** to get cheaper fares, and you may have to **stay over a Saturday night.** The lowest fare is subject to availability, and only a small percentage of the plane's total seats are sold at that price. It's good to **call a number of airlines, and when you are quoted a good price, book it on the spot**—the same fare on the same flight may not be available the next day. Airlines generally allow you to change your return date for a $25 to $50 fee, but most low-fare tickets are nonrefundable. However, if you don't use the ticket, you can apply the cost toward the purchase price of a new ticket, again for a small charge.

CONSOLIDATORS➣ Consolidators, who buy tickets at reduced rates from scheduled airlines, sell them at prices below the lowest available from the airlines directly—usually without advance restrictions. Sometimes you can even get your money back if you need to return the ticket. Carefully read the fine print detailing penalties for changes and cancellations. If you doubt the reliability of a consol-

idator, **confirm your reservation with the airline.**

CHARTER FLIGHTS➣ Charters usually have the lowest fares and the most restrictions. Departures are limited and seldom on time, and you can lose all or most of your money if you cancel. (The closer to departure you cancel, the more you lose, although sometimes you will be charged only a small fee if you supply a substitute passenger.) The flight may be canceled for any reason up to 10 days before departure (after that, only if it is physically impossible to operate). The charterer may also revise the itinerary or increase the price after you have bought the ticket, but only if the new arrangement constitutes a "major change" do you have the right to a refund. Before buying a charter ticket, **read the fine print** about the company's refund policies. Money for charter flights is usually paid into a bank escrow account, the name of which should be on the contract, and if you don't pay by credit card, **make your check payable to the carrier's escrow account** (unless you're dealing with a travel agent, in which case his or her check should be payable to the escrow account). The U.S. Department of Transportation's Office of Consumer Affairs has jurisdiction.

Charter operators may offer flights alone or with ground arrangements that constitute a charter package. You typically must book charters through your travel agent.

ALOFT

AIRLINE FOOD➤ If you hate airline food, **ask for special meals when booking.** These can be vegetarian, low-cholesterol, or kosher, for example; commonly prepared to order in smaller quantities than standard catered fare, they can be tastier.

SMOKING➤ Smoking is banned on all flights within the United States of less than six hours' duration and on all Canadian flights; the ban also applies to domestic segments of international flights aboard U.S. and foreign carriers. On U.S. carriers flying to the Caribbean and other destinations abroad, a seat in a no smoking section must be provided for every passenger who requests one, and the section must be enlarged to accommodate such passengers if necessary as long as they have complied with the airline's deadline for check-in and seat assignment. If smoking bothers you, request a seat far from the smoking section.

Foreign airlines are exempt from these rules

but do provide no-smoking sections; some nations have banned smoking on all domestic flights, and others may ban smoking on some flights. Talks continue on the feasibility of broadening no-smoking policies.

C
CAMERAS, CAMCORDERS, AND COMPUTERS

LAPTOPS

Before you depart, **check your portable computer's battery,** because you may be asked at security to turn on the computer to prove that it is what it appears to be. At the airport, you may prefer to **request a manual inspection,** although security X-rays do not harm hard disk or floppy-disk storage. Also, **register your foreign-made laptop with U.S. Customs.** If your laptop is U.S.-made, call the consulate of the country you'll be visiting to find out whether or not it should be registered with local customs upon arrival. You may want to **find out about repair facilities at your destination** in case you need them.

PHOTOGRAPHY

If your camera is new or if you haven't used it for a while, **shoot and develop a few rolls of film** before you leave. Always **store film in a cool, dry place**—never in the car's glove compartment or on the shelf under the rear window.

Every pass through an X-ray machine increases film's chance of clouding. To protect it, carry it in a clear plastic bag and **ask for hand inspection at security.** Such requests are virtually always honored at U.S. airports, and usually are accommodated abroad. Don't depend on a lead-lined bag to protect film in checked luggage—the airline may increase the radiation to see what's inside.

VIDEO

Before your trip, **test your camcorder, invest in a skylight filter to protect the lens, and charge the batteries.** (Airport security personnel may ask you to turn on the camcorder to prove that it's what it appears to be.) The batteries of most newer camcorders can be recharged with a universal or worldwide AC adapter charger (or multivoltage converter), usable whether the voltage is 110 or 220. All that's needed is the appropriate plug.

Videotape is not damaged by X-rays, but it may be harmed by the magnetic field of a walk-through metal detector, so **ask that videotapes be hand-checked.** Although most Caribbean islands operate on the National Television System Committee video standard (NTSC), used by the United States and Canada, Guadeloupe and Martinique use the Secam standard. On these islands, you will not be able to view your tapes through the local

TV set or view movies bought there in your home VCR. Blank tapes bought in the Caribbean can be used for camcorder taping, but they are pricey. Some U.S. audiovisual shops convert foreign tapes to U.S. standards; contact an electronics dealer to find one near you.

CHILDREN AND TRAVEL

Caribbean islands and their resorts are increasingly sensitive to families' needs. Many now have children's programs. Baby food is easy to find, but outside major hotels you may not find such items as high chairs and cribs. When choosing a destination, **consider whether or not English is spoken widely**; the language barrier can frustrate children.

BABY-SITTING

For recommended local sitters, **check with your hotel desk.**

DRIVING

If you are renting a car, **arrange for a car seat when you reserve.** Sometimes they're free.

FLYING

Always **ask about discounted children's fares.** On international flights, the fare for infants under age 2 not occupying a seat is generally either free or 10% of the accompanying adult's fare; children ages 2–11 usually pay half to two-thirds of the adult fare. On domestic flights, children under 2 not occupying a seat travel free, and older children currently travel on the "lowest applicable" adult fare. Some routes (including some in the Caribbean) are considered neither international nor domestic and have still other rules.

BAGGAGE➤ In general, the adult baggage allowance applies for children paying half or more of the adult fare. Before departure, **ask about carry-on allowances** if you are traveling with an infant. In general, those paying 10% of the adult fare are allowed one carry-on bag, not to exceed 70 pounds or 45 inches (length + width + height) and a collapsible stroller; you may be allowed less if the flight is full.

SAFETY SEATS➤ According to the FAA, it's a good idea to **use safety seats aloft.** Airline policy varies. U.S. carriers allow FAA-approved models, but airlines usually require that you buy a ticket, even if your child would otherwise ride free, because the seats must be strapped into regular passenger seats. Foreign carriers may not allow infant seats, may charge the child's rather than the infant's fare for their use, or may require you to hold your baby during takeoff and landing, thus defeating the seat's purpose.

FACILITIES➤ When making your reservation, **ask for children's meals or a freestanding bassinet** if you need them; the latter is available only to those with seats at the bulkhead, where there's enough legroom. If you don't need the bassinet, **think twice before requesting bulkhead seats**—the only storage for in-flight necessities is in the inconveniently distant overhead bins.

LODGING

Children are welcome in all except the most exclusive resorts; many hotels allow children under 12 or 16 to stay free in their parents' room (be sure to **ask the cutoff age** when booking). In addition, several hotel chains have children's programs, and many hotels and resorts arrange for baby-sitting. Representative of the services and activities available are the complimentary "Just Us Kids" program for children ages 5–12 at Aruba's Sonesta Resorts at Seaport Village; the camp available for children ages 5–12 all summer, at Christmastime, and at Easter at Puerto Rico's Hyatt Regency Cerromar Beach and Hyatt Dorado Beach; and the activities program for kids 5–12 at Puerto Rico's El San Juan Hotel and Casino.

Jamaica's all-inclusive Boscobel Beach specializes in families and offers a small army of SuperNannies, a petting zoo, crafts classes, and a disco for teens. On St. Thomas in the U.S. Virgin Islands, the Stouffer Grand Beach Resort has half-day and full-day programs for children ages 3–12. Club Med's St. Lucia and Dominican Republic resorts offer Mini

Club programs for children ages 2–11.

Also **consider apartment and villa rentals** (*see* Lodging, *below*). When you book, be sure to **ask about the availability of babysitters,** housekeepers, and medical facilities.

CRUISES

Cruising the Caribbean is perhaps the most relaxed and convenient way to tour this beautiful part of the world: You get all of the amenities of a Stateside hotel and enough activities to guarantee fun, even on rainy days. Cruising through the islands is an entirely different experience from staying on one island.

Cruise ships usually call at several Caribbean ports on a single voyage but are at each port for only one night. Thus, although you may be exposed to several islands, you don't get much of a feel for any one of them.

As a vacation, a cruise offers total peace of mind. All important decisions are made long before boarding. The itinerary is set, and the total cost of your vacation is known almost to the penny. For details, see *Fodor's Cruises and Ports of Call 1996;* the Cruise Primer chapter is particularly helpful if you're cruising for the first time.

To get the best deal on a cruise, **consult a cruise-only travel agency.**

CUSTOMS AND DUTIES

BACK HOME

IN THE U.S.➤ You may bring home $600 worth of foreign goods duty-free if you've been out of the country for at least 48 hours and haven't used the $600 exemption, or any part of it, in the past 30 days. This exemption, higher than the standard $400 allowance, applies to two dozen countries included in the Caribbean Basin Initiative. If you visit a CBI country and a non-CBI country, such as Martinique, you may still bring in $600 worth of goods duty-free, but no more than $400 can be from the non-CBI country. Travelers returning from the U.S. Virgin Islands are entitled to a $1,200 duty-free allowance. If your travel included the U.S.V.I. and another country—say, the Dominican Republic—the $1,200 allowance still applies, but at least $600 worth of goods must be from the U.S.V.I.

Travelers 21 or older may bring back 1 liter of alcohol duty-free, provided the beverage laws of the state through which they reenter the United States allow it. In addition, 100 non-Cuban cigars and 200 cigarettes are allowed, regardless of your age. Antiques and works of art more than 100 years old are duty-free.

Duty-free, travelers may mail packages valued at up to $200 to them-selves and up to $100 to others, with a limit of one parcel per addressee per day (and no alcohol or tobacco products or perfume valued at more than $5); outside, identify the package as being for personal use or an unsolicited gift, specifying the contents and their retail value. Mailed items do not count as part of your exemption.

IN CANADA➤ Once per calendar year, when you've been out of Canada for at least seven days, you may bring in C$300 worth of goods duty-free. If you've been away less than seven days but more than 48 hours, the duty-free exemption drops to C$100 but can be claimed any number of times (as can a C$20 duty-free exemption for absences of 24 hours or more). You cannot combine the yearly and 48-hour exemptions, use the C$300 exemption only partially (to save the balance for a later trip), or pool exemptions with family members. Goods claimed under the C$300 exemption may follow you by mail; those claimed under the lesser exemptions must accompany you.

Alcohol and tobacco products may be included in the yearly and 48-hour exemptions but not in the 24-hour exemption. If you meet the age requirements of the province through which you reenter Canada, you may bring in, duty-free, 1.14 liters (40 imperial ounces) of wine or liquor *or* 24 12-ounce cans or bottles of beer or ale. If you are 16 or older, you may bring in, duty-free, 200 cigarettes, 50 cigars or cigarillos, and 400 tobacco sticks or 400 grams of manufactured tobacco. Alcohol and tobacco must accompany you on your return.

An unlimited number of gifts valued up to C$60 each may be mailed to Canada duty-free. These do not count as part of your exemption. Label the package "Unsolicited Gift— Value Under $60." Alcohol and tobacco are excluded.

IN THE U.K.➣ From countries outside the EU, you may import duty-free 200 cigarettes, 100 cigarillos, 50 cigars, or 250 grams of tobacco; 1 liter of spirits or 2 liters of fortified or sparkling wine; 2 liters of still table wine; 60 milliliters of perfume; 250 milliliters of toilet water; plus £136 worth of other goods, including gifts and souvenirs.

D
FOR TRAVELERS
WITH DISABILITIES

In the Caribbean very few attractions and sights are equipped with ramps, elevators, or wheelchair-accessible rest rooms. However, major new properties are planning with the needs of travelers with disabilities in mind. Wherever possible in our lodging listings, we indicate whether special facilities are available.

When discussing accessibility with an operator or reservationist, **ask hard questions.** Are there any stairs, inside *or* out? Are there grab bars next to the toilet *and* in the shower/tub? How wide is the doorway to the room? To the bathroom? For the most extensive facilities, meeting the latest legal specifications, **opt for newer properties,** which more often have been designed with access in mind. Older properties or ships must usually be retrofitted and may offer more limited facilities as a result. Be sure to **discuss your needs before booking.**

DISCOUNT CLUBS

Travel clubs offer members unsold space on airplanes, cruise ships, and package tours at as much as 50% below regular prices. Membership may include a regular bulletin or access to a toll-free hot line giving details of available trips departing from three or four days to several months in the future. Most also offer 50% discounts off hotel rack rates. Before booking with a club, **make sure the hotel or other supplier isn't offering a better deal.**

DIVERS' ALERT

Scuba divers take note: **Do not fly within 24 hours of scuba diving.**

H
HEALTH
CONCERNS

There are few real hazards. The small lizards that seem to

have overrun the islands are harmless, and poisonous snakes are hard to find, although you should exercise caution while bird-watching in Trinidad. The worst problem may well be the tiny sand flies known as no-see-ums, which tend to appear after a rain, near wet or swampy ground, and around sunset. You may want to **bring along a good repellent.**

Sunburn or sunstroke can be serious. A long-sleeve shirt, a hat, and long pants or a beach wrap are essential on a boat, for midday at the beach, and whenever you go out sightseeing. **Use sunblock lotion** on nose, ears, and other sensitive areas, **limit your sun time** for the first few days, and be sure to **drink enough liquids.**

Since health standards vary from island to island, inquire about local conditions before you go. No special shots are required for most Caribbean destinations; where they are, we have made note of it.

I
INSURANCE

Travel insurance can protect your investment, replace your luggage and its contents, or provide for medical coverage should you fall ill during your trip. Most tour operators, travel agents, and insurance agents sell specialized health-and-accident, flight, trip-cancellation, and luggage insurance as well as comprehensive policies with some or all of these features. Before you make any purchase, **review your existing health and homeowner's policies** to find out whether they cover expenses incurred while traveling.

BAGGAGE

Airline liability for your baggage is limited by the terms of your ticket (*see* Packing for the Caribbean, *below*). Insurance for losses exceeding the terms of your airline ticket be bought directly from the airline at check-in for about $10 per $1,000 of coverage; note that it excludes a rather extensive list of items, shown on your airline ticket.

FLIGHT

You should **think twice before buying flight insurance.** Often purchased as a last-minute impulse at the airport, it pays a lump sum when a plane crashes, either to a beneficiary if the insured dies or sometimes to a surviving passenger who loses eyesight or a limb. Supplementing the airlines' coverage described in the limits-of-liability paragraphs on your ticket, it's expensive and basically unnecessary. Charging an airline ticket to a major credit card often automatically entitles you to coverage and may also embrace travel by bus, train, and ship.

HEALTH

If your own health insurance policy does not cover you outside the U.S., **consider buying supplemental medi-**

cal coverage. It can provide from $1,000 to $150,000 worth of medical and/or dental expenses incurred as a result of an accident or illness during a trip. These policies also may include a personal-accident, or death-and-dismemberment, provision, which pays a lump sum ranging from $15,000 to $500,000 to your beneficiaries if you die or to you if you lose one or more limbs or your eyesight, and a medical-assistance provision, which may either reimburse you for the cost of referrals, evacuation, or repatriation and other services, or may automatically enroll you as a member of a particular medical-assistance company. (*See* Health Issues in Important Contacts A to Z, *above*.)

FOR U.K. TRAVELERS➤ You can buy an annual travel-insurance policy valid for most vacations during the year in which it's purchased. If you go this route, make sure it covers you if you have a preexisting medical condition or are pregnant.

TRIP

Without insurance, you will lose all or most of your money if you must cancel your trip due to illness or any other reason. Especially if your airline ticket, cruise, or package tour is nonrefundable and cannot be changed, it's essential that you **buy trip-cancellation-and-interruption insurance.** When considering how much coverage you need, look for a policy

that will cover the cost of your trip plus the nondiscounted price of a one-way airline ticket should you need to return home early. Read the fine print carefully, especially sections defining "family member" and "preexisting medical conditions." Also **consider default or bankruptcy insurance,** which protects you against a supplier's failure to deliver. However, such policies often do not cover default by a travel agency, tour operator, airline, or cruise line if you bought your tour and the coverage directly from the firm in question.

L
LODGING

Plan ahead and **reserve a room well before you travel to the Caribbean.** If you have reservations but expect to arrive later than 5 or 6 PM, tell the management in advance. Unless so advised, some places will not hold your reservations after 6 PM. Also, be sure to **find out what the rate quoted includes**—use of sports facilities and equipment, airport transfers, and the like—and whether the property operates on the European Plan (EP, with no meals), Continental Plan (CP, with Continental breakfast), Breakfast Plan (BP, with full breakfast), Modified American Plan (MAP, with two meals), or Full American Plan (FAP, with three meals), or is All-inclusive (including three meals, all facilities, and drinks unless otherwise noted).

Be sure to **bring your deposit receipt** with you in case questions arise.

Decide whether you want a hotel on the leeward side of the island (with calm water, good for snorkeling) or the windward (with waves, good for surfing). Decide, too, whether you want to pay the extra price for a room overlooking the ocean or pool. Also **find out how close the property is to a beach;** at some hotels you can walk barefoot from your room onto the sand; others are across a road or a 10-minute drive away.

Nighttime entertainment is alfresco in the Caribbean, so if you go to sleep early or are a light sleeper, ask for a room away from the dance floor.

Air-conditioning is not a necessity on all islands, most of which are cooled by trade winds, but it can be a plus if you enjoy an afternoon snooze. Breezes are best in second-floor rooms, particularly corner rooms. If you like to sleep without air-conditioning, make sure that windows can be opened and have screens.

In this book, we categorize properties by price rather than quality. Prices are intended as a guideline only. Larger hotels with more extensive facilities cost more, but the Caribbean is full of smaller places with charm, individuality, and prices that make up for their lack of activities—which are gener-

ally available on a pay-per-use basis everywhere.

APARTMENT AND VILLA RENTALS

If you want a home base that's roomy enough for a family and comes with cooking facilities, **consider a furnished rental.** It's generally cost-wise, too, although not always— some rentals are luxury properties (economical only when your party is large). Home-exchange directories do list rentals—often second homes owned by prospective house swappers—and some services search for a house or apartment for you (even a castle if that's your fancy) and handle the paperwork. Some send an illustrated catalogue and others send photographs of specific properties, sometimes at a charge; up-front registration fees may apply.

To rent a villa, contact **Unusual Villas & Island Rentals** (101 Tempsford La., Penthouse 9, Richmond, VA 23226, ☎ 800/768–0280) or **Villas International** (605 Market St., #510, San Francisco, CA 94105, ☎ 415/281–0910 or 800/221–2260).

HOME EXCHANGE

If you would like to find a house, an apartment, or other vacation property to exchange for your own while on vacation, **become a member of a home-exchange organization,** which will send you its annual directories listing available exchanges and will in-

clude your own listing in at least one of them. Arrangements for the actual exchange are made by the two parties to it, not by the organization.

M

MEDICAL ASSISTANCE

No one plans to get sick while traveling, but it happens, so **consider signing up with a medical-assistance company.** These outfits provide referrals, emergency evacuation or repatriation, 24-hour telephone hot lines for medical consultation, dispatch of medical personnel, relay of medical records, cash for emergencies, and other personal and legal assistance.

MONEY AND EXPENSES

ATMS

Cirrus, Plus and many other networks connecting automated-teller machines operate internationally. Chances are that you can **use your bank card at ATMs** to withdraw money from an account and get cash advances on a credit-card account if your card has been programmed with a personal identification number, or PIN. Before leaving home, **check in on frequency limits** for withdrawals and cash advances. Also **ask whether your card's PIN must be reprogrammed** for use in the Caribbean. Four digits are commonly used overseas. Note that Discover is accepted only in the United States.

On cash advances you are charged interest from the day you receive the money from ATMs as well as from tellers. Although transaction fees for ATM withdrawals abroad may be higher than fees for withdrawals at home, Cirrus and Plus exchange rates are excellent because they are based on wholesale rates only offered by major banks.

COSTS

For information on costs, see individual island chapters.

TRAVELER'S CHECKS

Whether or not to buy traveler's checks depends on where you are headed; take cash to rural areas and small towns, traveler's checks to cities. The most widely recognized are American Express, Citicorp, Thomas Cook, and Visa, which are sold by major commercial banks for 1% to 3% of the checks' face value—it pays to shop around. Both American Express and Thomas Cook issue checks that can be countersigned and used by you or your traveling companion. Record the numbers of the checks, cross them off as you spend them, and keep this information separate from your checks.

WIRING MONEY

You don't have to be a cardholder to send or receive funds through MoneyGram(SM) from American Express. Just go to a MoneyGram agent, located in retail and convenience stores and in American Express Travel Offices. Pay up to $1,000 with cash or a credit card, anything over that in cash. The money can be picked up within 10 minutes in the form of U.S.-dollar traveler's checks or local currency at the nearest Money-Gram agent, or, abroad, the nearest American Express Travel Office. There's no limit, and the recipient need only present photo identification. The cost runs from 3% to 10%, depending on the amount sent, the destination, and how you pay.

You can also send money using Western Union. Money sent from the United States or Canada will be available for pickup at agent locations in 100 countries within 15 minutes. Once the money is in the system, it can be picked up at any one of 25,000 locations. Fees range from 4% to 10%, depending on the amount you send.

P
PACKAGES AND TOURS

A package or tour to the Caribbean can make your vacation less expensive and more convenient. Firms that sell tours and packages purchase airline seats, hotel rooms, and rental cars in bulk and pass some of the savings on to you. In addition, the best operators have local representatives to help you out at your destination.

A GOOD DEAL?

The more your package or tour includes, the better you can predict the ultimate cost of your vacation. Make sure you know exactly what is included, and beware of hidden costs. Are taxes, tips, and service charges included? Transfers and baggage handling? Entertainment and excursions? These can add up.

Most packages and tours are rated deluxe, first-class superior, first class, tourist, and budget. The key difference is usually accommodations. If the package or tour you are considering is priced lower than in your wildest dreams, be skeptical. Also, make sure your travel agent knows the hotels and other services. Ask about location, room size, beds, and whether it has a pool, room service, or programs for children, if you care about these. Has your agent been there or sent others you can contact?

BUYER BEWARE

Each year consumers are stranded or lose their money when operators go out of business—even very large ones with excellent reputations. If you can't afford a loss, take the time to check out the operator—find out how long the company has been in business, and ask several agents about its reputation. Next, don't book unless the firm has a consumer-protection program. Members of the United States Tour Operators Association and the National Tour Association are required to set aside funds exclusively to cover your payments and travel arrangements in case of default. Nonmember operators may instead carry insurance; look for the details in the operator's brochure—and the name of an underwriter with a solid reputation. Note: When it comes to tour operators, **don't trust escrow accounts.** Although there are laws governing those of charter-flight operators, no governmental body prevents tour operators from raiding the till.

Next, **contact your local Better Business Bureau and the attorney general's office** in both your own state and the operator's. Have any complaints been filed? Last, **pay with a major credit card.** Then you can cancel payment, provided that you can document your complaint. Always **consider trip-cancellation insurance** (*see* Insurance, *above*).

BIG VS. SMALL> An operator that handles several hundred thousand travelers annually can use its purchasing power to give you a good price. Its high volume may also indicate financial stability. But some small companies provide more personalized service; because they tend to specialize, they may also be experts on an area.

USING AN AGENT

Travel agents are an excellent resource. In fact, large operators accept bookings only through travel agents. But it's good to **collect brochures from several agencies,** because some agents' suggestions may be skewed by promotional relationships with tour and package firms that reward them for volume sales. If you have a special interest, **find an agent with expertise in that area;** the American Society of Travel Agents can give you leads in the United States. (Don't rely solely on your agent, though; agents may be unaware of small niche operators, and some special-interest travel companies only sell direct.)

SINGLE TRAVELERS

Prices are usually quoted per person, based on two sharing a room. If traveling solo, you may be required to pay the full double-occupancy rate. Some operators eliminate this surcharge if you agree to be matched up with a roommate of the same sex, even if one is not found by departure time.

PACKING FOR THE CARIBBEAN

Dress on the islands is light and casual. Bring loose-fitting clothes made of natural fabrics to see you through days of heat and humidity. Take a cover-up for the beaches, not only to protect you from the sun but also to wear to and from your hotel room. Bathing suits and immodest attire are frowned upon off the beach on many islands. A sun hat is advisable, but you don't have to pack one, since inexpensive straw hats are available everywhere. For shopping and sightseeing, bring walking shorts, jeans, T-shirts, long-sleeve cotton shirts, slacks, and sundresses. You'll need a light sweater for protection from the trade winds, and at higher altitudes. Evenings are casual, but "casual" can range from really informal to casually elegant, depending on the establishment. A tie is rarely required, but jackets are sometimes de rigueur in fancier restaurants and casinos.

Bring an extra pair of eyeglasses or contact lenses in your carry-on luggage, and if you have a health problem, **pack enough medication** to last the trip or have your doctor write a prescription using the drug's generic name, because brand names vary from country to country (you'll then need a prescription from a doctor in the country you're visiting). In case your bags go astray, **don't put prescription drugs or valuables in luggage to be checked.** To avoid problems with customs officials, carry medications in original packaging. Also don't forget the addresses of offices that handle refunds of lost traveler's checks.

ELECTRICITY

The general rule in the Caribbean is 110 and 120 volts AC, and the outlets take the same two-prong plugs found in the United States, but there are exceptions, particularly on the

French islands and those with a British heritage. Be sure to **check with your hotel** when making reservations. If you are traveling to an island that uses a foreign system, **bring a converter and an adapter.**

If your appliances are dual-voltage, you'll need only an adapter. Hotels sometimes have 110-volt outlets for low-wattage appliances marked "For Shavers Only" near the sink; don't use them for high-wattage appliances like blow-dryers. If your laptop computer is older, carry a converter; new laptops operate equally well on 110 and 220 volts, so you need only an adapter.

LUGGAGE

Because baggage carts are scarce at airports and luggage restrictions are tight, particularly on small island-hopper planes, **pack light.**

Free airline baggage allowances depend on the airline, the route, and the class of your ticket; ask in advance. In general, on domestic flights and on international flights between the United States and foreign destinations, you are entitled to check two bags— neither exceeding 62 inches, or 158 centimeters (length + width + height), or weighing more than 70 pounds (32 kilograms). A third piece may be brought aboard; its total dimensions are generally limited to less than 45 inches (114 centimeters), so it will fit easily under the seat in front of you or in the over-

head compartment. In the United States, the Federal Aviation Administration gives airlines broad latitude to limit carry-on allowances and tailor them to different aircraft and operational conditions. Charges for excess, oversize, or overweight pieces vary.

If you are flying between two foreign destinations, note that baggage allowances may be determined not by piece but by weight—generally 88 pounds (40 kilograms) in first class, 66 pounds (30 kilograms) in business class, and 44 pounds (20 kilograms) in economy. If your flight between two cities abroad *connects* with your transatlantic or transpacific flight, the piece method still applies.

SAFEGUARDING YOUR LUGGAGE➤ Before leaving home, **itemize your bags' contents** and their worth, and label them with your name, address, and phone number. (If you use your home address, cover it so that potential thieves can't see it.) Inside your bag, **pack a copy of your itinerary.** At check-in, **make sure that your bag is correctly tagged** with the airport's three-letter destination code. If your bags arrive damaged or not at all, file a written report with the airline before leaving the airport.

PASSPORTS AND VISAS

See individual island chapters for specific

requirements. If you don't already have one, you may need to **get a passport.** While traveling, **keep one photocopy of the data page** separate from your wallet and leave another copy with someone at home. If you lose your passport, promptly call the nearest embassy or consulate, and the local police; having the data page can speed replacement.

U.S. CITIZENS

New and renewal application forms are available at any of the 13 U.S. Passport Agency offices and at some post offices and courthouses. Passports are usually mailed within four weeks; allow five weeks or more in spring and summer.

CANADIANS

Passport application forms are available at 28 regional passport offices as well as post offices and travel agencies. Whether for a first or a subsequent passport, you must apply in person. Children under 16 may be included on a parent's passport but must have their own to travel alone. Passports are valid for five years and are usually mailed within two to three weeks of application.

U.K. CITIZENS

Some islands require passports; others do not but may require a British Visitor's Passport.

Applications for new and renewal passports are available from main post offices as well as at the passport offices, located in Belfast, Glasgow, Liverpool, London, Newport, and Peterborough. You may apply in person at all passport offices, or by mail to all except the London office. Children under 16 may travel on an accompanying parent's passport. All passports are valid for 10 years. Allow a month for processing.

R
RENTING A CAR

CUTTING COSTS

To get the best deal, **book through a travel agent and shop around.** When pricing cars, **ask where the rental lot is located.** Some off-airport locations offer lower rates—even though their lots are only minutes away from the terminal via complimentary shuttle. You may also want to **price local car-rental companies,** whose rates may be lower still, although service and maintenance standards may not be up to those of a national firm. Also **ask your travel agent about a company's customer-service record.** How has it responded to late plane arrivals and vehicle mishaps? Are there often lines at the rental counter, and, if you're traveling during a holiday period, does a confirmed reservation guarantee you a car?

Always **find out what equipment is standard** at your destination before specifying what you want; **do without automatic transmission or air-conditioning** if they're optional.

INSURANCE

When you drive a rented car, you are generally responsible for any damage or personal injury that you cause as well as damage to the vehicle. Before you rent, **see what coverage you already have** by means of your personal auto-insurance policy and credit cards. For about $14 a day, rental companies sell insurance, known as a collision damage waiver (CDW), that eliminates your liability for damage to the car; it's always optional and should never be automatically added to your bill.

REQUIREMENTS

For driver's license requirements, see individual island chapters.

SURCHARGES

Before picking up the car in one city and leaving it in another, **ask about drop-off charges or one-way service fees,** which can be substantial. Note, too, that some rental agencies charge extra if you return the car before the time specified on your contract. To avoid a hefty refueling fee, **fill the tank just before you turn in the car.**

S
SENIOR CITIZENS

Special facilities, rates, and package deals for older travelers are rare. When planning your trip, be sure to inquire about everything from senior-citizen discounts to available medical facilities. Focus on your vacation needs: Are you interested in sightseeing, activities, golf, eco-

tourism, the beach? Accessibility is an important consideration. When booking, inquire whether you can easily get to the things that you enjoy. The more remote islands have fewer options and amenities.

DISCOUNTS

To qualify for age-related discounts, **mention your senior-citizen status up front** when booking hotel reservations, not when checking out, and before you're seated in restaurants, not when paying your bill. Note that discounts may be limited to certain menus, days, or hours. When renting a car, **ask about promotional car-rental discounts**—they can net lower costs than your senior-citizen discount.

STUDENTS ON THE ROAD

The Caribbean is not as far out of a student's budget as you might expect. All but the toniest islands, such as St. Barthélemy, have camping facilities, inexpensive guest houses, or small no-frills hotels. You're most likely to meet students from other countries in the French and Dutch West Indies, where many go on holiday or sabbatical. Puerto Rico, Jamaica, Grenada, and Dominica, among others, have large resident international student populations at their universities.

To save money, **look into deals available through student-oriented travel agencies** to those with a bona fide student I.D. card, and to members of international student groups. *See* Students *in* Important Contacts A to Z, *above*.

T
TELEPHONES

LONG-DISTANCE

The long-distance services of AT&T, MCI, and Sprint make calling home relatively convenient and let you avoid hotel surcharges; typically, you dial an 800 number in the United States and a local number abroad). Before you go, **find out the local access codes** for your destinations.

W
WHEN TO GO

The Caribbean high season has traditionally been winter, usually extending from December 15 to April 14. This is when northern weather is at its worst, not necessarily when Caribbean weather is at its best. In fact, winter is when the Caribbean is at its windiest. It's also the most fashionable, the most expensive, and the most popular time to visit, and most hotels are heavily booked. You have to make your reservations at least two or three months in advance for the very best places (and sometimes a year in advance for the most exclusive spots). Hotel prices drop 20%–50% for summer (after April 15); cruise prices also fall. Saving money isn't the only reason to visit the Caribbean during

the off-season. Temperatures are only a few degrees warmer, and more and more hotels and restaurants are staying open year-round, so things aren't as dead-quiet as they used to be. September, October, and November are least crowded, but hotel facilities can be limited and some restaurants may be closed. Singles in search of partners should visit in high season or in summer, or choose a resort with a high year-round occupancy rate.

The flamboyant flowering trees are at their height in summer, and so are most of the flowers and shrubs of the West Indies. The water is clearer for snorkeling, and smoother for sailing in the Virgin Islands and the Grenadines, in May, June, and July. Generally speaking, there's more planned entertainment in winter. The peak of local excitement on many islands, most notably Trinidad, St. Vincent, and the French West Indies, is Carnival.

CLIMATE

The Caribbean climate is fairly constant. Average year-round temperature for the region is 78°F–85°F. The extremes of temperature are 65°F low, 95°F high, but as everyone knows, it's the humidity, not the heat, that makes you suffer, especially when the two go hand in hand. You can count on downtown shopping areas being hot at midday any time of the year, but air-conditioning provides some

respite. Stay near beaches, where water and trade winds can keep you cool, and shop early or late in the day.

High places can be cool, particularly when the Christmas winds hit Caribbean peaks (they come in late November and last through January). Since most Caribbean islands are mountainous (notable exceptions being the Caymans, Aruba, Bonaire, and Curaçao), the altitude always offers an escape from the latitude. Kingston (Jamaica), Port-of-Spain (Trinidad), and Fort-de-France (Martinique) swelter in summer; climb 1,000 feet or so and everything is fine.

Hurricanes occasionally sweep through the Caribbean in fall, and officials on many islands are not well equipped to warn locals, much less tourists. Check the news daily, and keep abreast of brewing tropical storms by reading Stateside papers if you can get them. The rainy season, usually in fall, consists mostly of brief showers interspersed with sunshine. You can watch the clouds come over, feel the rain, and remain on your lounge chair for the sun to dry you off. A spell of overcast days is "unusual," as everyone will tell you.

1 Destination: Caribbean

THE MANY FACES OF THE ISLANDS

I F YOU HAVE SEEN ONE ISLAND you have by no means seen them all. Tiny 5-square-mile Saba has less in common with the vast 19,000-square-mile Dominican Republic than Butte, Montana, has with Biloxi, Mississippi. Butte and Biloxi, however different in terrain and traits, sit in the same country and the citizenry speak more or less the same language. Saba, which is Dutch, and the Dominican Republic, whose roots are in Spain, simply sit in the same sea.

The Caribbean has towering volcanic islands, such as Saba; islands with forests, such as Dominica and Guadeloupe; and some islands, notably Puerto Rico, that have both rain forests and deserts. Glittering discos, casinos, and dazzling nightlife can be found on such islands as Aruba and the Dominican Republic, and throughout the region there are isolated cays with only sand, sea, sun, lizards, and mosquitoes. Some islands, St. Kitts among them, have ancient forts to view, while Puerto Rico and the Caicos Islands have caverns and caves to explore. There are also places like Grand Turk, where the only notable sights to see are beneath the translucent sea.

Different though they are in many ways, the islands are stylistically similar. The style-setter is the tropical climate. Year-round summertime temperatures and a plethora of beaches produce a pace that's known as "island time." Only the trade winds move swiftly. Operating on island time means, "I'll get to it when the spirit moves me."

Similarities are also attributable to the history of the region. The Arawaks paddled up from South America and populated the islands more than 1,000 years ago. In the early 14th century, the cannibalistic Caribs, who gave the area its name, arrived, probably from Brazil or Venezuela, then polished off the peaceful Arawaks and managed, for a time at least, to scare the living daylights out of the Europeans who sailed through in search of gold. (The original name of the Caribs was Galibi, a word the Spanish corrupted

to *Canibal*—the origin of the word "cannibal.") Christopher Columbus made four voyages through the region between 1492 and 1504, christening the islands while dodging the Carib arrows. He landed on or sailed past all of the Greater Antilles and virtually all of the eastern Caribbean islands.

From the 16th century until the early 19th century, the Dutch, Danes, Swedes, English, French, Irish, and Spanish fought bitterly for control of the islands. Some islands have almost as many battle sites as sand flies. Having gained control of the islands and annihilated the Caribs, the Europeans established vast sugar plantations and brought in Africans to work the fields. With the abolition of slavery in the mid-19th century, Asians were imported as indentured laborers. Today, the Caribbean population is a rich gumbo of nationalities, including Americans and Canadians who have retired to and invested in the islands.

It must be remembered that the Caribbean, like the European continent, is made up of individual countries, each with customs, immigration officials, and, in some instances, political difficulties. Most of the islands have opted for independence; others retain their ties to the mother country. They are developing nations, and many have severe economic and unemployment problems.

Virtually all of the islands depend upon tourism. And, human nature being what it is, many islanders resent their dependency on tourist dollars. Like as not, the person who serves you has stood in a long line, vying with other anxious applicants for the few available jobs. After serving your meals and cleaning your luxurious room, he or she returns to a tiny shack knowing full well that in less than a week you will have shelled out more than an islander makes in a month.

Some visitors object to encountering resentment, when all they seek is a pleasant vacation and they've paid dearly for it. Some feel rather keenly that they'd always like hot water—or at least *some* water—when they turn on the shower; in even the most luxurious resorts there are times when things simply don't work, and that's a fact of Caribbean life. And other visitors simply have no patience with island time.

On the other hand, there are those who travel to the Caribbean year after year. Some return to the same hotel on the same beach on the same island, while the more adventurous try to sample as much as this smorgasbord has to offer.

WHAT'S WHERE

Finding Your Own Place in the Sun

The Caribbean Sea, an area of more than a million square miles, stretches south of Florida down to the coast of Venezuela. In the northern Caribbean are the **Greater Antilles**—the islands closest to the United States—composed of Cuba, Jamaica, Haiti, the Dominican Republic, and Puerto Rico. (Due to the political unrest in Haiti and Cuba, they are not included in this book.) The **Cayman Islands** lie south of Cuba. The **Lesser Antilles**—greater in number but smaller in size than the Greater Antilles—are divided into three groups: the **Leewards** and the **Windwards** in the eastern Caribbean, and the islands in the **southern Caribbean.** The eastern Caribbean islands, from the Virgin Islands in the north all the way south to Grenada, form an arc between the Atlantic Ocean and the Caribbean Sea. Islands in the Leeward chain in order of appearance are the U.S. and British Virgin Islands, Anguilla, St. Martin/St. Maarten, St. Barthélemy, Saba, St. Eustatius, St. Kitts, Nevis, Antigua, Barbuda, Montserrat, Guadeloupe, and Dominica; the Windwards are composed of Martinique, St. Lucia, St. Vincent and the Grenadines, and Grenada. Barbados is just east of this group. In the southern Caribbean, off the coast of Venezuela, Trinidad and Tobago are anchored in the east, while Aruba, Bonaire, and Curaçao (known as the ABC Islands) bathe in the western waters. The **Turks and Caicos Islands,** which lie in the Atlantic Ocean between Florida and the north coast of Hispaniola (Haiti and the Dominican Republic), are part of the Bahamas but are included in this book because of their proximity to and affinity with the Caribbean islands.

PLEASURES & PASTIMES

Here are some suggestions on where to go for some of the Caribbean's major pleasures. Consult the Island-Finder chart on the following pages to help you choose your destination.

Boating and Sailing

Whether you charter a yacht with crew or captain a boat yourself, the waters of the Caribbean are excellent for sailing, and the many secluded bays and inlets provide ideal spots to drop anchor and picnic or explore. **Guadeloupe's** Port de Plaisance and the marinas on Tortola in the **British Virgin Islands, St. Vincent and the Grenadines,** and St. Thomas in the **U.S. Virgin Islands** are the starting points for some of the Caribbean's finest sailing. Yachtsmen also favor the waters around **Antigua** and put in regularly at Nelson's Dockyard, which hosts a colorful regatta in late April or early May.

Casinos and Nightlife

You can flirt with Lady Luck until the wee small hours in the dazzling casinos of Santo Domingo, **Dominican Republic;** San Juan, **Puerto Rico; St. Maarten;** and **Curaçao. Aruba** is loaded with lively night places, and San Juan's glittering floor shows are legendary. The merengue, born in the **Dominican Republic,** is exuberantly danced everywhere on the island. Both **Guadeloupe** and **Martinique** claim to have begun the beguine, and on both islands it is danced with great gusto, although the zouk (allnight revelry) is now the rage.

Cuisine

The cuisine on **Martinique** and **Guadeloupe** is a marvelous marriage of Creole cooking and classic French dishes; you'll find much of the same on the other French islands of **St. Martin** and **St. Barts.** You'll also find a fine selection of French wines in the French West Indies. **Grenada,** the spice island, has an abundance of seafood and an incredible variety of vegetables.

Diving

Jacques Cousteau named Pigeon Island, off the west coast of **Guadeloupe,** one of the 10 best dive sites in the world. The Wall

Island Finder

	Cost of Island	Number of rooms	Nonstop flights	Cruise ship port	U.S. dollars accepted	Historic sites	Natural beauty	Lush	Arid	Mountainous	Rain forest	Beautiful beaches	Good roads
Anguilla	$$$	978			•				•			•	
Antigua & Barbuda	$$$$	3317	•	•	•	•	•		•		•	•	
Aruba	$$	6150	•	•	•		•		•			•	•
Barbados	$$	5580	•	•	•	•						•	•
Bonaire	$$	803	•		•							•	
British Virgin Islands	$$$	1224		•	•	•	•	•		•	•	•	
Cayman Islands	$$$$	3453	•	•	•				•			•	•
Curaçao	$$	2200	•	•	•	•							•
Dominica	$	757					•	•			•	•	
Dominican Republic	$	28,000	•				•	•			•		•
The Grenadines	$	500					•	•			•	•	•
Grenada	$$$	1428		•	•	•	•	•			•	•	•
Guadeloupe	$$	7798		•		•	•	•			•	•	•
Jamaica	$$$	18,935	•	•	•		•	•			•		• •
Martinique	$$$	6960	•	•			•	•			•		•
Montserrat	$$	710		•	•		•	•			•	•	
Nevis	$$$	400		•	•		•	•			•		•
Puerto Rico	$	8581	•	•	•	•	•	•	•	•	•	•	•
Saba	$	138		•			•				•		•
St. Barthélemy	$$$$	715		•	•		•				•		•
St. Eustatius	$	83		•	•						•	•	
St. Kitts	$$	1200		•			•	•			•	•	•
St. Lucia	$$	2919	•	•	•		•	•			•	•	
St. Martin/St. Maarten	$$$	5300	•	•	•			•			•		•
St. Vincent	$$	730			•	•	•	•			•	•	
Trinidad	$	1600	•									•	
Tobago	$$	1100	•							•		•	•
Turks and Caicos	$$$	1139	•		•					•		•	
U.S. Virgin Islands:													
St. Croix	$$	1142		•	•	•		•			•		•
St. John	$$	763		•	•		•	•			•		• •
St. Thomas	$$	3217	•	•	•						•		• •

Public transportation	Fine dining	Local cuisine	Shopping	Music	Casinos	Nightlife	Diving and Snorkeling	Sailing	Golfing	Hiking	Ecotourism	Villa rentals	All-inclusives	Campgrounds	Luxury resorts	Secluded getaway	Good for families	Romantic hideaway
	•	•	•	•			•					•	•		•	•		•
•	•	•	•		•	•	•	•	•				•		•		•	
•	•	•	•	•	•	•	•						•		•		•	•
•	•	•	•	•		•	•		•	•		•			•		•	•
					•		•	•		•	•				•			
•	•	•	•			•	•	•		•	•	•	•		•	•	•	•
	•		•			•	•		•		•	•	•		•		•	
•	•	•	•		•	•	•	•		•					•			
		•					•			•	•	•				•		•
•	•	•			•	•	•	•		•					•		•	•
•		•					•	•		•	•	•	•		•	•	•	•
	•	•	•	•		•	•	•		•	•	•			•	•	•	•
•	•	•	•		•	•	•	•		•	•	•		•	•	•		•
•	•	•	•	•		•	•	•	•	•		•		•				
	•	•	•	•	•	•	•	•	•	•	•	•				•	•	
							•			•	•	•			•	•	•	
•	•	•	•	•	•	•	•	•		•	•	•	•		•	•	•	•
		•					•			•	•	•			•	•	•	•
	•	•	•				•					•			•	•	•	•
		•					•			•	•				•			
	•	•	•	•	•	•	•	•		•	•		•		•		•	•
•	•	•	•	•		•	•	•		•	•				•	•	•	•
•	•	•	•		•	•	•	•		•		•			•		•	•
•		•		•		•	•	•		•	•				•		•	•
•		•		•		•	•		•						•		•	•
		•		•		•	•		•							•		
							•	•		•			•		•			•
•	•	•	•			•	•		•	•	•				•			
	•	•					•			•	•	•		•	•	•	•	•
•	•	•	•			•	•	•	•			•	•		•			

off Grand Turk in the **Turks and Caicos Islands** is a sheer drop of 7,000 feet and has long been known by scuba divers. The eruption of **Martinique**'s Mt. Pelée at 8 AM on May 8, 1902, resulted in the sinking of several ships. **St. Eustatius** boasts an undersea "supermarket" of ships, as well as entire 18th-century warehouses, somewhat the worse for wear, below the surface of Oranjestad Bay. The waters surrounding all three of the **Cayman Islands** are acclaimed by experts, who also make pilgrimages to **Bonaire**'s 86 spectacular sites.

Pointers

While scuba (which stands for self-contained underwater breathing apparatus) looks and is surprisingly simple, *call your physician before your vacation and make sure that you have no condition that should prevent you from diving!* A full checkup is an excellent idea, especially if you're over 30. Since it can be dangerous to travel on a plane after diving, you should schedule both your diving courses and travel plans accordingly.

Learning to dive with a reputable instructor is also a must. In addition to training you how to resurface slowly enough, a qualified instructor can teach you to read "dive tables," the charts that calculate how long you can safely stay at certain depths.

Many resorts offer short courses consisting of two to three hours of instruction on land and time in a swimming pool or waist-deep water to get used to the mouthpiece and hose (known as the regulator) and the mask. A shallow 20-foot dive from a boat or beach, supervised by the instructor, follows.

Successful completion of this introductory course may prompt you to do further coursework to earn a certification card—often called a C-card—from one of the major accredited diving organizations: NAUI (National Association of Underwater Instructors), CMAS (Confederation Mondiale des Activités Subaquatiques, which translates into World Underwater Federation), NASE (National Association of Scuba Educators), or PADI (Professional Association of Diving Instructors). PADI offers a free list of training facilities (*see* Diving in Important Contacts A to Z, *above*).

Foreign Culture

African

Trinidad moves with the rhythm of calypso and is the stomping ground of a flat-out, freewheeling Carnival that rivals the pre-Lenten celebrations in Rio and New Orleans. The Trinidadians, whose African heritage has been augmented by many Asian races, have built up one of the most prosperous commercial centers in the Caribbean. Haiti was once another option. (It's now politically volatile and is not covered in this book.)

British

St. Kitts is known as the Mother Colony of the West Indies; it was from here that British colonists were dispatched in the 17th century to settle Antigua, Barbuda, Tortola, and Montserrat. If you're a history buff, you won't want to miss Nelson's Dockyard at **Antigua's** English Harbour or the hunkering fortress of Brimstone Hill on St. Kitts. Sports fans who understand the intricacies of cricket can watch matches between **Nevis** and St. Kitts teams. And the waters around Antigua and the **British Virgin Islands** are a mecca for serious sailors. **Barbados,** with its lovely tradewinds, has cricket, horseracing at Garrison Savannah, and rugby. A British colony from 1627, the island gained independence in 1966.

Dutch

Saba, St. Eustatius, St. Maarten, Bonaire, and **Curaçao** all fly the Dutch flag, but there the similarity ends. Saba is a tiny volcanic island known for its beauty, its friendly inhabitants, and its gingerbread-trimmed houses. Curaçao's colorful waterfront shops and restaurants are reminiscent of Amsterdam. Quiet St. Eustatius—affectionately called Statia—has well-preserved historical sites and is famed for being the first foreign nation to salute the new American flag in 1776. The main streets of Philipsburg, the capital of St. Maarten, are lined with colorful Dutch colonial buildings replete with fretwork and verandas. Bonaire is best known for its excellent scuba diving.

French

Martinique, Guadeloupe, St. Martin, and **St. Barthélemy** (often called St. Barts or St. Barths) compose the French West Indies. The language, the currency, the cuisine (the most imaginative in the Caribbean), the culture, and the style are très French. St. Barts is the quietest, Martinique the liveliest, St. Martin the friendliest, and Guadeloupe the lushest. And as an extra added attraction, you can wing over from Guadeloupe to see what life is like on the nearby islands of Les Saintes, Marie Galante, and Désirade.

Spanish

In the **Dominican Republic,** which occupies the eastern two-thirds of the island of Hispaniola, the language and culture are decidedly Spanish. The Colonial Zone of Santo Domingo is the site of the oldest city in the Western Hemisphere, and its restored buildings reflect the 15th-century Columbus period. One also gets a sense of the past in **Puerto Rico's** Old San Juan, with its narrow cobblestone streets and filigreed iron balconies.

Getting Away from It All

If you're looking to back out of the fast lane, you can park at one of the secluded, spartan mountain lodges on **Dominica,** which is one of the friendliest islands in the Caribbean. Or opt for the quiet grandeur of a renovated sugar plantation on **Nevis,** where you can feast in an elegant dining room or enjoy a barbecue on the beach. Tranquil **Anguilla,** with soft white beaches nudged by incredibly clear water, offers posh resorts as well as small, inexpensive, locally owned lodgings. From the low-key **Turks and Caicos Islands,** which lie in stunning blue-green waters, you can boat to more than a score of isolated cays to which even the term "low-key" would imply too fast a pace. **St. Kitts** is another peaceful green oasis, with lovely beaches and upscale, "great house" accommodations in the bargain. **St. Lucia** offers a plethora of places, from the simple to the simply elegant, for "liming" (we call it "hanging out"), the favorite local pastime. On tiny **Saba** there is little to do but tuck into a small guest house, admire the lush beauty of the island, and chat with the friendly Sabans. Nearby **St. Eustatius** is another friendly, laid-back island, as is **Montserrat.** The **Grenadines** offers three tiny, private-island luxury resorts: Young Island, Palm Island, and Petit St. Vincent.

Golf

According to those who have played it, the course at Casa de Campo in the **Dominican Republic** is one of the best in the Caribbean. The course at the Four Seasons Resort on **Nevis** is also challenging (and breathtaking). Golfers on St. Thomas, **U.S. Virgin Islands,** play the spectacular Mahogany Run. There are superb courses in **Puerto Rico,** including four shared by the Hyatt Dorado Beach and the Hyatt Regency Cerromar Beach. **Jamaica** has ten courses, including top-rated Tryall near Montego Bay, and the new Negril Hills Golf Club. The **Cayman Islands** now have an 18-hole championship golf course, The Links at Safehaven, and **Aruba** has its first 18-hole course, Robert Trent Jones–designed Tierra del Sol.

History

Antigua's well-preserved Nelson's Dockyard is a must for history aficionados. The ancient colonial zones of both Santo Domingo, **Dominican Republic,** and Old San Juan, **Puerto Rico,** should also be high on your "history" list. The Historical Society in **St. Eustatius** (Statia) publishes an excellent walking tour. Brimstone Hill on **St. Kitts** is a well-maintained fortress with several museums full of military memorabilia. **Nevis** has many sugar mills restored as comfortable hotels. Port Royal, outside Kingston, **Jamaica,** was a pirates' stronghold until an earthquake shook things up in 1692.

Luxury Resorts

A wealth of posh resorts awaits those who seek comfort in the lap of luxury. **Anguilla,** rapidly becoming one of the Caribbean's most popular destinations, has the dazzling Malliouhana and the Moroccan-style Cap Juluca. **Antigua's** elegant Curtain Bluff has a long list of well-heeled repeat guests. The Four Seasons resort on **Nevis** combines European elegance, state-of-the-art sports facilities, and Caribbean casualness. On **Jamaica** there's the well-established Half Moon Club, Montego Bay. **Puerto Rico's** new El Conquistador Resort and Country Club, with five individual hotels, is a luxurious world unto itself. On French **St. Martin,** La Samanna draws the rich and not-so-famous, and La Belle Creole re-creates a Mediterranean village, replete with a village square and opulent villas. For the ultimate in luxurious privacy, the **British Virgin Islands** has the Peter Island

Resort and Yacht Club on its own 1,300-acre private island. Intimate Le Toiny on **St. Barts** draws worldly personalities. And Caneel Bay resort on **St. John, U.S. Virgin Islands,** has seven beaches and takes up 170 acres adjacent to the Virgin Islands National Park.

Music

Calypso was born in **Trinidad; Jamaica** is the home of reggae; the **Dominican Republic** gave the world the merengue; and both **Martinique** and **Guadeloupe** claim to be the cradle of the beguine. The music of **Barbados** ranges from that heard during the Crop-Over Festival (mid-July–early August) to the hottest jazz. Steel drums, limbo dancers, and jump-ups are ubiquitous in the Caribbean. Jump-up? Simple. You hear the music, jump up, and dance.

Nature

Dominica, laced with rivers and streams, is a ruggedly beautiful island with arguably the lushest, most untamed vegetation in the Caribbean. **Puerto Rico's** luxuriant 28,000-acre El Yunque is the only rain forest in the U.S. forestry system. Little **Saba** is awash with giant vegetation, and the island's Mt. Scenery is justly named. **Guadeloupe's** 74,000-square-acre Natural Park boasts dramatic waterfalls, cool pools, and miles of hiking trails. Majestic Mt. Pelée, a not entirely dormant volcano, towers over **Martinique's** rain forest; on **St. Eustatius,** adventurers can crawl down into a jungle cradled within a volcanic crater; and on **St. Lucia** you can drive right through a volcano.

Snorkeling

Snorkeling requires no special skills, and most hotels that rent equipment have a staff member or, at the very least, a booklet offering instruction in snorkeling basics.

As with any water sport, it's never a good idea to snorkel alone, especially if you're out of shape. You don't have to be a great swimmer to snorkel, but occasionally currents come up that require stamina. The four dimensions as we know them seem altered underwater. Time seems to slow and stand still, so wear a water-resistant watch and let someone on land know when to expect you back.

Remember that taking souvenirs—shells, pieces of coral, interesting rocks—is forbidden. Many reefs are legally protected marine parks,

where removal of living shells is prohibited because it upsets the ecology.

Snuba

Not quite ready for scuba diving? Not to worry. For those kept from diving by poor health or claustrophobia, there is snuba, a combination of snorkeling and scuba diving. The snuba system consists of an inflatable raft that supports a tank of compressed air and a 20-foot air hose for one or two persons. The raft not only warns boats of your presence, but also provides a convenient resting place when you're tired. (There is even a clear window in the raft so you can still have an underwater view while taking a break.) The rental cost is approximately $45 an hour, and it takes only about an hour to become a certified snuba user.

Sunbathing

Just plain basking is one of the great pleasures of a Caribbean vacation, but before abandoning yourself to the tropics, you would be well advised to take precautions against the ravages of its equatorial sun. Be sure to use a sunscreen with a sun-protection factor, or SPF, of at least 15; if you're engaging in water sports, be sure the sunscreen is waterproof. At this latitude, the safest hours for sunbathing are 4–6 PM, but even then it is wise to limit exposure during your first few days to 15–20 minutes. Keep your system plied with fruit juices and water, and avoid coffee, tea, and alcohol.

Swimming

The calm, leeward, Caribbean side of most islands has the safest and most popular beaches for swimming. There are no big waves, there is little undertow, and the saltwater—which buoys the swimmer or snorkeler—makes staying afloat almost effortless.

The windward, or Atlantic, side of the islands, however, is a different story: Even strong, experienced swimmers should exercise caution here. The ocean waves are powerful and can be dangerous; unseen currents, strong undertows, and uneven, rocky bottoms may scuttle the novice. Some beaches post signs or flags daily to alert swimmers to water conditions. Pay attention to them! Where there are no flags, stick to wading and sunbathing.

Few beaches or pools in the Caribbean—even those at the best hotels—are protected by lifeguards, so you and your children swim at your own risk.

Waterskiing

Some large hotels have their own water-skiing concessions, with special boats, equipment, and instructors. Many beaches (especially those in Barbados), however, are patrolled by private individuals who own boats and several sizes of skis; they will offer their services through a hotel or directly to vacationers or can be hailed like taxis. Ask your hotel staff or other guests about their experiences with these entrepreneurs. Be *sure* they provide life vests and at least two people in the boat: one to drive and one to watch the skier at all times.

Windsurfing

Windsurfing is as strenuous as it is exciting, so it may not be the sport to try on your first day out, unless you're already in excellent shape. Always windsurf with someone else around who can go for help if necessary.

FODOR'S CHOICE

Beaches

★ **Shoal Bay, Anguilla.** This 2-mile L-shape beach of talcum-powder-soft white sand may get crowded, but that's only because it's one of the prettiest in the Caribbean.

★ **Green Cay, British Virgin Islands.** Sail to this little piece of heaven, off the shore of Jost Van Dyke, and pretend you were shipwrecked (while you drink a rum punch). There's absolutely nothing here, just intensely blue water, a couple of palm trees, and soft white sand.

★ **Seven Mile Beach, Grand Cayman.** It's actually 5½ miles of powdery white sand, litter- and peddler-free, and headquarters for the island's water sports concessions.

★ **Grand Anse Beach, Grenada.** Clear, gentle surf laps the gleaming sand of this 2-mile beach. To the north, you can see the narrow mouth of St. George's Harbour and the pastel houses, with their fish-scale tile rooftops, that climb the surrounding hillsides.

★ **Negril, Jamaica.** Although it's no longer untouched by development, this 7-mile stretch of sand is still a beachcomber's Eden. Nude beach areas are found along sections where no hotel or resort has been built.

★ **Macaroni Beach, Mustique.** Surfy swimming (be careful!), powdery white sand, a few palm huts and picnic tables, and very few people, are the draws here.

★ **Anse du Gouverneur, St. Barthélemy.** This beautiful, secluded spot offers good snorkeling and views of St. Kitts, Saba, and St. Eustatius.

Diving/Snorkeling

★ **Reefs around Bonaire.** An enormous range of coral, parrotfish, surgeon fish, angelfish, eels, snappers, and grouper are just some of the creatures you may see in the Bonaire Marine Park. The park encompasses the entire coastline around Bonaire and Klein Bonaire and includes more than 80 dive sites.

★ **Wreck of the *Rhone*, British Virgin Islands.** A Royal Mail Ship sunk by a hurricane in 1867, and still well preserved, makes for magnificent diving.

★ **Stingray City, Cayman Islands.** These islands are a diver's paradise, and this is one of their most unique sites. Dozens of unusually tame stingrays swim and twist around divers in the shallow waters.

★ **Scotts Head, Dominica.** Dramatic underwater walls and sudden drops line the coast here.

★ **Saba's Marine Park.** Encircling the entire island, the marine park features submerged pinnacles of land (at about the 70-foot depth mark), where all kinds of sea creatures rendezvous.

★ **Turks and Caicos Island's reefs.** More than 200 square miles of reefs surround these islands.

Hotels

★ **Cap Juluca, Anguilla.** This spectacular 179-acre resort wraps around the edge of Maunday's Bay and almost 2 miles of sugary white-sand beach. $$$$

★ **Curtain Bluff, Antigua.** The setting is breathtaking—high on a bluff between the wild Atlantic and calm Caribbean. The ambience is pure country-club elegance. $$$$

★ **Sandy Lane Hotel, Barbados.** Rooms are nothing short of spectacular, bathrooms are vast and luxurious, the beach is one of the best on the island, and the staff treats you like royalty. **$$$$**

★ **Bitter End Yacht Club and Marina, Virgin Gorda, British Virgin Islands.** Beautiful by any standard and heaven for sailors, whether you stay on a live-aboard yacht or in one of the exceptionally comfortable and appealing hillside or beachfront villas and chalets. **$$$$**

★ **Spice Island Inn, Grenada.** The spacious suites are great, but it's actually the bathrooms that steal the show, with spa Jacuzzis that could submerge a family of four, heaps of thick towels, and skylights for watching the moon rise. **$$$$**

★ **Coyaba Beach Resort and Club, Jamaica.** This plantation-style guest house with sunny rooms is decorated with lovely Colonial prints and hand-carved mahogany furniture. **$$–$$$$**

★ **Horned Dorset Primavera, Puerto Rico.** The emphasis here is on privacy and relaxation. The pounding of the surf and the squawk of the resident parrot are the only sounds you'll here as you lounge on the beach. **$$$$**

★ **Anse Chastanet Hotel, St. Lucia.** Rooms were designed to meld into the tropical mountainside, with louvered wooden walls open to stunning Piton and Caribbean vistas or to the deep shady-green of the forest. **$$$–$$$$**

★ **La Samanna, St. Martin.** This luxurious, secluded hotel overlooks the ravishing Baie Longue beach and offers accommodations that are perfect right down to their fresh flowers and potpourri. **$$$$**

★ **Grace Bay Club, Providenciales, Turks and Caicos.** Enjoy the views from your suite of Grace Bay's stunning turquoise waters, and take advantage of the expertly pampering service. **$$$**

Restaurants

★ **Malliouhana, Anguilla.** Sparkling crystal and fine china, exquisite service, and a spectacularly romantic, candlelit, open-air setting are the perfect match for this restaurant's exceptional haute French cuisine. **$$$$**

★ **Sandy Bay, Barbados.** Each morning a van is sent to scour the island for the freshest produce and seafood: The results—succulent grilled dolphin and lobster, lamb dressed with thyme and wild rosemary—are heavenly. **$$$$**

★ **Hemingway's, Grand Cayman.** Enjoy the breezes on Seven Mile Beach while sipping a Seven Mile Meltdown (dark rum, peach schnapps, pineapple juice, and fresh coconut) and savoring grouper stuffed with sweet corn and crab. **$$–$$$**

★ **Château de Feuilles, Guadeloupe.** A bit of a trip, but velvety sea urchin pâté, kingfish fillet with vanilla, and pineapple flan are worth every mile. **$$$**

★ **Le Fromager, Martinique.** From its perch above St-Pierre this beautiful restaurant offers views of the town's red roofs and the sea beyond, as well as delectable crayfish colombo, marinated octopus, and sole pecheur in a Creole sauce. **$$**

★ **Carl Gustaf, St. Barthélemy.** Sweeping views of Gustavia harbor and delectable classic French cuisine with an island accent are the draws here. **$$$–$$$$**

★ **Chez Martine, St. Martin.** Chef Thierry de Launay studied under Joël Robuchon; his fois gras claims a loyal following. **$$$$**

★ **Anacaona, Providenciales, Turks and Caicos.** This is a true gourmet dining experience, minus the attitude. Traditional French recipes are combined with Caribbean fruits, vegetables, and spices. **$$–$$$**

★ **Virgilio's, St. Thomas, U.S. Virgin Islands.** Come here for some of the best northern Italian cuisine in the islands, and don't leave without having a Virgilio's cappuccino, a chocolate-and-coffee drink so rich it's dessert. **$$$$**

FESTIVALS AND SEASONAL EVENTS

Regardless of when Carnival season starts on each island, it always means days and nights of continuous partying. There's a celebration going on from January through August, it's just a matter of being on the right island.

The first Carnival of the season is also the longest. **Martinique's** Carnival begins in early January and lasts through the first day of Lent, in mid-February. **Guadeloupe's** Carnival starts a day later and also continues until Lent, finishing with a parade of floats and costumes on Mardi Gras and a huge bash on Ash Wednesday. **Curaçao's** Carnival season lasts from late January to early February. All of these Carnivals feature music, dance, and a costumed parade.

February brings a flood of Carnival events, including those on **Bonaire, Puerto Rico, St. Lucia, St. Martin** (the French side of the island), **St. Barthélemy,** and **Trinidad and Tobago,** all of which combine feasting, dancing, music, and parades. During Carnival on **Trinidad and Tobago,** adults and children alike are swept up in the excitement of Playing Mas'—the state of surrendering completely to the rapture of fantastic spectacle, parades, music, and dancing.

Spring brings the **St. Thomas (U.S. Virgin Islands)** and the **Sint Maarten** (Dutch side of the island) Carnivals in April and the **Cayman Islands'** Carnival, which begins on Grand Cayman in May. In July, the season reaches **Saba** and the **Dominican Republic,** whose popular 10-day Merengue Festival features entertainment from outdoor bands and orchestras and the best cuisine from local hotel chefs. **Anguilla** and the **British Virgin Islands** start Carnival in early August with street dancing, calypso competitions, the Carnival Queen Coronation, and sumptuous beach barbecues. The **Turks and Caicos** islands finish the string of festivals during the last days of the month.

Many other festivals celebrate the islands' rich local cultures. Barbados's **Holetown Festival** commemorates the first settlement of Barbados on February 17, 1627, with a week of fairs, street markets, and revelry. The Historical and Cultural Foundations organize the **St. Martin Food Festival** in May. During the **Tobago Heritage Festival** in July, each village on Trinidad and Tobago mounts a different show or festivity. Beginning in July and continuing through August, Barbados celebrates the **Crop-Over Festival,** a monthlong cheer for the end of the sugarcane harvest. Calypsonians battle for the coveted Calypso Monarch award, and Bajan cooking abounds at the massive Bridgetown Market street fair. On a Sunday in early August, Guadeloupe holds a **Fête des Cuisinières** and celebrates the masters of Creole cuisine with a five-hour banquet that is open to the public. The **Hatillo Festival of the Masks,** held in December in Puerto Rico, is a carnival featuring folk music and dancing, as well as parades in which islanders don brightly colored masks and costumes.

Sports enthusiasts, tourists, and islanders enjoy the many regattas. Grenada's **New Year Fiesta Yacht Race** in late January is highlighted by the Around Grenada sailing contest.

Antigua's **Sailing Week** in April brings together more than 300 yachts from around the world. The British Virgin Islands' **Spring Regatta,** the **Curaçao Regatta,** the **Grenada Easter Regatta,** and the U.S. Virgin Islands' **International Rolex Cup Regatta** take place in April. Boat racing is the national sport in Anguilla, and the most important competitions take place on **Anguilla Day,** May 30. Just about every type of competition that can be held on or in water constitutes the weeklong **Aqua Action Festival** held in St. Lucia at the end of June. Canoe racing, Sunfish sailing, windsurfing, sportfishing, waterskiing, and a nonmariners race are some of the main attractions. The U.S. and British Virgin Islands share the **Hook In & Hold On Boardsailing Regatta** in June and July. Grenada's annual **Carriacou Regatta,** which takes place on this island some 16 miles to the north, brings a week of racing and partying at the end of July.

Martinique hosts the **Tour des Yoles Rondes** point-to-point yawl race in early August, and the annual **Sailing Regatta** in Bonaire takes place in October. The **Route du Rosé**, a transatlantic regatta of tall ships that set sail from St-Tropez in early November, is welcomed to St. Barts in December with a round of festivities.

Music lovers should also take note of several other annual events. In January, St. Barthélemy is host to an international collection of soloists and musicians as part of the **Annual St. Barts Music Festival.** The **Barbados Caribbean Jazz Festival** in Bridgetown features performances of original compositions and traditional jazz for three days at the end of May. At the end of June, the **Aruba Jazz and Latin**

Music Festival is held in Oranjestad, offering well-known entertainers performing Latin, pop, jazz, and salsa music at Mansur Stadium. And the **August Reggae Sunsplash International Music Festival** is getting hotter every year, as the best, brightest, and newest of the reggae stars gather to perform in open-air concerts in MoBay on Jamaica.

2 Anguilla

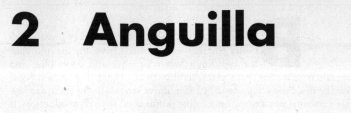

Updated by
Pamela
Acheson

BEACH LOVERS BECOME GIDDY when they first see Anguilla (rhymes with vanilla) from the air and spot the blindingly white beaches and neon blue and aquamarine waters that rim this scrubby piece of land. The highest point on the dry, limestone isle is 213 feet above sea level, and there are neither streams nor rivers, only saline ponds used for salt production. If you don't like beaches, you won't find a lot to do here. There are no glittering casinos or nightclubs and no duty-free shops stuffed with irresistible buys (although you're only about 30 watery minutes away from the bustle of St. Martin/St. Maarten's resorts and casinos).

Anguilla's beauty lies in its stunning beaches, its exceptionally clear waters, and its coral reefs. Peace, quiet, and pampering account for the island's popularity among travelers searching for a Caribbean getaway. You can swim, do some diving, practice your backhand, catch up on your reading, compare the merits of the beaches, or just find one that suits you and sink down on it to worship the sun. Times are slowly changing, however, and there are now six traffic lights on the island instead of the solitary signal of years past.

This is the most northerly of the Leeward Islands, lying between the Caribbean Sea and the Atlantic Ocean. Stretching from northeast to southwest, it's about 16 miles long and only 3 miles across at its widest point. *Anguilla* means "eel" in Italian, but the island's name may also be a derivative of either the Spanish *anguila* or French *anguille,* both of which also mean "eel". Archaeological evidence indicates that the island was inhabited as many as 2,000 years ago by Indians who named the island Malliouhana, a more mellifluous title that's been adopted by some of the island's shops and resorts.

In 1631, the Dutch built a fort here, but no one has been able to locate its site. English settlers from St. Kitts colonized the island in 1650, and, despite a brief period of independence with St. Kitts–Nevis in the 1960s, Anguilla has remained a British colony ever since.

There were the obligatory Caribbean battles between the English and the French, and in 1688 the island was attacked by a party of "wild Irishmen," some of whom settled on the island. But Anguilla's primary discontent was over its status vis-à-vis the other British colonies, particularly St. Kitts. In the 18th century, Anguilla, as part of the Leeward Islands, was administered by British officials in Antigua. In 1816, Britain split the islands into two groups, one of them composed of Anguilla, St. Kitts, Nevis, and the British Virgin Islands and administered by a magistrate in St. Kitts. For more than 150 years thereafter various island units and federations were formed and disbanded, with Anguilla all the while simmering over its subordinate status and enforced union with St. Kitts. Anguillans twice petitioned for direct rule from Britain, and twice were ignored. In 1967, when St. Kitts, Nevis, and Anguilla became an associated state, the mouse roared, kicked St. Kitts policemen off the island, held a self-rule referendum, and for two years conducted its own affairs. In 1968, a senior British official arrived and remained for a year working with the Anguilla Council. A second referendum in 1969 confirmed the desire of the Anguillans to remain apart from St. Kitts–Nevis, and the following month a British "peacekeeping force" parachuted down to the island, where it was greeted with flowers, fluttering Union Jacks, and friendly smiles. When the paratroopers were not working on their tans, they helped a team of royal engineers improve the port and build roads and schools.

Today Anguilla elects a House of Assembly and its own leader to handle internal affairs, while a British governor is responsible for public service, the police, and judiciary and external affairs.

The territory of Anguilla includes a few islets or cays, such as Scrub Island to the east, Dog Island, Prickly Pear Cays, Sandy Island, and Sombrero Island. The island's population numbers about 8,000, predominantly of African descent but also including descendants of Europeans, especially Irish. Historically, because the limestone land was hardly fit for agriculture, attempts at slavery and colonization never lasted long; thus Anguilla doesn't bear the scars of slavery found on so many Caribbean islands. Because the island couldn't be farmed, Anguillans became experts at making a living from the sea and are known for their boatbuilding and fishing skills. Tourism is the growth industry of the island's stable economy, but the government is determined to keep expansion at a slow and cautious pace to protect the island's natural resources and beauty. New hotels, scattered throughout the islands, are being kept small, select, and casino-free, and promotion of the island emphasizes its high-quality service, serene surroundings, and friendly people.

Before You Go

Tourist Information

Contact the very helpful **Anguilla Tourist Information and Reservation Office** (c/o Medhurst & Associates, 775 Park Ave., Huntington, NY 11743, ☎ 516/425–0900 or 800/553–4939, FAX 516/425–0903). In the United Kingdom, contact the **Anguilla Tourist Office** (3 Epirus Rd., London SW6 7UJ, ☎ 0171/937–7725).

Arriving and Departing

BY PLANE

American Airlines (☎ 800/433–7300) is the major airline with nonstop flights from the continental United States to its hub in San Juan, from which the airline's **American Eagle** flies three times daily (twice daily off-season) to Anguilla. **Windward Islands Airways** (Winair; ☎ 809/775–0183) wings in daily from St. Thomas and at least three times a day from St. Maarten's Juliana Airport. **LIAT** (☎ 809/465–2286) comes in from Antigua, Nevis, St. Kitts, St. Maarten, and St. Thomas. **Air Anguilla** (☎ 809/497–2643) offers several flights daily from St. Maarten, the U.S. Virgin Islands, and the British Virgin Islands and provides air-taxi service on request from neighboring islands, as does **Tyden Air** (☎ 809/497–2717).

FROM THE AIRPORT

At **Wallblake Airport** you'll find taxis lined up to meet the planes. A trip from the airport to Sandy Ground will cost about $8, to west-end resorts between $14 and $20. Fares, which are government regulated, should be listed in brochures the drivers carry. If you are traveling in a group, the fares apply to the first two people; each additional passenger adds $3 to the total. Tipping is welcome.

BY BOAT

Ferryboats run frequently between Anguilla and St. Martin. They leave from Blowing Point on Anguilla every half hour from 7:30 to 5 and from Marigot on St. Martin every half hour from 8 to 5:30. There are also evening ferries that leave from Blowing Point at 6 and 9:15 and from Marigot at 7 and 10:45. You pay the $9 one-way fare ($11 evenings) on board and a $2 departure tax before boarding. Don't buy a round-trip ticket, because it restricts you to the boat on which it is purchased. On very windy days the 20-minute trip can be bouncy, and if you suffer from motion sickness, you may want medication. An information booth outside the customs shed in Blowing Point, Anguilla, is usually open daily from 8:30 to 5, but sometimes the attendant wanders off.

FROM THE DOCKS
Taxis are always waiting to pick passengers up at the Blowing Point landing. It costs $12 to get to the Malliouhana Hotel, $15 to the Cap Juluca Hotel, and $17 to the most distant hotels. Taxi drivers should have a list of fares, which are fixed by the government.

Passports and Visas

U.S. and Canadian citizens need proof of identity. A passport is preferred (even one that has expired within the last five years). A photo ID, such as a driver's license, *along with* a birth certificate (with raised seal), voter registration card, or naturalization papers is also acceptable. Visitor's passes are valid for stays of up to three months. British citizens must have a passport. All visitors must also have a return or ongoing ticket.

Language

English, with a strong West Indian lilt, is spoken on Anguilla.

Precautions

The manchineel tree, which resembles an apple tree, shades many beaches. The tree bears poisonous fruit, and the sap from the tree causes painful blisters. Avoid sitting beneath the tree, because even dew or raindrops falling from the leaves can blister your skin.

Be *sure* to take along insect repellent—mosquitoes can be pesky in the late afternoon.

Anguilla is a quiet, relatively safe island, but there's no point in tempting fate by leaving your valuables unattended in your hotel room, on the beach, or in your car.

Staying in Anguilla

Important Addresses

Tourist Information: The **Anguilla Tourist Office** (Social Security Bldg., the Valley, ☎ 809/497–2759) is open weekdays 8–noon and 1–4.

EMERGENCIES
Police and **fire:** Emergency is now 911. For non-emergencies, dial 809/497–2333. **Hospital:** There is a 24-hour emergency room at the new **Princess Alexandra Hospital** (Stoney Ground, ☎ 809/497–2551). **Ambulance:** ☎ 809/497–2551. **Pharmacies:** The **Government Pharmacy** (the Valley, ☎ 809/497–2551) is located in Princess Alexandra Hospital; the **Paramount Pharmacy** (Waterswamp, ☎ 809/497–2366) is open Monday–Saturday 8:30–8:30 and has a 24-hour emergency service.

Currency

Legal tender here is the Eastern Caribbean dollar (E.C.), but U.S. dollars are widely accepted. (You'll often get change in E.C. dollars.) The E.C. dollar is fairly stable relative to the U.S. dollar, hovering between E.C.$2.60 and $2.70 to U.S.$1. Credit cards are not always accepted, and it's hard to predict where you'll need cash. Some resorts will only settle in cash; a few will also accept personal checks. Be sure to carry lots of small bills; change for a $20 bill is often difficult to obtain. Note: Prices quoted are in U.S. dollars unless indicated otherwise.

Taxes and Service Charges

The government imposes an 8% tax on accommodations. The departure tax is $10 at the airport, $2 if you leave by boat. A 10% service charge is added to all hotel bills and most restaurant bills. If you're not certain about the restaurant service charge, ask. If you are particularly pleased with the service, you can certainly leave a little extra. Tip taxi drivers 10% of the fare.

Guided Tours

A round-the-island tour by taxi will take about 2½ hours and will cost $40 for one or two people, $5 for each additional passenger. **Bennie's Tours** (Blowing Point, ☎ 809/497–2788) and **Malliouhana Travel and Tours** (the Valley, ☎ 809/497–2431) put together personalized package tours of the island.

Getting Around

TAXIS

Taxi rates are regulated by the government, and there are fixed fares from point to point. Posted rates are for one to two people; each additional person pays $3.

RENTAL CARS

This is your best bet for maximum mobility if you're comfortable driving on the left and don't mind some jostling. Anguilla's roads are generally paved (in a manner of speaking), but those that are not can be incredibly rutted, even those leading to a fancy hotel. Observe the 30 miles per hour speed limit, and watch out for the four-legged critters—goats, sheep, and cows—that amble across the road. To rent a car you'll need a valid driver's license and a local license, which can be obtained for $6 at any of the car rental agencies. Among the agencies are **Avis** (☎ 809/497–6221 or 800/331–2112), **Budget** (☎ 809/497–2217 or 800/527–0700), **Connors (National)** (☎ 809/497–6433 or 800/328–4567), and **Island Car Rental** (☎ 809/497–2723). Count on $35 to $45 per day's rental, plus insurance. Motorcycles and scooters are available for about $30 per day from **R & M Cycle** (☎ 809/497–2430).

Telephones and Mail

To call Anguilla from the United States, dial area code 809 + 497 + the local four-digit number. International direct dial is available on the island. **Cable & Wireless** (Wallblake Rd., ☎ 809/497–3100) is open weekdays 8–6, Saturday 9–1, Sunday and holidays 10–2 and sells Caribbean Phone Cards ($5, $10, $20 denominations) for use in specially marked phone booths. The card can be used for local calls and calls to other islands. You can also use the card to call the United States and, in this case, bill the call to a MasterCard or Visa. To make a local call on the island, just dial the four-digit number. Inside the departure lounge at the Blowing Point Ferry and at the airport, there is an AT&T USADirect access telephone for collect or credit card calls to the United States.

Airmail letters to the United States cost E.C.60¢; postcards, E.C.25¢.

Opening and Closing Times

Banks are open Monday–Thursday 8–3 and Friday 8–5. Shopping hours vary. No two shops seem to have the same hours, but many are certainly open between 10 and 4. Call, or ask at the tourist office for opening and closing times, or adopt the island way of doing things; if they're not open when you stop by, stop by again.

Exploring Anguilla

Numbers in the margin correspond to points of interest on the Anguilla map.

Exploring on Anguilla is mostly about checking out the spectacular beaches and classy resorts. There are only a few roads on the island, but none of them are marked, so it's still pretty easy to get lost your

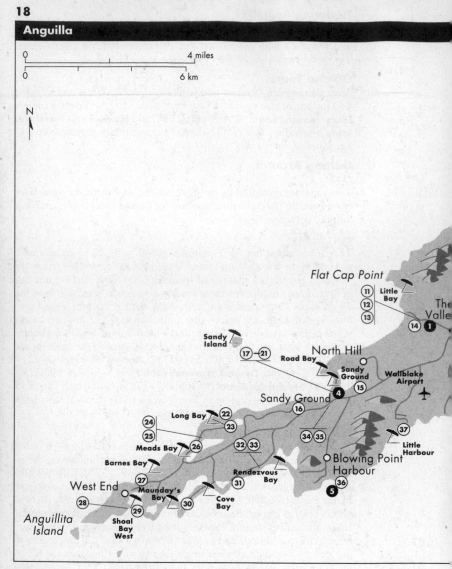

0 — 4 miles
0 — 6 km

N

Flat Cap Point
⑪ Little Bay
⑫
⑬
⑭ ①
The Valle

Sandy Island
⑰ — ㉑
Road Bay
North Hill
Sandy Ground
④ ⑮
Wallblake Airport

Sandy Ground
⑯

Long Bay
㉒
㉓
㉔
㉕
Meads Bay ㉖
Barnes Bay
㉜ ㉝
㉞ ㉟
⑦
Little Harbour

West End
㉗
Maunday's Bay
㉛
Rendezvous Bay
Blowing Point Harbour
㊱

Anguillita Island
㉘
㉙
Shoal Bay West
㉚
Cove Bay
⑤

Exploring
Blowing Point Harbour, **5**
The Fountain, **2**
Sandy Ground, **4**
Sandy Hill Bay, **3**
Wallblake House, **1**

Dining
Aquarium, **34**
Arlo's, **16**
Blanchard's, **22**
The Cafe at Cove Castles, **28**
Casablanca, **29**
Cross Roads, **11**

The Ferryboat Inn, **36**
Hibernia, **6**
Johnno's, **18**
Koal Keel, **10**
La Fontana, **9**
Le Bistro Creole, **23**

Lucy's Harbour View Restaurant, **35**
Malliouhana, **25**
The Old House, **15**
The Palm Court, **37**
Paradise Cafe, **29**
Pepper Pot, **12**
Pimms, **30**

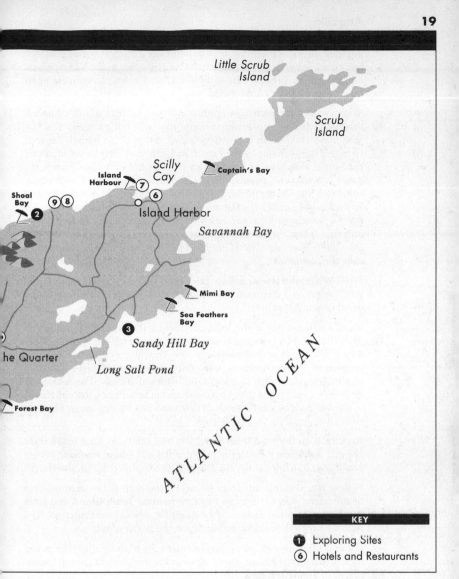

Little Scrub Island

Scrub Island

Scilly Cay

Island Harbour

Captain's Bay

Shoal Bay

Island Harbor

Savannah Bay

Mimi Bay

Sea Feathers Bay

Sandy Hill Bay

he Quarter

Long Salt Pond

Forest Bay

ATLANTIC OCEAN

KEY
- **1** Exploring Sites
- **6** Hotels and Restaurants

Riviera Bar & Restaurant, **17**
Roy's, **14**
Smuggler's Grill, **38**
Tropical Penguin, **21**

Lodging
Arawak Beach Resort, **7**
Cap Juluca, **30**
Casablanca Resort, **31**
Cinnamon Reef Beach Club, **37**

Coccoloba Plantation, **27**
Ferryboat Inn, **36**
Fountain Beach, **9**
Frangipani Beach Club, **26**
Inter-Island Hotel, **13**
La Sirena, **24**

Malliouhana, **25**
Mariners, **19**
Pineapple Beach Club, **32**
Rendezvous Bay Hotel, **33**
Shoal Bay Villas, **8**
Syd–an's, **20**

first time out. Having a map, and checking it frequently against passing landmarks, is essential. If you didn't get a map at the airport, the ferry dock, or your hotel, head to the tourist office in the Valley, where administrative offices, banks, markets, and a few boutiques, guest houses, and eateries are located.

 While you're in town you might want to visit the island's historic **Wallblake House,** a plantation house that was built around 1787 by Will Blake (Wallblake is probably a corruption of his name). Legends of murders, invasions by the French in 1796, and high living surround the house. Now owned and actively used by the Catholic Church, the estate has spacious rooms, some with tray ceilings edged with handsome carving. On the grounds are an ancient vaulted stone cistern and an outbuilding called the Bakery (which wasn't used for breadmaking but for baking turkeys and hams). The oven measures 12 feet across and rises 3 feet up through a stepped chimney. *Cross Roads, the Valley. Call Father John, ☎ 809/497–2405, to make an appointment to tour the plantation.*

From **Wallblake House** follow the sign to the Cottage Hospital, and you'll come to a dirt road that leads to **Crocus Bay** and several strips of white-sand beaches.

Head northeast out of the Valley, following the occasional marker to Shoal Bay and its beautiful beach. As you approach the coast at **Shoal Bay,** you'll pass near the **Fountain,** where Arawak petroglyphs have been discovered. Presently closed to the public, the area is being researched by the Anguilla Archaeological and Historical Society. The AAHS (☎ 809/497–2767) plans to open a museum in the former Customs House in the Valley. The next stretch of this road is a bumpy mess. Hang in there. The beach is worth the trip.

Backtrack on the road from Shoal Bay and take your first real left. In about 2 miles you'll reach the fishing village of **Island Harbour,** where you'll see colorful, handcrafted fishing boats pulled up on the shore.

Follow rutted dirt roads from Island Harbour to the easternmost tip of the island. On the way to the aptly named **Scrub Island** and **Little Scrub Island** off the eastern tip of Anguilla, you'll pass Captain's Bay, with its isolated, windswept beach, on the north coast.

If you want to skip the easternmost end of the island, follow the paved road south (not the road you came in on) from Island Harbour. It continues to **Sandy Hill Bay.**

Four miles farther down the coast, beyond the Long Salt Pond, is **Forest Bay,** a fit place for scuba diving. South of Forest Bay lies **Little Harbour,** with a lovely horseshoe-shape bay and the splendid **Cinnamon Reef Beach Club.**

From Little Harbour, follow the paved road past Wallblake Airport, just outside the Valley, and turn left on the main road. In about a mile, bear right, following signs for Sandy Ground, then continue for another 2 miles to **Sandy Ground,** one of the most active and most developed of the island's beaches. It is home to the **Mariners** resort, **Tamariain Watersports,** a dive shop, a commercial pier, and several small guest houses and restaurants. A ferry leaves frequently from here for Sandy Island, 2 miles offshore.

If you backtrack from Sandy Ground to the main road you were on and continue south, you pass (at the light) the turnoff to **Blowing**

Point Harbour, where you docked if you arrived by ferry from Marigot in St. Martin.

TIME OUT If you plan to picnic (on the beach or in your room), try the **Fat Cat** (George Hill, ☎ 809/497–2307) for escargots to go, as well as take-out quiche, soups, chili, chicken, and conch dishes. **Amy's Bakery** (Blowing Point, ☎ 809/497–6775) turns out homemade pies, cakes, tarts, cookies, and breads.

The main paved road continues more or less down the center of the island. Teeth-jarring dirt roads lead to the coasts, the beaches, and some of the best resorts on the island.

On the south coast, just west of Blowing Point, is the crescent-shape beach that's home to **Rendezvous Bay,** the island's first hotel, built in 1959.

Farther south, you'll pass a number of fancy resorts, all on gorgeous public beaches. Left-hand turnoffs will take you to the **Casablanca Resort** and to **Cap Juluca,** which is on beautiful **Maunday's Bay.** Right-hand turnoffs head to **Meads Bay,** where you'll find the **Malliouhana** and the **Frangipani Beach Club,** and to **Barnes Bay** and **Coccoloba Plantation.** At the very end of the road you'll come to **Shoal Bay West** and the striking architecture of **Cove Castles.**

Beaches

The island's star attractions are its dozens and dozens of dazzling, white-sand beaches. Each one is different. You'll find wild Atlantic waves, supercalm bays, dunes, long beaches that are great for walking, deserted beaches, and beaches lined with bars and restaurants. Good snorkeling is almost everywhere, but nude bathing is a no-no.

Unfortunately it's no longer a secret that **Shoal Bay** is one of the prettiest beaches in the Caribbean. But this 2-mile L-shape beach of talcum-powder-soft white sand is definitely still worth a visit. There are beach chairs, umbrellas, a backdrop of sea-grape and coconut trees, and for seafood and tropical drinks there's Trader Vic's, Uncle Ernie, and the Round Rock. Souvenir shops for T-shirts, suntan lotion, and the like abound. There's good snorkeling in the offshore coral reefs, and the water-sports center here can arrange diving, sailing, and fishing trips.

The calm waters of **Island Harbour** are surrounded by a long, slender beach. For centuries Anguillans have put out from these sands in colorful, handmade fishing boats to seek the day's catch. There are several beach bars and restaurants, and this is the departure point for the three-minute boat ride to **Scilly Cay.** You can get snorkeling equipment on the boat that goes to Scilly Cay, but at times the waters are too rough to see much. A beach bar on Scilly Cay serves drinks and grilled seafood.

Peaceful isolation at **Captain's Bay** rewards you for making the grueling, four-wheel-drive-only trip along the inhospitable dirt road that leads to the northeastern end of the island. The surf here slaps the sands with a vengeance, and the undertow is quite strong. Wading is the safest water sport.

Mimi Bay is a difficult-to-reach, isolated, ½-mile-long beach east of Sea Feathers. The trip is worth it. When the surf is not too rough, the barrier reef makes for great snorkeling.

Also not far from Sea Feathers is **Sandy Hill,** a base for fishermen. Here you can buy fresh fish and lobster right off the boats and snorkel in the warm waters. Don't plan to sunbathe—the beach is quite narrow here.

Rendezvous Bay is 1½ miles of pearl-white sand. Here the water is calm, and there's a great view of St. Martin. The Pineapple Beach Club's open-air beach bar is handy for snacks and frosty island drinks.

The good news and the bad news about **Cove Bay** is the same—it's virtually deserted. There are no restaurants or bars, just calm waters, coconut trees, and soft sand that stretches down to Maunday's Bay.

One of the most popular beaches, wide, mile-long **Maunday's Bay** is known for good swimming and snorkeling; you can rent water-sports gear at Tropical Watersports. Try Pimms at Cap Juluca for fine food and drink (*see* Dining, *below*).

Adjacent to Maunday's Bay is **Shoal Bay West,** a dazzling beach with several striking villa complexes, including the sculpturelike, futuristic Cove Castles. Stop for lunch at the Paradise Cafe (*see* Dining, *below*), and ask someone there to point out the best snorkeling spots. Beachcombers may find lovely conch shells here.

Barnes Bay is a superb spot for windsurfing and snorkeling. The elegant Coccoloba Plantation perches above and offers a poolside bar. In high season this beach can get a bit crowded with day-trippers from St. Martin.

The clear blue waters of **Road Bay** beach, in the area often referred to as Sandy Ground, are usually dotted with yachts. The Mariners resort, several restaurants (*see* Lodging, *below*), a water-sports center, and lots of windsurfing and waterskiing activity make this an active commercial area. It's a typical Caribbean scene daily, as fishermen set out in their boats and goats ramble the littoral at will. The snorkeling is not very good here, but do visit this bay for its glorious sunset vistas.

Sandy Island, nestled in coral reefs about 2 miles offshore from Road Bay, is a tiny speck of sand and sea and a few spindly palm trees. From the distance it has the look of a classic "deserted island," but it's got the modern-day comforts of a beach boutique, beach bar, and restaurant, and the use of snorkeling gear and underwater cameras here is free. There is a ferry that heads there every hour from Sandy Ground.

At **Little Bay** sheer cliffs embroidered with agave and creeping vines plummet to a small gray-sand beach, usually accessible only by water (it's a favored spot for snorkeling and night dives). But virtually assured of total privacy, the hale and hearty can clamber down a rope to explore the caves and surrounding reef.

Sports and the Outdoors

Cycling

There are plenty of flat stretches, making wheeling pretty easy. Bikes can be rented at **Boothes** (☎ 809/497–2075) and at **Boo's Cycle Rental** (☎ 809/497–2323), where you can also rent mopeds and scooters. **Multiscenic Tours** (☎ 809/497–5810) rents mountain bikes.

Deep-Sea Fishing

Albacore, dolphin, and kingfish are among the sea creatures angled after off Anguilla's shores. Trips can be arranged through Elbert or Trevor Richardson in Long Bay (☎ 809/497–6397); or you can head to Sandy Ground and see which of the many locals who provide trips is available. Fishing tackle, diving gear, and other sports equipment is available at the **Tackle Box Sports Center** (☎ 809/497–2896).

Fitness
Lest you go flabby lolling around on the beach, you'll find exercise equipment, aerobics, and martial arts instruction at **Highway Gym** (George Hill Rd., ☎ 809/497–2363).

Jogging
There are miles and miles of broad, flat beaches. Just pick one out and jog away.

Sea Excursions
Picnic, swimming, and diving excursions to Prickly Pear, Sandy Island, and Scilly Cay are available through **Sandy Island Enterprises** (☎ 809/497–6395), **Enchanted Island Cruises** (☎ 809/497–3111), **Suntastic Cruises** (☎ 809/497–3400), and **Tropical Watersports** (☎ 809/497–6666 or 809/497–6779). **Princess Soya** (☎ 809/497–2671) offers snorkeling trips and half-day sails on a 50-foot catamaran.

Tennis
For professional instruction, contact the Peter Burwash International pro at **Coccoloba Plantation** (☎ 809/497–6871), where there are two lighted courts. There are two courts at the **Carimar Beach Club** (☎ 809/497–6881); four Laykold (hard) courts at **Malliouhana** (☎ 809/497–6111); three (hard) courts at **Cap Juluca** (☎ 809/497-6666); two Deco Turf tournament courts at **Cinnamon Reef** (☎ 809/497–2727); two courts at the **Fountain Beach and Tennis Club** (☎ 809/497–6395) and **Rendezvous Bay** (☎ 809/497–6549); and one court each at **Cove Castles** (☎ 809/497-6801), the **Mariners** (☎ 809/497–2671), **Masara** (☎ 809/497–3400), **Pelicans** (☎ 809/497–6593), **Sea Grapes** (☎ 809/497–6433), and **Spindrift Apartments** (☎ 809/497–4164).

Water Sports
The major resorts offer complimentary Windsurfers, paddleboats, and water skis to their guests. If your hotel has no water-sports facilities, you can get in gear at **Tropical Watersports** (☎ 809/497–6666 or 809/497–6779), at Cap Juluca resort, or **Tamariain Watersports** (☎ 809/497–2020). Tamariain Watersports also has PADI instructors, short resort courses, and more than a dozen dive sites; and *Sundancer,* Tamariain's 30-foot powerboat, is available for charters. Tropical Watersports rents Sunfish and Hobie Cats. Sailboats and speedboats can be rented at **Sandy Island Enterprises** (☎ 809/497–6395).

Shopping

Shopping tips can be found in the informative free publications *Anguilla Life* and *What We Do in Anguilla,* but you have to be a really dedicated shopper to peel yourself off the beach and poke around in Anguilla's few shops. If you really want to shop, catch the ferry to Marigot on St. Martin and spend the day in chic boutiques showcasing the latest in Italian and French fashion.

Clothing
La Romana (Meads Bay, ☎ 809/497–6181), a miniversion of the well-known international specialty boutique, is the place to go for swimwear, Fendi fashions, fine luggage, and accessories. The **Boutique at Malliouhana** (Meads Bay, ☎ 809/497–6111) is the most upscale shop on Anguilla, selling such designer specialties as jewelry by Oro De Sol, La Perla swimwear, Go Silk resort wear, and Robert LaRoche sunglasses. **Whispers** (Cap Juluca, ☎ 809/497–6666) carries Caribbean handcrafts

and stylish resort wear for men and women. The **Sunshine Shop** (South Hill, ☎ 809/497–6964) stocks cotton *pareos* (Polynesian-style wraps), silk-screen items, cotton resort wear, and hand-painted Haitian wood items. **La Sirena Boutique** (Meads Bay, ☎ 809/467–6827) is bursting with colorful dresses, slacks, belts, and other accessories. **Beach Stuff** (Back St., South Hill, ☎ 809/497–6814), in its brightly painted building, attracts the younger crowd with bathing suits and cover-ups, sunglasses, T-shirts, and other sportswear. **The Valley Gap** (Shoal Bay Beach, ☎ 809/497–2754) sells a selection of local crafts, plus T-shirts and swimwear. **Vanhelle Boutique** (Sandy Ground, ☎ 809/497–2965) is a little shop with an appealing selection of gift items, as well as Brazilian swimsuits for men and women. **Java Wraps** (George Hill Rd., ☎ 809/497–5497), a small outpost of the Caribbean chain, carries superb batik clothing for the whole family. **Caribbean Style** (Rendezvous Bay, ☎ 809/497–6717) has a small but eclectic collection of everything from sandals to jewelry to furniture. **Oluwakemi's Afrocentric Boutique** (Lansome Rd., the Valley, ☎ 809/497–5411) sells books, sandals, umbrellas, jewelry, T-shirts, hats, and a variety of other garments. You can also choose from an array of fabrics and have virtually any item of apparel custom-made. **Objets D'Art Collectibles** (Warden's Place, the Valley, ☎ 809/497–2787) is a gallery that also sells "wearable art," sandals, jewelry, and fabrics.

Native Crafts

Anguilla Arts and Crafts Center (the Valley, ☎ 809/497–2200) carries a wide selection of island crafts. **Alicea's Place** (the Quarter, ☎ 809/497–3540), a small boutique, sells locally made ceramics and pottery. **New World Gallery** (the Valley, ☎ 809/407–5950) has frequent exhibits of local art and sells artwork, jewelry, textiles, and antiquities. **Scruples Gift Shop** (Social Security Bldg., ☎ 809/497–2800) offers simple gift items such as shells, handmade baskets, wood dolls, hand-crocheted mats, lace tablecloths, and bedspreads. **Devonish Cotton Gin Art Gallery** (the Valley, ☎ 809/497–2949) purveys the wood, stone, and clay creations of Courtney Devonish, an internationally known potter and sculptor, as well as works by other prominent local artists. **Cheddie's Carving Shop** (the Cove, ☎ 809/497–6027), just down the road from Coccoloba Plantation, showcases Cheddie's own fanciful creatures crafted out of wonderfully textured woods, including mahogany, walnut, and driftwood. Even the whimsically carved desk and balustrade in his studio testify to his vivid imagination. Many artists hold open studios; the tourist office can provide brochures.

Dining

Anguilla's eateries range from the truly elegant to down-home seaside shacks. Call ahead—in the winter to make a reservation and in the summer to see if the place you've chosen is open. Most restaurants not affiliated with a hotel tack on an additional 5% to the service charge if you pay by credit card.

What to Wear

During the day, casual clothes are widely accepted: Shorts will probably be fine, although many establishments don't allow bathing suits. In the evening, a sundress or nice casual pants are appropriate. Some hotel restaurants expect a degree of formality and may have a jacket requirement in high season; ask when you make reservations.

CATEGORY	COST*
$$$$	over $45
$$$	$35–$45
$$	$25–$35
$	under $25

per person, excluding drinks, service, and sales tax (8%)

$$$$ **The Cafe at Cove Castles.** Elegant, intimate dinners are served here overlooking beautiful Shoal Bay. Each season a new menu of consistently excellent dishes combines the best of Caribbean and French cooking. Past favorites include West Indian chicken stew, lobster medallions with ginger sauce, veal chops in truffle cream sauce, and fresh pasta with julienned vegetables. ✗ *Shoal Bay West,* ☎ *809/497–6801. Reservations advised. AE, MC. Closed Sept. and Oct. No lunch.*

$$$$ **Casablanca.** Multi-arched ceilings covered with pastel Moroccan mosaics—and nighttime views of the lights of St. Martin twinkling across the water—create a dramatic atmosphere. Grouper steamed with pepper and lime and served with cornmeal pancakes, Cornish hen roasted with almonds and raisins, and filet mignon with an onion and marsala compote are a few of the entrées found on the eclectic menu. Pistachio crème brûlée may sound a bit unorthodox, but it's the hit of the dessert list. ✗ *Rendezvous Bay,* ☎ *809/497–6779. Reservations advised. AE, MC, V.*

$$$$ **Malliouhana.** Sparkling crystal and fine china, exquisite service, and
★ a spectacularly romantic, candlelit, open-air setting are the perfect match for this restaurant's exceptional haute French cuisine. Michel Rostang, renowned for his Paris boîte, created the menu and is still the consulting chef. Try the goat cheese wrapped in fresh salmon or warm stewed lobster with pumpkin and French corn salad, then segue into lobster medallions with seasoned polenta or Bresse chicken breasts stuffed with asparagus. Don't pass up desserts, especially the roast pear in Sauternes with walnut brioche and cinnamon ice cream. The wine cellar contains about 25,000 bottles. ✗ *Meads Bay,* ☎ *809/497–6111. Reservations required. AE, MC, V. Closed Sept. and Oct.*

$$$$ **Pimms.** You expect Rudolph Valentino to sweep in beneath the domes, arches, and billowing canvas of this Arabian Nights setting on the edge of a half-moon bay. Water laps almost unnervingly close to the outer tables, but from them you can see brightly colored tropical fish swim up for a spare bit of your roll. French chefs prepare picture-perfect plates of mostly Continental-style items with a touch of Creole or West Indian flavor. Entrées include grilled Black Angus sirloin and fresh lobster or grouper in a spicy tomato sauce. ✗ *Cap Juluca, Maunday's Bay,* ☎ *809/497–6666. Reservations required. AE, MC, V.*

$$$ **Le Bistro Creole.** The owners of this appealing new spot are French,
★ and the menu offers a delightful blend of French and Caribbean cooking. Enjoy the open-air breezes wafting through the large open windows as you choose between an appetizer of tuna carpaccio or fried fish fritters. Entrées of fresh lobster and fish are menu standards, as are grilled filet mignon and lamb served in a garlic cream sauce. Bouillabaisse is the house specialty. ✗ *Long Bay,* ☎ *809/497–6700. Reservations advised in season. MC, V. No lunch.*

$$$ **Blanchard's.** Restaurateurs Bob and Melinda Blanchard's newest ven-
★ ture is set amidst lush tropical greenery. Start with a drink at the stunning mahogany-and-coral bar in the lounge. Your meal may include elements of Cajun, Caribbean, and Asian cooking. Green chili corn cakes, wild mushroom ragout, or Indonesian beef satay make good starters and can be followed by swordfish stuffed with leeks and fontina cheese or red snapper brushed with a balsamic mango glaze. Fish is the house

specialty, but you can also order Black Angus hand-cut steaks, free-range chicken, or one of the daily pasta specials. Desserts are tempting, especially the cappuccino brownies and a remarkable gingerbread box filled with warm bananas and cinnamon cream. There is also a 2,000-bottle wine cellar and a selection of fine Armagnacs and cognacs. ✕ *Long Bay,* ☎ *809/497–6100. Reservations advised. AE, MC, V. Closed Tues. No lunch.*

$$$ Hibernia. One of the island's most creative menus is served in this delightful cottage restaurant, with wood beams, bamboo furniture, raspberry-hued latticework, and East Indian paintings. Unorthodox yet delectable culinary pairings include fricassee of lobster in mustard cinnamon sauce and breast of chicken cooked with honey and mild chilis. There is also an unusual Thai-inspired bouillabaisse of assorted local seafood. For dessert, try the famous *pruneaux* in Armagnac chocolate sauce with homemade chestnut ice cream. ✕ *Island Harbour,* ☎ *809/497–4290. Reservations suggested. AE, D, MC, V. Closed Mon.*

$$$ Koal Keel. This restaurant, in a restored 18th-century great house that
★ was once part of a sugar and cotton plantation, provides a nice contrast to the island's ubiquitous beachfront eateries. The dining room is furnished with richly upholstered period furniture. The original handwrought stone walls are broken by window-size open spaces, creating a cool, breezy atmosphere. A replica of the house's original rock oven is used to bake fresh breads and to roast chickens and racks of lamb. The chefs have dubbed their cuisine "EuroCaribe"; the menu includes Anguilla pea soup, lobster crepes, smoked grouper on a bed of leeks, and grilled breast of duck. ✕ *The Valley,* ☎ *809/497–2930. Reservations required in season. AE, MC, V. Closed Sept.–mid-Oct.*

$$$ The Palm Court. This stylish eatery in the Cinnamon Reef Beach Club
★ is a long palm-lined corridor with red terra-cotta tile floors, Haitian furniture, a beautiful mural of the many varieties of local fish, and huge arched picture windows fronting the Caribbean. Frenchman Didier Rochat and Anguillan Vernon Hughes collaborate in the creation of an exciting nouvelle Caribbean menu. Char-grilled tuna with cinnamon tomato raisin sauce, queenfish roasted in phyllo and served with saffron cappellini, and swordfish steak in passion fruit salsa are house specialties. The mango puffs in caramel sauce are justly famous. ✕ *Cinnamon Beach Club, Little Harbour,* ☎ *809/497–2727. Reservations advised in season. AE, MC, V. Closed mid-Sept.–mid-Oct.*

$$$ Paradise Cafe. Seductive aromas from the kitchen and the tinkling of windchimes waft through this informal, breezy, beachfront restaurant. The chef draws from French and Asian influences in the preparation of seafood, chicken, and beef. Among the standouts are West Indian bouillabaisse, rack of lamb chinois in a black bean sauce, and rockfish fillet flash-fried in peanut oil and served with a sake and tamarind sauce. Hamburgers, salads, soups, and individual pizzas round out the lunch menu. ✕ *Shoal Bay West,* ☎ *809/497–6010. Reservations suggested in season. AE, MC, V. Closed Mon.*

$$ The Ferryboat Inn. Just a short walk from the Ferry Dock at Blowing
★ Point is this charming waterside restaurant. Tables are open to the breezes, and the nighttime view of St. Martin's glimmering lights creates a romantic atmosphere. The French onion and black bean soups, grilled lobster, lobster thermidor (the house specialty), and *entrecôte du vin au poivre* (a house version of steak au poivre with a red wine sauce) are all delicious. There are also veal and chicken dishes, hamburgers, and omelets. ✕ *Cul de Sac Road, Blowing Point,* ☎ *809/497–6613. Reservations advised in season. AE, MC, V. No lunch Sun.*

$$ La Fontana. Northern Italian dishes at this small restaurant have spicy island touches, thanks to the Rastafarian chef. Pasta possibilities include *fettuccine al limone* (with a sauce of black olives, lemon, parmesan, and butter), pasta with lobster and fresh herbs, and a daily Rasta pasta special, such as linguine with tomatoes and shrimp. Also on the menu are grilled duck, steak, fish, and chicken, and a fantastic lobster dish cooked with black olives, capers, and tomatoes. ✗ *Fountain Beach hotel, Shoal Bay, ☎ 809/497–3492. Reservations accepted. AE, MC, V. Closed Wed. and Sept.*

$$ Lucy's Harbour View Restaurant. A swinging gate forms the entrance to this terrace restaurant. Sweeping sea views and Lucy's delicious whole red snapper are the specialties here; curried and Creole dishes, such as conch and goat, are also favored selections. Be sure to try the sautéed potatoes (be very sparing with the tableside hot sauce!). A reggae band plays on Wednesday and Friday nights. ✗ *South Hill, ☎ 809/497–6253. Reservations accepted. No credit cards. Closed Sun.*

$$ Riviera Bar & Restaurant. The chef here has created an unusual menu of French, Creole, and Asian specialties—French cheeses, homemade pâté, sushi, oysters sautéed in soy sauce and sake, and dolphinfish in a spicy Creole sauce are typical offerings. The grilled lobster and fish soup à la Provençale are highly recommended. The beachside setting is relaxed and informal, and there's a very happy Happy Hour from 6 to 7 daily. Live bands play here frequently in season. ✗ *Sandy Ground, ☎ 809/497–2833. Reservations advised in season. AE, V.*

$$ Smuggler's Grill. Visit this romantic, somewhat-out-of-the-way restaurant on Forest Bay to sample one its 10 different preparations of fresh Anguillan lobster. The chef has based the recipes on cuisines from around the world, including French, Southeast Asian, Indian, and Tunisian. The menu also includes escargots, onion soup, and other French bistro fare, and a good selection of steaks and chops. The salad bar is amply stocked. ✗ *Forest Bay, ☎ 809/497–3728. MC, V. Closed Sun. and Aug.–Sept. No lunch.*

$–$$ ★ Arlo's. This popular Italian restaurant serves the best pizza on the island. If you don't want pizza as a main course, share one as an appetizer, then choose from a list of entrées that includes spaghetti Bolognese, lasagna, tortellini du jour, various preparations of fettuccine, and veal or chicken parmigiana. There's always a nightly appetizer and entrée special. The hilltop setting overlooks the sea; you can dine indoors or on the terrace. ✗ *South Hill, ☎ 809/497–6810. MC, V. Closed Sun. and Sept.–Oct. No lunch.*

$–$$ ★ The Old House. Guests enjoy the relaxing atmosphere at this lovely restaurant on a hill near the airport. Tables are covered with white and green tablecloths and are decorated with fresh flowers, even at breakfast, when those in the know order island fruit pancakes. For lunch or dinner try the conch simmered in lime juice and wine, curried local lamb with pigeon peas and rice, or Anguillan pot fish cooked in a sauce of limes, garlic, and tomatoes. ✗ *George Hill, ☎ 809/497–2228. Reservations advised. AE, D, MC, V.*

$ Aquarium. An upstairs terrace, the Aquarium is all gussied up with gingerbread trim, bright blue walls, and red tablecloths. The lunch menu lists sandwiches and burgers. Stewed lobster, curried chicken, barbecued chicken, and mutton stew are offered at night. This is a popular spot with locals. ✗ *South Hill, ☎ 809/497–2720. Reservations accepted. No credit cards. Closed Tues.*

$ Cross Roads. Millie Philip's roadside bar is a great place to get a hearty breakfast. At lunch, seafood salads, fish, and chicken are served. ✗ *Wallblake, the Valley, ☎ 809/497–2581. Reservations accepted. No credit cards.*

$ Johnno's. Performances by the island band Dumpa and the AnvVibes make this *the* place to be on Sunday afternoons, but the grilled or barbecued lobster, kingfish, snapper (all of which Johnno catches himself), and chicken are good anytime. This is a classic Caribbean beach bar, attracting a funky eclectic mix, from locals to movie stars. ✕ *Sandy Ground,* ☎ *809/497–2728. No credit cards.*

$ Pepper Pot. Cora Richardson's small eatery in the center of town serves some of the best rotis on the island. These Trinidadian specialties are made of boneless chicken, *tania* (a local vegetable), celery, pepper, onion, garlic, and peas, all wrapped in dough and baked. Dumpling dinners, lobster, whelk, and conch are also good choices. ✕ *The Valley,* ☎ *809/497–2328. Reservations accepted. No credit cards.*

$ Roy's. The dainty pink-and-white-covered deck belies the rowdy reputation of Roy and Mandy Bosson's pub, an Anguillan mainstay and one of the island's best buys. The menu's most popular items are Roy's fish-and-chips, cold English beer, pork fricassee, and a wonderful chocolate rum cake. Sunday's lunch special is roast beef and Yorkshire pudding. A faithful clientele gathers in the lively bar. ✕ *Crocus Bay,* ☎ *809/497–2470. Reservations accepted. MC, V. Closed Mon. No lunch Sat.*

$ Tropical Penguin. This is the newest addition to the bars and restaurants scattered along the shore at Sandy Ground. The yachting crowd and landlubbers alike head here for light lunches of salads, sandwiches, or hamburgers and come back at dinnertime for grilled chicken, pasta dishes, and fresh fish. ✕ *Sandy Ground,* ☎ *809/497–2253. No credit cards. Closed Sat.*

Lodging

Anguilla has a wide range of accommodations. There are grand and glorious resorts, apartments and villas from the deluxe to the simple, and small, very simple, locally owned guest houses. Because Anguilla has so many beautiful and uncrowded beaches, it is not necessary (the way it is on some other islands) for beach lovers to choose a property because of its beach. When you call to reserve a room in a resort, be sure to inquire about special packages. Meal plans are available, but the particulars vary from resort to resort.

CATEGORY	COST*
$$$$	over $400
$$$	$275–$400
$$	$150–$275
$	under $150

All prices are for a standard double room for two, excluding 8% tax and a service charge, which is typically 10%.

Hotels

$$$$ **Cap Juluca.** This spectacular 179-acre resort wraps around the edge of
★   Maunday's Bay and almost 2 miles of sugary white-sand beach. Its sparkling white, Moorish-style, two-story villas with domes, arches, and turrets are some of the most luxurious and oversize accommodations in the Caribbean. Rooms are minimally but elegantly decorated, with built-in, plumply cushioned seating areas, Moroccan fabrics, and Brazilian hardwood. The giant bathrooms vary, but many include private sunporches or gardens and two-person soaking tubs. Breakfast can be served on your private spacious terrace, and breakfast or a light lunch can be served poolside. At the end of the bay is Chatterton's, the hotel's casual Mediterranean-style grill, which overlooks the water and is open for lunch and dinner. Elegant dinners are served at the adjoining waterside restaurant, Pimms. The newest additions to the hotel are

a croquet court and a putting green. ☎ *Box 240, Maunday's Bay,* ☎ *809/497–6666/6779 or 800/235–3505,* FAX *809/497–6617. 98 units, 7 private villas. 3 restaurants, bar, boutique, room service, laundry service, library, VCRs and cassettes for rent, pool, 3 tennis courts, water-sports and fitness centers, croquet court, putting green. AE, V. CP, MAP.*

$$$$ **Malliouhana.** This ultrasophisticated resort, Anguilla's classiest, sits on
★ 25 lush tropical acres on a promontory that juts out between two exquisite beaches. The lobby entrance, boutique, restaurants, and bar are in a grand, multitiered, open-air building. Accommodations are sleekly decorated, with white walls and tile floors, rattan furniture, and Haitian prints; marble bathrooms have oversize tubs. All units and public areas have recently been repainted, and the Brazilian mahogany, which seems to be everywhere, has been stripped and oiled. The restaurant is the most elegant on the island. Peter Burwash International manages the tennis program here. Kids will like the small beachfront playground, which was recently added. ☎ *Box 173, Meads Bay,* ☎ *809/497–6111 or 800/372–1323,* FAX *809/497–6011. 20 doubles, 15 junior suites, 15 1-bedroom suites, 4 2-bedroom suites. Restaurant, bar, boutique, beauty salon, 3 pools, playground, 4 lighted tennis courts, exercise room, massage room, water-sports center, drugstore. No credit cards. EP, MAP.*

$$$ **Casablanca Resort.** This pink and green Moorish beachside fantasia is the largest, and by far the gaudiest-looking, resort on Anguilla. The entranceway to reception, restaurants, bars, and the 1,200-square foot pool is through a long, domed, open-air hallway of authentic Moroccan mosaics past a long reflecting pool. The rooms are done in pastel green and pink prints, pale green rattan furniture, and Moroccan throw rugs and have marble bathrooms with oversize tubs. The staff is friendly and obliging. On another, more developed, island, Casablanca might not seem so garish. ☎ *Box 444, Rendezvous Bay West,* ☎ *809/496–6999 or 800/231–1945,* FAX *809/496–6899. 88 rooms and suites. 2 restaurants, bar, pool, 2 lighted tennis courts, bicycles, boutique, library, jewelry store, sundry shop, piano bar, health club, water-sports center. AE, D, MC, V. BP, All-inclusive.*

$$$ **Cinnamon Reef Beach Club.** Low-key luxury sets the tone at this small,
★ appealing resort. Most of the whitewashed, split-level villas line the narrow beach, while five are tucked on a bluff. Each casually decorated villa has a living room, raised bedroom, dressing room, sunken shower, and patio, along with little extras such as a hammock, built-in hair dryer, and minibar. This is a friendly place with a gracious staff and lots of repeat guests. The restaurant chefs have won a number of the Anguilla Chefs of the Year awards, and the Friday-night barbecue is an island favorite. Meal plans and packages are available. ☎ *Box 141, Little Harbour,* ☎ *809/497–2727 or 800/223–1108; in Canada, 416/485–8724;* FAX *809/497–3727. 14 studios, 8 1-bedroom suites. Restaurant, lounge, pool, 2 tennis courts, room service, all water sports. AE, MC, V. EP, MAP.*

$$$ **Coccoloba Plantation.** Casual chic is the style of this resort set above a stunning beach. Guests stay in individual, gingerbread-trimmed villas that overlook the ocean and are done in bright Caribbean colors, with raised bedroom areas, marble bathrooms, and comfortable exposed patios. All rooms and one-bedroom suites have a small library of books, safe-deposit box, hair dryer, and complimentary fully stocked refrigerator and minibar. Most bathrooms have showers only. Peter Burwash International directs the tennis program, and tennis and other special packages are available. ☎ *Box 332, Barnes Bay,* ☎ *809/497– 6871 or 800/351–5656; in Canada, 800/468–0023;* FAX *809/497–*

6332. 44 rooms. Restaurant, 2 bars, library, boutique, 2 tennis courts, 2 pools, Jacuzzi, TV/reading room, sauna, massage, exercise rooms, water sports. AE, DC, MC, V. EP, MAP.

$$$ **Frangipani Beach Club.** This splashy, inviting spot on stunning Meads
★ Bay beach consists of pink, multilevel, Spanish Mediterranean–style buildings with archways, stone balustrades, wrought iron railings, and roofs of red clay tiles. Grounds are lushly landscaped with colorful tropical flowers and greenery. Each one-, two-, or three-bedroom suite is tastefully decorated with white rattan furniture and colorful fabrics. All units have marble bathrooms and doors that open out to spacious terraces or balconies. Many units have full kitchens. ☎ *Box 328, Meads Bay,* ☎ *809/497–6442 or 800/892–4564. 8–24 units (varies depending on number of bedrooms being used by one unit), luxury penthouse. Pool, restaurant, 2 bars, all water sports. AE. EP.*

$$–$$$ **Arawak Beach Resort.** Built on the site of an ancient Arawak village, this waterfront resort is perhaps the first in the Caribbean to showcase the Amerindian heritage of the region. Hexagonal, breezy, two-story villas are furnished with hand-carved replicas of Amerindian furniture. The restaurant serves Caribbean and Amerindian food, utilizing cassava, papaya, plantains, and other traditional island crops, some of which grow right in the restaurant's courtyard. A small museum displays artifacts uncovered during construction. Canoes are available in addition to the usual water sports. Although the hotel beach is not one of Anguilla's best, Scilly Cay and its beautiful beaches are just a minute away by launch. This is a no-smoking property; alcoholic beverages are not served, but you may bring your own. ☎ *Box 98, Island Harbour,* ☎ *809/497–4888,* 📠 *809/497–4898. 10 rooms, 3 junior suites, 1 luxury suite. Restaurant, pool, museum, boutique, all water sports. AE. EP.*

$$–$$$ **Fountain Beach.** The family who owns this tiny, delightful property along
★ beautiful Shoal Bay is of Italian descent, and their heritage is evident in the resort's Mediterranean–style white stucco buildings. Each unit comes with a fully equipped kitchen, a large bathroom with an open sunken shower (the studio also has a deep tub), and a view of the sea. Furnishings are rattan and colorfully painted wicker, and Haitian art decorates the walls. Despite the long bumpy road to the hotel, guests from all over the island head to La Fontana, the hotel's Italian restaurant, for dinner (*see* Dining, *above*). The construction of five new units, some with Jacuzzis, is planned for the next few years. *Shoal Bay,* ☎ *and* 📠 *809/497–3491. 8 1-bedroom suites, 2 junior suites. Restaurant, 2 pools, 2 tennis courts. AE, MC, V. EP, MAP. Closed Sept.*

$$–$$$ **Mariners.** Honeymooners and businesspeople on retreat make up much of the clientele of this popular casual resort. It's set at the far end of the beach at Sandy Ground, one of Anguilla's busiest stretches of sand, a short stroll from a number of beach bars and restaurants. The pervasive West Indian style of the Mariners includes the charm of 19th-century gingerbread cottages, and the occasional annoyance of service that, while friendly, is so laid-back it verges on lackadaisical. Accommodations vary considerably in size and price range, from deluxe two-bedroom, two-bath cottages with full kitchens to small rooms with twin beds, minibars, and shower baths. All units are light and airy, with tile floors, white rattan, and bright prints. Charter the resort's Boston whaler for picnics, snorkeling, and fishing trips. The Thursday-night barbecue and Saturday West Indian night in the beachfront restaurant are popular island events. ☎ *Box 139, Sandy Ground,* ☎ *809/497–2815, 809/497–2671, or 800/223–0079;* 📠 *809/497–2901. 25 1-bedroom suites, 25 studios. 2 restaurants, 2 bars, Jacuzzi, laundry service,* *boutique, pool, lighted tennis court, water-sports center. AE, MC, V. EP, MAP, FAP, all-inclusive (drinks not included).*

$$-$$$ Pineapple Beach Club. The new owners of this property (it was formerly known as the Anguilla Great House) have turned its one-bedroom suites into individual bedrooms, and rates here are now all-inclusive. White West Indian–style bungalows line Rendezvous Bay, one of Anguilla's longest beaches. From a chaise on your charming veranda, the view of the ocean is framed by vine-covered trellises and gingerbread trim. Each of the five rooms in each bungalow has mahogany furnishings, hand-embroidered linens, a huge tile shower, and ceiling fans (no air-conditioning). ☎ *Box 157, Rendezvous Bay,* ☎ *809/497–6061 or 800/223–0079,* FAX *809/497–6019. 27 rooms. Restaurant, pool, gallery/boutique, gym. AE, MC, V. All-inclusive.*

$$-$$$ Shoal Bay Villas. Palm trees and 2 miles of splendid sand surround this small condominium hotel. Units are brightly decorated in pink and blue, with painted rattan furniture; all but the poolside doubles have fully equipped kitchens. There's no air-conditioning, but all rooms have ceiling fans. The Reefside Beach Bar is an informal open-air restaurant open for breakfast, lunch, and dinner. All water sports can be arranged, and meal and room packages can be tailored to fit your needs. Children are not allowed during the winter. ☎ *Box 81, Shoal Bay,* ☎ *809/497–2051 or 800/722–7045; in NY, 212/535–9530; in Canada, 416/283–2621;* FAX *809/497–3631. 2 studios, 2 2-bedroom units, 7 1-bedroom units, 2 poolside doubles. Restaurant, bar, pool. AE, MC, V. EP, BP, MAP.*

$$ La Sirena. You'll find one of the island's best values at this personable,
★ well run hotel overlooking Meads Bay. La Sirena doesn't have the chic elegance of Malliouhana, but it lets you stay just down the beach for about a third of the cost. Choose one of the five spacious villas (a new three-bedroom villa was just completed) or one of the 20 guest rooms. The decor is typical Caribbean—rattan furniture and pastel-printed fabrics. Rooms are cooled by ceiling fans. The restaurant is on the second-floor and open to the sea breezes. A new Swiss chef prepares French cuisine with a Caribbean flair. ☎ *Box 200, Meads Bay,* ☎ *809/497–6827 or 800/331–9358; in NY, 212/251–1800;* FAX *809/497–6829. 20 rooms, 5 villas. 2 pools, restaurant, bar, car rental, picnic and snorkeling equipment. AE, MC, V. EP, MAP.*

$-$$ Rendezvous Bay Hotel. Anguilla's first resort, which opened more than 20 years ago, sits amid 60 acres of coconut groves on the fine white sand of Rendezvous Bay, just a mile from the ferry dock. The main building is simple and rather undecorated and has a breezy, broad front patio. Owner Jeremiah Gumb has turned the lounge into a showcase for his elaborate electric train set, complete with tunnels and multiple tracks. The original guest rooms are about 100 yards from the beach and are quite simple, with one double and one single bed, a private shower bath, Haitian art on the walls, and ceiling fans (no air-conditioning). New two-story villas along the shore contain spacious, air-conditioned, one-bedroom suites with refrigerators or kitchenettes. These are decorated with natural wicker and pastel prints and can be joined to form larger suites. There's a wide sand beach and a rocky stretch of coast that is great for snorkeling. ☎ *Box 31, Rendezvous Bay,* ☎ *809/497–6549; in the U.S., 908/738–0246 or 800/274–4893; in Canada, 800/468–0023;* FAX *809/497–6026. 20 rooms, 24 1-bedroom villa suites. Restaurant, lounge, game and TV room, 2 tennis courts, water-sports center. No credit cards. EP, MAP.*

$ Ferryboat Inn. The spacious apartments at this small family-run complex are a bargain. Each is simply decorated with white or pastel fabrics and has a full kitchen, dining area, cable TV, and ceiling fans. It's just a short walk from the ferry dock and on a small beach. The two-bedroom beach house is air-conditioned. All rooms and the open-air restaurant look out across the water toward hilly St. Martin, which is stunning at night, when it's covered with sparkling lights. ☎ *Box 189, Blowing Point,* ☎ *809/497–6613,* FAX *809/497–3309. 6 1- and 2-bedroom apartments, 1 beach house (air-conditioned). Restaurant, bar. AE, MC, V. EP.*

$ **Inter-Island Hotel.** Rooms and two small one-bedroom apartments at this modest establishment, are simply furnished with wicker and rattan. There is no air-conditioning, but some rooms have a breezy open balcony. Most rooms have refrigerators and all have cramped shower bathrooms that define the term "water closet." The homey restaurant serves hearty breakfasts and offers heaping servings at its West Indian dinners. The nearest beach is a two-minute drive away. ☎ *Box 194, the Valley,* ☎ *809/497–6259 or 800/223–9815; in Canada, 800/468–0023;* FAX *809/497–5381. 12 rooms, 2 1-bedroom apartments. Restaurant, bar, TV lounge, transportation to beach ½ mi away. AE, D, MC, V. EP.*

$ **Syd-an's.** These pleasant, clean efficiencies are a tremendous bargain. Each has a kitchenette and shower bath and is comfortably furnished. Road Bay, with all its bustling activity, is just across the street. ☎ *Sandy Ground,* ☎ *809/497–3180,* FAX *809/497–2332. 6 studios. Gift shop. AE, MC, V. EP.*

Villa and Apartment Rentals

The tourist office has a complete listing of vacation rentals. You can also contact **Sunshine Villas** (Box 142, Blowing Point, ☎ 809/497–6149, FAX 809/497–6021), the **Anguilla Connection** (Island Harbour, ☎ 809/497–4403, FAX 809/497-4402) or **Select Villas of Anguilla** (Box 256, George Hill, ☎ 809/497–5810). Housekeeping accommodations are plentiful and well organized. The following are a selection.

$$$$ **Cove Castles Villa Resort.** These glistening white, futuristic sculptures
★ on one of Anguilla's prettiest beaches are actually luxuriously comfortable, very private apartments. Each is decorated with custom-made wicker furniture, raw silk cushions, and hand-embroidered sheets. Kitchens are state of the art. Some units are air-conditioned. ☎ *Shoal Bay West, Box 248,* ☎ *809/497–6801 or 800/348–4716; in Canada, 800/468–0023;* FAX *809/497–6051. 4 3-bedroom villas, 8 2-bedroom villas. Restaurant, boutique, tennis court. No credit cards.*

$$$ **Paradise Cove.** From a distance, this group of luxury apartments looks a bit plain, but the interiors are spacious and elegant, and the units overlook water and are a very short walk to a quiet Cove Beach. One- or two-bedroom units have fully equipped kitchens and private laundry facilities. Maid service and private cooks are available. ☎ *Cove Beach, Box 135,* ☎ *809/497–2259 or 800/553–4939,* FAX *809/497–2149. 14 units. Restaurant, boutique, croquet court, children's play area. AE, MC, V.*

$$$ **Sea Grape Beach Club.** The attractive white stucco and red-tile-roofed buildings of this complex on Meads Bay hold luxurious 2,000-square-foot, two-bedroom condominiums. Each unit's blue-trimmed arched doorway leads to an airy common room, where enormous windows offer spectacular views of the beach. Each condo has three bathrooms, king-size beds, elegant furnishings, huge closets, and a spacious, very private deck. ☎ *Box 65, the Valley,* ☎ *809/497–6433, 809/497–6541, or 800/223–9815;* FAX *809/497–6410. 10 condos. Restaurant, bar, 2 tennis courts, satellite TV, water-sports center. AE, MC, V.*

$$ **Blue Waters.** These glistening white, Moorish-style buildings sit at the
★ far end of a spectacular beach, within walking distance of several excellent restaurants. Sunny one- and two-bedroom units are decorated

with pastel fabrics and have white tile floors, dining areas, full kitchens, and terraces. *Box 69, Shoal Bay West,* ☎ *809/497–6292,* ℻ *809/497–3309. 9 apartments. AE, MC, V.*

$$ **Easy Corner Villas.** These one-, two-, and three-bedroom apartments are adequately furnished and have well-equipped kitchens with microwaves. Only three of the units are air-conditioned; all have only shower baths. Number 10 is a deluxe two-bedroom villa. The location, on a bluff overlooking Road Bay, means you have to walk five minutes to the beach, but the price is right. *Box 65, South Hill,* ☎ *809/497–6433, 809/497–6541, or 800/223–8815;* ℻ *809/497–6410. 17 units. AE, MC, V.*

$$ **Rainbow Reef.** Three seaside acres provide a dramatically beautiful setting for this group of villas. Each self-contained unit has two bedrooms, a fully equipped kitchen, a spacious dining and living area, and a large gallery overlooking the sea. A gazebo with beach furniture and barbecue facilities perches right above the beach. *Box 130, Sea Feather Bay,* ☎ *809/497–2817 or 708/325–2299. 14 units. No credit cards.*

$$ **Skiffles Villas.** These self-catering villas, perched on a hill overlooking
★ Road Bay, are usually booked a year in advance. The one-, two-, and three-bedroom apartments have fully equipped kitchens, floor-to-ceiling windows, and pleasant porches. ✆ *Box 82, Lower South Hill,* ☎ *809/497–6619, 219/642–4855, or 219/642–4445;* ℻ *809/495–6110. 5 units. Pool. No credit cards.*

Nightlife

The **Mayoumba Folkloric Theater,** a group made up of the best performers in the Anguilla Choral Circle, performs song-and-dance skits depicting Antillean and Caribbean culture with African drums and a string band. They appear every Thursday night at **La Sirena** (Meads Bay, ☎ 809/497–6827). Be on the lookout for Bankie Banx, Anguilla's own reggae superstar. He has his own group called New Generations. If you're lucky, you'll catch him playing solo at the **Malliouhana** (Meads Bay, ☎ 809/497–6111) during cocktail hours. He's a true talent—no electronics, just a remarkable voice and great guitar playing. Other local groups include Keith Gumbs and the Mellow Tones, Spraka, Megaforce, Joe and the Invaders, Dumpa and the AnvVibes, and Sleepy and the All-Stars, a string-and-scratch band. Steel Vibrations, a pan band, often entertains at barbecues and West Indian evenings. Most of the major hotels feature some kind of live entertainment almost nightly in season. A Calypso combo plays most nights at **Cinnamon Reef Beach Club** (Little Harbour, ☎ 809/497–2727). The **Mariners** (Sandy Ground, ☎ 809/497–2671) has regularly scheduled Thursday-night barbecues and Saturday-night West Indian parties, both with live entertainment by local groups. During high season, **Pimms** and **Chatterton's** (Cap Juluca, ☎ 809/497–6666) have live music at dinner. Things are pretty loose and lively at **Johnno's** beach bar (☎ 809/497–2728) in Sandy Ground, which has live music and alfresco dancing Wednesday and Saturday nights and Sunday afternoons, when it feels as if the entire island population is in attendance. The **Dragon's Disco** (South Hill, ☎ 809/497–2687) is a hot spot on weekends after midnight. The **Coconut Paradise** restaurant (Island Harbour, ☎ 809/497–4150) has nightly entertainment ranging from disco to limbo. For soft dance music after a meal, go to **Lucy's Palm Palm** (☎ 809/497–2253) at Sandy Ground; there is usually a live band on Tuesday and Friday evenings. Sunday is the big night in restaurants. In addition to the above, **Uncle Ernie's** (Shoal Bay, no ☎), **Round Rock** (Shoal Bay, ☎ 809/497–2076), and **Smitty's** (Island Harbour, ☎ 809/497–4300) swing all day and well into the night.

3 Antigua

NE COULD SPEND AN ENTIRE YEAR—and a leap year, at that—exploring Antigua's beaches; the island has 366 of them, many with snow-white sand. All the beaches are public, some absolutely deserted and others with resorts stretching right along the water's edge and offering sailing, diving, windsurfing, and snorkeling. This is an island with hotels to please travelers of all kinds, from those seeking refined elegance, to those in search of casual beachfront merriment or quiet beachside snoozing, to those charmed by beautifully restored historic inns.

Updated by
Jordan Simon

Antigua (An-*tee*-ga), the largest of the British Leeward Islands (108 square miles), is an island with a strong sense of national identity and rich, historic inheritance. Its cricketers, like the legendary Viv Richards (arguably the greatest batsman the game has ever seen), are famous throughout the Caribbean. Its people are known for their sharp, commercial spirit; their wit; and, unfortunately at the government level, their corruption.

In the colonial era, Antigua was the headquarters of Lord Horatio Nelson's fleet. English Harbour, in the southeast of the island, is steeped in the history of that time. At its center is Nelson's Dockyard, now a national park. It is Antigua's answer to Williamsburg, Virginia—a carefully restored gem of British Georgian architecture. Accommodations here are generally in smaller, inn-type hotels. For Anglophiles and those interested in history, English Harbour and the surrounding villages and historic sites will be immensely rewarding.

Those in search of good beaches, plenty of nightlife, and a wide choice of restaurants will want to head to the northwestern end of the island, where resorts and hotels are scattered from Five Islands Harbour, south of St. John, to Dickenson Bay and the northwest shore. If you like to walk from one beach bar and restaurant to another, then Dickenson Bay and its long sliver of white sand is the spot for you.

One of the least-developed parts of the island is in the southwest, in the shadow of Antigua's highest mountain, Boggy Peak. At beaches like Fry's Bay and Darkwood Beach, visitors will find long, unspoiled beaches.

The original inhabitants of Antigua were a people called the Siboney. They lived here as early as 4,000 years ago and disappeared mysteriously, leaving the island unpopulated for about 1,000 years. When Columbus arrived in 1493, the Arawaks had set up housekeeping. The English took up residence 139 years later in 1632. After 30-odd years of bloody battles involving the Caribs, the Dutch, the French, and the English, the French ceded the island to the English in 1667. Unlike many other Caribbean islands, which spent centuries being reflagged like political Ping-Pong balls, Antigua remained under English control until achieving full independence, with its sister island Barbuda (26 miles to the north), on November 1, 1981.

The combined population of the two islands is about 90,000, only 1,200 of whom live on Barbuda. Tourism is the main industry here—there has been a recent building boom in tourism properties, with the construction of condominiums and the extensive renovation and expansion of the major hotels—and the government is seeking to broaden its monetary resources by reintroducing agriculture and manufacturing into the economy.

Before You Go

Tourist Information

Contact the **Antigua and Barbuda Tourist Offices** in the United States (610 5th Ave., Suite 311, New York, NY 10020, ☎ 212/541–4117, or 25 S.E. 2nd Ave., Suite 300, Miami, FL 33131, ☎ 305/381–6762), in Canada (60 St. Clair Ave. E, Suite 304, Toronto, Ontario M4T 1N5, ☎ 416/961–3085), and in the United Kingdom (Antigua House, 15 Thayer St., London W1M 5LD, England, ☎ 0171/486–7073).

Arriving and Departing

BY PLANE

American Airlines (☎ 800/433–7300) has daily direct service from New York and Miami, as well as several flights from San Juan that connect with flights from more than 100 U.S. cities. **BWIA** (☎ 800/JET–BWIA) has nonstop service from New York, Miami, and Toronto; **Air Canada** (☎ 800/422–6232) from Toronto; **British Airways** (☎ 800/247–9297) from London; and **Lufthansa** (☎ 800/645–3880) from Frankfurt. **LIAT** (☎ 809/462–0701) has daily flights from Antigua to Barbuda, 15 minutes away, as well as to and from many other Caribbean islands.

V. C. Bird International Airport is, on the tiniest of scales, to the Caribbean what O'Hare is to the Midwest. It's a major hub for traffic between Caribbean islands, and it is always busy with tiny planes taking off and landing.

FROM THE AIRPORT

Taxis meet every flight, and drivers will offer to guide you around the island. The taxis are unmetered, but rates are posted at the airport and drivers are required to carry a rate card with them. The fixed rate from the airport to St. John's is $12 in U.S. currency (although drivers have been known to *quote* Eastern Caribbean dollars) and from the airport to English Harbour, $24.

Passports and Visas

U.S. and Canadian citizens need proof of identity. A valid passport is most desirable, but a birth certificate is acceptable provided it has a raised or embossed seal and has been issued by a county or state (not a hospital) *and* provided that you also have some type of photo identification, such as a driver's license. A driver's license by itself is *not* sufficient. British citizens need a passport. All visitors must present a return or ongoing ticket.

Language

Antigua's official language is English.

Precautions

Some beaches are shaded by manchineel trees, whose leaves and applelike fruit are poisonous to touch. Most of the trees are posted with warning signs and should be avoided; even raindrops falling from them can cause painful blisters. If you should come in contact with one, rinse the affected area and contact a doctor.

Throughout the Caribbean, incidents of petty theft are increasing. Leave your valuables in the hotel safe-deposit box; don't leave them unattended in your room or on the beach. Also, the streets of St. John's are fairly deserted at night, so it's not a good idea to wander out alone.

Staying in Antigua

Important Addresses

Tourist Information: The **Antigua and Barbuda Department of Tourism** (Thames and Long Sts., St. John's, ☎ 809/462–0480) is open Monday–Thursday 8–4:30, Friday 8–3. There is also a tourist-information desk at the airport, just beyond the immigration checkpoint. The tourist office gives limited information. You may have more success with the **Antigua Hotels Association** (Long St., St. John's, ☎ 809/462–3703), which also provides assistance.

EMERGENCIES

Police: ☎ 809/462–0125. **Fire:** ☎ 809/462–0044. **Ambulance:** ☎ 809/462–0251. **Hospital:** There is a 24-hour emergency room at the 210-bed **Holberton Hospital** (Hospital Rd., St. John's, ☎ 809/462–0251/2/3). **Pharmacies: Joseph's Pharmacy** (Redcliffe St., St. John's, ☎ 809/462–1025), **City Pharmacy** (St. Mary's St., St. John's, ☎ 809/462–1363), and **Health Pharmacy** (Redcliffe St., St. John's, ☎ 809/462–1255).

Currency

Local currency is the Eastern Caribbean dollar (E.C.$), which is tied to the U.S. dollar and fluctuates only slightly. At hotels, the rate is E.C.$2.60 to U.S.$1; at banks, it's about E.C.$2.70. American dollars are readily accepted, although you will usually receive change in E.C. dollars. Be sure you understand which currency is being used, since most places quote prices in E.C. dollars. Most hotels, restaurants, and duty-free shops take major credit cards, and all accept traveler's checks. It's a good idea to inquire at the tourist office or your hotel about current credit-card policy. Note: Prices quoted are in U.S. dollars unless indicated otherwise.

Taxes and Service Charges

Hotels collect a 7% government room tax and usually add a 10% service charge to your bill. In restaurants, a 10% service charge is usually added to your bill, and it is customary to leave another 5% if you are pleased with the service. Taxi drivers expect a 10% tip. The departure tax is $10.

Guided Tours

Virtually all **taxi** drivers double as guides, and you can arrange an island tour with one for about $20 an hour. Every major hotel has a cabbie on call and may be able to negotiate a discount, particularly off-season.

Bryson's Travel (St. John's, ☎ 809/462–0223) offers personalized tours of the island, as well as cruises and deep-sea-fishing trips. **Alexander, Parrish Ltd.** (St. John's, ☎ 809/462–0387) specializes in island tours and can also arrange overnight stays. **Antours** (St. John's, ☎ 809/462–4788) gives half- and full-day tours of the island. Antours is also the **American Express** representative on the island.

Tropikelly (☎ 809/461–0383) and **Estate Safari Adventure** (☎ 809/462–4713) offer tours to the "wilds" of Antigua's interior, where there are few marked trails and roads are rough. Both operators charge about $55 per person and show you deserted plantation houses, rain-forest trails, and ruined sugar mills and forts. The luxuriant tropical forest around the island's highest point, Boggy Peak, is especially worth seeing. The cost of the tour includes lunch, and if you're with Estate Safari, snorkeling at a secluded beach.

Getting Around
BUSES
You'll see two bus stations in St. John's, near the Botanical Gardens and near Central Market, but don't expect to see many buses. Bus schedules here epitomize what is called "island time," which is to say they roll when the spirit (infrequently) moves them.

TAXIS
If you're uncomfortable about driving on the left or prone to getting lost, a taxi is your best bet, although fares mount up quickly. Taxis are unmetered, but rates are fixed from here to there, and drivers are required to carry a rate card at all times. They'll even take you from the St. John's area to English Harbour and wait for a "reasonable" amount of time (about a half hour) while you look around for about $40.

RENTAL CARS
To rent a car, you'll need a valid driver's license and a temporary permit ($12), which is available through the rental agent. Rentals average about $50 per day in season, with unlimited mileage. You'll probably get a better daily rate if you rent for several days. Most agencies rent automatic, stick-shift, and right- and left-hand-drive vehicles, as well as Jeeps ($55 per day). Although these four-wheel-drive vehicles will get you more places and are refreshingly open, beware that the roads are full of potholes, and a day in a Jeep can leave you feeling as if you've been through a paint-mixing machine! Remember to drive on the left (pay particular attention getting in and out of rotaries and making turns), and know that virtually all roads are unmarked. Fortunately, you will not have to deal with the incredibly steep curves that are on so many Caribbean islands.

Among the agencies are **Budget** (St. John's, ☎ 809/462–3009 or 800/648–4985), **National** (St. John's, ☎ 809/462–2113 or 800/468–0008), **Carib Car Rentals** (Hodges Bay, ☎ 809/462–2062), **Hertz** (St. John's, also Jolly Harbour, ☎ 809/462–4114), **Dollar** (St. John's, ☎ 809/462–0362), and **Avis** (at the airport or the St. James's Club, ☎ 809/462–2840).

Telephones and Mail
To call Antigua from the United States, dial 1, then area code 809, then the local seven-digit number. Few hotels have direct-dial telephones, but connections are easily made through the switchboard. The Caribbean Phone Card, available in $5, $10, and $20 amounts, can be used for local and long-distance calls and for access to AT&T USA Direct lines. There are now quite a few phones that accept the phone cards, and they work much better than the regular pay phones. You can purchase the card from most hotels or from a post office. Some phone card booths can now access Sprint and MCI. In addition, there are several **Boatphones** scattered throughout the island at major tourist sites; simply pick up the receiver and the operator will take your credit card number (any major card) and assign you a PIN (personal identification number). Calls using your PIN are then charged to that credit card.

To place a call to the United States, dial 1, the appropriate area code, and the seven-digit number, or use the phone card or one of the AT&T USA Direct phones, which are available at several locations including the airport departure lounge, the cruise terminal at St. John's, and the English Harbour Marina. To place an interisland call, dial the local seven-digit number.

In an emergency, you can make calls from Cable & Wireless (WI) Ltd. (42–44 St. Mary's St., St. John's, ☎ 809/462–9840, and Nelson's Dockyard, English Harbour, ☎ 809/463–1517).

Airmail letters to North America cost E.C.60¢; postcards, E.C.40¢. The post office is at the foot of High Street in St. John's.

Opening and Closing Times

Although some stores still follow the tradition of closing for lunch, most shops, especially in season, are open Monday–Friday 9–5 and Saturday 8–noon or 8–3. Hours vary from bank to bank, but generally they are open Monday–Thursday 8–2 and Friday 8–4.

Exploring Antigua

Numbers in the margin correspond to points of interest on the Antigua (and Barbuda) map.

St. John's

❶ The capital city of **St. John's,** home to some 40,000 people (nearly half the island's population), lies at sea level at the inland end of a sheltered bay on the northwest coast of the island. The city has seen better days, but it is in the midst of a face-lift, and there are some notable historic sights, pleasant shopping areas, and good restaurants. Although much of the city looks shabby, it is definitely worth a visit. Most of the gift stores and restaurants are near the waterfront. Up the hill is Antigua's downtown, with stores carrying major appliances, plumbing supplies, and other goods unlikely to be of interest to tourists.

All major hotels provide free maps and island brochures, or, if you happen to be in St. John's, stop in at the Tourist Bureau, at the corner of Long and Thames streets.

Cross Long Street and walk one block north and one block east to Church Street. The **Museum of Antigua and Barbuda** is a "hands-on history" opportunity. Signs say Please Touch, with the hope of welcoming both citizens and visitors into Antigua's past. Try your hand at the educational video games. Exhibits interpret the history of the nation from its geological birth to its political independence in 1981. There are fossil and coral remains from some 34 million years ago, a life-size replica of an Arawak house, models of a sugar plantation and a wattle-and-daub house, and a minishop with handicrafts, books, historical prints, and paintings. The colonial building that houses the museum is the former courthouse, which dates from 1750. *Church and Market Sts.,* ☎ *809/462–1469.* ☛ *Free.* ☉ *Weekdays 8:30–4, Sat. 10–1.*

Walk two blocks east on Church Street to the **Anglican Cathedral of St. John the Divine.** At the south gate, there are figures of St. John the Baptist and St. John the Divine said to have been taken from one of Napoléon's ships and brought to Antigua. The original church was built in 1681, replaced by a stone building in 1745, and destroyed by an earthquake in 1843. The present building dates from 1845. With an eye to future earthquakes, the parishioners had the interior completely encased in pitch pine, hoping to forestall heavy damage. The church was elevated to the status of cathedral in 1848. *Between Long and Newgate Sts.,* ☎ *809/461–0082.* ☛ *Free.*

Return to Long Street, walk one block south, and turn right on High Street. At the end of High Street, you'll see the **Cenotaph,** which honors Antiguans who lost their lives in World Wars I and II. Retrace your steps seven blocks to the **Westerby Memorial,** which was erected in 1888 in memory of the Moravian bishop George Westerby.

One block south of the memorial is **Heritage Quay,** a new multimillion-dollar shopping complex that keeps expanding. Two-story buildings showcase stores specializing in duty-free goods, sportswear, T-shirts, imports from down-island (paintings, T-shirts, straw baskets), and local crafts, plus several restaurants and a casino. Cruise ship passengers disembark here from the 500-foot-long pier.

Redcliffe Quay, set at the water's edge just south of Heritage Quay, is the most appealing part of St. John's. Attractively restored buildings in a riot of cotton-candy colors house shops, restaurants, and boutiques and are linked by courtyards and landscaped walkways. This is the shopping area favored by both residents and return guests. There are no duty-free shops, but there are many other interesting choices. There are also cafés where you can sit and ponder the scene of two centuries ago, when slaves were held here prior to being sold.

TIME OUT At **Hemingway's** (Jardine Court, ☎ 809/462–2763), a historic clapboard house in the center of St. John's, you can sit on the upstairs veranda and drink papaya and mango juice or have breakfast and watch the bustling life of the streets below.

At the far south end of town, where Market Street forks into Valley Road and All Saints Road, a whole lot of haggling goes on every Friday and Saturday, when locals jam the public **marketplace** to buy and sell fruits, vegetables, fish, and spices. Be sure to ask before you aim a camera; expect the subject of your shot to ask for a tip.

Elsewhere on the Island

After touring Fort James, divide the island into two more tours. First, you can take in English Harbour and Nelson's Dockyard on the south coast, returning to St. John's along the Caribbean (western) coast. Then travel to the eastern side of the island for sights ranging from historical churches to Devil's Bridge.

It's a good idea to wear a swimsuit under your clothes while you're sightseeing—one of the sights to strike your fancy may be an enticing secluded beach. Be sure to bring your camera along. There are some picture-perfect spots around the island.

Before you start, study your map for a minute or two. Road names are not posted, so you will need to have a sense of where you are heading if you hope to find it. The easiest way to get to anything is to see if a popular restaurant is near it, since easy-to-spot signs leading the way to restaurants are posted all over the island. (You'll see tons of them nailed to a post at every crossroad.) If you start to feel lost along the way, don't hesitate to ask anyone you see for directions. Bear in mind that locals generally give directions in terms of landmarks that may not seem much like landmarks to you (turn left at the yellow house, or right at the big tree).

FORT JAMES
Follow Fort Road northwest out of town, turn left at the Barrymore Hotel, turn left again when you reach the water, and follow the beach until the road ends (a total of 2 miles). You'll come to **Fort James,** named after King James II. The fort was constructed between 1704 and 1739 as a lookout point for the city and St. John's Harbour. The ramparts overlooking the small islands in the bay are in ruins, but 10 cannons still point out to sea.

ENGLISH HARBOUR

Take All Saints Road south out of St. John's (handmade signs point the way to English Harbour hotels and restaurants). Eight miles out ③ of town—almost to the south coast—is **Liberta,** one of the first settlements founded by freed slaves. East of the village, on Monk's Hill, is ④ the site of **Fort George,** built from 1689 to 1720. The fort wouldn't be of much help to anybody these days, but among the ruins you can make out the sites for its 32 cannons, its water cisterns, the base of the old flagstaff, and some of the original buildings.

⑤ **Falmouth,** 1½ miles farther south, sits on a lovely bay backed by former sugar plantations and sugar mills. **St. Paul's Church** was rebuilt on the site of a church once used by troops during the Nelson period.

⑥ **English Harbour** lies on the coast, just south of Falmouth. This is the most famous of Antigua's attractions. In 1671, the governor of the Leeward Islands wrote to the Council for Foreign Plantations in London pointing out the advantages of this landlocked harbor, and by 1704 English Harbour was in regular use as a garrisoned station.

In 1784, 26-year-old Horatio Nelson sailed in on HMS *Boreas* to serve as captain and second in command of the Leeward Island Station. Under his command was the captain of HMS *Pegasus,* Prince William Henry, duke of Clarence, who was to ascend the throne of England as William IV. The prince was Nelson's close friend and acted as best man when Nelson married the young widow Fannie Nisbet on Nevis in 1787.

The Royal Navy abandoned the station in 1889, and it fell into a state of decay. The Society of the Friends of English Harbour began restor- ⑦ ing it in 1951, and on Dockyard Day, November 14, 1961, **Nelson's Dockyard** was opened with much fanfare.

The dockyard is reminiscent, albeit on a much smaller scale, of Williamsburg, Virginia. Within the compound there are crafts shops, hotels, and restaurants. It is a hub for oceangoing yachts and serves as headquarters for the annual Sailing Week Regatta. A lively community of mariners keeps the area active in season. Beach lovers tend to stay elsewhere on the island, but visitors who enjoy history and who are part of (or like being around) the nautical scene often choose one of the hotels in the area of English Harbour. If you'd like to get a look at the area from the water, board the *Horatio Nelson* for a 20-minute guided cruise (Dockyard Divers, ☎ 809/464–8591). The tour costs $6 per person, and the boat leaves every half hour from 9 to 5 daily.

The **Admiral's House Museum** displays ship models, a model of English Harbour, silver trophies, maps, prints, and Nelson's very own telescope and tea caddy. *English Harbour,* ☎ *809/463–1053 or 809/ 463–1379.* ☛ *$2.* ⊙ *Daily 8–6.*

On a ridge overlooking the dockyard is **Clarence House** (☎ 809/463– 1026), built in 1787 and once the home of the duke of Clarence. Princess Margaret and Lord Snowdon spent part of their honeymoon here in 1960, and Queen Elizabeth and Prince Philip have dined here. It is now used by the governor-general as a country home; visits are possible when he is not in residence. The place is decorated pretty much as it was in the 18th century and is definitely worth a visit.

As you leave the dockyard, turn right at the crossroads and drive to ⑧ **Shirley Heights** for a spectacular view of English Harbour. The heights are named for Sir Thomas Shirley, the governor who fortified the harbor in 1787.

Exploring

Dining

Lodging

Antigua (and Barbuda)

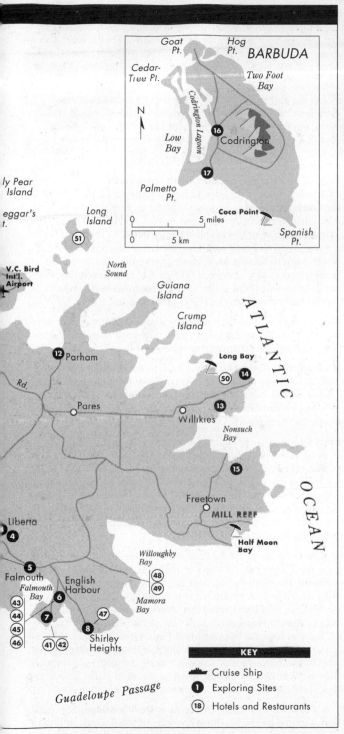

BARBUDA

Goat Pt.

Hog Pt.

Cedar-Tree Pt.

Two Foot Bay

Codrington Lagoon

N

Low Bay

16 Codrington

17

Palmetto Pt.

Coco Point

0   5 miles

0   5 km

Spanish Pt.

ly Pear Island

eggar's t.

Long Island

51

V.C. Bird Int'l. Airport

North Sound

Guiana Island

Crump Island

A T L A N T I C

12 Parham

Rd.

Pares

Long Bay
50 **14**

13

Willikies

Nonsuch Bay

15

Freetown

MILL REEF

O C E A N

Liberta

4

Half Moon Bay

5

Falmouth
Falmouth Bay

English Harbour

Willoughby Bay
48
49

43

6

Mamora Bay

44

45

7

47

46

41 **42**

8

Shirley Heights

Guadeloupe Passage

KEY
🚢 Cruise Ship
1 Exploring Sites
18 Hotels and Restaurants

Not far from Shirley Heights is the **Dows Hill Interpretation Centre.** Observation platforms afford excellent views of the whole English Harbour area, and there's a multimedia presentation on the island's history and culture, from the days of the Amerindians to the present. *For information, call the National Parks Authority at 809/460–1053.* ☛ *E.C.$15.* ⏲ *Daily 9–5.*

TIME OUT Cool off with the yachting crowd on the terrace of the **Admiral's Inn** (English Harbour, ☎ 809/460–1027), where the deeply tanned crews can keep an eye on their multimillion-dollar babies offshore—and on each other. The people-watching is first-rate, and so are the banana daiquiris (with or without Antiguan rum).

Drive back up to Liberta. Four and a half miles north of town, opposite the Catholic church, turn left and head southwest on **Fig Tree Drive** (*fig* is the Antiguan word for banana). The drive takes you through the rain forest, which is rich in mangoes, pineapples, and banana trees. This is also the hilliest part of the island—**Boggy Peak,** to the west, is the highest point, rising to 1,319 feet. Fig Tree Drive runs into Old Road, which leads down to **Curtain Bluff,** an unforgettable sight. At the tip of a tiny outcropping of land, between Carlisle Bay and Morris Bay, it offers dramatic views of the wonderful color contrasts where waters of the Atlantic Ocean meet those of the Caribbean Sea.

From here, the main road sweeps along the southwest coast, where there are lovely beaches and spectacular views. The road then veers away from the water and goes through the villages of Bolans and Jennings.

From Jennings, a road turns right and leads to the **Megaliths of Greencastle Hill,** an arduous climb away (you'll have to walk the last 500 yards). Some say the megaliths were set up by humans for the worship of the sun and moon; others believe they are nothing more than unusual geological formations.

THE EAST END

St. John's is 6 miles northeast of Jennings. To explore the other half of the island, take Parham Road east out of St. John's. Drive 5½ miles and turn left on the side road that leads 1¼ miles to the settlement of **Parham. St. Peter's Church,** built in 1840 by Thomas Weekes, an English architect, is an octagonal Italianate building whose facade was once richly decorated with stucco, though it suffered considerable damage during the earthquake of 1843.

Backtrack and continue east on Parham Road for about ¾ mile, to a fork in the road. One branch veers to the right in a southeasterly direction toward Half Moon Bay, and the other continues toward the northeast coast. The latter route runs through the village of Pares. If you have the time, take the marked dirt road on your right shortly after the village to **Betty's Hope,** Antigua's first sugar plantation, founded in 1650. You can tour the twin windmills and view exhibits on the island's sugar era. It isn't much now, but the private trust overseeing the restoration has ambitious plans. Continue along the main road through the village of Willikies to **Indian Town,** a national park, where archaeological digs have revealed evidence of Carib occupation.

Less than a mile farther along the coast is **Devil's Bridge,** a natural formation sculpted by the crashing breakers of the Atlantic at Indian Creek. This is now a national park. Blowholes have been carved by the waves. They may be hard to spot at first, but just wait until a wave bursts through!

Backtrack again to Parham Road and take the fork that runs south-east. You'll travel 9 miles to Half Moon Bay. Just before the coast are the village of **Freetown** and the **Mill Reef area,** where many pre-Columbian discoveries have been made.

⑮ **Harmony Hall,** northeast of Freetown (follow the signs), is an interesting art gallery. A sister to the Jamaican gallery near Ocho Rios, Jamaica, Harmony Hall is built on the foundation of a 17th-century sugar-plantation great house. Artists Graham Davis and Peter and Annabella Proudlock, who founded the Jamaican gallery, teamed up with local entrepreneur Geoffrey Pidduck to create an Antiguan art gallery specializing in high-quality West Indian art. A large gallery is used for one-man shows, and another exhibition hall displays watercolors. A small bar and an outside restaurant under the trees are open in season. *Brown's Mill Bay,* ☎ *809/463–2057.* ◷ *Daily 10–6.*

Barbuda

Twenty-six miles north of Antigua is Barbuda—a flat, 62-square-mile coral atoll with 17 miles of stunning pinkish white-sand beaches. Al-most all the island's 1,200 people live in **Codrington.** Barbuda's 8-mile
⑯ **Coco Point Beach** lures beachcombers, and the island is ringed by wrecks and reef, which makes it a great draw for divers and snorkelers. Ornithologists and bird lovers come here, too. The Bird Sanctuary, a wide mangrove-filled lagoon, is home to an estimated 170 species of birds, including frigate birds with 8-foot wingspans.

⑰ The sole historic ruin here is **Martello Tower,** which is believed to have been a lighthouse built by the Spaniards before the English occupied the island. LIAT (*see* Before You Go, *above*) has regularly scheduled daily flights from Antigua to Barbuda (with departure times just right for day-trippers); air and boat charters are also available (contact the Department of Tourism). Those wishing to overnight here can choose from two superluxury resorts and several guest houses.

Beaches

All of Antigua's beaches are public, and many are dotted with resorts that provide water-sports-equipment rentals and a place to grab a cool drink. Sunbathing topless or in the buff is strictly illegal except on one of the small beaches at Hawksbill Beach Club, where allover tans are possible. Beware that on the one or two days a week that cruise ships dock in St. John's (check with your hotel for specific dates), buses drop off loads of cruise ship passengers on virtually all the west-coast beaches. Choose this day to tour the island by car, visit one of the more remote east end beaches, or take a day trip to Barbuda.

Antigua

Dickenson Bay has a lengthy stretch of powder-soft white sand and exceptionally calm water. Here you'll find small and large hotels, super-casual beach bars, and beachfront restaurants. Water-sports equipment can be rented at the Halcyon Cove.

The white sand of **Runaway Beach** is home to the Barrymore Beach Hotel and the Runaway Beach Hotel, so it can get crowded. Refresh yourself with hot dogs and beer at the Barrymore's Satay Hut.

Five Islands Peninsula has four secluded beaches (including one for bathing in the buff) of fine tan sand and coral reefs for snorkeling. The Hawksbill Hotel is here.

Pigeon Point, near English Harbour, is a fine white-sand beach with very calm water. There are several restaurants and bars nearby.

Johnson's Point is a deliciously deserted beach of bleached white sand on the southwest coast.

A large coconut grove adds to the tropical beauty of **Carlisle Bay** and the two long snow-white beaches over which the estimable Curtain Bluff resort sits. Standing on the bluff of this peninsula, you can see the almost-blinding blue waters of the Atlantic Ocean drifting into the Caribbean Sea.

Half Moon Bay is a ¾-mile crescent of sand, a prime area for snorkeling and windsurfing. It is on the Atlantic side of the island and can be quite rough at times.

Long Bay, on the far eastern coast, has coral reefs in water so shallow that you can actually walk out to them. Along the lovely beach are the Long Bay Hotel and the rambling Pineapple Beach Club.

Barbuda
Coco Point, on Barbuda, is an uncrowded 8-mile stretch of white sand. Barbuda, encircled by reefs and shipwrecks, is great for scuba diving.

Sports and the Outdoors

Almost all the resort hotels can come up with fins and masks, Windsurfers, Sunfish, catamarans, and other water-related gear (*see* Lodging, *below*).

Bicycling
Try **Sun Cycles** (☎ 809/461–0324) for short- or long-term leases.

Boating
Halcyon Cove Watersports (Dickenson Bay, ☎ 809/462–0256), at Dickenson Bay, offers waterskiing and other water rides and rents small boats. **Sea Sports** (Dickenson Bay, ☎ 809/462–3355) rents Jet Skis and Sunfish and offers parasailing and waterskiing trips. **Shorty's** (☎ 809/462–6066), also at Dickenson Bay, offers some of the best water sports on the island and runs several daily glass-bottom-boat cruises. The atmosphere here can be hectic. **Nicholson Yacht Charters** (☎ 800/662–6066) are the real professionals. A long-established island family, they can charter you anything from a 20-foot ketch to a giant schooner.

Fitness Center
The **Benair Fitness Club** (Country Club Rd., Hodges Bay, ☎ 809/462–1540) has fitness equipment, Jacuzzi, aerobics classes, and a juice bar. The **Lotus Health Centre** (Dickenson Bay, ☎ 809/462–2231) offers spa treatments, including Swedish massage, foot reflexology, and various kinds of facials. The adjacent **Fitness Shack** (☎ 809/462–5223) has extensive fitness equipment and aerobics classes.

Golf
There is an 18-hole course at **Cedar Valley Golf Club** (☎ 809/462–0161) and a 9-hole course at the **Half Moon Bay Hotel** (☎ 809/460–4300).

Horseback Riding
First-rate Texas quarter horses and former racehorses are available for beach rides at the **St. James Stables,** attached to the St. James's Club (☎ 809/463–1430).

Sailing
The **Antigua School of Sailing** (St. John's, ☎ 809/462–2026) offers short resort courses.

Scuba Diving

With all the wrecks and reefs, there are lots of undersea sights to see. Contact **Dive Antigua** (☎ 809/462–3483), which offers certification courses and day and night dives from three separate locations: the St. James's Club (☎ 809/460–5000), Galleon Beach Club (☎ 809/460–1024), and the Royal Antiguan (☎ 809/462–3733). Dive packages are offered by the **Runaway Beach Club** (Runaway Bay, ☎ 809/462–2626). If you are in the English Harbour area, Captain A. G. Fincham, a British ex–merchant seaman and proprietor of **Dockyard Divers** (☎ 809/464–8591, FAX 809/460–1179), one of the oldest established outfits on the island, offers diving and snorkeling trips, PADI (Professional Association of Diving Instructors) courses, and dive packages with accommodations.

Sea Excursions

Join in the fun on a real pirate ship when you choose one of the *Jolly Roger* (☎ 809/462–2064) cruises, complete with "pirate" crew, limbo dancing, plank walking, and other pranks. Board the 45-foot Beneteau yacht *Paradise I* (☎ 809/462–4158) for a lunch or sunset cruise. Kokomo Cats (☎ 809/462–7245) runs several different cruises including one to deserted beaches, one to English Harbour, and one to gaze at the sunset. The crew of the *Titi 1* (☎ 809/460–1452), a 34-foot motorboat powered with twin 300 Evinrudes, will take you to nearby islets, remote beaches, or out for specially tailored snorkeling trips. They're based in Falmouth Harbour but will pick you up almost anywhere. **Wadadli Cats** (☎ 809/462–4792) offers various cruises, including a circumnavigation of the island, on its three sleek catamarans.

Tennis

The **Temo Sports Complex** (Falmouth Bay, ☎ 809/463–1781) has two floodlit tennis courts, three glass-backed squash courts, showers, a sports shop, and snack bars. Many of the larger resorts have their own tennis courts. The **St. James's Club** (☎ 809/460–5000) has seven (five lighted for night play); **Sandals** (☎ 809/462–0267) has two; **Halcyon Cove** (☎ 809/462 0256) four (lighted); and **Curtain Bluff** (☎ 809/462–8400) four Har-Tru and a grass court. Guests have top priority. For nonguests, court fees are about $30 an hour.

Waterskiing

Halcyon Cove Watersports (☎ 809/462–0256) and **Sea Sports** (☎ 809/462–3355), both at Dickenson Bay, will take you waterskiing.

Windsurfing

The **High Wind Centre** at the Lord Nelson Beach Hotel is the spot for serious board sailors, run by expert Patrick Scales (☎ 809/462–3094). Rentals and instruction are also available at **Halcyon Cove Watersports** (☎ 809/462–0256), and most major hotels offer boardsailing equipment.

Spectator Sports

For information about sports events, contact **Antigua Sports and Games** (☎ 809/462–1925).

CRICKET

Practically the only thing most Americans know about this game is that there's something called a sticky wicket. Here, as in Britain and all the West Indies, the game is a national passion. Youngsters play on makeshift pitches, which apparently are comparable to sandlots, and international matches are fought out in the stadium on Independence Avenue in St. John's.

Shopping

Antigua's duty-free shops are at Heritage Quay; they're the reason so many cruise ships call here. Bargains can be found on perfumes, liqueurs and liquor (including, of course, Antiguan rum), jewelry, china, and crystal. As for local items, look for straw hats, baskets, batik, pottery, and hand-printed cotton clothing.

Shopping Areas

Redcliffe Quay, on the waterfront at the south edge of St. John's, is by far the most appealing shopping area. Here several restaurants and over 30 boutiques, many with interesting one-of-a-kind items, are set around landscaped courtyards shaded by colorful trees. **Heritage Quay** (also in St. John's) has some 35 shops—including many that are duty-free—that cater primarily to the cruise ship crowd that docks almost at its doorstep. Outlets here include Benetton and Oshkosh B'Gosh. The main tourist shops in St. John's are along **St. Mary's, High,** and **Long streets.**

Good Buys

BOOKS AND MAGAZINES

It may be a flower shop, but the **Flower Basket** (Nevis Street—on the left, keep going, it's really there; ☎ 809/462–0411) also has the latest U.S. magazines, newspapers, and best-selling paperback books. A "must" buy at the **Map Shop** (St. Mary's St., ☎ 809/462–3993) for those interested in Antiguan life is the paperback *To Shoot Hard Labour: The Life and Times of Samuel Smith, an Antiguan Workingman.* Also check out any of the books of Jamaica Kincaid, whose works on her native Antigua have won international, albeit controversial, acclaim.

CIGARS, LIQUOR, AND LIQUEURS

The **Warehouse** (St. Mary's St., ☎ 809/462–0495) offers bargains on imported wines and liquor. **Manuel Diaz Liquor Store** (Long and Market Sts., ☎ 809/462–0440) is another spot for good buys, including a wide selection of Caribbean rums and liqueurs. You can buy Cuban cigars at the **Cigar Shop** (Heritage Quay, ☎ 890/462–2677), but it's illegal to bring them back to the United States.

CHINA AND CRYSTAL

Specialty Shoppe (St. Mary's St., ☎ 809/462–1198) has wares that make impressive presents. **Norma's Duty-Free Shop** (Heritage Quay Shopping Center and the Halcyon Cove, ☎ 809/462–0172) offers the usual range of delicate sets, from Lladro to Limoges. **Little Switzerland** (Heritage Quay, ☎ 809/462–3108) houses pricey buys in a luxurious, and air-conditioned, setting. **Bona** (Redcliffe Quay, ☎ 809/462–2036) presents antiques, select crystal and porcelain, leaf-of-lettuce pottery from Italy, and "wedding frogs" from Thailand, collected during the world travels of owners Bona and Martin Macy.

CLOTHING AND FABRICS

Base, in Redcliffe Quay (☎ 809/462–0920), is the brainchild of English designer Steven Giles, whose striped cotton-and-Lycra beachwear is now all the rage on the island. Janie Easton designs many of the original finds in her two **Galley Boutiques** (main shop in English Harbour, ☎ 809/462–1525; St. James's Club, ☎ 809/463–1333) with pizzazz and reasonable prices. The **CoCo Shop** (St. Mary's St., ☎ 809/462–1128) is a favorite source for Sea Island cotton designs, Daks clothing, and Liberty of London fabrics, along with the shop's own designs for the country-club set. **Karibbean Kids of Antigua** (Redcliffe Quay, ☎ 809/462–4566) has great gifts and clothing for youngsters. **A Thousand Flowers** (Redcliffe Quay, ☎ 809/462–4264) sells resort wear made of comfortable silks, linens, and batiks from all over the world and has many unusual items.

JEWELRY
Hans Smit is **The Goldsmitty** (Redcliffe Quay, ☎ 809/462–4601), an expert goldsmith who turns gold, black coral, and precious and semi-precious stones into one-of-a-kind works of art. (Be aware that environmental groups discourage tourists from purchasing corals that are designated as endangered species, because the reefs are often harvested carelessly.) **Colombian Emeralds** (Heritage Quay, ☎ 809/462–2086) is the largest retailer of Colombian emeralds in the world. Jewelry bargains are also at **Norma's Duty-Free Shop** (Heritage Quay Shopping Center and the Halcyon Cove, ☎ 809/462–0172).

LOCAL ART AND CRAFTS
Trinidadian Natalie White sells her sculptured cushions and wall hangings, all hand-painted on silk and signed, from her home-studio (☎ 809/463–2519) and from her **Craft Originals Studio** on the Coast Road. Artist-filmmaker Nick Maley and his wife, Gloria, have turned the **Island Arts Galleries** (Alton Pl., Sandy La., behind Hodges Bay Club, ☎ 809/461–3332; Heritage Quay, ☎ 809/462–2787; and St. James's Club, ☎ 809/460–5000) into a melting pot for Caribbean artists, with prices ranging from $10 to $15,000. **Harmony Hall** (at Brown's Bay Mill, near Freetown, ☎ 809/460–4120) is the Antiguan sister to the original Jamaica location. In addition to "Annabella Boxes," books, and cards, there are pottery and ceramic pieces, carved wooden fantasy birds, and an ever-changing roster of exhibits. John and Katie Shears have opened **Seahorse Studios** (at Cobbs Cross, en route to English Harbour, ☎ 809/463–1417), presenting the works of good artists in a bucolic setting. The **Handicraft Centre** (High and Thames Sts., St. John's, ☎ 809/462–0639) specializes in island products—straw bags, mahogany warri boards, pottery, and hand-painted T-shirts and sundresses. **La Boutique Africaine** (36 St. Mary's St., St. John's, ☎ 809/462–0119) is the place for Kenyan soapstone sculpture and woven bags, Masai flasks, Ibo ebony combs, exquisite ivory chess sets, colorful batiks, even Tibetan wall hangings at surprisingly good prices.

PERFUME
Try the **CoCo Shop** (St. Mary's St., ☎ 809/462–1128) for exotic island fragrances. The **Scent Shop** (High St., ☎ 809/462–0303) in downtown St. John's offers scent-sational buys in perfumes and cosmetics. In Heritage Quay, **La Parfumerie** (☎ 809/462–2601) offers high-priced imported scents. **Little Switzerland** (☎ 809/462–3108), also in Heritage Quay, has an extensive selection of European scents for men and women.

Dining

Antigua has a wide variety of restaurants, and you can find excellent food whether you feel like dressing up or dressing down. There are elegant Continental and French restaurants, casual waterfront bistros, and barefoot beach bars. It's impossible not to find fresh seafood on the menu, and virtually every chef incorporates local ingredients and elements of West Indian and Creole cuisine. Alas, the food is often overcooked, even in the tonier establishments.

Most menus list prices in E.C. dollars, but you should make sure which currency you're dealing with. It's also a good idea to ask if credit cards are accepted. Prices below are in U.S. dollars. Dinner reservations are needed during high season.

What to Wear

Perhaps because of the island's British heritage, Antiguans tend to dress more formally for dinner than is the custom on many of the other Caribbean islands. A few places, which will be noted, require a jacket. Wraps and shorts (no beach attire) are de rigueur for lunch, except at local hangouts.

CATEGORY	COST*
$$$$	over $50
$$$	$35–$50
$$	$20–$35
$	under $20

per person, excluding drinks, service, and 7% sales tax

$$$ **Alberto's.** Set above Willoughby Bay on Antigua's southeast side, this
★ superior Italian restaurant is a bit out of the way but popular nevertheless. The ebullient owner, Alberto, taught his culinary secrets to his English wife, Vanessa, and the two turn out delicious seafood prepared with an Italian accent. Try fresh island lobster (perhaps grilled with basil and garlic); cockles Alberto; the chef's creation of the evening (you're in luck if it's snapper marechiaro, in a tomato, olive, and caper sauce); or more traditional dishes such as eggplant parmigiana, osso buco, or linguine with clams. The ravioli in creamy walnut sauce and breadfruit in garlic parsley butter are sheer heaven. Tables line a balcony open to the breezes and hung with bougainvillea; marvelous painted china graces the walls (check out the octopuses and squids on the plates by the bar). ✗ *Willoughby Bay,* ☎ *809/460–3007 or via VHF 68. Reservations required. AE, MC, V. Closed Mon. and July–Oct. No lunch.*

$$$ **Chez Pascal.** The fun murals adorning the building (a chef in a toque taller than he is, a girl enjoying her wine) hint at the convivial ambience within this top-notch bistro. Cool jazz and French pop (Piaf, Montand, et al.) waft through the cozy rooms. The fanciful decor continues inside, with bold, colorful paintings (by the owner's mother), a bamboo bar, and copper pots hanging from the West Indian roof. You can sit outside on the lime-and-white trellised terrace surrounded by a virtual jungle of greenery. Then savor Pascal Milliat's refined classic Lyonnaise cuisine. You might start with the sublime *croustade de fruits de mer* (seafood puff pastry), chilled leek and breadfruit soup, or grouper marinated in lime, olive oil, and *fines herbes*. Entrées might include a marvelous rack of lamb in its own juice, grouper in red wine, snapper in a caper-lime sauce, or shrimp in tomato coulis and garlic butter. Pascal's sauces are delicate, while his pairings provide the perfect counterpoint of flavor and texture. Finish with an unimpeachable tarte *aux pommes* or profiteroles. The wine list is excellent, if overpriced. ✗ *Cross & Tanner Sts.,* ☎ *809/462–3232. Reservations advised. AE, MC, V. Closed Sun. No lunch.*

$$$ **Coconut Grove.** Coconut palms grow up through the roof of this open-air restaurant, and waves lap the white-coral sand a few feet away. For a romantic evening, head here when there's a full moon and reserve table 1, closest to the water and under the stars. The menu always includes freshly grilled local lobster and choices of other fresh fish, plus lamb, steak, a vegetarian dish, and marinated and grilled chicken breast. Unfortunately, standards had deteriorated a little recently. New management had taken over at press time and was expected to improve the service and the kitchen. ✗ *Siboney Beach Club, Dickenson Bay,* ☎ *809/462–1538. Reservations advised in peak season. MC, V.*

$$$ **Colombo's.** This open-air restaurant is on a small bay in English Harbour, with views of palm trees, historic cannons, and the water in the distance. Various pennants draped around the bar attest that this is a

big yachtie hangout. The extensive menu is condensed during the off-season, but you can still order such creative dishes as grouper carpaccio, gamberoni Antigua (shrimp flamed in rum in ginger sauce), lobster in basil sauce, and veal with wild mushrooms. At lunchtime there are also light salads, hamburgers, and sandwiches. On Wednesday nights a reggae band entertains. ✗ *Galleon Beach Club, English Harbour,* ☎ *809/460–1452. Reservations suggested. AE, MC, V.*

$$$ **La Perruche.** Antiguan Tyrone Baptiste marries local ingredients to
★ classic French preparations in this polished restaurant, perhaps the island's best. Among his inspirations are blackened shrimp in tomato-mango butter, a house-cured gravlax perfectly scented with dill, and medallions of beef in a shiitake-infused Bordelaise sauce. An avocado mousse with sweet potato wafers arranged like petals around the wooden serving bowl is typical of the restaurant's determination to please the eye as well as the taste buds. The fruit plate—rock-fig bananas, black pineapple, fresh kidney mango, and passion fruit arranged around a hub of Antiguan golden apple—is a work of art. The plant-filled patio itself is a pleasure, with pretty green-and-white trim, crystal glasses, and a profusion of painted wooden parrots that hang everywhere—hence, the restaurant's name. Careful division of the eating area gives the large space an intimate feel. Wherever you sit, the decor is humorously eclectic, including Buddhas, cupids, and cracked fountains that might seem in uncertain taste were the overall effect not so delightfully whimsical. Recent rumor has it that La Perruche will be sold, or might even close; it would be a great pity. ✗ *English Harbour,* ☎ *809/460–3040. AE, MC, V. Closed Sun. and Sept. No lunch.*

$$–$$$ **Lobster Pot.** A fishing boat sits in the center of this beachfront restau-
★ rant's flagstone dining room, and sea breezes sweep in through the open gallery. The best seats are those right on the water. The long (seven pages!) and diverse menu is a mix of fresh seafood, pasta, and Creole- and Caribbean-style dishes. Starters include lobster and pineapple phyllo with tamari and chili dips and grilled baby eggplant stuffed with cheese and herbs. Follow these with coconut-milk curry shrimp; baked breast of chicken stuffed with goat cheese, broccoli, and sun-dried tomatoes; herb-encrusted swordfish in tomato sauce; or of course, succulent lobster. For dessert try the apple crepes in honey and island spice sauce. The wine list is well considered and very fairly priced, with most selections in the $20s. ✗ *Runaway Bay,* ☎ *809/462–2856. Reservations advised. D, MC, V.*

$$–$$$ **Wardroom Restaurant.** An atmosphere of Olde England pervades in
this restaurant on the ground floor of the beautifully restored Copper and Lumber Store. The dining room, with massive brick walls and stained wood beams, opens out to a charming courtyard hung with bougainvillea and to views of the floodlit battlements of English Harbour. The menu is international, mixing dishes such as West African peanut soup with lobster in puff pastry, a good selection of local fish dishes, and even lamb cutlets. ✗ *Nelson's Dockyard,* ☎ *809/460–1058. Reservations advised. Closed Wed. No lunch.*

$$ **Admiral's Inn.** Known as the Ad to yachtsmen around the world, this
★ historic inn, in the heart of English Harbour, is a must for Anglophiles and mariners. At the bar inside, you can sit and soak up the centuries under dark, timbered wood (the bar top even has the names of sailors from Nelson's fleet carved into it), but most guests tend to sit on the terrace under shady Australian gums to enjoy the splendid views of the harbor complex and Clarence House opposite. Specialties include curried conch, fresh snapper with equally fresh limes, and lobster ther-

midor. The pumpkin soup is not to be missed. ✕ *Nelson's Dockyard,* ☎ *809/460–1027. Reservations required. AE, MC, V.*

$$ **Home.** When Carl Thomas came back to his native Antigua after years in New York, he decided to open a restaurant in his boyhood home, a '50s bungalow in a quiet suburb of St. John's. So he completely refurbished the original house, knocked down walls to create one large space, and planted an herb and vegetable garden. Modern, unfinished pine furniture and polished wood floors give the place an airy atmosphere. Unusual ceramic candlesticks adorn the tables, and walls are hung with African and Caribbean art. The menu, which Carl dubs "Caribbean haute cuisine," is ambitious for Antigua. Unfortunately, the quality is quite uneven. Carl could use a stronger hand with his seasonings. Grouper in herb sauce and other simpler offerings are more successful than such intriguing dishes as molasses pepper steak. Don't miss the smoked fish, a house specialty, and bread pudding with whisky sauce. ✕ *Gambles Terr., St. John's,* ☎ *809/461–7651. Reservations advised in high season. AE, MC, V. Closed Sun. Lunch Sat. only.*

$$ **Lemon Tree.** This air-conditioned, art-deco restaurant, on the second floor of a historic building in the old part of St. John's, is a smart, upbeat eating place, popular with cruise-ship guests. There's live music every night, varying from soft classical piano to funky reggae. The menu is eclectic, mixing minipizzas and ribs with beef Wellington, Cornish hen, lobster, vegetarian crepes, very spicy Cajun garlic shrimp, and pasta dishes. For those who like Mexican food, the Lemon Tree offers unbeatable burritos, as well as chili, nachos, and fajitas. ✕ *Long and Church Sts., St. John's,* ☎ *809/462–1969. Reservations advised on weekends. AE, DC, MC, V. Closed Sat. No lunch Sun.*

$$ **Redcliffe Tavern.** Every item on the tavern's part northern Italian, part
★   Continental, part Creole menu is wonderfully fresh. The dinner menu includes delicious pastas, marinated grilled chicken, fresh local lobster, spicy Creole crab puffs, and a smoked salmon and shellfish terrine in lime mousseline. The lunch menu also lists salads, sandwiches, and hamburgers. The dining room is on the second floor of a beautifully restored colonial warehouse set amid the courtyards of Redcliffe Quay. Brick and stone walls are decorated with antique water-pumping equipment still bearing the original English maker's crests. Salvaged from all over the island, the beautiful old machines, with their flywheels and pistons, have been imaginatively integrated into the restaurant's structure (one supports the buffet bar, for instance). You can also dine on the treetop-level terrace. ✕ *Redcliffe Quay, St. John's,* ☎ *809/461– 4557. Reservations advised. AE, MC, V.*

$$ **Shirley Heights Lookout.** This restaurant is set in an 18th-century fortification high on a bluff, with a breathtaking view of English Harbour below. The first-floor pub opens onto the lookout point. Upstairs, there's a cozy, windowed dining room with hardwood floors and beamed ceilings. Pub offerings include burgers, sandwiches, and barbecue, while upstairs you can order the likes of pumpkin soup and lobster in lime sauce. If you like to be at the center of things, come here Sunday around 3 PM or Thursday around 3:30 PM, when locals, yachters, and visitors troop up the hill for the barbecue. Livened by steel-band and reggae music, it lasts well into the evening. ✕ *Shirley Heights,* ☎ *809/463–1785. Reservations required in season in the dining room. AE, MC, V.*

$–$$ **Calypso.** The St. John's professional set frequents this cheerful outdoor spot. At lunchtime it is packed with smartly dressed lawyers and government functionaries smoking cigars and chatting over traditional Caribbean food. Tables are arranged under green umbrellas on a sunny trellised patio dominated by the remains of a brick kiln. Specials change every day, but you can usually count on stewed lamb, grilled lobster, and baked chicken served with rice, dumplings, and *fungi,* a pastelike vegetable dish made of cornmeal and okra. ✕ *Redcliffe St., St. John's,* ☎ *809/462–1965. AE, MC, V. Closed Sun. No dinner except Fri.*

$–$$ La Dolce Vita. This Italian charmer in Redcliffe Quay is a cool oasis, with crisp white napery and wood planters and chianti flasks everywhere. There's nothing wildly innovative here, just good, solid standards like pasta carbonara, Bolognese, Alfredo, and puttanesca; chicken or veal milanese; and yummy pizzas (try the unusual tuna or lobster). The bountiful salads are also reliable. ✕ *Redcliffe Quay 16,* ☎ *809/462–2016. AE, D, MC, V.*

$–$$ Russell's. Russell Hodge, the vivacious owner, had the brilliant idea of restoring a part of Fort St. James, with its gorgeous views of the bay and headlands, and converting it into an open-air restaurant. Potted plants and faux-Victorian gas lamps lend a romantic aura to the cool stone-and-wood terrace. The menu—all delectable local specialties with an emphasis on seafood—is listed on the blackboard. You might start with definitive conch fritters or whelks in garlic butter, then try an excellent snapper Creole. Live jazz is a lure Sunday nights. Russell's sister Valerie owns the estimable Shirley Heights Lookout (*see above*), and sister Patsy operates the delightful Pumpkin Runner, a fast-food van dispensing savory local dishes every night in St. John's. The Hodges might well be Antigua's first family of food. ✕ *Fort James,* ☎ *809/462–5479. AE, DC.*

$ Big Banana-Pizzas on the Quay. This tiny, often crowded spot is tucked ★ into one side of a beautifully restored warehouse with broad plank floors and stonework archways. It serves some of the best pizza on the island, topped with traditional and not-so-traditional items. You can also enjoy delectable specials like conch salad. It's a busy lunch and dinner spot, and there is live entertainment some evenings. ✕ *Redcliffe Quay, St. John's,* ☎ *809/462–2621. AE, MC, V.*

$ Brother B's. It's impossible to miss this funky restaurant in the appropriately named Soul Alley; a yellow-painted wooden fence and hand-painted boards advertise its fare. This is the place to try such local specialties as pepper pot; fungi; *pelleau,* a seasoned rice dish with chicken, meat, and peas; saltfish; *ducana,* a boiled dumpling filled with coconut and sweet potato; and bull's foot soup, a Caribbean variant of a 19th-century dish from Manchester, England. ✕ *Soul Alley, St. John's,* ☎ *809/462–0616. No credit cards. Also open for breakfast.*

Lodging

Scattered along Antigua's fine sandy beaches and tropical hillsides are resorts of all kinds, from exclusive, elegant hideaways and romantic restored inns to casual go-barefoot-everywhere places and all-inclusive hot spots for couples. Pick a spot near St. John's—anywhere between Dickenson Bay and Five Islands Harbour—if you want to be close to restaurants and shopping or want lots of action. If you stay right on Dickenson Bay you can easily walk to quite a few restaurants, beach bars, and resorts. English Harbour, though far from St. John's, has the best collection of inns, several excellent restaurants, and is the hangout for the yachting crowd. The resorts scattered elsewhere on the island tend to cater more to guests who want to stay put or are seeking seclusion. The price categories below reflect the room cost during high season.

CATEGORY	COST*
$$$$	over $350
$$$	$250–$350
$$	$150–$250
$	under $150

All prices are for a standard double room for two, excluding 7% tax and 10% service charge.

$$$$ ★ **Curtain Bluff.** Howard Hulford built this resort more than 30 years ago, and he's still very active in its management. You're likely to see him puttering around his beloved gardens or tasting a new wine for his legendary cellar of nearly 15,000 bottles. The resort is named for its spectacular setting, on a bluff bordered on one side by the wild Atlantic Ocean and on the other by the calm Caribbean. Spacious standard rooms are in two-story beachfront buildings facing the Caribbean, with terraces or balconies. They have wicker furnishings and a teal-and-white color scheme. The suites zigzag their way up the bluff on the Atlantic side and are some of the finest accommodations on Antigua—huge split-level apartments with two large balconies offering spectacular views, a large, tastefully decorated living room, and, up a flight of steps, a spacious and inviting bedroom. All accommodations have a safe and a phone. Swiss chef Reudi Portmann, who has ruled the kitchen here since the resort opened, prepares the meals served in the greenery-filled open-air restaurant. Jacket and tie are required for dinner, except on Wednesday and Sunday. Curtain Bluff may not be as distinctive as other Caribbean resorts in its class, but its exceptional service, casual elegance, and country-club ambience appeal to a select more mature crowd who return annually. ☎ *Box 288, St. John's,* ☎ *809/462–8400; in NY, 212/289–8888;* FAX *809/462–8409. 61 rooms and suites. 2 restaurants, lounge, 4 tennis courts, squash court, fitness center, pro shop, croquet, putting green, water-sports center. AE. Closed mid-May–mid-Oct. FAP.*

$$$$ **Galley Bay.** A beach of ravishing champagne-colored sand, a blue lagoon, and beautifully manicured gardens surround this quiet all-inclusive retreat. Beachfront villas have king-size beds, ceiling fans, showers, tiled floors, and tropical-print coverlets and drapes. Ten "executive rooms" are on the quietest section of the beach and offer slightly more space and a private patio with a hammock. Units in Gauguin Village consist of two small, round, thatch-roof Tahitian-style buildings linked by a patio. One room is a bedroom, the other a bathroom with a shower for two and a dressing table. Reviews of these accommodations are mixed: Some find them romantic cottages, while others think they're confining huts. All accommodations in the village have fridge, coffeemaker, and ceiling fan. The charming decor includes rattan furnishings, stucco walls, local artworks, and mosquito netting. ☎ *Box 305, St. John's,* ☎ *809/462–0302 or 800/223–6510,* FAX *809/462–4551. 30 rooms. Restaurant, bar, gift shop, tennis court, water-sports center. AE, MC, V. All-inclusive.*

$$$$ ★ **Jumby Bay.** Just 5 minutes by taxi and another 10 minutes by launch from Antigua is this exclusive, 300-acre, private island retreat. Spanish-style white stucco buildings with orange tile roofs line the beach. Rooms are in the two-story Pond Bay House and in individual rondavels (circular bungalows) and cottages spread around the property. All are spacious, and even those not labeled suites have separate sitting areas. Some bathrooms open out to small areas filled with tropical greenery. For an extra $600 per day, you can rent an expansive and well-furnished two-bedroom villa with a kitchen-dining room and a small swimming pool that's shared with several other villas. Lunch is an alfresco buffet, while the more elegant and formal dinner is in the old manor house's dining room, which is open to the ocean breezes. A few of the favored dishes are sautéed breast of chicken filled with wild mushrooms, Mediterranean seafood terrine sprinkled with saffron, and soufflé of scallops with basil purée. There are lots of walking trails, and everything is spread out, so if you hate to walk or bicycle, you might want to stay elsewhere. No children under age eight are permitted during high season. There is occasional jet noise from the nearby airport. ☎ *Box 243, St. John's, ☎ 809/462–6000 or 800/421–9016, FAX 809/462–6020. 38 suites, 18 villas. 2 restaurants, 3 bars, tennis, bicycles, sailboats, croquet, water-sports center. AE, MC, V. All-inclusive (including liquor and wine).*

$$$$ St. James's Club. This out-of-the-way hotel is on the 100-acre spit of land that helps form Mamora Bay. Rooms and one-bedroom suites are in the main buildings at the water's edge on the tip of the peninsula. Units are nicely furnished and painted in pastel colors; some have romantic canopy beds. You enter past the "villa village," a group of tightly clustered two-bedroom villas that rest on the top of the hills that spill down toward the main hotel. Although also well decorated, these villas include views of your neighbor's roof. You can dine at the three restaurants in the main building: the Rainbow Garden, an elegant spot for dinner; the Docksider Cafe, with an elegant menu but casual alfresco setting; or the Poolside Reef Deck, a breakfast and lunch spot. Also part of the resort is the Italian restaurant Piccolo Mondo, but the food there could be better. Overall, the St. James tends to live off its *renommé* (it is affiliated with other like-named resorts in London, Paris, and Los Angeles), rather than what it delivers. That said, the beaches and extensive sports facilities—and such amenities as a hotel helicopter that can be chartered for sightseeing—make this a fine, full-service resort. ☎ *Box 63, St. John's, ☎ 809/460–5000 or 800/274–0008, FAX 809/460–3015. 178 units. 3 restaurants, 5 bars, 24-hour room service, 3 swimming pools, Jacuzzi, minigym, 4 boutiques, beauty salon and masseuse, nightclub, casino, 7 tennis courts (5 hard, 2 omniturf; 5 lighted), water sports and scuba diving, lawn croquet, children's playground, golf privileges at the 18-hole Cedar Valley Golf Club, horseback riding. AE, MC, V. EP, MAP.*

$$$–$$$$ Pineapple Beach Club. A broad stone walk leads directly from the reception area to the beach of this bustling, beachside, all-inclusive resort. All rooms are on or very near the beach, but some have only partial ocean or garden views. Decor is typical Caribbean pastel, but redecoration was slated to take place by press time. There are no phones or TVs in rooms, but fax and phone service is available at the front desk. This is an activity-oriented place with a full array of water sports, nightly entertainment, and an electronic casino, but it does quiet down soon after midnight. Be sure to bring the letter confirming your reservation; the hotel has a bad habit of overbooking or losing reservation information. ☎ *Box 54, St. John's, ☎ 809/463–2006 or 800/345–0356, FAX 809/465–2452. 125 rooms. Restaurant, bar, pool, 4 tennis courts, kayaking, volleyball, horseshoes, croquet. AE, MC, V. All-inclusive.*

$$$ Blue Waters Beach Hotel. Although Blue Waters has drawn rave reviews in the past, both the charm and level of service there have unfortunately faded with time. Its setting on Antigua's northwest tip is stunning, with views across beautifully manicured tropical gardens to the sea, but the buildings are ordinary, the beach is small and not particularly good for swimming, and the service is mediocre at best. Accommodations are in several long, two-story buildings strung out above the beach (stairways at several locations lead to the beach below). Rooms are air-conditioned, decorated with rattan and pastel prints, have sliding doors that open onto a small patio or balcony (within easy earshot of your neighbors right and left), and nice ocean views. There are also several two- and three-bedroom villas. Breakfast is a haphazard affair, but lunch on the terrace is delightful, and there is nightly dancing under the stars. There are a variety of meal plans, and it is important that you fully understand them and agree to one when you check in. The gourmet restaurant, the Cacubi Room, offers a swooningly romantic, candlelit setting, but the food is disappointingly ordinary and the service uneven. ☎ *Box 256, St. John's (Boon Pt.),* ☎ *809/462–0290 or 800/372–1323; in the U.K., 0181/367–5175;* FAX *809/462–0293. 67 rooms. 2 restaurants, 2 bars, pool, 1 lighted tennis court, gift shop, water-sports center. AE, MC, V. EP, MAP.*

$$$ **Halcyon Cove.** Many European and American tour groups patronize this large, somewhat impersonal hotel on beautiful Dickenson Bay, so it's typically crowded, and your neighbor may be paying a third of what you are. Accommodations are in two- and three-story flat-roofed buildings scattered around the courtyard or along the beach. They have white tile floors and are decorated with blond wood and mint fabrics. All have air-conditioning and a private balcony or patio, but only higher-grade accommodations have full bath, TV, and refrigerator. A water-sports center on the busy beach offers excursions on a glass-bottom boat and waterskiing, in addition to the other usual water sports. The Wari Pier restaurant is set on stilts over the ocean and serves fine seafood and grilled items all day long. While you're on the walkway that connects it to the beach, be sure to look into the water—it's filled with schools of colorful fish. ☎ *Box 251, St. John's,* ☎ *809/462–0256,* FAX *809/462–0271. 194 rooms, 16 1-bedroom suites. 2 restaurants, 4 bars, ice-cream parlor, beauty salon, car rental, pool, 4 lighted tennis courts, boutiques, water-sports center. AE, D, DC, MC, V. EP, MAP.*

$$$ **Hawksbill Beach Hotel.** Thirty-seven acres of the bucolic Five Islands peninsula, including five beaches of fine tan sand (you can bathe in the buff at one), make up the grounds of this sprawling resort. The main building, reception area, and dining room are on a small bluff that commands a sweeping view of the sea and Montserrat beyond, set off by the restored ruins of a sugar mill in the foreground. Deluxe rooms are in gingerbread-trimmed, West Indian–style cottages surrounded by grass lawns and facing the sea, with a decor of wicker, tile floors, and light floral pastels. The less expensive rooms are in cottages with garden views. Most of these actually have restricted beach views and are the same size as the pricier beachfront units. Bedrooms, even in the deluxe category, are quite small, but guests here spend most of their time outside. There is no air-conditioning, TV, or phone. The classiest accommodations aren't the cottage guest rooms but the three-bedroom West Indian Great House, an old, colonial-style building with king-size beds, tile floors, wicker furniture, and kitchenette. Men are requested not to wear short sleeves into the dining room after 7 PM. And though children are more welcome than they used to be ("screamers" not included), Hawksbill is more a place for young couples and singles. Breakfast and the use of most water-sports facilities are complimentary. ☎ *Box 108, St. John's,* ☎ *809/462–0301 or 800/223–6510; in Canada, 416/622–8813;* FAX *809/462–1515. 90 rooms. 2 restaurants, 2 bars, pool, tennis court, boutique, water-sports center. AE, DC, MC, V. BP, MAP.*

$$$ **Hodges Bay Club.** A great snorkeling beach and proximity to both the airport and St. John's are good reasons to stay at this condominium property on the prestigious north shore, facing Prickley Pear Island. Connected, air-conditioned one- and two-bedroom villas line the beach or overlook the pool. All are spacious, comfortably decorated, and have

fully equipped kitchens, king-size beds, balconies, and daily maid service. Each bedroom has a private bath and can be closed off for rental as a hotel room. The Pelican Club restaurant here is considered one of the best hotel dining rooms on the island. ☎ *Box 1237, St. John's,* ☎ *809/462–2300 or 800/432–4229; in NY, 212/535–9530;* FAX *809/462–1962. 4 1-bedroom villas, 22 2-bedroom villas. Restaurant, pool, 2 tennis courts, water-sports center. AE, DC, MC, V. EP.*

$$–$$$ **Dickenson Bay Cottages.** There are only 13 units at this small, pleasant development on Marble Hill, just above Dickenson Bay. The two-story black- or gray-and-white villa-style buildings are surrounded by gardens and elegantly furnished with high-quality painted rattan, blond woods, and soft pastel fabrics. Downstairs is a well-equipped kitchen and a large living room area with a TV. The bedroom and bathroom are up a flight of stairs. Larger units have two bedrooms upstairs and a large veranda overlooking the ocean. One annoyance is the lack of a cross breeze, which obliges you to keep the air conditioner on. Guests have beach privileges at the excellent but busy beach at Halcyon Cove, just a five-minute walk away, and the resort has an arrangement for the use of the tennis and water-sports facilities there at a 20% discount. Several other resorts nearby give you a selection of entertainment and restaurants. ☎ *Box 1379, St. John's,* ☎ *809/462–4940,* FAX *809/462–4941. 13 rooms. Pool. AE, DC, MC, V. EP.*

$$–$$$ **Inn at English Harbour.** The reception area, bar and dining room, and
★ six of the guest rooms of this inn sit atop a hill with stunning views of English Harbour. The bar, with its green leather chairs, wooden floors, stone walls, and maritime prints, is one of the most pleasant on the island; and the flagstone terrace dining room offers an unparalleled romantic ambience and dependable Continental fare. Off to the side of the main house are the hilltop rooms, in individual, cottage-style units nestled amid typical English gardens. Down the steep hill, right on the beach, are 22 additional rooms in two-story wooden buildings surrounded by hibiscus and bougainvillea. The superior rooms are slightly larger, but all rooms have phones, wall safes, refrigerators, and hair dryers and are attractively furnished with rattan furniture and tropical or floral fabrics. Also on the beach is a second bar-restaurant that stays open until 6 PM. A shuttle bus runs guests up and down the hill. The beach, like all those in English Harbour, is not the best. During high season only MAP bookings are accepted. An air of quiet, laid-back refinement is cultivated by amiable second-generation owner Paul Deeth. ☎ *Box 187, St. John's,* ☎ *809/460–1014 or 800/223–6510; in Canada,* ☎ *800/424–5500;* FAX *809/460–1603. 28 rooms. 2 restaurants, 2 bars, water sports. AE, MC, V. EP, MAP.*

$$–$$$ **Royal Antiguan Resort.** This nine-story, high-rise hotel, possibly the island's ugliest, is set on the waterside a few miles south of St. John's. The hotel caters to groups and conventions and is by far the most "Stateside-like" hotel on Antigua. Rooms and suites are air-conditioned, with minibars and TVs, and there are numerous facilities: three restaurants, three bars, a huge ballroom used for meetings and cocktail parties, a shopping arcade, and a 5,500-square-foot casino with blackjack, roulette, craps, baccarat, and 130 slot machines, all played by Atlantic City rules. It was taken over in late 1994 by the Pineapple Beach Club management, which is expected to invest several million dollars in a complete renovation. The initial stage calls for brightening the drab decor. ☎ *Deep Bay, St. John's,* ☎ *809/462–3733 or 800/228–9898,* FAX *809/462–3732. 300 rooms. 3 restaurants, 4 bars, casino, swimming pool with swim-up bar, full water sports (snorkeling, Sunfish sailing, windsurfing, waterskiing, fishing), a certified dive master, 5 tennis*

courts, golf arranged at nearby 18-hole Cedar Valley course, a mini-crafts market on site. AE, D, MC, V. EP.

$$–$$$ **Sandals.** Pool competitions and beach volleyball, aerobics sessions, and
★ evening social events, including all kinds of group games, are just a
few of the things going on at this couples-only resort. The schedule of
events is organized by a "play maker," who will cajole (but not force)
you to join in the fun; but you can still enjoy the place if you just want
to read and relax. Everything, from the tennis coaching to the pedal
boats, the scuba diving to the swim-up pool-bars, discos, and meals,
is included in the price. For a little extra, you can even get married in
front of a miniature waterfall. Rooms, facing the beach or the garden,
and rondavels facing the beach are spacious. All units are air-conditioned and have phone, TV, safe, and hair dryer. Many have four-poster
or frilly beds, and all are light and fresh in seafoam green and bright
floral fabrics. Thirty-two units were scheduled to be added in time for
the 1995–96 season. You have a choice of four restaurants offering Continental, Indian, Japanese, and southwestern fare. Public areas are
handsome, especially the vast reception area with a rock grotto and
vaulting ficus that pierces the roof. All the place lacks is true island atmosphere. ☎ *Box 147, St. John's,* ☎ *809/462–0267; U.S. reservations,
800/726-3257;* FAX *809/462–4135. 195 rooms and suites. 4 restaurants,
4 bars, 5 pools, 5 Jacuzzis, health spa, gift shop, nightclub, 2 lighted
tennis courts, and water sports. AE. All-inclusive.*

$$–$$$ **Siboney Beach Club.** When Tony Johnson arrived in Antigua in the late
★ '50s, he planned to stay just a few weeks. Instead, he ended up building or refurbishing some of the island's finest resorts, and eventually
opened his own small gem set in an exquisite tropical garden on Dickenson Bay. Each suite has a small bedroom, a cleverly designed Pullman kitchen, a modestly furnished living room, and a plant-filled patio
or balcony that looks out to tropical greenery. Decor varies slightly,
but all feature rattan and rich tropical fabrics. Most units are air-conditioned. Room 9 is for those who revel in sea views, but the soothing sound of the surf permeates even those with partial views. A few
yards away is an excellent, although often busy, calm-water beach and
the Coconut Grove (*see* Dining, *above*), where guests can enjoy great
breakfasts and lunches as well as candlelight dinners at the water's edge.
The staff is exceptionally friendly, and Tony and his Trinidadian wife,
Ann, are always available to offer advice and good cheer, making Siboney your home away from home. ☎ *Box 222, St. John's,* ☎ *809/462–
0806 or 800/533–0234,* FAX *809/462–3356. 12 suites. Restaurant,
bar, pool. AE, MC, V. EP, MAP.*

$$ **Copper and Lumber Store Hotel.** Overlooking the marina at English
Harbour, this former supply store for Nelson's Caribbean fleet and fine
example of Georgian British architecture has been beautifully trans-
formed into a gracious inn. The warm brick, hardwood floors, tim-
bered ceilings, and burgundy leather, button armchairs and sofas give
it an Old World charm unique in the West Indies. Each of the 14 suites
is meticulously decorated with authentic Georgian period furnishings,
including antique washstands, secretaries, and four-poster canopy
beds; many sport such touches as wrought-iron chandeliers, old sail-
ing prints, mahogany steamer trunks, brass sinks, and faux gas lamps.
All suites have showers, and although they lack air-conditioning, ceil-
ing fans capture nice breezes. Unfortunately, many rooms have become
a bit frayed around the edges and could use a face-lift. A ferry service
shuttles guests to a beach on the other side of English Harbour. Be warned
that the hotel sits inside a national park and visitors stream through
the area during the day. ☎ *Box 184, St. John's,* ☎ *809/460–1058 or*

800/275–0877; in Canada, 800/463–0877; FAX *809/460–1529. 14 suites. 2 restaurants, pub. AE, MC, V. EP, MAP.*

$$ Yepton Beach Resort. This Swiss-designed, full-service, all-suites resort is set on Hog John Bay on the Five Islands peninsula, not far from St. John's. The Mediterranean-style white-stucco buildings are situated so that accommodations have views on one side of the resort's own attractive beach and on the other side of a lagoon dotted with pelicans and egrets. Some of the rooms are two-room suites, with a bedroom and large living-room-cum-kitchenette. Others are studios, with a folding Murphy bed and kitchenette. By putting together a double bedroom and a studio, one can also make an apartment that sleeps four. All rooms are air-conditioned. Live reggae, calypso, and jazz groups appear three nights a week. Many different packages are available. ✉ *Box 1427, St. John's,* ☎ *809/462–2520 or 800/361–4621,* FAX *809/462–3240. 38 units. Restaurant, 2 tennis courts, pool, Sunfish sailing, and snorkeling. AE, MC, V. EP, MAP.*

$ Admiral's Inn. This lovingly restored 18th-century Georgian inn is the
★ centerpiece of the magnificent Nelson's Dockyard complex. Once the engineers' office and warehouse (the bricks were originally used as ballast for British ships), the Admiral's Inn reverberates with history. The best rooms, upstairs in the main building, have the original timbered ceilings, complete with iron braces, hardwood floors, and massive whitewashed brick walls. Straw floor mats from Dominica and views through wispy Australian pines to the sunny harbor beyond complete the effect. The rooms in the garden annex are smaller and a bit airless. The Loft, which used to be the dockyard's joinery, has two big bedrooms, an enormous kitchen, and a magnificent view from the timbered living room onto the busy harbor. Be aware that this inn sits smack in the middle of a bustling daytime tourist attraction. The same owners run the simply furnished, breezy, self-contained Falmouth Beach Apartments. ✉ *Box 713, St. John's,* ☎ *809/460–1027, 800/223–5695, or 800/223–9815;* FAX *809/460–1534. 14 rooms, 1 2-bedroom apt. Restaurant, pub, complimentary beach shuttle and use of water sports at Falmouth Beach Apts. AE, MC, V. EP, MAP.*

$ Banana Cove. These one- and two-bedroom self-contained apartments are set in a relatively secluded part of Antigua, near Devil's Bridge. The units are airy and appealing, with hardwood floors, island prints, and bright pastel fabrics. Each has a complete kitchen and bath, a small terrace, and remarkably large closets. The best buys are the two-bedroom suites with pool views (ocean view is nearly twice as expensive). The beach is a small spit of land, but Long Bay is a short drive. ✉ *Dian Bay, Box 1389,* ☎ *809/463–2003 or 800/223–9815,* FAX *809/463–2425. 30 units. Restaurant, bar, pool. AE, MC, V. EP.*

$ Catamaran Hotel. Renovation in 1989 was careful to retain the historical ambience of this plantation-style house, with its attractive apricot, white, and black trim and wraparound veranda supported on white, classical-style pediments. The property sits on the water at Falmouth Harbour, on a beach lined with palm and almond trees. The best rooms are the eight first-floor suites, with four-poster beds, full baths, kitchenettes, and private balconies. None of the rooms has air-conditioning, TV, or telephone. English Harbour is only 2 miles away. There's also a restaurant (under different management), Captain Bruno's, serving à la carte meals and good pizzas. For those who want a low-key, low-priced, tranquil resort, this offers excellent value. ✉ *Box 958, Falmouth,* ☎ *809/460–1036,* FAX *809/460–1506. 16 rooms. Restaurant, bar, marina, shops. AE, MC, V. EP.*

$ **Falmouth Beach Apartments.** This is the sister hotel of the Admiral's Inn at English Harbour. The best accommodations are in an attractive colonial-style house at the water's edge on the hotel's own small palm-lined beach. These quiet, simple units are basically one large room—a bedroom-living-room-kitchenette combination—and a bathroom with a shower. All open onto the house's timbered wraparound veranda with a view of the water and the hilly peninsula opposite. Since the beach is very sheltered, it is perfect for toddlers and small children who are learning to swim. There is no air-conditioning and no telephones or TVs. (The upstairs units catch the breezes better.) Other rooms are located in four modern buildings perched on the hillside and have a separate kitchen, a bedroom with twin beds, and a bathroom with shower. Decor is the standard rattan and beige tiles, jazzed up by old maps or striking artworks. All apartments have daily maid service. ☎ *Box 713, Falmouth Harbour,* ☎ *809/460–1094 or 800/223–5695,* FAX *809/460–1534. 28 rooms. Water-sports center (Sunfish and paddleboats included in price). AE, MC, V. EP.*

$ **Lord Nelson Beach Hotel.** This small, weathered mom-and-pop resort
★ is run by the Fullers, expatriate Americans who have been here since 1949. As they have a vast, extended family of their own, it's a perfect place for children to scamper about and explore. If you don't mind a bit of chipped paint and organized chaos, you'll love it, too (as did Eugene Fodor when he once stayed here). An extensive collection of windsurfing boards, easy access to the water, and a dedicated pro have also made it a mecca for windsurfers. The best rooms are in a two-story, apricot-colored building looking directly onto the property's own horseshoe-shape beach. Each room is a slightly different hodgepodge (one has beautiful tiled floors and an ornately carved bed from Dominica that is so high you almost need to be a pole-vaulter to get into it). Several others have four-poster beds, antique armoires, and vivid local still lifes. Guests eat in the timbered dining room, draped with fish nets and dominated by a replica of the boat in which Captain Bligh was cast off from the *Bounty*; expect hearty dishes such as stuffed pork chops, wahoo, and snapper. Because the resort is fairly isolated (5 miles from St. John's), figure an extra E.C.$25 into your budget for cab fare to any meal you have elsewhere. ☎ *Box 155, St. John's,* ☎ *809/462–3094,* FAX *809/462–0751. 16 rooms. Restaurant, bar, maid service, dive shop, windsurfing. AE, MC, V. EP, MAP, FAP. Closed Sept.*

Nightlife

Most of Antigua's evening entertainment centers on the resort hotels, which feature calypso singers, steel bands, limbo dancers, and folkloric groups on a regular basis. Check with the Department of Tourism for up-to-date information.

Shirley Heights Lookout (Shirley Heights, ☎ 809/463–1785) does Sunday-afternoon barbecues that continue into the night with music and dancing. It's *the* place to be Sunday afternoons and Thursday evenings, when local residents, visitors, and the yachting crowd gather for boisterous fun and to exchange the latest gossip. **The Verandah** (St. Mary's St., St. John's, ☎ 809/462–5677) attracts an appreciative local crowd for live music Friday and Saturday nights. **Russell's** (Fort James, ☎ 809/462–5479) presents live jazz combos on Sunday nights. The **Crazy Cactus Cantina** (All Saints Rd., ☎ 809/462–1183) holds frequent Latin nights, when the sensuous rhythms of live merengue and salsa hold sway. On Wednesday nights, **Colombo's** (Galleon Beach Club, English Harbour, ☎ 809/460–1452) is the place to be for live reggae, and the **Lemon Tree** restaurant (Long and Church Sts., St. John's, ☎ 809/461–1969) swings every night but Sunday in season until at least 11 PM. The crowd at **Millers by the Sea** (Dickenson Bay, ☎ 809/462–2393) spills over onto the beach for its ever-popular happy hour and live nightly entertainment. This is the place to come and dance on the beach way into the night. The *Jolly Roger* (from Dickenson Bay, ☎ 809/462–2064) gets a boisterous group for its Saturday night cruises. Head out on this replica of a pirate ship for a four-hour sail under the stars with a barbecue, open bar, and dancing to live island music.

Casinos

There are four major casinos on Antigua, as well as several holes-in-the-wall that feature mainly one-armed bandits. Hours vary depending on the season and whether or not cruise ships are in, so it's best to inquire upon your arrival to the island. The "world's largest slot machine" as well as gaming tables are at the **King's Casino** (☎ 809/462–1727), at Heritage Quay. The **St. James's Club** (Mamora Bay, ☎ 809/463–1113) has a rather elegant casino with a European ambience. The casino at the **Royal Antiguan Resort** (☎ 809/462–3733) is a model of those in Atlantic City, New Jersey.

Discos

The Lime (Redcliffe Quay, St. John's, ☎ 809/462–2317) opens at 10:30 PM on Friday and Saturday and draws a frenetic mix of locals and visitors. **The Web** (Old Parham Rd., St. John's, ☎ 809/462–3186) and **Grasshopper** (Airport Rd., no ☎) attract a somewhat rowdier, more heavily local crowd.

4 Aruba

IMAGINE ARUBA AS ONE BIG LOVE BOAT CRUISE, with quite a few casinos to enliven the night or unburden your wallet. Most of its 38 hotels sit side by side down one major strip along the southwestern shore, with restaurants, exotic boutiques, fiery floor shows, and glitzy casinos right on their premises. Nearly every night there are organized theme parties, treasure hunts, beachside barbecues, and fish fries with steel bands and limbo dancers.

Updated by
Barbara Hults

Here, in a land whose symbol is a tree (the divi-divi) that is bent over like the ones Dorothy saw before her house took off to Oz, what's new? Why, smashing new golf and tennis clubs! Robert Trent Jones never saw wind like this before. But his designers have compensated, and so take your clubs and racket when you go.

The "A" in the ABC Islands, Aruba is small—only 19.6 miles long and 6 miles across at its widest point, approximately 70 square miles. Once a member of the Netherlands Antilles, Aruba became an independent entity within the Netherlands in 1986, with its own royally appointed governor, a democratic government, and a 21-member elected Parliament. With education, housing, and health care financed by an economy based on tourism, the island's population of 70,337 recognizes visitors as valued guests. The national anthem proclaims, "The greatness of our people is their great cordiality," and this is no exaggeration. Waiters serve you with smiles and solid eye contact, English is spoken everywhere, and hotel hospitality directors appear delighted to serve your special needs. Good direct air service from the United States makes Aruba an excellent choice for even a short vacation.

The island's distinctive beauty lies in its countryside—an almost extraterrestrial landscape full of rocky deserts, divi-divi trees, cactus jungles, secluded coves, and aquamarine vistas with crashing waves. With its low humidity and average temperature of 82°F, Aruba has the climate of a paradise; rain comes mostly during November. Sun, cooling trade winds, friendly and courteous service, modern and efficient amenities, and 11 modern casinos are Aruba's strong suit and help fill its more than 7,000 hotel rooms.

Before You Go

Tourist Information

Contact the **Aruba Tourism Authority,** 1000 Harbor Blvd. (Ground Level), Weehawken, NJ 07087, ☎ 201/330–0800 or 800/862–2782, FAX 201/330–8757; in Miami, 2344 Salzedo St., Miami, FL 33134, ☎ 305/567–2720, FAX 305/567–2721; in Canada, 86 Bloor St. W, Suite 204, Toronto, Ontario, M5S 1M5, ☎ 416/975–1950.

Arriving and Departing

BY PLANE

Aruba is 2½ hours away from Miami and 4 hours from New York. Flights leave daily to Aruba from New York area airports and Miami International Airport with easy connections from most American cities. **Air Aruba** (☎ 88/27822 or 800/882–7822), the island's official airline, flies nonstop to Aruba daily from Miami and Newark. Twice-weekly service has begun from Baltimore. **American Airlines** (☎ 800/433–7300) offers daily nonstop service from both Miami International and New York's JFK airport. American also offers economical packages to Aruba, especially in off-season (summer). **ALM** (☎ 800/327–7230), the major airline of the Dutch Caribbean islands, flies five days a week nonstop from Miami to Aruba; two nonstop and two direct flights a week leave out of Atlanta with connecting services (throughfares) to most major U.S. gateways tied in with Delta. Air Aruba and ALM also have connecting flights to Caracas, Bonaire, Curaçao, and St. Maarten as well as other Caribbean islands. ALM also offers a "Visit Caribbean Pass" for interisland travel. From Toronto and Montreal, you can fly to Aruba on American Airlines via San Juan. American also has connecting flights from several U.S. cities via San Juan. Viasa, the Venezuelan carrier (☎ 800/468–4272), flies direct from Houston.

Passports and Visas

U.S. and Canadian residents need only show proof of identity—a valid passport, birth certificate, naturalization certificate, green card, valid nonquota immigration visa, or a valid voter registration card. All other nationalities must submit a valid passport.

Precautions

Aruba is a party island, but only up to a point. A police dog sniffs for drugs at the airport.

The strong trade winds are a relief in the subtropical climate, but don't hang your bathing suit on a balcony—it will probably blow away. Help Arubans conserve water and energy: Turn off air-conditioning when you leave your room, and keep your faucets turned off.

Staying in Aruba

Important Addresses

Tourist Information: The **Aruba Tourism Authority** (L. G. Smith Blvd. 172, Eagle Beach, Aruba, ☎ 297/8–21019, or in Oranjestad at A. Schutte Str. 2, ☎ 297/8–23778) has free brochures and guides who are ready to answer any questions.

EMERGENCIES

Police: ☎ 100. **Hospital:** Horacio Oduber, ☎ 24300. **Pharmacy:** Botica del Pueblo, ☎ 21254. **Ambulance** and **fire:** ☎ 115. All hotels have house doctors on call 24 hours a day. Call the front desk.

Currency

Arubans happily accept U.S. dollars virtually everywhere, so there's no real need to exchange money, except for necessary pocket change (cigarettes, soda machines, or pay phones). The currency used, however, is the Aruban florin (AFl), which at press time exchanged to the U.S. dollar at AFl1.78 for cash, AFl1.80 for traveler's checks, and to the Canadian dollar at AFl1.30. The Dutch Antillean florin (used in Bonaire and Curaçao) is not accepted in Aruba. Major credit cards and traveler's checks are widely accepted, but you will probably be asked to show identification when cashing a traveler's check. Prices quoted here are in U.S. dollars unless otherwise noted.

Taxes and Service Charges

Hotels collect a 5% government tax and usually add an 11% service charge to room bills. Restaurants usually add a 15% service charge to your bill. The departure tax is $12.50. There is no sales tax.

Guided Tours

ORIENTATION

Aruba's highlights can be seen in a day. While most highways are in excellent condition, signs and directions are haphazard, making a guided tour your best option for exploring if you have only a short time. **De Palm Tours** (L. G. Smith Blvd. 142, ☎ 297/8–24400, 297/8–24545, or 800/766–6016; FAX 297/8–23012) has a near monopoly on the Aruban sightseeing business; reservations may be made through its general office or at hotel tour-desk branches. The basic 3½-hour tour hits the high spots of the island, including popular spots that are difficult to find on your own, such as the Ayo and Casibari rock formations (Jeep tours). Wear tennis or hiking shoes (there'll be optional climbing) and note that the air-conditioned bus can get cold. The tour, which begins at 9:30 AM, picks you up in your lobby and costs $17.50 per person. De Palm also offers full-day tours of Caracas, Venezuela ($225, passport required), and Curaçao ($185). Prices include round-trip airfare, transfers, sightseeing, and lunch; there is also free time for shopping. **Aruba Friendly Tours** (Cumana 20, Oranjestad, ☎ 297/8–25800) also offers guided tours of Aruba's main sights.

SPECIAL INTEREST
For a three-in-one tour of prehistoric Indian cultures, volcanic formations, and natural wildlife, contact archaeologist Eppie Boerstra of **Marlin Booster Tracking, Inc.,** at Charlie's Bar (☎ 297/8–45086 or 297/8–41513). The fee for a six-hour tour is $35 per person, including a cold picnic lunch and beverages. Tours can be given in English, Dutch, German, French, and Spanish.

Hikers will enjoy a guided three-hour trip to remote sites of unusual natural beauty accessible only on foot. The fee is $25 per person, including refreshments and transportation; a minimum of four people is required. Contact **De Palm Tours** (☎ 297/8–24400 or 297/8–24545).

You can now explore an underwater reef teeming with marine life without getting wet. **Atlantis Submarines** (Seaport Village Marina, ☎ 297/8–36090) operates a 65-foot, modern, air-conditioned sub that takes 46 passengers 50–90 feet below the surface along Aruba's Barcadera Reef. The 50-minute plunge costs $68 for adults, $34 for children. If you are not a scuba diver, the hour in the submarine is the next best thing to being down among the fish and coral.

BOAT CRUISES
If you try a cruise around the island, know that trimarans give a much smoother ride than monohull boats. Sucking on lemon or lime candy may help a queasy stomach; avoid going with an empty stomach. The most popular and reputable sailing cruises are offered by **De Palm Tours** (☎ 297/8–24400 or 297/8–24545), **MI Dushi** (☎ 297/8–26034), **Red Sail Sports** (☎ 297/8–24500), **Pelican Watersports** (☎ 297/8–31228), and **Wave Dancers** (☎ 297/8–25520).

Moonlight cruises offer stunning views and cost about $25 per person. (Be prepared to sail with a lot of sappy honeymooners.) Contact **Red Sail Sports** (☎ 297/8–24500), **Pelican Watersports** (☎ 297/8–31228) or **De Palm Tours** (☎ 297/8–24400 or 297/8–24545). De Palm Tours' three-hour trimaran cruise with an hour's stop for swimming and snorkeling runs daily except Sunday; the cost is $22.50 per person. Four-hour snorkel, sail, and lunch cruises aboard a 53-foot catamaran, plus sunset sails and a romantic dinner cruise, are among the on-the-water delights offered by Red Sail Sports (*see above*), at prices that range from $27.50 to $49.50 per person.

Getting Around
Remember, the island's winding roads are poorly marked, if at all. The major tourist attractions are fairly easy to find; others you'll happen upon only by sheer luck (or with an Aruban friend).

TAXIS

A dispatch office is located at Alhambra Bazaar and Casino (☎ 297/8–21604 or 297/8–22116); you can also flag down taxis on the street. Since taxis do not have meters, rates are fixed and should be confirmed before your ride begins. All Aruba's taxi drivers have participated in the government's Tourism Awareness Programs and have received their Tourism Guide Certificate. An hour's tour of the island by taxi will run you about $30, for a maximum of four people per car. A taxi from the airport to most hotels will run $8–$10.

RENTAL CARS

You'll need a valid U.S. or Canadian driver's license to rent a car, and you must be able to meet the minimum age requirements of each rental service, implemented for insurance reasons. **Budget Rent-A-Car** (☎ 800/527–0700) requires drivers to be between 25 and 65, **Avis** (☎ 800/331–2112) requires drivers to be between 23 and 70, and **Hertz** (☎ 800/654–3131) requires drivers to be older than 21. Insurance is available starting at $10 per day, and all companies offer unlimited mileage. Local car rental companies generally have lower rates.

Local addresses and phone numbers for the rental agencies are **Avis** (Kolibristraat 14, ☎ 297/8–28787; airport, ☎ 297/8–25496), **Budget Rent-A-Car** (Kolibristraat 1, ☎ 297/8–28600; airport, ☎ 297/8–25423; at Divi resorts, ☎ 297/8–35000), **Hertz, De Palm Car Rental** (L. G. Smith Blvd. 142, Box 656, ☎ 297/8–24545; airport, ☎ 297/8–24886), **Dollar Rent-a-Car** (Grendeaweg 15, ☎ 297/8–22783; airport, ☎ 297/8–25651; Manchebo, ☎ 297/8–26696), **National** (Tanki Leendert 170, ☎ 297/8–21967; airport, ☎ 297/8–25451; Holiday Inn, ☎ 297/8–63600), **Thrifty** (airport, ☎ 297/8–35335), and **Hedwina Car Rental** (airport, ☎ 297/8–37393; Fortheuvelstraat 32, ☎ 297/8–66442). Dollar and National require drivers to be at least 23 years old.

RENTAL MOTORCYCLES

Rates vary according to the make of the vehicle. For Suzuki scooters ($24 day, $132 week), contact **George's Cycle Center** (L. G. Smith Blvd. 136, ☎ 297/8–25975). Other moped, scooter, and motorcycle rental companies are **Ron's Motorcycle Rental** (Bakval 17A, ☎ 297/8–62090), **Nelson Motorcycle Rental** (Gasparito 10A, ☎ 297/8–26801), and **Semver Cycle Rental** (Noord 22, ☎ 297/8–66851).

BUSES

Buses run hourly trips between the beach hotels and Oranjestad. Round-trip fare is $1.50, and exact change is preferred. Buses also run down the coast from Oranjestad to San Nicolas for the same fare. Contact the Aruba Tourism Authority (☎ 297/8–21019) for a bus schedule, or inquire at the front desk of your hotel.

Telephones and Mail

To dial direct to Aruba from the United States, dial 011–297–8, followed by the number in Aruba. Local and international calls in Aruba can be made via hotel operators or from the Government Long Distance Telephone, Telegraph, and Radio Office, SETAR, which is in the post office building in Oranjestad. When dialing locally in Aruba, simply dial the five-digit number. To reach the United States, dial 001, then the area code and number.

Telegrams and telexes can be sent through SETAR, at the Post Office Building in Oranjestad or via your hotel. There is also a SETAR office in front of the Hyatt Regency hotel, adjacent to the hotel's parking lot (☎ 297/8–37138).

You can send an airmail letter from Aruba to anywhere in the world for AFl1.00, a postcard for AFl.70.

Opening and Closing Times

Shops are generally open between 8 AM and 6 PM, Monday through Saturday. Most stores stay open through the lunch hour, noon–2 PM. Many stores open when cruise ships are in port on Sundays and holidays. Nighttime shopping at the Alhambra Bazaar runs 5 PM–midnight. Bank hours are weekdays from 8 to noon and 1:30 to 4. The Aruba Bank at the airport is open on Saturday from 9 to 4 and on Sunday from 9 to 1.

Exploring Aruba

Numbers in the margin correspond to points of interest on the Aruba map.

Oranjestad

❶ Aruba's charming Dutch capital, **Oranjestad,** is best explored on foot. Take a taxi or bus from your hotel to the **Port of Call Marketplace,** a new shopping mall. After exploring the boutiques and shops, head up L. G. Smith Boulevard to the colorful **Fruit Market,** located along the docks on your right.

Continue walking along the harbor until you come to **Seaport Village,** a festive shopping, dining, and entertainment mall. Next door (one block southwest) is **Wilhelmina Park,** a small grove of palm trees and flowers overlooking the sea.

Cross L. G. Smith Boulevard to Oranjestraat and walk one block to **Fort Zoutman,** one of the island's oldest buildings. It was built in 1796 and used as a major fortress in the skirmishes between British and Curaçao troops. The Willem III Tower, named for the Dutch monarch of that time, was added in 1868. The fort's Historical Museum displays centuries' worth of Aruban relics and artifacts in an 18th-century Aruban house. *Oranjestraat, ☎ 297/8–26099. ☛ $1. ☉ Weekdays 9–4.*

Turn left onto Zoutmanstraat and walk two blocks to the **Archeology Museum,** where there are two rooms of Indian artifacts, farm and domestic utensils, and skeletons. *Zoutmanstraat 1, ☎ 297/8–28979. ☛ Free. ☉ Weekdays 7:30–noon and 1–4:30.*

Across the street you'll see the handsome Protestant Church. Turn right on Kazernestraat. On your left side are the Sonesta Hotel and Seaport Village Mall; on your right are the **Strada Complex I** and **Strada Complex II.** Both are shopping malls, and both are excellent examples of Dutch Colonial architecture. Behind Strada Complex II is the **Holland Aruba Mall,** a new shopping complex built to resemble a Dutch Colonial village. Upstairs is an international food court.

TIME OUT The motto at **Le Petit Café** (at Mainstreet, corner of Schlepstraat, ☎ 297/8–26511) is "Romancing the Stone"—referring to tasty cuisine cooked on hot stones. The low ceiling and hanging plants make this an intimate lunch spot for shoppers. Jumbo shrimps, sandwiches, ice cream, and fresh fruit dishes are light delights. *Open lunch and dinner Mon.–Sat.*

At the intersection of Kazernestraat and Caya G. F. Betico Croes, turn right. This is Oranjestad's main street. When you come to Hendrikstraat, turn left and continue walking until you come to the **St. Francis Roman Catholic Church.** Next to the church is the **Numismatic Museum,** displaying coins and paper money from more than 400 countries. *Iraussquilnplein 2-A,* ☎ *297/8–28831.* ☛ *Free.* ☉ *Weekdays 8:30– noon and 1–4:30.*

Diagonally across from the church is the **post office,** where you can buy colorful Aruban stamps. Next door is SETAR, where you can place overseas phone calls.

The Countryside

The "real Aruba"—what's left of a wild, untamed beauty—can be found only in the countryside. Rent a car, take a sightseeing tour, or hire a cab for $30 an hour (for up to four people). The main highways are well paved, but on the windward side of the island some roads are still a mixture of compacted dirt and stones. Although a car is fine, a Jeep will allow you to explore the unpaved interior. Traffic is sparse, and you can't get lost. If you do lose your way, just follow the divi-divi trees (because of the direction of the trade winds, the trees are bent toward the leeward side of the island, where all the hotels are).

Few beaches outside the hotel strip have refreshment stands, so take your own food and drink. And one more caution: Note that there are *no* public bathrooms—anywhere—once you leave Oranjestad, except in the infrequent restaurant.

EAST TO SAN NICOLAS

For a shimmering vista of blue-green sea, drive east on L. G. Smith Boulevard toward San Nicolas, on what is known as the Sunrise side of the island. Past the airport, you'll soon see the towering 541-foot peak of

❷ **Hooiberg** (Haystack Hill). If you have the energy, climb the 562 steps up to the top for an impressive view of the city.

Turn left where you see the drive-in theater (a popular hangout for Arubans). Drive to the first intersection, turn right, and follow the curve

❸ to the right to **Frenchman's Pass,** a dark, luscious stretch of highway arbored by overhanging trees. Local legend claims that the French and native Indians warred here during the 17th century for control of the

❹ island. Nearby are the cement ruins of the **Balashi Gold Mine** (take the dirt road veering to the right)—a lovely place to picnic, listen to the parakeets, and contemplate the towering cacti. A magnificent gnarled divi-divi tree guards the entrance.

Backtrack all the way to the main road, past the drive-in, and drive

❺ through the area called **Spanish Lagoon,** where pirates once hid to repair their ships.

❻ Back on the main highway, pay a visit to **San Nicolas,** Aruba's oldest village. During the heyday of the Exxon refineries, the town was a bustling port; now it's dedicated to tourism, with the main-street promenade full of interesting kiosks. The **China Clipper Bar** on Main Street used to be a famous "whore" bar frequented by sailors docked in port.

TIME OUT   Now an institution, **Charlie's Bar** has been a San Nicolas hangout for more than 50 years. During the oil-refinery days, it was a hopping bar for all kinds of rough-and-scruffs. Now it is owned by the second-generation Charlie, who is eager to promote San Nicolas as a historic town. Tourists flock here, if only to gawk at the unusual decor: License plates, hard hats, baseball pennants, and old credit cards cover and crowd every inch of the walls and ceiling. The specialty is "shrimps—jumbo and dumbo." Ask Charlie for his special "honeymoon sauce." The bus to San Nicolas stops right at the door. *Zeppenfeldstraat 56, San Nicolas,* ☎ *297/8–45086.* ☉ *Mon.–Sat. noon–10.*

Anyone looking for geological exotica should head for the northern coast, driving northwest from San Nicolas. Stop at the two old Indian **❼** caves **Guadirikiri** and **Fontein.** Both were used by the native Indians centuries ago, but you'll have to decide for yourself whether the "ancient Indian inscriptions" are genuine—rumor has it they were added by a European film company that made a movie here years ago. You may enter the caves, but there are no guides available, and bats are known to make appearances. Wear sneakers and take a flashlight or rent one from the soda vendor who has set up shop here. Just before the Fontein and Guadirikiri caves lies the **Tunnel of Love,** a heart-shape tunnel containing naturally sculpted rocks that look just like the Madonna, Abe Lincoln, even a jaguar. The climb through the tunnel is strenuous and should not be attempted by anyone not in good physical condition. It's definitely not recommended for elderly people or young children. Remember, admission is free to all three caves—don't be deterred by the occasionally pushy vendors.

❽ A few miles up the coast is the **Natural Bridge,** sculpted out of coral rock by centuries of raging wind and sea. To get to it, follow the main road inland and then the signs that lead the way. Nearby is a café overlooking the water and a souvenir shop stuffed with trinkets, T-shirts, and postcards for reasonable prices. The dirt road continues west a half mile to the massive ruins of the Bushiribana Gold Smelter, which resembles a crumbling fortress.

WEST OF PALM BEACH
Drive or take a taxi west from the hotel strip to Malmok, where Aruba's wealthiest families reside. Open to the public, **Malmok Beach** is considered one of the finest spots for shelling, snorkeling, and windsurfing (see Beaches, below). Right off the coast here is a favorite haunt for divers—the wreck of the German ship *Antilla*, which was **❾** scuttled in 1940. At the very end of the island stands the **California Lighthouse,** now closed, which is surrounded by huge boulders that look like extraterrestrial monsters; in this stark landscape, you'll feel as though you've just landed on the moon.

From here a rugged dirt road curls around the northwest corner of the island to the lonely Alto Vista Chapel. The wind whistles through the simple mustard-colored walls, eerie boulders, and looming cacti. Along the side of the road back to civilization are miniature coffins painted with depictions of the Stations of the Cross and hand-lettered signs exhorting PRAY FOR US, SINNER, and the like—a primitive yet powerful evocation of faith.

Off the Beaten Track

Aruba has another natural bridge on its desolate, magnificent east coast. To reach it, keep bearing east out of San Nicolas and continue uphill past the oil refinery and residential development of Seroe Colorado. Although the cathedral-like formation is not as spectacular as its celebrated sister, the raw elemental power of the sea that created it certainly is. The hike down to the best vantage point is fairly arduous, but you won't find a more pristine, isolated spot on Aruba for a picnic.

Beaches

Beaches in Aruba are legendary in the Caribbean: white sand, turquoise waters, and virtually no garbage, for everyone takes the "no littering" sign—NO TIRA SUSHI—very seriously, especially with an AFl500 fine.

Aruba

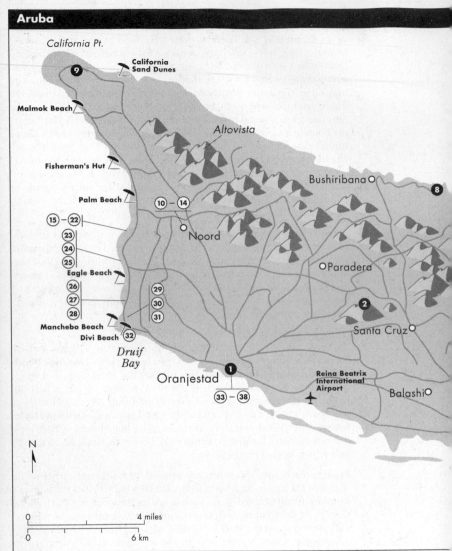

California Pt.

California Sand Dunes

Malmok Beach

Altovista

Fisherman's Hut

Bushiribana ○

Palm Beach

(10) — (14)

(15) — (22)
(23)
(24)
(25)

○ Noord

Eagle Beach

○ Paradera

(26)
(27)
(28)

(29)
(30)
(31)

Manchebo Beach
Divi Beach (32)

Santa Cruz ○

Druif Bay

Oranjestad

(33) — (38)

Reina Beatrix International Airport

Balashi ○

N

0		4 miles
0		6 km

Exploring
Balashi Gold Mine, **4**
California Lighthouse, **9**
Frenchman's Pass, **3**
Guadirikiri/Fontein caves, **7**
Hooiberg (Haystack Hill), **2**

Natural Bridge, **8**
Oranjestad, **1**
San Nicolas, **6**
Spanish Lagoon, **5**

Dining
Bon Appetit, **15**
Boonoonoonoos, **36**
Brisas del Mar, **39**

Buccaneer Restaurant, **10**
Chez Mathilde, **34**
Kowloon, **38**
La Paloma, **11**
Mi Cushina, **40**
The Old Cunucu House, **16**
The Old Mill, **24**

Papiamento, **12**
Talk of the Town Restaurant, **35**
Valentino's, **13**

Lodging
Americana Aruba Beach Resort & Casino, **17**

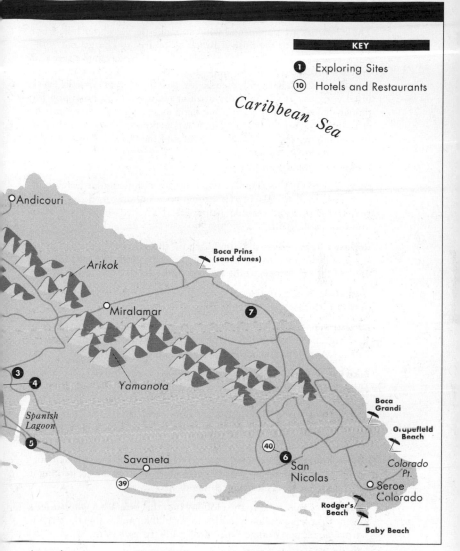

Amsterdam
Manor, **26**
Aruba Beach Club,
29
Aruba Hilton Hotel
and Casino, **19**
Aruba Palm Beach
Hotel & Casino, **18**
Bucuti Beach
Resort, **30**

Bushiri Beach
Resort, **33**
Caribbean Palm Vil-
lage, **14**
Casa del Mar Beach
Resort, **31**
Divi Aruba Beach Re-
sort, **32**
Holiday Inn Aruba
Beach Resort, **25**

Hyatt Regency Aruba
Resort & Casino, **20**
La Cabana All Suite
Beach Resort &
Casino, **27**
La Quinta Beach Re-
sort, **28**
The Mill Resort, **23**
Playa Linda Beach
Resort, **21**

Radisson Aruba
Caribbean Resort &
Casino, **22**
Sonesta Resorts at
Seaport Village, **37**

The influx of tourists in the past decade, however, has crowded the major beaches, which back up to the hotels along the southwestern strip. These beaches are public, and you can make the two-hour hike from the Holiday Inn to the Bushiri Beach Hotel free of charge and without ever leaving sand. If you go strolling during the day, make sure you are well protected from the sun—it scorches fast. Luckily, there's at least one covered bar (and often an ice-cream stand) at virtually every hotel you pass. If you take the stroll at night, you can hotel-hop for dinner, dancing, gambling, and late-night entertainment. On the northern side of the island, heavy trade winds make the waters too choppy for swimming, but the vistas are great and the terrain is wonderfully suited to sunbathing and geological explorations. Among the finer beaches are the following.

Baby Beach. On the island's eastern tip, this semicircular beach borders a bay that is as placid as a wading pool and only 4–5 feet deep—perfect for tots and terrible swimmers. Thatched shaded areas are good for cooling off.

Rodger's Beach. Next to Baby Beach on the eastern tip of the island, this is a beautiful curving stretch of sand only slightly marred by the view of the oil refinery at the far side of the bay.

Grapefield Beach. To the north of San Nicolas, this gorgeous beach is perfect for professional windsurfing.

Boca Grandi. Just west of Bachelor's Beach, on the northwest coast (near the Seagrape Grove and the Aruba Golf Club), Boca Grandi is excellent for wave jumping and windsurfing.

Boca Prins. Near the Fontein Cave and Blue Lagoon, this beach is about as large as a Brazilian bikini, but with two rocky cliffs and tumultuously crashing waves, it's as romantic as you get in Aruba. This is not a swimming beach, however. Boca Prins is famous for its backdrop of enormous vanilla sand dunes. Bring a picnic lunch, a beach blanket, and sturdy sneakers.

Malmok Beach. On the northwestern shore, this lackluster beach borders shallow waters that stretch out 300 yards from shore, making it perfect for beginners learning to windsurf.

Fisherman's Hut. Next to the Holiday Inn, this beach is a windsurfer's haven. Take a picnic lunch (tables are available) and watch the elegant purple, aqua, and orange Windsurfer sails struggle in the wind.

Palm Beach. Once called one of the 10 best beaches in the world by the *Miami Herald,* this is the stretch behind the Americana Aruba, Aruba Hilton Hotel and Casino, Aruba Palm Beach, and Holiday Inn hotels. It's the center of Aruban tourism, offering the best in swimming, sailing, and fishing. During high season, however, it's a sardine can.

Eagle Beach. Across the highway from what is quickly becoming known as Time-Share Lane is Eagle Beach on the southern coast. Not long ago, it was a nearly deserted stretch of pristine sands dotted with the occasional thatched picnic hut. Now that the new time-share resorts are completed, this beach is one of the more hopping on the island.

Manchebo Beach (formerly Punta Brabo Beach). In front of the Manchebo Beach Resort, this impressively wide stretch of white powder is where officials turn a blind eye to topless sunbathers. Elsewhere on the island, going topless is not permitted (though officials rarely enforce the ban).

Sports and the Outdoors

Bowling
The **Eagle Bowling Palace** (Pos Abou, ☎ 297/8–35038) has 12 lanes, a cocktail lounge, and a snack bar; it's open 10 AM to 2 AM.

Deep-Sea Fishing
With catches including barracuda, kingfish, bonito, and black and yellow tuna, deep-sea fishing is great sport on Aruba. Many charter boats are available. Sail for a half day or a full day. **De Palm Tours** (L. G. Smith Blvd. 142, Box 656, ☎ 297/8–24400) can arrange trips for up to six people, in boats that range from 24 to 27 feet. Half-day tours, including all equipment, can be arranged for $220–$250. Private yachts, manned by independent sea captains, can also be chartered. Check with the Aruba Tourism Authority or your hotel. Half-day tours run about $200, full-day about $425. **Pelican Tours** (☎ 297/8–31228 or 297/8–24739) and **Red Sail Sports** (☎ 297/8–24500) also arrange deep-sea fishing charters.

Golf
An all-new 18-hole par-71 golf course, **Tierra del Sol,** has opened, situated on the northwest coast near the California Lighthouse. Designed by Robert Trent Jones, the course combines Aruba's native beauty, such as the flora, cacti, and rock formations, with the lush greens of the world's best courses. Hyatt Resorts Caribbean is the manager. The installation of a water-irrigation system on this arid isle is costing about $10 million. It will allow 600,000 gallons of water to be distributed throughout the course over a five- to six-hour period. The **Aruba Golf Club** (Golfweg 82, near San Nicolas, ☎ 297/8–42006) has a nine-hole course with 25 sand traps, roaming goats, and lots of cacti. There are 11 AstroTurf greens, making 18-hole tournaments a possibility. The clubhouse contains a bar, storage rooms, workshop, and separate men's and women's locker rooms. The course's official U.S. Golf Association rating is 67; greens fees are $7.50 for 9 holes, $10 for 18 holes. There are no caddies, but golf carts are available.

Horseback Riding
One-hour jaunts ($15) arranged through **Rancho El Paso** (Washington 44, ☎ 297/8–23310) or **De Palm Tours** (☎ 297/8–24400) will take you through countryside flanked by cacti, divi-divi trees, and aloe vera plants; two-hour trips ($30) also go to the beach. Remember to wear a hat and take lots of suntan lotion.

Land Sailing
Carts with a Windsurfer-type sail are rented at **Aruba SailCart** (Bushiri 23, ☎ 297/8–35133) at $15 (single seater) and $20 (double seater) for 30 minutes of speeding back and forth across a dirt field. The sport is new to Aruba and thrilling for landbound sailors. Anyone can learn the rudiments of driving the cart in just a few minutes. Rentals are available from 10 AM to 7 PM; food and drinks are served until 10 PM.

Miniature Golf
Two elevated 18-hole minigolf courses surrounded by a moat are available at **Joe Mendez Adventure Golf** (Eagle Beach, ☎ 297/8–76625). There are also paddleboats and bumper boats, a bar, and a snack stand. Fees are $6 for a round of minigolf, $5 for 30 minutes of paddleboating, and $5 for 10 minutes of bumper boating.

Parasailing
Motorboats from Eagle and Palm beaches tow people up and over the water for about 15 minutes ($40).

Snorkeling and Scuba Diving

With visibility up to 90 feet, Aruban waters are excellent for snorkeling in shallow waters, and scuba divers will discover exotic marine life and coral. Certified divers can go wall diving or reef diving—or explore wrecks sunk during World War II. The *Antilla* shipwreck—a German freighter sunk off the northwest coast of Aruba near Palm Beach—is a favorite spot with divers and snorkelers.

De Palm Tours (L. G. Smith Blvd. 142, ☎ 297/8–24545 or 297/8–24400, FAX 297/8–23012) offers daily snorkeling and scuba-diving trips. However, its rates are the most expensive on the island.

Pelican Watersports (J. G. Emanstraat 1, Oranjestad, ☎ 297/8–31228 or 297/8–63600, ext. 329) also offers snorkeling and scuba diving.

Red Sail Sports (L. G. Smith Blvd. 83, ☎ 297/8–24500, ext. 109, or 800/255–6425) offers scuba packages, resort courses, PADI-certification courses, night diving, and underwater camera rental.

Aruba Pro Dive (Ponton 88, ☎ 297/8–25520) offers resort courses, daily one-tank dives, two-tank dives, and night dives. Other reputable dive operators offering daily one- and two-tank dives are **Charlie's S.E.A. Scuba** (San Nicolas, ☎ 297/8–34877) and **Mermaid Sports Divers** (Manchebo Beach Resort, ☎ 297/8–35546 or 800/223–1108).

Tennis

Aruba's winds add a certain challenge to the best of swings, but world-class tennis has just arrived, at the **Aruba Racquet Club** (☎ 297/8–60215). The $1.4 million club was designed by Stan Smith Design International and is located near the Aruba Marriott, which at press time was scheduled to open in the summer of 1995.

Windsurfing

Pelican Watersports (J. G. Emanstraat 1, ☎ 297/8–31228) rents equipment and offers instruction with a certified Mistral instructor. Stock boards and custom boards rent for $30 per two hours, $55 per day.

Red Sail Sports (☎ 297/8–24500 or 800/255–6425) offers two-hour beginner lessons for $44 and advanced lessons for $33 per hour. It also offers Fanatic board and regular windsurfing board rentals by the hour, day, and week.

Windsurfing instruction and board rental are also available through **Carib Asurf** (Manchebo Beach Resort, ☎ 297/8–23444), **Sailboard Vacation** (L. G. Smith Blvd. 462, ☎ 297/8–21072), **Roger's Windsurf Place** (L. G. Smith Blvd. 472, ☎ 297/8–21918), and **De Palm Tours** (L. G. Smith Blvd. 142, Box 656, ☎ 297/8–24545).

Shopping

Caya G. F. Betico Croes—Aruba's chief shopping street—makes for a pleasant diversion from the beach and casino life. *Duty-free* is a magic word here. Major credit cards are welcome virtually everywhere, U.S. dollars are accepted almost as often as local currency, and traveler's checks can be cashed with proof of identity. Shopping malls have arrived in Aruba, so when you finish walking the main street, stop in at a mall to browse through the chic new boutiques.

Aruba's souvenir and crafts stores are full of Dutch porcelains and figurines, as befits the island's Netherlands heritage. Dutch cheese is a good buy (you are allowed to bring up to 1 pound of hard cheese through U.S. customs), as are hand-embroidered linens and any products made from the native aloe vera plant—sunburn cream, face masks, and skin refresheners. Since there is no sales tax, the price you see on the tag is the price you pay. But one word of warning: Don't try to bargain. Arubans consider it rude to haggle.

Specialty Shops

Crafts can be found at several stores. At **Artesania Arubiano** (L. G. Smith Blvd. 142, next to the Aruba Tourism Authority, ☎ 297/8–37494) you'll find charming Aruban home-crafted pottery, silk-screened T-shirts and wall hangings, and folklore objects. The **Artistic Boutique** (Caya G. F. Betico Croes 25, ☎ 297/8–23142, with branches at the Aruba Hilton, ☎ 297/8–64466, ext. 3508; Seaport Village Mall, ☎ 297/8–32567; and the Holiday Inn, ☎ 297/8–33383) sells Aruban hand-embroidered linens, gold and silver jewelry, Persian carpets and dhurries, porcelain and pottery from Spain, and lots of antiques. **Mopa Mopa** (Havenstraat 5, ☎ 297/8–37125) sells intriguing items that look hand-painted but aren't. Buds from the mopa mopa tree are boiled to form a resin, to which artists add vegetable colors. This resin is then stretched by hand and mouth. Tiny pieces are cut and layered to form intricate designs on wooden shapes—truly unusual gifts. **Creative Hands** (Scotorolaan 5, Oranjestad, ☎ 297/8–35665) sells porcelain and ceramic *cunucu* houses and divi-divi trees, but the store's real draw is its exquisite Japanese dolls.

For duty-free perfumes and cosmetics, stop in at **Aruba Trading Company** (Caya G. F. Betico Croes 14, ☎ 297/8–22600), whose name is synonymous with old-fashioned reliability. ATC offers internationally known brand names at discounts, but you have to hunt for them. Perfumes and cosmetics are on the first floor, jewelry on the second. Both men's and women's clothes are also sold here.

Clothing is also sold at **Wulfsen & Wulfsen** (Caya G. F. Betico Croes 52, ☎ 297/8–23823). One of the highest-rated stores in the Netherlands Antilles for 25 years—and for much longer in Holland—Wulfsen's offers Italian, French, German, and Dutch fashions for both sexes. The Dutch-line Mexx is a favorite of hip teens; Betty Barkley and Mondo are popular for women. Men's clothes range from the conservative to the wild.

J. L. Penha & Son's (Caya G. F. Betico Croes 11, ☎ 297/8–24161), another venerated name in Aruban merchandising, also sells clothes and cosmetics and features Boucheron, Lanvin, Dior, and Cartier for women and Givenchy and Pierre Cardin for men.

For jewelry and watches, stop in at **Gandelman's Jewelers** (Caya G. F. Betico Croes 5-A, ☎ 297/8–34433) for Gucci and Swatch watches at reasonable prices, gold bracelets, pink and red coral, and a full line of Gucci accessories, from key chains to handbags. They have a customer service office in Connecticut (☎ 203/325–9786. More watches can be found at **Little Switzerland** (Caya G. F. Betico Croes 14, ☎ 297/8–21192). The Curaçao-based giant in china, crystal, and fine tableware offers good buys on Omega and Rado watches, Swarovski silver, Baccarat crystal, and Lladro figurines. If you don't see what you want, ask and they'll ship it to you.

Shopping Malls

Seaport Village Mall (located on L. G. Smith Blvd. across from the harbor, ☎ 297/8–23754) is landmarked by the Crystal Casino Tower. This covered mall is only five minutes away from the cruise terminal. It has more than 130 stores, boutiques, and perfumeries, with merchandise to meet every taste and budget. The arcade is lined with tropical plants and caged parrots, and there is a casino at the top of the escalator. **Arti**

has period-clad china dolls in a rainbow of skin tones. Made in Holland, the dolls stand 12 to 18 inches tall. Clown dolls in satin and lace and a very unusual tiny clay orchestra are collector's items. **Les Accessoires** sells purses made in Florence and exclusive leather designs, with prices ranging from $85 to $600. Their Venezuelan pareus come in handy as pool cover-ups. If green fire is your passion, **Colombian Emeralds** is located just over the inside and outside bridges to the mall. **Tropical Wave** has, in the back behind the junk, some nice Indonesian sculpture and handwoven duffel bags and sweaters from Ecuador. If couture is on your mind, **La Pomme** is the place for the latest Escada (typical suits from $900) and the charms of Louis Feraud.

There are several other shopping malls in Oranjestad, all of which are worth visiting. The **Holland Aruba Mall** (Havenstraat 6, right downtown) houses a collection of smart shops and eateries. Nearby are the **Strada I** and **Strada II,** two small complexes of shops in tall Dutch buildings painted in pastels. Strada II is home to **Fendi,** whose Etrusco striped vinyl luggage is available at a 45% discount.

Port of Call Marketplace (L. G. Smith Blvd. 17) features fine jewelry, perfumes, duty-free liquors, batiks, crystal, leather goods, and fashionable clothing.

Dining

Aruba's restaurants serve a cosmopolitan variety of cuisines, although most menus are specifically designed to please American palates—you can get fresh surf and New York turf almost anywhere. Make the effort to try Aruban specialties—*pan bati* is a delicious beaten bread that resembles a pancake, and plantains are similar to cooked bananas.

On Sunday, it may be difficult to find a restaurant outside of the hotels that's open for lunch. One of the best bets is the extensive buffet at the Holiday Inn.

For good or for bad, fast food has arrived in Aruba. For those who are homesick, there's McDonald's, Kentucky Fried Chicken, Burger King, and Wendy's. For breakfast and lunch, the restaurants in the hotels tend to be more expensive than the ones in town. Most hotels offer several food plans, which you can purchase either in advance or upon arrival. But before you purchase a Full American Plan (FAP), which includes breakfast, lunch, and dinner, remember that Aruba has numerous excellent and reasonably priced restaurants from which to choose. Nonetheless, most resorts here do offer better-than-average hotel dining; for more information consult the lodging listings.

What to Wear

Dress ranges from casual at less expensive restaurants to elegant in more expensive establishments and resort dining rooms. However, even the finest restaurants require at the most only a jacket for men and a sundress for women. The air-conditioning does get cold, so don't go bare-armed. And anytime you plan to eat in the open air, remember to douse yourself first with insect repellent—the mosquitoes can get unruly, especially in July and August, when the winds drop.

CATEGORY	COST*
$$$	over $30
$$	$20–$30
$	under $20

per person, for a main course only, excluding drinks and a 15% service charge

$$$ **Chez Mathilde.** This elegant restaurant occupies one of the last surviving
★ 19th-century houses in Aruba. Though the previous chef and maître
d' left to open another restaurant, the new Dutch chef maintains his
predecessor's high culinary standards. The French-style menu is con-
stantly being re-created. Feast on artfully presented smoked leg of
lamb in papaya-ginger-thyme dressing, crepes filled with roast duck
and spring onions in blueberry sauce, or veal chops topped with foie
gras and madeira sauce. The wine list is one of the best on the island.
Ask to sit in the swooningly romantic Pavilion Room, which has an
eclectic mix of turn-of-the-century Italian and French decor. ✕ *Haven-
straat 23, Oranjestad,* ☎ *297/8–34968. Reservations required. AE,
MC, V. No lunch Sun.*

$$$ **Valentino's.** The airy two-level dining room here is invitingly dressed
in sparkling white and shades of rose. The tables are placed comfort-
ably far apart, and the service is attentive without being overbearing.
The menu is Italian, and the *gamberoni di teresa* (shrimp sautéed in
garlic and fresh tomatoes) and fettuccine in smoked salmon cream sauce
are knockouts. The atmosphere is festive, since the restaurant is popular with celebrating Arubans. You'll find their gaiety infectious. ✕
Caribbean Palm Village, Noord 43E, ☎ *297/8–64777. Reservations
advised. AE, DC, MC, V.*

$$ **Bon Appetit.** With its white tablecloths, clay-potted plants, low light-
ing, and warm-looking wood beams, this restaurant glows like a beau-
tiful tan—but it's the savory smells that hook you. The international
cuisine wins acclaim—*Gourmet* magazine once requested the recipe for
keshi yena, baked cheese stuffed with meat and condiments. Gener-
ous portions of seafood and beef (especially the gargantuan prime rib)
fill the plates of this midpriced restaurant. The kitchen won a Dutch
award for being the cleanest in Aruba. Leave room for the flaming Max
dessert, named after owner and charming host Max Croes. ✕ *Palm
Beach 29,* ☎ *297/8–65241. Reservations advised. AE, D, DC, MC,
V. Closed Sun. No lunch.*

$$ **Buccaneer Restaurant.** Imagine you're in a sunken ship—fishnets and
turtle shells hang from the ceiling, and through the portholes you see
live sharks, barracudas, and groupers swimming by. That's the Buccaneer, a virtual underwater grotto snug in an old stone building,
flanked by heavy black chains and boasting a fantastic 5,000-gallon
saltwater aquarium, plus 12 more porthole-size tanks. The surf-and-
turf cuisine is prepared by the chef-owners with European élan, and
the tables are always full. Order the fresh catch of the day or more exotic fare, such as shrimps with Pernod; smoked pork cutlets with
sausage, sauerkraut, and potatoes; or the turtle steak with a light
cream sauce. Go early (around 5:45 PM) to get a booth next to the aquariums. ✕ *Gasparito 11-C, Noord,* ☎ *297/8–26172. AE, MC, V. Closed
Sun. No lunch.*

$$ **The Old Mill** (De Olde Molen). A gift from the queen of Holland, this
real Dutch mill was shipped brick by brick to Aruba in 1920 and re-
assembled here. For starters, try the seafood crepe Neptune, nestled in
a delicate cheese bed. Also excellent are the shrimp with spinach and
cream sauce and the Dutch fries—crunchy little nuggets of potato. Order
the ice cream with chocolate liqueur and take the bottle home as a sou-
venir of Aruba's oldest restaurant. ✕ *330 J.E. Irausquin Blvd., off Palm
Beach,* ☎ *297/8–22060. Reservations required. AE, MC, V. 2 dinner
seatings: 6:30 and 9 PM. Closed Sun.*

$$ **Papiamento.** Longtime restaurateurs Lenie and Eduardo Ellis decided
★ Aruba needed a bistro that was cozy yet elegant, intimate, and always
romantic. So they converted their 130-year-old home into just such a
dining spot. Guests can feast sumptuously indoors surrounded by an-

tiques, or outdoors in a patio garden decorated with enormous ceramics (designed by Lenie) and filled with ficus and palm trees adorned with lights. The service is impeccable at this family-run establishment. The chef utilizes flavors from both Continental and Caribbean cuisines to produce favorites that include seafood and meat dishes. Try the Dover sole, the Caribbean lobster, shrimp and red snapper cooked tableside on a hot marble stone, or the "claypot" for two—a medley of seafoods prepared in a sealed clay pot. ✗ *Washington 61, Noord,* ☎ *297/8-24544. Reservations advised. AE, MC, V. No lunch.*

$$ Talk of the Town Restaurant. Here you'll find candlelight dining and some of the best steaks in town: The owner comes from a family of Dutch butchers. This fine restaurant is also a member of the elite honorary restaurant society, Chaine de Rotisseurs. Saturday night is as-much-as-you-can-eat prime rib night ($18.95). Seafood specialties, such as the crabmeat crepes and the *escargots à la bourguignonne,* are popular, too. The restaurant adjoins the Best Western Talk of the Town Resort, between the airport and Oranjestad, where rates are quite reasonable. The poolside grill stays open until 2 AM. ✗ *L. G. Smith Blvd. 2, Oranjestad,* ☎ *297/8-23380. Reservations advised. AE, DC, MC, V.*

$-$$ Boonoonoonoos. The name—say it just as it looks!—means extraordinary, which is a bit of hyperbole for this Austrian-owned Caribbean bistro in the heart of town, but in the fiercely competitive Aruban restaurant business, you gotta have a gimmick. The specialty here is Pan-Caribbean cuisine. The decor is simple, but the tasty food, served with hearty portions of peas and rice and plantains, makes up for the lack of tablecloths, china, and crystal. The roast chicken Barbados is sweet and tangy, marinated in pineapple and cinnamon and simmered in fruit juices. The Jamaican jerk ribs (a 300-year-old recipe) are tiny but spicy, and the satin-smooth hot pumpkin soup drizzled with cheese and served in a pumpkin shell may as well be dessert. Avoid the place when it's crowded, since the service and the quality of the food deteriorate. ✗ *Wilhelminastraat 18A, Oranjestad,* ☎ *297/8-31888. Reservations advised. AE, V. Closed Sun. No lunch.*

$-$$ Brisas del Mar. This friendly 10-table place overlooking the sea makes
★ you feel as if you're dining in an Aruban home. Old family recipes use traditional indigenous ingredients like the aromatic *yerbiholé* leaf and the sizzling Mme. Jeanette pepper. Try the smashing steamy fish soup (which would do a Marseillaise proud), *keri keri* (shredded fish kissed with annatto seed), or some of the best pan bati on the island. The brightly hued fishing boats bobbing in the harbor attest to the freshness of the food. It's so good, it justifies the taxi ride needed to reach it—10 miles east of Oranjestad in the town of Savaneta. ✗ *Savaneta 22A,* ☎ *297/8-47718. Reservations advised. AE, D, MC, V. Closed Mon.*

$-$$ The Old Cunucu House. Situated on a small estate in a residential neighborhood, three minutes from the high-rise hotels, this 74-year-old white stucco home with slanting roofs, wood beams, and a terra-cotta courtyard filled with bougainvillea has been converted to a seafood-and-international restaurant of casual élan. Dine on red snapper, almond-fried shrimp with lobster sauce, Cornish hen, New York sirloin, or beef fondue à deux. An Aruban trio sings and plays background music every Friday, and on Saturday evening a mariachi band serenades the patrons. Happy hour is 5 to 6 PM. ✗ *Palm Beach 150,* ☎ *297/8-61666. Reservations advised. AE, DC, MC.*

$-$$ La Paloma. "The Dove" is a no-frills, low-key neighborhood joint decorated with hanging plants and chianti bottles, and it's usually packed. The cuisine is international and Italian, but you can order conch stew with pan bati and fried plantains. Caesar salad and minestrone soup are house specialties. This is not the place for a romantic interlude; come for the family atmosphere, American-style Italian food, and reasonable prices. ✗ *Noord 39,* ☎ *297/8–32770. AE, MC, V. Closed Tues.*

$ **Kowloon.** In addition to many Chinese provinces, Indonesia is also represented on the menu here. *Bami goreng,* a noodle-based dish with sheds of shrimp, pork, vegetables, and an Indonesian blend of herbs and spices, is a tasty reminder of Curaçao's Indonesian population. Have some *saté,* grilled chicken or pork with a peanut-based sauce. The modern Asian decor blends easily with the island's palms and sands. ✗ *Emmastraat 11,* ☎ *297/8–22587. AE, MC, V.*

$ **Mi Cushina.** The menu at "My Kitchen" lists such Aruban specialties as *sopi di mariscos* (seafood soup) and *kreeft stoba* (lobster stew). The walls are hung with antique farm tools, coffee bags, and old family photos, and there's a small museum devoted to the aloe vera plant. You'll need a car to get here, about a mile from San Nicolas. ✗ *NoordCura Cabai 24, San Nicolas,* ☎ *297/8–48335. Reservations advised. AE, MC, V. Closed Tues.*

Lodging

Hotels are fairly expensive in Aruba. To save money, go during the low season (summer) and/or check out the many good packages that American Airlines and other tour operators offer. Most of the hotels in Aruba are located west of Oranjestad along L. G. Smith Boulevard and are miniresort complexes, with their own drugstores, boutiques, health spas, beauty parlors, casinos, restaurants, pool bars, and gourmet delis. At press time Marriott's new Aruba hotel was scheduled to open in summer of 1995, near the very new Robert Trent Jones golf course. Plans for an eight-story atrium and glass lobby, two towers, and a casino, of course, suggest that the newcomer intends to start at the head of the class. Do not arrive in Aruba without a reservation; many hotels are booked months in advance, especially in the winter season. All hotels offer packages, and these are considerably less expensive than the one-night rate. Hotel restaurants and clubs are open to all guests on the island, so you can visit other properties no matter where you're staying. Most hotels, unless specified, do not include meals in their room rates. The meal plans offered are optional and incur an additional per-day expense. Off-season rates are discounted approximately 40%.

CATEGORY	COST*
$$$$	over $250
$$$	$200–$250
$$	$125–$200
$	under $125

All prices are for a standard double room for two, excluding 5% tax and 11% service charge.

$$$$ **Americana Aruba Beach Resort & Casino.** Teeming activity surrounds the new clover-leaf-shape pool with a waterfall and two Jacuzzis in its center. The buzz is indicative of the atmosphere in general: A social director is always cajoling you to participate in everything from beer-drinking contests to bikini shows. A daily children's activities program is free, as are most of the games in the video arcade. In the guest rooms, white bamboo and bleached-wood furniture are complemented by tropical blue, green, and peach fabrics. All rooms have cable TV and hair dryers. Americans and Canadians, mostly in tour groups, make up 80% of the clientele. The staff can be a tad lackadaisical. ▥ *L. G. Smith Blvd. 83, Palm Beach,* ☎ *297/8–64500 or 800/447–7462; in NY, 212/223–2848;* FAX *297/8–63191. 419 rooms. 2 restaurants, swimming pool with swim-up bar, TV, 2 lighted tennis courts, tour desk, water-sports concession,*

children's activities program, weight room/gym, casino, laundry/valet, 2 car rentals, company desks, telex/fax/typewriters, boutiques, beauty parlor/barbershop. AE, DC, MC, V. EP, MAP, All-inclusive.

$$$$ **Bushiri Beach Resort.** Two long, low buildings—built around a lush Jacuzzi garden and situated on a wide expanse of beach—make up this all-inclusive resort, Aruba's first. These buildings are old and nondescript, and although the rooms were renovated in 1992, they remain ordinary. But the Bushiri is a hotel-training school, a factor that shows in the enthusiastic staff. The best rooms are in the West Wing; "deluxe" rooms, the largest, have minifridges, safe-deposit boxes, and balconies that face the ocean. Where this resort shines is in its full daily activities program for adults. Snorkeling (with instruction and equipment), tennis, sailing, windsurfing, pool volleyball, and casino gambling classes are among the offerings. Kids are kept busy with their own day-long supervised program. Three sightseeing tours around the island, three meals daily, a poolside barbecue, and a midnight buffet, as well as all soft drinks and alcoholic beverages, are included in the single tab—and it still just reaches the most expensive category. In other words, this is quite a bargain. ☎ *L. G. Smith Blvd. 35, Oranjestad,* ☎ *297/8–25216, 800/462–6867, or 800/462–6868,* FAX *297/8–26789. 153 rooms. 2 restaurants, pool bar, cocktail lounge, piano bar, pool, satellite TV, 2 tennis courts, nightly entertainment, beach, water-sports center, drugstore, health club, 3 Jacuzzis, free nightly shuttle to the Holiday Inn casino. AE, DC, MC, V. All-inclusive.*

$$$$ **Hyatt Regency Aruba Resort & Casino.** This resort is a favorite among
★   Aruba's luxury properties. Now it has even more to brag about—the 18-hole Robert Trent Jones golf course that has just opened nearby under Hyatt management. Special packages for golfers are the Hyatt's new theme. The center of this $57 million resort looks like a Spanish grandee's palace with art deco flourishes and boasts a multilevel pool, with two-story waterslide, waterfalls, and a lagoon stocked with tropical fish and black swans. Beyond is a white-sand beach dotted with palms. All the spacious rooms here are the same size, so the view determines their price. The decor is southwestern, with rattan and bleached-wood furniture. All rooms are air-conditioned and have a digital safe, stocked minibar, color TV, clock radio, ceiling fan, voice mail, and oversize bathroom. There's a no-smoking floor. The top floor houses the hedonistic Regency Club rooms, each with two huge his-and-her marble bathrooms loaded with every amenity, plus a private-floor lounge where free breakfast, afternoon tea, and happy hour drinks are served. Camp Hyatt keeps children ages 3 to 15 busy day and night, so parents can enjoy time alone. Four excellent restaurants are on the premises, among them Olé and Ruinas del Mar. Their design is exquisite: stone and marble "ruins" surrounded by moats, waterfalls, and splashing fountains. The food is equally luscious. Lighted tennis courts with windscreens, a new basketball court, a comprehensive water-sports center, a sleek health-and-fitness center, two outdoor Jacuzzis, a shopping arcade, plus a host of well-managed services and a fine staff have turned this property into the top luxury resort on the island. ☎ *L. G. Smith Blvd. 85,* ☎ *297/8–61234 or 800/233–1234,* FAX *297/8–65478. 325 rooms and 25 suites. Pool with swim-up bar, 4 restaurants, 2 bars, snack bar, casino, fitness center, 2 lighted tennis courts, water-sports center, tour desk, baby-sitting, shops. AE, DC, MC, V. EP, MAP.*

$$$–$$$$ **Aruba Hilton Hotel and Casino.** The price tag thus far for this new (1994) Hilton is $42 million. Vast grand public areas are dazzling in ocher, apricot, and aqua. The rooms are done in dusty rose, peach, and sea-foam green; all feature ocean-view balcony, safe, and satellite TV, with superior and deluxe rooms adding a minibar and hair dryer. Fountains splash playfully into the free-form pool, and the Casablanca Casino has Rick's place in mind. A full-service spa, with all the muds and rubs, and a Red Sail water-sports facility on the beach have launched the project with vigor. ⌖ *Irausquin Blvd. 77, Palm Beach,* ☎ *297/8–64466 or 800/445–7667,* FAX *297/8–68217. 443 rooms. 3 restaurants, 3 cocktail lounges, nightclub, casino, spa, pool, children's wading pool, lighted tennis court, fitness center, games room, car rental, tour desk, water-sports facility, beach bar, ballroom with meeting and banquet rooms, shops, beauty parlor, deli. AE, DC, MC, V. EP, CP, MAP, FAP.*

$$$–$$$$ **Divi Aruba Beach Resort.** The motto at this popular Mediterranean-style low rise, taken over by Doral Resorts in 1993, remains "bare-foot elegance," which means you can streak through the lobby in your bikini. The main section of the resort has 90 standard guest rooms, 20 beachfront lanai rooms, and 40 casitas (garden bungalows) that look out onto individual courtyards amid astonishingly verdant grounds. A newer section, Divi Dos, contains 49 luxury rooms and a bridal suite, all with refrigerators and Jacuzzi bathtubs. The rooms were redecorated in 1992 in yellow, green, and creamy white, and they have balconies, cable TV, safe-deposit boxes, and air-conditioning. The Divi Dos section is known as a honeymoon haven: Special packages include champagne breakfast, "just married" signs, photo albums, colorful beach towels, and fruit baskets. Divi Dos's free-form pool includes a small island at the center, accessible by a bridge. Special theme nights include Tuesday's Carnival and Saturday's Beach BBQ Fiesta, with folkloric show and steel band. ⌖ *L. G. Smith Blvd. 93, Divi Beach,* ☎ *297/8–23300 or 800/554–2008,* FAX *297/8–31940. 203 rooms. 2 restaurants, 2 bars, 2 pools, Jacuzzi, tennis court, shuffleboard, shops, tour desk, water-sports concession, adult activities program, baby-sitting. AE, D, DC, MC, V. EP, MAP, FAP.*

$$$ **Casa del Mar Beach Resort.** This beachfront, low-rise time-share hotel has combined its facilities with its time-share neighbor, the Aruba Beach Club. As time-shares go, Casa del Mar's completely furnished suites are among the most expensive on the island. Each has a dining table seating six, and the kitchen comes fully stocked. Baby-sitters are on call, and there's a supervised children's program. ⌖ *L. G. Smith Blvd. 53, Punta Brabo Beach,* ☎ *297/8–27000 or 800/992–2015;* FAX *297/8–26557. 107 2-bedroom, 2-bath suites. Restaurant (2 restaurants and pool bar at sister property), lobby bar, TVs with in-room movie satellite, fitness center, sauna and massage, pool, 2 Jacuzzis, 4 lighted tennis courts, playground, games room, 2 pools, 2 kiddie pools, baby-sitting, shops. AE, DC, MC, V. EP.*

$$$ **Playa Linda Beach Resort.** Designed in a ziggurat of receding balconies, this all-suite time-share complex, sheathed in a facade of terra-cotta and cream, sits on one of the most beautiful and enticing sections of Palm Beach. Accommodations sleep four to six and are comfortable and stylishly appointed in peach and taupe with an abundance of mirrors. Each has cable TV, smallish bathroom, full kitchen or kitchenette, ocean-view veranda, and air-conditioning. All three hearty meals are served poolside, overlooking the ocean, at the open-air Linda Vista Restaurant. Water sports and tennis can be arranged. Entertainment, such as Carnival and Limbo Night, is arranged weekly. ⌖ *L. G. Smith Blvd. 87, Palm Beach,* ☎ *297/8–61000 or 800/346–7084; in NJ, 201/346–9095;* FAX *297/8–65210. 194 1-and 2-bedroom suites and studio apartments. 2 restaurants, 2 bars, activities center, adults' and children's pools, 3 lighted tennis courts, minimarket/gift shop. AE, MC, V. EP, MAP, FAP.*

$$$ Radisson Aruba Caribbean Resort & Casino. Called La Grande Dame of the Caribbean, this resort was the first high-rise on the island. Liz Taylor used to stay here when she was married to Eddie Fisher, and the queen of Holland still stays in the Royal Suite (available on request), so the staff is used to filling special needs. More than $5.6 million has been invested in a comprehensive renewal, begun in 1992, with the most obvious refreshment being the flowers, artwork, and generally festive air of the lobby, helped along by the lobby bar, Breezes. The sunny air-conditioned rooms, 66 with a full-ocean view, are scattered among four buildings. All have cable TV, safety-deposit box, and balcony. Scuba diving (including training), snorkeling, catamaran sailing, jet skiing, windsurfing, and waterskiing can be arranged on the resort's beach. The fitness center near the tennis courts offers a Universal weight system and aerobics classes. Bands play every Saturday night in the blue-and-gold nightclub. ✉ *L. G. Smith Blvd. 81, Palm Beach,* ☎ *297/8–66555 or 800/777–1700,* ℻ *297/8–63260. 378 rooms and suites. 4 restaurants, 4 bars, nightclub, meeting and banquet rooms, casino, pool, 4 lighted tennis courts, fitness center, tour desk, car rental, baby-sitting, water sports, video-game room, shops, beauty parlor, deli. AE, MC, V. EP, MAP. All-inclusive.*

$$–$$$ Holiday Inn Aruba Beach Resort & Casino. This is one of the larger properties on Palm Beach, but its size is camouflaged. Three buildings of seven stories each are set apart from each other along the shore, nicely landscaped with palm trees. Restaurants, bars, the El Spirit nightclub, and the Grand Holiday Casino keep the night lights shining. By day, swimming, tennis, windsurfing and other water sports, as well as shopping, keep the body beautiful. Children's activities are organized. ✉ *L. G. Smith Blvd. 230, Palm Beach,* ☎ *297/8–63600 or 800/465–4329,* ℻ *297/8–65870. 600 rooms. 4 restaurants, 6 bars, nightclub, casino, pool, tennis court, water-sports center, playground. AE, DC, MC, V. EP.*

$$–$$$ **Sonesta Resorts at Seaport Village.** If falling out of bed and onto a beach
★ isn't important to you, then Sonesta's in-town location is ideal—especially if you like to shop, eat, and gamble. There are actually two hotels, the new one with suites and the older (1992) with rooms. This modern resort stands out amid the Dutch architecture of Oranjestad. In one lobby, sleek low couches wrap around pink stucco pillars while glass elevators rise above the circular deep-water grotto; brilliantly hued toucans and parrots squawk at you from their baroque cages; and motor skiffs board guests headed for the resort's 40-acre private island. The 300 tropical green-and-pink guest rooms and suites are spacious and modern, with tiny balconies, cable TV, hair dryers, safe-deposit boxes, and stocked minibars. The free daily "Just Us Kids" program offers children ages 5 to 12 supervised activities, including kite flying, bowling, movies, storytelling, and field trips. For adults there are free casino classes, volleyball, and beach bingo. The gourmet restaurant, L'Escale, is one of Aruba's most creative—and expensive. The neighboring Crystal Casino houses the Caribbean's largest $1 slot machine. Dancers should head for the Desires Lounge, where there's live entertainment every night except Sunday. ✉ *L. G. Smith Blvd. 82,* ☎ *297/8–36000, 800/766–3782, or 800/343–7170;* ℻ *297/8–25317. Sonesta Resort & Casino, 300 rooms; Sonesta Suites & Casino, 275 suites. 4 restaurants, 4 bars, minispa and fitness center, pool, 40-acre private island with water-sports center, 2 casinos, nightclub, 85 shops, children's program, tour desk, beauty salon. AE, DC, MC, V. EP.*

$$ Aruba Beach Club. This attractive low-rise resort on Druif Beach doubles as a time-share. The open-air lobby leads to a patio, gardens, and pool, with the beach only a few steps beyond. Action centers on the pool bar, with a clientele that's mostly American, mostly young-to-mid-

dle-aged couples with children. The pastel rooms are more basic than
luxurious, even though they're refurbished every two years. Each has
a kitchenette, cable TV, room safe, and balcony. Guests may use all
the facilities at the Casa del Mar resort next door. ☎ *L. G. Smith Blvd.
53, Punta Brabo Beach,* ☎ *297/8–23000 or 800/223–6510,* FAX *297/8–
26557. 131 studio and 1-bedroom suites. 2 restaurants, cocktail lounge,
pool bar, ice-cream parlor, adults' and children's pools, 4 lighted tennis courts, playground, baby-sitting. AE, MC, V. EP.*

$$ Aruba Palm Beach Hotel & Casino. Formerly a Sheraton, this pink, eight-
story Moorish palazzo even has pink-swaddled palm trees dotting its
drive. The lobby, with its impressive grand piano, is a haze of pink and
purple underlaid with cool marble. The large backyard sunning grounds
are a well-manicured tropical garden, with a fleet of pesky parrots guard-
ing the entrance. The oversize guest rooms are cheerfully decorated in
either burgundy and mauve or emerald and pink. Each has a walk-in
closet, color cable TV, and a tiny balcony and overlooks the ocean, the
pool, or the gardens. For a peaceful meal, eat alfresco in the rock-gar-
den setting of the Seawatch Restaurant. For live music, try the Play-
ers Club lounge, open nightly until 3 AM. A limbo and steel-band show
is scheduled one night a week. ☎ *L. G. Smith Blvd. 79, Palm Beach,*
☎ *297/8–63900; in FL, 305/539–9933;* FAX *297/8–61941. 202 rooms.
2 restaurants, pizza parlor, deli, 2 bars, car rental desk, pool, coffee
shop, disco, theater, ballroom, shops, casino, 2 lighted tennis courts,
water sports, tour desk, beauty salon. AE, DC, MC, V. EP, MAP.*

$$ Bucuti Beach Resort. This is not your typical Best Western. The small,
★ European-style Bucuti Beach is a refreshing antidote to the impersonal
feel of some larger resorts. These hacienda-style buildings house enormous rooms with bright floral decor and sparkling tile floors. All have
cable TV, air-conditioning, minibar, microwave, coffeemaker, room safe,
and terrace or balcony with ocean view. The resort has an enviable location on a gleaming stretch of sand, just across from all the action at
the Alhambra Bazaar and Casino. The breezy oceanfront Pirate's Nest
restaurant is known islandwide for its excellent theme dinners, such
as Sunday's seafood cookout and limbo show. ☎ *Box 1299, Aruba,*
☎ *297/8–36141 or 800/528–1234,* FAX *297/8–25272. 63 rooms.
Restaurant, bar, pool. AE, DC, MC, V. EP, CP, MAP.*

$$ Caribbean Palm Village. In the giant strip mall that is Noord, this is
an unexpected oasis. The two-story Mediterranean-style buildings
sport porticoed balconies perfumed by frangipani and cooled by foun-
tains. All units have a full kitchen (including dishwasher and mi-
crowave), cable TV, safe, and air-conditioning; a standard room can
be closed off from the suite. What sets these suites apart from the stan-
dard sterile Caribbean room is the work of the original developer, who
animated the spacious suites with throw rugs, local artworks, potted
plants, and cleverly placed divans. Add to that a staff unusually cour-
teous and helpful by Aruban standards. If it weren't so far from the
beach, or at least offered a shuttle, it would qualify as Aruba's great-
est bargain. ☎ *Palm Beach Rd., Noord 43E,* ☎ *297/8–62700,* FAX
*297/8–62380. 170 units. 2 restaurants, bar, 2 pools, Jacuzzis, lighted
tennis court, exercise room. AE, DC, MC, V. EP, MAP.*

$$ La Cabana All Suite Beach Resort & Casino. At the top end of Eagle
Beach, across the road from the sand, is Aruba's largest time-sharing
condominium-hotel complex. The original four-story building faces the
beach and forms a horseshoe around a huge free-form pool complex
with a water slide, poolside bar, outdoor café, and water-sports center. One-third of the rooms have a full sea view; two-thirds have a partial view. All the oddly configured, but comfortable, rooms—studio suites
or one-bedroom suites—come with a fully equipped kitchenette, a

small balcony, and a Jacuzzi, and all have air-conditioning and ceiling fans. Suites have interconnecting doors so that three may be linked together to form two- and three-bedroom units. The ground-floor living rooms do not offer as much privacy as those on higher floors because they look out onto the pool area. The Grand Suites, in back of the original structure (some have sea views), opened in 1993, doubling the number of suites. However, the gracious staff makes it seem like a resort one-third its size. The resort has much to offer: a modern fitness and health center, an ice cream and espresso shop, a budget restaurant, a small grocery store, several shops, and an activities center in the main complex. Shuttle buses run guests over to the upscale casino, the Caribbean's largest, where the hotel has another three restaurants and the Tropicana nightclub, with comedians and Las Vegas–style shows. ⊡ *L. G. Smith Blvd. 250,* ☎ *297/8–79000 or 800/835–7193; in NY, 212/251–1710;* FAX *297/8–77208. 803 suites. 5 restaurants, 3 bars, one poolside; beach shops; casino; racquetball, squash, and 5 tennis courts; health and fitness center. AE, DC, MC, V. EP, MAP.*

$$ **The Mill Resort.** Two-story red-roof buildings flank the open-air common areas of this small condominium hotel, which opened in September 1990 and continues to expand. Unlike time-share resorts, this hotel sells each unit to an individual, who then leases the unit back to the resort for use as a hotel room. The decor is soft country French, with a delicate rose-and-white color scheme, white wicker furniture, and wall-to-wall silver carpeting. The junior suites have a king-size bed, sitting area, and kitchenette. The studios have a full kitchen, but only a queen-size convertible sofa bed and a tiny bathroom. There's no kitchen in the hedonistic Royal Den, but there's a marble Jacuzzi tub big enough for two. This resort is popular with couples seeking a quiet getaway and with families vacationing with small children. There is no restaurant on the premises, but the Old Mill is next door (*see* Dining, *above*). There are also (to the relief of many guests) no bars, no tour desk, and no organized evening activities. Action can be found at the nearby large resorts, and the beach is only a five-minute walk away. ⊡ *L. G. Smith Blvd. 330, Palm Beach,* ☎ *297/8–67700,* FAX *297/8–67271. 89 apartment-style rooms; suites are available by combining units. 2 lighted tennis courts, beach shuttle, exercise room and sauna, pool, kiddie pool, mini–food market, baby-sitting, car rental, snack bar. AE, DC, MC, V. EP.*

$–$$ **Amsterdam Manor Beach Resort.** This attractive gabled russet- and mustard-colored hotel looks like part of a Dutch Colonial village, by the ocean. You feel as if you're stepping back three centuries the moment you walk through the gate. Rooms are furnished either in Dutch modern or quaint provincial style and range from smallish studios with a balcony, cable TV, and kitchenette to deluxe two-bedroom suites with a Jacuzzi and full kitchen. Alas, this cozy enclave and its lovely pool with a waterfall are intruded upon by the noise of traffic from Palm Beach Road. At least that glorious beach is just across the street. ⊡ *L. G. Smith Blvd. 252,* ☎ *297/8–71492,* FAX *297/8–71463. 73 units. Restaurant, bar, pool, minimart. MC, V. EP.*

$–$$ **La Quinta Beach Resort.** Across the road from Eagle Beach is this moderately priced time-share complex with a friendly staff. The efficiency and one-bedroom units were completed in 1993 and are small but well designed and stylish, with full cooking facilities, TVs, and hair dryers in the tiled bathrooms. One-, two-, and three-bedroom units also have sleep sofas and VCRs; some also have a Jacuzzi. ⊡ *Eagle Beach,* ☎ *297/8–75010 or 800/223–9815,* FAX *297/8–76263. 54 units. Bar, 2 pools, cable TV, tennis courts. AE, DC, MC, V. EP.*

Nightlife

Casinos

Casinos are all the rage in Aruba. At last count there were 11. The crowds seem to flock to the newest of the new: As we went to press, the Marriott was planning its 1995 summer entry into this hotbed of high rollers. The Crystal Casino at the Sonesta enjoyed the business until the Hyatt Regency's ultramodern gaming room stole the show (the marquee above the bar at this casino opens to reveal a live band). Then it was the wildly popular **Royal Cabana Casino**—largest in the Caribbean— in La Cabana All Suite Beach Hotel (L. G. Smith Blvd. 250, ☎ 297/8– 9000) with its sleek interior, multitheme three-in-one restaurant and showcase Tropicana nightclub. Smart money's on the just-opened **Hilton Casablanca Casino,** quietly elegant with a Bogart theme (Irausquin Blvd. 77, ☎ 297/8–64466). One place where you'll always find some action is the **Alhambra Casino** (L. G. Smith Blvd. 93, Oranjestad, ☎ 297/8–35000), where a "Moorish slave" gives every gambler a hearty handshake upon entering.

The **Holiday Inn**'s casino (L. G. Smith Blvd. 230, ☎ 297/8–63600) is open 19 hours a day, with an adjacent New York–style deli open until 5 AM. The **Americana Aruba Beach Resort & Casino** (L. G. Smith Blvd. 83, ☎ 297/8–64500) opens daily at 1 PM for slots, 5 PM for all games. The **Aruba Palm Beach Hotel Casino** (L. G. Smith Blvd. 79, ☎ 297/8– 63900) opens at 10 AM for slots, 6 PM for all games. You can also woo Lady Luck at the Sonesta's **Crystal Casino** (L. G. Smith Blvd. 82, ☎ 297/8–36000), where the action is nonstop from 10 AM to 4 AM for slots, 1 PM to 4 AM for the gaming tables. And there's the expanded **Hyatt Regency's Copacabana Casino** (L. G. Smith Blvd. 85, ☎ 297/8– 61234), a 10,000 square-foot complex with a Carnival in Rio theme and live entertainment. Low-key gambling can be found at the new waterside **Seaport Casino** (L. G. Smith Blvd. 9, ☎ 297/8–35600). Most major hotels have casinos.

Discos and Dancing

Arubans usually start partying late, and action doesn't start till around midnight, mostly on the weekends. At **Papas & Beer** (L. G. Smith Blvd. 184, ☎ 297/8–60300), whose purple-and-pink neon signs can be seen lighting up the night from as far away as hotel row, live bands perform nightly, waiters in funky costumes do dance routines under flickering strobe lights, video screens flash, and food and drinks are served almost round-the-clock. Another popular nightclub is **Blue Wave** (Shellstraat, ☎ 297/8–38856) with live bands on Saturday nights and a "Ladies Night" drawing in the crowds on Thursday. For a young adult–style "amusement park," stop in at **La Visage** (L. G. Smith Blvd. 152A, ☎ 297/8–33418), the disco for the young set, both Arubans and tourists. Jazz lovers may prefer the quiet piano bar atmosphere of **La Nota** (Emmastraat 7, ☎ 297/8–32739), which gets lively from around 10 PM until closing at 2 AM.

One truly different evening out is **Chiva Parranda** (☎ 297/8–37643), which means "bus out on the town." Every Wednesday and Thursday at 6:30 PM, this nightlife tour boards up to 40 people on a handpainted 1947 Ford bus and whisks them off to the five hot local nightspots and a restaurant. The $49.50-per-person price includes a drink at each rum shop and a three-course dinner. You're picked up (and poured off) at your hotel. As your affable host remarks, "I finally learned how to cash in on being a party animal." Party animals can prowl farther now, with the **Cucunu,** a bus that offers them the chance to taste the pleasures of country bars. No dinner, but a snack and "jungle juice" are served aboard, for $29.50. It takes place Tuesday and Saturday from 8 till midnight. You're picked up and (fortunately, we'd guess) dropped off after the country crawl.

Specialty Theme Nights

One of the unique things about Aruba's nightlife is the number of specialty theme nights offered by the hotels: At last count there were more than 30. Each "party" features dinner and entertainment, followed by dancing. For a complete list, contact the Aruba Tourism Authority (☎ 297/8–23778 or 297/8–21019).

An Aruban must is the **Bon Bini Festival,** held every Tuesday evening from 6:30 to 8:30 PM in the outdoor courtyard of the Fort Zoutman Museum. *Bon Bini* is Papiamento for "welcome," and this tourist event is the Aruba Institute of Culture and Education's way of introducing you to all things Aruban. Stroll by the stands of Aruban foods, drinks, and crafts, or watch Aruban entertainers perform Antillean music and folkloric dancing. A master of ceremonies explains the history of the dances, instruments, and music. It's a fun event, and a good way to meet other tourists. Look for the clock tower. *Oranjestraat,* ☎ *297/8–22185. ☞ Afl2 adults, Afl1 children.*

Weekend evenings are lively all over town, so the theme-night pickings are fewer. The best ones are Divi Aruba Beach Resort's **Beach BBQ and Caribbean Party** (L. G. Smith Blvd. 93, ☎ 297/8–23300) on Saturday nights and the Mexican fiesta **Fajitas and 'ritas** (L. G. Smith Blvd. 85, ☎ 297/8–61234) held Friday nights at the beachside Palms Restaurant in the Hyatt Regency.

Theater

Aladdin Theater (L. G. Smith Blvd. 93, ☎ 297/8–35000), a cabaret tucked into the Alhambra Bazaar, hosts a variety of shows, including Broadway musicals.

Tropicana (L. G. Smith Blvd. 250, tel 297/8–39000), La Cabana All Suite's cabaret theater and nightclub, features first-class Las Vegas–style reviews and a special comedy series every weekend.

Twinklebone's House of Roast Beef (Noord 124, ☎ 297/8–26780) does serve succulent prime rib and the like. But it's best known for the fun cabaret put on by the staff twice nightly. Customers eat it up.

5　Barbados

Updated by
Jane E. Zarem

BARBADOS HAS A LIFE OF ITS OWN that continues after the tourists have packed their sun oils and returned home. The government is stable, business operations are sophisticated, and unemployment is relatively low, so the difference between haves and have-nots is less marked—or at least less visible—than on some islands. Visitors are neither fawned upon nor resented for their assumed wealth. Genuinely proud of their country, the quarter million Bajans (Barbadians) welcome visitors as privileged guests. Barbados is fine for people who want nothing more than to offer their bodies to the sun, yet travelers who want to discover Caribbean island life and culture will also find it ideal.

Barbados is 21 miles long, 14 miles wide, and relatively flat; the highest point is Mt. Hillaby, at 1,115 feet. Beaches along the tranquil West Coast—in the lee of the northwest trade winds—are backed by first-class resorts. More hotels are situated along the beaches on the South Coast. British and Canadian visitors often favor the posh hotels of St. James Parish. Americans (couples more often than singles) tend to congregate at the large South Coast resorts. Because the beaches of Barbados are open to the public, they lack the privacy that some visitors seek; but the beaches are lovely.

To the northeast are rolling hills and valleys covered by acres of impenetrable sugarcane. The Atlantic surf pounds gigantic boulders along the rugged East Coast, where the Bajans themselves have vacation homes. Elsewhere on the island, linked by almost 900 miles of good roads, are small villages, historic plantation houses, stalactite-studded caves, a wildlife preserve, and the Andromeda Gardens, one of the most attractive small tropical gardens in the world.

No one is sure whether the name Los Barbados ("the bearded ones") refers to the beardlike root that hangs from the island's fig trees or to the bearded natives who greeted the Portuguese "discoverer" of the island in 1536. The name Los Barbados was still current almost a century later when the British landed—by accident—in what is now Holetown in St. James Parish. They colonized the island in 1627 and remained until it achieved independence in 1966.

Barbados has retained a very British atmosphere. Afternoon tea is a ritual at numerous hotels. Cricket is the national sport (a religion, some say), and Barbados produces some of the world's top players. Polo is played in winter. The British tradition of dressing for dinner is firmly entrenched; a few luxury hotels request tie and jacket at dinner in season, and in good restaurants most women will consider themselves inappropriately dressed in anything less formal than a sundress. (A daytime stroll in a swimsuit is as inappropriate in Bridgetown as it would be on New York's 5th Avenue.) Yet the island's atmosphere is hardly stuffy. When the car you ordered for noon doesn't arrive until 12:30, you can expect a cheerful response, "He okay, mon, he just on Caribbean time."

Before You Go

Tourist Information

Contact the **Barbados Tourism Authority,** 800 2nd Ave., New York, NY 10017, ☎ 212/986–6516 or 800/221–9831, FAX 212/573–9850; 3440 Wilshire Blvd., Suite 1215, Los Angeles, CA 90010, ☎ 213/380–2198, FAX 213/384–2763. **In Canada:** 5160 Yonge St., Suite 1800, N. York, Ontario M2N–6L9, ☎ 416/512–6569 or 800/268–9122, FAX

416/512–6581; 615 René Levesque Blvd., Suite 460, Montreal, Québec H3B 1P5, ☎ 514/861–0085, ℻ 514/861–7917. **In the United Kingdom:** 263 Tottenham Court Rd., London W1P 9AA, ☎ 0171/636–9448, ℻ 0171/637–1496.

Arriving and Departing

BY PLANE

Grantley Adams Airport in Barbados is a Caribbean hub. There are daily flights from New York via San Juan, and **American Airlines** (☎ 800/433–7300) and **BWIA** (☎ 800/538–2942) both have nonstop flights from New York and direct flights from Miami. From Canada, **Air Canada** (☎ 800/776–3000) connects from Montreal through New York or Miami and flies nonstop from Toronto. From London, **British Airways** (☎ 800/247–9297) has nonstop service and BWIA connects through Trinidad.

Flights to St. Vincent, St. Lucia, Trinidad, and other islands are scheduled on **LIAT** (☎ 809/495–1187) and BWIA; Air St. Vincent/Air Mustique links Barbados with St. Vincent and the Grenadines.

FROM THE AIRPORT

Airport taxis are not metered. A large sign at the airport announces the fixed rate to each hotel or area, stated in both Barbados and U.S. dollars (about $20 to West Coast hotels, $13 to South Coast ones). A highway bypasses Bridgetown, which saves time getting to the West Coast.

BY BOAT

Bridgetown's Deep Water Harbour is on the northwest side of Carlisle Bay. Barbados is a popular cruise port—half of the annual visitors to the island are cruise passengers. Up to eight cruise ships can dock at one time at the snazzy new Cruise Ship Terminal, which opened in January 1994. Passengers can buy duty-free goods at the scores of shops in the terminal's attractive shopping arcade. Vendors display their handcrafts in colorful reproductions of chattel houses just outside the building. Downtown Bridgetown is a 15- to 20-minute walk from the pier; a taxi costs about $1.50 each way.

Passports and Visas

To enter Barbados, U.S. and Canadian citizens need proof of citizenship and a return or ongoing ticket. Acceptable proof of citizenship is a valid passport or an original birth certificate and a photo ID; a voter registration card or baptismal certificate is not acceptable. British citizens need a valid passport.

Language

English is spoken everywhere, often accented with the phrases and lilt of a Bajan dialect.

Precautions

Beach vendors of coral jewelry, handcrafts, and other items will not hesitate to offer you their wares. The degree of persistence varies, and sharp bargaining is expected on both sides. One hotel's brochure gives sound advice: "Please realize that encouraging the beach musicians means you may find yourself listening to the same three tunes over and over for the duration of your stay."

WATER

The water on the island is plentiful and safe to drink in both hotels and restaurants. It is naturally filtered through 1,000 feet of pervious coral.

INSECTS

Insects aren't much of a problem on Barbados, but if you plan to hike or spend time on secluded beaches, it's wise to use insect repellent.

TOXIC TREE

The little green apples that fall from the large branches of the manchineel tree may look tempting, but they are poisonous to eat and toxic to the touch. Even taking shelter under the tree when it rains can give you blisters. Most manchineels are identified with signs. If you do come in contact with one, go to the nearest hotel and have someone there phone for a physician.

CRIME

Don't invite trouble by leaving valuables unattended on the beach or in plain sight in your room, and don't pick up hitchhikers.

Staying in Barbados

Important Addresses

Tourist Information: The **Barbados Tourism Authority** is on Harbour Road in Bridgetown (☎ 809/427–2623, FAX 809/426–4080). Hours are 8:30–4:30 weekdays. There are also information booths, staffed by board representatives at Grantley Adams International Airport and at Bridgetown's Cruise Ship Terminal.

EMERGENCIES

Emergency and Police: ☎ 112. **Ambulance:** ☎ 115. **Fire department:** ☎ 113. **Scuba diving accidents:** Divers' Alert Network (DAN; ☎ 809/684–8111 or 809/684–2948). **24-hour decompression chamber:** Barbados Defence Force, St. Ann's Fort, Garrison, St. Michael Parish, ☎ 809/436–6185.

Currency

One Barbados dollar (BDS$1) equals about U.S.50¢. Because the value of the Barbados dollar is pegged to that of the U.S. dollar, the ratio remains constant. Both currencies and the Canadian dollar are accepted everywhere on the island. Prices quoted throughout this chapter are in U.S. dollars unless noted otherwise.

Taxes and Service Charges

At the airport you must pay a departure tax of BDS$25 (about U.S.$12) in either currency before leaving Barbados. A 5% government tax is added to hotel bills, and a 10% service charge is added to hotel bills and to most restaurant checks. Any additional tip recognizes extraordinary service. When no service charge is added, tip maids $1 per room per day, waiters 10% to 15%, taxi drivers 10%. Airport porters and bellboys expect BDS$2 (U.S.$1) per bag.

Guided Tours

Barbados has a lot to see. A half- or full-day bus or taxi tour is a good way to get your bearings and can be arranged by your hotel. The price varies according to the number of attractions included; an average full-day tour costs between $40 and $50 per person.

L. E. Williams Tour Co. (☎ 809/427–1043) offers an 80-mile island tour for about $50. A bus picks you up between 8:30 and 9:30 AM and takes you through Bridgetown, the St. James beach area, past the Animal Flower Cave, Farley Hill, Cherry Tree Hill, Morgan Lewis Mill, the East Coast, St. John's Church, Sam Lord's Castle, Oistin's fishing village, and to St. Michael Parish, with drinks along the way and a West Indian lunch at the Atlantis Hotel in Bathsheba.

Sally Shern operates **VIP Tours** (Hillcrest Villa, Upton, St. Michael Parish, ☎ 809/429–4617) and personalizes tours to suit your taste. Bajan-born Ms. Shern knows her island well and provides the unusual and unique: e.g., a champagne lunch at Sunbury Plantation House, a swim at her favorite beach. She picks up her clients in an air-conditioned Mercedes-Benz and charges $30 per hour for four people, with a minimum of five hours. **Bajan Helicopters** (the Wharf, Bridgetown, ☎ 809/431–0069) offers an eagle's-eye view of Barbados. Price per person ranges from U.S.$65 for a 20-minute half-island tour to U.S.$100 for a 30-minute full-island trip.

Highland Outdoor Tours (Canefield, St. Thomas Parish, ☎ 809/438–8069) specializes in adventure trips to the island's seldom-seen natural wonders. Visitors have the option of half-day or full-day horseback treks (including a bareback ride in the surf), scenic hiking expeditions, and tractor-drawn jitney rides through some of Barbados's great plantations. Prices range from $25 to $100 per person and include refreshments and transportation to and from your hotel.

Getting Around
TAXIS
Taxis operate at a fixed hourly rate of BDS$32. For short trips, the rate per mile (or part thereof) should not exceed BDS$2.50. Settle the rate before you start off, and be sure you agree on whether it's in U.S. or Barbados dollars. Most drivers will cheerfully narrate a tour.

BUSES
Blue buses with a yellow stripe are public, yellow buses with a blue stripe are private, and private maxi-taxis may be any color. They all travel constantly along Highway 1 (St. James Road) and are inexpensive (BDS$1.50, exact change appreciated), plentiful, reliable, and usually packed. Buses and vans provide a great opportunity to experience local color, and your fellow passengers will be eager to share their knowledge.

RENTAL CARS
It's a pleasure to explore Barbados by car, provided you take the time to study a map and don't mind asking directions frequently. The more remote roads are in good repair, yet few are well lighted at night, and night falls quickly—at about 6 PM. Even in full daylight, the tall sugarcane fields lining a road can make visibility difficult. Use caution: Pedestrians are everywhere. And remember, traffic keeps to the left.

To rent a car you must have an international driver's license, obtainable at the airport and major car-rental firms for $5 if you have a valid driver's license. More than 40 offices rent minimokes (open-air vehicles) for $35–$60 a day plus insurance (about $215 a week), usually with a three-day or four-day minimum; cars with automatic shift are $60–$65 a day, or approximately $260–$300 a week. Gas costs about $3 a gallon. The speed limit, in keeping with the pace of life, is 37 miles per hour (60 kilometers per hour) in the country, 21 miles per hour (40 kilometers per hour) in town.

The principal car-rental firms are **National** (Bush Hall, St. Michael, ☎ 809/426–0603), **Dear's Garage** (Christ Church, ☎ 809/429–9277 or 809/427–7853), **Sunny Isle** (Worthing, ☎ 809/435–7979), **Sunset Crest Rentals** (St. James, ☎ 809/432–1482), and **P&S Car Rentals** (St. Michael, ☎ 809/424–2052).

Telephones and Mail
The area code for Barbados is 809. Except for emergency numbers, all phone numbers have seven digits and begin with 42 or 43.

An airmail letter from Barbados to the United States or Canada costs BDS90¢ per half ounce; an airmail postcard costs BDS65¢. Letters to the United Kingdom are BDS$1.10; postcards are BDS70¢.

Opening and Closing Times

Stores are open weekdays 9–5, Saturday 8–1. Some supermarkets are open daily 8–6. Banks are open Monday to Thursday 8–3, Friday 8–5.

Exploring Barbados

The Barbados National Trust, headquartered at 10th Avenue, Belleville, St. Michael (☎ 809/426–2421), has designed the **Heritage Passport,** a 50% discounted admission to Barbados's most popular attractions and historic sites. A Full Passport includes 16 sites and costs $35; a Mini-Passport includes 5 sites and costs $12. Children under 12 are admitted free if accompanied by a Passport holder (maximum two children per passport). Passports may be purchased at hotels, Trust headquarters, or at the sites.

Bridgetown

Numbers in the margin correspond to points of interest on the Bridgetown map.

Bridgetown is a bustling city, complete with rush hours and traffic congestion. You'll avoid hassle by taking the bus or a taxi. Sightseeing will take only an hour or so, and the shopping area is compact.

In the center of town, overlooking the picturesque harbor known as
❶ the Careenage, is **Trafalgar Square.** Its monument to Lord Horatio Nelson predates Nelson's Column in London's Trafalgar Square by more than two decades. Several blocks inland, on Synagogue Lane, is the old-
❷ est synagogue in the Western Hemisphere. The **Jewish Synagogue** (☎ 809/426–5792) dates back to 1654 and has recently been restored to its original purpose as a house of prayer.

Bridgetown is a major Caribbean free port. The principal shopping
❸ area is **Broad Street,** which leads west from Trafalgar Square past the House of Assembly and Parliament buildings. A series of stained-glass windows depicting British monarchs from James I to Queen Victoria adorn these Victorian government buildings. Like so many smaller buildings in Bridgetown, they stand beside a growing number of modern office buildings.

❹ The **Careenage,** a finger of sea that made early Bridgetown a natural harbor and a gathering place, is where working schooners were careened (turned on their sides) to be scraped of barnacles and repainted. Today the Careenage serves mainly as a berth for pleasure yachts and charter boats.

Although no one has proved it conclusively, George Washington, on his only visit outside the United States, is said to have worshiped at
❺ **St. Michael's Cathedral** east of Trafalgar Square. The structure was nearly a century old when he visited in 1751, and it has since been destroyed by hurricanes and rebuilt twice, in 1780 and 1831. The two bridges over the Careenage are the Chamberlain Bridge and the Charles O'Neal Bridge, both of which lead to Highway 7.

❻ East of St. Michael's Cathedral, **Queen's Park** is home to one of the largest trees in Barbados: an immense baobab more than 10 centuries
❼ old. The historic **Queen's Park House,** former home of the commander of the British troops, has been converted into a theater—with an

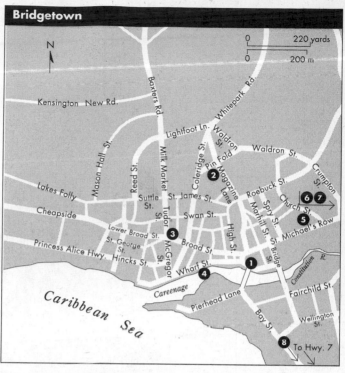

Bridgetown

exhibition room on the lower floor—and a restaurant. Queen's Park is a long walk from Trafalgar Square or the museum; you may want to take a taxi. ⊙ *Daily 9–5.*

8 About a mile south of Bridgetown on Highway 7, the intriguing **Barbados Museum** has artifacts and mementos of military history and everyday life in the 19th century. Here you'll see cane-harvesting implements, lace wedding dresses, ancient (and frightening) dentistry instruments, and slave sale accounts kept in a spidery copperplate handwriting. Wildlife and natural history exhibits, a well-stocked gift shop, and a good café are also here, in what used to be the military prison. *Hwy. 7, Garrison Savannah,* ☎ *809/427–0201.* ☞ *BDS$10 adults, BDS$5 children under 12.* ⊙ *Mon.–Sat. 9–5, Sun. 2–6.*

Central Barbados

Numbers in the margin correspond to points of interest on the Barbados map.

1 The **Folkstone Marine Park & Visitor Centre,** north of Holetown, has a land museum of marine life and an underwater snorkeling trail around Dottin's Reef (glass-bottom boats are available for nonswimmers). A dredge barge sunk in shallow water is the home to myriad fish, and it and the reef are popular with scuba divers. Huge sea fans, soft coral, and the occasional giant turtle are sights to see.

2 Highway 2 will take you to **Harrison's Cave.** These pale-gold limestone caverns, complete with subterranean streams and a 40-foot waterfall, are considered to be among the finest cave systems in the world. Open since 1981, the caves are so extensive that tours are made by electric tram (hard hats are provided, but all that may fall on you is a little dripping water). ☎ *809/438–6640.* ☞ *BDS$15 adults, BDS$7.50*

Exploring

Dining

Lodging

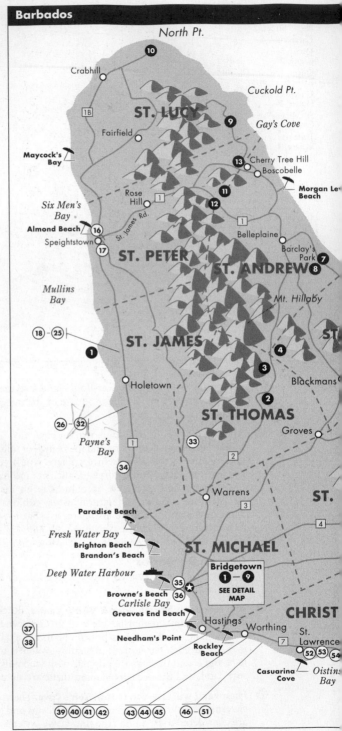

Barbados

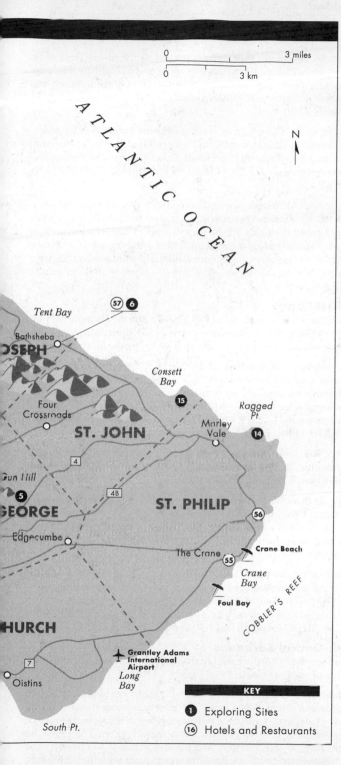

Benston Windsurfing Club Hotel, **54**

Casuarina Beach Club, **51**

Club Rockley Barbados, **42**

Cobblers Cove Hotel, **17**

Coconut Creek Club, **28**

Coral Reef Club, **18**

Crane Beach Hotel, **55**

Discovery Bay Hotel, **24**

Divi Southwinds Beach Resort, **49**

Glitter Bay, **20**

Grand Barbados Beach Resort, **36**

Little Bay Hotel, **46**

Marriott's Sam Lord's Castle, **56**

Ocean View, **39**

The Royal Pavilion, **21**

Sandy Beach Hotel, **43**

Sandy Lane Hotel, **29**

Settlers' Beach, **19**

Sichris Hotel, **44**

Southern Palms, **50**

Treasure Beach, **30**

KEY

❶ Exploring Sites

⑯ Hotels and Restaurants

dripping water). ☎ *809/438–6640.* ☛ *BDS$15 adults, BDS$7.50 children. Reservations recommended.* ⊙ *Daily 9–6.*

❸ The nearby **Welchman Hall Gully,** a part of the National Trust in St. Thomas, gives you another chance to commune with nature. Here are acres of labeled flowers and trees, the occasional green monkey, and great peace and quiet. ☎ *809/438–6671.* ☛ *BDS$10 adults, BDS$5 children.* ⊙ *Daily 9–5.*

❹ Continue along Highway 2 to reach the **Flower Forest,** 8 acres of fragrant flowering bushes, canna and ginger lilies, puffball trees, and more than a hundred other species of flora. The tranquil setting also offers beautiful views of Mt. Hillaby. ☎ *809/433–8152.* ☛ *BDS$10.* ⊙ *Daily 9–5.*

Go back toward Bridgetown and take Highway 4 and smaller roads ❺ to **Gun Hill** for a view so pretty it seems almost unreal: Shades of green and gold cover the fields all the way to the horizon, the picturesque gun tower is surrounded by brilliant flowers, and the white limestone lion behind the garrison is a famous landmark. Military invalids were once sent here to convalesce. ☎ *809/429–1358.* ☛ *BDS$5 adults, BDS$2.50 children.*

The East Coast

Take Highway 3 across the island to Bathsheba and the phenomenal view from the **Atlantis,** one of the oldest hotels in Barbados, where you may need help getting up from the table after sampling the lunch buffet.

❻ Nearby **Andromeda Gardens** (☎ 809/433–9384) is a fascinating collection of unusual and beautiful plant specimens from around the world, cultivated in beds set into the cliffs overlooking the sea. The plants were collected by the late horticulturist Iris Bannochie and are now administered by the Barbados National Trust. ☎ *809/426–2421.* ☛ *BDS$10 adults, BDS$5 children.* ⊙ *Daily 9–5.*

❼ North of Bathsheba, **Barclay's Park** also offers a view of the water, plus ❽ picnic facilities in a wooded seafront area. At the nearby **Chalky Mount Potteries,** you'll find craftspersons making and selling their wares.

A drive north to the isolated Morgan Lewis Beach (*see* Beaches, *below*) or to Gay's Cove, which every Bajan calls Cove Bay, will put you in ❾ reach of the town of **Pie Corner.** Pie Corner is known not for baked goods but for artifacts left by the Carib and Arawak tribes who once lived there.

❿ The **Animal Flower Cave** at North Point, reached by Highway 1B, displays small sea anemones, or sea worms, that resemble jewel-like flowers as they open their tiny tentacles. For a small fee you can explore inside the cavern and see the waves breaking just outside it. ☎ *809/439–8797.* ☛ *BDS$3 adults, BDS$1.50 children under 12.* ⊙ *Daily 9–4.*

North-Central Barbados

The attractions of north-central Barbados may easily be combined with the tour of the East Coast.

⑪ The **Barbados Wildlife Reserve** can be reached on Highway 1 from Speightstown on the West Coast. The reserve is home to herons, land turtles, a kangaroo, screeching peacocks, innumerable green monkeys, geese, brilliantly colored parrots, and a friendly otter. The fauna are not in cages, so step carefully and keep your hands to yourself. The preserve has been much improved in recent years with the addition of a giant walk-in aviary and natural-history exhibits. Terrific photo opportunities are everywhere. ☎ 809/422–8826. ☛ BDS$15 adults, BDS$10 children under 12 with adult. ⊘ Daily 10–5.

⑫ Just to the south is **Farley Hill,** a national park in northern St. Peter Parish; the rugged landscape explains why they call this the Scotland area. The imposing ruins of a once-magnificent plantation great house are surrounded by gardens, lawns, an avenue of towering royal palms, and gigantic mahogany, whitewood, and casuarina trees. Partially rebuilt for the filming of *Island in the Sun,* the structure was later destroyed by fire. ☛ BDS$2 per car; walkers free. ⊘ Daily 8:30–6.

⑬ **St. Nicholas Abbey,** near Cherry Tree Hill, was named for a former owner and is the oldest (ca. 1650) great house in Barbados. It's well worth visiting for its stone and wood architecture in the Jacobean style. Fascinating home movies, made by the present owner's father, record scenes of Bajan town and plantation life in the 1920s and 1930s. There are no set showing times; you need only ask to see them. ☎ 809/422–8725. ☛ $2.50. ⊘ Weekdays 10–3:30.

The South Shore

Driving east on Highways 4 and 4B, you pass many **chattel houses** along the route. The property of tenant farmers, these ever-expandable houses were built to be dismantled and moved when necessary. When you reach
⑭ the coast, you'll see the appropriately named **Ragged Point Lighthouse,** where the sun first shines on Barbados and its dramatic Atlantic seascape. About 4 miles to the northwest, in the eastern corner of St. John Parish, the coral-stone buildings and serenely beautiful grounds
⑮ of **Codrington Theological College** (☎ 809/433–1274), founded in 1745, stand on a cliff overlooking Consett Bay.

Take the smaller roads southeast to reach **Marriott's Sam Lord's Castle** (*see* Lodging, *below*), the Regency house built by the buccaneer. Most of the rooms are furnished with the fine antiques he is said to have acquired from passing ships (note the mahogany four-poster), but he had to hire Italian artisans to create the elaborate plaster ceilings. The tour is free to guests; others pay $2.50.

Beaches

Barbados is blessed with beautiful Caribbean beaches dotted with tall palms and shaded by leafy mahogany trees. All beaches are open to the public. (Access to hotel beaches may not always be public, but you can walk onto almost any beach from another one.)

West Coast Beaches

The West Coast has the stunning coves and white-sand beaches that are dear to postcard publishers—plus calm, clear water for snorkeling, scuba diving, and swimming. Beaches begin in the north at **Almond Beach Village** (about a mile of sand) and continue almost unbroken to Bridgetown at **Brighton Beach,** a popular spot with locals. The afternoon clouds and sunsets are breathtaking from any of the beaches along the West Coast.

While beaches here are seldom crowded, the West Coast is not the place to find isolation. Owners of private boats stroll by, offering waterskiing, parasailing, and snorkel cruises. There are no concession stands per se, but hotels welcome nonguests for terrace lunches (wear a coverup). Picnic items and necessities can be bought at the Sunset Crest shopping center in Holetown.

Good spots for swimming include **Paradise Beach; Brandon's Beach,** a 10-minute walk south; **Browne's Beach,** in Bridgetown; and **Greaves End Beach,** south of Bridgetown at Aquatic Gap, between the Grand Barbados Beach Resort and the Barbados Hilton in St. Michael Parish.

The West Coast is the area for scuba diving, sailing, and lunch-and-rum cruises on the red-sailed *Jolly Roger* "pirate" party ship (Fun Cruises, ☎ 809/436–6424). Somewhat more sedate sailing experiences can be had on the *Wind Warrior* (☎ 809/427–7245) and the *Secret Love* (☎ 809/432–1972).

You can go to depths of 150 feet off wrecks and reefs in the *Atlantis* (☎ 809/436–8929 or 809/436–8932), a Canadian-built 50-foot submarine that seats 28 passengers at a time, each at his or her own porthole. Classical music plays while an oceanography specialist informs. *Cost: $69.50 adults, $39.75 children 4–12.*

South Coast Beaches

The heavily traveled south coast of Christ Church Parish is much more built up than the St. James Parish coast in the west; here you'll find condos, high-rise hotels, beach parks, many places to eat and shop, and the traffic (including public transportation) that serves them. These busier beaches generally draw a younger, more active crowd. The quality of the beach itself is consistently good, the reef-protected waters safe for swimming and snorkeling.

Needham's Point, with its lighthouse, is one of Barbados's best beaches, crowded with locals on weekends and holidays. Two others are in the St. Lawrence Gap area, near **Casuarina Cove.** The **Benston Windsurfing Club Hotel** in Maxwell caters specifically to windsurfing aficionados, although most hotels and resorts provide boards or rent them for a nominal fee.

Crane Beach has for years been a popular swimming beach. As you move toward the Atlantic side of the island, the waves roll in bigger and faster; the waves at the nearby Crane Hotel are a favorite with bodysurfers. (But remember that this is the ocean, not the Caribbean, and exercise caution.)

Nearby **Foul Bay** lives up to its name only for sailboats; for swimmers and alfresco lunches, it's lovely.

East Coast Beaches

Those who love wild natural beauty will want to head north up the East Coast highway. With secluded beaches and crashing ocean waves on one side, rocky cliffs and verdant landscape on the other, the windward side of Barbados won't disappoint anyone who seeks dramatic views. But be cautioned: Swimming here is treacherous and *not* recommended. The waves are high, the bottom tends to be rocky, and the currents are unpredictable. Limit yourself to enjoying the view and watching the surfers—who have been at it since they were kids.

A worthwhile little-visited beach for those who don't mind trekking about a mile off the beaten track is **Morgan Lewis Beach,** on the coast east of Morgan Lewis Mill, the oldest intact windmill on the island. Turn east on the small road that goes to the town of Boscobelle (between Cherry Tree Hill and Morgan Lewis Mill), but instead of going to the town, take the even less-traveled road (unmarked on most maps; you will have to ask for directions) that goes down the cliff to the beach. What awaits is more than 2 miles of unspoiled, uninhabited white sand and sweeping views of the Atlantic coastline. You may see a few Barbadians swimming, sunning, or fishing, but for the most part you'll have privacy.

Return to your car, and cross the island's north point on the secondary roads until you reach the West Coast. About a mile west from the end of Highway 1B is **Maycock's Bay,** an isolated area in St. Lucy Parish about 2 miles north of Almond Beach Village, the island's northern-most resort complex.

Sports and the Outdoors

Golfing

Barbadians love golf, and golfers love Barbados. The **Royal West-moreland Golf Club** (☎ 809/422–4653), with a new and challenging Robert Trent Jones 18-hole course that meanders through the 480-acre Westmoreland Sugar Estate and overlooks the scenic West Coast, was brand-new for the 1995 season. Future construction is planned to add private villas, restaurants, and an additional 9 holes to the course. The prestigious **Sandy Lane Club** (☎ 809/432–1145) is also adding 9 holes to its present 18-hole championship course. Sandy Lane's dramatic 7th hole is famous for both its elevated tee and its incredible view. **Club Rockley Barbados** (☎ 809/435–7873), on the South Coast, has a challenging 9-hole course. **Almond Beach Village** (☎ 809/422–4900), the former Heywoods Resort, has a 9-hole course on the northwest corner of the island. The **Belair Par-3** (☎ 809/423–4653) course is on the rugged East Coast, near Sam Lord's Castle. All courses are open to nonguests. Greens fees range from $12.50 for 9 holes at Belair to $120 for 18 holes at Sandy Lane.

Hiking and Walking

Hilly but not mountainous, the interior of Barbados is ideal for hiking. The **Barbados National Trust** (No. 2, 10th Ave., Belleville, St. Michael, ☎ 809/426–9033) sponsors free 5-mile walks year-round on Sunday, from 6:30 AM to about 9:30 AM and from 3:30 PM to 5:30 PM, as well as special moonlight hikes when the heavens permit. Newspapers announce the time and meeting place (or you can call the Trust).

Horseback Riding

The **Caribbean International Riding Center** (St. Joseph, ☎ 809/433–1246) offers one-hour to half-day rides that range in price from BDS$55 to BDS$175. On the West Coast, **Brighton Stables** (☎ 809/425–9381) offers one-hour rides along beaches and palm groves for BDS$55. Prices for both operators include transportation to and from your hotel.

Parasailing

Parasailing, during which you wear a parachute harness and take off from a raft as you're towed by a speedboat, is available, wind conditions permitting, on the beaches of St. James and Christ Church. Just ask at any hotel, then flag down a speedboat (though it may have found you first). Rates are BDS$60–BDS$90 per flight.

Sailing and Fishing

Tiami, or *Wind Warrior* (☎ 809/425–5800), and *Irish Mist* (☎ 809/436–9201) are large catamarans that offer lunchtime and cocktail cruises. **Blue Jay Charters** (☎ 809/422–2098) has a 45-foot, fully equipped fishing boat, with a crew that knows the waters where blue marlin, sailfish, barracuda, and kingfish play.

Scuba Diving

Many dive shops provide instruction (the three-hour beginner's "resort courses" and the weeklong certification courses) followed by a shallow dive, usually on Dottin's Reef. Trained divers can explore reefs, wrecks, and the walls of "blue holes," the huge circular depressions in the ocean floor. Not to be missed by certified, guided divers is the *Stavronikita*, a 368-foot Greek freighter that was deliberately sunk at about 125 feet; hundreds of butterfly fish hang out around its mast, and the thin rays of sunlight that filter down through the water make exploring the huge ship a wonderfully eerie experience.

At the **Dive Shop, Ltd.** (Grand Barbados Beach Resort, ☎ 809/426–9947) experienced divers can participate in deep dives to old wrecks to look for bottles and other artifacts (and you can usually keep what you find). **Exploresub Barbados** (St. Lawrence Gap, Christ Church, ☎ 809/435–6542) offers a full range of daily dives. **Dive Boat Safari** (Barbados Hilton, ☎ 809/427–4350) offers full diving and instruction services.

Snorkeling

Snorkeling gear can be rented for a small charge from nearly every hotel.

Squash

Squash courts can be reserved at the **Club Rockley Barbados** (☎ 809/435–7880) and **Barbados Squash Club** (Marine House, Christ Church, ☎ 809/427–7913).

Submarining

Minisubmarine voyages are enormously popular with families and those who enjoy watching fish without getting wet, and the 28-passenger *Atlantis* turns the Caribbean into a giant aquarium. The 45-minute trip takes you as deep as 150 feet below the surface for a look at what even sport divers rarely see. The nighttime dives, using high-power searchlights, are spectacular. ☎ *809/436–8929 or 809/436–8932. Cost: $69.50 adults, $39.75 children 4–12.*

Surfing

The best surfing is available on the East Coast, and most wave riders congregate at the Soup Bowl, near Bathsheba. An annual international surfing competition is held on Barbados every October.

Tennis

Most hotels have tennis courts that can be reserved day and night. Be sure to bring your whites; appropriate dress is expected on the court.

Waterskiing

Waterskiing is widely available, often provided along St. James and Christ Church by the private speedboat owners. Inquire at your hotel, which can direct you to the nearest Sunfish sailing and Hobie Cat rentals as well.

Windsurfing

Windsurfing boards and equipment are often guest amenities at the larger hotels and can be rented by nonguests. The best place to windsurf is on the southeast coast of the island, at Silver Sands and Silver Rock Beach.

Spectator Sports

CRICKET

The island is mad for cricket, and you can sample a match at almost any time of year. While the season is June through late December, test matches are played in the first half of the year. The newspapers give the details of time and place.

HORSE RACING

Horse racing takes place on alternate Saturdays, from January to May and from July to November, at the **Garrison Savannah** in Christ Church, about 3 miles south of Bridgetown. Appropriate dress might be described as "casual elegant." ☎ *809/426–3980.* ☞ *BDS$10 adults, BDS$5 children under 12. Opens at 1:30 on race days.*

POLO

Polo, the sport of kings, is played seriously in Barbados. Matches are held at the **Polo Club** in St. James on Wednesday and Saturday from September to March. Hang around the club room after the match. That's where the lies, the legends, and the invitations happen. ☞ *About $2.50.*

RUGBY

The rough-and-tumble game of rugby is played at the Garrison Savannah; schedules are available from the **Barbados Rugby Club.** Contact Victor Roach (☎ 809/435–6543).

SOCCER

The "football," or soccer, season runs from January through June. For game schedules write to the **Barbados Football Association,** Box 1362, Bridgetown, Barbados.

Shopping

Traditionally, Broad Street and its side streets in Bridgetown have been the center for shopping action. Hours are generally weekdays 9–5 and Saturday 8–1. Many stores have an inbound (duty-free) department where you must show your travel tickets or a passport in order to buy duty-free goods.

The mall-like **Sheraton Centre** (at Sargeant's Village in Christ Church, ☎ 809/435–8115) has toys for tots, togs for teens, and temptations for all. The **Quayside Shopping Center** (at Rockley in Christ Church, ☎ 809/428–2474) is small and has a group of exclusive shops, such as Coconut Junction and Lazy Days, which has top-quality beachwear, beach accessories, and beach equipment—including surf and boogie boards.

Luxury Goods

Bridgetown stores have values on fine bone china, crystal, cameras, stereo and video equipment, jewelry, perfume, and clothing. **Broad Street** is the main shopping drag in Bridgetown. **De Lima's** and **Da Costa's Ltd** are here. Both are centerpieces of their own malls and stock high-quality imports. Among the specialty stores in these small malls are several jewelry stores—Louis Bayley (gold watches), Columbian Emeralds, and Correia's (diamonds, pearls, and semiprecious stones)—and a few crafts stores. **Cave Shepherd** and **Harrison's** department stores offer wide selections of goods at many locations, including Broad Street, the airport, and the Cruiseship Terminal.

Best 'N the Bunch (St. Lawrence Gap, 809/428–2474) is a wildly colored chattel house at the Chattel House Village and its own best advertisement. Here the expert jewelry of Bajan David Trottman is sold at reasonable prices.

Handicrafts

Island handicrafts are everywhere: woven mats and place mats, dresses, dolls, handbags, shell jewelry. The **Best of Barbados** shops (Mall 34, Broad St., Bridgetown, ☎ 809/436–1416, and six other locations) offer the highest-quality artwork and crafts, both "native style" and modern designs. A resident artist, Jill Walker, sells her watercolors and prints here. **Coffee & Cream Gallery** (Paradise Village, St. Lawrence Gap, ☎ 809/428–2708) displays and sells local artwork of all types.

At the **Pelican Village Handicrafts Center** on the Princess Alice Highway near the Cheapside Market in Bridgetown (☎ 809/426–4391), in a cluster of conical shops, you can watch goods and crafts being made before you purchase them. Rugs and mats made from pandanus grass and khuskhus are good buys.

For native Caribbean arts and crafts, including items from Barbados and elsewhere in the region, visit the **Verandah Art Gallery** (Broad St., Bridgetown, ☎ 809/426–2605).

Antiques

Antiques and fine memorabilia are the stock of **Greenwich House Antiques** (Greenwich Village, Trents Hill, St. James Parish, ☎ 809/432–1169). It's a whole plantation house full of antique Barbadian mahogany furniture, crystal, silver, china, and pictures and is open daily from 10:30 AM to 6 PM. **Antiquaria** (Spring Garden Hwy., St. Michael's Row, next to the Anglican cathedral, Bridgetown, ☎ 809/426–0635), a pink Victorian house, sells antique silver, brassware, mahogany furniture, and maps and engravings of Barbados. It's open every day but Sunday.

Chic Shops

Hidden in separate corners of Barbados are some very upscale, little-known shops that would be able to hold their own in New York or London. Carol Cadogan's **Cotton Days Designs** at Ramsgate Cottage (Lower Bay St., ☎ 809/427–7191) and on the Wharf in Bridgetown sets the international pace with all-cotton, collage creations that have been declared "wearable art." These are fantasy designs, with prices that begin at U.S.$250. Fortunately, she takes credit cards.

Another shop worth a visit on the Wharf is **Origins—Colours of the Caribbean** (☎ 809/436–8522), where original hand-painted and batik clothing, imported cottons, linens and silks for day and evening, and handmade jewelry and accessories are the order of the day. The hand-painted T-shirt dresses, priced at about U.S.$100, are fabulous.

At **Sunny Shoes Inc.** (Cave Shepherd's Broad St. store, ☎ 809/431–2121) concessionaire DeCoursey Clarke will make a pair of women's strap sandals while you wait—in any color(s) you wish—for about U.S.$26.

Dining

The better hotels and restaurants of Barbados have employed chefs trained in New York and Europe to attract and keep their sophisticated clientele. Gourmet dining here usually means fresh seafood, beef, or veal with finely blended sauces.

The native West Indian cuisine offers an entirely different dining experience. The island's West African heritage brought rice, peas, beans, and okra to its table, the staples that make a perfect base for slowly cooked meat and fish dishes. Many side dishes are cooked in oil (the pumpkin fritters can be addictive). And be cautious at first with the West Indian seasonings; like the sun, they are hotter than you think.

Most menus include dolphin, kingfish, snapper, and flying fish prepared every way imaginable. Shellfish abound; so does steak. For breakfast and dessert you'll find mangoes, soursop, papaya (pawpaw), and, in season, "mammy apples," a softball-sized, thick-skinned fruit with giant seeds.

Buljol is a cold salad of codfish, tomatoes, onions, sweet peppers, and celery, marinated and served raw.

Callaloo soup is made from okra, crabmeat, the spinachlike vegetable that gives the dish its name, and seasonings.

Christophines and **eddoes** are tasty, potatolike vegetables that are often served with curried shrimp, chicken, or goat.

Cou-cou is a mix of cornmeal and okra with a spicy Creole sauce made from tomatoes, onions, and sweet peppers; it is often served with steamed flying fish. A version served by the Brown Sugar restaurant, called "red herring," is smoked herring and breadfruit in Creole sauce.

Pepper-pot stew, a hearty mix of oxtail, beef chunks, and "any other meat you may have," simmered overnight, is flavored with *cassareep,* an ancient preservative and seasoning that gives the stew its dark, rich color.

Among the liquid refreshments of Barbados, in addition to the local and omnipresent Banks Beer and Mount Gay rum, there are **falernum,** a liqueur concocted of rum, sugar, lime juice, and almond essence, and **mauby,** a refreshing nonalcoholic beerlike drink made by boiling bitter bark and spices, straining the mixture, and sweetening it.

What to Wear
Barbados's British heritage and large resident population keep the island's dress code modest. While this does not always mean a tie and jacket, you'll find jeans, shorts, and beach shirts are frowned upon at dinnertime.

CATEGORY	COST*
$$$	over $40
$$	$25–$40
$	under $25

per person, excluding drinks and 10% service charge

$$$ **Bagatelle Great House.** Occupying a converted plantation house in a hilly area, Bagatelle Great House gives diners an impression of colonial life. The terrace allows intimate dining at tables for two, while inside the castlelike walls there are much larger round tables. The superb ambience is somewhat more memorable than the expensive Continental dishes. Upstairs is a gallery of Caribbean art. ✗ *St. Thomas Parish,* ☎ *809/421–6767. Reservations required. AE, MC, V.*

$$$ **Carambola.** Candlelight and a cliffside setting overlooking the Caribbean
★ make this alfresco restaurant in St. James Parish one of the most romantic on the island. It also happens to serve some of the best food in Barbados. The menu is a mix of Thai and Continental dishes, all prepared with a Caribbean touch. Start with a spicy, Caribbean-style crab tart, served with hollandaise sauce on a bed of sweet pepper coulis. For an entrée try fillet of kingfish broiled with ginger, coriander, and spring onions, or sliced duck breast with a wild mushroom fumet served with stuffed tomatoes and *gratin dauphinoise* (potatoes au gratin). When you think you can't eat another bite, the *citron gâteau* (lime mousse on a bed of lemon coulis) makes a light but superb finish. ✗ *Derricks, St. James Parish,* ☎ *809/432–0832. Reservations required. AE, MC, V. Closed Sun. No lunch.*

$$$ **La Cage aux Folles.** The restored Summerland Great House and its 2 acres of tropical gardens are the setting for one of the island's most acclaimed restaurants. The exotic five-course menu of international cuisine includes fresh fish with orange and Cointreau, sweet-and-sour shrimp, Malaysian satay, and sesame prawn pâté. ✗ *Prospect, St. James Parish,* ☎ *809/424–2424. Reservations necessary. Jacket and tie required. AE, D, DC, MC, V. Closed Tues. No lunch.*

$$$ **The Palm Terrace.** The Palm's young British chef, who came here from London's Le Gavroche, applies his talents to combine Barbadian produce with top-quality imports. The result is modern European creations,

such as mille-feuille of home-smoked chicken with tomato, chives, and carrots in a light mustard cream sauce. Fresh mint accents New Zealand rack of lamb, and panfried crab becomes a stuffing for the breast of chicken entrée. Widely spaced tables, comfortable chairs, and indoor palms swaying under floor-to-ceiling arches create an ambience that is formal yet relaxed, as you dine facing the Caribbean Sea. ✗ *Royal Pavilion, Porters, St. James Parish,* ☎ *809/422–4444. Reservations advised. AE, D, DC, MC, V. No lunch.*

$$$ **Raffles.** Young, international owners have made this one of Barbados's
★ top restaurants. Forty guests can be seated at beautifully decorated tables with a tropical safari theme. Main dishes may be shrimp saki, blackened fish, steak served in a wine-and-lime sauce, basil-curry chicken, and sweet-and-sour pork. The desserts are both delicious and decadent. ✗ *1st St., Holetown, St. James Parish,* ☎ *809/432–6557. Reservations necessary. AE, D, DC, MC, V. No lunch.*

$$$ **Sandy Bay Restaurant.** The renowned Sandy Lane Hotel is the perfect
★ place for an elegant meal overlooking one of the best beaches on the island. Munich-born chef Hans Schweitzer, formerly of the Midsummer House in Cambridge, England, has modernized the cuisine by introducing "art culinair" to this historic resort. His new dishes are mostly light fare, elegantly dressed with silky sauces, and accented with perfect fresh vegetables. Grilled dolphin, lobster and shrimp tempura, and lamb with honey, thyme, and wild rosemary are among the entrées. To ensure that the best produce is used, a van is sent out every morning to scour the island for the freshest vegetables and fish. Desserts are French, creamy, delicious, spectacular! Be sure to dress for the occasion. ✗ *Sandy Lane Hotel and Golf Club, St. James Parish,* ☎ *809/432–1311. Reservations advised. AE, MC, V.*

$$ **Brown Sugar.** A special-occasion atmosphere prevails at Brown Sugar, which is set in a restored West Indian wooden house across the road from the Grand Barbados Beach Resort outside Bridgetown. Dozens of ferns and hanging plants decorate the breezy multilevel restaurant. An extensive and authentic West Indian lunch buffet—everything from cou-cou to pepper-pot stew—served between noon and 2:30, is popular with local businessmen. The dinner menu adds entrées such as Creole orange chicken and homemade desserts, including angel food chocolate mousse cake, passion fruit or nutmeg ice cream, and lime cheesecake with guava sauce. ✗ *Aquatic Gap, Bay St., St. Michael Parish,* ☎ *809/426–7684. Reservations advised. AE, DC, MC, V. No lunch Sat.*

$$ **Fathoms.** The newest property of veteran restaurateurs Stephen and Sandra Toppin is open seven days a week for lunch and dinner, with 22 well-dressed tables scattered from the inside dining rooms to the patio's ocean edge. Dinner may bring a grilled lobster, island rabbit, jumbo baked shrimp, or cashew-crusted kingfish. Fathoms is casual by day, candlelit by night. ✗ *Payne's Bay, St. James Parish,* ☎ *809/432–2568. Reservations advised for dinner. AE, MC, V.*

$$ **Ile de France.** French owners Martine (from Lyon) and Michel (from
★ Toulouse) Gramaglia have adapted the pool and garden areas of the Windsor Arms Hotel and turned them into an island "in" spot. White latticework opens to the night sounds, soft taped French music plays, and a single, perfect hibiscus dresses each table. Specialties include foie gras, tournedos Rossini, lobster-and-crepe flambé, and filet mignon with a choice of pepper, béarnaise, or champignon sauce. ✗ *Windsor Arms Hotel, Hastings, Christ Church Parish,* ☎ *809/435–6869. Reservations required. No credit cards. Closed Mon. No lunch.*

$$ **Josef's.** Swede Nils Ryman created a menu from the unusual combination of Caribbean and Scandinavian fare. Blackened fish, rolled in Cajun spices and seared in oil, and toast Skagen, made from diced shrimp blended with mayonnaise and fresh dill, are menu favorites. Stroll around the garden before moving to the alfresco dining room downstairs or to the simply decorated room upstairs for a table that looks out over the sea. ✕ *Waverly House, St. Lawrence Gap, Christ Church Parish,* ☎ *809/435–6541. Reservations advised. AE, DC, MC, V.*

$$ **La Maison.** The elegant atmosphere in the colonial-style Balmore House
★ is created by English country furnishings and a paneled bar opening onto a seaside terrace for dining. The award-winning gourmet cuisine is nothing less than superb. A French chef from the Loire Valley creates seafood specials, including a flying-fish parfait appetizer. Passionfruit ice cream is a dessert special. ✕ *Holetown, St. James Parish,* ☎ *809/432–1156. Reservations advised. AE, D, MC, V. Closed Mon.*

$$ **Ocean View Hotel.** Barbados's oldest restaurant, the dining room of
★ this elegant pink grande dame hotel is dressed in fresh fabrics, with great bunches of equally fresh flowers and sparkling crystal chandeliers. Bajan dishes are served for lunch and dinner, and the Sunday-only Planter's Luncheon Buffet offers course after course of traditional dishes—callaloo, cou-cou, flying fish, and more. There's a cabaret and dancing on weekend evenings. ✕ *Hastings, Christ Church Parish,* ☎ *809/427–7821. Reservations advised. AE, MC, V.*

$$ **Pisces.** Fish is the way to go at this eatery at the water's edge in lively St. Lawrence Gap. Flying fish, dolphin, crab, kingfish, shrimp, prawns, and lobster are prepared any way from charbroiled to sautéed. There are also some chicken and beef dishes. Other items include conch fritters, tropical gazpacho, and seafood terrine with a mango sauce. Enjoy your meal in a contemporary setting filled with hanging tropical plants and twinkling white lights. ✕ *St. Lawrence Gap, Christ Church Parish,* ☎ *809/435–6564. Reservations advised. AE, MC, V. No lunch.*

$$ **Plantation.** Wednesday's Bajan buffet and entertainment on Wednesday, Friday, and Saturday are big attractions here. The Plantation is in a renovated Barbadian residence surrounded by spacious grounds above the Southwinds Resort. French and Barbadian cuisine is served either indoors or on the terrace. ✕ *St. Lawrence Gap, Christ Church Parish,* ☎ *809/428–5048. Reservations advised. AE, MC, V. No lunch.*

$$ **Rose and Crown.** A variety of fresh seafood is served in this casual eatery, but it's the local lobster that's high on diners' lists. Indoors is a paneled bar; outdoors are tables on a wraparound porch. ✕ *Prospect, St. James Parish,* ☎ *809/425–1074 Reservations advised. AE, MC, V. Closed Sat. No lunch.*

$$ **The Virginian.** Locals frequent this intimate restaurant for some of the island's best dining values. The lunch and dinner specialties are seafood, shrimp, and steaks. ✕ *Sea View Hotel, Hastings, Christ Church Parish,* ☎ *809/427–7963, ext. 121. Reservations advised. AE, MC, V.*

$$ **Witch Doctor.** The interior of the Witch Doctor is decorated with pseudo-African art that gives a lighthearted, carefree atmosphere to this casual hangout across the street from the sea. The menu includes traditional Barbadian dishes, American fare, and seafood. ✕ *St. Lawrence Gap, Christ Church Parish,* ☎ *809/435–6581. Reservations advised. MC, V. No lunch.*

$ **Atlantis Hotel.** While the surroundings may be simple, the seemingly endless buffet and the magnificent ocean view make this restaurant a real find. Owner-chef Enid Maxwell serves up an enormous Bajan buffet daily, where you're likely to find pickled souse (marinated pig parts and vegetables), pumpkin fritters, spinach balls, pickled breadfruit, fried "fline" (flying) fish, roast chicken, pepper-pot stew, and West Indian–style okra and eggplant. Among the homemade pies are an apple and a dense coconut. ✕ *Bathsheba, St. Joseph Parish,* ☎ *809/433–9445. Reservations advised. AE.*

$ David's Place. Come here for first-rate food in a first-rate location—
★ a black-and-white Bajan cottage overlooking St. Lawrence Bay. Baxters Road chicken, local flying fish, pepper-pot (salt pork, beef, and chicken boiled and bubbling in a spicy cassareep stock), curried shrimp, and other entrées are served with homemade cheesebread. Dessert might be banana pudding, coconut-cream pie, carrot cake with rum sauce, or cassava pone. ✕ *St. Lawrence Main Rd., Worthing, Christ Church Parish,* ☎ *809/435–6550. Reservations advised. AE, MC, V. No lunch Sat.–Mon.*

$ Nico's. Expatriates and tourists gather at this intimate second-floor bistro in Holetown. An oval bar surrounded by stools stands in the middle of the room, with the tables on the perimeter and a few more on the terrace above the street. Drop by for drinks and socializing, and order a snack (the fried Camembert is good); or try something more substantial, such as seafood thermidor. ✕ *Second St., Holetown, St. James Parish,* ☎ *809/432–6386. AE, MC, V. Closed Sun.*

$ Waterfront Cafe. Located on the Careenage, a sliver of sea in Bridgetown, this is the perfect place to enjoy a drink, snack, or meal. Locals and tourists gather at outdoor café tables for sandwiches, salads, fish, steak-and-kidney pie, and casseroles. The panfried flying-fish sandwich is especially tasty. In the evening, from the brick and mirrored interior, you can gaze through the arched windows, enjoy the cool trade winds, and let time pass. ✕ *Bridgetown, St. Michael Parish,* ☎ *809/427–0093. MC, V. Live music nightly. Closed Sun.*

Lodging

The southern and western shores of Barbados are lined with hotels and resorts of every size and price, offering a variety of accommodations ranging from private villas and elegant hotels to modest but comfortable rooms in simple inns. At the same time, apartment and home rentals and time-share condominiums have become widely available and are growing increasingly popular among visitors to the island. A few hotels are all-inclusive, though most still offer either EP or MAP meal plans.

Choosing the location of your hotel is important. Hotels to the north of Bridgetown, in the parishes of St. Peter, St. James, and St. Michael, tend to be self-contained resorts with stretches of empty road between them that discourage strolling to a neighborhood bar or restaurant. Southeast of Bridgetown, in Christ Church Parish, many of the hotels cluster near or along the busy strip known as St. Lawrence Gap, where dozens of small restaurants, bars, and nightclubs are close by.

Hotels listed here are grouped by parish, beginning with St. James in the west and St. Peter to the north, then St. Michael, Christ Church, St. Philip, and St. Joseph.

CATEGORY	COST*
$$$$	over $350
$$$	$250–$350
$$	$150–$250
$	under $150

All prices are for a standard double room, excluding 5% government tax and 10% service charge.

St. James Parish

$$$$ Coral Reef Club. Guests here spend their days relaxing on the white-sand beach or around the pool, taking time out for the hotel's superb afternoon tea. The public areas ramble along the beach and face the Caribbean Sea, and small coral-stone cottages are scattered over the surrounding 12 flower-filled acres. (The cottages farthest from the beach are a bit of a hike to the main house.) The accommodations are spacious, each with air-conditioning and ceiling fans, a small patio, and fresh flowers. The restaurant, under the direction of Bajan chef Graham Licorish, is noted for its inventive cuisine that combines local cooking with European flair. Most guests are on an MAP plan that includes a complimentary buffet lunch. Another convenience is the free shuttle into Bridgetown. ☎ *Porters,* ☎ *809/422–2372,* ℻ *809/422–1776. 68 rooms. Pool, entertainment. AE, MC, V. EP.*

$$$$ **Glitter Bay.** In the 1930s, Sir Edward Cunard, of the English shipping
★ family, bought this estate, built the main Great House and a beach house similar to his palazzo in Venice, and began hosting famous parties in honor of visiting aristocrats and celebrities, making Glitter Bay synonymous with grandeur. Today, new buildings, angled back from the beach, house 81 one- to three-bedroom suites with full kitchens, and the beach house has been transformed into five garden suites. Manicured, landscaped gardens separate the reception area and large, comfortable tea lounge from the pool, the alfresco dining room where evening entertainment is held, and a half mile of beach. Glitter Bay is more casual and family oriented than its next-door sister property, the Royal Pavilion; but they share facilities, including complimentary water sports. Guests at either resort have dining privileges at both. ☎ *Porters,* ☎ *809/422–4111,* ℻ *809/422–3940. 74 rooms. Restaurant, pool, water sports, 2 lighted tennis courts, golf course nearby. AE, DC, MC, V. EP, MAP.*

$$$$ **Royal Pavilion.** Of the 75 rooms here, 72 are oceanfront suites; the re-
★ maining three are nestled in a garden villa. The ground-floor oceanfront rooms allow guests simply to step through sliding doors, cross their private patio, and walk onto the sands. Second- and third-floor rooms, however, have the advantage of an elevated view of the sea. Breakfast and lunch are served alfresco along the edge of the beach. Afternoon tea and dinner are in the Palm Terrace (*see* Dining, *above*). The Royal Pavilion attracts sophisticated guests who want serenity (bringing children under the age of 12 is discouraged during the winter months). Recreational facilities are shared with the adjoining and more informal sister hotel, Glitter Bay. ☎ *Porters,* ☎ *809/422–4444,* ℻ *809/422–3940. 75 rooms. 2 restaurants; 2 bars; 2 lighted, artificial-grass tennis courts; supper-club entertainment; water-sports center; golf course nearby. AE, D, DC, MC, V. EP.*

$$$$ **Sandy Lane Hotel.** This prestigious hotel has set a standard for ele-
★ gance and style since 1961. Set on one of the best beaches in Barbados, with acres of well-tended grounds, Sandy Lane is one of the most impressive hotels in the Caribbean. The white coral structure, finished with Zandobbio marble throughout, with a staircase leading to the beach shaded with mahogany trees, will remind you of the *Great Gatsby.* All rooms overlook the sea and have private balconies for eating breakfast and watching magnificent sunsets. Rooms are nothing short of spectacular; bathrooms are vast and luxurious. Afternoon tea, fine dining, and personalized service all add to the charm. You'll be treated like royalty—in fact, royalty stays here when they visit Barbados. Plan to dress up, particularly in season—no jeans or shorts after 7 PM. ☎ *Hwy. 1,* ☎ *809/432–1311,* ℻ *809/432–2954. 90 rooms, 30 suites. 2 oceanfront restaurants, informal restaurant at Golf Club, 5 bars, live entertainment, fitness facility, free water sports, 18-hole golf course and club, pool, 5 tennis courts (4 lighted), Tree Top Club for children, complimentary baby-sitting. AE, DC, MC, V. EP, MAP.*

$$$$ **Settlers' Beach.** The accommodations at Settlers' Beach are two-story, two-bedroom homes with full kitchen and dining room, arranged asymmetrically around a large courtyard filled with towering palms and a pool. The property is small, squeezed between newer resorts, and attracts those seeking a quiet vacation. ⌂ *Hwy. 1,* ☎ *809/422–3052,* FAX *809/422–1937. 22 villas. Restaurant, pool. AE, MC, V. EP.*

$$$ **Coconut Creek Club.** A luxury cottage colony, the Coconut Creek Club is set on handsomely landscaped grounds with a small private beach and a bar pavilion for entertainment and dancing. The atmosphere here is more casual than that of its sister hotel, the Colony Club. Set on a low bluff, the hotel overlooks the ocean, and steps lead down to two secluded coves. Some rooms have ocean views; others overlook the garden or pool. Televisions are available on request for a small fee. ⌂ *Reservations: Box 249, Bridgetown; Hwy. 1,* ☎ *809/432–0803,* FAX *809/ 422–1726. 53 rooms. Dining room, pub, pool. AE, DC, MC, V. EP, MAP.*

$$$ **Discovery Bay Hotel.** Located in historic Holetown, site of the British "discovery" and settlement of the island, this quiet hotel—with a grand, white-columned, plantation-style entrance—is surrounded by 4½ acres of tropical gardens and bordered by a broad strand of Caribbean beach. Deluxe rooms have ocean views; others open onto a central lawn and pool area. A shuttle to Bridgetown is available to guests on weekdays. ⌂ *Hwy. 1, Holetown,* ☎ *809/432–1301,* FAX *809/422–1726. 87 rooms. Terrace restaurant, pool, table tennis, boutique. AE, D, DC, MC, V. EP.*

$$$ **Treasure Beach.** Most of the one-bedroom suites of this compact resort face the small garden and pool, although some have sea views, and all are just steps from the beach. Suites are spacious, with kitchenettes and sitting rooms that open onto large patios or verandas with louvered, full-length shutters for privacy. The atmosphere is quiet and pleasant, and the staff is equally so. ⌂ *Payne's Bay,* ☎ *809/432–1346,* FAX *809/432–1094. 24 1-bedroom, air-conditioned suites; 1 2-bedroom penthouse suite. Restaurant, pool, water sports. AE, DC, MC, V. EP, MAP.*

$$–$$$ **Almond Beach Club.** In this hotel, everything is included in the price of the room—all you want to eat and drink (including wine and liquor), water sports, boat trips, tennis, Bajan beach picnic, shopping excursions to Bridgetown, departure transportation to the airport, and service and taxes. Accommodations are in one-bedroom suites with balconies, two-bedroom duplex suites, and individual poolside or garden-view rooms. The food is excellent, from the breakfast buffet and a four-course lunch to the afternoon tea and pastries and the extensive dinner menu. The menus offer plenty of choice, but if your stay is seven days or more, the Almond Beach Club offers a dine-around program—dinner or lunch at a number of area restaurants with round-trip transportation included. There's an exchange program, which includes golf privileges, with Almond Beach Village; shuttle service is provided. The Almond Beach Club doesn't have the enforced-activity, "whistle-blowing" atmosphere of some all-inclusives. ⌂ *Vauxhall,* ☎ *809/432–7840 or 800/966–4737,* FAX *809/432–2115. 151 rooms. 2 restaurants, 3 pools, snorkeling, fishing, windsurfing, waterskiing, tennis, squash, sauna, fitness center. AE, MC, V. All-inclusive.*

St. Peter Parish

$$$$ **Cobblers Cove Hotel.** This all-suite hotel, located 12 miles up the West
★ Coast from Bridgetown, combines comfort and informal elegance. Each luxury suite has a balcony or patio and wet bar. The pink-and-white buildings contrasting with tropical gardens overlooking the sea

create a fine retreat that is now part of the Relais & Châteaux marketing group. The atmosphere is casual and smart, with a clublike lounge-library and a bar that becomes the evening gathering spot. For all-out luxury, you can stay in the Camelot Suite, with a king-size, four-poster bed; whirlpool bath; private splash pool; and lounge. ⌕ *Hwy. 1,* ☎ *809/422–2291 or 800/890–6060,* FAX *809/422–1460. 39 suites. Pool, floodlit tennis court, water sports, child care available, but no children under 12 allowed late Jan.–late Mar. Closed Sept. AE, MC, V. CP, MAP.*

$$–$$$ Almond Beach Village. The 30-acre property that used to be Heywoods reopened in late 1994 as the all-inclusive Almond Beach Village, sister hotel to Almond Beach Club in St. James. Renovated to the tune of $12 million, all rooms were gutted and completely redecorated. Pools were added, and the golf course was upgraded. Accommodations are in seven low-rise complexes that stretch along a mile of beach. A new 70-suite family section has junior and one-bedroom suites, a family restaurant, play area, kiddy pool, and children's program. All meals (including beverages), activities, and departure transfers are included in the rates. ⌕ *Hwy. 1,* ☎ *809/422–4900 or 800/425–6663,* FAX *809/422–1581. 288 rooms, including 70-suite family section. 9 pools, 4 restaurants, bars, 9-hole golf course, lighted tennis courts, squash courts, water sports, fitness center, entertainment. AE, MC, V. All-inclusive.*

St. Michael Parish

$$$ Grand Barbados Beach Resort. A mile from Bridgetown on Carlisle Bay, this convenient hotel has pleasant rooms and suites. The white-sand beach is lapped by a surprisingly clear sea, despite the oil refinery close by. The Aquatic Club executive floor has rooms whose rates include a Continental breakfast and secretarial services. Nightly live music, a dance floor, and a 260-foot-long pier that's perfect for romantic walks add to the enjoyment of a stay here. ⌕ *Box 639, Bridgetown,* ☎ *809/426–0890,* FAX *809/436–9823. 133 rooms. 2 restaurants, beach, pool, exercise room, whirlpool, sauna, shopping arcade, beauty salon/barber shop. AE, DC, MC, V. EP.*

$$–$$$ Barbados Hilton. This large resort, just five minutes from Bridgetown, is for those who like activity and having plenty of people around. Expect to rub shoulders with seminar attendees and conventioneers. You may detect an odor from the nearby oil refinery. Attractions here include an atrium lobby, a 1,000-foot-wide man-made beach with full water sports, and lots of shops. All rooms and suites have balconies. ⌕ *Needham's Point,* ☎ *809/426–0200,* FAX *809/436–8946. 184 rooms. Restaurant, lounge, pool, 4 lighted tennis courts, health club. AE, D, DC, MC, V. EP.*

Christ Church Parish

$$$ Divi Southwinds Beach Resort. In this resort, situated on 20 lush acres, the toss-up is whether to take one of the one-bedroom suites, with a balcony and kitchenette overlooking the gardens and pool, or one of the smaller and older-looking rooms, just steps from the white sandy beach. Though all the rooms are pleasant, the buildings themselves have a barracks appearance. Dining facilities next to the pool have the tour-package feel, with the emphasis on self-service. Guests come here for a rollicking good time that includes making full use of the scuba and water-sports facilities. ⌕ *St. Lawrence,* ☎ *800/367–3484,* FAX *809/428–4674. 166 rooms. 2 restaurants, 3 pools, 2 lighted tennis courts, putting green, shopping arcade. AE, MC, V. EP, MAP.*

$$$ Southern Palms. A plantation-style hotel on a 1,000-foot stretch of pink sand near the Dover Convention Center, Southern Palms is a convenient businessperson's hotel. You may choose from standard bedrooms, deluxe oceanfront suites with kitchenettes, and a four-bedroom penthouse. Each wing of the hotel has its own small pool. ⚅ *St. Lawrence,* ☎ *809/428–7171,* FAX *809/428–7175. 93 rooms. Dining room, 2 pools, duty-free shop, small conference center, miniature-golf course, tennis court, water sports. AE, D, DC, MC, V. EP.*

$$ **Casuarina Beach Club.** This luxury apartment hotel on 900 feet of pink sand takes its name from the casuarina pines that surround it. The quiet setting provides a dramatic contrast to that of other South Coast resorts. The bar and restaurant are on the beach. A new reception area includes small lounges where you can get a dose of TV—there aren't any in the bedrooms. Scuba diving, golf, and other activities can be arranged. The Casuarina Beach is popular with those who prefer self-catering holidays in a secluded setting, yet want to be close to nightlife and shopping. ⚅ *St. Lawrence Gap,* ☎ *809/428–3600,* FAX *809/428–1970. 134 rooms. Restaurant, bar, pool, tennis courts, squash courts, minimarket, duty-free shop. AE, D, DC, MC, V. EP.*

$$ **Club Rockley Barbados.** Some of these time-share condominiums have been transformed into an all-inclusive resort with air-conditioned one- and two-bedroom accommodations with balcony or patio. The extensive list of amenities includes a massage center, seven swimming pools, five tennis courts (three lighted), a nine-hole golf course, two air-conditioned squash courts, a shuttle bus to the beach (five minutes), a disco for late-night revelry, a children's program, and two dining rooms, one offering buffet dinners and another with an à la carte menu. ☎ *809/435–7880,* FAX *809/435–8015. 288 rooms. AE, D, DC, MC, V. All-inclusive.*

$$ **Sandy Beach Hotel.** On a wide, sparkling white beach, this comfortable hotel has a popular poolside bar and the Beachfront Restaurant, which serves a West Indian buffet Tuesday and Saturday nights. All rooms have kitchenettes. Water sports, at extra cost, include scuba-diving certification, deep-sea fishing, harbor cruises, catamaran sailing, and windsurfing. You can walk to St. Lawrence Gap for other restaurants and entertainment. ⚅ *Worthing,* ☎ *809/435–8000,* FAX *809/435–8053. 89 units. Restaurant, bar, entertainment, pool. AE, D, DC, MC, V. EP.*

$ **Benston Windsurfing Club Hotel.** A small hotel that began as a gathering place for windsurfing enthusiasts, the Benston Windsurfing Club is now a complete school and center for the sport. The rooms are spacious and sparsely furnished to accommodate the active and young crowd who choose this bare-bones hotel right on the beach. The bar and restaurant overlook the water. All sports can be arranged, but windsurfing (learning, practicing, and perfecting it) is king. ⚅ *Maxwell Main Rd.,* ☎ *809/428–9095,* FAX *809/435–6621. 14 rooms. Restaurant, bar, entertainment. AE, D, MC, V. EP.*

$ **Little Bay Hotel.** This small hotel is a find for anyone who wants to go easy on the wallet and yet sleep to the sounds of the sea. Each room has a private balcony, bedroom, small lounge, and kitchenette. There are no TVs in the rooms, but you can catch up on the news and watch sports in the small lounge next to the popular restaurant, Southern Accents. ⚅ *St. Lawrence Gap,* ☎ *809/435–7246,* FAX *809/435–8574. 10 rooms. Restaurant, lounge, bar. AE, MC, V. EP.*

$ **Ocean View.** Possibly the best-kept secret in the Caribbean, the 40 rooms
★ and suites of this individualistic hideaway are home to celebrities on their commute to private villas in Mustique. The rooms vary considerably, and their charm depends on whether you appreciate the eclectic furnishings. Although it lacks modern amenities, bear in mind that this is an old colonial building and enjoy it for that. Owner John Chandler places his personal collection of antiques throughout his

three-story grande dame nestled against the sea, adds great bouquets of tropical flowers everywhere, and calls it home. In season, the downstairs Club Xanadu presents very good, off-off-Broadway revues. ☎ *Hastings,* ☎ *809/427–7821,* FAX *809/427–7826. 40 rooms. Restaurant and bar, supper club. AE, MC, V. CP.*

$ **Sichris Hotel.** The Sichris is a real find. More attractive inside than seen from the road, it's a comfortable and convenient self-contained resort. Just minutes from the city, the air-conditioned one-bedroom suites all have kitchenettes and private balconies or patios. It's a walk of two or three minutes to the beach. ☎ *Worthing,* ☎ *809/ 435–7930,* FAX *809/435–8232. 24 rooms. Restaurant, bar, pool. AE, D, DC, MC, V. EP.*

St. Philip Parish

$$$ **Crane Beach Hotel.** This remote hilltop property on a cliff overlook-
★ ing the dramatic Atlantic coast remains one of the special places of Barbados. The Crane Beach has suites and one-bedroom apartments in the main building. Room rates vary considerably. Corner suite 1 is one of the nicest, with its two walls of windows and patio terrace. The Roman-style pool with columns separates the main house from the dining room. To reach the beach, you walk down some 200 steps onto a beautiful stretch of sand thumped by waves that are good for both bodysurfing and swimming. ☎ *Crane Bay,* ☎ *809/423–6220,* FAX *809/423–5343. 18 rooms. Restaurant, bar, pool. AE, D, DC, MC, V. EP, MAP.*

$$ **Marriott's Sam Lord's Castle.** Set on the Atlantic coast about 14 miles east of Bridgetown, Sam Lord's Castle is not a castle with moat and towers but a sprawling great house surrounded by 72 acres of grounds, gardens, and beach. The seven rooms in the main house have canopied beds; downstairs, the public rooms have furniture by Sheraton, Hepplewhite, and Chippendale—for admiring, not for sitting. Additional guest rooms in surrounding cottages have conventional hotel furnishings. The beach is a mile long, the Wanderer Restaurant offers Continental cuisine, and there are even a few slot machines, as befits a pirate's lair. ☎ *Long Bay,* ☎ *809/423–7350,* FAX *809/423–5918. 234 rooms. 3 restaurants, 3 pools, 7 lighted tennis courts, entertainment. AE, D, DC, MC, V. EP, MAP.*

St. Joseph Parish

$ **Atlantis Hotel.** The Atlantis provides a warm, pleasant atmosphere in a pastoral location overlooking a majestically rocky Atlantic coast. The hotel is modest, yet the congeniality and the Bajan food more than make up for that. ☎ *Bathsheba,* ☎ *809/433–9445. 16 rooms. Dining room. AE. EP.*

Rental Homes and Apartments

Private homes are available for rent south of Bridgetown in the Hastings–Worthing area, along the coast of St. James Parish, and in St. Peter Parish. The **Barbados Tourism Authority** (☎ 809/427–2623) has a listing of rental properties and prices.

Villas and private home rentals are also available through Barbados realtors. Among them are **Alleyne, Aguilar & Altman,** Rosebank, St. James (☎ 809/432–0840); **Bajan Services,** St. Peter (☎ 809/422–2618); and **Ronald Stoute & Sons Ltd.,** St. Philip (☎ 809/423–6800).

In the United States, contact **At Home Abroad** (☎ 212/421–9165) or Jan Pizzi at **Villa Vacations** (☎ 617/593–8885 or 800/800–5576).

The Arts and Nightlife

The Arts

Barbados Art Council. The gallery shows drawings, paintings, and other art, with a new show about every two weeks. *2 Pelican Village, Bridgetown,* ☏ *809/426–4385.* ☛ *Free.* ⏲ *Weekdays 10–5, Sat. 9–1.*

A selection of private art galleries offer Bajan and West Indian art at collectible prices. **The Studio Art Gallery** (Fairchild St., Bridgetown, ☏ 809/427–5463) exhibits local work (particularly that of Rachael Altman) and will frame purchases. The **Queen's Park Gallery** (Queen's Park, Bridgetown, ☏ 809/427–2345), the island's largest gallery, is run by the National Culture Foundation and presents changing, month-long exhibits.

Nightlife

When the sun goes down, the musicians come out, and folks go limin' in Barbados (anything from hanging out to a chat-up or jump-up). Competitions among reggae groups, steel bands, and calypso singers are major events, and tickets can be hard to come by—but give it a try.

Most of the large resorts have weekend shows aimed at visitors, and there is a selection of dinner shows. Interactive **comedy murder mysteries** are held at the Barbados Museum every Thursday night at 7 PM. Mingle and match wits with Inspector Clewlesse and his crew! A ticket includes all you can eat, all you can drink, and all you can laugh—and transportation is included. *Hwy. 7, Garrison Savannah,* ☏ *809/420–3409.* ☛ *$40. Show and drinks only, $20. Children half-price. Reservations recommended. MC, V.*

On Wednesdays, Thursdays, and Fridays at Plantation Garden, the **Barbados By Night** calypso cabaret show features dancing, fire-eating, limbo, steel-band music, and the award-winning sounds of Spice & Company. *St. Lawrence Rd., Christ Church Parish,* ☏ *809/428–5048. Reservations recommended. AE, DC, MC, V.*

Club Xanadu is a mid-December through April cabaret. On Thursday and Friday nights, it's the hottest ticket in town. David McCarty, who danced on Broadway and with the New York City Ballet, has joined forces with chanteuse Jean Emerson; along with local strutters, they put on a great show. Dinner—served in the upstairs flower-decked dining room—and show cost $44; cabaret admission only, approximately $12.50. *Ocean View Hotel, Hastings,* ☏ *809/427–7821. Reservations required.*

Island residents have their own favorite nightspots. The most popular one is still **After Dark** (St. Lawrence Gap, Christ Church, ☏ 809/435–6547), with the longest bar on the island, a jazz-club annex, and an outdoor area where headliners appear live.

Harbour Lights claims to be the "home of the party animal," and most any night features live music with dancing under the stars. *On the Bay, Marine Villa, Bay St., St. Michael,* ☏ *809/436–7225.*

Another "in" spot, **Front Line** (Wharf St., ☏ 809/429–6160) at the Wharf in Bridgetown, attracts a young crowd for its reggae music.

A late-night (after 11) excursion to **Baxter Road** is de rigueur for midnight Bajan street snacks, local rum, great gossip, and good lie-telling. **Enid & Livy's** and **Collins** are just two of the many long-standing favorites.

BARS AND INNS

Barbados supports the rum industry in more than 1,600 "rum shops," simple bars where people (mostly men) congregate to discuss the world's ills, and in more sophisticated inns, where you'll find world-class rum drinks and the island's renowned Mount Gay and Cockspur rums. The following offer welcoming spirits: the **Ship Inn** (St. Lawrence Gap, Christ Church Parish, ☎ 809/435–6961), the **Coach House** (Paynes Bay, St. James Parish, ☎ 809/432–1163), and **Harry's Oasis** (St. Lawrence, Christ Church Parish, no ☎). **Bert's Bar** at the Abbeville Hotel (Rockley, Christ Church Parish, ☎ 809/435–7924) serves the best daiquiris in town . . . any town. Also try the **Boat Yard** (Bay St., Bridgetown, ☎ 809/436–2622), the **Waterfront Cafe** (Bridgetown, ☎ 809/427–0093), the **Warehouse** (Bridgetown, ☎ 809/436–2897), and **Boomers Restaurant & Lounge** (St. Lawrence Gap, Christ Church Parish, ☎ 809/428–8439).

6 Bonaire

Updated by
Barbara Hults

ing is learned here,
plate says "A Diver's
Bonaire have remained n.
ernment, way back in 1971, when ... ... was just becoming a color to
be dealt with, designated all surrounding waters as a marine park and
threw in a ban on spearfishing and coral collecting. The underwater
park includes, roughly, the entire coastline, from the high-water tide-
mark to a depth of 200 feet, all of which is protected by strict laws.
Because the Bonairians desperately want to keep their paradise intact,
any diver with a reckless streak is firmly requested to go elsewhere.
Thanks to their foresight, the world can enjoy Bonaire's bounty.

Bonaire, on land, is a stark desert island, perfect for the rugged indi-
vidualist who is turned off by the overcommercialized high life of the
other Antillean islands. The island boasts a spectacular array of exotic
wildlife—from fish to fowl to flowers—that will keep nature watchers
awestruck for days. It's the kind of place where you'll want to rent a
Jeep and go dashing off madly in search of the wild flamingo, the wild
iguana, or even the wild yellow-winged parrot named the Bonairian lora.

This is not the island for connoisseurs of fine cuisine, shopping mani-
acs, beachcombers, or lounge lizards. The island itself may be lacking
in splendor, but what lies off its shores keeps divers enthralled. With
only 11,000 inhabitants, the island has the feeling of a small community with a gentle pace.

Before You Go

Tourist Information
Contact the Bonaire Government Tourist Office (10 Rockefeller Plaza,
Suite 900, New York, NY 10020, ☎ 212/956–5911 or 800/826–6247,
FAX 212/838–3407) for advice and information on planning your trip.
Ask about diving packages, either including accommodations or not.

Arriving and Departing

BY PLANE
ALM (☎ 800/327-7230) and Air Aruba (☎ 800/882–7822) will get
you to Bonaire. ALM has eight direct flights (through Curaçao), two
nonstop flights a week from Miami, and five flights a week from Atlanta through Curaçao, with connecting service (thoroughfares) to
most U.S. gateways tied in with Delta and other airlines, making ALM
Bonaire's major airline. ALM also flies to Caracas, Aruba, Curaçao,
and St. Maarten, as well as other Caribbean islands, using Curaçao as
its Caribbean hub. Air Aruba flies six days a week from Newark and
daily from Miami to Aruba with connecting service to Bonaire. **American Airlines** (☎ 800/433–7300) offers daily flights from New York
to Aruba, but you must connect to Bonaire through ALM or Air
Aruba. ALM also offers a Visit Caribbean Pass, which allows easy interisland travel.

FROM THE AIRPORT
Bonaire's Flamingo Airport is tiny, but you'll appreciate its welcoming
ambience. The customs check is perfunctory if you are arriving from another Dutch isle; otherwise you will have to show proof of citizenship,
plus a return or ongoing ticket. Rental cars and taxis are available at the

airport, but try to arrange the pickup through your hotel. A taxi will run between $8 and $12 (for up to four people) to most hotels.

Passports and Visas

U.S. and Canadian citizens need offer only proof of identity, so a passport, notarized birth certificate, or voter registration card will suffice. British subjects may carry a British Visitor's Passport, available from any post office; all other visitors must carry an official passport. In addition, any visitor who steps onto the island must have a return or ongoing ticket and is advised to confirm that reservation 48 hours before departure.

Language

The official language is Dutch, but few speak it, and even then only on official occasions. The street language is Papiamento, a mixture of Spanish, Portuguese, Dutch, English, African, and French—full of colorful Bonairian idioms that even Curaçaoans sometimes don't get. You'll light up your waiter's eyes, though, if you can remember to say *Masha danki* (thank you). English is spoken by most people working at the hotels, restaurants, and tourist shops, but a Spanish phrase book may come in handy.

Precautions

Because of violent trade winds pounding against the rocks, the windward (eastern) side of Bonaire is much too rough for diving. The *Guide to the Bonaire Marine Park* (available at dive shops around the island) specifies the level of diving skill required for 44 sites, and it knows what it's talking about. No matter how beautiful a beach may look, heed all warning signs regarding the rough undertow.

From October through December the mosquitoes in Bonaire are nearly vampiric. Spray your hotel room before you go to bed. Smart, happy people douse themselves, including their arms, legs, and face, with repellent all day long.

Get an orientation on what stings underwater and what doesn't. As the island's joke goes, you won't appreciate Bonaire until you've stepped on a long-spined urchin, but by then, you won't appreciate the joke.

Bonaire used to have a reputation for being the friendliest and safest island in the Caribbean, but lately, even residents are locking their car doors. Don't leave your camera in an open car, and leave your money, credit cards, jewelry, and other valuables in your hotel's safety-deposit box.

Staying in Bonaire

Important Addresses

Tourist Information: The **Bonaire Tourist Board** (Kaya Simon Bolivar 12, ☎ 599/7–8322 or 599/7–8649, FAX 599/7–8408).

EMERGENCIES

Police: For assistance call 7–8000; in an emergency, dial 11. **Ambulance:** ☎ 14. **Hospital: St. Franciscus Hospital,** Kralendijk (☎ 599/7–8900).

Currency

The great thing about Bonaire is that you don't need to convert your American dollars into the local currency, the NAf guilder. U.S. currency and traveler's checks are accepted everywhere, and the difference in exchange rates is negligible. Banks accept U.S. dollar banknotes at the official rate of NAf1.78 to the U.S. dollar, traveler's checks at NAf1.80. The rate of exchange at shops and hotels ranges from NAf1.75 to NAf1.80. The guilder is divided into 100 cents. Note: Prices quoted here are in U.S. dollars unless indicated otherwise.

Taxes and Service Charges

Hotels charge a room tax of $4.10 per person, per night, and many hotels (not all) add a 10%–15% maid service charge to your bill. Most restaurants add a 10% service charge to your bill. There's no sales tax on purchases in Bonaire. Departure tax when going to Curaçao is $5.75. For all other destinations it's $10.

Guided Tours

If you don't like to drive, **Bonaire Sightseeing Tours** (☎ 599/7–8778 or 599/7–8300, ext. 212; FAX 599/7–8118 or 599/7–8865) will chauffeur you around the island on various tours, among them a two-hour Northern Island Tour ($13) that visits the 1,000 steps; Goto Lake; and Rincon, the oldest settlement on the island; and a two-hour Southern Island Tour ($13) that covers Akzo Salt Antilles N.V., a modern salt-manufacturing facility where flamingos gather; Lac Bay; and the oldest lighthouse on the island. A half-day tour ($19) visits sites in both the north and south. For $30, you can take a half-day tour of Bonaire's Washington/Slagbaai National Park (entrance fee included), 13,500 acres of majestic scenery, wildlife, unspoiled beaches, and tropical flora. A full-day tour of the park costs $50. Day trips to Curaçao are offered for $125 per person and include round-trip airfare and transfers, an island tour of Curaçao, and lunch. **Ayubi's Tours** (☎ 599/7–5338) also offers several half- and full-day island tours.

Getting Around

You can zip about the island in a car or a Suzuki Jeep. Scooters and bicycles, which are also available, are less practical but can be fun, too. Just remember that there are at least 20 miles of unpaved road; the roller-coaster hills at the national park require a strong stomach; and during the rainy season, mud —called Bonairian snow—is unpleasant. All traffic stays to the right, and, delightfully, there is yet to be a single traffic light. Signs or green arrows are usually posted to leading attractions; if you stick to the paved roads and marked turnoffs, you won't get lost.

RENTAL CARS

Budget rents cars, Suzuki minivans, and Jeeps at its six locations, but reservations can be made only at the head office (☎ 599/7–8300, ext. 225). Pickups are at the airport (☎ 599/7–8315) and at several hotels. It's always a good idea to make advance reservations (FAX 599/7–8865 or 599/7–8118; in the U.S., ☎ 800/472–3325). Prices range from $31 a day for a Volkswagen to $60 a day for an automatic, air-conditioned four-door sedan. Other agencies are **Avis** (☎ 599/7–5795, FAX 599/7–5791, telex 1900 ROCAR), **Dollar Rent-A-Car** (☎ 599/7–8888; at the airport, ☎ 599/7–5588; FAX 599/7–7788), **Sunray** (☎ 599/7–5230, FAX 599/7–4888), and **AB Car Rental** (☎ 599/7–8980 or 599/7–5410, FAX 599/7–5034). There is also a government tax of $2 per day per car rental.

SCOOTERS

Two-seater scooters are available from **Bonaire Bicycle & Motorbike Rental** (☎ 599/7–8226) and **S. F. Wave Touch** (☎ 599/7–4246) for about $26 a day and $165 a week.

BICYCLES

Bonaire Bicycle & Motorbike Rental (☎ 599/7–8226) rents bicycles for $15 a day. **Captain Don's Habitat** (☎ 599/7–8290 or 599/7–8913) rents mountain bicycles for $6 per day plus a $250 deposit. **Harbour Village Beach Resort** (☎ 599/7–7500) rents Hybrid bikes for $11 a day to non-hotel guests, but hotel guests get first dibs.

TAXIS

Taxis are unmetered; they have fixed rates controlled by the government. A trip from the airport to your hotel will cost between $8 and $12 for up to four passengers. A taxi from most hotels into town costs between $5 and $8. Fares increase from 7 PM to midnight by 25% and from midnight to 6 AM by 50%. Taxi drivers are usually knowledgeable enough about the island to conduct half-day tours; they charge about $60 for a northern-route tour and $40 for a southern-route tour. Call **Taxi Central Dispatch** (☎ 599/7–8100 or dial 10), or inquire at your hotel.

Telephones and Mail

It's difficult for visitors to Bonaire to get involved in dramatic, heart-wrenching phone conversations or *any* phone discussions requiring a degree of privacy: Only about one-third of the major hotels have phones in their rooms, so calls must be made from hotel front desks or from the central telephone company office in Kralendijk. Telephone connections have improved, but static is still common. To call Bonaire from the United States, dial 011–599–7 + the local four-digit number. When making interisland calls, dial the local four-digit number. Local phone calls cost NAf25¢.

Airmail postage rates to the United States and Canada are NAf1.75 for letters and NAf.90¢ for postcards; to Britain, NAf2.50 for letters and NAf1.25 for postcards.

Opening and Closing Times

Stores in the Kralendijk area are generally open Monday through Saturday 8–noon and 2–6 PM. On Sundays and holidays, when cruise ships arrive, most shops open for a few extra hours. Most restaurants are open for lunch and dinner, but few not affiliated with hotels are open for breakfast. Banks stay open from 8:30 to 4 Monday through Friday.

Exploring Bonaire

Numbers in the margin correspond to points of interest on the Bonaire map.

Kralendijk

❶ Bonaire's capital city of **Kralendijk** (population: 2,500) is five minutes from the airport and a short walk from Bruce Bowker's Carib Inn and the Divi Flamingo Beach Resort. There's really not much to explore here, but there are a few sights worth noting in this small, very tidy city.

Kralendijk has one main drag, J. A. Abraham Boulevard, which turns into **Kaya Grandi** in the center of town. Along it are most of the island's major stores, boutiques, restaurants, duty-free shops, and jewelry stores (*see* Shopping, *below*).

Across Kaya Grandi, opposite the Spritzer & Fuhrmann jewelry store, is Kaya L. D. Gerharts, with several small supermarkets, the ALM office, a handful of snack shops, and some of the better restaurants, including Bistro des Amis and the Rendez-Vous (*see* Dining, *below*). Walk down the narrow waterfront avenue called Kaya C.E.B. Hellmund, which leads straight to the **North** and **South piers.** In the center of town, stop in at the new Harbourside Mall, which has 13 chic boutiques. Along this route you will see **Fort Oranje,** with cannons pointing to the sea. From December through April, cruise ships, including the *Seabourn Pride* and the *Regent Suns,* dock in the harbor every few days. The *Ocean Breeze* stops at Bonaire year-round. The elegant white structure that looks like a tiny Greek temple is the **Fish Market,** where local fishermen sell their early-morning haul, along with vegetables and fruits.

Elsewhere on the Island

Two tours, north and south, are possible of the 24-mile-long island; both will take from a few hours to a full day, depending upon whether you stop to snorkel, swim, dive, or lounge.

SOUTH BONAIRE

The trail south from Kralendijk is chock-full of icons—both natural and man-made—that tell the minisaga of Bonaire. Rent a Jeep (a car will do, but during the rainy months the roads can become muddy, making traction difficult) and head south along the Southern Scenic Route.

❷ The first landmark you'll come to is an unexpected symbol of modernism—the towering 500-foot antennas of **Trans-World Radio,** one of the most powerful stations in Christian broadcasting. From here, evangelical programs and gospel music are transmitted daily in five languages to all of North, South, and Central America, as well as the entire Caribbean.

❸ Keep on cruising past the salt pans until you come to the **salt flats,** voluptuous white drifts that look something like huge mounds of vanilla ice cream. Harvested twice a year, the "ponds" are owned by the Akzo Salt Antilles N.V. company, which has reactivated the 19th-century salt industry with great success. (One reason for that success is that the ocean on this part of the island is higher than the land—which makes irrigation a snap.) Keep a lookout for the three 30-foot obelisks—white, blue, and red—that were used to guide the trade boats coming to pick up the salt.

Along the sea just a bit farther south is **Pink Beach,** a half-mile-long stretch of incredibly soft sand that derives its name from the delicate pink hue of the sand at the shoreline (*see* Beaches, *below*).

The gritty history of the salt industry is revealed down the road in **Rode Pan,** the site of two groups of tiny slave huts. During the 19th century, the salt workers, imported slaves from Africa, worked the fields by day, then crawled into these huts at night to sleep. Each Friday afternoon, they walked seven hours to Rincon to weekend with their families, returning each Sunday to the salt pans. In recent years, the government has restored the huts to their original simplicity. Only very small people will be able to go inside, but take a walk around and put your head in for a look.

❹ Continue heading south to **Willemstoren,** Bonaire's first lighthouse, built in 1837 and still in use, but closed to visitors.

Rounding the tip of the island, head north and notice how the waves, driven by the trade winds, play a crashing symphony against the rocks. Locals make a habit of stopping here to collect pieces of driftwood in spectacular shapes. To the north are two more picturesque beaches— **Sorobon Beach** and **Boca Cai** at Lac Bay. The road here winds through otherworldly desert terrain, full of organ-pipe cacti and spiny-trunk mangroves—huge stumps of saltwater trees that rise out of the marshes like witches. At Boca Cai, you'll be impressed by the huge piles of sun-bleached conch shells discarded by local fishermen. On Sundays at Cai, live bands play from noon to 8, and there's beer and food available at the local restaurant. When the mosquitoes arrive at dusk, it's time to hightail it home.

Just before the entrance to the Sorobon Beach Resort, you'll note a sign for the Fundashon Marcultura. Because the conch had become an endangered species in these waters, a project was set up to raise conch in captivity. As a result, close to 3 million cultivated conch were re-

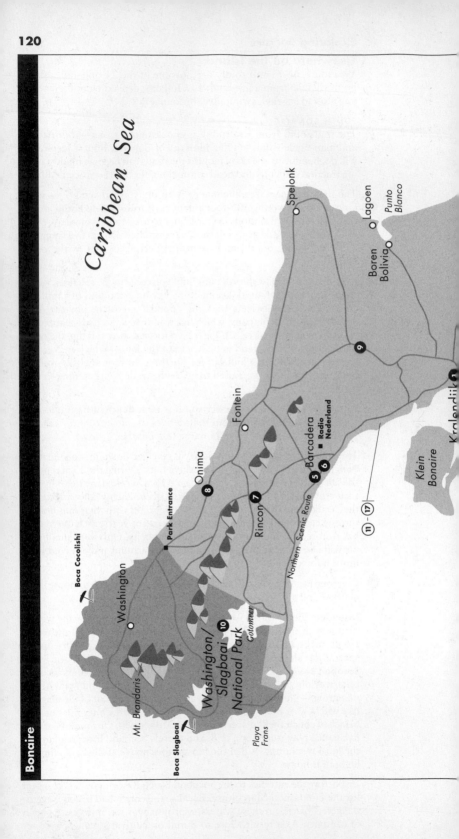

Bonaire

Caribbean Sea

Boca Cocolishi

Washington

Mt. Brandaris

Boca Slagbaai

Washington/
Slagbaai
National Park

10

Cotomeer

Playa
Frans

Park Entrance

Onima

8

Fontein

Rincon

7

Barcadera

■ Radio
Nederland

5 **6**

Northern Scenic Route

9

Spelonk

Lagoen

Punto
Blanco

Boren
Bolivia

Kralendijk **1**

Klein
Bonaire

⑪ - ⑰

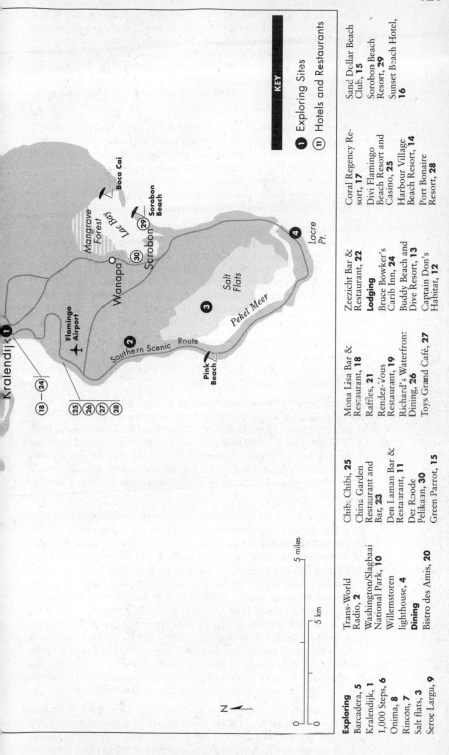

KEY

1 Exploring Sites

11 Hotels and Restaurants

Coral Regency Resort, **17**

Divi Flamingo Beach Resort and Casino, **25**

Harbour Village Beach Resort, **14**

Port Bonaire Resort, **28**

Sand Dollar Beach Club, **15**

Sorobon Beach Resort, **29**

Sunset Beach Hotel, **16**

Zeezicht Bar & Restaurant, **22**

Lodging

Bruce Bowker's Carib Inn, **24**

Buddy Beach and Dive Resort, **13**

Captain Don's Habitat, **12**

Mona Lisa Bar & Restaurant, **18**

Raffles, **21**

Rendez-Vous Restaurant, **19**

Richard's Waterfront Dining, **26**

Toys Grand Café, **27**

Chibi Chibi, **25**

China Garden Restaurant and Bar, **23**

Den Laman Bar & Restaurant, **11**

Der Roode Pelikaan, **30**

Green Parrot, **15**

Exploring

Barcadera, **5**

Kralendijk, **1**

1,000 Steps, **6**

Onima, **8**

Rincon, **7**

Salt flats, **3**

Seroe Largu, **9**

Trans-World Radio, **2**

Washington/Slagbaai National Park, **10**

Willemstoren lighthouse, **4**

Dining

Bistro des Amis, **20**

5 miles

5 km

N

leased to the wild. This success led to the Fundashon Maracultura. The research institute conducts experimental studies, cultivates and harvests shrimp and lobster for restaurants, and raises several species of colorful fish for sale to pet stores and aquariums. Tours are conducted weekdays at 10 AM and 1:30 PM, by appointment only. The foundation provides a fascinating and informative crash course in marine biology. *Sorobon,* ☎ *599/7–8595.* ☛ *$2 adults, $1 children under 12.*

NORTH BONAIRE

The northern tour takes you right into the heart of Bonaire's natural wonders—desert gardens of towering cacti, tiny coastal coves, dramatically shaped coral grottoes, and plenty of fantastic panoramas. A snappy excursion with the requisite photo stops will take about 2½ hours, but if you pack your swimsuit and a hefty picnic basket (forget about finding a Burger King), you could spend the entire day exploring this northern sector, including a few hours snorkeling in Washington Park.

Head out from Kralendijk on the Kaya Gobernador N. Debrot until it turns into the Northern Scenic Route, a one-lane, one-way street on the outskirts of town. Following the route northward, look closely for a yellow marker on your left just past the towering Radio Nederland antennas. A few yards ahead, you'll discover some stone steps that lead down into a cave full of stalactites and vegetation. Once used to trap

5 goats, this cave, called **Barcadera,** is one of the oldest in Bonaire; there's even a tunnel that looks intriguingly spooky.

Note that once you pass the antennas of Radio Nederland, you cannot turn back to Kralendijk. The road becomes one-way, and you will have to follow the cross-island road to Rincon and return via the main road through the center of the island.

The road weaves through spectacular eroded pink-and-black limestone walls and eerie rock formations with fanciful names like the Devil's Mouth and Iguana Head. Opposite the turnoff to the Bonaire Caribbean

6 Club is a site called **1,000 Steps,** a limestone staircase carved right out of the cliff on the left side of the road. If you take the trek down them, you'll discover a great place to snorkel and scuba dive. Actually, you'll climb only 67 steps, but it feels like 1,000 when you walk up them carrying scuba gear.

If you continue toward the northern curve of the island, the green storage tanks of the Bonaire Petroleum Corporation become visible. Follow the sign to **Goto Meer,** a saltwater lagoon that is a popular flamingo hangout. Bonaire is one of the few places in the world where pink flamingos nest. The spiny-legged creatures—affectionately called "pink clouds"— at first look like swizzle sticks. But they're magnificent birds to observe—and there are about 15,000 of them in Bonaire. The best time to catch them at home is January–June, when they tend to their gray-plumed young. For the best view of these shy birds, take the dirt access road to the left, which slices through a virtual jungle of cacti. Once you're back on the paved surface, the road will loop around and pass through

7 **Rincon,** a well-kept cluster of pastel cottages and century-old buildings that constitute Bonaire's oldest village. Watch your driving—both goats and dogs often sit right in the middle of the main drag.

Rincon was the original Spanish settlement on the island: It became home to the slaves brought from Africa to work on the plantations and salt fields. Superstition and voodoo lore still have a powerful impact here, more so than in Kralendijk, where they work hard at suppressing the old ways. Rincon has a couple of local eateries, but the real temptation is **Prisca's Ice Cream** (☎ 599/7–6334), to be found at her house on Kaya Komkomber.

Pass through Rincon on the road that heads back to Kralendijk, but ⑧ take the left-hand turn before Fontein to **Onima.** Small signposts direct the way to the **Indian inscriptions** found on a 3-foot limestone ledge that juts out like a partially formed cave entrance. Look up to see the red-stained designs and symbols inscribed on the limestone, said to have been the handiwork of the Arawak Indians when they inhabited the island centuries ago.

Backtrack to the main road and continue on to Fontein and then to ⑨ **Seroe Largu,** the highest point on the southern part of the island. During the day, a winding path leads to a magnificent view of Kralendijk's rooftops and the island of Klein Bonaire; at night, the twinkling city lights below make this a romantic stop.

WASHINGTON/SLAGBAAI NATIONAL PARK

Once a plantation producing divi-divi trees (whose pods were used for tanning animal skins), aloe (used for medicinal lotions), charcoal, and ⑩ goats, **Washington/Slagbaai National Park** is now a model of conservation, designed to maintain fauna, flora, and geological treasures in their natural state. Visitors may easily tour the 13,500-acre tropical desert terrain along the dirt roads. As befits a wilderness sanctuary, the well-marked, rugged roads force you to drive slowly enough to appreciate the animal life and the terrain. A four-wheel-drive is a must. (Think twice about coming here if it rained the day before—the mud you may encounter will be more than inconvenient.) If you are planning to hike, bring a picnic lunch, camera, sunscreen, and plenty of water. There are two different routes. The long one, 22 miles (about 2½ hours), is marked by yellow arrows; the short one, 15 miles (about 1½ hours), is marked by green arrows. Goats and donkeys may dart across the road, and if you keep your eyes peeled, you may catch sight of large iguanas, camouflaged in the shrubbery.

Bird-watchers are really in their element here. Right inside the park's gate, flamingos roost on the salt pad known as **Salina Mathijs,** and exotic parakeets dot the foot of **Mt. Brandaris,** Bonaire's highest peak at 784 feet. Some 130 species of colorful birds fly in and out of the shrubbery in the park. Keep your eyes open and your binoculars at hand. (For choice beach sites in the park, *see* Beaches, *below.*) Swimming, snorkeling, and scuba diving are permitted, but visitors are requested not to frighten the animals or remove anything from the grounds. There is absolutely no hunting, fishing, or camping allowed. A useful guidebook to the park is available at the entrance for about $6. ☛ *$5 adults, $1 children under 15. The park is open daily 8–5, but you must enter before 3:30.*

What to See and Do with Children

Captain Don's Habitat offers all-inclusive **Family Weeks** in August, with packages that provide a variety of activities, in and out of the water, for both children and adults (*see* Lodging, *below*).

The Sand Dollar Beach Club resort has the daily, year-round **Sand Penny Club** for the children (ages 3–15) of guests. The kids can learn to snorkel and will have a chance to participate in a number of activities and games (*see* Lodging, *below*).

The **Sunset Beach Hotel** and the **Divi Flamingo Beach Resort** also offer family packages and programs for children (*see* Lodging, *below*).

Beaches

Beaches in Bonaire are not the island's strong point. Don't come expecting Aruba-length stretches of glorious white sand. Bonaire's beaches are smaller, and though the water is indeed blue (several shades of it, in fact), the sand is not always white. You can have your pick of beach in Bonaire according to color: pink, black, or white. The best hotel beaches are found at Harbour Village, Sunset Beach, and Sorobon (*see* Lodging, *below*).

Hermit crabs can be found along the shore at **Boca Cocolishi,** a black-sand beach in Washington/Slagbaai National Park on the northeast coast. The dark hues of tiny bits of dried coral and shells form the basin and beach, giving the sand an unusual look. This beach gives new meaning to the term windswept: Cooling breezes whip the water into a frenzy as the color of the sea changes from midnight blue to aquamarine. This being the windward side of the island, the water is too rough for anything more than wading; however, the spot is perfect for an intimate picnic *à deux*. To get there, take the Northern Scenic Route to the park, then ask for directions at the gate.

Also inside Washington Park is **Boca Slagbaai,** a beach of coral fossils and rocks with interesting coral gardens that are good for snorkeling just offshore. Bring scuba boots or canvas sandals to walk into the water, because the "beach" is rough on bare feet. The gentle surf makes it an ideal place for picnicking or swimming, especially for children.

The exquisite ocher-and-russet building here was constructed by the first plantation owner and included a customs office and slaughterhouse. Today it houses a restaurant serving fine lunches Thursday–Sunday.

Playa Funchi, another Washington Park beach, is notable for the lagoon on one side where flamingos nest, and the superb snorkeling on the other, where iridescent green parrotfish swim right up to shore.

As the name suggests, the sand at **Pink Beach** boasts a pinkish tint that takes on a magical shimmer in the late-afternoon sun. The water is suitable for swimming, snorkeling, and scuba diving. Take the Southern Scenic Route on the western side of the island, past the Trans-World Radio station, close to the slave huts. A favorite hangout for Bonairians on the weekend, it is virtually deserted during the week.

For uninhibited sun worshipers who'd rather enjoy the rays in the altogether, the private, "clothes-optional" beach, at the **Sorobon Beach Resort,** offers calm water, soft clean sand, and delightfully strong tropical breezes. Nonguests are welcome and can purchase a $15 day pass at the entrance gate.

Boca Cai is across Lac Bay, which is an ideal spot for windsurfing.

If you enjoy water sports, find out which beaches are best for a specific sport (*see* Sports and the Outdoors, *below*).

Sports and the Outdoors

Scuba Diving

Bonaire has some of the best reef diving this side of Australia's Great Barrier Reef. In fact, the island is unique primarily for its incredible dive sites; it takes only 5–25 minutes to reach your site, the current is usually mild, and while some reefs have very sudden, steep drops, most begin just offshore and slope gently downward at a 45° angle. General visibility runs 60 to 100 feet, except during surges in October and

November. An enormous range of coral can be seen, from knobby brain and giant brain coral to elkhorn, staghorn, mountainous star, gorgonian, and black coral. You're also likely to encounter schools of parrotfish, surgeonfish, angelfish, eels, snappers, and groupers. Beach diving is excellent just about everywhere on the leeward side of the island.

The well-policed Bonaire Marine Park, which encompasses the entire coastline around Bonaire and Klein Bonaire, remains an underwater wonder because visitors take the rules here seriously. Do not even think about (1) spearfishing, (2) dropping anchor, or (3) touching, stepping on, or collecting coral. Divers must pay an admission charge of $10, for which they receive a colored plastic tag (to be attached to an item of scuba gear) entitling them to one calendar year of unlimited diving in the Marine Park. The fees are used to maintain the underwater park. Tags are available at all scuba facilities and from the marine park headquarters in the Old Fort in Kralendijk (☎ 599/7–8444). All dive operations on Bonaire now offer free buoyancy-control, advanced buoyancy-control, and photographic buoyancy-control classes. Check with any dive shop for the schedule.

There is a hyperbaric decompression chamber located next to the hospital in Kralendijk (☎ 599/7–8187 or 599/7–8900 for emergencies).

DIVE OPERATIONS

Bonaire hotels frequently offer dive packages, which include accommodations, boat trips, shore diving, air, and use of tanks. Ask the Bonaire tourist office for a brochure describing the various packages. Organized tours are not necessary on Bonaire, as many dive sites are easily accessible from shore and clearly marked by yellow stones on the roadside. Most of the hotels listed in this guide have dive centers. The competition for quality and variety is fierce. Before making a room reservation, inquire about specific dive/room packages that are available. Many of the dive shops also have boutiques where you can purchase T-shirts, color slides showing underwater views, postcards, and tropical jewelry. **Peter Hughes Dive Bonaire** (Divi Flamingo Beach Resort, ☎ 599/7–8285 or 800/367–3484), **Sand Dollar Dive and Photo** (Sand Dollar Beach Club, Kaya Gobrenador Debrot 79, ☎ 599/7–8738), and **Habitat Dive Center** (Captain Don's Habitat, Kaya Gobrenador Debrot 103, ☎ 599/7–8290) are all PADI (Professional Association of Diving Instructors) five-star dive facilities qualified to offer both PADI and NAUI (National Association of Underwater Instructors) certification courses. Sand Dollar Dive and Photo is also qualified to certify dive instructors. Other centers include **Bonaire Scuba Center** (Black Durgon Inn, ☎ 599/7–5736; in the U.S., write Box 775, Morgan, NJ 08879, or call 908/566–8866 or 800/526–2370), **Buddy Dive Resort** (Kaya Gobrenador N., Debrot 85, ☎ 599/7–8647), **Dive Inn** (close to South Pier, Kaya C.E.B. Hellmund, ☎ 599/7–8761), **Neal Watson's Bonaire Undersea Adventures** (Coral Regency Resort, Kaya Gobrenador Debrot 90, ☎ 599/7–5580 or 800/327–8150), **Great Adventures Bonaire** (Harbour Village Beach Resort, ☎ 599/7–7500 or 800/424–0004), and **Bruce Bowker's Carib Inn Dive Center** (Bruce Bowker's Carib Inn, ☎ 599/7–8819; ℻ 599/7–5295).

Americans Jerry Schnabel and Suzi Swygert of **Photo Tours N.V.** (Kaya Grandi 68, ☎ 599/7–8060) specialize in teaching and guiding novice-through-professional underwater photographers. They also offer land-excursion tours of Bonaire's birds, wildlife, and vegetation. **Dee Scarr's Touch the Sea** (Box 369, ☎ 599/7–8529) is a personalized (two people at a time) diving program that provides interaction with marine life; it is available to certified divers.

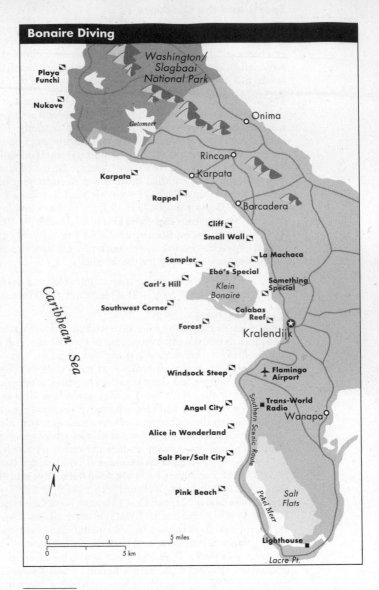

Bonaire Diving

Washington/
Slagbaai
National Park

Playa
Funchi

Nukove

Gotomeer

Onima

Rincon

Karpata

Karpata

Rappel

Barcadera

Cliff

Small Wall

La Machaca

Sampler

Ebo's Special

Carl's Hill

Klein
Bonaire

Something
Special

Southwest Corner

Forest

Calabas
Reef

Kralendijk

Caribbean Sea

Windsock Steep

Flamingo
Airport

Angel City

Trans-World
Radio

Wanapa

Alice in Wonderland

Southern Scenic Route

Salt Pier/Salt City

N

Pink Beach

Salt
Flats

Pekel Meer

0   5 miles
0   5 km

Lighthouse

Lacre Pt.

DIVE SITES

The *Guide to the Bonaire Marine Park* lists 44 sites that have been identified and marked by moorings. In the past few years, however, an additional 42 designated mooring and shore diving sites have been added
through a conservation program called Sea Tether. Guides associated
with the various dive centers can give you more complete directions.
The following are a few popular sites to whet your appetite; these and
selected other sites are pinpointed on our Bonaire Diving map.

Take the track down to the shore just behind the Trans-World Radio
station; dive in and swim south to **Angel City,** one of the shallowest
and most popular sites in a two-reef complex that includes **Alice in Wonderland.** The boulder-size green-and-tan coral heads are home to black
margates, Spanish hogfish, gray snappers, and large purple tube sponges.

Calabas Reef, located off the Divi Flamingo Beach Resort, is the island's most popular dive site. All divers using the hotel's facilities take their warm-up dive here where they can inspect the wreck sunk by Don Stewart for just this purpose. The site is replete with Christmas-tree sponges and fire coral adhering to the ship's hull. Fish life is frenzied, with the occasional octopus putting in an appearance.

You'll need to catch a boat to reach **Forest,** a dive site off the coast of Klein Bonaire, so named for the abundant black-coral forest found there. Responsible for occasional currents, this site gets a lot of fish action, including what's been described as a "friendly" spotted eel that lives in a cave.

Small Wall is one of Bonaire's only complete vertical wall dives. Located off the Black Durgon Inn, it is one of the island's most popular night-diving spots. Access is made by boat (Black Durgon guests can access it from shore). The 60-foot wall is frequented by seahorses, squid, turtles, tarpon, and barracudas and has dense hard and soft coral formations; it also allows for excellent snorkeling.

Rappel is one of the most spectacular dives, near the Karpata Ecological Center. The shore is a sheer cliff, and the lush coral growth is home to an unusual variety of marine life, including orange seahorses, squid, spiny lobsters, and a spotted trunkfish named Sir Timothy that will befriend you for a banana or a piece of cheese.

Something Special, just south of the entrance of the marina, is famous for its garden eels, which slither around the relatively shallow sand terrace.

Windsock Steep, situated in front of the small beach opposite the airport runway, is an excellent first-dive spot and a popular place for snorkeling close to town.

Deep-Sea Fishing

Captain Rich (☎ 599/7–1111) will take you on his 30-foot twin diesel sportfishing boat, the *Slamdunk,* to fish for wahoo, marlin, tuna, and sailfish. Rates are $275 for a half day, $375 for a full day (maximum six people). **Piscatur Charters** (☎ 599/7–8774) offers light-tackle angler reef fishing for jacks, barracudas, and snappers from a 15-foot skiff. Rates are $125 for a half day, $225 for a full day. The 30-foot sportfisherman *Piscatur* is available for charter at $275 for a half day, $375 for a full day.

Sailing Cruises

The *Samur* (☎ 599/7–5433), the *Oscarina* (☎ 599/7–8290 or 599/7–8819), and the *Woodwind* (☎ 599/7–8285) offer a variety of cruises for snorkeling, picnicking, and watching the sunset. A private day's cruise on the sailboat *Oscarina* (☎ 599/7–8290) is $350 for a party of four. Glass-bottom-boat trips are offered on the *Bonaire Dream.* The 1½-hour trip costs $15 for adults, $7.50 for children, and leaves daily, except Sunday, from the Harbour Village Marina.

Snorkeling

Don't consider snorkeling the cowardly diver's sport; in Bonaire the experience is anything but elementary. For only $6–$11 per day, you can rent a mask, fins, and snorkel at any hotel with a water-sports center (*see* Lodging, *below*). The better spots for snorkeling are on the leeward side of the island, where you have access to the reefs.

Swimming

Beaches good for swimming can be found anywhere along the western coast of the island. Excellent sites are **Pink Beach, Sorobon,** and **Boca Cai.** The best resort beaches are found at **Harbour Village Beach Resort, Sunset Beach Hotel,** and **Divi Flamingo Beach Resort and Casino.** Or take a water taxi ($12 round-trip) to **Klein Bonaire,** an islet where you can spend the day playing king of the dune. Except for a few forgotten sneakers, there is absolutely *nothing* on Klein Bonaire, so remember to take some food along. And don't miss the boat back home.

Tennis

Tennis is available for free to the guests at the **Sunset Beach Hotel, Divi Flamingo Beach Resort,** and the **Sand Dollar Beach Club.** Nonguests can play for free during the day at the **Divi Flamingo Beach Resort** and even take the free tennis clinics on Tuesday and Wednesday mornings (8:30–10). At night, there's an hourly charge.

Waterskiing

To stay above the water—with luck—learn to waterski. Call **Goodlife Watersport** (☎ 599/7–4588) to arrange a lesson.

Windsurfing

Lac Bay, a protected cove on the east coast, is ideal for windsurfing. Novices will find it especially comforting since there's no way to be blown out to sea. **Windsurfing Bonaire,** known locally as "Jibe City" (☎ and FAX 599/7–5363; U.S. representative, 800/748–8733), offers courses for beginning to advanced board sailors. Lessons cost $20; board rentals start at $20 an hour, $40 for a half day. There are regular pickups at all the hotels at 9 AM and 1 PM; ask your hotel to make arrangements.

Shopping

You can get to know all the shops in Bonaire in a matter of a few hours, but sometimes there's no better way to enjoy some time out of the sun and sea than to go shopping, particularly if your companion is a dive fanatic and you're not. Almost all the shops are situated on the Kaya Grandi or in adjacent streets and tiny malls. There are several snazzy boutiques worth a browse. One word of caution: Buy as many flamingo T-shirts as you want, but don't take home items made of goatskin or tortoiseshell; they are not allowed into the United States.

Cigars, Havana Style

Cigar smokers will find friends at **Little Holland** (Harborside Mall, ☎ 599/7–5670) as they breathe in the smoky splendor of Havana cigars. Montecristo, H. Upmann, Romeo & Juliet, and Cohiba are in residence. Far from being banished to the porch, cigar smokers will be welcomed into a special acclimatized Cedar Cigar Room. Someone understands!

Clothing

Benetton (19 Kaya Grandi, ☎ 599/7–5107) has added Bonaire to its list of franchises in the Caribbean and makes the claim that prices here are 30% less than in New York. At **Caro's Boutique** (34 Kaya Grandi, ☎ 599/7–8308) men can find designs by LaCoste and Guy LaRoche.

One shop that's sure to inspire a purchase is the **Ki Bo Ke Pakus,** or **What Do You Want?** (Divi Flamingo Beach Resort, ☎ 599/7–8239), with an exquisite line of batiks, material for dashikis, island-made jewelry, and chic designer swimsuits and beach cover-ups.

Perfume and Cosmetics

D'Orsy's (Harborside Mall, ☎ 599/7–5288) sells name-brand, duty-free perfumes and makeup from Lancôme, Clinique, Estée Lauder, Chanel, Nina Ricci, and Ralph Lauren, to name a few.

Souvenirs and Crafts

The hippest boutique in Bonaire is **Birds of Paradise** (Bonaire Shopping Gallery, 36 Kaya Grandi, ☎ 599/7–8998), with merchandise ranging from wooden fish earrings and other desert-chic jewelry to Esprit sportswear and stylish swimsuits. **Dalila Shop** (Bonaire Shopping Gallery, 36-A Kaya Grandi, ☎ 599/7–8460) specializes in decorations for the home, including locally made *chibichibi* (sugar birds), tile paintings, Dutch souvenirs, and unusual stuffed fish and cloth parrots. **Littman Gifts** (35 Kaya Grandi, ☎ 599/7–8091) is the place for batik cloth by the yard, European costume jewelry, T-shirts, framed underwater pictures, wooden divers, and glass flamingos. **Caribbean Arts and Crafts** (38-A Kaya Grandi, ☎ 599/7–5051) offers unique Mexican onyx, papier-mâché clowns, woven wall tapestries, painted wooden fish and parrots, straw bags, and handblown glass vases. **Things Bonaire** (Kaya Grandi 38C, ☎ 599/7–8423) offers T-shirts, shorts, colorful earrings, batik dresses, souvenirs, and guidebooks. A government-funded crafts center, **Fundashon Arte Industri Bonairiano** (J. A. Abraham Blvd., Kralendijk, next to the post office, no ☎), sells locally made necklaces of black coral in a variety of colors, hand-painted shirts and dresses, and the "fresh craft of the day."

Dining

Gourmets have not been sneaking off to Bonaire for five-star cuisine, but with a healthy variety of dining experiences, visitors should not go home hungry.

What to Wear

Dress on the island is casual but conservative. Most restaurants don't allow beachwear; even casual poolside restaurants prefer a sarong or cover-up. The fanciest restaurants may require a jacket. If a restaurant requires reservations, it's a good idea to ask about the dress code.

CATEGORY	COST*
$$$	over $25
$$	$15–$25
$	under $15

per person, excluding drinks and service. There is no sales tax.

$$$ **Bistro des Amis.** The Bistro's creative French menu and its simple yet elegant setting are both designed by owner Lucille Martyn. Try to get this engaging Dutch woman to talk about her specialties, then savor the Dutch chef's unforgettable sweet red-pepper soup, carpaccio in mustard-dill sauce, duck with orange sauce, smoked salmon in honey-lemon sauce, and grouper sautéed in dill and white wine. Or just have a drink at the mahogany bar. ✗ *4 Kaya L. D. Gerharts,* ☎ *599/7–8003. Reservations required. AE, MC, V. Closed Sun. No lunch.*

$$$ **Der Roode Pelikaan.** The Red Pelican is by far the most soigné eatery
★ on Bonaire: a harmonious blend of white tile floors, heavy wood beams, comfortable rattan furnishings, coral pink napery, and the owner's splendid collection of medieval Dutch crafts, from chamber pots to ale steins, all imaginatively incorporated into the decor. Add to that constantly changing art exhibits and tinkling ivories, and you have the stuff of a most civilized evening out. The Dutch chefs weave culinary magic with their light versions of such traditional Dutch fare

as marinated fish salad, *stoofpot* (a thick sultry seafood stew), and chicken in walnut sauce. Connected to the new Lac Bay development, this is a quietly glamorous enclave. ✕ *Kaminda Sorobon 64, Lac Bay,* ☎ *599/7–5686. Reservations advised. AE, MC, V.*

$$$ Raffles. Sir Thomas Raffles, born somewhere in the Caribbean Sea in 1781, grew up to become the colonial ruler of Jamaica, founder of Singapore, and governor of Java in the early 1800s. Hoteliers and restaurateurs have been inspired to name their establishments—such as this eatery in one of the oldest two-story houses on Bonaire—in his honor. Seekers of a romantic tête-à-tête flock to this air-conditioned oasis of green and white, where soft jazz plays, tables are intimate and candlelit, and the service is unobtrusive. The bar is boat-shaped. More casual, café-style dining can be found outside on the terrace, where you can watch the strolling passersby. There's an à la carte menu, imaginatively blending Caribbean influences with Continental standards, and three fixed-priced complete dinners. The seven-seafood soup and the fish pâté make excellent starters. As an entrée, order the Seafood Platter Caribe (lobster tail, shrimp, scallops, and a fillet of grouper) or the salmon cascade, but save room for a mango parfait, dark and white chocolate mousse, or a homemade fruit sherbet. Look for the landmark red British phone booth that sits outside the door. ✕ *Kaya C.E.B. Hellmund 5,* ☎ *599/7–8617. Reservations advised. AE, MC, V. Closed Mon. No lunch.*

$$–$$$ Mona Lisa Bar & Restaurant. Here you'll find Continental fare, along with a few authentic Dutch and Indonesian dishes. The most famous plate is the pork tenderloin *sate* drizzled with a peanut-butter sauce. Somehow, Mona Lisa has become renowned for fresh vegetables, though who knows where they come from, since nearly everything in Bonaire has to be imported. Lunch prices are more reasonable than those on the dinner menu. This is also a late-night hangout for local schmoozing and light snacks, which are served until about 2 AM in the colorful bar adorned with various team and business baseball-style caps. The intimate dining room is decorated with brick-and-iron grillwork, lace curtains, and whirring ceiling fans. ✕ *15 Kaya Grandi,* ☎ *599/7–8718. Reservations advised. MC, V. Closed Sun.*

$$ Chibi Chibi. In an unusual, open-air, beach-facing wooden structure—with balustrade and open planking—the Chibi Chibi is praised for its menu of local, American, and Continental fare. Try the fettuccine Flamingo (this is one of the Divi Flamingo Resort's restaurants) or the baked Edam cheese stuffed with meat. Fish is also a specialty. ✕ *Divi Flamingo Beach Resort, J. A. Abraham Blvd.,* ☎ *599/7–8285. Reservations advised. AE, D, MC, V. No lunch.*

$$ Den Laman Bar & Restaurant. A 6,000-square-foot aquarium provides the backdrop to this casual, nautically decorated, sea-breeze-cooled restaurant. Eat indoors next to the glass-enclosed "ocean show" (request a table in advance) or outdoors on the noisier patio overlooking the sea. Pick a fresh Caribbean lobster from the tank, or order red snapper Creole, which is a hands-down winner. Homemade cheesecake is a draw. ✕ *77 Gobrenador Debrot, next to the Sunset Beach Hotel,* ☎ *599/7–8599. Reservations advised. AE, MC, V. No lunch.*

$$ Rendez-Vous Restaurant. The terrace of this café, draped with a canopy of electric stars, is the perfect place to watch the world of Bonaire go by as you fill up on warm freshly baked French bread with garlic butter, hearty homemade soups, seafood, steaks, and vegetarian specialties. Or munch on light pastries accompanied by steamy espresso. ✕ *3 Kaya L. D. Gerharts,* ☎ *599/7–8454. Reservations advised. AE. Closed Tues. No lunch.*

$$ **Richard's Waterfront Dining.** Animated and congenial owner Richard
★   Beady's alfresco eatery on the water is casually romantic and has be-
come the most recommended restaurant on the island—a reputation
that's well deserved. Richard, originally from Boston, sets the tone
by personally checking on every table. Although the menu is limited,
the food is consistently excellent, catering to American palates with
flavorful, not spicy, preparations. Among the best dishes are conch
alajillo (fillet of conch with garlic and butter), shrimp primavera, and
grilled wahoo. Filet mignon béarnaise satisfies the palette already
sated with creatures of the deep. For a touch of seafood, start with
the fish soup, a tasty broth with chunks of the catch of the day. A new
pier lets you arrive by boat. The Sunset Happy Hour is popular with
locals. ✕ *60 J. A. Abraham Blvd., a few houses away from Bruce
Bowker's Carib Inn,* ☎ *599/7–5263. Reservations advised. AE, MC,
V. Closed Mon. No lunch.*

$$ **Toy's Grand Café.** Restaurants don't come much more playful than this
★   hip Dutch paean to high camp. Murals of everyone from Elvis to
Chaplin to Mickey Mouse enliven the walls. Toy trains and crazy pup-
pets jut out from the walls, and jack-in-the-boxes seem poised for assault at any minute. Potted plants engulf the wicker chairs. The food
is equally eclectic: French, barbecue, or Indonesian. Try the snails in
blue cheese, the *nasi goreng* (fried rice), or the pork medallions in peach
sauce. ✕ *J. A. Abraham Blvd., Kralendijk,* ☎ *599/7–6666. Reservations advised. No credit cards.*

$–$$ **Green Parrot.** This family-run restaurant, on the dock of the Sand Dol-
lar Beach Club, features the biggest hamburgers and the best strawberry margaritas on the island. Try the onion string appetizer, which
consists of onion rings shaped into a small bread loaf. Bagels with cream
cheese, char-grilled steaks, Creole fish, and barbecued chicken and ribs
are also served. This is where you'll find both the American expatriates and tourists hanging out. It's also a good place for viewing the
setting sun. ✕ *Sand Dollar Beach Club,* ☎ *599/7–5454. Reservations
advised in high season. AE, MC, V.*

$–$$ **Zeezicht Bar & Restaurant.** Zeezicht (pronounced *zay-zeekt* and mean-
ing sea view) is one of the better restaurants in town that are open for
three meals a day. At breakfast and lunch you'll get basic American
fare with an Antillean touch, such as a fish omelet. Dinner is either on
the terrace overlooking the harbor or in the homey, rough-hewn main
room. Locals are dedicated to this hangout, especially for the ceviche,
conch sandwiches, snails in hot sauce, and the Zeezicht special soup
with conch, fish, shrimps, and oysters. After dessert, stop in the garden to see the monkey and parrots. ✕ *10 Kaya Corsow, across from
Karel's Beach Bar,* ☎ *599/7–8434. AE, MC, V.*

$ **China Garden Restaurant and Bar.** Despite its name, this place has an
everything-you-could-ever-want menu, from American sandwiches to
shark's-fin soup, steaks, lobster, even omelets. But Cantonese dishes
are still the specialty. Try the goat Chinese-style, anything in black-bean
sauce, or one of the sweet-and-sour dishes. Lots of locals turn up between 5 and 7 PM to have a drink and watch the latest in sports on the
bar's cable TV. The decor is brightened with Chinese lanterns and scarlet tablecloths. ✕ *47 Kaya Grandi,* ☎ *599/7–8480. Reservations advised in season. AE, DC, MC, V. Closed Tues.*

Lodging

Hotels on Bonaire, with the exception of Harbour Village, cater primarily to avid divers who spend their days underwater and come up
for air only for evening festivities. Hence, hotel facilities tend to be mod-

est with small swimming pools and limited service. Groomed sandy beaches are not a requisite for a hotel, but an efficient dive shop is. Many resort accommodations have fully equipped kitchens. Although the larger hotels offer a variety of meal plans, most are on the European Plan. As a general rule, hotel restaurants can be significantly more expensive than restaurants in town. Divers can take advantage of very good prices by comparing the packages offered by the hotels. Ask the tourist office for a listing by calling 800/826–6247.

The **Bonaire Government Tourist Office** (☎ 800/826–6247) can help you locate suitable guest houses and smaller rental apartments in Bonaire. Rental apartments are also available through **Bonaire Sunset Villas** (☎ 800/223–9815, FAX 599/7–8118), **Sunset Oceanfront Apartments** (☎ 800/223–9815, FAX 599/7–8865), **Club Laman Caribe** (☎ 599/7–6840, FAX 599/7–7741), or **Black Durgon Inn Properties** (☎ 599/7–5736; in the U.S., 800/526–2370; FAX 599/6–8846).

CATEGORY	COST*
$$$$	over $225
$$$	$150–$225
$$	$100–$150
$	under $100

All prices are for a standard double room for two in high season, excluding a $4.10 per-person, per-night, government room tax and a 10% to 15% service charge.

$$$$ **Harbour Village Beach Resort.** This is the resort for divers who want
★ both an upscale resort and a dive vacation. If Armani designs a scuba mask, it will sell here. Wide walkways bordered by lush foliage and blooming tropical flowers separate eight low-rise, southwestern-style buildings, with Moorish arches, red barrel-tile roofs, and a pastel color scheme. The palm tree–lined beach is wide and inviting. While not as impressive as the grounds or building exteriors, the pleasant rooms and suites are done in dusty rose and aqua and have French doors leading to a terrace or patio (except for second-story courtyard rooms), white tile floors, and pale wood and wicker furniture. Each room also has a hair dryer, cable TV, amenity package, and direct-dial phone. Price category is determined by view—garden courtyard, marina, or ocean. There is a full-service dive shop and a water-sports concession that offers sailing, windsurfing, deep-sea fishing, kayaking, and powerboat rentals at the resort's marina. A new fitness center offers an air-conditioned state-of-the-art workout. At press time, a spa with every mud and rub was poised to open in 1995, with special spa packages already in place. On the horizon is a golf course and a casino. There will soon be no reason to go elsewhere. It's so well run that even seekers of the quiet life will be satisfied. The Kasa Coral restaurant, which overlooks the pool, serves full American buffet breakfasts, international à la carte lunches, and gourmet, fixed-price, multicourse dinners. ✉ *Box 312, ☎ 599/7–7500 or 800/424–0004, FAX 599/7–7507. 60 rooms, 8 oceanfront suites, 30 condominium units. 2 restaurants, 2 bars/lounges, dive center, dive lockers at beach, fitness center, meeting room, water-sports center, pool, bicycles, baby-sitting, marina, gift shop. AE, DC, MC, V. EP, MAP, FAP.*

$$$ **Captain Don's Habitat.** With its recent (1992) expansion and massive renovation, the Habitat, once a sort of extended home of Captain Don Stewart, the island's wildest sharpshooting personality, can no longer pass itself off as a mere guest house for divers. Stewart's Curaçaon partners have poured money into this resort, adding a set of upscale rooms (junior suites) and then a long row of private villas (the Hamlet section) that rank among the island's best: All are spacious, with ocean-view verandas, full kitchens, and stylish appointments. The rooms in the original 11 cottages are also spacious but in need of refurbishing. The atmosphere at the Habitat is laid-back and easygoing, with the emphasis on the staff's personal warmth rather than on spick-and-span efficiency. This is also one of few dive resorts that welcome families. The beachfront property units—with glorious views of Klein Bonaire— are spaced widely apart, and the grounds have been landscaped with rocks and cacti. Be sure to meet Captain Don, who shows up twice a week just to say hello, shoot the breeze, and tell his incredible tales, most of which are actually true. A full dive center with seven boats, complete with a resident photo pro, rounds out the picture. ⊡ *Kaya Gobrenador Debrot 103, Box 88,* ☎ *599/7–8290. U.S. representative: Habitat North American,* ☎ *800/327–6709,* FAX *599/7–8240. 11 cottages, 11 villas, 16 rooms. 2 bars, restaurant, gift shop, pool, cruises, baby-sitting, laundry facilities, bicycles, dive center, photo labs. AE, DC, MC, V. EP, MAP, FAP.*

$$$ Coral Regency Resort. This time-share resort's 32 studios and one- and two-bedroom suites are in 10 coral-pink, two-story buildings set around a quadrangle containing a small pool and sunbathing area— there's no beach for lounging. As a result, for privacy, the rooms on the second floor are more desirable than those on the first. The studio apartments have a small but complete kitchen, while the suites have a spacious living room with overhead fan, a large balcony looking out to sea (wonderful for morning breakfasts), and a fully equipped kitchen—including microwave and blender. All units have cable TV, direct-dial phone, and air-conditioning. The plain but clean bedrooms are compact, with little space left over after the huge king-size bed or two twins, but the marble-tiled bathrooms are large. Paul's Oceanfront Bar & Restaurant and the dive shop, a Neal Watson Undersea Adventures affiliate, add to the offerings. More villa units are planned, but these will be in a separate area several hundred yards from the waterfront. ⊡ *Kaya Gobrenador, Debrot 90, Box 380,* ☎ *599/7–5580; in the U.S.,* ☎ *800/327–8150;* FAX *599/7–5680. 32 units. Bar, restaurant, pool, dive center. AE, DC, MC, V. CP, MAP, FAP.*

$$$ Sand Dollar Beach Club. These elegant, spacious time-share apart-
★ ments combine a European design with a tropical rattan decor, though this varies according to the individual owner's taste. Each has cable TV, air-conditioning, a full kitchen, a large bathroom, a couch that turns into a queen-size bed, and a private patio or terrace that looks out to the sea (though the views from the ground-floor units are obstructed by foliage). Some units also have telephones. This American enclave is popular with serious divers and their families. There's daily maid service, and the maids will even do your laundry for $4 a load. There's an on-premise PADI five-star dive center, a limited activities club for children, and two lighted tennis courts. There is a beach, but it's minuscule and disappears at high tide. The resort's waterfront Green Parrot restaurant serves breakfast, lunch, and dinner, and there's a grocery store for those who like to cook. ⊡ *Kaya Gobrenador Debrot 79,* ☎ *599/7–8738,* FAX *599/7–8760. 77 studio, 1-, 2-, and 3-bedroom units and 8 2-bedroom town houses. Restaurant, bar, dive center, photo lab, pool, 2 lighted tennis courts, outdoor showers, strip shopping center, grocery/convenience store. AE, DC, MC, V. EP, MAP, FAP.*

$$$ Sorobon Beach Resort. Here's the perfect place for acting out all your *Swept Away* fantasies. The Sorobon is a secluded cluster of cottages on a lovely private sandy beach at Lac Bay, on the southeast shore. This delightfully unpretentious small resort is for "naturalists" who take its "clothing-optional" motto literally. Guests are a fair mix of Europeans and Americans. The chalets are arranged in a "V" shape to give the resort more openness and access to the beach. Each chalet consists of two small one-bedroom units, each with simple light-wood Scandinavian furnishings, an older-style kitchen, and a shower-only bath. In keeping with the get-away-from-it-all concept, there's no air-conditioning, TV, or telephone. A daily shuttle will take you to town. Relax sitting around full-moon bonfires, playing Ping-Pong, or enjoying a shiatsu massage, all right on the beach. The heady windsurfing in Lac Bay, a result of the unbeatable combo of shallow bay and strong trade winds, draws raves. Restaurant, bar, volleyball, nature-oriented book and video library, even a telescope to view the stunning night skies are all for the asking. But act blasé when the manager arrives wrapped in a towel. ⊡ *Box 14,* ☎ *599/7–8080 or 800/828–9356,* 🖷 *599/7–5363. 25 cottages. Kitchenettes, restaurant, bar, library. AE, MC, V. EP.*

\$\$–\$\$\$ **Divi Flamingo Beach Resort and Casino.** The Divi Flamingo is the closest thing you'll find to a small village on Bonaire—a plantation-style resort that will serve your every need. No matter which hotel you're staying at, reserve a table at the Chibi Chibi restaurant (*see* Dining, *above*), where you can hear ocean waves pounding beneath the floorboards. The resort consists of the hotel and the Club Flamingo studio apartments, which have the newest and nicest rooms. This is the oldest hotel on the island—a former internment camp for German POWs during World War II, and even those rooms that have been "renovated" still cry out for new furnishings and another coat of fresh paint. Though the resort is definitely showing signs of age, because of its dive facility and upbeat activities programs it still receives a fair share of repeat guests. Dive Bonaire was founded by world-class expert Peter Hughes and features some of the best photo labs in the Caribbean. Several rooms are accessible to travelers using wheelchairs, and the dive operation even has specially trained masters who teach scuba diving to individuals with disabilities and dive with them. The on-premise tennis pro offers free clinics every Tuesday and Wednesday morning, there's a daily activities program, live bands perform several nights a week, and the island's only casino—billed as the world's only barefoot gaming center—is here as well. The all-inclusive package offers great value for the price. ⊡ *J. A. Abraham Blvd.,* ☎ *599/7–8285. U.S. representative: Divi Hotels,* ☎ *800/367–3484,* 🖷 *599/7–8238. 105 rooms, 40 time-share units. 2 restaurants, 3 bars, casino, 2 pools, 2 dive shops, photo shop, jewelry store, lighted tennis court, 2 car-rental desks, tour desk, Jacuzzi, boutique. AE, D, MC, V. EP, MAP, All-inclusive.*

\$\$–\$\$\$ **Port Bonaire Resort.** Just opened at the end of 1994, Port Bonaire is a group of luxury apartments, penthouses, and beach houses, all with patios or balconies that look out on the ocean. The overall design, with tile roofs and pastel exteriors, is called Dutch Mediterranean. Families will find the fully equipped kitchens handy; they even have microwaves and dishwashers. Daily maid service and a room safe are also welcome. A dive center will open in 1995. ⊡ *Box 269, Kaya International,* ☎ *599/7–5636,* 🖷 *599/7–5639. 26 units. Bar, snack bar, pool, sundeck, kiddie pool, dive center. AE, DC, MC, V, EP.*

\$\$ **Sunset Beach Hotel.** In 1990 a group of businessmen purchased this hotel (then called the Bonaire Beach Hotel) and began renovations. New beds and drapes were brought in, walls painted, and wood floors polished. Each sizable room got a digital safety vault, direct-dial telephone, remote-control color TV, minirefrigerator, and coffeemaker. Age, however, has its drawbacks, and here the drawback is the location of the original buildings: They are all set back from the shore, giving even the best rooms only garden views. And in spite of the new amenities, the old-looking rooms and bathrooms lack brightness and appeal. Still, the 12 acres encompass one of the island's better hotel beaches (in contrast to the swimming pool, which is tiny), a miniature golf course, a water-sports concession that offers more than any other on the island, and a romantic thatch-roof restaurant overlooking the sea. Unfortunately, the food is not the island's best, and although the service is superfriendly, it is not always efficient. Divers come for the complete scuba center, Dive Inn, which has three dive boats. You can also rent Sunfish, Windsurfers, and snorkeling gear, or go parasailing or boogie boarding. The Bonairian Theme night, with native buffet, folkloric dance show, steel band, and dancing waitresses, costs $20 per person. ☎ *Kaya Gobrenador Debrot 75, Box 333,* ☎ *599/7–8448,* ℻ *599/7–8118. U.S./Canada representative:* ☎ *800/333–1212, 800/344–4439, or 800/223–9815. 142 rooms, 3 1-bedroom suites. Restaurant, bar/lounge, pool, 3 hot tubs, dive center, watersports center, water taxi to Klein Bonaire, miniature golf, shuffleboard, 2 lighted tennis courts, game room, tour desk, gift shop, car rental. AE, D, DC, MC, V. EP, MAP.*

$ ★ **Bruce Bowker's Carib Inn.** American diver Bruce Bowker started his small diving lodge out of a private home, continually adding onto and refurbishing the air-conditioned inn, about a mile from the airport. New rattan furnishings, cable TVs, completely renovated kitchens, and a family-style atmosphere have turned his homey hostelry into one of the island's best bets, albeit one that gets booked far in advance by repeat guests. Bowker knows everybody by name and loves to fill special requests. The two units with no kitchen have a refrigerator and electric kettle, but for more involved dining, you'll have to leave the premises—there's no restaurant. (Richard's Waterfront Restaurant is right next door.) Those who prefer to cook can shop for supplies at the grocery store just across the street. Nervous virgin divers will enjoy Bowker's small scuba classes (one or two people); PADI certification is available. You'll have to drive about a mile to the nearest beach. ☎ *Box 68,* ☎ *599/7–8819,* ℻ *599/7–5295. U.S. representative: ITR,* ☎ *212/545–8619 or 800/223–9815. 9 units. Pool, scuba classes, dive center, retail dive store. AE, MC, V. EP.*

$ **Buddy Beach and Dive Resort.** Those who eschew luxury, requiring only basic amenities with matching rates, enjoy this growing complex situated on the beach. The original 10 apartments are tiny but clean, with a kitchenette, tile floors, twin beds, a sleep sofa, and a shower-only bathroom. In keeping with the no-frills style, the five units on the ground level have no air conditioning and no TV; the five second-floor units have air-conditioning. In the 20 new luxury units, guests have a choice of a studio or a one- to three-bedroom apartment, all with sea views, TV, air-conditioned bedrooms, full kitchen, plus dishwasher and microwave. A dive operation and pool are also on the premises. ☎ *Kaya Gobrenador Debrot, Box 231,* ☎ *599/7–8065 or 800/786–3483,* ℻ *599/7–8647. 10 apartments and 20 studio and 1- to 3-bedroom condominium units. Pool with bar, dive shop. AE, MC, V. EP.*

The Arts and Nightlife

The Arts

Slide shows of underwater scenes keep both divers and nondivers fascinated in the evenings. Dee Scarr, a dive guide, presents the fascinating "Touch the Sea" show Monday night at 8:45, from the beginning of November to the end of June, at **Captain Don's Habitat** (☎ 599/7–8290). Check with the Habitat for other shows throughout the week. **Sunset Beach Hotel** (☎ 599/7–8448) offers a free one-hour slide show every Wednesday evening at 7. **Divi Flamingo Beach Resort** (☎ 599/7–

8285) offers a free underwater video, "Discover the Caribbean," on Sunday night at 7 PM.

The best singer on the island is guitarist **Cai-Cai Cecelia,** who performs with his duo Monday night at the **Divi Flamingo Beach Resort,** Wednesday night at **Sunset Beach Hotel,** and Thursday night at **Captain Don's Habitat.** He sings his own compositions, as well as Harry Belafonte classics. A local duo also sings and plays music every Thursday night at the **Divi Flamingo Beach Resort.** The Kunuku Band plays every Friday and Sunday for happy hour at **Captain Don's Habitat.** The M & M Duo also entertains three nights a week at the Chibi Chibi Restaurant at the **Divi Flamingo Beach Resort.**

Nightlife

Most divers are exhausted after they finish their third, fourth, or fifth dive of the day, which probably explains why there's only one disco in Bonaire. Nevertheless, **E Wowo** (Kralendijk, at the corner of Kaya Grandi and Kaya L. D. Gerharts, no ☎) is usually packed in high season, so get there early. The name E Wowo means "eye" in Papiamento and is illustrated with two flashing op-art eyes on the wall. Recorded music is loud, and the large circular bar seats a lot of action. The entrance fee varies according to the season.

The popular bar **Karel's** (☎ 599/7–8434), on the waterfront across from the Zeezicht Restaurant, sits on stilts above the sea and is *the* place for mingling with islanders, dive pros, and tourists, especially Friday and Saturday nights, when there's live music.

Mi Ramada (Rincon, ☎ 599/7–6338) is a hopping joint, splashed with neon colors and adorned with everything from license plates to creatively carved driftwood, that serves fine local Creole food to the accompaniment of top bands from all three ABC islands. Friday and Saturday nights are party time, when Bonairians gather along the main street of Kralendijk to dance to informal bands that set up on the sidewalk.

The island has only one casino, the **Divi Flamingo Beach Casino,** which opens at 8 PM and is closed on Sunday.

7 The British Virgin Islands

*Tortola, Virgin Gorda, and
Outlying Islands*

Updated by
Pamela
Acheson

T SEVERAL POINTS, the British Virgin Islands are less than a mile from the U.S. Virgin Islands, yet the B.V.I. have remained happily free of the runaway development that has detracted from the charm of so many West Indian islands. Here you will find about 50 islands, islets, and cays that are serene, seductive, and spectacularly beautiful. The pleasures to be found here are of the understated sort—sailing around the multitude of tiny, nearby islands; diving to the wreck of the RMS *Rhone,* sunk off Salt Island by a nasty hurricane in 1867; snorkeling in one of hundreds of wonderful spots; walking empty beaches; seeing some spectacular views from the island's peaks; and settling down on some breeze-swept terrace to admire the sunset.

One reason the B.V.I. have retained this sense of blissful simplicity is their strict building codes. No building can rise higher than the surrounding palms—two stories is the limit. The lack of direct air flights from the mainland United States also helps the British islands retain the endearing qualities of yesteryear's Caribbean. One first has to get to Puerto Rico, 60 miles to the west, or to nearby St. Thomas in the United States Virgin Islands and catch a small plane to the little airports on Beef Island/Tortola and Virgin Gorda. Many of the travelers who return year after year prefer arriving by water, either aboard their own ketches and yawls or on one of the convenient ferryboats that cross the turquoise waters between St. Thomas and Tortola.

Tortola, about 10 square miles, is the largest of the islands, and Virgin Gorda, with 8 square miles, ranks second. The islands scattered around them include Jost Van Dyke, Great Camanoe, Norman, Peter, Salt, Cooper, Ginger, Dead Chest, and Anegada, among others.

Sailing has always been a popular activity in the B.V.I. The first arrivals here were a romantic seafaring tribe, the Siboney Indians. Christopher Columbus was the first European to visit, during his second voyage to the New World, in 1493. The redoubtable "Admiral of the Ocean Seas," impressed by the number of islands dotting the horizon, named them *Las Once Mil Virgines* (The 11,000 Virgins) in honor of the 11,000 virgin-companions of Saint Ursula, martyred in the 4th century.

In the ensuing years, the Spaniards passed through these waters seeking gold, and, finding none, they quickly moved on to the richer pastures of Mexico. The next seafarers to arrive were a number of pirates who found the islands' hidden coves and treacherous reefs an ideal base from which to prey on passing galleons crammed with Mexican and Peruvian gold, silver, and spices. Among the most notorious of these predatory men were Blackbeard Teach; Bluebeard; Captain Kidd; and Sir Francis Drake, who lent his name to the channel that sweeps through the two main clusters of the B.V.I.

In the 17th century, these colorful cutthroats were replaced by the Dutch. The Dutch, in turn, were soon sent packing by the British, who retained control of the islands for nearly three centuries. The British established a plantation economy, and for the next 150 years they developed the sugar industry. African slaves were brought in to work the cane fields while the plantation owners and their families reaped the benefits. When slavery was abolished in 1838, the plantation economy quickly faltered, and the majority of the white population returned to Europe.

The islands dozed, a forgotten corner of the British empire, until the early 1960s. In 1966, a new constitution, granting greater autonomy to the islands, was approved. While the governor is still appointed by the queen of England, his limited powers concentrate on external affairs and local security. Other matters are administered by the legislative council, consisting of representatives from nine island districts. General elections are held every four years. The arrangement seems to suit the British Virgin Islanders just fine: The mood is serene, with none of the occasional political turmoil found on other islands. Having had tacit control over their destinies for more than a century and a half, local residents now have no reason to feel that visitors are more than welcome guests.

The 1960s also saw the arrival of a few profit-seeking souls, notably Laurance Rockefeller and American-expatriate Charlie Cary, who became convinced that the islands' balmy weather, powder-soft beaches, and splendid sailing would make them an ideal holiday destination. Attempts at building a small tourist industry began in 1965, when Rockefeller set about creating the Little Dix resort on Virgin Gorda. A few years later, Cary and his wife, Ginny, established the Moorings marina complex on Tortola, and sailing in the area burgeoned. Today the majority of jobs on the islands are tourism-related. British Virgin Islanders love their unspoiled tropical home and are determined to maintain its easygoing charms, for both themselves and the travelers who are their guests. The cruise ship dock in Road Harbour officially opened in the end of 1994, and it remains to be seen what effect this will have on the island.

Before You Go

Tourist Information

Information about the B.V.I. is available through the **British Virgin Islands Tourist Board** (370 Lexington Ave., Suite 416, New York, NY 10017, ☎ 212/696–0400 or 800/835–8530) or at the **British Virgin Islands Information Office** in San Francisco (1686 Union St., Suite 305, San Francisco, CA 94123, ☎ 415/775–0344 or 800/232–7770). British travelers can write or visit the **BVI Information Office** (110 St. Martin's La., London WC2N 4DY, ☎ 0171/2404259).

Arriving and Departing

BY PLANE

No nonstop service is available from the United States to the B.V.I.; connections are usually made through San Juan, Puerto Rico, or St. Thomas, U.S.V.I. Airlines serving both San Juan and St. Thomas include **American** (☎ 800/433–7300), **Continental** (☎ 800/231–0856), and **Delta** (☎ 800/323–2323). **American Eagle** (☎ 800/433–7300) flies from San Juan to Tortola. Regularly scheduled service between the B.V.I. and most other Caribbean islands is provided by **Leeward Islands Air Transport (LIAT)** (☎ 809/495–1187). Many Caribbean islands can also be reached via **Gorda Aero Service** (Tortola, ☎ 809/495–2271), a charter service.

BY BOAT

Various ferries connect St. Thomas, U.S.V.I., with Tortola and Virgin Gorda. **Native Son, Inc.** (☎ 809/495–4617), operates three ferries— (**Native Son, Oriole,** and **Voyager Eagle**)—and offers service between St. Thomas and Tortola (West End and Road Town) daily. **Smiths Ferry Services** (☎ 809/494–4430 or 809/494–2355) carries passengers between downtown St. Thomas and Road Town and West End on Monday through Saturday, offers daily service between Red Hook on St. Thomas and Tortola's West End, and travels between St. Thomas and Spanish Town Tuesday, Thursday, and Sunday. **Inter-Island Boat**

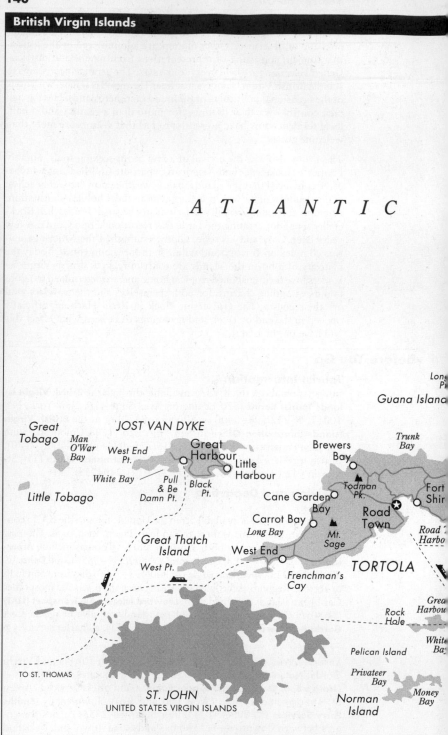

ATLANTIC

Long
Pt
Guana Island

Great
Tobago

Man
O'War
Bay

JOST VAN DYKE

West End
Pt.

Great
Harbour

Brewers
Bay

Trunk
Bay

Little
Harbour

White Bay

Pull
& Be
Damn Pt.

Black
Pt.

Cane Garden
Bay

Todman
Pk.

Fort
Shir

Little Tobago

Road
Town

Carrot Bay

Long Bay

Mt.
Sage

Road
Harbo

Great Thatch
Island

West End

TORTOLA

West Pt.

Frenchman's
Cay

Grea
Harbou

TO ST. THOMAS

Rock
Hole

White
Ba

Pelican Island

Privateer
Bay

ST. JOHN
UNITED STATES VIRGIN ISLANDS

Norman
Island

Money
Bay

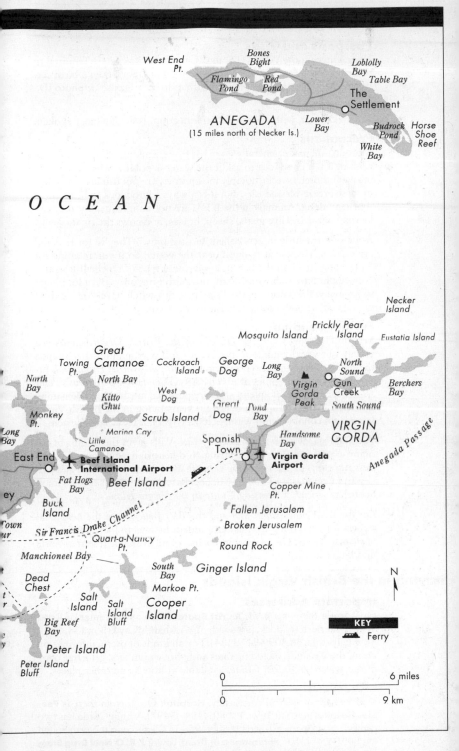

West End
Pt.

Bones
Bight

Loblolly
Bay

Table Bay

Flamingo
Pond

Red
Pond

The
Settlement

ANEGADA
(15 miles north of Necker Is.)

Lower
Bay

Budrock
Pond

Horse
Shoe
Reef

White
Bay

O C E A N

Necker
Island

Prickly Pear
Island

Mosquito Island

Eustatia Island

Great
Camanoe

Towing
Pt.

North Bay

Cockroach
Island

George
Dog

Long
Bay

North
Sound

Gun
Creek

Berchers
Bay

North
Bay

Kitto
Ghut

West
Dog

Virgin
Gorda
Peak

South Sound

Monkey
Pt.

Scrub Island

Great
Dog

Pond
Bay

VIRGIN
GORDA

Marina Cay

Little
Camanoe

Spanish
Town

Handsome
Bay

East End

**Beef Island
International Airport**

**Virgin Gorda
Airport**

Anegada Passage

Fat Hogs
Bay

Beef Island

Copper Mine
Pt.

Buck
Island

Sir Francis Drake Channel

Fallen Jerusalem

Town

Quart-a-Nancy
Pt.

Broken Jerusalem

Manchioneel Bay

South
Bay

Round Rock

Dead
Chest

Ginger Island

Salt
Island

Salt
Island
Bluff

Markoe Pt.

Cooper
Island

N

Big Reef
Bay

KEY

Peter Island

Ferry

Peter Island
Bluff

0   6 miles

0   9 km

Services' *Sundance II* (☎ 809/776–6597) connects St. John and West End on Tortola daily.

Passports and Visas

Upon entering the B.V.I., U.S. and Canadian citizens are required to present some proof of citizenship—if not a passport, then a birth certificate or voter-registration card with a driver's license or photo ID.

Language

British English, with a West Indian inflection, is the language spoken.

Precautions

Although there are generally no perils from drinking the water in these islands, it is a good idea to ask if the water is potable when you check into your hotel. Insects, notably mosquitoes, are not usually a problem in these breeze-blessed isles, but it is always a good idea to bring some repellent along. Animals in the B.V.I. are not dangerous, but they can be road hazards. Give goats, sheep, horses, and cows the right of way.

Beware of the little insects called "no-see-ums." They're for real and are especially pesky at twilight near the water. So if you're going for an evening stroll on the beach, apply some type of repellent liberally. No-see-um bites itch worse than mosquito bites and take a lot longer to go away. Prevention is the best cure, but witch hazel (or a dab of gin or vodka) offers *some* relief if they get you.

Further Reading

Vernon Pickering's *Concise History of the British Virgin Islands* is a wordy but worthy guide to the events and personalities that shaped the region. Pickering also produces the *Official Tourist Handbook* for the B.V.I. Look for copies of *A Place Like This: Hugh Benjamin's Peter Island,* a charming, eloquent, and very personal tale by Hugh Benjamin, a Kittitian who has spent the last 20 years living in the British Virgin Islands, in collaboration with Richard Myers, a New York writer.

For linguists, *What a Pistarckle!* by Lito Valls gives the origins of the many expressions you'll be hearing, and historians will enjoy *Eyewitness Accounts of Slavery in the Danish West Indies* by Isidor Paiewonsky and *Conquest of Eden* by Michael Paiewonsky. For sailors, Simon Scott has written a *Cruising Guide to the Virgin Islands.*

On the B.V.I., the *Island Sun* and the *BVI Beacon* are the best local papers for everything from entertainment listings to local gossip. The *Welcome Tourist Guide* is comprehensive and available free at airports and larger hotels.

Staying in the British Virgin Islands

Important Addresses

On Tortola there is a **B.V.I. Tourist Board Office** at the center of Road Town near the ferry dock, just south of Wickham's Cay I (Box 134, Road Town, Tortola, ☎ 809/494–3134). For all kinds of useful information about these islands, including rates and phone numbers, get a free copy of the *Welcome Tourist Guide,* available at hotels and other places.

EMERGENCIES
Dial 999 for a medical emergency. **Hospital:** On Tortola there is **Peebles Hospital** in Road Town (☎ 809/494–3497). Virgin Gorda has two clinics, one in Spanish Town (☎ 809/495–5337) and one at North Sound (☎ 809/495–7310). **Pharmacies:** in Road Town, **J. R. O'Neal Drug Store** (☎ 809/494–2292) and **Lagoon Plaza Drug Store** (☎ 809/494–2498).

Currency

British though they are, the B.V.I. have the U.S. dollar as the standard currency.

Taxes and Service Charges

Hotels collect a 7% accommodations tax, which they will add to your bill along with a 10% service charge. Restaurants may put a similar service charge on the bill, or they may leave it up to you. For those leaving the B.V.I. by air, the departure tax is $8; by sea it is $5.

Guided Tours

If you'd like to do some chauffeured sightseeing on Tortola, get in touch with the **B.V.I. Taxi Association** (three-person minimum, ☎ 809/494–2875, 809/494–2322, or 809/495–2378), **Style's Taxi Service** (☎ 809/494–2260 during the day or 809/494–3341 at night), or **Travel Plan Tours** (☎ 809/494–2872). **Scato's Bus Service** (☎ 809/494–2365), in Road Town, provides public transportation, special tours with group rates, and beach outings. Guided tours on Virgin Gorda can be arranged through **Andy's Taxi and Jeep Rental** (☎ 809/495–5252) or **Mahogany Rentals and Island Tours** (☎ 809/495–5469).

Getting Around

BOATS

Speedy's Fantasy (☎ 809/495–5240) makes the run between Road Town, Tortola, and Spanish Town, Virgin Gorda, daily. Running daily between Virgin Gorda's North Sound (Bitter End Yacht Club) and Beef Island, Tortola, are **North Sound Express** (☎ 809/494–2746) boats. There are also daily boats between Peter Island's private dock on Tortola just east of Road Town and Peter Island. **Jost Van Dyke Ferry Service** (☎ 809/495–2997) makes the Jost Van Dyke–Tortola run several times a day via the **When** ferry.

CARS

Driving on Tortola and Virgin Gorda is not for the timid. Roller-coaster roads with breathtaking ascents and descents and tight turns that give new meaning to the term "hairpin curves" are the norm. It's a challenge well worth trying, however; the ever-changing views of land, sea, and neighboring islands are among the most spectacular in the Caribbean. Most people will strongly recommend renting a four-wheel-drive vehicle. Driving is on the left side of the road. It's easy to become accustomed to it if you drive slowly, think before you make a turn, and pay attention when driving in and out of the occasional traffic circle, locally called a "roundabout." Speed limits are 30–40 mph outside town and 10–15 mph in residential areas. A valid B.V.I. driver's license is required and can be obtained for $10 at car-rental agencies. You must be at least 25 and have a valid driver's license from another country to get one.

On Tortola, car rentals are available from **Avis** (☎ 809/494–3322), **Budget** (☎ 809/494–2639), **Hertz** (☎ 809/495–4405), and **National** (☎ 809/494–3197). On Virgin Gorda, try **Mahogany Rentals** (☎ 809/495–5469) or **Andy's Taxi and Jeep Rental** (☎ 809/495–5252).

TAXIS

Your hotel staff will be happy to summon a taxi for you. On Tortola, there are B.V.I. Taxi Association stands in Road Town near the ferry dock (☎ 809/494–2875) and Wickham's Cay I (☎ 809/494–2322); there's one on Beef Island at the airport (☎ 809/495–2378). You can also usually find a taxi at the Sopers Hole ferry dock, West End, where ferries from St. Thomas arrive. On Virgin Gorda, Mahogany and Andy's (*see above*) also provide taxi service.

BUSES
For information about rates and schedules on Tortola, call **Scato's Bus Service** (☎ 809/494–2365).

MOPEDS AND BICYCLES
On Virgin Gorda, **Honda Scooter Rental** (☎ 809/495–5212) rents mopeds and bikes.

Telephones and Mail

The area code for the B.V.I. is 809. To call anywhere in the B.V.I. once you've arrived, dial only the last five digits: Instead of dialing 494–1234, just dial 4–1234. A local call from a public pay phone costs 25¢. Coin-operated pay phones are frequently on the blink, but phones that use the **Caribbean Phone Card,** available in $5, $10, and $20 denominations, are a handy alternative. The cards are sold at most major hotels and many stores and can be used in special Phone Card telephones. You can call anywhere in the world with them (although rates to the U.S. are cheaper if you use AT&T; *see below*). For credit-card or collect long-distance calls to the United States, look for special USA Direct phones that are linked to an AT&T operator, or dial 111 from a pay phone and charge the call to your MasterCard or Visa. USA Direct and pay phones can be found at most hotels and in towns.

There are post offices in Road Town on Tortola and in Spanish Town on Virgin Gorda. Postage for a first-class letter to the United States is 35¢ and for a postcard 20¢. (It might be noted that postal efficiency is not first class in the B.V.I.) For a small fee, **Rush It** in Road Town (☎ 809/494–4421) or Spanish Town (☎ 809/495–5821) offers most U.S. mail and UPS services via St. Thomas the next day.

Opening and Closing Times

Stores are generally open from 9 to 5 Monday through Saturday. Bank hours are Monday through Thursday 9–2:30 and Friday 9–2:30 and 4:30–6.

Exploring Tortola

Numbers in the margin correspond to points of interest on the Tortola map.

The drives on Tortola are dramatic, with dizzying roller-coaster dips and climbs and glorious views. Leave plenty of time to negotiate the hilly roads and drink in the irresistible vistas at nearly every hairpin turn. Distractions are the real danger here, from the glittering mosaic of azure sea, white skies, and emerald islets to the ambling cattle and grazing goats roadside.

Before setting out on your tour of Tortola, you may want to devote an hour or so to strolling down Main Street and along the waterfront ① in **Road Town,** the laid-back island capital. A good place to start is at the General Post Office facing **Sir Olva Georges Square,** across from the ferry dock and customs office. (Locals don't use street names much because they *know* where everything is, so if you ask directions, ask how to get to such-and-such restaurant or store, rather than how to find the street.) The hands of the clock atop this building permanently point to 10 minutes to 5, rather appropriate in this drowsy town, where time does seem to be standing still.

The eastern side of Sir Olva Georges Square is open to the harbor, and a handful of elderly Tortolans can generally be found enjoying the breeze that sweeps in from the water here. The General Post Office is at the opposite side of the square. From the front of the post office follow

Main Street to the right past a number of small shops housed in traditional pastel-painted West Indian buildings with high-pitched, corrugated tin roofs, bright shutters, and delicate fretwork trim.

On the left, about half a block from the post office, you'll encounter the **British Virgin Islands Folk Museum.** Founded in 1983, the museum has a large collection of artifacts from the Arawak Indians, some of the early settlers of the islands. Of particular interest are the triangular stones called *zemis,* which depict the Arawak gods Julihu and Yuccahu. The museum also has a display of a number of bottles, bowls, and plates salvaged from the wreck of the RMS *Rhone,* a British mail ship sunk off Salt Island in a hurricane in 1867. *Main St., no ☎. ☞ Free. ☉ Mon., Tues., Thurs., Fri. 10–4; Sat. 10–1, though hours may vary.*

From Main Street, turn right onto Challwell Street, cross Waterfront Drive, and proceed a few hundred yards to **Wickham's Cay** to admire the boats moored at **Village Cay Marina.** Enjoy a broad view of the wide harbor, home of countless sailing vessels and yachts and a base of the well-known yacht-chartering enterprise the Moorings. You'll find a **B.V.I. Tourist Board** office to serve you right here as well as banks, a post office, and more stores and boutiques.

When you've finished wandering about Wickham's Cay, take Fishlock Road up to the courthouse, and make a right to get back on Main Street. At the police station, turn left onto Station Avenue and follow it to the **J. R. O'Neal Botanic Gardens.** These 2.8 acres of lush gardens include hothouses for ferns and orchids, gardens of medicinal herbs, plants that bloom around Christmas, and plants and trees indigenous to the seashore. *Station Ave., ☎ 809/494–4557. ☞ Free. ☉ Mon.–Sat. 8–4, Sun. noon–5.*

Retrace your steps to Sir Olva Georges Square to pick up your car. From Road Town, head southwest along Waterfront Drive. Follow the coastline for 5 miles or so of the easiest driving in the B.V.I.: no hills; little traffic; lots of curves to keep things interesting; and the lovely, island-studded channel on your left. At Sea Cows Bay the road bends inland just a bit to pass through a small residential area, but it soon rejoins the water's edge. Sir Francis Drake Channel provides a kaleidoscope of turquoise, jade green, and morning glory blue on your left, and further entertainment is provided by pelicans diving for their supper.

The next development you come to is **Nanny Cay.** Jutting out into the channel, this villagelike complex, with brightly painted buildings trimmed with lacy wood gingerbread, also contains a marina that can accommodate more than 200 yachts.

From Nanny Cay the route continues westward as St. John, the smallest of the three main U.S.V.I., comes into view across the channel. The road curves into **West End** past the ruins of the 17th-century Dutch **❷ Fort Recovery,** a historic fort 30 feet in diameter, on the grounds of Fort Recovery Villas. There are no guided tours, but the public is welcome to stop by. The road ends at **Sopers Hole.** The waterfront here is dominated by the boat terminal and customs office that service the St. Thomas/St. John/Tortola ferries. Turn around and head back, taking **❸** your very first right over a bridge; follow signs to **Frenchman's Cay** and bear right on the other side of the bridge. There's a marina and a captivating complex of pastel-hued West Indian–style buildings with shady second-floor balconies, colonnaded arcades, shuttered windows, and gingerbread trim that showcase art galleries, boutiques, and restaurants. **Pusser's Landing** is a lively place where you can stop for a cold

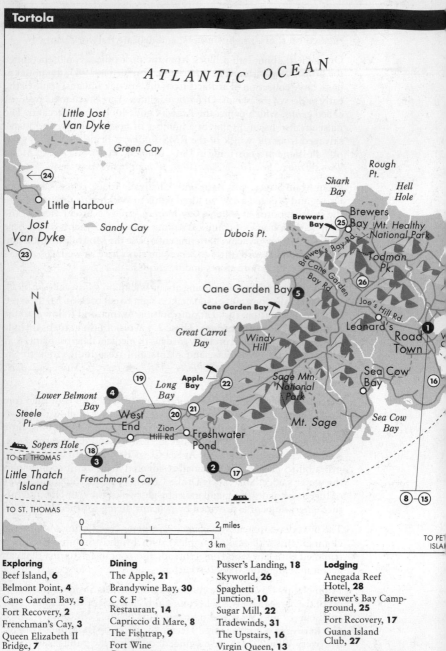

ATLANTIC OCEAN

Little Jost
Van Dyke

Green Cay

24

Little Harbour

Jost
Van Dyke

Sandy Cay

23

Dubois Pt.

Rough
Pt.

Shark
Bay

Hell
Hole

Brewers
Bay

Brewers
Bay

25

Mt. Healthy
National Park

N

Cane Garden Bay

5

Todman
Pk.

26

Joe's Hill Rd.

Leonard's

Road
Town

1

Cane Garden Bay

Great Carrot
Bay

Windy
Hill

Sage Mtn.
National
Park

Sea Cow
Bay

16

Lower Belmont
Bay

4

19

Long
Bay

Apple
Bay

22

21

Sea Cow
Bay

Steele
Pt.

West
End

20

Zion
Hill Rd

Freshwater
Pond

Mt. Sage

Sopers Hole

18

TO ST. THOMAS

3

2

17

Little Thatch
Island

Frenchman's Cay

8 — 15

TO ST. THOMAS

| 0 | | | 2 miles |
| 0 | | | 3 km |

TO PE
ISLA

Exploring
Beef Island, **6**
Belmont Point, **4**
Cane Garden Bay, **5**
Fort Recovery, **2**
Frenchman's Cay, **3**
Queen Elizabeth II
Bridge, **7**
Road Town, **1**

Dining
The Apple, **21**
Brandywine Bay, **30**
C & F
Restaurant, **14**
Capriccio di Mare, **8**
The Fishtrap, **9**
Fort Wine
Gourmet, **15**

Pusser's Landing, **18**
Skyworld, **26**
Spaghetti
Junction, **10**
Sugar Mill, **22**
Tradewinds, **31**
The Upstairs, **16**
Virgin Queen, **13**

Lodging
Anegada Reef
Hotel, **28**
Brewer's Bay Camp-
ground, **25**
Fort Recovery, **17**
Guana Island
Club, **27**

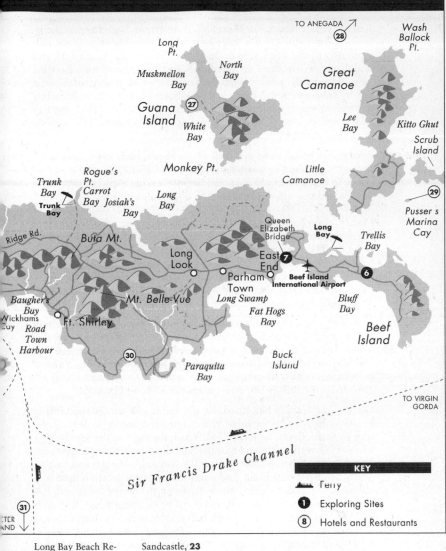

TO ANEGADA ↗
(28)

Wash
Ballock
Pl.

Long
Pt.

North
Bay

*Great
Camanoe*

Muskmellon
Bay

*Guana
Island*

(27)

White
Bay

Lee
Bay

Kitto Ghut

Scrub
Island

Monkey Pt.

*Little
Camanoe*

Rogue's
Pt.

Trunk
Bay

Carrot
Bay Josiah's
Bay

Long
Bay

(29)

Pusser's
Marina
Cay

**Trunk
Bay**

Queen
Elizabeth
Bridge

**Long
Bay**

Trellis
Bay

Ridge Rd.

Buta Mt.

Long
Look

East
End

(7)

(6)

Parham
Town

**Beef Island
International Airport**

Baugher's
Bay

Mt. Belle-Vue

Long Swamp

Bluff
Bay

Wickhams
Cay

Ft. Shirley

Fat Hogs
Bay

*Beef
Island*

Road
Town
Harbour

(30)

*Paraquita
Bay*

Buck
Island

TO VIRGIN
GORDA

(31)
TER
AND ↓

Sir Francis Drake Channel

KEY	
⛴ Ferry	
❶ Exploring Sites	
⑧ Hotels and Restaurants	

Long Bay Beach Resort, **19**
Moorings-Mariner Inn, **11**
Peter Island Resort and Yacht Harbour, **31**
Prospect Reef Resort, **16**
Pusser's Hotel, **29**

Sandcastle, **23**
Sandy Ground Estates, **24**
Sebastian's on the Beach, **20**
Sugar Mill Hotel, **22**
Treasure Isle Hotel, **12**

drink (many are made with Pusser's famous rum) and a sandwich and watch the boats come and go from the harbor.

Retrace your route out of West End, turn left, and head across the island on Zion Hill Road, a steep byway that rises and then drops precipitously to the other side of the island. Follow the road to the end and then turn left, drive up a steep hill, and be prepared for a dazzling view of **Long Bay,** a mile-long stretch of white sand secured on the west end by **Belmont Point,** a sugar-loaf promontory that has been described as "a giant, green gumdrop." On this stretch of beach is the Long Bay Beach Resort, one of Tortola's more appealing resorts. The large island visible in the distance is Jost Van Dyke.

TIME OUT   After you've had a swim or a walk on the beach, head to the beach restaurant at **Long Bay Beach Resort** (☎ 809/495–4252), where you can dine inside in an old sugar mill or outside around the beachfront pool, where you are welcome to swim after you've dined.

Once you are back in the car continue following the road, which hugs the shore, and look out for a shack on the left festooned with everything from license plates to crepe paper leis to colorful graffiti. It's hard to believe that this ramshackle place is the **Bomba Shack,** one of the liveliest nightspots on Tortola and home of the famous Bomba Shack "Full Moon" party. Every full moon, bands play here all night long and people flock here from all over Tortola and from other islands.

Continue along the shore past the **Sugar Mill Hotel** and over **Windy Hill,** a gripping climb that affords splendid vistas of the sea and sky. You'll descend to sea level at **Cane Garden Bay**: Its crystalline water and silky stretch of sand make this enticing beach one of Tortola's most popular getaways. Its existence is no secret, however, and it can get crowded, especially when cruise ships are in Road Harbour.

Go up Cane Garden Bay Road, up, up, and up. When the road finally levels out high up on the ridge, you can decide what to do next. To return to Road Town, take Joe's Hill Road, the right at the sign to Skyworld. Follow this right and bear left (and down) when you come to the "Y." The road's steep grade may make you gasp, but the spectacular, nearly aerial view of Road Town and the harbor is worth a little nervousness. If you'd rather continue exploring the rest of the island, follow that first sign to Skyworld, and you'll be on Ridge Road. Stay on it and you'll twist and turn through hills until you finally drop down at East End, the sleepy village that is the entryway to **Beef Island,** and the Beef Island International Airport. The narrow **Queen Elizabeth II Bridge** connects Tortola and Beef Island, and you'll have to pay a toll to cross (50¢ for passenger cars, $1 for vans and trucks). It's worth it if only for the sight of the toll taker extending a tin can attached to the end of a board through your car window to collect the fee. If you like interesting seashells, **Long Bay** on Beef Island has them for the picking.

From East End, head back along the south shore by bearing left on Blackburn Highway to Sir Francis Drake Highway, then west along the coast back to Road Town.

Exploring Virgin Gorda

Numbers in the margin correspond to points of interest on the Virgin Gorda map.

Virgin Gorda's main settlement, located on the island's southern wing, is **Spanish Town,** a peaceful village so tiny that it barely qualifies as a town at all. Also known as the Valley, Spanish Town is home to a marina, a small cluster of shops, and a couple of car-rental agencies. Just north of town is the ferry slip. At the **Virgin Gorda Yacht Harbour** you can enjoy a stroll along the dockfront or do a little browsing in the shops there.

Having rented a vehicle (you'll find a four-wheel drive the most satisfactory for negotiating some of the rougher terrain; remember that many of the roads are unmarked, so be prepared to stop and ask for directions), turn right from the marina parking lot onto Lee Road and head through the more populated, flat countryside of the south for about 10 minutes. You'll pass the Fischer's Cove Beach Hotel on your right. Keep driving until the road ends in a round parking area. From here it's a 35-yard walk to **the Baths,** Virgin Gorda's most celebrated site. Giant boulders, brought to the surface eons ago by a vast volcanic eruption, are scattered about the beach and in the water. They are the size of small houses and form remarkable grottoes. Climb between these rocks to swim in the many pools. Early morning and late afternoon are the best times to visit, since the Baths and the beach here are usually crowded with day-trippers visiting from Tortola.

TIME OUT   There is a small bar called **Mad Dog's** (☎ 809/495–5830) just before the parking area where you may want to pause for a cool drink and a BLT or hot dog after making the climb back from the Baths. Piña coladas are the specialty.

If it's privacy you crave, follow the shore north for a few hundred yards to reach several other quieter bays—Spring, the Crawl, Little Trunk, and Valley Trunk—or head south to Devil's Bay. These beaches have the same giant boulders as those found at the Baths.

Back in the car, retrace your route along Lee Road until you reach the southern edge of Spanish Town. After you pass a school and sports field on your right, take the next right and proceed to a T-intersection, then make another right and follow Copper Mine Road, part of it un- paved, to **Copper Mine Point.** Here you will discover a tall, stone shaft silhouetted against the sky and a small stone structure overlooking the sea. These are the ruins of a copper mine established here 400 years ago and worked first by the Spanish, then by English miners until the early 20th century. This is one of the few places in the B.V.I. where you won't see islands along the horizon.

Pass through town and continue north to **Savannah Bay** and **Pond Bay,** two pristine stretches of sand that mark the thin neck of land connecting Virgin Gorda's southern extension to the larger northern half. The view from this scenic elbow, called **Black Rock,** is of the Sir Francis Drake Channel to the northeast and the Caribbean Sea to the southwest. The road forks as it goes uphill. The unpaved left prong winds past the Mango Bay Club resort (and not much else) to Long Bay and not quite to Mountain Point. To continue exploring, take the road on the right, which winds uphill and looks down on beautiful South Sound. You'll notice nary a dwelling nor sign of mundane civilization up here, only a green mountain slope on your left and a spectacular view down to South Sound on the right. From here, too, you can also look back and get a wonderful sense of Virgin Gorda's stringy, crooked shape: Back there, looking flat and almost like a separate island, is the Valley, which you've just left. Because of this shape, Virgin Gorda is one of those places where you can get a bird's-eye (or map's-eye) view of things from right inside your car.

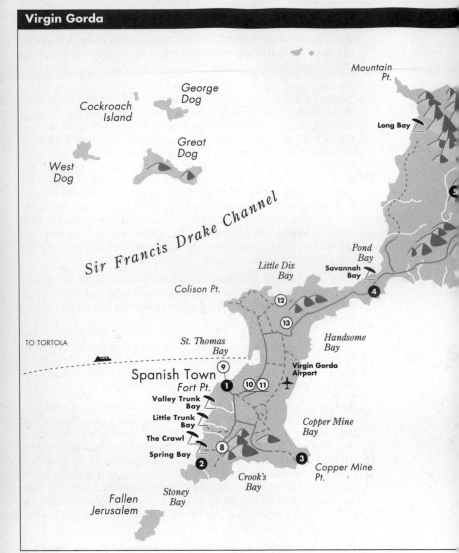

Exploring
The Baths, **2**
Black Rock, **4**
Copper Mine Point, **3**
Eustatia Sound, **7**
Saba Rock, **6**
Spanish Town, **1**
Virgin Gorda Peak, **5**

Dining
Bath and Turtle, **9**
Crab Hole, **10**
Drake's Anchorage, **14**
Olde Yard Inn, **13**

Lodging
Biras Creek, **16**
Bitter End Yacht Club and Marina, **17**
Drake's Anchorage, **14**
Guavaberry Spring Bay Vacation Homes, **8**

Leverick Bay Resort, **15**
Little Dix Bay, **12**
Olde Yard Inn, **13**
The Wheelhouse, **11**

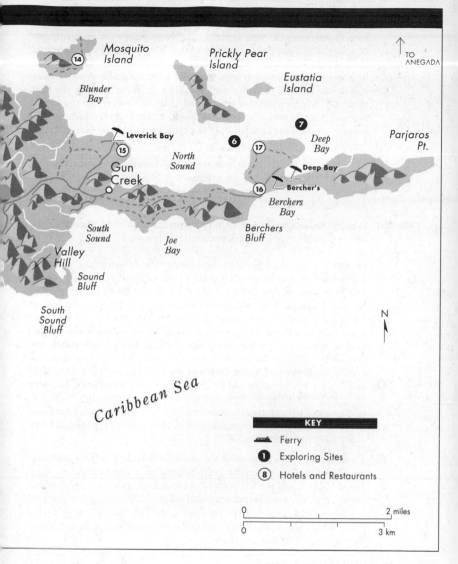

TO
ANEGADA

Mosquito
Island

Prickly Pear
Island

Eustatia
Island

Blunder
Bay

14

Parjaros
Pt.

7

Leverick Bay

15

6

17

Deep
Bay

North
Sound

Gun
Creek

16

Deep Bay

Bercher's

Berchers
Bay

South
Sound

Joe
Bay

Berchers
Bluff

Valley
Hill

Berchers
Bluff

Sound
Bluff

South
Sound
Bluff

N

Caribbean Sea

KEY

Ferry

1 Exploring Sites

8 Hotels and Restaurants

0 ————————————— 2 miles

0 ————————————— 3 km

⑤ You should see a small sign on the left for the trail up to the 265-acre **Virgin Gorda Peak National Park** and the island's summit at 1,359 feet. (Sometimes the sign is missing, so keep your eyes open for a set of stairs that disappears into the trees.) It's about a 15-minute hike up to a small clearing, where you can climb a ladder to the platform of a wood observation tower. If you're keen for some woodsy exercise or just want to stretch your legs, go for it. Unfortunately, the view at the top is somewhat tree-obstructed. A bit farther on, the road forks again. The right fork leads to **Gun Creek,** where launches pick up passengers for the Bitter End and Biras Creek, two of Virgin Gorda's most appealing hostelries.

The left fork will bring you to **Leverick Bay. Leverick Bay Resort** is here, plus a cozy beach and marina, a restaurant, a cluster of shops, and some luxurious hillside villas to rent. This is also where a launch picks up passengers for Drake's Anchorage, a resort on nearby Mosquito Island.

TIME OUT Stop by **Pusser's Beach Bar** for a snack and browse in the nearby stores before your return trip to your vacation headquarters.

Low-gear your way up one of the narrow hillside roads (you're not on a driveway, it only seems that way) to one of those topmost Leverick dwellings, where you can park for a moment. Out to the left, across Blunder Bay, you'll see **Mosquito Island,** home of Drake's Anchorage Resort; the hunk of land straight ahead is **Prickly Pear,** which has been named a national park to protect it from development. At the neck of land to your right, across from Gun Creek, is **Biras Creek Hotel,** and around the bend to the north of that you'll see the Danish-roof buildings of the **Bitter End Yacht Club and Marina.** Between the Bitter End
⑥ and Prickly Pear you should be able to make out **Saba Rock,** home of one of the Caribbean's best-known diving entrepreneurs, Bert Kilbride—a colorful character who knows where all the wrecks are and who is recognized and commissioned by the queen of England as Honorary Keeper of the Wrecks.

⑦ That magical color change in the sea near Prickly Pear reveals **Eustatia Sound** and its extensive reef. Beyond that are Horseshoe Reef, Necker Island, and the flat coral island of Anegada some 20 miles north, where most of those wrecks are and where bare-boaters are not permitted to sail because of the perilous reefs. But you can easily take a boat to Biras Creek, the Bitter End, or Drake's Anchorage. In fact, that's the only way you can get there.

Other British Virgin Islands

Just across the channel from Road Town on Tortola is **Peter Island,** an 1,800-acre island known for its exclusive resort. **Jost Van Dyke,** the sizable island north of Tortola's western tip, is a good choice for travelers in search of isolation and good hiking trails; it has several hostelries and two campgrounds, but only two small settlements, few cars, and small generators for electricity. Guests of the resort on **Guana Island** also enjoy the nature trails and wildlife sanctuary on this private island just above the eastern tip of Tortola. **Pusser's Marina Cay** is a snug 6-acre islet near Great Camanoe, just north of Beef Island, east of Tortola, with a Pusser's Store, Restaurant, and Hotel. **Cooper Island** is a green, hilly island on the south side of Sir Francis Drake Channel. It has a restaurant and a four-room hotel and has long been a popular anchorage. **Necker** is a private island just north of Virgin Gorda with accommodations for 20 that can only be rented as a block. Anegada, about 16 miles north of Virgin Gorda's North Sound, is a flat mass of coral 11 miles long and 3 miles wide with a population of only about 160. Visitors are chiefly scuba divers, snorkelers, lovers of deserted beaches, and fishermen, some of whom come for the bonefishing here. (For more information on these islands, *see* Lodging, *below.*)

Off the Beaten Track

Sage Mountain National Park. At 1,716 feet, Tortola's Sage Mountain is the highest peak in the B.V.I. The best unobstructed views up here are from the top, which has recently been cleared. From the parking area, a trail will lead you in a loop not only to the peak itself but also to the island's rain forest, sometimes shrouded in mist. Most of the island's forest was cut down over the centuries to clear land for sugarcane, cotton, and other crops, as well as pastureland and timber. But in 1964 this park was established to preserve the remaining rain forest. Up here you can see mahogany trees, white cedars, mountain guavas, elephant-ear vines, mamey trees, and giant bulletwoods, to say nothing of such birds as mountain doves and thrushes. Take a taxi from Road Town or drive up Joe's Hill Road and make a left onto Ridge Road toward Chalwell and Doty villages. The road dead-ends at the park. *Ridge Rd., no ☎ (contact the tourist office for information).* ☞ *Free.*

Beaches

Beaches here are less developed than, say, on St. Thomas or St. Croix. You'll also find fewer people. Try to get out on a boat at least one day during your stay in these islands, whether a dive-snorkeling boat or a day-trip sailing vessel. It's sometimes the best way to get to the most virgin Virgin beaches (some have no road access).

Tortola

Tortola's north side has a number of postcard-perfect, palm-fringed white-sand beaches that curl luxuriantly around turquoise bays and coves. Nearly all are accessible by car (preferably with four-wheel drive), albeit down bumpy roads that corkscrew precipitously. Facilities range from none to several beach bars with rest rooms.

If you want to surf, the area of **Apple Bay, Little Apple Bay,** and **Cappoon's Bay** is the spot, although the beach itself is pretty narrow. Sebastian's, the very appealing hotel here, caters especially to those in search of the perfect wave. Good waves are never a sure thing, but January and February are usually high times here. **Josiah's Bay** is another favored place to hang-10. The beach is wide, very often deserted, and a nice place to come for a quiet picnic.

The water at **Brewers Bay** is good for snorkeling. There's a campground here, but in the summer you'll find almost nobody around. The beach and its old sugar mill and rum-distillery ruins are just north of Cane Garden Bay (up and over a steep hill), just past Luck Hill.

Cane Garden Bay rivals St. Thomas's Magens Bay in beauty but is Tortola's most popular beach (it's the closest beach to Road Town—one steep up- and down-hill drive) and one of the B.V.I.'s best-known anchorages. It's a grand beach for jogging if you can resist staying out of that translucent water. You can rent sailboards and such, and for noshing or sipping you have a choice of going to Stanley's Welcome Bar; Rhymer's the Wedding; or Quito's Gazebo, where local recording star Quito Rhymer sings island ballads four nights a week. For true romance, nothing beats an evening of stargazing from the bow of a boat, listening to Quito's love songs drift across the bay.

Long Bay (West) is a stunning mile-long stretch of white sand, and the road that leads to it offers panoramic views of the bay (bring your camera). Long Bay Beach Resort sits along part of it, but the whole beach is open to the public. The water is not as calm as that at Cane Garden or Brewer's Bay, but it is still very swimmable.

Long Bay (East) on Beef Island offers scenery that draws superlatives and is visited only by a knowledgeable few. The view of Little Camanoe and Great Camanoe islands is appealing, and if you walk around the bend to the right, you can see little Marina Cay and Scrub Island. Take the Queen Elizabeth II Bridge to Beef Island and watch for a small dirt turnoff on the left before the airport. Drive across that dried-up marsh flat— there really is a beach (with interesting seashells) on the other side.

After bouncing your way to beautiful **Smuggler's Cove** (Lower Belmont Bay), you'll really feel as if you've found a hidden paradise (although don't expect to be alone on weekends). Have a beer or a toasted cheese sandwich, the only items on the menu, at the *extremely casual* snack bar. There is a fine view of the island of Jost Van Dyke, and the snorkeling is good.

About the only thing you'll find moving at **Trunk Bay** is the surf. It's directly north of Road Town, midway between Cane Garden Bay and Beef Island, and you'll have to hike down a *ghut* (gully) from the high Ridge Road.

Virgin Gorda

The best beaches are most easily reached by water, although they are accessible on foot, usually after a moderately strenuous hike of 10 to 15 minutes.

Anybody going to Virgin Gorda must experience swimming or snorkeling among its unique boulder formations. But why go to the **Baths,** which is usually crowded, when you can catch some rays just north at **Spring Bay** beach, which is a gem, and, a little farther north, at the **Crawl**? Both are easily reached from the Baths on foot or by swimming.

Leverick Bay is a small, busy beach-cum-marina that fronts a resort restaurant and pool. Don't come here to be alone or to jog. But if you want a lively little place and a break from the island's noble quiet, take the road north and turn left before Gun Creek. The view of Prickly Pear Island is an added plus, and there's a dive facility right here to motor you out to beautiful Eustatia Reef just across North Sound.

It's worth going out to **Long Bay** (near Virgin Gorda's northern tip, past the Diamond Beach Club) for the snorkeling (Little Dix Bay resort has outings here). Going north from Spanish Town, go left at the fork near Pond Bay. Part of the route there is dirt road.

The North Shore has many nice beaches. From Biras Creek or Bitter End you can walk to **Bercher's** and **Deep Bay** beach. Two of the prettiest beaches in North Sound are accessible only by boat: Mosquito Island's **Hay Point Beach** and Prickly Pear's **Vixen Point Beach.**

Savannah Bay is a lovely long stretch of white sand, and though it may not always be deserted, it's wonderfully private for a beach just north of Spanish Town (on the north side of where the island narrows, at Black Rock). From town it's about 30 minutes on foot.

Other Islands

Beaches on other islands, reachable only by boat, include Jost Van Dyke's **Great Harbour** and **White Bay; Marina Cay;** Peter Island's **Big Reef Bay, White Bay,** and **Dead Man's Bay;** Mosquito Island's **Limetree Beach,**

Long Beach, and **Honeymoon Beach**; and Cooper Island's **Manchioneel Bay.** Farther off, and reachable by plane as well as by boat, is beach-ringed, reef-laced **Anegada.**

Sports and the Outdoors

Horseback Riding
On Tortola, equestrians should get in touch with **Shadow Stables** (☎ 809/494–2262) or Mr. Thomas at his **Ellis Thomas Riding School** (☎ 809/494–4442).

Sailboarding
One of the best spots for sailboarding is at Trellis Bay on Beef Island. **Boardsailing B.V.I.** (Trellis Bay, Beef Island, ☎ 809/495–2447) has rentals, private lessons, and group rates. On Virgin Gorda, the **Nick Trotter Sailing School** (Bitter End Yacht Club, North Sound, ☎ 800/872–2392) has beginner and advanced courses.

Sailing and Boating
The B.V.I. offer some of the finest sailing waters in the world, with hundreds of boats available for charter—with or without crew—as well as numerous opportunities for day sails. For help in chartering a boat and crew for an extended trip, contact **Virgin Island Sailing** (Box 146, Road Town, Tortola, B.V.I., ☎ 800/233–7936), a top brokerage house. For sailors interested in renting a bare boat, contact the **Moorings** (1305 U.S. 19 S, Suite 402, Clearwater, FL 34624, ☎ 800/535–7289). Based in Road Town, it is the largest operator in the Caribbean and offers sailboats in a wide range of sizes, with or without crew.

Scuba Diving and Snorkeling
The famed wreck of the RMS *Rhone,* off Salt Island, is reason enough to dive during your B.V.I. stay. For snorkelers, perhaps the most popular spot is at the famed Baths on Virgin Gorda. Dive and snorkel sites also abound near the smaller islands of Norman, Peter, Cooper, Ginger, the Dogs, and Jost Van Dyke; the North Sound area of Virgin Gorda; Brewer's Bay and Frenchman's Cay on Tortola; and the wreck-strewn waters off Anegada. In addition to renting equipment, many of the dive operators here also offer instruction, hotel-dive packages, and snorkeling excursions. On Tortola, contact **Baskin-in-the-Sun** (Box 108, Road Harbour, ☎ 809/494–2858 or 800/233–7938) or **Underwater Safaris Ltd.** (Box 139, Road Town, ☎ 809/494–3235 or 800/537–7032). **Dive BVI** (VG Yacht Harbour, ☎ 809/495–5513 or 800/848–7078) has locations on Virgin Gorda and Peter Island.

Sportfishing
A number of companies can transport and outfit you for fishing. On Tortola try **Charter Fishing Virgin Islands** (Prospect Reef, ☎ 809/494–3311). On Virgin Gorda contact **Captain Dale** (☎ 809/495–5225), who operates the 38-foot Bertram *Classic* out of Biras Creek.

Tennis
Several resorts on Tortola have tennis courts for guests' use. For a fee, nonguests may use courts at **Prospect Reef** (Road Town, ☎ 809/494–3311). **Peter Island Resort and Yacht Harbour** (☎ 809/494–2561), which is a 20-minute ferry ride from Road Town) has courts available to nonguests for a fee and offers tennis lessons (reservations advised). On Virgin Gorda, nonguests can use the courts at **Biras Creek** (☎ 809/494–3555) for a fee.

Shopping

The British Virgins are not known as a shopping haven, but there are interesting finds, particularly artwork. Don't be put off by an informal shop entrance. Some of the best finds in the B.V.I. lie behind a shop-worn door.

Shopping Districts

Most of the shops and boutiques on Tortola are clustered on and off Road Town's **Main Street** and at **Wickham's Cay** shopping area, adjacent to the Marina. There is also an ever-growing group of art, jewelry, clothing, and souvenir stores at **Soper's Hole** on Tortola's West End. On Tortola's resort-crested sister isles, boutiques are located within the individual hotel complexes. Several of the best are at **Little Dix Bay** and **Bitter End Yacht Club** on Virgin Gorda. Other properties on the same island—**Biras Creek** and **Olde Yard Inn**—have small but equally select boutiques. There is a small collection of shops at Leverick Bay and there's a diverse scattering of stores in the minimall adjacent to the bustling yacht harbor in Spanish Town.

Specialty Stores

ART AND ANTIQUES

Collector's Corner (Columbus Centre, Wickham's Cay, ☎ 809/494–3550) carries antique maps; watercolors by local artists; gold and silver jewelry; coral; and larimar, a pale blue Caribbean gemstone. Visit the **Courtyard Gallery** (Main St., Road Town, no ☎) for its exclusive Carinia Collection, delicate crushed-coral sculptures created on the premises and depicting hummingbirds, angelfish, pelicans, and flowers. **Islands Treasures** (Soper's Hole Marina, ☎ 809/495–4787) is the place to find watercolors, paintings, pottery, sculpture, model ships, coffee-table books on the Caribbean, and prints of Caribbean maps and scenes. **Caribbean Fine Arts Ltd.** (Main St., Road Town, ☎ 809/494–4240) is a small shop that carries a wide range of Caribbean art, including original watercolors, oils, and acrylics, as well as signed prints, limited-edition serigraphs, and turn-of-the-century sepia photographs. At **Sunny Caribbee Art Gallery** (Main St., Road Town, ☎ 809/494–2178) you'll find one of the largest displays of paintings in the Caribbean, along with a large selection of island spices and sauces and bath products made from natural ingredients.

CLOTHING

Trendy **Bonker's Gallery** (Main St., Road Town, ☎ 809/494–2535) carries resort wear for women, including cotton and washable-silk tops and bottoms and cover-ups. There is also a small collection of pants and shirts for men. **Next Wave** (Virgin Gorda Yacht Harbour, ☎ 809/495–5623) has bathing suits, T-shirts, and canvas tote bags. The **Pelican's Pouch Boutique** (Virgin Gorda Yacht Harbour, ☎ 809/495–5599) has a large selection of swimsuits plus cover-ups, beach hats, T-shirts, and accessories. Both locations of **Sea Urchin** (Columbus Centre, Road Town, ☎ 809/494–2044; Soper's Hole Marina, ☎ 809/495–4850) have a great selection of island-living designs: print shirts and shorts, slinky swimsuits, sandals, and T-shirts. Stop by **Violet's** (Wickham's Cay I, ☎ 809/494–6398) to check out the beautiful silk lingerie and the small line of designer dresses.

FOOD AND DRINK

Ample Hamper (Village Cay Marina, Wickham's Cay, ☎ 809/494–2494; Soper's Hole Marina, ☎ 809/495–4684) sells cheeses, wines, fresh fruits, and canned goods from the United Kingdom and the United States. It will provision yachts and rental villas. **Fort Wine Gourmet** (Main St.,

Road Town, ☎ 809/494–3036), a café-cum-store, carries a remarkably sophisticated selection of gourmet items and fine wines, including Petrossian caviars and Hediard goods from France. **Gourmet Galley** (Wickham's Cay II, Road Town, ☎ 809/494–6999) stocks a fine selection of wines, cheeses, and fresh fruits and vegetables and provides full provisioning for yachtspeople and villa renters. **Bitter End's Emporium** (Bitter End Yacht Club, North Sound, ☎ 809/494–2745) is a great place to stop for such edible treats as local fruits, bakery goods, and cheeses. You get a whiff of the fresh breads before you even get in the door of the **Virgin Island Bakery** (Virgin Island Yacht Harbour, no ☎). Stop in for freshly baked loaves, rolls, muffins, and cookies, and sandwiches and sodas to go.

GIFTS

J. R. O'Neal, Ltd. (Main St., Road Town, ☎ 809/494–2292) carries fine crystal, Royal Worcester china, a wonderful selection of hand-painted Italian dishes, hand-blown Mexican glassware, ceramic housewares from Spain, and woven rugs and tablecloths from India. Check out the **Pink Pineapple** (Prospect Reef Resort, ☎ 809/494–3311) for a remarkable array of gift items, from wearable artwork and hand-painted jewelry to watercolors and batik fabric. **The Pusser's Company Store** (Main St. and Waterfront Rd., Road Town, ☎ 809/494–2467; Soper's Hole Marina, ☎ 809/495–4603; Leverick Bay, ☎ 809/495–7369) draws crowds with its selection of nautical memorabilia, an entire line of clothes and gift items bearing the Pusser's logo, and handsome decorator bottles of Pusser's rum. **The Sunny Caribbee Herb and Spice Company** (Main St., Road Town, ☎ 809/494–2178), located in a brightly painted West Indian house, packages its own herbs, teas, coffees, herb vinegars, hot sauces, natural soaps, skin and suntan lotions, Caribbean art, and hand-painted decorative accessories. A small branch of this store is located at the Skyworld Restaurant (see Dining, below). **Turtle Dove Boutique** (Flemming St., Road Town, ☎ 809/494–3611) is among the best in the B.V.I. for French perfume, international swimwear, and silk dresses, as well as gifts and accessories for the home.

JEWELRY

The outside of **Felix Gold and Silver Ltd.** (Main St., ☎ 809/494–2406) is not much to look at, but inside jewelers handcraft exceptionally fine jewelry. Choose from island or other themes, or have something custom made; in most cases, the shop will make it for you within 24 hours. **Samarkand** (Main St., Road Town, ☎ 809/494–6415) specializes in handmade gold and silver pendants, earrings, bracelets, and pins.

LOCAL CRAFTS

Artists at **Caribbean Handprints** (Main St., Road Town, ☎ 809/494–3717) create silk-screened fabrics, which you can buy by the yard or fashioned into dresses, shirts, pants, bathrobes, beach cover-ups, and beach bags. Local artists display their works at the **Virgin Gorda Craft Shop** (Virgin Gorda Yacht Harbour, no ☎). Choose among West Indian jewelry and crafts styled in straw, shells, and other local materials, or pick up clothing and paintings by Caribbean artists.

TEXTILES

Zenaida (Frenchman's Cay, ☎ 809/495-4867) displays the fabric finds of Argentinean Vivian Jenik Helm, who travels through South America, Africa, and India in search of batiks, hand-painted and hand-blocked fabrics, and interesting weaves. You can choose from her fabulous pareus and wall hangings, unusual bags, belts, sarongs, scarves, and ethnic jewelry.

Dining

The most popular choices in B.V.I. restaurants are seafood dishes. You'll find a greater range of eateries on Tortola than on more remote Virgin Gorda and the other islands, where most hotels offer a meal plan.

What to Wear

Casual but neat is the way to go on both Tortola and Virgin Gorda. Beachwear is a bit too casual, but nice shorts are fine during the day. In the evening diners tend to don nice pants and sundresses. Resort dining rooms may require a jacket; ask when you make your reservations.

CATEGORY	COST*
$$$$	over $35
$$$	$25–$35
$$	$15–$25
$	under $15

per person for three courses, excluding drinks and service; there is no sales tax in the B.V.I.

Tortola

$$$$ Tradewinds. Catch the ferry for a 25-minute ride to this elegant restau-
★ rant on Peter Island, and dine and dance under the stars. The excellent à la carte menu offers Continental selections prepared with
Caribbean flair. Appetizers such as grilled assorted vegetables or medallions of cold lobster are followed by entrées that may include grilled
local grouper, baby lamb chops, pasta with slices of grilled chicken in
a tomato-basil sauce, or a veal chop with shiitake mushrooms. For a
truly decadent finish, choose one of the sinfully rich desserts (maybe
Strawberry Romanoff) *and* have a tasty Sprat Bay Coffee. ✕ *Peter Island*, ☎ *809/494–2561. Reservations essential. AE, MC, V. Closed Mon.*

$$$ Brandywine Bay. For the best in romantic dining, don't miss this hill-
★ side gem, where candlelit alfresco tables have a sweeping view of
neighboring islands. Italian owner-chef Davide Pugliese prepares food
the Tuscan way—grilled with lots of fresh herbs. The remarkable
menu, which hostess Cele Pugliese describes tableside, can include
homemade mozzarella, grilled portobello mushrooms, grilled local
wahoo, and grilled veal chops with ricotta and sun-dried tomatoes. Roast
duck, a house specialty, is always served with an exotic sauce such as
berry, mango, orange-and-ginger, or passion fruit. The lemon tart and
the tiramisù are irresistible. There's also an excellent wine list. ✕ *Sir
Francis Drake Hwy., east of Road Town,* ☎ *809/495–2301. Reser-
vations advised. AE, MC, V. Closed Sun. No lunch.*

$$$ Skyworld. You'll want to arrive early for dinner at this mountaintop
aerie; the sunset views are breathtaking. Watch the western horizon
become ablaze with color, then settle back in the casually elegant dining room to feast on some delectable offerings. Try the veal in lemon
caper sauce, the local swordfish with sun-dried-tomato pesto, or the
passion-fruit sorbet. This is also a special place for lunch. Not only
are the sandwiches on home-baked bread delicious, but both the restaurant and the observation tower above offer the B.V.I.'s highest (and
absolutely breathtaking) 360-degree view of numerous islands and
cays. Even St. Croix (40 miles away) and Anegada (20 miles away) can
be seen on a clear day. ✕ *Ridge Rd.,* ☎ *809/494–3567. Reservations
advised. AE, MC, V.*

$$$ Sugar Mill Restaurant. The candles gleam and the background music
is pleasingly mellow in this well-known restaurant. The lovely stone
dining room is built in the ruins of a centuries-old sugar mill. The cop-
per cauldron that is now a bubbling fountain was once used for the

mill's rum production. Well-prepared selections on the à la carte menu include pasta and vegetarian entrées. House favorites are the spicy Caribbean sausage with Creole sauce, the mahogany glazed duck with sesame noodles, and His Majesty's West Indian Regimental beef curry. ✗ *Apple Bay,* ☎ *809/495–4355. Reservations advised. AE, MC, V.*

$$$ **The Upstairs.** Ask for a window table here and you'll be bathed in gen-
★ tle tropical breezes as you gaze out at the stars. Excellent service and food are hallmarks of this elegant and romantic restaurant overlooking a small marina. For a truly exceptional meal, try the filet mignon served with peaches and an outstanding port wine sauce. Other specialties include a delicious lobster au gratin appetizer, grilled local fish, roast duck, and key lime pie. A 10% service charge is included in the bill. ✗ *On Prospect Reef Hotel grounds (turn left just after the entrance), Road Town,* ☎ *809/494–2228. Reservations accepted. AE, MC, V.*

$$–$$$ **Pusser's Landing.** Yachters flock to the two-story home of this popular waterfront restaurant. Downstairs, belly up to the large, comfortable mahogany bar or choose a waterside table for drinks, sandwiches, or a light dinner. Head upstairs for quieter alfresco dining and a delightfully eclectic menu that includes homemade black bean soup, freshly grilled local fish, pasta, and such pub favorites as "bubble and squeak" (mashed potatoes with sautéed onions). The air-conditioned Dinner Theater, with its 15-foot screen, features fixed-price, three-course meals and showings of movies and sports events. ✗ *Soper's Hole,* ☎ *809/495–4554. Reservations accepted. AE, MC, V.*

$$ **The Apple.** This small, inviting restaurant is in a West Indian house. Soft candlelight creates a relaxed atmosphere for diners as they sample fish steamed in lime butter, conch or whelks in garlic sauce, and other local seafood dishes. There is a traditional West Indian barbecue and buffet every Sunday evening from 7 to 9. The excellent lunch menu includes a variety of sandwiches, meat and vegetarian lasagna, lobster quiche, seafood crepes, and croissants with ham and Swiss or spinach and feta. ✗ *Little Apple Bay,* ☎ *809/495–4437. Reservations accepted. AE, MC, V.*

$$ **C and F Restaurant.** Just outside Road Town, on a side street past the Moorings, is one of the island's most popular restaurants. Crowds head here for the best barbecue in town (chicken, fish, and ribs), fresh local fish prepared any way you wish, and excellent curries. Sometimes you have to wait for a table, but it is worth it. ✗ *Purcell Estate,* ☎ *809/494–4941. No reservations. No lunch. AE, MC, V.*

$$ **The Fishtrap.** Dine alfresco at this restaurant, which serves grilled local fish, steaks, and chicken. Friday and Saturday there's a barbecue with a terrific salad bar; Sunday prime rib is the special. ✗ *Columbus Centre, Wickham's Cay, Road Town,* ☎ *809/494–2636. Reservations accepted. AE, MC, V. No lunch Sun.*

$$ **Spaghetti Junction.** This funky spot is a hit with the boating crowd. Nightly specials complement the tasty and traditional Italian menu (veal or chicken parmigiana, pastas, etc.), and sun-dried tomato in the Caesar salad is a nice twist. Check out the gorilla in the rest room. ✗ *Waterfront Dr., Road Town,* ☎ *809/494–4880. No credit cards. Closed holidays and Sept. No lunch.*

$$ **Virgin Queen.** The sailing and rugby crowd and locals gather here to
★ play darts, drink beer, and eat Queen's Pizza (some say it's the best pizza in the Caribbean) or some of the excellent West Indian and English fare. A delicious menu includes saltfish, barbecued ribs with beans and rice, bangers and mash, shepherd's pie, and chili. ✗ *Fleming St., Road Town,* ☎ *809/494–2310. No reservations. No credit cards. Closed Sun.*

$–$$ **Capriccio di Mare.** The owners of the well-known Brandywine Bay restau-
★   rant (*see above*) also run this authentic Italian café. You can stop by
for cappuccino and a fresh pastry, or have a delicious meal of toast
Italiano (grilled ham and Swiss cheese sandwiches), perfectly cooked
linguine or penne with a variety of sauces, or crispy-crust tomato-and-
mozzarella pizza topped with hot Italian sausage or fresh grilled eggplant. Try the Mango Bellini, a mango and Italian sparkling wine
mixture that's a variation on the famous Bellini Cocktail served by
Harry's Bar in Venice. ✗ *Waterfront Dr., Road Town,* ☎ *809/494–
5369. No reservations. No credit cards.* ⊘ *8 AM–8 PM. Closed Sun.*

$–$$ **Fort Wine Gourmet.** French doors open onto a little outdoor café at
★   this charming spot. It's open all day and is a great spot for an espresso
or a cappuccino, a fresh pastry, or a tasty salad or sandwich. ✗ *Main
St., Road Town,* ☎ *809/494–3036. No reservations.* ⊘ *8 AM–6 PM.*

Virgin Gorda

$$$ **Drake's Anchorage.** You come by boat (provided free) to this serene
★   and romantic candlelit spot right at the water's edge. Dine on lobster,
dorado encrusted with bananas and bread crumbs, rack of lamb, or
steak au poivre. ✗ *North Sound,* ☎ *809/494–2252. Reservations
necessary. AE, MC, V.*

$$$ **Olde Yard Inn.** Civilized and charming, the dining room here is suf-
fused with gentle classical melodies and the scent of herbs. A cedar roof
covers the breezy, open-air room decorated with old-style Caribbean
charm. The French-accented cuisine includes lamb chops with mango
chutney, chicken breast in a rum cream sauce, and grilled local fish and
steaks. ✗ *The Valley, north of the marina,* ☎ *809/495–5544. Reservations advised. AE, MC, V.*

$$ **Bath and Turtle.** You can really sit back and relax at this informal
★   patio tavern with its friendly staff. Choose from the simple menu's
burgers, well-stuffed sandwiches, pizzas, pasta dishes, and daily spe-
cials. Live entertainment is presented on Wednesday and Sunday
nights. ✗ *Virgin Gorda Yacht Harbour,* ☎ *809/495–5239. Reser-
vations accepted. MC, V.*

$–$$ **Crab Hole.** Callaloo soup, saltfish, stewed goat, rice and peas, green
bananas, curried chicken roti, and other West Indian specialties are the
draw at this homey hangout. ✗ *The Valley,* ☎ *809/495–5307. Reservations accepted. No credit cards.*

Lodging

The number of rooms available in the B.V.I. is small compared with
that at other destinations in the Caribbean; what is available is also
often in great demand, and the prices are not low. The top-of-the-line
resorts here are among the most expensive in the Caribbean and are
sometimes difficult to book even off-season. Even the more moderately
priced hotels command top dollar during the season; off-season, however, they are legitimate bargains at about half the price. In addition,
many of the hotels offer rates that include all three meals.

CATEGORY	COST*
$$$$	over $300
$$$	$200–$300
$$	$100–$200
$	under $100

*All prices are for a standard double room in high season, excluding 7%
hotel tax and 10% service charge.*

Tortola

$$$ **Long Bay Beach Resort.** The mile-long arc of white sand from which
★ this resort gets its name graces the front of many a B.V.I. postcard. A
wide variety of accommodations includes 32 deluxe beachfront rooms,
with two queen-size beds or one king-size four-poster bed, marble-top
wet bars, and showers with Italian tiles. There are also smaller beach
cabanas, 10 rustic, tropical hideaways set on stilts at the water's edge.
Hillside choices include small but adequate rooms, studios with a
comfortable seating area, and roomy one- and two-bedroom villas; all
have balconies with lovely views. The Beach restaurant offers all-day
dining, and the Garden restaurant serves fixed-price three-course din-
ners in a romantic, candlelit setting. ☎ *Box 433, Road Town,* ☎
809/495–4252 or 800/729–9599, FAX *809/495–4677. 105 rooms. 2
restaurants, 2 bars, beach, pool, pitch-and-putt golf, small tennis court,
commissary. AE, MC, V. EP, MAP.*

$$$ **Sugar Mill Hotel.** The owners of this small, out-of-the-way hotel, Jeff
and Jinx Morgan, opened it two decades ago after becoming well-es-
tablished travel and food writers. The reception area, bar, and restaurant are in the ruins of a centuries-old sugar mill and are decorated
with bright Haitian artwork. Rather plain guest houses are scattered
on the hillside; the rooms are furnished in soft pastels and rattan and
have ceiling fans but no air conditioners. (Light sleepers may be disturbed by the roosters, who start crowing long before dawn.) There's
a circular swimming pool set into the hillside and a tiny beach where
lunch is served on a shady terrace. The Sugar Mill Restaurant is well
known on the island (*see* Dining, *above*). ☎ *Box 425, Road Town,* ☎
809/495–4355, FAX *809/495–4696. 20 rooms. Restaurant, 2 bars,
beach, pool, water sports. AE, MC, V. EP, MAP.*

$$–$$$ **Prospect Reef Resort.** A much-needed face-lift of this sprawling resort
overlooking Sir Francis Drake Channel included a fresh coat of paint
in bright pinks, purples, blues, and yellows and new fabrics in light
tropical prints to brighten the rooms. There are 11 types of units, including variously sized rooms with kitchenettes and two-story, two-
bedroom units with private interior courtyards. All have a balcony, patio,
or both and may face either the water or the hotel's gardens. There
are 7 acres of neatly manicured grounds with creative rock paths and
a network of lagoons. In addition to a large swimming pool and diving pool, Prospect Reef has a saltwater pool sectioned off from the sea
with large rocks and a narrow, artificial beach. The resort also has its
own harbor, where sailboats are available for day trips or longer excursions. ☎ *Box 104, Road Town,* ☎ *809/494–3311,* FAX *809/494–
5595. 131 rooms. 2 restaurants, beach, beachside snack bar, 2 bars, 3
pools, children's splash pool, 6 tennis courts, pitch-and-putt golf,
water sports, hair salon, gift shop, beachwear shop, commissary, conference center. AE, MC, V. EP.*

$$ **Fort Recovery.** The appealing one- to four-bedroom bungalows here are
★ built around the remnants of a Dutch fort, along a small beach facing
Sir Francis Drake Channel. The grounds are bright with tropical flow-
ers. All units have patios, kitchens, and equally excellent views. There's
no restaurant, but a new kitchen prepares elegant gourmet meals, which
waiters will deliver to your room. Yoga classes, exercise classes, mas-
sages, and fitness packages are available. ☎ *Box 239, Road Town,* ☎
809/495–4467, FAX *809/495–4036. 10 units. Beach, commissary sell-
ing basic food supplies and frozen homemade entrées. AE, MC, V. EP.*

$$ **Moorings-Mariner Inn.** Headquarters for the Moorings Charter operation and popular with yachting folk who find its full-service facilities
convenient and the companionship of fellow "boaties" congenial, this
is also a good choice for those who want to be within easy walking

distance of town. The atmosphere is a combination of laid-back and lively, and the rooms, including four suites, are large and comfortable. Rooms have peach tile floors and bright, tropical-print bedspreads and curtains; all also have a small kitchenette (with sink, refrigerator, and two-burner stove) and a balcony. Most rooms face the water, except for eight, which overlook the pool or the tennis court. ☎ *Box 139, Road Town,* ☎ *809/494–2331,* FAX *809/494–2226. 40 rooms. Restaurant, bar, pool, tennis court, volleyball court, dive shop, gourmet shop. AE, MC, V. EP.*

$$ Sebastian's on the Beach. Airy white rooms, simply decorated with flo-
★ ral-print curtains and bedspreads, have either terraces or balconies, some with great ocean views. Bathrooms have only stall showers, and there is no air-conditioning; but ceiling fans and louvered windows keep the rooms cool, and you are lulled to sleep by the sound of the ocean. The nonbeachfront rooms lack views and can be noisy, but they are just as big and are quite a bit cheaper than the beachfront rooms. The restaurant here is excellent. ☎ *Box 441, Road Town,* ☎ *809/495–4212,* FAX *809/495–4466. 26 rooms. Restaurant, bar, beach, water sports, commissary. AE. EP.*

$$ Treasure Isle Hotel. Paint in bright shades of lemon, violet, and mango pink covers the exterior of this pretty hillside property, which overlooks the harbor. The proximity of Road Town and several marinas makes this hotel a handy base. The air-conditioned rooms are spacious and accented with fabrics printed with Matisse-like patterns. Open to the breezes and the heady aroma of tropical flowers, the Spy Glass Bar with its comfortable lounge is the perfect place to relax and look out at a stunning view of the harbor and islands in the distance. There is daily transportation to Cane Garden Bay and Brewer's Bay. ☎ *Box 68, Road Town,* ☎ *809/494–2501,* FAX *809/494–2507. 40 rooms. Restaurant, 2 bars, pool, water sports. AE, MC, V. EP.*

$ Brewer's Bay Campground. If you care to camp, both prepared and bare sites are located on Brewer's Bay, one of Tortola's prime snorkeling spots. Check out the ruins of the distillery that gave the bay its name. There are public bathrooms but no showers. ☎ *Box 185, Road Town,* ☎ *809/494–3463. Beach, bar, restaurant, commissary, water sports, baby-sitters available.*

Virgin Gorda

$$$$ Biras Creek Hotel. You can reach this 150-acre secluded hideaway only by launch. The hilltop open-air bar and restaurant area is made of stonework and offers stunning views of North Sound. Each guest cottage has a bedroom, a living room, and a bathroom that opens out to a sensuous, open-air, walled shower. You can explore the grounds on foot or on bicycles provided by the hotel. There's a pool set right at the edge of the sea; and there's a beach for swimming, although it's a bit grassy. Sailing, boardsailing, and snorkeling equipment is available, and there are two lighted tennis courts. The atmosphere is one of casual elegance. ☎ *Box 54, North Sound,* ☎ *809/494–3555,* FAX *809/494–3557. 34 rooms. Restaurant, bar, 2 beaches, 2 lighted tennis courts, marina, pool, water sports, hiking and biking trails. AE, MC, V. FAP.*

$$$$ Bitter End Yacht Club and Marina. Stretching along the coastline of North
★ Sound, the BEYC enjoys panoramic views of the sound, Leverick Bay, and nearby islands. Accommodations range from exceptionally comfortable and appealing hillside or beachfront villas and chalets to liveaboard yachts. Also inviting about this property is the friendly, unpretentious welcome the staff extends to all its guests. The resort organizes daily snorkeling and diving trips to nearby reefs, windsurfing lessons, and excursions to local attractions, but the BEYC is most

touted for its Nick Trotter Sailing School. Judged by many to offer the best sailing instruction in the Caribbean, the school helps both seasoned salts and beginners sharpen their skills. When the sun goes down, the festivities continue at either the elegant Carvery, where themed buffets are served on special occasions, or at the Clubhouse, an open-air restaurant overlooking the sound. The hotel's character is one of the liveliest and most convivial in the B.V.I. ✆ *Box 46, North Sound,* ☎ *809/494–2746,* FAX *809/494–3557. 100 rooms. 2 restaurants, bar, beach, marina, pool. AE, MC, V. FAP.*

$$$$ **Little Dix Bay.** The luxury resort that first set the standards for under-
★ stated elegance in the B.V.I. was taken over by Rosewood Resorts and closed for the fall of 1993 for refurbishing. Telephones, new fabrics, and new furniture have been added to all rooms, and air-conditioning has been added to many rooms. There's a sophisticated Italian restaurant in the Sugar Mill; and dining in the open, peak-roofed Pavilion restaurant is a memorable experience. There are beautifully manicured lawns, the reef-protected beach is long and silken, and tennis, sailing, snorkeling, waterskiing, and bicycling are included in the rate. Popular with honeymooners and older couples who have been coming back for years, Little Dix may leave the single traveler feeling slightly left out. Nonetheless, the accommodations are superb, the service is thoughtful and attentive, and the setting is unforgettable. ✆ *Box 70,* ☎ *809/495–5555,* FAX *809/495–5661. 102 rooms. 3 restaurants, 2 bars, beach, water sports, marina, 7 tennis courts, boutique. AE, MC, V. EP, MAP, FAP.*

$$ **Guavaberry Spring Bay Vacation Homes.** These unusual hexagonal cottages are perched on stilts. You'll feel like you're in a tree house, amid the swaying branches and chirping birds. One- and two-bedroom units are situated on a hill, a short walk from a tamarind-shaded beach and not far from the mammoth boulders and cool basins of the famed Baths. ✆ *Box 20, Virgin Gorda,* ☎ *809/495–5227,* FAX *809/495–7367. 16 units. Commissary, beach. No credit cards. EP.*

$$ **Leverick Bay Resort.** The 16 hillside rooms of this small hotel are decorated in pastels and hung with original artwork. All rooms have refrigerators, balconies, and lovely views of North Sound. Four two-bedroom condos are also available. A Spanish colonial–style main building houses a restaurant operated by Pusser's of Tortola. A dive operation, crafts shop, commissary, coin-operated laundry, and beauty salon are also on-site. ✆ *Box 63,* ☎ *809/495–7421,* FAX *809/495–7367. 20 rooms. Restaurant, bar, beach, marina, pool, shopping arcade, water sports. AE, D, MC, V. EP.*

$$ **Olde Yard Inn.** Owners Charlie Williams and Carol Kaufman have cultivated a refreshingly unique atmosphere at this quiet retreat just outside Spanish Town. Classical music plays in the small bar; a large and varied collection of books lines the walls of the octagonal library cottage. The restaurant's French-accented menu is lovingly prepared and served with style in the high-ceilinged dining rooms. The guest rooms are cozy and simply furnished. At the end of 1994, a pool, a lunch restaurant that overlooks the pool, and a health club where you can work out, take exercise classes, and have massages were added. The inn is not on the beach; Savannah Bay and Pond Bay are a 20-minute walk away. You may want to request one of the air-conditioned rooms; the hotel's location in the Valley means trade winds are less noticeable here. ✆ *Box 26, Spanish Town,* ☎ *809/495–5544,* FAX *809/495–5986. 14 rooms. Restaurant, bar, library, horseback riding. AE, MC, V. EP, MAP.*

$ **The Wheelhouse.** You won't find any frills at this hotel, but it certainly is easy on the pocketbook, and it's conveniently close to the Virgin Gorda marina and shopping center. The cinder-block building has rooms that are air-conditioned and decorated with pastel print bedspreads and curtains. However, the rooms are still small, and the restaurant and bar can get noisy. ☎ *Box 66,* ☎ *809/495–5230. 12 rooms. Restaurant, bar. AE, MC, V. CP.*

Anegada

$$$ **Anegada Reef Hotel.** This hotel is away from it all in every sense of the phrase: It's the only hotel on Anegada, and the island itself is off the beaten path. Rooms are motel-like and rustic, but people come here for peace rather than luxury. Snorkeling and diving are as good here as anywhere else in the islands. Bonefishing in the flats is a favorite activity, and deep-sea fishing trips can be arranged. If you favor true laid-back living and absolutely no schedules, this is the spot for you. ☎ *Anegada,* ☎ *809/495–8002,* FAX *809/495–9362. 16 rooms. Restaurant, bar, beach, gift shop, water sports. MC, V. FAP.*

Guana Island

$$$$ **Guana Island Club.** Fifteen guest rooms are spread among seven houses scattered along a hillside on this totally private island. The houses are simply decorated in Caribbean style, with rattan furniture and ceiling fans, and each has a porch. The island's many trails make it a favorite spot for hikers, and it's a bird-watching paradise. ☎ *Box 32, Road Town, Tortola,* ☎ *809/494–2354,* FAX *914/967–8048. 15 rooms. Restaurant, wildlife sanctuary, tennis, croquet, hiking trails, water sports. No credit cards. FAP.*

Jost Van Dyke

$$ **Sandcastle.** This tiny, four-cottage hideaway (with a staff of five) is on a half mile of white beach on remote White Bay. There's "nothing" to do here, except maybe snooze in a hammock, read, gaze, walk, swim, rest, and savor sophisticated cuisine by candlelight. Arrangements can be made for diving, sailing, and sportfishing trips. ☎ *White Bay,* ☎ *809/775–5262,* FAX *809/775–5262. Restaurant, bar, beach. No credit cards.*

$$ **Sandy Ground Estates.** Tucked into the foliage along the edge of one of Jost Van Dyke's East End beaches is this collection of eight privately owned one- and two-bedroom houses. Each one is architecturally different, and interiors range from spartan to stylish. Kitchens are fully equipped and can be prestocked (you'll want to do this, since supplies are limited on the island), and there are four very casual restaurants within walking distance. ☎ *Sandy Ground, East End of Jost Van Dyke,* ☎ *809/495–3391. Beach. No credit cards.*

Mosquito Island

$$$$ **Drake's Anchorage.** Manager Albert Wheatley ensures that this small,
★ secluded getaway offers true privacy and the pampering of the more elegant resorts without the formality. Changing for dinner here means switching from a bathing suit to comfortable cottons. The three West Indian–style, waterfront bungalows contain 10 comfortably furnished rooms, including two suites. There are also two fully equipped villas for rent. There are hiking trails, water-sports facilities, four delightful beaches with hammocks here and there, and a highly regarded restaurant—a truly peaceful, rejuvenating experience. ☎ *Box 2510, North Sound, Virgin Gorda,* ☎ *809/494–2254 or 800/624–6651,* FAX *809/494–2254. Restaurant, bar, 4 beaches, water sports, hiking trails, gift shop. AE, MC, V. FAP.*

Necker Island

$$$$ **Necker Island.** You and 19 of your closest friends can rent this whole island. In fact, that's the only way you can stay at this ultraexpensive, ultrachic getaway, vacation spot of the likes of Princess Di and Oprah Winfrey. There are five beaches, many walks, a tennis court, and a luxurious villa with 20 spacious guest rooms. ⌘ *Necker Island,* ☎ *809/494–2757. 5 beaches, several sportfishing boats. AE, MC, V.*

Peter Island

$$$$ **Peter Island Resort and Yacht Harbour.** This luxury resort includes an
★ elegant restaurant, stunning freshwater pool, and tennis courts complete with a resident pro. There are also small sailboats, Sunfish, kayaks, mountain bicycles, Windsurfers, Hobie Cats, a 20-station fitness trail, an exercise room, 10 miles of walking trails, a dive shop, and a masseuse. The 50 beautiful guest rooms are in quadriplex cottages that are tucked among beds of radiant tropical flowers either at the edge of the beach or near the pool. This is a perfect romantic getaway. ⌘ *Box 211, Road Town, Tortola,* ☎ *809/494–2561 or 800/346–4451,* FAX *809/494–2313. 50 rooms, 2 villas. 2 restaurants, 2 bars, 5 beaches, pool, 4 lighted tennis courts, tennis pro, 2 gift shops, fitness trail, 5-star PADI dive facility, marina (limited services), helicopter pad. AE, MC, V. EP, MAP, FAP.*

Pusser's Marina Cay

$$ **Pusser's Hotel.** Pusser's took over Marina Cay in 1994, and now it's home to a Pusser's Restaurant, Pusser's Store, and this hotel. Six units are available—four rooms and two suites. Rooms are on the small side but are comfortably furnished and perched above the water's edge. The islet is quite small, and there's not much to do but relax. It's a great place to lie on the beach, get some sun, and snorkel. Ferry service is free from the dock on Beef Island. Call for ferry times, which vary with the season. ⌘ ☎ *809/494–2174. 6 units. Beach. AE, MC, V.*

Nightlife

Check the *Limin' Times,* which is published weekly, for current schedules. Generally, in-season schedules are close to what is listed below.

On Tortola, live bands play at **Pusser's Landing** (Soper's Hole, ☎ 809/494–4554) Thursday through Sunday, at the **Jolly Rodger** (West End, ☎ 809/495–4559) Friday and Saturday, at **Sebastian's** (Apple Bay, ☎ 809/495–4214) Saturday and Sunday, and at **Bomba's Shack** (Apple Bay, ☎ 809/495–4148) on Sunday, Wednesday, and every full moon. At **Quito's Gazebo** (Cane Garden Bay, ☎ 809/495–4837), B.V.I. recording star Quito Rhymer sings his own island ballads Sunday, Tuesday, Thursday, and Friday nights, starting at 8:30. **Stanley's Welcome Bar** (Cane Garden Bay, ☎ 809/495–4520) gets rowdy when crews stop by to party. On Virgin Gorda, **Andy's Chateau de Pirate** (Fischer's Cove Beach Hotel, The Valley, ☎ 809/495–5252) has live music and dancing on the weekends, and the **Bath and Turtle** has local bands Wednesday and Sunday evenings. One of the busiest nocturnal spots in the B.V.I. is little Jost Van Dyke. Check out **Rudy's Mariner Rendezvous** (☎ 809/495–9282), **Foxy's Tamarind** (☎ 809/495–9258), and **Sydney's Peace and Love** (☎ 809/495–9271).

8 Cayman Islands

Updated by
Melissa Rivers

THE VENERABLE OLD *SATURDAY EVENING POST* dubbed them "the islands that time forgot." But the past decade has changed all that: The Cayman Islands, a British Crown colony that includes Grand Cayman, Cayman Brac, and Little Cayman, are now one of the Caribbean's hottest destinations.

Why do metropolis-weary visitors trek 480 miles south of Miami, filling the hotels and condominiums that line famed Seven Mile Beach, even during the traditionally slow summer season? Their dollars certainly go farther in other Caribbean destinations, for in Grand Cayman—which positively reeks of suburban prosperity, bulging as it does with some 554 offshore banks located in George Town, the capital—the U.S. dollar is worth 80 Cayman cents, and the cost of living is 20% higher than in the United States.

Effective advertising accounts for some visitors, but the secret is word-of-mouth testimonials. The Cayman Islanders—the population is around 31,000, almost all of it residents of Grand Cayman—are renowned for the courteous and civil manners befitting their British heritage. Visitors will find no hasslers or panhandlers and no need to look apprehensively over their shoulder on dark evenings, for the colony enjoys a very low crime rate. Add to that permanent political and economic stability, and you have a fairly rosy picture.

The Caymans fully deserve their reputation as a paradise for divers: Translucent waters and a colorful variety of marine life are protected by the government, which has created a marine parks system in all three islands.

Columbus is said to have sighted the islands in 1503, but he didn't stop off to explore. He did note that the surrounding sea was alive with turtles, so the islands were named Las Tortugas. The name was later changed to Cayman.

The islands stayed largely uninhabited until the late 1600s, when Britain took over the Cayman Islands and Jamaica from Spain under the Treaty of Madrid. Cayman attracted a mixed bag of English, Dutch, Spanish, and French settlers, pirates, refugees from the Spanish Inquisition, shipwrecked sailors, and deserters from Oliver Cromwell's army in Jamaica. Today's Caymanians are the descendants of those nationalities.

The caves and coves of the islands—still fascinating to explore—were a perfect hideout for pirates like Blackbeard and Sir Henry Morgan, who plundered Spanish galleons hauling riches from the New World of South America to Spain. Many a ship also fell afoul of the reefs surrounding the islands, often with the help of the Caymanians, who lured the vessels to shore with beacon fires. Some of the old pioneer homes on the islands were made from the remains of those galleons.

The legend of the Wreck of the Ten Sails was to have a lasting effect on the Caymanians. In 1794, a convoy of 10 Jamaican ships bound for England foundered on the reefs, but the islanders managed to rescue everyone. Royalty was purportedly aboard, and a grateful George III decreed that Caymanians should forever be exempt from conscription and never have to pay taxes; however, research completed in 1994 shows this tale to be purely fictional.

The Cayman Islands are still a British colony. A governor appoints three official members to the Legislative Assembly and has to accept the advice of the Executive Council in all matters except foreign affairs, defense, internal security, and civil service appointments.

Before You Go

Tourist Information

For the latest information on activities and lodging, write or call any of the following offices of the **Cayman Islands Department of Tourism**: 6100 Waterford Bldg., 6100 Blue Lagoon Dr., Suite 150, Miami, FL 33126–2085, ☎ 305/266–2300; 2 Memorial City Plaza, 820 Gessner, Suite 170, Houston, TX 77024, ☎ 713/461–1317; 420 Lexington Ave., Suite 2733, New York, NY 10170, ☎ 212/682–5582; 9525 West Bryn Mawr Ave., Suite 160, Rosemont, IL 60018, ☎ 708/678–6446; 3440 Wilshire Blvd., Suite 1202, Los Angeles, CA 90010, ☎ 213/738–1968; 234 Eglinton Ave. E, Suite 306, Toronto, Ont. M4P 1K5, ☎ 416/485–1550; Trevor House, 100 Brompton Rd., Knightsbridge, London SW3 1EX, ☎ 0171/581–9960.

Arriving and Departing

BY PLANE

Cayman Airways (☎ 800/422–9626) flies nonstop to Grand Cayman from Miami two or three times daily, from Tampa four times a week, and from Houston and Atlanta three times a week. **American Airlines** (☎ 800/433–7300) has daily nonstop flights from both Miami and Raleigh/Durham, North Carolina. **Northwest** (☎ 800/447–4747) has regularly scheduled nonstop flights from Miami. **USAir** (☎ 800/428–4322) flies daily nonstop from Tampa and three times a week from Pittsburgh and Charlotte, North Carolina. **Cayman Airtours** (☎ 800/247–2966) offers package deals. Air service from Grand Cayman to Cayman Brac and Little Cayman is offered via Cayman Airways and **Island Air** (☎ 809/949–5152 or 800/922–9606). Flights land at Owen Roberts Airport, Gerrard-Smith Airport, or Edward Bodden Airfield. **Airport Information**: For flight information, call 809/949–5252.

Upon arrival, some hotels offer free pickup at the airport. Taxi service and car rentals are also available.

Passports and Visas

American and Canadian citizens do not have to carry passports, but they must show some proof of citizenship, such as a birth certificate or voter registration card, plus a return ticket. British and Commonwealth subjects do not need a visa but must carry a passport. Visitors to the islands cannot be employed without a work permit.

Language

English is spoken everywhere; all local publications are in English as well.

Precautions

Locals make a constant effort to conserve fresh water, so don't waste a precious commodity. Caymanians also strictly observe and enforce laws that prohibit collecting or disturbing endangered animal, marine, and plant life and historical artifacts found throughout the islands and surrounding marine parks; simply put, take only pictures and don't stand on reefs.

Penalties for drug and firearms importation and possession of controlled substances include large fines and prison terms.

Theft is not widespread, but be smart: Lock up your room and car and secure valuables as you would at home. Outdoors, marauding blackbirds called "ching chings" have been known to carry off jewelry if it is left out in the open.

There are several poisonous plants on the island—the maiden plum, the lady hair, and the manchineel tree. If in doubt, don't touch. The leaves

and applelike fruit of the machineel are poisonous to touch and should
be avoided; even raindrops falling from them can cause painful blisters.

Staying in the Cayman Islands

Important Addresses

Tourist Information: The main office of the **Department of Tourism** is
located in the Harbour Center (N. Church St., ☎ 809/949–0623). Information booths are at the airport (☎ 809/949–2635); in the George
Town Craft Market, on Cardinal Avenue, open when cruise ships are
in port (☎ 809/949–8342); and in the kiosk at the cruise ship dock
in George Town (no ☎). There is also an islandwide tourist hot line
(☎ 809/949–8989). You can also contact the **Tourist Information and
Activities Service** (☎ 809/949–6598, FAX 809/947–6222) day or night
for complete tourist information and free assistance in booking island
transportation, tours, charters, cruises, and other activities.

EMERGENCIES

Police and Hospitals: 911. **Ambulance**: 555. **Pharmacy**: Island Pharmacy (☎ 809/949–8987) in West Shore Centre on Seven Mile Beach.
Divers' Recompression Chamber: Call 809/949–4234 or 555.

Currency

Although the American dollar is accepted everywhere, you'll save
money if you go to the bank and exchange U.S. dollars for Cayman
Island (C.I.) dollars, which are worth about $1.20 each. The Cayman
dollar is divided into a hundred cents with coins of 1¢, 5¢, 10¢, and
25¢ and notes of $1, $5, $10, $25, $50, and $100. There is no $20
bill. Prices are often quoted in Cayman dollars, so it's best to ask. All
prices quoted here are in U.S. dollars unless otherwise noted.

Taxes and Service Charges

Hotels collect a 6% government tax and add a 10% service charge to
your bill. Many restaurants add a 10%–15% service charge. At press
time, the departure tax was C.I. $8. (U.S. $10).

Guided Tours

LAND TOURS

Guided day tours of the island can be arranged with **A.A. Transportation Services** (☎ 809/949–7222; ask for Burton Ebanks), **Majestic
Tours** (☎ 809/949–7773), **Reids Premier Tours** (☎ 809/949–6531),
Rudy's Travellers Transport (☎ 809/949–3208), and **Tropicana Tours**
(☎ 809/949–0944). Half-day tours average $25–$45 a person and generally include a visit to the Turtle Farm and Hell in West Bay, drives
along Seven Mile Beach and through George Town, and time for shopping downtown. In addition to those stops, full-day tours, which average $50–$65 per person and include lunch, also visit Bodden Town
to see pirate caves and graves and the East End to see blow holes on
the ironshore and the site of the famous Wreck of the Ten Sails.

AIR TOURS

Cayman Helicopter Tours (☎ 809/949–4400) operates a six-passenger,
air-conditioned helicopter that makes quick work of taking in the ge-
ographical features of Grand Cayman. The waters around the island
are so clear that you can see shipwrecks, stingrays, and shallow reefs
from the air. Fares start at around $150 per person.

WATER TOURS

The most impressive sights are underwater. Don't miss a trip on **Atlantis Submarines** (☎ 809/949–7700), which takes 48 passengers, a
driver, and a guide down along the Cayman Wall to depths of up to

100 feet for close-up views of the abundant, colorful marine life. This $2.8 million submarine has entertained hundreds of thousands of passengers, has all sorts of safety features, including a constantly circling surface monitor boat, and is air-conditioned. Through its large windows, you can see huge barrel sponges, corals in extraterrestrial-like configurations, strange eels, and schools of beautiful and beastly fish. Night dives are quite dramatic, because the artificial lights of the ship make the colors more vivid than they are in daytime excursions. Costs range from around $60 to $80 per person for trips from 45 minutes to an hour in length. The company also operates private trips on a research submersible that reaches depths of 800 feet. In the **Seaworld Explorer** (☎ 809/949–8534), passengers sit before windows in the hull of the boat just 5 feet below the surface, observing divers who swim around with food, attracting fish to the craft. The cost of this hour-long trip is $29, $19 for children 2–12.

Guided snorkeling trips, available through **Charter Boat Headquarters** (☎ 809/947–4340), **Captain Eugene's Watersports** (☎ 809/949–3099), and **Kirk Sea Tours** (☎ 809/949–6986), usually include stops at Stingray City Sandbar, Coral Garden, and Conch Bed, the top snorkel sites. Full-day trips include lunch prepared on the boat or onshore and cost under $40 per person; half-day trips average $25. Glass-bottom-boat trips cost around $23 and are available through **Aqua Delights** (☎ 809/947–4786), **Cayman Mermaid** (☎ 809/949–8100), and **Kirk Sea Tours** (☎ 809/949–6986).

Sunset sails, dinner cruises, and other themed (dance, booze, pirate, etc.) cruises are available aboard the *Jolly Roger* (☎ 809/949–8534), a replica of a 17th-century Spanish galleon; *Blackbeard's Nancy* (☎ 809/949–8988), a 1912 topsail schooner; and the *Spirit of Ppalu* (☎ 809/949–1234), a 65-foot glass-bottom catamaran. Party cruises typically run $15–$50 per person.

Getting Around

If your accommodations are along Seven Mile Beach, you can walk or bike to the shopping centers, restaurants, and entertainment spots along West Bay Road. George Town is small enough to see on foot. If you're touring Grand Cayman by car, there's a well-maintained road that circles the island; it's hard to get lost. If you want to see the sights or simply get away from the resort, you'll need a rental car or moped on Little Cayman and Cayman Brac; your hotel can make the arrangements for you. Otherwise, airport transfers are included in most resort rates, and many resorts offer bicycles for local sightseeing.

TAXIS

Taxis offer islandwide service. Fares are determined by an elaborate rate structure set by the government, and although it may seem pricey for a short ride (fare from Seven Mile Beach for four people to the airport ranges from $10 to $15), cabbies rarely try to rip off tourists. Ask to see the chart if you want to double-check the quoted fare. **A.A. Transportation** (☎ 809/949–7222), **Cayman Cab Team** (☎ 809/947–1173), and **Holiday Inn Taxi Stand** (☎ 809/947–4491) offer 24-hour service.

RENTAL CARS

Grand Cayman is relatively flat and fairly easy to negotiate if you're careful of the traffic. To rent a car, bring your current driver's license, and the car-rental firm will issue you a temporary permit ($5). Most firms have a range of models available, from compacts to Jeeps to minibuses. Rates range from $35 to $55 a day. The major agencies have offices in a plaza across from the airport terminal, where you can pick up and drop off vehicles. Just remember, driving is on the left.

Car-rental companies are **Ace Hertz** (☎ 809/949–2280 or 800/654–3131), **Budget** (☎ 809/949–5605 or 800/527–0700), **Cico Avis** (☎ 809/949–2468 or 800/331–1212), **Coconut** (☎ 809/949–4037 or 800/262–6687), **Dollar** (☎ 809/949–4790), **Economy** (☎ 809/949–9550), **Soto's 4X4** (☎ 809/945–2424), and **Thrifty** (☎ 809/949–6640 or 800/367–2277).

BICYCLES AND SCOOTERS
When renting a motor scooter or bicycle, don't forget the sunblock and that driving is on the left. Bicycles ($10–$15 a day) and scooters ($25–$30 a day) can be rented from **Bicycles Cayman** (☎ 809/949–5572), **Cayman Cycle** (☎ 809/947–4021), and **Soto Scooters** (☎ 809/947–4363).

Telephones and Mail

For international dialing to Cayman, the area code is 809. To call outside, dial 0 + 1 + area code and number. You can call anywhere, anytime, through the cable and wireless system and local operators. To make local calls, dial the seven-digit number. To place credit-card calls, dial 110.

Beautiful stamps are available at the main post office in downtown George Town and at the philatelic office in West Shore Plaza. Both are open weekdays from 8:30 to 3:30 and Saturday from 8:30 to 11:30. Sending a postcard to the United States, Canada, the Caribbean, or Central America costs C.I.15¢. An airmail letter is C.I.30¢ per half ounce. To Europe and South America, the rates are C.I.20¢ for a postcard and C.I.40¢ per half ounce for airmail letters.

Opening and Closing Times

Banking hours are generally Monday–Thursday 9–2:30 and Friday 9–1 and 2:30–4:30. Shops are open Monday–Friday 9–5, and on Saturday in George Town from 10 to 2; in outer shopping plazas, from 10 to 5. Shops are usually closed on Sunday except in hotels.

Exploring the Cayman Islands

Numbers in the margin correspond to points of interest on the Grand Cayman map.

George Town

❶ Begin exploring **George Town** at the **Cayman Islands National Museum** on Harbour Drive, slightly south of the Cruise Ship Dock Gazebo. Built in 1833, this building was used as a courthouse, a jail (where the gift shop is now), a post office, and a dance hall before being reopened in 1990 as a museum. It is small but fascinating, with excellent displays and videos illustrating the history of Cayman plant, animal, human, and geological life. Pick up a walking tour map of George Town at the museum gift shop before leaving. *Harbour Dr.,* ☎ *809/949–8368.* ☛ *$5 adults, $2.50 students and senior citizens.* ⊙ *Weekdays 9–5, Sat. 10–4.*

From the museum, turn right onto Harbour Drive for a leisurely stroll along the waterfront. The circular gazebo is where visitors from the cruise ships disembark. Diagonally across the street is the **Elmslie Memorial United Church,** named after Scotsman James Elmslie, the first Presbyterian missionary to serve in the Caymans. The church was the first concrete block building built in the Cayman Islands. Its vaulted ceiling, wood arches, and sedate nave reflect the quietly religious nature of island residents.

Continue north on Harbour Drive (which becomes North Church Street) past the **War Memorial** erected in memory of the Caymanian Royal Navy volunteers who died in defense of Great Britain during World Wars I and II. Next you come to **Fort George Park,** established to preserve the stone wall remnants of the circa-1790 fort, reputedly one of the smallest ever built in the Caribbean.

TIME OUT   Follow your nose north on North Church Street to the **Wholesome Bakery and Café** (☎ 809/949-7588), which adds the homey smell of baking bread to the sea breezes off George Town Harbour. Stop in here for the delectable meat patties, generous slices of pie, and coconut or rum raisin ice cream.

Backtrack and turn left onto **Fort Street,** a main shopping street where you'll find the People's Boutique, the Kennedy Gallery, and a whole row of jewelry shops featuring black coral, gold and silver, gemstones, and treasure coins—Peter Davey, Bernard Passman, Smith's, Savoy Jewellers, and the Jewellery Centre.

At the end of the block is the heart of downtown George Town. At the corner of Fort Street and **Edward Street,** notice the small clock tower dedicated to Britain's King George V and the huge fig tree manicured into an umbrella shape. Here, too, is a new statue (unveiled in 1994) of national hero James Bodden, the father of Cayman tourism. Across the street is the **Cayman Islands Legislative Assembly Building,** next door to the 1919 **Peace Memorial Building.**

Turning right on Edward Street, you'll find the charming **library,** built in 1939; it has English novels, current newspapers from the United States, and a small reference section. It's worth a visit just for the Old World atmosphere and a look at the shields depicting Britain's prominent institutions of learning that decorate the ceiling beams. Across the street is the **courthouse.** Down the next block is the financial district, where banks from all over the world have offices.

Straight ahead is the **General Post Office,** also built in 1939, with its strands of decorative colored lights and some 2,000 private mailboxes on the outside. (Mail is not delivered on the island.) Behind the post office is **Elizabethan Square,** a shopping and office complex on Shedden Road that houses various food, clothing, and souvenir establishments. The courtyard, with benches around a pleasant garden and fountain, is a good place to rest your feet.

Exiting Elizabethan Square onto Shedden Road and walking past Anderson Square and Caymania Freeport, turn right back onto Edward Street, then left at the Royal Bank of Canada onto **Cardinal Avenue.** This is the main shopping area. On the right is the chic Kirk Freeport Plaza, known for its fine jewelry, plus duty-free china, crystal, Gucci items, perfumes, and fine cosmetics.

Turn left on Harbour Drive and make your way back to Shedden Road, passing the English Shoppe, a souvenir outlet that looks more as if it belongs on Shaftesbury Avenue in London than in the West Indies, and Artifacts, with its maritime antiques.

 The **Cayman Maritime Treasure Museum,** a quick taxi ride away on West Bay Road, in front of the Hyatt Regency, is a real find. Dioramas show how Caymanians became seafarers, boatbuilders, and turtle breeders. An animated figure of Blackbeard the Pirate spins salty tales about the pirates and buccaneers who "worked" the Caribbean. Since the museum is owned by a professional treasure-salvaging firm, it's not surprising that there are a lot of artifacts from shipwrecks. *West Bay Rd.,* ☎ *809/947–5033.* ☛ *$5 adults, $3 children 6–12.* ☺ *Mon.–Sat. 9–5.*

The Outer Districts

To see the rest of the island, rent a car or scooter, or take a guided tour (*see above*). A full-day guided tour (sufficient to see the major sites) is comparable in cost to a single day of car rental. The flat road that circles the island is in good condition, with clear signs; you'd have to work to get lost here. Venturing away from the Seven Mile Beach strip, you'll encounter the more down-home character of the islands.

At the other end of the island is the **West Bay** community, home to numerous gingerbread-trimmed homes of historic interest (a walking tour brochure is available from the tourist office). One such home is ❸ the **Old Homestead,** formerly known as the West Bay Pink House and probably the most photographed home in Grand Cayman. The picturesque pink-and-white Caymanian cottage was built in 1912 of wattle and daub around an ironwood frame, and tours, led by cheery Mac Bothwell, who grew up in the house, present a nostalgic and touching look at life in Grand Cayman before the tourism and banking boom. *West Bay Rd.,* ☎ *809/949–7639.* ☛ *$5.* ☺ *Mon.–Sat. 8–5.*

❹ The **Cayman Island Turtle Farm,** started in West Bay in 1968, is the most popular attraction on the island today, with some 200,000 visitors a year. There are turtles of all ages, from Ping-Pong-ball-size eggs to day-old hatchlings to huge 600-pounders that can live to be 100 years old. The Turtle Farm was set up both as a conservation and a commercial enterprise; it releases about 5% of its stock back out to sea every year, harvests turtles for local restaurants, and exports the by-products. (Note: U.S. citizens cannot take home any turtle products because of a U.S. regulation banning their import.) In the adjoining café, you can sample turtle soup or turtle sandwiches while looking over an exhibit about turtles. *West Bay Rd.,* ☎ *809/949–3893.* ☛ *$5 adults, $2.50 children 6–12.* ☺ *Daily 8:30–5.*

The other area of West Bay that is of brief interest is the tiny village ❺ of **Hell,** which is little more than a patch of incredibly jagged rock formations called ironshore. The big attraction here is a small post office, which sells stamps and postmarks cards from Hell, and lots of T-shirt and souvenir shops. Almost unbelievably, a nearby nightclub, called the Club Inferno, is run by the McDoom family.

Head south to South West Point on South Church Street, then east as the road becomes South Sound Road for a straight shot along the is-❻ land's southern edge. In the Savannah district, **Pedro's Castle,** built in 1780, lays claim to being the oldest structure on the island. Legends linked to the structure abound, but what is known is that the building was struck by lightning in 1877 and left in ruins until bought by a restaurateur in the 1960s. Gutted once again by fire in 1970, the building was purchased by the government in 1991 for restoration as a historic landmark and remains cordoned off by a chain-link fence, closed to the public until restoration is complete (perhaps in 1996).

❼ At **Bodden Town**—the island's original capital—you'll find an old cemetery on the shore side of the road. Graves with A-frame structures are said to contain the remains of pirates, but, in fact, they may be those of early settlers. A curio shop serves as the entrance to what's called the **Pirate's Caves,** partially underground natural formations that are

Grand Cayman

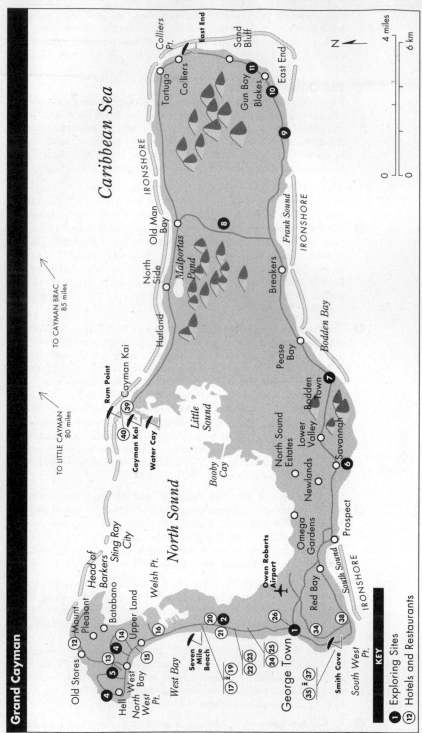

Caribbean Sea

TO CAYMAN BRAC
85 miles

TO LITTLE CAYMAN
80 miles

East End

Sand
Bluff

Colliers
Pt.

Colliers

Tortuga

East End

Gun Bay
Blakes

East End

11

10

9

IRONSHORE

IRONSHORE

*Malportas
Pond*

Old Man
Bay

Breakers

Frank Sound

North
Side

IRONSHORE

8

Hutland

Bodden Bay

Pease
Bay

Bodden
Town

Lower
Valley

7

Savannah

6

North Sound
Estates

Newlands

Prospect

South Sound

Omega
Gardens

Rum Point

39

Cayman Kai

40

Cayman Kai

Water Cay

North Sound

*Little
Sound*

*Booby
Cay*

Head of
Barkers

*Sting Ray
City*

Batabano

Mount
Pleasant

Old Stores

12

13

5

4

Hell

North
West
Pt.

West
Bay

4

14

Upper Land

15

16

Welsh Pt.

West Bay

**Seven
Mile
Beach**

20

2

21

17 **19**

22 **23**

24 **25**

26

**Owen Roberts
Airport**

Red Bay

George Town

1

34

35 **37**

Smith Cove

38

*South West
Pt.*

IRONSHORE

N

4 miles

6 km

0

0

KEY

1 Exploring Sites

12 Hotels and Restaurants

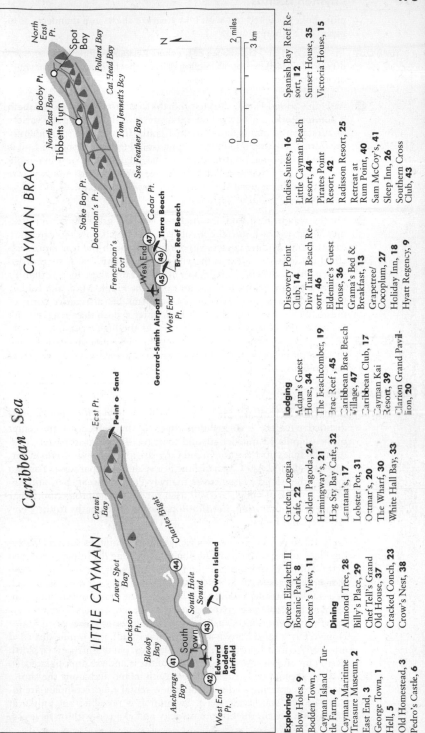

Caribbean Sea

LITTLE CAYMAN

CAYMAN BRAC

Exploring
Blow Holes, 9
Bodden Town, 7
Cayman Island Turtle Farm, 4
Cayman Maritime Treasure Museum, 2
East End, 3
George Town, 1
Hell, 5
Old Homestead, 3
Pedro's Castle, 6
Queen Elizabeth II Botanic Park, 8
Queen's View, 11

Dining
Almond Tree, 28
Billy's Place, 29
Chef Tell's Grand Old House, 37
Cracked Conch, 23
Crow's Nest, 38
Garden Loggia Cafe, 22
Golden Pagoda, 24
Hemingway's, 21
Hog Sty Bay Cafe, 32
Lantana's, 17
Lobster Pot, 31
Ortmar's, 20
The Wharf, 30
White Hall Bay, 33

Lodging
Adam's Guest House, 34
The Beachcomber, 19
Brac Reef, 45
Caribbean Brac Beach Village, 47
Caribbean Club, 17
Cayman Kai Resort, 39
Clarion Grand Pavilion, 20
Discovery Point Club, 14
Divi Tiara Beach Resort, 46
Eldemire's Guest House, 36
Grama's Bed & Breakfast, 13
Grapetree/Cocoplum, 27
Holiday Inn, 18
Hyatt Regency, 9
Indies Suites, 16
Little Cayman Beach Resort, 44
Pirates Point Resort, 42
Radisson Resort, 25
Retreat at Rum Point, 40
Sam McCoy's, 41
Sleep Inn, 26
Southern Cross Club, 43
Spanish Bay Reef Resort, 12
Sunset House, 35
Victoria House, 15

more hokey (decked out with fake treasure chests and mannequins in pirate garb) than spooky.

TIME OUT   The large and airy **Lighthouse at Breakers Restaurant** (Breakers, ☎ 809/947–2047) has booth seating around spectacular waterfront windows and offers seafood and Italian cuisine.

⑧ At Frank Sound Road, turn left (north) to get to the **Queen Elizabeth II Botanic Park,** a 60-acre wilderness preserve showcasing the variety of habitats and plants native to the islands. Interpretive signs identify the flora along the mile-long walking trail. Halfway along the trail is a walled compound housing the rare blue iguana found only in remote sections of the Caymans. You will also see native orchids and, if you're lucky, the brilliant green Cayman parrot. *Frank Sound Rd.,* ☎ *809/947–9462.* ✆ *$3.* ☺ *Daily 7:30–5:30.*

⑨ On the way to East End are the **Blow Holes,** a great photo opportunity as waves crash into the fossilized coral beach, forcing water into caverns and sending geysers shooting up through the ironshore (cal-
⑩ cified coral ledge). Next is the village of **East End,** the first recorded settlement on the island. Its major claim to fame these days is that it's where a renowned local musician called the Fiddle Man, aka Radley Gourzong, lives and occasionally performs his distinctive form of music (more akin to Louisiana's backwater zydeco than reggae) with his band, the Happy Boys. Farther on, as the highway curves north,
⑪ you'll come to **Queen's View** lookout point and a monument dedicated by Queen Elizabeth in 1994 to commemorate the legendary **Wreck of the Ten Sails,** which took place just offshore.

Cayman Brac

Brac, the Gaelic word for "bluff," aptly identifies this island's most distinctive feature, a rugged limestone cliff that runs down the center of the island's 12-mile length and soars to 140 feet at its eastern end. Lying 89 miles northeast of Grand Cayman, accessible via Cayman Airways and Island Air, Cayman Brac is a spelunker's paradise: You can explore the island's large **caves** (namely Peter's, Great, Bat, and Rebeka's), some of which are still used for hurricane protection. Wear sneakers for exploring, not flip-flops; some of the paths to the caves are steep and rocky.

Only 1,200 people live on this island, in communities such as Watering Place and Spot Bay. In addition to displaying the implements used in the daily lives of Bracers in the 1920s and 1930s, the two-room **Cayman Brac Museum** (☎ 809/948–2622) showcases a few oddities, such as a 4,000-year-old Viking ax. The variety of Brac flora includes unusual orchids, mangoes, papaya, agave, and cacti. The endangered Cayman Brac parrot is most easily spotted in the **Parrot Preserve** on Major Donald Drive (also known as Lighthouse Road); this 6-mile dirt road also leads to ironshore cliffs that offer the best panoramic view of North East Point and the open ocean. Parts of the island are unpopulated, so you can explore truly isolated areas both inland and along the shore. Two hotels catering to divers and a new rental condo complex are located on the southwest coast. Swimming is possible, but unlike at Seven Mile Beach, the bottom is rocky and clogged with turtle grass.

Little Cayman

Only 7 miles away from Cayman Brac is Little Cayman Island, which has a population of about 50 (only 20 or so full-timers) on its 12 square miles. This is a true hideaway: few phones, fewer shops, no nightlife—just spectacular diving, great fishing, and laid-back camaraderie. Visitor accommodations are mostly in small lodges. In addition to privacy, the real attractions of Little Cayman are diving in spectacular **Bloody Bay,** off the north coast, and fishing, which includes angling for tarpon and bonefish. You can also go birding at the **Governor Gore Bird Sanctuary,** established in 1994 and home to 5,000 pairs of red-footed boobys (the largest colony in the Western Hemisphere) and 1,000 magnificent frigate birds.

And if Little Cayman ever gets too busy, there is one final retreat—**Owen Island,** which is just 200 yards offshore. Accessible by rowboat, it is in the middle of a blue lagoon and has a sandy beach. Take your own picnic if you plan to spend the day.

What to See and Do with Children

The kids won't want to miss a dive on **Atlantis Submarine** (*see* Guided Tours, *above*); rides on the **Seaworld Explorer** or glass-bottom boats run a close second. They are also usually pleased with a visit to West Bay's **Hell** (perhaps because the name makes them snicker) and the **Turtle Farm** (*see* Exploring the Cayman Islands, *above*). **Pirate's Caves** in Bodden Town (*see* Exploring the Cayman Islands, *above*) may keep the little ones entertained but probably won't interest teens.

Older children can enjoy many of the water sports and beach games available. Only the Hyatt Regency has a children's program. Other hotels politely say that they do not organize children's activities; be prepared to do so yourself.

Off the Beaten Track

If you are driving around, stop by the conch house, an architectural oddity located across from the power plant. The house was constructed of conch shells years ago, but a recent renovation has added modern skylights and a garish satellite dish in the front yard.

Carey Cayman Coral (no ☎) is a workshop out on South Sound Road, east of the Crow's Nest Restaurant, run by Carey Hurlstone. Carey, a gentle bear of a man with tattoos covering his skin, professes he was a biker with the Hell's Angels before coming home to Cayman to work as a craftsman. He makes black coral jewelry and figurines and carves glass. Carey's workmanship is superb, and his prices are quite reasonable for the quality.

Beaches

Grand Cayman

You may read or hear about the "dozens of beaches" of these islands, but that's more exaggeration than reality. Grand Cayman's west coast, the most developed area of the entire colony, is where you'll find its famous **Seven Mile Beach** (actually 5½ miles long) and its expanses of powdery white sand. The beach is litter-free and sans peddlers, so you can relax in an unspoiled, hassle-free (if somewhat crowded) atmosphere. This is also Grand Cayman's busiest vacation center, and most of the island's accommodations, restaurants, and shopping centers are on this strip. You'll find headquarters for the island's aquatic activities in various places along the strip (*see* Sports and the Outdoors, *below*).

Grand Cayman has several smaller beaches that may better be called coves, including **Smith Cove,** off South Church Street, south of the Grand Old House—a popular bathing spot with residents on weekends.

The best shore-entry snorkeling locations are off the ironshore south of George Town, at **Eden Rock** (☎ 809/949–7243) and **Parrot's Landing** (☎ 809/949–7884); north of town, at the reef just off the **West Bay Cemetery** on Grand Cayman's west coast; and in the reef-protected shallows of the island's north and south coasts, where coral and fish life are much more varied and abundant.

The best windsurfing is just off the beaches in **East End,** at Colliers, by Morritt's Tortuga Club. The beach can be lovely if it's kept clean of seaweed tossed ashore by trade winds, but the windsurfing is the real draw here. Seldom discovered by visitors unless they're staying here are the beautiful beach areas of **Cayman Kai** (which was undergoing some development at press time), **Rum Point,** and, even more isolated and unspoiled, **Water Cay.** These are favored hideaways for residents and popular Sunday picnic spots.

Cayman Brac

The resorts and rental condos on the **southwest coast** have fine small beaches, better for sunning than for snorkeling because of the abundance of turtle grass in the water. Excellent snorkeling can be found immediately offshore of the now-defunct **Buccaneer's Inn** on the north coast.

Little Cayman

The beaches **Point o' Sand,** on the eastern tip, and **Owen Island,** off the south coast, are isolated patches of powder that are great for sunbathing and worth every effort to reach by car, bike, or boat.

Sports and the Outdoors

Deep-Sea Fishing

If you enjoy action fishing, Cayman waters have plenty to offer—blue and white marlin, yellowfin tuna, sailfish, dolphin, and wahoo. Bonefish and tarpon are also plentiful off Little Cayman. Some 25 boats are available for charter, offering fishing options that include deep-sea, reef, bone, tarpon, light-tackle, and fly-fishing. Grand Cayman charter operators to contact are **Charter Boat Headquarters** (☎ 809/947–4340), **Crosby Ebanks** (☎ 809/947–4049), **Island Girl** (☎ 809/947–3029), and **Bayside Watersports** (☎ 809/949–3200). Little Cayman operators are **Sam McCoy's Fishing & Diving** (☎ 809/949–2891 or 800/626–0496) and **Southern Cross Club** (☎ 800/899–2582). In 1984 June was dubbed Million Dollar Month; registered anglers can win cash and vacation prizes by landing record-breaking catches. Five tournaments are held, each with its own rules, records, and entrance fees. For information and applications, write to the Million Dollar Month Committee (Box 878 GT, Grand Cayman, Cayman Islands, B.W.I.).

Diving and Snorkeling

To say that the Cayman Islands are a scuba diver's paradise is not overstating the case. Jacques Cousteau called Bloody Bay (off Little Cayman) one of the world's top dives, and the famed Cayman Wall, off Grand Cayman, ranks up there as well. Pristine water (often exceeding 100-foot visibility), breathtaking coral formations, and plentiful and exotic marine life await divers. A host of top-notch dive operations offer a variety of services, instruction, and equipment. A Grand Cayman must-see for adventurous souls is **Stingray City,** which has been called the best 12-foot dive (or snorkel) in the world. Here are dozens of unusually tame stingrays who, accustomed to being fed first by fishermen and now by divers, suction squid off divers' outstretched palms and gracefully swim and twist around the divers in the shallow waters.

Divers are required to be certified and possess a "C" card or take a short resort or full certification course. A certification course, including classroom, pool, and boat sessions as well as checkout dives, takes four to six days and costs $350–$400. A short resort course usually lasts a day and costs about $80–$100. It introduces the novice to the sport and teaches the rudimentary skills needed to make a shallow, instructor-monitored dive.

All dive operations on Cayman are more than competent; among them are **Aquanauts** (☎ 809/945–1990 or 800/357–2212), **Bob Soto's** (☎ 809/947-4631 or 800/262–7686), **Don Foster's** (☎ 809/949–5679 or 800/833–4837), **Eden Rock** (☎ 809/949–7243), **Parrot's Landing** (☎ 809/949–7884 or 800/448–0428), **Red Sail Sports** (☎ 809/949–8745 or 800/ 255–6425), and **Sunset Divers** (☎ 809/949–7111 or 800/854– 4767). Request full information on all operators from the Department of Tourism (*see* Before You Go, *above*). A single-tank dive averages $45; a two-tank dive, about $55. Snorkel-equipment rental runs from $5 to $15 a day, so consider purchasing your own before you come.

On Cayman Brac, **Brac Aquatics** (☎ 809/949–1429 or 800/544– 2722) and **Divi Tiara** (☎ 809/948–1553 or 800/367–3484) offer scuba and snorkeling. On Little Cayman, contact **Paradise Divers** (☎ 809/948– 0004 or 800/450 2084), **Reef Divers** (☎ 809/948–1033), **Sam McCoy's Fishing & Diving** (☎ 809/949–2891 or 800/626–0496), or the **Southern Cross Club** (☎ 800/899–2582). Each hotel also has its own instructors.

Most operations can rent all diving gear, including equipment for underwater photography; Bob Soto's, Don Foster's, Fisheye Photographic, and Sunset U/W Photo have facilities for film processing and underwater photo courses.

One-week live-aboard dive cruises are available aboard the 110-foot *Cayman Aggressor III* (☎ 800/348–2628) and the luxury yacht *Little Cayman Diver II* (☎ 800/458–2722).

Fitness

Most hotels and resorts offer fitness facilities. **Nautilus Fitness Center** (Seven Mile Beach, Grand Cayman, ☎ 809/949–5132) has machines, weights, a sauna, and a whirlpool. Daily membership is $10; weekly, $25.

Golf

The **Grand Cayman–Britannia** golf course (☎ 809/949–8020), next to the Hyatt Regency, was designed by Jack Nicklaus. The course is really three in one—a 9-hole par-70 regulation course, an 18-hole par-57 executive course, and a Cayman course (played with a Cayman ball that goes about half the distance of a regulation ball). Greens fees range from $40 to $80. Golf carts ($15–$25) are mandatory.

Windier, and therefore more challenging, is the **Links at Safe Haven** (☎ 809/949–5988), Cayman's first 18-hole championship golf course. The Roy Case–designed par-71, 6,519-yard course also has an aqua driving range (the distance markers and balls float), a two-story clubhouse, locker rooms, a pro shop, a patio bar with live jazz happy hours on weekends, and a fine restaurant serving Continental and Caribbean cuisine daily for lunch and dinner. Greens fees run to $60. Golf carts ($15–$20 per person) are mandatory.

Tennis

Most hotels and condo complexes have tennis courts for guests.

Water Sports

Water skis, Windsurfers, Hobie Cats, and Jet Skis are available at many of the aquatic shops along Seven Mile Beach (*see* Diving, *above*). **Sailboards Caribbean** (☎ 809/949–1068) offers windsurfing rentals, lessons for beginners, and a full gamut of courses through high-wind advanced levels. **Cayman Windsurf** (☎ 809/947–7492) offers windsurfing lessons and rentals at the East End of the island at Morritt's Tortuga Club and on North Sound by Safe Haven.

Shopping

Grand Cayman has two money-saving attributes—duty-free merchandise and the absence of a sales tax. Prices on imported merchandise—English china, Swiss watches, French perfumes, and Japanese cameras and electronic goods—are often lower than elsewhere, but not always. To make sure you get a bargain, come prepared with a price list of items you are thinking of buying and comparison shop. Unusual jewelry can also be found, ranging from authentic sunken treasure and ancient coins made into necklaces and pins to relatively inexpensive rings and earrings made from semiprecious stones, coral, and seashells. **Tortuga Rum Company's** (☎ 809/949–7701 or 949–7866/7) scrumptious rum cake makes a great souvenir.

Good Buys

ARTS AND CRAFTS

Debbie van der Bol runs an arts-and-crafts shop called **Pure Art** (☎ 809/949–9133) on South Church Street and at the Hyatt Regency (☎ 809/947–5633). She sells watercolors, wood carvings, and lacework by local artists, as well as her own sketches and cards. Original prints, paintings, and sculpture with a tropical theme are found at **Island Art Gallery** (☎ 809/949–9861) in the Anchorage Shopping Center in George Town. The **Kennedy Gallery** (☎ 809/949–8077), in West Shore Center and on Fort Street in George Town, features primarily limited edition pastel watercolors of typical Cayman scenes by Robert E. Kennedy.

The **Heritage Crafts Shop** (☎ 809/949–7093), near the harbor in George Town, sells local crafts and gifts. The **West Shore Shopping Center,** on Seven Mile Beach near the Radisson, offers good-quality island art, beachwear, ice cream, and more. The **Queen's Court Shopping Center,** on Seven Mile Beach close to town, was just opening at press time and promises to offer an array of souvenirs, crafts, and gifts.

BLACK CORAL

Black coral products are exquisite and a popular choice. However, environmental groups discourage tourists from purchasing any coral that is designated as endangered species, because the reefs are not always harvested carefully. If you feel differently, there are a number of local craftsmen who create original designs and finish their own work. The coral creations of **Bernard Passman** (Fort St., George Town, ☎ 809/949–0123) won the approval of the English royal family. Beautiful coral pieces are also found at **Richard's Fine Jewelry** (Harbour Dr., George Town, ☎ 809/949–7156), where designers Richard and Rafaela Barile attract their fair share of celebrities.

Dining

Grand Cayman's restaurants satisfy every palate and pocketbook. Gourmet Continental cuisine is available to the high rollers; ethnic food can be had at moderate prices. West Indian fare in dining spots serving locals is the best in taste and value.

Seafood, not surprisingly, appears on most restaurant menus. Fish—including grouper, snapper, dolphin, tuna, wahoo, and marlin—is served either simply (baked, broiled, steamed) or Cayman-style, with peppers, onions, and tomatoes. Conch, the meat of a large pink mollusk, is ubiquitous in stews and chowders and as fritters or panfried ("cracked"). Caribbean lobster is available but is often quite expensive, and other shellfish are in short supply in local waters. The only traditional culinary treat of the islands is turtle soup, stew, or steak, but fewer restaurants carry it these days (all that do purchase it from the Turtle Farm).

Dining out on Grand Cayman can be expensive, so replenish your billfold, because some places do not accept plastic. Many restaurants add a 10%–15% service charge to the bill, so check before leaving an additional tip.

What to Wear

Smart casual wear (slacks and sundresses) is acceptable throughout the Caymans for dinner in all but a few places. The nicer resorts and more expensive restaurants may require a jacket, especially in high season; ask when making reservations. Shorts are usually acceptable during the day, but unless you're going to an ultracasual beach bar, beachwear (bathing suits, cover-ups, tank tops, etc.) is a no-no. Most restaurants have an alfresco dining section, and if you plan to dine under the stars, do take advantage of the bug spray they provide—the mosquitoes are fierce after sunset.

All the restaurants reviewed below are on Grand Cayman, because there are few to none on the sister islands (visitors eat at the resorts and guest houses).

CATEGORY	COST*
$$$	over $30
$$	$20–$30
$	under $20

per person, excluding drinks and service charge

$$$ **Chef Tell's Grand Old House.** ★ TV celebrity chef Tell Erhardt has been running this popular establishment since 1986. His menu features Continental entrées and a few local specialties. Among the spicier appetizer choices is fried coconut shrimp with mustard apricot sauce. On the milder side are entrées such as lobster "The Chef's Way," dipped in egg batter and sautéed with shallots, mushrooms, and white wine, and coffee lacquered duck with fresh pear chutney. The oceanside gazebos, surrounded by palms and cooled by ceiling fans, are the liveliest and best spots for dining. The excellent service adds to this gracious dining experience. ✕ *S. Church St.,* ☎ *809/949–9333. Reservations required for dinner, advised for lunch. DC, MC, V. Closed Sun. No lunch Sat.*

$$$ **Garden Loggia Cafe.** The Hyatt's indoor-outdoor café opens onto the most beautifully landscaped garden courtyard on the island. The Caribbean decor includes pastel colors, ceiling fans, and marble-top tables. The restaurant, serving Italian and Oriental cuisine, opens for dinner only during high season (mid-Dec.–May), but it's the weekly

Sunday champagne brunch, featuring everything from fresh seafood to waffles and custom-made omelets, that draws a crowd. Reserve a seat as early as possible to avoid disappointment. ✕ *Hyatt Regency Grand Cayman, West Bay Rd.,* ☎ *809/949–1234. Reservations required. AE, D, DC, MC, V.*

$$$ **Ottmar's.** This quietly elegant restaurant is styled after a West Indian
★ great house. Jade carpeting, peach walls, linen, trickling fountain, mahogany furniture, and glass chandeliers create an attractive setting for the excellent service. Favorites on the far-reaching international menu include bouillabaisse, chicken breast Oscar (topped with crab, asparagus, and hollandaise), French pepper steak (flamed in cognac and doused with green peppercorn sauce and crème fraîche), Florida red snapper (broiled, poached, panfried, or Provençal), and Indonesian rijsttafel (platter of seafood and rice in curry sauce with traditional condiments). ✕ *Clarion Grand Pavilion, West Bay Rd.,* ☎ *809/941– 5879 and 809/947–5882. Reservations required. AE, D, DC, MC, V. No lunch.*

$$$ **The Wharf.** Stylishly decorated in blue and white, the Wharf looks onto a veranda and the nearby sea. On the surf-and-turf menu are conch fritters, home-smoked salmon, "Seafood a L'aneth" (lobster and scallops in dill sauce), veal scaloppine, and steak fillet Béarnaise; anything on the fresh daily menu is recommended. Live Paraguayan music entertains diners. The Ports of Call bar is a perfect spot from which to watch the sun set, and tarpon feeding off the deck is a nightly (9 PM) spectacle here. ✕ *West Bay Rd.,* ☎ *809/949–2231. Reservations advised. AE, D, MC, V. No lunch weekends.*

$$–$$$ **Hemingway's.** Sea views and breezes attract diners to this classy open-
★ air restaurant on Seven Mile Beach. In the evening, candlelight and a guitarist (except Sunday) complete the romantic atmosphere. Nouvelle Caribbean and seafood dishes include pumpkin-coated mahimahi with mango jus, macadamia-crusted pork loin, and grouper stuffed with crab and sweet corn in a jerk cream sauce. Portions are large, and service is superb. For a tropical drink, try the Seven Mile Meltdown, with dark rum, peach schnapps, pineapple juice, and fresh coconut. ✕ *West Bay Rd. across from the Hyatt,* ☎ *809/949–1234, ext. 2009. Reservations accepted. AE, D, DC, MC, V.*

$$–$$$ **Lantana's.** Alfred Schrock, longtime chef at the Wharf Restaurant, now
★ creates excellent American-Caribbean lunches and dinners here. Enjoy lobster quesadillas, house-made lamb sausage, or blackened king salmon over cilantro linguine with banana fritters and cranberry relish. If you come for nothing else, *don't* miss the incredible roasted garlic soup and the apple pie. The decor of the bilevel restaurant—potted plants, teak furniture, painted wooden fish—is as imaginatively authentic as the food. ✕ *Caribbean Club, West Bay Rd.,* ☎ *809/947–5595. Reservations advised for dinner. AE, D, MC, V. No lunch weekends.*

$$–$$$ **Lobster Pot.** The second-floor terrace of this cozy restaurant overlooks the bay downtown, so the sunsets are an extra attraction. The menu includes both Continental dishes and such Caribbean specialties as conch chowder, seafood curry, and, of course, lobster. This place is popular, and the constant turnover creates a rather frenzied atmosphere. If you can't make it for dinner, drop by the pub and have a frozen banana daiquiri. ✕ *N. Church St.,* ☎ *809/949–2736. Reservations advised. AE, D, MC, V.*

$$ **Crow's Nest.** With the ocean right in its backyard, this secluded seafood restaurant, located about a 15-minute drive south of George Town, is a great spot for snorkeling as well as lunching. The shark du jour, herb-crusted dolphin with lobster sauce, and shrimp and conch dishes are excellent, as is the chocolate fudge rum cake. ✕ *South Sound Rd.,* ☎ *809/949–9366. Reservations advised. AE, MC, V. No lunch Sun.*

$$ Golden Pagoda. The well-known Chinese restaurant in the Caymans features Hakka-style cooking. Among its specialties are moo goo gai pan, butterfly shrimp, and chicken in black-bean sauce. Takeout (takie-outie, they call it) is now available, as are showy Japanese teppanyaki dinners (minimum two persons) Tuesday through Saturday night. ✕ *West Bay Rd.,* ☎ *809/949–5475. Reservations required for Japanese dinner. AE, MC, V. No lunch weekends.*

$$ White Hall Bay. Formerly the Cook Rum, the White Hall Bay has moved across the street to a restored waterfront Caymanian house, but it hasn't lost any of its casual ambience and charm. The hearty West Indian menu includes turtle and conch stews, salt beef and beans, crab backs, and pepper-pot stew. Follow up with dessert specials, such as cook rum cake and coconut cream pie. ✕ *N. Church St.,* ☎ *809/949–8670. AE, D, MC, V.*

$$$–$$$ Cracked Conch. Specialties of this popular, often-crowded seafood restaurant, the originator of cracked (tenderized and panfried) conch, include conch fritters, conch chowder, spicy Cayman-style snapper, turtle steak, and other seafood offerings. The key lime pie is divine. Locals flock here on weekdays for the low-priced lunch buffet—hot entrée, soup, and salad for C.I.$6.50. The bar, a prime local hangout, has karaoke, dive videos, and great happy-hour specials. ✕ *West Bay Rd. near the Hyatt,* ☎ *809/947–5217. MC, V.*

$ Almond Tree. Looking for authentic island atmosphere in modern Grand Cayman? This eatery combines architecture from the South Seas isle of Yap with bones, skulls, and bric-a-brac from Africa, South America, and the Pacific. Sample good-value seafood entrées, including turtle steak and fresh grouper, with "All-U-Can-Eat" entrées for C.I.$11 on Wednesday and Friday. ✕ *N. Church St.,* ☎ *809/949–2893. Dinner reservations advised. AE, MC, V. Closed Sun.*

$ Billy's Place. Who comes to the Caribbean without trying jerk food? Billy's, the yellow and blue diner in the Kirk Supermarket parking lot, is the place to do it in Grand Cayman. In addition to hearty servings of jerk chicken, pork, goat, shrimp, conch, fish, lobster, and burgers, you can order Indian *pakoras* (vegetable fritters), tandoori chicken or shrimp, and several curried selections. Service tends to be abrupt, but the crowds don't seem to mind. ✕ *N. Church St.,* ☎ *809/949–0470. AE, D, MC, V. Closed Sun.*

$ Hog Sty Bay Cafe. Lots of socializing goes on in the casual atmosphere of this English-style café on the harbor in George Town. A simple menu of sandwiches, hamburgers, and Caribbean dishes will satisfy you for lunch and dinner. Many believe the conch fritters served here are the best in town. Come and watch the sun set from the seaside patio or for the weekday happy hour. ✕ *N. Church St.,* ☎ *809/949–6163. AE, MC, V.*

Lodging

The success of the Cayman Islands as a resort destination means you should book ahead for holidays. Most lodgings require a 7- or 14-day minimum stay at Christmastime. During the summer season, it's possible to find suitable lodging even on short notice. If you choose to stay in a condominium, you can book on a daily basis and stay any length of time. While about a third of the visitors come for the diving, a growing number are young honeymooners. There are few accommodations in the economy range, so guests must be prepared for resort prices. Money-saving packages (everything from honeymoon trips to air-hotel deals) are offered through hotels and through **TourScan, Inc.** (☎ 800/962–2080 or 203/655–8091) and **Cayman Airtours** (☎ 800/247–2966).

Most of the larger hotels along Seven Mile Beach don't offer meal plans. The smaller properties that are more remote from the restaurants usually offer MAP or FAP. The rates for most hotels on Cayman Brac and Little Cayman include meals, and in some cases drinks and diving as well, making them a better value than their prices reveal at first glance. Over half the Caymans' rooms are rental condos and villas; all are equipped with fully stocked kitchens, telephones, satellite television, air-conditioning, living and dining areas, patios, and are individually decorated (most following a pastel tropical scheme). **Cayman Islands Reservation Service**: 800/327–8777.

Note: At press time, a new oceanfront luxury resort, the Grand Cayman Marriott Resort (☎ 800/228–9290), was under construction on Seven Mile Beach. Completion is scheduled for November 1995.

CATEGORY	COST*
$$$$	over $260
$$$	$200–$260
$$	$145–$200
$	under $145

All prices are for a standard double room for two in winter, excluding 6% tax and 10% service charge. To estimate rates for hotels offering MAP/FAP, add about $40 per person per day to the average price ranges above.

Grand Cayman

HOTELS

$$$$ **Hyatt Regency Grand Cayman.** Painted sky blue and white and set amid
★ gorgeous grounds, the Hyatt is adjacent to the Britannia Golf Course. The rooms, moderate in size and renovated in 1995, have a marble entranceway, oversize bathtub, minibar, French doors, and a veranda. Regency Club accommodations include complimentary Continental breakfast, early-evening hors d'oeuvres, and 24-hour concierge service. Across the street on Seven Mile Beach, the Hyatt's beach club offers every water sport imaginable. At Camp Hyatt, kids 3–12 can participate in a supervised activities program for a cost of around $50 a child per day. ☎ *Box 1698, Grand Cayman,* ☎ *809/949–1234 or 800/553–1300,* FAX *809/949–8528. 225 rooms, 10 suites; 44 rooms in Regency Club; 35 1-, 2-, 3-, and 4-bedroom villas. 3 restaurants, 4 bars, 4 pools, hot tub, dive shop, marina, water-sports center, golf course, 4 lighted tennis courts, croquet lawn, boutiques, beauty salon, massage, car rental, handicap-accessible room, conference rooms. AE, D, DC, MC, V. EP, BP, MAP.*

$$$$ **Spanish Bay Reef.** Grand Cayman's only all-inclusive resort is by far the most secluded of any property along the west shore. Pale pink two-story stucco units are surrounded by flowering trees and bushes on their own small sandy beach. An outdoor dining-bar area around the pool and overlooking the ocean includes tables under a semicircular white-latticed arcade. There's also a spacious, coral-stone indoor bar and dining area. Simple but comfortable guest units, with bright Caribbean print bedspreads and curtains, are connected by boardwalks. The resort is on the northwest tip of the island, several miles past Seven Mile Beach in West Bay. Spanish Bay Reef itself is a deep drop-off, which means superior beach diving and snorkeling; instruction in both is offered. Rates include round-trip transfers, all taxes and gratuities, unlimited shore diving, boat dives, and use of bicycles (not in mint condition). ☎ *Box 903,*

Grand Cayman, ☎ 809/949–3765, FAX 809/949–1842. 50 units. Restaurant, bar, pool, hot tub, dive shop, fishing charters. AE, D, DC, MC, V. All-inclusive.

$$$ Clarion Grand Pavilion. While it is across the street from Seven Mile Beach (it shares the beach club with the Hyatt), this intimate property is wrapped around a beautiful courtyard with waterfall and fountains cascading into the pool. Rooms in teal and peach offer all the modern comforts and a lot of well-thought-out extras you won't find at the other bustling resorts—daily newspaper, coffee/tea machine, minibar, bathrobes, an amazing array of toiletries, pants press, even an in-room fax on request. ✉ *Box 30117, Grand Cayman, ☎ 809/947–5656 or 800/252–7466, FAX 809/947–5353. 88 rooms, 5 2- and 3-bedroom suites. Restaurant, café, pool bar, cocktail lounge, pool, fitness room, sauna, hot tub, water-sports center, golf privileges at Safe Haven, gift shop, laundry facilities. AE, D, DC, MC, V. EP.*

$$$ Holiday Inn Grand Cayman. This hotel, home of the Coconuts Comedy Club, was the pioneer resort establishment on the beach, and it's still loose and fun. The property is cheerful yet unpretentious, a sprawling modern hotel with bright tropical colors in the spacious public rooms and one of the widest and nicest beaches on the strip. The guest rooms, given a fresh new face during a 1994 renovation, are standard Holiday Inn: comfortable, if not luxurious, with pool or ocean views. The huge breakfast buffet is a good value, and don't miss the "Barefoot Man," who performs four nights a week outside on the patio. ✉ *Box 904, Seven Mile Beach, Grand Cayman, ☎ 809/947–4444 or 800/421–9999, FAX 809/947–4213. 215 rooms. 3 restaurants, 2 bars, ice cream parlor, water-sports center, dive shop, pool, car rental, conference facilities. AE, DC, MC, V. EP, BP, MAP.*

$$$ ★ Indies Suites. Cayman's first and only all-suite hotel is attractive, comfortable, and across the road from the beach at the quieter north end of the Seven Mile stretch. One- or two-bedroom suites are done in cream and burnt orange, with contemporary wood furniture. Each has a fully equipped modern kitchen with a microwave oven, a living-dining room (with a sleeper sofa), a terrace, and a storeroom for dive gear. Free Continental buffet breakfast daily, a complimentary sunset cruise once a week, and a live band that entertains in the lushly landscaped courtyard twice a week are nice extras. ✉ *Box 2070 GT, Seven Mile Beach, Grand Cayman, ☎ 809/947–5025 or 800/654–3130, FAX 809/947–5024. 40 suites. Water-sports shop, pool, poolside bar, snack shop, convenience store, hot tub, laundry facilities, maid service, dive shop, snorkeling, conference facilities. AE, MC, V. CP.*

$$$ ★ Radisson Resort Grand Cayman. This is a five-story luxury property on Seven Mile Beach, just 1 mile from George Town. Designed in colonial style with arched doorways, the hotel's airy pale yellow and marble lobby opens onto a plant-filled courtyard. Families like the large adjoining rooms done in bright tropical colors; all have balconies facing either the ocean or a garden court. There's an inviting beach bar near the pool, a dive shop offering every possible water sport, and a good snorkeling reef just 50 feet offshore. A full-service spa was added in late 1994. ✉ *Box 30371, Seven Mile Beach, Grand Cayman, ☎ 809/949–0088 or 800/333–3333, FAX 809/949–0288. 315 rooms, 4 suites. Restaurant, snack bar, bar, pool, hot tub, dive shop/water-sports center, boutiques, spa, beauty salon, car rental. AE, DC, MC, V. EP.*

$$ Cayman Kai Resort. Nestled next to a coconut grove, each sea lodge has a full kitchen, dining and living areas, and a screened-in porch overlooking the ocean. The hotel is on a beach at the north-central tip of the island—quite remote. You need a car to get anywhere, but many guests are content to stay put and dive. Not all rooms have air-conditioning, so be sure to request it if it's important to you. ☎ *Box 201, North Side,* ☎ *809/947–9055 or 800/223–5427,* FAX *809/947–9102. 17 units. Restaurant, 2 bars. AE, MC, V. EP.*

$$ **Sleep Inn.** This two-story Choice Hotels affiliate is a stroll from Seven
★ Mile Beach, close to the airport, and just a mile from George Town's shops. Air-conditioned rooms are motel-modern, with peaches-and-cream pastels and modern wood furnishings. The Dive Inn dive shop is here, as are tours and car and motorcycle rentals. ☎ *Box 30111, Grand Cayman,* ☎ *809/949–9111,* FAX *809/949–6699. 124 rooms. Pool, whirlpool, poolside bar and grill, water-sports shop, boutique. AE, D, MC, V. EP.*

$–$$ **Sunset House.** Low-key and laid-back describe this resort with sparse, motel-style rooms on the ironshore south of George Town, 4 miles from Seven Mile Beach. A congenial staff, popular bar, and seafood restaurant are pluses, but it's the diving that attracts most guests. Full dive services include free waterside lockers, two- and three-tank dives at the better reefs around the island, and Cathy Church's U/W Photo Center. There are also excellent dive packages. It's a 5-minute walk to a sandy beach, 10 minutes to George Town, ☎ *Box 479, S. Church St., Grand Cayman,* ☎ *809/949–7111 or 800/854–4767,* FAX *809/949– 7101. 59 rooms. Restaurant, bar, dive shop and underwater photo center, fresh and seawater pools, whirlpool. AE, D, DC, MC, V. EP, BP, MAP.*

CONDOMINIUMS AND VILLAS

The **Cayman Islands Department of Tourism** provides a complete list of condominiums and small rental apartments in the *$$* range. Many of these are multibedroom units that become affordable when shared by two or more couples. Rates are higher during the winter season, and there may be a three- or seven-night minimum, so check before you book. The following complexes bear a marked similarity to one another: All are equipped with fully stocked kitchens, telephones, satellite television, air-conditioning, living and dining areas, and patios, and are individually decorated (most following a pastel tropical scheme). Differences arise in property amenities and proximity to town. All are well maintained and directly on the beach, though you will need a car for grocery shopping. **Cayman Islands Reservation Service** (6100 Blue Lagoon Dr., Suite 150, Miami, FL 33126, ☎ 800/327–8777), **Cayman Villas** (Box 681, Grand Cayman, ☎ 809/947–4144 or 800/235–5888, FAX 809/949–7471), and **Hospitality World Ltd.** (Box 30123, Grand Cayman, ☎ 809/949–8098 or 800/232–1034, FAX 809/949–7054) can also make reservations.

$$$$ **The Beachcomber.** Set in the middle of Seven Mile Beach 3 miles from George Town, each of the simply furnished apartments in this older condo community has a view of the ocean from a private, screened patio. There is a grocery store just across the street and countless shopping and dining outlets within walking distance, so once you're here, you don't really need a car. The Beachcomber reef is just offshore for snorkeling, and palapas on the beach provide shade when the sun gets a bit too warm. ☎ *Box 1799, Seven Mile Beach, Grand Cayman,* ☎ *809/947–4470,* FAX *809/947–5019. 23 units. Pool, beach huts, outdoor grills, laundry facilities. AE, MC, V.*

$$$$ **Caribbean Club.** Eighteen one- and two-bedroom villas (six on the beach) make up this quiet island condominium getaway. All units were renovated in 1994. While secluded, these units are not quite on a par with the truly deluxe properties on the island. Children under age 11 are not allowed in the winter season. ☎ *Box 30499, Seven Mile Beach, Grand Cayman,* ☎ *809/947–4099 or 800/327–8777,* FAX *809/947–4443. 18 villas. Restaurant (open for lunch and dinner), bar, tennis court, maid service. AE, MC, V. EP.*

$$$$ Discovery Point Club. At the quiet, far north end of Seven Mile Beach in West Bay 6 miles from George Town, this complex offers the same lovely beach with more peace and seclusion and is within walking distance of great snorkeling in the protected waters of Cemetery Reef. Tennis courts, a hot tub, and a pool for relaxation are part of the appeal here. Kids 12 and under stay for free during the off-season (Apr.–Dec.). ☎ *Box 439, West Bay, Grand Cayman,* ☎ *809/947–4724,* FAX *809/947–5051. 45 units. Pool, hot tub, 2 tennis courts, outdoor grills, laundry facilities. AE, MC, V.*

$$$$ Victoria House. The one-, two-, and three-bedroom units in this squarish white building have white tile floors and white walls and are decorated with muted Caribbean prints and rattan furniture. You may choose from a range of activities, including tennis and water sports. The Victoria is 3 miles north of town on a quiet stretch of Seven Mile Beach; if you're an early riser, you may catch a glimpse of giant sea turtles on the sand. ☎ *Box 30571, Seven Mile Beach (near West Bay), Grand Cayman,* ☎ *809/947–4233,* FAX *809/947–5328. 25 units. Scuba, snorkeling, tennis, hammocks, laundry facilities. AE, MC, V.*

$$$–$$$$ Grapetree/Cocoplum. A half-mile from George Town on Seven Mile Beach, these sister condo units are adjacent to one another. Grapetree's two-bedroom, two-bath units are carpeted, with traditional wicker furnishings and a beige and brown decor. Cocoplum's units are similar, with Caribbean pastel prints; its grounds have more plants and trees. The two share two pools and tennis courts. ☎ *Box 1802, Seven Mile Beach, Grand Cayman,* ☎ *809/949–5640 or 800/635–4824,* FAX *809/949–0150. 51 units. 2 pools, tennis courts, outdoor grills. AE, MC, V.*

$$$–$$$$ Retreat at Rum Point. It has its own narrow beach with casuarina trees, far from the madding crowd on the north-central tip of Grand Cayman, 27 miles from town. Up to six people can rent a two-bedroom villa here. Two or three people are comfortable in the one-bedroom units. Spacious rooms have blue-lavender upholstered furniture. There are dive facilities nearby, where you can take advantage of superb offshore diving, including the famed North Wall. You'll be stranded without a car; it's a 35-minute drive to George Town or the airport. ☎ *Box 46, North Side, Grand Cayman,* ☎ *809/947–9535 or 800/423–2422,* FAX *809/947–9058. 23 units. Restaurant, bar, pool, tennis courts, exercise room, sauna, racquetball court, laundry facilities. MC, V.*

GUEST HOUSES AND B&BS

Away from the beach and short on style and facilities, these nevertheless offer rock-bottom prices (all fall well below our $ category), a friendly atmosphere, and your best shot at getting to know the locals. Rooms are clean and simple, often with cooking facilities, and most have private bathrooms. Many establishments have outdoor grills and picnic tables for guest use. A rental car is recommended. These places do not accept personal checks or credit cards but do take reservations through the **Cayman Islands Reservation Service:** ☎ 800/327–8777.

Grama's Bed & Breakfast (Box 198, Crescent Close of Town Hall Crescent, West Bay, Grand Cayman, ☎ 809/949–3798), 8 miles from town and the airport, has five rooms and a pool. **Adam's Guest House** (Box 312, on Melnac Ave. near the Seaview Hotel, Grand Cayman, ☎ 809/949–2512 or ☎/fax 809/949–0919), a mile south of George Town and 4 miles from the beach, also has five rooms. **Eldemire's Guest House**

(Box 482, on South Church St., Grand Cayman, ☎ 809/949–5387, FAX 809/949–6987), Grand Cayman's first guest house, has seven rooms and is a 15-minute drive to Seven Mile Beach, but less than a mile south of pretty Smith Cove Bay.

Cayman Brac

HOTELS

$$–$$$$ **Brac Reef Beach Resort.** Designed, built, and owned by Bracer Linton Tibbets, the resort lures divers and vacationers who come to savor the special ambience of this tiny island. The recently (1994) renovated rooms with private balconies, pool, pretty beach, snorkeling, guest bicycles, new dive shop, and two-story covered dock are additional reasons to stay here. The modest all-inclusive package rates include three buffet meals daily, all drinks, airport transfers, and taxes and service charges. There's even an all-inclusive dive package. ☎ *Box 56, Cayman Brac,* ☎ *809/948–7323; in FL, 813/323–8727 or 800/327–3835; FAX 809/948–7207. 40 rooms. Restaurant, bar, pool, hot tub, dive shop, lighted tennis court, bicycles. AE, D, MC, V. EP, MAP, FAP, All-inclusive.*

$$–$$$ **Divi Tiara Beach Resort.** This older resort is dedicated to divers. It has a top-quality diving facility complemented by the Divi chain's standards: tile floors, rattan furniture, louvered windows, balconies, and ocean views (from most rooms). Some of the more expensive rooms have whirlpool bathtubs. A shuttle takes guests across the island to a great snorkeling spot. Kids 16 and under stay free in their parents' room. ☎ *Box 238, Cayman Brac,* ☎ *809/948–1553; in the U.S., 919/419–3484 or 800/801–5550; FAX 809/948–7316 or 919/419–2075 in the U.S. 70 rooms. Restaurant, bar, pool, lighted tennis court, volleyball, dive shop, water-sports center, underwater photo shop, snorkeling, fishing. AE, MC, V. EP, MAP, FAP, All-inclusive.*

CONDOMINIUMS AND VILLAS

$$ **Caribbean Brac Beach Village.** This small condo complex built in 1992 ★   enjoys the same pretty beach as the other resorts, but for the money you get a two-bedroom, 2½-bath fully furnished apartment right on the beach. Kids 11 and under stay free with their parents, making this a family money saver. Beige walls and rattan furniture, white tile floors, and pastel floral prints give the units a bright, airy look. With advance notice, the management company will stock your kitchen with groceries and arrange for dive packages, rental cars, and maid service (each at minimal additional cost). A pool, restaurant, bar, gift shop, and six more condos were scheduled for addition during a 1995 expansion. ☎ *Box 4, Stake Bay, Cayman Brac,* ☎ *809/948–2265 or 800/791–7911, FAX 809/948–2206. 16 rooms. Pier, laundry room. MC, V. EP.*

Little Cayman

HOTELS

$$–$$$$ **Little Cayman Beach Resort.** This two-story property, on the south side ★   of the island, opened in early 1993. Considerably less rustic than those of other Little Cayman resorts, the air-conditioned, water-view rooms here have modern furnishings in jewel-tone tropical colors. The dining room overlooking the bar area seats 50 for family-style buffet meals. Double hammocks are slung under beach palapas. The resort offers diving and fishing packages and also caters to bird-watchers and soft-adventure ecotourists. Paddleboats, sailboats, kayaks, a complete dive operation, tennis, and free bicycles provided for exploring the island keep guests busy. All-inclusive packages are available for both divers and nondivers and include three meals daily, all alcoholic and soft drinks, airport transfers, taxes, and gratuities. ☎ *Blossom Village, Little Cay-*

man, ☎ 809/948–1033 or 800/327–3835, 🖷 809/948–1045. 32 rooms. Restaurant, bar, dive shop, pool, hot tub, tennis court, gift shop, deep-sea fishing charters, bicycles, dive packages available. AE, D, MC, V. EP, MAP, FAP. All-inclusive.

$$–$$$ **Pirates Point Resort.** The guest house feel of this comfortably informal
★ resort generates almost instant camaraderie among the guests, and many come back year after year. The charming, individually decorated rooms have tiled floors, white rattan and wicker furnishings, ceiling fans, and louvered windows. Owner Gladys Howard, a native Texan, leads nature walks and is a cordon bleu chef; her small restaurant is open to nonguests, too. "Relaxing" rates (for nondivers) include the mouth-watering meals and wine; all-inclusive rates include meals, alchoholic beverages, two daily boat dives, fishing, and picnics on uninhabited Owen Island. Sunset wine-and-cheese parties are held weekly on the beach-side dock. ☎ Little Cayman, ☎ 809/948–1010 or 800/654–7537, 🖷 809/948–1011. 10 rooms. Restaurant, bar, bikes, dive operation, fishing, complimentary airport transfers. MC, V. FAP, All-inclusive.

$$ **Southern Cross Club.** Three family-style meals a day are included in the rates at this older retreat that caters to fishers and divers. The rooms, in cottages spread along a pretty beach, have a simple white-on-white decor with wicker furniture, ceiling fans (no air-conditioning), and painted cement floors. Diving and fishing (deep-sea, light-tackle, bottom, and bonefishing) are the draw here. A motorboat makes trips to uninhabited Owen Island nearby. There's been a lot of turnover in staff and management lately, and service is suffering for it. ☎ Little Cayman, ☎ 809/948–1099 or 800/899–2582; in the U.S., 317/636–9501, 🖷 317/636–9503. 10 rooms. Restaurant, beach bar, bicycles, diving and fishing packages, snorkeling, complimentary airport transfers. No credit cards. FAP.

$–$$ **Sam McCoy's Diving and Fishing Lodge.** Be prepared for an ultracasual experience: This is an ordinary family house with very simple bedrooms and baths. There's no bar or restaurant per se; guests just eat at a few tables outdoors or with Sam and his family in the dining room. Fans like it for its owner's infectious good nature, the superb diving and snorkeling just offshore, and the family atmosphere. "Relaxing" rates (for nondivers) include three meals a day and airport transfers; all-inclusive rates also include beach and boat diving. Sam's son, Chip, is the most experienced local fishing guide on the island; his bonefishing trips are around $20 an hour. ☎ Little Cayman, ☎ and 🖷 809/948–0026 or 800/626–0496. 6 rooms. Pool, beach barbecue. No credit cards. FAP, All-inclusive.

Nightlife

Each of the island hot spots attracts a different clientele. The **Holiday Inn** (☎ 809/947–4444) offers something for everyone: **Coconuts** (☎ 809/ 947–5757), the hotel's original comedy club, features young American stand-up comedians who entertain year-round every Wednesday through Sunday. Crowds also gather poolside, where the island-famous "Barefoot Man" sings and plays four nights a week. Dancing is spontaneous and welcome, and it's a great spot to people-watch.

Long John Silver's Nightclub (☎ 809/949–7777), at the Treasure Island Resort, is a spacious, tiered club that is usually filled to capacity when the island's top bands play there. **Island Rock Nightclub** (Falls Shopping Center, Seven Mile Beach, ☎ 809/947–5366), a popular disco and bar with occasional live bands, had been converted to a teen club at press time but may revert to an adult club during high season; call to check before venturing out. Latest to hit the hot-spot list is **Rumheads** (☎ 809/949–7169), featuring nightly drink specials, live entertainment, and theme nights; the youngish crowd can get pretty rowdy, and brawls aren't exactly out of the ordinary here.

Locals and visitors frequent the **Cracked Conch** (West Bay Rd. near the Hyatt, ☎ 809/947–5217) for karaoke, classic dive films, and the great happy hour with hors d'oeuvres Tuesday–Friday evenings.

For current entertainment, look at the freebie magazine, *What's Hot,* or check the Friday edition of the *Caymanian Compass* for listings of music, movies, theater, and other entertainment possibilities.

9 Curaçao

Updated by
Barbara Hults

CURAÇAO IS AN ISLAND FOR EXPLORERS. Its charming Dutch capital, underwater park, Seaquarium, floating market, and dozens of little cove beaches give it a taste of everything, and it is apt to please most tastes. Thirty-five miles north of Venezuela and 42 miles east of Aruba, Curaçao is the largest of the islands in the Netherlands Antilles. The sun smiles down on the island, but it's never stiflingly hot: The gentle trade winds refresh. Water sports attract enthusiasts from all over the world, and some of the best reef diving is here. Though the island claims 38 beaches, it doesn't have long stretches of sand or enchanting scenery. The island is dominated by an arid countryside, rocky coves, and a sprawling capital situated around a natural harbor. Until recently, the economy was based not on tourism but on oil refining and catering to offshore corporations seeking tax hedges. Although tourism has become a major economic force in the past five years or so, with millions of dollars invested in restoring old colonial landmarks and modernizing hotels, Curaçao's atmosphere remains comparatively low-key—offering an appealing alternative to the commercialism found on many other Caribbean islands.

As seen from the Otrabanda of Willemstad by the first-time visitor, Curaçao's "face" will be a surprise—spiffy rows of pastel-colored town houses that look as though they were transplanted from Holland. Although the gabled roofs and red tiles show a Dutch influence, the absurdly gay colors of the facades, as novelist Christopher Isherwood once described them, are peculiar to Curaçao. It is said that the first governor of Curaçao developed a terrible allergy to the color white (it gave him migraines), so all the houses were painted in colors. The dollhouse look of the *landhuizen* (plantation houses) makes a cheerful contrast to the stark cacti and the austere shrubbery dotting the countryside.

The history books still cannot agree on who discovered Curaçao—one school of thought believes it was Alonzo de Ojeda, another says it was Amerigo Vespucci—but they seem to agree that it was around 1499. The first Spanish settlers arrived in 1527. In 1634, the Dutch came via the Netherlands West India Company. They promptly shipped off the Spaniards and the few remaining Indians—survivors of the battles for ownership of the island, famine, and disease—to Venezuela. Eight years later, Peter Stuyvesant began his rule as governor, which lasted until he left for New York around 1645. Twelve Jewish families arrived from Amsterdam in 1651, and in 1732 members of the community they started here built a synagogue; today, it is the oldest synagogue still in use in the Western Hemisphere. Over the years, the city built massive fortresses to defend itself against French and British invasions—many of those ramparts now house unusual restaurants and hotels. The Dutch claim to Curaçao was finally recognized in 1815 by the Treaty of Paris. In 1954, Curaçao became an autonomous part of the Kingdom of the Netherlands, with an elected parliament and island council. It is ruled by a governor appointed by the queen.

Today Curaçao's population is derived from more than 50 nationalities blending together in an exuberant mix of Latin, European, and African roots and a Babel of tongues, resulting in a legacy of superb restaurants and an active cultural scene. The island, like its Dutch settlers, is known for its religious tolerance, and tourists are warmly welcomed.

Before You Go

Tourist Information

Contact the **Curaçao Tourist Board** (475 Park Ave. S, Suite 2000, New York, NY 10016, ☎ 212/683–7660 or 800/270–3350, ℻ 212/683–9337; 330 Biscayne Blvd., Suite 808, Miami, FL 33132, ☎ 305/374–5811 or 800/445–8266, ℻ 305/374–6741) for information.

Arriving and Departing

BY PLANE

American Airlines (☎ 800/624–6262) flies direct daily from Miami. **ALM** (☎ 800/327–7230), Curaçao's national airline, maintains frequent service from Miami and Atlanta. For Atlanta departures, ALM has connecting services (throughfares) to most U.S. gateways with Delta. ALM also offers a Visit Caribbean Pass, allowing easy interisland travel. **Air Aruba** (☎ 800/882–7822) has daily direct flights to Curaçao (flights make brief stops in Aruba) from both Miami and Newark airports. Air Aruba also has regularly scheduled service to Curaçao from Baltimore, and to Aruba and Bonaire. **E Liner Airways** (☎ 599/9–697270 or 599/9–604773) has started interisland service, including sightseeing and a beach tour of Aruba and of Bonaire.

Passports and Visas

U.S. and Canadian citizens traveling to Curaçao need only proof of citizenship and a valid photo ID. A voter's registration card or a notarized birth certificate (not a photocopy) will suffice—a driver's license will *not*. British citizens must produce a passport. All visitors must show an ongoing or return ticket.

Language

Dutch is the official language, but the vernacular is Papiamento—a mixture of Dutch, Portuguese, Spanish, and English. Developed during the 18th century by Africans, Papiamento evolved in Curaçao as the mode of communication between landowners and their slaves. These days, however, English, as well as Spanish, and, of course, Dutch, are studied by schoolchildren. Anyone involved with tourism—shopkeepers, restaurateurs, and museum guides—speaks English. But a Spanish phrase book may help.

Precautions

Mosquitoes on Curaçao do not seem as vicious and bloodthirsty as they do on Aruba and Bonaire, but that doesn't mean they don't exist. To be safe, keep perfume to the minimum, be prepared to use insect repellent before dining alfresco, and spray your hotel room at night—especially if you've opened a window.

If you plan to go into the water, beware of long-spined sea urchins, which can cause pain if you come in contact with them.

Do not eat any of the little green applelike fruits of the manchineel tree: They're poisonous. In fact, steer clear of the trees altogether; raindrops or dewdrops dripping off the leaves can blister your skin. If contact does occur, rinse the affected area with water and, in extreme cases, get medical attention. Usually, the burning sensation won't last longer than two hours.

Staying in Curaçao

Important Addresses

Tourist Information: The **Curaçao Tourism Development Foundation** has three offices on the island where multilingual guides are ready to answer questions. You can also pick up maps, brochures, and a copy of *Curaçao Holiday*. The main office is located in Willemstad at Pietermaai No. 19 (☎ 599/9–616000); other offices are in the Waterfort Arches (☎ 599/9–613397), across from the Van Der Valk Plaza Hotel, and at the airport (☎ 599/9–686789).

EMERGENCIES
Police or **fire:** ☎ 114. The **main police station** number is 599/9–611000. **Hospitals:** For medical emergencies, call **St. Elisabeth's Hospital** (☎ 599/9–624900) or an ambulance (☎ 112). **Pharmacies: Botica Popular** (Madurostraat 15, ☎ 599/9–611269), or ask at your hotel for the nearest one.

Currency

U.S. dollars—in cash or traveler's checks—are accepted nearly everywhere, so there's no need to worry about exchanging money. However, you may need small change for pay phones, cigarettes, or soda machines. The currency in the Netherlands Antilles is the guilder, or florin, as it is also called, indicated by an fl. or NAf. on price tags. The U.S. dollar is considered very stable; the official rate of exchange at press time was NAf1.75 to U.S. $1. Note: Prices quoted here are in U.S. dollars unless indicated otherwise.

Taxes and Service Charges

Hotels collect a 7% government tax and add a 12% service charge to the bill; restaurants add 10%–15%. The airport departure tax is U.S. $10 ($5.75 for Bonaire).

Guided Tours

To see Willemstad with an architect's eye, call Anko van der Woude (☎ 599/9–613554), at **Old City Tours,** who guides tours to the old sections, Otrabanda (on Thursday, $6) and Punda (on Tuesday, $8, including admission to mansion). He points out the similarities of street names with New Amsterdam (New York), which was being created at about the same time. The **Curaçao Museum** (☎ 599/9–623873) conducts architectural and historical walking tours of the town on Wednesday and Thursday afternoons. The tours start at Brionplein and cost $5.75 a person (a drink at a typical bar is included). To see the rest of the island, a guided tour can save you time and energy, though it is easy to cover the island yourself in a rented car. Most hotels have tour desks where arrangements can be made with reputable tour operators. For very personal, amiable service, try **Casper Tours** (☎ 599/9–653010 or 599/9–616789). For $25 per person, you'll be escorted around the island in an air-conditioned van, with stops at the Juliana Bridge, the salt lakes, Knip Bay for a swim, the grotto at Boca Tabla, and lunch at Jaanchi Restaurant, which is famous for its native cuisine. **Taber Tours** (☎ 599/9–376637) offers a 3½-hour city and country tour ($10) that includes visits to the Curaçao Liqueur Factory, the Curaçao Museum, and the Bloempot shopping center. A full-day tour includes a visit to the Seaquarium and a snorkel trip; it costs $25 per person. Taber Tours also offers a two-hour sunset cruise ($29.50 for adults and $20 for children) with a feast of French bread, cheese, and wine. A day trip to Aruba or Bonaire is also available. **Curven Tours** (☎ 599/9–379806) offers island tours and special packages to Venezuela.

Getting Around

TAXIS
Taxi drivers have an official tariff chart, with fares from the airport vicinity running about $10–$15 to Willemstad and the nearby beach hotels. Taxis tend to be moderately priced, but since there are no meters,

you should confirm the fare with the driver before departure. There is an additional 25% surcharge after 11 PM. Taxis are readily available at hotels; in other cases, call Central Dispatch at ☎ 599/9–616711.

RENTAL CARS

You can rent a car from **Budget** (☎ 599/9–683420), **Avis** (☎ 599/9–681163), **Dollar** (☎ 599/9–690262), or **National Car Rental** (☎ 599/9–683489) at the airport or have one delivered free to your hotel. Rates typically range from about $46 a day for a Toyota Starlet to about $73 for a four-door sedan. If you're planning to do country driving or rough it through Christoffel Park, a Jeep is best. All you'll need is a valid U.S. or Canadian driver's license. Scooters ($20), mopeds ($15), and bikes ($12.50) can be rented from **Easy Going** (☎ 599/9–695056).

Telephones and Mail

Phone service through the hotel operators in Curaçao is slow, but direct-dial service, both on-island and to the United States, is fast and clear. Hotel operators will put the call through for you, but if you make a collect call, do check immediately afterward that the hotel does not charge you as well. To call Curaçao direct from the United States, dial 011–599–9 plus the number in Curaçao. To place a local call on the island, dial the six-digit local number. An airmail letter to anywhere in the world costs NAf2.50, a postcard NAf1.25.

Opening and Closing Times

Most shops are open Monday–Saturday 8–noon and 2–6. Banks are open weekdays 8–3:30.

Exploring Curaçao

Numbers in the margin correspond to points of interest on the Curaçao map.

Willemstad

❶ What does the capital of Curaçao, **Willemstad,** have in common with New York City? Broadway, for one. Here it's called Breedestraat, but the origin is the same. Dutch settlers came here in the 1630s, the same period when they sailed through the Narrows to Manhattan. Willemstad is a favorite cruise stop for two reasons: The shopping is considered among the best in the Caribbean, and a quick tour of most of the downtown sights can be managed within a six-block radius. Santa Anna Bay slices the city down the middle: On one side is the Punda, and on the other is the Otrabanda (literally, the "other side"). Think of the Punda as the side for tourists, crammed with shops, restaurants, monuments, and markets. Otrabanda is less touristy, with lots of narrow winding streets full of private homes notable for their picturesque gables and Dutch-influenced designs.

There are three ways to make the crossing from one side to the other: (1) drive or take a taxi over the Juliana Bridge, (2) traverse the Queen Emma Pontoon Bridge on foot, or (3) ride the free ferry, which runs when the bridge is open for passing ships. All the major hotels outside of town offer free shuttle service to town twice daily. Shuttles coming from the Otrabanda side leave you at Rif Fort. From there it's a short walk north to the foot of the Pontoon Bridge. Shuttles coming from the Punda side leave you near the main entrance to Fort Amsterdam.

Our walking tour of Willemstad starts at the **Queen Emma Bridge,** affectionately called the Lady by the natives. During the hurricane season in 1988, the 700-foot floating bridge practically floated right out to sea; it was later taken down for major reconstruction. If you're stand-

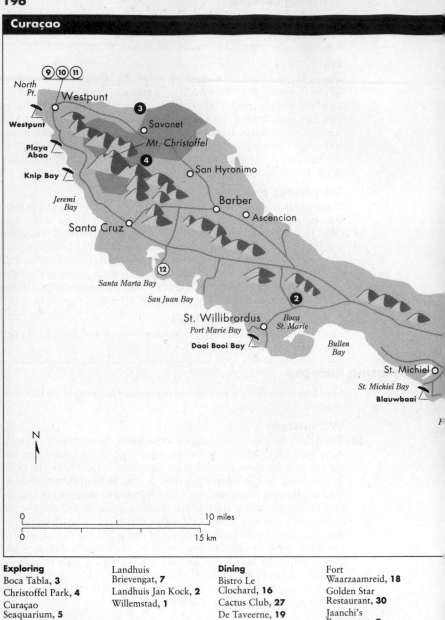

North
Pt.

Westpunt

Westpunt

Playa
Abao

Knip Bay

Jeremi
Bay

Santa Cruz

⑨ ⑩ ⑪

❸

Savonet

Mt. Christoffel

❹

San Hyronimo

Barber

Ascencion

⑫

Santa Marta Bay

San Juan Bay

St. Willibrordus

Port Marie Bay

Daai Booi Bay

*Boca
St. Marie*

❷

*Bullen
Bay*

St. Michiel

St. Michiel Bay

Blauwbaai

N

0 _____ 10 miles

0 _____ 15 km

Exploring
Boca Tabla, **3**
Christoffel Park, **4**
Curaçao
Seaquarium, **5**
Curaçao Underwater
Marine Park, **6**
Hato Caves, **8**

Landhuis
Brievengat, **7**
Landhuis Jan Kock, **2**
Willemstad, **1**

Dining
Bistro Le
Clochard, **16**
Cactus Club, **27**
De Taveerne, **19**
Fort Nassau Restaurant, **20**

Fort
Waarzaamreid, **18**
Golden Star
Restaurant, **30**
Jaanchi's
Restaurant, **9**
L'Alouette, **31**
La Pergola, **23**

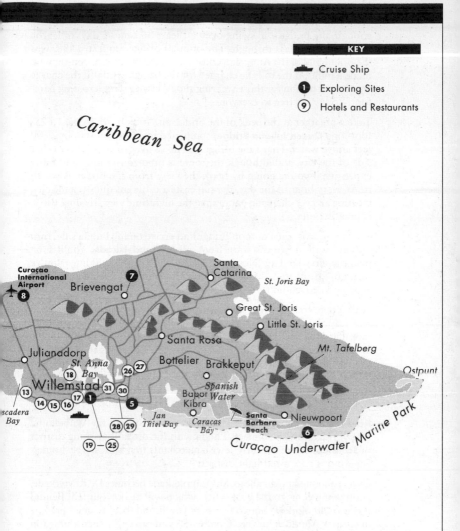

KEY

Cruise Ship

① Exploring Sites

⑨ Hotels and Restaurants

Caribbean Sea

Curaçao International Airport ✈ ⑧

Brievengat ⑦

Santa Catarina

St. Joris Bay

Great St. Joris

Little St. Joris

Julianadorp

St. Anna Bay

Santa Rosa

Bottelier   Brakkeput

Mt. Tafelberg

Ostpunt

Willemstad ⑱   ㉖ ㉗

㉛ ㉚

scadera Bay   ⑬

⑭ ⑮ ⑯ ⑰ ①

⑤

Bapor Kibra

Spanish Water

Jan Thiel Bay

Caracas Bay

Santa Barbara Beach

Nieuwpoort

⑥

㉘ ㉙

⑲ — ㉕

Curaçao Underwater Marine Park

Pirates, **14**
Rijstaffel Indonesia Restaurant, **26**
Seaview, **25**

Lodging
Avila Beach Hotel, **21**
Coral Cliff Resort and Beach Club, **12**
Curaçao Caribbean Hotel and Casino, **14**
Holiday Beach Hotel and Casino, **15**

Kadushi Cliffs, **10**
Landhaus Daniel, **11**
Lions Dive Hotel & Marina, **29**
Otrabanda Hotel & Casino, **17**
Princess Beach Hotel and Casino, **28**

Porto PaseoHotel and Casino, **22**
Sonesta Beach Hotel & Casino, **13**
Van Der Valk Plaza Hotel and Casino, **24**

ing on the Otrabanda side, take a few moments to scan Curaçao's multicolored "face" on the other side of Santa Anna Bay. If you wait long enough, the bridge will swing open (at least 30 times a day) to let the seagoing ships pass through. The original bridge, built in 1888, was the brainchild of the American consul Leonard Burlington Smith, who made a mint off the tolls he charged for the bridge. Initially, the charge was 2¢ per person for those wearing shoes, free to those crossing barefoot. Today it's free to everyone.

Take a breather at the peak of the bridge and look north to the 1,625-foot-long **Queen Juliana Bridge,** completed in 1974 and standing 200 feet above water. That's the bridge you drive over to cross to the other side of the city, and although the route is time-consuming (and more expensive if you're going by taxi), the view from the bridge is worth it. At every hour of the day, the sun casts a different tint over the city, creating an ever-changing panorama; the nighttime view, rivaling Rio's, is breathtaking.

When you cross the Pontoon Bridge and arrive on the Punda side, turn left and walk down the waterfront, along **Handelskade.** You'll soon pass the ferry landing. Now take a close look at the buildings you've seen only from afar; the original red tiles of the roofs came from Europe and arrived on trade ships as ballast.

Walk down to the corner and turn right at the customs building onto Sha Caprileskade. This is the bustling **floating market,** where each morning dozens of Venezuelan schooners arrive laden with tropical fruits and vegetables. Fresh mangoes, papayas, and exotic vegetables vie for space with freshly caught fish and herbs and spices. It's probably too much to ask a tourist to arrive by 6:30 AM, when the buying is best, but there's plenty of action to see throughout the afternoon. Any produce bought here, however, should be thoroughly washed before eating.

Keep walking down Sha Caprileskade. Head toward the Wilhelmina Drawbridge, which connects Punda with the once-flourishing district of **Scharloo,** where the early Jewish merchants first built stately homes. Scharloo is now a red-light district.

If you continue straight ahead, Sha Caprileskade becomes De Ruyterkade. Soon you'll come to the post office, which will be on your left. Behind it is the **Old Market** (Marche), where you'll find local women preparing hearty Antillean lunches. For $4–$6 you can enjoy such Curaçaon specialties as *funghi* (cornbread), *kesi yena* (Gouda cheese stuffed with meat), goat stew, fried fish, peas and rice, and fried plantains. After lunch, return to the intersection of De Ruyterkade and Columbusstraat and turn left.

Walk up Columbusstraat to the **Mikveh Israel-Emanuel Synagogue,** built in 1732 by the Jewish community that came from Amsterdam in 1651 to establish a new congregation. Jews from Portugal and Brazil, fleeing persecution, soon joined them, and by the early 1700s more than 2,000 Jews were in residence. This temple, the oldest still in use in the Western Hemisphere, is one of the most important sights in Curaçao and draws 20,000 visitors a year. Enter through the Spanish-tiled courtyard around the corner on Hanchi Di Snoa, and ask the front office to direct you to the guide on duty. A unique feature is the brilliant white sand covering the synagogue floor, a remembrance of Moses leading his people through the desert and of the Diaspora. The Hebrew letters on the four pillars signify the names of the Four Mothers of Israel: Sarah, Rebecca, Rachel, and Leah. The fascinating Jewish Cultural Museum (☎ 599/9–611633, ☛ $2) in the back displays Jewish antiques (including a set of circumcision instruments) and artifacts from Jewish families collected from all over the world. The gift shop near the gate has excellent postcards and commemorative medallions. *Hanchi Di Snoa 29,* ☎ *599/9–611067.* ☾ *Weekdays 9–11:45 AM and 2:30–5 PM. English and Hebrew services conducted by an American rabbi are held Fri. at 6:30 PM and Sat. at 10 AM. Jacket and tie required.*

Continue down Columbusstraat and cross Wilhelminaplein (Wilhelmina Park). Now you will be in front of the courthouse, with its stately balustrade, and the impressive Georgian facade of the Bank of Boston. The statue keeping watch over the park is of Queen Wilhelmina, a deceased popular monarch of the Netherlands, who gave up her throne to her daughter Juliana after her Golden Jubilee in 1948. Cut back across the park and turn left at Breedestraat, Punda's main street and a window-shopper's delight. Take Breedestraat down to the Pontoon Bridge, then turn left at the waterfront. At the foot of the bridge are the mustard-colored walls of **Fort Amsterdam.** Take a few steps through the archway and enter another century. The entire structure dates from the 1700s, when it was actually the center of the city and the most important fort on the island. Now it houses the governor's residence, the Fort Church, the ministry, and several other government offices. Outside the entrance a series of majestic gnarled *wayaka* trees are fancifully carved with a dragon, giant squid, mermaid, and a portrait of the queen—the work of noted local artist Mac Alberto, who can be seen strolling the streets impeccably garbed in blinding white suits, a courtly boutonniere in his lapel. Next door is the **Plaza Piar,** dedicated to Manuel Piar, a native Curaçaoan who fought for the independence of Venezuela under the liberator Simon Bolívar. On the other side of the plaza is the **Waterfort,** a bastion dating from 1634. The original cannons are still positioned in the battlements. The foundation, however, now forms the walls of the Van Der Valk Plaza Hotel. Following the sidewalk around the plaza, you'll discover one of the most delightful shopping areas on the island, newly built under the **Waterfort Arches** (*see* Shopping, *below,* for details).

Western Side

The road through the village of Soto that leads to the northwest tip of the island winds through landscape that Georgia O'Keeffe might have painted—towering cacti, flamboyant dried shrubbery, and aluminum-roof houses. Throughout this *cunucu,* or countryside, you'll see native fishermen hauling in their nets, women pounding cornmeal, and an occasional donkey blocking traffic. Landhouses, large plantation houses from centuries past, dot the countryside, though most are closed to the public. Their facades, though, can often be glimpsed from the highway. For a splendid view, and some unusual island tales of ghosts, follow Wespunt Highway to the intersection at Cunucu Abao, then veer

❷ left onto Weg Naar San Willibrordo until you come to **Landhuis Jan Kock** (☎ 599/9–648087), located across from the salt pans. Since the hours are irregular, be sure to call ahead to arrange a tour of this reputedly haunted mid-17th-century plantation house, or stop by on Sunday mornings, when the proprietor occasionally opens the small restaurant behind her home and serves delicious Dutch pancakes.

Continuing north on this road, you'll come to the village of Soto. From here the road leads to the northwest tip of the island, where it becomes

❸ Wespunt Highway again and heads south to **Boca Tabla,** where the sea has carved a magnificent grotto. Safely tucked in the back, you can watch and listen to the waves crashing ferociously against the rocks. A short

❹ distance farther is **Christoffel Park,** a fantastic 4,450-acre garden and wildlife preserve with the towering Mt. Christoffel at its center. Open to the public since 1978, the park consists of three former plantations with individual trails that take about 1 to 1½ hours each to traverse. You may drive your own car (heavy-treaded wheels) or rent a Jeep with an accompanying guide ($15). Start out early (by 10 AM the park starts to feel like a sauna), and if you're going solo, first study the *Excursion Guide to Christoffel Park* that's sold at the front desk of the elegant, if dilapidated, Landhuis Savonet (the plantation house turned Natural History Museum); it outlines the various routes and identifies the flora and fauna found here. No matter what route you take, you'll be treated to interesting views of hilly fields full of prickly pear cacti, divi-divi trees, bushy-haired palms, and exotic flowers that bloom unpredictably after April showers. There are also caves—the strong at heart will revel in the rustling of bat wings and the sight of scuttling scorpion spiders (scary but not poisonous)—and ancient Indian drawings.

As you drive through the park, keep a lookout for tiny deer, goats, and other small wildlife that might suddenly dart in front of your car. The whip snakes and minute silver snakes you may encounter are not poisonous. White-tail hawks may be seen on the green route, white orchids and crownlike passion flowers on the yellow route. Climbing the 1,239-foot Mt. Christoffel on foot is an exhilarating experience and a definite challenge to anyone who hasn't grown up scaling the Alps. The guidebook claims the round-trip will take you one hour, and Curaçaoan adolescent boys do make a sport of racing up and down, but it's really more like 2½ (sweaty) hours for a reasonably fit person who's not an expert hiker. And the last few feet are deadly. The view from the peak, however, *is* thrilling—a panorama of the island, including Santa Marta Bay and the tabletop mountain of St. Hironimus. On a clear day, you can even see the mountain ranges of Venezuela, Bonaire, and Aruba. *Savonet,* ☎ *599/9–640363.* ☛ *$5 adults, $3 children 6–15.* ☉ *Mon.–Sat. 8–5, Sun. 6–3.*

Eastern Side

To explore the eastern side of the island, take the coastal road—Martin Luther King Boulevard—out from Willemstad about 2 miles to Bapor Kibra. There you'll find the Seaquarium and the Underwater Park.

❺ The **Curaçao Seaquarium** is *the* place to see the island's underwater treasures without getting your feet wet. It's now more fun than ever, thanks to the *Seaworld Explorer,* a semisubmersible submarine that leaves from near the Seaquarium entrance (4:30 PM) to take its daily hour-long tour of the coral reefs and submerged wrecks offshore, with their kaleidoscope of fish who are happy to emerge when the diver empties their daily meal into the water. Queen angelfish, yellowtail snapper, porcupine fish, and the ever-popular barracuda are among the denizens. The craft, with a barge top that submerges only 5 feet underwater, has wide glass windows in the submerged section, which extends down to about 100 feet. Call for reservations 24 hours in advance (☎ 599/7–604892; $29 adults, $19 children under 12), and get your ticket before going into the Seaquarium.

Don't neglect the Seaquarium itself. It's the world's only public aquarium where sea creatures are raised and cultivated totally by natural methods. Where else can you hand-feed a shark (or watch a diver do it)? The new section called Animal Encounters consists of several large, open water enclosures that bring you face to face with a variety of jaws. If you want to snorkel among them, you're welcome. In one pool, snorkelers and divers swim freely with stingrays, tarpon, groupers, and such. In the other, Shark Encounter, divers and snorkelers can feed sharks

by hand in perfect safety, they say, through thick mesh fencing that separates diver and shark. In between these two busy tanks is an underwater observatory where you can watch, if shark feeding isn't your hobby.
The cost is $50 for divers, $30 for snorkelers, which includes admission to the Seaquarium and food for the sharks. Reservations for Animal Encounters must be made 24 hours in advance.

You can spend several hours in Seaquarium, mesmerized by the 46 freshwater tanks full of more than 400 varieties of exotic fish and vegetation found in the waters around Curaçao, including sharks, lobsters,
turtles, corals, and sponges. Look out for the more than 5-foot-long mascot, Herbie the lugubrious jewfish. Four sea lions from Uruguay are the
most recent pride of the aquarium. If you get hungry, stop at the excellent Italian restaurant or the steak house–cum–Mexican eatery. There
are also glass-bottom-boat tours, fun feeding shows, and a viewing platform overlooking the wreck of the steamship SS *Oranje Nassau*, which
sank in 1906 and now sits in 10 feet of water. A nearby 495-yard man-
made beach of white sand is well suited to novice swimmers and children, and bathroom and shower facilities are available. A souvenir
shop sells some of the best postcards and coral jewelry on the island.
☎ 599/9–616666. ☛ *$6 adults, $3 children.* ☉ *Daily 9 AM–10 PM.*

❻ **Curaçao Underwater Marine Park** (☎ 599/9–618131) consists of
about 12½ miles of untouched coral reefs that have been granted the
status of national park. Mooring buoys have been placed at the most
interesting dive sites on the reef to provide safe anchoring and to prevent damage to the reef. Several sunken ships lie awaiting visitors in
the deep. The park stretches along the south shore from the Princess
Beach Hotel in Willemstad to the eastern tip of the island.

❼ **Landhuis Brievengat** (☎ 599/9–378344) is a 10-minute drive northeast of Willemstad, near the Centro Deportivo sports stadium. On the
last Sunday of the month (from 10 AM to 3 PM), this old estate holds
an open house with crafts demonstrations and folkloric shows. You
can see the original kitchen still intact, the 18-inch-thick walls, fine antiques, and the watchtowers once used for lovers' trysts. The restaurant, which is open only on Wednesday and Friday, serves a fine
rijsttafel (Indonesian smorgasbord). Every Friday night a party is held
on the wide wraparound terrace, with two bands and plenty to drink.

Head northwest toward the airport (take a right onto Gosieweg, follow the loop right onto Schottegatweg, take another right onto Jan Nor-
duynweg, a final right onto Rooseveltweg, and follow the signs) to the
❽ island's newest attraction, **Hato Caves.** Hour-long guided tours wind
down into the various chambers to the water pools, voodoo chamber,
wishing well, fruit bats' sleeping quarters, and Curaçao Falls, where a
stream of silver joins with a stream of gold (they're colored by lights)
and is guarded by a limestone "dragon" perched nearby. Hidden lights
illuminate the limestone formations and gravel walkways. This is one
of the better Caribbean caves open to the public. ☎ 599/9–68037. ☛
$4.25 adults, $2.75 children. ☉ *Tues.–Sun. 10–5.*

What to See and Do with Children

The **Curaçao Seaquarium,** *see* Exploring, *above.*

Beaches

Curaçao has some 38 beaches, but unfortunately many are extremely
rocky and litter-strewn. The best way to find "your" beach is to rent
a Jeep, motor scooter, or heavy-treaded car. Ask your hotel to pack

a picnic basket for you and go exploring. Getting lost and ending up in some undiscovered cove is half the fun. Curaçao doesn't have Aruba's long, powdery stretches of sand; instead, you'll discover the joy of inlets: tiny bay openings to the sea marked by craggy cliffs, exotic trees, and scads of interesting pebbles. Imagine a beach that's just big enough for your party of four—or a party of just two. Beware of thorns and keep an eye out for flying fish. They propel their tails through the water until they reach a speed of 44 mph, then spread their fins and soar.

Hotels with the best beach properties include the new **Sonesta Beach Hotel** (impressively long), the **Princess Beach** (impressively sensuous), and the **Coral Cliff Resort** (impressively deserted). No matter which hotel you're staying at, beach hopping to other hotels can be fun. Nonguests are supposed to pay the hotels a beach fee, but often there is no one to collect.

One of the largest, more spectacular beaches on Curaçao is **Blauwbaai** (Blue Bay). There's plenty of white sand and lots of shady places, showers, and changing facilities, but since it's a private beach, you'll pay an entrance fee of about $2.50 per car. Take the road that leads past the Holiday Beach Hotel and the Curaçao Caribbean north toward Julianadorp. At the end of the stretch of straight road, a sign will instruct you to bear left for Blauwbaai and the fishing village of St. Michiel. The latter is a good place for diving.

Starting from the church of St. Willibrordus, signs will direct you to **Daai Booi Bay,** a sandy shore dotted with thatched shelters. The road to this public beach is a small paved highway flanked on either side by thick lush trees and huge organ-pipe cacti. The beach is curved, with shrubbery rooted into the side of the rocky cliffs—a great place for swimming.

Knip Bay has two parts: Big (Groot) Knip and Little (Kleine) Knip. Only Little Knip is shaded with trees, but these are manchineels, so steer clear of them. Also beware of cutting your feet on beer bottle caps. Both beaches have alluring white sand, but only Big Knip has changing facilities. Big Knip also has several tiki huts for shade and calm turquoise waters that are perfect for swimming and lounging. The protected cove, flanked by sheer cliffs, is usually a blast on Sundays, when there is live music. To get there, take the road to the Knip Landhouse, then turn right. Signs will direct you.

Playa Forti, just south of Westpunt (the island's northwest point), is a double cove of beige sand with a splendid view of Westpunt Church, colorful fishing boats bobbing in the turquoise water, and a little café in the shade where you can watch local boys dive from the cliffs on weekends.

Playa Lagun, farther southeast, is dotted with powder-blue camping huts and caught between towering gunmetal gray cliffs. Cognoscenti know this is one of the best places to snorkel—you may even go nose to nose with the resident giant squid.

To reach **Santa Barbara,** a popular family beach on the eastern tip, you'll drive through one of Curaçao's toniest neighborhoods, Spanish Water, where gleaming white yachts replace humble fishing fleets. The beach has changing facilities and a snack bar but charges a small admission fee, usually around $3.35 per car. Around the bend, **Caracas Bay** is a popular dive site, with a sunken ship so close to the surface that snorkelers can balance their flippers on the helm.

Sports and the Outdoors

Fitness Centers

Turkish bath, sauna, whirlpool, massage, beauty treatments—all the gentle luxuries can be found at the **Sundance Health & Fitness Center** (John F. Kennedy Blvd., ☎ 599/9–62770). Professional medical staff is on tap. The **Ooms Sports Institute** (Jan Thiel Bay, ☎ 599/9–618100), at the Lions Dive Hotel, is open to nonguests for a fee. It schedules exercise classes and is equipped with the latest fitness equipment.

Golf

Visitors are welcome to play golf at the **Curaçao Golf and Squash Club** (☎ 599/9–373590) in Emmastad. The nine-hole course offers a challenge because of the stiff trade winds and the sand greens. ⊘ 8–12:30.

Horseback Riding

Ashari's Ranch (☎ 599/9–686254) is the only stable to offer romps to the beach ($15 an hour).

Jogging

The **Rif Recreation Area,** locally known as the *corredor,* stretches from the water plant at Mundo Nobo to the Curaçao Caribbean Hotel along the sea. It consists of more than 1.2 miles of palm-lined beachfront, a wading pond, and a jogging track with an artificial surface, as well as a big playground. There is good security and street lighting along the entire length of the beachfront.

Sailing

Sail Curaçao (Yachtclub Asiento, Spanish Water, ☎ 599/9–676003) offers day sails, sailing instruction, snorkeling trips and windsurfing.

Tennis

Most hotels (including Sonesta Beach, Curaçao Caribbean, Las Palmas, Princess Beach, and Holiday Beach) offer well-paved courts, illuminated for day and night games. These courts are usually occupied by guests of the hotels. Your best bet if you're not staying at one of these properties is the **Santa Catherina Sports and Country Club** (☎ 599/9–677028), where forty-five minutes of court time costs $7 during the day, $10 after 6 PM.

Water Sports

Curaçao has facilities for all kinds of water sports, thanks to the government-sponsored **Curaçao Underwater Marine Park** (☎ 599/9–618131), which includes almost a third of the island's southern diving waters. Scuba divers and snorkelers can enjoy more than 12½ miles of protected reefs and shores, with normal visibility from 60 to 80 feet (up to 150 feet on good days). With water temperatures ranging from 75° to 82°F, wet suits are generally unnecessary. No coral collecting, spearfishing, or littering is allowed. An exciting wreck to explore is the SS *Oranje Nassau,* which ran aground more than 80 years ago and now hosts hundreds of exotic fish and unusually shaped coral.

Most hotels either offer their own program of water sports or will be happy to make arrangements for you. An introductory scuba resort course usually runs about $50–$65.

Underwater Curaçao (☎ 599/9–618131) offers complete vacation-dive packages in conjunction with the Lions Dive Hotel & Marina. Its fully stocked dive shop, located between the Lions Dive Hotel and the Curaçao Seaquarium, offers equipment for both sale and rental. Personal instruction and group lessons are conducted on state-of-the-art dive boats personally designed by "Dutch" Schrier. One dive will run you

$33; dive-only packages are available. Take a dive-snorkeling trip on the *Coral Sea,* a 40-foot twin diesel yacht-style dive boat. Landlubbers can see beneath the sea aboard *The Coral View,* a monohull flat-top glass-bottom boat that makes four excursions a day. (*See also Seaworld Explorer* in Exploring, *above.*)

Seascape (☎ 599/9–625000, ext. 177), at the Curaçao Caribbean Hotel and Casino, specializes in snorkeling and scuba-diving trips to reefs and underwater wrecks in every type of water vehicle—from pedal boats and water scooters to waterskis and Windsurfers. A six-dive package costs $155 and includes unlimited beach diving plus one free night dive. Snorkeling gear costs about $5 an hour or $10 a day to rent. Die-hard fishermen with companions who prefer to suntan will enjoy the day trip to Little Curaçao, the "clothes optional" island between Curaçao and Bonaire, where the fish are reputed to be lively: Plan on $25 per person. Deep-sea fishing for a maximum of six people can also be arranged; it costs $300 for a half day, $500 for a full day.

Peter Hughes Divers (☎ 599/9–367888, ext. 5047), at the Princess Beach Hotel, rents equipment and conducts diving and snorkeling trips. Also available is a cabin cruiser for half-day ($200) or full-day ($500) deep-sea fishing excursions.

For windsurfing, check out the **Curaçao High Wind Center** (Princess Beach Hotel, ☎ 599/9–614944). Lessons cost $20 an hour.

Coral Cliff Diving (☎ 599/9–642822) offers scuba certification courses ($320), a one-week windsurfing school ($170), a one-week basic sailing course ($255), and a full schedule of dive and snorkeling trips to Curaçao's southwest coast. It also rents pedal boats, Hobie Cats, and underwater cameras.

Spectator Sports

Soccer matches and baseball games, from March through October, are held in the modern and comfortable **Centro Deportivo** stadium, located about 10 minutes from town at Bonamweg 49. ☎ 599/9–376620. ☺ *Daily 9:30–12:30 and 3–6.*

Shopping

Curaçao has long enjoyed the reputation of having some of the best shops in the Caribbean, but don't expect posh Madison Avenue boutiques. With a few exceptions (such as Benetton, which recently moved into the Caribbean with a vengeance), the quality of women's fashions here lies along the lines of sales racks, although not paying a VAT or other taxes sweetens any purchase. Be aware that many shops are closed on Sunday.

If you're looking for bargains on Swiss watches, cameras, crystal, perfumes, or electronic equipment, do some comparison shopping back home and come armed with a list of prices. Willemstad is no longer a free port.

Shopping Areas

Most of the shops are concentrated in **Willemstad's Punda** within about a six-block area. The main shopping streets are **Heerenstraat, Breedestraat,** and **Madurostraat. Heerenstraat** and **Gomezplein** are pedestrian malls, closed to traffic, and their roadbeds have been raised to sidewalk level and covered with pink inlaid tiles.

The hippest shopping area lies under the **Waterfort Arches,** along with a variety of restaurants and bars. One of our two favorite shops under the arches is **Bamali** (☎ 599/9–612258), which sells Indonesian batik clothing, leather bags, and charming handicrafts. Our other favorite at Waterfort is **Clarisa & Laura Kemper** (☎ 599/9–618313), which specializes in exquisite leather and silk creations.

Good Buys

Julius L. Penha & Sons (Heerenstraat 1, ☎ 599/9–612266), in front of the Pontoon Bridge, sells French perfumes, Hummel figurines, linen from Madeira, delftware, and handbags from Argentina, Italy, and Spain. The store also has an extensive cosmetics counter. **Boolchand's** (Heerenstraat 4B, ☎ 599/9–616233) handles an interesting variety of merchandise behind a facade of red-and-white-checked tiles. Stock up here on French perfumes, British cashmere sweaters, Italian silk ties, Dutch dolls, Swiss watches, and Japanese cameras.

CLOTHING

Benetton (Madurostraat 4, ☎ 599/9–614619, and other addresses) has winter stock in July and summer stock in December; all stock is 20% off the retail price. **Crazy Look** (Madurostraat 6, ☎ 599/9–611440) has French, Italian, and Dutch fashions with a hip Eurotrash look, as well as trendy sweatshirts and baggy pants. **Boutique Liska** (Schottegatweg Oost 191-A, ☎ 599/9–613111) is where local residents shop for smart women's fashions. **Boutique Aquarius** (Breedestraat 9, ☎ 599/9–612618) sells Fendi merchandise for 25% less than in the United States. Fendi fanatics can stock up on belts, shoes, pocketbooks, wallets, and even watches. If you've always longed for Dutch clogs, tulips, delftware, Dutch fashions, or chocolate, try **Clog Dance** (De Rouvilleweg 9B, ☎ 599/9–623280).

DELICACIES

Toko Zuikertuintje (Zuikertuintjeweg, ☎ 599/9–370188), a supermarket built on the original 17th-century Zuikertuintje Landhuis, is where most of the local elite shop. Enjoy the free tea and coffee while you stock up on all sorts of European and Dutch delicacies. Shopping here for a picnic is a treat in itself.

JEWELRY AND WATCHES

The leading jeweler in the Netherlands Antilles, **Spritzer & Fuhrmann** (Gomezplein 1, ☎ 599/9–612600) carries gold jewelry, watches, French crystal, diamonds, emeralds, and china. **Gandelman** (Breedestraat 35, ☎ 599/9–611854) has watches by Cartier and Piaget, leather goods by Prima Classe, and Lallique, Baccarat, and Daum crystal. **La Zahav N.V.** (Curaçao International Airport, ☎ 599/9–689594) is one of the best places to buy gold jewelry—with or without diamonds, rubies, and emeralds—at true discount prices. The shop is located in the airport transit hall, just at the top of the staircase.

LINENS

New Amsterdam (Gomezplein 14, ☎ 599/9–613823) is the place to price hand-embroidered tablecloths, napkins, and pillowcases.

Tablecloths begin at $32, double bedspreads at $100.

LOCAL CRAFTS

Native crafts and curios are on hand at **Fundason Obra di Man** (Bargestraat 57, ☎ 599/9–612413). Particularly impressive are the posters of Curaçao's architecture. **Black Coral** (Princess Beach Hotel, ☎ 599/9–614944) is owned by Dutch-born artisan Bert Knubben, one of Curaçao's true characters. For the past 30 years, he's been designing and sculpting the most exciting black-coral jewelry in the Caribbean—and he even dives for the coral himself, with special permission from the government. Dolphin pendants and twiglike earrings finished in 14-karat gold are excellent buys. Call before you drop by. Artisans with disabilities at **Landhuis Groot Santa Martha** (☎ 599/9–641950) fashion handicrafts of varying types. **Arawak Clay Products** (Cruise Terminal, Otrabanda, ☎ 599/9–627249) has a factory showroom of native-made crafts. You can purchase a variety of tiles, plates, pots, and tiny replicas of landhouse. **Gallery 86** (☎ 599/9–613417), in the Bloksteeg (Punda) opposite the Bank of the Netherlands Antilles, features the works of local artists and occasionally those of South Americans and Africans.

Dining

Restaurateurs in Curaçao believe in whetting appetites with a variety of cuisines and intriguing ambience: Dine under the boughs of magnificent old trees, in the romantic gloom of wine cellars in renovated landhouses, or on the ramparts of 18th-century forts. Curaçaoans partake of some of the best Indonesian food in the Caribbean, and they also find it hard to resist the French, Swiss, Dutch, and Swedish delights.

What to Wear

Dress in restaurants is almost always casual, but if you feel like putting on your finery, there will always be a place for you. Some of the resort dining rooms and nicer restaurants do require that men wear jackets, especially in high season; ask when you make reservations. Do take a wrap or a light sweater with you—for some reason, most restaurants have their air conditioners going full blast.

CATEGORY	COST*
$$$$	over $40
$$$	$30–$40
$$	$15–$30
$	under $15

per person, excluding drinks and service charge

$$$$ **De Taveerne.** From the intricate detail of its antiques and brickwork
★ to its impressive Continental menu, this restaurant is the most elegant, romantic spot on the island. Dining is in the whitewashed wine cellar of this magnificent renovated octagonal country estate, built in the 1800s by an exiled Venezuelan revolutionary. The best appetizer is the salmon carpaccio with laurel bay dressing en brioche. The entrées are as rich and decadent as the ambience: velvety lobster bisque finished with Armagnac, sautéed goose liver in plum sauce, and smoked eel with horseradish. For dessert, there's the absolutely unforgettable broiled pears, topped with vanilla ice cream and drenched with Curaçao chocolate liqueur. ✕ *Landhuis Groot Davelaar, on Silena, near the Promenade Shopping Center,* ☎ *599/9–370669. Reservations required. AE, DC, MC, V. Closed Sun.*

$$$–$$$$ **Bistro Le Clochard.** A romantic gem, the bistro is built into the 18th-century Rif Fort and is suffused with the cool, dark atmosphere of ages past—an oasis of arched doorways, exposed brickwork, wood beams, and lace curtains. Cocktails and hors d'oeuvres are now served on the new Waterside Terrace, with its merry view of the floating bridge and harbor. The use of fresh ingredients in the consistently well prepared French and Swiss dishes makes dining here a dream, though a pricey one. Try the fresh-fish platters or the tender veal in mushroom sauce. The chef is especially adroit at preparing game, such as the wild boar cutlet in honey and sesame. Savor the fondue and let yourself get carried away by the unusual setting; just save room for the chocolate mousse. Avoid visits on weekends, when an inexplicably hokey duo regales din-

ers with a violin and jarring electric piano. But you might enjoy the complimentary snacks on Friday at Hungry Hour from 5 to 7. ✗ *On the Otrabanda Rif Fort,* ☎ *59/9–625666. Reservations required. AE, DC, MC, V. Closed Sun. off-season. No lunch Sat.*

$$$–$$$$ **L'Alouette.** With only eight tables, this cozy space defines intimate. Taste-
★ ful touches include stained glass, fanciful stemware, art-deco lamps, and severe black-and-white tables that provide a stunning contrast to the peach walls and voluminous lushly folded drapery. Maria Eugenia Saban's cooking is equally subtle and sophisticated, wonderfully tex-tured; everything is carefully prepared and slow-cooked in its own juices. You might begin with two cheese flans (goat cheese–leek and Gruyère-mushroom), perfectly complemented by a tomato sauce perfumed with basil, or a seafood sausage in lobster velouté. Your entrée might be the sublime salmon in lime and *ciboulette* (chive) sauce. Maria is an am-ateur chef in the best sense of the word: She cooks because she loves it. Her exquisite presentations and creative counterpoints can't fail to seduce even the most discriminating palate. ✗ *Orionweg 12,* ☎ *599/9 –618222. Reservations required. AE, DC, MC, V.*

$$$ **Fort Nassau Restaurant.** This is *the* place from which to witness the twinkling magic of Curaçao at night. High on a hilltop overlooking Willemstad, the restaurant is built into an 18th-century fort and gives a 360-degree view of the city's rooftops. Go for a drink in the breezy, couple-filled Battery Terrace bar or dine in air-conditioned comfort in front of the huge bay windows. The menu is diverse, from duck with a molasses sauce to lightly broiled fish (ask the waiter what's fresh—and not on the menu), but the price that you pay is more for the views and ambience. Avoid the enticing yet overly complex stabs at innova-tive cuisine, such as roast hare in sesame oil drizzled with star anise sauce: The simple selections are the best here. ✗ *Near Juliana Bridge,* ☎ *599/9–613086. Reservations required. AE, DC, MC, V.*

$$$ **La Pergola.** Built into the stuccoed walls of the Waterfort, with huge picture windows fronting the rambunctious sea and a pretty pink-and-white arbor wound with bunches of grapes, La Pergola offers creative variations on Italian standards. Try the smoked salmon drizzled with olive oil and studded with cloves; grouper siciliana with capers, olives, anchovies, tomatoes, and garlic; and the tiramisù and *zuppa inglese,* both some of the most authentic in the Caribbean. ✗ *Waterfort Arches, Willemstad,* ☎ *599/9–613482. Reservations advised. AE, DC, MC, V. No lunch Sat.*

$$–$$$ **Pirates.** A friendly and efficient waitstaff delivers dish after dish of su-perb seafood, including such delicacies as oyster soup, seviche, paella, and conch. The sea bass Creole-style is delicious, as is the red snapper in almond sauce. Diners with a hearty appetite are likely to accumu-late a large tab. The decor is lighthearted nautical, with an anchor, a watchtower, and, of course, a presiding mermaid. The dominant color scheme is olive and periwinkle. ✗ *Curaçao Caribbean Hotel,* ☎ *599/9– 625000. Reservations advised. AE, DC, MC, V.*

$$ **Fort Waarzaamreid.** High on a hill overlooking Willemstad and the harbor, this fort was captured by Captain Bligh of HMS *Bounty* two centuries ago. Now it is controlled by an Irishman, Tom Farrel, who operates an open-air restaurant and bar in the evening. The atmosphere is informal, and the food is primarily barbecued seafood and steaks decorated with your own makings from a salad bar. You will be equally well greeted if you go just for cocktails and snacks—and the sunsets are magnificent. ✗ *Seru Domi, Willemstad,* ☎ *599/9–623633. Located off the main highway on the Otrabanda side of the suspension bridge. Reservations advised. AE, V. No lunch.*

$$ Rijstaffel Indonesia Restaurant. An antique rickshaw guarding the entrance sets the mood for this tranquil spot. No steaks or chops here, just one dish after another of exotic delicacies that make up the traditional Indonesian banquet called rijstaffel. Choose from 16 to 25 traditional dishes that are set buffet-style around you. You can also order from an à la carte menu, which includes fried noodles, fresh jumbo shrimp in garlic, and combination meat-and-fish platters. Desserts are nearly mystical: A "ladies only" ice cream comes with a red rose, and the coconut ice cream comes packed in a coconut shell. The walls are hung with beautiful Indonesian puppets ($25–$40) that make stunning gifts. ✕ *Mercurriusstraat 13–15, Salinja,* ☎ *599/9–612606. Reservations required. AE, DC, MC, V. No lunch Sun.*

$$ Seaview. Seaview is nestled snugly in the corner of the Waterfort Arches, where the surf pounds against the rocks—you expect the sea to drench you at any minute. This casual terrace eatery offers sterling fresh seafood. Try the tangy *salpicon de mariscos,* a version of seviche that includes everything from octopus to shrimp seasoned with a saffron, bay leaf, and lime vinaigrette. Landlubbers won't be disappointed by the tender pepper fillet. The chef can surprise with such specialties as green-and-white asparagus en brioche kissed by a delicate fragrant herbal cream sauce. It's a marvelous place to watch the pyrotechnics of the sun at dusk. ✕ *Waterfort Arches, Willemstad,* ☎ *599/9–616688. AE. No lunch Sun.*

$ Cactus Club. A veritable grove of aloe and cacti greets you in the courtyard of this Caribbean version of Bennigan's or TGIFriday's. The inside is surprisingly subdued: faux Tiffany lamps, hanging plants, whirring ceiling fans—hardly the honky-tonk atmosphere the name leads you to expect. Food is cheap and filling, tending toward favorites like fettuccine Alfredo, fajitas, buffalo wings, and Cajun snapper. And of course there are burgers, prepared to your liking. It's predictably popular with both locals and homesick Americans. ✕ *Mahaai,* ☎ *599/9– 371600. DC, MC, V.*

$ Golden Star Restaurant. This place looks and feels more like a friendly
★ roadside diner than a full-fledged restaurant, but the native food here is among the best in town. Owner Marie Burke turns out such Antillean specialties as *bestia chiki* (goat stew), shrimp Creole, and delicately seasoned grilled conch, all served with generous heaps of rice, fried plantains, and avocado. Steaks and chops can be had for the asking. ✕ *Socratestraat 2,* ☎ *599/9–654795. AE, DC, MC, V.*

$ Jaanchi's Restaurant. Tour buses stop regularly at this open-air restaurant for lunches of mouthwatering native dishes. The main-course specialty is a hefty platter of fresh-caught fish, potatoes, and vegetables. Curaçaoans joke that Jaanchi's "iguana soup is so strong it could resurrect the dead"—truth is, it tastes just like chicken soup, only better. But Jaanchi Jr. says, if you want iguana, you must order in advance "because we have to go out and catch them." He's not kidding. ✕ *Westpunt 15,* ☎ *599/9–640126. AE, DC, MC, V.*

Lodging

Hotels in Curaçao all have their pluses and minuses. If you're a business traveler, you'll appreciate the modest Van Der Valk Plaza, Otrabanda, and new Porto Paseo, with easy access to the city center, but you'll have a long trek to the beach. Guests at the sophisticated Avila Beach, Sonesta Beach, Curaçao Caribbean, Princess Beach, and Holiday Beach hotels enjoy their own beaches, but they're a 10-minute drive from town. The Curaçao Caribbean and the Sonesta Beach Hotel are across the road from the International Trade Center. Most hotels offer free shuttle bus services to the downtown area. They also either include breakfast or offer a large buffet breakfast at a reasonable price. Full American Plans are not popular because of the abundance of good restaurants in all price ranges.

There are many rentals available on the island. Your best bet is to contact the **Curaçao Tourism Development Foundation** (Box 3266, Curaçao, Netherlands Antilles, ☎ 599/9–616000, FAX 599/9–612305) at least two months before you plan to go; it will send you a list of available properties.

CATEGORY	COST*
$$$	over $175
$$	$110–$175
$	under $110

All prices are for a standard double room for two and include tax and service charges.

$$$ **Curaçao Caribbean Hotel and Casino.** This five-story complex is self-contained, with one of the best organized activities programs on the island, including rum-swizzle parties, volleyball, T-shirt painting contests, Papiamento lessons, walking tours, and special theme nights for dinner and dancing. The lovely champagne-colored coves can become crowded, but there is a lounging area above them that is perfect for sunbathing. Water sports include everything imaginable. Guest rooms on the first four floors are less than striking, in spite of the new burgundy rugs and a minor face-lift. The top floor, dedicated to business guests, has its own reception area, breakfast area, and fax and computer capabilities. It's the only floor that was completely renovated, yet it still appears unfinished, though nice extras include hair dryers and coat presses. All the hotel rooms have small balconies, but only half face the sea. Plans are being developed to extend the hotel's beach area and build new town-house time-sharing units. ⊠ *Box 2133, Piscadera Bay, Willemstad,* ☎ *599/9–625000 or 800/344–1212,* FAX *599/9–625846. 200 rooms. 3 restaurants, 24-hr coffee shop, 2 bars, pool, casino, beauty salon, barbershop, 2 lighted tennis courts, health spa, boutiques, drugstore, secretarial services, telex, meeting and convention rooms. AE, D, DC, MC, V. EP, MAP.*

$$$ **Kadushi Cliffs.** If you're staying for a week or more, you might want to rent a condo away from town, in the beautifully lush western part of the island. There are 22 modern two-bedroom villas here, all beautifully furnished. A pool and a restaurant are the only real facilities (there's a tiny beach), but this dearth helps keep the noise level down. The management will arrange for sports and boating. A car is required. ⊠ *Westpunt,* ☎ *599/9–640200 or 800/448–8355,* FAX *599/9–640282. 22 villas. Restaurant, pool. AE, DC, MC, V.*

$$$ **Princess Beach Hotel and Casino.** You can't beat the location: You're on one of the most beautiful beaches in Curaçao and right in front of the Underwater Marine Park. The hotel has recently been renovated, and two new ocean-view wings have added space gracefully. Most rooms are huge, with breathtaking ocean or garden views. All rooms include a hair dryer, air-conditioning, color cable TV, and either a balcony or a patio. The pathway to guest rooms is through lush, tropical grounds full of chirping birds. The freshwater pool has the added bonus of a staff to offer drinks to guests as they paddle about on floats. The casino is one of the more exciting ones in Curaçao. This is a high-energy place, with lively happy hours, popular theme buffet dinners, and a slew of sports activities to keep guests busy, including those offered by the Curaçao High Wind Center. ⊠ *Martin Luther King Blvd. 8,* ☎

599/9–367888 or 800/327–3286, ⚏ *599/9–614131. 341 rooms. Restaurant, pool with bar, boutiques, drugstore, dive shop, tour desk, car- and scooter-rental agent, casino, beauty salon, baby-sitting services. AE, DC, MC, V. EP, BP, MAP, FAP.*

$$$ **Sonesta Beach Hotel & Casino.** Curaçao's newest resort is a sprawling,
★   burnished ocher low rise, built to blend in with the surrounding Dutch Colonial–style architecture. The approach, through lushly landscaped grounds brimming with oleander, hibiscus, and gently swaying palms, is impressive; and the beach is one of Curaçao's finest. The air-conditioned accommodations have a muted tropical pastel color scheme, TVs, minibars, tiled showers and baths, and either a terrace or a balcony. Striking contemporary artworks adorn the walls. Price is determined solely by view, though all rooms boast at least a partial ocean vista. Two children under age 12 stay free when sharing the room with their parents, and the free daily "Just Us Kids" program offers supervised activities for children ages 5 to 12. ⚏ *Box 6003, Piscadera Bay,* ☎ *599/9–368800 or 800/766–3782,* ⚏ *599/9–627502. 214 rooms, 34 suites. 3 restaurants, 2 bars, casino, water-sports and dive center, free-form swimming pool with swim-up bar, children's wading pool, 2 lighted tennis courts, health club, shopping arcade, 2 whirlpools, baby-sitting service, children's program. AE, DC, MC, V. EP.*

$$ **Avila Beach Hotel.** The royal family of Holland and its ministers stay
★   at this 200-year-old mansion overlooking the ocean for three good reasons: the privacy, the personalized service, and the austere elegance. The reception area is cooled by whirring fans and graced with brass lanterns, porcelain statuary, and a baby grand, suggesting colonial plantation living at its ultimate. The original guest rooms (in the mansion) are charming but basic-looking, with hardwood or tile floors and small baths with showers only. Most guests will prefer the newer La Belle Alliance section, on its own beach adjacent to the main property. These Mediterranean-style yellow-and-gold low-rise buildings, with Dutch red-gabled roofs and lighted walkways, hold 45 rooms and 18 one- and two-bedroom apartments. All of these units have either balconies or patios with sea views. Half of the rooms are equipped with kitchenettes; all of the apartments have full kitchens. Although this section lacks the Old World ambience of the original structure, the accommodations are larger and have more modern amenities. The restaurant has a unique outdoor dining area shaded by an enormous tree. The Danish chefs, who specialize in a Viking pot, local dishes, and weekly smorgasbord, also smoke their own fish and bake their own bread. Recent additions to the Avila include a new café-jazz club with an open-air sea view, a tennis court, and a conference room. The double quarter-moon-shape beach is enchanting. Many consider this hotel the best buy on the island and a welcome change from the new megaresorts. ⚏ *Box 791, Penstraat 130134, Willemstad,* ☎ *599/9–614377 or 800/448–8355,* ⚏ *599/9–611493. 95 rooms. Restaurant, coffee shop, tennis court, bar, baby-sitting service, cable TV, conference room, shuttle bus to city center. AE, DC, MC, V. EP.*

$$ **Holiday Beach Hotel and Casino.** This ex–Holiday Inn is a four-story, 27-year-old, U-shape, aquamarine-colored building surrounding a pool area. Over the past four years, the rooms have been completely renovated and refurnished in a beige, emerald, and rose color scheme, with bleached wood and rattan furniture. All have TV, shower and bath, and balcony. Half the rooms face the parking lot; most of the others face the pool area, and only a few have sea views. The air-conditioned lobby is spacious to permit the assembly of tour groups, and one of the island's largest casinos, Casino Royale, is off to the lobby's left. The hotel's

outstanding feature is its crescent beach, quite large for Curaçao and dotted with palm trees. There's also a water-sports concession and a tiki-hut beach bar. Guests are encouraged to join in the voluminous daily selection of activities. The lobby bar happy hour is one of the most popular on the island. While this is an older property, the renovation, along with the friendly service, makes it a good choice for people seeking good value on a middle-of-the-road budget. ☎ *Box 2178, Otrabanda, Pater Euwensweg, Willemstad,* ☎ *599/9–625400 or 800/223–9815,* FAX *599/9–624397. 200 rooms. Playground, 2 tennis courts, water sports, beauty shop, boutique, drugstore, gift shop, car-rental agent, baby-sitting service, casino. AE, DC, MC, V. EP.*

$ **Coral Cliff Resort and Beach Club.** Seclusion and rustic simplicity are everything here. A 45-minute ride from the center of Willemstad, the grounds of the resort boast a beach so alluring that it attracts even native islanders seeking a weekend retreat. (The beach is open to the public for a $5 admission charge.) The resort exudes a European atmosphere—wood beams accent the lavender, mint, olive, cream, and teal colors—and is very popular with Dutch tourists. Guests used to luxurious or amenity-laden resorts will find the rooms stark and in sore need of modernizing. However, all are air-conditioned, have spectacular views of the sea, and are equipped with satellite TV, direct-dial phone, and an old but functional kitchenette. The hotel recently installed a children's playground and miniature golf course, a tennis court, and slot machines in the bar. All guests receive complimentary airport transfers. ☎ *Box 3782, Santa Marta Bay,* ☎ *599/9–641820 or 800/ 223–9815,* FAX *599/9–641781. 35 units. Restaurant, bar, pool, car-rental agent, miniature golf, marina, water-sports center, and PADI 4-star dive shop. AE, DC, MC, V. EP, BP, MAP, FAP.*

$ **Landhaus Daniel.** Dating back to 1630, this plantation house was never a farm, but it served as an inn for travelers going east or west on the island. The property, at the west end of the island, has a restaurant, a pool, and a dive center as well. Rooms are nicely furnished. A few have private baths; only one is air-conditioned, but the trade winds usually take care of excessive heat at night. ☎ *Wegnaar Westpunt,* ☎ *599/9– 648400. 9 rooms. Restaurant, dive center. No credit cards. EP.*

$ **Lions Dive Hotel & Marina.** This recent addition to the Curaçao vacation scene is a hop, skip, and plunge away from the Seaquarium. The pink-and-green caravansary is set next to a quarter mile of private beach. The rooms are airy, modern, and light-filled, with tile floors, large bathrooms, and lots of windows. A pair of French doors leads out to a spacious balcony or terrace, and every room has a view of the sea. The Sunday-night happy hour is especially festive, with a local merengue band playing poolside. By midnight, however, the only sound to be heard is the whir of your room's air conditioner. Pluses include a young, attractive staff who are eager to please and a top-notch scuba center. Dive packages are offered with Underwater Curaçao, and most, if not all, of the guests are dive enthusiasts. ☎ *Bapor Kibra, Curaçao,* ☎ *599/9– 618100 or 800/223–9815,* FAX *599/9–618200. 72 air-conditioned rooms with color TV. Restaurant, terrace bar, pool, scuba-diving center with 2 dive boats, water-sports concession, windsurfing center, video-rental shop. AE, DC, MC, V. CP.*

$ **Otrabanda Hotel & Casino.** Built in 1991, this city hotel is across the harbor from downtown Willemstad, in the historic Otrabanda section. Rooms are tiny but appealing, decorated with rattan furnishings and light pastels and paintings of country life, with smashing harbor views. All have cable TV, air-conditioning, and full bath. If you're watching your budget, this hotel offers superior value. ☎ *Breedestraat (O),*

Otrabanda, ☎ 599/9–627400, ℻ 599/9–627299. 45 rooms. Coffee shop, restaurant, bar, casino. AE, V. CP.

$ **Porto Paseo Hotel and Casino.** The tropical gardens, lamplit flagstone
★ courtyard, rock walls, and mustard-colored red-tile-roof buildings of
this charming new (1993) property on the Otrabanda side of the harbor were designed to duplicate a typical landhaus. At its center is the hotel, a restored 17th-century building. It's a remarkably peaceful, private place amid the city's bustle. Squawking white cockatoos preside over the entrance to an open-air bar splashed with murals depicting island life and overlooking Santa Anna Bay. The unadorned but pleasant rooms shimmer in silver, mauve, and ecru and have satellite TV, air-conditioning, and a shower bath. 🖂 De Rouvilleweg 47, Willemstad, ☎ 599/9–627878 or 800/287–2226, ℻ 599/9–627969. 50 rooms. Restaurant, bar, dive center, pool, casino. AE, DC, MC, V.

$ **Van Der Valk Plaza Hotel and Casino.** "Please don't touch the passing ships" is the slogan of the Van Der Valk Plaza, the only hotel in the world with marine-collision insurance. The ships do come close to the island's first high-rise hotel, which is built right into the massive walls of a 17th-century fort at the entrance of Willemstad's harbor. At the Plaza, you give up beachfront (you have beach privileges at major hotels, however) for walking access to the city's center. Consequently, it's a business traveler's oasis, complete with secretarial service, fax and telex machines, and typing and translation services. The ramparts rising from the sea offer a fantastic evening view of the twinkling lights of the city. A new, enlarged casino has been completed, the fine restaurants are a splendid place to watch the ships anchor in the harbor, and the lobby is now a vision in marble, with handsomely upholstered furniture, vaulting trees, and a winding lagoon and waterfall. Regrettably, the rooms are sorely lacking in style and decor. One hundred and thirty-five of the rooms are in the tower, many with a sea view and some with balconies. All rooms have cable TV, air-conditioning, and a minifridge. 🖂 Box 229, Plaza Piar, Willemstad, ☎ 599/9–612500 or 800/447–7462, ℻ 599/9–616543. 254 rooms. Restaurant, coffee shop, 3 bars, casino, room service, dive shop, drugstore, gift shop, car-rental agent, tour desk, pool. Baby-sitter and house physician on call. AE, DC, MC, V. CP.

The Arts and Nightlife

The Arts

The Curaçao Museum, housed in a century-old former plantation house, is filled with artifacts, paintings, and antique furnishings that trace the island's history. Across from the Holiday Beach Hotel, off Pater Euwensweg, ☎ 599/9–623873. ☛ $1.50. ☉ Tues.–Fri. 9–noon and 2–5, Sat. 10–4.

Nightlife

Friday is the big night out, with rollicking happy hours, most with live music, at several hotels, most notably the Holiday Beach and Avila Beach (see Lodging, above). The once-a-month open house at Landhuis Brievengat (see Exploring, Curaçao, Eastern Side, above) is a great way to meet interesting locals—it usually offers a folkloric show, snacks, and local handicrafts. Every Friday night the landhouse holds a big party with two bands. Check with the tourist board for the schedule of folkloric shows at various hotels. The Sonesta Beach, Van Der Valk Plaza, Curaçao Caribbean, Holiday Beach, Otrabanda, and Princess Beach hotels all have casinos that are open 1 PM–4 AM.

The Salinja district is the spot for clubbing: You'll find everything from merengue to house. **The Pub** (Salinja 144A, ☎ 599/9–612190) is a crowded, energetic dancing-and-drinking club. It's the place for the loud, the hip, the young, and the wanna-bes checking on the latest Curaçao fads. The dress is casual to funky, so leave your heels at home. ⊙ *Fri. 8 PM–4 AM, Sat. 9 PM–4 AM, Mon.–Thurs. and Sun. 9 PM–3 AM.*

Considered the most colorful disco in town, **Facade** (Lindbergweg 32, Salina, ☎ 599/9–614640) is about as hip as Curaçao gets. It's dark and cool, with huge bamboo chairs for lounging. The men cruise and the women are dressed to kill. There are two disco floors with flashing lights and an intense aural assault, sometimes from a live band. It's packed on Thursday, Friday, and Saturday nights from 10 PM to 4 AM. Friday happy hour is from 6 to 8 PM and 10 to 11 PM. Facade is closed Tuesday.

L'Aristocrat (Lindbergweg-Salina, ☎ 599/9–614353) attracts the more mature crowd seeking late-night pleasures, and on Saturday night the line to get in stretches down the block. Inside, the trendy clientele gyrates to a heavy beat while silent large-screen TVs flash sensual images. This is the place to see and be seen. There's a $9 cover charge, and it's open Friday and Saturday 10 PM to 4 AM, closed Monday. The island sometimes offers a "Curaçao Vacation Bonus Book" containing coupons good for substantial discounts on food, drink, and merchandise. Check with the **Curaçao Tourist Hotline** (☎ 800/332–8266) before you go.

Rum Runners (Otrobanda Waterfront, De Rouvilleweg 9, ☎ 599/9–623038) is another casual hot spot. This well-lit indoor-outdoor bar and eatery serves up tapas in an atmosphere that's reminiscent of a college fraternity hall. There's music nightly. The crowd stays until about midnight, after which the majority switch to **Facade, The Pub,** or **L'Aristocrat.**

10 Dominica

THE NATIONAL MOTTO emblazoned on the coat of arms of the Commonwealth of Dominica reads *"Après Bondi, c'est la ter."* It is a French-Creole phrase mean-
Updated by
Jordan Simon
ing "After God, it is the land." On this unspoiled isle, the land is indeed the main attraction: It turns and twists, towers to mountain crests, then tumbles to falls and valleys. It is a land that the Smithsonian Institution called a giant plant laboratory, unchanged for 10,000 years. Indeed, after a heavy rain you half expect to see things grow before your very eyes; the island is a virtual rainbow in entirely green hues.

The grandeur of Dominica (pronounced dom-in-*ee*-ka) is not man-made. This untamed, ruggedly beautiful land, located in the eastern Caribbean between Guadeloupe to the north and Martinique to the south, is a 305-square-mile nature retreat; 29 miles long and 15 miles wide, the island is dominated by some of the highest elevations in the Caribbean and is laced with 365 rivers, "one for every day of the year." Much of the interior is covered by a luxuriant rain forest, a wild place where you almost expect Tarzan to swing howling by on a vine. Straight out of Conan Doyle's *Lost World,* everything here is larger than life, from the towering tree ferns to the enormous insects. This exotic spot is home to such unusual critters as the Sisserou (or Imperial) parrot and the red-necked (or Jacquot) parrot, neither of which can be found anywhere else in the world.

Dominica is home, too, to the last remnants of the Carib Indians, whose ancestors came paddling up from South America more than a thousand years ago. The fierce Caribs kept Christopher Columbus at bay when he came to call during his second voyage to the New World. Columbus turned up at the island on Sunday, November 3, 1493. In between Carib arrows he hastily christened it Dominica (Sunday Island) and then sailed on.

For almost two centuries the British and French tried unsuccessfully to subdue the Caribs, and in 1748 they agreed to let the Caribs keep the island. However, French and English planters, unable to resist the lure of the fertile land, began to fight one another for squatter's rights. The Caribs had named their island *waitukubuli* ("tall is her body"), but it was *Dominica* that remained in history. In 1805, the English paid a "ransom" of £12,000 to the French, and Dominica became a British possession. In 1967, the British colony became self governing, and on November 3, 1978, Dominica became a fully independent republic, officially called the Commonwealth of Dominica. Despite (or perhaps because of) its ferocious past, Dominica today is a quiet, peaceful place. There are about 75,000 people living on the island, and they are some of the friendliest people in all of the Caribbean.

Before You Go

Tourist Information
Contact the **Caribbean Tourism Organization** (20 E. 46th St., New York, NY 10017, ☎ 212/682–0435). In the United Kingdom, contact the **Dominica Tourist Office** (1 Collingham Gardens, London SW5 0HW, ☎ 0171/835–1937 or 0171/370–5194).

Arriving and Departing
BY PLANE
No major airlines fly into Dominica (although at press time **American** was planning to begin service in late 1995), but **LIAT** (☎ 809/462–

0700) connects with flights from the United States on Antigua, Barbados, Guadeloupe, Martinique, St. Lucia, St. Maarten, and San Juan. **Air Martinique** (☎ 809/448–2181) flies from Fort de France, and **Air Guadeloupe** (☎ 809/448–2181) from Pointe-à-Pitre. **Air BVI** (☎ 809/774–6500) connects from Tortola, BVI. **BWIA** (☎ 809/462–0262) connects from Antigua, and **Winair** (☎ 809/448–2181) connects from St. Maarten.

FROM THE AIRPORT
Canefield Airport (about 3 miles north of Roseau) handles only small aircraft and daytime flights; landing here can be a hair-raising experience for those uneasy about flying. Cab fare is about $8 to Roseau. **Melville Hall Airport,** on the northeast coast, handles larger planes; although interesting, the 90-minute drive through the island's rain forest to Roseau is bumpy, exhausting, and costs about $50 by private taxi or $17 per person by co-op cab.

BY FERRY
The **Caribbean Express** (c/o Whitchurch Shipping & Tours, ☎ 809/448–5787) has scheduled service Monday, Wednesday, Friday, and Saturday from Guadeloupe in the north to Martinique in the south, with stops at Les Saintes and Dominica. **Madikera** (c/o Trois Pitons Travel, ☎ 809/448–6977) began offering similar service in 1993, stopping in Roseau on Wednesday, Friday, Saturday, and Sunday.

Passports and Visas

U.S. and Canadian citizens must present a driver's license or passport and a return or ongoing ticket. British citizens must show a passport.

Language

The official language is English, but most Dominicans also speak a French-Creole patois.

Precautions

Be sure to bring insect repellent. Bring along pills for motion sickness; the roads twist and turn dramatically, and the local drivers barrel across them at a dizzying pace. If you plan on hiking even the simplest trail, bring along extra clothing and hiking boots or athletic sneakers to change into; trails are very rugged and often very muddy.

Staying in Dominica

Important Addresses

Tourist Information: Contact the main office of the **Division of Tourism** (National Development Corp., Valley Rd., Box 293, Roseau, ☎ 809/448–2045). The tourist desk at the **Old Market Plaza** (Roseau, ☎ 809/448–2186) is open Monday 8–5, Tuesday–Friday 8–4, Saturday 9–1. The offices at **Canefield Airport** (☎ 809/449–1242) and **Melville Hall Airport** (☎ 809/445–7051) are open weekdays 6:15–11 AM and 2–5:30 PM.

EMERGENCIES
Police, fire, and ambulance: Call 999. **Hospital: Princess Margaret Hospital** (Federation Dr., Goodwill, ☎ 809/448–2231 or 809/448–2233). **Pharmacy: Jolly's Pharmacy** (12 King George V St., Roseau, ☎ 809/448–3388).

Currency

The official currency is the Eastern Caribbean dollar (E.C.$). Figure about E.C.$2.60 to U.S.$1. U.S. dollars are readily accepted, but you'll usually get change in E.C. dollars. Major credit cards are widely accepted, as are traveler's checks. Prices quoted here are in U.S. dollars unless indicated otherwise.

Taxes and Service Charges

Hotels collect a 5% government tax; restaurants a 3% tax. The departure tax is $10 or E.C.$25. Most hotels and restaurants add a 10% service charge to your bill. Taxi drivers appreciate a 10% tip.

Guided Tours

A wide variety of hiking and photo safari tours are conducted by **Dominica Tours** (☎ 809/448–2638) in sturdy four-wheel-drive vehicles. Prices range from $15 to $100 per person, depending upon the length of the trip and whether picnics and rum punches are included. There are also boat tours, which include snorkeling, swimming, and rum or fruit drinks. The latest rage in Dominica is whale-watching; the knowledgeable diver-photographer Fitzroy Armour leads three- to four-hour expeditions November through April, when surprisingly graceful schools of sperms, humpbacks, and orcas patrol the surrounding waters.

Rainbow Rover Tours (☎ 809/448–8650) are conducted in air-conditioned Land Rovers. You can take in the island for a half or full day at a cost of $30–$60, which includes food and drink. **Ken's Hinterland Adventure Tours** (☎ 809/448–4850) provides tours in vans with knowledgeable guides and can design expeditions to fit your needs. If you're uneasy about some of the more dangerous hikes, Ken's is the best choice: They use two way radios at all times, which you'll appreciate if ever there's an emergency. Ken's offers another activity zooming in popularity among visitors: sea kayaking. It's a wonderful opportunity to challenge the crashing surf and explore the scalloped coast.

Any taxi driver will be happy to offer his services as a guide at the cost of $18 an hour, with tip extra. It's a good idea to get a recommendation from your hotel manager or the Dominica Division of Tourism (*see* Tourist Information, *above*) before selecting a guide and driver. **Mally's Tour & Taxi Service** (☎ 809/448–3114) and **Julius John's** (☎ 809/449–1968) are two of the better operators.

Getting Around

VANS

This is a cheap, though not always dependable, means of transportation. Minivans cruise the island and, like taxis, will stop when hailed. You can also catch a minivan in Roseau by the bridges crossing the Roseau River.

RENTAL CARS

If it doesn't bother you to drive on the left on potholed mountainous roads with hairpin curves, rent a car and strike out on your own. Daily car-rental rates begin at $35 (weekly about $190), plus collision damage insurance at $6 a day and personal accident insurance at $2 a day, and you'll have to put down a deposit and purchase a visitor's driving permit for E.C.$20. You can rent a car from **Avis** (4 High St., Roseau, ☎ 809/448–2481), **Wide Range Car Rentals** (79 Bath Rd., Roseau, ☎ 809/448–2198), **Valley Rent-A-Car** (Goodwill Rd., Roseau, ☎ 809/448–3233), **Anselm's Car Rental** (3 Great Marlborough St., Roseau, ☎ 809/448–2730), or **S.T.L. Rent-A-Car** (Goodwill Rd., Roseau, ☎ 809/448–2340 or 809/448–4525). **Budget Rent-A-Car** (Canefield Industrial Estate, Canefield, ☎ 809/449–2080) offers daily rates, three-day specials, and weekly and monthly rates.

Telephones, Electricity, and Mail

To call Dominica from the United States, dial area code 809 and the local access code, 44, followed by the five-digit local number. On the island, you need to dial only the five-digit number. The island has efficient direct-dial international service. All pay phones are equipped for local and overseas dialing.

Electric voltage is 220/240 AC, 50 cycles. American appliances require an adaptor.

First-class (airmail) letters to the United States and Canada cost E.C.95¢; postcards cost E.C.50¢.

Opening and Closing Times

Business hours are weekdays 8–1 and 2–4, Saturday 8–1. Banks are open Monday–Thursday 8–3, Friday 8–5.

Exploring Dominica

Numbers in the margin correspond to points of interest on the Dominica map.

Despite the small size of this almond-shape island, it can take a couple of hours to get between many of the island's popular destinations; roads are in poor shape and travel is relatively slow. The amount of time you spend hiking, mountain climbing, bird-watching, or just enjoying the scenery will determine how much you can see during one round-the-island trip. It takes about four days of solid trekking to take in the whole of Dominica. The highways ringing most of the island's perimeter have been upgraded in recent years; but more remote destinations remain somewhat inaccessible, and it's wise to hire a car and driver or to take an escorted tour (*see* Guided Tours, *above*).

Roseau

All the hotels and virtually all the island's population are on the leeward, or Caribbean, side of the island. Twenty thousand or so people

❶ reside in the capital, **Roseau** (pronounced rose-*oh*). This noisy, ragged town on the flat delta of the Roseau River reminds one of a somewhat more tattered version of New Orleans's French Quarter. A new waterfront and pier have upgraded the coastal side of town, but Roseau, which is one of the poorest capitals in the Caribbean, lacks the grand colonial architecture and the regal layout typical of the region. Walking through town you will notice the French West Indian construction of most homes and shops—small wood-and-stone or wood-and-concrete shanties, many with balustrades and French doors. One impressive sight, on Victoria Street, is the **Fort Young Hotel,** built as a fort in the 18th century. Directly across the street is the **state house**; the **public library** and the **old court house** are both nearby.;

The **national park office,** fittingly located in the 40-acre Botanical Gardens in Roseau, can provide tour guides and a wealth of printed information. ☎ *809/448–2401, ext. 417.* ☉ *Mon. 8–1 and 2–5, Tues.–Fri. 8–1 and 2–4.*

TIME OUT   Sit in the garden of the late Jean Rhys, the Dominican-born novelist who won Britain's Royal Literary Award. The garden has now been turned into an informal garden eatery, the **World of Food** (Queen Mary St. and Field's La., ☎ 809/448–6125). If you've never read Rhys, stop off at **Paperbacks** (6 Cork St., ☎ 809/448–2370) and purchase her *Wide Sargasso Sea* or any of her many other books.

Elsewhere on the Island

2 **Morne Trois Pitons** is a blue-green hill of three peaks, the highest of which is 4,403 feet. The mountain is usually veiled in swirling mists and clouds, and the 16,000-acre national park over which it looms is awash with cool mountain lakes, waterfalls, and rushing rivers. Ferns grow 30 feet tall, and wild orchids sprout from trees. Sunlight leaks through green canopies, and a gentle mist rises over the jungle floor.

3 The road from the capital to the Morne Trois Pitons National Park runs through the **Roseau River valley** toward Laudat. About 5 miles out of Roseau, the Wotton Waven Road branches off toward the **Sulphur Springs,** where you'll see the belching, sputtering, and gurgling release of hot springs along a river and nearby field—evidence of the area's restless volcanic activity. Double back and continue up the road

4 to Laudat, taking the next side road to the spectacular twin **Trafalgar Falls.** The road ends at **Papillote Wilderness Retreat** (*see* Dining and Lodging, *below*). Both are visible from a viewing platform that is an easy hike from Papillote's driveways—guides there will happily show you the way. If you're in decent shape and possess agility and balance, it's worth hiking up the riverbed to the cool pools at the bases of both falls. The taller of the two is where hot, orange-colored sulfuric and ferric waters mix with the crash of cold river water; taking a dip is an exhilarating experience.

5 Again, double back to the main road from Roseau and continue to **Laudat,** a small mountaintop village about 7 miles from Roseau and a good starting point for a venture into the national park. Two miles north-

6 east of Laudat, at the base of **Morne Micotrin** (4,006 feet), you'll find **Freshwater Lake,** and farther on, **Boeri Lake,** which is fringed with greenery and has purple hyacinths floating on its surface.

Laudat is the starting point for the most talked about—and most

7 treacherous—hike in Dominica: the trek to **Boiling Lake** and the **Valley of Desolation.** You should go only with a guide (*see* Hiking, *below*) and will have to leave at about 8 AM for this steep and slippery, all-day, 6-mile (round-trip) trek. You will return covered with mud, nicks, and scrapes; exhausted; and satisfied that you've seen one of the world's true wonders. Guides keep small groups of hikers (usually six to eight maximum) under their eye at all times. This is for serious hikers only: Make sure you're in excellent condition, and bring your own drinking water. The lake, the world's second-largest boiling lake, is like a caldron of gurgling gray-blue water. It's 70 yards wide, and the temperature of the water ranges from 180°F to 197°F. Its depth is unknown. It is believed that the lake is not a volcanic crater but a flooded fumarole—a crack through which gases escape from the molten lava below.

On your way to the lake, you'll pass through the Valley of Desolation, a sight that definitely lives up to its name. Harsh sulfuric fumes have destroyed virtually all the vegetation in what was once a lush forested area. Stay on the trail to avoid breaking through the crust that covers the hot lava below.

You'll have to backtrack to Roseau and head north toward the Pont

8 Casse rotary to reach **Emerald Pool.** At the rotary, follow signs for Castle Bruce for about 3½ miles until you come to the trail that leads to Emerald Pool. Lookout points along this short 20-minute trail provide sweeping views of the windward (Atlantic) coast and the forested interior. Emerald Pool is a swirling, fern-bedecked basin into which a 50-foot waterfall splashes. This is the most accessible of Dominica's natural wonders—and fittingly its least wondrous.

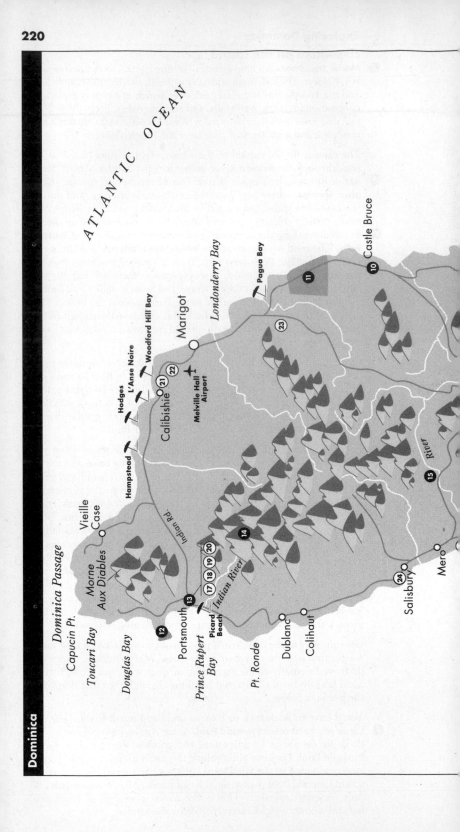

ATLANTIC OCEAN

Castle Bruce ⑩

⑪

Pagua Bay

㉓

Londonderry Bay

Marigot

Woodford Hill Bay

L'Anse Noire ㉑ ㉒

Calibishie

Melville Hall Airport

Hodges

Hampstead

River

⑮

Vieille Case

Morne Aux Diables

Dominica Passage

Capucin Pt.

Toucari Bay

Douglas Bay

⑫

Portsmouth ⑬

Prince Rupert Bay

Picard Beach

Indian River

⑰ ⑱ ⑲ ⑳

⑭

Indian Rd.

Pt. Ronde

Dublanc

Colihaut

Salisbury ㉔

Mero

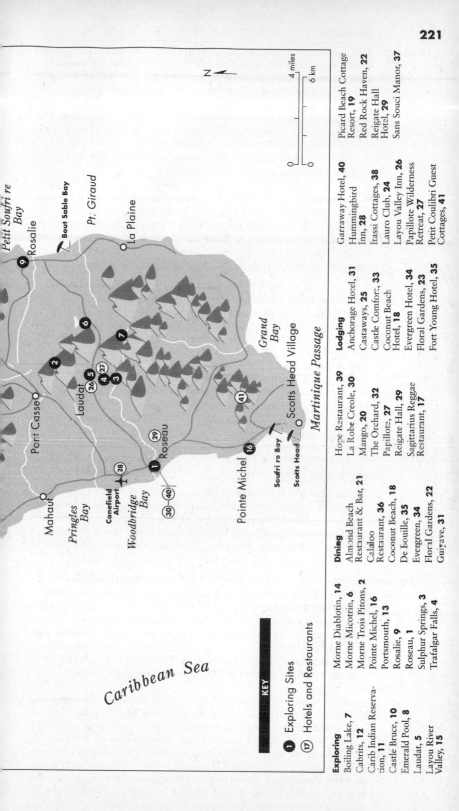

Caribbean Sea

Petit Soufrière Bay

Bout Sable Bay

Pt. Giraud

Rosalie

La Plaine

Port Casse

Laudat

Roseau

Mahaut

Pringles Bay

Canefield Airport

Woodbridge Bay

Pointe Michel

Grand Bay

Scotts Head Village

Soufrière Bay

Scotts Head

Martinique Passage

N

0   4 miles
0   6 km

KEY

⦿ Exploring Sites

⑰ Hotels and Restaurants

Exploring
Boiling Lake, **7**
Cabrits, **12**
Carib Indian Reservation, **11**
Castle Bruce, **10**
Emerald Pool, **8**
Laudat, **5**
Layou River Valley, **15**

Morne Diablotin, **14**
Morne Micotrin, **6**
Morne Trois Pitons, **2**
Pointe Michel, **16**
Portsmouth, **13**
Rosalie, **9**
Roseau, **1**
Sulphur Springs, **3**
Trafalgar Falls, **4**

Dining
Almond Beach Restaurant & Bar, **21**
Calaloo Restaurant, **36**
Coconut Beach, **18**
De Fouille, **35**
Evergreen, **34**
Floral Gardens, **22**
Guiyave, **31**

Hope Restaurant, **39**
La Robe Creole, **30**
Mango, **20**
The Orchard, **32**
Papillote, **27**
Reigate Hall, **29**
Sagittarius Reggae Restaurant, **17**

Lodging
Anchorage Hotel, **31**
Castaways, **25**
Castle Comfort, **33**
Coconut Beach Hotel, **18**
Evergreen Hotel, **34**
Floral Gardens, **23**
Fort Young Hotel, **35**

Garraway Hotel, **40**
Hummingbird Inn, **28**
Itassi Cottages, **38**
Lauro Club, **24**
Layou Valley Inn, **26**
Papillote Wilderness Retreat, **27**
Petit Coulibri Guest Cottages, **41**

Picard Beach Cottage Resort, **19**
Red Rock Haven, **22**
Reigate Hall Hotel, **29**
Sans Souci Manor, **37**

TIME OUT Peter Kaufmann and his friendly dogs are the proprietors of a terrific diversion a short drive from the Emerald Pool: Welcome to the **Emerald Bush Bar–Restaurant–Bush Hotel–Nature Park** (☎ 809/448–4545, answering machine). Here you can stop for a glass of fresh juice or a rum punch, wander along a couple hours' worth of unbelievably lush trails, or spend the night in an A-frame cottage that is barely a cut above camping (rooms cost as little as $18 per night). The list of nonamenities is long: no electricity, no phone, no TV, etc. Be prepared to rough it—but this is one of the most beautiful settings in Dominica. The bar and restaurant are open only until about sundown.

A good map and steady nerves are necessary for driving along the rugged, ragged windward coast. If you head back from the Emerald Pool toward Pont Casse and turn left at the intersection a couple miles before ⑨ the rotary, the road leads to **Rosalie,** where there is a river for swimming, a black-sand beach, an old aqueduct, and a waterwheel. There is also a waterfall that dashes down a cliff into the ocean.

From here, head north along the coast to the little fishing village of ⑩ **Castle Bruce.** On the beach here you can watch dugout canoes being made from the trunks of gommier trees using traditional Carib methods (after the tree is cut it gets stretched). About 6 miles north of Cas- ⑪ tle Bruce lies the **Carib Indian Reservation,** which was established in 1903 and covers 3,700 acres. Don't expect a lot in the way of ancient culture and costume. The folks who gave the Caribbean its name live pretty much like other West Indians, as fishermen and farmers. However, they have maintained their traditional skills at wood carving, basket weaving, and canoe building. Their wares are displayed and sold in little thatch-top huts lining the road. The reservation's Roman Catholic church at Salibia has an altar that was once a canoe. Another point of interest on the reservation is **L'Escalier Tête Chien** ("trail of the snake staircase" in Creole patois)—a hardened lava flow that juts down to the ocean.

The Atlantic here is particularly fierce and roily, the shore marked with countless coves and inlets. The Carib still tell wondrous colorful legends of the island's origins: La Roche Pagua, they say, is home to a fragrant white flower; bathe in its petals and your loved one will obey your every command. By night, Londonderry Islets metamorphose into grand canoes to take the spirits of the dead out to sea.

TIME OUT Stop for an hour or an overnight at the **Carib Territory Guesthouse** (☎ 809/445–7256), a very basic wayside Carib house owned by Caribs Charles and Margaret Williams, who live on the premises with their children. There are eight very bare and inexpensive bedrooms here for the adventurous traveler—the three new ones added in 1994 have their own baths and are comfiest. You can also get lunch and a cold drink, not to mention a good selection of Carib crafts. Call Williams in advance and schedule a half-day or full-day walk with him through the territory.

Continuing north from the reservation, you'll go past lovely **Pagua Bay,** with its beach of dark sand. A bit farther along, near Melville Hall Airport, is **Marigot,** the largest (population: 5,000) settlement on the east coast. On the northeast coast, steep cliffs rise out of the Atlantic, which flings its frothy waters over dramatic reefs, and rivers crash through forests of mangroves and fields of coconut. The beaches at **Woodford Hill, Hampstead, Anse Noir,** and **Hodges** are excellent for snorkeling and scuba diving, though all this wind-tossed beauty can be dangerous to swimmers, since there are strong underwater currents as well as whipped-cream waves. From here you can see the French island of Marie Galante in the distance.

The road continues across the top of the island through banana plantations to Portsmouth, but a side road leads up to the village of **Vieille Case** and **Capucion Pointe,** at the northernmost tip of the island. **Morne Aux Diables** soars 2,826 feet over this area and slopes down to **Toucari Bay** and **Douglas Bay** on the west coast, where you'll find long stretches of dark-sand beach.

⑫ In northern Portsmouth, you'll find the 250-acre **Cabrits National Park,** surrounded on three sides by the Caribbean Sea. Local historian Lennox Honychurch has restored **Fort Shirley,** a military complex built between 1770 and 1815. You can tour the restored buildings and visit the small museum that highlights the natural and historic aspects of the park. The park is connected to the mainland by a freshwater swamp, verdant with ferns, grasses, and trees, where you can see a variety of migrant birds. Smaller cruise ships sometimes dock here instead of at Woodbridge Bay, near Roseau. The new cruise-ship facility here offers a cooperative crafts shop, a continuously screened film about Fort Shirley, and occasional live dance or music performances.

TIME OUT The bar in the **Purple Turtle Guest House** (Portsmouth, ☎ 809/445-5296) is a fine place for a rum punch before or after a tour of Portsmouth, especially at sunset.

⑬ **Portsmouth** is a small town of about 5,000; it's most popular with the yachting set. **Prince Rupert Bay,** site of a naval battle in 1782 between the French and the English, is far and away the island's most beautiful harbor. There are more than 2 miles of sandy beaches fringed with coconut trees and a few small hotels. The **Indian River** flows through here on its way from the mountains down into the sea, and a canoe ride takes you through a lush rain forest thick with mangrove trees and exotic bird life. Board a rowboat (not power) for total tranquillity, to be able to hear fish jumping and birds calling. The guides here are notoriously overeager: Choose carefully or ask your hotel to recommend someone.

⑭ Just south of Indian River is **Pointe Ronde,** the starting point for an expedition to **Morne Diablotin,** at 4,747 feet the island's highest summit. This is not an expedition you should attempt alone; the uninhabited interior is an almost impenetrable primeval forest. You'll need a good guide (see Hiking, below), sturdy shoes, a warm sweater, and firm resolve.

Heading back to Roseau, the west-coast road dips down through the little villages of **Dublanc** (with a side road off to the Syndicate Estate), **Colihaut,** and **Salisbury** before reaching the mouth of the Layou River. ⑮ The **Layou River valley** is rich with bananas, cacao, citrus fruits, and coconuts. The remains of Hillsborough Estate, once a rum-producing plantation, are here. The river is the island's longest and largest, with deep gorges, quiet pools and beaches, waterfalls and rapids—a great place for a full day's outing of swimming and shooting the rapids, or just sunning and picnicking.

The road at the bend near Dublanc that leads to the Syndicate Estate also leads to the 200-acre site of the **Project Sisserou.** This protected site has been set aside with the help of some 6,000 schoolchildren, each of whom donated 25¢ for the land where the endangered Sisserou parrot (found only in Dominica) flies free. At last estimate, there were only about 60 of these shy and beautiful birds, covered in rich green feathers with a mauve front.

Just south of Roseau the road forks, with a treacherous prong leading east to **Grand Bay,** where bay leaves are grown and distilled. If you continue due south from Roseau you'll go through **Pointe Michel,** settled decades ago by Martinicans who fled the catastrophic eruption of Mont Pelée. The stretch all the way from Roseau to **Scotts Head** at the southernmost tip of the island has excellent beaches for scuba diving and snorkeling.

Beaches

Don't come to Dominica in search of powdery white-sand beaches. The travel-poster beaches do exist on the northeast coast, but this is still an almost totally undeveloped area. You'll see mostly dark-sand beaches, evidence of the island's volcanic origins, the best of which sit at the mouths of rivers and in protected bays. Scuba diving, snorkeling, and windsurfing are all excellent here.

Layou River has the best river swimming on the island, and in some places, you can sunbathe on its banks.

Picard Beach, on the northwest coast, is the island's best beach. Great for windsurfing and snorkeling, it's a 2-mile stretch of brown sand fringed with coconut trees. The Picard Beach Cottage Resort and Coconut Beach hotel are along this beach.

Pagua Bay, a quiet, secluded beach of dark sand, is on the Atlantic coast.

Woodford Hill Bay, Hampstead, L'Anse Noir, and **Hodges,** all on the northeast coast, are excellent beaches for snorkeling and scuba diving.

In the southeast, near La Plaine, **Bout Sable Bay** is not much good for swimming, but the surroundings are stirringly elemental: Towering red cliffs challenge the rollicking Atlantic.

The beaches south of Roseau to **Scotts Head** at the southernmost tip of the island are good for scuba diving and snorkeling because of the dramatic underwater walls and sudden drops.

The scuba diving is excellent at **Soufrière Bay,** a sandy beach south of Roseau. Volcanic vents puff steam into the sea; the experience has been described as "swimming in champagne."

Sports and the Outdoors

Boating

Motorboat and sailing trips can be arranged through **Dominica Tours** (☎ 809/448–2638) and the **Castaways Beach Hotel** (☎ 809/449–6245).

Hiking

Trails range from the easygoing to the arduous. For the former, all you'll need are sturdy, rubber-soled shoes and an adventurous spirit.

For the hike to Boiling Lake or the climb up Morne Diablotin you will need hiking boots, a guide, and water. Guides will charge about $30–$35 per person and can be contacted through the Dominica Tourist Office or the Forestry Division (☎ 809/448–2401 or 809/448–2638).

Scuba Diving

Skin Diver magazine recently ranked Dominica among the top five Caribbean dive destinations. **Dive Dominica** (Castle Comfort, ☎ 809/448–2188 or 800/544–7631, FAX 809/448–6088) has three boats and is one of the oldest dive shops on the island. Owners Derek and Ginette Perryman, NAUI-approved instructors, offer snorkeling and resort dives for beginners and, for the advanced set, dives on drop-offs, walls, and pinnacles—by day or night. The owners of the **Dominica Dive Resorts, Waitukubuli** (there are two: one at the Anchorage Hotel, ☎ 809/448–2638, the other at the Portsmouth Beach Hotel, ☎ 809/445–5142) are PADI-certified and offer both resort courses and full certification. The **Castaways Beach Hotel,** 11 miles north of Roseau, has diving at its watersports center (☎ 809/449–6245 or 800/525–3833). The latest addition to the scene is **Nature Island Dive** (Soufrière, ☎ 809/449–8181), run by three friendly couples, one local, one American, one British/American. They also offer sea kayaking and mountain bike tours and rentals. Future plans include building a casual dive resort that will incorporate old plantation ruins on the hill overlooking the bay. The going rate at all of the above is about $60–$65 for a two-tank dive or $80–$90 for a resort course with two open-water dives.

Snorkeling

Major island operators rent equipment: **Anchorage Hotel** (☎ 809/448–2638), **Castaways Beach Hotel** (☎ 809/449–6245), **Coconut Beach Hotel** (☎ 809/445–5393), **Sunshine Village** (☎ 809/445–5066), and **Picard Beach Cottage Resort** (☎ 809/445–5131).

Swimming

River swimming is extremely popular on Dominica, and the best river to jump into is the Layou River (*see* Exploring Dominica, *above*). *See also* Beaches, *above,* for our pick of the best beaches at which to swim, snorkel, or surf.

Windsurfing

Contact either **Anchorage Hotel, Picard Beach Cottage Resort,** or **Castaways Beach Hotel** (*see* Snorkeling, *above*).

Shopping

Gift Ideas

The distinctive handicrafts of the Carib Indians include traditional baskets made of dyed *larouma* reeds and waterproofed with tightly woven *balizier* leaves. These crafts are sold on the reservation, as well as in Roseau's shops. Dominica is also noted for its spices, hot peppers, bay rum, and coconut-oil soap; its vetiver-grass mats are sold all over the world.

Starbrite Industries (Canefield Industrial Estate, ☎ 809/449–1006) makes great candles, including some in the shape of the Dominican parrot, cupids, and trees. It's open weekdays 8–4. The **Old Mill Culture Centre and Historic Site** (Canefield Rd., no ☎) presents exhibits on the historical, cultural, and political development of Dominica. In addition, the center exhibits and sells wood carvings by a master carver, Louis Desire, and those of his students—all lovingly carved from Dominican woods. The center is open weekdays 9–1 and 2–4. The gift shop at the **Papillote Wilderness Retreat** (Roseau, ☎ 809/448–2286) has a magnificent selection of wood carvings.

Stop in at **Caribana Handcrafts** (31 Cork St., Roseau, ☎ 809/448–2761) for ceramics, woodcarvings, and baskets. **Fadelle's** (28 Kennedy Ave., Roseau, ☎ 809/448–2686) offers still more straw and woodwork, as well as soaps, sauces, and perfumes. You can watch the local ladies weaving in the back room at **Tropicrafts** (41 Queen Mary St., Roseau, ☎ 809/448–2747; Bay St., Portsmouth, ☎ 809/445–5956), where you'll find wood carvings, rum, hot sauces, and local perfumes, in addition to traditional Carib baskets, hats, and woven mats. **Balisier** (35 Great George St., no ☎) is the spot for charming sunbonnets, carnival dolls, island jewelry, and hand-painted T-shirts. A local priest runs **Dominica**

Pottery (Bayfront St. and Kennedy Ave., Roseau, no ☎), whose products are fashioned with various local clays and glazes.

At their studio-home (54 Queen Mary St., ☎ 809/448–3740), siblings **Arnold** and **Roberta Toulon** hand-paint T-shirts that sell so well that stock is always limited. They will, however, make up a special order within two days. Arnold's canvases of fine art are also on display.

The government actively encourages local artisans and helped open the new **NDFD Small Business Mini Mall** (9 Great Marborough St., Roseau, ☎ 809/448–0412). Among the more notable booths are **Linx Jewelry**, where Dyanna hand-paints T-shirts and creates unusual African-influenced earrings, bracelets, necklaces, and pins from coconut husks, seashells, clay, wood and pods; **Caribbean Perfumes**, fragrant with teas, scents, and potpourri from vanilla to vetiver; and the **Blow Kalbass Healing Center**, which hawks natural products touted to cure everything from acne to rheumatism (locals swear by the skin creams, clay baths, and hair pomade).

Proof that the old ways live on in Dominica can be found in the number of herbal doctors setting up shop in the streets of Roseau. One stimulating memento of your visit is rum steeped with Bois Bandé (scientific name Richeria Grandis), a tree whose bark is reputed to have aphrodisiacal properties. You can find it at Tropicrafts (*see above*) and in the supermarkets (try **Whitchurch** on Kennedy Ave.). Macoucherie distills the best-known elixir.

Dining

The fertile Dominican soil produces a cornucopia of fresh vegetables, and chefs here utilize them to great advantage, most often with a Creole flair. There are sweet green plantains, *kushkush* yams, breadfruit, and dasheen (a tuber similar to the potato called taro elsewhere)—these and other staples are known as ground provisions. You'll find fresh fish on virtually every menu, and occasionally "mountain chicken"— a euphemism for a large frog called *crapaud*. Two rare delicacies for the intrepid diner are *manicou* (a small opossum) and the tender, gamey *agouti* (a large, indigenous rodent)—both are best smoked or stewed. You will not find fast-food restaurants or a variety of ethnic options, but the local cuisine is delicious.

What to Wear

Dominica is far from the chic fashion world. Clothes here are practical and traditional—for dinner it's shirt and trousers for men and modest dresses for women. During the day, nice shorts are acceptable at most places, but beach attire is frowned upon.

CATEGORY	COST*
$$$	over $35
$$	$15–$35
$	under $15

per person, excluding drinks, service charge, and 3% tax

$$$ **La Robe Creole.** Take your pick from an eclectic à la carte menu.
★ Callaloo and crab soup, made with dasheen and coconut, is a specialty. Other tasty options include lobster and conch crepes, charcoal-grilled fish and meats, barbecued chicken, and a selection of salads. The dining room is a cozy place, with wood rafters, ladder-back chairs, and colorful madras tablecloths. The downstairs take-out annex, the Mouse Hole, is an inexpensive place to stock up for your picnic. ✗ *3 Victoria St., Roseau, ☎ 809/448–2896. Reservations advised. AE. Closed Sun.*

$$$ Reigate Hall. In this stylish but rustic restaurant with an old-fashioned waterwheel, green linen napery, and formal place settings—a rarity in Dominica—guests and perhaps a few locals mingle over some of the better hotel food on the island. Although some low-fat, low-cholesterol dishes have been added, favored specialties remain mountain chicken in champagne sauce and coq au vin. ✕ *Reigate Hall Hotel, Roseau,* ☎ *809/448–4031. Reservations advised. AE, MC, V.*

$$ De Bouille. The upscale, attractive dining room at the Fort Young Hotel—with its stone walls and wood-raftered ceiling—is usually filled with the businesspeople who frequent the hotel. The Indian chef adds a touch of his homeland cuisine to Continental and Dominican dishes (the special may be mountain chicken tandoori). The menu includes callaloo and pumpkin soup, grilled lobster, steak, and curried chicken. ✕ *Fort Young Hotel, Roseau,* ☎ *809/448–5000. Reservations advised. AE, MC, V.*

$$ Evergreen. Enjoy a relaxing meal on a large airy terrace overlooking the sea. It's decorated with bright tropical prints, crystal teardrop chandeliers, and a striking art deco–ish bar in stark gray, black, and white. Delicious dinners include a choice of soup and salad; the entrées of chicken, fish, and beef are served with local fruits and vegetables, such as kushkush and plantains. Homemade desserts include fresh fruit, cake, and ice cream. ✕ *Evergreen Hotel, Roseau,* ☎ *809/448–3288. Reservations advised. AE, MC, V.*

$$ Floral Gardens. You may feel as if you're eating in a private home at
★ this warm, welcoming restaurant with its wood-paneling, rough-hewn timber beams, and vetiver mats. The food is delectable. This is the place to sample local specialties, such as crapaud and agouti. Finish with luscious homemade coconut or rum raisin ice cream. ✕ *Floral Gardens Motel, Concord,* ☎ *809/445–7636. Reservations advised in high season. AE, MC, V.*

$$ Guiyave. Have a drink at the second-floor bar and then repair to the table-filled balcony for a scrumptious lunch. Spareribs, lobster, rabbit, and mountain chicken are offered, along with homemade beef or chicken patties, spicy rotis (Caribbean burritos), and a variety of light snacks and sandwiches. This restaurant is noted for its fresh tropical fruit juices (cherry, guava, passion fruit, and barbadine) and its homemade pies, tarts, and cakes. ✕ *15 Cork St., Roseau,* ☎ *809/448–2930. No credit cards. No dinner.*

$$ Mango. Vases overflowing with fresh flowers and a beautiful mural depicting the Indian River enliven this unassuming new restaurant frequented by locals. Diners enjoy both the comparatively refined ambience and Peter Pascal's solid home cooking. The lambi (conch) is tender as can be, the goat colombo has quite a kick, and the mountain chicken is succulent. This is one of the few places where you can find breego, a tiny flavorful conch. ✕ *Bay St., Portsmouth,* ☎ *809/445–3099. No credit cards.*

$$ The Orchard. A spacious, unadorned dining room opens onto a pleasant, covered courtyard, surrounded by latticework. Chef Joan Cools-Lartique whips up Creole-style coconut shrimp, lobster, black pudding, mountain chicken, callaloo soup with crabmeat, and other island delicacies, as well as an assortment of sandwiches, for the changing menu. ✕ *31 King George V St., Roseau,* ☎ *809/448–3051. AE, D, MC, V.*

$$ Papillote. The indefatigable Anne Jean-Baptiste has constructed a beautiful new stone-and-tile restaurant. Fans of the original Papillote needn't worry: The botanical gardens are still right outside, a hot-spring pool still bubbles merrily (just the spot to savor a lethal rum punch before or after dinner), and it's just as popular with birds, butterflies—and tour groups—as ever. Try the bracing callaloo soup, dasheen puffs, chicken rainforest (marinated with papaya and wrapped in banana leaves), and, if they're on the menu, the succulent *bouk* (tiny, delicate river shrimp). ✕ *Papillote Wilderness Retreat,* ☎ *809/448–2287. Reservations advised in high season. AE, D, MC, V.*

$–$$ Almond Beach Restaurant & Bar. If you're visiting one of the island's northeast beaches, stop here for a lunch of callaloo soup, lobster, or octopus. Select from tantalizing fruit juices, including guava, passion fruit, tangerine, soursop, and papaya, or one of the bewitching spice rums steeped for more than two months in various herbs and spices. Try the *pweve* (patois for pepper), the aniselike *nanie,* or *lapsenth,* a violet-scented pick-me-up and digestive. The setting and ambience are delightful: Murals painted by local artists adorn the back wall, and you dine in a series of gazebos overlooking the Atlantic. The genial owners, Mr. and Mrs. Joseph, are experts on local culture and custom and sometimes arrange a traditional belé dance or jing ping concert on busy weekends. ✕ *Calibishi,* ☎ *809/445–7783. AE, D, MC, V.*

$–$$ Calaloo Restaurant. Up the stairs of a verandaed building on a busy
★ Roseau street is this small, informal eatery decorated with local crafts. Mrs. Marge Peters is the vivacious hostess who holds court at the postage-stamp-size bar. She takes great pride in age-old cooking traditions and uses only the freshest local produce. (What she does with breadfruit alone—roasted slabs, puffs, creamy velouté, juice, pie—could fill a cookbook.) Changing lunch and dinner specials, served with heaping helpings of provisions such as pumpkin, plantain, yams, and yucca, might include pepper-pot soup, curried conch, or the signature crab callaloo, fragrant with cumin, coconut cream, lime, clove, and garlic. Most everything here is homemade, including juices (try the sea moss—"puts lead in your pencil") and ice cream (the soursop is marvelous). ✕ *63 King George V St., Roseau,* ☎ *809/448–3386. No credit cards.*

$ Coconut Beach. This casual, low-key beachfront restaurant and bar is popular with both visiting yacht owners (moorings are available), expatriate medical students from the nearby school, and anyone interested in an afternoon on a stretch of white-sand beach. Fresh tropical drinks and local seafood dishes are the specialty here; sandwiches and rotis are also served. ✕ *Coconut Beach Hotel, Portsmouth,* ☎ *809/445– 5393. AE, D, MC, V.*

$ Hope Restaurant. The owners did their best to cheer up the unprepossessing interior, painting the walls a bright turquoise and strewing fresh flowers around the three cramped dining rooms. But you don't come here for the ambience. You come for genuine Creole cooking at rock-bottom prices. Mountain chicken (E.C.$35) and agouti (E.C.$25) are served with generous sides of provisions—for barely half the price charged at fancier restaurants. Savory pork, goat, and chicken are even cheaper. Hope provides local flavor in every sense of the phrase: It's filled with old men playing dominoes and cabbies whose runs have just ended (they always know a good deal). It's open every day for breakfast, lunch, and dinner. ✕ *15 Steber St., Roseau,* ☎ *809/448–2019. No credit cards.*

$ Sagittarius Reggae Restaurant. Astrological paraphernalia covers the walls of this place. The johnnycakes have Egg McMuffins beat by a country mile, and the fruit juices are sublime. Weekends, a disc jockey blasts reggae and soca, transforming the restaurant into a hopping club. ✕ *Portsmouth, no* ☎. *No credit cards.*

Lodging

Most hotels here are locally owned, and standards are often not up to what seasoned Caribbean travelers expect. Rooms may be dark—even creepy—bathrooms simple, and linens a bit threadbare at some properties. On the plus side, prices are low, and staffs are usually friendly and down-to-earth. It pays to compare rates and call for hotel brochures, as everything from bare-bones motels to charming hilltop retreats is comparably priced here.

The only beachfront hotels are in the Portsmouth area, the one exception being the Castaways on Mero Beach. Roseau's seaside facilities have splendid Caribbean views but are beachless. Since you're on this lush, tropical island, try to spend at least two nights at one of the wonderful nature retreats set in the rain forest: These are Dominica's greatest assets, at least where lodging is concerned.

Most hotels offer a MAP plan; considering the uniformity of Dominica's restaurants and the difficulty of getting around, this option makes sense. Dominican hoteliers seldom differentiate between high and low season—though a few have caught on.

CATEGORY	COST*
$$$	over $100
$$	$65–$100
$	under $65

All prices are for a standard double room for two, excluding 5% tax, 3% sales tax, and 10%–15% service charge.

Hotels

$$$ Castaways Beach Hotel. A young crowd, many of them divers, flocks to this beachfront hotel in Mero, 11 miles north of Roseau. Daytime activity centers on its mile-long, dappled gray beach; evenings, the focus is on the restaurant and terrace, which are attractive, although the food leaves something to be desired. The festive Sunday brunch with live music packs them in. Rooms are spacious and have balconies overlooking the beach. However, it's hard to tell that they were refurbished in 1992, since they are still dark, a bit musty, and decorated in 1970s colors and styles. Some have air-conditioning and cable TV. ☎ *Box 5, Roseau,* ☎ *809/449–6245 or 800/742–4276,* FAX *809/449–6246. 27 rooms. Restaurant, 2 bars, beach, tennis, water-sports center, scuba, dive packages offered. AE, MC, V. EP, MAP.*

$$$ Fort Young Hotel. Once the island's main military installation, Fort
★ Young is now Roseau's top downtown hotel. The fort was built in the late 1700s, and Dominican paintings and prints from that era decorate the massive stone walls. The cliffside setting offers dramatic views; it's worth paying extra for a room facing the ocean. Rooms have small balconies, air-conditioning, ceiling fans, shower baths, cable TV, and modern furnishings. ☎ *Box 519, Roseau,* ☎ *809/448–5000,* FAX *809/448–5006. 73 rooms. Restaurant, bar, pool, entertainment, disco. AE, MC, V. EP, MAP, FAP.*

$$$ Garraway Hotel. This rather garish lime-green structure in downtown Roseau by the waterfront is Dominica's first international standard business hotel. The owner proudly compares it to a Ramada or Marriott. It's an apt comparison. Rooms are large and decorated mainly in soft seashell colors like seafoam, coral, and powder blue; all have direct-dial phones, cable TV, and air-conditioning. Suites have sitting rooms of varying sizes and sofa beds. The higher floors survey a colorful jumble of rooftops that seems straight from a Chagall canvas. Local paintings and vetiver mats add a distinctive touch to the decor of the public spaces. The Garraway is unusually tasteful and elegant for a business hotel. Still, those seeking true Dominican flavor are better off in a small inn or guest house. At press time, an additional 17 rooms were slated to be completed in late 1995. The restaurant specializes in creative Creole cuisine. ☎ *Bay Front, Box 789, Roseau,* ☎ *809/449–8800,* FAX

809/449–8807. *20 rooms, 11 suites. Restaurant, bar, Jacuzzi, conference room. AE, MC, V. EP.*

$$$ **Lauro Club.** From the dining room's bright linen napery, cheerful wall
★ mural, and fresh flowers to the cottages' bold colors and contemporary furniture, the Lauro Club has a neat European feel that, oddly enough, works well in the Caribbean. Each unit has a sitting area, a daybed, and a kitchenette on a large veranda, but none has a TV or air-conditioning. Six units have direct sea views; the other four are up the hill a bit but still catch a glimpse of the water. Below are a swimming pool and a sandy beach area; a long wooden staircase twists down to the ocean. The Club is in Salisbury, between Roseau and Portsmouth and about 13 miles from each, so you'll probably need to rent a car. ⊠ *Box 483, Roseau, ☎ 809/449–6602, FAX 809/449–6603. 10 units. Restaurant, bar, pool. AE, MC, V. EP, MAP.*

$$$ **Petit Coulibri Guest Cottages.** You need a four-wheel-drive vehicle to
★ reach this aerie, perched high above Soufrière at the end of one of the worst access roads in the Caribbean. It's worth it: Once there on top of the world, you won't want to come down. Loye and Barney Barnard (she's from Savannah, he's a Yankee from the Berkshires) have created Dominica's choicest lodging. They designed the three individual stone-and-wood duplex cottages, then decorated them tastefully with stained-glass windows, local crafts and watercolors, Mexican serapes, maple beds swathed in mosquito netting, and ceramic-and-straw lamps. This is an ecotourist's delight: Everything is solar-powered or run on batteries, water comes from cisterns, and trees grow through the living room. Each cottage has two bedrooms, a kitchenette, and a huge balcony affording sweeping views of the sea. Travelers on a budget might consider the studio, but it's dark and spartan. The Barnards (who once ran a nearby aloe vera plantation and factory) can suggest many hikes in the rugged surrounding mountains. Save one night for dinner in the main house. Loye's a marvelous cook, much of the food is grown on the property, and the conversation sparkles like the lights on far-off Martinique. ⊠ *Petit Coulibri Estate near Soufrière, Box 331, Roseau, ☎ 809/446–3150, FAX 809/449–8182. 3 cottages, 1 studio. Dining room, pool. AE, MC, V. EP.*

$$$ **Picard Beach Cottage Resort.** Eight small wood cottages dot the grounds of this former coconut plantation on the island's northwest coast. Units have a simple, rustic appeal, with louvered windows, locally made furniture, small porches, and kitchenettes. The restaurant serves large breakfasts as well as lunch and dinner. The beach is right out your door, and you can use the pool at the Portsmouth Beach Hotel next door. The place is a bit overpriced but offers what are probably the best rooms in Portsmouth. ⊠ *Box 34, Roseau, ☎ 809/445–5131 or 800/424–5500, FAX 809/445–5599. 8 cottages. Restaurant, bar, beach, pool, dive center with scuba, snorkeling, and windsurfing. AE, MC, V. EP.*

$$$ **Red Rock Haven.** These stylish self-contained cottages fronting the rollicking Atlantic are a good bet for those who want to get away from it all. All have terrace, kitchenette, and bath and are charmingly furnished with local crafts and designer linens. Well-stocked bookshelves are a wonderful bonus (you're encouraged to make a contribution when you leave). You can walk to the small private sliver of beach, but you'll need a car to reach everything else. ⊠ *Pointe Baptiste, Calibishie, mailing address: Box 71, Roseau, ☎ 809/448–2181, FAX 809/448–5787. 3 cottages. Bar, pool, sauna, gift shop. AE, MC, V. EP.*

$$$ **Reigate Hall Hotel.** It is known as the fanciest hotel in Dominica, but, unfortunately, the service and standards at Reigate Hall have deteriorated of late, and the property is not as impeccably maintained as in the past. The lovely stone-and-wood dwelling is perched high on a steep

wooded cliff, a mile above Roseau and the ocean. Rooms have locally made furnishings, air-conditioning, and private balconies; the higher-priced rooms 17 and 18 have sea views. Some rooms have exposed brick, beam ceilings, and antiques; others have wet bars and refrigerators. Room amenities and arrangement are sort of a hodgepodge, with every room a bit different. ✉ *Reigate, Roseau,* ☎ *809/448–4031; in the U.S., 800/223–9815; in Canada, 800/468–0023;* FAX *809/448–4034. 14 rooms, 2 suites, 1 apartment. Restaurant, 2 bars, pool, tennis, sauna. AE, MC, V. EP, MAP.*

$$$ **Sans Souci Manor.** Three luxury apartments and one bungalow sit in
★ a prosperous suburb high above Roseau. All units have clay-tile floors, locally made wood and wicker furniture, fully equipped kitchens, large verandas with sweeping views of Roseau and the hills, and museum-quality Caribbean and Latin American art. Urbane owner John Keller hosts a sophisticated crowd of Americans and Europeans. Dinners—for those who wisely opt for the MAP plan—are three-course affairs prepared by Mr. Keller, a gourmet cook, and served house-party style on his plant-filled terrace. ✉ *Box 373, St. Aromet, Roseau,* ☎ *809/448– 2306,* FAX *809/448–6202. 3 apartments, 1 bungalow. Dining, honor bar, pool, airport transfers. AE, MC, V. EP, MAP.*

$$–$$$ **Anchorage Hotel.** Years of wear have taken their toll on this hotel, although it still becomes an active scene during the season. Make sure you reserve one of the renovated rooms, which have clay-tile floors and madras fabrics, in the two-story galleried section; don't bother with any of the other dark, lifeless units until they've seen a refurbishment—hopefully soon. ✉ *Box 34, Roseau,* ☎ *809/448–2638,* FAX *809/448–5680. 36 rooms. Restaurant, bar, pool, squash court. AE, D, MC, V. EP, MAP, FAP.*

$$–$$$ **Evergreen Hotel.** A recent expansion added six bright, modern rooms
★ with balconies and an airy bar and restaurant with terrace to this small hotel 2 miles from downtown Roseau. While the squeaky-clean new annex is somewhat lacking in authentic island charm, it's still where you want to stay. Air-conditioned rooms have bright print fabrics, rattan furnishings, cable TV, large shower baths, and lovely sea views. Other new additions include a pool, Italian ceramic tiles in the public areas, and a small garden. The older building, a stone-and-wood structure with a red roof, has more character. Rooms here are less expensive but are plain and lack sea views. Public rooms contain paintings and wood carvings by noted local artist Carl Winston. The restaurant is excellent and another good reason to stay here. ✉ *Box 309, Roseau,* ☎ *809/448–3288,* FAX *809/448–6800. 16 rooms. Restaurant, bar, pool, dive shop, yacht moorings. AE, D, MC, V. CP, MAP.*

$$ **Coconut Beach Hotel.** This continually expanding Portsmouth hotel received a much-needed face-lift in 1994. The original self-contained beachfront units have been brightened with frilly floral linens, still-life paintings, and vases of fresh flowers daily, but baths here are bare and depressing, and amenities are nonexistent (only those staying a week get utensils to use in their kitchenettes). The newer suites are simple, fresh, white-tiled affairs with air-conditioning and full bath to compensate for the lack of ocean view and access. All units have cable TVs. The hotel fronts the island's best beach, lovely Picard. Another plus is an open-air bar and restaurant where a crowd of yachties (moorings are available here) and locals keeps things lively. The staff is friendly and laid-back. ✉ *Box 37, Roseau,* ☎ *809/445–5393,* FAX *809/445–5693. 22 rooms. Restaurant, bar, dive shop, yacht moorings. AE, D, MC, V. EP, MAP.*

$ **Papillote Wilderness Retreat.** Picture a magical retreat in the middle
★ of a rain forest: Lush greenery abounds, geese and guinea fowl ramble the grounds, surreal stone animals crop up everywhere, a nearby
river beckons you to take a dip, and 200-foot Trafalgar Falls is a short
hike from your room. Papillote Wilderness Retreat claims this spectacular natural setting, as well as a bubbling hot-spring pool and
owner Anne Jean-Baptiste's botanical garden. She has cultivated a
mind-boggling assortment of plants and flowers, which she may graciously use to brew you a soothing herbal infusion—bergamot to combat insomnia or l'oiselles for a cold. Rooms are not as spectacular as
their surroundings; they're low-ceilinged, bare, and somewhat dark,
with a rustic, log-cabin feel. The restaurant serves good, moderately
priced meals. ✉ *Box 67, Roseau,* ☎ *809/448–2287,* FAX *809/448–2286.
10 rooms. Restaurant, bar, gift shop. AE, DC, MC, V. EP, MAP.*

Guest Houses and Lodges

$$ **Castle Comfort Lodge.** This small dive lodge, sandwiched between the
Anchorage and Evergreen hotels and run by the enthusiastic Derek and
Ginette Perryman, wins a loyal following for its first-rate dive shop and
excellent-value dive packages. Rooms are nothing special, although the
five oceanfront units are more modern and cheerful than many you
will find on the island. The back rooms are smaller but have cable TV
and phone. As a bonus, the home-cooked meals are bountiful and delicious. The Perrymans can also arrange various inland adventures and
nature walks. ✉ *Box 63, Roseau,* ☎ *809/448–2188,* FAX *809/448–6088.
10 rooms. Restaurant, dive shop. AE, MC, V. EP, MAP.*

$$ **Hummingbird Inn.** This simple hilltop retreat is just a short drive from
★ Roseau and Canefield Airport. Two hillside bungalows with outstanding Caribbean views hold 10 rooms. Interiors are simple—white walls,
terra-cotta-tile floors, and peaked wooden ceilings. Varnished wooden
hurricane windows can be left open all night to let in fresh breezes and
the sounds of tree frogs and the ocean a few hundred yards below. There's
no air-conditioning, TV, or phones. Ceiling fans were added in 1994.
Other nice touches include handmade quilts, hammocks slung strategically on the wraparound terraces, and tables fashioned out of the trunks
of local gommier trees. One large suite also has a four-poster bed and
kitchen. The Hummingbird's cook is perhaps the best of any guest
house on Dominica, and nonguests can arrange for dinner here if they
call a day in advance. ✉ *Box 20, Roseau,* ☎ *or fax 809/449–1042. 9
rooms, 1 suite. Restaurant, bar. AE, MC, V. EP, MAP.*

$–$$ **Itassi Cottages.** The brochure pretty well lives up to its promise: ". . . for
★ discerning travelers who are not necessarily loaded." These three self-contained cottages can hold from two to six people each. They're
much homier than most island lodgings, with a mix of antiques, straw
mats, beautiful handmade floral bedspreads, calabash lamps, and
wraparound porches with hammocks and sweeping views of Roseau,
Scotts Head, and the Caribbean. These are ideal for long-term stays.
Each has a kitchen, ceiling fans, and cable TV, and there is a shared
laundry facility. Grounds are beautifully landscaped and include a tennis court. ✉ *Box 319, Roseau,* ☎ *809/448–4313,* FAX *809/448–3045.
3 cottages. Kitchens, laundry facility, tennis court. AE, MC, V.*

$–$$ **Layou Valley Inn.** Tamara Holmes and her late husband built this
tasteful house in the foothills of the national park, under the peaks of
Morne Trois Pitons. She's a Russian who once translated for NASA
but now devotes her talents to the kitchen, where she whips up excellent Creole food, as well as the occasional French or Russian specialty—
coq au vin or chicken Kiev. The rooms are simple and clean, and the
sunken lounge (an oasis of hand-hewn mosaics, stone floors, exquisite

wood carvings, and lush hanging plants) and glass-fronted dining area are comfortable, attractive places where guests mingle. Unless you plan on going nowhere (which suits some guests just fine), you'll need a car—even buses pass only infrequently. ☎ *Box 196, Roseau,* ☎ *809/449–6203,* FAX *809/448–5212. 10 rooms. Restaurant, bar, swimming in nearby rivers. AE, MC, V. EP, MAP.*

$ **Floral Gardens.** This motel looks like a Swiss chalet—complete with latticed windows and flower boxes—plunked down on the edge of Dominica's rain-forest reserve, on the island's windward side. Although rooms are carefully decorated with island crafts and homey fabrics, they are small and dark, with a slightly claustrophobic feel. New, larger units overlooking the beautiful Layou River were completed in 1994; 10 more "luxury suites" are on the drawing board. The restaurant here (*see* Dining, *above*) is a favorite among residents and tour groups, and the hotel's location is convenient for river bathing, hiking, and relaxing on northeast coast beaches. Congenial O. J. Seraphin, the former interim prime minister, is the enterprising owner. Never content to leave things alone, he's added an exquisite waterfall pool and botanical garden, and future plans include expanding the already large gift shop into six galleries, each one showcasing a different island craft or product, from pottery to potpourri. ☎ *Concord,* ☎ *809/445–7636,* FAX *809/445–7636. 18 rooms. Restaurant, gift shop. AE, MC, V. EP, MAP.*

Nightlife

Discos

If you're not too exhausted from mountain climbing, swimming, and the like, you can join the locals on weekends at the **Warehouse** (☎ 809/449–1303), outside Roseau toward the airport, or the **Night Box** (Goodwill Rd., no ☎), which attracts a rowdier clientele. Another favorite with locals is the easygoing **Good Times** (2 mi north of Roseau in Checkhall, ☎ 809/449–1660), a reggae bar with an outdoor patio and a sizable crowd on weekends. Indeed, Checkhall is known as a partying spot, so much so that cabbies cruise the streets for passengers well into the wee hours.

Nightclubs

When the moon comes up, most visitors go down to the dining room in their resident hotel for the music or chat offered there, which is always liveliest on weekends. The Fort Young has upscale entertainment, as do many of the better hotels—the Castaways, Anchorage, Garraway, and Reigate Hall in particular.

The **Shipwreck,** in the Canefield industrial area (☎ 809/449–1059), has live reggae and taped music on weekends and a Sunday bash that starts at noon and continues into the night.

The best insider's spot is definitely **Wykie's La Tropical** (51 Old St., Roseau, ☎ 809/448–8015). This classic Caribbean hole-in-the-wall is a gathering spot for the island's movers and shakers, especially during Friday's happy hours from 5 to 7, when they nibble on stewed chicken or black pudding, then stay on for a local calypso band or some jing ping—a type of folk music featuring the accordion, the *quage* (a kind of washboard instrument), drums, and a boom boom (a percussive instrument). Another resident favorite is **Lenville** (☎ 809/446–6598), a very basic rum shop with barbecued chicken and dancing in the village of Coulivistrie.

11 Dominican Republic

Updated by
Jordan Simon

SPRAWLING OVER TWO-THIRDS OF THE ISLAND of Hispaniola, the Dominican Republic is the spot where European settlement of the Western Hemisphere really began. Santo Domingo, its capital, is the oldest continuously inhabited city in this half of the globe, and history buffs who visit have difficulty tearing themselves away from the city's 16th-century Colonial Zone. Sun-seekers head for the beach resorts of Puerto Plata, Barahona, Samaná, and La Romana; at Punta Cana, beachcombers tan on the Caribbean's longest stretch of white-sand beach. The highest peak in the West Indies is here: Pico Duarte (10,128 feet) lures hikers to the central mountain range. Ancient sunken galleons and coral reefs divert divers and snorkelers.

Columbus happened upon this island on December 5, 1492, and on Christmas Eve his ship, the *Santa María,* was wrecked on the Atlantic shore. He named it La Isla Española ("the Spanish island"), established a small colony, and sailed back to Spain on the *Pinta.* A year later he returned, only to find that the Spanish colony had been destroyed by the Taino Indians, the island's original inhabitants. But Columbus established another colony nearby, leaving his brother Bartholomew in charge. Santo Domingo, which is located on the south coast where the Río Ozama spills into the Caribbean Sea, was founded in 1496 by Bartholomew Columbus and Nicolás de Ovando and during the first half of the 16th century became the bustling hub of Spanish commerce and culture in the New World.

Hispaniola (a derivation of *La Isla Española*) has had an unusually chaotic history, replete with bloody revolutions, military coups, yellow-fever epidemics, invasions, and bankruptcy. In the 17th century, the western third of the island was ceded to France. A slave revolt in 1804 resulted in the establishment there of the first black republic, Haiti. Dominicans and Haitians battled for control of the island on and off throughout the 19th century. The Dominicans declared themselves independent from Haiti in 1844 and from Spain in 1865. The country was, however, bankrupt by the turn of the century. The United States helped to administer the island's finances, and eventually U.S. Marines occupied the country from 1916 to 1924, until a new Dominican constitution was signed. Rafael Trujillo ruled the Dominican Republic with an iron fist from 1930 until his assassination in 1961. A short-lived democracy was overthrown soon thereafter, followed by another occupation by the U.S. Marines in 1965. The country has been relatively stable since the early 1970s, and administrations have been staunch supporters of the United States.

American influence looms large in Dominican life. If Dominicans do not actually have relatives living in the United States, they know someone who does; and many speak at least rudimentary English. Still, it is a vibrantly Latin country, and the Hispanic flavor contrasts sharply with the culture of the British, French, and Dutch islands in the Caribbean.

Dominican towns and cities are generally not quaint, neat, or particularly pretty. Poverty is everywhere, but the country is also alive and chaotic, sometimes frenzied, sometimes laid-back. Dominicans love music — there is dancing in the streets every summer at Santo Domingo's Merengue Festival—and they have a well-deserved reputation for being one of the friendliest people in the region. This is a tropical country; there is less urgency to get things done, and tempers don't flare up quickly.

Blackouts, for instance, are a daily occurrence in much of the country, but this does not cause much discomfort for visitors, since most major hotels have emergency generators.

In recent years, tourism has played an increasingly important role in the government's scheme of things. Like Puerto Rico, its cousin to the east across the Mona Channel, the Dominican Republic used the 500th anniversary of its "discovery" by Christopher Columbus to give the tourist industry a much-needed boost. Its tourist zones are incredibly varied and include extravagant Casa de Campo, the manicured hotels of Playa Dorada, Santa Domingo's exquisite Colonial Zone, the neglected streets of Jarabacoa in its gorgeous mountain setting, and the world-weary beauty of the Samaná peninsula.

Before You Go

Tourist Information

Contact the **Dominican Republic Department of Tourism,** Dominican Consulate, 1 Times Sq., 11th Floor, New York, NY 10036, ☎ 212/768–2480; 2355 Salzedo Ave., Suite 305, Coral Gables, FL 33134, ☎ 305/444–4592; 1464 Crescent St., Montreal, Québec, Canada H3A 2B6, ☎ 514/933–6126. The best source of information is the **Dominican Tourist Information Center** in Santo Domingo (☎ 800/752–1151). Be prepared to wait at least two weeks to get requested material sent to you.

Arriving and Departing

BY PLANE

The Dominican Republic has two major international airports: Las Américas International Airport, about 20 miles outside Santo Domingo, and La Unión International Airport, about 15 miles east of Puerto Plata on the north coast. **American Airlines** (☎ 800/433–7300) has the most extensive service to the Dominican Republic. It flies nonstop from New York and Miami to Santo Domingo and Puerto Plata and offers connections to both Santo Domingo and Puerto Plata from San Juan, Puerto Rico. American Eagle has two flights a day from San Juan to La Romana and several flights weekly to Punta Cana. **Continental** (☎ 800/231–0856) flies nonstop from New York to Puerto Plata, and from Newark, New Jersey, to Santo Domingo. It also offers connecting service from Puerto Plata to Santo Domingo. **Carnival** (☎ 800/437–2110) offers daily service to Santo Domingo from New York, Miami, and Orlando. By press time, **United** (☎ 800/241–6522) should have service from Miami to Santo Domingo and Puerto Plata. Minneapolis-based **TransGlobal Tours** (☎ 800/338–2160) offers weekly charters from the Twin Cities to Puerto Plata.

Several regional carriers serve neighboring islands. **ALM** (☎ 800/327–7230) connects Santo Domingo to St. Maarten and Curaçao. There is also limited domestic service available from La Herrera Airport in Santo Domingo to smaller airfields in La Romana, Samaná, and Santiago. The new Barahona International Airport is slated to open by mid-1995 (but this is Caribbean time). It will handle large jet aircraft, mostly charters and domestic flights.

The remodeled and enlarged Las Américas (Santo Domingo) and La Unión (Puerto Plata) facilities are sophisticated by Latin American standards. Still, overworked customs and immigration officials are often less than courteous, and luggage theft is rife. Try to travel with carry-on luggage, and keep a sharp eye on it. Be prepared for a daunting experience as you leave customs. However, some order is being imposed—taxis now line up and, for the most part, charge the official established rates. If you have arranged for a hotel transfer, a representative should be waiting for you in the immigration hall.

Taxis are available at the airport, and the 25-minute ride into Santo Domingo averages R.D.$250 (about U.S.$21). Taxi fares from the Puerto Plata airport average R.D.$200.

Passports and Visas

U.S. and Canadian citizens must have either a valid passport or proof of citizenship, such as an original (not photocopied) birth certificate, and a tourist card. Legal residents of the United States must have an alien registration card (green card), a valid passport, and a tourist card. British citizens need only a valid passport; no entry visa is required. The requisite tourist card costs $10, and you should be sure to purchase it at the airline counter when you check in and then fill it out on the plane. You can purchase the card on arrival at the airport, but you may encounter long lines. Keep the bottom half of the card in a safe place because you'll need to present it to immigration authorities when you leave. There is also a U.S.$10 departure tax (payable only in U.S. dollars).

Language

Before you travel to the Dominican Republic, you should know at least a smattering of Spanish. Guides at major tourist attractions and front-desk personnel in the major hotels speak a fascinating form of English, though they often have trouble understanding tourists. Traffic signs and restaurant menus, except at popular tourist establishments, are in Spanish. Using smiles and gestures will help, but a nodding acquaintance with the language or a phrase book is more useful.

Precautions

Beware of the *buscones* at the airports. They offer to assist you, and do so by relieving you of your luggage and disappearing with it. Also avoid the black marketers, who will offer you a tempting rate of exchange for your U.S. dollars. If the police catch you changing money on the street, they'll haul you off to jail (the *calabozo*). Also, buy amber only from reputable shops. The attractively priced piece offered by the street vendor is more than likely plastic. Guard your wallet or pocketbook in Santo Domingo, especially around the Malecón (waterfront boulevard), which teems with pickpockets.

Staying in the Dominican Republic

Important Addresses

Tourist Information: The **Secretary of Tourism** is in Santo Domingo in a complex of government offices at the corner of Avenida Mexico and Avenida 30 de Marzo (Officinas Guberbamentales Bldg. D, ☎ 809/221–4660, FAX 809/682–3806). Unless you are seeking special assistance, it is not worth making the trek here for the limited material offered to tourists. The **tourist office** is in Puerto Plata (Playa Long Beach, ☎ 809/586–3676). Both offices are open weekdays 9–2:30, but the Puerto Plata office often opens late and closes early.

Police: In Santo Domingo, call 711; in Puerto Plata, call 586–2804; in Sosúa, call 571–2233. However, do not expect too much from the police, aside from a bit of a hassle and some paperwork that they will consider the end of the matter. In general, the police and government bureaucrats take a hostile approach to visitors.

Hospitals: Santo Domingo emergency rooms that are open 24 hours are **Centro Médico Universidad Central del Este** (UCE) (Av. Máximo Gómez 68, ☎ 809/221–0171), **Clínica Abreu** (Calle Beller 42, ☎ 809/688–4411), and **Clínica Gómez Patino** (Av. Independencia 701, ☎ 809/685–9131). In Puerto Plata, you can go to **Clínica Dr. Brugal** (Calle José del Carmen Ariza 15, ☎ 809/586–2519). In Sosúa, try the **Centro Médico Sosúa** (Av. Martinez, ☎ 809/571–3949).

Pharmacies: Pharmacies that are open 24 hours a day are, in Santo Domingo, **San Judas Tadeo** (Av. Independencia 57, ☎ 809/689–6664); in Puerto Plata, **Farmacia Deleyte** (Av. John F. Kennedy 89, ☎ 809/586–2583).

Currency

The coin of the realm is the Dominican peso, which is divided into 100 centavos. It is written R.D.$ and fluctuates relative to the U.S. dollar. At press time, U.S.$1 was equivalent to R.D.$12.50. Always make certain you know in which currency any transaction is taking place (any confusion will probably not be to your advantage). There is a growing black market for hard currency, so be wary of offers to exchange U.S. dollars at a rate more favorable than the official one. Prices quoted here are in U.S. dollars unless noted otherwise.

Taxes and Service Charges

Hotels and restaurants add a service charge (15% in hotels, 10% in restaurants) and 8% government tax. Although hotels add the 15% service charge, it is customary to leave a dollar per day for the hotel maid. At restaurants and nightclubs you may want to leave an additional 5%–10% tip for a job well done. Taxi drivers expect a 10% tip. Skycaps and hotel porters expect at least R.D.$5 per bag. U.S. visitors must buy a $10 tourist card before entering the Dominican Republic, and all foreign visitors must pay a $10 departure tax. Both must be paid in U.S. dollars.

Guided Tours

Prieto Tours (☎ 809/685–0102 or 809/688–5715) operates Gray Line of the Dominican Republic. It offers half-day bus tours of Santo Domingo, nightclub tours, beach tours, tours to Cibao Valley and the Amber Coast, and a variety of other tours. **Turinter** (☎ 809/685–4020) tours include dinner and a show or casino visit, a full-day tour of Samaná, and specialty tours (museum, shopping, fishing). **Cafemba Tours** (☎ 809/586–2177) runs various tours of the Cibao Valley and the Amber Coast, including Puerto Plata, Sosúa, and Río San Juan. **Apolo Tours** (☎ 809/586–5329) offers a full-day tour of Playa Grande and tours to Santiago (including a casino tour) and Sosúa. It will also arrange transfers between your hotel and the airport, day sightseeing tours, and custom and small-group tours along the north coast, which include stops along the way for swimming and an overnight stay at Samaná. **Ecoturista** (☎ 809/221–4104) arranges ecological tours and cultural and scientific expeditions, many of them tailored to the clients' needs. **Caribbean Jeep Safaris** (☎ 809/571–1924) is an English-speaking outfit that runs Jeep tours in the mountains behind Puerto Plata and Sosúa, ending up at the new Cabarete Adventure Park, where you can swim in an underground pool and explore caves with Taino rock paintings. Buffet lunch and unlimited drinks are included in the R.D.$600 price.

Getting Around

TAXIS

Taxis, which are government regulated, line up outside hotels and restaurants. The taxis are unmetered, and the minimum fare within Santo Domingo is about R.D.$50 (U.S.$4), but you can bargain for less if you order a taxi away from the major hotels. Hiring a taxi by the hour and with any number of stops is R.D.$125 (U.S.$10) per hour with a minimum of two hours. Be sure to establish the time that you start; drivers like to advance the time a little. You should also be certain that it is clearly understood in advance which currency is to be used in the agreed-upon fare. Taxis can also drive you to destinations outside the city. Rates are posted in hotels and at the airport. Sample fares are R.D.$1,000 (U.S.$80) to La Romana and R.D.$1,900 (U.S.$150) to Puerto Plata. If you're negotiating, the going rate is R.D.$5 per kilometer. Round-trips are considerably less than twice the one-way fare. Call **Taxi Anacaona** (☏ 800/530–4800), **Taxi la Paloma** (☏ 809/531–6892), **Taxi Raffi** (☏ 809/689–5468), or **Centro Taxi** (☏ 809/685–9248).

In a separate category are radio taxis, which are convenient if you'd like to schedule a pickup—and a wise choice if you don't speak Spanish. The fare is negotiated over the phone when you make the appointment. The most reliable company is **Apolo Taxi** (☏ 809/541–9595). The standard charge is R.D.$100 per hour during the day, R.D.$120 at night, no minimum, with as many stops as you like.

Avoid unmarked street taxis—there have been numerous incidents of assaults and robberies, particularly in Santo Domingo.

BUSES

Públicos are small blue-and-white or blue-and-red cars that run regular routes, stopping to let passengers on and off. The fare is R.D.$2. Competing with the públicos are the *conchos* or *colectivos* (privately owned buses), whose drivers tool around the major thoroughfares, leaning out of the window or jumping out to try to persuade passengers to climb aboard. It's a colorful, if cramped, way to get around town. The fare is about R.D.$1. Privately owned air-conditioned buses make regular runs to Santiago, Puerto Plata, and other destinations. Avoid night travel, because the country's roads are full of potholes. You should make reservations by calling **Metro Buses** (Av. Winston Churchill, in Santo Domingo, call 809/566–7126; in Puerto Plata, 809/586–6062; in Santiago, 809/587–4711) or **Caribe Tours** (Av. 27 de Febrero at Leopoldo Navarro, ☏ 809/221–4422). One-way bus fare from Santo Domingo to Puerto Plata is R.D.$75 (U.S.$6). *Voladoras* ("fliers") are vans that run from Puerto Plata's Central Park to Sosúa and Cabarete a couple of times each hour for R.D.$10. They don't run on a reliable schedule and are not always labeled with their destination.

MOTORBIKE TAXIS

Known as *motoconchos*, these bikes are a popular and inexpensive way to get around such tourist areas as Puerto Plata, Sosúa, and Jarabacoa. Bikes can be flagged down both on the road and in town; rates vary from R.D.$3 to R.D.$20 per person, depending upon distance.

RENTAL CARS

You'll need a valid driver's license from your own country and a major credit card and/or cash deposit. Cars can be rented at the airports and at many hotels. Among the known names are **Avis** (☏ 809/535–7191), **Budget** (☏ 809/562–6812), **Hertz** (☏ 809/221–5333), and **National** (☏ 809/562–1444). Rates average U.S.$70 and up per day, depending upon the make and size of the car. Driving is on the right. Many Dominicans drive recklessly, often taking their half of the road out of the middle, but they will flash their headlights to warn against highway patrols.

If for some unavoidable reason you must drive on the narrow, unlighted mountain roads at night, exercise extreme caution. Many local cars are without headlights or taillights, bicyclists do not have lights, and cows stand by the side of the road. Traffic and directional signs are less than adequate, and unseen potholes can easily break a car's axle. The 80-kph (50-mph) speed limit is strictly enforced. Finally, keep in mind that gas stations are few and far between in some of the remote regions. Police supplement their income by stopping drivers on various pretexts and expecting a "gift." Locals give R.D.$20 or R.D.$40.

PLANE
If you lack the time to travel overland, you can charter a small plane for trips around the island and to neighboring countries, and for surprisingly inexpensive rates. Contact Jimmy or Irene Butler at **Air Taxi** (Núñez de Cáceres 2, Santo Domingo, ☎ 809/227–8333 or 809/567–1555).

Telephones and Mail
To call the Dominican Republic from the United States, dial area code 809 and the local number. Connections are clear and easy to make. Fortunately, service from the Dominican Republic is much improved. There is direct-dial service to the United States; just dial 1, followed by area code and number.

Airmail postage to North America for a letter or postcard costs R.D.$2, to Europe, R.D.$4, and may take up to three weeks to reach the destination.

Opening and Closing Times
Regular office and shop hours are weekdays 8–12:30 and 2:30–5, Saturday 8–noon. Government offices are open weekdays 7:30–2:30. Banking hours are weekdays 8:30–4:30.

Exploring the Dominican Republic

Numbers in the margin correspond to points of interest on the Santo Domingo map.

Santo Domingo
We'll begin our tour where Spanish civilization in the New World began, in the 12-block area of **Santo Domingo** called the Colonial Zone. This historical area is now a bustling, noisy district with narrow cobbled streets, shops, restaurants, residents, and traffic jams. Ironically, all the noise and congestion make it somehow easier to imagine this old city as it was when the likes of Columbus, Cortés, Ponce de León, and pirates sailed in and out and colonists were settling themselves in the New World. Tourist brochures boast that "history comes alive here"—a surprisingly truthful statement.

A quick taxi tour of the old section takes about an hour, but if you're interested in history, you'll want to spend a day or two exploring the many old "firsts," and you'll want to do it in the most comfortable shoes you own. Wearing shorts, miniskirts, and halters in churches is considered inappropriate. (Note: Hours and ☛ charges are erratic; check with the tourist office for up-to-date information.)

One of the first things you'll see as you approach the Colonial Zone is a statue, only slightly smaller than the Colossus of Rhodes, staring out over the Caribbean Sea. It is **Montesina,** the Spanish priest who came to the Dominican Republic in the 16th century to appeal for human rights for Indians.

② **Parque Independencia** (Independence Park), on the far western border of the Colonial Zone, is a big city park dominated by the marble and concrete **Altar de la Patria.** The impressive mausoleum was built in 1976 to honor the founding fathers of the country (Duarte, Sánchez, and Mella).

③ To your left as you leave the square, the **Concepción Fortress,** within the old city walls, was the northwest defense post of the colony. *Calle Palo Hincado at Calle Isidro Duarte, no* ☎. ☛ *Free.* ⊙ *Tues.–Sun. 9–6.*

From Independence Park, walk eight blocks east on Calle El Conde **④** and you'll come to **Parque Colón.** The huge statue of Columbus dates from 1897 and is the work of French sculptor Gilbert. On the west side of the square is the **old town hall** and, on the east, the **Palacio de Borgella,** residence of the governor during the Haitian occupation of 1822–44 and presently the seat of the Permanent Dominican Commission for the **Fifth Centennial of the Discovery and Evangelization of the Americas.** Gallery spaces house architectural and archaeological exhibits pertaining to the fifth centennial.

Towering over the south side of the square is the coral limestone fa- **⑤** cade of the **Catedral Santa María la Menor,** the first cathedral in America. Spanish workmen began building the cathedral in 1514 but left off construction to search for gold in Mexico. The church was finally finished in 1540. Its facade is composed of architectural elements from the late Gothic to the plateresque style. Inside, the high altar is made of beaten silver, and in the treasury there is a magnificent collection of gold and silver. Some of its 14 lateral chapels serve as mausoleums for noted Dominicans, including Archbishop Meriño, who was once president of the Dominican Republic. Of interest is the Chapel of Our Lady of Antigua, which was reconsecrated by John Paul II in 1984. In the nave are four baroque columns, carved to resemble royal palms, which for more than four centuries guarded the magnificent bronze and marble sarcophagus containing (say Dominican historians) the remains of Christopher Columbus, whose last wish was to be buried in Santo Domingo. The sarcophagus has recently been moved to the Columbus Memorial Lighthouse (*see below*)—only the latest in the Great Navigator's posthumous journeys. *Calle Arzobispo Meriño,* ☎ *809/689–1920.* ☛ *Free.* ⊙ *Mon.–Sat. 9–1; Sun. masses begin at 6 AM.*

When you leave the cathedral, turn right, walk to Columbus Square, and turn left on Calle El Conde. Walk one more block and turn right on Calle Hostos and continue for two more blocks. You'll see the ruins **⑥** of the **Hospital de San Nicolás de Bari,** the first hospital in the New World, which was built in 1503 by Nicolás de Ovando. *Calle Hostos, between Calle de Las Mercedes and Calle Luperon, no* ☎.

Continue along Calle Hostos, crossing Calle Emiliano Tejera, up the hill, **⑦** and about midblock on your left you'll see the majestic ruins of the **San Francisco Monastery.** Constructed between 1512 and 1544, the monastery contained the church, chapel, and convent of the Franciscan order. Sir Francis Drake's demolition squad significantly damaged the building in 1586, and in 1673 an earthquake nearly finished the job, but when it's floodlit at night, the old monastery is indeed a dramatic sight.

Walk east for two blocks along Calle Emiliano Tejera. Opposite the **⑧** Telecom building on Calle Isabel la Católica, the **Casa del Cordón** is recognizable by the sash of the Franciscan order carved in stone over

Dominican Republic

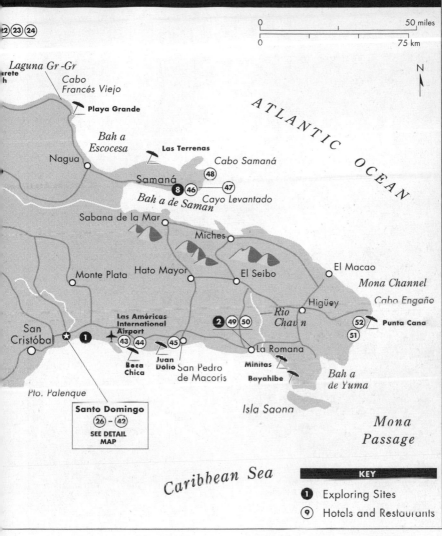

㉒ ㉓ ㉔

Laguna Gr -Gr

Cabo
Francés Viejo

Playa Grande

Bah a
Escocesa

Las Terrenas

Cabo Samaná

Nagua

㊽

Samaná

❽ ㊻

㊼

Bah a de Saman

Cayo Levantado

ATLANTIC OCEAN

N

Sabana de la Mar

Miches

Monte Plata

Hato Mayor

El Seibo

El Macao

Mona Channel

Cabo Engaño

**Las Américas
International
Airport**

❷ ㊾ ㊿

Rio
Chav n

Higüey

㊼

㊾ ㊾

Punta Cana

San
Cristóbal

❶

㊸ ㊹

㊺

**Boca
Chica**

**Juan
Dolio**

San Pedro
de Macorís

Minitas

Bayahibe

La Romana

Bah a
de Yuma

Pto. Palenque

Santo Domingo
㉖ – ㊷
**SEE DETAIL
MAP**

Isla Saona

Mona
Passage

Caribbean Sea

KEY

❶ Exploring Sites

⑨ Hotels and Restaurants

Caribbean Village
Club and Resort, **14**
Casa de Campo, **49**
Cayo Levantado, **47**
Club Marina, **24**
Dorado Naco and
Playa Naco, **11**
Flamenco Beach
Resort, Villas
Doradas, and Playa
Dorada Beach
Resort, **19**

Gran Hotel Lina
and Casino, **28**
Hamaca Beach
Hotel, **43**
Hostal Palacio
Nicolás
de Ovando, **37**
Hotel Cofresi, **9**
Hotel El Embajador
and Casino, **36**
Hotel Gran Bahía, **48**
Hotel Montemar, **15**

Hotel Santo
Domingo, **26**
Inter-Continental
Hotel V
Centenario, **38**
Jaragua
Renaissance Resort
and Casino, **35**
Paradise Beach
Resort and Club, **12**
Playa Chiquita, **21**

Puerto Plata
Beach Resort and
Casino, **13**
Punta Cana Beach
Resort, **52**
Sand Castle, **22**
Santo Domingo
Sheraton Hotel and
Casino, **27**

Santo Domingo

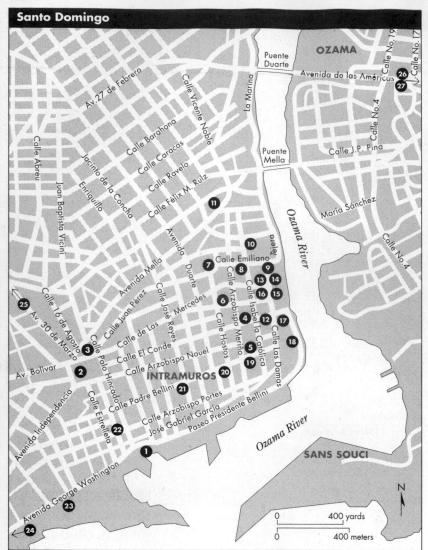

Acuario Nacional, **26**
Alcázar de Colón, **9**
Calle Las Damas, **12**
Capilla de los Reme-
dios, **14**
Casa de Bastidas, **17**
Casa de Tostado, **19**
Casa del Cordón, **8**
Catedral Santa María
la Menor, **5**

Concepción
Fortress, **3**
El Faro a Colón, **27**
Hospital de San
Nicolás de Bari, **6**
Hostal Palacio
Nicolás de
Ovando, **15**
Iglesia y Convento
Domínico, **20**
Jardín Botánico Na-
cional Dr. Rafael

M. Moscoso, **25**
La Atarazana, **10**
La Iglesia de Regina
Angelorum, **21**
Malecón, **23**
Montesina, **1**
Museo de las
Casas Reales, **13**
National
Pantheon, **16**
Parque Colón, **4**

Parque Independen-
cia, **2**
Plaza de la
Cultura, **24**
Puerta de la Miseri-
cordia, **22**
San Francisco
Monastery, **7**
Santa Bárbara
Church, **11**
Torre del
Homenaje, **18**

the arched entrance. This house, built in 1503, is the Western Hemisphere's oldest surviving stone house. Columbus's son Diego Colón, viceroy of the colony, and his wife lived here until the Alcázar was finished. It was in this house, too, that Sir Francis Drake was paid a ransom to prevent him from totally destroying the city. The house is now home to the Banco Popular. *Corner of Calle Emiliano Tejera and Calle Isabel la Católica, no ☎. ☞ Free. ☉ Weekdays 8:30–4:30.*

⑨ Walk one block east along Calle Emiliano Tejera to reach the imposing **Alcázar de Colón,** with its balustrade and double row of arches. The Renaissance structure has strong Moorish, Gothic, and Isabelline influences. The castle of Don Diego Colón, built in 1514, was painstakingly reconstructed and restored in 1957. Forty-inch-thick coral limestone walls were patched and shored with blocks from the original quarry. There are 22 rooms, furnished in a style to which the viceroy of the island would have been accustomed—right down to the dishes and the viceregal shaving mug. Many of the period paintings, statues, tapestries, and furnishings were donated by the University of Madrid. *Just off Calle Emiliano Tejera at the foot of Calle Las Damas,* ☎ 809/687–5361. ☞ *R.D.$10.* ☉ *Mon. and Wed.–Fri. 9–5, Sat. 9–4, Sun. 9–1.*

⑩ Across from the Alcázar, **La Atarazana** (the Royal Mooring Docks) was once the colonial commercial district, where naval supplies were stored. There are eight restored buildings, the oldest of which dates from 1507. It now houses crafts shops, restaurants, and art galleries.

TIME OUT If your walking tour leads you to La Atarazana by midday, join the Reserve Bank and Telecom staff at the **Café Montesinos** (Calle La Atarazana 23, ☎ 809/689–0580) for a typical Dominican noonday meal. For R.D.$60 you can try fish or beef in a succulent Creole sauce, a tasty bean soup with plantains, or one of the other hearty dishes on the menu. If you happen to be in the area in the late afternoon, stop in for a pizza and a drink at **Drake's Pub** (Calle La Atarazana 25, ☎ 809/687–8089). There's a fine view of the Alcázar from here, and the place fills up with congenial locals and foreigners.

⑪ To reach the **Santa Bárbara Church,** go back to Calle Isabel la Católica, turn right, and walk several blocks. This combination church and fortress, the only one of its kind in Santo Domingo, was completed in 1562. *Av. Mella, between Calle Isabel la Católica and Calle Arzobispo Meriño, no* ☎. ☞ *Free.* ☉ *Weekdays 8–noon. Sun. masses begin at 6 AM.*

⑫ Retrace your steps to Calle Isabel la Católica, turn left on Calle de Las Mercedes, and walk one block right to **Calle Las Damas,** where you'll make a right turn to the New World's oldest street. The "Street of the Ladies" was named after the elegant ladies of the court who, in the Spanish tradition, promenaded in the evening.

On your left you'll see a sundial dating from 1753 and the **Casa de los Jesuitas,** which houses a fine research library for colonial history as well as the Institute for Hispanic Culture. ☞ *Free.* ☉ *Weekdays 8–4:30.*

⑬ Across the street is the **Museo de las Casas Reales** (Museum of the Royal Houses). The collections in the museum are displayed in two early-16th-century palaces that have been altered many times over the years. Exhibits cover everything from antique coins to replicas of the *Niña,* the *Pinta,* and the *Santa María.* There are statue and cartography galleries, coats of armor and coats of arms, coaches and a royal court room, gilded furnishings, and Indian artifacts. The first room of the former Governor's Residence has a wall-size map marking the routes sailed by Columbus's ships on expeditions beginning in 1492. *Calle Las Damas,* *corner Calle Mercedes,* ☎ *809/682–4202.* ☛ *R.D.$10.* ☉ *Tues.–Sat. 9–4:45, Sun. 10–1.*

⑭ Across the street is the **Capilla de los Remedios** (Chapel of Our Lady of Remedies), which was originally built in the 17th century as a private chapel for the family of Francisco de Dávila. Early colonists also worshiped here before the completion of the cathedral. Its architectural details, particularly the lateral arches, are evocative of the Castilian-Romanesque style. *Calle Las Damas, at the foot of Calle Mercedes, no* ☎. ☛ *Free.* ☉ *Mon.–Sat. 9–6; Sun. masses begin at 6 AM.*

⑮ Just south of the chapel on Calle Las Damas, the **Hostal Palacio Nicolás de Ovando** (*see* Lodging, *below*), now a highly praised hotel, was once the residence of Nicolás de Ovando, one of the principal organizers of the colonial city.

⑯ Across the street from the hotel looms the massive **National Pantheon.** The building, which dates from 1714, was once a Jesuit monastery and later a theater. Trujillo had it restored in 1955 with an eye toward being buried there. (He is buried instead at Père Lachaise in Paris.) An allegorical mural of his assassination is painted on the ceiling above the altar, where an eternal flame burns. The impressive chandelier was a gift from Spain's Generalissimo Franco. *Calle Las Damas, near the corner of Calle Mercedes, no* ☎. ☛ *Free.* ☉ *Mon.–Sat. 10–5.*

⑰ Continue south on Calle Las Damas and cross Calle El Conde. Look on your left for the **Casa de Bastidas,** where there is a lovely inner courtyard with tropical plants and temporary exhibit galleries. *Calle Las Damas, just off Calle El Conde, no* ☎. ☛ *Free.* ☉ *Tues.–Sun. 9–5.*

⑱ You won't have any trouble spotting the **Torre del Homenaje** (Tower of Homage) in the Fort Ozama. The fort sprawls two blocks south of the Casa de Bastidas, with a brooding crenellated tower that still guards the Ozama River. The fort and its tower were built in 1503 to protect the eastern border of the city. The sinister tower was the last home of many a condemned prisoner. *On Paseo Presidente Bellini, overlooking Río Ozama, no* ☎. ☛ *R.D.$10.* ☉ *Tues.–Sun. 8–7.*

⑲ When you leave the fortress, turn left off Calle Las Damas onto Calle Padre Bellini. A two-block walk will bring you to **Casa de Tostado.** The house was built in the first decade of the 16th century and was the residence of writer Don Francisco Tostado. Its twin Gothic windows are the only ones that are still in existence in the New World. It now houses the **Museo de la Familia Dominicana** (Museum of the Dominican Family), which features exhibits on the well-heeled Dominican family in the 19th century. *Calle Padre Bellini, near Calle Arzobispo Meriño,* ☎ *809/689–5057.* ☛ *R.D.$10.* ☉ *Thurs.–Tues. 9–2.*

⑳ Walk two blocks west on Calle Padre Bellini to the corner of Avenida Duarte. The graceful building with the rose window is the **Iglesia y Convento Domínico** (Dominican Church and Convent), founded in 1510. In 1538, Pope Paul III visited here and was so impressed with the lectures on theology that he granted the church and convent the title of university, making it the oldest institution of higher learning in the New World. *Calle Padre Bellini and Av. Duarte,* ☎ *809/682–3780.* ☛ *Free.* ☉ *Tues.–Sun. 9–6.*

㉑ Continue west on Calle Padre Bellini for two blocks, and at the corner of Calle José Reyes you'll see another lovely church, **La Iglesia de Regina Angelorum** (Church of Regina Angelorum), which dates from 1537. The church was damaged during the Haitian regime, from 1822 to 1844, but you can still appreciate its Baroque dome, Gothic arches, and traceries. *Corner of Calle Padre Bellini and Calle José Reyes,* ☎ *809/682–2783.* ☛ *Free.* ☉ *Mon.–Sat. 9–6.*

 Walk four blocks west on Calle Padre Bellini, turn left on Calle Palo Hincado, and keep going straight till you reach the **Puerta de la Misericordia** (Gate of Mercy), part of the old wall of Santo Domingo. It was here on the plaza, on February 27, 1844, that Ramón Mata Mella, one of the country's founding fathers, fired the shot that began the struggle for independence from Haiti.

Parque Independencia separates the old city from the new. Avenidas 30 de Marzo, Bolívar, and Independencia traverse the park and mingle with avenues named for George Washington, John F. Kennedy, and Abraham Lincoln. Modern Santo Domingo is a sprawling, noisy city with a population of close to 2 million.

 Avenida George Washington, which is lined with tall palms and Las Vegas–style tourist hotels, breezes along the Caribbean Sea. The Parque Litoral de Sur, better known as the **Malecón,** borders the avenue from the colonial city to the Hotel Santo Domingo, a distance of about 3 miles. The seaside park, with its cafés and places to relax, is a popular spot, but beware of pickpockets.

 Avenida Máximo Gómez comes down from the north. Take a right turn on it, cross Avenida Bolívar, and you'll come to the landscaped lawns, modern sculptures, and sleek buildings of the **Plaza de la Cultura.** Among the buildings are the **National Theater** (☎ 809/687–3191), which stages performances in Spanish; the **National Library,** in which the written word is Spanish; and museums and art galleries, whose notations are also in Spanish. The following museums on the plaza are open Tuesday–Saturday from 10 to 5, and admission to each is R.D.$10. The **Museum of Dominican Man** (☎ 809/687–3622) traces the migrations of Indians from South America through the Caribbean islands. The **Museum of Natural History** (☎ 809/689–0106) examines the flora and fauna of the island. In the **Gallery of Modern Art** (☎ 809/682–8260), the works of 20th-century Dominican and foreign artists are displayed.

North of town in the Arroyo Hondo district is the **Jardín Botánico Nacional Dr. Rafael M. Moscoso** (Dr. Rafael M. Moscoso National Botanical Gardens), the largest garden in the Caribbean. Its 445 acres include a Japanese garden, a great ravine, a glen, a gorgeous display of orchids, and an enormous floral clock. You can tour the gardens by train, boat, or horse-drawn carriage. *Arroyo Hondo, no* ☎. ☛ *R.D.$2.* ☉ *Daily 10–6.*

In the 320-acre **Parque Zoológico Nacional** (National Zoological Park), not far from the botanical gardens, animals roam free in natural habitats. There is an African plain, a children's zoo, and what the zoo claims is the world's largest birdcage. *Av. Máximo Gómez at Av. de los Próceres,* ☎ *809/562–2080.* ☛ *R.D.$10.* ☉ *Daily 10–6.*

Now head east and cross the Río Ozama at Puente Duarte. Take Avenida de las Américas to the **Acuario Nacional** (National Aquarium). The largest aquarium in the Caribbean, with an impressive collection of tropical fish and dolphins, its construction was a controversial public expenditure. *In the Sans Souci district on the Av. de las Américas.* ☛ *R.D.$10.* ☉ *Daily 10–6.*

Follow the signs to the nearby **El Faro a Colón** (Columbus Memorial Lighthouse). This striking lighthouse monument and museum dedicated to the Great Navigator is shaped like a pyramid cross. The lighthouse complex was completed in 1992, its inauguration coinciding with the 500th anniversary of Christopher Columbus's landing on the island. Along with its showpiece laser-powered lighthouse, the complex holds the tomb of Columbus (recently moved there after 400 years in the Catedral Santa María la Menor) and six museums featuring exhibits related to Columbus and early exploration of the New World. One museum focuses on the long, rocky, and often controversial history of the lighthouse memorial itself and another on the Great Navigator's posthumous peregrinations (Cuba, Spain, and the Dominican Republic have all laid claim to—and hosted—his remains, which even today are a subject of controversy). *Av. España,* ☎ 809/591–1492. ☛ *R.D.$5 adults, R.D.$1 children under 12.* ☉ *Tues.–Sun. 9–4.*

The East Coast
Numbers in the margin correspond to points of interest on the Dominican Republic map.

❶ Continue east on Las Américas Highway toward La Romana, about a two-hour drive along the southeast coast. All along the highway are small resort-hotel complexes where you can find refreshments or stay overnight. About 1½ miles outside the capital, you'll come to the **Parque de los Tres Ojos** (Park of the Three Eyes). The "eyes" are cool blue pools peering out of deep limestone caves, and it's actually a four-eyed park. If you've a mind to, you can look into the eyes more closely by climbing down into the caves.

About 20 minutes east of the city is **Boca Chica Beach,** popular because of its proximity to the capital. Another 45 minutes or so farther east is the city of **San Pedro de Macorís,** where the national sport and the national drink are both well represented. Some of the country's best *béisbol* games are played in **Tetelo Vargas Stadium,** which you can see off the highway to your left. The grander homes in the area most likely belong to Dominican baseball stars like George Bell. The **Macorís Rum distillery** is on the eastern edge of the city. Outside town is Juan Dolio, another beach popular with *capitaleños.*

The two big businesses around La Romana used to be cattle and sugarcane. That was before Gulf & Western created (and subsequently sold) the **Casa de Campo** resort (*see* Lodging, *below*), which is a very big business, indeed, and **Altos de Chavón,** a re-creation of a 16th-century village and art colony on the resort grounds.

❷ **Altos de Chavón** sits on a bluff overlooking the Río Chavón, about 3 miles east of the main facility of Casa de Campo. You can drive there easily enough, or you can take one of the free shuttle buses from the resort. In this re-creation of a medieval Spanish village, there are cobblestone streets lined with lanterns, wrought-iron balconies, and courtyards swathed with bougainvillea. More than a museum piece, this village is a place where artists live, work, and play. There is an art school, affiliated with New York's Parsons School of Design; a disco; an archaeological museum; five restaurants; and a 5,000-seat outdoor amphitheater (used about four times a year), where Frank Sinatra and Julio Iglesias have entertained. The focal point of the village is **Iglesia St. Stanislaus,** which is named after the patron saint of Poland in tribute to the Polish pope John Paul II, who visited the Dominican Republic in 1979 and left some of the ashes of St. Stanislaus behind.

From here the road continues east to Punta Cana and Bavaro, glorious beaches on the sunrise side of the island. On the way you'll pass through Higüey, an undistinguished collection of ramshackle buildings notable only for its controversial church, consecrated by Pope John Paul II in 1984, which resembles a pinched McDonald's arch.

The Cibao Valley

The road north from Santo Domingo, known as Autopista Duarte, cuts through the lush banana plantations, rice and tobacco fields, and royal poinciana trees of the Cibao Valley. All along the road there are stands where, for a few centavos, you can buy ripe pineapples, mangoes, avocados, *chicharrones* (either fried pork rinds or chicken pieces), and fresh fruit drinks. To the west is **Pico Duarte,** at 10,128 feet the highest peak in the West Indies.

In the heart of the Cibao is La Vega. Founded in 1495 by Columbus, it is the site of one of the oldest settlements in the New World. The inquisitive will find the tour of the ruins of the original settlement, **La Vega Vieja** (The Old La Vega), a rewarding experience. About 3 miles north of La Vega is **Santo Cerro** (Holy Mount), site of a miraculous apparition of the Virgin and therefore many local pilgrimages. The **Convent of La Merced** is there, and the views of the Cibao Valley are breathtaking. The new town boasts a remarkable church of its own, **Concepcion de la Vega,** constructed in 1992 to commemorate the 500th anniversary of the discovery (and evangelization) of America. The unusual modern Gothic style—all curvaceous concrete columns, arches, and buttresses—is striking indeed.

La Vega is also celebrated for its Carnival, featuring the haunting, disturbing *Diablos Cojuelos*—"devil masks." These papier-mâché creations are incredibly intricate, fanciful gargoyle demons painted in surreal colors with real cow's teeth contributing eerie authenticity. The skill is usually passed down for generations; several artisans work in dark cramped studios throughout the area. The studio closest to downtown is that of José Luis Gomez. Ask any local (tip them 10–20 pesos) to guide you to his atelier (no ☎). José speaks no English but will show you the stages of mask development. He sells the masks, which make extraordinary wall hangings, for U.S.$50–$60, a great buy considering the craftsmanship.

About 90 miles north of the capital, you'll come to the industrial city of **Santiago de los Caballeros,** where a massive monument honoring the restoration of the republic guards the entrance to the city. Many past presidents were born in Santiago, and it is currently a center for processing tobacco leaf. You can gain an appreciation of the art and skill of Cuban cigar-making with a tour of **E. Leon Jimenez Tabacalera** (☎ 809/563–1111). The best hotel in town is the **Gran Almirante.**

The Amber Coast

The Autopista Duarte ultimately leads (in three to four hours from Santo Domingo) to the Amber Coast, so called because of its large, rich, and unique deposits of amber. The coastal area around Puerto Plata is a region of splashy resorts and megadevelopments like Costambar and Playa Dorada. The north coast boasts more than 70 miles of beaches, with condominiums and villas going up fast.

Puerto Plata, although now quiet and almost sleepy, was a dynamic city in its heyday. You can get a feeling for this past in the magnificent Victorian **Glorieta** (Gazebo) in the central **Parque Independencia.** Next to the park, the recently refurbished **Catedral de San Felipe** recalls a simpler, colonial past. On Puerto Plata's own Malecón, the **Fortaleza de San Felipe** protected the city from many a pirate attack and was later used as a political prison. The fort is most dramatic at night.

Puerto Plata is also the home of the **Museum of Dominican Amber,** a lovely galleried mansion and one of several tenants in the Tourist Bazaar. The museum displays and sells the Dominican Republic's national stone. Semiprecious, translucent amber is actually fossilized pine resin that dates back about 50 million years, give or take a few millennia. The north coast of the Dominican Republic has the largest deposits of amber in the world (the only other deposits are found in Germany and the former U.S.S.R.), and jewelry crafted from the stone is the best-selling item on the island. *Calle Duarte 61,* ☎ *809/586–2848.* ☛ *R.D.$15.* ☉ *Mon.–Sat. 9–5.*

Southwest of Puerto Plata (follow the signs from the Autopista), you can take a cable car (when it is working) to the top of **Mt. Isabel de Torres,** which soars 2,600 feet above sea level. On the mountain there is a botanical garden, a huge statue of Christ, and a spectacular view. The cable was first laid in 1754, although rest assured that it's been replaced since then. Lines can be long, and once on top of the mountain you will wonder if it was worth the time. Don't eat at the restaurant at the top—the food is awful. *No phone. Cable car operates Tues., Thurs., Fri., Sat., and Sun. 8–6. Round-trip is R.D.$20.*

7 Take the Autopista east from Puerto Plata about 15 miles to **Sosúa,** a small community settled during World War II by 600 Austrian and German Jews. After the war, many of them returned to Europe or went to the United States, and most of those who remained married Dominicans. Only a few Jewish families reside in the community today, and there is only one small one-room synagogue. The flavor of the town is decidedly Spanish. (Note: The roads off the Autopista are horribly punctured with potholes.)

Sosúa has become one of the most frequently visited tourist destinations in the country, favored by French Canadians and Europeans. Hotels and condos are going up at breakneck speed. It actually consists of two communities, **El Batey,** the modern hotel development, and **Los Charamicos,** the old quarter, separated by a cove and one of the island's prettiest beaches. The sand is soft and white, the water, crystal clear and calm. The walkway above the beach is packed with tents filled with souvenirs, pizzas, and even clothing for sale—a jarring note in this otherwise idyllic setting.

TIME OUT **P.J.'s International Pub Café** (Calle Pedro Clisante, no ☎), in the center of Sosúa, is a shack seemingly glued together by old license plates, business cards, beer posters, and yellowing calendars. Fifteen pesos will buy you a pint of draft. The ambience, courtesy of colorful expatriates and scruffy young Europeans, is free.

Continue east on the Autopista past **Cabarete,** a popular windsurfing haunt, and **Playa Grande.** The powdery white beach remains miraculously undisturbed and unspoiled by development.

8 The Autopista rolls along eastward and rides out onto a "thumb" of the island, where you'll find **Samaná.** Back in 1824, a sailing vessel called the *Turtle Dove,* carrying several hundred escaped American slaves from the Freeman Sisters' underground railway, was blown ashore in Samaná. The escapees settled and prospered, and today their descendants number several thousand. The churches here are Protestant; the worshipers live in villages called Bethesda, Northeast, and Philadelphia; and the language spoken is an odd 19th-century form of English.

The wealth of marine life in the surrounding waters is beginning to attract more specialty tourists. Sportfishing at Samaná is considered to be among the best in the world. In addition, about 3,000 humpback whales winter off the coast of Samaná from December to March. Major whale-watching expeditions like those out of Massachusetts are being organized and should boost the region's economy without scaring away the world's largest mammals.

Samaná makes a fine base for exploring the area's natural splendors. Most hotels on the peninsula arrange tours to the **Los Haitises National Park,** a remote unspoiled rain forest with limestone knolls, crystal lakes, mangrove swamps teeming with aquatic birds, and caves stippled with Taino petroglyphs. **Las Terrenas,** a remote stretch of beautiful, nearly deserted beaches on the north coast of the Samaná peninsula, is barely known to North American tourists, although French Canadians and Europeans, especially Germans, have begun making the long trek to this latter-day hippie haven that also attracts surfboarders and windsurfers. There are several modest seafood restaurants (the best is **Boca Fina,** no ☎), a dusty main street in the town of Las Terrenas, a small airfield, the comparatively grand all-inclusive **El Portillo Beach Club** (☎ 809/688–5785), and several congenial hotels right on the beach at Punta Bonita. If you're seeking tranquillity and are happy just hanging out drinking beer and soaking up sun, this is the place for you. The road from Samaná, even though it is longer and not paved, is a lot less strenuous than coming over the hills from Sanchez.

What to See and Do with Children

Acuario Nacional (*see* Exploring the Dominican Republic, *above*).

Agua Splash Caribe is a new aquapark across from the aquarium featuring the usual waterslides, "river rapids," and wave pools. A schedule of spectacular water revues is planned for the evenings. *Av. Espana,* ☎ *809/591–5927.* ☉ *Tues.–Sun. 10–7 year-round.* ☞ *Adults R.D.$80 Sat. and Sun., R.D.$50 Tues.–Fri.; children under 12 R.D.$50 Sat. and Sun., R.D.$30 Tues.–Fri.*

Columbus Memorial Lighthouse (*see* Exploring the Dominican Republic, *above*) fascinates kids, who especially love the hourly changing of the guard.

Parque Zoológico Nacional (*see* Exploring the Dominican Republic, *above*).

Parque de los Tres Ojos (*see* Exploring the Dominican Republic, *above*).

Off the Beaten Track

The Dominican Republic offers vastly different microclimates in an area that is only twice the size of Massachusetts.

Laguna Grí-Grí is a swampland smack out of the Louisiana bayou country, with the added attraction of a cool blue grotto that almost outdoes the Blue Grotto of Capri. Laguna Grí-Grí is only about 90 minutes west of Puerto Plata, in Río San Juan (ask for directions off the Autopista).

Nature lovers should consider a trip to **Jarabacoa,** in the mountainous region known rather wistfully as the Dominican Alps. There is little to do in the town itself but eat and rest up for excursions on foot, horseback, or by motorbike taxi to the surrounding waterfalls and forests—quite incongruous in such a tropical country. Accommodations in the area are rustic but comfortable. Recommended are **Alpes Dominicanos** (☎ 809/581–1462), which offers both hotel rooms with kitchenettes and individual self-service cottages, and the hacienda-style motel **Pinar Dorado** (☎ 809/574–2820).

Less accessible and vastly different is the largest lake in the Antilles, **Lago Enriquillo,** near the Haitian border. The salt lake is also the lowest point in the Antilles: 114 feet below sea level. It encircles wild, arid, and thorny islands that serve as sanctuary to such exotic birds and reptiles as the flamingo, the iguana, and the caiman—the indigenous crocodile.

Equally wild and pristine is **Barahona,** just to the south and the latest area to be developed. Here mountains carpeted with emerald rain forests and laced with silvery streams slope down into sugary white stretches of sand. The best places to stay are the intimate country inn, **Casa Bonita** (☎ 809/685–5184), and the deluxe **Bohoruco Beach Resort** (☎ 809/685–5184).

Just off the east coast of Hispaniola lies **Isla Saona,** now a national park inhabited by sea turtles, pigeons, and other wildlife. Caves on the island were once used by Indians. The beaches are beautiful, and legend has it that Columbus once strayed ashore here.

Beaches

The Dominican Republic has more than 1,000 miles of beaches, including the Caribbean's longest strip of white sand—Punta Cana. Many beaches are accessible to the public and may tempt you to stop for a swim. Be careful: Some have dangerously strong currents.

Boca Chica is the beach closest to Santo Domingo (2 miles east of Las Américas Airport, 21 miles from the capital), and it's crowded with city folks on weekends. This beach was once a virtual four-lane highway of fine white sand. "Progress" has since cluttered it with plastic beach tables, chaise longues, pizza stands, and beach cottages for rent. But the sand is still fine, and you can walk far out into clear blue water, which is protected by natural coral reefs that help keep the big fish at bay.

About 20 minutes east of Boca Chica is another beach of fine white sand, **Juan Dolio.** The Metro Hotel and Marina, the all-inclusive Decameron, Villas del Mar Hotel, and Punta Garza Beach Club are on this beach.

Moving counterclockwise around the island, you'll come to the La Romana area, with its miniature **Minitas** beach and lagoon, and the long, white-sand, palm-lined crescent of **Bayahibe** beach, which is accessible only by boat. La Romana is the home of the 7,000-acre Casa de Campo resort (*see* Lodging, *below*), so you're not likely to find any private place in the sun here.

The gem of the Caribbean, **Punta Cana** is a 20-mile strand of pearl-white sand shaded by trees and coconut palms. Located on the easternmost coast, it is the home of several top resorts.

Las Terrenas, on the north coast of the Samaná peninsula, looks like something from *Robinson Crusoe*: Tall palms list toward the sea, away from the mountains; the beach is narrow but sandy; and best of all, there is nothing man-made in sight—just vivid blues, greens, and yellows. Two adjacent hotels are right on the beach at nearby Punta Bonita.

Playa Grande, on the north coast, is a long stretch of powdery sand that is slated for development. The new Playa Grande Hotel has already disturbed the solitude. With this exception, the entire northeast coast seems like one unbroken golden stretch, unmaintained and littered with kelp, driftwood, and the occasional beer bottle. If you don't mind the lack of facilities and upkeep, you have your pick of deserted beaches.

The ideal wind and surf conditions of **Cabarete Beach,** also on the north coast, have made it an integral part of the international wind surfing circuit.

Farther west is the lovely beach at **Sosúa,** where calm waters gently lap at long stretches of soft white sand. Unfortunately the backdrop here is a string of tents, with hawkers pushing cheap souvenirs. You can, however, get snacks and rent water-sports equipment from the vendors.

On the north Amber Coast, still-developing **Puerto Plata** is about to outdo San Juan's famed Condado strip. The beaches are of soft beige or white sand, with lots of reefs for snorkeling. The Atlantic waters are great for windsurfing, waterskiing, and fishing expeditions.

About an hour west of Puerto Plata lies **Luperón Beach,** a wide white-sand beach fit for snorkeling, windsurfing, and scuba diving. The Luperón Beach Resort is handy for rentals and refreshments.

Sports and the Outdoors

Although there is hardly a shortage of outdoor activities here, the resorts have virtually cornered the market on sports, including every conceivable water sport. In some cases, facilities may be available only to guests. You can check with the tourist office for more details. Listed below is a mere smattering of the island's athletic options:

Bicycling
Pedaling is easy on pancake-flat beaches, but there are also steep hills in the Dominican Republic. Bikes are available at **Villas Doradas** (Playa Dorada, Puerto Plata, ☎ 809/586–3000), **Dorado Naco** (Dorado Beach, ☎ 809/586–2019), **Jack Tar Village** (Puerto Plata, ☎ 809/586–3800), and the **Hotel Cofresi** (Puerto Plata, ☎ 809/586–2898).

Boating
Hobie Cats and pedal boats are available at **Heavens** (Playa Dorada, ☎ 809/586–5250). Check also at **Casa de Campo** (La Romana, ☎ 809/523–3333) and **Club Med** (Punta Cana, ☎ 809/567–5228).

Deep-Sea Fishing
Marlin and wahoo are among the fish that folks angle for here. Arrangements can be made through **Casa de Campo** (La Romana, ☎ 809/682–2111Tel in Lodging is 523-3333) or **Actividas Acuaticás** (Playa Dorada, ☎ 809/506–3988). Fishing is best between January and June.

Golf
Casa de Campo has two 18-hole Pete Dye courses that are open to the public and a third for the private use of villa owners. The **Bávaro Beach** resort complex shares an 18-hole course. The **Playa Dorada** hotels have their own 18-hole Robert Trent Jones–designed course; there is also a 9-hole course nearby at the **Costambar** complex. Guests in Santo Domingo hotels are usually allowed to use the 18-hole course at the **Santo Domingo Country Club** on weekdays—*after* members have teed off. There is a 9-hole course outside of town, at Lomas Lindas. A new Pete Dye course is under construction outside Santo Domingo.

Horseback Riding
Casa de Campo (La Romana) has a dude ranch on its premises, saddled with 2,000 horses. You can even arrange for polo lessons (it's a major stop on the international circuit). In Puerto Plata, **Gran Chapparal** (☎ 809/320–4250) offers beach rides.

Sailing

Sailboats are available at **Club Med** (Punta Cana) and **Casa de Campo** (La Romana).

Scuba Diving

Ancient sunken galleons, undersea gardens, and offshore reefs are the lures here. For equipment and trips, contact **Mundo Submarino** (Santo Domingo, ☎ 809/566–0344).

Tennis

There must be a million nets laced around the island, and most of them can be found at the large resorts (*see* Lodging, *below*).

Windsurfing

Between June and October, **Cabarete Beach** offers what many consider to be optimal windsurfing conditions: wind speeds at 20–25 knots and 3- to 15-foot waves. The Professional Boardsurfers Association has included Cabarete Beach in its international windsurfing slalom competition. The novice is also welcome to learn and train on modified boards stabilized by flotation devices. **CaribBIC on Windsurfing Center,** on Caberete Beach (☎ 800/635–1155 or 800/243–9675), offers accommodations, equipment, training, and professional coaching.

Spectator Sports

BASEBALL

Baseball is the national pastime and passion. Major leaguers hone their skills in the Professional Winter League, which plays from late October through January. Call **Liga de Béisbol** (☎ 809/567–6371) for details on the five teams and their schedule of play. You can also consult newspaper listings, or your hotel can reserve tickets. You may not reach an English-speaking representative at Liga de Béisbol.

GREYHOUND RACES

The dogs make tracks every Monday, Wednesday, Friday, and Sunday at **Canódromo El Coco.** *Av. Monumental, La Yuca—about 15 min north of the capital,* ☎ *809/560–6968 or 560–8342.* ☛ *R.D.$1– R.D.$4. Races Mon., Wed., Fri. 7:30 PM, Sun. and holidays 4 PM.*

HORSE RACING

There are races year-round at the **Hipódromo Perla Antillana.** *Av. San Cristóbal, Santo Domingo,* ☎ *809/565–2353.* ☛ *Free. Post time: Tues., Thurs., Sat. 3 PM.*

POLO

The ponies pound down the field at **Sierra Prieta** (Santo Domingo) and at **Casa de Campo** (La Romana). The season runs from October through May. For information about polo games, call 809/565–6880.

Shopping

The hot ticket in the Dominican Republic is amber jewelry. This island has the world's largest deposits of amber, and the prices here for the translucent, semiprecious stones, which range in color from pale lemon to dark brown, are unmatched. The most valuable stones are those in which tiny insects or small leaves are embedded. (Don't knock it till you've seen it.)

The Dominican Republic is the homeland of designer Oscar de la Renta, and you may want to stop at some of the chic shops that carry his creations. In the crafts department, hand-carved wood rocking chairs are big sellers, and they are sold unassembled and boxed for easy transport. La Vega is famous for its *diablos cojuelos* (devil masks) and

Santiago for its cigars, which rival the best Havanas (*see* Exploring, *above*). Look also for the delicate ceramic lime figurines that symbolize the Dominican culture.

Bargaining is both a game and a social activity in the Dominican Republic, especially with street vendors and at the stalls in El Mercado Modelo. Vendors are disappointed and perplexed if you don't haggle. They also tend to be tenacious, so unless you really have an eye on buying, don't even stop to look—you may get stuck buying a souvenir just to get rid of an annoying vendor.

Shopping Districts

El Mercado Modelo in Santo Domingo is a covered market in the Colonial Zone bordering Calle Mella. The restored buildings of **La Atarazana** (across from the Alcázar in the Colonial Zone) are filled with shops, art galleries, restaurants, and bars. The main shopping streets in the Colonial Zone are **Calle El Conde,** which has been transformed into an exclusively pedestrian thoroughfare, and **Calle Duarte.** (Some of the best shops on Calle Duarte are north of the Colonial Zone, between Calle Mella and Avenida de Las Américas.) **Plaza Criolla** (corner of Av. 27 de Febrero and Av. Anacaona) is filled with shops that sell everything from scents to nonsense. Duty-free shops selling liquors, cameras, and the like are at the **Centro de los Héroes** (Av. George Washington), the **Hotel El Embajador,** the **Santo Domingo Sheraton,** and at **Las Américas Airport.** The two major commercial malls in Santo Domingo are **Unicentro** (406 Av. Abraham Lincoln) and **Plaza Central** (Avs. Bolívar and 27 de Febrero). The latter includes such top boutiques as **Jenny Polanco, Nicole B,** and **Benetton,** which includes a coffeehouse on its second level with rotating exhibit by up-and-coming young artists.

In Puerto Plata, the seven showrooms of the **Tourist Bazaar** (Calle Duarte 61) are in a wonderful old galleried mansion with a patio bar. Another cluster of shops is at the **Plaza Shopping Center** (Calle Duarte at Av. 30 de Marzo). A popular shopping street for jewelry and local souvenirs is **Calle Beller.**

In **Altos de Chavón,** art galleries and shops are grouped around the main square.

Good Buys

AMBER

Ambar Tres (La Atarazana 3, Colonial Zone, Santo Domingo, ☎ 809/688–0474) carries a wide selection of the Dominican product.

DOMINICAN ART

In Santo Domingo, the **Arawak Gallery** (Av. Pasteur 104, ☎ 809/685–1661) specializes in pre-Columbian artifacts and contemporary pottery and paintings. **Galería de Arte Nader** (La Atarazana 9, Colonial Zone, ☎ 809/688–0969) showcases top Dominican artists in a variey of medias. **Novo Atarazana** (Atarazana 21, ☎ 809/689–0582) has an assortment of local artwork.

Visit the stalls of **El Mercado Modelo** in the Colonial Zone for a dizzying selection of Dominican crafts. **El Conde Gift Shop** (Calle El Conde 153, Santo Domingo, ☎ 809/682–5909) is the spot for exquisite mahogany carvings.

In Puerta Plata, **Macaluso's** (Calle Duarte 32, and in Plaza Turisol, ☎ 809/586–3433) specializes in Dominican and Haitian paintings and wood carvings. The **Collector's Corner Gallery and Gift Shop** (Plaza Shopping Center, Calle Duarte at Av. 30 de Marzo, no ☎) offers a wide range of souvenirs, including amber.

In Santiago, try **Artesanía Lime** (Autopista Duarte, Km 2½, Santiago, ☎ 809/582–3754) for mahogany carvings as well as Carnival masks.

Check out the Dominican fashions at **Jenny Polanco's** boutiques in the Santo Domingo Sheraton (☎ 809/686–6666, ext. 2270), Plaza Central (☎ 809/541–5929), and the Paradise Beach Resort in Playa Dorada (☎ 809/586–3663, ext. 314).

Dining

Most restaurants begin serving dinner around 6 PM, but the locals don't generally turn up until 9 or 10. There are Spanish, French, Italian, and Chinese restaurants, as well as those serving traditional Dominican fare. (Regrettably, many local restaurants in heavily touristed areas like the Amber Coast are closing, victims of the all-inclusive craze.) Hotel restaurants are uniformly good; consult lodging listings for additional recommendations. Some favorite local dishes you should sample are paella, *sancocho* (a thick stew usually made with five different meats, though sometimes as many as seven), *arroz con pollo* (rice with chicken), *plátanos* (plantains) in all their tasty varieties, and *tortilla de jamón* (spicy ham omelet). Country snacks include *chicharrones* (fried pork rinds or chicken pieces) and *galletas* (flat biscuit crackers). Many a meal is topped off with *majarete,* a tasty cornmeal custard. Presidente, Bohemia, and Quisqueya are the local beers, Barceló, Bermúdez, and Brugal the local rums. Wine is on the expensive side because it has to be imported.

What to Wear

In resort areas, shorts and beach wraps are acceptable at lunch; for dinner, especially at gourmet restaurants, long pants, skirts, and collared shirts are the norm. Dress tends to be more formal in Santo Domingo, both at lunch and dinner, with long pants and dresses suggested. Ties are not required anywhere.

CATEGORY	COST*
$$$	over $30
$$	$20–$30
$	under $20

per person, excluding drinks, 10% service charge, and 8% sales tax

Boca Chica

$–$$ **Neptuno's Club.** This breezy seaside eatery is little more than a shack perched above the water, seemingly held together by the barnacles of marine memorabilia. While you can order good local preparations of chicken and pork, it goes without saying that seafood reigns supreme. Try the Neptuno's fish casserole in coconut water or kingfish in béchamel sauce. ✕ *Boca Chica Beach,* ☎ *809/523–4703. MC, V. Closed Mon.*

La Romana

$$$ **Casa del Rio.** Look out over the virtual jungle of the banks of the Rio
★   Chavón while you dine in an the ultraromantic, candlelit stone cellar of a 16th-century-style castle. The elegant decor is a mere backdrop for the imaginative creations put forth by chef Philippe Mongereau. His new Caribbean cuisine is a combination of classic French methods of preparation and savory indigenous ingredients and culinary traditions. The seasonally changing menu may include such standouts as leg of lamb baked in Creole marmalade, lobster tail glazed with vanilla vinaigrette, and mango Napoleon on a bed of julienne shrimp and artichoke hearts. Mongereau is experimenting with Asian ingredients like lemongrass, coriander, and garam masala, and the subtle counterpoint

of textures and flavors is truly heavenly. The restaurant's success is measured not only by the heavy repeat clientele but by the capitaleños who swear it's worth the two-hour drive from Santo Domingo. ✕ *Altos de Chavón,* ☎ *809/523–3333, ext. 2345. Reservations required. Jacket required. AE, DC, MC, V. No lunch.*

The Amber Coast

$$–$$$ **De Armando.** You may feel that you're dining in a proper old relative's dining room in this charmingly old-fashioned eatery. In a pretty aqua-and-white house, the dining room has high-backed embroidered chairs, crisp white napery, and dark-wood tables. Steak, seafood, and Continental dishes are all served to the tune of a guitar trio. Try the snapper in green peppercorn sauce or sea bass in champagne mushroom velouté. ✕ *Av. Mota 23, at Av. Separación,* ☎ *809/586–3418. Reservations required. MC, V.*

$$ **Another World.** It defines hokey and kitschy. The brochures exhort you to "spend an unforgettable evening with Stuart and his charming mother Jeanette, from Miami, Florida, in their 120-year-old restored Victorian 'haunted' farmhouse." (Stuart is a former singer-actor known to belt his rendition of "My Way." Jeanette calls the ghosts their "friendly boarders.") And then there's the minizoo, including a 350-pound Bengal tiger, a honey bear, and a capuchin monkey appropriately named Hanky Panky. The food selection is straight from Noah's Ark as well: Frogs' leg tempura, river prawns, escargots, rabbit, and quail are just a few choices from the enormous —and surprisingly well-prepared—menu. Free pickup and return to Puerto Plata hotels, as well as complimentary hors d'oeuvres and cordials, make this a pitch difficult to resist. ✕ *Puerto Plata,* ☎ *809/543–8116. Reservations advised. MC, V. No lunch.*

$ $$ **Caribae.** Aquariums teeming with all kinds of sea creatures decorate the dining room of this warm, unassuming spot. You can choose your own lobster, shrimp, and oysters for the barbecue. Costs are low, because the restaurant raises its own shrimp at a farm and grows its own 100% organic vegetables. ✕ *Camino Libre 70, Sosúa,* ☎ *809/571–3138. MC, V.*

$ **Guajiro's Caribbean Cafe.** Visit this casual Sosúa eatery for some of the best inventive local cuisine in the area. Try the green plantain soup or *yuca* (an island tuber) in *mojo* (a lime, garlic, and olive oil marinade) to start, then *pollo à la merengue* (sweet and spicy coriander chicken) or *filetillo saltado* (catch of the day, usually kingfish, in *sofrito,* a savory sauce of garlic and green pepper rouged with tomato). For a filling meal, order the cubano sandwich, bursting with roast pork, ham, cheese, and pickles. Thatching, nautical paraphernalia dangling from the rafters, rough-hewn wood tables and chairs, and traditional hats, shirts, and machetes hanging on the walls give the place a rustic country feel. Latin Jazz nights are scheduled regularly and draw a rollicking crowd. ✕ *Calle Pedro Clisande, El Batey, Sosúa,* ☎ *809/571–2161. No reservations. AE, MC, V.*

$ **Roma II.** Surprisingly delicious pizzas, cooked in a wood-burning oven, come from this unassuming wood shack. The pizza dough and pasta are made fresh daily. Other specialties include *spaghetti con pulpo* (octopus), *filete chito* (steak with garlic), and there's a host of other pastas and sauces. ✕ *Corner Calle E. Prudhomme and Calle Beller,* ☎ *809/586–3904. No reservations. No credit cards.*

Samaná

$$ **Café de France.** Local aficionados swear the beef here (try the fillet in mushroom or peppercorn sauce) is among the best in the Dominican Republic. Seafood here is also dependable: One standout is shrimp (or grouper) in garlic-coconut sauce. The small bistro is on the waterfront and is simply decorated, with white stucco walls and red tablecloths. An even more casual annex serves knockout pizzas. ✕ *Malecon, Samaná, no ☎. Reservations advised (stop by the restaurant). MC, V.*

Santo Domingo

$$$ **Vesuvio.** Capital-city denizens flock to this superb Italian restaurant, where
★   everything on the lengthy menu is either freshly caught, homemade, or homegrown. On most islands it's a struggle to get (and keep) things fresh, and the crisp vegetables here are nothing short of miraculous. Vesuvio has spent 40 years as the best in its business, yet refuses to rest on its laurels. Part of the restaurant's appeal is the lively ambience created by Dominican families relishing their meal. The chef doesn't shy away from combining strong, bold flavors. Start with antipasti—kingfish carpaccio dancing in zesty capers, onions, and basil-infused olive oil or *calamares al vino blanco* (squid in white-wine sauce)—then segue into *scaloppina al tarragon* (veal with tarragon), or, if they have it, succulent river crayfish grilled simply with butter and garlic. The pièce de résistance is the dessert cart—maybe it can also come by to roll you out! (**Vesuvio II** is at Av. Tiradentes 17, ☎ 809/562–6090.) ✕ *Av. George Washington 521,* ☎ *809/689–2141. No reservations. Jacket required. DC, MC, V.*

$$–$$$ **El Caserio.** An extensive menu lists such specialties as paella valenciana (rice casserole with chicken, seafood, and sausage), seafood zarzuela (a mix of fish and shellfish in a green herbal sauce), bluefish with anchovies, and leg of lamb Segovia. For dessert, forget your diet and order chocolate cake Caserio. Adjacent to the formal dining room and reminiscent of a whitewashed Andalusian cottage is **Aranjuez,** a bistrolike place that serves an appetite-whetting range of *tapas* (appetizers). ✕ *Av. George Washington 459,* ☎ *809/685–3392. Reservations required. Jacket required. AE, DC, MC, V.*

$$–$$$ **La Briciola.** The owners of this upscale Milan restaurant chain combined three venerable eateries housed in adjoining 16th-century colonial buildings to create this stunner. They did an exemplary job of modernizing the interiors while preserving their architectural integrity. The arch-ceilinged stone-and-brick main dining room and more casual piano bar/pizzeria overlook an interior courtyard whose trees are romantically illuminated at night. Cerise upholstery, mahogany furnishings, wooden chandeliers, and Italian tile work create a warm atmosphere. Excellent fresh pastas include velvety *gnocchi fume* (with Scamorze cheese, ham, and cream), tortellini al salmone, and *maccheroni capriccio* (in a tomato sauce enlivened by capers, pine nuts, and parsley). The risotto dell'oza, with salmon caviar and vodka, is superb. Meat dishes take a backseat to the deftly prepared seafood, such as grouper al limone, tuna in balsamic vinegar, and salmon in three sauces (mayonnaise, tartar, and mint). Delicious tiramisù and zabaglione complete the feast (but save room for the gratis cherry marzipan and lemon or chocolate cookies offered with the bill). The all-Italian wine list is extensive and fairly priced. ✕ *Calle Arzobispo Merino 152-A at Padre Bellini,* ☎ *809/688–5055. Reservations advised. Jacket required. AE, DC, MC, V. Closed Mon.*

$$–$$$ **Lina.** Lina was the personal chef of Trujillo, and she taught her secret
★   recipes to the chefs of this stylish contemporary restaurant, still a favorite of Santo Domingo movers and shakers. Brass columns, mirrored ceiling, planters, art naif, Villeroy & Boch china, and a pianist tickling the ivories set the elegant tone. The extensive menu favors Continental and haute Dominican dishes. Paella is the best-known specialty, but other offerings include filet mignon Roquefort, red snapper in co-

conut or almond cheese sauce, and a casserole of mixed seafood flavored with Pernod. ✕ *Gran Hotel Lina, Av. Máximo Gómez at Av.
27 de Febrero,* ☎ *809/686–5000. Reservations required. Jacket required.
AE, DC, MC, V.*

$$–$$$ Mesón de la Cava. The capital's most unusual restaurant is more than
50 feet below ground in a natural cave complete with stalagmites and
stalactites. You must descend a circular staircase, ducking rock pro-
trusions, to dine on Continental standards like prime fillet with Dijon
flambé, and tournedos Roquefort. Seafood preparations tend to be more
adventurous, such as red snapper poached in white wine and served
with coconut sauce, but the food takes a backseat to the spectacular
setting. There is live music and dancing nightly until 1 AM, although
sometimes you may wish they'd stop playing Jackson Five renditions
and allow a majestic silence to fall over the cathedralesque grotto. ✕
Av. Mirador del Sur, ☎ *809/533–2818. Reservations required. Jacket
required. AE, DC, MC, V.*

$$–$$$ Pappalapasta. Delicious Italian food and a location around the cor-
★ ner from the Presidential Palace combine to make this eatery popular
with politicians, diplomats, and the businessmen seeking favors from
them. A series of intimate dining rooms are handsomely decorated with
rattan and polished hardwood furnishings, abstract artworks, richly
colored Tiffany-style lamps, and cut-glass windows. Start with a classic selection of antipasto—carpaccio, eggplant Parmesan, and tuna with
capers. Pumpkin ravioli in almond-amaretto butter, gnocchi al pesto,
and spaghetti with lobster sauce are standouts in the pasta selection.
You may also opt for the sublime seabass *à la meunière* (breaded and
topped with butter, parsley, and lemon juice), snapper *chiaro di mare*
(with olives, capers, garlic, tomato, and peppers), or the unimpeach-
able fillet in cognac mushroom sauce. The service is surprisingly
leisurely; maybe they're waiting discreetly for your deal to be con-
summated. ✕ *Dr. Baez 23,* ☎ *809/682–4397. Reservations advised.
Jacket required. AE, MC, V. Closed Mon.*

$$ Café St. Michel. The decor is rather odd, sort of a contemporary in-
door take on a gazebo, but the menu of French-bistro–style dishes and
local fare keeps diners coming back. Cream of pumpkin soup and steak
tartare are specialties. Desserts include a prize-winning chocolate torte
and spectacular soufflés. ✕ *Av. Lope de Vega 24,* ☎ *809/562–4141
Reservations advised. Jacket required. AE, MC, V.*

$$ Fonda de la Atarazana. Dinner and dancing on the brick patio of a
17th-century building in the Colonial Zone make for a very romantic
evening. Try the kingfish, shrimp, or *chicharrones de pollo* (bits of fried
chicken). ✕ *La Atarazana 5,* ☎ *809/689–2900. Reservations advised
on weekends. AE, MC, V.*

$ El Conuco. Conuco means countryside—and it's hard to believe that
★ this open-air thatched hut, alive with hanging plants, hibiscus, and frangipani and decorated with basketry, sombreros, license plates, and graffiti, is smack in the center of Santo Domingo. This is a superb place
to sample typical Dominican cuisine, from *la bandera* (white rice, kid-
ney beans, and stewed beef duplicating the colors of the flag) to a magnificent, delicately flaky *bacalao de la comai* (cod in white cream sauce
with garlic and onions). The ambience is always celebratory; waiters
occasionally take to makeshift drum sets to accompany the merengue
tapes. ✕ *152 Casimiro de Moya,* ☎ *809/221–3231. MC, V.*

$ La Bahía. The catch of the day is always tops at this unpretentious spot.
Try the kingfish in coconut sauce. The conch, which appears in a variety of dishes, is also good. For starters, try the *sopa palúdica,* a thick
soup made with fish, shrimp, and lobster and served with tangy garlic bread. The decor strikes a nautical note, with fishing nets and

seashells. ✗ *Av. George Washington 1,* ☎ *809/682–4022. No reservations. AE, MC, V.*

$ **Ludovino's** and **Joaquin's.** Shacks and stands serving cheap eats for peo-
★ ple on the run are a Dominican tradition, as much a part of the culture and landscape as the Colonial Zone. Two such shacks have become legends in Santo Domingo; both are located in working-class districts outside the normal tourist loop. El Palacio de los Yaniqueques (everyone calls it Ludovino's after the nutty owner) is famed for its johnny-cakes—fried dough stuffed with everything from chicken to seafood. You pay the cashier when you order and get a free thimbleful of strong, sweet coffee while you wait for your food. Joaquin's serves up the best pork sandwich—laden with onions, tomatoes, pickles, and seasonings—in the Western world (yes, even Texas barbecue takes a backseat). The price for a filling meal? Two bucks at either. ✗ *Ludovino's: 19 Summer Wells, no* ☎. ⊘ *Daily 7* AM*–8* PM. *Joaquin's: Av. Abraham Lincoln and Max Henríquex Ureña St., no* ☎. ⊘ *Nightly 7* PM*–2* AM.

Lodging

Your options here vary from the New World's first hotel to some of the world's newest and poshest resorts. An ambitious development plan continues, especially on the north coast. The Dominican Republic has the largest hotel inventory (28,000 rooms and growing) in the Caribbean. Puerto Plata alone has 9,000 rooms and hosts 250,000 tourists a year. There are already so many adjoining resorts that when you go out for a stroll you have to flag landmarks to find your way back to the one where your luggage is. The fierce competition translates into some of the best hotel buys in the Caribbean. Be sure to inquire about special packages when you call to reserve; arranging your room as a package through a tour operator will cost considerably less. Be aware that many hotels, especially on the north coast, turn their water supply off at midnight as a conservation measure. Rooms are air-conditioned unless otherwise noted.

Hotels in Santo Domingo base their tariffs on the EP and maintain the same room rates through the year. In contrast, resorts have high winter and low summer rates, with the low rate reducing the room prices by as much as 50%. All-inclusive properties are concentrated along the north coast. More and more hotels are turning all-inclusive, but those that haven't offer EP or MAP. Our prices, in U.S. dollars, are based on a double room during the high season. For meal plans, add $20–$30 per person to the room-only rate listed below; for all-inclusive, add $40–$45 per person.

CATEGORY	COST*
$$$$	over $175
$$$	$125–$175
$$	$75–$125
$	under $75

All prices are for a standard double room for two, excluding 15% service charge and 8% tax.

Boca Chica/Juan Dolio

$$$ **Hamaca Beach Hotel.** This all-inclusive resort is a half hour east of Santo Domingo and just a few minutes from Las Américas Airport. The impressive reception area has terra-cotta floors, wicker furnishings, and water walls; its teal and yellow decor is picked up beautifully by huge floral arrangements. Guest rooms have full baths and cable TV and are furnished in painted rattan and dark woods. Floral linens coordinate with pale green tile floors. There's a lovely champagne-colored beach. The food at the restaurants, while good, is mostly standard Continental fare. ☎ *Boca Chica Beach,* ☎ *809/523–4455 or 800/828–8895,* FAX *809/523–4438. 209 rooms. 3 restaurants, 2 bars, grill, terrace, 2 tennis courts, scuba diving, archery, bicycling, horseback riding, snorkeling, sailing, windsurfing, excursions to Catalina Island, transportation to Santo Domingo casinos. AE, MC, V. All-inclusive.*

$$ **Capella Beach Hotel.** This new deluxe resort opened in 1994 on a section of Juan Dolio Beach it ostentatiously calls Villas Del Mar, and it's striving to become the top southern-coast destination, with the exception, of course, of Casa de Campo. It's built on a grand scale, with beautiful tile and mosaic work in the elegant public spaces and a hodgepodge of architectural styles from Victorian (white colonnaded porticoes) to Moorish (arches and red-tile roofs) to South Pacific (two of the restaurants sit in cathedralesque thatched huts). Rooms are large and handsomely appointed with ceramic lamps, pictures of local plants, and pink and mint green fabrics. Most have balconies and huge walk-in closets; some have ocean view. Unfortunately, service does not yet meet exacting international standards, food is not as good as it might be, and the property already requires upkeep (bathrooms seem rather cheaply done and elevators have stained carpets). Nonetheless, the vast array of amenities and facilities is bound to please travelers seeking something a cut above most Dominican resorts, especially at the surprisingly reasonable rates. ☎ *Villas Del Mar, Box 4750, Santo Domingo,* ☎ *809/526–1080 or 800/468–3571,* FAX *809/526–1088. 261 rooms, 21 suites. 3 restaurants, 3 bars, 2 pools, 2 (lighted) tennis courts, fitness center with sauna and massage, water-sports center (including dive shop and 46-ft yacht), game room, shopping arcade, nightly entertainment. AE, D, MC, V. EP, MAP.*

The Amber Coast

$$ $$$ **Bayside Hill Resort and Beach Club.** Part of the Costambar development—a 15-hotel complex including a nine-hole golf course, residential community, and supermarket—this hotel is an adroit blend of classic and contemporary elements: modern artworks and Corinthian columns, marble floors and metal sculptures. The centerpiece is a split-level pool and Jacuzzi with waterfalls and cavorting mermaid statuary. The Cafemba restaurant is highly respected for its innovative Continental cuisine. The rooms, decorated in olive, yellow, and peach, have tile floors, cable TV, and a small terrace or balcony. They are pleasant enough but disappointing compared to the public areas. The best rooms are those with stunning panoramic vistas of Puerto Plata. A free shuttle runs guests from the hillside development to the beach. Costambar is pleasantly quiet compared to Playa Dorada. ☎ *Costambar, Puerto Plata,* ☎ *809/586–5260 or 800/322–2388,* FAX *809/586–5545. 150 rooms. 2 restaurants, 3 bars, beach club and water-sports center, pool, golf, beauty parlor, gift shop, disco. AE, MC, V. All-inclusive.*

$$–$$$ **Sand Castle.** The name says it all. This resort is a fantasy of curves, balconies, and balustrades set high above coral cliffs. Royal palms rise majestically from the beachside gardens. Rooms are simple and comfortable in muted green and yellow pastels; some have a stained-glass window or decorative stained-glass above the bathroom door. All rooms have cable TV. Your stay here will be more enjoyable if you have a room with a view, especially of the small curving beach below. Though the hotel is by itself on a peninsula, lots of organized activities and the nearby village of Sosúakeep guests busy. Service is polite but distant. ☎ *Puerto Chiquito, Sosúa,* ☎ *809/571–2420 or 800/445–5963,* FAX *809/571–2000. 240 rooms. 3 restaurants, 5 bars, 2 pools, Jacuzzi, shopping ar-*

cade, disco, convention center, water-sports center including dive shops, horseback riding, bicycling. AE, MC, V. EP, MAP.

$$ Caribbean Village Club and Resort. Rooms in the newer Royale building have kitchenettes and cable TV and are simply decorated in peach tones. The older Tropicale is a series of small houses with connecting skywalks. Rooms here are more like miniapartments, perfect for families, all with terrace or balcony, kitchenette, small sitting area, marble floors, and light pastel decor. One free-form pool has a swim-up terrace. The beach is a 10-minute hike away, but there's free shuttle service. The hotel's La Tortuga restaurant, a snack bar, and water-sports facilities are right on the sand. Nightly entertainment and dancing take place in the patio lounge and lobby bar. The staff genuinely works hard to compensate for the off-beach location. *Playa Dorada,* ☎ *809/586– 5350,* FAX *809/320–5386. 310 rooms, 26 suites. 3 restaurants, 3 bars/lounges, grill, 2 pools, 2 lighted tennis courts, minimart, disco, child care, beach club and water-sports center, medical clinic, shopping arcade, golf. AE, MC, V. CP, MAP.*

$$ Dorado Naco and Playa Naco. These two sister hotels make up a sprawling complex. Dorado Naco is a cluster of villas containing spacious, carpeted one- and two-bedroom apartments. In the living and dining area are a sofa bed, cable TV, two phones, dining table that seats four, and a counter bar. Each apartment has a large patio or terrace surrounded by tropical flowers and plants. The larger, more expensive rooms have views of the pool and the restaurants that surround it (there are no ocean views here). Hacienda-style Playa Naco went all-inclusive in 1994. The main lobby and standard hotel rooms overlook the pool and tennis courts and are a five-minute walk from the sands. More expensive one- and two-bedroom units are in two-story buildings along the path to the beach. The pleasing decor includes tile floors and mauve, lavender, and olive tones. The bustling free-form pool has several waterfalls. ✉ *Box 162, Playa Dorada. Dorado Naco:* ☎ *809/586– 2019,* FAX *809/320–3608. Playa Naco:* ☎ *809/320–6226,* FAX *809/320–6225. U.S. reservations for both,* ☎ *800/322–2388. 496 units. 6 restaurants, 3 bars, coffee shop, 2 pools, shopping arcade, beauty salon, car rental, game room, minimarket, bicycle rental, horseback riding, 4 lighted tennis courts, golf, disco, pub, 3 Jacuzzis, beach club and water-sports center, convention center. AE, DC, MC, V. EP, MAP, FAP (Dorado Naco), All-inclusive (Playa Naco).*

$$ Flamenco Beach Resort, Villas Doradas, and **Playa Dorada Beach Re-
★ sort.** Guests can use the facilities at all three of these hotels that are lined up one after the other on the mile-long white-sand beach. They're all known for their lively nightlife and variety of social and sports programs, but the similarities end there. Rooms at the older, all-inclusive Playa Dorada are dowdy and sadly in need of refurbishment. Service is efficient but unenthusiastic. Villas Doradas, also all-inclusive, is a step up. Rooms are decorated in earth tones (a refreshing change of pace) and hung with abstract paintings, and all have cable TV, safe, and minibar. The Chinese restaurant here is surprisingly good. The newer Flamenco is the real jewel. The glorious public spaces include cobblestone and Andalusian brick floors, hand-painted tiles, stuccoed walls, and antique carved doors. There are four magnificent restaurants including Via Veneto, a lively trattoria, and gourmet Spanish El Cortijo. The main free-form pool (with swim-up bar) is designed to resemble a lake, complete with waterfall and lapping waves. Rooms and suites have tasteful hardwood furnishings, terra-cotta floors, bright floral upholstery, minibar, cable TV, and a balcony or terrace. Club Miguel Angel is a hotel within a hotel offering premium concierge service. The only thing missing at the Flamenco is an ocean view. ✉ *Flamenco: Playa*

Dorada, Puerto Plata, ☎ *809/320–5084,* ᶠᴬˣ *809/320–6319. 518 units. 4 restaurants, 3 bars, pizzeria, 2 pools, water-sports center, 2 lighted tennis courts, shopping arcade. Villas Doradas: Box 1370, Puerto Plata,* ☎ *809/320–3000,* ᶠᴬˣ *809/320–4790. 207 rooms. 5 restaurants, 2 bars, pool, water-sports center, car rental, 3 tennis courts, gift shop. Playa Dorada: Box 272, Puerto Plata,* ☎ *809/586–3988 or 800/423–6902,* ᶠᴬˣ *809/320–1190. 252 rooms, 1 suite. 4 restaurants, 2 bars, pool, disco, casino, ice-cream parlor, golf, tennis courts, horseback riding, bikes, jogging trail, water-sports center. AE, DC, MC, V. EP, MAP, FAP (Flamenco), All-inclusive (Playa and Villas Doradas).*

$$ **Paradise Beach Resort and Club.** Of the 12 hotels in the Playa Dorada
★ complex, this hotel stands out on two counts: It is one of the few that front the beach and it has a unique design. Its cluster of low-rise buildings with white-tile roofs and latticed balconies and windows follows winding paths through palms, birds-of-paradise, and hibiscus from the reception area down to the beach. Rooms are decorated in a carefully chosen palette of pastel greens and blues. Standard rooms have one double or two twin beds; some of the one-bedroom apartments have kitchens. In the center of the resort is a free-form pool, with a water channel that winds its way from the pool to the beach. Two of the resort's three restaurants (not the gourmet Italia) are open-air and on the beach. ⌧ *Box 337, Playa Dorada,* ☎ *809/586–3663 or 800/752–0836,* ᶠᴬˣ *809/320–4858. 216 rooms, 186 suites. 3 restaurants, 3 bars, boutiques, 2 lighted tennis courts, golf, horseback riding, water-sports center, bicycles, scooters. AE, DC, MC, V. All-inclusive.*

$$ **Playa Chiquita.** A broad breezeway leads from the registration desk, past the free-form pool with swim-up bar and shallow children's section, right to the delightful private cove. The rooms have a contemporary tropical decor, with pastel upholstery, rattan furnishings, and terra-cotta floors. All have cable TVs, double or king-size beds, and wet bars; most have a patio or balcony. The recently added casino has proved wildly popular with local and tourists alike. ⌧ *Sosúa,* ☎ *809/689–6191 or 800/922–4272,* ᶠᴬˣ *809/571–2460. 90 rooms. Restaurant, coffee shop, pool, gift shop, nightclub, casino, water sports. AE, MC, V. EP, MAP.*

$$ **Puerto Plata Beach Resort and Casino.** More of a village than a resort, Puerto Plata's 7 acres hold cobblestone pathways, colorful gardens, and suites in 23 porticoed two- and three-story buildings. Accommodations have terra-cotta floors and a primarily mint and jade decor, with cable TV, minifridge, and balcony or terrace. An activities center sets up water-sports clinics, arranges horseback rides, and so forth. The resort also caters to the little ones, with children's games and enclosures for them at the shallow end of the pool. Bogart's is the glitzy disco. Ylang-Ylang, named after the evening flower that blooms here, is a highly rated gourmet restaurant and catering service. The Neptune restaurant across the road on the beach is good for seafood. This resort is just outside of town and a ways from Playa Dorada, which will be an added attraction to some. ⌧ *Box 600, Av. Malecón, Puerto Plata,* ☎ *809/586–4243 or 800/223–9815,* ᶠᴬˣ *809/586–4377. 216 units. 4 restaurants, bar, pool, outdoor Jacuzzi, horseback riding, casino, gift shop, nightclub, 4 lighted tennis courts, water-sports center. AE, MC, V. MAP, All-Inclusive.*

$–$$ **Cabarete Beach Hotel.** This delightful small hotel is set right on a tantalizing curve of golden sand ideal for windsurfing and swimming (the surrounding reef protects it from fierce breakers). Deluxe rooms are those with full ocean view and air-conditioning. Standards (some with air-conditioning) are slightly smaller and noisier. All rooms are decorated with bright framed prints and blond woods and have charming touches such as rocking chairs. The lovely terrace restaurant is known for its bountiful breakfast buffets of luscious homemade breads, muffins, and pastries. The Tropical Bar—a riot of painted gourds and coconuts, colorful murals, and thatching—prides itself on its eight fresh fruit juices daily and more than 50 exotic libations. The BIC Windsurf Center (though not part of the hotel) is right next door. The staff is unfailingly helpful and courteous. ☎ *Cabarete,* ☎ *809/571–0755,* FAX *809/571–0831. 24 rooms. Restaurant, bar, gift shop. AE, MC, V. EP, MAP.*

$–$$ **Hotel Cofresi.** Rooms here are rather basic and somewhat cramped, but the staff is courteous and the setting is breathtaking. The resort is built on the reefs along the Atlantic, and the sea spritzes its waters into the peaceful man-made lagoon and pools along the beach. Most rooms have cable TV, hair dryer, safe, and kitchenette. There are jogging and exercise trails, paddleboats for the lagoon, scuba-diving clinics, and evening entertainment, including a disco. The restaurants specialize in flavorful Dominican fare. ☎ *Box 327, Costambar,* ☎ *809/586–2898,* FAX *809/586–8064. 145 rooms, 5 suites. 2 restaurants, 2 bars, disco, 3 pools (1 saltwater), bicycling, horseback riding, paddleboats, 2 lighted tennis courts, game room, water-sports center. AE, MC, V. All-inclusive.*

$ **Club Marina.** Eduardo de Lora, a master stained-glass craftsman, designed this charming beige stucco and red tile hotel. Everything displays his creative touch: The pool is landscaped with rocks, giving it a natural grotto feel, and spiral staircases are embedded with shards of glass (there are no exposed edges!). The rooms themselves are plain but impeccably neat, with a well-worn integrity. The blue-and-white tiles, lilac bedspreads, and closets painted jade green brighten them up. The restaurant serves wonderful home cooking, and its prices are sensational. All units have cable TV, private bath, and a small balcony. The beach is a five-minute walk away. The hotel is owned by the beachfront Casa Marina resort, and although you're paying only half as much as guests there, you get the use of all its facilities! ☎ *Alejo Martínez St., Sosúa,* ☎ *809/571–3939. 36 rooms. Restaurant, pool. AE, MC, V.*

$ **Hotel Montemar.** If you don't mind the lackadaisical upkeep—some rooms have soiled or burned carpets and broken tiles—the Montemar is a good choice for a cost-conscious holiday. It's on the Malecón, between Puerto Plata and Playa Dorada, a five-minute walk from the town's Long Beach. Prices are low, there's a daily schedule of activities, and transportation is provided to the beaches of Playa Dorada. All rooms have air-conditioning, cable TV, safe, direct-dial phone, and private bath. Small standard rooms lack an ocean view. A staff of hotel-school trainees gives the place an appealingly warm atmosphere. ☎ *Box 382, Puerto Plata,* ☎ *809/586–2800 or 800/332–4872,* FAX *809/586–2009. 95 rooms. Restaurant, bar, 2 tennis courts, beach club, pool, boutique, gift shop, beauty parlor. AE, MC, V. All-inclusive.*

La Romana

$$$$ **Casa de Campo.** "House in the country" is an interesting appellation
★   for this resort, which sprawls over 7,000 acres and accommodates some 3,000 guests. It includes 350 casitas, casita-suites, and one-, two-, and three-bedroom villas and offers two public golf courses (one of them, called Teeth of the Dog, has seven holes that skirt the sea), 16 tennis courts, horseback riding, polo, archery, trapshooting, and every imaginable water sport. Minibuses provide free transportation around the resort, but you can also rent electric carts, scooters, and bicycles. Oscar de la Renta designed much of the resort, owns a villa, and has

a boutique in Altos de Chavón, the re-created medieval village and art colony on the property (*see* Exploring the Dominican Republic, *above*). Some rooms and villas are decorated in Laura Ashley style, others with bolder, more abstract touches. The resort is—in a word—awesome. The advantage of staying here is that American Eagle flies in twice a day from San Juan to the La Romana airstrip. The disadvantage is that there are few attractions in the vicinity of the hotel other than the hotel's own campus—not that most guests mind. ⌖ *Box 140, La Romana,* ☎ *809/523–3333 or 800/223–6620,* FAX *809/523–8548. 740 rooms. 9 restaurants, 8 bars, 13 pools, 16 tennis courts (6 lighted), fitness center, Jacuzzi, sauna, polo fields, horseback riding, shooting and archery ranges, 2 18-hole golf courses, boutiques, marina, airstrip. AE, DC, MC, V. EP, MAP.*

Punta Cana

$$$ Bavaro Beach Resort. This four-star luxury resort, actually part of a complex of five low-rise hotels, is situated on the glorious 20-mile stretch of Punta Cana beach. Each room has a private balcony or terrace, cable TV, and refrigerator. The biggest rooms are at the Bavaro Beach Hotel, with hemp and wood furnishings and bright striped upholstery. The Bavaro Gardens is decorated in vivid primary colors. The Bavaro Casino Hotel has several duplex suites ideal for families. All of the accommodations at the Bavaro Golf Hotel are suites with kitchenettes— a real money saver if you're willing to cook. The Bavaro Palace is the most refined and subdued, with such touches as marble vanities. A social director coordinates a wide variety of daily activities, but it is a very impersonal resort. ⌖ *Higüey,* ☎ *809/682–2162 or 800/336–6612,* FAX *809/682–2169. 1,001 rooms. 8 restaurants, 12 bars, 2 grills, 5 pools, 3 discos, casino, nightclub, shopping arcade, beauty salon, medical center, golf, archery, bicycles, horseback riding, 6 lighted tennis courts, watersports center. AE, MC, V. MAP, FAP.*

$$–$$$ Punta Cana Beach Resort. Several pretty coral-and-aquamarine buildings dot the lush grounds of this rambling resort. Expansion is planned for the 1996–97 season, including the addition of a golf course and a 350-room hotel. The handsome lobby sets a civilized tone with Dominican crafts, birdcages, and lots of plants. Rooms are spare but pleasant, primarily in jade, coral, and cream, with wicker furnishings. The half-mile private beach is gorgeous, and there are nature walks into the mahogany forest, where you can take a dip in a natural freshwater pool. There are lots of activities here, too, including nightly musical entertainment by the staff. ⌖ *Punta Cana Beach,* ☎ *809/686–0084,* FAX *809/689–8745. Write to Box 1083, Santo Domingo. 341 units. 5 restaurants, 2 bars, disco, boutique, gift shop, beauty parlor, minimart, medical clinic, pool, water-sports center, 4 lighted tennis courts, playground, day care and children's minicamp. AE, DC, MC, V. EP, MAP.*

Samaná

$$ Cayo Levantado. This tranquil hotel is tucked into the lush greenery of the tiny island national park just off the Samaná coast. The exquisite fringe of pearly white beach is overrun weekends with day-trippers, but the makeshift stalls hawking T-shirts, paintings, beer, and delicious grilled items do create a party atmosphere. There's another, smaller beach on the other side of the island for the romantically inclined. The rooms, either in the main building or bungalows, are simple and appealing, with writing desks, wicker furnishings, and bright pastel fabrics. There are no TVs or phones. The food is good, solid Creole: a fortunate thing, since the hotel now operates as an all-inclusive. ⌖ *Cayo Levantado,* ☎ *809/538–3131. 44 rooms. Restaurant, bar, pool, boutique, water sports. AE, MC, V. FAP.*

$$ Hotel Gran Bahía. Overdevelopment has not yet reached the pretty
★ water's edge where this small, elegant all-inclusive resort sits. The modern colonial Victorian has graceful verandas and balconies looking out
over the pool and the sea beyond; you can see schools of whales frolicking offshore during the winter. The superb views make breakfast on
your room's private terrace or balcony a treat. Guest rooms are large,
with cheerful floral prints, tiled floors, and pastel watercolor paintings.
The grand yet welcoming reception area and three-story white colonnaded atrium surround a spectacular fountain flanked with numerous
cozy nooks for cocktails or reading. Dining alfresco is pleasant, though
you would be wise to stay with the fresh seafood rather than try the
meat dishes. The delightfully European ambience here appeals to a select, chic crowd. ☎ *Box 2024, Santo Domingo,* ☎ *809/538–3111 or
800/372–1323,* FAX *809/538–2764. 98 rooms. 2 restaurants, bar, pool,
2 tennis courts, gym, archery, 9-hole golf course, beauty salon, boutique,
whale-watching arranged. AE, MC, V. All-inclusive.*

Santo Domingo

$$$–$$$$ Jaragua Renaissance Resort and Casino. Fourteen acres of gardens, wa-
★ terfalls, and fountains surround this ultramodern complex. Top-name
entertainers are booked into the 800-seat nightclub, master chefs from
four countries tend to the cuisine, and a staff doctor supervises the diet
program in the spa. The resort was featured on *Lifestyles of the Rich
and Famous* and is still the class act in town, although some rooms are
a bit frayed at the edges. Spacious rooms have three phones, 21-channel satellite TV, minibar, and hair dryer. Each floor has a different
decor, one in peach and burgundy, another apricot and mint. Rates are
based on view (garden, pool, or ocean). Twelve cabanas surround the
Olympic-size free-form pool, and the casino covers 20,000 square feet.
☎ *Av. George Washington 367, Santo Domingo,* ☎ *809/221–2222 or
800/331–3542,* FAX *809/686–0528. 337 rooms, 18 suites. 6 restaurants, 5 bars, casino, pool, 4 tennis courts (1 lighted), golf (at the Santo
Domingo Country Club), and European spa with exercise/diet programs,
saunas, Jacuzzis, whirlpool. AE, MC, V. EP, MAP, FAP.*

$$$ Inter-Continental Hotel V Centenario. Santo Domingo's newest five-star
hotel opened in late 1992 on the Malecón. Marble floors and pillars
give the reception area a crisp, fresh feel. The rooms are a refreshing
change, furnished in attractive earth tones, Dominican handicrafts, and
burnished rattans. Each has a minifridge, cable TV, and an electronic
safe. You can try your luck at the casino or take time out to relax in
the lounge-bar area with its subdued lighting and enticing easy chairs.
The cellar tapas bar has become a favorite after-work hangout for locals. A casual coffee shop looks out over the Caribbean, and the pool
shares a terrace with a bar and an alfresco seafood restaurant. ☎ *Av.
George Washington 218, Santo Domingo,* ☎ *809/221–0000,* FAX
*809/221–2020. 167 rooms, 33 suites. 3 restaurants, 2 bars, pool,
shops, casino, 1 tennis and 2 squash courts, sauna, gym, parking. AE,
MC, V. EP, MAP, FAP.*

$$$ Santo Domingo Sheraton Hotel and Casino. This 11-story modern
hotel is on Avenida George Washington in the center of the Malecón
action. Rooms are average in size and decorated in taupe and teal; many
have French balconies (more like a ledge) overlooking the sea, and all
have minibar and cable TV. The two restaurants are superior in all respects: Antoine's for gourmet Continental fare in a romantic setting,
and the cozy La Casa for expertly prepared local specialties. This Sheraton's service is disorganized, but the staff tries to be helpful. ☎ *Box
1493, Santo Domingo,* ☎ *809/686–6666 or 800/325–3535,* FAX
809/687–8150. 260 rooms. 2 restaurants, coffee shop, bar, casino, pool,

disco, 2 lighted tennis courts, beauty salon, shops, health club. AE, DC, MC, V. EP, MAP, FAP.

$–$$$ **Hotel Santo Domingo.** This complex actually consists of two different
★ hotels: **Hotel Hispaniola** and **Hotel Santo Domingo.** Catering to a
younger crowd, the Hispaniola has 165 rooms, with an active pool, a
modern disco favored by capitaleños, and a casino filled with striking
paintings, stained glass, and towering floral arrangements. There are
two restaurants here, Las Cañas and La Pizetta, as well as the Hispaniola
Bar, which has a small dance area. The bar is very dark, very intimate,
and very, very red. Guest rooms are spacious, furnished mostly in
chintz, wicker, and blond woods, but they're a tad worn. In dramatic
juxtaposition is the Hotel Santo Domingo. This is the epitome of an
haute hotel. Oscar de la Renta designed the interiors: with the black-
and red-lacquered hall lamps, conch-shell mirrors, bold colors, and hand-
crafted Dominican furniture. The rooms have balconies and cable
TVs, and most have double beds. Located on 14 delicately manicured
acres overlooking the Caribbean, the hotel caters to the executive. Many
VIPs check into the Premier Club for extra perks. The elegant Alcázar
restaurant serves excellent Continental meals in de la Renta's roman-
tic Moorish dining room. The regular merengue combo at dimly lit Las
Palmas makes it a local favorite for music and dancing. The hotels are
at the western edge of the Malecón—often more convenient for busi-
nesspeople who want to be close to the new commercial section of town
than for tourists who prefer being closer to the historic area. ☎ *Av.
Independencia and Abraham Lincoln. Box 2112, Santo Domingo,* ☎
809/535–1511 or 800/223–6620, ℻ *809/535–4050. 220 rooms. 3
restaurants, 2 bars, pool, sundeck, sauna, 3 lighted tennis courts, con-
ference rooms, helipad. AE, MC, V. EP, MAP, FAP.*

$$ **Gran Hotel Lina and Casino.** The whitewashed modern cinder-block
structure of this hotel gives little hint of its stylish, exquisite interior,
which gleams with marble floors, mirrored brass colonnades, and
striking modern artworks. The rather plain rooms, mostly in dusky rose,
are air-conditioned with double beds, minifridges, huge marble baths,
and cable TVs and exude a staid secure ambience. The staff is friendly
and helpful. ☎ *Box 1915, Santo Domingo,* ☎ *809/686–5000 or
800/942–2461,* ℻ *809/686–5521. 205 rooms, 15 suites. Restaurant,
piano bar, casino, nightclub, coffee shop, health club, 2 tennis courts,
pool. AE, DC, MC, V. EP, MAP, FAP.*

$$ **Hotel El Embajador and Casino.** This hotel radiates an air of faded gen-
tility; it seems caught in a '50s time warp—Hollywood's idea of a top
hotel in an exotic locale. But though the exterior needs sprucing up,
the public rooms are imposing by Dominican standards. The bed-
rooms are spacious but spare, with tatty carpeting, old-fashioned desks
and wardrobes, and bare walls. All have minibar, cable TV, and pri-
vate balcony with either a mountain or an ocean view (choose the lat-
ter). An executive concierge floor is good for business travelers. The
Jardin de Jade serves marvelous Chinese food. The pool is open to the
public and is a popular weekend gathering place for resident foreign-
ers. You can try your luck at the casino, or just listen to the live bands
that play there throughout the day and night. ☎ *Av. Sarasota 65, Santo
Domingo,* ☎ *809/221–2131 or 800/457–0067,* ℻ *809/532–4494.
304 rooms, 12 suites. 2 restaurants, 2 bars, casino, pool, free trans-
port to beach, 4 tennis courts (1 lighted), nightclub, shopping arcade.
AE, DC, MC, V. EP, MAP.*

$ **Hostal Palacio Nicolás de Ovando.** The oldest hotel in the New World,
★ and one of the few in the Colonial Zone, was home to the first gov-
ernor in the early 1500s. The decor is Spanish, with carved mahogany
doors, beamed ceilings, tapestries, arched colonnades, and three court-

yards with splashing fountains. The spartan rooms are reminiscent of monks' cells but have views of the port, the pool, or the Colonial Zone. Dominican specialties are served in the restaurant. This is Santo Domingo's only hotel with the charm of antiquity. Its disadvantage is its location: At night, the area can be deserted and unpleasant for walking alone. ☎ *Calle Las Damas 44, Apdo. 89-2, Santo Domingo,* ☎ *809/687–3101,* ℻ *809/686–5170. 55 rooms. Restaurant, bar, pool. AE, MC, V. EP.*

The Arts and Nightlife

Get a copy of the magazine *Vacation Guide* and the newspaper *Touring,* both of which are available free at the tourist office and at hotels, to find out what's happening around the island. Also look in the *Santo Domingo News* and the *Puerto Plata News* for listings of events. The monthly *Dominican Fiesta!* also provides up-to-date information.

Cafés

Café Atlántico (J.A. Aybar at Abraham Lincoln, ☎ 809/565–1841) is responsible for bringing happy hour and Tex-Mex cooking to the Dominican Republic. (Its sister restaurant of the same name is a hot spot in Washington, D.C.) Usually young, very lively, and very friendly, the late-afternoon yuppie crowd comes for the music, the food, the exotic drinks, and the energetic atmosphere.

Exquesito (Av. Tiradentes 8, ☎ 809/541–0233) is in a striking setting that mixes traditional Dominican decor with deconstructivist provincial Italian. The fare includes French cheeses, Italian antipasti, and a local version of the deli. Talk, relax, and try the fondue at this top gathering spot that appeals to the young and terminally hip.

A recent annex to the Café St. Michel, the **Grand Café** (Av. Lope de Vega 26, ☎ 809/562–4141) attracts a relaxed local crowd. You can escape the music by going upstairs to the Tree House. The menu is informal and generally light, but try the Creole oxtail served with crabmeat patties.

The **Museo del Jamon** (La Atarazana 9, no ☎) is a casual boîte (with displays on curing ham, hence the name) that is popular Thursday and Sunday evenings after 10 for its folkloric dance shows, with the brilliantly lit Alcazar as a thrilling backdrop.

Casinos

Most of the casinos are concentrated in the larger hotels of Santo Domingo, but there are others here and there, and all offer blackjack, craps, and roulette. Casinos are open daily 3 PM–4 AM. You must be 18 to enter, and jackets are required. In Santo Domingo, the most popular casinos are in the **Jaragua** (Av. Independencia, ☎ 809/686–2222), the **Embajador** (Av. Sarasota, ☎ 809/533–2131), the **Gran Hotel Lina** (Av. Máximo Gómez, ☎ 809/686–5000), the **Naco Hotel** (Av. Tiradentes 22, ☎ 809/562–3100), and the **Hispañiola** (Av. Independencia, ☎ 809/535–1511).

You'll soon discover that there is no such thing as last call in the Dominican Republic. Customers usually decide when closing time will be.

Music and Dance

An active and frenzied young crowd dances to new wave, house, and, of course, merengue at **Alexander's** club (Av. Pasteur 23, ☎ 809/685–9728). An institution, it is open till all hours.

The neon palm tree outside **Bella Blue** (Av. George Washington 165, ☎ 809/689–2911) is a noticeable night beacon for a fun time. The crowd at this Malecón dance club is definitely over 21, and no jeans are allowed.

Happy hours are joyous indeed at Santo Domingo's top hotels, thanks to two-for-one drinks and energetic bands. A favorite of locals for its performances by local merengue bands, **Las Palmas** (Hotel Santo Domingo, Av. Independencia at Abraham Lincoln, ☎ 809/535–1511) has a happy hour from 6 to 8 PM. The newest sensation is **Guácara Taína** (655 Rómulo Betancourt Ave., ☎ 809/530–2666), a cultural center/disco set in a cave, hosting folkloric dances during the early evening and transforming into the city's hottest night spot later on. The world's only disco grotto, it boasts two dance floors, three bars, and lots of nooks and crannies.

An aptly named club, **Tops** (Plaza Hotel, Av. Tiradentes, ☎ 809/541–6226) offers excellent views of the city. Located on the 12th floor of the hotel, it features a variety of special events, from lingerie fashion shows to the latest bands.

When all the partying is over, capitaleños will guide you to **La Aurora** (Av. Hermanos Deligne, ☎ 809/685–6590), a lush after-hours supper club in a rustic garden setting. Savor typical dishes, even sancocho, at 4 in the morning. Here you'll see not only party goers but also the musicians who entertained them. It's a spot of preference for Santo Domingo's hottest band, 4:40.

Nearly every hotel in Puerto Plata has a disco and frequent live entertainment. Among the most popular spots are **La Roca Club** (Sosúa, ☎ 809/571–2179), **Crazy Moon** (Paradise Beach Resort and Club, ☎ 809/320–3663), and **Andromeda** (Heavens, ☎ 809/586–5250).

12 Grenada

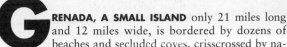

Updated by
Jane E. Zarem

GRENADA, A SMALL ISLAND only 21 miles long and 12 miles wide, is bordered by dozens of beaches and secluded coves, crisscrossed by nature trails, and filled with spice plantations, tropical forests, and select hotels that cling to hillsides and overlook the sea.

Known as the Isle of Spice, Grenada is a major producer of nutmeg, cinnamon, mace, cocoa, and many other common household spices. The pungent aroma of spices fills the air: at the outdoor markets, where they're sold from large burlap bags; in the restaurants, where chefs believe in using them liberally; and in the pubs, where cinnamon and nutmeg are sprinkled on the rum punches. If the Irish hadn't beaten them to the name, Grenadians might have called their land the Emerald Isle, for the lush rain forests and the thick vegetation on the hillsides give it a great, green beauty that few Caribbean islands can match.

Located in the Eastern Caribbean 90 miles north of Trinidad, Grenada is the most southerly of the Windward Islands. It is a nation composed of three inhabited islands and a few uninhabited islets: Grenada island is the largest of the three, with 120 square miles and about 91,000 people; Carriacou, 16 miles north of Grenada, has 13 square miles and a population of about 5,000; and Petit Martinique, 5 miles northeast of Carriacou, has 486 acres and a population of 700.

Although Carriacou and Petit Martinique are popular for day trips and fishing and snorkeling excursions, most of the tourist action is on Grenada. Here, too, you will find the nation's capital, St. George's, and its largest harbor, St. George's Harbour.

Until 1983, when the United States/Eastern Caribbean intervention catapulted tiny Grenada into the forefront of international news, it was a relatively obscure island providing a quiet hideaway for those who love fishing, snorkeling, or simply lazing in the sun.

Today, Grenada is a safe and secure vacation spot with enough good shopping, restaurants, and pubs to make it a regular port of call for major cruise lines and plenty of beaches and coves for those who want to scuba dive, snorkel, or just sit and stare at the waves.

Although Grenada's tourism industry is undergoing an expansion, it is a controlled expansion counterbalanced by the island's West Indian flavor. No building can stand taller than a coconut palm, and new construction on the beaches must be at least 165 feet from the high-water mark. The hotels, resorts, and restaurants remain, for the most part, small and family-owned by people who get to know their guests and pride themselves on giving personalized service. They're typical of the islanders as a whole—friendly and hospitable.

Grenada was sighted by Columbus in 1498. Although he never set foot on the island, he named it Concepción. Throughout the 17th century, it was the scene of bloody battles between the indigenous Carib Indians and the French. The Caribs finally lost to the French in 1651, committing mass suicide by leaping off a cliff rather than submitting to their captors. The French, however, lost the island again in 1762 to the British, thus beginning the seesaw of power between the two nations that became a familiar tale on many of the Windward Islands.

In 1967, Grenada became part of the British Commonwealth. Seven years later, it was granted total independence. The New Jewel Movement (NJM) seized power in 1979, formed the People's Revolutionary Government, and named as prime minister Maurice Bishop, who established controversial ties with Cuba. Bishop's prime ministry lasted until 1983, when a coup d'état led to his execution, along with those of many of his supporters. NJM Deputy Prime Minister Bernard Coard and Army Commander Hudson Austin took over the government. U.S. troops invaded the island on October 25, 1983, and evacuated the American students who were attending St. George's University Medical School. Coard and Austin were arrested, and resistance to the invasion was quickly put down. Since then, the annual number of U.S. residents alone traveling to this splendid isle has more than tripled.

Herbert A. Blaize was elected prime minister in December 1984. With $57.2 million in U.S. aid, his government began reorganizing Grenada's economy to focus on agriculture, light manufacturing, and tourism. The country started to rebuild roads, and a new telephone system, with direct dial from the United States, replaced the outdated one. Point Salines International Airport opened in 1984, enabling jets to land on the island and allowing night landings, both firsts for Grenada. It now has one of the longest runways in the Caribbean.

The election of Nicholas Brathwaite as prime minister, in March 1990, brought peaceful progress to this island nation and a stable and U.S.-friendly government.

Before You Go

Tourist Information
Contact the **Grenada Board of Tourism**: in the United States (820 2nd Ave., Suite 900D, New York, NY 10017, ☎ 212/687–9554 or 800/927–9554, FAX 212/573–9731); in Canada (Suite 820, 439 University Ave., Toronto, Ontario M5G 1Y8, ☎ 416/595–1339, FAX 416/595–8278); or in the United Kingdom (1 Collingham Gardens, Earl's Court, London SW5 0HW, ☎ 0171/370–5164 or 0171/370–5165, FAX 0171/370–7040).

Arriving and Departing
BY PLANE
American Airlines (☎ 800/433–7300) has daily flights during high season from major U.S. and Canadian cities via its San Juan hub. **BWIA** (☎ 800/327–7401 or 800/538–2942 in Miami) flies from New York, Miami, Toronto, and London to Barbados, where **LIAT** (Leeward Islands Air Transport, ☎ 809/440–2796 or 809/440–2797) connects with flights to Grenada. **Air Canada** (☎ 800/776–3000) flies from Toronto to Barbados, as well. LIAT has scheduled service between Grenada and Carriacou and also serves Trinidad, St. Lucia, Martinique, Antigua, Dominica, Guadeloupe and Venezuela.

FROM THE AIRPORT
Taxis are readily available at the airport. Rates to St. George's and the hotels of Grand Anse and L'Anse aux Epines are $10–$12. Rides taken between 6 PM and 6 AM incur a 33.3% surcharge.

Passports and Visas
Passports are not required of U.S., Canadian, or British citizens, provided they have two proofs of citizenship (one with photo) and a return air ticket. A passport, even an expired one, is the best proof of citizenship. A driver's license with photo *and* an original birth certificate or voter registration card will also suffice.

Language
English is the official language of Grenada.

Precautions
Secure your valuables in the hotel safe. Avoid walking late at night in the Grand Anse/L'Anse aux Epines hotel districts; it's dark enough to bump into things, maybe even into one of the cows that graze silently by the roadside. Starving mosquitoes adore tourists, especially after heavy rains; bring repellent.

Staying in Grenada

Important Addresses
Tourist Information: The **Grenada Board of Tourism** is located on the Carenage, in St. George's (☎ 809/440–2001, FAX 809/440–6637). It has maps, brochures, and information on accommodations, tours, and other services.

EMERGENCIES

Police and fire: Call 911. **Ambulance:** In St. George's, Grand Anse, and L'Anse aux Epines, call 434. For other areas, check with your hotel. **Hospital: St. George's Hospital** (☎ 809/440–2051; 809/440–2052; 809/440–2053). **Pharmacies: Gitten's** (Halifax St., St. George's, ☎ 809/440–2165; after hours 809/440–2340) and **Gitten's Drugmart** (Grand Anse, ☎ 809/444–4954; after hours 809/440–2340) are both open weekdays and Saturday 9–8, Sunday and public holidays 9–noon. **Parris' Pharmacy Ltd.** (Victoria St., Grenville, ☎ 809/442–7330), on the windward side of the island, is open Monday–Wednesday and Friday 9–4:30, Thursday 9–1, and Saturday 9–7.

Currency
Grenada uses the Eastern Caribbean (E.C.) dollar. At press time, the exchange rate was E.C.$2.67 to U.S.$1. Money can be exchanged at any bank or hotel. U.S. currency and traveler's checks are widely accepted, but be sure to ask which currency is referred to when you make purchases and business transactions. Prices are usually quoted in E.C. dollars. Hotels are unable by law to give foreign currency in change or on departure. Most hotels and major restaurants accept credit cards. *Note:* Prices quoted here are in U.S. dollars unless indicated otherwise.

Taxes and Service Charges
Hotels add an 8% government tax; restaurants add a 10% tax. Hotels—and some restaurants—add an additional 10% service charge to your bill. If not, a 10%–15% gratuity should be added for a job well done.

The departure tax is E.C.$35 for adults and E.C.$17.50 for children ages 5 to 12. Children under 5 are exempt.

Guided Tours
Arnold's Tours (☎ 809/440–0531 or 809/440–2213) offers several land, sea, and "Lan-Sea" combination tours. Prices typically range from $25 for a island tour, hiking trip, or sunset cruise to $140 for an all-day cruise to Carriacou. Dennis Henry of **Henry's Safari Tours** (☎ 809/444–5313) knows Grenada like the back of his hand. He offers a program of adventurous hikes and Jeep safaris, or you can design your own tour. **Spiceland Tours** (☎ 809/440–5180) offers several five- and seven-hour island tours, from an "Urban/Suburban" tour of St. George's and the South Coast to an "Emerald Forest Tour" highlighting Grenada's natural beauty.

A most unusual way to see Grenada is to join a scientific research project for a day. Options offered by the **Foundation for Field Research** (Box 771, St. George's, ☎ 809/440–8854, FAX 809/440–2330) include an underwater excavation of a 17th-century town and recording the social behavior of Mona monkeys in the wild. This is no tourist bus trip; you donate labor as well as a portion of the project cost, which is tax deductible. Write for more details.

Getting Around

BUSES

Privately owned minivans ply the winding road between St. George's and Grand Anse Beach, where many of the hotels are located. Hail one anywhere along the way, pay E.C.$1, and hold on to your hat. They pass by frequently from about 6 AM to 8 PM daily except Sundays and public holidays. You can get anywhere on the island by these minivans for E.C.$1–E.C.$6—a bargain by any standard—but be prepared for packed vehicles, unpredictable schedules, and some hair-raising maneuvers on mountainous roads and byways.

TAXIS

Taxis are plentiful, and rates (set by the government) are posted at the hotels and at the pier on the Carenage in St. George's. The trip between Grand Anse and St. George's costs about E.C.$20. A surcharge of 33.3% is added to all fares for rides taken between 6 PM and 6 AM. Cabs are plentiful at all hotels, at the cruise passenger Welcome Center, and on the Carenage.

RENTAL CARS

To rent a car, you will need a valid driver's license with which you may obtain a local permit from the traffic department (at the fire station on the Carenage) or some car-rental firms, at a cost of E.C.$30. Driving is on the left. Rental cars cost about $50 a day or $260 a week with unlimited mileage. A Jeep or automatic-drive car runs about $55 a day and $285 a week. Gas costs about $2.60 per gallon. Your hotel can arrange a rental for you. Car-rental agencies in St. George's are numerous. **David's** (☎ 809/444–3399 or 809/444–3038, FAX 809/444–4404) maintains four offices: Point Salines International Airport, Grenada Renaissance Resort, Rex Grenadian Hotel, and the Limes in Grand Anse. **Avis** is at Spice Isle Rental (☎ 809/440–3936 or 809/440–2624, FAX 809/440–4110; after hours ☎ 809/444–4563) on Paddock and Lagoon roads in St. George's. In the True Blue area, call **McIntyre Bros. Ltd.** (☎ 809/444–3944 or 809/440–2901; after hours ☎ 809/443–5319).

Telephones and Mail

Grenada can be dialed directly from the United States and Canada. The area code is 809. Long-distance calls from Grenada can be dialed directly from pay phones and most hotel rooms, as well.

Airmail rates for letters to the United States and Canada are E.C.75¢ for a half-ounce letter and E.C.35¢ for a postcard.

Opening and Closing Times

Stores are generally open from 8 to 4 weekdays, 8 to 1 on Saturday. Most are closed Sunday. Banks in St. George's are open Monday–Thursday 8–1:30 or 2, Friday 8–5. The main post office, on Lagoon Road in St. George's, is open 8–3:30 weekdays.

Exploring Grenada

Numbers in the margin correspond to points of interest on the Grenada (and Carriacou) map.

St. George's

Grenada's capital city and major port is one of the most picturesque and authentic West Indian towns in the Caribbean. Pastel warehouses cling to the curving shore along the Carenage, the horseshoe-shape harborside thoroughfare. Rainbow-colored houses rise above it and disappear into steep green hills. A walking tour of **St. George's** can be made in about two hours.

Start on the Carenage, a walkway along St. George's Harbour and the town's main thoroughfare. Cruise ships and windjammers dock at the pier at the eastern end, next to the **Welcome Center** and **Grenada Board of Tourism** office. The **Delicious Landing** restaurant (☎ 809/440–3948), with outdoor tables, is at the western end. In between are the **National Library,** a number of warehouses and small **shops,** and two more good restaurants, **Rudolf's** and **The Nutmeg** (*see* Dining, *below*). The Nutmeg has a huge open window that provides a great view of the harbor.

You can reach the **Grenada National Museum** by walking along the west end of the Carenage and taking Young Street west to Monckton Street. The museum has a small, interesting collection of archaeological and colonial artifacts and recent political memorabilia. *Young and Monckton Sts., ☎ 809/440–3725.* ☛ *$1 adults, 25¢ children under 18.* ☉ *Weekdays 9–4:30, Sat. 10–1:30.*

Continue west along Young Street past tile-roofed warehouses, turn left at the Traffic Police Control Station onto Cross Street, and you'll reach the **Esplanade,** the thoroughfare that runs along the ocean side of town. (The fastest way between the Carenage and the Esplanade is through the **Sendall Tunnel,** slightly north of Fort George. Take it if you're too tired to walk up the steep hill.)

At the intersection of Cross Street and the Esplanade is the **Yellow Poui Art Gallery** (☎ 809/440–3001), which displays artwork from Grenada, Jamaica, Trinidad, and Guyana and canvases by expatriate British, German, and French artists. ☉ *Weekdays 9:15–12:15 and 1:15–3:15, Sat. 9:15–12:15.*

Take the Esplanade north and turn right onto Granby Street, which will take you downhill to **Market Square.** The square comes alive every Saturday morning from 8 to noon with vendors selling baskets, spices, brooms, clothing, knickknacks, and fresh produce, including tropical fruit you can eat on the spot. (Other days feature a much-reduced selection.) Don't miss it!

Walk back up Granby Street to Halifax, and turn left. At the intersection of Halifax and Church streets is **St. Andrew's Presbyterian Church,** built in 1830. Follow Church Street east to Gore Street and **St. George's Anglican Church,** built in 1828. It's lined with plaques depicting Grenada in the 18th and 19th centuries. Continue up Church Street to the **York House,** built around 1800. Now home to the Senate and Supreme Court, it's open to the public for unstructured visits. Return to Market Square and turn left to reach **St. George's Methodist Church,** built in 1820, on Green Street near Tyrrel Street.

Take Tyrrel Street east to the corner of Park Lane to see the **Marryshow House.** Built in 1917, it combines Victorian and West Indian architecture. The Marryshow also houses the **Marryshow Folk Theatre,** Grenada's first cultural center. Plays, West Indian dance and music, and poetry readings are presented here on occasion. *Tyrrel St., near Bain Alley,* ☎ *809/440–2451.* ☛ *Free.* ☉ *Weekdays 8:30–4:30, Sat. 9–1.*

Head back west on Tyrrel Street and turn left onto Church Street. **Fort George** is high on the hill at the southern tip of Church Street. The fort, rising above the point that separates the harbor from the ocean, was built by the French in 1705. The fort now houses the police headquarters. *Church St., no* ☎. ☛ *Free.* ☉ *Daily during daylight hours.*

② Just outside town, **Bay Gardens** is a private horticultural paradise where 450 species of flowers and plants that grow on the island are cultivated in patterns mimicking their growth in the wild. Eight acres of paths are open to visitors. *In the suburb of St. Paul's, a short drive from town.* ☛ *$1.* ☉ *Daily during daylight hours.*

The West Coast

The coast road north from St. George's winds past soaring mountains and valleys covered with banana and breadfruit trees, palms, bamboo, **③** and tropical flowers. You can stop at **Concord Falls,** about 8 miles north of St. George's, which has a small visitor center, a viewing platform, and a changing room for donning your bathing suit (☛ $1). During the dry months, when the currents aren't too strong, you can take a dip under the cascades. If you're up to it, hike 2 miles through tropical forest to a second, spectacular waterfall which thunders down over huge boulders and creates a small swimming pool. The path is clear, but it's smart to use a guide. The boulders, as well as the path, are slippery as you get close to the falls, and maneuvering can be tricky.

About 15 minutes farther north is the town of **Gouyave,** center of the nutmeg industry. A tour of the three-story **Nutmeg Processing Plant,** which turns out 3 million pounds of Grenada's most famous export per year, makes a fragrant and fascinating half hour. *Gouyave, no* ☎. ☛ *$1.* ☉ *Weekdays 10–1 and 2–4.*

④ **Dougaldston Estate,** at the edge of town, has a spice factory where you can see cocoa, nutmeg, mace, cloves, cinnamon, and other spices laid out on giant trays drying in the sun. Pick up a bag of cinnamon bark, cloves, bay leaves, mace, or nutmeg for $2. *Gouyave, no* ☎. ☛ *$1.* ☉ *Weekdays 9–4.*

Continuing along the coast road to the northernmost tip of the island brings you to Sauteurs, the French word for leapers. It was off the 100-foot cliff called Leapers Hill that the Carib Indians flung themselves in 1651, preferring to die rather than submit to the French invaders.

TIME OUT For lunch take the short drive to the **Mount Rodney Estate,** just 1 mile from Sauteurs. The house was built in the 1870s and has a magnificent view of the Grenadines. Lunches are served in the breezy gazebo on weekdays from noon to 3 PM. Afterward, take a leisurely tour of the home and 6 acres of gardens. Reservations are essential, as lunch is restricted to 30 guests per day (☎ 809/442-9420).

The East Coast

⑤ Start your tour at **Westerhall,** a residential area about 5 miles southeast of St. George's, known for its beautiful villas, gardens, and panoramic **⑥** views. From here, take a dirt road north to **Grand Bacolet Bay,** a jagged peninsula on the Atlantic where the surf pounds against deserted **⑦** beaches. A little more than 2 miles north, **Grenville,** the island's second-largest city, is reminiscent of a French market town. From here, you can watch schooners set sail for the outer islands. As in St. George's, Saturday is market day, and the town fills with local people doing their shopping for the week. Cooking enthusiasts may want to see the town's spice-processing factory, which is open to the public.

If you take the interior route back to St. George's, you'll get a full sense of the lush, mountainous nature of the island. Only one paved road cuts across the island. Leaving Grenville and heading for St. George's, you'll wind upward through the rain forest until you're surrounded by mist. Then you'll descend onto the sunny hillsides. In the middle of **⑧** the island is **Grand Etang National Park.** Visit the informative Welcome Center to view displays on the local flora and fauna. A forest manager is on hand to answer questions. Crater Lake, in the crater of an extinct volcano, is a 13-acre glasslike expanse of cobalt blue water. The area is a bird sanctuary and forest reserve, where you can fish and hike. *Main interior road, between Grenville and St. George's,* ☎ *809/442–7425.* ☛ *$1.* ☉ *Daily 8:30–4.*

⑨ Another place to visit is **Annandale Falls and Visitors' Centre,** where a mountain stream cascades 50 feet into a pool surrounded by such exotic tropical flora as liana vines and elephant ears. This is a good swimming and picnicking spot. *Main interior road, 15 min east of St. George's,* ☎ *809/440–2452.* ☉ *Daily 9–5.*

Levera National Park and Bird Sanctuary is the newest addition to Grenada's protected parkland. The park encompasses 450 acres at the northeastern tip of the island, where the Caribbean meets the Atlantic. Facilities include a visitor center, changing rooms, a small amphitheater, and a gift shop. The first of the Grenadines is visible in the distance. The thick mangroves here provide food and protection for nesting seabirds and seldom-seen tropical parrots. Some fine Arawak ruins and petroglyphs can be seen, as well.

Grand Anse and the South End
Most of the island's hotels and nightlife are in Grand Anse or the adjacent community of L'Anse aux Epines, which means Cove of Pines. **⑩** At press time, **St. George's University Medical School** was planning to vacate its prime location on Grand Anse Beach, consolidating the school at its new campus in True Blue.

True Blue, a residential area on a picturesque cove between Grand Anse and L'Anse aux Epines, can be reached from the Grand Anse Road by turning left onto an unnamed road just before the airport.

The **Grand Anse Shopping Centre** has a supermarket/liquor store, clothing store, shoe store, fast-food joint, and several small gift shops with good-quality souvenirs and such luxury items as English china and Swedish crystal (*see* Shopping, *below*).

Grenada's Grenadines
Carriacou, Petit Martinique, and a handful of uninhabited specks that are included in the nation of Grenada are north of Grenada island and part of the Grenadines, an archipelago of 32 tiny islands and cays.

Carriacou is a little island (13 square miles) with a lot of punch. With more than a hundred rum shops and only one gas station, this island hideaway will bring the fastest metabolism down to a quiet purr. Carriacou exudes the kind of ebullient spirit and goodwill that you want to find in a Caribbean retreat but usually find only in a travel brochure. Come here if you want peace. Don't bother if you want luxurious amenities or if you would suffer coldly a parrot on your breakfast table!

Grenada (and Carriacou)

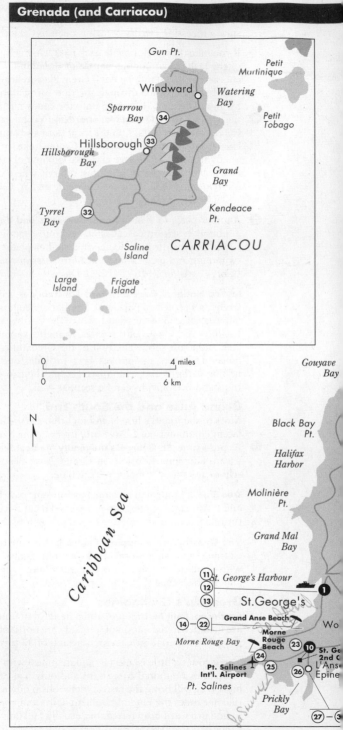

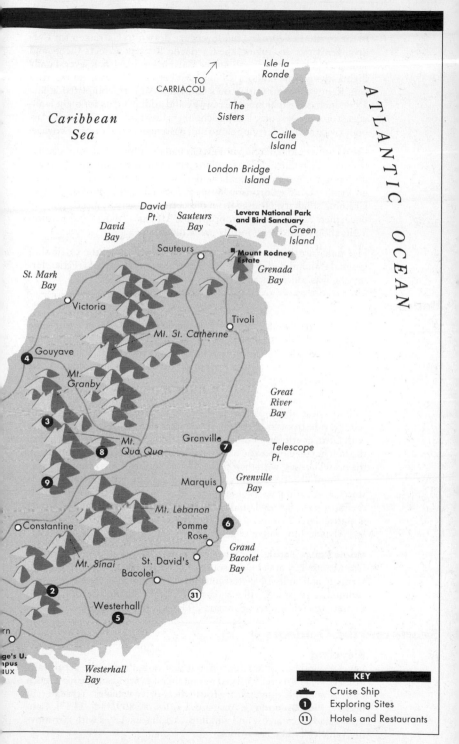

Isle la Ronde

The Sisters

Caille Island

London Bridge Island

Caribbean Sea

ATLANTIC OCEAN

TO CARRIACOU

David Pt.

David Bay

Sauteurs Bay

Levera National Park and Bird Sanctuary

Green Island

Sauteurs

■ **Mount Rodney Estate**

Grenada Bay

St. Mark Bay

Victoria

Mt. St. Catherine

Tivoli

4 Gouyave

Mt. Granby

Great River Bay

3

Granville **7**

Telescope Pt.

8 *Mt. Qua Qua*

9

Marquis

Grenville Bay

Mt. Lebanon

6

Constantine

Pomme Rose

Mt. Sinai

St. David's

Grand Bacolet Bay

Bacolet

2

31

Westerhall

5

ge's U.
pus
UX

Westerhall Bay

KEY

Cruise Ship

1 Exploring Sites

11 Hotels and Restaurants

Hillsborough is Carriacou's main town. Rolling hills cut a wide swath through the island's center, from Gun Point in the north to Tyrrel Bay in the south. In February, fun lovers are drawn to Carriacou for Carnival festivities. In August, the Carriacou Regatta attracts yachts and sailing vessels from throughout the Caribbean. LIAT has several daily flights (flying time is about 18 minutes) between Grenada and Carriacou. Renovations to Carriacou's Lauriston Airport, completed in late 1994, included expanding the runway and adding lights for night landings. You can also come by sea. Schooners leave from St. George's Harbour twice a week, ferrying cargo and passengers on a 4½-hour voyage.

Carriacou's colonial past parallels Grenada's, although its tiny size has restricted its political role to a minor part in the area's history. The only museum in the eastern Caribbean that is owned by the people, not the government, is the **Carriacou Museum,** located in Hillsborough behind Gramma's Bakery. Housed in an old cotton ginnery, it has displays of unearthed Amerindian, European, and African artifacts and features a gift shop loaded with locally made items.

Five miles northeast of Carriacou is Petit Martinique, the smallest of Grenada's inhabited islands. Like Carriacou and Grenada, Petit Martinique was settled by the French.

Beaches

Grenada has some 80 miles of coastline, 65 bays, and 45 white-sand beaches—many in secluded little coves. All the beaches are public and within an easy cab ride of St. George's. Most front the Caribbean, south of St. George's in the Grand Anse and L'Anse aux Epines areas, where most of the hotels are clustered. Virtually every hotel, apartment complex, and residential area has its own beach or tiny cove.

The loveliest and most popular beach is **Grand Anse,** about a 10-minute ride from St. George's. It's a gleaming, 2-mile curve of sand with clear, gentle surf. At its southern end is a palm-covered point; to the north, you can see the narrow mouth of St. George's Harbour and the pastel houses, with their fish-scale-tile rooftops, that climb the surrounding hillsides. Vendors selling spices, palm hats and baskets, T-shirts, and coral jewelry punctuate a day on this beach. They are, for the most part, licensed, and their wares are worth a look. The sunset is particularly beautiful at Grand Anse—enjoy it over cocktails at Spice Island Inn, where tables overlook the beach.

Morne Rouge Beach is on the Caribbean side, about 1 mile south of Grand Anse Bay and 3 miles south of St. George's Harbour. The beach forms a half-mile-long crescent and has a gentle surf excellent for swimming. A small café serves light meals during the day. In the evening, there's a disco, Fantazia 2001 (*see* Nightlife, *below*).

Sports and the Outdoors

Bicycling

Level ground is rare in Grenada, but that doesn't stop the aerobically primed. What's more, 15-speed mountain bikes are available for a much more reasonable rate than are four-wheel-drive vehicles. You can rent bikes at **Ride Grenada** (L'Anse aux Epines, ☎ 809/444–1157). Caution: Roads are narrow and winding, and sharing lanes with fast-moving vehicles can be hazardous.

Fishing

Deep-sea fishing around Grenada is excellent, with marlin, sailfish, yellowfin tuna, and dolphin fish topping the list of good catches. The annual **Spice Island Game Fishing Tournament** is held in late January. Half-day and full-day sportfishing excursions are available through **Evans Chartering Services** (☎ 809/444–4422 or 809/444–4217).

Golf

The **Grenada Golf and Country Club** in Grand Anse (☎ 809/444–4128) has a nine-hole course. Greens fees are E.C.$7. Your hotel will make arrangements for you.

Sailing, Diving, and Snorkeling

The **Moorings' Club Mariner Watersports Center** (☎ 809/444–4439 or 809/444–4549), at the Secret Harbour Hotel on the southeast shore, has half- and full-day charter yachts and a range of Shore 'n' Sail programs, developed by America's Cup racer Steve Colgate, for beginning and experienced sailors. You can rent sailing or power yachts, with or without crew, from **Seabreeze Yacht Charters** at the Spice Island Marine Centre (☎ 809/444–4924; from the U.S., 800/387–3998). **Starwind** (☎ 809/440–3678 or 809/440–2508) offers day, half-day, and sunset sailing trips along Grenada's southwest coast.

Diving in this area is excellent, with visibility as far as 200 feet. Hundreds of varieties of fish and more than 40 species of coral await underwater explorers. The best snorkeling is found around Carriacou's offshore islands. A superb spot for scuba diving is at the site of what is sometimes dubbed the *Titanic* of the Caribbean. The *Bianca C,* a 600-foot cruise ship that caught fire and sank in 1961, settled in waters more than 100 feet deep and is now home to giant turtles, spotted eagle rays with 15-foot wingspans, and a 350-pound grouper that lives in the ship's smokestack.

At Grand Anse Beach, **Dive Grenada** (Grenada Renaissance Resort, ☎ 809/444–4371, ext. 638) and **Grand Anse Aquatics Ltd.** (Coyaba Beach Resort, ☎ 809/444–4129) offer scuba and snorkeling trips to reefs and shipwrecks. Single dives are $40; Bianca C dives, $55, snorkeling trips, $18. They also offer diving instruction, including resort courses for novices. On Carriacou, **Silver Beach Diving** (☎ 809/443–7882), near Hillsborough, offers scuba diving at more than 20 sites.

Other Water Sports

The major hotels on Grand Anse Beach have water-sports centers where you can rent small sailboats, Windsurfers, and Sunfish. The centers are located on the beach in front of the hotels. Your hotel can make arrangements for you, or you can call one of the major hotels for information.

Tennis

Several hotels have tennis courts that are free to their guests: **Calabash** (☎ 809/444–4234), **Secret Harbour** (☎ 809/444–4548), **Coyaba Beach Resort** (☎ 809/444–4129), **Spice Island Inn** (☎ 809/444–4258), **Grenada Renaissance** (☎ 809/444–4371), **Coral Cove** (☎ 809/444–4217), **La Source** (☎ 809/444–2556), **Rex Grenadian** (☎ 809/444–3333), and **Twelve Degrees North** (☎ 809/444–4580). Visitors may also play on the Richmond Hill and Tanteen Tennis Club courts. Your hotel desk clerk can contact them for you.

Triathlon

Each January, triathletes from around the world compete in Grenada's annual International Triathlon. The competition starts and finishes at Grand Anse Beach. Participants compete in a 1.5-kilometer swim, a 25-kilometer cycling race, and a 5-kilometer run.

Shopping

The best souvenirs of Grenada are little spice baskets filled with cinnamon, nutmeg, mace, bay leaf, vanilla, "saffron" (turmeric), and ginger. You can buy them in practically every shop or from vendors who stroll the beach in Grand Anse. Vendors also sell fabric dolls, T-shirts, coral jewelry, fans, and hats and baskets woven from green palm. (Environmental groups discourage tourists from buying black coral.)

Good Buys

ST. GEORGE'S

Art Fabrik (Young St., ☎ 809/440–0568) is a batik studio, where you can watch the fabric being designed and decorated. Look for the blue door! A unique selection of batik art, clothing, and accessories is for sale in the boutique. The two branches of **Gifts Remembered** (Cross St., ☎ 809/440–2482; Coyaba Beach Resort, ☎ 809/444–4129) are crammed with wonderful, inexpensive stuff, including brightly painted ceramic boats, houses, and trucks laden with fruit and smiling people and T-shirts that are better quality than usual. **Spice Island Perfumes** on the Carenage (☎ 809/440–2006) is a treasure trove of local perfumes, body oils, and natural extracts of spices and herbs. Best of all are its tiny wooden pots of solid fragrances, including bitter orange, jasmine, or spice for around $8. At the far end of the Carenage, **White Cane Industries** (☎ 809/444–2014) stocks bargain baskets, hats, and spectacularly colored rag rugs, all handwoven locally by blind craftspeople. Pricier is **Tikal** (Young St., ☎ 809/440–2310), a long-established boutique well known for its exquisite handicrafts and fashions, both local and imported from Africa and Latin America. For the latest reggae, calypso, soca, and steel-band music, try **Turbo Charge Records & Tapes** (St. John's St., ☎ 809/440–0586).

GRAND ANSE

The **Grand Anse Shopping Centre** houses the **Gift Shop** (☎ 809/444–4408), an outlet for imported luxury items such as watches, leather goods, fine jewelry, crystal, and china, at duty-free prices, and **Imagine** (☎ 809/444–4028), which specializes in island handicrafts, including batik fabrics.

CARRIACOU

In L'Esterre on Carriacou, hand-painted signs announce "This way to the great artist," **Canute Calliste.** If you get lost, one of his many (more than 20) grandchildren will lead the way. Works by Calliste, colorful watercolors of island scenes, are also available at the Carriacou Museum.

Dining

Unlike most Caribbean islands, which have a scarcity of fresh produce, Grenada has everything from cabbages and tomatoes to bananas, mangoes, papaya (called pawpaw), plantains, melons, callaloo (similar to spinach), breadfruit, oranges, tangerines, limes, christophines (similar to squash), and avocados—the list is endless. Fresh seafood of all kinds, including lobster and oysters, is also plentiful. Conch, known here as *lambi,* is very popular and appears on most menus in some form, usually as a stew. Be sure to try one of the exotic ice creams made from guava or nutmeg. Almost all Grenadian restaurants serve local dishes.

Rum punches are served everywhere, but no two places make them exactly alike—except that nutmeg is always grated on top. The local beer, Carib, is also very popular and quite good.

What to Wear

Dining in Grenada is a casual experience. Collared shirts and casual sundresses are apropos, but even the nicest restaurants don't require a jacket.

CATEGORY	COST*
$$$	over $40
$$	$20–$40
$	under $20

per person, excluding drinks, service, and 10% sales tax

Grenada

$$$ **Canboulay.** Trinidadians Erik and Gina-Lee Johnson put Canboulay
★ on the map with their exciting reconfigurations of local cuisine. The menu changes often, but regular items include crab crepes with a puree of callaloo, breadfruit vichyssoise, grilled tuna steak with citrus-pepper sauce, African *bobotie* (spiced, raisin-studded ground beef topped with a baked custard), and five-star versions of the ubiquitous nutmeg ice cream and *roti* (curried meat, potatoes, and beans wrapped in a giant tortilla). The frozen chocolate-mocha cheesecake has broken hearts, and anything the Johnsons do with shrimp—coconut-beer-batter-it, or peanut-sauce-it—is memorable. The dining room's shutters are opened to hilltop breezes and a view of Grand Anse. The more casual Verandah restaurant is open for lunch. ✕ *Morne Rouge, St. George's,* ☎ *809/411–4401. Reservations advised. AE, D, MC, V. Closed Sun. No lunch Sat.*

$$$ **Cicely's at the Calabash.** The open-air restaurant (named for chef Cicely Roberts) at the Calabash hotel is small and pretty, surrounded by palms and tropical flowers. The prix fixe dinner is a good deal; past menus have included fillet of kingfish with roast potatoes, mixed vegetables, and fried plantains, and chicken with ginger and chive sauce, accompanied by a salad and cauliflower in mustard sauce. Cheese and English-style biscuits with coffee, tea, or cocoa top off your meal ✕ *L'Anse aux Épines,* ☎ *809/444–4234. Reservations advised. AE, MC, V.*

$$$ **La Belle Creole.** Creative West Indian cuisine and a wraparound view
★ of Grand Anse are the claims to fame of this romantic hillside restaurant. The lunch and dinner menus are always changing, but reappearing favorites include Grenadan caviar (roe of the white sea urchin), soursop mousse, and lobster-egg flan on the appetizer list and entrées of stuffed baked rainbow runner, Creole saffron pork chops, and callaloo quiche. On Sunday, a local band plays at the lunchtime poolside barbecue. The graciousness with which you are served at this restaurant is bound to impress even the most jaded traveler. ✕ *Blue Horizons Cottage Hotel, Morne Rouge, St. George's,* ☎ *809/444–4316. Reservations required for nonhotel guests. AE, MC, V.*

$$$ **Spice Island Inn.** Diners tend to dress for the five-course, fixed-price
★ evening meal at this nicest of hotel dining rooms (reservations for nonhotel guests are limited). The ivy-hung terrace is separated from Grand Anse beach by the narrowest of paths. Roast beef or calves' liver are as likely to appear on the menu as local fare, of which the unlikely sounding grapefruit consommé is a sublime example. Lobster usually appears in some form, taking the title role at the Saturday "Seafood Night" buffet, upstaged only by a dessert table groaning with pineapple pie, nutmeg ice cream, chocolate truffle torte, and the like. Wednes-

day is "Grenadian Night," when crab back, sea egg, roast suckling pig, and all the trimmings are on the table, followed by dancing under the stars. Fridays feature an equally festive barbecue and steel-band music. ✕ *Grand Anse,* ☎ *809/444–4258 or 809/444–4423. Reservations required in season. AE, D, MC, V.*

$$ The Boatyard. Embassy personnel and expatriates fill this lively restaurant, which sits smack in the middle of a marina. Burgers, fish-and-chips, and deep-fried shrimp are served at lunchtime. At dinner you may order club steaks, lobster, and different types of meat and seafood brochettes. In season there's disco music on Friday night, a steel band on Saturday, and live jazz on Sunday. ✕ *L'Anse aux Epines,* ☎ *809/444–4662. MC, V. Closed Mon.*

$$ Coconut's Beach, The French Restaurant. Take local seafood, add butter, wine, and Grenadian herbs, and you have excellent French Creole cuisine. Throw in a beautiful setting at the northern end of Grand Anse Beach, and this little cottage becomes a delightful spot for lunch or dinner. Lambi curry is a hit. Lobster may be wrapped in a crepe, dipped in garlic butter, or added to spaghetti. In season, there's a beach barbecue with live music each Wednesday, Friday, and Sunday night. ✕ *Grand Anse Beach,* ☎ *809/444–4644. Reservations advised. Free transportation arranged. AE, MC, V.*

$$ The Nutmeg. Fresh seafood is the specialty at this restaurant. Try the grilled turtle steaks, lobster, or shrimp, or just stop by for a drink, a chicken roti, and a great view of the harbor. ✕ *The Carenage, St. George's,* ☎ *809/440–2539. AE, D, MC, V.*

$$ Red Crab. Average, somewhat overpriced food hasn't kept this pub from being a favorite meeting and eating spot, especially on Saturday night. Seafood, particularly lobster, and steak are the staples of the menu; hot garlic bread comes with all orders. You can eat inside or under trees and stars. There's live music Monday and Friday in season. ✕ *L'Anse aux Epines (near The Calabash),* ☎ *809/444–4424. AE, MC, V. Closed Sun.*

$$ Rudolf's. This informal pub offers fine West Indian fare, as well as sandwiches and burgers. Skip the attempts at haute cuisine "Viennoise" or "Parisienne," and enjoy the crab back, lambi, and delectable nutmeg ice cream. This is *the* place for eavesdropping on local gossip. Even for Grenada, the rum punches are lethal. ✕ *The Carenage, St. George's,* ☎ *809/440–2241. No credit cards. Closed Sun.*

$$ Tabanca at Journey's End. Dine on the open terrace overlooking the sea and St. George's Harbour. Sunbathers are lured to this bistro from Grand Anse Beach, just below, for luncheon of sandwiches, crisp salads, or seafood specialties. Fillet of kingfish topped with a poached egg wins raves, Carib beer is on tap, and the special rum punch hits the spot. Dinners of steak, fish, and lobster are delicious. Homemade desserts—tortes and other pastries—are inspired by the Austrian heritage of the owner. ✕ *Grand Anse,* ☎ *809/444–1300. AE, D, DC, MC, V. Closed Tues.*

$ Cot Bam. "Club on the Beach at Morne Rouge" is on Grand Anse Beach next to the Coyaba Beach Resort, within walking distance of all the Grand Anse hotels. The casual atmosphere of this bar-restaurant-nightclub, with its tin roof and bamboo railings, makes it a great place to kick back and relax. You can stroll in wearing shorts, after a long day at the beach, to dance or chat the night away. Order a chicken roti served with coleslaw for E.C.$6 and a Carib beer, and you're set for the evening. The staff is a delight. ✕ *Grand Anse,* ☎ *809/444–2050. AE.*

$ La Sagesse. A perfect spot to soothe the most frazzled of souls, this open-air restaurant and beach bar is on a secluded cove 20 minutes from Grand Anse. Come for a swim, hike, and a meal—or just a meal!

Select from sandwiches, salads, or lobster for lunch. Lambi, smoked marlin or dolphin, fillet of grouper, and tuna steak are joined on the dinner menu by a daily vegetarian special. Transportation to and from your hotel is provided. ✕ *La Sagesse Nature Center, St. David's,* ☎ *809/444-6458. Reservations advised. AE, MC, V.*

$ **Mamma's.** One of Mamma's daughters will set generous helpings of local specialties before you—roast turtle, lobster salad, christophine salad, cabbage salad, or fried plantain, as well as such exotica as armadillo, opossum, and sea urchin. Sixteen to 19 native dishes are served family style at a fixed E.C.$45 per person. You will not leave hungry, although word is that standards have slipped a little since Mamma passed away. ✕ *Lagoon Rd., St. George's,* ☎ *809/440-1459. Reservations required. No credit cards.*

CARRIACOU

$ **Scraper's.** Good things are happening at Tyrrel Bay. Scraper's serves up lobster, conch, and an assortment of fresh catches, along with a simple spirit and decor seasoned with occasional calypsonian serenades (owner Steven Gay "Scraper" is a pro). Order a rum punch and exercise your right to do nothing. ✕ *Tyrrel Bay,* ☎ *809/443-7403. AE, D, MC, V.*

Lodging

Grenada's accommodations range from simply furnished kitchenette apartments to suites of overwhelming Caribbean-style elegance. Most of the hotels are owned and operated by Grenadians; those that aren't are usually run by British or American expatriates who thrive on the simplicity of Grenadian life. The hotels tend to be small (10 to 20 rooms in most cases) and intimate, with friendly managers and owners.

Reservations at any of the 24 members of the **Grenada Hotel Association** can be made by calling 800/223-9815 in the United States or Canada, 212/545-8469 in New York State.

Most posted daily room rates at Grenadian hotels are quoted in U.S. currency and represent the room rate only, without meals. Visitors can often opt for CP or MAP, depending on the season. The plans specified in the individual listings below apply year-round unless otherwise noted. Prices during the summer are discounted by 20% to 40%.

CATEGORY	COST*
$$$$	over $200
$$$	$150–$200
$$	$100–$150
$	under $100

All prices are for a standard double room for two during high season, excluding 8% tax and 10% service charge.

Hotels
GRENADA

$$$$ **The Calabash.** Rooms in this all-suite hotel are scattered over 8 acres of tropical gardens overlooking a curved beach, a yacht harbor, and charter-boat anchorage in "Prickly Bay," L'Anse aux Epines, a few minutes away from the hotel row of Grand Anse. A recent renovation included the addition of a casual beach bar and restaurant. Fourteen suites have whirlpool baths, and eight suites each have a private pool. All have air-conditioning and a veranda, where breakfast is delivered. You'll have to live with the noise generated by the nearby Point Salines International Airport: Early-morning flights can bounce you out of bed. 🏠 *Box 382, St. George's,* ☎ *809/444-4234,* FAX *809/444-4804. 28*

suites. Restaurant, beach bar-restaurant, pool, water-sports center, tennis. AE, MC, V. BP, MAP.

$$$$ **La Source.** Just minutes from Point Salines airport is Grenada's only all-inclusive resort. A towering, louvered wood-and-stained-glass reception hall leads into a courtyard around which spa treatment rooms, an excellent restaurant (dine on the mint-and-raspberry colonnaded terrace or in the colonial teak and plush Great Room), piano bar, and pool are ranged. The bedrooms have Persian rugs on Italian marble floors, Jamaican mahogany furniture and woodwork, high ceilings, balconies, and marble bathrooms with hair dryers and illuminated makeup mirrors. Rooms are in several four-story buildings on or above the main beach. Be prepared to walk up and down lots of stairs to get to your room. Rates seem steep at first glance, but they include *everything*—three meals, snacks, drinks at the bar, wine with dinner, tipping (it's banned), sports, plus, of course, spa treatments. Massages, facials, and saunas are scheduled for you upon arrival and are augmented by creams and oils made from lemons, limes, papayas, or whatever's in season. The array of sports facilities is impressive—the best on Grenada. You're truly supposed to be getting away from it all: There's no television on the property. ☎ *Pink Gin Beach, Box 852, St. George's, ☎ 809/444–2556 or 800/544–2883, FAX 809/444–2561. 100 rooms. 2 restaurants, full spa with treatment rooms, sauna, hot tub, hair salon, piano bar, 2 beaches, pool, poolside bar service, water sports, gym (aerobics, yoga, stretch, and meditation classes), par-3, 9-hole golf course, 2 lighted tennis courts, fencing, archery, volleyball, cycling, table tennis, entertainment. AE, MC, V. All-inclusive.*

$$$$ **Spice Island Inn.** If you want luxurious accommodations in the best
★ location Grenada has to offer, this resort on Grand Anse beach is the place to go. There are three types of suites here, all spacious, brightly decorated with the colors of sand and coral, and equipped with air-conditioning, ceiling fan, phone, hair dryer, minibar, vast mirrored closets, and a patio. Some suites are right on Grand Anse Beach. Others have white-ballustraded terraces overlooking garden, sea, and sunset. Then there are the private pool suites, each with its own private plunge pool. What really distinguishes Spice Island from the pack, though, are the fabulous bathrooms. They're equipped with spa Jacuzzis that could submerge a family of four, heaps of thick towels, and skylights for watching the moon rise. Since Grand Anse is Grenada's prime stretch of sand, the location is perfect for beach lovers. And with the restaurant (*see* Dining, *above*) and bar at the edge of the sand in the center of the complex, your feet need never touch concrete. ☎ *Box 6, Grand Anse, St. George's, ☎ 809/444–4258 or 800/223–9815, FAX 809/444–4807. 39 whirlpool suites and 17 private-pool suites. Restaurant, bar, tennis courts, water-sports center, boutique, fitness center, entertainment most nights, golf course privileges. AE, D, DC, MC, V. CP, MAP.*

$$$–$$$$ **Grenada Renaissance Resort.** The beach location (across from the Grand Anse shopping center) is convenient, the grounds are beautiful, the rooms are comfortable, and the list of amenities is long—but the decor is ho-hum American-motel. The ceilings are low and the rooms less spacious than those at competing resorts. Still, all rooms have king-size or large twin beds, satellite TV, and hair dryers. ☎ *Box 441, Grand Anse, St. George's, ☎ 809/444–4371, FAX 809/444–4800. 184 doubles, 2 luxury suites. 2 restaurants, lounge, pool, tennis, barber shop/beauty salon, 2 gift shops. AE, DC, MC, V. EP, MAP.*

$$$ **Coyaba Beach Resort.** Coyaba means "heaven" in the Arawak Indian language. Situated right on Grand Anse Beach, certainly a heavenly spot, Coyaba is comfortable, popular, and well equipped. Leading off the lawns are tennis and volleyball courts, a sizable pool with swim-up bar, and a bamboo-walled terrace restaurant. The carpeted rooms, housed in four two-story, tile-roofed buildings, have air-conditioning, satellite TV, phone, hair dryer, and a balcony (or strip of grass with lounge chair). Most rooms are set back too far to overlook the beach, but sand and sea are only a brief amble away. Plants, dark-stained wood, and Arawak-inspired folk art adorn both rooms and public areas. ☎ *Box 336, Grand Anse, St. George's, ☎ 809/444–4129 or 800/223–9815, FAX 809/444–4808. 40 rooms. Restaurant, bar, pool with swim-up bar, tennis courts, water-sports center, lounge boutique. AE, D, DC, MC, V. EP, CP, BP, MAP, FAP.*

$$-$$$ Rex Grenadian. You're likely to be vacationing alongside a convention group at this massive British-owned resort near the airport; the Rex has overtaken the Grenada Renaissance in size and business facilities. The resort is also very popular with European tour groups. The central building is a faux-Palladian white palace of lofty, pink-limed oak ceilings, vast arched windows, trellised walkways, and tiled terraces. The snazziest rooms and suites are the ones conveniently located adjacent to the central building. Other rooms are in eight two-story cliffside blocks of buildings with either a garden or ocean view. All rooms are decorated in robin's-egg blue and taupe with rattan furniture, king or large twin beds, and balconies. Basic garden-view rooms are equipped with a fan and shower. For an extra $25 you can have air-conditioning, tub, and hair dryer. Enthusiastic landscaping includes a lake and fountain, which many rooms overlook, and a pool terrace with restaurant and bar above one of two beaches. All manner of activity is laid on—water sports, rainy-day programs (bingo, local dialect classes, dance lessons), evening shows, happy hours. ☎ *Point Salines, Box 893, St. George's, ☎ 809/444–3333 or 800/255–5859, FAX 809/444–1111. 212 rooms, 3 restaurants, café, lounge, 2 beaches, beach bar, pool with bar-restaurant, piano bar, executive lounge, conference facilities, water sports, fitness center, tennis, entertainment. AE, D, DC, MC, V. EP.*

$$ Blue Horizons Cottage Hotel. Spice Island Inn's sister hotel is an es-
★   pecially good value. Each comfortable, air-conditioned suite has a kitchenette, private terrace, TV, phone, and hair dryer. Handsome mahogany furniture is set off by white walls and cool, tiled floors. Palms stud the large, sunny lawn around the swimming pool. Grand Anse beach, where the Spice Island Inn sprawls along 1,600 feet of sand, is a short walk down the hill. Water sports are free for guests of either hotel. Guests may eat at Blue Horizon's La Belle Creole or at Spice Island. ☎ *Box 41, Grand Anse, St. George's, ☎ 809/444–4316 or 809/444–4592; in the U.S., 800/223–9815; FAX 809/444–2815. 26 deluxe and 6 superior suites. Restaurant, 2 bars, lounge, pool. AE, MC, V. EP, CP, MAP.*

$$ Flamboyant Hotel and Cottages. Not just a good value, the friendly Flamboyant is also home of the famous Monday-night crab-racing spectacular. The rooms and suites of this Grenadian-owned cross between hotel and self-catering resort have one of the island's best views, sweeping over the entire Grand Anse Bay to St George's. All rooms are simply furnished with air-conditioning, minibar, satellite TV, phone, and balcony. One-bedroom suites and two-bedroom cottages each have a kitchen and lounge. You can take a dip in the freshwater pool or continue down a rather steep stairway to the beach. A cabana bar serves snacks and is the site of frequent barbecues. ☎ *Box 214, St. George's, ☎ 809/444–4247, FAX 809/444–1234. 16 rooms, 20 suites, and 2 cottages. Restaurant, bar, beach bar, pool, cable TV, free snorkeling equipment. AE, D, MC, V. EP, BP, MAP.*

$ **La Sagesse Nature Center.** This is a secluded getaway on a lovely bay 10 miles east of Point Salines International Airport. The grounds include a salt-pond bird sanctuary, thick growths of mangroves, and several hiking trails. A main guest house, recently renovated, has two high-ceilinged suites with kitchenettes, ceiling fans, and hot-water baths. There is also a two-bedroom beach cottage, and two less-expensive rooms are tucked in behind the restaurant. Mike Meranski, the cheerful American owner-manager, will run guests into town for grocery supplies and shopping. ⚏ *Box 44, St. David's,* ☎ *809/444–6458,* ℻ *809/444–6458. 6 double rooms. Restaurant, bar, satellite TV. MC, V. EP.*

$ **True Blue Inn.** Although the "blue" in the inn's name comes from the history of the residential area that was once an indigo plantation, the title could just as easily have come from the beautiful views of blue bay and ocean. Four spacious one-bedroom apartment units are perched cliffside, among the trees, each with a private veranda overlooking the sea. Three two-bedroom island cottages, nestled in private seaside gardens, are air-conditioned and have ceiling fans. Kitchens in both the apartments and the cottages are large and fully equipped. You can swim in the pool or the bay. Sunsets are spectacular from Indigo's, the inn's deck restaurant. Boaters frequently come for dinner, tying up at the inn's private dock. For a special treat, you can book a day sail on the owner's yacht. ⚏ *True Blue Inn, Box 308, St. George's (Old Mill Ave., True Blue),* ☎ *809/444–2000 or 800/742–4276,* ℻ *809/444–1247. 7 units. Restaurant, bar, pool, full maid/laundry service daily, docking facilities, yacht charter and dinghy service. AE, MC, V.*

CARRIACOU

$$ **Silver Beach Resort.** Stretches of pristine beach surround this 18-room hotel on Carriacou, Grenada's sister isle. All rooms have private patios and ocean views (but no TVs). The scuba facilities here are the biggest in the Grenadines. The open-air restaurant by the water is the best place on the island for a hearty, early-morning breakfast. ⚏ *Silver Beach,* ☎ *809/443–7337,* ℻ *809/443–7165. 12 doubles (2 with kitchenettes) and 6 cottages. Restaurant, snorkeling, windsurfing, spearfishing, day trip to offshore islets, boutique, gift shop, floating dock, moorings, docking facilities, showers and garbage disposal for yachts, scuba certification course, island bus service, car rental. AE, MC, V. EP, CP, MAP.*

$ **Cassada Bay Resort.** In addition to a breathtaking panorama of the ocean, this resort gives you the use of a private offshore island (a five-minute boat ride from the beach) for snorkeling and windsurfing. Cabins here, on the south side of Carriacou, cascade down the side of a hilltop overlooking the sea and offer an unadorned but peaceful sea-sprayed hideaway. ⚏ *Belmont,* ☎ *809/443–7494,* ℻ *809/443–7672. 20 doubles. Restaurant, bar, water-sports center. AE, DC, MC, V. EP, CP, MAP.*

Apartment Hotels

These fully equipped units often represent a great budget alternative, especially for families. Contact the tourist office for additional listings.

$$–$$$ **Twelve Degrees North** is top of the line (and most expensive), with eight one- and two-bedroom apartments, maid service (which includes cooking your breakfast and lunch and doing your laundry), private beach, pool, and tennis. A minimum stay of one week is required during high season, and children under 12 are not allowed. ⚏ *Box 241, L'Anse aux Epines, St. George's,* ☎ *809/444–4580,* ℻ *809/444–4580. 8 apartments. Pool, water sports, tennis. AE, V. EP.*

$ Wave Crest Holiday Apartments. Owner-manager Joyce Dabrieo runs a tight ship. She and her husband take great pains to keep all 20 air-conditioned, sunny rooms and apartments, some of which are self-catering, spotless and well maintained. Grand Anse beach is only a five-minute walk away. ⌨ *Box 278, St. George's,* ☎ *809/444–4116,* FAX *809/444–4847. 14 1-bedroom apartments, 2 2-bedroom apartments, 4 double rooms. AE, D, MC, V.*

Villa and Private-Home Rentals

Several local agencies handle rentals of villas and private homes: The most reliable is **Grenada Property Management** (Melville St., St. George's, ☎ 809/440–1896). In-season rates range from about $600 a week for a two-bedroom home with a pool to about $3,500 for a six-bedroom home on the beach.

Nightlife

Grenada's nightlife is centered mainly on the resort hotels. During winter, many have steel, reggae, and pop bands in the evenings. **Spice Island Inn, The Calabash, Coyaba,** and the **Grenada Renaissance** are among the most lively, but check out the new **Rex Grenadian,** too (*see* Lodging, *above*). Check with your hotel or the tourist information office to find out where various bands are performing on a given night.

Fantazia 2001 (Gem Apartments premises, Morne Rouge Beach, ☎ 809/444–4224) is a popular disco on the beach, where soca and reggae are played, along with international favorites. It's dark and loud and fun, with a mix of locals and tourists. There is a small cover charge (E.C.$5) on Friday and Saturday nights. **Le Sucrier** (The Sugar Mill, Grand Anse, ☎ 800/444–1068) is open on Wednesday, Thursday, Friday, and Saturday from 9 PM to 3 AM and attracts a young crowd with local comedy and a disco on Thursday and "oldies" night on Wednesday. Friday night is "the" night at the **Boatyard Restaurant and Bar** (L'Anse aux Epines beach in the Marina, ☎ 809/444–4662), from 11 PM till sunup, with international discs spun by a smooth-talkin' local DJ. Check out **Cot Bam** (☎ 809/444–2050) on Grand Anse beach for a night of dancing, dining, and socializing. The place is open until 3 AM on Friday and Saturday, and it definitely hits the spot for visitors who want something simple, lively, and friendly for little money. Don't forget the **Beachside Terrace** (St. George's, ☎ 809/444–4247) at the Flamboyant Hotel in Grand Anse. Crab racing on Monday nights, a live steel band on Wednesdays, and a beach barbecue with calypso music on Friday evenings draw an international set who savor a casual, unpretentious environment.

Brave the twin otter to Carriacou, then buy yourself a drink at the **Hillsborough Bar** (Carriacou, ☎ 809/443–7932). The bar is a small, white, flat-topped structure on the main street of the island's seat of government, a town populated by no more than about 600 citizens, including owner Edward Primus. Rum flows freely.

13 Guadeloupe

Updated by
Jordan Simon

T'S A STEAMY HOT SATURDAY in August. There may be a tropical depression brewing somewhere to the west— it's that time of year. But the mood in Pointe-à-Pitre, Guadeloupe's commercial center, is anything but depressing. Amid music and laughter, women adorned with gold jewelry and dressed in clothes made of the traditional madras and foulard parade through the streets. Balanced on their heads are huge baskets decorated with miniature kitchen utensils and filled with mangoes, papayas, breadfruits, christophines, and other island edibles. The procession wends its way to the Cathédrale de St-Pierre et St-Paul, where a high mass is celebrated. A five-hour feast with music, song, and dance will follow.

The Fête des Cuisinières (Cooks' Festival) takes place annually in honor of St. Laurent, patron saint of cooks. The parading *cuisinières* are the island's women chefs, an honored group. This festival gives you a tempting glimpse of one of Guadeloupe's stellar attractions—its cuisine. The island's more than 200 restaurants serve some of the best food in the Caribbean.

But there is more here than meets the palate. Night owls and nature enthusiasts, hikers and bikers, scuba divers, sailors, mountain climbers, beachcombers, and hammock potatoes all can indulge themselves in Guadeloupe.

Sugar, not tourism, is Guadeloupe's primary source of income. As a result, the island's attractions are less commercialized than are those of neighboring isles. However, Guadeloupe is eager to pull in a larger share of the tourist trade, and each year more field workers opt for jobs in resorts and restaurants. Currently, about 10% of the workforce is employed in the tourism industry, compared with the situation in St. Martin/St. Maarten, where the whole island is sold to tourists. At harvesttime here in late January, the fields teem with workers cutting the sugarcane, and the roads are clogged with trucks taking the cane to distilleries.

French is Guadeloupe's official language. But even if your tongue twirls easily around a few French phrases, you will sometimes receive a bewildered response. The Guadeloupeans' Creole patois greatly affects their French pronunciation. However, their friendliness allows for repeated attempts at communication, so eventually you'll be understood. If not, don't despair—most hotels and many of the restaurants have some English-speaking staff.

Guadeloupe looks like a giant butterfly resting on the sea between Antigua and Dominica. Its two wings—Basse-Terre and Grande-Terre— are the two largest islands in the 659-square-mile Guadeloupe archipelago, which includes the little islands of Marie-Galante, La Désirade, and Les Saintes, as well as French St. Martin and St. Barthélemy to the north. Mountainous 312-square-mile Basse-Terre ("low land") lies on the leeward side, where the winds are "lower." Smaller, flatter Grande-Terre (218 square miles) gets the "bigger" winds on its windward side. The Rivière Salée, a 4-mile seawater channel flowing between the Caribbean and the Atlantic, forms the "spine" of the butterfly. A drawbridge over the channel connects the two islands. Driving around the islands is the best way to fully appreciate their diversity.

If you're seeking resort hotels, casinos, and white sandy beaches, your target is Grande-Terre. By contrast, Basse-Terre's national park, laced with mountain trails and washed by waterfalls and rivers, is a 74,100-acre haven for hikers, nature lovers, and anyone yearning to peer into the steaming crater of an active volcano. If you want to get away from it all, head for the islands of Les Saintes, La Désirade, and Marie-Galante.

Christopher Columbus "discovered" Guadeloupe on November 4, 1493, when he landed at Ste-Marie on the southern shore of Basse-Terre. He named the island for Santa Marie de Guadeloupe de Estremadura. The Carib inhabitants, who had already polished off the peaceful Arawaks, had no intention of relinquishing the land they called Karukéra (Island of Beautiful Waters), and the Spaniards gave up on the island in 1604. In 1635, the French laid claim to it. They ran the Caribs off and brought in African slaves to work their sugar plantations, and in 1674 Guadeloupe was annexed by France. The British also had designs on the island, and they controlled it from 1759 until 1763, when they relinquished it in exchange for all French rights to Canada. During the French Revolution, battles broke out between royalists and revolutionaries on the island. In 1794, Britain responded to the call from Guadeloupe royalists to come to their aid, and that same year France dispatched Victor Hugues to sort things out. (In virtually every town and village you'll run across a "Victor Hugues" street, boulevard, or park.) After his troops banished the British, Hugues issued a decree abolishing slavery and guillotined recalcitrant planters. The ones who managed to keep their heads fled to Louisiana or hid in the hills of Grande-Terre, where their descendants now live. Hugues was soon relieved of his command, slavery was reestablished by Napoléon, and the French and English continued to battle over the island. The 1815 Treaty of Paris restored Guadeloupe to France, and in 1848, due largely to the efforts of Alsatian Victor Schoelcher, slavery was permanently abolished. The island has been a full-fledged *département* of France since 1946, and in 1974 it was elevated to a *région,* administered by a prefect appointed from Paris by the minister of the interior.

Before You Go

Tourist Information

For information contact the **French West Indies Tourist Board** by calling France-on-Call at 900/990–0040 (50¢ per minute 9 AM–7 PM EST), or write to the **French Government Tourist Office,** 610 5th Ave., New York, NY 10020; 9454 Wilshire Blvd., Beverly Hills, CA 90212; 645 N. Michigan Ave., Chicago, IL 60611. In Canada contact the French Government Tourist Office, 1981 McGill College Ave., Suite 490, Montreal, Québec H3A 2W9, ☎ 514/288–4264 or 30 St. Patrick St., Suite 700, Toronto, Ontario M5T 3A3, ☎ 416/593–6427. In the United Kingdom the tourist office can be reached at 178 Piccadilly, London, United Kingdom W1V 0AL, ☎ 0171/499–6911.

Arriving and Departing

BY PLANE

American Airlines (☎ 800/433–7300) is usually the most convenient, with year-round daily flights from more than 100 U.S. cities direct to San Juan and nonstop connections to Guadeloupe via American Eagle. **Air Canada** (☎ 800/422–6232) flies direct from Montreal and Toronto. **Air France** (☎ 800/237–2747) flies nonstop from Paris and Fort-de-France and has direct service from Miami and San Juan. **Air Guadeloupe** (☎ 590/87–53–74) flies daily from St. Martin and St. Maarten, St. Barts, Marie-Galante, La Désirade, and Les Saintes. **LIAT** (☎ 212/251–1717) flies from St. Croix, Antigua, and St. Maarten in the north and is your best bet from Dominica, Martinique, St. Lucia, Grenada, Barbados, and Trinidad.

FROM THE AIRPORT

You'll land at La Raizet International Airport, 2½ miles from Pointe-à-Pitre. Cabs are lined up outside the airport. The metered fare is about 60F to Pointe-à-Pitre, 90F to Gosier, and 200F to St-François. Fares go up 40% on Sundays and holidays and from 9 PM to 7 AM nightly. For 5F, you can take a bus from the airport to downtown Pointe-à-Pitre.

BY BOAT

Major cruise lines call regularly, docking at berths in downtown Pointe-à-Pitre about a block from the shopping district. **Trans Antilles Express** (☎ 590/83–12–45) and **Transport Maritime Brudey Frères** (☎ 590/90–04–48) provide ferry service to and from Marie-Galante and Les Saintes. The *Jetcat* and *Madras* ferries depart daily from the pier at Pointe-à-Pitre for Marie-Galante starting at 8 AM (check the schedule). The trip takes one hour, and the fare is 160F round-trip. For Les Saintes, Trans Antilles Express connects daily from Pointe-à-Pitre at 8 AM and from Terre-de-Haut at 4 PM. The trip takes 45 minutes and costs 160F round-trip. The *Socimade* (☎ 590/88–48–63) runs between La Désirade and St-François, departing daily at 8 AM and 4 PM. Return ferries depart daily at 3:30 PM. These schedules are subject to change and should be verified through your hotel or at the tourist office. The **Caribbean Express** (☎ 590/83–04–43) operates from Guadeloupe's Pointe-à-Pitre to Dominica and Martinique. The fare to Dominica is 450F, and the ride takes 2½ hours; the fare to Martinique is 450F and takes 4 hours. The ferry departs from Pointe-à-Pitre at 8 AM four days a week, but check the schedules because they frequently change.

Passports and Visas

U.S. and Canadian citizens need only proof of citizenship. A passport is best (even one that expired up to five years ago). Other acceptable documents are a notarized birth certificate with a raised seal (not a photocopy) or a voter registration card accompanied by a government-authorized photo ID. A free temporary visa, good only for your stay in Guadeloupe, will be issued to you upon your arrival at the airport. British citizens need a valid passport, but no visa. In addition, all visitors must hold an ongoing or return ticket.

Language

The official language is French. Everyone also speaks a Creole patois, which you won't be able to understand even if you're fluent in French. In the major tourist hotels, most of the staff knows some English. However, communicating may be more difficult in the smaller hotels and restaurants in the countryside. Some taxi drivers speak a little English. Arm yourself with a phrase book, a dictionary, patience, and a sense of humor.

Precautions

Put your valuables in the hotel safe. Don't leave them unattended in your room or on the beach. Keep an eye out for motorcyclists riding double, as they sometimes play the notorious game of veering close to the sidewalk and snatching shoulder bags. It isn't a good idea to walk around Pointe-à-Pitre at night, because it's almost deserted after dark. If you rent a car, always lock it with luggage and valuables stashed out of sight.

The rough Atlantic waters off the northeast coast of Grande-Terre are dangerous for swimming.

Ask permission before taking a picture of an islander, and don't be surprised if the answer is a firm "No." Guadeloupeans are also deeply religious and traditional. Don't offend them by wearing short shorts or swimwear off the beach.

Staying in Guadeloupe

Important Addresses

Tourist Information: The **Office Départemental du Tourism** has an office in Pointe-à-Pitre (5 Square de la Banque B.P. 1099, 97181 Cedex, ☎ 590/82–09–30). The office is open weekdays 8–5, Saturday 8–noon. A tourist information booth is at the airport.

EMERGENCIES

Police: In Pointe-à-Pitre (☎ 590/82–00–17), in BasseTerre (☎ 590/81–11–55). **Fire:** In Pointe-à-Pitre (☎ 590/83–04–76), in Basse-Terre (☎ 590/81–19–22). **SOS ambulance:** ☎ 590/82–89–33. **Hospitals:** There is a 24-hour emergency room at the main hospital, **Centre Hopitalier de Pointe-à-Pitre** (Abymes, ☎ 590/89–10–100). There are 23 clinics and five hospitals located around the island. The tourist office or your hotel can assist you in locating an English-speaking doctor. **Pharmacies:** Pharmacies alternate in staying open around the clock. The tourist office or your hotel can help you locate the one that's on duty.

Currency

Legal tender is the French franc, which is equal to 100 centimes. At press time (spring 1995), U.S.$1 bought 5.20F and £1 bought 8.10F, but currencies fluctuate daily. Check the current rate of exchange around the time of your departure. Some places accept U.S. dollars, but it's best to change your money into the local currency. Credit cards are accepted in most major hotels, restaurants, and shops, less so in smaller places and in the countryside. Prices are quoted here in U.S. dollars unless otherwise noted.

Taxes and Service Charges

The *taxe de séjour* varies from hotel to hotel but never exceeds $1.50 per person, per day. Most hotel prices include a 10%–15% service charge; if not, it will be added to your bill.

Restaurants are legally required to include 15% gratuity in the menu price, and no additional gratuity is necessary. Tip skycaps and porters about 5F. Many cab drivers own their own cabs and don't expect a tip. You won't have any trouble ascertaining if a 10% tip is expected.

Guided Tours

There are set fares for taxi tours to various points on the island. The tourist office or your hotel can arrange for an English-speaking taxi driver and even organize a small group for you to share the cost of the tour.

Norbert Noel Robert (Pointe-à-Pitre, ☎ 590/82–97–86) speaks excellent English, loves to talk, knows *everybody,* and is a font of information (practical or not). **George-Marie Gabrielle** (Pointe-à-Pitre, ☎ 590/82–05–38) offers half- and full-day excursions around the island. A modern bus with an English-speaking guide will pick you up at your hotel. **Organisation des Guides de Montagne de la Caraibe,** O.G.M.C. (Maison Forestière, Matouba, ☎ 590/94–29–11), provides guides for hiking tours in the mountains. **Parfum d'Aventure** (St-François, ☎ 590/88–47–62) offers adventure excursions in Basse-Terre, including canyoning, canoeing on the Lézarde, sea kayaking, hikes from easy to grueling, and four-wheel drives.

Getting Around

TAXIS

Taxis are metered and fairly pricey. During the day you'll pay about 60F from the airport to Pointe-à-Pitre, about 90F to Gosier, and about 200F to St-François. On Sundays, holidays, and between 9 PM and 7 AM, fares increase 40%. If your French is in working order, you can contact radio cabs at 590/82–00–00, 590/82–13–67, and 590/20–74–74.

BUSES

Modern public buses run from 5:30 AM to 7:30 PM. They stop along the road at bus stops and shelters marked ARRET-BUS, but you can also flag one down along the route.

VESPAS OR BIKES

If you opt to tour the island by bike, you won't be alone. Biking is a major sport here (*see* Sports and the Outdoors, *below,* for rental information).

Vespas (motorbikes) can be rented at **Vespa Sun** (many locations in Pointe-à-Pitre, ☎ 590/82–17–80) and **Equator Moto** (Gosier, ☎ 590/90–36–77). A scooter generally costs 200F per day including insurance. You'll need to put down a 1,000F deposit.

RENTAL CARS

Your valid driver's license will suffice for up to 20 days, after which you'll need an international driver's permit. Guadeloupe has 1,225 miles of excellent roads (marked as in Europe), and driving around Grande-Terre is relatively easy. On Basse-Terre it will take more effort to navigate the hairpin bends that twist through the mountains and around the eastern shore. Guadeloupeans are skillful drivers, but they do like to drive fast. Cars can be rented at **Avis** (☎ 590/82–33–47 or 800/331–1212), **Budget** (☎ 590/82–95–58 or 800/527–0700), **Hertz** (☎ 590/84–57–94 or 800/654–3131), **Thrifty** (☎ 590/91–55–66), and **Eurorent** (☎ 590/91–42–16). There are rental offices at the airport as well as at the major resort areas. Car rentals cost a bit more on Guadeloupe than on the other islands: Count on about $60 a day for a small rental car. Insist on a Peugeot or Ford rather than a Citroen, which seem to break down more easily on rutted roads and in the rain forest.

Telephones and Mail

To call from the United States, dial 011–590, then the local six-digit number. (To call person-to-person, dial 01–590.) It is not possible to place collect or credit card calls to the United States from Guadeloupe. Coin-operated phones are rare but can be found in restaurants and cafés. If you need to make many calls outside of your hotel, purchase a Telecarte at the post office or other outlets marked "Telecarte en Vente Ici." Telecartes look like credit cards and are used in special booths labeled "Telecom." Local and international calls made with the cards are cheaper than operator-assisted calls.

To call the United States from Guadeloupe, dial 19 + 1 + the area code and phone number. To dial locally in Guadeloupe, simply dial the six-digit phone number.

Postcards to the United States cost 3.70F; letters up to 20 grams, 4.60F. Stamps can be purchased at the post office, *café-tabacs,* hotel newsstands, and souvenir shops. Postcards and letters to the United Kingdom cost 3.60F.

Opening and Closing Times

Banks are open weekdays 8–noon and 2–4. Credit Agricole, Banque Populaire, and Société Générale de Banque aux Antilles have branches that are open Saturday. During the summer most banks are open 8–3. Banks close at noon the day before a legal holiday that falls during the week. As a rule, shops are open weekdays 8 or 8:30–noon and 2:30–6, but hours are flexible when cruise ships are in town.

Exploring Guadeloupe

Numbers in the margin correspond to points of interest on the Guadeloupe map.

Pointe-à-Pitre

 Pointe-à-Pitre is a city of some 100,000 people in the southwest of Grande-Terre. It lies almost on the "backbone" of the butterfly, near the bridge that crosses the Salée River. In this bustling, noisy city, with narrow streets, honking horns, and traffic jams, there is a faster pulse than in many other Caribbean capitals, though at night the city streets are deserted.

Life has not been easy for Pointe-à-Pitre. The city has suffered severe damage over the years as a result of earthquakes, fires, and hurricanes. The most recent damage was done in 1979 by Hurricane Frederick, in 1980 by Hurricane David, and in 1989 by Hurricane Hugo. Standing on the rue Frébault, you can see on one side the remaining French colonial structures and on the other, the modern city. However, downtown is rejuvenating itself while maintaining its old charm. Completion of the Centre St-John Perse has meant the transformation of old warehouses into a new cruise-terminal complex that consists of a hotel (the Hotel St-John), three restaurants, space for 80 shops, and the headquarters for Guadeloupe's Port Authority.

Stop at the tourist office, in Place de la Victoire across from the quays where the cruise ships dock, to pick up maps and brochures. *Bonjour, Guadeloupe* and *Living in Guadeloupe,* the free visitors' guides, are very useful. Outside the office, stalls take over the sidewalk, selling everything from clothes to kitchen utensils. Across the road along the harbor, a gaggle of colorfully dressed women sells fruits and vegetables.

When you leave the office, turn left, walk one block along rue Schoelcher, and turn right on rue Achille René-Boisneuf. Two more blocks will bring you to the **Musée St-John Perse.** The restored colonial "Steamboat Gothic" house is dedicated to the Guadeloupean poet who won the 1960 Nobel Prize in literature. (Nearby, at No. 54 rue René-Boisneuf, a plaque marks his birthplace.) The museum contains a complete collection of his poetry, as well as some of his personal belongings. There are also works written about him and various mementos, documents, and photographs. *Corner rues Noizières and Achille René-Boisneuf,* ☎ *590/90–01–92.* ☛ *10F.* ☼ *Thurs.–Tues. 9–5.*

Rues Noizières, Frébault, and Schoelcher are Pointe-à-Pitre's main shopping streets. In sharp contrast to the duty-free shops is the bustling **marketplace,** which you'll find by backtracking one block from the museum and turning right on rue Frébault. Located between rues St-John Perse, Frébault, Schoelcher, and Peynier, the market is a cacophonous and colorful place where housewives bargain for papayas, breadfruits, christophines, tomatoes, and a bright assortment of other produce.

Take a left at the corner of rues Schoelcher and Peynier. The **Musée Schoelcher** honors the memory of Victor Schoelcher, the 19th-century Alsatian abolitionist who fought against slavery in the French West Indies. The museum contains many of his personal effects, and the exhibits trace his life and work. *24 rue Peynier,* ☎ *590/82–08–04.* ☛ *10F.* ☼ *Weekdays 8:30–11:30 and 2–5.*

Walk back along rue Peynier past the market for three blocks. You'll come to **Place de la Victoire,** surrounded by wood buildings with balconies and shutters. Many sidewalk cafés have opened up on this revitalized square, making it a good place for lunch or light refreshments. The square was named in honor of Victor Hugues's 1794 victory over the British. The sandbox trees in the park are said to have been planted by Hugues the day after the victory. During the French Revolution, Hugues's guillotine in this square lopped off the heads of many a white aristocrat. Today the large palm-shaded park is a popular gathering place. The tourist office is at the harbor end of the square.

Rue Duplessis runs between the southern edge of the park and La Darse, the head of the harbor, where fishing boats dock and fast motorboats depart for the choppy ride to Marie-Galante and Les Saintes.

Rue Bebian is the western border of the square. Walk north along it (away from the harbor) and turn left on rue Alexandre Isaac. You'll see the imposing **Cathédrale de St-Pierre et St-Paul,** which dates from 1847. Mother Nature's rampages have wreaked havoc on the church, and it is now reinforced with iron ribs. Hurricane Hugo took out many of the upper windows and shutters, but the lovely stained-glass windows survived intact.

Grande-Terre

This round-trip tour of **Grande-Terre** will cover about 85 miles. Drive south out of Pointe-à-Pitre on Route N4 (named the "Riviera Road" in honor of the man-made beaches and resort hotels of Bas-du-Fort). The road goes past the marina, which is always crowded with yachts and cabin cruisers. The numerous boutiques and restaurants surrounding the marina make it popular in the evening.

The road turns east and heads along the coast. In 2 miles you'll sight ❷ **Fort Fleur d'Epée,** an 18th century fortress that hunkers on a hillside behind a deep moat. This was the scene of hard-fought battles between the French and the English. You can explore the well-preserved dungeons and battlements and, on a clear day, take in a sweeping view of Iles des Saintes and Marie-Galante.

❸ The **Guadeloupe Aquarium** is just past the fort off the main highway. This aquarium, one of the Caribbean's largest and most modern, also ranks fourth in all of France. *Place Créole (just off Rte. N4),* ☎ *590/90–92–38.* ☛ *38F adults, 20F children 5 and older.* ☉ *Daily 9–7.*

❹ **Gosier,** a major tourist center 2 miles farther east, is a busy place indeed, with big hotels and tiny inns, cafés, nightclubs, shops, a casino, and a long stretch of sand. The Creole Beach, the Auberge de la Vieille Tour, and the Canella Beach are among the hotels here.

Breeze along the coast through the little hamlet of St-Felix and on to ❺ **Ste-Anne,** about 8 miles east of Gosier. Only ruined sugar mills remain from the days in the early 18th century when this village was a major sugar-exporting center. Sand has replaced sugar as the town's most valuable asset. The soft white-sand beaches here are among the best in Guadeloupe. On a more spiritual note, you'll pass Ste-Anne's lovely cemetery with stark-white aboveground tombs.

Don't fret about leaving the beaches of Ste-Anne behind you as you head eastward. The entire south coast of Grande-Terre is scalloped with white-sand beaches. Eight miles along, just before coming to the blue-❻ roof houses of **St-François,** you'll come to the Raisins-Clairs beach, another beauty.

Guadeloupe

KEY

⛴ Cruise Ship
⛴ Ferry
❶ Exploring Sites
㉟ Hotels and Restaurants

Le Corsaire, **62**
Le Côte Jardin, **52**
Le Flibustier, **63**
Le Karacoli, **37**
Le Touloulou, **79**
Les Gommiers, **40**
Les Oiseaux, **66**
Relais des Iles, **44**

Lodging
Auberge de la Distillerie, **49**
Auberge de la Vieille Tour, **54**
Bois Joli, **47**
Canella Beach Residence, **60**
Cap Sud Caraibes, **59**
Club Méditerranée La Caravelle, **64**
Domaine de Petite Anse, **41**
Fleur d'Epée Novotel, **53**
Fort Royal Touring Club, **38**
Golf Marine Club Hotel, **72**
Grand Anse Hotel, **42**
Hamak, **71**
La Cocoteraie, **69**
La Créole Beach Hotél, **57**
La Plantation Ste Marthe, **73**
La Sucrerie du Comté, **36**
L'Auberge Les Petits Saints aux Anacardies, **46**
Le Domaine de l'Anse des Rochers, **67**
Le Meridien St. François, **70**
L'Orchidée, **58**
Relais du Moulin, **65**
Tropical Club Hotel, **75**
Village Créole, **45**

St-François was once a simple little village primarily involved with fishing and tomatoes. The fish and tomatoes are still here, but so are some of the island's ritziest hotels. This is the home of the Hamak and Le Méridien's extension, La Cocoteraie, two very plush properties. Avenue de l'Europe runs between the well-groomed 18-hole Robert Trent Jones municipal golf course and the man-made marina. On the marina side, a string of shops, hotels, and restaurants caters to tourists.

7 To reach **Pointe des Châteaux,** take the narrow road east from St-François and drive 8 miles out onto the rugged promontory that is the easternmost point on the island. The Atlantic and the Caribbean waters join here and crash against huge rocks, carving them into castlelike shapes. The jagged, majestic cliffs are reminiscent of the headlands of Brittany. The only human contribution to this dramatic scene is a white cross high on a hill above the tumultuous waters. From this point there are spectacular views of the south and east coasts of Guadeloupe and the distant cliffs of La Désirade.

TIME OUT   **Paillote** (☎ 590/88–63–61) is a tiny roadside stand right on the *pointe* where you can get libations and light bites, such as lobster and fish grilled on a wood fire.

About 2 miles from the farthest point, a rugged dirt road crunches off to the north and leads to the nudist beach Pointe Tarare.

Take Route N5 north from St-François for a drive through fragrant silvery-green seas of sugarcane. About 4 miles beyond St-François
8 you'll see **Zévalos,** a handsome colonial mansion that was once the manor house of the island's largest sugar plantation.

9 Four miles northwest you'll come to **Le Moule,** a port city of about 17,000 people. This busy city was once the capital of Guadeloupe. It was bombarded by the British in 1794 and 1809 and by a hurricane in 1928. Canopies of flamboyants hang over narrow streets, where colorful vegetable and fish markets do a brisk business. The small buildings are of weathered wood with shutters, balconies, and bright awnings. The town hall, with graceful balustrades, and a small 19th-century neoclassical church are on the main square. Le Moule also has a beautiful crescent-shape beach. A mile to the east is an excellent beach protected by a reef, making it perfect for windsurfing; boards may be rented from the Tropical Club Hotel (☎ 590/93–97–97).

10 North of Le Moule, archaeologists have uncovered the remains of Arawak and Carib settlements. The **Edgar-Clerc Archaeological Museum,** 3 miles out of Le Moule in the direction of Campêche, contains Amerindian artifacts from the personal collection of this well-known archaeologist and historian. There are several rooms with displays pertaining to the Carib and Arawak civilizations. *La Rosette,* ☎ 590/23–57–57. ☛ Free. ☉ *Thurs.–Tues. 9–12:30 and 2–5.*

From Le Moule you can turn west on Route D101 to return to Pointe-à-Pitre or continue northwest to see the rugged north coast.

To reach the coast, drive 8 miles northwest along Route D120 to Campêche, going through Gros-Cap.

TIME OUT   **Château de Feuilles** (☎ 590/22–30–30), between Le Moule and Campêche (nearer Gros-Cap), is an absolutely superb place for a long lunch. A mini-estate, the château has style and excellent cuisine. Bring your swimming togs and use the pool while lunch is being prepared (*see* Dining, *below*).

🕕 Turn north on Route D122 1½ miles north of Campêche. **Porte d'Enfer** (Gate of Hell) marks a dramatic point on the coast where two jagged cliffs are stormed by the wild Atlantic waters. One legend has it that a Madame Coco strolled out across the waves carrying a parasol and vanished without a trace.

🕘 Four miles from Porte d'Enfer is **La Pointe de la Grande Vigie,** the northernmost tip of the island. Park your car and walk along the paths that lead right out to the edge. There is a splendid view of Porte d'Enfer from here, and on a clear day you can see Antigua, 35 miles away.

🕚 **Anse Bertrand,** the northernmost village in Guadeloupe, lies 4 miles south of La Pointe de la Grande Vigie along a gravel road. Drive carefully. En route you'll pass Anse Laborde, another good beach. The area around Anse Bertrand was the last refuge of the Caribs. Most of the excitement these days takes place in the St-Jacques Hippodrome, where horse races and cockfights are held.

🕝 Route N6 will take you 5 miles south to **Port-Louis,** a fishing village of about 7,000. As you come in from the north, look for the turnoff to the Souffleur beach. It was once one of the island's prettiest, but it has become a little shabby. Still, the sand is fringed by flamboyant trees whose brilliant orange-red flowers bloom during the summer and early fall, and though the beach is crowded on weekends, it's blissfully quiet during the week. The sunsets here are something to write home about.

TIME OUT *Poisson d'Or* is a rustic seaside restaurant that serves spicy Creole dishes. *Rue Sadi Carnot, Port-Louis,* ☎ *590/22–88–75. No credit cards.*

From Port-Louis the road leads 5 miles south through mangrove swamps and turns inland at Petit Canal. Three miles east of Petit Canal, turn
🕞 right on the main road. Head 6 miles south to **Morne-à-l'Eau,** an agricultural city of about 16,000 people. Morne-à-l'Eau's unusual amphitheater-shape cemetery is the scene of a moving (and photogenic) candlelight service on All Saints' Day. Take Route N5 out of town along gently undulating hills past fields of sugarcane and dairy farms.

Just south of Morne-à-l'Eau are the villages of **Jabrun du Sud** and **Jabrun du Nord,** which are inhabited by the descendants of the "Blancs Matignon," the whites who hid in the hills and valleys of the Grands Fonds after the abolition of slavery.

Continue on Route N5 to Pointe-à-Pitre.

Basse-Terre

There is high adventure on the butterfly's west wing, which swirls with mountain trails and lakes, waterfalls, and hot springs. Basse-Terre is the home of the Old Lady, as the Soufrière volcano is called locally, as well as of the capital, also called Basse-Terre.

Guadeloupe's de rigueur tour takes you through the 74,100-acre **Parc National de la Guadeloupe,** a sizable chunk of Basse-Terre. (The park's administrative headquarters is in Basse-Terre, ☎ 590/80–24–25.) Before going, pick up a *Guide to the National Park* from the tourist office, which rates the hiking trails according to difficulty.

The Route de la Traversée (La Traversée) is a good paved road that runs east–west, cutting a 16-mile-long swath through the park to the west-coast village of Mahaut. La Traversée divides Basse-Terre into two almost equal sections. The majority of mountain trails are in the southern half. Allow a full day for the following excursion. Wear rubber-soled shoes, and take along both swimsuit and sweater, and perhaps food for a picnic. Try to get an early start to remain ahead of the hordes of cruise-ship passengers that descend on La Traversée and the park for the day.

Begin your tour by heading west from Pointe-à-Pitre on Route N1, crossing the Rivière Salée on the Pont de la Gabare drawbridge. At the Destrelan traffic circle turn left and drive 6 miles south through sweet-scented fields of sugarcane to the Route de la Traversée (aka D23), where you'll turn west.

As soon as you cross the bridge you'll begin to see the riches produced by Basse-Terre's fertile volcanic soil and heavier rainfall. La Traversée is lined with masses of thick tree ferns, shrubs, flowers, tall trees, and green plantains that stand like soldiers in a row.

Five miles from where you turned off Route N1 you'll come to a junction. Turn left and go a little over a mile south to **Vernou.** Many of the old mansions you'll see in this area remain in the hands of the original aristocratic families, the Bekés (whites in Creole), who can trace their lineage to before the French Revolution. Traipsing along a path that leads beyond the village through the lush forest you'll come to the

⑯ pretty waterfall at **Saut de la Lézarde** (Lizard's Leap), the first of many you'll see.

⑰ Back on La Traversée, 3 miles farther, you'll come to the next one, **Cascade aux Ecrevisses** (Crayfish Falls). Park your car and walk along the marked trail that leads to a splendid waterfall dashing down into the Corossol River (a fit place for a dip). Walk carefully—the rocks along the trail can be slippery.

⑱ Two miles farther along La Traversée you'll come to the **Parc Tropical de Bras-David,** where you can park and explore various nature trails. The **Maison de la Forêt** (☞ Free; open daily 9–5) has a variety of displays that describe (for those who can read French) the flora, fauna, and topography of the national park. There are picnic tables where you can enjoy your lunch in tropical splendor.

⑲ Another 2½ miles will bring you to the two mountains known as **Les Mamelles**—Mamelle de Petit-Bourg at 2,350 feet and Mamelle de Pigeon at 2,500 feet. (*Mamelle* means "breast," and when you see the mountains you'll understand why they are so named.) There is a spectacular view of the two mountains from the pass that runs between them; the vista includes a smaller mountain to the north. From this point, trails ranging from easy to arduous lace up into the surrounding mountains. There's a glorious view from the lookout point 1,969 feet up Mamelle de Pigeon. If you're a climber, you'll want to spend several hours exploring this area.

You don't have to be much of a hiker to climb the stone steps leading
⑳ from the road to the **Zoological Park and Botanical Gardens.** Titi the Raccoon is the mascot of the park. There are also cockatoos, iguanas, and turtles. The cramped cages are a sorrowful sight (you'll want to liberate the residents immediately), but the setting and views are stunning. A snack bar is open for lunch daily except Monday. *La Traversée,* ☎ 590/98–83–52. ☞ *30F adults, 20F children.* ☉ *Daily 9–5.*

On the winding 4-mile descent from the mountains to **Mahaut** you'll see patches of the blue Caribbean through the green trees. In the village of Mahaut turn left on Route N2 for the drive south along the coast. In less than a mile you'll come to **Malendure.** The big attraction here is offshore, where **Pigeon Island** sits surrounded by the Jacques Cousteau Marine Reserve. Les Heures Santes and Chez Guy, both on the Malendure Beach, conduct diving trips, and the glass-bottom *Aquarium* and *Nautilus* make daily snorkeling trips to this spectacular site.

TIME OUT Though there are a couple of café-bars on Malendure Beach, the restaurant for lunch is **Le Rocher de Malendure** (☎ 590/98–70–84), that rare tourist trap that lives up to its billing. Perched on a bluff overlooking Pigeon Island, the open-air restaurant is a gem, with dining on a series of flower-bedecked terraces affording marvelous views. Fresh seafood is the obvious lure, although you can get fine tournedos in three sauces or veal in raspberry vinaigrette. The owner can also arrange deep-sea fishing expeditions.

㉑ From Malendure continue through neighboring **Bouillante,** where hot
㉒ springs burst up through the earth, and **Vieux-Habitants,** one of the oldest settlements on the island. Pause to see the restored church, which dates from 1650, before driving 8 miles south to the capital city.

㉓ **Basse-Terre,** the capital and administrative center, is an active city of about 15,000 people. Founded in 1640, it has had even more difficulties than Pointe-à-Pitre. The capital has endured not only foreign attacks and hurricanes but sputtering threats from La Soufrière as well. More than once it has been evacuated when the volcano began to hiss and fume. The last major eruption was in the 16th century. But the volcano seemed active enough to warrant the evacuation of more than 70,000 people in 1975.

The centers of activity are the port and the market, both of which you'll pass along boulevard Général de Gaulle. The 17th-century **Fort St. Charles,** at the extreme south end of town, and the **Cathedral of Our Lady of Guadeloupe,** to the north across the Rivière aux Herbes, are worth a short visit. Drive along boulevard Felix Eboué to see the colonial buildings that house government offices. Follow the boulevard to the **Jardin Pichon** to see its beautiful gardens. Stop off at **Champ d'Arbaud,** an Old World square surrounded by colonial buildings. Continue along the boulevard to the **botanical gardens.** A steep, narrow
㉔ road leads 4 miles up to the suburb of **St-Claude,** on the slopes of La Soufrière. In St-Claude there are picnic tables and good views of the volcano. You can also get a closer look at the volcano by driving up to the Savane à Mulets. From there leave your car and hike (with an experienced guide) the strenuous two-hour climb to the summit at 4,813 feet, the highest point in the Lesser Antilles. Water boils out of the eastern slope of the volcano and spills into the Carbet Falls.

㉕ Drive 2 miles farther north from St-Claude to visit **Matouba,** a village settled by East Indians whose descendants still practice ancient rites, including animal sacrifice. If you've an idle 10 hours or so, take off from Matouba for a 19-mile hike on a marked trail through the Monts Caraibes to the east coast.

Descend and continue east on Route N1 for 4 miles to **Gourbeyre.** Visit
㉖ **Etang As de Pique.** Reaching this lake, 2,454 feet above the town, is another challenge for hikers, but you can also get to it in an hour by car via paved Palmetto Road. The 5-acre lake, formed by a lava flow, is shaped like an *as de pique* (ace of spades).

From Gourbeyre you have the option of continuing east along Route N1 or backtracking to the outskirts of Basse-Terre and taking the roller coaster–like Route D6 along the coast. Either route will take you through lush greenery to **Trois-Rivières.**

㉗ Not far from the ferry landing for Les Saintes is the **Parc Archéologique des Roches Gravées,** which contains a collection of pre-Columbian rock engravings. Pick up an information sheet at the park's entrance. Displays interpret the figures of folk and fauna depicted on the petroglyphs. The park is set in a lovely botanical garden that is off the beaten track for many tourists, so it remains a haven of tranquillity. *Bord de la Mer, Trois-Rivières,* ☎ 590/92–91–88. ☞ *4F.* ☉ *Daily 9–5.*

㉘ Continue for 5 miles, through banana fields and the village of Bananier, to reach the village of **St-Sauveur,** gateway to the magnificent **Chutes du Carbet** (Carbet Falls). Three of the chutes, which drop from 65 feet, 360 feet, and 410 feet, can be reached by following the narrow, steep, and spiraling Habituée Road for 5 miles up past the **Grand Etang** (Great Pond). At the end of the road you'll have to proceed on foot. Well-marked but slippery trails lead to viewing points of the chutes.

TIME OUT   You can have a hearty lunch of Creole chicken, curried goat, or crayfish at **Chez Dollin-Le Crepuscule** (Habituée Village, ☎ 590/86–34–56) before or after viewing the falls. There's also a four-course menu.

㉙ Continue along Route N1 for 3 miles toward **Capesterre-Belle-Eau.** You'll cross the Carbet River and come to **Dumanoir Alley,** lined with century-old royal palms.

㉚ Three miles farther along, through fields of pineapples, bananas, and sugarcane, you'll arrive at **Ste-Marie,** where Columbus landed in 1493. In the town there is a monument to the Great Discoverer.

Seventeen miles farther north you'll return to Pointe-à-Pitre.

Iles des Saintes

㉛ This eight-island archipelago, usually referred to as **Les Saintes,** dots the waters off the south coast of Guadeloupe. The islands are Terre-de-Haut, Terre-de-Bas, Ilet à Cabrit, Grand Ilet, La Redonde, La Coche, Le Pâté, and Les Augustins. Columbus discovered the islands on November 4, 1493, and christened them Los Santos in honor of All Saints' Day.

Of the islands, only Terre-de-Haut and Terre-de-Bas are inhabited, with a combined population of 3,260. Many of les Saintois, as the islanders are called, are fair-haired, blue-eyed descendants of Breton and Norman sailors. Fishing is the main source of income for les Saintois, and the shores are lined with their fishing boats and *filets bleus* (blue nets dotted with burnt-orange buoys). The fishermen wear hats called *salakos,* which look like inverted saucers or coolie hats. They are patterned after a hat said to have been brought here by a seafarer from China or Indonesia.

With 5 square miles and a population of about 1,500, Terre-de-Haut is the largest island and the most developed for tourism. Its "big city" is Bourg, which boasts one street and a few bistros, cafés, and shops. Clutching the hillside are trim white houses with bright red or blue doors, balconies, and gingerbread frills.

Getting to Terre-de-Haut is an exhilarating affair, whether by land or sea. Air Guadeloupe has regularly scheduled flights, and your whole life may flash before your eyes as you soar down to the tiny airstrip. However, the flight is mercifully brief, and you may prefer it to the choppy 35-minute ferry crossing from Trois-Rivières or the 60-minute ride from Pointe-à-Pitre. Ferries leave Trois-Rivières at about 8:30 AM (7:30 AM on Sunday) and return about 3 PM. From Pointe-à-Pitre the usual departure time is 8 AM, with return at 4 PM. The round-trip fare from either point is 160F. Check with the tourist office for up-to-date ferry schedules.

Terre-de-Haut's ragged coastline is scalloped with lovely coves and beaches, including the nudist beach at Anse Crawen. The beautiful bay, complete with sugarloaf, has been called a mini Rio. This is a quiet, peaceful getaway, but it may not remain unspoiled. Tourism is increasing and now accounts for 50% of the economy. Although government plans call for a total of only 250 hotel rooms, the tourist-related industries are making a major pitch for more facilities for tourists. Although it makes a great day trip, you'll really get a feel for Les Saintes only if you stay over.

There are three paved roads on the island, but don't even think about driving here. The roads are ghastly, and backing up is a minor art form, choreographed on those frequent occasions when two vehicles meet on one of the steep, narrow roads. The four minibuses that transport passengers from the airstrip and the wharf double as tour buses. However, the island is so small you can get around by walking. It's a mere five-minute stroll from the airstrip and ferry dock to downtown Bourg.

32 **Fort Napoléon** is a relic from the period when the French fortified these islands against the Caribs and the English, but nobody has ever fired a shot at or from it. Inside is a museum whose galleries hold a collection of 250 modern paintings, heavily influenced by Cubism and Surrealism and hung at odd angles, and an exhaustive exhibit on the important naval Battle of Les Saintes (history buffs may recall Admiral de Grasse from the American Revolution). You can also visit the well-preserved barracks and prison cells and admire the surrounding botanical gardens, which specialize in cacti of all sizes and descriptions. From the fort you can see Fort Josephine across the channel on the Ilet à Cabrit. *Bourg, no* ☎. ☛ *15F adults, 5F children 6–12.* ⊙ *Daily 9–12:30.*

For such a tiny place, Terre-de-Haut offers a variety of hotels and restaurants. For details, *see* Dining and Lodging, *below.* There are also the **Centre Nautique des Saintes** (Plage de la Coline, ☎ 590/99–54–25) and **Espace Plongé Caraibes** (Bourg, ☎ 590/99–51–84), should you wish to scuba dive off the islands.

Marie-Galante

Columbus sighted this flat island on November 3, 1493, the day before he landed at Ste-Marie on Basse-Terre. He named it for his flagship, the *Maria Galanda*, and sailed on.

The ferry departs from Pointe-à-Pitre at 8 AM, 2 PM, and 5 PM with returns at 6 AM, 9 AM, and 3:45 PM. (Schedules often change, especially on the weekends, so check them at the tourist office or the harbor offices.) The round-trip costs 160F. You'll put in at Grand Bourg, the major city, with a population of about 8,000. A plane will land you 2 miles from Grand Bourg. If your French or phrase book is good enough, you can negotiate a price with the taxi drivers for touring the island.

33 Covering about 60 square miles, **Marie-Galante** is the largest of Guadeloupe's islands. It is dotted with ruined 19th-century sugar mills, and sugar is still one of its major products—the others are cotton and rum. One of the last refuges of the Caribs when they were driven from the mainland by the French, the island is now a favorite retreat of Guadeloupeans, who come on weekends to enjoy the beach at Petit-Anse.

You'll find dramatic coastal scenery, with soaring cliffs holding an angry ocean at bay, such as the Gueule Grand Gouffre (Mouth of the Giant Chasm) and Les Galeries (where millennia of erosion have sculpted a natural arcade), and enormous sun-dappled grottoes like Le Trou à Diable, whose underground river can be explored with a guide. Don't miss the **Château Murat** (☏ 590/97–03–79; ☛ 10F adults, 5F children 6–12; open daily 9:15–5), a restored 17th-century sugar plantation and rum distillery that houses exhibits on the history of rum-making and sugarcane production, as well as the admirable Ecomusée, whose displays celebrate local crafts and customs. And do visit the distilleries, especially Père Labat, whose rum is considered one of the finest in the Caribbean and whose atelier turns out lovely pottery.

There are several places near the ferry landing where you can get an inexpensive meal of seafood and Creole sauce. If you want to stay over, you can choose from Au Village de Ménard (5 bungalows, ☏ 590/97–77–02) in St-Louis, Auberge de l'Arbre à Pain (7 rooms, ☏ 590/97–73–69) in Grand Bourg, or Hotel Hajo (6 rooms, ☏ 590/97–32–76) in Capesterre. An entertainment complex in Grand Bourg called El Rancho has a 400-seat movie theater, a restaurant, terrace grill, snack bar, disco, and a few double rooms.

La Désirade

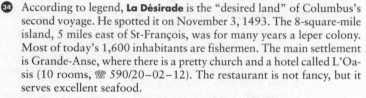

According to legend, **La Désirade** is the "desired land" of Columbus's second voyage. He spotted it on November 3, 1493. The 8-square-mile island, 5 miles east of St-François, was for many years a leper colony. Most of today's 1,600 inhabitants are fishermen. The main settlement is Grande-Anse, where there is a pretty church and a hotel called L'Oasis (10 rooms, ☏ 590/20–02–12). The restaurant is not fancy, but it serves excellent seafood.

There are good beaches here, notably Souffleur and Baie Mahault, and there's little to do but loll around on them. The island is virtually unspoiled by tourism and is likely to remain so in the foreseeable future.

Three or four minibuses meet the flights and ferries, and you can negotiate with one of them to get a tour. Ferries depart from St-François daily at 8 and 4. The return ferry departs daily at 3:30. However, be sure to check schedules.

Off the Beaten Track

Far fewer tourists explore the northern half of Basse-Terre, yet there are several worthwhile attractions, not the least of which is the magnificent coastal road, skirting cliffs and tiny coves, dancing in and out of thick stands of mahogany and gommier trees, and weaving through unspoiled fishing villages with boats and ramshackle houses as brightly colored as a child's fingerpainting. Just north of Mahaut is Pointe-Noire, where you can visit La Maison du Bois (☏ 590/98–17–09; ☛ 5F; open Tues.–Sun. 9:30–5:30), for a glimpse into the traditional use of wood on the island. Superbly crafted musical instruments and furnishings are on sale. Just across the road is La Maison du Cacao (☏ 590/98–21–23; ☛ 25F adults, 15F children under 12; open daily 9–5), a working cocoa plantation. Farther north, Ste-Rose offers Le Domaine de Severin, a rum distillery (☏ 590/28–91–86; ☛ Free; open daily 8:30–12:30); the restaurant is well known for its fine lunches. The nearby Musée du Rhum (Bellevue, Ste-Rose, ☏ 590/28–70–04; open Mon.–Sat. 9–1) is interesting, but expensive at 40F (25F children). It features the usual exhibits on the history of rum distillation and an extensive collection of insects from the grotesque to the luminous upstairs. On the way back to Pointe-à-Pitre on N4, you'll see signs to the Ravine Chaude (Lamentin, ☏ 590/25–75–92; ☛ 20F; open daily 8–8), a superlative spa that draws upon the area's healthful geothermal waters. The ultramodern establishment caters almost entirely to locals; massage, sauna, kinesotherapy, algae masks, and hydrotherapy are some of the available treatments.

Beaches

Guadeloupe's beaches, all free and open to the public, generally have no facilities. For a small fee, hotels allow nonguests to use changing facilities, towels, and beach chairs. You'll find long stretches of white sand on Grande-Terre. On the south coast of Basse-Terre the beaches have gray volcanic sand, and on the northwest coast the color is golden-tan. There are several nudist beaches (noted below), and topless bathing is commonplace at the resort hotels. Note that the Atlantic waters on the northeast coast of Grande-Terre are too rough for swimming.

Ilet du Gosier is a little speck off the shore of Gosier where you can bathe in the buff. Make arrangements for water-sports rentals and boat trips to the island through the Creole Beach Hotel in Gosier (☎ 590/ 90–46–46). Take along a picnic for an all-day outing. *Beach closed weekends.*

Some of the island's best beaches of soft white sand lie on the coast of Grande-Terre from Ste-Anne to Pointe des Châteaux. One of the longest and prettiest stretches is just outside the town of Ste-Anne at **Caravelle Beach,** though there are rather dilapidated shacks and cafés scattered about the area. Protected by reefs, the beach makes a fine place for snorkeling. Club Med, with its staggering array of activities, occupies one end of this beach.

Just outside of St-François is **Raisin-Clairs,** home of Le Méridien (☎ 590/88–51–00), which rents Windsurfers, water skis, and sailboats.

Between St-François and Pointe des Châteaux, **Anse de la Gourde** is a beautiful stretch of sand that becomes very popular on weekends. **La Langouste** (☎ 590/88–52–19), a lunch spot popular on the weekends, guards the entrance to the beach.

Tarare is a secluded strip just before the tip of Pointe des Châteaux; many bathe naked there. There is a small bar-café located where you park, a four-minute walk from the beach.

Just outside of Deshaies, on the northwest coast of Basse-Terre, **La Grande Anse** is a secluded beach of soft beige sand sheltered by palms. There's a large parking area but no facilities other than the Karacoli restaurant, which sits with its "feet in the water," ready to serve you rum punch and Creole dishes.

All along the western shore of Basse-Terre you'll see signposts to small beaches. The sand starts turning gray as you reach Pigeon Island; it becomes volcanic black as you work your way farther south.

Malendure beach lies on the west coast of Basse-Terre, across from Pigeon Island. Jacques Cousteau called it one of the 10 best diving places in the world. Several scuba operations are based here (*see* Sports, *below*). There are also glass-bottom-boat trips for those who prefer keeping their heads above water.

Souffleur, on the west coast of Grande-Terre north of Port-Louis, has brilliant flamboyant trees that bloom in the summer. There are no facilities on the beach, but you can buy the makings of a picnic from nearby shops. Be sure to stick around long enough for a super sunset.

Place Crawen, Les Saintes's quiet, secluded beach for skinny-dipping, is a half mile of white sand on Terre-de-Haut. Facilities are within a five-minute walk at Bois Joli hotel (☎ 590/99–50–38). The other popular Les Saintes beach is **Les Pompierres,** a palm-fringed stretch of tawny sand.

Petit-Anse, on Marie-Galante, is a long gold-sand beach crowded with locals on weekends. During the week it's quiet, and there are no facilities other than the little seafood restaurant, La Touloulou.

Sports and the Outdoors

Bicycling

The relatively flat terrain of Grande-Terre makes for easy wheeling. You can rent bikes in Pointe-à-Pitre at **Velo Tout Terrain** (☎ 590/97–85–40), which also offers mountain-bike tours in Basse-Terre and Marie-Galante. In St-François you can rent from **Espace VTT** (☎ 590/88–79–91).

Boating

If you plan to sail these waters, you should be aware that the winds and currents of Guadeloupe tend to be strong. There are excellent, well-equipped marinas in Pointe-à-Pitre, Bas-du-Fort, Deshaies, St-François, and Gourbeyre. Bareboat or crewed yachts can be rented in Bas-du-Fort at **Jet Sea Touring** (☎ 590/90–82–95), **Moorings** (☎ 590/90–81–81), **Star Voyages Antilles** (☎ 590/90–86–26), and **ATM Yachts** (☎ 590/90–92–02). Most beachfront hotels rent Hobie Cats, Sunfish, pedal boats, motorboats, and water skis.

Deep-Sea Fishing

Half- and full-day trips in search of bonito, dolphin, captainfish, barracuda, kingfish, and tuna can be arranged through **Le Rocher de Malendure** (Pigeon, Bouillante, ☎ 590/98–70–84) and **Caraibe Peche** (Marina, Bas-du-Fort, ☎ 590/90–97–51). Count on about 3,500F for a half-day's boat charter and 4,500F for a full day.

Fitness

The **PLM-Azur Marissol** (Bas-du-Fort, ☎ 590/90–84–44) offers gym space for calisthenics and stretching, water exercise classes in the pool or the sea, yoga classes, and beauty care. **Viva Forme** (Bas-du-Fort, ☎ 590/90–98–74) has two squash courts and weights and machines for muscle toning.

Flying

ULMs (Ultra Léger Motorisés) are popular with European tourists. The extremely lightweight seaplanes soar along the coast at approximately 100 feet. Go for a ride at **Holywind** (Canella Beach Residence, Pointe de la Verdure, Gosier, ☎ 590/90–44–00). The cost is 170F for 10 minutes.

Golf

Golf Municipal Saint-François (St-François, ☎ 590/88–41–87) has an 18-hole Robert Trent Jones course, an English-speaking pro, a clubhouse, a pro shop, and electric carts for rental. The greens fee is 250F.

Hiking

Basse-Terre's national park is laced with fascinating trails, many of which should be attempted only with an experienced guide. Trips for up to 12 people are arranged by **Organisation des Guides de Montagne de la Caraibe** (Maison Forestière, Matouba, ☎ 590/94–29–11).

Horseback Riding

Beach rides, picnics, and lessons are available through **Le Criolo** (St-Felix, Gosier, ☎ 590/84–04–06).

Scuba Diving

The main diving area is the Cousteau Underwater Park off Pigeon Island (west coast of Basse-Terre). Guides and instructors here are certified under the French CMAS rather than PADI or NAUI. To explore the wrecks and reefs, contact **Chez Guy et Christian** (Malendure, ☎ 590/98–82–43). This outfit also arranges dives elsewhere around Guadeloupe and weekly packages that include accommodations in bungalows. Other leading operations include **Caraibes Plongées** (Gosier, ☎ 509/90–44–90), **Les Heures Saines** (Malendure, ☎ 590/98–86–63), and **Marine Anse Plongée** (Bouillante, ☎ 590/98–78–78). On Isle des Saintes, the **Centre Nautique des Saintes** (Plage de la Coline, Terre-de-Haut, ☎ 590/99–54–25) and **Espace Plongé Caraibes** (Bourg, ☎ 590/99–51–84) arrange dives.

Sea Excursions and Snorkeling

Most hotels rent snorkeling gear and post information about excursions. The ***King Papyrus*** (Marina Bas-du-Fort, ☎ 590/90–92–98) is a catamaran you can snorkel from that offers full-day outings replete with rum, dances, and games, as well as moonlight sails. **Nautilus** (Plage de Malendure, ☎ 590/98–89–08) offers glass-bottom-boat tours and snorkeling.

Tennis

Courts are located at many hotels, including **Auberge de la Vieille Tour** (two courts), **Caravelle/Club Med** (six courts), **La Créole Beach** (two courts), **Golf Marine Club Hotel** (two courts), **Hamak** (one court), **Le Méridien St. François** (two courts), and **Relais du Moulin** (one court). You can also play at the **Marina Club** in Pointe-à-Pitre (☎ 590/90–84–08) and at the **Tennis League of Guadeloupe** at the Centre Lamby-Lambert Stadium in Glosier (☎ 590/90–90–97).

Windsurfing

Windsurfing is immensely popular here. Rentals and lessons are available at all beachfront hotels. Windsurfing buffs congregate at the **UCPA Hotel Club** (☎ 590/88–64–80) in St-François. You can also rent a *planche-à-voile* (Windsurfer)—try the **Callinago** (Gosier, ☎ 590/84–25–25).

Shopping

If shopping is your goal and you want to do it on a French island, head for Martinique—selection is better and you are more likely to be understood. But shopping can be fun in Pointe-à-Pitre at the street stalls around the harbor quay, in front of the tourist office, and at the market. Moreover, numerous small boutiques selling unique designs have opened in town. The more touristy shops are down at the St-John Perse cruise terminal, where an attractive mall is home to two dozen shops. Get an early start, because it gets very hot and sticky around midday.

Many stores offer a 20% discount on luxury items purchased with traveler's checks or, in some cases, major credit cards. You can find good buys on anything French—perfumes, crystal, china, cosmetics, fashions, scarves. As for local handcrafted items, you'll see a lot of junk, but you can also find wood carvings, madras table linens, island dolls dressed in madras, finely woven straw baskets and hats, and salako hats made of split bamboo. Of course there's the favorite Guadeloupean souvenir—rum.

Shopping Areas

In Pointe-à-Pitre the main shopping streets are **rue Schoelcher, rue de Noizières,** and **rue Frébault.** Bas-du-Fort's two shopping districts are the **Mammouth Shopping Center** and the **Marina,** where there are 20 or so boutiques and several restaurants. In **St-François** there are also several shops surrounding the marina. Many of the resorts have fashion boutiques. There are also a number of duty-free shops at Raizet Airport.

Good Buys

CHINA, CRYSTAL, AND SILVER

For Baccarat, Lalique, Porcelaine de Paris, Limoges, and other upscale tableware, check **Selection** (rue Schoelcher, Pointe-à-Pitre, no ☎). **Rosebleu** (5 rue Frébault, Pointe-à-Pitre, ☎ 590/82–93–44) offers similar buys on crystal and silver by top lines, including Christoffle.

COSMETICS AND LINGERIE

Guadeloupe's exclusive purveyor of Stendhal and Germaine Monteil is **Vendome** (8–10 rue Frébault, Pointe-à-Pitre, ☎ 590/83–42–84). Tickle someone's fancy with the delicate, fanciful, and very French lingerie found at **Soph't** (41, Immeuble Lesseps, Centre St-John Perse, Pointe-à-Pitre, ☎ 590/83–07–73).

LOCAL CRAFTS

Tim Tim (15 rue Henri IV, ☎ 590/83–48–71) is a nostalgia shop with elegant (and expensive) antiques ranging from Creole furniture to maps. For dolls, straw hats, baskets, and madras table linens, try **Au Caraibe** (4 rue Frébault, Pointe-à-Pitre, no ☎). Anthuriums and other plants that pass muster at U.S. customs are packaged at **Floral Antilles** (80 rue Schoelcher, ☎ 590/82–18–63). For imaginative art, visit the **Centre d'Art Haitien** (Rue Delgres, Pointe-à-Pitre, ☎ 590/82–54–46, and 65 Montauban, Gosier, ☎ 590/84–04–84). **L'Atelier de l'Art** (Gosier, Rte. des Hotels, no ☎) offers fanciful creations of wood and straw. **Chritiane Boutique** (Blvd. Général de Gaulle, Gosier, ☎ 590/84–52–51) offers a mind-boggling jumble ranging from tacky tchotchkes like "fertility" sculptures to sublime art naif canvases for as little as $20. The small town of Vieux Fort on the southern coast of Basse-Terre is renowned for its lacework. The **Centre de Broderie** (☎ 590/92–04–14) is built into the ruins of Fort L'Olive, and you can watch local ladies at work tatting intricate tablecloths, napkins, and place mats, according to traditions passed down over generations. This kind of stitchery is rare; unfortunately with the devaluation of the dollar, prices are *très cher*: $30 for a doily. In Ste-Anne, **La Case à Soie** (☎ 590/88–11–31) creates flowing silk dresses and scarves in Caribbean colors. On Terre-de-Haut, **Maogany Artisanat** (Bour, ☎ 590/99–50–12) sells Yves Cohen's batik and hand-painted T-shirts in luminescent seashell shades. **Pascal Foy** (Rte. à Pompierres, ☎ 590/99–52–29) produces stunning homages to traditional Creole architecture: painted houses incorporating collage and objets trouvés that make marvelous wall hangings. Prices begin at $90 and are well worth it. On Terre-de-Bas, contact **José Beaujour** (☎ 590/99–80–20) for an authentic salako.

PERFUMES

Sweet buys can be found at **Phoenicia** (Bas-du-Fort, Gosier, ☎ 590/90–85–56; 8 rue Frébault, Pointe-à-Pitre, ☎ 590/83–50–36; and 121 bis rue Frébault, Pointe-à-Pitre, ☎ 590/82–25–75). **Au Bonheur des Dames** (49 rue Frébault, Pointe-à-Pitre, ☎ 590/82–00–30) offers an array of cosmetics and skin care products, in addition to its perfumes. **L'Artisan Parfumeur** (rue Schoelcher, Pointe-à-Pitre, no ☎) sells both top French and American brands and tropical scents.

RUM AND TOBACCO

Delice Shop (45 rue Achille René-Boisneuf, Pointe-à-Pitre, ☎ 590/82–98–24) is the spot for island rums and gourmet items from France, from cheese to chocolate. **Comptoir sous Douane** (Raizet Airport, ☎ 590/82–22–76) has a good selection of island rums and tobacco.

Dining

The food here is superb. Many of Guadeloupe's restaurants feature seafood (shellfish is a great favorite), often flavored with rich herbs and spices à la Creole. Favorite appetizers are *accras* (codfish fritters), *boudin* (highly seasoned pork sausage), and *crabes farcis* (stuffed land crabs). Christophines, a type of vegetable pear, are prepared in a variety of ways. Plantains, served as a side dish, are considered a vegetable banana. *Blaff* is a spicy fish stew. Lobster, turtle steak, and *lambi* (conch) are often among the main dishes, and homemade coconut ice cream is a typical dessert. The island boasts more than 200 restaurants, including those serving classic French, Italian, African, Indian, Vietnamese, and South American fare. The quality of hotel dining rooms is superior; consult the lodging listings for recommendations. The local libation of choice is the *petit punch* ("'ti poonch," as it is pronounced)—a heady concoction of rum, lime juice, and sugarcane syrup. The innocent-sounding little punch packs a powerful wallop.

What to Wear

Dining is casual at lunch, but beach attire is a no-no. Except at the more laid-back marina and beach eateries, dinner is slightly more formal. Long pants, collared shirts, and skirts or dresses are appreciated, although not required.

CATEGORY	COST*
$$$	over $40
$$	$25–$40
$	under $25

per person, excluding drinks

Grande-Terre

$$$ ★ **Auberge de la Vieille Tour.** Lionel Péan's superb cuisine is artistically presented in a stylish room with intimate lighting, stone walls, grand floral arrangements, and crisp mango and taupe napery. Request a window table when you make your reservations; there's a splendid view of Ilet du Gosier. It's hard to choose from the constantly changing menu, with entrées such as smoked swordfish with a two-pepper mousse and blinis, noisettes of lamb in honey and lime, and sea bream kissed with passion-fruit vinegar. You may want to opt for the *menu dégustation,* for a representative sampling of Péan's work. There is an extensive (and expensive) wine list. A band plays cool jazz Wednesday–Saturday evenings. ✕ *Gosier,* ☎ 590/84–23–23. *Reservations advised. AE, DC, MC, V.*

$$$ **Auberge de St-François.** Claude Simon's country home is set in an orchard, and his tables are set with Royal Doulton china and fine crystal. Dining is indoors or on one of the flower-filled patios, with a superb view of Marie-Galante and Pointe des Châteaux. The house specialty is crayfish prepared in several different ways (the unusual fricassee with bacon and scallops is a standout). The brochette of smoked shark with a pepper sauce and the conch dishes are also good. A *menu touriste* (180F) of three courses, each with a choice of three dishes, is an affordable alternative to the à la carte offerings. Monsieur Simon has a superior wine cellar to complement his cuisine. ✕ *St-François,* ☎ 590/88–51–71. *Reservations advised. MC, V. Closed Sun. and Mon.*

$$$ **Château de Feuilles.** This restaurant is worth a special trip. You will
★ savor no finer luncheon than one served in this relaxed, stylish coun-
try setting by Martine and Jean-Pierre Dubost. While waiting for your
meal you can take a dip in the pool or stroll around the 2-acre farm.
For an aperitif, about 20 different punch concoctions are made with
different juices and flavors: Sample all if you dare. The changing menu
may include goose *rillettes* (pâté), velvety sea urchin pâté, kingfish fil-
let with vanilla, swordfish with sorrel, or the deep-sea fish *capitan* grilled
with lime and green pepper. For dessert, try the pineapple flan. The es-
tate is 9 miles from Le Moule on the Campêche road, between Gros-
Cap and Campêche. ✗ *Campêche,* ☎ *590/22–30–30. Reservations
advised. MC, V. Closed Mon. No dinner (except for groups of 10 or
more by reservation).*

$$$ **La Canne à Sucre.** A favorite over the years for its innovative Creole
★ cuisine, La Canne à Sucre has a reputation for being the best restau-
rant in Pointe-à-Pitre. It has a commanding position at the corner of
the quay, in the complex adjacent to the cruise-ship terminal, and hulking ships cast a shadow over the terrace. Take time to admire the lovely
murals of a sugarcane harvest that adorn the building. There are two
dining rooms with separate menus. Meals upstairs are more elaborate
and twice as expensive. Try the *foie gras frais de canard au vieux rhum*
(fresh duck liver in old rum) or red snapper in a cucumber coulis. The
views here are wide-ranging. In the main-floor Brasserie, you can order
such classic bistro dishes as duck à l'orange, grouper in red wine butter, and a puff pastry of skate with saffron sauce. A jacket is required
for dinner upstairs. ✗ *Quai No. 1, Port Autonome, Pointe-à-Pitre,* ☎
590/82–10–19. Reservations advised. AE, MC, V. No lunch Sat.

$$$ **La Louisiane.** The owner, chef Daniel Hogon, who hails from the Carl-
★ ton in Cannes, prepares such traditional favorites as duck-liver confit
with raspberry vinaigrette or smoked fish as starters, then crayfish flambé,
fillet of beef in green pepper sauce, or roast rack of lamb. For dessert,
try the charlotte of exotic fruits. The Menu Creole at 120F is a fine
buy. The dozen tables of this small restaurant are on a terrace deco-
rated with paintings and flower-filled hanging pots. The restaurant is
on the road to Ste-Marthe, about 2 miles from St-François, and Mon-
sieur Hogon will send a car for you upon request. You'll receive far
better service if you speak adequate French. ✗ *St-François,* ☎ *590/88–
44–34. Reservations advised. MC, V. Closed Mon.*

$$$ **Le Balata.** This commanding restaurant sits high on a bluff above the
★ main Gosier Bas-du-Fort highway. If you're traveling from Gosier in
the direction of Fort-de-France, you'll find the winding, pitted entrance road off the highway, at the Elf gas station. Pretty flowered linens
and trellises woven with hanging vines create a pastoral setting.
Madame Guynamant presents classic French cuisine and a selection
of good French wines at reasonable prices. A fixed menu, including
wine, is available at 155F. Choose a table by the window (reserve early)
and enjoy the magnificent view of Fort Fleur d'Epée. ✗ *Route de
Labrousse, Gosier,* ☎ *590/90–88–25. Reservations advised. AE, MC,
V. Closed Sun. and Aug. No lunch Sat.*

$$$ **Le Côte Jardin.** The marina between Bas-du-Fort and Pointe-à-Pitre is
a lively evening venue with a dozen restaurants, bar lounges, and
shops around the quay. You can take your pick from pizzas to ham-
burgers, but for something more formal, try the creative cuisine at Le
Côte Jardin. The plant-filled intimate restaurant is very pretty indeed,
with white lace curtains, enormous white wicker peacock chairs, and
coral and white napery. A menu of haute French Creole lists dishes that
range from basic lamb Provençal and baked red snapper to more ex-

otic *escargots de la mer* with garlic butter. ✕ *La Marina,* ☎ 590/90–
91–28. *Reservations advised. AE, MC, V.*

$$–$$$ **Le Flibustier.** This rustic hilltop farmhouse is a favorite with staffers
from neighboring Club Med. It's a lively, fun place that warms up after
8 PM, when the G.O.'s (*general organisateurs*—the staffers who force
you to limbo) hold court, smoke up a storm, and serenade attractive
guests with ribald ditties. You can order a complete dinner—mixed salad,
grilled lobster, coconut ice cream, petit punch, and half a pitcher of
wine—or à la carte off the blackboard menu. ✕ *La Colline, Fonds
Thézan (between Ste-Anne and St-Felix),* ☎ 590/88–23–36. *No credit
cards. Closed Mon. No lunch Sun.*

$$–$$$ **Les Oiseaux.** The delights of this restaurant begin with its setting, a
★ stucco-and-stone house nestled amid a tangle of gardens overlooking
the sea. The dining room is filled with potted plants and dressed with
colorful madras linens and local crafts. Owner-chefs Claudette and
Arthur Rolle have developed a menu of such dishes as *entrecôte Roquefort* (shark with coconut) and *marmite de Robinson* (a stew of dorado,
kingfish, tuna, shrimp, and local vegetables). Shellfish aficionados
should try *cassoulet de fruits de mer* (a seafood casserole). Ask Claudette
to show you her book of local remedies. If your French is *very* good
she might even prepare a special infusion for your particular complaint.
Even if it isn't, be sure to sample a homemade *digestif* such as *rhum
d'amour,* which aids the circulation, helps sweat out colds, and improves
"la force, pour marcher le sexe," as Claudette slyly comments. ✕
Anse des Rochers, ☎ 590/88–56–92. *Reservations required. AE, MC,
V. Usually closed Oct. No lunch Mon.–Wed.*

$$ **La Grande Pizzeria.** Open late and very popular, this simple seaside spot
serves pizza, pasta, salads, and some Milanese, Bolognese, and other
Italian seafood specialties, including a smashing risotto aux fruits de
mer and tagliatelle with shrimp scampi. Plastic tables and chairs are
set on the terrace and spruced up with colorful napery. ✕ *Bas-du-Fort,*
☎ 590/90–82–64. *MC, V. No lunch.*

$–$$ **Chez Violetta–La Creole.** The late Violetta Chaville established this
restaurant's à la carte Creole menu when she was head of Guadeloupe's
association of cuisinières (female chefs). Her brother has carried on her
cooking traditions, dishing up specials such as red snapper in Belle
Doudou sauce, a Creole mix of onions, tomatoes, peppers, and spices.
The food, while still good, has been eclipsed by other island kitchens,
but the restaurant remains a stop on many tourist itineraries and is popular with American visitors. ✕ *Eastern outskirts of Gosier Village,* ☎
590/84–10–34. *AE, MC, V.*

$–$$ **La Table Creole.** Carmélite Jeanne rules the kitchen of this little terrace
★ eatery, turning out dazzling Creole cuisine that is deceptively mild yet
will heat you up like the noonday sun. Sea urchin gratin, succulent kingfish and snapper blaff, and goat colombo are among her memorable
specialties. The menus at 80F and 100F are fabulous bargains. Sprays
of fresh flowers are everywhere, and Madame Jeanne usually dresses
colorfully to match. ✕ *St. Félix, outside Gosier,* ☎ 590/84–28–28.
MC, V. Closed Sept. No dinner Sun.

$–$$ **Le Corsaire.** Restaurants on Gosier's main drag and the Route des Ho-
tels leading to the Pointe de la Verdure vie with one another to offer
the best-value menus. Family-run Le Corsaire rates highly, thanks not
only to its fine fare at finer prices but also to its fun-loving ambience.
The waitstaff affects a piratical look with ponytails, earrings, and goa-
tees. A *vivier* (lobster tank) and a flamboyant mural of a buccaneer
and his ship dominate the decor. Maman is a sweetie, singing out
"C'est bon?" from the kitchen and nodding approvingly as you eat.

For 99F you get a set menu, which might start with a conch tart or stuffed crab, then segue into beef brochette, octopus fricassee, or chicken colombo. The King Creole menu at 120F nets you a large lobster. You can also order a pizzas for 40–52F. ✗ *Rte. des Hotels, Gosier,* ☎ *590/84–17–39. AE, MC, V. No lunch Mon.*

$ **Chez Mimi.** This intimate boîte is an appealing clutter of handmade butterflies, flower baskets and hats, plastered with postcards and businesscards, and splashed with vivid murals. Mimi is as colorful as the decor, and the food (try the luscious clam blaff for 70F) is delectable. ✗ *81 rue St-Jean, Le Moule, tel 590/23–64–87. No credit cards. Closed Sun.*

$ **Folie Plage.** This lovely spot, north of Anse-Bertrand, is especially popular with families on weekends. Prudence Marcelin prepares reliable Creole food; superb court bouillon and imaginative curried dishes are among the specialties. There is a children's wading pool here. ✗ *Anse Laborde,* ☎ *590/22–11–17. Reservations advised. No credit cards.*

Basse-Terre

$–$$ **Chez Clara.** Clara Laseur, who gave up a jazz-dancing career in Paris
★ to run her family's seaside restaurant with her mother, dishes out delicious Creole meals. Seating is on the inviting terrace of a gorgeous Creole house adorned with lacy gingerbread trim. Clara takes the orders (her English is excellent), and the place is often so crowded (even in the off-season) with her friends and fans that you may have to wait at the octagonal wooden bar before being seated. The food is worth the wait, however—check the daily specials listed on the blackboard, for example the succulent octopus or sublime ginger carambola sorbet. ✗ *Ste-Rose,* ☎ *590/28–72–99. Reservations advised. MC, V. Closed Wed. and Oct. No dinner Sun.*

$–$$ **Le Karacoli.** Lucienne Salcede's rustic seaside restaurant is well estab-
★ lished and well regarded. It has its feet firmly planted in the sands of Grande-Anse, a great place for a swim, and Lucienne won't mind if you come in shirtless off the beach. She'll even graciously direct you to a shower (really!), so you don't track up the gleaming tile floors. Order a bottle of muscadet and some delicious Creole specialties, and you're set for a perfect afternoon. Creole boudin is a hot item here (in more ways than one), as are accras. Other offerings include coquilles Karacoli, court bouillon, fried chicken, and turtle ragout. For dessert, try the banana flambé, heavily perfumed with rum, followed by a homemade *digestif* (after-dinner liqueur). ✗ *Grande-Anse, north of Deshaies,* ☎ *590/28–41–17. MC, V. No dinner Sat.–Tues.*

$ **Chez Jackye.** Jacqueline Cabrion serves Creole and African dishes in her cheerful plant-filled, seaside restaurant. Creole boudin is a house specialty, as are lobster (grilled, vinaigrette, or fricassee), fried crayfish, clam blaff, and goat in port sauce. There's also a wide selection of omelets, sandwiches, and salads. For dessert, try peach melba or banana flambé. The 120F menu will have you waddling out happily. ✗ *Anse Guyonneau, Rue de la Bataille, Pte. Noire,* ☎ *590/98–06–98. DC, MC, V. Closed Sun.*

$ **Les Gommiers.** A changing menu here may list crayfish soup, octopus fricassee, pork chops with banana, goat colombo, seafood paella, and grilled entrecôte. Banana splits and profiteroles are on the dessert list. For lunch, salade Niçoise and other light dishes are offered. Fixed menus at 70F and 100F are sensational values. Lovely peacock chairs grace the bar, and polished wood furnishings and potted plants fill the dining room. ✗ *Rue Baudot, Pte. Noire,* ☎ *590/98–01–79. MC, V. No dinner Sun.–Tues.*

Iles des Saintes, Terre-de-Haut

$$ **Le Banc de Sable.** Jacques and Odette Chan run this superb restaurant.
★ Dine on a charming open-air terrace built into the old stone house or in the tiny garden overlooking the sea. Jacques's father is Chinese and his mother Breton; he artfully blends their native cuisines in such mouth-watering dishes as chicken in ginger, duck in honey, and a *panaché de poissons* (a mix of the day's fresh catch, perhaps tuna, kingfish, and snapper) in sea urchin sauce. For dessert, try the *tarte crouistillante* (crusty pastry brimming with custard and tropical fruits in a passion-fruit coulis). ✕ *Bourg,* ☎ *590/99–54–76. MC, V. No dinner Sun.*

$–$$ **La Saladerie.** This delightful seaside terrace restaurant serves a so-phisticated mélange of Creole and Continental dishes. Begin with *rillettes* of smoked fish, crabes farcis, or a warm crepe filled with lobster, conch, octopus, and fish. House specialties include an assortment of smoked fish served cold and stuffed fish fillet served in a white-wine sauce. The wine list is pleasantly varied. This is the place for a light meal with a fabulous view. ✕ *Anse Mirre,* ☎ *590/99–50–92. MC, V.*

$–$$ **Relais des Iles.** Select your lobster from the *vivier* and enjoy the splen-
★ did view from this hilltop eatery while your meal is expertly prepared by Bernard Mathieu. Interesting preparations of local vegetables—christophines au gratin, breadfruit purée—accompany each entrée. For dessert, try the melt-in-your-mouth white chocolate mousse. The wine list is excellent. ✕ *Rte. de Pompierre,* ☎ *590/99–53–04. Reservations advised in high season. MC, V. Closed Tues.*

Marie-Galante

$ **Le Touloulou.** The ultracasual Le Touloulou, set on the curve of Petite Anse beach, serves sumptuous seafood at down-to-earth prices. Chef Patrice Pillet's standouts include conch *feuilleté* (in puff pastry) with yams and the very local *bébélé* (tripe with breadfruit, plantains, and dumplings). There are good set menus for 60F, 90F, and 140F. ✕ *Petite Anse,* ☎ *590/97–32–63. MC, V. Closed Mon. and mid-Sept.–mid-Oct.*

Lodging

Guadeloupe doesn't have the selection of elegant, tasteful hotels found on other islands, but you can opt for a splashy hotel with a full complement of resort activities or head for a small inn called a Relais Creole. If French is not your forte, you'll fare better in the large hotels. Gosier and Bas-du-Fort have been the main venues for resort hotels, but the areas around Ste-Anne and St-François also have their fair share of resorts. There are also small hotels throughout Basse-Terre and on Iles des Saintes and Marie-Galante. Most hotels include buffet breakfast in their rates. Prices decline 25% to 40% in the off-season.

For information about villas, apartments, and private rooms in modest houses, contact **Gîtes de France** (☎ 590/91–64–33). For additional information about apartment-style accommodations, contact the **ANTRE Association** (☎ 590/88–53–09).

CATEGORY	COST*
$$$$	over $300
$$$	$225–$300
$$	$150–$225
$	under $150

All prices are for a standard double room for two, excluding a taxe de séjour, which varies from hotel to hotel, and a 10%–15% service charge.

$$$$ **Hamak.** Five landscaped acres, a private white-sand beach, and atten-
★ tive service make this one of the smartest places on Guadeloupe, a peren-

nial favorite of Americans. Golfers will be delighted that Guadeloupe's municipal golf course is across the street, and gardeners appreciate the hotel's array of flowers and shrubs. One-bedroom suites are in bungalows; each unit has a living room, a small bedroom, a private rear patio with outdoor freshwater shower, and a front terrace with a hammock. All are air-conditioned, with twin beds, hair dryers, and international direct-dial phones. Some have small kitchenettes with hand stenciling. TVs and videos are available. Blond wood and wicker furnishings are accented by local artworks. You pay a high price for the bungalows, which have small rooms, bathrooms no bigger than closets, and a tiny and crowded beach, but the pampering service and seclusion compensate. ☎ *St-François 97118,* ☎ *590/88-59-99 or 800/633-7411,* ℻ *590/88-41-92. 56 units. Restaurant, 2 bars, lighted tennis court, hot tub, water-sports center. AE, MC, V. BP, MAP.*

$$$$ **La Cocoteraie.** You get the most luxury the island has to offer here, and
★ you pay for it—between $300 and $600 a night. This very private annex to Le Méridien consists of 52 suites. Each has a television, a minibar, a safe, and a private balcony with a view of either the marina or the pool. Large bathrooms have a round tub and separate shower. The decor is a handsome blend of bright pastels (lavender, mauve, turquoise, and taupe), mahogany furnishings, glazed ceramic lamps, and madras upholstery. A restaurant, two tennis courts, an extravagantly large multilevel pool surrounded by columns and enormous Chinese vases, and a very small beach are all for the exclusive use of La Cocoteraie guests, and you have full use of the facilities of Le Méridien (*see below*). The only drawback is a management that caters to the French bourgeois— the booking office is in Paris—and expresses little interest in attracting English-speaking guests. ☎ *Ave. de l'Europe, St-François 97118,* ☎ *590/88-79-81 or 800/543-4300,* ℻ *590/88-78-33. 52 suites. Restaurant, pool, 2 lighted tennis courts, access to Méridien's facilities. AE, DC, MC, V. CP, MAP.*

$$$ **Auberge de la Vieille Tour.** The addition of an arc-shape row of town houses increased the room count here to 160, too high to be a true auberge (inn). The personal flavor and individual service have diminished. Nevertheless, the hotel still has a desirable location three blocks from the Gosier center. The main building occupies the hilltop of a 4-acre estate. Steep steps go down to the pool and beach. The older rooms are in the main building and another long building facing Ilet du Gosier. They are rather small and dully furnished, though this may be forgiven if your room has a sea view. The new rooms, in the town houses on the other side of the pool, are larger and have cheerful contemporary furnishings. In high season, breakfast, lunch, and barbecues are served in the terrace restaurant at the pool level, and Robert Zarkis's orchestra plays nightly in the formal dining room. Water-sports equipment is available for guests at the sister hotel, Callinago. ☎ *Montauban Gosier 97190,* ☎ *590/84-23-23 or 800/223-9862,* ℻ *590/84-33-43. 160 rooms. 2 restaurants, bar, boutiques, 2 lighted tennis courts, pool. AE, DC, MC, V. BP, MAP.*

$$$ **La Creole Beach Hotel.** Ten acres of tropical greenery and two beaches are the lush setting for this hotel. Rooms are spacious and have individually controlled air conditioners, TVs, radios, international direct-dial phones, and sliding glass doors that open onto a balcony. Decor is dominated by vivid jungle fabrics. Mazelike corridors and pathways can be somewhat confusing. The water-sports center offers excursions to Ilet du Gosier. ☎ *Box 19, Gosier 97190,* ☎ *590/90-46-46 or 800/755-9313,* ℻ *590/90-46-96. 321 rooms. 2 restaurants, bar, pool, 2 lighted tennis courts, car-rental desk, boat excursions, water-sports center. AE, DC, MC, V. CP.*

$$-$$$ Club Méditerranée La Caravelle. This version of the well-known club chain has air-conditioned twin-bed rooms, some with balconies, and 50 secluded acres at the western end of a magnificent white-sand beach. Nice extras include a volleyball court, calisthenics classes, and a French-English language lab where you can take French classes and use a tape recorder and headphones to practice. The property draws a fun-loving, younger crowd, most of whom are from France, and serves as the home port for Club Med's sailing cruises. ☎ *Ste-Anne 97180,* ☎ *590/88–21–00 or 800/258–2633,* FAX *590/88–06–06. 275 rooms. Restaurant, pub, boutique, pool, 6 lighted tennis courts (with pro), watersports center. AE, MC, V. All-inclusive (drinks extra).*

$$-$$$ Fleur d'Epée Novotel. The atrium-style Novotel won't win any architectural awards for aesthetics, but it is vastly superior to the next-door Marissol, with whom it shares a crowded strip of blinding white sand. The two hotels frequently exchange spillover during high season, so beware. All rooms have air-conditioning, TV, minibar, and terrace (most with sea view). The decor is a refreshing combination of powder-blue fabrics, white tiles, and subdued rattan furnishings. Tour groups are the primary clientele. ☎ *Bas-du-Fort,* ☎ *590/90–40–00,* FAX *590/90–99–07. 191 rooms. 2 restaurants, bar, water-sports center, pool, boutique. AE, DC, D, MC, V. CP, MAP.*

$$-$$$ La Plantation Ste-Marthe. You are a few miles inland from the coast
★ here, but the 15 acres of grounds are lovely, the ocean can be seen from some guest rooms, and there is shuttle service to the beach. The august, almost baroque reception area has columns of pale blue and mango, vast murals, a winding, polished-wood double staircase, and black-and-white patterned marble floors. The accommodations are nearly as sumptuous. In four three-story Creole-style buildings, the guest rooms open onto spacious terraces that overlook the large pool. Most rooms are standard doubles, and all have minibar, TV, air-conditioning, phone, and safe. Thirty-four duplex suites have loft-style bedrooms looking down upon a salon. Bathrooms, with separate toilets, are cheerfully decorated with red-and-blue tiles. Throughout the hotel, tasteful furniture is a unique modern adaptation of French period pieces that incorporates cane work. Mahogany beds and aquamarine and coral tile work contribute to the refined aura. Next to the large free-form pool, designed to resemble a lake, is the main restaurant, dressed in Belle Epoque style, with indoor and terrace dining. The chef is from Paris, where his most recent position was at the renowned Taillevent. ☎ *St-François 97110,* ☎ *590/88–43–58 or 800/333–1970,* FAX *590/88–72–47. 96 rooms and 24 duplexes. Restaurant, bar, pool, conference rooms. AE, MC, V. EP, MAP.*

$$-$$$ Le Méridien St. François. You couldn't pack more activity into one vacation than is offered by this hotel. The 150-acre resort puts out its own *A to Z Leisure Guide* and broadcasts from Télé Méridien to let you know what's going on. The activities director organizes everything from boccie to book lending. The beach hut is a busy place even off-season (partly because the Air France crews use the hotel). The spacious, breezy lobby has a trompe l'oeil mural of an arcade and is filled with Haitian artwork and fresh flowers. Standard rooms are modest, and wear and tear has taken its toll, but all are air-conditioned with double or twin beds, radios, direct-dial phones, and balconies, about half of which face the sea. Odd-numbered rooms have the best views. Decor is standard to the Méridien chain, right down to the mint-and-orange fabrics and boxy configuration. This one at least sports a few individual touches, such as flowerpots on the balconies. ☎ *St-François 97118,* ☎ *590/88–51–00 or 800/543–4300,* FAX *590/88–40–71. 265 rooms, 10 suites. 3 restaurants, 2 bars, disco, boutiques, pool, 2 lighted*

tennis courts, car-rental desk, water-sports center. AE, DC, MC, V. CP,
MAP.

$$ **Canella Beach Residence.** In this 150-room resort built to resemble a
Creole village, you have a choice of single-level and duplex studios and
junior and duplex suites. Each has its own terrace or balcony with a
small kitchenette. Ask for a room on the top floor for the best views.
Decor is a pleasant departure from pastels, with earth tones comple-
menting the white tile floors and rattan furnishings. Each unit has a
phone, and you are assigned your own phone number when you check
in, so calls don't have to go through the front desk. Unlike the other
Pointe de la Verdure hotels, the Canella Beach enjoys its own semipri-
vate cove. Water sports are free, and there is a beach bar for refresh-
ments. Set back from the beach are the swimming pool and tennis courts.
The staff, with inspiration from Jean-Pierre Reuff, the general man-
ager, is enthusiastic (and sometimes disorganized) and enjoys speak-
ing English. Another plus is the Verandah restaurant, which offers dining
indoors with air-conditioning or outdoors cooled by the sea breezes.
The menu includes Creole and French dishes; the salad with warm goat
cheese makes an excellent light meal or an appetizer. ⛫ *Pointe de la
Verdure, Gosier 97190,* ☎ *590/90–44–00 or 800/223–9815,* ☒ *590/
90–44–44; in NY, 212/251–1800. 146 rooms. Restaurant, pool, 4 ten-
nis courts, water sports, excursions arranged to nearby islands. AE,
DC, MC, V. EP, MAP.*

$$ **Cap Sud Caraibes.** This is a tiny Relais Creole on a country road between Gosier and Ste-Anne, just a five-minute walk from a quiet beach.
The staff does its best to make you feel at home. Individually decorated rooms are air-conditioned, and each has a balcony and either a
shower or an enormous bath. ⛫ *Gosier 97190,* ☎ *590/85–96–02,*
☒ *590/85–80–39. 12 rooms. Transfer from airport to hotel, bar, dry
cleaning, laundry, snorkeling equipment. AE, MC, V. CP.*

$$ **Fort Royal Touring Club.** This is by far the most elegant, comfortable
lodging on Basse-Terre. The modern white structure overlooks two pris-
tine beaches. Spacious rooms all have TV, air-conditioning, phone, hair
dryer, and terrace or balcony with sea views. White tile floors contrast
nicely with azure fabrics, and there are handsome wicker and rattan
furnishings and mahogany beds. The hotel offers tours into the national
park and plenty of activities, most of them beach-related. ⛫ *Pointe
du Petit Bas-Vent, Deshaies 97126,* ☎ *590/25–50–00,* ☒ *590/25–
50–01. 198 rooms. Restaurant, bar, 2 pools, 4 lighted tennis courts,
4-hole minigolf, water-sports center including dive shop. AE, MC, V.
EP, CP, MAP.*

$$ **Golf Marine Club Hotel.** Near the town's newer shops and restaurants,
this small hotel offers a more moderately priced alternative to Hamak
and Le Méridien. But the hotel's name overpromises: It is not a club,
the municipal golf course is across the street, and it has neither marina nor beach. You must walk two blocks to the nearest public beach.
The rooms, however, are pristine and pleasingly decorated in soft
blues. Each has a balcony, but those facing the street tend to be noisy,
so reserve one looking onto the gardens. A third of the rooms are called
mezzanine suites and have loft bedrooms and a roll-out couch in the
lounge. These are pleasant for two people, and a small family can squeeze
in. On the patio terrace facing the small pool is a relaxed, informal
restaurant where meals are served. ⛫ *Ave. de l'Europe, B.P. 204, St-
François 97118,* ☎ *590/88–60–60,* ☒ *590/88–68–98. 42 rooms, 32
suites. Restaurant, pool, 2 tennis courts. AE, MC, V. CP, MAP.*

$$ **Le Domaine de l'Anse des Rochers.** The 27 acres of this resort are spread
along the coast a few miles from St-François. Rooms are either in Cre-
ole-style buildings or in 34 villas that climb the rise behind them. All

rooms have terra-cotta floors, rich russet-patterned bedspreads, ceramic lamps, and original touches like antique radios. Bathrooms are merely functional, but terraces and kitchenettes are pluses. The formal restaurant offers à la carte dining, but most evenings, guests attend the theme buffet dinner at the Blanc Mangé restaurant, where performers entertain on the large piazza. Across the piazza is an open-sided disco, good for late-night revelry. The complex is so large that the trek to the man-made beach at one end can prompt you to use the car. And though Anse des Rochers may not have the best beach on the island, it does boast the largest swimming pool. Dramatically designed, the pool creates the effect of water cascading into the sea. Your travel agent should be able to obtain discounted rates for you, which can make this hotel very reasonable. ⊠ *Anse des Rochers, St-François 97118,* ☎ *590/93–90–00,* FAX *590/93–91–00. 356 rooms. 2 restaurants, beach snack bar, pool, disco, minimart, gift shop, car rental, 2 lighted tennis courts, archery, conference rooms. MC, V. EP, MAP.*

$$ **L'Orchidée.** Right in the center of Gosier, this hotel is perfect for the business person who does not need resort facilities or a beach. Its spotless, air-conditioned studios have a small kitchenette, a balcony, and a direct-dial phone. The decor consists of dark-wood furnishings, teal fabrics, and sparkling white tile floors. On the ground floor a small shop serves morning coffee. Owner-manager Madame Karine Chenaf speaks English and can help you arrange your day. ⊠ *32 blvd. Général de Gaulle, Gosier 97130,* ☎ *590/84–54–20,* FAX *590/84–54–90. 21 rooms, 3 apartments. Dining room, boutique, indoor parking, free membership in local recreation center with pool, tennis, water sports. MC, V. EP.*

$$ **Relais du Moulin.** A restored windmill serves as the reception room for this Relais Creole tucked in Châteaubrun, near Ste-Anne. A spiral staircase leads up to a TV/reading room, from which there is a splendid view. Accommodations are in air-conditioned bungalows. Rooms are immaculate but claustrophobic, somehow managing to pack in twin beds, small terraces, and kitchenettes. The hotel is on a small hill, and there is usually a pleasant, cooling breeze. The restaurant overlooks the restored windmill. By day, sunlight floods through large windows, while at night candlelight flickers on crisp white cloths. The nouvelle cuisine served here includes the house specialty: grouper and lobster served with Creole sauce or stuffed with fresh homemade pâté. Crème caramel in coconut sauce is among the sumptuous desserts. A *menu dégustation* for 220F offers seven courses and is a good way to sample Creole cooking. The beach is a 10-minute hike away. It's best to have your own rental car. Bikes are available. The owner-manager speaks English. ⊠ *Châteaubrun, Ste-Anne 97180,* ☎ *590/88–23–96 or 800/223–9815,* FAX *590/88–03–92. 40 rooms. Restaurant, bar, pool, tennis court, archery. AE, DC, MC, V. CP, MAP.*

$$ **Tropical Club Hotel.** Great windsurfing and swimming are big draws for this hotel on the northeastern coast of Grand-Terre. The golden beach catches cooling trade winds from the Atlantic, but a reef about 100 yards offshore keeps the waves gentle. Set back from the beach is an almond-shaped pool, adjacent to an open-sided dining room that serves French and Creole fare. The guest rooms are in three buildings on a rise at the back of the main hotel building. Each room has a double bed, two bunk beds, TV, air-conditioning, telephone, and fan. The bunk beds are in an entrance annex—ideal for children (those under 21 stay free). The bathroom has a shower only, and the toilet is in a separate area. Every room has a private balcony with a small kitchenette, table and chairs, and a view of the sea. The best views are from the rooms on the top (third) floor. The decor, in tired rattan and seafoam colors, won't win any awards, and the setting is remote, but

the property compensates with a host of activities and an energetic staff.
🕾 *Le Moule, 97160,* ☎ *590/93–97–97,* 🖷 *590/93–97–00. 72 rooms.
Restaurant, bar, pool, windsurfing, pétanque area, gym, boutique,
and 3 lighted tennis courts nearby. AE, MC, V. CP, MAP.*

$ **Auberge de la Distillerie.** This homey country inn is an excellent choice
★ for those who want to be close to the national park and its hiking trails.
The 12 rooms in the 19th-century house are individually and charm-
ingly decorated, with wicker furnishings, tile floors, wood beams, ceramic lamps, and local artworks. Apricot, mint, olive, silver, and rose
are the dominant colors of the decor. All have air-conditioning, TV,
phone, and terrace; some have a fridge. The slightly larger bungalows
have larger terraces and open onto the extravagantly overgrown gardens. There's also a rustic wood chalet that sleeps two to four people.
The restaurant, noted for its delectable Creole cuisine, is built around
the partially enclosed pool. Boat trips on the Lézarde River can be arranged; you can also swim in the river. 🕾 *Vernou 97170, D23, Petit-
Bourg,* ☎ *590/94–25–91 or 800/223–9815,* 🖷 *590/94–11–91. 14
rooms. Restaurant, bar, pool, bakery. AE, MC, V. CP, MAP.*

$ **Domaine de Petite Anse.** The ocher, red-roofed buildings of this resort
spill down lushly landscaped hills overlooking the ocean. The location
is perfect: You're near a beach and close to the national park. Accommodations are either in hotel rooms or bungalows and are decorated with dark rattan and bright floral fabrics. Rooms are simple and
small, but well outfitted with TV, phone, air-conditioning, safe, and
fridge. Be sure to request one with a balcony and sea view (they're the
same price). Bungalows have a terrace, full bath, and kitchenette in addition to the amenities listed above. This is one of Guadeloupe's premier spots for an active vacation, and very popular with young French
couples and families. The resort is noted for its dive shop and nature
tours. The staff, although friendly, speaks limited English. 🕾 *Plage de
Petite Anse, Monchy, Bouillante 97125,* ☎ *590/98–78–78,* 🖷 *590/98–
80–28. 135 rooms, 40 bungalows. Restaurant, bar, boutique, pool,
catamaran, archery, volleyball, water-sports center including sea kayaking and dive shop. AE, DC, MC, V. EP.*

$ **Grand Anse Hotel.** Less than a mile from a black-sand beach, and of-
fering spectacular mountain views, this Relais Creole is a good choice
for nature lovers. It's also near the ferry landing from which you leave
for Les Saintes. Air-conditioned bungalows have shower bath, phone,
TV, refrigerator, and small balcony. The heavy polished wood furnishings
should achieve antique status in a few years. Water sports and nature
hikes can be arranged. 🕾 *Trois-Rivières 97114,* ☎ *590/92–90–47,*
🖷 *590/92–93–69. 16 bungalows. Restaurant, pool, bar. MC, V. CP,
MAP.*

$ **La Sucrerie du Comté.** The ruins and rusting equipment (including a
★ locomotive) of a 19th-century sugar factory litter the lawns and gardens here like hulking abstract sculptures. In fact, it is the historically
significant grounds, along with the attractive public areas, that are the
main attraction of this resort. The interiors of the fine restaurant and
bar re-create gracious plantation living, with wood beams, stone walls,
lace lamp shades, and towering floral arrangements. The nearest beach
is a 10-minute stroll through a tangle of greenery. Twenty-six bungalows duplicate the gingerbread architecture of the turn of the century.
Inside, the air-conditioned rooms are small but pretty, with white tile
floors, peach walls, and aqua and pale green linens. The enthusiastic
French owner, Monsieur Girard Jean-Luc, will have you speaking
French in no time, as you try the homemade fruit punches lined up in
great jars on the bar in the evening. 🕾 *Comté de Lohéac, Ste-Rose 97115,*

☎ 590/28–60–17, FAX 590/28–65–63. *50 rooms. Restaurant, bar, pool, 1 tennis court. AE, DC, MC, V. CP, MAP.*

Iles des Saintes

$–$$ **Village Creole.** Baths by Courrèges, dishwashers, freezers, satellite TV,
★ videos, and international direct-dial phones are among the amenities
in this apartment hotel. Somewhat isolated, it appeals to the likes of
models and high-powered business titans looking for a peaceful retreat.
Units are decorated simply but chicly, with white tile floors, unvarnished
rattan, powder-blue accents, and framed posters. Ghyslain Laps, the
English-speaking owner and would-be chef, will help you whip up meals
in the kitchen. If you'd prefer not to cook, he can provide you with a
cook and housekeeper for an extra charge. A sailboat is available for
excursions to Marie-Galante and Dominica. The small beach is too rough
for swimming. 🖅 *Pte. Coquelet 97137, Terre-de-Haut,* ☎ *590/99–53–
83,* FAX *590/99–55–55. 22 duplexes. Airport shuttle service, daily
maid service, safe deposit, business center, scooter and boat rentals,
water-sports center. MC, V. EP.*

$ **L'Auberge les Petits Saints aux Anacardies.** Ten air-conditioned rooms
★ are tucked into this inn, which is trimmed with trellises and topped by
dormers. Each room has twin beds, a phone, and casement windows
that open to a splendid view of gardens, hills, and the bay. Some also
have sea views (Room 2's is extraordinary), and most have a private
bath. A glorious clutter greets you in the reception area, which is
crammed with antiques and objets d'art culled from owners Jean Paul
Coles and Didier Spindler's world travels—porcelain lions, birdcages,
cigar-store Indians. Furnishings are a similarly odd assortment of antiques. There's a one-bedroom bungalow next to the main house. Steak
au poivre, grilled lobster, and smoked local fish are among the restaurant's offerings. The hotel's private boat makes excursions around the
islands. This is one of the most distinctive properties in the archipelago.
🖅 *La Savane 97137, Terre-de-Haut,* ☎ *590/99–50–99,* FAX *590/99–
54–51. 10 rooms (9 with private interior bath). Restaurant, boutique,
bar, pool, sauna. AE, MC, V. CP, MAP.*

$ **Bois Joli.** A beautiful setting, right on the bay overlooking the "sug-
arloaf," is the attraction here. Most of the rooms, either in the inn or
one of the bungalows, are air-conditioned but rather drab. The hotel
restaurant serves wonderful clams in Creole sauce on a terrace that overlooks the sea. Water sports can be arranged, and the Anse Crawen nudist beach is a five-minute walk away. Pets are allowed. 🖅 *Terre-de-Haut
97137,* ☎ *590/99–50–38 or 800/223–9815,* FAX *590/99–55–05. 29
rooms. Restaurant, bar, pool, airport transfers. MC, V. CP, MAP.*

The Arts and Nightlife

Cole Porter notwithstanding, Guadeloupeans maintain that the beguine
began here (the Martinicans make the same claim for their island). Discos come, discos go, and the current music craze is "zouk," but the
beat of the beguine remains steady. Many of the resort hotels feature
dinner dancing, as well as entertainment by steel bands and folkloric
groups.

Bars and Nightclubs

There's nightly entertainment at **Lele Bar** (Le Méridien, St-François,
☎ 590/88–51–00) and **Au Bar du Minuit** (Montauban, Gosier, ☎
590/84–53–77). **Le Jardin Brésilien** (Marina, Bas-du-Fort, ☎ 590/90–
99–31) has light music in a relaxed setting on the waterfront. **Le Figuier Vert** (Mare Galliard, Gosier, ☎ 590/85–85–51) offers live jazz Friday
and Saturday nights. Right at the pier in Bourg, Terre-de-Haut, sultry

Brazilian chanteuse Nilce Laps holds sway nightly at **Nilce's** (no ☎),
in a charming waterfront bistro decorated with assorted authentic
bistro antiques. Locals also congregate at the **Cafe de la Marina** (☎
590/99–53–78) after the day-trippers leave; there's always someone
playing the Santois version of a bagpipe.

Casinos

There are two casinos on the island. Both have American-style roulette,
blackjack, and chemin de fer. Admission is $10. The legal age is 21,
and you'll need a photo ID. Tie and jacket are not required, but
"proper attire" means no shorts. The **Casino de Gosier les Bains**
(Gosier, ☎ 590/84–18–33) has a bar and restaurant and is open Monday–Saturday 9 PM–dawn. Slot machines open at 10 AM. The **Casino
de St-François** (Marina, St-François, ☎ 590/88–41–31) has a snack
bar and nightclub and is open Tuesday–Sunday 9 PM–3 AM.

Discos

A mixed crowd of locals and tourists frequents the discos. Night owls
should note that carousing is not cheap. Most discos charge an ☛ of
at least $8, which includes one drink (drinks cost about $5 each). Some
of the enduring hot spots are **Le Foufou** (Fleur d'Epée Novotel, Bas-
du-Fort, ☎ 590/84–35–59), the very Parisian **Elysée Matignon** (Rte.
des Hôtels, Bas-du-Fort, ☎ 590/90–89–05), **Le Caraibe** (Salako,
Gosier, ☎ 590/84–22–22), **Caraibes 2** (Carrefour de Blanchard, Bas-
du-Fort, ☎ 590/90–97–16), **La Victoria** (Rte. de Bas-du-Fort, ☎ 590/
90–97–76), and **New Land** (Rte. Riviera, Gosier, ☎ 590/84–37–91).
The only disco of note on Basse-Terre is the **Espace Vaneau** (Mahaut,
Bouillante, ☎ 590/98–25–72).

14 Jamaica

Updated by
Melissa Rivers

THE THIRD-LARGEST ISLAND in the Caribbean (after Cuba and Puerto Rico), the English-speaking nation of Jamaica enjoys a considerable self-sufficiency based on tourism, agriculture, and mining. Its physical attractions include jungle mountaintops, clear waterfalls, and unforgettable beaches, yet the country's greatest resource may be the Jamaicans themselves. Although 95% of the population trace their bloodlines to Africa, their national origins lie in Great Britain, the Middle East, India, China, Germany, Portugal, South America, and many of the other islands in the Caribbean. Their cultural life is a wealthy one; the music, art, and cuisine of Jamaica are vibrant, with a spirit easy to sense but as hard to describe as the rhythms of reggae or a flourish of the streetwise patois.

In addition to its north-coast pleasure capitals—Montego Bay and Ocho Rios—Jamaica has a real capital in Kingston. For all its congestion and for all the disparity between city life and the bikinis and parasails to the north, Kingston is the true heart and head of the island. This is the place where politics, literature, music, and art wrestle for acceptance in the largest English-speaking city south of Miami, its actual population of nearly 1 million bolstered by the emotional membership of virtually all Jamaicans.

The first people known to have reached Jamaica were the Arawaks, Indians who paddled their canoes from the Orinoco region of South America about a thousand years after the death of Christ. Then, in 1494, Christopher Columbus stepped ashore at what is now called Discovery Bay. Having spent four centuries on the island, the Arawaks had little notion that his feet on their sand would mean their extinction within 50 years.

What is now St. Ann's Bay was established as New Seville in 1509 and served as the Spanish capital until the local government crossed the island to Santiago de la Vega (now Spanish Town). The Spaniards were never impressed with Jamaica; their searches found no precious metals, and they let the island fester in poverty for 161 years. When 5,000 British soldiers and sailors appeared in Kingston Harbor in 1655, the Spaniards did not put up a fight.

The arrival of the English, and the three centuries of rule that followed, provided Jamaica with the surprisingly genteel underpinnings of its present life—and the rousing pirate tradition fueled by rum that enlivened a long period of Caribbean history. The British buccaneer Henry Morgan counted Jamaica's governor as one of his closest friends and enjoyed the protection of His Majesty's government no matter what he chose to plunder. Port Royal, once said to be the "wickedest city of Christendom," grew up on a spit of land across from present-day Kingston precisely because it served so many interests. Morgan and his brigands were delighted to have such a haven, and the people of Jamaica profited by being able to buy pirate booty there at terrific bargains.

Morgan enjoyed a prosperous life; he was knighted and made lieutenant governor of Jamaica before the age of 30, and, like every good bureaucrat, he died in bed and was given a state funeral. Port Royal fared less well. On June 7, 1692, an earthquake tilted two-thirds of the city into the sea, the tidal wave that followed the last tremors washed away millions in pirate treasure, and Port Royal simply disappeared. In recent years divers have turned up some of the treasure, but most of it still lies in the depths, adding an exotic quality to the water sports pursued along Kingston's reefs.

The very British 18th century was a time of prosperity in Jamaica. This was the age of the sugar baron, who ruled his plantation great house and made the island the largest sugar-producing colony in the world. Because sugar fortunes were built on slave labor, however, production became less profitable when the Jamaican slave trade was abolished in 1807 and slavery was ended in 1838.

As was often the case in colonies, a national identity came to supplant allegiance to the British in the hearts and minds of Jamaicans. This new identity was given official recognition on August 6, 1962, when Jamaica became an independent nation with loose ties to the Commonwealth. The island today has a democratic form of government led by a prime minister and a cabinet of fellow ministers.

Before You Go

Tourist Information

Contact the **Jamaica Tourist Board,** 801 2nd Ave., 20th Floor, New York, NY 10017, ☎ 212/856–9727, 800/233–4JTB; FAX 212/856–9730; 500 N. Michigan Ave., Suite 1030, Chicago, IL 60611, ☎ 312/527–1296, FAX 312/527–1472; 1320 S. Dixie Hwy., Suite 1100, Coral Gables, FL 33146, ☎ 305/665–0557, FAX 305/666–7239; 8214 Westchester, Suite 500, Dallas, TX 75225, ☎ 214/361–8778, FAX 214/361–7049; 3440 Wilshire Blvd., Suite 1207, Los Angeles, CA 90010, ☎ 213/384–1123, FAX 213/384–1123. In Canada: 1 Eglinton Ave. E, Suite 616, Toronto, Ontario M4P 3A1, ☎ 416/482–7850, FAX 416/482–1730. In the U.K.: 1–2 Prince Consort Rd., London, SW7 2BZ, ☎ 0171/224–0505, FAX 0171/224–0551.

Arriving and Departing

BY PLANE

Donald Sangster International Airport in Montego Bay (☎ 809/952–3009) is the most efficient point of entry for visitors destined for Montego Bay, Ocho Rios, Runaway Bay, and Negril. **Norman Manley International Airport** in Kingston (☎ 809/924–8231) is better for visitors to the capital or Port Antonio. **Trans Jamaica Airlines** (☎ 809/952–5401 in Montego Bay, 809/924–8850 in Kingston) provides shuttle services on the island. Be sure to reconfirm your departing flight a full 72 hours in advance.

Air Jamaica (☎ 800/523–5585) and **American Airlines** (☎ 212/619–6991 or 800/433–7300) fly nonstop daily from Raleigh-Durham and Miami. Air Jamaica provides the most frequent service from U.S. cities, including Atlanta, Philadelphia, Baltimore, and Orlando. American also flies in from San Juan. **Continental** (☎ 800/231–0856) flies in four times a week from Newark, **Northwest Airlines** (☎ 212/563–7200 or 800/447–4747) has daily direct service to Montego Bay from Minneapolis and Tampa, and **Aeroflot** (☎ 809/929–2251) flies in from Havana. **Air Canada** (☎ 800/776–3000) offers daily service from Toronto and Montreal in conjunction with Air Jamaica, and both **British Airways** (☎ 800/247–9297) and Air Jamaica connect the island with London.

Passports and Visas

Passports are not required of visitors from the United States or Canada, but every visitor must have proof of citizenship, such as a birth certificate or a voter registration card (a driver's license is not enough). British visitors need passports but not visas. Each visitor must possess a return or ongoing ticket. Declaration forms are distributed in flight to keep customs formalities to a minimum.

Language

The official language of Jamaica is English. Islanders usually speak a patois among themselves, a lyrical mixture of pidgeon English, Spanish, and various African languages.

Precautions

Do not let the beauty of Jamaica cause you to relax the caution and good sense you would use in your own hometown. Never leave money or other valuables in your hotel room; use the safe-deposit boxes that most establishments make available. Carry your funds in traveler's checks, not cash, and keep a record of the check numbers in a secure place. Never leave a rental car unlocked, and never leave valuables, even in a locked car. Finally, resist the call of the wild when it presents itself as a scruffy-looking native offering to show you the "real" Jamaica. Jamaica on the beaten path is wonderful enough; don't take chances by wandering far from it. And ignore efforts, however persistent, to sell you a ganja joint.

Staying in Jamaica

Important Addresses

Tourist Information: The main office of the **Jamaica Tourist Board** is in Kingston (2 St. Lucia Ave., New Kingston, Box 360, Kingston 5, ☎ 809/929–9200). There are also JTB desks at both Montego Bay and Kingston airports and JTB offices in all resort areas.

EMERGENCIES
Police, fire, and ambulance: Police and air-rescue is 119; fire department and ambulance is 110. **Hospitals: University Hospital** at Mona in Kingston (☎ 809/927–1620), **Cornwall Regional Hospital** (Mt. Salem, in Montego Bay, ☎ 809/952–5100), **Port Antonio General Hospital** (Naylor's Hill in Port Antonio, ☎ 809/993–2646), and **St. Ann's Bay Hospital** (near Ocho Rios, ☎ 809/972–2272). **Pharmacies: Pegasus Hotel in Kingston** (☎ 809/926–3690), **McKenzie's Drug Store** (16 Strand St. in Montego Bay, ☎ 809/952–2467), and **Great House Pharmacy** (Brown's Plaza in Ocho Rios, ☎ 809/974–2352).

Currency

The Jamaican government abolished the fixed rate of exchange for the Jamaican dollar, allowing it to be traded publicly and subject to market fluctuations. At press time the Jamaican dollar was worth about J\$30 to U.S.\$1. Currency can be exchanged at airport bank counters, exchange bureaus, or commercial banks. Prices quoted below are in U.S. dollars unless otherwise noted.

Taxes and Service Charges

Hotels collect a 10% government consumption tax on room occupancy. The departure tax is J\$400, or approximately \$14. Most hotels and restaurants add a 10% service charge to your bill. If not, a 10% to 20% tip is appreciated.

Guided Tours

Half-day tours are offered by a variety of operators in the important areas of Jamaica. The best great-house tours include Rose Hall, Greenwood, and Devon House. Plantations to tour are Prospect and Sun Valley. The Appleton Estate Express Tour uses a bus to visit villages, plantations, and a rum distillery. The increasingly popular waterside folklore feasts are offered on the Dunn's, Great, and White rivers. The significant city tours are those in Kingston, Montego Bay, and Ocho Rios. Quality tour operators include **Glamour Tours** (☎ 809/979–8207), **Tropical Tours** (☎ 809/952–1110), **Greenlight Tours** (☎ 809/952–2650), **SunHoliday Tours** (☎ 809/952–5629), and **Jamaica Tours** (☎ 809/952–8074) The highlight of the Hilton High Day Tour (☎ 809/952–3343), which has been dubbed "Up, Up, and Buffet," is a meet the people, experience Jamaican food, and learn some of its history day, all on a private estate (around $65, including transportation). **Helitours Jamaica Ltd.** offers a way to see Jamaica from the air, with helicopter tours ranging from 15 minutes to an hour aloft at prices that vary accordingly ($65–$225). Contact the Ocho Rios office (☎ 809/974–2265). **South Coast Safaris Ltd.** has guided boat excursions up the Black River for some 10 miles (round-trip), into the mangroves and marshlands, aboard the 25-passenger *Safari Queen* and 25-passenger *Safari Princess* (☎ 809/965–2513 or, after 7 PM, 809/962–0220). **Calico Sailing** (☎ 809/952–5860, FAX 809/979–0843) offers snorkeling trips and sunset cruises on the waters of MoBay; costs are $50 and $25 respectively. The **Touring Society of Jamaica** (☎ and fax 809/975–7158) offers several ecotours, from birding in the Blue Mountains to the natural history of Cockpit Country.

Getting Around
TAXIS
Some but not all of Jamaica's taxis are metered. If you accept a driver's offer of his services as a tour guide, be sure to agree on a price before the vehicle is put into gear. All licensed taxis display red Public Passenger Vehicle (PPV) plates. Cabs can be summoned by telephone or flagged down on the street. Rates are per car, not per passenger, and 25% is added to the metered rate between midnight and 5 AM. Licensed minivans are also available and bear the red PPV plates.

RENTAL CARS
Jamaica has dozens of car-rental companies throughout the island. Because rentals can be difficult to arrange once you've arrived, you must make reservations and send a deposit before your trip. (Cars are scarce, and without either a confirmation number or a receipt you may have to walk.) Best bets are **Avis** (☎ 800/331–1212), **Dollar** (☎ 800/800–4000), **Hertz** (☎ 800/654–3131), and **National** (☎ 800/227–3876). In Jamaica, try the branch offices in your resort area or try **United Car Rentals** (☎ 809/952–3077) or **Jamaica Car Rental** (☎ 809/952–5586). You must be at least 21 years old to rent a car (at least 25 years old at several agencies), have a valid driver's license (from any country), and have a valid credit card. You may be required to post a security of several hundred dollars before taking possession of your car; ask about it when you make the reservation. Rates average $75–$90 a day.

Traffic keeps to the left in Jamaica, and those who are unfamiliar with driving on the left will find that it takes some getting used to. Be cautious until you are comfortable with it.

TRAINS
At press time, rail service between Kingston and Montego Bay was suspended.

BUSES
Buses are the mode of transportation Jamaicans use most, and consequently buses are *extremely* crowded and slow. They're also not air-conditioned, and rather uncomfortable. Yet the service is fairly frequent between Kingston and Montego Bay and between other significant des-

tinations. Schedule or route information is available at bus stops or from the bus driver.

The front desks of most major hotels can arrange the rental of bicycles, mopeds, and motorcycles. Daily rates run from about $45 for a moped to $70 for a Honda 550. Deposits of $100–$300 or more are required. However, we highly recommend that you *NOT* rent a moped or motorcycle. The strangeness of driving on the left, the less-than-cautious driving style that prevails on the island, the abundance of potholes, and the prevalence of vendors who will approach you at every traffic light are just a few reasons to skip cycles. If you want to venture out on your own, rent a car.

Telephones and Mail
The area code for all Jamaica is 809. Direct telephone, telegraph, telefax, and telex services are available.

At press time, airmail postage from Jamaica to the United States or Canada was J$1.50 for letters, J$1.20 for postcards.

Opening and Closing Times
Normal business hours for stores are weekdays 8–4, Saturday 8–1. Banking hours are generally Monday–Thursday 9–2, Friday 9–noon and 2:30–5.

Exploring Jamaica

Numbers in the margin correspond to points of interest on the Jamaica map.

Montego Bay
❶ The number and variety of its attractions make **Montego Bay,** on the island's north coast, the logical place to begin an exploration of Jamaica. Confronting the string of high-rise developments that crowd the water's edge, you may find it hard to believe that little of what is now Montego Bay (the locals call it MoBay) existed before the turn of the century. Today many explorations of Montego Bay are conducted from a reclining chair on Doctor's Cave Beach, with a table nearby to hold frothy drinks.

Rose Hall Great House, perhaps the greatest in the West Indies in the 1700s, enjoys its popularity less for its architecture than for the legend surrounding its second mistress, Annie Palmer, who was credited with murdering three husbands and a plantation overseer who was her lover. The story is told in two novels sold everywhere in Jamaica: *The White Witch of Rose Hall* and *Jamaica White.* The great house is east of Montego Bay, just across the highway from the Rose Hall resorts. There's a pub on site for snacks and drinks. ☎ *809/953–2323.* ☛ *$10 adults, $6 children.* ☉ *Daily 9–6.*

Greenwood Great House, 15 miles east of Montego Bay, has no spooky legend to titillate visitors, but it's much better than Rose Hall at evoking the atmosphere of life on a sugar plantation. The Barrett family, from which the English poet Elizabeth Barrett Browning was descended, once owned all the land from Rose Hall to Falmouth, and the family built several great houses on it. The poet's father, Edward Moulton Barrett ("the Tyrant of Wimpole Street"), was born at Cinnamon Hill, currently the private estate of country singer Johnny Cash. Highlights of Greenwood include oil paintings of the Barretts, china made especially for the family by Wedgwood, a library filled with rare books printed as early as 1697, fine antique furniture, and a collection of exotic musical instruments. There's a pub on site for snacks and drinks here as well. ☎ 809/953–1077. ✔ *$10 adults, $5 children.* ◷ *Daily 9–6.*

② One of the most popular excursions in Jamaica is rafting on the **Martha Brae River.** The gentle waterway takes its name from that of an Arawak Indian who killed herself because she refused to reveal the where-abouts of a local gold mine to the Spanish. According to legend, she finally agreed to take them there and, on reaching the river, used magic to change its course, drowning herself along with the greedy Spaniards. Her duppy (ghost) is said to guard the mine's entrance to this day. Book-ings are made through hotel tour desks. The trip costs just under $40 per raft (two per raft) for the 1½-hour river run, about 25 miles from most hotels in Montego Bay. The ticket office, gift shops, a bar-restau-rant, and swimming pool are at the top of the river. To make ar-rangements call 809/952–0889.

The **Appleton Estate Express** (☎ 809/952–3692 or 809/952–6606), an air-conditioned bus, takes you through the lush hills and country-side around Montego Bay. You'll get a look at Jamaican villages, plan-tations growing banana and coconut, coffee groves, and the facility that turns out Appleton Rum. The $70 fare includes transfers to and from your hotel, Continental breakfast, buffet lunch, and open bar.

There is also **Mountain Valley Rafting** on the River Lethe, approximately 12 miles (about 50 minutes) southwest of Montego Bay. The trip is $40 per raft (two per raft), lasting an hour or so, through unspoiled hillside country. Bookings are made through hotel tour desks or by call-ing 809/952–0527.

An Evening on the Great River is a must for tour groups, yet fun nonetheless. The adventure includes a boat ride up the torchlit river, a full Jamaican dinner, a native folklore show, and dancing to a reg-gae band. It costs around $60 per person with hotel pickup and re-turn, less if you arrive via your own transport. ☎ 809/952–5047 or 809/952–5097. *Offered Sun., Tues., and Thurs.*

Ocho Rios

③ Perhaps more than anywhere else in Jamaica, **Ocho Rios**—67 miles east of Montego Bay—presents a striking contrast of natural beauty and recreational development. The Jamaicans can fill the place by them-selves, especially on a busy market day, when cars and buses from the countryside clog the heavily traveled coastal road that links Port An-tonio with Montego Bay. Add a tour bus or three and the entire pas-senger list from a cruise ship, and you may find yourself mired in a considerable traffic jam.

TIME OUT   **Double V Jerk Centre** (109 Main St., ☎ 809/974-2084) is a good place to park yourself for frosty Red Stripe beer and fiery jerk pork or chicken. It's lively at lunch, when you can tour the adjacent minizoo, with fish and tropical birds.

Yet a visit to Ocho Rios is worthwhile, if only to enjoy its two chief attractions—Dunn's River Falls and Prospect Plantation. A few steps away from the main road in Ocho Rios are waiting some of the most charming inns and oceanfront restaurants in the Caribbean. Lying on the sand of what will seem to be your private cove or swinging gently in a hammock with a tropical drink in your hand, you'll soon forget the traffic that's only a brief stroll away.

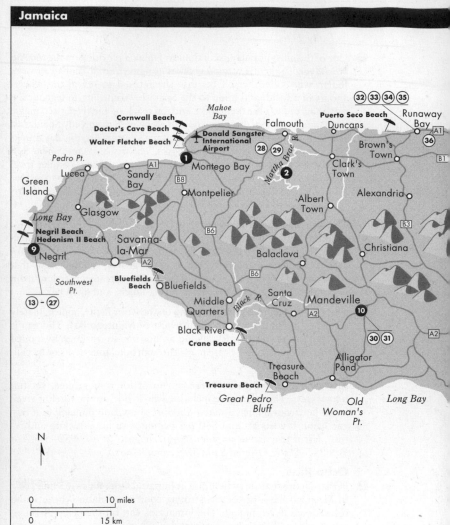

Mahoe Bay

Falmouth

Cornwall Beach
Doctor's Cave Beach
Walter Fletcher Beach

Donald Sangster
International
Airport

Puerto Seco Beach
Duncans

Runaway
Bay

A1

Pedro Pt.

Lucea

Green
Island

Sandy
Bay

A1

B8

Montego Bay

Montpelier

Martha Brae R.

Brown's
Town

B1

Clark's
Town

Albert
Town

Alexandria

B3

Long Bay

Negril Beach
Hedonism II Beach

Glasgow

Savanna-
la-Mar

A2

Christiana

Southwest
Pt.

Bluefields
Beach

Bluefields

B6

Balaclava

B6

Santa
Cruz

Black R.

Mandeville

A2

A2

Middle
Quarters

Black River

Crane Beach

Alligator
Pond

Treasure
Beach

Treasure Beach

Great Pedro
Bluff

Old
Woman's
Pt.

Long Bay

N

| 0 | | 10 miles |
| 0 | | 15 km |

Exploring
Firefly, **5**
Golden Eye, **4**
Kingston, **11**
Mandeville, **10**
Martha Brae River, **2**
Montego Bay, **1**
Negril, **9**
Ocho Rios, **3**
Port Antonio, **6**
Port Royal, **12**
Rio Grande River, **7**
Somerset Falls, **8**

Dining
Almond Tree, **39**
Blue Mountain
Inn, **54**
Cafe au Lait, **14**
Cosmo's Seafood
Restaurant
and Bar, **22**
Evita's, **40**
Hot Pot, **56**
Hotel Four
Seasons, **58**
Ivor Guest House, **62**
Jade Garden, **59**

Le Pavillon, **55**
Palm Court, **57**
Paradise Yard, **16**
Peppers, **67**
Rick's Cafe, **13**
The Ruins, **41**
Sweet Spice, **17**
Tan-ya's, **20**

Lodging
Astra Country Inn &
Restaurant, **30**
Bonnie View Planta-
tion Hotel, **63**
Boscobel Beach, **50**
Charela Inn, **19**
Chukka Cove, **36**
Ciboney, Ocho
Rios, **52**
Club Caribbean, **34**
Club Jamaica
Beach Resort, **43**
Couples, **49**

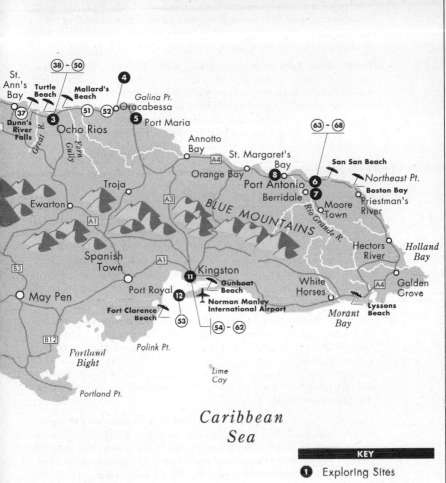

St.
Ann's
Bay

**Turtle
Beach**

**Mallard's
Beach**

(38) – (50)

4

Galina Pt.
Oracabessa

51   52

3

37

**Dunn's
River
Falls**

Ocho Rios

Great R.

Fern Gully

5   Port Maria

Annotto
Bay

A4

St. Margaret's
Bay

Orange Bay

8

Port Antonio

Berridale

Troja

Ewarton

A3

BLUE MOUNTAINS

A1

(63) – (68)

6

7

San San Beach

Northeast Pt.

Boston Bay
Priestman's
River

Moore
Town

Rio Grande R.

Hectors
River

Holland
Bay

Spanish
Town

A1

A1

Kingston

11

Port Royal

12

**Gunboat
Beach**

B3

May Pen

**Fort Clarence
Beach**

53

**Norman Manley
International Airport**

(54) – (62)

White
Horses

A4

Golden
Grove

**Lyssons
Beach**

Morant
Bay

B12

Portland
Bight

Polink Pt.

Portland Pt.

Lime
Cay

*Caribbean
Sea*

KEY

❶ Exploring Sites

⑬ Hotels and Restaurants

Devine Destiny, **15**
Dragon Bay, **68**
Enchanted
Garden, **38**
FDR, Franklyn D. Resort, **35**
Fisherman's Inn Dive
Resort, **28**
Goblin Hill, **67**
Grand Lido, **26**
H.E.A.R.T.
Country Club, **33**
Hedonism II, **25**

Hibiscus Lodge, **44**
Hotel Mocking
Bird Hill, **66**
Jamaica Grande, **42**
Jamaica Inn, **47**
Jamaica, Jamaica, **32**
Jamaica Palace, **65**
Jamaica Pegasus, **55**
Mandeville Hotel, **31**
Morgan's Harbour
Hotel, Beach Club,
and Yacht Marina, **53**
Negril Cabins, **27**

Negril Gardens, **18**
Plantation Inn, **46**
Poinciana Beach Resort, **23**
Sandals Dunn's
River, **37**
Sandals Negril, **24**
Sandals Ocho
Rios, **45**
Sans Souci Lido, **51**
Shaw Park
Beach Hotel, **48**
Swept Away, **21**

Terra Nova, **60**
Trelawny Beach
Hotel, **29**
Trident Villas
and Hotel, **64**
Wyndham New
Kingston, **57**

The dispute continues as to the origin of the name Ocho Rios. Some claim it's Spanish for "eight rivers"; others maintain that the name is a corruption of *chorreras,* which describes a seemingly endless series of cascades that sparkle from the limestone rocks along this stretch of coast. For as long as anyone can remember, Jamaicans have favored Ocho Rios as their own escape from the heat and the crowds of Kingston.

Dunn's River Falls is an eye-catching sight: 600 feet of cold, clear mountain water splashing over a series of stone steps to the warm Caribbean. The best way to enjoy the falls is to climb the slippery steps. Don a swimsuit, take the hand of the person ahead of you, and trust that the chain of hands and bodies leads to an experienced guide. The leaders of the climbs are personable fellows who reel off bits of local lore while telling you where to step. *Immediately off Main Rd. (A-1), between St. Ann's and Ocho Rios,* ☎ *809/974–5015.* ☛ *$5 adults, $2 children 2–11.*

Prospect Plantation Tour is the best of several offerings that delve into the island's former agricultural lifestyle. It's not just for specialists; virtually everyone enjoys the beautiful views over the White River Gorge and the tour by jitney (a canopied open-air cart pulled by a tractor) through a plantation with exotic fruits and tropical trees planted over the years by such celebrities as Winston Churchill and Charlie Chaplin. Horseback riding over 1,000 acres is available as is minigolf, and there's a pub on site for drinks. ☎ *809/974–2058.* ☛ *$12 adults and children over 12.* ☾ *Daily 10:30–2.*

The only major historic site in Ocho Rios is the **Old Fort,** built in 1777 as a defense against invaders from the sea. The original "defenders" spent much of their time sacking and plundering as far afield as St. Augustine, Florida, and sharing their bounty with the local plantation owners who financed their missions. Fifteen miles west is Discovery Bay, site of Columbus's landing, with a small museum of artifacts and Jamaican memorabilia.

Ocho Rios's newest attraction is **Coyaba River Garden and Museum,** which features exhibits on Jamaica's many cultural influences (the national motto is "Out of Many One People"). The museum covers the island's history from the time of the Arawak Indians up to the modern day. The complex includes an art gallery, a crafts shop, and a snack bar and offers the Moonshine Festival, a dinner-entertainment package, on Wednesday, and the Jamaica Music Review every Friday night. *Shaw Park Rd., Ocho Rios,* ☎ *809/974–6235.* ☛ *$4.50 adults and children over 12.* ☾ *Daily 8:30–5.*

Other excursions of note are the one to Runaway Bay's Green Grotto Caves (and a boat ride on an underground lake); a ramble through the Shaw Park Botanical Gardens; a visit to Sun Valley, a working plantation with banana, coconut, and citrus trees; and a drive through Fern Gully, a natural canopy of vegetation filtered by sunlight (Jamaica has the world's largest number of fern species, more than 500).

❹ Two area residences are of more than passing interest. **Golden Eye,** between Oracabessa and Port Maria, just east of Ocho Rios on the main coast road, was used in wintertime by Ian Fleming, the creator of James Bond, from 1946 until his death in 1964. Later Golden Eye served as home to reggae legend Bob Marley and to the founder of Island Records, Chris Blackwell. Today it can be seen only by those who can afford to rent it from the record company; however, at press time there was talk of opening to the public as a museum (phone Firefly, *below,* for more information). It's an airy complex of deep-blue buildings, walls, and bookcases bursting with Bond memorabilia, and a private cove reached by stone steps that would have delighted 007.

❺ **Firefly,** about 20 miles east of Ocho Rios in Port Maria, was once Sir Noël Coward's vacation residence and is now preserved in all its hill top wonder by the Jamaican National Heritage Trust. Coward used to entertain jet-setters and royalty in the surprisingly spartan digs in an Eden-like setting. He wrote *High Spirits, Quadrille,* and other plays here. Coward's simple grave is on the grounds next to a small stage where his plays are occasionally performed. Recordings of Coward singing of mad dogs and Englishmen echo over the lawns. Guided tours include time in the photo gallery and a walk through the house and grounds, the viewing of a biographical video on Coward, and a drink in the gift shop. *Port Maria,* ☎ *809/997-7201.* ☛ *$10.* ⊙ *Daily 8:30-5:30.*

Also in **Port Maria** is St. Mary's Parish Church, a handsome stone building that sits stolidly on the waterfront. Just across the street are the burned-out remains of the courthouse.

Further information on Ocho Rios is available from the Ocho Rios Jamaica Tourist Board office (☎ 809/974-2570).

Port Antonio

❻ Every visitor's presence in **Port Antonio** pays homage to the beginnings of Jamaican tourism. Early in the century the first tourists arrived here on the island's northeast coast, 133 miles east of Montego Bay, drawn by the exoticism of the island's banana trade and seeking a respite from the New York winters. The original posters of the shipping lines make Port Antonio appear as foreign as the moon, yet in time it became the tropical darling of a fast-moving crowd and counted Clara Bow, Bette Davis, Ginger Rogers, Rudyard Kipling, J. P. Morgan, and William Randolph Hearst among its admirers. Its most passionate devotee was the actor Errol Flynn, whose spirit still seems to haunt the docks, devouring raw dolphin fish and swigging gin at 10 AM.

Although the action has moved elsewhere, the area can still weave a spell. Robin Moore wrote *The French Connection* here, and Broadway's tall and talented Tommy Tune found inspiration for the musical *Nine* while being pampered at Trident.

A stroll through the town suggests a step into the past. **Queen Street,** in the residential Titchfield area, a couple of miles north of downtown Port Antonio, has several fine examples of Georgian architecture. **De-Montevin Lodge** (21 Fort George St., on Titchfield Hill, ☎ 809/993-2604), owned by the Mullings family (the late Gladys Mullings was Errol Flynn's cook), and the nearby **Musgrave Street** (the Craft Market is here) are in the traditional sea-captain style that one finds along coasts as far away as New England.

The town's best-known landmark is **Folly,** on the way to Trident, a Roman-style villa in ruins on the eastern edge of East Harbor. The creation of a Connecticut millionaire in 1905, the manse was made almost entirely of concrete. Unfortunately, the cement was mixed with seawater, and it began to crumble as it dried. According to local lore, the millionaire's bride took one look at her shattered dream, burst into tears, and fled forever. Little more than the marble floor remains today. Note that Folly becomes something of a ganja hangout after sundown and should be avoided then.

TIME OUT **Navy Island Resort and Marina** is the 64-acre island made famous by Errol Flynn when he bought it. The present operator welcomes visitors, who catch the private launch to his restaurant for lunch (or dinner, by prior reservation: ☎ 809/993-2667). Lunch can be as simple as a thick pepper-pot soup and grilled fish with lime; dinner can be a five-course spectacular.

 Rafting on the **Rio Grande River** (yes, Jamaica has a Rio Grande, too) is a must. This is the granddaddy of the river-rafting attractions, an 8-mile-long swift green waterway from Berrydale to Rafter's Rest. Here the river flows into the Caribbean at St. Margaret's Bay. The trip of about three hours is made on bamboo rafts pushed along by a raftsman who is likely to be a character. You can pack a picnic lunch and eat it on the raft or along the riverbank; wherever you lunch, a vendor of Red Stripe beer will appear at your elbow. A restaurant, bar, and souvenir shops are at Rafter's Rest (☎ 809/993-2778). The trip costs about $40 per two-person raft.

Another interesting excursion takes you 8 miles west of Port Antonio to **Somerset Falls,** a sun-dappled spot crawling with flowering vines, where you can climb the 400 feet with some assistance from a concrete staircase. A brief raft ride takes you part of the way. **Athenry Gardens,** a 3-acre tropical wonderland, and **Nonsuch Cave** are some 6 miles northeast of Port Antonio in the village of Nonsuch. The cave's underground beauty has been made accessible by concrete walkways, railed stairways, and careful lighting. *Somerset Falls,* ☎ *809/993-3740.* ☛ *$2.* ☉ *Daily 10-5. Athenry/Nonsuch,* ☎ *809/993-3740.* ☛ *$5.* ☉ *Daily 9-5.*

A short drive east from Port Antonio deposits you at **Boston Bay,** which is popular with swimmers and has been enshrined by lovers of jerk pork. The spicy barbecue was originated by the Arawaks and perfected by runaway slaves called the Maroons. Eating almost nothing but wild hog preserved over smoking coals enabled the Maroons to survive years of fierce guerrilla warfare with the English.

For as long as anyone can remember, Port Antonio has been a center for some of the finest deep-sea fishing in the Caribbean. Dolphins (the delectable fish, not the lovable mammal) are the likely catch here, along with tuna, kingfish, and wahoo. In October the weeklong Blue Marlin Tournament attracts anglers from around the world. By the time enough beer has been consumed, it's a bit like the running of the bulls at Pamplona, except that fish stories carry the day.

Further information on Port Antonio is available from the Port Antonio Jamaica Tourist Board office (☎ 809/993-3051).

Crystal Springs, about 18 miles west of Port Antonio, has more than 15,000 orchids, and hummingbirds dart among the blossoms, landing on visitors' outstretched hands. Hiking and camping are available here. *Buff Bay,* ☎ *809/993-2609.* ☛ *50¢.* ☉ *Daily 9-6.*

Negril

Situated 52 miles southwest of Montego Bay on the winding coast road, **Negril** is no longer Jamaica's best-kept secret. In fact, it has begun to shed some of its bohemian, ramshackle atmosphere for the attractions and activities traditionally associated with Montego Bay. Applauding the sunset from Rick's Cafe may still be the highlight of a day in Negril, yet increasingly the hours before and after have come to be filled with conventional recreation.

One thing that has not changed around this west-coast center (whose only true claim to fame is a 7-mile beach) is the casual approach to life. As you wander from lunch in the sun to shopping in the sun to sports in the sun, you'll find that swimsuits are common attire. Want to dress for a special meal? Slip a caftan over your bathing suit.

Negril's newest attraction is the **Anancy Family Fun & Nature Park** (☎ 809/957–4100), just across the street from the family-oriented Poinciana Beach Resort. Named after the mischievous spider character in Jamaican folktales, the 3-acre site features an 18-hole miniature golf course, go-cart rides, a fishing pond, a nature trail, and three small museums (craft, conservation, and heritage). Another new attraction is the **Negril Hills Golf Club** (☎ 809/957–4638). The 18-hole championship course, designed by Roy Case and Robert Simons, is slated for completion in mid-1995. At press time, 9 holes were open.

Even though you may be staying at one of the charming smaller inns in Negril, you may enjoy spending a day at **Hedonism II** (*see* Lodging, *below*), a kind of love poem to health, Mother Nature, and good (mostly clean) fun. The owners love to publicize the occasional nude volleyball game in the pool at 3 AM, but most of the pampered campers are in clothes and in bed well before that hour. And what if Hedonism II is not the den of iniquity it likes to appear to be? What it is, and what your day pass ($70) gets you, is a taste of the spirit as well as the food and drink—and participation in water sports, tennis, squash, and daily activities.

Next to Hedonism II is a sister resort, the **Grand Lido** (*see* Lodging, *below*), that offers a "day and night pass" for nonguests that includes daily activities, dinner at the Cafe Lido, live entertainment, and dusk-to-dawn dancing. The price is a hefty $70, and reservations are a must.

After sunset, activity centers on **West End Road**, Negril's main (and only) thoroughfare, which comes to life in the evening with bustling bistros and ear-splitting discos. West End Road leads to the town's only building of historical significance, the **Lighthouse.** All anyone can tell you about it, however, is that it's been there for a while. Even historians find it hard to keep track of the days in Negril.

Negril today stretches along the coast south from the horseshoe-shaped **Bloody Bay** (named during the period when it was a whale-processing center) along the calm waters of **Long Bay** to the Lighthouse section and the landmark **Rick's Cafe** (☎ 809/957–4335). Sunset at Rick's is a Negril tradition. Divers spiral downward off 50-foot-high cliffs into the deep green depths as the sun turns into a ball of fire and sets the clouds ablaze with color.

In the 18th century Negril was where the English ships assembled in convoys for the dangerous ocean crossing. Not only were there pirates in the neighborhood, but the infamous Calico Jack and his crew were captured right here, while they guzzled the local rum. All but two of them were hanged on the spot; Mary Read and Anne Bonney were pregnant at the time, and their execution was delayed.

Mandeville

More than a quarter of a century after Jamaica achieved its independence from Great Britain, **Mandeville** seems like a hilly tribute to all that is genteel and admirable in the British character. At 2,000 feet above sea level, 70 miles southeast of Montego Bay, Mandeville is considerably cooler than the coastal area 25 miles to the south. Its vegetation is more lush, thanks to the mists that drift through the mountains. The people of Mandeville live their lives around a village green, a Georgian courthouse, tidy cottages and gardens, even a parish church. The entire scene could be set down in Devonshire, were it not for the occasional poinciana blossom or citrus grove.

Mandeville is omitted from most tourist itineraries even though its residents are increasingly interested in showing visitors around. It is still much less expensive than any of the coastal resorts, and its diversions include horseback riding, cycling, croquet, hiking, tennis, golf, birdwatching, and people-meeting.

The town itself is characterized by its orderliness. You may stay here several days, or a glimpse of the lifestyle may satisfy you and you'll scurry back to the steamy coast. **Manchester Club** features tennis, nine holes of golf, and well-manicured greens; **Mrs. Stephenson** conducts photographic tours of her **Gardens** (☎ 809/962–2328), an arboretum filled with lovely orchids and fruit trees; and the natural **Bird Sanctuary** at **Marshall's Penn Great House** (☎ 809/962–2260) is visited by more than 25 species indigenous to Jamaica. Tours of this bird sanctuary are by appointment only and are led by owner Robert Sutton, one of Jamaica's leading ornithologists. Other sites worth visiting are **Lover's Leap,** where legend has it that two slave lovers leapt off the 1,700-foot-high cliff rather than be recaptured by their plantation owner, and the **High Mountain Coffee Plantation** (☎ 809/963–4211) in nearby Williamsfield, where free tours (by appointment only) show how coffee beans are turned into one of American's favorite morning drinks.

Kingston

The reaction of most visitors to the capital city, situated on the southeast coast of Jamaica, is anything but love at first sight. In fact, only a small percentage of visitors to Jamaica see it at all. **Kingston,** for the tourist, may seem as remote from the resorts of Montego Bay as the loneliest peak in the Blue Mountains. Yet the islanders themselves can't seem to let it go. Everybody talks about Kingston, about their homes or relatives there, about their childhood memories. More than the sunny havens of the north coast, Kingston is a distillation of the true Jamaica. Parts of it may be dirty, crowded, often raucous, yet it is the ethnic cauldron that produces the cultural mix that is the nation's greatest natural resource. (Note, however, that when the sun sets even Kingstonians beat a quick path out of downtown Kingston, which is considered unsafe after dark.) Kingston is a cultural and commercial crossroads of international and local movers and shakers, art-show openings, theater (from Shakespeare to pantomime), and superb shopping. Here, too, the University of the West Indies explores Caribbean art and literature, as well as science. As one Jamaican put it, "You don't really know Jamaica until you know Kingston."

The first-time business or pleasure traveler may prefer to begin with New Kingston, which glistens with hotels, office towers, apartments, and boutiques. Newcomers may feel more comfortable settling in here and venturing forth from comfort they know will await their return.

Kingston's colonial past is very much alive away from the high-rises of the new city. **Devon House,** our first stop, is reached through the iron gates at 26 Hope Road. Built in 1881 and bought and restored by the government in the 1960s, the mansion has period furnishings. Shoppers will appreciate Devon House, for the firm Things Jamaican has converted portions of the space into some of the best crafts shops on the island. On the grounds you'll find one of the few mahogany trees to survive Kingston's ambitious but not always careful development. *Devon House,* ☎ 809/929–7029. ☛ $2. ⊙ *Tues.–Sat. 9:30–5. Shops open Mon.–Sat. 10–6.*

Once you have accepted the fact that Kingston doesn't look like a travel poster—too much life goes on here for that—you may see your trip here for precisely what it is, the single best introduction to the people of Jamaica. Near the waterfront, the **Institute of Jamaica** is a museum and library that traces the island's history from the Arawaks to current events. The charts and almanacs here make fascinating browsing; one example, famed as the Shark Papers, is made up of damaging evidence tossed overboard by a guilty sea captain and later recovered from the belly of a shark. *12 East St.,* ☎ *809/922–0620.* ☛ *Free.* ☾ *Mon.–Thurs. 9–5, Fri. 9–4.*

From the institute, push onward to the **University of the West Indies** (☎ 809/927–1660) in the city's Mona section. A cooperative venture begun after World War II by several West Indian governments, the university is set in an eye-catching cradle of often misty mountains. The place seems a monument to the conviction that education and commitment lead to a better life for the entire Caribbean. There's a bar and disco on the campus where you can meet the students. Jamaica's rich cultural life is evoked at the **National Gallery,** which was once at Devon House and can now be found at Kingston Mall near the reborn waterfront section. The artists represented here may not be household names in other nations, yet the paintings of such intuitive masters as John Dunkley, David Miller, Sr., and David Miller, Jr., reveal a sensitivity to the life around them that transcends academic training. Among other highlights from the 1920s through the 1980s are works by Edna Manley and Mallica Reynolds, better known as Kapo. Reggae fans touring the National Gallery will want to look for Christopher Gonzalez's controversial statue of Bob Marley. *12 Ocean Blvd.,* ☎ *809/922–1561.* ☛ *Fees charged for special exhibits.* ☾ *Weekdays 11–4.*

Reggae fans will also want to see the **Bob Marley Museum.** Painted in Rastafarian red, yellow, and green, this recording studio was built by Marley at the height of his career. The house has since become the museum, with impromptu tours given by just about anyone who may be around (Bob's famous son, Ziggy, a reggae star in his own right, was the guide on our last visit). Certainly there is much here to help the outsider understand Marley, reggae, and Jamaica itself. The Ethiopian flag is a reminder that Rastas consider the late Ethiopian emperor Haile Selassie to be the Messiah, a descendant of King Solomon and the Queen of Sheba. A striking mural by Everald Brown, *The Journey of Superstar Bob Marley,* depicts the hero's life from its beginnings in a womb shaped like a coconut to enshrinement in the hearts of the Jamaican people. *56 Hope Rd.,* ☎ *809/927–9152.* ☛ *$4 adults, 50¢ children ages 4–12.* ☾ *Mon., Tues., Thurs., and Fri. 9:30–5, Wed. and Sat. 12:30–6.*

TIME OUT After touring the museum, stop to rest your feet and sip fresh fruit juice at the **Queen of Sheba,** an Ethiopian restaurant on the museum grounds. If you're hungry, you can sample local Jamaican dishes such as rice and peas or Ethiopian fare (strictly vegetarian) here as well.

There is also a fine **statue** of Bob Marley on Arthur Wint Drive across from the **National Stadium.**

While no longer lovingly cared for, the **Royal Botanical Gardens at Hope** is a nice place to picnic or while away an afternoon. Donated to Jamaica by the Hope family following the abolition of slavery, the garden consists of 50 acres filled with tropical trees, plants, and flowers, most clearly labeled for those taking a self-guided tour. Free concerts are given here on the first Sunday of each month. Park in the lot and walk or pay J$50 to drive through the park. *Hope Rd.,* ☎ *809/927–1085.* ☛ *J$10 adults, J$5 children.* ✆ *Weekdays 10–5, weekends 10–6.*

Another good picnic spot is the **Rockfort Mineral Baths,** listed on the Jamaica National Heritage Trust after being restored by the Caribbean Cement Company (which is next door). Named for the stone fort set above Kingston Harbour in 1694 by the British to guard against invasion, and for the natural mineral spring that emerged following a devastating earthquake in 1907, this complex draws Kingstonians who come to cool off in the invigorating spring water in the public swimming pool or to unwind tense muscles in private whirlpool tubs. You can also have a massage and visit the juice bar or the cafeteria before staking out your picnic spot on the landscaped grounds. *Kingston (on A-1, just outside town),* ☎ *809/938–5055.* ☛ *Pool: $J40 adults, $J20 children; private baths start at $J250.* ✆ *Weekdays 6:30–6, weekends 8–6.*

⓬ Unless your visit must be very brief, you shouldn't leave Kingston without a glimpse of "the wickedest city in the world." **Port Royal** has hardly been that since an earthquake tumbled it into the sea in 1692, yet the spirits of Henry Morgan and other buccaneers add a great deal of energy to what remains. The proudest possession of St. Peter's Church, rebuilt in 1726 to replace Christ's Church, is a silver communion plate said to have been donated by Morgan himself. A ferry from the Square in downtown Kingston goes to Port Royal at least twice a day, and the town is small enough to see on foot.

You can no longer down rum in Port Royal's legendary 40 taverns, but you can take in a draft of the past at the **National Museum of Historical Archaeology** and explore the impressive remains of **Fort Charles,** once the area's major garrison. On the grounds is the small **Fort Charles Maritime Museum** and **Giddy House,** an old artillery storehouse that gained its name after being permanently tilted by the earthquake of 1907. Nearby is a graveyard in which rests a man who died twice. According to the tombstone, Lewis Galdy was swallowed up in the great earthquake of 1692, spewed into the sea, rescued, and lived another four decades in "Great Reputation." *Old Naval Hospital, Port Royal,* ☎ *809/924–8782.* ☛ *$2 adults, $1 children.* ✆ *Daily 9:30–5:30.*

TIME OUT **Gloria's Rendezvous** (5 Queen St., ☎ 809/924–8578), the brightly painted, ramshackle eatery next to the Port Royal Police Station, is wildly popular with Kingston locals escaping the sultry city heat on weekends. Delectable grilled fish and chicken are the draw.

If you drove out, you'll pass several sites of interest on the way back to Kingston, including **remains of old forts** virtually covered over by vegetation, an **old naval cemetery,** which has some intriguing headstones, and a bit farther on, a **monument** commemorating **Jamaica's first coconut tree,** planted in 1863 (there's no tree there now, just plenty of cactus and scrub brush).

Further information on Kingston is available at the Kingston Jamaica Tourist Board office (☎ 809/929–9200).

Off the Beaten Track

The **Cockpit Country,** 15 miles inland from Montego Bay and one of the most primitive areas in the West Indies, is a terrain of pitfalls and potholes carved by nature in limestone. For nearly a century after 1655 it was known as the Land of Look Behind because British soldiers rode their horses back-to-back in pairs, looking out for the savage freedom fighters known as Maroons. Fugitive slaves who refused to surrender to the invading English, the Maroons eventually won a treaty of independence and continue to live apart from the rest of Jamaica in the Cockpit Country. The government leaves them alone, untaxed and ungoverned by outside authorities. Minibus tours from Montego Bay to Maroon headquarters at Accompong are offered through the **Maroon Tourist Attraction Co.** (☎ 809/952–4546).

The **Blue Mountains** are lush, with deep valleys and soaring peaks that climb into the clouds. Admirers of Jamaica's wonderful coffee may wish to take a tour to **Pine Grove** or to the Jablum coffee plant at **Mavis Bank.** Unless you are traveling with a local, do not rent a car and go on your own, as the mountain roads wind and dip, hand-lettered signs blow away, and a tourist can easily get lost—not just for hours, but for days. Pine Grove, a working coffee farm that doubles as an inn, has a restaurant that serves owner Marcia Thwaites's Jamaican cuisine. Mavis Bank is delightfully primitive—especially considering the retail price of the beans it processes. There is no official tour; ask someone to show you around.

If your calf muscles are in good shape, another way to see the Blue Mountains is by the **downhill bicycle tour** offered by Paul and Becky Lemoine (☎ 809/974–0635). The daylong adventure costs $80 and includes lunch. Or visit Gloria Palomino's café restaurant **The Gap** (☎ and fax 809/923–5617; open for lunch Tues.–Sun.), 4,200 feet above sea level, adjacent to several well-defined nature walking trails. Her gift shop sells the coveted Blue Mountain coffee. On your way up (or back) stop in World's End for a free tour of **Dr. Sangster's Rum Factory** (call ahead, ☎ 809/926–8888; open weekdays 9–4). The small factory produces wonderful liqueurs flavored with local coffee beans, oranges, coconuts, and other Jamaican produce; samples are part of the tour.

Spanish Town, 12 miles west of Kingston on A1, was the island's capital under Spanish rule. The town boasts the tiered Georgian **Antique Square,** the **Jamaican People's Museum of Crafts and Technology** (in the Old King's House stables), and the oldest cathedral (**St. James**) in the Western Hemisphere. Spanish Town's original name was Santiago de la Vega, which the English corrupted to St. Jago de la Vega, both meaning St. James of the Plains.

Beaches

Jamaica has 200 miles of beaches, some of them still uncrowded. The beaches listed below are public places (there is usually a small admission charge), and they are among the best Jamaica has to offer. In addition, nearly every resort has its own private beach, complete with towels and water sports. Some of the larger resorts sell day passes to nonguests. Generally, the farther west you travel, the lighter and finer the sand.

Doctor's Cave Beach at Montego Bay shows a tendency toward population explosion, attracting Jamaicans and tourists alike; at times it may resemble Fort Lauderdale at spring break. The 5-mile stretch of sugary sand has been spotlighted in so many travel articles and brochures over the years that it's no secret to anyone. On the bright side, Doctor's Cave is well fitted for all its admirers with changing rooms, colorful if overly insistent vendors, and a large selection of snacks.

Two other popular beaches in the Montego Bay area are **Cornwall Beach,** farther up the coast, which is smaller, also lively, with lots of food and drink available and a water-sports concession, and **Walter Fletcher Beach,** on the bay near the center of town. Fletcher offers protection from the surf on a windy day and therefore unusually fine swimming; the calm waters make it a good bet for children, too.

Ocho Rios appears to be just about as busy as MoBay these days, and the busiest beach is usually **Mallards.** The **Jamaica Grande** hotel, formerly the Mallards Beach and Americana hotels, is here, spilling out its large convention groups at all hours of the day. Next door is **Turtle Beach,** which islanders consider the place for swimming in Ocho Rios.

In Port Antonio, head for **San San Beach** or **Boston Bay.** Any of the shacks spewing scented smoke along the beach at Boston Bay will sell you the famous peppery delicacy, jerk pork.

Puerto Seco Beach at Discovery Bay is sunny and sandy.

There are no good beaches in Kingston. Beachgoers can travel outside of the city, but the beaches there, as a rule, are not as beautiful as those in the resort areas. The most popular stretch of sand is **Hellshire Beach** in Bridgeport, about a 20- to 30-minute drive from Kingston. **Fort Clarence,** a beach in the Hellshire Hills area southwest of the city, has changing facilities and entertainment. Sometimes Kingstonians are willing to drive 32 miles east to the lovely golden **Lyssons Beach** in Morant Bay or, for a small negotiable fee, to hire a boat at the Morgan's Harbor Marina at Port Royal to ferry them to **Lime Cay.** This island, just beyond Kingston Harbor, is perfect for picnicking, sunning, and swimming.

Not too long ago, the 7 miles of white sand at **Negril Beach** offered a beachcomber's vision of Eden. Today much of it is fronted by modern resorts, although the 2 miles of beach fronting Bloody Bay remain relatively untouched. The nude beach areas are found mostly along sections of the beach where no hotel or resort has been built, such as the area adjacent to Cosmo's (*see* Dining, *below*). A few resorts have built accommodations overlooking their nude beaches, thereby adding a new dimension to the traditional notion of "ocean view."

Those who seek beaches off the main tourist routes will want to explore Jamaica's unexploited south coast. Nearest to "civilization" is **Bluefields Beach** near Savanna-La-Mar, south of Negril along the coast. **Crane Beach** at Black River is another great discovery. And the best of the south shore has to be **Treasure Beach,** 20 miles farther along the coast beyond Crane.

Sports and the Outdoors

The tourist board licenses all operators of recreational activities, which should ensure you of fair business practices as long as you deal with companies that display the decals.

Fishing

Deep-sea fishing can be great around the island. Port Antonio gets the headlines with its annual Blue Marlin Tournament, and Montego Bay and Ocho Rios have devotees who talk of the sailfish, yellowfin tuna, wahoo, dolphin, and bonito. Licenses are not required. Boat charters can be arranged at your hotel.

Golf

The best courses are found around Montego Bay at **Tryall** (☎ 809/956–5681), **Half Moon** (☎ 809/953–2560), **Rose Hall** (☎ 809/953–2650), and **Ironshore** (☎ 809/953–2800). Good courses are also found at **Caymanas** (☎ 809/926–8144) and **Constant Spring** (☎ 809/924–1610) in Kingston and at **SuperClubs Runaway Bay** (☎ 809/973–2561) and

Sandals Golf and Country Club (☎ 809/974-2528), formerly Upton, in Ocho Rios. A 9-hole course in the hills of Mandeville is called **Manchester Club** (☎ 809/962-2403). Great golf and spectacular scenery also go hand in hand at the new **Negril Hills Golf Club** (☎ 809/957-4638) in Negril, which was scheduled to open fully by mid-1995 but has only managed to get half the course (9 holes) up and running so far. **Prospect Plantation** (☎ 809/974-2058) in Ocho Rios and the **Anancy Family Fun and Nature Park** (☎ 809/957-4100) in Negril have 18-hole minigolf courses.

Horseback Riding

Jamaica is fortunate to have the best equestrian facility in the Caribbean, **Chukka Cove** (write Box 160, Ocho Rios, St. Ann, ☎ 809/972-2506), near Ocho Rios. The resort, complete with stylishly outfitted villas, offers full instruction in riding, polo, and jumping, as well as hour-long trail rides, three-hour beach rides, and rides to a great house. Weekends, in season, this is the place for hot polo action and equally hot social action. **Rocky Point Stables** (☎ 809/953-2286), just east of the Half Moon Club in Montego Bay, **Rhodes Hall Plantation Ltd.** (☎ 809/957-4258), between Green Island and Negril, and **Prospect Plantation** (☎ 809/974-2058) also offer rides.

Tennis

Many hotels have tennis facilities that are free to their guests, but some will allow nonguests to play for a fee. The sport is a highlight at **Tryall** (☎ 809/956 5660), **Round Hill Hotel and Villas** (☎ 809/952-5150), **Sandals Montego Bay** (☎ 809/952-5510), and **Half Moon Club** (☎ 809/953-2211) in Montego Bay; **Swept Away** (☎ 809/957-4061) in Negril; and **Sandals Dunn's River** (☎ 809/972-1610), **Sans Souci Lido** (☎ 809/974-2353), and **Ciboney** (☎ 809/974-1027) in Ocho Rios.

Water Sports

The major areas for swimming, windsurfing, snorkeling, and scuba diving are Negril in the west and Port Antonio in the east. All the large resorts rent equipment for a deposit and/or a fee. Diving is perhaps the only option that requires training, because you need to show a C-card in order to participate. However, some dive operators on the island are qualified to certify you. Jamaica Tourist Board-licensed dive operators include **Resort Divers** (Swept Away, Negril, ☎ 809/957-4061; San Souci Lido, Ocho Rios, ☎ 809/974-2353; Jamaica/Jamaica, Runaway Bay, ☎ 809/973-2436), **Sun Divers** (Poinciana Beach Resort, Negril, ☎ 809/957-4069, and Ambiance Hotel, Runaway Bay, ☎ 809/973-2346), **Garfield Dive Station** (Ocho Rios, ☎ 809/974-5749), **North Coast Marine** (Half Moon Club, Montego Bay, ☎ 809/953-2211), and **Sandals Beach Resort Watersports** (Montego Bay, ☎ 809/979-0104). All of these operators offer certification courses and dive trips. Most all-inclusive resorts offer free scuba diving to their guests. **Lady Godiva** (San San Beach, Port Antonio, ☎ 809/993-3281) offers scuba diving, snorkeling, windsurfing, a glass-bottom boat, and sailing; excursions start at $25 per person.

Shopping

Shopping in Jamaica goes two ways: things Jamaican and things imported. The former are made with style and skill; the latter are duty-free luxury finds. Jamaican crafts take the form of resort wear, hand-loomed fabrics, silk screens, wood carvings, paintings, and other fine arts.

Jamaican rum is a great take-home gift. So is Tia Maria, Jamaica's world-famous coffee liqueur. The same goes for the island's prized Blue Mountain and High Mountain coffees and its jams, jellies, and marmalades.

Some bargains, if you shop around, include Swiss watches, Irish crystal, jewelry, cameras, and china. The top-selling French perfumes are also available alongside Jamaica's own fragrances.

Shopping Areas

KINGSTON

A shopping tour of the Kingston area should begin at **Constant Spring Road** or **King Street.** No matter where you begin, keep in mind that the trend these days is shopping malls, and in Jamaica they caught on with a fever. The ever-growing roster includes **Twin Gates Plaza, New Lane Plaza,** the **New Kingston Shopping Centre, Tropical Plaza, Manor Park Plaza,** the **Village,** the **Springs,** and the newest (and some say nicest), **Sovereign Shopping Centre.**

A day at **Devon House** (26 Hope Rd., Kingston, ☎ 809/929–6602) should be high on your shopping list. This is the place to find old and new Jamaica. The great house is now a museum with antiques and furniture reproductions and the Lady Nugent's Coffee Terrace outside. There are boutiques in what were once the house's stables: a branch of Things Jamaican, Tanning and Turning for leather finds, first-rate furnishings and antique reproductions at Jacaranda, silver and pewter re-creations (many from centuries-old patterns) at the Olde Port Royal, and some of the best tropical-fruit ice cream (mango, guava, pineapple, and passion fruit) at I-Scream.

MONTEGO BAY AND OCHO RIOS

While you should not rule out a visit to the "crafts market" on Market Street in MoBay, you should consider first how much you like pandemonium and haggling over prices and quality. The crafts markets in Ocho Rios are less hectic unless a cruise ship is in port, and the crafts markets in Port Antonio and Negril are good fun. You'll find a plethora of T-shirts; straw hats, baskets, and place mats; carved wood statues; colorful Rasta berets; and cheap jewelry.

If you're looking to spend money, head for **City Centre Plaza, Overton Plaza, Miranda Ridge Plaza, St. James's Place,** and **Westgate Plaza** in Montego Bay; in Ocho Rios, the shopping plazas are **Pineapple Place, Ocean Village,** the **Taj Mahal, Coconut Grove,** and **Island Plaza.** It's also a good idea to chat with salespeople, who can enlighten you about the newer boutiques and their whereabouts.

Specialty Shops

ARTS AND CRAFTS

Silk batiks, by the yard or made into chic designs, are at **Caribatik** (A-1, 2 mi east of Falmouth, ☎ 809/954–3314), the studio of the late Muriel Chandler. Drawing on patterns in nature, Chandler translated the birds, seascapes, flora, and fauna into works of art.

The **Gallery of West Indian Art** (1 Orange La., MoBay, ☎ 809/952–4547 and at Round Hill, ☎ 809/952–5150) is the place to find Jamaican and Haitian paintings. A corner of the gallery is devoted to hand-turned pottery (some painted) and beautifully carved and painted birds and jungle animals.

Harmony Hall (an 8-minute drive east on A1 from Ocho Rios; ☎ 809/975–4222), a restored great house, is where Annabella Proudlock sells her unique wood Annabella Boxes. The covers feature reproductions of Jamaican paintings. Larger reproductions of paintings, lithographs, and signed prints of Jamaican scenes are also for sale, along with hand-carved wood combs—all magnificently displayed. Harmony Hall is also well known for its year-round art shows by local artists.

Belts, bangles, and beads are the name of the game at the factory of **Ital-Craft** (Shop 8, Upper Manor Park Shopping Plaza, 184C Spring Rd., Kingston, ☎ 809/931–0477). Belts are the focus of this savvy operation, but it also produces some intriguing jewelry and purses (many made from reptile skins). While Ital-Craft's handmade treasures are sold in boutiques throughout Jamaica, we recommend a visit to the factory for the largest selection of these belts, made of spectacular shells, combined with leather, feathers, or fur. (The most ornate belts sell for about $75.)

Sprigs and Things (Miranda Ridge Plaza, Gloucester Ave., MoBay, ☎ 809/952–4735) is where artist Janie Soren sells T-shirts featuring her hand-painted designs of birds and animals. She also paints canvas bags and tennis dresses.

Things Jamaican (Devon House, 26 Hope Rd., Kingston, ☎ 809/929–6602, and 44 Fort St., MoBay, ☎ 809/952–5605) has two outlets and two airport stalls that display and sell some of the best native crafts made in Jamaica, with items that range from carved wood bowls and trays to reproductions of silver and brass period pieces.

BIKINIS

Teeny-weeny bikinis, which more than rival Rio's, are designed by Sonia Vaz and sold at her manufacturing outlet, **Vaz Enterprises, LTD.** (77 East St., Kingston, ☎ 809/922–9200), at Sandals, and other resorts (see Lodging, *below*).

JEWELRY

L. A. Henriques (Shop 11, Upper Manor Park Plaza, Kingston, ☎ 809/931–0613) sells high-quality jewelry made to order.

RECORDS

Reggae tapes by world-famous Jamaican artists, such as Bob Marley, Ziggy Marley, Peter Tosh, and Third World, can be found easily in U.S. or European record stores, but a pilgrimage to **Randy's Record Mart** (17 N. Parade, Kingston, ☎ 809/922–4859) should be high on the reggae lover's list. Also worth checking are the **Record Plaza** (Tropical Plaza, Kingston, ☎ 809/926–7645), **Record City** (14 King St., Port Antonio, ☎ 809/993–2836), and **Top Ranking Records** (Westgate Plaza, Montego Bay, ☎ 809/952–1216). While Kingston is the undisputed place to make purchases, the determined somehow (usually with the help of a local) will find **Jimmy Cliff's Records** (Oneness Sq., MoBay, no ☎), owned by reggae star Cliff.

SANDALS

Cheap sandals are good buys in shopping centers throughout Jamaica. While workmanship and leathers don't rival the craftsmanship of those found in Italy or Spain, neither do the prices (about $20 a pair). In Kingston, **Lee's** (New Kingston Shopping Centre, ☎ 809/929–8614) is a good place to sandle-shop. In Ocho Rios, the **Pretty Feet Shoe Shop** (Ocean Village Shopping Centre, ☎ 809/974–5040) is a good bet. In Montego Bay, try **Overton Plaza** or **Westgate Plaza**.

Gift Ideas

Fine Macanudo handmade cigars make great gifts and are easily carried. They can be bought on departure at Montego Bay airport (call 809/925–1082 for outlet information). Blue Mountain coffee can be found at **John R. Wong's Supermarket** (1–5 Tobago Ave., Kingston, ☎ 809/926–4811). The **Sovereign Supermarket** (Sovereign Center, 106

Hope Rd., ☎ 809/927–5955) has a wide selection of coffee and other goods; it is somewhat easier to find and is closer to other shopping and dining. You can also look for the magic beans at **Magic Kitchen Ltd.** (Village Plaza, Kingston, ☎ 809/926–8894). If the stores are out of Blue Mountain, you may have to settle for High Mountain coffee, the natives' second-preferred brand.

Jamaican-brewed rums and Tia Maria can be bought at either the Kingston or MoBay airports before your departure. As a general rule, only rum factories, such as Sangster's, are less expensive than the airport stores, and if you buy at the airport there's no toting of heavy, breakable bottles from your hotel.

Dining

Sampling the island's cuisine introduces you to virtually everything the Caribbean represents. Every ethnic group that has made significant contributions on another island has made them on Jamaica, too, adding to a Jamaican stockpot that is as rich as its melting pot. So many Americans have discovered the Caribbean through restaurants owned by Jamaicans that the very names of the island's dishes have come to represent the region as a whole.

Jamaican food represents a true cuisine, organized, interesting, and ultimately rewarding. It would be a terrible shame for anyone to travel to the heart of this complex culture without tasting several typically Jamaican dishes. Here are a few:

Rice and Peas. This traditional dish is known also as Coat of Arms and is similar to the *moros y christianos* of Spanish-speaking islands: white rice cooked with red beans, coconut milk, scallions, and seasoning.

Pepper Pot. The island's most famous soup—a peppery combination of salt pork, salt beef, okra, and the island green known as callaloo—it is green, but at its best it tastes as though it ought to be red.

Curry Goat. Young goat is cooked with spices and is more tender and has a gentler flavor than the lamb for which it was substituted by immigrants from India.

Ackee and Saltfish. Salted fish was once the best islanders could do between catches, so they invented this incredibly popular dish that joins saltfish (in Portuguese, *bacalao*) with ackee, a vegetable (introduced to the island by Captain Bligh of Bounty fame) that reminds most people of scrambled eggs.

Jerk Pork. Created by the Arawaks and perfected by the Maroons, jerk pork is the ultimate island barbecue. The pork (the purist cooks the whole pig) is covered with a paste of hot peppers, pimento berries (also known as allspice), and other herbs and cooked slowly over a coal fire. Many think that the "best of the best" jerk comes from Boston Beach in Port Antonio.

Patties. These spicy meat pies elevate street food to new heights. Although they in fact originated in Haiti, Jamaicans can give patty lessons to anybody.

Where restaurants are concerned, Kingston has the widest selection; its ethnic restaurants offer Italian, French, Rasta natural foods, Cantonese, German, Thai, Indian, Korean, and Continental fare. There are fine restaurants as well in all the resort areas, and the list includes many that are in large hotels. Most of the restaurants outside the hotels in

MoBay and Ocho Rios will provide complimentary transportation when you call for reservations.

What to Wear

Dress is casual chic (just plain casual at the local hangouts), except at the top resorts, some of which require semiformal wear in the evening during high season. People tend to dress up a little for dinner—just because they feel like it—so you may feel more comfortable in nice slacks or a sundress. Ask about the dress code when making your reservations.

CATEGORY	COST*
$$$$	over $40
$$$	$30–$40
$$	$20–$30
$	Under $20

per person, excluding drinks and service charge (or tip)

Kingston

$$$–$$$$ ★ **Blue Mountain Inn.** The elegant Blue Mountain Inn is a 30-minute taxi ride from New Kingston and worth every penny of the fare. On a former coffee plantation, the antique-laden inn complements its English Colonial atmosphere with Continental cuisine. All the classics of the beef and seafood repertoires are here, including chateaubriand béarnaise and lobster thermidor. ✗ *Gordon Town Rd.,* ☎ *809/927–1700 or 809/927–2606. Reservations required. Jacket required. AE, MC, V.*

$$$ **Le Pavillon.** Lunch, afternoon tea, and dinner are all well done at Le Pavillon. The setting, just off the Jamaica Pegasus lobby, is sophisticated. The menu is international with a Jamaican flair and is complemented by an excellent (and costly) wine list. Service is top-notch. A value-packed seafood buffet lunch is served on Friday. Even during the day this place is a little formal: Shorts are a no-no. ✗ *Jamaica Pegasus hotel,* ☎ *809/926–3690. Reservations required. AE, DC, MC, V.*

$$–$$$ **Palm Court.** Nestled on the mezzanine floor of the Wyndham New Kingston, the elegant Palm Court is open for lunch and dinner (lunch is noon to 3 PM; dinner from 6 PM). The menu is Continental, with a heavy Italian accent: tagliatelle Alfredo, with ham and fresh mushrooms; tricolor pasta with shrimp, fish, and lobster; and a seafood kebab. There's also a reasonably priced pasta bar. ✗ *Wyndham New Kingston,* ☎ *809/926–5430. Reservations advised. AE, DC, MC, V.*

$$ **Hotel Four Seasons.** The Four Seasons has been pleasing local residents for more than 25 years with cuisine from the German and Swiss schools as well as local seafood. The setting tries to emulate Old World Europe without losing its casual island character. ✗ *18 Ruthven Rd.,* ☎ *809/926–8805. Reservations advised. AE, DC, MC, V.*

$$ **Ivor Guest House.** This elegant yet cozy restaurant has an incredible view of Kingston from 2,000 feet above sea level. Go for dinner, when the view is dramatically caught between the stars and the glittering brooch of Kingston's lights. International and Jamaican cuisine is served. Owner Helen Aitken is an animated and cordial hostess. Afternoon tea here is a treat. ✗ *Jack's Hill,* ☎ *809/977–0033. Reservations required. AE, MC, V. Closed Sept.*

$$ ★ **Jade Garden.** Located on the third floor of the Sovereign Centre, the Jade Garden, with its shiny black lacquer chairs and views of the Blue Mountains, garners rave reviews for its Cantonese and Thai menu. Favorites include steamed fish in black bean sauce, black mushrooms stuffed with shrimp, and shrimp with lychee. There is an inexpensive lunch buffet every Friday afternoon (J$460 per person) and dim sum on the last Sunday of each month. ✗ *106 Hope Rd.,* ☎ *809/978–3476/9. Reservations advised on weekends. AE, MC, V.*

$ **Hot Pot.** Jamaicans love the Hot Pot for breakfast, lunch, and dinner.
★   Fricassee chicken is the specialty, along with other local dishes, such as mackerel run-down (salted mackerel cooked down with coconut milk and spices) and ackee and salted cod. The restaurant's fresh juices "in season" are the best—tamarind, sorrel, coconut water, soursop, and cucumber. ✕ *2 Altamont Terr.,* ☎ *809/929–3906. MC, V.*

$ **Peppers.** This casual outdoor bar is the "in" spot in Kingston, particularly on weekends. Sample the grilled lobster or jerk pork and chicken with the local Red Stripe beer. ✕ *31 Upper Waterloo Rd.,* ☎ *809/925–2219. MC, V.*

Montego Bay

$$$–$$$$ **Georgian House.** A landmark restaurant in the heart of town, the Georgian House occupies a restored 18th-century building set in a shady garden courtyard. An extensive wine cellar complements the Continental and Jamaican cuisines, the best of which are the steaks and the dishes made with the local spiny lobster. Don't miss the gallery of Jamaican art. ✕ *Union and Orange Sts.,* ☎ *809/952–0632. Reservations required. AE, D, DC, MC, V.*

$$$ **Julia's.** Couples flock to this romantic Italian restaurant set up in the hills overlooking the twinkling lights of MoBay. Diners choose from an à la carte or five-course fixed-price menu ($33 per person) that includes homemade soups and pastas; entrées of fish, chicken, and veal; and scrumptious desserts. Don't expect the meal to equal the stupendous view, and you won't be disappointed. ✕ *Bogue Hill,* ☎ *809/952–1772 or 809/979–0744. Reservations accepted. AE, MC, V.*

$$$ **Sugar Mill.** Seafood is served with flair at this terrace restaurant set on
★   the grounds of the Half Moon Golf Course. Caribbean specialties, steak, and lobster are usually offered in a pungent sauce that blends Dijon mustard with Jamaica's own Pickapeppa. Otherwise choices are the daily à la carte specials and anything flamed. Live music and a well-stocked wine cellar round out the experience. ✕ *At Half Moon Golf Course,* ☎ *809/953–2228. Reservations required for dinner, advised for lunch. AE, DC, MC, V.*

$$–$$$ **Norma at the Wharf House.** This sister property to creative chef and entrepreneur Norma's successful Kingston restaurant has gathered rave reviews as a supper club. The setting is a converted 300-year-old stone sugar warehouse on the water, decorated in blue and white. Innovative Jamaican cuisine ranges from Caribbean lobster steamed in Red Stripe beer to jerk chicken with mangoes flambé. On Friday nights a jazz band enlivens the bar and sometimes plays out on the wharf. ✕ *10 minutes west of MoBay in Reading (on the road to Negril),* ☎ *809/979–2745. Reservations required for dinner. MC, V. Closed May–Aug. and Mon. No lunch Tues.–Wed.*

$$–$$$ **Pier 1.** Despite the fact that it shares a name with the American imports store, Pier 1 writes the book daily on waterfront dining. After tropical drinks at the deck bar, you'll be ready to dig into the international variations on fresh seafood, the best of which are the grilled lobster and any preparation of island snapper. Several party cruises leave from the marina here, and the restaurant is mobbed by locals who come to dance on Friday night. ✕ *Just off Howard Cooke Blvd.,* ☎ *809/952–2452. Reservations advised for dinner. AE, MC, V.*

$$ **Town House.** Most of the rich and famous who have visited Jamaica over the decades have eaten at the Town House. You will find specials of the day and good versions of standard ideas (red snapper papillote is the specialty, with lobster, cheese, and wine sauce), along with many Jamaican favorites (curried chicken with breadfruit and ackee) in an 18th-century Georgian house adorned with original Jamaican and

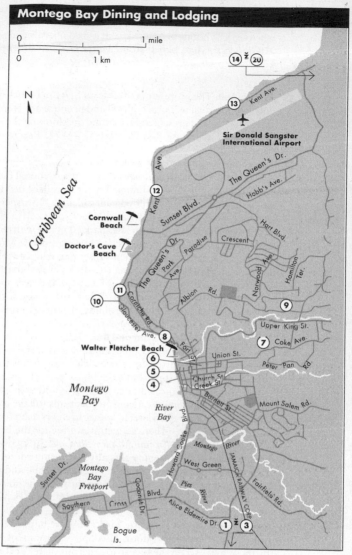

Montego Bay Dining and Lodging

Haitian art. There's alfresco dining on the stone patio as well. ✗ *16 Church St.,* ☎ *809/952–2660. Reservations advised. AE, DC, MC, V.*

$ **Hemingway's Pub.** The local business community enjoys the pub lunches and dinners at this casual bar and restaurant. The fish-and-chips here is a classic. The terrace is a great place to set and watch the sun go down. ✗ *Miranda Ridge Plaza, Gloucester Ave., tel 809/952–8606/7. No credit cards.*

$ **Le Chalet.** Don't let the French name fool you. This Denny's look-alike,
★ set in a nondescript shopping mall, serves heaping helpings of some of the best Chinese and Jamaican food in MoBay. Tasty lobster Cantonese costs only $9. ✗ *32 Gloucester Ave.,* ☎ *809/952–5240. AE, MC, V.*

$ **Pork Pit.** This open-air hangout, across the street from popular Wal-
★ ter Fletcher Beach and not far from the airport, must introduce more travelers to Jamaica's fiery jerk pork than any other place on the is-

land. The Pork Pit is a local phenomenon down to the Red Stripe beer, yet it's accessible in both location and style. Plan to arrive around noon, when the jerk begins to be lifted from its bed of coals and pimento wood. ✕ *Gloucester Ave., across from Walter Fletcher Beach,* ☎ *809/952–1046. No reservations. No credit cards.*

Negril

$$ **Cafe au Lait.** The proprietors of Cafe au Lait are French and Jamaican, and so is the cuisine. Local seafood and produce are prepared with delicate touches and presented in a setting overlooking the sea. ✕ *Mirage Resort on Lighthouse Rd.,* ☎ *809/957–4471. Reservations advised. MC, V.*

$$ **Tan-ya's.** This alfresco restaurant is on the edge of the beach at the Seasplash hotel. Jamaican delicacies with an international flavor are served for breakfast, lunch, and dinner. Try the excellent deviled crab backs or the snapper Florentine stuffed with callaloo. ✕ *Seasplash Hotel, Norman Manley Blvd.,* ☎ *809/957–4041. AE, DC, MC, V.*

$–$$ **Rick's Cafe.** Here it is, the local landmark complete with cliffs, cliff divers, and powerful sunsets, all perfectly choreographed. Most folks come for the drinks and the renowned sunset party, since the standard pub menu seems pricey. In the sunset ritual, the crowd toasts Mother Nature with rum drinks, shouts and laughter, and ever-shifting meeting and greeting. When the sun slips below the horizon, there are more shouts, more cheers, and more rounds of rum. ✕ *Lighthouse Rd.,* ☎ *809/957–4335. No credit cards.*

$ **Cosmo's Seafood Restaurant and Bar.** Owner Cosmo Brown has made
★ this seaside open-air bistro a pleasant place to spend a lunch, an afternoon, and maybe stay on for dinner. The fresh fish is the main attraction, and the conch soup that's the house specialty is a meal in itself. There's also lobster (grilled or curried), fish-and-chips, and a catch-of-the-morning. Customers often drop cover-ups to take a dip before coffee and dessert and return later to lounge in chairs scattered under almond and sea-grape trees. (There's an entrance fee for the beach alone, but it's less than $1.) ✕ *Norman Manley Blvd.,* ☎ *809/957–4330. MC, V.*

$ **Paradise Yard.** Locals enjoy this alfresco restaurant on the Savanna-La-Mar side of the roundabout in Negril. Sit back and relax in the casual atmosphere while eating Jamaican dishes or the house special Rasta Pasta. It's open for breakfast, lunch, and dinner. ✕ *White Hall Rd.,* ☎ *809/957–4006. MC, V.*

$ **Sweet Spice.** When Paradise Yard is full (it happens) turn to Sweet Spice, immediately next door. This open-air mom-and-pop diner run by the Whytes serves inexpensive, generous plates of conch steak, fried or curried chicken, fresh-catch fish, oxtail in brown stew sauce, and other down-home specialties. The fresh juices are quite satisfying. Drop by for breakfast, lunch, or dinner. ✕ *1 White Hall Rd.,* ☎ *809/957–4621. MC, V.*

Ocho Rios

$$–$$$ **Almond Tree.** One of the most popular restaurants in Ocho Rios, the
★ Almond Tree has a menu of Jamaican and Continental favorites: pumpkin and pepper-pot soups, many wonderful preparations of fresh fish, veal piccata, fondue, spaghetti Bolognese. The swinging rope chairs of the terrace bar and the tables perched above a lovely Caribbean cove are great fun. ✕ *83 Main St., Ocho Rios,* ☎ *809/974–2813. Reservations required. AE, DC, MC, V.*

$$ **The Ruins.** A 40-foot waterfall dominates the open-air Ruins restaurant, and in a sense it dominates the food as well. Surrender to local preference and order the Lotus Lily Lobster, a stir-fry of the freshest local shellfish, then settle back and enjoy the tree-shaded deck and the

Reality check. Call home.

―― *AT&T USADirect® and World Connect.® The fast, easy way to call most anywhere.* ――

Take out AT&T Calling Card or your local calling card.** Lift phone. Dial AT&T Access Number for country you're calling from. Connect to English-speaking operator or voice prompt. Reach the States or over 200 countries. Talk. Say goodbye. Hang up. Resume vacation.

Anguilla 1-800-872-2881	French Antilles 19011
Antigua (Public Card Phones)......................#1	Grenada†. 1-800-872-2881
Bahamas......................**1-800-872-2881**	**Haiti†■**....................**001-800-972-2883**
Barbados•••■..............**1-800-872-2881**	Jamaica†† 0-800-872-2881
Bermuda†■...........…**1-800-072-2881**	**Netherland Antilles**...**001-800-872-2881**
Bonaire **001-800-872-2881**	St. Kitts/Nevis 1-800-872-2881
British V.I. 1-800-872-2881	St. Lucia ....Special USADirect Dedicated Locations
Cayman Islands 1-800-872-2881	St. Vincent ••• 1-800-872-2881
Dom. Rep.††■ **1-800-872-2881**	**Trinidad&Tobago**..Special USADirect Dedicated Locations
Dominica 1-800-872-2881	Turks & Caicos••• 1-800-872-2881

AT&T
Your True Choice

For a free wallet sized card of all AT&T Access Numbers, call: 1-800-241-5555.

All the best trips start with **Fodor's**.

EXPLORING GUIDES

At last, the color of an art book combined with the usefulness of a complete guide.

"As stylish and attractive as any guide published." —*The New York Times*

"Worth reading before, during, and after a trip." —*The Philadelphia Inquirer*

More than 30 destinations available worldwide. $19.95 each.

BERKELEY GUIDES

The budget traveler's handbook

"Berkeley's scribes put the funk back in travel." —*Time*

"Fresh, funny, and funky as well as useful." —*The Boston Globe*

"Well-organized, clear and very easy to read." —*America Online*

14 destinations worldwide. Priced between $13.00 - $19.50. ($17.95 - $27.00 Canada)

AFFORDABLES

"All the maps and itinerary ideas of Fodor's established gold guides with a bonus—shortcuts to savings." —*USA Today*

"Travelers with champagne tastes and beer budgets will welcome this series from Fodor's." —*Hartfort Courant*

"It's obvious these Fodor's folk have secrets we civilians don't." —*New York Daily News*

Also available: Florida, Europe, France, London, Paris. Priced between $11.00 - $18.00 ($14.50 - $24.00 Canada)

At bookstores, or call **1-800-533-6478**

Fodor's
The name that means smart travel.™

graceful footbridges that connect the dining patios. There's live entertainment on weekends. ✕ *DaCosta Dr.,* ☎ *809/974–2442. Reservations advised. AE, D, DC, MC, V.*

$–$$ **Evita's.** The setting here is a sensational, nearly 100-year-old ginger-
★ bread house high on a hill overlooking Ocho Rios Bay (but also convenient from MoBay). Large, open windows provide cooling mountain breezes and stunning views of city and sea. More than 18 kinds of pasta are served here, ranging from lasagna Rastafari (vegetarian) to *rotelle alla Eva* (crabmeat with white sauce and noodles). There are also excellent fish dishes—sautéed fillet of red snapper with orange butter, red snapper stuffed with crabmeat—and several meat dishes, among them grilled sirloin with mushroom sauce and barbecued ribs glazed with honey-and-ginger sauce. ✕ *Mantalent Inn, Ocho Rios,* ☎ *809/974–2333. Reservations advised. AE, MC, V.*

Lodging

The island has a variety of destinations to choose from, each of which offers its own unique expression of the Jamaican experience. **Montego Bay** has miles of hotels, villas, apartments, and duty-free shops. Although lacking much in the way of cultural stimuli, MoBay presents a comfortable island backdrop for the many conventions and conferences it hosts.

Ocho Rios, on the northeast coast halfway between Port Antonio and Montego Bay, is hilly and lush, with rivers, riotous gardens, and a growing number of upscale resorts, many of which are all-inclusive. Ocho Rios's hotels and villas are all situated within short driving distance of shops and one of Jamaica's most scenic attractions, Dunn's River Falls.

Port Antonio, described by poet Ella Wheeler Wilcox as "the most exquisite port on earth," is a seaside town nestled at the foot of verdant hills toward the east end of the north coast. The two best experiences to be had here are rafting the Rio Grande and a stop at the Trident, arguably the island's classiest resort. Today, Port Antonio enjoys the reputation of being Jamaica's most favored out-of-the-way resort.

Negril, some 50 miles west of Montego Bay, was long a sleepy Bohemian retreat. In the last decade the town has bloomed considerably and added a number of classy all-inclusive resorts (Sandals Negril, Grand Lido, and Swept Away), with a few more on the drawing board. Negril itself is only a small village, so there isn't much of historical significance to seek out. Then again, that's not what brings the sybaritic singles and couples here. The crowd is young, hip, laid-back, and here for the sun, the sand, and the sea.

Mandeville, 2,000 feet above the sea, is noted for its cool climate and proximity to secluded south-coast beaches. Most accommodations don't have air-conditioning (it's simply not needed) but are close to golf, tennis, horseback riding, and bird-watching areas.

The smallest of the resort areas, **Runaway Bay** has a handful of modern hotels and an 18-hole golf course.

Kingston is the most culturally active place on Jamaica. Some of the island's finest business hotels are here, and those high towers are filled with rooftop restaurants, English pubs, serious theater and pantomime, dance presentations, art museums and galleries, jazz clubs, upscale supper clubs, and disco dives.

Jamaica was the birthplace of the Caribbean all-inclusive, the vacation concept that took the Club Med idea and gave it a lusty, excess-in-the-tropics spin. The all-inclusive resort has become the most popular vacation option on Jamaica, offering incredible values with rates from $145 to $350 per person per night. Rates include airport transfers; hotel accommodations; three meals a day plus snacks; all bar drinks, often including premium liquors; wine, beer, and soft drinks; a plethora of land and water sports, including instruction and equipment; and all gratuities and taxes. The only surcharges are usually for such luxuries as massages, souvenirs, sightseeing tours, and weddings or vow-renewal ceremonies (though these are often included at any of the high-end all-inclusives). At times they may feel a bit like Pleasure Island, as all of your needs and most of your wants are taken care of. The all-inclusives have branched out, some of them courting families, others going after an upper crust that would not even have picked up a brochure a few years ago. Most require a three-night minimum stay.

If you're the exploring type who likes to get out and about, you may prefer an EP property. Many places offer MAP or FAP packages that include extras like airport transfers and sightseeing tours. Even if you don't want to be tied down to a meal plan, it pays to inquire, because the savings can be considerable. Rooms at most hotels come equipped with cable or satellite TV, air-conditioning, direct-dial phone, clock radio, and, in many cases, a safe. Larger properties usually have no-smoking rooms and rooms accessible to travelers with disabilities, as well room service, a beauty parlor, a tour desk, and car rentals.

Please note that the price categories listed below are based on winter rates. As a general rule, rates are reduced anywhere from 10% to 30% from April 30 to December 15. The **Jamaica Reservation Service** (☎ 800/526–2422) can book resorts, hotels, and guest houses throughout the country.

At press time, two new properties were just opening: the luxury all-inclusive, adults-only **Braco Village Resort** (☎ 800/654–1337) in Rio Bueno just west of Runaway Bay, and **Comfort Suites Resort** (☎ 800/228–5150), set on a beautifully landscaped hillside in Ocho Rios, overlooking the bay and the cruise-ship terminal. We were unable to visit the properties in fully operational state, but initial reports have been good. Surprisingly, both fall in our $–$$ range.

CATEGORY	COST EP*	COST MAP**	COST AI***
$$$$	over $245	over $250	over $275
$$$	$175–$245	$190–$250	$225–$275
$$	$105–$175	$130–$190	$175–$225
$	under $105	under $130	under $175

EP prices are for a standard double room for two in winter, excluding 10% tax and any service charge.
**MAP prices include breakfast and dinner for two daily in winter. Often MAP packages come with use of nonmotorized water sports and other benefits.*
***All-inclusive (AI) winter prices are per person, double occupancy, and include tax, service, all meals, drinks, facilities, lessons, and airport transfers.*

Falmouth

$$$ **Trelawny Beach Hotel.** The dependable Trelawny Beach resort offers seven stories of pale pink rooms overlooking 4 miles of beach. Off the beaten path, it's run as an all-inclusive resort with an emphasis on families. During the off-season, one child under 15 gets free room and board when sharing accommodations with his or her parents. There are daily activities programs for children and adults, a free shopping shuttle into

MoBay, and a designated area of beach for nude sunbathing. ☎ *Box 54, Falmouth, ☎ 809/954–2450 or 800/336–1435, FAX 809/954–2149. 350 rooms. 2 dining rooms, 4 lighted tennis courts, pool, daily activities, water-sports equipment, shopping arcade, beauty salon, disco, nightly entertainment, MoBay shopping shuttle. AE, DC, MC, V. MAP, FAP, All-Inclusive.*

$$ **Fisherman's Inn Dive Resort.** A charming red-tile-and-stucco building
★ fronts a phosphorescent lagoon at this welcoming, well-run hotel. At night the hotel restaurant offers a free boat ride to diners; dip your hand in the water, and the bioluminescent microorganisms glow. The bright breezy rooms all face the water; pale carpets and walls are enhanced by floral curtains and bedspreads. The inn is a good deal, whether you dive (excellent packages are available) or not. Rates include three dives daily and MAP meal plan; nondivers do get a slight discount. ☎ *Rock District, ☎ 809/954–4078, FAX 809/954–3427. 12 rooms. Restaurant, bar, pool, private beach across lagoon, water-sports center/PADI dive shop. AE, MC, V. MAP.*

Kingston

$$$ **Jamaica Pegasus.** The Jamaica Pegasus is one of two business-class hotels in the New Kingston area. The 17-story complex near downtown has an efficient and accommodating staff, meeting rooms, a top-notch restaurant, a café, Old World decor, a pampering ambience, and an international crowd in the lobby. Other advantages here include an excellent business center, duty-free shops, and 24-hour room service. The rooms, all with balcony and voice mail, were scheduled to have desperately needed face-lifts in 1995. ☎ *81 Knutsford Blvd., Box 333, Kingston, ☎ 809/926–3690 or 800/225–5843, FAX 809/929–5855. 334 rooms, 16 suites. 2 restaurants, cocktail lounge, coffee shop, boutiques, beauty salon, Olympic-size pool, kids' pool, jogging track, health club, 2 lighted tennis courts. AE, DC, MC, V. EP, MAP.*

$$-$$$ **Wyndham New Kingston.** The high-rise Wyndham New Kingston, the
★ second of Kingston's business-beat hotels, underwent major renovations in 1994. All facilities were upgraded, giving everything a pleasant new look, from the expansive marble lobby to the peach, teal, and green decor in the well-appointed guest rooms. Lots of extras were thrown in, such as secured-access elevators and in-room hair dryers and coffee/tea setup. Rates include a massage at the spa and admission to Jonkanoo, the hotel's hot nightclub (*see* Nightlife, *below*). ☎ *Box 112, Kingston, ☎ 809/926–5430 or 800/526–2422, FAX 809/929–7439. 284 rooms, 13 suites, 6 1- and 2-bedroom housekeeping units. 2 restaurants, 3 bars, Olympic-size pool, art gallery, shopping arcade, gaming room, 2 lighted tennis courts, health club, beauty salon/spa, nightclub. AE, DC, MC, V. EP, MAP.*

$$ **Morgan's Harbour Hotel, Beach Club, and Yacht Marina.** A favorite of the sail-into-Jamaica set, this small property has 22 acres of beachfront at the very entrance to the old pirate's town. Done in light tropical prints, the rooms are very basic, but many have a balcony and minifridge. Ask for one in the new wing. Because the hotel is so close to the airport, passengers on delayed or canceled flights are often bused here to wait. ☎ *Port Royal, Kingston, ☎ 809/924–8464 or 800/526–2422, FAX 809/924–8562. 39 rooms, 6 suites. Restaurant, pier bar, disco, water-sports center, complimentary airport shuttle, full-service marina, deep-sea-fishing charters, access to Lime Cay and other cays. AE, MC, V. EP.*

$$ **Terra Nova.** Set in the quieter part of New Kingston, 1 mile from the commercial district and within walking distance of Devon House, is the intimate Terra Nova hotel. Guest rooms are decked out in classical mahogany furniture and fine art. The El Dorado restaurant offers

international cuisine and reasonably priced buffets (seafood on Wednesday and Jamaican on Friday). ☎ *17 Waterloo Rd., Kingston 10,* ☎ *809/926–9334,* 𝔽𝔸𝕏 *809/929–4933. 35 rooms. Restaurant, coffee shop, bar, pool. AE, DC, MC, V. EP.*

Mandeville

$ **Astra Country Inn & Restaurant.** Country is the key word in the name of this retreat, which is 2,000 feet up in the mountains. The low price reflects the nature of the very basic rooms here: They define spartan but are immaculately clean. There is no air-conditioning, but you shouldn't miss it this high in the mountains. The small restaurant is open from 7 AM to 9 PM and serves snacks in addition to breakfast, lunch, and dinner. The food is billed as "home cooking" and emphasizes fresh produce—lots of vegetables and fruit juices. ☎ *Ward Ave., Box 60, Mandeville,* ☎ *809/962–3265 or 800/526–2422,* 𝔽𝔸𝕏 *809/962–1461. 20 rooms, 2 housekeeping suites. Restaurant and bar, swimming pool, sauna, AE, MC, V. EP.*

$ **Mandeville Hotel.** Tropical gardens wrap around the building, and flowers spill onto the terrace where breakfast and lunch are served. Rooms are simple and breeze-cooled; suites have full kitchens. You'll need a car to get around town, go out for dinner, and get to the beach, which is an hour away. ☎ *Box 78, Mandeville,* ☎ *809/962–2460 or 800/233–4582,* 𝔽𝔸𝕏 *809/962–0700. 46 rooms, 17 1-, 2-, and 3-bedroom housekeeping suites. Restaurant, bar, coffee shop, pool, golf privileges at nearby Manchester Club. AE, MC, V. EP.*

Montego Bay

$$$$ **Round Hill Motel and Villas.** The Hollywood set frequents this peace-
★   ful resort, 8 miles west of town on a hilly peninsula. Twenty-seven villas housing 74 suites are scattered over 98 acres, and there are 36 motel rooms in Pineapple House, a two-story building overlooking the sea. Rooms are done in a refined Ralph Lauren style, with mahogany furnishings and terra-cotta floors. The villas are leased back to the resort by private owners and vary in decor, but jungle motifs are a favorite. All come with a personal maid and a cook to make your breakfast (or all three meals for an extra charge), and several have private pools. The restaurant serves creative combinations of light sauces, fresh produce, seafood, and meat. The good food and elegant presentation make feasting in the dining room, or better yet on the seaside terrace, a memorable treat. ☎ *Box 64, Montego Bay,* ☎ *809/952–5150 or 800/237–3237,* 𝔽𝔸𝕏 *809/952–2505. 36 rooms, 27 housekeeping villas. Restaurant, pool, 5 tennis courts (2 lighted), fitness center, watersports center. AE, DC, MC, V. EP, MAP, FAP, All-inclusive.*

$$$$ **Tryall Golf, Tennis, and Beach Club.** Part of a posh residential development 13 miles west of Montego Bay, Tryall clings to a hilltop overlooking a golf course and the Caribbean. You choose between rooms in the former great house of a 2,200-acre island plantation and one of the private villas dotting the landscape, each with its own pool and full staff (butler, cook, maid, laundress, and gardener). You provide the grocery list, and the villa staff will do all the food preparation. All accommodations are individually and plushly decorated. There are two fine dining rooms in the great house: One is elegant and serves Continental and Jamaican cuisine, and the other serves more casual fare. The beautiful seaside golf course is one of this resort's more memorable features. It's also reputed to be one of the meanest courses in the world and as such hosts big-money tournaments. ☎ *Box 1206, Montego Bay,* ☎ *809/956–5660/7 or 800/742–0498,* 𝔽𝔸𝕏 *809/956–5673. 47 rooms, 55 villas. 2 restaurants, golf course, 9 tennis courts (5*

lighted), pool with swim-up bar, water sports, golf packages available. AE, DC, MC, V. EP, MAP, FAP, All-inclusive.

$$$–$$$$ **Half Moon Golf, Tennis, and Beach Club.** For four decades the 400-acre
★ Half Moon Club resort has been a destination unto itself with a repu-
tation for doing the little things right. Although it has mushroomed from
30 to more than 300 units, it has maintained its intimate, luxurious feel.
The rooms, suites, and villas, whether in modern or Queen Anne style,
are decorated in exquisite taste, with such flourishes as Oriental throw
rugs and antique radios. Several villas have private pools, and the mile-
long stretch of beach is just steps away from every guest room. Expansion
in 1994–95 added an upscale shopping mall, four new restaurants, large
conference facilities, 20 more luxury villas with pools, and a nature re-
serve. Kids under 12 are given a 50% discount on meal plans. ⌸ *Box
80, east of Montego Bay (7 mi),* ☎ *809/953–2211 or 800/227–3237,
FAX 809/953–2731. 53 individual rooms, 279 rooms in housekeeping
suites and villas. 7 restaurants, 3 bars, golf course, minigolf, croquet,
4 squash courts, 13 tennis courts (7 lighted), horseback riding, health
spa, gym, water-sports center, 39 pools (2 open to guests without pri-
vate pools), nature reserve, art gallery, 40 boutiques, children's program,
bicycles. AE, DC, MC, V. EP, MAP, FAP, All-inclusive.*

$$–$$$$ **Coyaba Beach Resort and Club.** Owners Joanne and Kevin Robertson
★ live on the property, interacting with guests daily, giving this $4 million
oceanfront retreat the feel of an intimate and inviting country inn. Located just east of Montego Bay, Coyaba is also very family friendly. The
plantation-style great house is a successful blend of modern amenities
and Old World grace: Guest rooms are decorated with lovely Colonial
prints and hand-carved mahogany furniture, and sunshine from the tall
windows pours over terra-cotta floors and potted plants. Ocean-view
rooms are considerably more expensive than those with a mountain view.
Airport transfers, banana cake and rum baskets, afternoon tea, and Continental breakfast are part of the package. ⌸ *Little River, St. James,* ☎
*809/953–9150 or 800/223–9815, FAX 809/953–2244. 50 rooms. Restau-
rant, 2 bars, pool, whirlpool, fitness room, lighted tennis court, masseuse,
gift shop, water-sports equipment, scuba diving and fishing charters,
golf packages. MC, V. EP.*

$$ **Atrium at Ironshore.** Fifteen moderately priced, fully furnished apart-
ments make up this small complex. Decor varies, but each of the
charming units has pastel floral prints, beige tile floors, beige rattan
furniture, a patio or balcony, and a private housekeeper/cook on call.
Large saltwater tanks full of tropical fish brighten the alfresco dining
terrace near the waterfall-fed pool, and you'll often find lively games
of darts or skittles under way in the English-style pub. A shopping mall
with supermarket, cinema, and several boutiques is within walking dis-
tance, but you'll have to take a shuttle to the beach. Children under
12 stay free with their parents. ⌸ *1084 Morgan Rd.,* ☎ *809/953–2605,
FAX 809/952–5641. 15 1½-, 2-, and 3-bedroom housekeeping suites.
Restaurant, pub, pool, laundry facilities, beach and shopping shuttle.
AE, DC, MC, V. EP.*

$$ **Holiday Inn Rose Hall.** The hotel chain has done much to raise a run-
down campground to the level of a full-service property, with activi-
ties day and night and many tour facilities (and large tour groups as
well). Although the rooms are cheerful enough, the hotel is big and
noisy, with drab hallways and public areas. Perhaps by press time the
renovations scheduled for late 1995 will have resulted in positive
changes. The quietest rooms are those farthest from the pool. The beach
is just a sliver. There's live entertainment nightly near the pool and in
the bars and restaurants. Kids under 19 stay free; those under 12 eat
free as well. ⌸ *Box 480, Montego Bay,* ☎ *809/953–2485 or 800/352–*

0731, FAX *809/953–2840. 520 rooms. 3 restaurants, 4 bars, pool, water-sports center, exercise room, kids' camp, shuffleboard, 4 tennis courts (2 lighted), gaming room with slot machines, disco, shops. AE, DC, MC, V. EP, MAP, All-Inclusive.*

$$ Royal Jamaican. Another all-inclusive resort for couples only, the Royal Jamaican is distinguished by Jamaican-style architecture arranged in a semicircle around attractive gardens. It's a sister in both theme and quality to other Sandals resorts. While sportive and activity-laden, this property is a bit quieter and more genteel than the other Sandals and draws a nicely mixed international crowd. Standard rooms have lacquered furniture in light colors and mauve carpeting and bedspreads; bathrooms are small. The deluxe oceanfront rooms and suites are more elegant and inviting, with mahogany four-poster beds and floral print fabrics. All accommodations are air-conditioned, but the breezes that come in the slat windows do a nice job of keeping things cool. A colorful "dragon boat" carries guests across to Sandals's private island to dine at the new Indonesian restaurant. ✆ *Box 167, Montego Bay,* ☎ *809/953–2231 or 800/726–3257,* FAX *809/953–2788. 190 rooms. 4 restaurants, 4 bars, 4 pools, 5 whirlpools, 2 saunas, gym, beauty salon, disco, private offshore island, beach, 3 tennis courts (2 lighted). 3-night minimum stay. AE, DC, MC, V. All-inclusive.*

$$ Sandals Montego Bay. The largest private beach in Montego Bay is the
★ spark that lights Sandals Montego Bay, one of the most popular couples resorts in the Caribbean. The all-inclusive format includes airport transfers, all taxes and tips, a plethora of water and land sports, including scuba diving, all sports equipment and lessons, aerobics classes, meals, theme parties, and other entertainment. It's a bit like a cruise ship that remains in port, with rooms overlooking the bay. The revelers don't seem to mind the zooming planes (the airport is next door), and the atmosphere here remains one of a great big fun party. Even the staff seem happy as they hum or sing their way through the workday. Rooms are comfortable enough, but the revelers here are seldom in them because there is so much to do. The new Oleandor Restaurant is probably the best fine-dining outlet in the Sandals chain. ✆ *Box 100, Montego Bay,* ☎ *809/952–5510 or 800/726–3257,* FAX *809/952–0816. 243 rooms. 4 restaurants, snack bar, 4 bars (1 swim-up), 2 pools, 3 whirlpools, 4 plunge pools, gym, body shop, water-sports center, 4 lighted tennis courts, 1 racquetball court, nightclub, gift shop, concierge service. 3-night minimum stay. AE, DC, MC, V. All-inclusive.*

$$ Wyndham Rose Hall. The veteran Wyndham Rose Hall, a self-contained resort built on the 400-acre Rose Hall Plantation, mixes recreation with a top-flight conference setup. A bustling business hotel popular with groups, it has all the resort amenities: tennis courts, golf course, three interconnected pools, a nightclub, a water-sports center, and a shopping arcade. Rooms in shades of deep blue and rose are comfortable but somewhat sterile. A "Kid's Klub" with daily supervised activities is included in the rates. The thin crescent of beach is good for sailing and snorkeling. Indoor and outdoor restaurants serve Continental, Italian, and Jamaican fare. ✆ *Box 999, Montego Bay,* ☎ *809/953–2650 or 800/996–3426,* FAX *809/953–2617. 489 rooms, 19 suites. 4 restaurants, coffee shop, 3 pools, water-sports center, 6 lighted tennis courts, golf course, nightclub, lounge, fitness center, shopping arcade. AE, DC, MC, V. EP, MAP, All-inclusive.*

$ Richmond Hill Inn. The hilltop Richmond Hill Inn, a quaint, 200-year-old great house originally owned by the Dewars clan, attracts repeat visitors by providing spectacular views of the Caribbean and a great deal of peace, compared with MoBay's hustle. Decor tends toward the dainty and is a bit dated, with frilly lace curtains and doilies, lots of lavenders and mauves, and crushed-velevet furniture here and there. A free shuttle will take you to shopping and beaches, about 10–15 minutes away. ☎ *Union St., Box 362, Montego Bay,* ☎ *809/952–3859 or 800/423–4095. 15 rooms, 4 suites. Dining room, coffee shop, bar, pool, free MoBay shuttle. AE, MC, V. MAP, FAP.*

$ ★ **Sandals Inn.** If you're willing to do without a private beach (there's a public one across the street), you can stay here for much less than at the other couples-only Sandals resorts. The inn is more intimate and far quieter than the other Sandals; it's managed more as a small hotel than a large resort. Full room service is one of the nice touches here not found at the other Sandals properties on Jamaica. The charming rooms are compact; most have balconies facing the pool. Dark carpet contrasts with white lacquered furniture and tropical print fabrics. There's plenty to do here, and you can get in on the action at the other two MoBay Sandals by hopping aboard the free hourly shuttle. The in-town location makes the inn convenient to shopping and tours. ☎ *Box 412, Montego Bay,* ☎ *809/952–4140 or 800/726–3257, FAX 809/952–6913. 52 rooms. 2 restaurants, 2 bars, gift shop, pool, lighted tennis court, fitness center, water-sports center. 3-night minimum stay. AE, DC, MC, V. All-inclusive.*

Negril

$$$$ ★ **Grand Lido.** The opening of the SuperClubs' all-inclusive Grand Lido in 1989 broke new ground by extending this popular concept to the upper-income bracket. The dramatic entrance of marble floors and columns sets a tone of striking elegance. The well-appointed ocean-front and garden rooms (split-level and arguably the most spacious and stylish of the all-inclusives), sports facilities, and 24-hour room service follow up in high style. For some, the pièce de résistance is a sunset cruise on the resort's 147-foot yacht, *Zien,* which was a wedding gift from Aristotle Onassis to Prince Rainier and Princess Grace of Monaco. Grand Lido attracts a slightly more mature and settled crowd than does the usual Negril resort. The gourmet restaurant, Piacere, is one of Jamaica's best, and an atmosphere of cool elegance prevails throughout. ☎ *Box 88, Negril,* ☎ *809/957–4010 or 800/859–7873, FAX 809/957–4317. 182 rooms, 18 suites. 3 restaurants, 9 bars, disco, game room, 24-hour room service, water-sports center including scuba diving, 2 pools, 5 whirlpools (1 clothing optional), clothed and nude beaches, 4 tennis courts (2 lighted), fitness center, beauty salon, spa, art gallery, video and book library, video theater, boutiques, complimentary laundry service, complimentary manicure and pedicure, complimentary weddings. 3-night minimum stay. AE, DC, MC, V. All-inclusive.*

$$$ ★ **Hedonism II.** Here is the resort that introduced the Club Med–style all-inclusive to Jamaica years ago. Still wildly successful, Hedonism appeals most to single (60% of guests are), uninhibited vacationers who like a robust mix of physical activities. You can try everything from scuba diving to a trampoline clinic. Wood-trimmed public areas are filled with potted plants (and scantily clad guests). Handsome guest rooms have modern blond wood furniture. It's too wild for some, party-animal heaven to others. ☎ *Box 25, Negril,* ☎ *809/957–4200 or 800/859–7873, FAX 809/957–4289. 280 rooms. Restaurant, 5 bars (including piano bar, laser karaoke bar, and disco), clothed and nude beaches, pool, 2 hot tubs, water-sports center with scuba diving, fitness center, aerobics, trapeze and trampoline clinics, horseback riding, 6 lighted tennis courts, 2 squash courts, bicycles, basketball, volleyball, game room. AE, DC, MC, V. All-inclusive.*

$$$ **Sandals Negril.** One of the best and longest stretches of Negril's 7-mile beach is a tempting reason to choose this Sandals resort. Couples looking for an upscale, sportive getaway and a casual atmosphere (you can wear dressy shorts to dinner) flock here. Water sports, including scuba diving, are emphasized; and the capable staff is happy both to teach neophytes and take out guests who are already certified. One pool is designated for scuba training. There's an offshore island, a huge swim-up pool bar, and a range of spacious accommodations. Both rooms and staff are sunny and appealing. ⌨ *Box 10, Negril,* ☎ *809/957–4216 or 800/726–3257,* FAX *809/957–4338. 215 rooms. 4 restaurants, 4 bars (including swim-up, piano, and disco), 3 pools, 2 whirlpools, water-sports center, dive shop, shuffleboard, volleyball, basketball, squash, and racquetball courts, 4 lighted tennis courts, croquet lawn, water-skiing, saunas, fitness center, movies. 3-night minimum stay. AE, DC, MC, V. All-inclusive.*

$$$ **Swept Away.** Fitness and health-conscious couples are the target mar-
★ ket for this all-inclusive, which emphasizes sports and healthy cuisine. Twenty cottages containing 134 suites are spread along half a mile of drop-dead gorgeous beach. Each cottage has a private inner-garden atrium. The 10-acre sports complex across the road outclasses the competition by a long shot. The Feathers Continental Restaurant is open to nonguests. The compound's chefs concentrate on healthful dishes with lots of fish, white meat, fresh fruits, and vegetables. ⌨ *Long Bay, Negril,* ☎ *809/957–4040 or 800/545–7937,* FAX *809/957–4060. 134 suites. 2 restaurants, 4 bars, 10 lighted tennis courts, 2 squash courts, 2 racquetball courts, fitness center, spa, jogging track, aerobics room, yoga classes, 2 steam rooms and saunas with plunge pools, 2 hot tubs, pool with lap lines, water-sports center including scuba diving, golf privileges at Negril Hills. 3-night minimum stay. AE, DC, MC, V. All-inclusive.*

$$ **Charela Inn.** Each quiet, elegantly appointed room here has a private
★ balcony or a covered patio. The owners' French-Jamaican roots find daily expression in the kitchen, and there's an excellent selection of wines. The small beach here is part of the glorious 7-mile Negril crescent. Kids under 10 stay free with parents, but they aren't allowed in deluxe rooms. ⌨ *Box 33, Negril, Westmoreland,* ☎ *809/957–4277 or 800/423–4095,* FAX *809/957–4414. 35 rooms, 4 suites. Restaurant, pool, beach, sailboats and Windsurfers, day cruise, cocktail party. 5-night minimum stay. MC, V. EP, MAP.*

$$ **Negril Cabins.** These timber cottages are nestled amid lush vegetation and towering royal palms. Rooms are unadorned, but natural wood paneling gives them a fresh look. Only "superior" rooms have air-conditioning; other rooms are cooled by ceiling fans and the breezes that come through the slatted windows. Televisions are also found only in the superior rooms. The gleaming beach is across the road. A most convivial place, this property is popular with young Europeans. Reasonably priced dive packages are available, and kids under 16 stay free in their parents' room. ⌨ *Norman Manley Blvd., Box 118, Negril,* ☎ *809/957–4350 or 800/382–3444,* FAX *809/957–4381. 100 rooms. 3 restaurants, 3 bars (including piano and swim-up), pool, hot tub, small gym, laundry, dive shop, tennis court, game room, children's program, gift shop. AE, MC, V. EP.*

$$ **Poinciana Beach Resort.** The management here has created all-inclusive packages with families in mind. A stay at Poinciana includes a "Fun-Pass" to Anancy Park across the street, a supervised children's activity program, a playground, and baby-sitting during meal hours. Up to two children under 14 (one per parent) can stay free. One- and two-bedroom housekeeping suites with kitchens are a good choice for families. Rooms and suites have cream-colored walls and tile floors. Bright jewel tones in the Jamaican prints that adorn the walls are echoed in the floral bedspreads. One of Jamaica's prettiest palm-speckled sandy beaches awaits, along with a water-sports center (scuba diving costs extra). There are also slot machines, tennis, a sunset cruise, a disco, a sports/piano bar, and a poolside bar with unlimited drinks. The open-air restaurant serves Caribbean cuisine, while the second floor café offers faster fare—burgers, hot dogs, and fries. ☎ *Box 44, Negril,* ☎ *809/957–4100 or 800/468–6728,* FAX *in FL 305/749–6794. 90 rooms including studios and 1- and 2-bedroom housekeeping suites. 2 restaurants, disco, bar, 2 pools, whirlpool, 2 lighted tennis courts, water-sports center, dive shop, basketball court, volleyball, lawn chess, gaming room, gym, shuffleboard, laundry facility, playground, library, beauty salon, masseuse, grocery store, duty-free shops, golf package. AE, MC, V. All-inclusive.*

$ ★ **Devine Destiny.** Lush tropical forest surrounds this terra-cotta tile-roofed resort set 500 yards from the West End cliffs. Spacious guest rooms are decorated in aqua and terra-cotta. All have refrigerators, but there are no ☎s, radios, or televisions. Some rooms have kitchenettes, some have air-conditioning; some both, some neither. Be sure to state your preferences when making your reservations. Most rooms overlook what the resort claims is the largest pool in Negril. Whether or not the claim is true matters little, for the free-form pool with graceful arched bridges, half-moon swim-up bar, and dining terrace is lovely. Up to two children under 12 stay free with their parents, and there's a game room to keep them occupied. The beach is 20 minutes away on foot, but a daily shuttle makes it easily accessible. ☎ *Summerset Rd. (Box 117, West End, Negril),* ☎ *and fax 809/957–9184. 40 rooms. 2 restaurants, bar, pool, sundeck, game room, TV room, beach shuttle. AE, MC, V. EP.*

$ **Negril Gardens.** Towering palms and well tended gardens surround the pink and white buildings of this hotel. Half of the rooms are beachside, half across the street overlooking the pool; all are attractive, with tile floors and rattan furniture in light colors (no ☎s or televisions). The beach is nice, and water sports are available. ☎ *Box 58, Negril,* ☎ *809/957–4408 or 800/752–6824,* FAX *809/957–4374. 65 rooms. Restaurant, 2 bars (including disco), lighted tennis court, small gym, game room, pool, water sports. AE, MC, V. EP, MAP, FAP.*

Ocho Rios

$$$$ **Boscobel Beach.** This is a parent's dream of a Jamaican vacation, an all-inclusive that makes families feel welcome. Everybody is kept busy all week for a single package price, and everyone leaves happy. The cheery day-care centers group children by age. Thoughtfully, there is an adults-only section of the resort (for when the kids want to get away). Up to two children (one per parent) under 14 stay free in their parent's room. Bedspreads in a bright pink, purple, and green shell print spice up the white tile floors, white curtains, and creamy walls of the rooms and suites. Breakfast and lunch are served at long buffets, and snacks are offered all day at the beach bar. Only the adults can dine at Allegro, a romantic Italian restaurant (kids get a supervised dinner elsewhere). Families can dine together at the Pavillion restaurant, which has a Continental menu. ☎ *Box 63, Ocho Rios,* ☎ *809/975–7330 or 800/859–7873,* FAX *809/975–7370. 208 rooms, half of them junior suites. 3 restaurants, 5 bars (including disco and piano), gym, 2 pools, 2 hot tubs, water-sports center with scuba diving, children's activity and nanny care programs, nursery, playground, petting zoo, game room, bicycles, shopping and sightseeing tours, boutique, 4*

lighted tennis courts, volleyball, golf greens fees and transportation, aerobics. AE, DC, MC, V. All-inclusive.

$$$$ **Chukka Cove.** The battle cry at Chukka Cove is "Saddle Up." The resort earns its horse feed by maintaining some of the best equestrian facilities in the Western Hemisphere. In addition to polo, experienced riders will want to investigate Chukka Cove's Jamaican Riding Holiday, an exploration of the north coast on horseback. Riders also have a choice of trail rides, mountain trail rides, beach rides, or an overnight escorted ride to the Lillyfield Great House. ☎ *Box 160, Ocho Rios,* ☎ *809/974–2593,* FAX *809/974–5568. 3 2-bedroom villas with cook and maid. Stables, equestrian instruction (all levels), swimming from rocks. No credit cards. EP, MAP, FAP.*

$$$$ **Sans Souci Lido.** This pastel-pink cliffside fantasyland looks and feels
★ like a dream, if indeed the dreamer had perfect taste and no need to fret over the bill. Romantic oceanfront suites are equipped with oversize whirlpool tubs. Soothing, light colors are the base of the decor; blond wood furniture, cool tile floors, and sheer curtains are accented by pastel watercolors and Jamaican prints on the walls. The Caribbean and Continental cuisine at the Casanova Restaurant delights, as does the pampering guests receive at Charlie's Spa in the form of a complimentary massage, body scrub, reflexology session, facial, manicure, and pedicure. A stay here is a wonderfully luxurious experience and a hands-down favorite in Jamaica. Children under 16 are not allowed. ☎ *Box 103, Ocho Rios,* ☎ *809/974–2353 or 800/859–7873,* FAX *809/974–2544. 13 rooms, 98 suites. 3 restaurants, 4 bars, 24-hour room service, full-service health spa and fitness center, yoga classes, freshwater and mineral pools, mineral-water hot tub, 2 lighted tennis courts, scuba diving, water-sports center, golf greens fees and transportation, croquet lawn, badminton and basketball courts, bicycles, game room, gift shops, complimentary shopping and sightseeing trips, complimentary laundry and dry cleaning service, complimentary weddings. 3-night minimum stay. AE, DC, MC, V. All-inclusive.*

$$$–$$$$ **Ciboney, Ocho Rios.** A Radisson Villa, Spa and Beach Resort, this stately plantation property has 36 rooms in its great house and 264 spacious one-, two-, and three-bedroom villa suites on 45 lush hillside acres overlooking the Caribbean. It is operated as a luxury all-inclusive geared toward affluent adults, both singles and couples; no children under the age of 16 are allowed. Outstanding features are the European-style spa and four signature restaurants, including the Orchids restaurant, whose menu was developed by the Culinary Institute of America. Every villa has a private attendant and pool, giving guests the ultimate in privacy and pampering. A casual contemporary decor is found throughout—light-colored rattan, tile floors, and pastel fabrics. All guests receive complimentary massage, manicure, and pedicure: Book your treatments early (even before you arrive) if you want to get a spot on the spa's roster. If there's a drawback here it's how busy the place is. The bustle creates a crowded feel. The private beach is a shuttle ride away. ☎ *Box 728, Main St., Ocho Rios,* ☎ *809/974–1027 or 800/333–3333,* FAX *809/974–5838. 264 1-, 2-, and 3-bedroom suites, 36 rooms. 4 restaurants, 7 bars (including disco and 2 swim-ups), 2 public pools, 90 private pools, 6 lighted tennis courts, full-service spa, 2 steam rooms, 2 saunas, 20 hot tubs, 2 cold plunges, golf greens fees and transportation, shuffleboard, croquet, lawn chess, horseback riding, aerobics classes, basketball court, squash court, racquetball court, water-sports center including scuba diving, beach shuttle to private beach club, boutiques, beauty salon, jogging track, nightly entertainment, art gallery. AE, DC, MC, V. All-inclusive.*

$$$–$$$$ **Jamaica Grande.** Ramada bought the Americana (Divi-Divi) and Mallards Beach resorts and created Jamaica Grande, now the largest conference hotel in Jamaica. The property attracts families (kids under 12 stay free with parents), couples, singles (there's no added singles supplement), conference attendees, and incentive-travel winners. Even though it's a beachfront resort, the focal point is definitely the tiered and winding pool with waterfall, swaying bridge, and swim-up bar. Accommodations in the south building are a bit roomier, whereas those in the north have slightly better views. The staff is quite friendly for such a large and rather overwhelming property. Kids are kept busy in the daily Club Mongoose activity program (included in the rates). The hotel's disco, Jamaica Me Crazy (see Nightlife, below), is very popular. ⌕ Box 100, Ocho Rios, ☎ 809/974–2201 or 800/228–9898, FAX 809/974–5378. 691 rooms, 21 suites. 5 restaurants, 9 bars, 3 swimming pools, water-sports center, fitness center, disco, 4 tennis courts (2 lighted), supervised children's program, gaming parlor with slot machines, kids' game room, shopping arcade, beauty salon. AE, DC, MC, V. EP, MAP, All-inclusive.

$$$–$$$$ **Jamaica Inn.** A combination of class and quiet attracts a privileged crowd to this vintage property. There are weeks in season when every single guest is on at least his or her second visit. Each room has its own veranda (larger than most hotel rooms) on the private cove's powdery champagne-color beach. The colonial decor is on the dark side, with mahogany furniture, terrazzo floors, and walls hung with oil paintings. There are no TVs or radios. Jacket and tie are de rigueur after 7 PM. ⌕ Box 1, Ocho Rios, ☎ 809/974–2514 or 800/243–9420, FAX 809/974–2449. 44 rooms, 1 suite with private pool. Restaurant, bar, pool, fitness room, library, afternoon tea. No children under 14. AE, MC, V. FAP.

$$$–$$$$ **Plantation Inn.** This plantation actually looks like one—the Deep South variety à la Gone with the Wind. The whole place conjures up an existence as soft as a southern drawl. All the big, breezy rooms have private balconies, and each has a dramatic view down to the sea. Jamaican cuisine is served at the popular restaurant, where dining and dancing by candlelight round out the romantic experience. Up to two children under 12 stay free in their parents' room. ⌕ Box 2, Ocho Rios, ☎ 809/974–5601 or 800/752–6824, FAX 809/974–5912. 76 rooms, 2 villas. Restaurant, pool, water-sports center and dive shop, 2 tennis courts (1 lighted) with daily tennis clinics, health club, sauna, lawn croquet, golf packages, afternoon tea, nightly entertainment, shops. AE, DC, MC, V. EP, MAP, All-inclusive.

$$$ **Sandals Dunn's River.** Twenty-three acres of gardens surround this lux-
★ ury couples-only all-inclusive. The Continental-Italian masterpiece, set on a wide sugary beach, is the finest of Sandals' Jamaican resorts. The rooms are larger than at most Sandals and are decorated in light pink, blue, turquoise, and cream. Most have a balcony or patio overlooking the sea or the lush grounds. Oceanfront suites have four-poster beds. There are Italian, West Indian, Continental, and even a Japanese teppanyaki restaurant to choose from, in addition to the buffet dining room on the terrace. The resort draws a well-heeled crowd in their thirties and forties and prides itself on catering to every guest's every whim. ⌕ Box 51, Ocho Rios, ☎ 809/972–1610 or 800/726–3257, FAX 809/972–1611. 246 rooms, 10 suites. 4 restaurants, 7 bars (including beach bar, 2 swim-ups, disco, piano, and nightclub), 2 pools, 3 hot tubs, beach, 2 saunas and steam rooms, water sports including scuba diving, 9-hole pitch-and-putt golf green, spa and fitness center, jogging course, 4 tennis courts (2 lighted), gaming parlor, TV room,

shuffleboard, basketball court, garden chess, beauty salon, gift shop. AE, MC, V. All-inclusive.

$$$ **Sandals Ocho Rios.** The Sandals concept follows its successful formula at yet another couples-only, all-inclusive resort, this one on 12½ acres of beachfront property. The white- and sand-colored buildings contrast nicely with the vegetation and the sea. The accommodations are airy, but generic motel decor and white plastic furniture on the balconies create an impersonal atmosphere. Guests enjoy meandering paths through lush foliage, hammocks for two strung between trees, and cozy benches nestled amid flower beds for private stargazing. ⊞ *Ocho Rios,* ☎ *809/974–5691 or 800/726–3257,* FAX *809/974–5700. 237 units. 3 restaurants, 4 bars (including 2 swim-ups, piano, and disco), 2 pools, hot tub, 2 lighted tennis courts, gym, spa, 2 saunas, game room, basketball court, garden chess, water-sports center with scuba diving, golf greens fees and transportation, sightseeing tour, gift shop. AE, DC, MC, V. All-inclusive.*

$$–$$$ **Couples.** No singles, no children: The emphasis at Couples is on romantic
★   adventure for just the two of you, and the all-inclusive concept eliminates the decision making that can intrude on social pleasure. One-bedroom suites are designed for romance, with two-person hot tubs in the bathroom that peek through a window at the four-poster king-size bed. Continental breakfast is served in bed. The favorite dining spot is Bayside, an open-air restaurant with seating in graceful gazebos that stretch out over the water on stilted platforms. There's a lovely white beach for relaxation or water sports, and a private island where you can sunbathe in the buff. Couples has the highest occupancy rate of any resort on the island—and perhaps the most suggestive logo as well. There may be a correlation. ⊞ *Tower Isle, St. Mary,* ☎ *809/975–4271 or 800/268– 7537,* FAX *809/975–4439. 161 rooms, 11 suites with whirlpool bathtubs. 3 restaurants, 3 bars, 2 pools, 5 whirlpools, island for nude sunbathing, 5 tennis courts (3 lighted), gym, 2 air-conditioned squash courts, water-sports center that includes scuba diving, horseback riding, nightly entertainment, golf greens fees and transfers, shopping arcade, sunset cruise, sightseeing tour. AE, DC, MC, V. All-inclusive.*

$$ **Shaw Park Beach Hotel.** Another popular property, Shaw Park offers an alternative to downtown high-rises. Hallways are dimly lit and uninviting, and rooms are fairly nondescript but comfortable enough. The grounds are colorful and well tended, and the Silks disco is a favorite for late-night carousing. Up to two children under 12 stay free in their parents' room. ⊞ *Cutlass Bay, Box 17, Ocho Rios,* ☎ *809/974– 2552 or 800/243–9420,* FAX *809/974–5042. 118 rooms. Restaurant, bar, pool, water sports and dive shop, beach, kids' play area, fitness room, library, game/TV room, beauty salon, disco. AE, DC, MC, V. EP.*

$ **Club Jamaica Beach Resort.** This intimate all-inclusive has been reborn
★   after extensive renovations. There are only 95 rooms here, ensuring guests plenty of personal attention from the young, cheerful staff. The rooms are refreshing, with gleaming white tile floors, comfortable modern furnishings, and gem-tone color schemes; more than half look out on the ocean. Guests, identified by their plastic, hospital-style bracelets, tend to be active middle-agers and can be seen seen participating in the resort's daily activities (including nonmotorized water sports on the public beach) and dancing the night away to live entertainment. Children under 12 are not allowed. ⊞ *Box 342, Turtle Beach, Ocho Rios,* ☎ *809/974-6632/42 or 800/818–2964,* FAX *809/974–6644. 95 rooms. Restaurant and dining terrace, pool bar, cocktail lounge, disco, pool, whirlpool, public beach, water-sports center, daily activities and entertainment, gift shops. AE, MC, V. All-inclusive.*

$ **Enchanted Garden.** Twenty stunning acres of gardens, filled with tropical plants and flowers and punctuated with a dramatic series of streams and waterfalls, certainly are enchanting. There is an aviary and a seaquarium where you can enjoy a delicatessen lunch or tea surrounded by tanks of fish and hanging orchids. The futuristic cinder-block villas seem regrettably incongruous amid the natural splendor, but the rooms are comfortable, if somewhat small, and you're never far from the soothing sound of rushing water. There's a free shuttle to the beach, which is several minutes away. ☎ *Box 284, Ocho Rios,* ☎ *809/974–5346 or 800/323–5655,* FAX *809/974–5823. 112 villa rooms and suites (some housekeeping units), 30 with private plunge pool. 5 restaurants, pool, library, spa, disco, gift shop, beauty parlor, aviary, 2 lighted tennis courts, beach shuttle. AE, MC, V. EP, MAP, All-inclusive.*

$ **Hibiscus Lodge.** This gleaming white building with a blue awning sits amid beautifully manicured lawns laced with trellises and adorned by peacocks, not too far from its tiny private beach. The impeccably neat, cozy rooms all have at least a partial sea view, terrace, and shower-bath but no phone or TV. This German-run property may be Jamaica's best bargain, attracting a discriminating (and jubilant) crowd. ☎ *Box 52, Ocho Rios,* ☎ *809/974–2676 or 800/526–2422,* FAX *809/974–1874. 26 rooms. Restaurant, piano bar, pool, hot tub, lighted tennis court, TV room. AE, DC, MC, V. EP, MAP.*

Port Antonio

$$$$ **Trident Villas and Hotel.** If a single hotel had to be voted the most likely
★ for coverage by *Lifestyles of the Rich and Famous,* this would have to be it. Peacocks strut the manicured lawns; colonnaded walkways wind through whimsically sculpted topiary; and the pool, buried in a rocky bit of land jutting out into crashing surf, is a memory unto itself. The luxurious Laura Ashley–style rooms, many with turrets and bay windows, are awash in mahogany and local art; they do not have TVs or clocks. The truly gracious living and white-gloved dining will transport you back to the days of Empire. ☎ *Box 119, Port Antonio,* ☎ *809/993–2602 or 800/237–3237,* FAX *809/993–2590. 12 rooms, 14 villas. Restaurant, bar, TV room, game room, nonmotorized water sports, boutique, 2 tennis courts, swimming pool, small private beach, helipad. AE, MC, V. EP, MAP, FAP, All-inclusive.*

$$–$$$ **Goblin Hill.** For a while this was known as the Jamaica Hill resort, but
it is once again going by its original, evocative name. It's a lush 12-acre estate atop a hill overlooking San San Bay. Each attractively appointed villa comes with its own dramatic view, plus a housekeeper-cook. They are not equipped with phones or TVs. You'll need a car to get to the beach. Excellent villa and car-rental packages are available. ☎ *Box 26, Port Antonio,* ☎ *809/925–8108 or 800/472–1148,* FAX *809/925–6248. 28 housekeeping villas. Bar, pool, beach, 2 lighted tennis courts, water sports, reading and game room, play area, children's activity program, nature trail. AE, MC, V. EP.*

$$ **Dragon Bay.** Set on a scenic private cove, Dragon Bay is an idyllic group-
★ ing of villas surrounded by tropical gardens. The property underwent major renovations in 1994, upgrading the grounds, amenities, and each of the stunning, individually decorated villas. An orchid house is slated to be added off the main dining terrace, providing a romantic spot for weddings. Villa 35 has a private pool, a large living room, and two bedrooms with separate sitting rooms that have sofa beds: You could conceivably squeeze two families in. ☎ *Box 176, Port Antonio,* ☎ *809/993–3281/3,* FAX *809/993–3284. 30 1-, 2-, and 3-bedroom villas. Restaurant, bar, disco, pool, gym, sauna, private beach. AE, MC, V. EP, MAP, FAP, All-inclusive.*

$$ **Hotel Mocking Bird Hill.** With dogs running around the hillside property and only 10 rooms overlooking the sea and the Blue Mountains, Mocking Bird Hill feels more like a cozy bed-and-breakfast than a hotel. Owners Barbara Walker and Shireen Aga run an extremely environmentally sensitive operation: They've used bamboo instead of hardwood for furniture, solar panels to heat water, ceiling fans instead of ozone-depleting air-conditioning systems, local produce for meals in their Mille Fleurs dining terrace, and natural landscaping on their 7 acres. They also offer an array of eco-tour options in conjunction with other like-minded community members. The tasteful blue-on-white rooms do not have phones or televisions. ▣ *Box 254, Port Antonio,* ☎ *809/993–3370,* ℻ *809/993–7133. 10 rooms. Restaurant, bar, pool, TV room, art gallery, art classes, hiking tours, scuba diving and fishing charters available. MC, V. EP, MAP.*

$$ **Jamaica Palace.** Built in 1988 to resemble a 17th-century Italian Colonial mansion, this imposing property rises in an expanse of white-pillared marble, with a black-and-white theme continued on the interior, including black lacquer and gilded oversize furniture. Each room has a semicircular bed and original European objets d'art and Oriental rugs; some are more lavish than others. Although the hotel is not on the beach, there is a 114-foot swimming pool shaped like Jamaica. ▣ *Box 227, Port Antonio,* ☎ *809/993–2021 or 800/423–4095,* ℻ *809/993– 3459. 24 rooms, 56 suites. 2 restaurants, 2 bars, pool, boutiques, garden chess, beach shuttle, golf packages. AE, MC, V. EP, FAP, MAP.*

$ **Bonnie View Plantation Hotel.** Accommodations here are spartan, mattresses are a tad lumpy, and the furnishings a bit frayed. But the hotel certainly lives up to its name: Guests come for the sublime views and air of tranquillity. The nicest rooms (more expensive) are those with private verandas. But you can open your window for a burst of invigorating mountain air or hang out in the restaurant and savor the unparalleled water panoramas. Beachcombers are forewarned: It's a 25-minute drive to the ocean. ▣ *Box 82, Port Antonio,* ☎ *809/993– 2752 or 800/423–4095,* ℻ *809/993–2862. 20 rooms. Restaurant, pool, sundeck. AE, DC, MC, V. EP.*

Runaway Bay

$$$ **FDR, Franklyn D. Resort.** Jamaica's first all-suite, all-inclusive resort for
★ families, this fabulous answer to parents' prayers opened in 1990. Upscale yet unpretentious, the pink buildings house spacious and well-thought-out one-, two-, and three-bedroom villas and are grouped in a horseshoe around the swimming pool. Best of all, a "girl Friday" is assigned to each suite, filling the role of nanny, housekeeper, and (when desired) cook. She'll even baby-sit at night for a small charge. Most parents are so impressed that they wish they could take their girl Friday home with them when they leave. Children and teens are kept busy with daylong supervised activities and sports, while parents are free to join in, lounge around the pool, play golf, go scuba diving, or just enjoy uninterrupted time together. Kids under 16 stay and play free with their parents. ▣ *Runaway Bay,* ☎ *809/973–3067 or 800/654– 1337,* ℻ *809/973–3071. 76 suites. 2 restaurants, 4 bars (including disco and piano), pool, water-sports center, clothed and nude beaches, gym, game room, lighted tennis court, miniclub for children with supervised activities, glass-bottom-boat tour, gift and crafts shops. AE, MC, V. All-inclusive.*

$$ **Jamaica, Jamaica.** This all-inclusive was a pioneer in emphasizing the
★ sheer Jamaican-ness of the island. The cooking is particularly first-rate, with an emphasis on Jamaican cuisine and fresh seafood. Rooms are dominated by carved wooden headboards and a massive Jamaican

wooden chair. For more upscale accommodations, request a beachfront one-bedroom suite. Guests—often Germans, Italians, and Japanese—flock here for the psychedelically colored reef surrounding the beach and the superb golf school. Children under 16 are not allowed. ☎ *Box 58, Runaway Bay,* ☎ *809/973–2436 or 800/859–78/3,* FAX *809/973–2352. 238 rooms, 4 suites. 2 restaurants, beach grill, 4 bars (including piano/karaoke, disco, and nightclub), clothed and nude beaches, swimming pool and lap pool, 3 whirlpools, water-sports center, 2 lighted tennis courts, horseback riding, dive center, gym, TV room, game room, 18-hole golf course with golf school nearby, sightseeing tours, sundry and gift shops. AE, DC, MC, V. All-inclusive.*

$ **Club Caribbean.** This all-inclusive markets itself to families on a budget. A series of typically Caribbean cottages, half with kitchenette, lines the long but narrow beach. The rooms are very simple and clean, with ceiling fans, worn rattan furnishings, and floral print fabrics, but no ☎ or TV. Those with air-conditioning cost a bit extra. Ask for one of the new cottages added in late 1994. The place is very popular with European families. Children under six stay free, and 30 cottages feature bunk beds instead of kitchenettes. While most water sports are included, scuba diving costs extra. ☎ *Box 65, Runaway Bay,* ☎ *809/973–3507 or 800/223–9815,* FAX *809/973–3509. 130 rooms. Restaurant, 3 bars, pool, shopping arcade, dive center, water-sports center, 2 tennis courts, day-care center with children's program, gift shop. AE, MC, V. All-inclusive.*

$ **H.E.A.R.T. Country Club.** It's a shame more visitors don't know about this place, perched above Runaway Bay and brimming with Jamaica's true character. While training young islanders interested in the tourism industry—H.E.A.R.T. stands for Human Employment And Resource Training—it also provides a quiet and pleasant stay for guests. The employees make an effort to please. Rooms seem somewhat worn around the edges but are equipped with all the basics and have either an ocean or pretty garden view. The tranquil restaurant serves delicious local and Continental specialties. Kids under 12 stay free with their parents. An excellent beach is a 20-minute hike (uphill coming back) or a 5- to 10-minute drive away. ☎ *Box 98, St. Ann,* ☎ *809/973–2671,* FAX *809/973–2693. 20 rooms. Restaurant, piano bar, golf, beach shuttle. AE, MC, V. EP, MAP.*

The Arts and Nightlife

Jamaica—especially Kingston—supports a lively community of musicians. For starters there is reggae, popularized by the late Bob Marley and the Wailers and performed today by son Ziggy Marley, Jimmy Tosh (the late Peter Tosh's son), Gregory Isaacs, Third World, Jimmy Cliff, and many others. If your experience of Caribbean music has been limited to steel drums and Harry Belafonte, then the political, racial, and religious messages of reggae may set you on your ear; listen closely and you just might hear the heartbeat of the people. Those who already love reggae may want to plan a visit in mid-July to August for the Reggae Sunsplash. The four-night concert at the Bob Marley Performing Center (a field set up with a temporary stage), in the Freeport area of Montego Bay, showcases local talent and attracts such performers as Rick James, Gladys Knight and the Pips, Steel Pulse, Third World, and Ziggy Marley and the Melody Makers.

Discos and Clubs

For the most part, the liveliest late-night happenings throughout Jamaica are in the major resort hotels. Some of the best music will be found in Negril at **De Buss** (☎ 809/957–4405) and of course at the hot, hot spot, **Kaiser's Cafe** (☎ 809/957–4070), as well as the disco at **Hedonism II** (☎ 809/957–4200), and **Compulsion Disco** (☎ 809/957–4416). The most popular spots in Kingston are **Godfather** (Knutsford Blvd., ☎ 809/929–5459), **Mingles** at the Courtleigh (☎ 809/929–5321), **Illusions** in the New Lane Plaza (☎ 809/929–2125), **Jonkanoo** in the Wyndham New Kingston (☎ 809/929–3390), and **Mirage** (☎ 809/978–8557), the hot new disco in Sovereign Centre.

In Port Antonio, if you have but one night to disco, do it at the **Roof Club** (11 West St., no ☎). On weekends, from elevenish on, this is where it's all happening. If you want to "do the town," check out **CenterPoint** (Folly Rd., ☎ 809/993–3377), **Shadows** (40 West St., ☎ 809/993–3823), or the Jamaican cultural show on Friday nights at **Fern Hill Club** (☎ 809/993–3222). The principal clubs in Ocho Rios are **Jamaica Me Crazy** at the Jamaica Grande (☎ 809/974–2201), **Acropolis** (70 Main St., ☎ 809/ 974–2633), **Silks** in the Shaw Park Beach Hotel (☎ 809/974–2552), and the **Little Pub on Main Street** (☎ 809/974–2324), which produces Caribbean revues. The hottest places in Montego Bay are the **Cave** disco at the Seawinds Beach Resort (☎ 809/952–4070), **Sir Winston's Reggae Club** (Gloucester St., ☎ 809/952–2084), and the **Rhythm Nightclub** at the Holiday Inn Rose Hall (☎ 809/953–2485). After 10 PM on Friday nights, the crowd gathers at **Pier 1** on Howard Cooke Boulevard, opposite the straw market (☎ 809/952–2452). Some of the all-inclusives offer a dinner and disco pass from about $50.

15 Martinique

Updated by
Jordan Simon

 OT FOR NAUGHT did the Arawaks name Martinique *Madinina,* which means "Island of Flowers." This is one of the most beautiful islands in the Caribbean, lush with exotic wild orchids, frangipani, anthurium, jade vines, flamingo flowers, and hundreds of vivid varieties of hibiscus. Trees bend under the weight of such tropical treats as mangoes, papayas, bright red West Indian cherries, lemons, limes, and bananas. Acres of banana plantations, pineapple fields, and waving green seas of sugarcane show the bounty of the island's fertile soil.

The towering mountains and verdant rain forest in the north lure hikers, while underwater sights and sunken treasures attract snorkelers and scuba divers. Martinique appeals as well to those whose idea of exercise is turning over every 10 or 15 minutes to get an even tan or whose adventuresome spirit is satisfied by finding booty in a duty-free shop. Francophiles in particular will find the island enchanting.

The 425-square-mile island, the largest of the Windward Islands, is 4,261 miles from Paris, but its spirit (and language) is French, with more than a mere soupçon of West Indian spice. Tangible, edible evidence of that fact is the island's cuisine—a tempting blend of classic French and Creole dishes.

Columbus sailed near Martinique in 1493, but it was not until his fourth voyage, in 1502, that he came ashore at Le Carbet. He paused long enough to remark, "My eyes would never tire of contemplating such vegetation," and to put ashore a number of goats to provide fresh meat for future visits. His eyes very quickly tired of the snakes he saw slithering about in his newfound Eden, so he weighed anchor and put water between him and them, never to return.

By the time Columbus made his way to Martinique, the cannibalistic Caribs had long since arrived on the island and eaten the Island of Flowers's Arawaks. Carib arrows kept outsiders at bay until 1635, when Pierre Belain d'Esnambuc, a Norman nobleman and adventurer, landed with a group of 100 settlers at the mouth of the Roxelane River. The French promised the Caribs the western half of the island, but instead polished them off and imported African slaves to work their sugarcane plantations.

By the mid-17th century, Martinique was an important sugar-producing island. Britain wanted to pluck the pearl away from the French, and the two nations fought over the island until the early 19th century. In 1815, the island was ceded by treaty to France, and French it has remained ever since.

Martinique became an overseas department of France in 1946 and a *région* in 1974, a status not unlike that of an American state vis-à-vis the federal government. The Martinicans vote in French national elections and have all the benefits of France's social and economic systems. The island is governed by a prefect who is appointed by the French minister of the interior. Martinique has one of the highest standards of living in the Caribbean.

Though the majority of tourists are from France, Martinique is encouraging North Americans to visit the island. Efforts are being made to teach taxi drivers a few important words in English; the tourist office has a number of free guide booklets written in English; and most hotels, restaurants, and shops have English-speaking staff.

Before You Go

Tourist Information

For information contact the **French West Indies Tourist Board** by calling 800/391–4909. You can also contact the **French Government Tourist Office, Martinique Promotion Bureau,** 444 Madison Ave., New York, NY 10022, ☎ 212/757–1125; 9454 Wilshire Blvd., Beverly Hills, CA 90212, ☎ 310/271–2358; or 676 N. Michigan Ave., Chicago, IL 60611, ☎ 312/751–7800. In Canada the tourist office can be reached at 1981 McGill College Ave., Suite 490, Montreal, Québec H3A 2W9, ☎ 514/288–4264, or 1 Dundas St. W, Suite 2405, Toronto, Ontario M5G 1Z3, ☎ 416/593–4723 or 800/361–9099; in the United Kingdom, at 178 Piccadilly, London W1V 0AL, ☎ 0181/124–4123.

Arriving and Departing

BY PLANE

The most frequent flights from the United States are on **American Airlines** (☎ 800/433–7300), which has year-round daily service from more than 100 U.S. cities to San Juan. From there, the airline's American Eagle flies on to Martinique with a stop first at Guadeloupe. **Air France** (☎ 800/237–2747) flies direct from Miami and San Juan; **Air Canada** (☎ 800/422–6232) has service from Montreal and Toronto; **LIAT** (☎ 809/462–0700), with its extensive coverage of the Antilles, flies in from Antigua, St. Maarten, Guadeloupe, Dominica, St. Lucia, Barbados, Grenada, and Trinidad and Tobago. **Council Charter** (☎ 212/661 4546 or 800/765–6065) provides Saturday–Saturday flights out of New York's JFK, and offers flight-lodging packages, during high season.

FROM THE AIRPORT

You'll arrive at Lamentin International Airport, which is about a 15-minute taxi ride from Fort-de-France and about 40 minutes from the Trois-Ilets peninsula, the first of many resort areas on the southern beaches where most hotels are located.

Passports and Visas

U.S. and Canadian citizens must have a passport (an expired passport may be used as long as the expiration date is no more than five years ago) or proof of citizenship, such as an original (not photocopied) birth certificate or a voter registration card accompanied by a government-authorized photo identification. British citizens are required to have a passport. In addition, all visitors must have a return or ongoing ticket.

Language

Many Martinicans speak Creole, a mixture of Spanish and French. Try *sa ou fe* for hello. In major tourist areas you'll find someone who speaks English, but the courtesy of using a few French words, even if it is *Parlez-vous anglais?,* is appreciated. The people of Martinique are extremely courteous and will help you through your French. Even if you do speak fluent French, you may have a problem understanding the accent of the country people. Most menus are written in French, so a dictionary is helpful.

Precautions

Exercise the same safety precautions you would in any other big city: Leave valuables in the hotel safe-deposit vault and lock your car, with luggage and valuables stashed out of sight. Also, don't leave jewelry or money unattended on the beach.

Beware of the *mancenillie* (manchineel) trees. These pretty trees with little green fruits that look like apples are poisonous. Sap and even raindrops falling from the trees onto your skin can cause painful, scarring blisters. The trees have red warning signs posted by the Forestry Commission.

If you plan to ramble through the rain forest, be careful where you step. Poisonous snakes, cousins of the rattlesnake, slither through this lush tropical Eden.

Except for the area around Cap Chevalier and the Tartane peninsula, the Atlantic waters are rough and should be avoided by all but expert swimmers.

Staying in Martinique

Important Addresses

Tourist Information: The **Martinique Tourist Office** (Blvd. Alfassa, ☎ 596/63–79–60) is open Monday–Thursday 8–5, Friday 7:30–5, Saturday 8–noon. The office's free maps and booklets, *Choubouloute* and *Martinique Info*, are useful. The Tourist Information Booth at Lamentin International Airport is open daily until the last flight has landed.

EMERGENCIES
Police: Call 17. **Fire:** Call 18. **Ambulance:** Call 70–36–48 or 71–59–48. **Hospital:** There is a 24-hour emergency room at **Hôpital La Meynard** (Châteauboeuf, just outside Fort-de-France, ☎ 596/55–20–00). **Pharmacies:** Pharmacies in Fort-de-France include **Pharmacie de la Paix** (corner rue Victor Schoelcher and rue Perrinon, ☎ 596/71–94–83) and **Pharmacie Cypria** (Blvd. Général de Gaulle, ☎ 596/63–22–25).

Currency

The coin of the realm is the French franc, which consists of 100 *centimes*. At press time, the rate was 5.30F to U.S. $1, but check the current exchange rate before you leave home. U.S. dollars are accepted in some hotels, but for convenience, it's better to convert your money into francs. Banks give a more favorable rate than do hotels. A currency exchange service that also offers a favorable rate is **Change Caraibes,** in the arrivals building at Lamentin International Airport (☎ 596/51–57–91; open weekdays 7 AM–9 PM, Sat. 8:30–2, closed Sun.), and in Fort-de-France (rue Ernest Deproge, across from the Tourist Office, ☎ 596/60–28–40; open weekdays 8–7, Sat. 8–12:30, closed Sun.). Note: Prices quoted here are in U.S. dollars unless indicated otherwise.

Major credit cards are accepted in hotels and restaurants in Fort-de-France and the Pointe du Bout areas; few establishments in the countryside accept them. There is a 20% discount on luxury items paid for with traveler's checks or with certain credit cards.

Taxes and Service Charges

A resort tax varies from hotel to hotel; the maximum is $1.50 per person per day. Rates quoted by hotels usually include a 10% service charge; some hotels add 10% to your bill. All restaurants include a 15% service charge in their menu prices.

Guided Tours

For a personalized tour of the island, ask the tourist office to arrange a tour with an English-speaking taxi driver. There are set rates for tours to various points on the island, and if you share the ride with two or three other sightseers, the price will be whittled down.

Madinina Tours (☎ 596/61–49–49) offers half- and full-day jaunts, with lunch included in the all-day outings. Boat tours are also available, as are air excursions to the Grenadines and St. Lucia. Madinina has tour desks in most of the major hotels.

Parc Naturel Regional de la Martinique (9 blvd. Général de Gaulle, Fort-de-France, 97206, ☎ 596/73–19–30) organizes inexpensive guided hiking tours year-round. Descriptive folders are available at the tourist office.

Getting Around

TAXIS

Stands are located at Lamentin International Airport, in downtown Fort-de-France, and at major hotels. Taxis are expensive. Rates are regulated by the government, but local taxi drivers are an independent lot, and prices often turn out to be higher than the minimum "official" rate. The official rate is established at the beginning of each year and is listed in the tourist brochures, available at the airport tourist office. When taxi drivers overcharge, passengers have little recourse. You can either cause a fuss by contacting the police or show the driver the "officially quoted rate" in the brochure and hope that he accepts it. The cost from the airport to Fort-de-France is about 70F; from the airport to Pointe du Bout, about 150F. A 40% surcharge is in effect between 8 PM and 6 AM and on Sunday. This means that if you arrive at Lamentin at night, depending on where your hotel is, it may be cheaper to rent a car from the airport and keep it for 24 hours than to take a one-way taxi to your hotel.

BUSES

Public buses and eight-passenger minivans (license plates bear the letters TC) are an inexpensive means of transportation. Buses are always crowded and are not recommended for the timid traveler. In Fort-de-France, the main terminal for the minivans is at Pointe Simon on the waterfront. There are frequent departures from early morning until 8 PM; fares range from $1 to $5.

FERRIES

Weather permitting, *vedettes* (ferries) operate daily between Fort-de-France and the Marina Méridien in Pointe du Bout and between Fort-de-France and Anse-Mitan and Anse-à-l'Ane (all trips take about 25 minutes). The Quai d'Esnambuc is the arrival and departure point in Fort-de-France. At press time, the one-way fare was 16F; round-trip, 27F.

The **Caribbean Express** (☎ 596/63–12–11) offers scheduled interisland service aboard a 128-foot, 227-passenger motorized catamaran, linking Martinique with Guadeloupe and Dominica. Fares run approximately 25% below economy airfares.

BICYCLES AND MOTORBIKES

Bikes and motorbikes can both be rented from **Funny** (☎ 596/63–33–05) or **T. S. Location Sarl** (☎ 596/63–42–82), both in Fort-de-France, **Discount** (☎ 596/66–54–37) in Pointe du Bout, and **Scootonnerre** (☎ 596/76–41–12) in Le Diamant.

RENTAL CARS

Having a car will make your stay in Martinique much more pleasurable. You will be limited to the environs of your hotel otherwise, and most of the better beaches are away from the hotel complexes. Martinique has about 175 miles of well-paved and well-marked roads (albeit with international signs). Streets in Fort-de-France are narrow and clogged with traffic; country roads are mountainous with hairpin curves. The Martinicans drive with aggressive abandon but are surprisingly courteous and will let you into the flow of traffic. When driving up-country, take along the free map supplied by the tourist office. If you want a detailed map, the *Carte Routière et Touristique* is available at bookstores. There are plenty of gas stations in the major towns, but a full tank of gas will get you all the way around the island with gallons to spare.

If you book a rental car from the United States at least 48 hours in advance, you can qualify for a hefty discount.

A valid driver's license is needed to rent a car for up to 20 days. After that, you'll need an International Driver's Permit. Major credit cards are accepted by most car-rental agents. Rates are about $60 per day (unlimited mileage). Lower daily rates with per-mile charges, which usually turn out to be higher overall rates, are sometimes available. Question agents closely. Among the many agencies are **Avis** (☎ 596/70–11–60 or 800/331–1212), **Budget** (☎ 596/63–69–00 or 800/527–0700), and **Hertz** (☎ 596/60–64–64 or 800/654–3131).

Telephones and Mail

To call Martinique station-to-station from the United States, dial 011 plus 596 plus the local six-digit number.

It is not possible to make collect or credit-card calls from Martinique to the United States. There are few coin telephone booths on the island, and those are usually in hotels and restaurants. Most public telephones now use the Telecarte. Units are deducted from your card according to how long and far a phone call you make. Telecartes may be purchased from post offices, café-tabacs, and hotels. Long-distance calls made with Telecartes are less costly than are operator-assisted calls.

To place an interisland call, dial the local six-digit number. To call the United States from Martinique, dial 19–1, area code, and the local number. For Great Britain, dial 19–44, area code (without the first zero), and the number.

Airmail letters to the United States cost 4.60F for up to 20 grams; postcards, 3.70F. For Great Britain, the costs are 4.40F and 3.60F, respectively. Stamps may be purchased from post offices, café-tabacs, and hotel newsstands.

Opening and Closing Times

Stores that cater to tourists are generally open weekdays 8:30–6, Saturday 8:30–1. Banking hours are weekdays 7:30–noon and 2:30–4.

Exploring Martinique

Numbers in the margin correspond to points of interest on the Martinique map.

The starting point of the tour is the capital city of Fort-de-France, where almost a third of the island's 360,000 people live. From here, we'll tour St-Pierre, Mont Pelée, and other points north; go along the Atlantic coast; and finish with a look at the sights in the south.

Fort-de-France

❶ **Fort-de-France** lies on the beautiful Baie des Flamands on the island's Caribbean (west) coast. With its narrow streets and pastel buildings with ornate wrought-iron balconies, the capital city is reminiscent of the French Quarter in New Orleans. However, where New Orleans is flat, Fort-de-France is hilly. Public and commercial buildings and residences cling to its hillsides behind downtown.

Stop first at the **tourist office,** which shares a building with Air France on the boulevard Alfassa, right on the bay near the ferry landing. English-speaking staffers provide excellent, free material, including detailed maps and an 18-page booklet in English with a series of seven self-drive tours.

Thus armed, walk across the street to **La Savane.** The 12½-acre landscaped park is filled with gardens, tropical trees, fountains, and benches. It's a popular gathering place and the scene of promenades, parades, and impromptu soccer matches. A statue of Pierre Belain d'Esnambuc, leader of the island's first settlers, is upstaged by Vital Dubray's flattering white Carrara marble statue of the empress Joséphine, Napoléon's first wife. Sculpted in a high-waisted Empire gown, Joséphine gazes toward Trois-Ilets across the bay, where in 1763 she was born Marie-Joseph Tascher de la Pagerie. Near the harbor is a **marketplace** where high-quality local crafts are sold. Across from the Savane, you can catch the **ferry** for the beaches at Anse-Mitan and Anse-à-l'Ane and for the 20-minute run across the bay to the resort hotels of Pointe du Bout. The ferry is more convenient than a car for travel between Pointe du Bout and Fort-de-France.

Rue de la Liberté runs along the west side of La Savane. Look for the main post office (rue de la Liberté, between rue Blénac and rue Antoine Siger). Just across rue Blénac from the post office is the **Musée Départementale de Martinique,** which contains exhibits on the pre-Columbian Arawak and Carib periods, including pottery, beads, and part of a skeleton that turned up during excavations in 1972. One exhibit examines the history of slavery; costumes, documents, furniture, and handicrafts from the island's colonial period are on display. *9 rue de la Liberté,* ☎ *596/71–57–05.* ☛ *15F adults, 5F children 5–12.* ☉ *Weekdays 8:30–1 and 2:30–5, Sat. 9–noon.*

Leave the museum and walk west (away from La Savane) on rue Blénac along the side of the post office to rue Victor Schoelcher. There you'll see the Romanesque **St-Louis Cathedral,** whose steeple rises high above the surrounding buildings. The cathedral has lovely stained-glass windows. A number of Martinique's former governors are interred beneath the choir loft.

Rue Schoelcher runs through the center of the capital's primary shopping district, a six-block area bounded by rue de la République, rue de la Liberté, rue de Victor Severe, and rue Victor Hugo. Stores feature Paris fashions (at Paris prices) and French perfume, china, crystal, and liqueurs, as well as local handicrafts.

TIME OUT **Couleur Café** (corner rues Victor Severe and Gallieni, ☎ 596/71–54–41) is a hip, open-sided hangout, with a bamboo ceiling, African tapestries, and roughly painted turquoise counter and chairs. It's always jammed with gorgeous, impoverished young French people, who congregate to gossip, smoke like chimneys, and scarf down fine salads, quiches, and croque monsieurs, every day from 10 AM to 2:30 PM.

Three blocks north of the cathedral, make a right turn on rue Perrinon and go one block. At the corner of rue de la Liberté is the **Bibliothèque Schoelcher,** the wildly elaborate Byzantine-Egyptian-Romanesque–style public library. It's named after Victor Schoelcher, who led the fight to free the slaves in the French West Indies in the 19th century. The eye-popping structure was built for the 1889 Paris Exposition, after which it was dismantled, shipped to Martinique, and reassembled piece by ornate piece at its present location.

The **Galerie de Biologie et de Géologie** at the **Parc Floral et Culturel** will acquaint you with the variety of exotic flora on this island. There's also an aquarium showing fish that can be found in these waters. The park

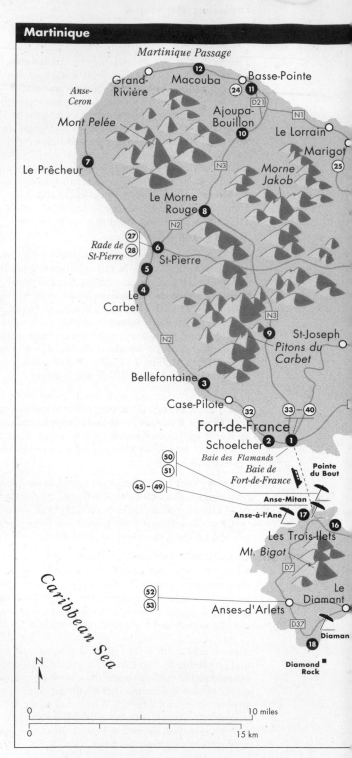

Martinique

KEY

1 Exploring Sites

24 Hotels and Restaurants

Lodging

Anse Caritan, **64**
Baie du Galion, **31**
Club Med/Buccaneer's Creek, **63**
Diamant Les Bains, **58**
Diamant Marine, **59**
Diamant-Novotel, **57**
Fregate Bleue, **44**
Habitation Lagrange, **26**
Hameau de Beauregard, **65**
Impératrice, **39**
La Batelière Hotel, **32**
La Riviera, **43**
Lafayette, **40**
Le Bakoua, **49**
Le Méridien Trois-Ilets, **48**
Leyritz Plantation, **24**
Martinique Cottages, **42**
PLM Azur La Pagerie, **45**
Relais Caraibes, **60**
Rivage Hotel, **46**
Saint Aubin, **29**

contains the island's official cultural center, where there are sometimes free evening concerts. Wandering about the grounds, you'll run into musicians and artists, who may give you an impromptu lesson on playing the steel drum or working with driftwood. *Pl. Jose-Marti, Sermac,* ☎ *596/71–66–25.* ☛ *Grounds free; aquarium 35F adults, 28F children under 12; botanical/geological gallery 5F adults, 1F children under 12. Park open daily dawn to 10 PM; aquarium open daily 9–7; gallery open Tues.–Fri. 9:30–12:30 and 3:30–5:30, Sat. 9–1 and 3–5.*

The Rivière Madame meanders through the park and joins the bay at **Pointe Simon,** where yachts can be chartered. The river divides the downtown area from the ritzy residential district of Didier in the hills. Fronting the river, on avenue Paul Nardal, are the vibrantly noisy, messy, smelly vegetable and fish markets. One of the best shows in town occurs around 4 PM, when fishermen return with their catch, effortlessly tossing 100-pound bundles of rainbow-hued fish.

The North

The tour of the north is divided into two sections: a short day's trip and a long day's (even overnight) excursion. Martinique's "must do" is the drive north along the coast from Fort-de-France to St-Pierre. The 40-mile round-trip to St-Pierre can be made in an afternoon, although there is enough to see to fill an entire day. The drive farther north, from St-Pierre to the north coast, will appeal primarily to nature lovers, hikers, and mountain climbers. If you are interested in climbing Mont Pelée or hiking, plan to spend at least a night on the road (*see* Sports and the Outdoors, *below,* for guided hikes). Bear in mind that a 20-mile mountain drive takes longer than driving 20 miles on the prairie.

② Head west out of Fort-de-France on Route N2. You'll pass through the suburb of **Schoelcher,** home of the University of the French West Indies and Guyana. La Batelière Hotel, noted for its sports facilities, is also here.

Just north of Schoelcher is Fond-Lahaye, where the road begins to climb sharply. About 4½ miles farther along, you'll come to the fishing village of **Case-Pilote,** named after a Carib chief to whom the French took kindly and called Pilote.

③ Continuing along the coastal road, you'll see red-roof houses clinging to the green mountainside on the way to **Bellefontaine,** 4 miles north. This is another fishing village, with pastel houses on the hillsides and colorful *gommier* canoes (fishing boats made from the gum tree) bobbing in the water. One of the houses here is built in the shape of a boat.

④ Continue north along the coast until you get to **Le Carbet.** Columbus is believed to have landed here on June 15, 1502. In 1635, Pierre Belain d'Esnambuc arrived here with the first French settlers.

Le Carbet is home to the **Zoo de Carbet,** also called the Amazona Zoo, which features animals from the Caribbean, Amazonas, and Africa, including rare birds, snakes, wildcats, and caimans. *Le Coin, Le Carbet,* ☎ *596/78–00–64.* ☛ *20F adults, 10F children under 12.* ☉ *Daily 9–6.*

Just north of Carbet is **Anse-Turin,** where Paul Gauguin lived for a short time in 1887 with his friend and fellow artist Charles Laval. The
⑤ **Musée Gauguin** traces the history of the artist's Martinique connection through documents, letters, and reproductions of some of the paintings he did while on the island. There is also a display of Martinican costumes and headdresses. *Anse Turin, Le Carbet,* ☎ *596/78–22–66.* ☛ *15F adults, 5F children under 12.* ☉ *Daily 10–5.*

From here follow signs for the **Vallée des Papillons,** a botanical garden and butterfly compound constructed around the 16th-century stone ruins of the Habitation Anse Latouche sugar plantation. You can tour the greenhouse and insectarium, or simply wander the grounds looking for iridescent flashes of color fluttering through the greenery. The best time to view the butterflies is from 10 AM to 3 PM. You can lunch at the excellent on-site restaurant, Le Poids du Roy. *Habitation Anse Latouche,* ☎ *596/78–19–19.* ☛ *30F adults, 10F children under 12.* ⊙ *Daily 9:30–4:15.*

⑥ Retrace your route back to N2, turn right, and continue to **St-Pierre,** the island's oldest city, which now has a population of about 6,000. At the turn of this century, St-Pierre was a flourishing city of 30,000 and was called the Paris of the West Indies. In spring 1902, Mont Pelée began to rumble and spit out ash and steam. By the first week in May, all wildlife had wisely vacated the area. City officials, however, ignored the warnings, needing voters in town for an upcoming election. At 8 AM on May 8, 1902, the volcano erupted, belching forth a cloud of burning ash with temperatures over 3,600°F. In the space of three minutes, Mont Pelée transformed the Paris of the West Indies into Martinique's Pompeii. The entire town was destroyed, and its inhabitants were instantly calcified. There was only one survivor, a prisoner named Cyparis, who was saved by the thick walls of his underground cell. (He was later pardoned and for some years afterward was a sideshow attraction at the Barnum & Bailey Circus.) You can wander through the site to see the ruins of the island's first church, built in 1640; the theater; the toppled statues; and Cyparis's cell. The Cyparis Express is a small tourist train that runs through the city, hitting the important sights with a running narrative (in French). *Departs from Pl. des Ruines du Figuier,* ☎ *596/55–50–92. Fare: 30F adults, 10F children under 12. Runs every 45 min weekdays 9:30–1 and 2:30–5:30 (call for exact times).*

The **Musée Vulcanologique** was established in 1932 by American volcanologist Franck Perret. His collection includes photographs of the old town, documents, and a number of relics—some gruesome—excavated from the ruins, including molten glass, melted iron, and contorted clocks stopped at 8 AM, the time of the disaster. *St-Pierre,* ☎ *596/78–15–16.* ☛ *15F adults, 5F children.* ⊙ *Daily 9–5.*

In St-Pierre, Route N2 turns inland toward Morne Rouge, but before going there, you may want to follow the coastal road 8 miles north to
⑦ **Le Prêcheur.** En route, you'll pass what is called the Tomb of the Carib Indians. The site is actually a formation of limestone hills from which the last of the Caribs are said to have flung themselves to avoid capture by the French. The village of Le Prêcheur was the childhood home of Françoise d'Aubigné, later to become the Marquise de Maintenon and the second wife of Louis XIV.

⑧ Return to St-Pierre and drive 4 miles east on Route N2 to reach **Le Morne Rouge.** Lying on the southern slopes of Mont Pelée, the town of Morne Rouge, too, was destroyed by the volcano. It is now a popular resort spot, with spectacular mountain scenery. This is the starting point for a climb up the 4,600-foot mountain, but you must have a guide (*see* Sports and the Outdoors, *below*).

At this point, you have the option of returning to Fort-de-France or continuing on for a tour of the north and Atlantic coasts.

If you choose to return to the capital, take the Route de la Trace (Rte. N3) south from Le Morne Rouge. The winding, two-lane paved road is one of the Caribbean's great drives, a roller-coaster ride snaking through dense tropical rain forests.

⑨ La Trace leads to **Balata,** where you can see the **Balata Church,** an exact replica of Sacré-Coeur Basilica in Paris, and the **Jardin de Balata** (Balata Gardens). Jean-Philippe Thoze, a professional landscaper and devoted horticulturist, spent 20 years creating this collection of thousands of varieties of tropical flowers and plants. There are shaded benches where you can relax and take in the panoramic views of the mountains. *Rte. de Balata,* ☎ *596/72–58–82.* ☛ *30F adults, 10F children.* ☉ *Daily 9–5.*

From Balata, Route N3 continues 8 miles south to the capital city.

⑩ If you've opted to continue exploring the north and Atlantic coasts, take Route N3 north from Morne Rouge. You'll pass through Petite Savane and wind northeast to the flower-filled village of **Ajoupa-Bouillon,** a 17th-century settlement in the midst of pineapple fields.

⑪ A mile and a half east of Ajoupa-Bouillon, Route N3 dead-ends at Route N1, which runs north–south. Turn left, and head through sugarcane, pineapple, and banana fields toward **Basse-Pointe,** which lies at sea level on the Atlantic coast (about a 3-mile drive). Soon after you turn onto N1, you'll see a small road (D21) off to the left. This road leads to the estimable **Leyritz Plantation,** which has been a hotel for several years. When tour groups from the cruise ships are not swarming over the property, the rustic setting, complete with sugarcane factory and gardens, is delightful. Visit the plantation's **Musée de Poupées Végétales,** which contains a collection of exotic sculptures made by local artisan Will Fenton. He has used bananas, balisier (a tall grass), and other local plants to create the figures of women of French history, all in extravagant period costumes. *Musée de Poupées Végétales, Leyritz Plantation,* ☎ *596/78–53–92.* ☛ *15F.* ☉ *Daily 7–5:30.*

Go back to Route N1 and continue north. Just before Basse-Pointe you'll pass a Hindu temple, one of the relics of the East Indians who settled in this area in the 19th century. The view of the eastern slope of Mont Pelée is lovely from here. There's not much to do in Basse-Pointe, although on its outskirts, just before you leave, is the **JM Distillery** (☎ 596/78–92–55; open weekdays 7 AM–noon and 1:30–3:30). It produces fine *rhum vieux,* and a tour and samples are free.

⑫ Continue down the road to **Macouba** on the coast. From here, the island's most beautiful drive leads 6 miles to **Grand-Rivière,** on the northernmost point. Perched on high cliffs, this village affords magnificent views of the sea, the mountains, and, on clear days, the neighboring island of Dominica. From Grand-Rivière, you can trek 11 miles on a well-marked path that leads through lush tropical vegetation to the beach at Anse-Ceron on the northwest coast. The beach is lovely and the diving is excellent, but the currents are very strong and swimming is not advised.

TIME OUT Stop in at **Yva Chez Vava** (Rte. 1 on the eastern edge of Grand-Rivière, ☎ 596/55–72–72) for a rum punch and a lunch of seafood and Creole dishes, including an excellent fish soup and a tasty fricassee of crayfish.

From Grand-Rivière, backtrack 13 miles to the junction of Routes N1 and N3.

⑬ From the junction, continue 10 miles on Route 1 along the Atlantic coast, driving through the villages of Le Lorrain and Marigot to **Ste-Marie,** a town of about 20,000 Martinicans and the commercial capital of the island's north. There is a lovely mid-19th-century church in the town and, on a more earthy note, a rum distillery.

The **Musée du Rhum,** operated by the St. James Rum Distillery, is in a graceful galleried Creole house. Guided tours of the museum take in displays of the tools of the trade and include a visit to the distillery. And, yes, you may sample the product. *Ste-Marie,* ☎ *596/69–30–02.* ☛ *Free.* ☉ *Weekdays 9–6, weekends 9–1.*

⑭ **La Trinité,** a northern subprefecture, is 6 miles to the south in a sheltered bay. From La Trinité, the **Caravelle Peninsula** thrusts 8 miles into the Atlantic Ocean. Much of the peninsula is under the auspices of the Regional Nature Reserve and offers places for trekking, swimming, and sailing. This is the home of the **Morne Pavilion,** an open-air sports and leisure center operated by the nature reserve (*see* Sports and the Outdoors, *below*). To reach it, turn right before Tartane on the Spoutourne Morne Pavilion road. Tartane has a popular beach with cool Atlantic breezes.

At the eastern tip of the peninsula, you can root through the ruins of ⑮ the **Dubuc Castle.** This was the home of the Dubuc de Rivery family, who owned the peninsula in the 18th century. According to legend, young Aimée Dubuc de Rivery was captured by Barbary pirates, sold to the Ottoman Empire, became a favorite of the sultan, and gave birth to Mahmud II.

Return to La Trinité and take Route N4, which winds about 15 miles through lush tropical scenery to Lamentin. There you can pick up Route N1 to Fort-de-France or Route N5 to D7 and the southern resort areas.

The South

The loop through the south is a round-trip of about 100 miles. This excursion will include the birthplace of the empress Joséphine, Pointe du Bout and its resort hotels, a few small museums, and many large beaches. You can spend an afternoon, a day, or a couple of weeks exploring this region, depending on the time at your disposal and your frame of mind.

From Fort-de-France, take Route N1 to Route N5, which leads south through Lamentin, where the airport is located. A 20-mile drive will bring you to Rivière-Salée, where you'll make a right turn on Route ⑯ D7 and drive 4½ miles to the village of **Les Trois-Ilets.**

TIME OUT Euromarche (Lamentin) is one of the most complete supermarkets in the Western Hemisphere. For under $15, two of you can stagger out with hot French breads, pâtés, cheeses, and salmon flown in from Europe. Add some Creole boudin from the deli counter and a chilled bottle of wine or the local dark Rhum St. James, and have a gourmet picnic. *Closed Sun.*

Les Trois-Ilets, named after the three rocky islands nearby, is a lovely little village with a population of about 3,000. It's known for its pottery, straw, and woodworks and as the birthplace of Napoléon's Empress Joséphine. On the village square, you can visit the simple church where she was baptized Marie-Joseph Tascher de la Pagerie. To reach the museum and the old sugar plantation on which she was born, drive a mile west on Route D7 and turn left on Route D38.

A stone building that held the kitchen of the estate is now home to the **Musée de la Pagerie.** (The main house blew down in the hurricane of 1766, when Joséphine was three.) It contains an assortment of memorabilia pertaining to Joséphine's life and loves (she was married at 16 in an arranged marriage to Alexandre de Beauharnais). There are family portraits; documents, including a marriage certificate; a love letter written to her in 1796 by Napoléon; and various antique furnishings, including the bed she slept in as a child. *Trois-Ilets,* ☎ *596/68–38–34.* ☛ *15F adults, 3F children.* ۞ *Tues.–Sun. 9–5.*

Return to D7 and turn right, passing the D38 turnoff and continuing on to the village of Trois-Ilets. The **Maison de la Canne** (at Pointe Vatable, as you leave town) will teach you everything you ever wanted to know about sugarcane. Exhibits take you through three centuries of sugarcane production, with displays of tools, scale models, engravings, and photographs. *Trois-Ilets,* ☎ *596/68–32–04.* ☛ *15F adults, 5F children under 12.* ۞ *Tues.–Sun. 9–5:30.*

⑰ You can reach **Pointe du Bout** and the beach at **Anse-Mitan** by turning right on Route D38 west of Trois-Ilets and just past the **Golf de l'Impératrice Joséphine** (a golf course). This area is filled with resort hotels, among them the Bakoua and the Méridien. The Pointe du Bout marina is a colorful spot where a whole slew of boats are tied up. The ferry to Fort-de-France leaves from this marina. More than anywhere else on Martinique, Pointe du Bout caters to the vacationer. A cluster of boutiques, ice-cream parlors, and rental-car agencies forms the hub from which restaurants and hotels of varying caliber radiate. If you are looking for resort life and action, what little there is in Martinique will be found here.

When you return to Route D7, turn right and head west. Less than 5 miles down the road you will reach **Anse-à-l'Ane,** where there is a pretty white-sand beach complete with picnic tables. There are also numerous small restaurants and inexpensive guest-house hotels here.

South from Anse-à-l'Ane, Route D7 turns into a 10-mile roller coaster en route to **Anse-d'Arlets,** a quiet backwater fishing village. You'll see fishermen's nets strung up on the beach to dry and pleasure boats on the water. In recent years, the activity has centered on the restaurants and small shops lining the shore. You may want to stop for dinner and a wonderful view of the sunset.

From the center of town, take Route D37 along the coast down to Morne Larcher and on to **Le Diamant,** a small, friendly village with a little fruit-and-vegetable market on its town square. The road—narrow, twisting, and hilly—offers some of the best shoreline views in Martinique. Be sure to pull to the side at a scenic spot from which you can stare ⑱ out at **Diamond Rock,** a mile or two offshore.

In 1804, during the squabbles over possession of the island between the French and the English, the latter commandeered the rock, armed it with cannons, christened it HMS *Diamond Rock,* and proceeded to use it as a warship. For almost a year and a half, the British held the rock, bombarding any French ships that came along. The French got wind of the fact that the British were getting cabin fever on their isolated ship-island and arranged a supply of barrels of rum for those on the rock. The French easily overpowered the inebriated sailors, ending one of the most curious engagements in naval history.

TIME OUT   On the main drag of Le Diamant, with *les pieds dans l'eau* (its feet in the water), is **Pizza Pepe** (☎ 596/76-40-49). A pretty jade-colored rattan bar, boldly hued napery, and a few plants enliven this simple terrace, where you can order such creative pizzas as oceanique (crab, onions, olives) and Ingrid (crème fraîche, salmon, olives). You can also get a

plate of roast chicken or grilled shark served with heaping helpings of
rice and fresh vegetables for 60F.

Back on the road (D7), it's about 5 miles to the junction of the island's
main highway to the south (N5). If you go to the north, you'll be back
in Fort-de-France within a half hour. Instead, go south along the coast.

Some 10 miles down the coastline lies **Ste-Luce,** another fishing village
with a pretty white beach. From Ste-Luce, you can take Route D17
north 1 mile to the **Forêt de Montravail,** where arrows point the way
to Carib rock drawings.

The recently repaved and straightened D7 can quickly take you from
Ste-Luce to Ste-Anne. For a more scenic route, say good-bye to Route
D7 in Ste-Luce and hook up with Route D18, which will take you northeast 4 miles to **Rivière-Pilote,** a town of about 12,000 people. From
there, Route D18A trickles down south to **Pointe Figuier,** where the
scuba diving is excellent. If you have time, stop by the **Ecomusée de
Martinique,** despite its name more a historical than a natural museum,
whose holdings include artifacts from Arawak and Carib settlements
through the plantation years. *Anse Figuier,* ☎ *596/62–79–14.* ☛ *15F
adults, 5F children under 12.* ☼ *Tues.–Sun. 9–5.*

Stay with Route D18A and curve around the beautiful Cul-de-Sac
inlet through **Le Marin.** Just east of Le Marin, turn right on Route D9
and drive all the way down to the sea. En route you'll pass the turnoff
to Buccaneer's Creek/Club Med and drive through the pretty village
of **Ste-Anne,** where a Roman Catholic church sits on the square facing a lovely white beach. Not far away, at the southernmost tip, is the
island's best beach, **Les Salines.** It's 1½ miles of soft white sand, calm
waters, and relative seclusion (except on weekends).

In sharp contrast to the north, this section of the island is dry. The soil
does not hold moisture for long. A rutted track—suitable for vehicles
but not for queasy stomachs—leads from Ste-Anne all the way to
Pointe des Salines and slightly beyond. The gnarled, stubby trees have
given the area the name **Petrified Forest,** in part because the sight is
unexpected in a place known as the Island of Flowers.

Backtrack 9 miles to Le Marin. The adventuresome should take a detour a mile before reaching town. Take the small road on your right that
leads to **Cap Chevalier.** After less than 2 miles, the road forks. The road
to the left dead-ends at a small community and does not justify the 4
miles of driving. The fork to the right, however, runs for about 4 miles
to a tiny cove with five or six one-man fishing boats and racks where
the fishermen dry their nets. The scene is definitely worth a photograph.

To get out of Cap Chevalier, you must go back toward Le Marin. On
the outskirts of Le Marin, Route N6 branches off to the right and goes
north 7 miles to **Le Vauclin,** skirting the highest point in the south, **Mt.
Vauclin** (1,654 feet). Le Vauclin is an important fishing port on the Atlantic coast, and the return of the fishermen shortly before noon each
day is a big event.

Continue north 9 miles on Route N6 to **Le François,** a sizable city of
some 16,000 Martinicans. Admission is free to its greatest attraction,
the **Habitation Clément** (☎ 596/54–62–07, open daily 9–6), an 18th-
century mansion and working rum distillery that together provide a
vivid portrait of plantation life. Tastings are included. Le François is
also noted for its snorkeling. Offshore, between the reefs, are a number of shallow basins called *fond blancs* because of their white-sand

bottoms. Group boat tours leave from the harbor ($30 per person includes lunch and drinks). You can also haggle with a fisherman to take you out for a while on his boat to indulge in the uniquely Martinican custom of standing waist-deep in the calm water, sipping a 'ti punch, and gossiping.

There is a lovely bay 6 miles farther along at **Le Robert.** You'll also come to the junction of Route N1, which will take you west to Fort-de-France, 12½ miles away.

Beaches

All of Martinique's beaches are open to the public, but hotels charge a fee for nonguests to use changing rooms and facilities. There are no official nudist beaches, but topless bathing is prevalent at the large resort hotels. Unless you're an expert swimmer, steer clear of the Atlantic waters, except in the area of Cap Chevalier and the Caravelle Peninsula. The soft, white-sand beaches begin south of Fort-de-France; to the north the beaches are hard-packed gray volcanic sand.

The soft white beaches of **Pointe du Bout** are man-made, superb, and lined with luxury resorts, among them the Méridien and the Bakoua.

Anse-Mitan was created by Mother Nature, who placed it just to the south of Pointe du Bout and sprinkled it with golden sand. The waters around this beach offer superb snorkeling opportunities. Small, family-owned bistros are half hidden in palm trees nearby.

On the beach at **Anse-à-l'Ane,** you can spread your lunch on a picnic table, browse through the nearby shell museum, and cool off in the bar of the Le Calalou hotel.

Diamant, the island's longest beach (2½ miles), has a splendid view of Diamond Rock, but the waters are sometimes rough and the currents are strong. This area is home to the Diamant-Novotel, Diamant Les Bains, Diamant Marine, and Relais Caraibes hotels.

Anse-Trabaud is on the Atlantic side, across the southern tip of the island from Ste-Anne. There is nothing here but white sand and the sea.

Les Salines is a 1½-mile cove of soft white sand lined with coconut palms. A short drive south of Ste-Anne, Les Salines is awash with families and children during holidays and on weekends but quiet and uncrowded during the week—even at the height of the winter season. This beach, especially the far end, is the most peaceful and beautiful. Take along a picnic, including plenty of liquids; there is only one restaurant, Aux Delices de la Mer (☎ 596/62–50–12), close to Pointe des Salines.

Near Les Salines, **Pointe Marin** stretches north from Ste-Anne. A good windsurfing and waterskiing spot, it also has restaurants, campsites, sanitary facilities, and a 10F ☛ charge. Club Med occupies the northern edge, and Ste-Anne, with several good restaurants, is near at hand.

Sports and the Outdoors

Bicycling

The **Parc Naturel Régional de la Martinique** (☎ 596/73–19–30) has designed biking itineraries off the beaten track. Bikes can be rented from **Funny** (☎ 596/63–33–05) and **T. S. Location Sarl** (☎ 596/63–42–82), both in Fort-de-France, **Discount** (☎ 596/66–54–37) in Pointe du Bout, and **Scootonnerre** (☎ 596/76–41–12) in Le Diamant. Mountain biking is popular in mainland France. Now it has reached Martinique. VTT (Vélo Tout Terrain) bikes specially designed with 18 speeds to handle all terrains may be rented from **V.T.Tilt** (Anse-Mitan, ☎ 596/66–01–01).

Boating

For boat rentals and yacht charters, check with **ATM Yachts** (Port de Plaisance du Marin, ☎ 596/74–98–17; in the U.S., ☎ 909/678–2250 or 800/227–5317), **Caraibes Evasion** (Pointe du Bout Marina, ☎ 596/66–02–85), **Moorings Antilles Françaises** (Port de Plaisance du Marin, ☎ 596/74–75–39), **Star Voyages** (Port de Plaisance du Marin, ☎ 596/66–00–72), and **Tropic Yachting** (Marina Pointe du Bout, ☎ 596/66–03–85).

Deep-Sea Fishing

Fish cruising these waters include tuna, barracuda, dolphin, kingfish, and bonito. For a day's outing on the 37-foot *Egg Harbor,* with gear and breakfast included, contact **Bathy's Club** (Méridien, ☎ 596/66–00–00). Charters of up to five days can be arranged on Captain Réné Alaric's 37-foot *Rayon Vert* (Auberge du Vare, Case-Pilote, ☎ 596/78–80–56). **Bleu Marine Evasion** (Le Diamant, ☎ 596/76–46–00) and **Caribtours** (Pointe du Bout, ☎ 596/66–02–56) also offer excursions. In Le Carbet, **Le Monde des Pêcheurs** (☎ 596/78–03–72) can arrange a memorable day's outing with local fishermen.

Golf

At **Golf de l'Impératrice Joséphine** (☎ 596/68–32–81) there is an 18-hole Robert Trent Jones course with an English-speaking pro, fully equipped pro shop, a bar, and restaurant. Located at Trois-Ilets, a mile from the Pointe du Bout resort area and 18 miles from Fort-de-France, the club offers special greens fees for hotel guests and cruise-ship passengers.

Hiking

Inexpensive guided excursions are organized year-round by the **Parc Naturel Régional de la Martinique** (9 blvd. Général de Gaulle, Fort-de-France, ☎ 596/73–19–30).

Horseback Riding

Excursions and lessons are available at **Ranch Jack** (near Anse-d'Arlets, ☎ 596/68–37–67), the **Black Horse Ranch** (near La Pagerie in Trois-Ilets, ☎ 596/68–37–80), **Ranch Val d'Or** (Ste-Anne, ☎ 596/76–70–58), and **La Cavale** (near Diamant on the road to the Novotel hotel, ☎ 596/76–22–94).

Sailing

Hobie Cats, Sunfish, and Sailfish can be rented by the hour from hotel beach shacks. Also check **Club Nautique du Marin** (☎ 596/74–92–48), **Cercle Nautique de Schoelcher** (Anse Madame, ☎ 596/61–15–21), **Hotel Frantour** (☎ 596/66–04–04), and **ATM Yachts** (Port de Plaisance du Marin, ☎ 596/74–98–17; in the U.S., ☎ 909/678–2250 or 800/227–5317).

Scuba Diving

To explore the old shipwrecks, coral gardens, and other undersea sites, you must have a medical certificate and insurance papers. Among the island's dive operators are **Club Subaquatique** (Le Port, Case-Pilote, ☎ 596/78–73–75), **Bathy's Club** (Méridien, ☎ 596/66–00–00), **Marine Hotel** (Le Diamant, ☎ 596/76–46–00), **Planete Bleue** (La Marina, Trois-Ilets, ☎ 596/66–08–79), **Sub Diamant Rock** (Novotel, ☎ 596/76–42–42), and **Okeonos Club** (Le Diamant, ☎ 596/76–21–76).

Sea Excursions and Snorkeling

The glass-bottom boat **Seaquarium** (Fort-de-France, ☎ 596/61–49–49) and the semisubmersible **Aquascope** (Pointe du Bout, ☎ 596/68–36–09) do 45- to 60-minute excursions. A relatively new attraction is the 50-passenger submarine *Mobilis* (St-Pierre, ☎ 596/78–18–18), which plunges to a depth of more than 300 feet in the waters surrounding St-Pierre, touring the many shipwrecks and the rainbow-hued sea gardens that are found there. The hour-long voyage is like something out of Jules Verne and costs 350F for adults, 175F for children. For information on other sailing, swimming, snorkeling, and beach picnic trips, contact **Affaires Maritimes** (☎ 596/71–90–05).

Sports Center

The **Morne Pavilion** (☎ 596/73–19–30), on the Caravelle Peninsula, is an open-air sports and leisure center offering sailing, tennis, and other activities.

Tennis and Squash

In addition to its links, the **Golf de l'Impératrice Joséphine** (Trois-Ilets, ☎ 596/68–32–81) has three lighted tennis courts. There are also two courts at **Le Bakoua** (☎ 596/66–02–02), six courts at **La Batelière Hotel** (☎ 596/61–49–49), seven courts (six lighted) at **Club Med/Buccaneer's Creek** (☎ 596/76–74–52), two courts at **Diamant-Novotel** (☎ 596/76–42–42), one court at the **Leyritz Plantation** (☎ 596/78–53–92), and two courts at **Le Méridien Trois-Ilets** (☎ 596/66–00–00). Several other hotels have tennis courts that are available to nonguests when empty, including the **Primerêve Hotel** (☎ 596/69–40–40), **Anchorage Hotel** (☎ 596/76–92–32), and **Diamant Marine** (☎ 596/76–46–00). For additional information about tennis on the island, contact **La Ligue Régionale de Tennis** (Petit Manoir, Lamentin, ☎ 596/51–08–00). An hour's court time averages 50F for nonguests. There are also three squash courts at the modern, aptly named **Squash Hotel** (☎ 596/63–00–01), just outside Fort-de-France.

Shopping

French fragrances and designer scarves, fine china and crystal, leather goods, and liquors and liqueurs are all good buys in Fort-de-France. Purchases are further sweetened by the 20% discount on luxury items when paid for by traveler's checks or certain major credit cards. Among local items, look for Creole gold jewelry, such as loop earrings, heavy bead necklaces, and slave bracelets; white and dark rum; and handcrafted straw goods, pottery, and tapestries. In addition, U.S. Customs allows you to bring some of the local flora into the country.

Shopping Areas

The area around the cathedral in Fort-de-France has a number of small shops carrying luxury items. Of particular note are the shops on **rue Victor Hugo, rue Moreau de Jones, rue Antoine Siger,** and **rue Lamartine.** There is also a duty-free shop at the airport. On the outskirts of Fort-de-France, shopping malls include **Centre Commercial de Cluny, Centre Commercial de Dillon, Centre Commercial de Bellevue,** and more than 60 boutiques at **La Galleria** in Le Lamentin.

Good Buys

CHINA AND CRYSTAL

Look for Lalique, Limoges, and Baccarat at **Cadet Daniel** (72 rue Antoine Siger, Fort-de-France, ☎ 596/71–41–48). **Roger Albert** (7 rue Victor Hugo, Fort-de-France, ☎ 596/71–71–71) also carries crystal from all the major designers.

FLOWERS

Anthuriums, torch lilies, and lobster claws are packaged for shipment at **MacIntosh** (31 rue Victor Hugo, Fort-de-France, ☎ 596/70–09–50, and at the airport, ☎ 596/51–51–51). **Les Petites Floralies** (75 rue Blénac, Fort-de-France, ☎ 596/71–66–16) is another florist with a wide selection.

LOCAL HANDICRAFTS

The **Galerie d'Art** (89 rue Victor Hugo, ☎ 596/63–10–62) has some unusual and excellent Haitian art—paintings, sculptures, ceramics, and intricate jewelry cases—at reasonable prices.

Following the peeling roadside signs advertising *ateliers artisanales* (art studios) can yield unexpected treasures, many of them reasonably priced. **Art et Nature** (Ste-Luce, ☎ 596/62–59–19) features Joel Gilbert's unique wood paintings, daubed with 20–30 shades of earth and sand. Robert Manscour's **L'Eclat de Verre** (Hwy. N4, outside Gros Morne, ☎ 596/58–34–03) specializes in all manner of glittering glassworks. **Victor Anicet** (Monésie, 596/68–25–42) fashions lovely ceramic masks and vases. You can watch the artisans at work at **La Paille Caraibe** (Morne des Esses, 596/69–83–74), weaving straw baskets, mats, hats, and amphorae. While at **Le poterie-briqueterie des Trois-Ilets** (Trois-Ilets, ☎ 596/68–17–12) you can watch the creation of pots, vases, and jars patterned after ancient Arawak and Carib traditions.

Just outside Le Diamant is **Atelier Ceramique** (☎ 596/76–42–65). The owners and talented artists, David and Jeannine England, have lived in the Caribbean for more than a decade and are members of the small British expatriate community on the island. Whether or not you like their products—ceramics, paintings, and miscellaneous souvenirs—it's a rare chance to brush up on your English.

PERFUMES

Dior, Chanel, and Guerlain are among the popular scents at **Roger Albert** (7 rue Victor Hugo, Fort-de-France, ☎ 596/71–71–71). Airport minishops sell the most popular scents at in-town prices, so there's no need to carry purchases around.

RUM

Rum can be purchased at the various distilleries, including **Duquesnes** (Fort-de-France, ☎ 596/71–91–68), **St. James** (Ste-Marie, ☎ 596/69–30–02), **Clément** (Le François, ☎ 596/54–62–07), and **Trois Rivières** (Ste-Luce, ☎ 596/62–51–78).

Dining

It used to be argued that Martinique had the best food in all the Caribbean, but many believe this top-ranking position has been lost to some of the other islands of the French West Indies—Guadeloupe, St. Barts, even St. Martin. Nevertheless, Martinique remains an island of restaurants serving classic French cuisine and Creole dishes, its wine cellars filled with fine French wines. Hotel restaurants are predictably good—consult the lodging listings for more recommendations—but some of the best restaurants are tucked away in the countryside, and therein lies a problem. The farther you venture from tourist hotels, the less likely you are to find English-speaking folk. But that shouldn't stop you from savoring the countryside cuisine. The local Creole specialties are *colombo* (curry), *accras* (cod or vegetable fritters), *crabes farcis* (stuffed land crab), *écrevisses* (freshwater crayfish), *boudin* (Creole blood sausage), *lambi* (conch), *langouste* (clawless Caribbean lobster), *soudons* (sweet clams), *blaff* (fish or shellfish plunged into seasoned stock), and *oursin* (sea urchin). The local favorite libation is *le 'ti punch*, a "little punch," concocted of four parts white rum, one part sugarcane syrup (some people like a little more syrup), and a squeeze of lime.

Most restaurants offer a prix fixe menu, often with several choices of entrées and wine, that represents tremendous value. For additional savings, pick up a copy of the *Ti Gourmet* booklet, available at the tourist office and larger hotels; most of the restaurants listed offer a free drink or discount upon presentation.

What to Wear
As in Guadeloupe, people dress for dinner in casual resort wear. Men don't wear jackets but do wear collared shirts. Women typically wear light cotton sundresses. Nice shorts are fine for lunch, but at dinnertime beach attire is too casual for most restaurants.

CATEGORY	COST*
$$$	over $50
$$	$30–$50
$	under $30

per person, excluding drinks

Anse-d'Arlets

$-$$ **Tamarin Plage Restaurant.** The lobster *vivier* in the middle of the room gives you a clue to the specialty here, but there are other recommendable offerings as well. Fish soup or Creole boudin are good starters; then consider court bouillon, chicken fricassee, and curried mutton. The beachfront bar is a popular local hangout. ✗ *Anse-d'Arlets,* ☎ *596/68–67–88. Reservations accepted. No credit cards.*

$ **Bidjoul.** Many modest restaurants line the small side street that is actually Anse-d'Arlets's main drag. The street borders the water, and fishermen sail right up to the eateries with their latest catch. Bidjoul has a tiny dining room; opt for one of the tables set up under the canopy on the beach across the road. The salads (try the smoked salmon, or the *pecheur,* with tuna, shrimp, crab, and rice) are huge, and the grilled fish as fresh as could be. So, too, is the fish at the neighboring restaurants, but the enthusiasm of Bidjoul's owner makes it stand out. It has become the popular gathering spot for watching the sun set into the Caribbean Sea. ✗ *Anse-d'Arlets,* ☎ *596/68–65–28. No reservations. MC, V.*

Anse-Mitan/Pointe du Bout

$$ **La Villa Creole.** The steak béarnaise, curries, conch, court bouillon, and ★ other dishes are all superb. However, the real draw here is owner Guy Bruère-Dawson, a popular singer and guitarist who entertains during dinner. The setting is romantic at this very popular place, with ceiling fans whirring and oil lamps flickering on the tables. Ask to be seated in the lush back garden. ✗ *Anse-Mitan,* ☎ *596/66–05–53. Reservations required. AE, DC, V. Closed Sun. No lunch Mon.*

$ **Au Poisson d'Or.** This typical Creole restaurant offers several excellent set menus. You might choose fried conch, poached local fish, fried sea urchin, or scallops sautéed in white wine. The decor is attractive: bamboo walls, straw thatching, madras napery, a veritable jungle of potted plants, and clever paintings of seafood. The only drawback is its position on the "wrong side" of the road, away from the beach. Choose a table in the front area of the terrace to benefit from any passing breezes. ✗ *Pointe du Bout,* ☎ *596/66–01–80. No reservations. No credit cards. Closed Mon.*

$ **La Marina.** Beckoning red-and-white awnings and colorful murals give this breezy terrace a cheerful atmosphere. Views are of the yachts cruising in and out of their berths. Top choices include seafood risotto and lambi fricassee. Tasty pizzas and salads are the best budget options. ✕ *Pointe du Bout, no* ☎. *No reservations. AE, MC, V.*

Basse-Pointe

$$–$$$ **Leyritz Plantation.** The pride of Martinique is *the* place all the cruise
★ passengers head to as soon as they disembark. The restored 18th-century plantation has exquisite stone walls, the ambience of a country inn, and a dramatic view of Mont Pelée. The menu is mostly Creole, featuring boudin, chicken with coconut, and several curried dishes. ✕ *Basse-Pointe,* ☎ *596/78–53–92. Reservations necessary. AE, DC, MC, V.*

Fort-de-France

$$$ **La Fontane.** Mango trees shade the wraparound veranda of this lovely
★ gingerbread house on the road to Balata. Inside you'll find Oriental rugs, fresh flowers, and a display of antiques that includes a handsome gramophone and a grandfather clock. Try *Le Bambou de la Fontane,* a salad of fish, tomato, corn, melon, and crayfish. Other options are cream soup with crab, lobster stewed with basil, *noisettes d'agneau* (medallions of lamb) with boletus mushrooms and mango, red snapper with lemon-lime sauce, *magret de canard* (breast of duck), and steak au poivre. ✕ *Km 4, Rte. de Balata,* ☎ *596/64–28–70. Reservations required. Jacket and tie required. AE. Closed Sun. and Mon.*

$$$ **La Grand' Voile.** Crisp white cloths, fine china and crystal, and lots of
★ windows overlooking the harbor give a formal air to this lovely dining room. Starters include chilled chicken-liver mousse, crayfish ravioli, and fresh steamed mussels. These can be followed with such dishes as lobster in Creole sauce and rabbit in tarragon sauce. Finish off your feast with a memorable soufflé or guava mousse with raspberry sauce. The *menu dégustation* (a variety of sample-size portions) is an affordable way to savor the restaurant's specialties. Service is sometimes on the slow side. ✕ *Pointe Simon,* ☎ *596/70–29–29,* FAX *596/61–85–02. Reservations advised. AE, MC, V. Closed Sun.*

$$ **Le Coq Hardi.** Crowds flock here for the best steaks and grilled meats in town. You can pick out your own steak and feel confident that it will be cooked to perfection. Steak tartare is the house specialty, but tournedos Rossini (with artichoke hearts, foie gras, truffles, and Madeira sauce), entrecôte Bordelaise, prime rib, and T-bone steaks are also on the menu. For dessert, there's a selection of sorbets, profiteroles, and pear Belle Hélène. ✕ *Km 0.6, rue Martin Luther King,* ☎ *596/71–59–64. Reservations advised. AE, MC, V. Closed Wed. No lunch Sat.*

$ **Chez Gaston.** The Creole menu of this cozy upstairs dining room includes such items as ox-foot soup, conch in parsley sauce, and simmered sea urchins. The brochettes are especially recommended. The kitchen stays open late, and there's a piano bar and small dance floor. Downstairs, snacks are served all day. A French phrase book will be very helpful. ✕ *10 rue Felix Eboue,* ☎ *596/71–59–71. Reservations accepted. No credit cards.*

$ **Le Marie Sainte.** Warm wood paneling, exposed beams, colorfully tiled
★ tables, and bright napery create a homey ambience in this wildly popular lunchtime spot. It's worth waiting on the occasional line for the scrumptious *daube de poissons* (braised fish), crayfish, and banana beignets. ✕ *160 rue Victor Hugo,* ☎ *596/70–00–30. No credit cards. Closed Sun. and Mon. No dinner.*

$ **Le Second Soufflé.** The chef uses fresh produce to make soufflés rang-
★ ing from *aubergine* (eggplant) to *filet de ti-nain* (small green bananas) with chocolate sauce. He also whips up such nonsoufflé items as eggplant ragout and okra quiche. The food echoes the famous Voltaire line painted on the wall: "Tu ne possèdes rien si tu ne digères pas bien:

You have nothing if you don't have good digestion." Even the decor pays tribute to the Martinican table, with colorful murals of fruits and vegetables. ✕ *27 rue Blénac,* ☎ *596/63–44–11. No reservations. No credit cards. No lunch Sat.*

Lamentin

$$–$$$ **Le Verger.** An orchard is the setting for this green-and-white country
★   house, not far from the airport. The terrace has a lovely view of the pool and garden (romantic when lit up at night). Pheasant, duck (try the perfect *magret* with green peppercorns), and other game are on the extensive menu along with classic French and Creole dishes (the sea urchin blaff is justly famous). Follow the signs for La Trinité; the entrance to the restaurant is on the right immediately after the Esso and Shell stations. ✕ *Pl. d'Armes,* ☎ *596/51–43–02. Reservations advised. AE, DC, MC, V. Closed Sun.*

Le Diamant

$$$ **Relais Caraibes.** Parisians Monsieur and Madame Senez opened this
★   individual bungalow colony *avec* restaurant, and they spend enough time in Paris to gather original objets d'art for decor and for sale. Lunch or dinner choices include chicken Antilloise, a half lobster in two sauces, fish fillet in a basil sauce, and fricassee of country shrimp. The crisply decorated dining room, awash in fresh flowers, commands a clear view of Diamond Rock. ✕ *La Cherry, Diamant,* ☎ *596/76–44– 65. AE, MC, V. Closed Mon.*

$$ **L'Écrin Bleu.** The breathtaking views of the sea and St. Lucia would be reason enough to visit this terrace eatery, but you hardly need more incentive than is provided by the delectable and affordable seafood. Choose your own lobster or try the salmon tartare, sea bream in spiced beurre blanc, swordfish with saffron, or conch *en feuilleté* (in puff pastry). The gourmet menu (260F) includes crayfish in ginger or saffron sauce, half a grilled lobster, and John Dory in sweet pepper sauce, not to mention dessert. ✕ *Rte. des Anse-d'Arlets,* ☎ *596/76–41–92. Reservations advised in high season. AE.*

$–$$ **Le Diam's.** For an inexpensive meal of anything from crisp, tasty pizzas to grilled fish of the day, this casual, open-sided restaurant facing the village square is hard to beat. More creative preparations include grouper in vanilla, salmon in tarragon sauce, and duck with olives. There's also a 40F children's menu—chopped steak or ham, rice or fries, and ice cream, a rarity on this island. Checkered tablecloths and wicker furniture are the only elements of the simple decor; an overhead fan keeps a breeze going through the dining room. ✕ *Pl. de l'Eglise,* ☎ *596/76–23–28. No reservations. MC, V. Closed Tues. No lunch Wed.*

$ **Chez Christiane.** Don't be deceived by the seedy front bar (which rocks
★   during pool tournaments and free Friday rum tastings). The back dining room is delightful, with bamboo walls, fresh flowers, and local artist Roland Brival's imaginative paintings of local fauna (he adds texture with shards of green glass). The Creole cuisine is magnificent. The 70F menu might offer boudin, fried fish in caper sauce, and a *coupe glacée* (sundae). Other top choices are a smoky callaloo soup (here called *soupe verte aux crabes*), braised ray with ginger, and smoked chicken colombo. ✕ *Rue Diamant,* ☎ *596/76–49–55. Reservations advised. No credit cards.*

Le François

$ **Club Nautique.** While this little place is not going to turn up in *Architectural Digest,* the food—which comes fresh daily out of the sea—is exquisitely prepared. Have the house specialty drink, a *décollage* (it means "takeoff" in French—and this potent herb-infused rum will have you jetting sky high), then dig into turtle steak or charcoal-broiled lobster. The restaurant is right on the beach, and boat trips depart from here for snorkeling in the nearby coral reefs. ✕ *Le François,* ☎ 596/54–31–00. *Reservations accepted. AE, DC, MC, V. No dinner Sun.*

Morne-des-Esses

$$ ★ **Le Colibri.** Jules Palladino, a large, gregarious man who clearly loves his food, has established his culinary domain in this spot in the northwestern reaches of the island. Choice seating is at one of the seven tables on the cheerful back terrace. For starters, try *buisson d'écrevisses,* a pyramid of six giant freshwater crayfish accompanied by a tangy tomato sauce flavored with thyme, scallions, and tiny bits of crayfish. This is one of the few places to get traditional *cochon au lait* (suckling pig) and *gibier* (game), such as rabbit in prune sauce and tender, smoky *manicou* (cousin to the opossum). ✕ *Morne-des-Esses,* ☎ 596/69–91–95. *Reservations required. AE, DC, MC, V. Closed Mon. off-season.*

Ste-Anne

$$$ **Aux Filets Bleus.** In addition to dining at this open-air eatery on the beach, you can go for a swim and dance to live music on top of the underground lobster tank. The cheerful decor takes its cue from the surrounding waters, rippling in various shades of blue from azure to teal. Be sure to check out the astonishing, angry mural outside the restaurant, all upraised fists and Picasso-esque profiles, (à la *Guernica*). Turtle or fish soup, stuffed crab, and avocado vinaigrette are all good opening bids. In addition to an assortment of lobster entrées, there is grilled or steamed fish and octopus with red beans and rice. Prices are slightly above what you'd expect for basically straightforward cooking and beachfront ambience. ✕ *Pointe Marin,* ☎ 596/76–73–42. *Reservations required. V. Closed Mon.*

$–$$ **Athanor.** Pizza, grilled fish, Creole dishes, and meats with French sauces are some of the choices on the Athanor's extensive menu. Recommended are octopus, blaff, and grilled lobster. Choose a table either in the casual plant-filled dining room, splashed with bright floral napery and colorful murals, or in the small garden. ✕ *Rue de Bord de Mer, Ste-Anne,* ☎ 596/76–72–93. *Reservations advised in high season. MC, V.*

$–$$ **La Dunette.** Dinner at this restaurant, in the small Ste-Anne hotel of the same name, is served on a plant-hung terrace overlooking the sea. Wrought-iron chairs and tables and bright blue awnings add to the refreshing garden atmosphere. Your choices for lunch or dinner include fish soup, grilled fish or lobster, snapper stuffed with sea urchin, conch fricassee, and several colombos and tandooris. ✕ *Ste-Anne,* ☎ 596/76–73–90. *Reservations advised in high season. MC, V. Closed Wed.*

$–$$ **Poï et Virginie.** Facing the jetty in the center of Ste-Anne is this popular restaurant with bamboo walls, bright art naif, ceiling fans, and colorful, fresh-cut flowers. The menu is extensive—from meats to fish—but the specialty is the lobster and crab salad. Other noteworthy dishes are lemon chicken in coconut milk, tuna with green peppers, and crayfish in saffron. Lunchtime is busy, especially on weekends; get here soon after noon if you want a table facing the bay, with views of St. Lucia in the distance. ✕ *Rue de Bord de Mer, Ste-Anne,* ☎ 596/76–72–22. *No reservations. AE, DC, MC, V. Closed Mon. No lunch Tues.*

Ste-Luce

$$–$$$ **La Corniche.** It's a dizzying climb up to this charming small hotel, but once you catch your breath you can enjoy the fine vistas of emerald hills and sapphire sea and even finer fare. Start with the marinated kingfish with mustard sauce, then segue into a delicate, flaky John Dory with coconut sauce or juicy quail stuffed with passion fruit. ✕ *Monésie, Ste-Luce,* ☎ *596/62–47–48. Reservations advised in high season. MC, V. Closed Mon. No dinner Sun.*

$$ **La Petite Auberge.** This country inn is hidden behind a profusion of tropical flowers, just across the main road from the beach. Fresh seafood is turned into such dishes as *filet de poisson aux champignons* (fish cooked with mushrooms), conch flamed in aged rum, *crabe farci,* and fresh langouste in a Creole sauce. Or sample *magret à la mangue* (duck breast with mango), veal stuffed with spinach, or entrecôte Creole. They're all winners. The inn has 12 guest rooms, all with rustic decor—pink-and-white tile floors, wood paneling, hardwood beds, white wicker furnishings, floral linens—air-conditioning, balcony, and minifridge, for an unbeatable 330F a night EP. ✕ *Plage du Gros Raisins, Ste-Luce,* ☎ *596/62–59–70. Reservations advised in high season. AE.*

St-Pierre

$$ **Le Fromager.** This beautiful restaurant is perched high above St-Pierre,
★ with smashing views of the town's red roofs and the sea beyond from the breezy terrace. Dining inside is also pleasant, thanks to the gleaming ecru tile floors, white wicker, polished hardwood furnishings, lace tablecloths, old rum barrels, and potted plants. Superlative choices include crayfish colombo, marinated octopus, and duck fillet with pineapple. You may also opt for the 100F chef's choice menu, which might include avocado vinaigrette and sole sauce pecheur (in a Creole sauce), as well as fruit or crème caramel. ✕ *On the road toward Fond St. Denis,* ☎ *596/78–19–07. Reservations advised in high season. AE, DC, MC, V.*

$ **La Factorérie.** The food is appealing and the views sweeping at this open-air restaurant alongside the ruins of the Eglise du Fort. Fresh vegetables from the nearby agricultural training school accompany grilled langouste, grilled chicken in a piquant Creole sauce, *fricassee de lambi* (conch), and the fresh catch of the day. This is a convenient spot to have lunch when visiting St-Pierre, but it is not worth a special trip. ✕ *Quartier Fort, St-Pierre,* ☎ *596/78–12–53. No credit cards. No dinner Sat. and Sun.*

Tartane

$$ **Le Vieux Galion.** This seaside restaurant plays up the nautical theme, with a huge aquarium and murals of old sailing ships complementing fantastic Atlantic views. The crashing surf serenades diners on the terrace. Owner Jean-Pierre Maur does wonders with seafood. Especially memorable are grouper rouged with peppers, Tahitian *poisson cru* (marinated raw fish), and conch *à l'armoricaine,* with tomato, garlic, crème fraîche, and cognac. ✕ *Rte. du Tartane, Anse Bellune,* ☎ *596/58–20–58. AE, MC, V. Closed Mon. No dinner Sun.*

Lodging

Martinique's range of accommodations runs from tiny French inns called Relais Creoles to splashy tourist resorts, with an 18th-century plantation to round things out. The majority of the hotels are clustered in Pointe du Bout and Anse-Mitan on the Trois-Ilets peninsula across the bay from Fort-de-France, Le Diamant, and Ste-Anne. You will also find other notable lodgings scattered around the island. Attractive packages are offered by many of the hotels during the year, and it's a good idea to ask what's available when you call to reserve. Martinique is not an island known for its hotels. Expect functional accommodations and friendly but laid-back service. Most of the major hotels include a large buffet breakfast in their rates or will arrange an MAP plan. Perhaps because there are so many good restaurants on the island, hotels have refrained from developing all-inclusive packages.

The **Villa Rental Service** (☎ 596/71–56–11, ꜰᴀх 596/63–11–64) can assist with rentals of homes, villas, and apartments. Most are in the south of the island near good beaches and can be rented on a weekly or monthly basis.

CATEGORY	COST*
$$$$	over $240
$$$	$150–$240
$$	$85–$150
$	under $85

All prices are for a standard double room for two with Continental breakfast, excluding $1.50 per person per night tax and 10% service charge.

Anse-Mitan/Pointe du Bout

$$$$ **Le Bakoua.** Rooms here are relatively small, given the $275-a-night tar-
★ iff (higher if you're on the beach), but this elegant enclave *is* Martinique's chicest address, and the service is pampering. Accommodations are in three hillside buildings and a fourth on the man-made white-sand beach. The decor is cushy-cum-rustic, with polished hardwood furnishings, frilly floral linens, and white tile floors. All rooms have a balcony or patio; bathroom with hand-painted tile walls, marble vanity, and hair dryer; and the usual deluxe amenities, including minibar, TV, radio, king-size bed, direct-dial phone, and air-conditioning. The beach is compact and adjoins that of the Méridien. The pool, referred to as a *piscine trompe de l'oeil*, is above the beach, and the water flows over one side, giving the impression that the pool is part of the ocean. Entertainment consists of live music and shows nightly, including dancing, limbo, and Friday-night performances of Les Grands Ballets de la Martinique. Most of the staff speaks commendable English. Be sure to inquire about special package deals. ⊡ ☎ *596/66–02–02 or 800/221–4542; in the U.K., 0171/730–7144; ꜰᴀх 596/66–00–41. Write to Box 589, Fort-de-France 97200. 140 rooms, including 2 1-bedroom suites. 2 restaurants, bar, pool, 2 lighted tennis courts, boutique, flower shop, beauty salon, water-sports center. AE, DC, MC, V. CP, MAP.*

$$$$ **Le Méridien Trois-Ilets.** There is a great deal of activity here, even in the low season, much of it revolving around the always-congested pool and man-made beach. Unfortunately, the hotel has aged. Despite sporadic redecorations, the boxy, oddly configured rooms, done in blond woods and floral fabrics, remain patchworked with repairs. They are air-conditioned and have wall-to-wall carpeting, built-in hair dryers, TVs, and minibars. Some have balconies with a splendid view of the bay and of Fort-de-France. La Case Créole offers some of the better hotel dining on the island. The hotel staff speaks excellent English, the atmosphere is the island's most convivial, and there's live entertainment nightly. ⊡ *Trois-Ilets 97229, ☎ 596/66–00–00 or 800/543–4300, ꜰᴀх 596/66–00–74; in NY, 212/245–2920. 295 rooms, 2 luxury suites, 4 1-bedroom suites. 2 restaurants, bar, casino, pool, 2 lighted tennis courts, duty-free shops, marina, car-rental desk, tour desk, water-sports center. AE, DC, MC, V. BP, MAP.*

$$ **PLM Azur La Pagerie.** La Pagerie looks as if it were plucked out of the
★ Côte d'Azur and planted near the marina in Pointe du Bout. The hotel has small air-conditioned rooms and studios, all with private bath and trim little balcony, and some with kitchenette. The decor is handsome throughout, with dark-wood furnishings, planters, and lace curtains.

Although the hotel has no beach or water-sports activities, it is within a short stroll of the resort hotels, restaurants, and activity. Lunch and dinner are served alfresco by the pool. The PLM's lively, cheerful atmosphere has made it a favorite evening water hole of local expatriates and the sailing crowd. ☎ *Pointe du Bout 97229, ☎ 596/66–05–30,* FAX *596/66–00–99; U.S. reservations, 800/221–4542; in NY, 212/757–6500. 98 rooms. Restaurant, bar, pool. AE, MC, V. EP, MAP.*

$ **Rivage Hotel.** You get good value for your money at Maryelle and Jean Claude Riveti's small hotel. The place does have the air of a motor inn circa the Eisenhower years, but it's immaculately maintained, and the studios give you much more room than neighboring hotels at about a third of the cost. Each garden-view unit has air-conditioning, TV, phone, private bath, and either a kitchenette (not always as clean as the rest of the property) or a minifridge. Breakfast and light meals are served in the friendly, informal snack bar. You should have no difficulty communicating: English, Spanish, and French are spoken. The beach is right across the road. ☎ *Anse-Mitan 97229, ☎ 596/66–00–53,* FAX *596/66–06–56. 17 rooms. Snack bar, car rental, pool. MC, V. EP.*

Basse-Point

$–$$ **Leyritz Plantation.** Sleeping on a former sugar plantation, in the an-
★ tiques-furnished rooms of the manor house or cottages or in a renovated slave cabin, is certainly a novelty. Leyritz is isolated in the northern part of the island, on 16 acres of lush vegetation, with manicured lawns and stunning views of Mont Pelée. Nicest are the 10 cottage rooms, which have rough wood beams, mahogany four-poster beds, marble-top armoires, secretaries, and other antiques. The slightly larger former slave quarters have eaves, stone-and-stucco walls, more contemporary furnishings, and madras linens. Ironically, it's the newer bungalows that are cramped and lacking in individuality. All accommodations have air-conditioning, TV, phone, and hair dryer. Except for periodic invasions of cruise-ship passengers, it is very quiet here—a sharp contrast to the frenzied level of activity at the hotels in Pointe du Bout. You may not want to spend your entire vacation here, but it makes an interesting overnight stay while visiting the northern part of the island. There's free transportation to the beach, which is about 30 minutes away. ☎ *Basse-Pointe 97218, ☎ 596/78–53–92,* FAX *596/78–92–44. 67 rooms. Restaurant, bar, tennis court, pool. DC, MC. CP, MAP.*

Fort-de-France

$$ **Impératrice.** The slightly musty rooms of the Impératrice are in a 1950s five-story building that overlooks La Savane park in the heart of the city. The rooms in the front are either the best or the worst, depending upon your sensibilities: They are noisy, but they overlook the city's center of activity. All rooms have air-conditioning, TV, four-poster bed, and private bath and are decorated with bright Creole prints; 20 have balconies. Children under 8 stay free in the room with their parents, children 8–15 stay at a 50% discount. The hotel also has a popular sidewalk café. ☎ *Fort-de-France 97200, ☎ 596/63–06–82 or 800/223–9815; in Canada, 800/468–0023; in NY, 212/251–1800;* FAX *596/72–66–30. 24 rooms. Restaurant, bar. AE, DC, MC, V. CP.*

$ **Lafayette.** This hotel's claim to fame is its superb second-story restaurant, an oasis of indoor greenery, white latticework, and rich Haitian paintings overlooking the Savane, where you can dine on impeccably prepared Continental fare. If you want to be right in the heart of town, this place is a real find. The choicest rooms are those with French windows. All of the comfortable but rather old-fashioned rooms have heavy wood furnishings, teal linens, and floral curtains, and all have TV and phone. ☎ *5 rue de la Liberté, Fort-de-France 97200, ☎ 596/73–*

80–50 or 800/223–9815, FAX *596/60–97–75. 24 rooms. Restaurant, bar, use of Le Bakoua hotel beach facilities. AE, DC, V. CP.*

Lamentin

$ **Martinique Cottages.** These garden bungalows in the countryside have kitchenettes, terraces, cable TVs, and phones. La Plantation restaurant is a gathering spot for gourmets. It specializes in *nouvelle cuisine Creole*, with such inventive delicacies as yellow banana and foie gras mille-feuille. The beaches are a 15-minute drive away. The cottages are difficult to find; take advantage of the property's airport transfers. ✉ *Lamentin 97232,* ☎ *596/50–16–08,* FAX *596/50–26–83. 8 rooms. Restaurant. AE, MC, V. EP.*

La Trinité

$$ **Saint Aubin.** This restored coral-colored colonial house, with pretty gables and intricate gingerbread trim, is in the countryside above the Atlantic coast. Each modern, if musty, room has wicker furnishings, air-conditioning, TV, phone, and private bath. Those on the top floor are larger and ideal for families; five second-floor rooms open onto a shared balcony with sweeping views of the sea. This is a peaceful retreat, and only 3 miles from La Trinité, 2 miles from the Spoutourne sports center and the beaches on the Caravelle Peninsula. The inn's restaurant, which serves estimable Creole fare, is closed during June and October. Owner Guy Foret is an engaging host. ✉ *Box 52, La Trinité, 97220,* ☎ *596/69–34–77 or 800/223–9815; in Canada, 800/468–0023; in NY, 212/840–6636,* FAX *596/69–41–14. 15 double rooms. Restaurant, bar, pool. AE, DC, MC, V. CP.*

Le Diamant

$$$$ **Diamant-Novotel.** This self-contained resort occupies half an island in an ideal windsurfing location. Just beyond the registration area, a footbridge spans a large pool on the way to the air-conditioned, spacious guest rooms, each of which has a TV, phone, hair dryer, and small balcony facing either the sea or the pool. Furnishings are cane and wicker painted pastel peach and green, and the floors are tile. The dining room is large and unromantic, set up to accommodate groups, but there is a pleasant terrace bar where a local band plays on most nights. A smaller, more formal restaurant is open during peak season. The four beaches on the 5-acre property are small. Scuba packages are offered. Children under 16 stay free with their parents. The staff speaks English and maintains a surprising level of enthusiasm and efficiency, given the hotel's size and the large number of tour groups. ✉ *Le Diamant 97223,* ☎ *596/76–42–42 or 800/221–4542,* FAX *596/76–22–87. 180 rooms. 2 restaurants, 3 bars, 2 tennis courts, pool, dive shop, car-rental desk, watersports center, boutiques, beauty salon. AE, DC, MC, V. CP, MAP.*

$$ **Diamant Les Bains.** Although manager Hubert Andrieu and his fam-
★ ily go all out to make their guests comfortable, you won't feel quite at home here unless you speak at least a little French. A few of the rooms are in the main house, along with the superb Creole restaurant, but most are in bungalows, some just steps away from the sea. The bungalows are lovely, with gleaming white tiles, wood ceilings, local artwork, bright blue fabrics, and olive rattan furnishings. Each has air-conditioning, phone, TV, terrace, and minifridge. The standard rooms are simpler, but still colorful, and are without terrace and fridge. ✉ *Le Diamant 97223,* ☎ *596/76–40–14 or 800/223–9815; in Canada, 800/468–0023; in NY, 212/251–1800;* FAX *596/76–27–00. 24 rooms. Restaurant, bar, pool, water-sports center. MC, V. CP, MAP. Closed Sept.*

$$ **Diamant Marine.** Miniapartments—one room with bed, kitchenette, and balcony—are in rows of pristine stucco buildings that progress down the hillside to the beach. The rooms are painted in mint, aqua, and periwinkle and decorated with bright abstract prints. The main building, which contains the restaurant, front desk, boutique, and flower shop, is 100 feet above the beach, and the pool is at the bottom of the hill, just above the beach. This arrangement is visually attractive, but the climb up the steps from the pool and beach to the main house and restaurant is strenuous. The hotel caters to French families on tour packages, and the high turnover and large-group clientele contribute to the wear and tear on facilities, although management works hard at maintenance. As at other Marine properties, the staff tends to be youthful and energetic, but things can get impersonal during high season. ☎ *Pointe de la Chery 97223 (near Diamant),* ☎ *596/76–46–00 or 800/221–4542,* ℻ *596/76–25–99. 149 rooms. Restaurant, 2 bars, 2 pools (1 for children), free use of water-sports equipment at Diamant-Novotel, deep-sea fishing, 2 lighted tennis courts, dive shop, boutique, flower shop. AE, DC, MC, V. CP, MAP.*

$$ **Relais Caraibes.** Of all the hotels on Martinique, this one comes clos-
★   est to having the individuality and authenticity of a country inn, as well as good food and attractive accommodations. A note of immediate chic is struck in the thatched public rooms, awash in interior gardens, white wicker furnishings, and antiques ranging from bronze Indian elephants to African masks, culled from the world travels of amiable Parisian owners Monsieur et Madame Senez. Twelve bungalows, decorated in a similar eclectic style, are spread over the manicured grounds, which offer views of the sea and Diamond Rock. Each has a bedroom, a small salon with a sofa bed, a kitchenette, and a bathroom. There are also three standard rooms in the main house, which have unusual touches like hand-painted headboards, straw birdcages and Chinese fans. The pool is perched at the edge of a cliff that drops to the sea. The hotel is a mile off the main road, and you need a car to get around. The beach, however, is a short walk away. ☎ *Pointe de la Chery, Diamant 97223,* ☎ *596/76–44–65 or 800/223–9815,* ℻ *596/76–21–20. 15 rooms. Restaurant, bar, pool, boat, scuba instruction. AE, MC, V. CP, MAP.*

Le François

$$$ **Fregate Bleue.** This is another of Martinique's rare distinctive inns. The
★   owner, Madame Yveline de Lucy de Fossarieu, left the management of Leyritz Plantation, because she wanted the quiet life. In 1991 she opened the Fregate Bleue, an eight-room, glorified bed-and-breakfast. The house itself is captivating, filled with light, plants, trompe l'oeil paintings, and hand-carved parrots. The rooms are delightful—their spaciousness accentuated by off-white furnishings, patterned carpets, and the occasional antique. Each also has a balcony, most of which overlook Les Islets de l'Impératrice. (Two rooms and the small cottage have limited sea views.) All rooms have a small kitchenette and a modern bathroom with such niceties as bathrobes. Madame de Lucy serves elegant dinners and *petit déjeuner* (breakfast). The nearest restaurants are a 10-minute drive away, and you must negotiate a rather rutted road to get to the highway. Though the sea is a stone's throw away, there is no beach nearby, and the Fregate Bleue's pool is small. ☎ *Le François 97240 (5 mi south of Le François on Vauclin Rd.),* ☎ *596/54–54–66 or 800/633–7411,* ℻ *596/54–78–48. 7 rooms. Small pool. AE, MC, V. BP.*

$ **La Riviera.** Three pretty whitewashed buildings with red tile roofs overlook Le François Bay and do indeed look as if they were transported straight from St. Tropez. All rooms have air-conditioning, TV, minibar, phone, and a balcony opening onto breathtaking water views. Decor is contemporary and fresh, mostly in floral patterns. Owner-manager Marie-Anne Prian and her husband, Jacques, speak English and are most helpful. The restaurant serves marvelous Continental-tinged Creole cuisine; try the blaff of sea urchins or the omelet flamed with aged rum. A long private pier makes La Riviera popular with yachties. ⊞ *Rte. du Club Nautique, Le François 97240,* ☎ *596/54–68–54,* ⨏ᴬˣ *596/54–30–43. 14 rooms. Restaurant, bar, boat rentals (canoes free to guests). AE, MC, V. CP, MAP.*

Marigot

$$$$ **Habitation Lagrange.** This unexpected find, an 18th-century manor
★   house, stands amid the crumbling stone buildings of a former sugar plantation, 1½ miles off the main road north of Marigot. High ceilings, austere furnishings, and polished wood floors set a degree of colonial formality. The grand reception is lit by brass chandeliers and decorated with huge murals of 18th-century genre scenes, Oriental umbrella stands, and African sculptures. Three master bedrooms have stone walls, parquet floors, and four-poster canopy beds. Bathrooms have modern fixtures but maintain the 18th-century style, from the gold-plated taps to the bathtubs encased in wood. Two new two-story buildings house 12 rooms with gabled ceilings, furnished with mahogany armoires and wicker chaise longues, and hung with chintz curtains. Three more rooms are in an original stone building facing the pool and are decorated rather sparsely, with little more than a canopy bed on white parquet floors. All rooms have a phone and a refrigerator. Meals are a suitably elaborate affair. Dinner is served at polished tables in the dining room, followed by a brandy in the small library. The chef, Jean-Charles Brédas, is perhaps Martinique's finest homegrown chef and uses French technique and island ingredients. The sumptuous set menu is a fabulous bargain at 250F. The young owners are extremely enthusiastic, but you may need to understand a little French to appreciate their hospitality. ⊞ *Marigot 97225,* ☎ *596/53–60–60,* ⨏ᴬˣ *596/53 50–58. 17 rooms, 1 suite. Dining room, bar, library, pool, tennis court. AE, DC, MC, V. BP, MAP. Closed Sept. 1–Oct. 15.*

Schoelcher

$$$–$$$$ **La Batelière Hotel.** The island's largest rooms and some of its nicest tennis courts are good reasons to stay at La Batelière. The beachfront location, north of Fort-de-France and away from most of the island's resort activity, can be a positive or negative, depending on what you're looking for. Many guest rooms overlook the sea. All have new contemporary furniture; suites have canopy beds. All accommodations are air-conditioned and have direct-access phone, cable TV, radio, and private balcony or patio. The smart, if sober, reception area and lounge face the sea. One level below the lounge is the semicircular pool and pool bar, and below that is a small beach sheltered from the waves by a breakwater. With these upgraded facilities and its proximity to Fort-de-France, the hotel should be attractive to business travelers. Ask about the scuba and honeymoon packages. ⊞ *Schoelcher 97233,* ☎ *596/61–49–49 or 800/223–6510,* ⨏ᴬˣ *596/61–70–57. 192 rooms, 5 duplexes, and 2 suites. 2 restaurants, 2 bars, pool, 6 lighted tennis courts, shopping arcade, conference rooms, water-sports center. AE, DC, MC, V. CP, MAP.*

Ste-Anne

$$$ **Anse Caritan.** This appealing property combines the amenities of a large hotel with the service and ambience of a more intimate one. It's nestled amid exquisite tropical gardens fronting a ribbon of champagne-colored sand. Management does its best to give the hotel an "island" feel. A large traditional fishing boat, or *gommier,* sits next to the pool; and rooms, though nothing exceptional in soft colors like periwinkle, mauve, and gray, have unusual touches like hand-painted leaves and bamboo on the walls. Rooms have air-conditioning, phones, safes, hair dryers and a rough wood terrace or balcony, most with sea view. The restaurant is known for its innovative Creole fare, and there's live music nightly. The staff is remarkably friendly and diligent. The Rasta gardener, for example, will pick herbs to soothe your sunburn, and the managers actually encourage guests' comments. ☎ *Pte. des Salines, Ste-Anne 97227,* ☎ *596/76–74–12,* FAX *596/76–72–59. 96 rooms. Restaurant, snack bar, bar, pool, water-sports center, dive shop, deep-sea fishing, disco. AE, MC, V. CP, MAP.*

$$–$$$ **Club Med/Buccaneer's Creek.** Occupying 48 landscaped acres, Martinique's Club Med is an all-inclusive village with plazas, cafés, restaurants, boutique, and a small marina. Air-conditioned pastel cottages contain twin beds and private shower bath. The only money you need spend here is for bar drinks, personal expenses, and excursions into Fort-de-France or the countryside. There's a white-sand beach, a plethora of water sports, and plenty of nightlife. ☎ *Pointe Marin 97180,* ☎ *596/ 76–72–72 or 800/258-2633; in NY, 212/750–1670;* FAX *596/72–76– 02. 300 rooms. 2 restaurants and bars, 7 tennis courts (6 lighted), fitness and water-sports center, nightclub, disco. AE, MC, V. All-inclusive (except drinks).*

$$ **Hameau de Beauregard.** This pastel-colored, Mediterranean-style village offers self-contained time-share apartments, all with TV, phone, kitchenette, and air-conditioning. One-bedroom units have a sofa bed, making them a good bet for families. Interiors are decorated in jade and bright jungle prints. Most of the activity revolves around the pool, though the beach is a short stroll away. ☎ *Pte. des Salines 97227,* ☎ *596/76–75–75,* FAX *596/76–97–13. 90 units. Restaurant, bar, pool. MC, V. EP, CP, MAP.*

Tartane

$$ **Baie du Galion.** This new hotel, a member of the Best Western chain, is on the lovely, wild Presqu'ile du Caravelle (Caravelle Peninsula). The medium-sized rooms are furnished in a charming Creole style, with polished dark-wood furnishings and bright fabrics. All have air-conditioning, TV, phone, safe, fridge, and balcony (50 also have kitchenette). Hiking is good in the adjacent nature reserve. The beach, though on the Atlantic, is relatively good for swimming, and the enormous pool is a focal point for guests. ☎ *Anse Tartane 97220,* ☎ *596/58–65–30 or 800/223–9815,* FAX *596/58–25–76. 146 rooms. Restaurant, bar, pool, tennis court. AE, MC, V. BP, MAP.*

The Arts and Nightlife

The island is dotted with lively discos and nightclubs, but entertainment on Martinique is not confined to partying. Most leading hotels offer nightly entertainment in season, including the marvelous **Les Grand Ballets de Martinique,** one of the finest folkloric troupes in the Caribbean. In addition, many restaurants offer live combos, usually on weekends.

Discos

Your hotel or the tourist office can put you in touch with the current "in" places. It's also wise to check on opening and closing times and ☛ charges. For the most part, the discos draw a mixed crowd of locals and tourists, the young and the not so young. Some of the currently popular places are **Blue Night** (20 blvd. Allègre, Fort-de-France, 596/71–58–43), **Le New Hippo** (24 blvd. Allègre, Fort-de-France, ☎ 596/71–74–60), **Le Sweety** (rue Capitaine Pierre Rose, Fort-de-France, no ☎), **VonVon** (Méridien, ☎ 596/66–00–00), **La Cabane de Pêcheur** (Diamant-Novotel, ☎ 596/76–42–42), **L'Oeil** (Petit Cocotte, Ducos, ☎ 596/56–11–11), and **Zipp's Dupe Club** (Dumaine, Le François, ☎ 596/54–47–06).

Zouk and Jazz

Currently the most popular music is the zouk, which mixes the Caribbean rhythm and an Occidental tempo with Creole words. Jacob Devarieux (Kassav) is the leading exponent of this style and is occasionally on the island. More likely, though, you will hear zouk music played by one of his followers at the hotels and clubs. Jazz musicians, like the music, tend to be informal and independent. They rarely hold regular gigs. The **Neptune** (Diamant, ☎ 596/76–34–23) is a hot spot for zouk. In season, you'll find one or two combos playing at clubs and hotels, but it is only at **Coco Lobo** (☎ 596/63–63–77, located next to the tourist office in Fort-de-France), that there are regular jazz sessions.

Other Music

Las Tapas (7 rue Garnier Pages, Fort-de-France, ☎ 596/63–71–23) presents flamenco or salsa and merengue bands. At Pointe du Bout, **La Villa Creole** (*see* Dining, *above*) is a charming bistro whose owner, Guy Dawson, entertains nightly on the guitar—everything from Brel and Piaf to original ditties. **L'Amphore** (behind the Le Bakoua hotel, ☎ 596/ 66–03–09) is a late-night hangout with a popular piano bar.

Casinos

The **Casino Trois-Ilets** (Méridien, ☎ 596/66 00–00) is open from 9 PM to 3 AM Monday to Saturday. You must be at least 21 (with a picture ID) to enter, and there is a 70F admission charge (admission to slot-machine room is free). Try your hand at American and French roulette or blackjack.

16 Montserrat

Updated by
Pamela
Acheson

CHRISTOPHER COLUMBUS SAILED BY the leeward coast of this Caribbean island in 1493, and, seeing the jagged mountains, he named it Montserrat, after the Santa Maria de Montserrate monastery near Barcelona, which is surrounded by similar terrain.

The Carib Indians who inhabited the island then were still there in 1632, when dissident Irish Catholics fleeing persecution arrived from nearby St. Kitts. These new settlers found a green and luxuriant island whose topography strongly resembled that of their native Ireland, prompting Montserrat's nickname, the Emerald Isle of the Caribbean. Today the Irish influence is much diminished. Still, your passport is stamped with a shamrock upon arrival, the phone book is loaded with Irish places and surnames, and St. Patrick's Day is celebrated enthusiastically (albeit to commemorate a major 18th-century slave uprising).

Actually, the African influence is more pronounced, thanks to Montserrat's comparatively low profile. Newborns are still given "jumbie" nicknames to fool the evil spirits, and the related jumbie dances, designed to ward off or propitiate those spirits, are lusty and vibrant. The rollicking Carnival, two weeks of merrymaking held during the Christmas season, is a riot of color in traditional authentic costumes.

On the map Montserrat looks like a flint-ax head with the sharp end pointing north. The island is divided along the center by a range of switchback hills, the highest of which is Chance's Peak in the south, which rises to a height of 3,002 feet. Also in the southern hills is the volcano known as Galway's Soufrière. It is long extinct, but steam pouring from vents in the dramatic yellow-and-pink rock and the lush tropical vegetation circling the rim of the crater make this a powerful, evocative sight.

Measuring only 11 miles by 7 miles, Montserrat is a small, friendly island that has escaped much of the large-scale development common in other parts of the Caribbean. It tends to attract independent travelers who want a low-key, away-from-it-all vacation. If you want to pump iron, drink piña coladas, and boogie till dawn, you'll probably be bored. If you like seclusion, nature, and peace and quiet, you'll love it. Despite the island's small size, there are an unusually large number of nature walks, hiking trails, and scenic vistas. This is the island to visit when you want to see rare birds, bubbling volcanic springs, waterfalls, and dense forest.

Most visitors arrive at Blackburn Airport on the Atlantic (east) coast of the island and then drive to the Caribbean (west) coast. Since there are no roads that traverse the island from east to west or circle it to the south, this will mean a trip around the northern tip. On the way, you will notice that the landscape changes considerably. The Atlantic coast is rockier, more windswept, and less fertile. Steep cliffs make most of the beaches on that side of the island inaccessible.

The best beaches, as well as the capital, Plymouth, and most of the villas and hotels are concentrated in a small area, measuring about 5 miles by 2 miles, on the Caribbean coast. Here Montserrat's vegetation is most luxuriant. Hibiscus and bougainvillea, giant philodendron and avocado trees, mango trees, christophines (a kind of squash), and many other species all thrive on the terracelike hills that slope down to the water. There are also spectacular views across the Caribbean to Antigua's mysterious island of Rodondo and, a bit farther away, Nevis and St. Kitts, a sequence of indigo blue peaks on the northern horizon.

Despite the fact that Montserrat now has a brand-new $30 million seaport, big enough to accommodate small cruise ships, the island still retains its peaceful, unhurried, completely nontouristy atmosphere. For now, the island is on the itinerary of only a few cruises, mostly the oversize sailing vessels. It remains to be seen what changes will occur as more and more ships come calling and as plans go ahead for a shopping development alongside the port.

Before You Go

Tourist Information
You can get information about Montserrat through the **Caribbean Tourism Organization** (20 E. 46th St., New York, NY 10017, ☎ 212/682–0435).

Arriving and Departing
BY PLANE
Although Antigua is not the only gateway, it's the best way to reach Montserrat. **BWIA** (☎ 800/538–2942) flies nonstop on Thursdays and Saturdays (plus Mondays in season) to Antigua from New York and on Thursday, Saturday, and Sunday from Miami; it also has regularly scheduled nonstop service from Toronto, Canada, and Heathrow Airport, London. **American Airlines** (☎ 800/433–7300) has connecting service from a number of U.S. cities through San Juan, Puerto Rico. **Air Canada** (☎ 800/776–3000) offers service from Toronto; **British Airways** (☎ in Britain, 0181/897–4000; in the U.S., 800/247–9297) from Gatwick Airport, London; and **Lufthansa** (☎ 800/645–3880 in the U.S.) transports visitors from Frankfurt via Puerto Rico.

From Antigua's V. C. Bird International Airport, you can make your connections with **LIAT** (☎ 809/491–2200 or 800/253–5011) or **Montserrat Airways** (☎ 809/491–5342 or 809/491–6494) for the 15-minute flight to Montserrat.

You will land on the 3,400-foot runway at Blackburne Airport, on the Atlantic coast, about 11 miles from Plymouth.

FROM THE AIRPORT
Taxis meet every flight; the government-regulated fare from the airport to Plymouth is E.C.$29 (U.S.$11).

Passports and Visas
U.S. and Canadian citizens only need proof of citizenship, such as a passport, a notarized birth certificate, or a voter registration card plus a photo ID, such as a driver's license. A driver's license by itself is *not* sufficient. British citizens must have a passport; visas are not required. All visitors must hold an ongoing or return ticket.

Language
It's English with more of a lilt than a brogue. You'll also hear a patois that's spoken on most of the islands.

Precautions
Ask for permission before taking pictures. Some residents may be reluctant photographic subjects, and they will appreciate your courtesy.

Most Montserratians frown at the sight of skimpily dressed tourists; do not risk offending them by strolling around town in shorts and swimsuits.

Staying in Montserrat

Important Addresses

Tourist Information: The **Montserrat Department of Tourism** (Church Rd., Plymouth, ☎ 809/491–2230) is open weekdays 8–noon and 1–4.

EMERGENCIES

Police: ☎ 999 or 809/491–2555. **Hospital:** There is a 24-hour emergency room at **Glendon Hospital** (Plymouth, ☎ 809/491–2552). **Pharmacies: Lee's Pharmacy** (Evergreen Dr., Plymouth, ☎ 809/491–3274) and **Daniel's Pharmacy** (George St., Plymouth, ☎ 809/491–2908).

Currency

The official currency is the Eastern Caribbean dollar (E.C.$), often called beewee. At press time, the exchange rate was E.C.$2.70 to U.S.$1. U.S. dollars are readily accepted, but you'll often receive change in beewees. Note: Prices quoted here are in U.S. dollars unless noted otherwise.

Taxes and Service Charges

Hotels collect a 7% government tax and add a 10% service charge. Most restaurants add a 10%–15% service charge. If restaurants do not add the service charge, it's customary to leave a 10% or 15% tip. Taxi drivers should be given a 10% tip. The departure tax is E.C.$25 (about U.S.$9).

Guided Tours

Guides are recommended when you are heading to Mount Chance, Galway's Soufrière, and the Great Alps Falls. Prices for two people range from $10 to $30. Guides and tours can be arranged by calling Cecil Cassell, president of the **Montserrat Tour Guide Association** (☎ 809/491–3160, FAX 809/491–2052). Or you can call **John Ryner** (☎ 809/491–2190) and the aptly named **Bo-Beep Taylor** (☎ 809/491–3787). Prices (fixed by the department of tourism) are E.C.$30 per hour (U.S. $12) or E.C.$130–$150 (U.S. $50–$58) for a five-hour day tour. Refreshments are extra. For further information, contact the Department of Tourism.

Getting Around

TAXIS

Taxis, private vehicles, or the M11 (a play on the local registration numbers, meaning your own two legs) are the main means of transport on the island. A loosely organized network of minibuses travels between the villages and Plymouth, but schedules are erratic and unreliable. Taxis are always available at the airport, the main hotels, and the taxi stand in Plymouth (☎ 809/491–2261). The Department of Tourism publishes a list of taxi fares to most destinations.

CAR RENTALS

The island has more than 115 miles of paved (but potholed) roads. Unless you're uncomfortable about driving on the left, you won't have any trouble exploring. You'll need a valid driver's license, plus a Montserrat license, which is available at the airport or the Treasury Department on Strand Street in Plymouth. The fee is E.C.$30 (U.S.$12). Rental cars cost about $35–$40 per day. The smaller companies, whose prices are generally 10%–25% cheaper, will negotiate, particularly off-season. **Pauline Car Rentals** (Plymouth, ☎ 809/491–2345) is a local rental company. Other agencies are **Jefferson's Car Rental** (Dagenham, ☎ 809/491–2126), **Budget** (Blackburne Airport, ☎ 809/491–6065), **Reliable** (Plymouth, ☎ 809/491–6990), and **Fenco** (Plymouth, ☎ 809/491–4901).

MOUNTAIN BIKES

Montserrat is good mountain-bike country: small, with relatively traffic-free roads and lots of challenging hills to try out all those gears. Potholes will present a constant challenge, as will the heat and steep gradients. Even so, biking is a great way to get around this island, where the majority of facilities, shops, and accommodations are concentrated in a small area on the west coast. At **Island Bikes** (Harney St., Plymouth, ☎ 809/491–4696, FAX 809/491–5552), Butch Miller and Susan Goldin, the bustling, can-do Americans who run the outfit, are self-confessed biking junkies and know the island like the backs of their own saddles. Rentals are $25 a day, $140 a week. The couple also conducts guided tours, which include refreshments and a sag wagon for the faint of heart, and can arrange bed-and-bike package tours. They also sponsor two international cycle races each year.

Telephones and Mail

To call Montserrat from the United States, dial area code 809 and access code 491 plus the local four-digit number. International direct dial is available on the island; both local and long-distance calls come through clearly. To call locally on the island, you need to dial the seven-digit number, the first three digits of which are always 491.

Airmail letters and postcards to the United States and Canada cost E.C.$1.15 each. Montserrat is one of several Caribbean islands whose stamps are of interest to collectors. You can buy them at the main post office in Plymouth (open Mon., Tues., Thurs., Fri. 8:15–3:55, Wed. and Sat. 8:15–11:25 AM).

Opening and Closing Times

Most shops are open Monday to Saturday 8–5. Banking hours are Monday to Thursday 8–3 and Friday 3–5.

Exploring Montserrat

Numbers in the margin correspond to points of interest on the Montserrat map.

Plymouth

About a third of the island's population of 11,000 lives in the capital city of **Plymouth,** which faces the Caribbean on the southwest coast. The town is neat and clean, its narrow streets lined with trim Georgian structures built mostly of stones that came from Dorset as ballast on old sailing vessels. Most of the town's sights are located right along the water, and you can easily explore the whole town in less than two hours. On the south side, a bridge over Fort Ghaut ("gut," or ravine) leads to Wapping, where most of the restaurants are located.

We'll begin at **Government House,** on the south side of town just above Sugar Bay. The frilly Victorian house, painted green with white trim and decorated with a shamrock, dates from the 18th century. Beautifully landscaped gardens surround the building, which is the residence of the governor of Montserrat. The grounds are open to visitors Monday, Tuesday, Thursday, and Friday, from 10:30 AM to 12:30 PM and are worth a visit.

Follow Peebles Street north and cross the bridge. Just over the bridge, at the junction of Harney, Strand, and Parliament streets, you'll see the **Plymouth Market,** where islanders bring their produce on Friday and Saturday mornings—a very colorful scene of great piles of local vegetables and fruits and vendors in brightly colored outfits.

From the market, walk along Strand Street for one block to the tall, white **war memorial** with a bell turret. The memorial is a tribute to the soldiers of both world wars. Next to the monument is the **post office and treasury,** a galleried West Indian–style building by the water, where you can buy stamps that make handsome souvenirs.

Walk away from the water on George Street, which runs alongside the war memorial. The town's main thoroughfare, Parliament Street, cuts diagonally north–south through the town. A left turn onto Parliament Street, at the corner of George Street, will take you to the Methodist church and the courthouse. If you continue straight on George Street, you'll come to the Roman Catholic church. From back in Plymouth, if you cross the bridge heading east toward Amersham, you will come across the **American University of the Caribbean,** a medical school with many American students.

Elsewhere on the Island
From here on, you'll need wheels. Take Highway 2, the main road north out of Plymouth. On the outskirts of town there's a stone marker that commemorates the first colony in 1632.

TOUR 1

2 **St. Anthony's Church,** which is just north of town, was consecrated sometime between 1623 and 1666. It was rebuilt in 1730 following one of the many clashes between the French and the English in the area. Two silver chalices displayed in the church were donated by freed slaves after emancipation in 1834.

3 Richmond Hill rises north of town. Here you will find the **Montserrat Museum** in a restored sugar mill. The museum contains maps, historical records, artifacts (including some Arawak and Carib items), and all sorts of memorabilia pertaining to the island's growth and development. *Richmond Hill,* ☎ *809/491–5443.* ☛ *Free (donations accepted).* ☺ *Sun. and Wed. 2:30–5 (but telephone to be sure).*

4 Take the first left turn past the museum to Grove Road; it will take you to the **Fox's Bay Bird Sanctuary,** a 15-acre mangrove swamp. The marked trail through the sanctuary begins right near Fox's Bay beach. Watch for green herons, the rare blue herons, coots, egrets, and kingfishers plus many lizards and iguanas.

The **Bransby Point Fortification** is also in this area and contains a collection of restored cannons.

5 Backtrack on Grove Road to Highway 2, drive north, and turn right on Highway 4 to **St. George's Fort.** It's overgrown and of little historical interest, but the view from the hilltop is well worth the trip.

6 Highway 2 continues north past the Belham Valley Golf Course to **Vue Pointe** hotel, on the coast at Old Road Bay. Head east to the green slopes of Centre Hills. Here you'll find the site of the former **Air Studios,** the recording studio founded in 1979 by former Beatles producer George Martin. Sting, Boy George, and Paul McCartney have all cut records here, but Hurricane Hugo damaged the facility severely and it never reopened.

7 About 1½ miles farther north, near Woodland's Bay, a scenic drive takes you along **Runaway Ghaut.** More than two centuries ago, this peaceful green valley was the scene of bloody battles between the French and the English. Local legend has it that "those who drink its water clear they spellbound are, and the Montserrat they must obey." Next, you will come to **Carr's Bay, Little Bay,** and **Rendezvous Bay,** the is-

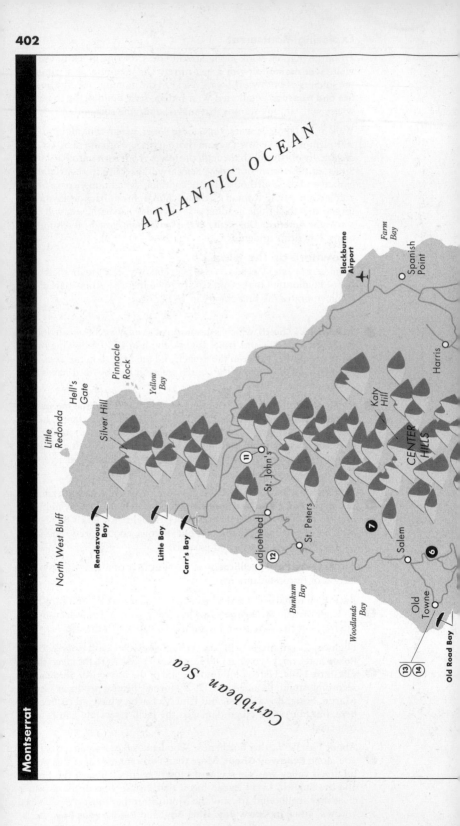

ATLANTIC OCEAN

Caribbean Sea

Little
Redonda

North West Bluff

Rendezvous
Bay

Hell's
Gate

Silver Hill

Pinnacle
Rock

Yellow
Bay

Little Bay

Carr's Bay

Cudjoehead

⑪ St. John's

⑫

St. Peters

Bunkum
Bay

Woodlands
Bay

CENTER
HILLS

Katy
Hill

Harris

Salem

⑦

⑥

Old
Towne

⑬ ⑭

Old Road Bay

Blackburne
Airport ✈

Farm
Bay

Spanish
Point

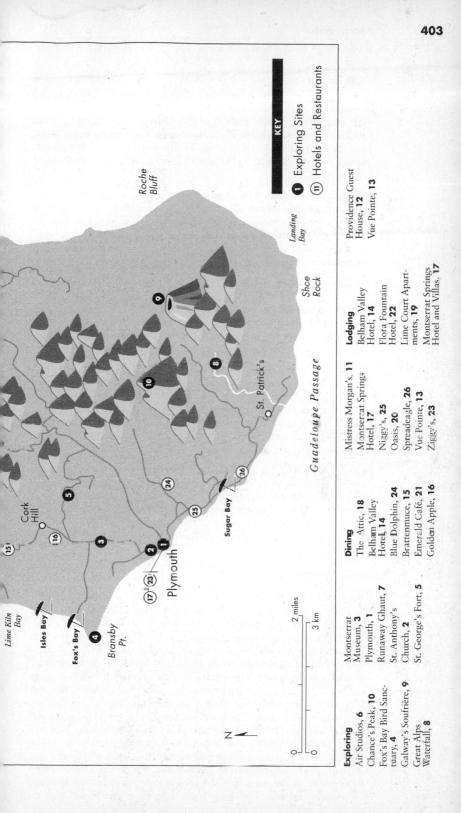

KEY

● Exploring Sites

⑪ Hotels and Restaurants

Roche Bluff

Landing Bay

Shoe Rock

Guadeloupe Passage

St. Patrick's

Lodging
Belham Valley
Hotel, **14**
Flora Fountain
Hotel, **22**
Lime Court Apart-
ments, **19**
Montserrat Springs
Hotel and Villas, **17**
Providence Guest
House, **12**
Vue Pointe, **13**

Dining
The Attic, **18**
Belham Valley
Hotel **14**
Blue Dolphin, **24**
Brattenmuce, **15**
Emerald Café, **21**
Golden Apple, **16**
Mistress Morgan's, **11**
Montserrat Springs
Hotel, **17**
Niggy's, **25**
Oasis, **20**
Spreadeagle, **26**
Vue Pointe, **13**
Ziggy's, **23**

Sugar Bay

Plymouth

Cork Hill

Lime Kiln Bay

Isles Bay

Fox's Bay

Bransby Pt.

N

0 — 2 miles
0 — 3 km

Exploring
Air Studios, **6**
Chance's Peak, **10**
Fox's Bay Bird Sanc-
tuary, **4**
Galway's Soufrière, **9**
Great Alps
Waterfall, **8**
Montserrat
Museum, **3**
Plymouth, **1**
Runaway Ghaut, **7**
St. Anthony's
Church, **2**
St. George's Fort, **5**

land's three most popular beaches, which are along the northwest coast.

<u>TOUR 2</u>

The next tour of the island will be considerably more arduous, taking in the mountains, rain forests, and *soufrières* (volcanic craters with sulfuric springs) to the south and east of Plymouth. To hire a knowledgeable guide, contact Cecil Cassell at the **Montserrat Tour Guides Association,** contact the department of tourism, or ask at your hotel. The guide's fee will be about $6 (E.C.$15) per person to the waterfall. Wear sturdy rubber-soled shoes.

A 15-minute drive south of Plymouth on Old Fort Road will bring you to the village of **St. Patrick's.** From there, a scenic drive takes you to the starting point of the moderately strenuous 30- to 45-minute hike through **8** thick rain forests to **Great Alps Waterfall.** The falls plunge 70 feet down the side of a rock and splash into a shallow pool. For a refreshing break, step in the pool and let the waters cascade right over you.

9 A rugged road leads eastward to **Galway's Soufrière,** where another hike is involved, this one lasting about a half hour. Once there, you'll see reddish and yellow-brown volcanic rock and springs and fumaroles of gurgling, bubbling (and quite smelly) molten sulfur. Everyone's heard the phrase "so hot you could fry an egg on it." Here your guide will almost certainly fry an egg to demonstrate the intense heat of the rocks.

10 The island's highest point, **Chance's Peak,** pokes up 3,002 feet through the rain forests. The climb to the top is arduous, but there are now 2,000 makeshift stairs (thanks to Cable & Wireless, who added the wooden stairs after Hugo to ease access to their mountaintop radio tower). If you do make it to the top, what little breath you may have left will be taken away by the view, *if* the clouds have parted. (Go early in the morning, when the clouds are least likely to be there.)

Also in this area is the old **Galway's Estate,** a plantation built in the late 17th century by the prosperous Irishmen John and Henry Blake, who came to Montserrat from Galway. It has been earmarked as an important archaeological site by the Smithsonian. Amateur archaeologists come here annually in the summer, and the sugar boiling house and parts of both a wind-driven and cattle-driven sugar mill have been partially restored.

Off the Beaten Track

Head for the **South Soufrière Hills** at the southern tip of the island. It is the wildest and least spoiled part of Montserrat and includes, among its highlights, the **Bamboo Forest,** a large tract of semi–rain forest inhabited by birds, frogs, and plants. It is home to many of the 100 species of birds that visit Montserrat, among them the national emblem, *iaterus oberi,* or Montserrat oriole, also known locally as the tannia bird, which is found nowhere else on earth. You will also see bromeliads, tulip and breadfruit trees, and a plethora of other tropical plants. Because no roads lead into the area and there are no marked paths, you are advised to go with a guide. The most knowledgeable guide is **Joseph Peters,** a young man who will take you on a two- to three-hour tour and fill you in on the wildlife and botany. He can be reached at his home (☎ 809/491–6850) or via the Department of Tourism in Plymouth. You can also call the **Department of Agriculture** (☎ 809/491–2546). Plans have been afoot for years for some sort of low-impact, ecotourism development in the area, but things move very slowly on Montserrat.

Beaches

The sand on the beaches on Montserrat's south coast is of volcanic origin; usually referred to as black, it's actually light to dark gray. On the northwest coast, the sand is beige or white. The three most popular destinations for swimming and sunning are **Rendezvous Bay** (Montserrat's only white-sand beach), **Little Bay,** and **Carr's Bay,** all on the northwest coast. Though it is possible to drive to both Carr's Bay and Little Bay and to hike from Little Bay over the hill to Rendezvous Bay, it is certainly more relaxing to reach any of these beaches via the sailing and snorkeling excursions arranged by the **Vue Pointe** hotel (☎ 809/491–5210).

Fox's Bay has a lovely strip of gray sand on the bay just north of the bird sanctuary. **Old Road Bay** and **Isles Bay** are on the coast north of Fox's Bay (4 miles north of Plymouth) and also have stretches of gray-sand beaches.

Sugar Bay, to the south of Plymouth, is a beach of fine gray volcanic sand. The Yacht Club overlooks this beach.

Sports and the Outdoors

Boating

Captain Martin (☎ 809/491–5738) takes guests out on his 46-foot trimaran for a full-day sail to the white-sand beach at **Rendezvous Bay** for swimming and snorkeling at the nearby reef. The boat leaves about 10 AM and returns about 5 PM; the cost is $45 and includes an open bar and snorkeling equipment. **Vue Pointe** hotel (☎ 809/491–5210) offers sailing and snorkeling excursions to Rendezvous Bay, Little Bay, and Carr's Bay. The cost is $25 a person and includes a sandwich lunch and snorkeling equipment.

Golf

The **Montserrat Golf Course** (☎ 809/491–5220), in the picturesque Belham Valley, is "slope rated" by the USGA (in other words, it's incredibly hilly) and must be one of the few golf courses in the world that can list gopher holes and iguanas among its hazards. The number of holes (11) is also somewhat eccentric, though by playing a number of them twice, you can get your 18. Four fairways run along the ocean. The rest are up hill and down dale. Watch out for the iguanas—they collect golf balls.

Mountain Biking

Montserrat is perfect mountain-bike country (*see* Getting Around, in Staying in Montserrat, *above*).

Sailing, Snorkeling, and Scuba Diving

Snorkeling equipment is provided on the day cruises to the white-sand coves on the west coast; boats usually have an open bar. Arrangements can be made through the **Vue Pointe** hotel (☎ 809/491–5210) or **Captain Martin** (☎ 809/491–5738).

Sea Wolf Diving School (☎ 809/491–7807) in Plymouth and **Aquatic Discoveries** (☎ 809/491–3474), located next to the Vue Pointe hotel, both offer one- or two-tank dives, night dives, and instruction from PADI-certified instructors. Costs are about $40 for a one-tank dive and $60 for a two-tank dive. Aquatic Discoveries also offers snorkel tours, whale-watching trips, and deep-sea-fishing excursions.

Danny Water Sports (☎ 809/491–5645), operating out of the Vue Pointe hotel, rents snorkel equipment and Windsurfers and also offers fishing, Sunfish sailing, and waterskiing.

Tennis

There are lighted tennis courts at the **Vue Pointe** hotel (☎ 809/491–5210), the **Montserrat Springs Hotel** (☎ 809/491–2481), and the **Montserrat Golf Club** (☎ 809/491–5220).

Windsurfing

Contact **Danny Water Sports** (☎ 809/491–5645) to rent boards (about $10 per 45 minutes).

Spectator Sports

Cricket is the national passion. Cricket and soccer matches are held from February through June in **Sturge Park. Shamrock Car Park** is the venue for netball and basketball games. Contact the Department of Tourism (☎ 809/491–2230) for schedules.

Shopping

Montserrat's sea-island cotton is famous for its high quality, but, unfortunately, there is only a limited amount and it is not cheap. There are good buys on hand-turned pottery, straw goods, ceramic jewelry, and jewelry made from shells and coral. Montserratian stamps can be purchased at the post office or at the Philatelic Bureau, just across the bridge in Wapping. Two lip-smacking local food products are Cassell's hot sauce, available at most supermarkets, and Perk's Punch, an effervescent rum-based concoction manufactured by **J. W. R. Perkins, Inc.** (☎ 809/491–2596).

Good Buys

CLOTHES

The **Jus' Looking** (George St., Plymouth, ☎ 809/491–4076; small branch at airport, open in afternoons only, ☎ 809/491–4040) boutique features "sculpted," hand-painted pillows from Antigua; painted and lacquered boxes from the Dutch West Indies; Sunny Caribbee's jams, jellies, and packaged spices from the British Virgin Islands (including an Arawak love potion and a hangover cure); special teas; and Caribelle Batik's line of richly colored fabrics, shirts, skirts, pants, and dresses. The shop also has an excellent selection of local poetry and history books. **Montserrat Shirts** (Parliament St., ☎ 809/491–2892) has a good selection of men's tropical cotton shirts, plus T-shirts and sandals for the whole family. **Etcetera** (John St., ☎ 809/491–3299) is a little shop carrying colorful, lightweight cotton dresses and a small but fine selection of local crafts. (If you're lucky, you may see someone making a hat of coconut palm fronds.)

The **Montserrat Sea Island Cotton Co.** (corner of George and Strand Sts., Plymouth, ☎ 809/491–7009), long famous for its cotton creations, has dresses, shirts, and other clothing items plus table linens, much of it made from local sea island cotton.

CRAFTS

The **Tapestries of Montserrat** (Parliament St., ☎ 809/491–2520), on the second floor of the John Bull Shop, offers a floor-to-ceiling display of hand-tufted creations—from wall hangings and pillow covers to tote bags and rugs—all with fanciful yarn adornments of flowers, carnival figures, animals, and birds. Owners Gerald and Charlie Handley will even help you create your own design for a small additional fee. At **Carol's Corner** (Vue Pointe hotel, ☎ 809/491–5210), Carol Osborne sells everything related to Montserrat—stamps, copper bookmarks, the *Montserrat Cookbook*, Frane Lessac's books of prose, and paintings. Drop by **Dutcher's Studio** (Olveston, ☎ 809/491–5253) to see hand-cut, hand-painted objects made from glass, ceramics, and old bottles, and some very appealing ceramic jewelry. If Paula Dutcher is there, ask about the morning iguana feeding at her house. Anywhere from 5 to 50 reptiles converge on her lawn, sunning themselves and eating hibiscus from your hand. **Island House** (☎ 809/491–3938), on John Street, stocks a fine collection of Haitian art, Caribbean prints, and clay pottery.

Dining

Despite its size, Montserrat offers a variety of dining options to fit all budgets. Most of the more inexpensive eateries are found in small cafés, some of which look like the proverbial hole-in-the-wall. Don't be deceived, as most offer delicious Caribbean home cooking. The island also has a lively assortment of rum shops—the Caribbean version of local bars—packed with islanders on Friday nights; you can join in and get a drink and a simple meal.

Montserrat's national dish is goatwater stew, made with goat meat and vegetables and similar to Irish stew. Goat meat is strong but tasty. Mountain "chicken" (actually enormous frogs) is also a great favorite. Yams, breadfruit, christophines (a kind of squash), limes, mangoes, papayas, and a variety of seafood are served in most restaurants. Home brewed ginger beer, one of the finest traditional drinks of the West Indies, is widely available.

What to Wear

In general, neat casual clothing is the norm at lunch and dinner. Beach attire is too casual. Although jackets are not required, shorts and jeans are not acceptable at the fancier restaurants for dinner.

CATEGORY	COST*
$$$	over $30
$$	$20–$30
$	under $20

per person, excluding drinks and service. If the service charge is not added to the bill, leave a 10%–15% tip.

$$$ **Montserrat Springs Hotel.** The split-level cathedral-ceilinged dining room, enclosed on three sides, faces a large pool and a sundeck, beyond which you can see the ocean. A menu of West Indian and Continental cuisine includes an excellent goat-water stew, local snapper with a Creole sauce, grilled tenderloin steak, and an excellent Spanish omelet. ✕ *Richmond Hill, Plymouth,* ☎ *809/491–2481. Reservations advised in season. AE, MC, V.*

$$$ **Vue Pointe.** Candlelit dining in the hillside hotel's restaurant overlook-
★ ing the sea makes for a very romantic evening. There is a nightly five-course table d'hôte menu, or you can order à la carte. West Indian–style mountain chicken, kingfish, beef Wellington, and red snapper with Creole sauce are favorites. For dessert, it's hard to choose between the lime pie and the guava cheesecake. The Wednesday-night barbecue, accompanied by music from a steel band, is a popular island event. ✕ *Old Towne,* ☎ *809/491–5210. Reservations advised for dinner. AE, MC, V.*

$$–$$$ **Belham Valley Hotel.** Considered by many to be the best restaurant
★ on the island, this former private home offers intimate, elegant dining. The best tables are on the open-air terrace; hung with ferns and croton plants, it looks down over picturesque Belham Valley and the lights of Isle Bay Hill. The sound of tree frogs and the rhythm of the

ocean mingle with the clink of glasses and the recorded music of Stan Getz, Astrud Gilberto, and other jazz greats. Hibiscus tumbles over stone walls and sprouts from table vases; ceilings and floors are timbered. The beautiful setting is accompanied by one of the best menus on the island. Start with conch fritters or liver pâté, and progress to Seafood Delight (sautéed lobster, red snapper, and sea scallops in a vermouth sauce) or broiled baby lobster tails. Scrumptious desserts are mango or lime mousse, lemon cake, and a tropical fruit sundae with a ginger sauce. At lunchtime, the offerings are lighter: omelets, salads, and sandwiches. ✕ *Old Towne,* ☎ *809/491–5553. Reservations required for dinner. AE, MC, V. Closed Mon. No lunch weekends.*

$$ **Emerald Café.** Dining is relaxed at 10 tables inside and on the terrace, where there are white tables shaded by blue umbrellas. Burgers, sandwiches, salads, and grilled chicken and fish are served at lunchtime. For dinner you can order tournedos sautéed in spicy butter, broiled or sautéed Caribbean lobster, T-bone steak, mountain chicken Diable, and giant swordfish steaks. The Island Coconut Pie and other homemade pastries are superb. There's also an ample list of liqueurs and wines, a full bar, and entertainment on weekends. ✕ *Wapping, Plymouth,* ☎ *809/491–3821. Dinner reservations advised in season. MC. Closed Sun.*

$$ **Oasis.** A 200-year-old stone house is the setting for this charming restaurant. You can dine indoors in the intimate bar and lounge, but most choose the outdoor patio, which looks out onto colorful tropical flowers. Calypso mountain chicken, jumbo shrimp Provençale, red snapper with lime butter, and grilled sirloin steak are house specialties. Owners Eric and Mandy Finnamore are also well known for their British-style fish-and-chips. ✕ *Wapping, Plymouth,* ☎ *809/491–2328. Reservations advised in season. No credit cards. Closed Wed.*

$ **The Attic.** The (formerly) third-story Attic had a sister restaurant on the second story called the Pantry. Compliments of Hurricane Hugo, the Attic ended up in the Pantry, where owners John and Jeanne Fagon decided it would stay! For breakfast, lunch, and dinner, 12 busy tables supply town folk with specialties of ocean perch, pork chops with pantry sauce (made from whatever's in the pantry), breaded shrimp, and lobster tail. ✕ *Marine Dr., Plymouth,* ☎ *809/491–2008. No credit cards.*

$ **Blue Dolphin.** The inside is short on ambience—the chairs are Naugahyde,
★ and the menu is scrawled on a blackboard without prices or descriptions—but the seductive aromas wafting from the kitchen announce that the Blue Dolphin serves some of the best food on the island, including luscious pumpkin fritters, mouthwatering lobster, and meltingly tender mountain chicken. And this hilltop-perched eatery has a fabulous view of the town and sea. ✕ *Amersham,* ☎ *809/491–3263. No credit cards.*

$ **Brattenmuce.** About 10 minutes by car above the road from Plymouth to Belham Valley, you can't miss the canary-yellow facade and brightly colored croton bushes of this restaurant. The name is a play on the name of the owners, Matt Hawthorne and Bruce Munro, two Canadian expats who have been in Montserrat since 1985. They serve no-frills, North American cuisine—meat loaf and creamed potatoes, pork chops, and chicken cordon bleu. On Wednesday nights they have a Games Night, which is popular with "the snow birds," retirees from the North. A three-course meal for E.C.$25 includes free use of the Scrabble boards and Trivial Pursuit. For those who want to stay over, Rogie's, above the restaurant, has simple rooms to let. In the off-season Brattenmuce is open on Wednesday, Friday, and Saturday in the evening. In season, it closes only on Monday. ✕ *Belham Valley,* ☎ *809/ 419–7564. Reservations advised. No credit cards.*

$ **Golden Apple.** In this large, galleried stone building, you'll be served huge plates of good, local cooking. The restaurant's specialty is goat-water stew, which is cooked on weekends only, outside over an open fire. Souse; *pelau* (chicken-and-rice curry); conch, stewed or curried; and mountain chicken are also excellent. Tables are covered with cheerful red-and-white-checked tablecloths, and the atmosphere is relaxed. There's also a grocery store attached. ✗ *Cork Hill,* ☎ *809/491–2187. No credit cards.*

$ **Mistress Morgan's.** Friday and Saturday are goat-water-stew days at Mistress Morgan's, and from 11:30 onward you can join the carloads of locals who make the trek up here to the north of the island to eat their fill. Order yourself a hearty bowl of the stew, which costs only E.C.$8 (U.S.$3.50), and plunk yourself down at one of the four picnic tables in the simple, unadorned room. The stew is just the way it should be—with the flesh falling off the bone, brimming with dumplings and innards. If that doesn't sound appetizing, try the souse, baked chicken, or any of the other down-home specialties. ✗ *Airport Rd., St. John's,* ☎ *809/491–5419. No credit cards.*

$ **Niggy's.** In his previous life, the owner was a British character actor
★ in Hollywood. That was before he decided to trade the smell of grease-paint and the roar of the crowd for a place behind the bar in this extremely popular restaurant (the British governor eats here regularly). The setting is a simple clapboard cottage with yellow bella flowers trailing over the gate, and the food, served at picnic style benches under a trellis of flowering plants, is excellent and a good value. Try the grilled steaks and chops, shrimp scampi, or one of the pasta specials. Inside at the bar, you'll be regaled with tales of Hollywood, and the whole place feels like a set for a Caribbean remake of *Casablanca.* There's entertainment weekends, and for those who want to stay over, there are two simple but clean rooms in the back. The property is a 10-minute drive from the center of Plymouth. ✗ *Kinsale,* ☎ *809/491–7489. No credit cards. No lunch.*

$ **Spreadeagle.** This is a tiny place that you'll be glad you found if you visit Galway's Soufrière or Great Alps Falls. Peter "Bobb," the owner, keeps beer on ice and serves all sorts of beverages and light snacks. ✗ *German's Bay,* ☎ *809/491–7503. No credit cards.* ☉ *Daily 9–5.*

$ **Ziggy's.** On top of a barrel at the entrance to their restaurant, John
★ and Marcia Punter display all the fruits and vegetables that grow on the island, among them ginger, nutmeg, yams, plantain, christophine, and coconuts. This is one of the first clues that what used to be a simple waterfront café and bar has become one of the best bistros on the island. The furnishings are sparse, but the waterside setting is very pleasant, and the menu—everything from curried mutton and rice to lasagna—one of the most varied on the island. ✗ *Wapping, Plymouth,* ☎ *809/491–2237. Reservations advised. No credit cards. Closed Wed.*

Lodging

Accommodations on Montserrat are limited in terms of hotels, but there are many villas of all sizes available for rent. The two largest hotels—the Vue Point and Montserrat Springs—are also the island's only real resorts. Small hotels that cater to businesspeople, guest houses, and a few bed-and-breakfasts are also available. Be aware that most hotels are still "tropical-breeze-cooled": Only a few have rooms that are air-conditioned.

Villas are not only affordable here; given their comforts and conveniences, many consider them preferable to the hotels. You can even request the properties where your favorite rock stars—from Sting to Elton John—relaxed.

Most of Montserrat's hotels operate on the Modified American Plan (MAP: breakfast and dinner are included in the rate).

CATEGORY	COST*
$$$	over $145
$$	$75–$145
$	under $75

All prices are for a standard double room for two in winter, excluding 7% tax and 10% service charge.

Hotels

$$$ **Montserrat Springs Hotel and Villas.** Spacious air-conditioned rooms in this, the largest of the island's hotels, are in one wing of the main building and in cottages scattered along the steep hillside sloping down to the beach. All rooms have excellent views of the water and Chance's Peak and are bright and airy. The decor is primarily cream and white. Rooms have private balconies and cable TV; suites have separate living rooms and full kitchens. From the terrace surrounding the beautiful outdoor pool, you can take in sweeping views of the ocean in one direction and Chance's Peak in the other. There are two lighted tennis courts. At the beach bar you can luxuriate in a whirlpool filled with piping-hot mineral water direct from a soufrière. The restaurant is recommended (*see* Dining, *above*). ☎ *Box 259, Plymouth,* ☎ *809/491–2481 or 800/253–2134,* ℻ *809/491–4070. 40 rooms and 6 suites. Restaurant, 2 bars, room service, pool, hot/cold mineral-water Jacuzzi, beach, 2 lighted tennis courts, AE, MC, V. EP, MAP.*

$$–$$$ **Vue Pointe.** The moment you arrive here you feel as though both the
★ staff and the owners, Cedric and Carol Osborne, really care about your well-being. The gracious Monday-night cocktail parties that the Osbornes host at their house, with drinks, delicious homemade hors d'ouevres, and good conversation, are a perfect example. (Cedric Osborne comes from one of the island's first families and is a mine of information about local goings-on.) The breeze-cooled accommodations include 12 rooms in the main building and 28 hexagonal rondavels that spill down to the gray-sand beach on Old Road Bay. Each rondavel has a large bedroom, cable TV, phone, hair dryer, minifridge, spacious bathroom, and great view. In the main building a large lounge and bar overlook the pool; the Wednesday-night barbecue, with steel bands and other entertainment, is an event well attended by locals and guests alike. In the adjacent sea-view restaurant, you can have a candlelight dinner of local and international specialties (the chef is one of the most skilled on the island). A 150-seat conference center serves as a theater and disco. For water-sports enthusiasts, there is scuba diving, snorkeling, and fishing. ☎ *Box 65, Plymouth,* ☎ *809/491–5210 or 800/235–0709,* ℻ *809/491–4813. 12 rooms, 28 rondavels. Restaurant, bar, gift shop, pool, 2 lighted tennis courts, water-sports center, shuffleboard, game room. AE, MC, V. EP, MAP.*

$$ **Flora Fountain Hotel.** This is a hotel for people coming on business (only 35% of the clientele are tourists) or for those who appreciate an old, rambling hotel in the heart of town. The two-story structure has been created around an enormous fountain that's sometimes lighted at night, with small tables scattered in the inner courtyard. There are 18 plainly decorated but adequate rooms, all with tile bath, air-conditioning, most with balconies. All rooms have phones but not all have TVs, so ask if it's important to you. The restaurant has a chef from Bombay who serves simple sandwiches and fine Indian dishes. Friday night's Indian buffet includes several meat and fish dishes, at least two kinds of rice, vegetable and pork dishes with spices, *raita* (a yogurt sauce), and *samosa* (spicy meat patties). ⌧ *Box 373, Church Rd., Plymouth,* ☎ *809/491–6092,* ℻ *809/491–2568. 18 rooms. Restaurant, bar AE, D, MC, V. EP, CP, MAP.*

$–$$ **Providence Guest House.** On an island where it is almost impossible to
★ find good bed-and-breakfast accommodations, this two-unit guest house, perched on a bluff high above the ocean with spectacular views of St. Kitts and Redonda, stands out. The present owners lovingly restored the former plantation house, and the beautiful stone-and-wood building, with a wraparound veranda, is now one of the finest examples of traditional Caribbean architecture on the island. The two guest rooms—one has a bath as well as a shower and is considerably larger—are on the ground floor and open directly onto the pool area, where gleaming water is edged with tiles from Trinidad. Both rooms have the original timbered ceilings and massive stone walls, which keep them cool in the summer, and are decorated with red quarry tiles and pastel fabrics. If there is any drawback to this idyll, it is the location. The nearest restaurant is 3 miles away in Belham Valley, and the nearest beach is a hike down the hillside. But the owners are willing to make evening meals on request, and they have also installed a kitchenette by the pool, where you can prepare your own meals. A large breakfast of eggs, oatmeal, and fruits from the garden (in season) is included in the room rate. ⌧ *Providence Estate House, Montserrat,* ☎ *809/491 6476. 2 rooms. Swimming pool, kitchenette, cable TV. No credit cards. CP.*

$ **Belham Valley Hotel.** On a hillside overlooking Belham Valley and the Belham Valley River, this hotel has a cottage and two apartments (a studio and a newer two-bedroom). All have a stereo, cable TV, a fully equipped kitchen, and a phone; none are air-conditioned. It's the restaurant here that's the big draw, with its lovely views and great food (*see* Dining, *above*). The beach is an eight-minute walk away. ⌧ *Box 409, Plymouth,* ☎ *809/491–5553. 3 units. Restaurant, maid service. AE, MC. EP.*

$ **Lime Court Apartments.** Right in the center of town, opposite the Parliament building, you'll find this slightly run-down, large white colonial-style apartment building. The downstairs apartments tend to be dark and airless, and with the sound of the generator and the puttering of the fridges, not very peaceful. But the large, well-equipped, two-bedroom, two-bath "penthouse," up a flight of steps at the top of the building, has a fine view from its balcony of the town's red rooftops and the sea beyond. It can sleep two couples and is reasonable at $45 per night. All apartments have kitchenettes with a stove and microwave, and private bathrooms (showers only). ⌧ *Box 250, Parliament St., Plymouth,* ☎ *809/491–3656. 8 apartments. Maid service, cable TV. AE, MC, V. EP.*

Villas and Condominiums

Luxury villas sprang up all over Montserrat in the 1980s, and there's a great range to choose from if you want a do-it-yourself vacation on the island. All the villa developments are on the west coast of the island, within 20 minutes of Plymouth by car. The majority are in the districts of Old Towne, Olveston, and Woodlands. The latter is particularly noteworthy for its magnificent views of the ocean and its steep hillsides covered in lush vegetation. Prices are high for just two people (a one-bedroom is around $1,000 per week) but become more reasonable when the cost can be split among more people. Two-bedroom villas with a pool range from $1,000 to $2,400 per week; three-bedroom villas from $1,500 to $2,500; and four-bedroom villas from

$2,500 to $3,000. There are villas of all sizes that are the ultimate in luxury and exceed even these prices. Off-season rates are as much as 50% lower (and usually negotiable), and some excellent bargains can be picked up by summer travelers. All villas come with maid service.

Caribbean Connection Plus (☎ 203/261–8603; FAX 203/261–8295) is a Stateside reservation service for about 50 one- to four-bedroom villas and some condos. It also has an on-island representative to ensure that all goes well. **Montserrat Enterprises Ltd** (Box 58, Marine Dr., Plymouth, ☎ 809/491–2431 [ask for Mr. Edwards], FAX 809/491–4660) has 22 villas in Old Towne, Woodlands, and Isles Bay. **Neville Bradshaw Agencies** (Box 270, Plymouth, ☎ 809/491–5270, FAX 809/491–5069) has a wide range of villas, mostly in Old Towne and Isles Bay. **Isles Bay Plantation** (Box 64, Plymouth, ☎ 809/491–5248, FAX 809/491–5016; in London, ☎ and fax 0171/482–1071), known locally as the Beverly Hills of Montserrat, has the crème de la crème of Montserrat's villas. Each house is set on approximately ½ acre of tropical landscaped gardens, has its own 40-foot pool, and is only a 10-minute walk from the beach. **Shamrock Villas** (Box 180, Plymouth, ☎ 809/491–2431) are one- and two-bedroom apartments and town-house condominiums in a hillside development minutes from Plymouth.

Nightlife

The hotels offer regularly scheduled barbecues and steel bands, and the small restaurants feature live entertainment in the form of calypso, reggae, rock, rhythm and blues, and soul.

Niggy's (Kinsale, ☎ 809/491–7489) usually has a vocalist Friday and Saturday nights, and there is often also live jazz on weekends. The **Yacht Club** (Wapping, ☎ 809/491–2237) has live island music on Friday, while the **Plantation Club** (Wapping, upstairs over the Oasis, ☎ 809/491–2892) is a lively late-night place with taped rhythm and blues, soul, and *soca* (Caribbean music). **La Cave** (Evergreen Dr., Plymouth, no ☎), featuring West Indian–style disco and Caribbean and international music, is popular among the young locals. **Nepcoden** (Weekes, no ☎), with its ultraviolet lights, peace signs, and black walls, is a throwback to the '60s. In this cellar restaurant you can eat rotis or chicken for $6. **Colors** (Fox's Bay, no ☎) is one of the island's most popular nightclubs, with live bands and lots of dancing on weekends.

17 Puerto Rico

NO CITY IN THE CARIBBEAN is as steeped in Spanish tradition as Puerto Rico's Old San Juan. Originally built as a fortress enclave, the old city has

Updated by
Marcy
Pritchard

myriad attractions, including restored 16th-century buildings, museums, art galleries, bookstores, and 200-year-old houses with balustraded balconies of filigreed wrought iron overlooking narrow cobblestone streets. This Spanish tradition also spills over into the island's countryside, from its festivals celebrated in honor of various patron saints in the little towns to the *paradores,* those homey, inexpensive inns whose concept originated in Spain.

Puerto Rico boasts hundreds of beaches with every imaginable water sport and acres of golf courses and tennis courts. It has, in San Juan's sophisticated Condado and Isla Verde areas, glittering hotels; flashy, Las Vegas–style shows; casinos; and frenetic discos. It has the ambience of the Old World in the seven-square-block area of the old city and in its quiet colonial towns. Out in the countryside lie its natural attractions, including the extraordinary, 28,000-acre Caribbean National Forest, more familiarly known as the El Yunque rain forest, with 100-foot-high trees (more than 240 species of them) and dramatic mountain ranges. You can hike through forest reserves laced with trails, go spelunking in vast caves, and explore coffee plantations and sugar mills. Having seen every sight on the island, you can then do further exploring on the islands of Culebra, Vieques, Icacos, and Mona, where aquatic activities, such as snorkeling and scuba diving, prevail.

Puerto Rico, 110 miles long and 35 miles wide, was populated by several tribes of Indians when Columbus landed on the island on his second voyage in 1493. In 1508, Juan Ponce de León, the frustrated seeker of the Fountain of Youth, established a settlement on the island and became its first governor, and in 1521, he founded Old San Juan. For three centuries, the French, Dutch, and English tried unsuccessfully to wrest the island from Spain. In 1897, Spain granted the island dominion status. In 1899, as a result of the Spanish American War, Spain ceded the island to the United States, and in 1917, Puerto Ricans became U.S. citizens. In 1952, Puerto Rico became a semiautonomous commonwealth territory of the United States.

If you're a U.S. citizen, you need neither passport nor visa when you land at the bustling Luis Muñoz Marín International Airport, outside San Juan. You don't have to clear customs, and you don't have to explain yourself to an immigration official. English is widely spoken, though the official language is Spanish.

Before You Go

Tourist Information

Contact the **Puerto Rico Tourism Company** (Box 6334, San Juan, PR 00914, ☎ 800/866–7827). Other branches: 575 5th Ave., 23rd Floor, New York, NY 10017, ☎ 800/223–6530 or 212/599–6262, FAX 212/818–1866; 3575 W. Cahuenga Blvd., Suite 560, Los Angeles, CA 90068, ☎ 800/874–1230 or 213/874–5991, FAX 213/874–7257; 901 Ponce de Leon Blvd., Suite 604, Coral Gables, FL 33134, ☎ 305/445–9112 or 800/815–7391, FAX 305/445–9450. In the United Kingdom, contact the tourism office at 11a W. Halkin St., London SW1X 8JL, ☎ 0171/333–0333.

Addresses of representatives in other cities can be obtained by calling the toll-free numbers above.

Arriving and Departing

BY PLANE

The Luis Muñoz Marín International Airport (☎ 809/462–3147), east of downtown San Juan, is the Caribbean hub for **American Airlines** (☎ 800/433–7300). American has daily nonstop flights from New York, Newark, Miami, Boston, Philadelphia, Chicago, Nashville, Los Angeles, Dallas, Baltimore, Hartford, Raleigh-Durham, Washington, D.C., and Tampa. **Delta** (☎ 800/221–1212) has nonstop service from Atlanta and Orlando, as well as connecting service from other major cities. **Northwest** (☎ 800/447–4747) has nonstop flights from Detroit and Minneapolis to San Juan. **TWA** (☎ 800/892–4141) flies nonstop from New York, Miami, and St. Louis. **United** (☎ 800/241–6522) flies nonstop from Miami, and Chicago. **USAir** (☎ 800/428–4322) offers nonstop flights from Philadelphia and Charlotte. Puerto Rico–based **Carnival Airlines** (☎ 800/437–2110) operates daily nonstop flights from New York, Newark, Miami, and Orlando to San Juan, Ponce, and Aguadilla.

Foreign carriers include **Air France** (☎ 800/237–2747), **British Airways** (☎ 800/247–9297), **BWIA** (☎ 800/327–7401), **Iberia** (☎ 800/772–4642), **LACSA** (☎ 800/225–2272), **LIAT** (☎ 800/468–0482), and **Lufthansa** (☎ 800/645–3880).

Connections between Caribbean islands can be made through **Air Jamaica** (☎ 800/523–5585), **Dominicana Airline** (☎ 800/327–7240), and **Sunaire Express** (☎ 800/595–9501).

FROM THE AIRPORT

Airport Limousine Service (☎ 809/791–4745) provides minibus service to hotels in the Isla Verde, Condado, and Old San Juan areas at basic fares of $2.50, $3.50, and $4.50, respectively; the fares vary, depending on the time of day and number of passengers. Limousines of **Dorado Transport Service** (☎ 809/796–1214) serve hotels and villas in the Dorado area for $15 per person. Taxi fare from the airport to Isla Verde is about $8–$10; to the Condado area, $12–$15; and to Old San Juan, $18–$20. Be sure the taxi driver starts the meter, or agree on a fare beforehand; you may also be charged a small fee per piece of luggage.

Passports and Visas

Puerto Rico is a commonwealth of the United States, and U.S. citizens do not need passports to visit the island. British citizens must have passports. Canadian citizens need proof of citizenship (preferably a passport).

Language

Puerto Rico's official language is Spanish, and although English is widely spoken, you will probably want to take a Spanish phrase book along if you rent a car to travel around the island.

Precautions

San Juan, like any other big city and major tourist destination, has its share of crime, so guard your wallet or purse on the city streets. Puerto Rico's beaches are open to the public, and muggings occur at night even on the beaches of the posh Condado and Isla Verde tourist hotels. Don't leave anything unattended on the beach. Leave your valuables in the hotel safe, and stick to the fenced-in beach areas of your hotel. Always lock your car and stash valuables and luggage out of sight. Avoid deserted beaches day or night.

Staying in Puerto Rico

Important Addresses

The government-sponsored **Puerto Rico Tourism Company** (Paseo la Princesa, Old San Juan, Puerto Rico 00902, ☎ 809/721–2400) is an excellent source for maps and printed tourist materials. Pick up a free copy of *qué pasa*, the official visitors' guide.

Information offices are also found at **Luis Muñoz Marín International Airport** in Isla Verde (☎ 809/791–1014 or 809/791–2551); **La Casita,** near Pier 1 in Old San Juan (☎ 809/722–1709); at the Plaza de Armas in **City Hall** (☎ 809/724–7171 ext. 2392); in the **Covadonga Bus Terminal** (☎ 809/725–1260) across from Pier 4; and in **Condado,** next to the Condado Plaza Hotel (☎ 809/721–2400). Out on the island, information offices are located in **Ponce** (Fox Delicias Mall, 2nd Floor, Plaza Las Delicias, ☎ 809/840–5695); **Aguadilla** (Rafael Hernández Airport, ☎ 809/890–3315); and in many towns' city halls on the main plaza. Offices are usually open weekdays from 8 to noon and 1 to 4:30.

EMERGENCIES

Police, fire, and medical emergencies: Call 911. **Hospitals:** Hospitals in the Condado/Santurce area with 24-hour emergency rooms are **Ashford Community Hospital** (1451 Av. Ashford, ☎ 809/721–2160) and **San Juan Health Centre** (200 Av. De Diego, ☎ 809/725–0202). **Pharmacies:** In San Juan, **Walgreens** (1130 Av. Ashford, Condado, ☎ 809/725–1510) operates a 24-hour pharmacy; in Old San Juan, try **Puerto Rico Drug Company** (157 Calle San Francisco, ☎ 809/725–2202). Walgreens operates more than 30 pharmacies on the island.

Currency

The U.S. dollar is the official currency of Puerto Rico.

Taxes and Service Charges

The government tax on room charges is 7% (9% in hotels with casinos). Some hotels automatically add a 10%–15% service charge to your bill. In restaurants, a 15%–20% tip is expected. There is no departure tax.

Guided Tours

Old San Juan can be seen either on a self-guided walking tour or on the free trolley. To explore the rest of the city and the island, consider renting a car. (We do, however, recommend a guided tour of the vast El Yunque rain forest.) If you'd rather not do your own driving, there are several tour companies you can call. Most San Juan hotels have a tour desk that can make arrangements for you. The three standard half-day tours (at $15–$30) are of Old and New San Juan; Old San Juan and the Bacardi Rum Plant; and Luquillo Beach and El Yunque rain forest. All-day tours ($25–$45) can include a trip to Ponce, a day at El Comandante Racetrack, or a combined tour of the city and El Yunque rain forest.

Leading tour operators include **Loose Penny Tours** (☎ 809/261–3030), **Gray Line of Puerto Rico** (☎ 809/727–8080), **Normandie Tours, Inc.** (☎ 809/722–6308), **Rico Suntours** (☎ 809/722–2080 or 809/722–6090), and **United Tour Guides** (☎ 809/725–7605 or 809/723–5578). **Cordero Caribbean Tours** (☎ 809/786–9114 or 809/780–2442 evenings) does tours in air-conditioned limousines for an hourly rate.

Getting Around

If you are staying in San Juan, you can get around by walking, bus, taxi, or hotel shuttle. However, if you venture out on the island, a rental car is your best transportation option.

Roads in Puerto Rico are generally well marked; however, a good road map is helpful when traveling to more remote areas on the island. Some car-rental agencies distribute free maps of the island when you pick up your car. These maps lack detail and are usually out-of-date due to new construction. The simplest thing to do is head to the nearest gas station—most of them sell better maps. Good maps are also available at **The Book Store** (257 Calle San José, Old San Juan, ☎ 809/724–1815).

TAXIS

Metered cabs authorized by the **Public Service Commission** (☎ 809/751–5050) start at $1 and charge 10¢ for every additional tenth of a mile, 50¢ for every suitcase, and $1 for home or business calls. Waiting time is 10¢ for each 45 seconds. Be sure the driver starts the meter. You can also call **Major Taxicabs** in San Juan (☎ 809/723–2460) and **Ponce Taxi** (☎ 809/840–0088).

BUSES

The **Metropolitan Bus Authority (AMA)** (☎ 809/250–6064) operates *guaguas* (buses) that thread through San Juan. The fare is 25¢, and the buses run in exclusive lanes, *against the traffic* on major thoroughfares, stopping at magenta, orange, and white signs marked *Parada* or *Parada de Guaguas*. The main terminals are Covadunga parking lot and Plaza de Colón, in Old San Juan, and Capetillo Terminal in Rio Piedras, next to the central business district.

PÚBLICOS

Públicos (literally, "public cars"), with yellow license plates ending in "P" or "PD," scoot to towns throughout the island, stopping in each town's main plaza. These 17-passenger vans operate primarily during the day, with routes and fares fixed by the Public Service Commission. In San Juan, the main terminals are at the airport and at Plaza Colón on the waterfront in Old San Juan.

TROLLEYS

If your feet fail you in Old San Juan, climb aboard the free open-air trolleys that rumble and roller-coast through the narrow streets. Departures are from La Puntilla and from the marina, but you can board anywhere along the route.

LINÉAS

Linéas are private taxis you share with three to five other passengers. There are more than 20 companies, each usually specializing in a certain region. Most will arrange door-to-door service. Check local yellow pages listings under Linéas de Carros. They're a cheaper method of transport and a great way to meet people, but be prepared to wait: They usually don't leave until they have a full load.

FERRIES

The ferry between Old San Juan (Pier 2) and Cataño costs a mere 50¢ one-way. The ferry runs every half hour from 6 AM to 10 PM. The 400-passenger ferries of the **Fajardo Port Authority** (☎ 809/863–0852), which carry cargo as well as passengers, make the 90-minute trip between Fajardo and the island of Vieques twice on weekdays and three times on weekends (one-way $2 adults, $1 children 3–12). They make the 90-minute run between Fajardo and the island of Culebra once a day Monday–Thursday and twice a day Friday–Sunday (one-way $2.25 adults, $1 children 3–12).

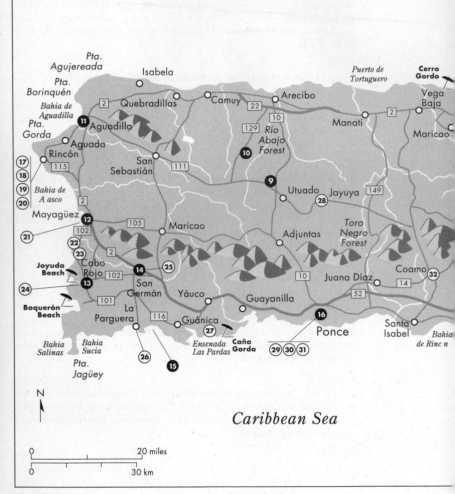

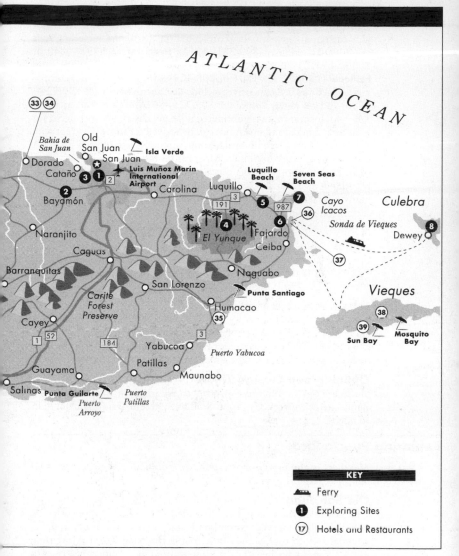

ATLANTIC OCEAN

Bahia de San Juan

33 34

Dorado
Cataño
Old San Juan
San Juan
Isla Verde

3 1 2

Luis Muñoz Marín International Airport

Carolina

Bayamón

2

Luquillo
Luquillo Beach

Seven Seas Beach

5 987 7

Cayo Icacos

36

Culebra

Sonda de Vieques

8

Dewey

Naranjito

6

Fajardo

Ceiba

191 3

4

El Yunque

Caguas

Barranquitas

Naguabo

37

San Lorenzo

Carite Forest Preserve

Punta Santiago

Humacao

35

Vieques

38

39

Sun Bay

Mosquito Bay

Cayey

1 52

184

3

Yabucoa

Patillas

Puerto Yabucoa

Guayama

Maunabo

Salinas Punta Guilarte

Puerto Arroyo

Puerto Patillas

KEY

🚢 Ferry

❶ Exploring Sites

⑰ Hotels and Restaurants

Pastrami Palace, **18**
Restaurant El Ancla, **31**

Lodging
Casa del Francés, **39**
Copamarina Beach Resort, **27**

El Conquistador Resort and Country Club, **36**
Horned Dorset Primavera, **19**
Hyatt Dorado Beach, **34**
Hyatt Regency Cerromar Beach, **33**

Mayagüez Hilton and Casino, **21**
Palmas del Mar, **35**
Parador Baños de Coamo, **32**
Parador Boquemar, **24**
Parador Hacienda Gripiñas, **28**

Parador Oasis, **25**
Parador Villa Parguera, **26**
Ponce Hilton and Casino, **30**
Sea Gate (Vieques), **38**

RENTAL CARS

U.S. driver's licenses are valid in Puerto Rico for three months. All major U.S. car-rental agencies are represented on the island, including **Avis** (☎ 809/721–4499 or 800/331–1212), **Hertz** (☎ 809/791–0840 or 800/654–3131), **Budget** (☎ 809/791–3685 or 800/527–0700), and **National** (☎ 809/791–1805 or 800/328–4567). Local rental companies, sometimes less expensive, include **Caribbean Rental** (☎ 809/724–3980) and **L & M Car Rental** (☎ 809/725–8416). Prices start at about $30 (plus insurance), with unlimited mileage. Discounts are offered for long-term rentals, and insurance can be waived for those who rent with American Express credit cards. Some discounts are offered for AAA or 72-hour advance bookings. Most car rentals have shuttle service to or from the airport and the pickup point. If you plan to drive across the island, arm yourself with a good map and be aware that there are many unmarked roads up in the mountains. Many service stations in the central mountains do not take credit cards. Speed limits are posted in miles, distances in kilometers, and gas prices in liters.

PLANES

From the Isla Grande Airport, you can take a **Vieques Air-Link** (☎ 809/722–3736) flight to Vieques ($30 one-way), or a **Flamenco Airways** (☎ 809/725–7707) flight to Culebra for ($25 one-way).

Telephones and Mail

The area code for Puerto Rico is 809. Puerto Rico uses U.S. postage stamps and has the same mail rates (22¢ for a postcard, 32¢ for a first-class letter). Post offices in major Puerto Rican cities offer Express Mail next-day service to the U.S. mainland and to Puerto Rican destinations.

Opening and Closing Times

Shops are open from 9 to 6 (from 9 to 9 during Christmas holidays). Banks are open weekdays from 8:30 to 2:30 and Saturday from 9:45 to noon.

Exploring Puerto Rico

Numbers in the margin correspond to points of interest on the Old San Juan Exploring map.

Old San Juan

Old San Juan, the original city founded in 1521, contains authentic and carefully preserved examples of 16th- and 17th-century Spanish colonial architecture, some of the best in the New World. More than 400 buildings have been beautifully restored in a continuing effort to preserve the city. Graceful wrought-iron balconies, decorated with lush green hanging plants, extend over narrow streets paved with blue-gray stones (*adequines,* originally used as ballast for Spanish ships). The old city is partially enclosed by the old walls, dating from 1633, that once completely surrounded it. Designated a U.S. National Historic Zone in 1950, Old San Juan is chockablock with shops, open-air cafés, private homes, tree-shaded squares, monuments, plaques, pigeons, and people. The traffic is awful. Get an overview of the inner city on a morning's stroll (bearing in mind that this "stroll" includes some steep climbs). However, if you plan to immerse yourself in history or to shop, you'll need two or three days.

El Morro and Fort San Cristóbal are described in our walking tour: You may want to set aside extra time to see them, especially if you're an aficionado of military history. UNESCO has designated each fortress a World Heritage Site; each is also a National Historic Site. Both are

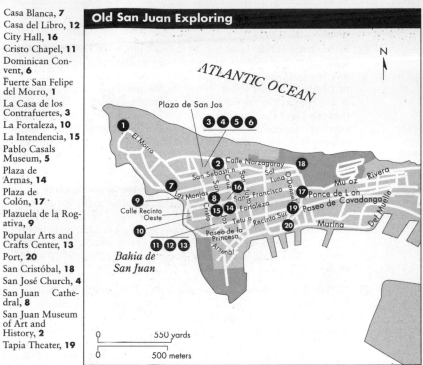

administered by the National Park Service; you can take one of its tours or wander around on your own.

① Sitting on a rocky promontory on the northwestern tip of the old city is **Fuerte San Felipe del Morro** ("El Morro"), a fortress built by the Spaniards between 1540 and 1783. Rising 140 feet above the sea, the massive six-level fortress covers enough territory to accommodate a nine-hole golf course. It is a labyrinth of dungeons, ramps and barracks, turrets, towers, and tunnels. Built to protect the port, El Morro has a commanding view of the harbor. Its small, air-conditioned museum traces the history of the fortress. *Calle Norzagaray, ☎ 809/729–6960.* ☛ *Free.* ☉ *Daily 9:15–6.*

② San José Plaza is two short blocks from the entrance to El Morro, but for the moment we'll bypass it and head for the **San Juan Museum of Art and History,** which is a block east of the tour's path but a must. A bustling marketplace in 1855, this handsome building is now a modern cultural center that houses exhibits of Puerto Rican art. Multi-image audiovisual shows present the history of the island; concerts and other cultural events take place in the huge courtyard. *Calle Norzagaray, at the corner of Calle MacArthur, ☎ 809/724–1875.* ☛ *Free.* ☉ *Tues.–Sat. 9–5.*

③ Turn back west toward San José Plaza to **La Casa de los Contrafuertes,** on Calle San Sebastián. This building is also known as the Buttress House because wide exterior buttresses support the wall next to the plaza. The house is one of the oldest remaining private residences in Old San Juan. Inside is the Pharmacy Museum, a re-creation of an 18th-century apothecary shop, and the Latin American Graphic Arts Museum and Gallery, which hosts occasional exhibitions. *101 Calle San Sebastián,*

Plaza de San José, ☎ *809/724–1844.* ☛ *Free.* ☺ *Tues.–Sat. 9–noon and 1–4:30.*

④ In the center of the plaza, next to the museum, is the **San José Church.** With its series of vaulted ceilings, it is a splendid example of 16th-century Spanish Gothic architecture. The church, which is one of the oldest Christian houses of worship in the Western Hemisphere, was built in 1532 under the supervision of the Dominican friars. The body of Ponce de León, the Spanish explorer who came to the New World seeking the Fountain of Youth, was buried here for almost three centuries before being removed in 1913 and placed in the San Juan Cathedral. *Calle San Sebastián,* ☎ *809/725–7501.* ☛ *Free.* ☺ *Mon.–Sat. 8:30–4; mass Sun. at 12:15 PM.*

⑤ Also on the plaza, take a look through the **Pablo Casals Museum,** which contains memorabilia of the famed cellist, who made his home in Puerto Rico for the last 16 years of his life. The museum holds manuscripts, photographs, and his favorite cellos, in addition to recordings and videotapes of Casals Festival concerts (the latter shown on request). *101 Calle San Sebastián, Plaza de San José,* ☎ *809/723–9185.* ☛ *Free.* ☺ *Tues.–Sat. 9:30–5.*

⑥ Next door is the **Dominican Convent.** Built by Dominican friars in 1523, the convent often served as a shelter during Carib Indian attacks and, more recently, as headquarters for the Antilles command of the U.S. Army. Now home to the Institute of Puerto Rican Culture, the beautifully restored building contains an ornate 18th-century altar, religious manuscripts, artifacts, and art. The Institute also maintains a bookshop here. The convent is the intended future home of the city's museum of fine arts. Classical concerts are occasionally held here. *98 Calle Norzagaray,* ☎ *809/724–1844.* ☛ *Free.* ☺ *Weekdays 10–5, Sat. 9–5.*

⑦ From San José Plaza, walk west on Calle Beneficencia to **Casa Blanca.** The original structure on this site, not far from the ramparts of El Morro, was a frame house built in 1521 as a home for Ponce de León. But Ponce de León died in Cuba, never having lived in it, and it was virtually destroyed by a hurricane in 1523, after which Ponce de León's son-in-law had the present masonry home built. His descendants occupied it for 250 years. From the end of the Spanish-American War in 1898 to 1966, it was the home of the U.S. Army commander in Puerto Rico. A museum devoted to archaeology is on the second floor. The lush surrounding gardens, cooled by spraying fountains, are a tranquil spot for a restorative pause. *1 Calle San Sebastián,* ☎ *809/724–4102.* ☛ *Free.* ☺ *Wed.–Sat. 9–noon and 1–4:30.*

⑧ Head east on Calle Sol and down Calle Cristo to **San Juan Cathedral.** This great Catholic shrine of Puerto Rico had humble beginnings in the early 1520s as a thatch-topped wood structure. Hurricane winds tore off the thatch and destroyed the church. It was reconstructed in 1540, when the graceful circular staircase and vaulted Gothic ceilings were added, but most of the work on the church was done in the 19th century. The remains of Ponce de León are in a marble tomb near the transept. *153 Calle Cristo,* ☎ *809/722–0861.* ☺ *Daily 8–4. Masses: Sat. 7 PM, Sun. 9 AM and 11 AM, weekdays 12:15 PM.*

Across the street from the cathedral you'll see the Gran Hotel El Convento (*see* Lodging, *below*), which was a Carmelite convent more than 300 years ago. Go west alongside the hotel on Caleta de las Monjas
⑨ toward the city wall to the **Plazuela de la Rogativa.** In the little plaza, statues of a bishop and three women commemorate a legend, accord-

ing to which the British, while laying siege to the city in 1797, mistook the flaming torches of a *rogativa* (religious procession) for Spanish reinforcements and beat a hasty retreat. The monument was donated to the city in 1971 on its 450th anniversary.

🔟 One block south on Calle Recinto Oeste you'll come to **La Fortaleza,** which sits on a hill overlooking the harbor. La Fortaleza, the Western Hemisphere's oldest executive mansion in continual use and official residence of the present governor of Puerto Rico, was built as a fortress. The original primitive structure, built in 1540, has seen numerous changes over the past four centuries, resulting in the present collection of marble and mahogany, medieval towers, and stained-glass galleries. Guided tours are conducted every hour on the hour in English, on the half hour in Spanish. ☎ *809/721–7000.* ☞ *Free.* ⊘ *Weekdays 8:30–5.*

⓫ At the southern end of Calle Cristo is **Cristo Chapel.** According to legend, in 1753 a young horseman, carried away during festivities in honor of the patron saint, raced down the street and plunged over the steep precipice. A witness to the tragedy promised to build a chapel if the young man's life could be saved. Historical records maintain the man died, though legend contends that he lived. Inside is a small silver altar, dedicated to the Christ of Miracles. ⊘ *Tues. 10–3 and on most Catholic holidays.*

⓬ Across the street from the chapel, the 18th-century **Casa del Libro** has exhibits devoted to books and bookbinding. The museum's 5,000 books include many rare volumes. *255 Calle Cristo,* ☎ *809/723–0354.* ☞ *Free.* ⊘ *Tues.–Sat. 11–4:30.*

⓭ The new **Popular Arts and Crafts Center,** run by the Institute of Puerto Rican Culture, is in a colonial building next door. The center is a superb repository of island craftwork, some of which is for sale. *253 Calle Cristo,* ☎ *809/722–0621.* ☞ *Free.* ⊘ *Mon.–Sat. 9:30–5.*

⓮ Follow the wall east one block and head north on Calle San José two short blocks to **Plaza de Armas,** the original main square of Old San Juan. The plaza, bordered by calles San Francisco, Fortaleza, San José, and Cruz, has a lovely fountain with 19th-century statues representing the four seasons.

⓯ West of the square stands **La Intendencia,** a handsome three-story neoclassical building. From 1851 to 1898, it was home to the Spanish Treasury; now it is the headquarters of Puerto Rico's State Department. *Calle San José, at the corner of Calle San Francisco,* ☎ *809/722–2121, ext. 230.* ☞ *Free. Tours at 2 and 3 in Spanish, 4 in English.* ⊘ *Weekdays 8–noon and 1–4:30.*

⓰ On the north side of the plaza is **City Hall,** called the *Alcaldía,* built between 1604 and 1789. In 1841, extensive renovations were done to make the Alcaldía resemble Madrid's city hall, with arcades, towers, balconies, and a lovely inner courtyard. A tourist information center and an art gallery are on the first floor. ☎ *809/724–7171, ext. 2391.* ⊘ *Weekdays 8–4; tourist center also open Sat. 8–4.*

TIME OUT **La Bombonera** (259 Calle San Francisco, ☎ 809/722-0658), established in 1903, is known for its strong Puerto Rican coffee and *Mallorca*— a Spanish pastry made of light dough, toasted, buttered, and sprinkled with powdered sugar. Breakfast, for under $5, is served until 11. It's a favorite Sunday-morning gathering place in Old San Juan.

Four blocks east, on the pedestrian mall of Calle Fortaleza, you'll find
⑰ **Plaza de Colón,** a bustling square with a statue of Christopher Columbus atop a high pedestal. Originally called St. James Square, it was renamed in honor of Columbus on the 400th anniversary of the discovery
of Puerto Rico. Bronze plaques in the base of the statue relate various
episodes in the life of the great explorer. On the north side of the plaza
is a terminal for buses to and from San Juan.

Walk two blocks north from Plaza de Colón to Calle Sol and turn right.
⑱ Another block will take you to **San Cristóbal,** the 18th-century fortress
that guarded the city from land attacks. Even larger than El Morro,
San Cristóbal was known as the Gibraltar of the West Indies. ☎ 809/
729–6960. ☛ Free. ⊙ Daily 9–5.

⑲ Just south of Plaza de Colón is the magnificent **Tapia Theater** (Calle
Fortaleza at Plaza de Colón, ☎ 809/722–0407), named after the
Puerto Rican playwright Alejandro Tapia y Rivera. Built in 1832 and
remodeled in 1949 and again in 1987, the municipal theater is the site
of ballets, plays, and operettas. Stop by the box office to find out what's
showing and if tickets are available.

⑳ Stroll from Plaza de Colón down to the **port,** where the **Paseo de la
Princesa** is spruced up with flowers, trees, benches, and street lamps.
Take a seat and watch the boats zip across the water.

San Juan

*Numbers in the margin correspond to points of interest on the San Juan
Exploring, Dining, and Lodging map.*

You'll need to resort to taxis, buses, públicos, or a rental car to reach
the points of interest in "new" San Juan.

Avenida Muñoz Rivera, Avenida Ponce de León, and Avenida Fernández
Juncos are the main thoroughfares that cross Puerta de Tierra, just east
of Old San Juan, to the business and tourist districts of Santurce, Condado, and Isla Verde.

 In Puerta de Tierra is Puerto Rico's **Capitol,** a white marble building
that dates from the 1920s. The grand rotunda, with mosaics and
friezes, was completed a few years ago. The seat of the island's bicameral
legislature, the Capitol contains Puerto Rico's constitution and is
flanked by the modern buildings of the Senate and the House of Representatives. There are spectacular views from the observation plaza
on the sea side of the Capitol. Pick up a booklet about the building
from the House Secretariat on the second floor. Guided tours are by
appointment only. *Av. Ponce de León,* ☎ *809/721–7305 or 809/721–
7310.* ☛ *Free.* ⊙ *Weekdays 8:30–5.*

 At the eastern tip of Puerta de Tierra, behind the splashy Caribe Hilton,
the tiny **Fort San Jeronimo** is perched over the Atlantic like an af-
terthought. Added to San Juan's fortifications in the late 18th century,
the structure barely survived the British attack of 1797. Restored in
1983 by the Institute of Puerto Rican Culture, it is now a military museum. At press time, however, the museum was closed for repairs, and
no reopening date had been announced, so visitors could only view the
fort from the outside. ☎ *809/724–1844.*

Dos Hermanos Bridge connects Puerta de Tierra with Miramar, Condado, and Isla Grande. Isla Grande Airport, from which you can take
short hops, is on the bay side of the bridge.

On the other side of the bridge, the Condado Lagoon is bordered by
Avenida Ashford, which threads past the high-rise Condado hotels and

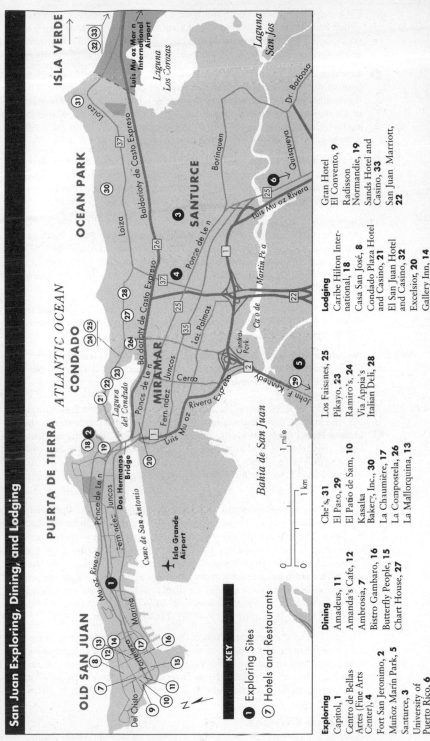

El Centro Convention Center, and Avenida Baldorioty de Castro Expreso, which barrels all the way east to the airport and beyond. Due south of the lagoon is Miramar, a primarily residential area with fashionable turn-of-the-century homes and a cluster of hotels and restaurants.

③ Santurce, which lies between Miramar on the west and the Laguna San José on the east, is a busy mixture of shops, markets, and offices. The classically designed **Sacred Heart University** is the home of the **Museum of Contemporary Puerto Rican Art,** which showcases the works of such modern masters as Rodon, Campeche, and Oller. *Barat Bldg.,* ☎ *809/268–0049.* ☛ *Free.* ⊙ *Weekdays 9–4:30, Sat. 10–4.*

④ Internationally acclaimed performers appear at the **Centro de Bellas Artes** (Fine Arts Center). This completely modern facility, the largest of its kind in the Caribbean, has a full schedule of concerts, plays, and operas. *Corner of Av. De Diego and Av. Ponce de León,* ☎ *809/725–7338.*

Southeast of Miramar, Avenida Muñoz Rivera skirts along the northern side of the mangrove-bordered **San Juan Central Park,** a convenient place for jogging and tennis. The park was built for the 1979 Pan-American Games. *Cerra St. exit on Rte. 2, Santurce,* ☎ *809/722–1646.* ☛ *Free.* ⊙ *Mon. 2–9:45, Tues.–Fri. 6:30 AM–9:45 PM, weekends 6:30 AM–6 PM.*

South of Santurce is the "Golden Mile"—Hato Rey, the city's bustling financial hub. Isla Verde, with its glittering beachfront hotels, casinos, discos, and public beach, is to the east, near the airport.

TIME OUT   **Pescadería Atlántica** (81 Calle Loiza, ☎ 809/726–6654) is a combination seafood restaurant and retail store. Stop in for a cool drink at the bar and a side dish of *calamares,* lightly breaded squid in a hot, spicy sauce.

Las Américas Expressway, heading south, goes by Plaza Las Américas, the largest shopping mall in the Caribbean, and takes you to the **⑤ Muñoz Marín Park,** an idyllic tree-shaded spot dotted with gardens, lakes, playgrounds, and picnic areas. Cable cars connect the park with the parking area. *Next to Las Américas Expressway, west on Av. Piñero, Hato Rey,* ☎ *809/763–0568.* ☛ *Free; parking $1 per vehicle.* ⊙ *Tues.–Sun. 8–5.*

⑥ Río Piedras, a southern suburb of San Juan, is home to the **University of Puerto Rico,** located between Avenida Ponce de León and Avenida Barbosa. The university's campus is one of two sites for performances of the Puerto Rico Symphony Orchestra. Theatrical productions and other concerts are also scheduled here throughout the year. The **University Museum** has permanent archaeological and historical exhibits and occasionally mounts special art displays. *Next to the university's main entrance on Av. Ponce de León,* ☎ *809/764–0000, ext. 2452 or 2456.* ⊙ *Mon.–Wed. and Fri. 9–4:30, Thurs. 9–9, Sat. 9–3:30.*

The university's main attraction is the **Botanical Garden,** a lush forest of more than 200 species of tropical and subtropical vegetation. Footpaths lead to a graceful lotus lagoon, a bamboo promenade, an orchid garden, and a palm garden. *Intersection of Rtes. 1 and 847 at the entrance to Barrio Venezuela,* ☎ *809/763–4408.* ☛ *Free.* ⊙ *Tues.–Sun. 9–5.*

San Juan Environs

Numbers in the margin correspond to points of interest on the Puerto Rico map.

From San Juan, follow Route 2 west toward Bayamón, and you'll spot
1 the **Caparra Ruins,** where, in 1508, Ponce de León established the island's first settlement. The ruins are that of an ancient fort. Its small
Museum of the Conquest and Colonization of Puerto Rico contains historical documents, exhibits, and excavated artifacts. (You can see the
museum's contents in less time than it takes to say the name.) *Rte. 2,
Km 6.6, Guaynabo,* ☎ *809/781–4795.* ☛ *Free.* ☉ *Wed.–Sun. 9–4.*

2 Continue on Route 2 to **Bayamón.** In the central park, across from
Bayamón's city hall, there are some historical buildings and a 1934 sugarcane train that runs through the park (☎ 809/798–8191; open daily
8 AM–5 PM). On the plaza, in the city's historic district, stands the 18th-
century Catholic church of Santa Cruz and the old neoclassical city hall,
which now houses the **Francisco Oller Art and History Museum.** ☎ *809/
787–8620.* ☛ *Free.* ☉ *Tues.–Sat. 9–4.*

3 Along Route 5 from Bayamón to Catano, you'll see the **Barrilito Rum
Plant.** On the grounds are a 200-year-old plantation home and a 150-
year-old windmill, which is listed in the National Register of Historic
Places.

The **Bacardi Rum Plant,** along the bay, conducts 45-minute tours of the
bottling plant, museum, and distillery, which has the capacity to produce 100,000 gallons of rum a day. There is a gift shop. (Yes, you'll be
offered a sample.) *Rte. 888, Km 2.6, Cataño,* ☎ *809/788–1500.* ☛ *Free.
Tours every 20 minutes Mon.–Sat, 9:30–10:30 and noon–4.*

Out on the Island

Puerto Rico's 3,500 square miles is a lot of land to explore. While you
can get from town to town via *público,* we don't recommend traveling that way unless your Spanish is good and you know exactly where
you're going. The public cars stop in each town's main square, leaving you on your own to reach the beaches, restaurants, paradores, and
sightseeing attractions. You'll do much better if you rent a car. Most
of the island's roads are excellent. However, there is a tangled web of
roads through the mountains, and they are not always well marked.
It helps to buy a good road map.

EAST AND SOUTH

Our first excursion out on the island will take us east, down the coast
to the south, and back up to San Juan. The first leg of the trip—to
4 Luquillo Beach and the nearby **Caribbean National Forest,** commonly
known as **El Yunque,** can easily be done in a day. (There will be heavy
traffic and a crowded beach on weekends, when it seems as if the whole
world heads for Luquillo.) The full itinerary will take two to three days,
depending upon how long you loll on the beach and linger over the
mountain scenery.

To take full advantage of the 28,000-acre El Yunque rain forest, go
with a tour. Dozens of trails lead through the thick jungle (it sheltered
the Carib Indians for 200 years), and the tour guides take you to the
best observation points, bathing spots, and waterfalls. Some of the trails
are slippery, and there are occasional washouts.

However, if you'd like to drive there yourself, take Route 3 east from
San Juan and turn right (south) on Route 191, about 25 miles from
the city. The **Sierra Palm Visitor Center** is on Route 191, Km 11.6 (open
daily 9–5, until 4 in winter). Nature talks and programs at the center
are in Spanish and English and by appointment only—another good
reason to go with a tour group.

El Yunque, named after the good Indian spirit Yuquiyu, is in the Luquillo mountain range. The rain forest is verdant with feathery ferns, thick ropelike vines, white tuberoses and ginger, miniature orchids, and some 240 different species of trees. More than 100 billion gallons of rainwater fall on it annually. Rain-battered, wind-ravaged dwarf vegetation clings to the top peaks. (El Toro, the highest peak in the forest, is 3,532 feet.) El Yunque is also a bird sanctuary and the base of the rare Puerto Rican parrot. Millions of tiny, inch-long *coquis* (tree frogs) can be heard singing (or squawking, depending on your sensibilities). *For further information call the Catalina Field Office,* ☎ *809/887–2875 or 809/766–5335; or write Caribbean National Forest, Box B, Palmer, PR 00721.*

⑤ To reach **Luquillo Beach,** take Route 191 back to Route 3 and continue east 5 miles to Km 35.4. One of the island's best and most popular beaches, Luquillo was once a flourishing coconut plantation. Coral reefs protect its calm, pristine lagoon, making it an ideal place for a swim. The entrance fee is $1 per car, and there are lockers, showers, and changing rooms, as well as stands selling savory Puerto Rican delicacies (*see* Beaches, *below*).

If you want to continue exploring, get back on Route 3 and drive 5
⑥ miles to **Fajardo,** a major fishing and sailing center with thousands of boats tied and stacked in tiers at its three large marinas. Boats can be rented or chartered here, and the *Spread Eagle* catamaran (☎ 809/863–1905) can take you out for a full day of snorkeling, swimming, and sunning. Fajardo is also the embarkation point for ferries to the islands of Culebra (a $2.25 fare) and Vieques ($2).

North of Fajardo on Route 987, just past the Seven Seas Recreational
⑦ Area, is the entrance to **Las Cabezas de San Juan Nature Reserve.** Opened in 1991, the reserve contains mangrove swamps, coral reefs, beaches, and a dry forest—all of Puerto Rico's natural habitats rolled into a microcosmic 316 acres. Nineteenth-century El Faro, one of the island's oldest lighthouses, is restored and still functioning; its first floor contains a small nature center that has an aquarium and other exhibits. The reserve is open by reservation only to the general public Friday–Sunday and to tour groups Wednesday, Thursday, and Friday morning. Tours are given on request (in advance, by telephone) four times a day. *Rte. 987, Km 5.8,* ☎ *809/722–5882; weekends, 809/860–2560.* ☛ *$5 adults, $2 children under 12, $2.50 senior citizens.*

⑧ **Culebra** has lovely white-sand beaches, coral reefs, and a wildlife refuge. In the sleepy town of Dewey, on Culebra's southwestern side, check at the visitor information center at city hall (☎ 809/742–3291) about boat rentals. On **Vieques,** Sun Bay public beach has picnic facilities; Blue Beach is superb for snorkeling; and Mosquito Bay is luminous even on moonless nights, thanks to the millions of bioluminescent organisms that glow when disturbed—it's like swimming in a cloud of fireflies. Seventy percent of Vieques is owned by the U.S. Navy, ensuring it will remain unspoiled. The deserted beaches—Green, Red, Blue, Navia, and Media Luna—are among the Caribbean's loveliest; you might see a wild *paso fino* horse galloping in the surf. The visitor information center (☎ 809/741–5000) is in the fishing village of Esperanza. Both islands are havens for colorful "expatriates" escaping the rat race Stateside. This is pure old-time Caribbean: fun and funky, the kind of getaway that is fast disappearing.

Back on the main island, resume your ramble on Route 3, heading south past the U.S. Naval Base, and ride through the sugarcane fields to Humacao. South of Humacao (take Route 906) is the 2,700-acre Palmas del Mar, the island's largest residential resort complex.

Stay on Route 3 through Yabucoa, tucked up in the hills, and on through Maunabo and Patillas, where you can pick up routes that will take you through the Cayey Mountains. Route 184 north skirts Lake Patillas and cuts smack through the Carite Forest Reserve. Stay on Route 184 until it meets Route 1, where you'll shoot northward back to San Juan.

WESTERN ISLAND

If you're short of time, drive the 64 miles from San Juan to Ponce in 90 minutes. Take the Las Américas Expressway, Route 52, which cuts through the splendid mountains of Cordillera Central.

If time is not a problem, take a three- or four-day tour exploring the western regions of the island. This route covers Aguadilla, Rincón, Mayagüez, San Germán, and Ponce. There's much to see along the way— caves and coves, karst fields and coffee plantations, mountains, beaches, and even a zoo.

Start out going west on Route 2. Arecibo is home to one of the world's largest telescopes. You can take a self-guided tour of the **Arecibo Observatory,** where groundbreaking work in astronomy, including SETI (the search for extraterrestrial intelligence) continues. A new visitor center is under construction for an early 1996 opening. *Rte. 625,* ☎ *809/ 878–2612.* ☛ *Free.* ☺ *Tues.–Fri. 2–3, Sun. 1–4:30.*

9 In Arecibo pick up Route 10 and go south. Make a right on Route 111, and you'll find the **Caguana Indian Ceremonial Park,** used 800 years ago by the Taíno tribes for recreation and worship. Mountains surround a 13-acre site planted with royal palms and guava. According to Spanish historians, the Taínos played a game similar to soccer, and in this park there are 10 courts bordered by cobbled walkways. There are also stone monoliths, some with colorful petroglyphs; a small museum; and a souvenir shop. *Rte. 111, Km 12.3,* ☎ *809/894–7325.* ☛ *Free.* ☺ *Daily 9:00–4:30.*

10 Drive west on Route 111 and then north on Route 129 through the spectacular karst country, an alien landscape of collapsed limestone sinkholes, to Km 18.9, where you'll find the **Río Camuy Cave Park,** a 268-acre reserve that contains one of the world's largest cave networks. Guided tours take you on a tram down through dense tropical vegetation to the entrance of the cave, where you continue on foot over underground trails, ramps, and bridges. The caves, sinkholes, and subterranean streams are all spectacular (the world's second-largest underground river runs through here), but this trip is not for those with claustrophobia. Be sure to call ahead; the tours allow only a limited number of people. *Rte. 129, Km 18.9,* ☎ *809/898–3100 or 809/756– 5555.* ☛ *$10 adults, $7 children under 12. Parking $1.* ☺ *Tues.–Sun. 8–4. Last tour starts at 3:40.*

11 Backtrack to Route 111, which twists westward to **Aguadilla** on the northwest coast. In this area, somewhere between Aguadilla and Añasco, south of Rincón, Columbus dropped anchor on his second voyage in 1493. Both Aguadilla and **Aguada,** a few miles to the south, claim to be the spot where his foot first hit ground, and both towns have plaques to commemorate the occasion.

Route 115 from Aguadilla to **Rincón** is one of the island's most scenic drives, through rolling hills dotted with pastel-colored houses. Rincón, perched on a hill, overlooks its beach, which was the site of the World Surfing Championship in 1968. Skilled surfers flock to Rincón during the winter, when the water is rough and challenging. The town is also increasingly popular with divers. Locals boast that the best diving and snorkeling in Puerto Rico (and some even say the Caribbean) is off the Rincón coast, particularly around the offshore island of Desecheo, a federal wildlife preserve. Whale-watching is another draw for this town; humpback whales winter off the coast from December through February.

⑫ Continue on 115 to Route 2 for the 6-mile drive to **Mayagüez,** Puerto Rico's third-largest city, with a population approaching 100,000. Although bypassed by the mania for restoration that saw Ponce and Old San Juan spruced up for the Columbus quincentennial, Mayagüez is graced by some lovely turn-of-the-century architecture, such as the landmark Art Deco Teatro Yagüez and the Plaza de Colón.

North of town visit the **Mayagüez Zoo,** a 45-acre tropical compound that's home to about 500 animals. In addition to Bengal tigers, reptiles, and birds, there's a lake and a children's playground. *Rte. 108 at Barrio Miradero,* ☎ *809/834–8110.* ☛ *$1 adults, 50¢ children. Parking $1.* ☉ *Tues.–Sun. 9–4:30.*

⑬ Due south of Mayagüez, via the coastal route 102, is **Cabo Rojo,** once a pirates' hangout and now a favorite resort area of Puerto Ricans. The area has long stretches of white-sand beaches on the clear, calm Caribbean Sea, as well as many seafood restaurants, bars, and hotels. There are also several paradores in the region. If you want a side trip, take Route 100 south and then Route 101 to its westernmost point— tiny **Boquerón,** a funky, pastel village with sidewalk oyster vendors, bars, restaurants serving fresh seafood, and several of the standard T-shirt shops. There are also diving and snorkeling tours at the Boquerón Dive Shop on Main Street. Boquerón's *balneario* (public beach) is one of the best beaches on the island. Parking is $1 per car, and two-room cabins are for rent.

⑭ From Cabo Rojo continue east on Route 102 to delightfully quaint **San Germán,** a quiet and colorful Old World town that's home to the oldest intact church under the U.S. flag. Built in 1606, Porta Coeli (Gates of Heaven) overlooks one of the town's two plazas (where the townspeople continue the Spanish tradition of promenading at night). The church is now a museum of religious art, housing 18th- and 19th-century paintings and wooden statues. ☎ *809/892–5845.* ☛ *Free.* ☉ *Tues.–Sun. 9–noon and 1–4.*

The fishing village of **La Parguera,** an area of simple seafood restaurants, mangrove cays, and small islands, lies south of San Germán at the end of Route 304. This is an excellent scuba-diving area, but the

⑮ main attraction is **Phosphorescent Bay.** Boats tour the bay, where microscopic dinoflagellates (marine plankton) light up like Christmas trees when disturbed by any kind of movement. The phenomenon can be seen only on moonless nights. Boats leave for the hour-long trip nightly between 7:30 and 12:30, depending on demand, and the trip costs $8 per person. You can also rent or charter a small boat to explore the numerous cays.

From San Germán, Route 2 traverses splendid peaks and valleys; pastel houses cling to the sides of steep green hills. The Cordillera Central mountains run parallel to Route 2 here and provide a stunning backdrop to the drive. East of Yauco, the road dips and sweeps right

⑯ along the Caribbean and into **Ponce.**

Puerto Rico's second-largest city (population 300,000) is undergoing a massive restoration in anticipation of the 300th anniversary, in 1996, of the city's first settlement. Leave the traffic and strip malls on Route 2, and wander around Ponce's historic downtown.

The town's 19th-century style has been recaptured with pink marble-bordered sidewalks, gas lamps, painted trolleys, and horse-drawn carriages. You have not seen a firehouse until you've seen the red-and-black–striped **Parque de Bombas,** a structure built in 1882 for an exposition and converted to a firehouse the following year. The city hired architect Pablo Ojeda O'Neill to restore it, and it is now a museum of Ponce's history, which, not surprisingly, has a display of Fire Brigade memorabilia. *Plaza Las Delicias, ☎ 809/284–4141, ext. 342. ☛ Free. ☉ Wed.–Mon. 9:30–6.*

Ponce's charm stems from a combination of neoclassical, Ponce Creole, and art-deco styles. The tiny streets lined with wrought-iron balconies are reminiscent of New Orleans's French Quarter. Stop in and pick up information about this seaside city at the columned **Casa Armstrong-Poventud,** the home of the Institute of Puerto Rican Culture and a Tourism Information Office (open weekdays 8–noon and 1–4:30; use the side entrance). Stroll around the **Plaza Las Delicias,** with its perfectly pruned India-laurel fig trees, graceful fountains, gardens, and park benches. View **Our Lady of Guadelupe Cathedral** (masses are held daily), and walk down Calles Isabel and Christina to see turn-of-the-century wooden houses with wrought-iron balconies.

Two superlative examples of early-20th-century architecture house the **Ponce History Museum** (Museo de la Historia de Ponce), where 10 rooms of exhibits vividly re-create Ponce's golden years, providing especially fascinating glimpses into the worlds of culture, high finance, and journalism during the 19th century. *53 Calle Isabel, ☎ 809/844–7071. ☛ $3 adults, $2 senior citizens, $1.50 children under 12. ☉ Mon. and Wed.–Fri. 10–5, Sat. and Sun. 10–6.*

Continue as far as Calles Mayor and Christina to the white stucco **La Perla Theater,** with its Corinthian columns. Be sure to allow time to visit the **Ponce Museum of Art** (Museo de Arte de Ponce). The architecture alone is worth seeing: The modern, two-story building designed by Edward Durell Stone (who designed New York's Museum of Modern Art) has seven interconnected hexagons, glass cupolas, and a pair of curved staircases. The collection includes late Renaissance and Baroque works from Italy, France, and Spain, as well as contemporary art by Puerto Ricans. *Av. Las Américas, ☎ 809/848–0505. ☛ $3 adults, $2 children under 12. ☉ Daily 10–5.*

Another fine museum is **Castillo Serrallés,** a splendid Spanish Revival mansion perched on El Vigía Hill, with smashing views of Ponce and the Caribbean. This former residence of the Serrallés family, owners of the Don Q rum distillery, has been restored with a mix of original furnishings and antiques that recall the era of the sugar barons, including a baronial dining room with heavy carved mahogany and wrought-iron doors. A short film details the history of the sugar and rum industries. The unusual, rather ugly 100-foot-tall cross (La Cruceta del Vigía) looming behind the museum is being restored; when finished (a completion date had not been set at press time), visitors will be able to climb to its observation tower. *El Vigía Hill, ☎ 809/259–1774. ☛ $3 adults, $2 senior citizens, $1.50 children under 12. ☉ Tues.–Thurs. 9:30–4:30, Fri.–Sun. 10–5.*

There are two intriguing historical sights just outside the city. **Hacienda Buena Vista** is a 19th-century coffee plantation, restored by the Conservation Trust of Puerto Rico, with much of the authentic machinery and furnishings intact. Reservations are required for the 90-minute tours; tours in English are given on request (in advance) once a day. *Rte. 10, Km. 16.8, north of Ponce,* ☎ *809/722–5882 weekdays; 809/848–7020 weekends.* ☛ *$5 adults, $2.50 senior citizens, $2 children under 12.* ⊙ *Wed.–Fri. to tour groups; Fri.–Sun. to public.*

The **Tibes Indian Ceremonial Center** is the oldest cemetery in the Caribbean. It is a treasure trove of pre-Taíno ruins and burials, dating from AD 300 to AD 700. Some archaeologists, noting the symmetrical arrangement of stone pillars, surmise the cemetery may have been of great religious significance. The complex includes a detailed re-creation of a Taíno village and a museum. *Rte. 503, Km 2.7,* ☎ *809/840–2255.* ☛ *$2 adults, $1 children.* ⊙ *Tues.–Sun. 9–4.*

What to See and Do with Children

El Morro and **San Cristóbal** forts.
El Yunque rain forest.
The **Ponce Hilton, Hyatt Regency Cerromar Beach,** and **Hyatt Dorado Beach** offer activities for children on weekends, during the summer, and during the Christmas and Easter holidays. The **El Conquistador Resort and Country Club** offers Camp Coquí for kids from 9 to 3 daily.
Las Cabezas de San Juan Nature Reserve, near Fajardo.
Mayagüez Zoo, Mayagüez.
Muñoz Marín Park, San Juan.
Río Camuy Caves, near Utuado.
Trolleys, Old San Juan.

Off the Beaten Track

Mona Island, 50 miles west of Mayagüez in the turbulent shark-infested Mona Passage, is nicknamed the Galápagos of the Caribbean, thanks to the plethora of endangered and unique indigenous species that call it home. The variety of marine and bird life is especially breathtaking. The coastline is rimmed with imposing limestone cliffs up to 200 feet high pocked with caves that are said to contain buried treasure; the many perfectly preserved Taíno hieroglyphs and rock paintings there are of great archaeological value.

Access to the island is only via private plane or boat. Very limited camping facilities are available on the pristine beaches. Call the Department of Natural Resources for information and camping reservations (☎ 809/723–1616).

Beaches

By law, all of Puerto Rico's beaches are open to the public (except for the Caribe Hilton's man-made beach in San Juan). The government runs 13 *balnearios* (public beaches), which have dressing rooms, lifeguards, parking, and in some cases picnic tables, playgrounds, and camping facilities. Admission is free, parking $1. Most balnearios are open 9–5 daily in summer and Tuesday through Sunday the rest of the year. Listed below are some major balnearios. You can also contact the Department of Recreation and Sports (☎ 809/722–1551, ext. 341).

Boquerón Beach is a broad beach of hard-packed sand fringed with coconut palms. It has picnic tables, cabin rentals, bike rentals, basketball court, minimarket, scuba diving, and snorkeling. *On the southwest coast, south of Mayagüez, Rte. 101, Boquerón.*

A white sandy beach bordered by resort hotels, **Isla Verde** offers picnic tables and good snorkeling, with equipment rentals nearby. It's a lively beach popular with city folk. *Near metropolitan San Juan, Rte. 187, Km 3.9, Isla Verde.*

Crescent-shape **Luquillo Beach** comes complete with coconut palms, picnic tables, and tent sites. Coral reefs protect its crystal-clear lagoon from the Atlantic waters, making it ideal for swimming. It's one of the largest and most well-known beaches on the island, and it gets crowded on weekends. *30 mi east of San Juan, Rte. 3, Km 35.4.*

An elongated beach of hard-packed sand, **Seven Seas** is always popular with bathers. It has picnic tables and tent and trailer sites; snorkeling, scuba diving, and boat rentals are nearby. *Rte. 987, Fajardo.*

Sun Bay, a white-sand beach on the island of Vieques, has picnic tables and tent sites and offers snorkeling and scuba diving. Boat rentals are nearby. *Rte. 997, Vieques.*

Surfing

The best surfing beaches are along the Atlantic coastline from Borinquén Point south to Rincón, where there are several surf shops. Surfing is best from November through April. Aviones and La Concha beaches in San Juan and Casa de Pesca in Arecibo are summer surfing spots and have nearby surf shops.

Sports and the Outdoors

Bicycling

The broad beach at Boquerón makes for easy wheeling. You can rent bikes at **Boquerón Balnearios** (Rte. 101, Boquerón, Dept. of Recreation and Sports, ☏ 809/722–1551, ext. 341). In the Dorado area on the north coast, bikes can be rented at the **Hyatt Regency Cerromar Beach** (☏ 809/796–1234) or the **Hyatt Dorado Beach** (☏ 809/796–1234). Bikes are for rent at many of the hotels out on the island, including the **Ponce Hilton** (☏ 809/259–7676) and the **Copamarina Beach Resort** (☏ 809/821–0505).

Boating

Virtually all the resort hotels on San Juan's Condado and Isla Verde strips rent paddleboats, Sunfish, Windsurfers, kayaks, and the like. Contact **Condado Plaza Hotel Watersports Center** (☏ 809/721–1000, ext. 1361), the **El San Juan Hotel Watersports Center** (☏ 809/791–1000), or the **Caribe Hilton** (☏ 809/721–0303). Out on the island, your hotel will be able either to provide rentals or recommend rental outfitters.

Fishing

Half-day, full-day, split charters, and big- and small-game fishing can be arranged through **Benitez Deep-Sea Fishing** (Club Náutico de San Juan, Miramar, ☏ 809/723–2292), **Castillo Watersports** (ESJ Towers, Isla Verde, ☏ 809/791–6195 or 809/726–5752), and **Caribe Aquatic Adventures** (Radisson Normandie, ☏ 809/729–2929, ext. 240)

Golf

There are four Robert Trent Jones–designed 18-hole courses shared by the **Hyatt Dorado Beach** and the **Hyatt Regency Cerromar Beach** hotels (Dorado, ☏ 809/796–1234, ext. 3238 or 3016). You'll also find 18-hole courses at the **Palmas del Mar resort** (Humacao, ☏ 809/852–6000), **Club Riomar** (Río Grande, ☏ 809/887–3964), and **Punta Borinquén**

(Aguadilla, ☎ 809/890–2987). The **Bahia Beach Plantation** (Río Grande, ☎ 809/256–5600) is Puerto Rico's newest course. There are two 9-hole courses out on the island, one at the **Club Deportivo del Oeste** (Cabo Rojo, ☎ 809/851–8880), and one at the **Aguirre Golf Club** (Aguirre, ☎ 809/853–4052). The **Ponce Hilton** (Ponce, ☎ 809/259–7676) has a new driving range. Be sure to call ahead when you plan to play; public hours at these courses vary, and you should schedule a tee time.

Hiking

Dozens of trails lace **El Yunque** (information is available at the Sierra Palm Visitor Center, Rte. 191, Km 11.6). You can also hit the trails in **Río Abajo Forest** (south of Arecibo) and **Toro Negro Forest** (east of Adjuntas). Each reserve has a ranger station.

Horseback Riding

Beach-trail rides can be arranged at **Palmas del Mar Equestrian Center** (Palmas del Mar, Humacao, ☎ 809/852–6000). **Hacienda Carabalí** (Rte. 992, Km 4, Luquillo, ☎ 809/889–5820) offers beach riding and rain-forest trail rides.

Sailing

Sailing instruction is offered by **Palmas Sailing Center** (Palmas del Mar, Humacao, ☎ 809/852–6000, ext. 10310) and most of the large resort hotels. Trips are offered by **Caribe Aquatic Adventures** (Radisson Normandie, ☎ 809/729–2929, ext. 240) and **Castillo Watersports** (ESJ Towers, Isla Verde, ☎ 809/791–6195 or 809/726–5752). Rentals are available at many hotels around the island.

Snorkeling and Scuba Diving

There is excellent diving off Puerto Rico's coast. Some outfits offer package deals combining accommodations with daily diving trips; check when making your arrangements. Snorkeling and scuba-diving instruction and equipment rentals are available at **Caribbean School of Aquatics** (☎ 809/728–6606), **Caribe Aquatic Adventures** (*see* Sailing, *above*), **Coral Head Divers** (Palmas del Mar, Humacao, ☎ 809/852–6000 or 800/468–3331), **Parguera Divers Training Center** (La Parguera, ☎ 809/899–4171), **Captain Bill's Dive & Surf Shop** (R. 413, Rincón, ☎ 809/823–0390 or evenings 809/823–2672; hotel-dive packages available), **Dive Copamarina** (Copamarina Beach Resort, R. 333, Guánica, ☎ 809/821-6009; hotel-dive packages available), and **Boquerón Dive Shop** (Main St., Boquerón, ☎ 809/851–2155).

Escorted half-day dives range from $35 to $70 and generally include two tanks of air. Packages, which include lunch and other extras, start at $60. Night dives are often available at close to double the price. Snorkeling excursions, which include equipment rental and sometimes lunch, start at $25. Snorkel equipment rents at beaches for about $5.

Caution: Coral-reef waters and mangrove areas can be dangerous to novices. Unless you're an expert or have an experienced guide, avoid unsupervised areas and stick to the water-sports centers of major hotels.

Tennis

If you'd like to use the courts at a property where you are not a guest, call in advance for information about reservations and fees.

There are 17 lighted courts at **San Juan Central Park** (Calle Cerra exit on Rte. 2, ☎ 809/722–1646); 6 lighted courts at the **Caribe Hilton Hotel** (Puerta de Tierra, ☎ 809/721–0303, ext. 1730); 8 courts, 4 lighted, at **Carib Inn** (Isla Verde, ☎ 809/791–3535, ext. 6); and 2 lighted courts at the **Condado Plaza Hotel** (Condado, ☎ 809/721–1000, ext. 1775).

Out on the island, there are 14 courts, 2 lighted, at **Hyatt Regency Cerromar Beach** (Dorado, ☎ 809/796–1234, ext. 3040); 7 courts, 2 lighted, at the **Hyatt Dorado Beach** (Dorado, ☎ 809/796–1234, ext. 3220); 20 courts, 4 lighted, at **Palmas del Mar** (Humacao, ☎ 809/852–6000, ext. 51); 3 lighted courts (and a practice wall) at the **Mayagüez Hilton** (Mayagüez, ☎ 809/831–7575, ext. 2150); 4 lighted courts at the **Ponce Hilton** (Ponce, ☎ 809/259–7676); and 4 lighted courts at **Punta Borinquén** (Aguadilla, ☎ 809/891–8778).

Windsurfing

Many resort hotels rent Windsurfers to their guests, including the **El San Juan,** the **El Conquistador, Palmas del Mar,** the **Hyatts,** and the **Condado Plaza.** If your hotel doesn't provide them, they can probably help you make arrangements with a local outfitter.

Spectator Sports

HORSE RACING

Thoroughbred races are run year-round at **El Comandante Racetrack.** On race days the dining rooms open at 12:30 PM. *Rte. 3, Km 15.3, Canóvanas,* ☎ *809/724–6060.* ☉ *Wed., Fri., Sun., and holidays.*

BASEBALL

The island's season runs October–February. Many major-league ballplayers in the United States got their start in Puerto Rico's baseball league, and some return in the off-season to hone their skills. Stadiums are in San Juan, Santurce, Ponce, Caguas, Arecibo, and Mayagüez; the teams also play once or twice in Aguadilla. Contact the tourist office for details or call **Professional Baseball of Puerto Rico** (☎ 809/765–6285).

Shopping

San Juan is not a free port, and you won't find bargains on electronics and perfumes. You can, however, find excellent prices on china, crystal, fashions, and jewelry.

Shopping for local Caribbean crafts can be great fun. You'll run across a lot of tacky things you can live without, but you can also find some treasures, and in many cases you'll be able to watch the artisans at work. (For guidance, contact the Puerto Rico Tourism Company's Artisan Center, ☎ 809/721–2400, ext. 2201, or the Fomento Crafts Project, ☎ 809/758–4747, ext. 2291).

Popular souvenirs and gifts include *santos* (small, hand-carved figures of saints or religious scenes), hand-rolled cigars, handmade *mundillo* lace from Aguadilla, Carnival masks (papier-mâché from Ponce and fierce *veijigantes* made from coconut husks in Loíza, an African-American enclave near San Juan), and fancy men's shirts called *guayaberas.* Also, some folks swear that Puerto Rican rum is the best in the world.

Shopping Districts

Old San Juan is full of shops, especially on Cristo, Fortaleza, and San Francisco streets. The **Las Américas Plaza** south of San Juan is the largest shopping mall in the Caribbean, with 200 shops, restaurants, and movie theaters. Other malls out on the island include **Plaza del Caribe** in Ponce, **Plaza del Carmen** in Caguas, and the **Mayagüez Mall.** A new mall is currently under construction in Aguadilla, right on Route 2.

Good Buys

CLOTHING

You can get discounts on Hathaway shirts and Christian Dior clothing at **Hathaway Factory Outlet** (203 Calle Cristo, ☎ 809/723–8946). Discounts on Ralph Lauren apparel are found at the **Polo/Ralph Lau-**

ren **Factory Store** (201 Calle Cristo, ☏ 809/722–2136). The **London Fog Factory Outlet** (156 Calle Cristo, ☏ 809/722–4334) offers reductions on men's, women's, and children's raincoats. People are lining up to enter the new **Marshalls** (Plaza de Armas, ☏ 809/722–0874) in Old San Juan. Try the **Bikini Factory** (3 Palmar Norte, Isla Verde, ☏ 809/726–0016) for stylish men's and women's swimwear.

<u>JEWELRY</u>

There is gold, gold, and more gold at **Reinhold** (201 Calle Cristo, ☏ 809/725–6878). For brand-name watches visit the **Watch and Gem Palace** (204 Calle San José, Old San Juan, ☏ 809/722–2136).

<small>LOCAL CRAFTS</small>

For one-of-a-kind buys, head for **Puerto Rican Arts & Crafts** (204 Calle Fortaleza, Old San Juan, ☏ 809/725–5596). You should also pay a visit to the **artisan markets** in Sixto Escobar Park (Puerta de Tierra, ☏ 809/722–0369) and Luis Muñoz Marín Park (next to Las Américas Expressway west on Piñero Ave., Hato Rey, ☏ 809/763–0568). The **Haitian Gallery** (367 Calle Fortaleza, ☏ 809/725–0986) carries Puerto Rican crafts and a selection of folksy, often inexpensive paintings from around the Caribbean. In Ponce, consult the **Casa Paoli Center of Folkloric Investigations** (14 Calle Mayor, ☏ 809/840–4115).

<small>PAINTINGS AND SCULPTURES</small>

Galería Gotay (212 Calle San Francisco, Old San Juan, ☏ 809/722–5726) carries contemporary art in many medias. **Galería Botello** (208 Calle Cristo, Old San Juan, ☏ 809/723–9987; Plaza Las Américas, ☏ 809/754–7430) exhibits and sells antique *santos* (religious sculptures).

Another gallery worth visiting is the **Galería San Juan** (Gallery Inn, 204–206 Calle Norzagaray, Old San Juan, ☏ 809/722–1808; *see* Lodging, *below*). **Corinne Timsit International Galleries** (104 Calle San Jose, Old San Juan, ☏ 809/724–0994) features work by contemporary Latin American painters.

Dining

The quality of restaurants on the island is uniformly excellent. In San Juan, you'll find everything from Italian to Thai, as well as superb local eateries serving *comidas criollas* (traditional Caribbean-Creole meals). Hotel food in Puerto Rico sets a standard for the Caribbean. Consult the lodging listings for additional recommendations. Wherever you go, dress is casual to casually elegant; few establishments require a jacket. It is *always* a good idea to make reservations in the busy season, from mid-November through April.

Puerto Rican cooking emphasizes local vegetables: Plantains are cooked a hundred different ways—*tostones* (fried green), *amarillos* (baked ripe), and chips. Rice and beans with tostones or amarillos are basic accompaniments to every dish. Locals cook white rice with *achiote* (annatto seeds) or saffron, brown rice with *gandules* (pigeon peas), and black rice with *frijoles negros* (black beans). Garbanzos and white beans are served in many daily specials. A wide assortment of yams is served baked, fried, stuffed, boiled, mashed, and whole. *Sofrito*—a garlic, onion, sweet pepper, coriander, oregano, and tomato puree—is used as a base for practically everything.

Beef, chicken, pork, and seafood are all rubbed with *adobo*, a garlic-oregano marinade, before cooking. *Arroz con pollo* (chicken with rice), *sancocho* (beef and tuber soup), *asopao* (a soupy rice with chicken or seafood), and *encebollado* (steak smothered in onions) are all typical plates.

Fritters, also popular, are served in snack places along the highways as well as at cocktail parties. You may find *empanadillas* (stuffed fried turnovers), *surrullitos* (cheese-stuffed corn sticks), *alcapurias* (stuffed green banana croquettes), and *bacalaitos* (codfish fritters).

Local *pan de agua* is an excellent French loaf bread, best hot out of the oven. It is also good toasted and should be tried in the *Cubano* sandwich (roast pork, ham, Swiss cheese, pickles, and mustard).

Local desserts include flans, puddings, and fruit pastes served with native white cheese. Homegrown mangoes and papayas are sweet, and *pan de azucar* (sugar bread) pineapples make the best juice on the market. Fresh *parcha* (passion fruit), *guarapo* (sugarcane), and *guanabana* (a fruit similar to papaya) juice are also sold cold from trucks along the highway. Puerto Rican coffee is excellent served espresso-black or generously cut *con leche* (with hot milk).

To sample local cuisine, consult the listing of *mesones gastrónomicos* in the *¿Qué Pasa?* guide. These are restaurants cited by the government for preserving island culinary traditions and maintaining high standards.

The best frozen piña coladas are served at the Caribe Hilton and the Hyatt Dorado Beach, although local legend has it that the birthplace of the piña colada is the Gran Hotel El Convento. Rum can be mixed with cola (known as a *cuba libre*), soda, tonic, juices, water, served on the rocks, or even up. Puerto Rican rums range from light white mixers to dark, aged sipping liqueurs. Look for Bacardi, Don Q, Ron Rico, Palo Viejo, and Barillito.

What to Wear

The dress code for restaurants in Puerto Rico varies greatly. The price category of a restaurant is usually a good indicator of its formality. For less expensive places, anything but beachwear is generally fine. Ritzier hotel dining rooms and expensive eateries will expect collared shirts and sundresses, although jacket and tie requirements are rare. However, Puerto Ricans enjoy dressing up for dinner, so chances are you'll never feel overdressed.

CATEGORY	COST*
$$$$	over $45
$$$	$30–$45
$$	$15–$30
$	under $15

per person, excluding drinks and service

Old San Juan

$$$–$$ La Chaumière. Reminiscent of an inn in the French provinces, this intimate restaurant with black-and-white floors, heavy wood beams, and floral curtains serves respected onion soup, oysters Rockefeller, rack of lamb, scallops Provençale, and veal Oscar (layered with lobster and asparagus in béarnaise sauce) in addition to daily specials. ✕ *367 Calle Tetuan, ☎ 809/722–3330. Reservations advised. AE, DC, MC, V. Closed Sun. No lunch.*

$$ Amanda's Cafe. This airy café, across from San Cristobal on the north side of the city, offers seating inside or out with a view of the Atlantic and the old city wall. The cuisine is Mexican, French, and Caribbean, and the nachos, refreshing fruit frappés, and margaritas are the best in town. ✕ *424 Calle Norzagaray. AE, MC, V.*

$$ Bistro Gambaro. A virtual shrine to the creative impulse, this serene, unpretentious spot has whimsically carved and painted chairs and tables draped with colorful textiles. The food is equally imaginative, running from an impeccable pasta pesto to chicken in mango-cognac sauce. The three-course fixed-price menus range in price from $17 to $28 and are an excellent buy. ✕ *320 Fortaleza,* ☎ *809/724–4592. AE, MC, V.* ☉ *Dinner Tues.–Sat. and Sun. brunch.*

$$ **La Mallorquina.** The oldest restaurant in Puerto Rico (it is said to date to 1848) is recommended more for its atmosphere than for its food. Pale pink walls and whirring ceiling fans are pleasant, and the nattily attired waitstaff is friendly. The food is good but basic Puerto Rican and Spanish fare, such as asopao and paella. ✕ *207 Calle San Justo,* ☎ *809/722–3261. Reservations advised. AE, MC, V.*

$–$$ **Amadeus.** In an atmosphere of gentrified Old San Juan, this charm-
★   ing restaurant offers a nouvelle Caribbean menu. The front dining room is attractive—whitewashed walls, dark wood, white napery, and ceiling fans—but go through the outside passage to the back dining room where printed cloths, candles, and exposed brick make for even more romantic dining. The roster of appetizers includes buffalo wings and plantain mousse with shrimp. Chicken breast stuffed with sun-dried tomatoes, cheese ravioli with a goat-cheese-and-walnut sauce, and Cajun-grilled mahimahi are a few of the delectable entrées. ✕ *106 Calle San Sebastián,* ☎ *809/722–8635. Reservations advised. AE, MC, V. Closed Mon.*

$–$$ **Butterfly People.** The tables in this restored mansion look onto a lush tropical indoor courtyard. The food is simple and well prepared, including basics, such as burgers and sandwiches, as well as sautéed plantains stuffed with spiced beef and grilled kingfish dressed with olive oil and green peppercorns. The real reason for visiting is the gallery, which holds the largest collection of iridescent rainbow-hued butterflies in the world. Save room for the double chocolate mousse dessert. ✕ *152 Fortaleza St.,* ☎ *809/723–2432. D, MC, V. Closed Sun. No dinner.*

$–$$ **El Patio de Sam.** A warm dark-wood and faux-brick interior and a wide selection of beers make Sam's a popular late-night gathering place. The menu is mostly steaks and seafood, with a few native dishes like asopao mixed in. Try the Samueles Special pizza: mozzarella, tomato sauce, beef, pepperoni, and black olives: It feeds two or three adults. The dessert flans melt in your mouth. ✕ *102 Calle San Sebastián,* ☎ *809/723–1149. AE, D, DC, MC, V.*

$ **Ambrosia.** Order frozen fresh fruit drinks at the bar, or have a seat and order from a selection of pastas, veal, and chicken. The daily lunch specials are a good value and usually include quiche and lasagna served with large mixed salads. ✕ *250 Calle Cristo,* ☎ *809/722–5206. AE, MC, V. Closed Sun.*

San Juan

$$$$ **La Compostela.** Contemporary Spanish food and a serious 9,000-bot-
★   tle wine cellar are the draws to La Compostela, a restaurant with a dark-wood interior and many plants. Specialties include mushroom pâté and Port *pastelillo* (meat-filled pastries), grouper fillet with scallops in salsa verde, rack of lamb, duck with kiwi sauce, and paella. This is a favorite restaurant with the local dining elite, and it is honored yearly in local competitions. ✕ *106 Av. Condado, Santurce,* ☎ *809/724–6088. Reservations advised. AE, DC, MC, V. Closed Sun.*

$$$$ **Ramiro's.** Step into a soft sea green dining room for some imaginative
★   Castilian cuisine. Chef-owner Jesus Ramiro is known for his artistic presentation: flower-shape peppers filled with fish mousse, a mix of seafood caught under a vegetable net, roast duckling with sugarcane honey, and, if you can stand more, a kiwi dessert sculpted to resemble twin palms. ✕ *1106 Av. Magdalena, Condado,* ☎ *809/721–9049. Reservations advised. AE, DC, MC, V. No lunch Sat.*

$$$–$$$$ **Los Faisanes.** This Continental stunner is one of San Juan's most dis-
★ tinguished eateries. Mahogany doorways, faux-Tiffany lamps, crisp white
and ecru napery, and Bernadaud china set a refined tone, carried
through by the equally elegant cuisine. Feast on roast duck with guava
and cinnamon, veal chops with scallion and mushroom sauce, and won-
derfully light soufflés. ✕ *1108 Av. Magdalena, Condado,* ☎ *809/725–
2801. Reservations advised. AE, MC, V.*

$$$ **Chart House.** It's no secret that the graceful veranda of this restored
Ashford mansion across from the Marriott is a perfect spot for cock-
tails, and a lively crowd gathers here in the evening. The upstairs open-
air dining rooms are splashed with bright marine-themed artworks. The
menu includes prime rib, steak, shrimp teriyaki, Hawaiian chicken, and
the signature dessert: mud pie. ✕ *1214 Av. Ashford, Condado,* ☎ *809/
728–0110. Reservations advised. AE, D, DC, MC, V. No lunch.*

$$$ **Pikayo.** Chef Wilo Benet is the new darling in the foodie firmament,
thanks to his artful fusion of classic French, Caribbean Creole, and Cal-
ifornia nouvelle cuisine. The beautifully presented dishes, which change
regularly, are a feast for the eye as well as the palate. Your meal might
consist of popcorn shrimp in an apple-ginger rémoulade, followed by
fillet of beef with Roquefort in a red-wine sauce. The decor is smartly
contemporary, with lots of black-and-white accents and comfortable
banquettes. ✕ *Tanama Princess Hotel, 1 Joffre St., Condado,* ☎ *809/
724–4160. Reservations advised. AE, MC, V. Closed Sun. and Mon.
No lunch Sat.*

$$ **Che's.** Juicy *churrasco* (barbecued steaks), lemon chicken, and grilled
sweetbreads are specialties at this casual Argentinean restaurant. The
hamburgers are huge, and the french fries are fresh. The Chilean and
Argentinean wine list is also decent. ✕ *35 Calle Caoba, Punta Las
Marias,* ☎ *809/726–7202. Reservations advised on weekends. AE,
D, DC, MC, V.*

$ **El Paso.** This family-run restaurant serves genuine Creole food seasoned
for a local following. Specialties include asopao, pork chops, and
breaded empanadas. There's always tripe on Saturday and arroz con
pollo on Sunday. ✕ *405 Av. De Diego, Puerto Nuevo,* ☎ *809/781–
3399. AE, DC, MC, V.*

$ **Kasalta Bakery, Inc.** Make your selection from rows of display cases
★ offering a seemingly endless array of tempting treats. Walk up to the
counter and order from an assortment of sandwiches (try the Cubano),
meltingly tender octopus salad, savory *caldo gallego* (a soup jammed
with fresh vegetables, sausage, and potatoes), cold drinks, strong café
con leche, and luscious pastries. ✕ *1966 Calle McLeary, Ocean Park,*
☎ *809/727–7340. AE, MC, V.*

$ **Via Appia's Italian Deli.** The only true sidewalk café in San Juan, this
eatery serves pizzas, sandwiches, cold beer, and pitchers of sangria. It
is a good place to people-watch, and the staff is friendly. ✕ *1350 Av.
Ashford, Condado,* ☎ *809/725–8711. AE, MC, V.*

Out on the Island

Dining out on the island is always a casual experience; although you
may wish to phone ahead for reservations on a weekend in high season, it is generally not required.

$$ **Black Eagle.** The inconsistent quality of the food here hasn't dimmed
its status as a Rincón dining landmark. It's on the water's edge, and
you dine on the veranda, listening to the lapping waves. The steak-and-
seafood menu lists breaded conch fritters, a fresh fish of the day, lob-
ster, and imported prime meats. ✕ *Hwy. 413, Km 1, Rincón,* ☎ *809/
823–3510. AE, DC, MC, V.*

$$ **El Molino del Quijote Restaurante.** Amid beautifully landscaped gardens just off the beach, this festive, colorful restaurant with tile-topped tables and local artwork serves Spanish and Puerto Rican cuisine. Try the *bolas de pescado* (fish balls) appetizer and one of the paellas as an entrée, or combine several appetizers for a meal. The sangria is highly recommended. Two one-bedroom cabanas are available to rent. ✕ *Rte. 429, Km 3.3, Rincón,* ☎ *809/823–4010. AE, MC, V.* ☼ *Fri.–Sun.*

$$ **La Casona de Serafin.** This informal, oceanside bistro is a *mesón gastronómique* and specializes in steaks, seafood, and Puerto Rican *criolla* (Creole) dishes. The indoor dining room has bleached walls, mahogany furniture, and subdued red napery. Try the tostones, asopao, and surrullitos, and follow up with the pumpkin-custard dessert. The somewhat dilapidated palm-fringed patio sits right on the beach, so you can listen to the waves lap the shore. ✕ *Hwy. 102, Km. 9, Cabo Rojo,* ☎ *809/851–0066. AE, MC, V.*

$$ **Restaurant El Ancla.** The seafood and Puerto Rican specialties here are served with tostones, *papas fritas* (french fries), and garlic bread. The menu ranges from lobster and shrimp to chicken, beef, and asopao. The piña coladas, with or without rum, and the flan are especially good. ✕ *Av. Hostos Final 9, Playa-Ponce,* ☎ *809/840–2450. AE, DC, MC, V.*

$–$$ **Anchor's Inn.** From the windows of this unadorned seaside eatery, you can watch the flotillas of brightly colored yachts and fishing boats in Fajardo harbor. The latter must head straight for the restaurant with their catch, for the seafood is as fresh and succulent as it gets. A *mesón gastronómico,* Anchor's Inn specializes in such Puerto Rican specialties as surrullitos, asopao, and lobster mofongo. There are seven guest rooms upstairs. ✕ *Rte. 987, Km 2.4, Fajardo,* ☎ *809/863–7200. AE, MC, V. Closed Tues.*

$–$$ **El Bohio.** A local favorite, this informal restaurant 15 minutes south of Mayagüez serves steak and a variety of seafood—all cooked just about any way you want it. You can dine on the large, enclosed wooden deck that juts out over the sea or in the dining room inside. ✕ *Hwy. 102, Playa Joyuda, Cabo Rojo,* ☎ *809/851–2755. AE, DC, MC, V.*

$ **Lupita's.** A fine mariachi band patrols the mezzanine and courtyard of this festive Mexican restaurant Thursday through Sunday nights. The handsome arched dining room has an Aztec decor, with panchos and serapes hung on the walls for added color. The food—Mexican-American standards like nachos, tacos, and chicken mole—is quite good, the margaritas and shooters even better, and the ambience festive. ✕ *Calle Isabel 60, Ponce,* ☎ *809/848–8808. AE, MC, V.*

$ **Pastrami Palace.** A favorite ex-pat hangout, this friendly, small restaurant and lunch counter in downtown Rincón serves up American basics from omelets, pancakes, and sandwiches to homemade pies, ice cream, and excellent coffee. The colorful decor includes local artwork, and there's a small library for lunchtime reading. An outdoor café is being added. ✕ *Calle Parque, Rincón,* ☎ *809/823–0102. No credit cards. No dinner.*

Lodging

Accommodations on Puerto Rico come in all shapes and sizes. Self-contained luxury resorts cover hundreds of acres. San Juan's high-rise beachfront hotels likewise cater to the epicurean; several target the business traveler. Out on the island, the government-sponsored paradores are lodgings modeled after Spain's successful parador system. Some are rural inns, some offer motel-style (no-frill) apartments, and some are large hotels. They are required to meet certain standards, such as proximity to a sightseeing attraction or beach and a kitchen serving native cuisine. Parador prices range from $50 to $125 for a double room. Reservations for all paradores can be made by calling 800/443–0266 in the United States, 809/721–2884 in San Juan, or 800/981–7575 elsewhere in Puerto Rico. They are a phenomenal bargain but tend to get noisy and raucous on weekends, when families descend from the cities for a minivacation.

Most hotels in Puerto Rico operate on the European Plan. In some larger hotels, however, packages are available that include several or all meals, while others offer all-inclusive deals.

CATEGORY	COST*
$$$$	over $225
$$$	$150–$225
$$	$75–$150
$	under $75

All prices are for a standard double room for two, excluding 7% tax (9% for hotels with casinos) and 10%–15% service charge.

Old San Juan

$$$–$$$$
★ **Casa San José.** Unassuming elegance defines the character of this quiet, intimate bed-and-breakfast. Black-and-white marble floors grace the foyer. Each of the 10 rooms is individually decorated with hand-picked Spanish, French, and English colonial antiques and opens onto or overlooks an interior courtyard with a trickling fountain and tropical plants. The rooms have phones but no televisions. The second-floor salon, where breakfast is served, is furnished with beautiful antiques and a grand piano and includes a small library. The hotel is just steps from Plaza de Armas in the center of Old San Juan. Children under 12 are not accommodated. ☎ *159 Calle San José, 00901, ☎ 809/723–1212, FAX 809/723–7620. 10 units. Breakfast room. AE, DC, MC, V. CP.*

$$–$$$ Gallery Inn. Owners Jan D'Esopo and Manuco Gandia restored this rambling, classically Spanish house, one of the oldest private residences in the area, and turned it into an inn. It's full of quirky architectural details—winding, uneven stairs, private balconies, and small interior gardens. The rooms are individually decorated and have telephones but no televisions; most are air-conditioned. Views here are some of the best in the old city, a panorama of the El Morro and San Cristóbal forts and the Atlantic. Galería San Juan, a small gallery and working studio in the inn, features work in various medias (including sculpture and silk screen) by Jan D'Esopo, Bruno Lucchesi, and Teresa Spinner. The inn even offers a package that combines a five-night stay with the creation of your portrait bust. There is no restaurant, but meals can be cooked for groups upon request. ☎ *204–206 Calle Norzagaray, 00901, ☎ 809/722–1808, FAX 809/724–7360. 3 suites, 5 rooms. Self-service bar. AE, MC, V. EP.*

$$–$$$ Gran Hotel El Convento. This is one of Puerto Rico's most famous hotels. On Calle Cristo right across from the San Juan Cathedral, the light brown stucco building, with its dark-wood paneling and arcades, was a Carmelite convent in the 17th century. Alas, the heavy dour furnishings seem not to have been refurbished since. All the rooms are air-conditioned, with TV, phone, and wall-to-wall carpeting. Fourteen rooms have tiny balconies (ask for one with a view of the bay). ☎ *100 Calle Cristo, 00902, ☎ 809/723–9020 or 800/468–2779, FAX 809/721–2877. 99 rooms. Restaurant, 2 bars, pool, Jacuzzi, free transport to beach weekdays. AE, D, DC, MC, V. EP.*

San Juan

$$$$ **Caribe Hilton International.** Built in 1949, this property occupies 17
★ acres on Puerta de Tierra. Rooms have been modernized and refurbished
over the years and have a crisp, pastel decor and balconies with ocean
or lagoon views; the higher the floor, the better the view. Executive levels provide services such as private check-in and checkout, complimentary
evening cocktails, and complimentary Continental breakfast for business travelers. The spacious atrium lobby is decorated with rose marble, waterfalls, and lavish tropical plants. Restaurants include Batey
del Pescador for seafood and Peacock Paradise for Chinese cuisine. The
hotel has San Juan's only private beach, complete with a boardwalk
at its edge. ⚇ *Box 1872, San Juan 00902,* ☎ *809/721–0303 or
800/468–8585,* ℻ *809/724–6992. 668 rooms and suites. 6 restaurants,
private beach, 2 pools, 6 lighted tennis courts, gym, air-conditioned
squash and racquetball courts, business center. AE, D, DC, MC, V. EP,
MAP.*

$$$$ **Condado Plaza Hotel and Casino.** The Atlantic and the Condado Lagoon border this property. Two wings, appropriately named Ocean and
Lagoon, are connected by an enclosed, elevated walkway over Avenida
Ashford. Standard rooms have walk-in closets and separate dressing
areas. There are a variety of suites, including spa suites with oversize
Jacuzzis, and a fully equipped business center. The Plaza Club floor
has 24-hour concierge service and a private lounge, and guests there
receive complimentary Continental breakfast, afternoon hors d'oeuvres, and evening coffee. The Ocean wing sits on a small strip of public beach, and there are two pools. This is the sister hotel of the El San
Juan resort, and you have access to all of the facilities there via a complimentary shuttle bus (the bus will also drop you off in Old San
Juan). Dining options include Tony Roma's (a branch of the American chain) and an informal restaurant poolside. ⚇ *Box 1270, 999 Av.
Ashford, Condado 00907,* ☎ *809/721–1000 or 800/468–8588,* ℻
*809/721–4613. 589 rooms and suites. 5 pools, Jacuzzi, casino, 2
lighted tennis courts, 7 restaurants, 3 bars, fitness center (there is a fee
for use), water-sports center, business center, ATM machine. AE, D,
DC, MC, V. EP, MAP.*

$$$$ **El San Juan Hotel and Casino.** An immense chandelier shines over the
★ hand-carved mahogany paneling, rose marble, and French tapestries
in the huge lobby of this 12-acre resort on the Isla Verde beach. The
casino is right off the lobby. You'll be hard pressed to decide if you
want a suite in the main tower, with whirlpool bath and wet bar; a
garden lanai room, with private patio and whirlpool bath; or a casita,
with a sunken Roman bath. (Some of the tower rooms have no balcony or ocean view; be sure to check.) All rooms have CD player, three
phones, TV with VCR, minibar, and walk-in closets with an iron and
board. The furnishings are dark rattan, and there are rich carpets and
tropical-print spreads and drapes. This luxurious hotel attracts a mon-
eyed mix of international business and leisure travelers. The posh Dar
Tiffany restaurant, an oasis of potted palms, etched glass, and Tiffany
lamps, serves impeccable Continental fare. The intimate, romantic La
Piccola Fontana is one of San Juan's better Italian restaurants. Don't
miss the informal rooftop bar; watching the sun drop down is a splendid end to a day of sightseeing. ⚇ *Av. Isla Verde, Box 2872, San Juan
00902,* ☎ *809/791–1000 or 800/468–2818,* ℻ *809/791–0390. 389
rooms. 5 restaurants, 8 bars, 2 pools (1 with swim-up bar), children's
pool, 3 Jacuzzis, disco, casino, 3 lighted tennis courts, activity center,
game room, water-sports center, shopping arcade, health club (not complimentary), business center, no-smoking rooms, facilities for people*

with disabilities, complimentary shuttle bus to Condado Plaza Hotel and Old San Juan, concierge. AE, DC, MC, V. EP, MAP.

$$$$ **Sands Hotel and Casino.** One of Puerto Rico's largest casinos glitters
★ just off the lobby, stunning artworks from around the world grace the public rooms, and a huge free-form pool lies between the hotel and its beach. Rooms are air-conditioned and have tiny balconies (ask for one with an ocean view). The decor is basic tropical, with a green, peach, and white color scheme and white rattan furniture. The exclusive Plaza Club section is that rare executive level worth the added expense, offering garden suites, a masseuse, a small gym, and other entice-ments. ⊞ *187 Isla Verde Rd., Isla Verde 00979,* ☎ *809/791–6100 or 800/544–3008,* ℻ *809/791–8525. 418 rooms. 4 restaurants, pool, 2 lounges, casino, concierge, water-sports center, business center, valet parking. AE, D, DC, MC, V. EP.*

$$$$ **San Juan Marriott.** The red neon sign atop San Juan's newest hotel is a beacon to its excellent Condado location, seen for miles. The hotel opened in January 1995, and parts of it—the fitness room, for exam-ple—were still incomplete when we visited. Rooms have soothing pas-tel carpeting, flowered spreads, and balconies overlooking the ocean, the pool, or both. Restaurants include Tuscany, for northern Italian cuisine, and the more casual La Vista, popular for dining alfresco. On weekends, there's live entertainment in the enormous lobby, which, com-bined with the persistent ringing of slot machines from the adjoining casino, makes the area quite noisy (rooms are soundproofed). Gorgeous Condado beach is right outside. ⊞ *1309 Av. Ashford, San Juan 00907,* ☎ *809/722–7000 or 800/228–9290,* ℻ *809/722–6800. 510 rooms, 15 suites. 3 restaurants, 2 lounges, pool, 2 lighted tennis courts, casino, health club, sauna, beauty salon, meeting rooms, business center, video arcade, whirlpool, no smoking rooms, children's programs. AE, D, DC, MC, V. EP, FAP, MAP.*

$$$ **Radisson Normandie.** This oceanfront, art-deco style hotel is a national landmark. It was built in 1939, in the shape of the fabled ocean liner of the same name. Rooms have minibars, cable TV, coffeemakers, and hair dryers; some have sunrooms. Additional frills and pampering can be found at the seventh-floor executive club, where you receive com-plimentary Continental breakfast and evening hors d'oeuvres. You can make reservations to use the tennis courts at the Hilton next door. ⊞ *Corner of Av. Muñoz Rivera and Av. Rosales, Puerta Tierra, Box 50059, San Juan 00902,* ☎ *809/729–2929 or 800/333–3333,* ℻ *809/ 729–3083. 177 rooms. Restaurant, pool, lounge, business center, health club, diving, jogging track, water-sports available. AE, D, DC, MC, V. EP, MAP.*

$$ **Excelsior.** Room decor here is lackluster, but the rates are an excellent value. Each room has a phone and a private bath with a hair dryer; some have kitchenettes. Fine carpets adorn the corridors, and sculptures dec-orate the lobby. Augusto's, one of the hotel's restaurants, is well respected for its international cuisine. Complimentary coffee, newspaper, and shoe shine are offered each morning. ⊞ *801 Av. Ponce de León, Mi-ramar 00907,* ☎ *809/721–7400 or 800/223–9815,* ℻ *809/723–0068. 140 rooms. Cocktail lounge, 2 restaurants, pool, fitness room, free park-ing, free transportation to beach. AE, DC, MC, V. EP.*

Out on the Island

CABO ROJO

$ **Parador Boquemar.** You can walk to the Boquerón public beach (one of the island's best) from this small parador at the end of Route 101. Rooms are comfortable. Each has air-conditioning, TV, minifridge, phone, and private bath and is decorated in the island uniform of tropical prints and rattan. Ask for a third-floor room with a balcony overlooking the water. La Cascada, a *mesón gastronomique*, is well known for its scrumptious traditional native cuisine. ☎ *Box 133, Boquéon 00622, ☎ 809/851–2158 or 800/443–0266, FAX 809/851–7600. 64 rooms. Restaurant, pool, laundry across street, lounge. AE, D, DC, MC, V. EP.*

<u>COAMO</u>

$ **Parador Baños de Coamo.** On Route 546, Km 1, northeast of Ponce, this mountain inn is located at the hot sulfur springs that are said to be the Fountain of Youth of Ponce de León's dreams. Rooms open onto latticed wooden verandas and have a pleasing blend of contemporary and period furnishings. All are air-conditioned and have private bath. The parador can make arrangements for you to ride Puerto Rico's glorious, unique paso fino horses. ☎ *Box 540, 00769, ☎ 809/825–2186 or 800/443–0266, FAX 809/825–4739. 48 rooms. Restaurant, lounge, pool, horseback riding. AE, DC, MC, V. EP.*

<u>DORADO</u>

$$$–$$$$ **Hyatt Dorado Beach.** The ambience is a bit more subdued and family
★ oriented at this resort than at its sister, the Cerromar Beach. A variety of elegant accommodations are in low-rise buildings scattered over 1,000 lavishly landscaped acres. Most rooms have private patios or balconies, and all have polished terra-cotta floors, marble baths, and air-conditioning. Upper-level rooms in the Oceanview Houses have a view of the two half-moon beaches. ☎ *Rte. 693, 00646, ☎ 809/796–1234 or 800/233–1234, FAX 809/796–2022. 298 rooms. 3 restaurants, 2 lounges, 2 18-hole Robert Trent Jones golf courses, 7 tennis courts, bike rentals, hiking and jogging trails, 2 pools, wading pool, casino, water-sports center. AE, DC, MC, V. EP, MAP.*

$$$–$$$$ **Hyatt Regency Cerromar Beach.** One of the best sports-oriented resorts
★ in the Caribbean, the Cerromar has two Robert Trent Jones golf courses, 14 tennis courts, a spa and health club, jogging and biking trails, and a 900-foot river pool with waterfalls, a Jacuzzi in a manmade cavern, a swim-up bar, and a three-story-high water slide. It's 22 miles west of San Juan, right on the Atlantic, and has a lovely reef-protected beach. The modern seven-story hotel is done up in tropical style. Rooms have tile floors, marble baths, air-conditioning, and a king-size or two double beds. You'll find quieter rooms on the west side, away from the pool activity. Guests at the Cerromar and its sister facility, the Hyatt Dorado Beach a mile down the road, have access to the facilities of both resorts, and colorful red trolleys (free, of course) make frequent runs between the two. Sushi Wong's serves delicious pan-Asian cuisine, and Medici's is an ultrasophisticated northern Italian eatery. ☎ *Rte. 693, Km 11.8, 00646, ☎ 809/796–1234 or 800/233–1234, FAX 809/796–4647. 506 rooms. 4 restaurants, 2 bars, casino, disco, 2 18-hole Robert Trent Jones golf courses, 14 tennis courts (2 lighted), pool, spa and health club, bike rentals, jogging and hiking trails. AE, DC, MC, V. EP, MAP.*

<u>GUÁNICA</u>

$$ **Copamarina Beach Resort.** Sprawling across 18 acres between the sea and the Guánica Dry Forest is this quiet, landscaped resort. The pool is the centerpiece of the property, surrounded by the open-air reception area, manicured lawns, the outdoor Las Palmas Cafe, the elegant Ballena restaurant and bar, and the building wings. The bay bottom on this section of beach is covered in seaweed, but secluded beaches with clear water can be found a few minutes down the road. The spotless rooms have small terraces with water views, one queen-size or two

double beds, TV, phone, and air conditioner. The furniture is bleached-wood-and-rattan, and the bedspreads are the ubiquitous tropical print. Try the red snapper in the dining room, and stop in the bar for the bartender's straight-up margarita. Arrange a snorkeling excursion to Gilligan's Island, an offshore key. Kayaks, sailboats, paddleboats, and tennis rackets are some of the gear for rent. There are plans to add 55 rooms, 15 villas, and a convention center to the complex. ☎ *Rte. 333, Km. 6.5, Caña Gorda, Box 805, 00653, ☎ 809/821–0505 or 800/468–4553, FAX 809/821–0070. 70 rooms. 2 restaurants, 2 bars, pool, Jacuzzi, volleyball net, gift shop, activity center, 2 tennis courts, meeting rooms, game room, scuba-diving packages, bike rentals. AE, D, DC, MC, V. EP.*

HUMACAO

$$ –$$$$ **Palmas del Mar.** This is a luxurious resort community, on 2,750 acres
★ of a former coconut plantation on the sheltered southeast coast (about an hour's drive from San Juan). Two hotels, the 23-suite Palmas Inn and 100-room Candelero Hotel, are the centerpieces of the complex. In the rustic yet elegant Candelero, rooms are airy and spacious. Ask for a room on the third floor, where there are cathedral ceilings. The Palmas Inn suites, all with stunning sea or garden views, evoke luxurious Mediterranean villas, with pastel-pink connecting walkways, cobblestone plazas, and fountains adorned with hand-painted tile work. The resort includes private homes and condominium villas. ☎ *Box 2020, Rte. 906, 00792, ☎ 809/852–6000 or 800/468–3331, FAX 809/852–6330. 100 rooms; 140 villas; 23 1-, 2-, and 3-bedroom suites. 10 restaurants, beach, 18-hole Gary Player golf course, 20 tennis courts (4 lighted), casino, equestrian center, pool, bike rentals, fitness center, water-sports center, marina, diving, sailing, fishing. AE, DC, MC, V. EP, MAP.*

JAYUYA

$ **Parador Hacienda Gripiñas.** Don't stay here if you're looking for a beach
★ vacation: The sea is more than 30 miles away, so this white hacienda is for those looking for a romantic mountain hideaway. Polished wood and beam ceilings warm the interior. Large airy rooms are decorated with native crafts. Relaxation beckons at every turn: Rocking chairs nod in the spacious lounge, hammocks swing on the porch, and splendid gardens invite a leisurely stroll. Your morning coffee is grown on the adjacent working plantation, and its aroma seems to fill the grounds, as does the chirp of the ubiquitous coquis (tree frogs). ☎ *Rte. 527, Km 2.5, Box 387, 00664, ☎ 809/828–1717 or 800/443–0266, FAX 809/828–1719. 19 rooms. Restaurant, lounge, pool, hiking and horseback-riding trails. AE. EP.*

LA PARGUERA

$$ **Parador Villa Parguera.** This parador is a stylish hotel on Phosphorescent Bay. Large, colorfully decorated rooms have TV, phone, air-conditioning, private bath, and balcony or terrace. A spacious dining room, overlooking the swimming pool and the bay beyond, serves excellent native and international dishes. Children under 10 stay free in their parents' room. Ask about honeymoon packages. ☎ *Rte. 304, Box 273, Lajas 00667, ☎ 809/899–3975 or 800/443–0266, FAX 809/899–6040. 63 rooms. Restaurant, saltwater pool, lounge, nightclub, ATM machine. AE, D, DC, MC, V. EP.*

LAS CROABAS

$$$$ **El Conquistador Resort and Country Club.** This massive $250-million complex is a world unto itself, divided into five self-contained hotels. It's perched dramatically atop a 300-foot bluff overlooking the

Caribbean, the Atlantic, and the El Yunque rain forest. The architecture is a harmonious blend of Moorish and Spanish colonial: cobblestone streets, white stucco and terra-cotta buildings, open-air plazas with soaring arches and tinkling fountains, tiled benches, and gas lamps. Plants and colorful caged parrots decorate many of the open spaces. One of the five hotels, Las Olas, is actually built into the cliff face. In all of the hotels, the stylish, elegant decor in the large rooms runs toward the ubiquitous Caribbean rattan and pastels, spiced with native artworks. Each room has a seating area with couch, glass-top coffee table, desk, chairs, and entertainment center. Enormous bathrooms have sunken tub, long marble countertop, makeup mirror, and walk-in closet. Nice extras include dimmer switches on bedside lamps, well-stocked minibars, CD players, and VCRs. The hotel's beach is an offshore island, which you reach via shuttle boat. The pampering begins at LMM International Airport: The resort is the only one on the island to operate a private lounge and provide deluxe motor coach transfers. The ride is a little over an hour. ☎ *Av. El Conquistador, Box 70001, Las Croabas 00738,* ☎ *809/863–1000 or 800/468–5228,* FAX *809/863–6500. 918 rooms and suites. 7 restaurants, 3 bars, lounge, business center, car rentals, casino, convention center, nightclub, marina, fishing, diving, water-sports center, 5 pools, 7 lighted tennis courts, 18-hole Arthur Hills golf course, fitness center, spa, shopping arcades, ATM machine, supervised children's program. AE, D, DC, MC, V. EP.*

MAYAGÜEZ

$$$–$$$$ **Mayagüez Hilton and Casino.** Built on 20 acres about 2 miles north of the city of Mayagüez, this pink stucco resort on the island's west coast is about a 2½-hour drive from San Juan. The casino has a new Player's Bar, to get around the no-alcohol-in-casinos law. The superb Rotisserie restaurant is known for its lavish theme buffets and top-notch steaks and seafood. Rooms are air-conditioned and have minibar, TV, and telephone. The decor is typical tan-and-muted-pastel. Many rooms overlook the parking lot, although poolside rooms view the tropical gardens and Mayagüez harbor in the distance. The hotel caters mainly to businesspeople, and a new business center, with private check-in and secretarial services, is in the works. ☎ *Rte. 2, Km 152.5, Box 3629, 00709,* ☎ *809/831–7575, 800/445–8667, or in Puerto Rico, 800/462–3954;* FAX *809/834–3475. 141 rooms, 4 suites, 10 junior suites. Restaurant, lounge, bar, Olympic-size pool, baby pool, playground, game room, 3 lighted tennis courts, minigym, Jacuzzi, meeting rooms, ATM machine, no-smoking rooms, casino, disco. AE, D, DC, MC, V. EP.*

PONCE

$$–$$$$ **Ponce Hilton and Casino.** By far the class hotel act on the south coast, ★ this cream-and-turquoise resort, nestled amid 80 acres of landscaped gardens, caters to a corporate clientele. Completely self-contained, it offers three fine restaurants (La Hacienda's antiques mimic an old coffee plantation; the romantic and elegant La Cava has a working wine cellar and can be reserved for a private dinner), access to a public beach, casino, shopping arcade, pool, four tennis courts, a driving range, and a new disco with pool tables and live music on weekends. The huge rooms are decorated in sky blue, teal, and peach, and furnished with modern rattan. All have a minibar, safe, TV, phone, and balcony. The views are best from the fourth-floor rooms. The only drawback is its out-of-town location (a 10-minute cab ride from town). ☎ *Rte. 14, Av. Santiago de los Caballeros, Box 7419, 00732,* ☎ *809/259–7676 or 800/445–8667,* FAX *809/259–7674. 156 rooms, 8 suites. 3 restaurants, 2 bars, casino, disco, pool, Jacuzzi, volleyball, 4 lighted tennis courts, ½ basketball court, Ping-Pong table, ATM machine, baby-sit-*

ting, *business center, meeting rooms, fitness room, shopping arcade, beauty salon. AE, D, DC, MC, V. EP.*

RINCÓN

$$$$ **Horned Dorset Primavera.** The emphasis here is on privacy and re-
★ laxation. The Spanish neocolonial-style resort is tucked away amid lush landscaping overlooking the sea. Lounging on the long secluded beach, the only sounds you're likely to hear are the crash of the surf and the occasional squawk of the enormous parrot in the lounge. Suites have private balconies and are exquisitely furnished with antiques, includ-ing handsome mahogany four-poster beds, dressers, and nightstands. A new villa, Casa Escondido, contains eight rooms and is designed as a typical turn-of-the-century Puerto Rican hacienda, with tile or wood floors, mahogany furnishings, private terraces, and marble baths. There are no radios, no televisions, and no telephones in any of the rooms. The elegant restaurant serves Continental cuisine in surroundings befitting royalty. A delightful Continental breakfast is served in the open-air lounge. The hotel is a member of the prestigious Relais & Châteaux group. Children under 12 are not permitted. *Rte. 429, Km 3, Box 1132, 00743,* ☎ *809/823–4030 or 809/823–4050,* FAX *809/823–5580. 8 rooms, 22 suites. Restaurant, pool, library, lounge. AE, MC, V. EP.*

SAN GERMÁN

$ **Parador Oasis.** The Oasis, not far from the town's two plazas, was a family mansion 200 years ago; the lobby retains a taste of the house's history with peppermint-pink walls and white-wicker furniture. The older rooms are convenient—right off the lobby—but show their age. The newer rooms in the rear lack character but are functional, clean, and a little roomier. All have TV, phone, and air-conditioning. ☎ *72 Calle Luna, Box 144, 00683,* ☎ *809/892–1175 or 800/443–0266,* FAX *809/892–1175, ext. 200. 52 rooms. Restaurant, pool, Jacuzzi, lounge, small gym, sauna. AE, D, DC, MC, V. EP.*

VIEQUES

$$ **Casa del Francés.** Self-professed curmudgeon Irving Greenblatt, a for-mer Bostonian, runs this atmospheric guest house in a restored French sugar plantation great house. Rooms are rather plain but enormous, with vaulted 17-foot ceilings. The food is good, the pool inviting, the guests an eclectic mix, and Irving a true character who will regale you with hor-ror stories of running a Caribbean hotel. The sightseeing boat for the phosphorescent bay leaves from here. ☎ *Box 458, Esperanza 00765,* ☎ *809/741–3751,* FAX *809/741–2330. 18 rooms. Restaurant, bar, pool, snorkeling. AE, MC, V. EP, MAP (compulsory in season).*

$ **Sea Gate.** Occupying 2 acres of a hilltop on the island of Vieques, this whitewashed hotel is a family-run operation. Friendly, helpful propri-etors John, Ruthye, and Penny Miller will meet you at the airport or ferry, drive you to the beaches, arrange scuba-diving and snorkeling trips, and give you a complete rundown on island goings-on. Accom-modations include three-room units with terraces (some have kitchens) and two separate two-bedroom cottages, which offer more privacy. All have fans but no air-conditioning (the hilltop breezes are just fine), and no ☎s; TVs are available on request. There is no restaurant, but the owners will cook for you on request. *Box 747, 00765,* ☎ *809/741–4661. 18 units. No credit cards.*

Villa and Apartment Rentals

Villa and condominium or apartment rentals are becoming increasingly popular in Puerto Rico, particularly outside San Juan. If you are trav-eling with several people, these are often a very affordable option. Call the tourist information office in the area where you are interested in staying, or try the options listed below.

If you're part of a large group or you'd like to investigate off-season rates at higher-end properties in the Isla Verde area of San Juan, contact **Condo World** (26645 W. Twelve Mile Rd., Southfield, MI 48034, ☎ 800/521–2980). For rentals out on the island, try **Island West Properties** (Rte. 413, Km 1.3, Box 700, Rincón 00677, ☎ 809/823-2323, FAX 809/823–3254). It has weekly and monthly vacation rentals that fall into the $ to $$ range.

$–$$ **Desecheo Inn.** This house is connected with Captain Bill's Dive & Surf Shop (*see* Sports and the Outdoors, *above*) and often part of dive-accommodation packages. The house is on a hillside and looks over El Faro lighthouse and the surfing beaches. You can roll out of bed each morning and look out the window for a wave check. There are three units: one two-floor, two-bedroom apartment with a large living room and kitchen (sleeps up to eight), and two smaller apartments with kitchenettes (one sleeps four, one sleeps three). The smallest ground-floor unit uses an outdoor shower. The furniture is functional if worn. Each unit has air-conditioning and TV; the top two have balconies. The units share a backyard and a wooden deck with a covered grill and bar. Nightly and weekly rates are available. Check-in is at the Dive Shop. ☎ *R. 413, Km. 2.5, Box 4181, Rincón,* ☎ *809/823–0390 or 809/823–2672 (evenings),* FAX *809/823–0390. 3 apartments. TV, washer/dryer, garage. AE, MC, V.*

$$ **Lemontree Vacation Rentals.** These sparkling, large apartments sit right on the beach, with staircases from their decks to the sand. There are four units, each with a fully equipped kitchen, TV, telephone, and large deck with mahogany-topped wet bar and gas grill. The owner-managers, Mary Jeanne and Paul Hellings, have put their personal touches on the apartments: Paul creates all the detailed woodwork, and Mary Jeanne designs the interiors. The bright tropical decor includes local artwork on the walls. There is one three-bedroom unit with two baths, one two-bedroom unit, and two brand-new one-bedroom units. The new units have wooden cathedral ceilings and picture windows. The beach is small, but larger ones are close by. It's a 10-minute drive to downtown Rincón. The owners hope to accept credit cards soon; call ahead and check. ☎ *Rte. 429, Box 200, Rincón,* ☎ *809/823–6452,* FAX *809/823–5821. 4 units. Weekly maid service, laundry service available, linens provided. No credit cards.*

The Arts and Nightlife

¿Qué Pasa?, the official visitors' guide, has current listings of events in San Juan and out on the island. Also, pick up a copy of the *San Juan Star, Quick City Guide,* or *Sunspots,* and check with the local tourist offices and the concierge at your hotel to find out what's doing.

Music, Dance, and Theater

LeLoLai is a year-round festival that celebrates Puerto Rico's Indian, Spanish, and African heritage. Performances take place each week, moving from hotel to hotel, showcasing the island's music, folklore, and culture. Because it is sponsored by the Puerto Rico Tourism Company and major San Juan hotels, passes to the festivities are included in some packages offered by participating hotels. You can also purchase tickets to a weekly series of events for $10. *Contact the El Centro Convention Center,* ☎ *809/723–3135. Reservations can be made by telephoning 809/722–1513.*

La Tasca del Callejon (Calle Fortaleza 317, ☎ 809/721–1689) is renowned for its tapas bar and the cabaret show (usually including flamenco guitar) performed by its engaging, talented staff.

Bars

Calle San Sebastian in Old San Juan is lined with trendy bars and restaurants; if you're in the mood for barhopping, head in that direction—it's pretty crazy on weekend nights. The Gran Hotel El Convento's **Ponce de León Salon** (☎ 809/723–9020) also has a pleasant bar. The **Blue Dolphin** (2 Calle Amapola, Isla Verde, ☎ 809/791–3083) is a hangout where you can rub elbows with some offbeat locals and enjoy some stunning sunset happy hours. While strolling along the Isla Verde beach, just look for the neon blue dolphin on the roof—you can't miss it.

El Patio de Sam (102 Calle san Sebastián, ☎ 809/723–1149) is an Old San Juan institution whose expatriate clientele claims it serves the best burgers on the island. The dining room is awash in potted plants and strategically placed canopies that create the illusion of dining on an outdoor patio.

Casinos

By law, all casinos are in hotels, primarily in San Juan. The government keeps a close eye on them. Dress for the larger casinos tends to be on the formal side, and the atmosphere is refined. The law permits casinos to operate noon–4 AM, but individual casinos set their own hours.

Casinos are located in the following San Juan hotels (*see* Lodging, *above*): **Condado Plaza Hotel, Caribe Hilton, Dutch Inn & Tower** (999 Ashford Ave., Condado), **Sands, El San Juan, Holiday Inn Crowne Plaza** (Rte. 187, Isla Verde), and **Radisson Ambassador** (1369 Ashford Ave., Condado). Elsewhere on the island, there are casinos at the **Hyatt Regency Cerromar** and **Hyatt Dorado Beach hotels,** and at **Palmas del Mar,** the **Ponce Hilton,** the **El Conquistador,** and the **Mayagüez Hilton.**

Discos

Fridays are big nights in San Juan. Dress to party: If you try to go out in jeans, sneakers, and a T-shirt, you will probably be refused entry at most nightclubs.

Young professionals gather at **Peggy Sue** (1 Av. Roberto H. Todd, ☎ 809/722–4664), where the design is 1950s and the music includes oldies and current dance hits.

In San Juan, the gay crowd flocks to **Krash** (1257 Av. Ponce de León, Santurce, ☎ 809/722–1390). **Lazers** (251 Calle Cruz, ☎ 809/721–4479) attracts different crowds on different nights.

In Condado and Isla Verde, the thirty-something crowd heads for **Sirenas** (La Concha Hotel, ☎ 809/721–6090) and **Amadeus** (El San Juan Hotel, ☎ 809/791–1000).

Out on the island nightlife is hard to come by, but there are discos in the **Mayagüez** and **Ponce Hiltons.**

Nightclubs

The Sands Hotel's **Players Lounge** brings in such big names as Joan Rivers, Jay Leno, and Rita Moreno. Try El San Juan's **El Chico** to dance to Latin music in a western saloon setting. The Condado Plaza Hotel's **La Fiesta Lounge** sizzles with steamy Latin shows, and the **Casino Lounge** offers live jazz Wednesday through Saturday. The El Centro Convention Center offers the festive **Olé Latino** Latin revue (☎ 809/722–8433).

18 Saba

Updated by
Marcy
Pritchard

THIS 5-SQUARE-MILE FAIRY-TALE ISLE is not for everybody. If you're looking for exciting nightlife or lots of shopping, forget Saba, or make it a one-day excursion from St. Maarten. There are only a handful of shops on Saba, even fewer inns and eateries, and the island's movie theater closed with the arrival of cable. Saba has only 1,200 friendly but shy inhabitants; everyone knows everyone and crime is virtually nonexistent, as is unemployment. Beach lovers should also take note that Saba is an essentially beachless volcanic island: Steep cliffs ring the island and plummet sharply to the sea.

So, why Saba? Saba is a perfect hideaway, a challenge for adventurous hikers (Mt. Scenery rises to a height of 2,855 feet), a haven for divers, and, for Sabans, heaven on water. It's no wonder they call their island the Unspoiled Queen.

The capital of Saba (pronounced SAY-ba) is the Bottom, which is at the top, not the bottom, of a hill. Meandering goats have the right of way on the Road (there's only one); chickens cross at their own risk. In tiny, toylike villages, flower-draped walls and neat picket fences border narrow paths. Tidy houses with red roofs and gingerbread trim are planted on the mountainside among the bromeliads, palms, hibiscus, orchids, and Norwegian pines. Saba may be the prettiest island in the Caribbean; it's certainly the most immaculate and has an enchanting fairy-tale air to it. Despite such modern additions as television sets (since 1965) and 24-hour electricity (installed in 1970), the island's uncomplicated lifestyle has persevered. Saban ladies still hand-embroider delicate Saba lace—a reminder of Saban gentility that has flourished since the 1870s—and brew the potent rum-based liquor, Saba Spice, sweetened with secret herbs and spices. Families still follow the generations-old tradition of burying their dead in their neatly tended gardens.

Saba is part of the Netherlands Antilles Windward Islands and is 28 miles—a 15-minute flight—from St. Maarten. The island is a volcano that has been extinct for 5,000 years (no one even knows where the crater was). Carib Indians may have lived here around AD 800. Columbus spotted the little speck in 1493, but somehow Saba remained uninhabited until the first Dutch settlers arrived from Statia in 1640. In the 17th, 18th, and early 19th centuries the French, Dutch, English, and Spanish vied for control of the island. Saba changed hands 12 times before permanently raising the Dutch flag.

Sabans are a hardy lot. To get from Fort Bay to the Bottom, the early Sabans carved 900 steps out of the mountainside. Everything that arrived on the island, from a pin to a piano, had to be hauled up. Those rugged steps remained the only way to travel until the Road was built by Josephus Lambert Hassell (a carpenter who took correspondence courses in engineering) in the 1940s. An extraordinary feat of engineering, the handmade road took 25 years to build, and if you like roller coasters, you'll love it. The 9-mile, white-knuckle route begins at sea level in Fort Bay, zigs up to 1,968 feet, and zags down to 131 feet above sea level at the airport, constructed on the island's only flat point, called (what else?) Flat Point.

Before You Go

Tourist Information

For help planning your trip, contact the **Caribbean Tourism Organization** (20 E. 46th St., New York, NY 10017–2452, ☎ 212/682–0435) or the **Saba Tourist Office** (Windwardside, ☎ 599/4 -62231, FAX 599/4– 62350). In Canada, contact **New Concepts in Travel** (2455 Cawthra Rd., Suite 70, Mississauga, Ontario L5A 3PI, ☎ 905/803–0131, FAX 905/803–0132).

Book reservations through a travel agent or over the telephone; mail can take a week or two to reach the island.

Arriving and Departing

BY PLANE

Unless you parachute in, you'll arrive from St. Maarten via **Windward Islands Airways** (☎ 599/5–54210). The approach to Saba's tiny airstrip is the stuff of which nightmares are made. The strip is only a quarter mile long, but the STOL (Short Takeoff and Landing) aircrafts are built for it, and the pilot needs only half of it. Try not to panic; remember that the pilot knows what he is doing and wants to live just as much as you do. (If you're nervous, don't sit on the right. The wing just misses grazing the cliffside on the approach.) Once you've touched down on the airstrip, the pilot taxis an inch or two, turns, and deposits you just outside a little shoe box called the Juancho E. Yrausquin Airport.

BY BOAT

The Edge, a high-speed ferry, leaves St. Maarten's Pelican Marina in Simpson Bay three times weekly at 9 AM and returns by 5 PM. The trip to Saba's Fort Bay takes an hour, and the round-trip fare is $60 (☎ 599/5–42640 in St. Maarten). If you take the watery way, however, you'll have lost more than an hour of sightseeing time on Saba.

Passports and Visas

U.S. citizens need proof of citizenship. A passport is preferred, but a birth certificate or voter registration card will do (a driver's license will *not*). British citizens must have a British passport. All visitors must have an ongoing or return ticket.

Language

Saba's official language is Dutch, but everyone on the island speaks English.

Precautions

Take along insect repellent, sunscreen, and sturdy, no-nonsense shoes that get a good grip on the ground.

Staying in Saba

Important Addresses

Tourist Information: The amiable Glenn Holm is at the helm of the **Saba Tourist Office** (Windwardside, ☎ 599/4–62231, FAX 599/4–62350) weekdays 8–noon and 1–5, and Sunday 10–2. The tourist office can help you make guest-house reservations.

EMERGENCIES

Police: Call 599/4–63237 in the Bottom, 599/4–62221 in Windwardside. **Hospital:** The **A. M. Edwards Medical Center** (The Bottom, ☎ 599/4–63288) is a 10-bed hospital with a full-time physician. **Pharmacy:** the **Pharmacy** (The Bottom, ☎ 599/4–63289).

Currency

U.S. dollars are accepted everywhere, but Saba's official currency is the Netherlands Antilles florin (NAf; also called the guilder). The exchange rate fluctuates but is around NAf1.80 to U.S.$1. Prices quoted here are in U.S. dollars unless noted otherwise. **Barclays Bank** and **Commercial Bank** in Windwardside are the only banks on the island. Barclays is open weekdays 8:30–2; Commercial, 8:30–4.

Taxes and Service Charges

Hotels collect a 5% government tax. Most hotels and restaurants add a 10%–15% service charge to your bill. You must pay a $2 departure tax when leaving Saba for either St. Maarten or St. Eustatius.

Guided Tours

All 12 of the taxi drivers who meet the planes at Yrausquin Airport also conduct tours of the island. The cost for a full-day tour is $8 per person with a minimum of four people. If you're just in from St. Maarten for a day trip, have your driver make lunch reservations for you at **Scout's Place** or the **Captain's Quarters** (*see* Dining, *below*) before starting the tour. After a full morning of sightseeing, your driver will drop you off for lunch, complete the tour afterward, and return you to Yrausquin in time to make the last flight back to St. Maarten. Guides are available for hiking; arrangements may be made through the tourist office.

Getting Around

RENTAL CARS

Saba's one and only road—the Road—is serpentine, with many a hairpin (read hair-raising) curve. However, if you dare to drive, there are nine rental cars at **Doc's Car Rentals** (Windwardside, ☎ 599/4–62271). Cars can also be rented at **Scout's Place** (Windwardside, ☎ 599/4–62205) and at **Johnson's Rent A Car** (Juliana's, Windwardside, ☎ 599/4–62469). A car rents for about $40 per day, with a full tank of gas and unlimited mileage. (If you run out of gas, call the island's only gas station, down at Fort Bay, ☎ 599/4–63272. It closes at noon.) Scooters can be rented at **Steve's Rent A Scoot** (☎ 599/4–62507), next to Sandra's Salon & Boutique, for $10 per hour or $30 per day, less by the week.

HITCHHIKING

Carless Sabans get around the old-fashioned ways—walking and hitchhiking (very popular and safe). If you choose to get around by thumbing rides, you'll need to know the rules of the Road. To get a ride from the Bottom (which actually is near the top of the island), sit on the wall opposite the Anglican church; to catch a ride in Fort Bay, sit on the wall opposite Saba Deep dive center, where the road begins to twist upward.

Telephones and Mail

To call Saba from the United States, dial 011/599/4 followed by the five-digit number, which always begins with a 6. On the island, it is only necessary to dial the five-digit number. Telephone communications are excellent on the island, and you can dial direct long distance.

Airmailing a letter to the United States costs NAf1.30; a postcard, NAf.60.

Opening and Closing Times

Businesses and government offices on Saba are open weekdays 8 AM to 5 PM. Most shops are closed on Sunday.

Exploring Saba

Numbers in the margin correspond to points of interest on the Saba map.

Begin your driving tour with a trip from Flat Point, at the airport, up to Hell's Gate. Because there is only one road, the tour continues along its hairpin curves up to Windwardside and then on to the Bottom and down to Fort Bay. This cross-island tour will give you a quick overview of tiny Saba, its limited cultural sights, and varied natural settings.

There are 20 sharp curves on the Road between the airport and Hell's Gate. On one of these curves, poised on Hell's Gate's hill, is the stone **Holy Rosary Church,** which looks medieval but was built in 1962. In the **community center** behind the church, village ladies sell blouses, handkerchiefs, tablecloths, and tea towels embellished with the delicate and unique Saba lace. The same ladies make innocent-sounding Saba Spice, each according to her old family recipe. The rum-based liqueur will knock your socks off.

The Road spirals past banana plantations, oleander bushes, and stunning views of the ocean below. In **Windwardside,** the island's second-largest village, perched at an altitude of 1,968 feet, you'll find rambling lanes and narrow alleyways winding through the hills and a cluster of tiny, neat houses and shops.

On your right as you enter the village is the **Church of St. Paul's Conversion,** a colonial building with a red-and-white steeple. Your next stop should be the **Saba Tourist Office** (just down the road), where you can pick up brochures and books about Saba. You may want to spend some time browsing through the **Square Nickel,** the **Breadfruit Gallery, Saba Tropical Arts,** and **Around the Bend** (*see* Shopping, *below*).

The **Saba Museum,** surrounded by lemongrass and clover, lies just behind the Captain's Quarters. There are small signs marking the way to the 150-year-old house that has been set up to look much as it did when it was a sea captain's home. Period pieces on display include a handsome mahogany four-poster bed with pineapple design, an antique organ, and, in the kitchen, a rock oven. You can also look at old documents, such as a letter a Saban wrote after the hurricane of 1772, in which he sadly says, "We have lost our little all." The first Sunday of each month, the museum holds croquet matches on its grounds; all-white attire is requested at this formal but fun social event. *Windwardside, no phone.* ☛ *$1 donation requested.* ⊙ *Weekdays 10–4.*

Near the museum are the stone and concrete steps—1,064 of them—that rise to **Mt. Scenery.** The steps lead past giant elephant ears, ferns, begonias, mangoes, palms, and orchids up to a mahogany grove at the summit: six identifiable ecosystems in all. New, helpful signs have been posted naming the trees, plants, and shrubs, and the tourist office can provide a field guide describing what you'll see along the way. On a cloudless day the view is spectacular. Have your hotel pack a picnic lunch, wear nonslip shoes, take along a jacket and a canteen of water, and hike away. The round-trip excursion will take about three hours and is best begun in the early morning.

TIME OUT   **Corner Deli and Gourmet Shop** is *the* place to pick up picnic provisions and local gossip. It was opened by native New Yorker Alan Slatky, who spent 20 years as executive chef at four-star hotels, and offers fresh salads, homemade breads, roast chicken, charcuterie, and a little bit of SoHo in Saba.

❹ Zigzag downhill from Windwardside, past the small settlement of St. John's, to **The Bottom,** which sits in a bowl-shape valley 820 feet above the sea. The Bottom is the seat of government and the home of the lieutenant governor. The gubernatorial mansion, next to Wilhelmina Park, has fancy fretwork, a high-pitched roof, and wraparound double galleries. In 1993, Saba University opened a medical school in the Bottom, at which about 70 students are enrolled.

On the other side of town is the **Wesleyan Holiness Church,** a small stone building with white fretwork, dating from 1919. Stroll by the church, beyond a place called the Gap, to a **lookout point** where you can see the 400 rough-hewn steps leading down to Ladder Bay. Ladder Bay and Fort Bay were the two landing sites from which Saba's first settlers had to haul themselves and their possessions. Sabans sometimes walk down to Ladder Bay to picnic. Think long and hard before you do: It's 400 steps back *up* to the Road.

❺ The last stop on the Road is **Fort Bay,** the jumping-off place for all of the island's dive operations (*see* Scuba Diving and Snorkeling, *below*) and the location of the St. Maarten ferry docks. There's also a gas station, a 277-foot deep-water pier that accommodates the tenders from ships that call here, and the information center for the **Saba Marine Park** (*see* Scuba Diving and Snorkeling, *below*). On the quay is a recompression chamber, one of the few in the Caribbean, and **Saba Deep's** dive shop, above which is its new snack bar, **In Two Deep.** It's a good place to catch your breath over some refreshment while enjoying the view of the water.

Off the Beaten Track

Well's Bay, Saba's famous black-sand beach, is usually around for a few months in the summer. (The sand is washed in and out by not-always-predictable ocean tides.) **Cove Bay,** a 20-foot-long strip of rocks and pebbles laced with gray sand, is now the only place for sunning (and moonlit dips after a Saturday night out). There's a picnic area there, and a small tidal pool encircled by rocks for children to swim in. The truly intrepid can then take the Road back to Lower Hell's Gate, where the Old Sulphur Mine Walk leads to bat caves (with typical sulphuric stench) that can—with caution—be explored.

Sports and the Outdoors

Boating
Saba Deep (☎ 599/4–63347) occasionally conducts one-hour, round-island cruises that include cocktails, hors d'oeuvres, and a marvelous view of the sunset.

Deep-Sea Fishing
Saba is not a big fishing destination, but a few Sabans will take you out on their boats. Keep in mind that these are not big, fancy vessels. If you want to arrange a fishing trip, contact the tourist office or Saba Deep, or ask your hotel to arrange it for you.

Hiking
You can't avoid some hiking, even if you just go to mail a postcard. The big deal, of course, is Mt. Scenery, with 1,064 slippery steps leading up to the top (*see* Exploring Saba, *above*).

For information about Saba's 18 recommended botanical hiking trails, check with the Tourist Office. Botanical tours are available upon re-

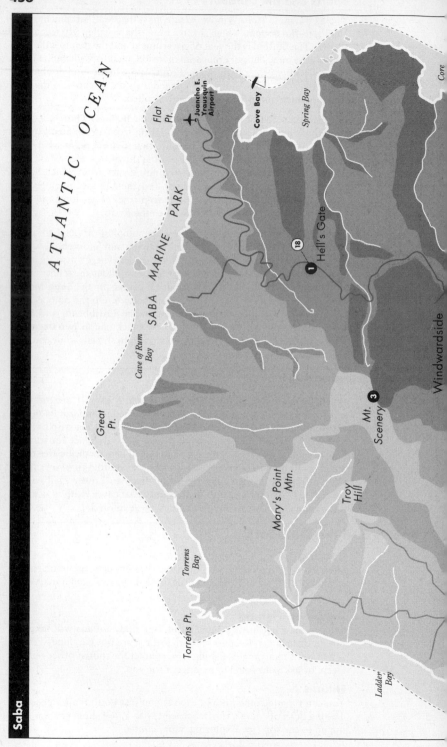

ATLANTIC OCEAN

Flat Pt.

Juancho E. Yrausquin Airport

Cove Bay

Spring Bay

Core

SABA MARINE PARK

Cave of Rum Bay

Great Pt.

Hell's Gate

18

1

3

Mt. Scenery

Windwardside

Mary's Point Mtn.

Troy Hill

Torrens Bay

Torrens Pt.

Ladder Bay

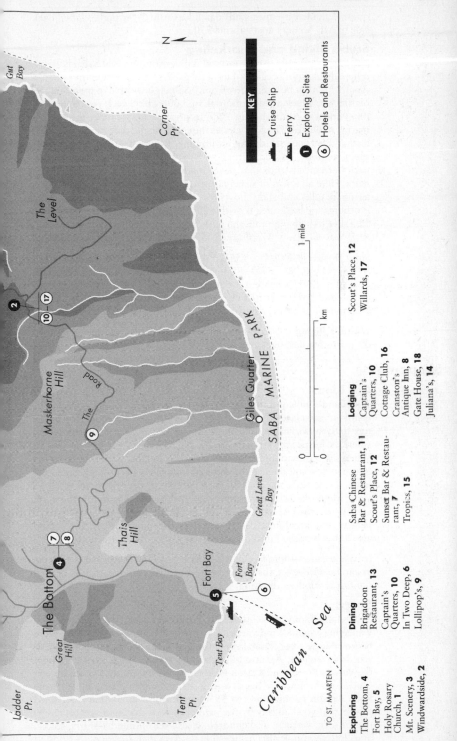

KEY

🚢 Cruise Ship

⛴ Ferry

① Exploring Sites

⑥ Hotels and Restaurants

1 mile

1 km

Exploring

The Bottom, **4**
Fort Bay, **5**
Holy Rosary
Church, **1**
Mt. Scenery, **3**
Windwardside, **2**

Dining

Brigadoon
Restaurant, **13**
Captain's
Quarters, **10**
In Two Deep, **6**
Lollipop's, **9**

Saba Chinese
Bar & Restaurant, **11**
Scout's Place, **12**
Sunset Bar & Restaurant, **7**
Tropics, **15**

Lodging

Captain's
Quarters, **10**
Cottage Club, **16**
Cranston's
Antique Inn, **8**
Gate House, **18**
Juliana's, **14**

Scout's Place, **12**
Willards, **17**

Caribbean
Sea

TO ST. MAARTEN

SABA MARINE PARK

Giles Quarter

Great Level
Bay

Fort Bay

Tent Bay

Tent Pt.

Great Hill

The Bottom

Thais Hill

The Road

Maskerhorne Hill

The Level

Corner Pt.

Gut Bay

Ladder Pt.

N

quest. A guided strenuous full-day hike through the undeveloped back side of Mt. Scenery costs about $50.

Scuba Diving and Snorkeling

Saba Bank, a fertile fishing ground 3 miles southwest of Saba, is an excellent diving spot because of its coral gardens and undersea mountains. As other islands become "dived out," Saba is dedicated to preserving its marine life, which attracts more than 3,000 divers each year. **Saba Marine Park** was established in 1987 to preserve and manage the island's marine resources. The park circles the entire island, dipping down to 200 feet, and is zoned for diving, swimming, fishing, boating, and anchorage. One of the unique features of Saba's diving is the submerged pinnacles of land (islands that never made it) at about the 70-foot depth mark. Here all forms of sea creatures rendezvous. The information center offers talks and slide shows for divers and snorkelers and provides brochures and literature on marine life. (Divers are requested to contribute $2 a dive to help maintain the park facilities.) *Harbor Office, Fort Bay,* ☎ *599/4–63295.* ☯ *Weekdays 8–5. Call first to see if anyone's around.*

Saba Deep (☎ 599/4–63347, ℻ 599/4–63397) and **Sea Saba** (☎ 599/4–62246, ℻ 599/4–62362) will take you to explore Saba's 26 dive sites. Both offer rental equipment, SSI- (Scuba Schools International) and PADI-certified instructors, and dive packages that include accommodations anywhere on the island.

Wilson's Diving (☎ 599/4–63334) in Fort Bay specializes in shorter dive trips for day-trippers.

Shopping

Gift Ideas

The island's most popular purchases are Saba lace and Saba Spice. The history of Saba lace (also called Spanish lace) goes back more than a century to Saban Gertrude Johnson, who attended a Caracas convent school where she learned the art of drawing and tying threads to adorn fine linens. When she returned home in the 1870s, she taught lacemaking to other Saban ladies, and the art has endured ever since. Every weekday Saban ladies display and sell their creations at the community center in Hell's Gate. Many also sell their wares from their houses; just follow the signs. Collars, tea towels, napkins, and other small items are relatively inexpensive, but larger items, such as tablecloths, can be pricey. You should also know that the fabric requires some care—it is not drip-dry.

Saba Spice may *sound* as delicate as Saba lace, and the aroma is as sweet as can be. However, the base for the liqueur is 151-proof rum, and all the rest is window dressing.

Shops

Saba's famed souvenirs can be found in almost every shop. While you're wandering around Windwardside, stop in at **Saba Tropical Arts,** the **Square Nickel, Peggy's Boutique, Lynn's Gallery,** the **Breadfruit Gallery, Windwardside Gallery, Around the Bend,** the **Variety Store,** the **Little Shop,** the **Variety Store,** and **Cotton Pickins.** Most of the shops (with the exception of Around the Bend) are closed on Sunday. In the Bottom, the **Saba Artisan Foundation** (☎ 599/4–63260) turns out hand-screened fabrics that you can buy by the yard or already made into resort clothing for men, women, and children. It also sells printed T-shirts, spices, and clothing. Look also for the superlative *Saban Cottages: A Book of Watercolors,* sold at the tourist office and several stores.

Dining

In most of Saba's restaurants you pretty much have to take potluck. If you don't like what's cooking in one place, you can check out the other restaurants. However, it won't take you long to run out of options, and it's tough to find gourmet cooking.

What to Wear

Restaurants here are quite informal wherever you go. Shorts or a nice cover-up over your swimsuit are a good idea during the day. For dinner you may want to put on pants or a casual sundress, but you won't find any dress requirements.

CATEGORY	COST*
$$$	over $25
$$	$20–$25
$	under $20

per person, excluding drinks and service

$$–$$$ **Captain's Quarters.** Dine in comfort, on a breezy porch surrounded by flowers and mango trees. The chef artfully blends Dutch, Indonesian, French, and Creole cuisines. Try the chicken breast served in spicy Indonesian-style peanut sauce. The fish (whatever's fresh that day) is prepared with a variety of sauces, including lime butter. On Saturday night the owner takes over the grill and barbecues steaks, chicken, and fish. Service is pleasant but can be slow. ✗ *Windwardside,* ☎ *599/4–62201. Reservations required. AE, MC, V.*

$$ **Tropics.** A black-and-white-checked tile floor, crisp black and white napery, and gleaming silver flatware create a chic, if not exactly tropical, atmosphere in this poolside restaurant. The entrées, a mix of Continental and West Indian dishes, can be on the bland side; stick with steak and simply prepared fresh seafood. Try the croquette appetizer: a spicy blend of meat lightly breaded and deep-fried. ✗ *Windwardside,* ☎ *599/4–62469. Reservations advised. MC, V. Closed Sun. No dinner Mon.–Tues.*

$–$$ ★ **Brigadoon Restaurant.** Dining in this open-front restaurant, on the first floor of a colonial building, you can enjoy the passing action on the street. Fresh fish grilled and served with a light Creole sauce is the specialty, but there are also chicken and steak dishes, lobster, and flavorful creations such as shrimp encrusted with salt and pepper. Monday night is Mexican night. ✗ *Windwardside,* ☎ *599/4–62380. AE, D, MC, V. No lunch.*

$–$$ **Lollipop's.** Owner Carmen was nicknamed Lollipop in honor of her sweet disposition. Sample her fine land crab, goat, and fresh grilled fish. Meals are served on the outdoor terrace, where stonework and a charming aqua-and-white trellis create a tranquil atmosphere. If you make a reservation, Carmen will pick you up and drop you off at your hotel after dinner. ✗ *St. John's,* ☎ *599/4–63330. No credit cards.*

$–$$ **Scout's Place.** Chef and manager Diana Medero cooks up braised steak with mushrooms, curried goat, and chicken cordon bleu. You can also opt for a simple sandwich—the crab is best. Tables covered with flowered plastic cloths are arranged on the porch and have stunning views of the water. Wednesday breakfast serves as the unofficial town meeting for expatriate locals. There is a lunch seating at 12:30 and a dinner seating at 7:30; only snacks and drinks are served during the rest of the day. ✗ *Windwardside,* ☎ *599/4–62295. Reservations required for the scheduled seatings. MC, V.*

$ **In Two Deep.** The owners of Saba Deep run this delightful harborside spot, with its stained-glass window and mahogany bar. The soups, sandwiches (especially the Reuben), and smoothies (try the lemon pucker) are excellent. The bar is plastered with humorous sayings, and customers are usually high-spirited—most have just come from a dive. ✕ *Fort Bay,* ☎ *599/4–63438. MC, V.*

$ **Saba Chinese Bar & Restaurant.** In this plain little house with plastic tablecloths you can get, among other things, sweet-and-sour pork or chicken, cashew chicken, and curried dishes. ✕ *Windwardside,* ☎ *599/4–62268. Reservations advised. No credit cards. Closed Mon.*

$ **Sunset Bar & Restaurant.** Artificial flowers and colorful place mats enliven this humble, homey place. Authentic Creole food—heavenly johnnycakes, bread tart pudding, and lip-smacking ribs—is served. ✕ *The Bottom,* ☎ *599/4–63332. No credit cards.*

Lodging

Like everything else on Saba, the guest houses are tiny and tucked into tropical gardens. The selection is limited, and because most restaurants are located in the guest houses, you would do well to take advantage of meal plans. Accommodations are invariably neat and quite reasonably priced. Saba has experienced a (relative) boom in hotel development of late. Three new properties are reviewed below, including Saba's first luxury hotel.

CATEGORY	COST*
$$$	over $125
$$	$75–$125
$	under $75

All prices are for a standard double room in high season, excluding 5% tax and 10%–15% service charge.

Hotels

$$$ **Captain's Quarters.** All the rooms here are spacious and airy, fur-
★ nished with Victorian antiques (including four-poster beds in most rooms), and decorated with floral print fabrics. Two choice bedrooms are in the small main house, which was built by a Saban sea captain in 1832. Across the parking lot from the pool is a long bungalow unit holding six rooms; numbers 7 through 10 can easily sleep four. Two rooms with stunning views of the sea were added in 1994 in a building behind the bar, and there are plans to add more rooms and a new dining area. For now, dining is in a shaded garden pavilion surrounded by hibiscus, poinsettia, and papaya trees. ⌷ *Windwardside,* ☎ *599/4–62201,* ℻ *599/4–62377, in NY* ☎ *212/289–6031. 10 rooms. Restaurant, bar, pool. AE, MC, V. CP.*

$$$ **Willards.** This is the most luxurious place to stay on the island, set on the side of a cliff with stunning panoramic vistas of the Caribbean. Spacious rooms and bungalows are individually decorated, but all have tile floors, white walls, ceiling fans, rattan furniture, and a balcony. The three types of room—bungalow, luxury, and VIP—vary in size, furnishings, and whether the bathroom contains a tub or shower. Willards does not allow children younger than 14. ⌷ *Box 515, Windwardside,* ☎ *599/4–62498 or 800/223–9815,* ℻ *599/4–62482. 10 rooms. Restaurant, bar, heated pool, hot tub, tennis court. AE, MC, V. EP, MAP.*

$$ **Cottage Club.** Local brothers Dean and Mark Johnson run this new property. Ten gingerbread bungalows are nestled amid rainbow-hued tropical gardens, their balconies overlooking either the water or the village of English Quarter. Interiors are large and breezy, with gleaming tile floors and high beamed ceilings. Pastel shell prints are used for drapes and spreads, and local art decorates the walls. Each bungalow has its own fully equipped kitchen, dining area, bath (shower only),

balcony, telephone, and cable TV. The stone, colonial-style main house holds the reception area and is a showplace for antiques from the owners' collection, accented with potted plants and Saban-lace curtains. Bungalows 1 and 2 have the best views. A pool is planned, as is a conference room. If you give the owners a shopping list, they'll stock your kitchen for you. ⊞ *Windwardside,* ☎ *599/4–62486,* FAX *599/4–62476. 10 units. Grocery delivery. MC, V. EP.*

$$ **Gate House.** Two ex–New Yorkers run this secluded six-room inn in the tiny village of Hell's Gate. The secluded location, between the airport and Windwardside, makes this somewhat of a getaway, even for Saba. Spacious rooms have whitewashed walls and tile floors and are decorated with crisp pinstripe and checked fabrics and colorful art. Two units have kitchenettes. The new restaurant off the lobby looks out to the sea and is creating an admiring buzz on the island. Chef Beverly changes the menu of local specialties daily; the prix fixe dinner is $20. ⊞ *Hell's Gate,* ☎ *599/4–62416; in U.S., 708/354–9641;* FAX *599/4– 62415. 6 rooms. Restaurant. MC, V. CP, MAP.*

$$ **Juliana's.** Juliana and Franklin Johnson's comfortable, tidy studios have tile floors, light wood furnishings, and floral print spreads. One has a queen-size bed; the others have doubles or twins. There's also a 2½-room apartment (Flossie's Cottage) with a kitchenette, a living-dining room, and a bedroom, as well as a large porch facing the sea. Almost every window has fabulous views of the Caribbean. Across the street is the pool, and the café, Tropics (*see* Dining, *above*). ⊞ *Windwardside,* ☎ *599/4–62269; in U.S., 800/223–981;* FAX *599/4–62289. 11 studios, 1 apartment. Restaurant, pool. MC, V. EP.*

$–$$ **Scout's Place.** Accurately billed as "Bed 'n Board, Cheap 'n Cheerful," Scout's Place makes up in convenience and value what it lacks in luxury. Staying here puts you in the center of Windwardside, within walking distance of Sea Saba dive center. The four original rooms are extremely plain and have no hot water; two even share a bath. Ten newer rooms do have hot water (in private bathrooms), as well as four-poster beds and balconies. The restaurant serves a full breakfast. ⊞ *Windwardside,* ☎ *599/4–62205,* FAX *599/4–62388. 14 rooms, 12 with private bath. Restaurant, pool, bar, gift shop, car rentals. MC, V. EP, CP.*

$ **Cranston's Antique Inn.** The six rooms of this slightly run-down spot are popular digs for the diving set. The shared baths are far from luxurious (dingy decor à la early '70s), but the rooms have attractive hardwood floors and are neatly decorated with pink or blue fabrics and dark wood antiques; most have four-poster beds. The pool bar is festive, and the Inner Circle disco is practically across the street. There are plans to add private baths, but don't expect them anytime soon. ⊞ *The Bottom,* ☎ *and fax 599/4–63203. 6 rooms, 1 with private bath. Restaurant, pool, bar. D, MC, V. EP.*

Apartment Rentals

Twelve apartments, cottages, and villas, all with hot water and modern conveniences, are available for daily, weekly, and monthly rentals. For a listing of all rental properties, check with the **Saba Tourist Office** (*see* Important Addresses, *above*).

Nightlife

Guido's Pizzeria (Windwardside, ☎ 599/4–62330) is transformed into the Mountain High Club disco on Friday and Saturday nights, and you can dance till 2 AM. Do the nightclub scene at the **Inner Circle** (The Bottom, ☎ 599/4–62240), or just hang out at **Scout's Place** or the **Captain's Quarters.** Consult the bulletin board in each village for a listing of the week's events.

19 St. Barthélemy

T. BARTHÉLEMY'S MAGIC lies in the way this tiny tropical isle blends the essence of the Caribbean with the essence of France. You can spend the day on a deserted beach lying under a palm tree, then shower and choose from more than 50 excellent restaurants for an elegant meal. When you tire of the sun, you can easily drive all over the island, taking in the vistas and the soft breezes, and then stop off for an exquisitely prepared gourmet lunch. Or you can head to one of the three shopping areas for duty-free French perfumes and the latest in French fashion.

Updated by
Marcy
Pritchard

The island itself is a mere 8 square miles, with lots of hills and sheltered inlets. Gustavia, the only real town, wraps itself neatly around a lilliputian harbor. Red-roof bungalows dot the hillsides. And beaches that run the gamut from calm to "surfable," shell to fine white sand, and crowded to deserted encircle the island. The French cuisine here is tops in the Caribbean, and gourmet lunches and dinners are rallying points of island life. A French *savoir vivre* pervades, and the island is definitely for the style conscious—casual but always chic. This is no place for the beach-bum set.

Rothschild owns property and Rockefeller built an estate here, and for a long time the island, 15 miles from St. Martin in the French West Indies, was the haunt of the well heeled and well informed. While the island still has cachet, and remains largely a retreat for the wealthy, the tourist base has expanded in the last decade. Last year almost 200,000 visitors stopped by, including day-trippers from nearby islands and passengers from cruise ships that anchor just outside the harbor.

Longtime visitors speak wistfully of the old, quiet St. Barts. While development *has* quickened the pace, the island has not been overrun with prefab condos or glitzy resorts. The largest hotel has fewer than 100 rooms, and the remaining rooms are scattered in about 40 small hotels around the island; no high-rises are allowed. The tiny airport accommodates nothing bigger than 19-passenger planes (and these only during daylight hours), and there aren't any casinos or flashy late-night attractions. Moreover, St. Barts is generally not a destination for the budget-minded. Development has largely been in luxury lodgings and gourmet restaurants.

When Christopher Columbus "discovered" the island in 1493, he named it after his brother, Bartholomeo. A small group of French colonists arrived from nearby St. Kitts in 1656 but were wiped out by the fierce Carib Indians who dominated the area. A new group from Normandy and Brittany arrived in 1694. This time the settlers prospered—with the help of French buccaneers, who took full advantage of the island's strategic location and well-protected harbor. In 1784 the French traded the island to King Gustav III of Sweden in exchange for port rights in Göteborg. He dubbed the capital Gustavia, laid out and paved streets, built three forts, and turned the capital into a prosperous free port. The island thrived as a major shipping and commercial center until the 19th century, when earthquakes, fire, and hurricanes brought financial ruin. Many residents fled for newer lands of opportunity, and in 1878 France agreed to repurchase its beleaguered former colony.

Today the island is still a free port and, as a dependency of Guadeloupe, is part of an overseas department of France. Dry, sunny, and stony, St. Barts was never one of the Caribbean's "sugar islands" and thus never developed an industrial slave base. Most natives are descendants of those tough Norman and Breton settlers of three centuries ago. They are feisty, industrious, and friendly but insular. However, you will find many new, young French arrivals—predominantly from northwestern France—who speak English well.

You may hear some old timers speak the old Norman patois of their ancestors or see the older women dressed in the traditional garb of provincial France. They have prospered with the tourist boom, but some are worried that the upward swing of prices may threaten business, especially tour groups and families. So far, though, this gem of an island continues to draw an ever-widening circle of fans.

Be aware that timing here is very important. A larger number of hotels and restaurants here have seasonal closings than on other islands. There are still some places open in August, but your selections will be more limited; places begin reopening at the end of October. Fortunately, the gorgeous beaches never close. The advantage of traveling in the off-season is enormous savings—sometimes half of the high-season rate.

Before You Go

Tourist Information
Information can be obtained by writing the **French West Indies Tourist Board** (610 5th Ave., New York, NY 10020) or by calling France-on-Call at 900/990–0040 (50¢ per minute). You can also write to or visit the **French Government Tourist Office** (444 Madison Ave., 16th Floor, New York, NY 10022; 9454 Wilshire Blvd., Suite 303, Beverly Hills, CA 90212; 645 N. Michigan Ave., Suite 3360, Chicago, IL 60611; 1981 McGill College Ave., Suite 490, Montreal, Québec H3A 2W9, ☎ 514/288–4264; 30 St. Patrick St., Suite 700, Toronto, Ontario M5T 3A3, ☎ 416/593–4723; and 178 Piccadilly, London W1V OAL, ☎ 0171/629–9376).

Arriving and Departing
BY PLANE
The principal gateway from North America is St. Maarten's Juliana International Airport. Although it is only 10 minutes by air to St. Barts, the last 2 may take your breath away. Don't worry when you see those treetops out your window. You're just clearing a hill before dropping down to the runway. Flights leave at least once an hour between 7:30 AM and 5:30 PM on either **Windward Islands Airways** (☎ 590/27–61–01 or 599/5–4230) or **Air St. Barthélemy** (☎ 590/87–73–46 or 599/5–3150). **Air Guadeloupe** (☎ 599/5–4212 or 590/87–53–74) and **Air St. Barthélemy** offer daily service from Espérance Airport in St. Martin, the French side of the same island. Air Guadeloupe also has direct flights to St. Barts from Guadeloupe and San Juan, while **Air St. Thomas** (☎ 590/27–71–76) operates daily flights between St. Barts and both St. Thomas and San Juan. You must reconfirm your return interisland flight, even during off-peak seasons, or you may very well lose your reservation.

FROM THE AIRPORT
Airport taxi service costs $5–$15 (to the farthest hotel). Since the cabs are unmetered, you may be charged more if you make stops on the way. Cabs meet some flights, and a taxi dispatcher (☎ 590/27–66–31) is there some of the time, but if you plan to rent a car, which most people do, it's really easiest to do it at the airport. Many hotels offer free pickup and drop-off.

BY BOAT

Catamarans leave Philipsburg in St. Maarten at 9 AM daily, arriving in Gustavia's harbor around 11 AM. These are one-day, round-trip excursions (about $50, including open bar), with departures from St. Barts at 3:30 PM. If there's room, one-way passengers ($25) are often taken as well. The seas can be choppy, and it is not uncommon for passengers to get seasick. Contact **Bobby's Marina** in Philipsburg (☎ 599/5–23170) for reservations. The *St. Barth Express* (☎ 590/27–77–24) sails between Gustavia, Philipsburg (Bobby's Marina), and Marigot (Port la Royale) at 7:30 AM and leaves Marigot at 3:30 PM for the return trip (stopping at Philipsburg). The *Dauphin II* (☎ 590/27–84–38) leaves Gustavia for Marigot at 7:15 AM and 3:45 PM; the crossing takes a little over an hour. The boat departs from Marigot at 8:45 AM and 5:15 PM and goes directly to St. Barts. One-way fare is $35 and round-trip $50. **St. Barth Yachting Service** (☎ 590/27–64–49), **Sibarth** (☎ 590/27–62–38), **Marine Service** (☎ 590/27–70–34), and **OcéanMust Marina** (☎ 590/27–62–25) in Gustavia have boats for private charter.

Passports and Visas

U.S. and Canadian citizens need either a passport (one that expired no more than five years ago will suffice) or a notarized birth certificate with a raised seal accompanied by photo identification. A valid passport is required for stays of more than three months. British and other EU citizens need a national identity card. All visitors need a return or ongoing ticket.

Language

French is the official language, though a Norman dialect is spoken by some longtime islanders. Most hotel and restaurant employees speak some English—at least enough to help you get or find what you want or need.

Precautions

Roads are frequently unmarked, so be sure to get a map. Instead of road signs, look for signs pointing to a destination. These will be nailed to posts at all crossroads. Roads are narrow and sometimes very steep, so check the brakes and gears of your rental car *before* you drive away. St. Barts drivers seem to be in some kind of unending grand prix and keep their minimokes (the car of choice on this island) maxed out at all times. Prepare yourself for cars charging every which way, making sudden changes in direction while honking wildly, and backing up at astonishingly high speeds. They pause for no one. Some hillside restaurants and hotels have steep entranceways and difficult steps that require a bit of climbing or negotiating. If this could be a problem for you, ask about accessibility ahead of time.

Staying in St. Barthélemy

Important Addresses

Tourist Information: The **Office du Tourisme** (☎ 590/27–87–27, FAX 590/27–74–47) is in a white building on the Gustavia pier; the people who work there are most eager to please. Hours are Monday through Friday from 8:30 to 6 and Saturday from 9 to noon.

EMERGENCIES

Hospital: Gustavia Clinic (☎ 590/27–60–35) is on the corner of rue Jean Bart and rue Sadi Carnot. For the doctor on call, dial 590/27–76–03. **Pharmacies:** There is a pharmacy in Gustavia on quai de la République (☎ 590/27–61–82) and one in St. Jean at the La Savane Commercial Center (☎ 590/27–66–61).

Currency

The French franc is legal tender. Figure about 5.5F to the U.S. dollar. U.S. dollars are accepted in most establishments, but you may receive change in francs. Credit cards are accepted at most shops, hotels, and restaurants. Note: Prices quoted here are in U.S. dollars unless indicated otherwise.

Taxes and Service Charges

A 10F departure tax is charged for departure to other French islands, and a 16F departure tax is charged to all other destinations. Some hotels add a 10%–15% service charge to bills; others include it in their tariffs. Most restaurants include a 15% service charge in their published prices. It is especially important to remember this when your credit-card receipt is presented to be signed with the tip space blank (just draw a line through it), or you could end up paying a 30% service charge.

Most taxi drivers own their vehicles and do not expect a tip.

Guided Tours

Tours are by minibus or taxi. There are three tours offered by the tourist office (approximately 45 minutes, 1 hour, or 1½ hours in length); these are less expensive—about $10 per person for the shortest one—than private tours. A private five-hour island tour costs about $100 per vehicle (three–four people); an hour-long tour costs about $40 for up to three people and $50 for up to eight people. Itineraries are negotiable.

Tours can be arranged at hotel desks, through the tourist office, or by calling any of the island's taxi operators, including **Hugo Cagan** (☎ 590/27–61–28) and **Florian La Place** (☎ 590/27–63–58). If you don't speak French, be sure to request a driver whose English is good.

Helicopter tours are offered by **Trans Helico Caraibes** (☎ 590/27–40–68) for about $65 per person.

Getting Around

TAXIS

Taxis are expensive and not particularly easy to arrange, especially in the evening. There are two taxi stations on the island, in Gustavia and at the airport. You may also arrange cab service by calling 590/27–66–32, 590/27–60–59, or 590/27–63–12. There is a flat rate of 25F for rides up to five minutes long. Each additional three minutes is 20F. Fares are 50% higher from 8 PM to 6 AM and on Sunday and holidays.

RENTAL CARS

Most people opt to rent cars. There are excellent beaches, restaurants, and vistas all around the island. Beware the steep, curvy, haphazardly paved roads; get a map; and check the rental car's brakes before you drive away. The most common rental car is a minimoke, a small open-air vehicle with a bumper-car feel. **Avis** (☎ 590/27–71–43), **Budget** (☎ 590/27–67–43), **Hertz** (☎ 590/27–71–14), and **Europcar** (☎ 590/27–73–33) are represented at the airport, among others. Check with several of the rental counters for the best price. All accept credit cards. You must have a valid driver's license, and in high season there may be a three-day minimum (or no cars available). In February especially, arrange for your car rental ahead of time. Your choices will most likely be limited to minimokes, Suzuki Jeeps, and open-sided Gurgels (VW Jeep)—all with stick shift only, which rent in season for $40–$45 a day, with unlimited mileage and limited collision insurance. You may find a Jeep, which is sturdier, preferable to the chic but rickety minimokes. A few hotels have their own car fleets, and a car should be rented at the time you make your room reservation. The choice of vehicles may be limited, but many hotels offer 24-hour emergency road service, which most rental companies do not. There are only two gas stations on the island, one near the airport and one in Lorient. They are not open on Sunday or after 5 PM, but you can use the one near the airport with a credit card at any time.

MOTORBIKES

Motorbike companies rent motorbikes, scooters, mopeds, and mountain bikes. Motorbikes go for about $30 per day and require a $100 deposit. Call **Rent Some Fun** (☎ 590/27–70–59).

HITCHHIKING

Hitching rides is a popular, legal, and interesting way to get around; it is widely practiced in the more heavily trafficked areas on the island.

Telephones and Mail

To phone St. Barts from the United States, dial 011–590 and the local six-digit number. To call the United States from St. Barts, dial 19–1, the area code, and the local number. For St. Martin, dial just the six-digit number; for St. Maarten, dial 3 plus the five-digit number. For local information, dial 12. Public telephones do not accept coins; they accept Telecartes, a type of prepaid credit card that you can purchase from the post offices at Lorient, St. Jean, and Gustavia, as well as at the gas station next to the airport. Making an international call with a Telecarte is less expensive than making the call from your hotel.

Mail is slow. It can take up to three weeks for correspondence between the United States and the island. Post offices are in Gustavia, St. Jean, and Lorient. It costs 3.10F to mail a postcard to the United States, 3.90F to mail a letter.

Opening and Closing Times

Businesses and offices close from noon to 2 during the week and are closed on Saturday and Sunday. Shops are generally open weekdays 8:30–noon and 2–5, and Saturday 8:30 to noon. Some of the shops across from the airport and in St. Jean also open on Saturday afternoon and until 7 PM on weekdays. The banks are open weekdays 8–noon and 2–3:30.

Exploring St. Barthélemy

Numbers in the margin correspond to points of interest on the St. Barthélemy map.

Gustavia and the West

❶ With just a few streets on three sides of its tiny harbor, **Gustavia** is easily explored in a two-hour stroll. Here you will find excellent shopping, many restaurants and cafés, and a museum. Remember that most shops close from noon to 2, so you might want to combine shopping with an enjoyable lunch at one of the restaurants overlooking the harbor.

A good place to park your car is harborside on the rue de la République, where flashy catamarans, yachts, and sailboats are moored. If you haven't gotten a map or have some questions, head to the **tourist office** on the pier, where you can pick up an island map and a free copy of *St. Barth Magazine*, a monthly publication on island happenings. If you feel like stopping for a café au lait and a croissant, settle in at either **Bar de l'Oubli** or **Le Select** (*see* Nightlife, *below*), two cafés just a few steps away. As you stroll through the little streets, you will notice that plaques sometimes spell out names in both French and Swedish, a reminder of the days when the island was a Swedish colony. Small shops along **rue du**

Roi Oscar II, rue de la France, rue du Bord de Mer, and **rue du Général de Gaulle** sell French perfumes, the latest in French and Italian designer wear for men and women, resort wear, crystal, gold jewelry, and other luxury items.

If you feel like a swim, drive to the end of the harbor, turn onto **rue Victor Hugo,** turn right on **rue de l'Eglise,** and follow the road to **Petit Anse de Galet.** This quiet little *plage* is also known as Shell Beach because of the tiny shells heaped ankle-deep in some places.

On the far side of the harbor known as **Le Pointe** is the charming **Municipal Museum,** where you will find watercolors, portraits, photographs, and historic documents detailing the island's history as well as displays of the island's flowers, plants, and marine life. ☎ *599/27–89–07.* ☞ *10F.* ☉ *Mon.–Thurs. 8–noon and 1:30–5:30, Fri. 8–noon and 1:30–5, Sat. 8:30–noon.*

For a good beach and some spectacular vistas, head south out of town, following the signs to Lurin. (You'll head up the hill past the Carl Gustaf Hotel.) The views of the harbor get better and better the higher up you go. After about five minutes, look for a sign to Plage du Gouverneur. A small rocky route off to the right will take you bumping and grinding down a steep incline to **Anse du Gouverneur,** one of St. Barts's most beautiful beaches, where pirate's treasure is said to be buried. If the weather is clear, you will be able to see the islands of Saba, St. Eustatius, and St. Kitts.

TIME OUT   The hilltop **Sante Fe Restaurant** (Morne Lorne, at the turnoff to Gouverneur's Beach, ☎ 590/27–61–04) is a popular spot for sunsets and American-style hamburgers. Sunday afternoons it's jammed with Americans and Brits cheering their favorite teams on the TV.

Corossol, Colombier, Flamands
Starting at the intersection on the hilltop overlooking the airport (known as Tourmente), take the road to Public Beach and on to
 Corossol, a two-street fishing village with a little beach. Corossol is where the island's French provincial origins are most evident. Residents speak an old Norman dialect, and some of the older women still wear traditional garb—ankle-length dresses, bare feet, and starched white sunbonnets called *quichenottes* (kiss-me-not hats). The women don't like to be photographed. However, they are not shy about selling you some of their handmade straw work—handbags, baskets, broad-brim hats, and delicate strings of birds—made from lantana palms. The palms were introduced to the island 100 years ago by foresighted Father Morvan, who planted a grove in Corossol and Flamands, thus providing the country folk with a living that is still pursued today. Here, too, is the **Inter Oceans Museum,** which features more than 7,000 seashells from around the world. ☎ *590/27–62–97.* ☞ *20F.* ☉ *Daily 9–5.*

③ From Corossol, head down the main road about a mile to **Anse des Flamands,** a wide beach with several small hotels, including the St. Barth Isle de France, and many rental villas. From here, take a brisk hike to the top of the now-extinct volcano that is believed to have given birth to St. Barts. From the peak you can take in the gorgeous view of the islands.

A drive to the end of Flamands Road brings you to a rocky footpath that leads to the island's most remote beach, **Anse de Colombier.**

St. Jean, Grand Cul de Sac, Saline

4 Brimming with bungalows, bistros, sunbathers, and windsurfing sails, the half-mile crescent of sand at **St. Jean** is the island's most popular beach. Informal restaurants are scattered here and there along the shore, and windsurfers skim along the water, catching the strong breezes. If you walk as far to the west as possible, you can get a close look at the little planes taking off from the airport. For respite from the sun, cross the street near Eden Rock and you will find many branches of Gustavia boutiques and several restaurants.

5 Leaving St. Jean, take the main road to **Lorient.** On your left are the royal palms and rolling waves of Lorient Beach. Lorient, site of the first French settlement, is one of the island's two parishes, and a restored church, historic headstones, a school, post office, and gas station mark the spot.

Turn right before the gleaming white Lorient cemetery. In a short while you'll reach a dusty cutoff to your right. The pretty little Creole house on your left is home to Ligne de Cosmetiques M (*see* Shopping, *below*). Behind it is one of St. Barthélemy's treasured secrets, **Le Manoir.** The 1610 Norman manor was painstakingly shipped from France and reconstructed here in 1984 by the charming Jeanne Audy Rowland in tribute to the island's Viking forebears. The tranquil surrounding courtyard and garden contain a waterfall and a lily-strewn pool. Madame Rowland graciously allows visitors. The manor guest rooms and its cottage are also available at a very reasonable daily or weekly rate (☎ 590/27–79–27), "but you must have an artist's soul," she requests sweetly and earnestly. It also helps if you speak some French.

Retrace your route back to Lorient and continue along the coast. Turn left at the Mont Jean sign. Your route rolls around the island's pretty windward coves, past **Pointe Milou,** an elegant residential colony, and on to **Marigot,** where you can pick up a bottle of fine wine at **La Cave.** The bargain prices may surprise you (*see* Shopping, *below*).

The winding road passes through the mangroves, ponds, and beach of **Grand Cul de Sac,** where there are plenty of excellent beachside restaurants and water-sports concessions.

TIME OUT **Chez Pompi** (Petit Cul de Sac, ☎ 590/27–75–67), on the road to Toiny, is a delightful cottage straight from a Cézanne painting. Pompi (aka Louis Ledee) is an artist of some repute, whose naive, slightly abstract artwork clutters the walls of his tiny studio. You can browse and chat with the amiable Monsieur Pompi while enjoying his fine Creole and country French cuisine.

6 Over the hills beyond Grand Cul de Sac is the much-photographed **Toiny coast.** Drystone fences crisscross the steep slopes of Morne Vitet along a rocky shoreline that resembles the rugged coast of Normandy. The road turns inland and up the slopes of Morne de Grand Fond. At the first fork (less than a mile), the road to the right leads back to Lorient. A left-hand turn at the next intersection will bring you within a **7** few minutes to a dead end at **Grande Saline.** The big salt ponds of Grande Saline are no longer in use, and the place looks desolate, but climb the short hillock behind the ponds for a surprise—the long arc of **Anse de Grande Saline.**

Beaches

There are nearly 20 *plages* (beaches) scattered around the island, each with a distinctive personality and all of them public. Even in season,

St. Barthélemy

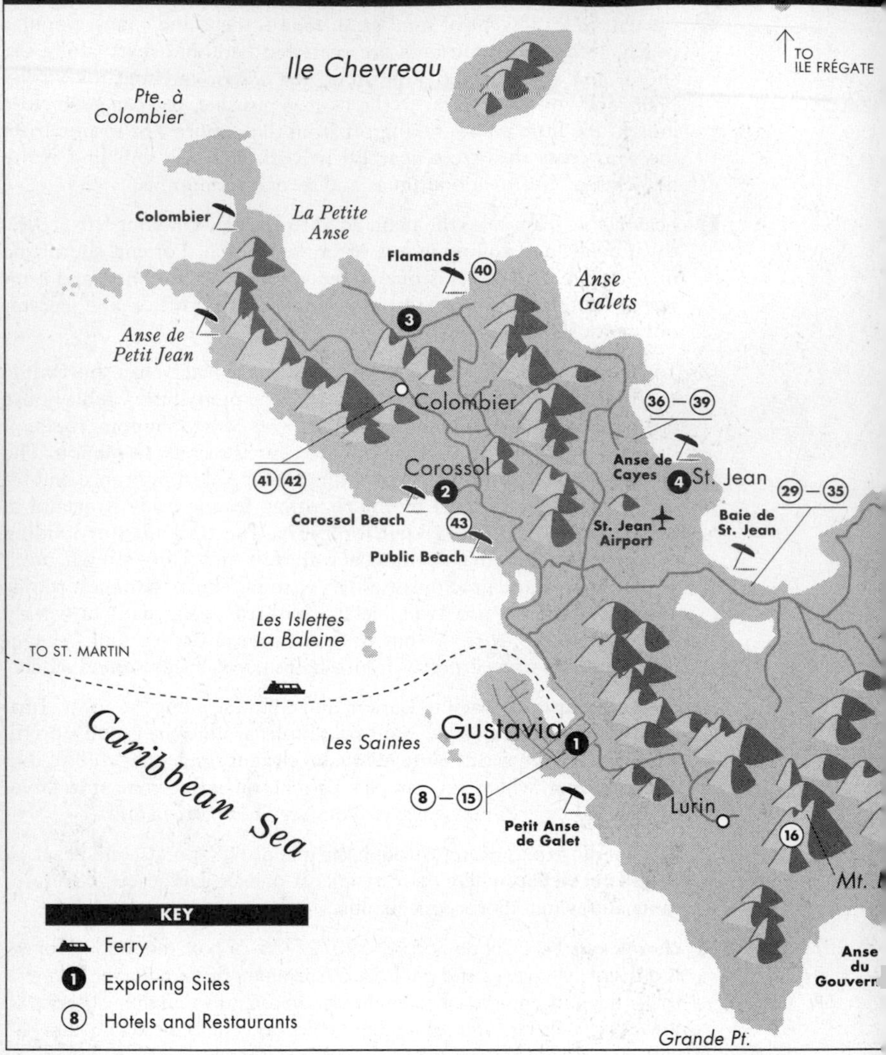
Ile Chevreau
TO ILE FRÉGATE
Pte. à Colombier
Colombier
La Petite Anse
Flamands
40
Anse Galets
Anse de Petit Jean
3
Colombier
36–39
41 42
Corossol
2
Anse de Cayes
4
St. Jean
29–35
Corossol Beach
43
St. Jean Airport
Baie de St. Jean
Public Beach
Les Islettes La Baleine
TO ST. MARTIN
Caribbean Sea
Les Saintes
Gustavia
1
8–15
Petit Anse de Galet
Lurin
16
Anse du Gouverr
Grande Pt.
KEY
Ferry
Exploring Sites
Hotels and Restaurants

Exploring
Anse des Flamands, **3**
Corossol, **2**
Grande Saline, **7**
Gustavia, **1**
Lorient, **5**
St. Jean, **4**
Toiny coast, **6**

Dining
Adam, **29**
Brasserie La Creole, **30**
Carl Gustaf, **12**
Eddy's Ghetto, **11**
François Plantation, **41**
Gloriette, **19**
L'Escale, **8**
L'Orchidée, **26**
Lafayette Club , **18**
La Marine, **15**
La Toque Lyonnaise, **20**
Le Flamboyant, **21**
Le Gaiac, **17**
Le Patio, **38**
Le Repaire, **9**
Le Rivage, **22**
Le Sapotillier, **13**
Marigot Bay Club, **24**
Maya's, **43**
New Born, **36**
Pasta Paradise, **10**
Topolino, **32**
Wall House, **14**

↑ TO
ILE TOC VERS

ATLANTIC OCEAN

Les Grenadiers

La Tortue

Pte. Milou (26)

(27)(28) **Lorient**

Lorient

Marigot (24) (23) **Marechal Beach**

Marigot

(18)—(22)

Grand Cul de Sac

(5)

Petit Cul de Sac

Mt. du Grand Fond

(25)

Vitet (25)

Toiny

○ *Morne de Grand Fond*

Morne Vitet (17)

(6)

Grande Saline (7)

Pt. à Toiny

Anse de Grand Fond

N

Grande Saline

Lurin

eur

Pt. du Gouverneur

0 — 1 mile

0 — 1 km

Lodging

Baie des Flamands, **40**
Carl Gustaf, **12**
Castelets, **16**
Club La Banane, **27**
Eden Rock, **31**
El Sereno Beach Hotel and Villas, **20**

Filao Beach, **33**
François Plantation, **41**
Guanahani, **23**
Hostellerie des Trois Forces, **25**
Hotel Christopher, **26**
Hotel Manapany Cottages, **37**

Hotel St. Barth Isle de France, **40**
Hotel Yuana, **39**
La Normandie, **28**
Le P'tit Morne, **42**
Le Toiny, **17**
Tropical Hotel, **34**
Village St. Jean, **35**

it is possible to find a nearly empty beach. Topless sunbathing is common, but nudism is forbidden. Here are the main attractions:

St. Jean is like a mini Côte d'Azur—beachside bistros, bungalow hotels, bronze beauties, windsurfing, and lots of day-trippers. The reef-protected strip is divided by Eden Rock promontory, and there's good snorkeling west of the rock. **Lorient** is popular with St. Barts's families and surfers, who like its rolling waves. **Marigot** is a tiny, calm beach with good snorkeling along the rocky far end. Shallow, reef-protected **Grand Cul de Sac** is especially nice for small children and windsurfers; it has excellent lunch spots and lots of pelicans. Around the point, next to the Guanahani Hotel, is tiny **Marechal Beach,** which offers some of the best snorkeling on the island. Secluded **Grande Saline,** with its sandy ocean bottom, is just about everyone's favorite beach and is great for swimmers. Despite the law, young and old alike go nude on this beach. It can get windy here, so go on a calm day. **Anse du Gouverneur** is even more secluded and equally beautiful, with good snorkeling and views of St. Kitts, Saba, and St. Eustatius.

A five-minute walk from Gustavia is **Petit Anse de Galet,** named after the tiny shells on its shore. Both **Public Beach** and **Corossol Beach** are best for boat- and sunset-watching. The beach at **Colombier** is the least accessible but the most private; you'll have to take either a rocky footpath from La Petite Anse or brave the 30-minute climb down a cactus-bordered trail from the top of the mountain behind the beach. **Flamands** is the most beautiful of the hotel beaches—a roomy strip of silken sand.

Sports and the Outdoors

Boating
St. Barts is a popular yachting and sailing center, thanks to its location midway between Antigua and St. Thomas. Gustavia's harbor, 13 to 16 feet deep, has mooring and docking facilities for 40 yachts, with good anchorages available at Public, Corossol, and Colombier. **Loulou's Marine** (☎ 590/27–62–74) is the place for yachting information and supplies. **Marine Service** (☎ 590/27–70–34) offers full-day outings on a 40-foot catamaran to the uninhabited Ile Fourchue for swimming, snorkeling, cocktails, and lunch; the cost is $90 per person. Marine Service also arranges deep-sea-fishing trips, with a full-day charter of a 32-foot crewed cabin cruiser running $800; an unskippered motor rental runs about $260 a day. You can also take an hour's cruise on the glass-bottom boat *L'Aquascope* by contacting Marine Service. **Sibarth's** yacht charter agency (☎ 590/27–62–38) offers sunset and half- and full-day sails. **OcéanMust Marina** (☎ 590/27–62–25) in Gustavia also has charters.

Diving and Deep-Sea Fishing
Deep-sea fishing can be arranged through **Sibarth's** yacht charter agency (☎ 590/27–62–38), **Marine Service** (☎ 590/27–70–34), or **OcéanMust Marina** (☎ 590/27–62–25). Marine Service also operates a PADI-certified diving center, with scuba-diving trips for about $50 per person, gear included. The CMAS-certified **Club La Bulle** (☎ 590/27–62–25) and PADI-certified **Dive with Dan** (☎ 590/27–64–78) are other scuba options. Small groups should call **St. Barth Plongée** (☎ 590/27–63–33) in Gustavia for dive or snorkeling excursions.

Horseback Riding
Laure Nicolas leads two-hour excursions for $35 per person from **Ranch des Flamands** (Anse des Flamands, ☎ 590/27–80–72).

Tennis

If you wish to play tennis at a hotel at which you are not a guest, be sure to call ahead to inquire about fees and reservations. There are two lighted tennis courts at the **Guanahani** (☎ 590/27–66–60), **Le Flamboyant Tennis Club** (☎ 590/27–69–82), and the **Sports Center of Colombier** (☎ 590/27–61–07). There is one lighted court each at the **Hotel Manapany Cottages** (☎ 590/27–66–55), the **Taiwana** (☎ 590/27–65–01), the **St. Barth's Beach Hotel** (☎ 590/27–60–70), and the **St. Barth Isle de France** (☎ 590/27–61–81), which also has the island's only squash court. **Les Ilets de la Plage** (590/27–62–38) has one unlighted court.

Windsurfing

Windsurfing fever has definitely caught on here. Boards can be rented for about $20 an hour at water-sports centers along St. Jean and Grand Cul de Sac beaches. Lessons are offered for about $40 an hour at **St. Barth Wind School** (St. Jean, ☎ 590/27–71–22) and at **Wind Wave Power** (St. Barths Beach Hotel, ☎ 590/27–60–70), which also has parasailing.

Shopping

St. Barts is a duty-free port, and there are especially good bargains in jewelry, porcelain, imported liquors, and French perfumes, cosmetics, and designer resort wear.

Shopping Areas

Shops are clustered in **Gustavia, La Savane Commercial Center,** which is across from the airport, and **La Villa Creole,** an appealing shopping complex in St. Jean. A gourmet supermarket is located across from the airport, and there is a second one just east of the airport that specializes in fresh fruits and vegetables.

Good Buys

CLOTHING

A number of boutiques in all three shopping areas carry the latest in French and Italian sportswear and haute couture fashion items. The price tags may astound you (even after you convert the francs to dollars you may still be in high three-figures), but these prices are actually well below the Paris price for the same item, and so they are considered bargains by some. Shops to look for include Stéphane & Bernard, Kokonuts, Libertine, Hermès, Gucci, and Black Swan, all of which are in Gustavia and have branches either across from the airport or in St. Jean or both; but there are many other stores and boutiques to be found. At both St. Jean's La Villa Creole and La Savane (across from the airport), it is worth working your way from one end of the shopping complex to the other.

ISLAND CRAFTS

Stop in Corossol to pick up some of the intricate straw work (wide-brim beach hats, mobiles, handbags) that the ladies of Corossol create by hand (see Exploring St. Barthélemy, above). In Gustavia, look for hand-turned pottery at **St. Barts Pottery** (☎ 590/27–62–74). You'll see coral and exotic shell jewelry at the **Shell Shop** (no ☎). Superb local skin-care products are available at **Ligne de Cosmetiques M** (☎ 590/27–82–63) in Lorient (see Exploring St. Barthélemy, above). Gustavia also has a new market, **Le 'Ti Marché,** dedicated to art and crafts handmade on the island. Open every day except Sunday, the market is set up in stalls on the corner of rue du Roi Oscar II near the city hall. The much-sought-after Belou's P line of aromatic oils is available here. For details call 590/27–83–72 or the tourist office.

WINE AND GOURMET SHOPS

Wine lovers will enjoy **La Cave** (Marigot, ☎ 590/27–63–21), where an excellent collection of French vintages is stored in temperature-controlled cellars. Also check out **La Cave du Port Franc** (☎ 590/27–65–27), on the far side of the harbor, for vintage wines, contemporary paintings, and objets d'art.

For exotic groceries or picnic fixings, stop by one of St. Barts's fabulous gourmet delis—**La Rotisserie** (☎ 590/27–63–13) on rue du Roi Oscar II (branches in St. Jean and Pointe Milou).

Dining

The French reverence for food is evident everywhere on St. Barts, from the most expensive classic French restaurant to the simplest beachside café. If you enjoy exquisitely prepared cuisine served at an enjoyable pace (and don't mind paying for it), then you may never want to leave St. Barts. A la carte prices at the well-known French restaurants are very high, but many offer a prix fixe menu for a very reasonable price—a nice way to sample the cuisine. Lunch prices are usually cheaper than evening prices, and Italian, Creole, and French-Creole restaurants tend to be less expensive day and night. Beware that restaurants here typically charge for drinking water (a French custom), which comes by the bottle, both sparkling and flat, and costs about $4. *Accras* (salt cod fritters) with Creole sauce (minced hot peppers in oil), spiced christophine (a kind of squash), *boudin Créole* (a very spicy blood sausage), and a lusty *soupe de poissons* (fish soup) are some of the delicious and ubiquitous Creole dishes.

Reservations are always recommended; on weekend nights in season, they're required almost everywhere.

What to Wear

Jackets are rarely required, but this is a tony island and people here are fashionably dressed. You may feel uncomfortable in jeans. For men, a sports jacket and khakis will take you anywhere. For women, dress pants, a skirt, or even nice walking shorts are acceptable everywhere. If you're unsure, ask about the dress code when making reservations.

CATEGORY	COST*
$$$$	over $60
$$$	$45–$60
$$	$30–$45
$	under $30

per person, excluding drinks, service, and 4% sales tax

$$$–$$$$
★ **Carl Gustaf.** Not even the sweeping views of the harbor can detract from the sublime creations of Patrick Gateau. Monsieur Gateau, who trained at the Crillon in Paris, deftly weaves tropical influences into his classical cuisine. Among his standouts are warm goat-cheese salad, lobster spring rolls, lobster ravioli in shellfish cream sauce, and grilled swordfish steak with stewed aubergines, tomatoes, sweet peppers, and onions. You choose your dessert when you order your meal to allow time for it to be prepared. Look no further than the warm chocolate praline cake—it will reduce a chocolate lover to tears. The $35 prix fixe lunch menu is a great bargain, and a $50 menu is available at dinner. The large, breezy, white dining room has a new open-air terrace that looks over Gustavia harbor. ✕ *Rue des Normands, Gustavia,* ☎ *590/27–82–83. Reservations advised. AE, MC, V. No lunch Sun. in summer.*

$$$ **François Plantation.** A flower-draped, lantern-hung arborway leads to
★ this elegant restaurant. Inside, mahogany tables and chairs are sur-
rounded by beautiful plants. Chef Christophe Picard's cuisine legère,
a lighter version of classic French cuisine, draws guests from all over
the island; locals consistently rate it in their top three. Try his ravioli
of red mullet appetizer, and move on to roasted sea bass spiced with
vanilla or lamb fillet roasted in a light crust with basil and Gorgonzola
cheese and served with sautéed fennel and tomato. You can also order
the rare Coutancie beef: The cattle must drink three liters of beer and
receive a 20-minute rubdown twice daily, among other strict guidelines,
to qualify. Dessert specials include a remarkable warm dark chocolate
tart served with vanilla ice cream. ✗ *Colombier,* ☎ *590/27–78–82.
Reservations required. AE, D, MC, V. Closed Sept.–Oct. No lunch.*

$$$ **Lafayette Club.** Despite outrageous prices, this lunch-only, beachside
bistro is such an in-season "in" spot that reservations are necessary if
you want to eat between noon and 2. Expect to pay about $14 for a
green salad with bacon and croutons or goat cheese and sliced tomatoes, $30 and up for grilled local fish, fillet of duck, shrimp with fresh
pasta, and grilled lobster. ✗ *Grand Cul de Sac,* ☎ *590/27–62–51. Reservations advised. No credit cards. No dinner. Closed May–mid-Nov.*

$$$ **Le Gaiac.** Cool breezes waft through this open-air restaurant at the el-
egant, out-of-the-way Le Toiny hotel. Pale blue napery and blue can-
vas chairs beautifully complement the blue bay view. New chef Maxime
Des Champs hails from France, and he has lightened the restaurant's
cuisine with an emphasis on combining local ingredients and traditional
French cooking techniques. Appetizers at lunch include duck carpac-
cio with coffee-flavored vinaigrette and chilled spicy mango soup. En-
trées include club sandwiches and grilled fish and shellfish. The dinner
menu expands with roast saddle of lamb with a plantain and sweet
potato pie, fillet of sole poached in a creamy mussel sauce with fresh
garden vegetables, and steamed red mullet with a fennel and tomato
marinade. ✗ *Anse de Toiny,* ☎ *590/27–88–88. Reservations advised.
AE, DC, MC, V. Closed Sept.–mid-Oct. and Tues. in summer.*

$$$ **Le Sapotillier.** Dining in this cozy boîte or in the courtyard under a grand
★ old sapodilla tree, you may feel like a guest in the owners' house—yet
the food is anything but down-home. This long-established French
restaurant serves fresh local fish Provençale style, veal stew with Roquefort and vegetables, red snapper in ginger sauce with gnocchi, and young
rabbit in puff pastry. The sumptuous black-and-white-chocolate mousse
is a house favorite. ✗ *Rue de Centenaire, Gustavia,* ☎ *590/27–60–28.
Reservations required. MC, V. Closed May–mid-Oct. No lunch.*

$$$ **L'Orchidée.** This elegant French-Creole restaurant with coral stucco walls
and mahogany archways is in the Hotel Christopher. Have a seat in a
casual captain's chair on the deck, amid the white napery and gleam-
ing silver, and listen to the waves on the rocky shore. The staff is
friendly and solicitous, the atmosphere romantic, and the food beau-
tifully presented. Try grilled mahimahi with lime or chicken with curry-
and-coconut sauce served with two kinds of mashed potatoes. A prix
fixe menu is available for about $45. ✗ *Hotel Christopher, Pointe Milou,*
☎ *590/27–63–63. Reservations advised. AE, MC, V. No lunch.*

$$–$$$ **Adam.** Vincent Adam, a graduate of the Culinary Academy of France,
★ opened this haute cuisine gem in the hills just off St. Jean beach. Din-
ner is served in the Creole-style house or in the garden. Many locals
insist it's one of the top restaurants on the island. There are both an
à la carte menu with wonderful choices and a very reasonable priced
prix fixe menu (about $38). Offerings include lobster tabouli, salmon
tartare with caviar and oysters, terrine of sweetbreads, and fillet of beef.

Vegetarian selections are also available. ✗ *St. Jean,* ☎ *590/27–93– 22. Reservations advised. AE, MC, V. No lunch.*

$$–$$$ **La Toque Lyonnaise.** Chef Michel Fredric apprenticed with masters Bo-
★   cuse, Troigros, and Veras before taking charge of the kitchen at this pleasant outdoor dining spot at the El Sereno. He wows diners with adaptations
of classic French recipes. A la carte choices include marinated salmon
in ginger cream, grilled lobster flavored with vanilla beans, and rack of
lamb in tapenade. There is also a three-course *menu dégustation* for 240F
(about $43). Courses vary, but you might start with a Roquefort ter-
rine with pears poached in Sauternes, followed by salmon steak in mustard sauce and a warm apple-cinnamon tart. ✗ *El Sereno Beach Hotel
and Villas, Grand Cul de Sac,* ☎ *590/27–64–80. Reservations advised. AE, DC, MC, V. Closed June–Aug. No lunch.*

$$–$$$ **Le Flamboyant.** In the hills above Grand Cul du Sac is this small restau-
rant famous for its French and Creole cuisine. The menu is not extensive
but includes duck, beef, and seafood, and there is always a Creole plat
du jour such as curried goat. You can dine inside, but most guests opt
for the breezy terrace with a fine view of the countryside and the sea
in the distance. Reservations are not required, but they're a good idea
if you want to sit outside. ✗ *Grand Cul de Sac,* ☎ *590/27–75–65.
MC, V. No lunch.*

$$–$$$ **Maya's.** Locals, visitors, and celebs keep returning to this informal,
open-air restaurant, just outside of Gustavia on the north end of Public Beach. Relax in a colorful deck chair, and watch the boats in Gustavia's harbor as you contemplate the Creole, Vietnamese, and Thai
menu. You choose from five selections for each of three courses. The
menu changes nightly, but you might find christophine au gratin, several fresh salads, canard à l'orange, salmon teriyaki, and shrimp curry.
✗ *Public Beach,* ☎ *590/27–75–73. Reservations advised. AE, D,
MC, V. Closed Sun. and June–Oct. No lunch.*

$$–$$$ **Wall House.** Consistently excellent French cuisine is the hallmark of
this restaurant on the far end of the far side of Gustavia's harbor. The
interior is glistening white—shiny white wicker furniture, white tile floors,
white tablecloths and walls—with pots of greenery here and there. Owner
Gerard Began is unobtrusively on-site most evenings; the staff is gracious and will make enthusiastic recommendations. Start with marinated salmon with dill, gazpacho, grilled mahimahi over sliced
cucumbers, foie gras, or cold eggplant mousse. For your main course,
try fillet of shark in lobster sauce, duck in cassis sauce with sautéed
potatoes, or beef with pepper sauce. Three prix fixe menus offer excellent value. The lunch menu features lighter fare. ✗ *Gustavia,* ☎ *590/
27–71–83. Reservations advised. AE, MC, V.*

$$ **Le Patio.** Some of the best classic Italian food on the island is served
★   by candlelight at this pleasant hillside restaurant, where you can dine
inside or on the terrace. Entrées change weekly, but you may find grouper
medallions rolled in black peppercorns with a light ginger and lime sauce
or salmon fillet with both a mustard and a crushed tomato sauce, in
addition to six or seven pasta offerings. Children will enjoy holiday
menus—such as red snapper in phantom sauce at Halloween. There
are nice views of the bay, and the atmosphere is romantic and intimate.
Service is unhurried, despite the remarkably reasonable prices. ✗ *Vil-
lage St. Jean hotel,* ☎ *590/27–61–39. MC, V. Closed Wed. and June.
No lunch.*

$$ **New Born.** For authentic Creole cuisine, head down the bumpy road
that leads to the Hotel Manapany. The dark-wood restaurant is some-
what devoid of decoration except for a large aquarium in the back;
ask for a table near it if you want to watch the sharks, turtles, and trop-

ical fish swim while you eat. The fresh seafood is caught at the beach, just steps away. This is the place to sample such Creole specialties as accras, boudin, curried goat or shrimp, and salt cod salad. For dessert try the coconut custard or bananas flambé. ✕ *Anse des Cayes,* ☎ *590/27–67–07. Reservations advised. AE, MC, V. Closed Sun. in off-season. No lunch.*

$–$$ **Eddy's Ghetto.** The combination of imaginatively prepared, modestly priced
★ fare—crab salad, ragout of beef, crème caramel—and a disarmingly fun-loving atmosphere has made Edward Stakelborough's open-air restaurant a hit. The crowd is lively, and the wine list is impressive. ✕ *Gustavia, just off rue du Général de Gaulle. No phone. No credit cards.*

$–$$ **La Marine.** Mussels from France arrive on Thursday, and in-the-know islanders are there to eat them at the very popular dockside picnic tables. The lunch menu always includes fresh fish, hamburgers, and omelets; dinner adds more grilled meat and fish. ✕ *Rue Jeanne d'Arc, Gustavia,* ☎ *590/27–70–13. No credit cards.*

$–$$ **Le Repaire.** This busy brasserie looks out over Gustavia's harbor and is a popular spot from early breakfast until late in the evening. Grab a cappuccino, pull a captain's chair up to the front window, and watch cruise-ship passengers come off the boats to descend upon the town. The menu includes everything from cheeseburgers to foie gras and grilled fish and lobster. There is a billiards table and live music on weekends. ✕ *Gustavia (Quai de la République),* ☎ *590-27–72–48. D, MC, V.* ☺ *Daily 6 AM–midnight. Closed Sun,*

$ $$ **Le Rivage.** Bathing suits are acceptable attire at this popular and very
★ casual Creole establishment on the beach at Grand Cul de Sac. Delicious lobster salad, sandwiches, and fresh grilled fish are served at indoor and outdoor tables. The relaxed atmosphere and surprisingly low prices can make for an enjoyable meal, but the service gets frantic when the restaurant is busy. ✕ *Grand Cul de Sac.* ☎ *590/27–82–42. Reservations advised. AE, MC, V. Closed Thurs.*

$–$$ **L'Escale.** Great food, ambience, and views draw locals and visitors alike
★ to this open-air restaurant, at the water's edge on the far side of Gustavia's harbor. The varied menu includes a wide range of pasta (lasagna, tortellini, ravioli, plus spaghetti with marinara, Bolognese, and other sauces), as well as fresh local fish, veal scallopine in an assortment of sauces, steak tartare, chicken, and 12 kinds of pizza. Many dishes are cooked in a wood-burning oven. ✕ *Gustavia,* ☎ *590/27–81–06. Reservations required in season. MC, V. No lunch.*

$–$$ **Marigot Bay Club.** Have a seat at the dark-wood bar or at a table on the beam-ceiling patio, and take in the views of the colorful sailboats moored in the bay. The owner of this casual spot loves to fish and often reels in the catch of the day himself. It might be grouper, tuna, red snapper, or yellowtail and is frequently served with a Creole sauce. Other specials here include veal sautéed with mushrooms and wine, filet mignon with green peppercorn sauce, chicken breast in creamy lime sauce, and fresh local lobster baked in the shell with Gruyère cheese. In season, lunch is also served. ✕ *Marigot,* ☎ *590/27–75–45. Reservations required. AE, MC, V. No dinner Sun.; no lunch Mon. in season.*

$–$$ **Topolino.** This lesser-known but excellent (and very reasonably priced) Italian restaurant is set back from the road, within easy walking distance of St. Jean beach. Linen tablecloths, freshly cut flowers, and dim lighting create a romantic evening atmosphere. The menu includes fresh seafood, grilled chicken and steaks, various veal dishes, a number of pasta choices, and thin-crusted pizzas. There is a happy hour from 6 to 7 and live entertainment almost every night. The wine list has a number of fine, inexpensive choices. ✕ *St. Jean,* ☎ *590/27–70–92. Reservations advised. MC, V. No lunch.*

$ Brasserie La Creole. Right in the center of the St. Jean shopping arcade is this casual brasserie with indoor seating, a comfortable bar, and outdoor umbrella tables. Drop by in the morning for freshly baked croissants and magnificent coffee. At lunch try the *croque-monsieur,* a hot sandwich of thin-sliced ham and Gruyère cheese. There is a full breakfast menu, and from noon until late in the evening the restaurant serves sandwiches, salads, and various beef, chicken, and fish entrées. ✕ *St. Jean,* ☎ *590/27–68–09. AE.* ⊙ *Daily 7 AM–midnight.*

$ Gloriette. This beachside spot serves delicious local Creole dishes, such as crunchy accras and grilled red snapper with Creole sauce, as well as light salads. ✕ *Grand Cul de Sac,* ☎ *590/27–75–66. AE, MC, V. Closed Sun.*

$ Pasta Paradise. Eight kinds of homemade pasta and a selection of sauces are served each day at this friendly eatery in a historic Creole building. There are other items on the menu, including grilled mahimahi with pepper and vinegar sauce and veal kidney sautéed in mustard sauce. Sit in the air-conditioned dining room or on the breezy terrace. ✕ *Gustavia (rue du Roi),* ☎ *590/27–80–78. AE, MC, V. No lunch Sun.*

Lodging

Expect to be shocked at the prices that you must pay for accommodations. You pay for the privilege of staying on the island rather than for the hotel. Even at $500 a night, bedrooms tend to be small, but that does not detract from the lure of St. Barts for those who can afford it. Away from the beaches are a number of small hotels and a multitude of rental bungalows that offer less expensive accommodations. Most hotels offer either the Continental (CP) or European (EP) meal plan, although the Modified American Plan (MAP) is sometimes available.

Hotels may have as many as six different rate periods during a year. The highest rates are in effect from mid-December to early January, and hotels are booked far in advance for this holiday period. Rates used for the listings below are for the second highest period, early January through April—still in season, but not the holiday peak. At all other times, rates are usually lower. If you are flexible in your planning, you can save a good deal of money.

CATEGORY	COST*
$$$$	$400–$550
$$$	$300–$400
$$	$200–$300
$	under $200

All prices are for a standard double room for two, excluding a 10%–15% service charge; there is no government room tax.

Hotels

$$$$ **Carl Gustaf.** Red-tile-roofed buildings spill down the hillside at this very
★ expensive, small luxury resort at the head of Gustavia harbor. Each one- and two-bedroom suite looks out across a deck with a small, private plunge pool to spectacular views of the harbor, the quaint town of Gustavia, and the hilly coastline of the island. Units have spacious, gleaming-white bedrooms and living rooms stylishly highlighted with pastel prints, plus marble floors, high ceilings, tiny but state-of-the-art kitchens, fax machines, two TVs, two stereos, VCR, minibar, and marble bath. The glittering nighttime view from the piano-bar lounge and elegant, open-air restaurant (known for its classic French cuisine; *see* Dining, *above*) is one of the most spectacular on the island. 🏠 *Box 700, rue des Normands, Gustavia 97133,* ☎ *590/27–82–83 or 800/932–3222,*

FAX 590/27–82–37. 14 1- and 2-bedroom suites. Restaurant, pool, private plunge pools, fitness club, sauna. AE, DC, MC, V. CP.

$$$$ Filao Beach. One of St. Barts's most popular beaches and excellent service win many repeat guests at this casual resort. Rooms are in two-
★ unit bungalows set back from the beach amidst lush gardens. Although simple and smallish, they are brightly decorated with rattan furniture and pastel print fabrics; all have air-conditioning, TV, and phone. Each room has a patio, some of which are made more private by thick banks of sea-grape vines. Rooms closer to the beach rise accordingly in price, but the garden rooms are still only steps away from the sand. Bathrooms are compact but neat and fully stocked with toiletries. A restaurant, open for breakfast and lunch, is on the raised wooden deck that surrounds the pool. The bartender is well known for his killer cocktails. The hotel is a member of the prestigious Relais & Chateaux organization. ☎ Box 667, St. Jean 97099, ☎ 590/27–64–84 or 800/372–1323, FAX 590/27–62–24. 30 rooms. Restaurant, bar, pool. CP.

$$$$ Guanahani. This elegant 7-acre resort, the island's largest, is set between two beaches, one sheltered and one open to ocean waves. The lobby is a riot of color—deep greens, soothing blues, and rich plaids; have a drink on the terrace here. Rooms and one-bedroom suites are in tightly clustered bungalows, expensively decorated with bright tropical fabrics and Georgian-style furniture. Some newer units are done in a stunning contemporary style, with wood floors and dark wood furniture, colorful walls, funky art and sculpture, a sunken seating area, and a partial curved wall between the sleeping and bath areas. Suites have either private pools or Jacuzzis. Units vary tremendously in terms of privacy, views, and distance from activities; there are just six rooms on the beach. To avoid disappointment, be sure to make your preference known when making your reservation. A poolside restaurant is open for breakfast and lunch. The more formal Bartolomeo is open for dinner and serves classic French cuisine in both an indoor dining room and outside in a tropical garden. The resort is a member of the Leading Hotels of the World. ☎ Box 609, Grand Cul de Sac 97098, ☎ 590/27–66–60 or 800/223–6800, FAX 590/27–70–70. 17 double rooms, some with ocean views; 39 deluxe rooms; 8 1-bedroom suites; 13 1-bedroom suites with private pool. 2 restaurants, 2 lighted tennis courts, 2 pools, Jacuzzi, windsurfing, water-sports center, dive shop, beauty salon. AE, MC, V. CP.

$$$$ Le Toiny. Luxury awaits at this comfortable little hideaway tucked
★ into the hillside at a remote end of the island. Twelve spacious, green-roofed villas, each with a private patio and pool (10 by 20 feet), are arranged for maximum privacy. Each is exquisitely appointed, with a massive four-poster mahogany bed and armoire, Chinese porcelain vases, Italian fabrics, and fine linens, and has a minibar, two TVs, VCR, hair dryer, fax, safe, stereo, air-conditioning, and three telephones. You can also request either a Stairmaster or a Lifecycle. The bathroom has a walk-in shower as well as a tub. The elegant, alfresco restaurant, Le Gaiac, overlooks the Italian-tiled communal swimming pool and offers sweeping views of the distant ocean. A windy beach, Saline, is a five-minute drive away. ☎ Anse de Toiny 97133, ☎ 590/27–88–88 or 800/932–3222, FAX 590/27–89–30. 12 villas. Restaurant, bar, pool, laundry, fitness equipment. AE, DC, MC, V. CP.

$$$–$$$$ Club La Banane. If you're looking for privacy, you may like this intimate hideaway, where guests keep pretty much to themselves. The nine unique units are decorated with plants, antique furniture, and a bit of whimsy. There are four-poster beds, sunken bath areas, all kinds of antiques, Haitian artwork, and unusual pottery. Rooms look out to dense tropical greenery. There are two small swimming pools (one with a waterfall), and it's a three-minute walk to the beach. The restaurant is open only to hotel guests for breakfast and lunch. Visitors come from around the island for dinner, served alfresco around the pool, and for the nightly after-dinner show in which the entire staff participates, including owner Jean-Marie Rivière, a Parisian cabaret producer. ☎ *Quartier Lorient 97133,* ☎ *590/27–68–25,* FAX *590/27–68–44. 9 rooms. Restaurant, bar, 2 pools, Jacuzzi. AE, MC, V. CP.*

$$$-$$$$ **Hotel St. Barth Isle de France.** Even the pool furniture is elegant at this intimate luxury enclave, which is on one of the island's prettiest beaches. Enormously spacious rooms and suites are either beachfront, in the two-story clubhouse, or across the street, in bungalows facing gardens and one of the hotel's two pools. All units are decorated with mahogany furniture, island prints, and white cotton bedspreads. Each has a patio or balcony, a private bath with two sinks and a tub, a minifridge, cable TV, and a phone. Some garden bungalows have a kitchenette. The restaurant serves breakfast and lunch, and you may opt for breakfast in your room. ☎ *Box 612, Baie des Flamands 97098,* ☎ *590/27–61–81,* FAX *590/27–86–83. 35 rooms, 5 1-bedroom suites. Restaurant, bar, 2 pools, 1 lighted tennis court, 1 squash court, fitness center. AE, MC, V. CP.*

$$$ **Hotel Christopher.** Sofitel Resorts manages this full-service hotel. Four two-story colonial-style buildings overlooking the water (but not on the beach) hold beautifully furnished, air-conditioned rooms with panoramic views of St. Martin and nearby islets. Each room has a private terrace or balcony with sitting area, minifridge, and contemporary marble bath. Some bathrooms have small gardens: If the sight of a small lizard in here will ruin your vacation, ask for a bath sans greenhouse. There is a giant (4,500-square-foot) swimming pool—by far the largest on the island—with islands and footbridges. L'Orchidée serves French and Creole cuisine at dinner, and the poolside restaurant, Le Mango, has a lunch menu that includes selections for the calorie-conscious. In season, there is a complimentary shuttle to St. Jean beach twice daily except Sunday. Many packages are available, so be sure to inquire when you book. ☎ *Pointe Milou 97133,* ☎ *590/27–63–63 or 800/763–4835,* FAX *590/27–92–92. 40 suites. 2 restaurants, pool, room service, fitness room. AE, DC, MC, V. EP, CP, MAP, FAP.*

$$$ **Hotel Manapany Cottages.** A ramshackle entry road ends at this luxury enclave of closely spaced units that stretch back from a narrow and not very swimmable beach. Accommodations vary from rather snug St. Barts–style cottages and suites tucked into the hillside to much-in-demand beachfront suites with marble baths and four-poster beds. Bronze bodies ring the pretty but small pool, and outsiders drop in regularly to dine at the hotel's two restaurants. The atmosphere here is sophisticated and cosmopolitan, and there are many repeat guests. Airport transfers are complimentary, and rates include breakfast. ☎ *Box 114, Anse des Cayes 97133,* ☎ *590/27–66–55 or 800/847–4249,* FAX *590/ 27–75–28. 32 cottages. 2 restaurants, 2 bars, pool, hot tub, exercise room, boutique, lighted tennis court, water-sports center. AE, D, DC, MC, V. CP.*

$$-$$$ **Castelets.** The views are breathtaking at this exclusive retreat atop Morne Lurin. Antiques-furnished rooms are in terraced chalets (with the exception of two in the main house) connected by steep paths. The size of the rooms varies greatly, as does their price: The smallest are actually in the inexpensive ($) category, while the largest suites slip into the very expensive ($$$$) range. Since the hotel is inland and off by itself, you will need a car. It's a very steep five-minute drive down to Gustavia or the nearest beach. The well-known hotel restaurant now

serves lighter (and less expensive) fare than in the past. ⊞ *Box 60, Morne Lurin 97133,* ☎ *590/27–61–73 or 800/223–1108,* FAX *590/27–85–27. 10 rooms, 1 2-bedroom suite. Restaurant, small pool. AE, MC, V. CP.*

$$–$$$ François Plantation. A colonial-era graciousness pervades this elegant hillside complex of West Indian–style cottages. It's owned and managed by longtime island habitués Françoise and François Beret. Monsieur Beret is a passionate gardener, and the grounds are an intensely colorful display of tropical flowers and greenery. The smallish, air-conditioned rooms are dominated by the antique mahogany queen-size four-poster beds and decorated with brightly colored fabrics. Two units are larger and can accommodate an extra bed. All have minifridge, telephone, and TV. The pool is at the very top of the hill, with magnificent views of the beach below, the hills of St. Barts, and nearby islets. You'll need a car to get to the beach and to go out for lunch (the restaurant is open only for breakfast and dinner); some packages include a rental car. You'll also need reservations for dinner at the gourmet restaurant (*see* Dining, *above*). ⊞ *Colombier 97133,* ☎ *590/27–78–82; in the U.S., 800/932–3222;* FAX *590/27–61–26. 4 garden- and 8 sea-view rooms. Restaurant, pool. AE, MC, V. CP.*

$$ Eden Rock. Set on a craggy bluff that abruptly splits St. Jean Beach is St. Barts's first hotel, opened in the '50s by Rémy de Haenen and lovingly restored by his granddaughter. The six rooms have been spiffed up with four poster beds, tropical print fabrics, mosquito netting, sparkling silver fixtures, and minibar. The terra-cotta floors are original, as are the stunning views of St. Jean Bay. You can breakfast in the restaurant or in your room. The open-air bar and French-Creole barbecue restaurant, which stretch along the top of the rock, are great places to enjoy the sea breeze and watch the frigate birds dive bomb for fish. ⊞ *St. Jean 97133,* ☎ *590/27–72–94,* FAX *590/27–88–37. 6 rooms. Restaurant, bar. MC, V. CP.*

$$ **El Sereno Beach Hotel and Villas.** The quiet, casual chic and reason-
★ able rates of this compact resort attract many repeat guests. The small, simply furnished rooms, with whitewashed walls and blue beams, have either a sea or garden view. They don't get much of a breeze, but they are air-conditioned and have a minifridge, satellite TV, telephone, and patio. High walls and plants provide privacy. The beach, with its exceptionally calm waters, is just steps away. There are also nine comfortably furnished one-bedroom, gingerbread-trimmed villas. A new West Indian café was slated to open at press time. ⊞ *Box 19, Grand Cul de Sac 97133,* ☎ *590/27–64–80,* FAX *590/27–75–47. 20 rooms (3 sea-view), 9 1-bedroom villas. 2 restaurants, bar, pool, beach with water-sports center, boutique. AE, DC, MC, V. EP.*

$–$$ Baie des Flamands. Families and tour groups frequent this motel-style hotel. Upper-level rooms have balconies, and lower-level ones, which are right on the beach, have terrace kitchenette units. All rooms have phones and air-conditioning, but upper-level rooms do not have TVs. One of the first hotels on the island, it is still run by a St. Barts family and has a gentle, laid-back island ambience. It has a good restaurant, La Frégate, and an outstanding beach location. A rental car is often included in the rate, and children under eight stay free with a parent. ⊞ *Box 582, Anse des Flamands 97098,* ☎ *590/27–64–85 or 800/447–7462,* FAX *590/27–83–98. 24 rooms. Restaurant, bar, pool, rental cars. AE, MC, V. CP.*

$–$$ Hotel Yuana. Green-roofed West Indian–style cottages are strung along a flowery hillside at this small complex overlooking Anse des Cayes. Appealing rooms have white walls, white tile floors, colorful tile baths, blue or peach painted wicker furniture, floral print fabrics, a kitchenette, and a wide terrace overlooking the ocean. Each unit has both a ceiling fan and air-conditioning, plus a TV/VCR and a phone. A 30-foot boat is available to rent. Airport transfers are included, package rates are available, and children under 12 stay free. ⌧ *Anse des Cayes 97133,* ☎ *590/27–80–84 or 800/645–6030,* FAX *590/27–78–45. 12 rooms. Bar, breakfast room, pool. AE, MC, V. EP.*

$–$$ **Tropical Hotel.** This complex is straight up the hill from St. Jean Beach. Rooms are in a motel-like, one-story, L-shape building and open out to patios and views of either the ocean or thick tropical foliage. They are simple but well-maintained and have air-conditioning, TV, telephone, and minifridge. White walls and furniture create an airy atmosphere. The main building houses reception, a TV/game room, and an appealing open-air bar and lounge. ⌧ *Box 147, St. Jean 97133,* ☎ *590/27–64–87,* FAX *590/27–81–74. 20 rooms. Bar, snack bar, small pool. AE, MC, V. CP.*

$–$$ **Village St. Jean.** The second generation of the Charneau family now ★ runs this popular cottage colony, which has acquired a strong following over the years. The accent is on service and affordability, and this is one of the best values on the island. Air-conditioned cottages are spacious, although a bit sparsely furnished (except for the newly refurbished two-bedroom cottages), and have open-air kitchenettes and patios. There are also six hotel rooms without kitchenettes but with refrigerators. Rooms are slowly being done over with elegant natural fabrics and dark wood furniture, including some teak pieces from Bali; some have beam ceilings and cheerful striped awnings, and most have king-size beds. Renovations should be completed by press time. Units have a variety of views, from full ocean to almost none, and the units closest to the road are subject to the ongoing noise of minimoke engines struggling with the steep terrain. The open-air restaurant, Le Patio, serves excellent Italian fare. From the hotel it is an easy five-minute walk down to popular St. Jean Beach and to a variety of stores and restaurants (the walk back up is a bit more strenuous). ⌧ *Box 623, St. Jean 97098,* ☎ *590/27–61–39 or 800/633–7411,* FAX *590/27–77–96. 6 rooms, 20 cottages. Restaurant, bar, pool, small grocery, boutique, games room, library. MC, V. EP.*

$ **Hostellerie des Trois Forces.** This rustic, fairly isolated mountaintop inn ★ is an idiosyncratic delight, with a string of tiny, gingerbread-trimmed West Indian–style cottages charmingly decorated according to astrological color schemes (Libra is soft blue; Leo, bright red; etc.). All have a minibar, a terrace with a breathtaking ocean view, and air-conditioning or a ceiling fan. Most have four-poster beds. The tinkle of chimes floats through the pleasant restaurant. Astrologer Hubert de la Motte (he's a Gemini, by the way) is the personable owner and talented chef, and he may even arrange a reading for you. The slogan of the rustic restaurant is Food Is Love. ⌧ *Morne Vitet,* ☎ *590/27–61–25,* FAX *590/27–81–38. 8 rooms. Restaurant, bar, pool. AE, MC, V. EP.*

$ **La Normandie.** This small, family-run hotel offers very modestly furnished rooms that are far from the beach but extremely inexpensive. All are air-conditioned; some have TVs. ⌧ *Lorient 97133,* ☎ *590/27–61–66,* FAX *590/27–68–64. 8 rooms. Pool. No credit cards. EP.*

$ **Le P'tit Morne.** There is good value in these modestly furnished moun- ★ tainside studios, each with a private balcony, air-conditioning, and panoramic views of the coastline below. Small kitchenettes are adequate for creating light meals or packing picnic lunches. The snack bar serves breakfast. It's relatively isolated here, and the beach is a 10-minute drive away. ⌧ *Box 14, Colombier 97133,* ☎ *590/27–62–64,* FAX *590/27–84–63. 14 rooms. Snack bar, small pool, reading room. AE, MC, V. CP.*

Villas, Condos, Apartments

On St. Barthélemy, "villa" is used generically to describe anything from a small cottage to a truly luxurious house with a cook, a maid, and a pool. You get what you pay for. In-season rates range from $1,000 to $10,000 a week. For the price of a moderately expensive hotel room, you can get a condo or a small cottage. If you get a group of friends together, you can get a villa with a number of rooms and a private pool for significantly less than it would cost for each person to stay in one of the expensive hotels. How to choose between a villa and a hotel? It may depend on whether you want the full kitchen that comes with a villa or would rather pay the sometimes expensive restaurant tabs to sample the island's exceptional food. You can strike a compromise by opting for a hotel whose rooms have kitchenettes. Whether you stay in a villa or a hotel you will almost always want to rent a car, so be sure to figure this as part of your budget, no matter where you stay.

Villas, apartments, and condos can be rented through **Sibarth** (☎ 590/27–62–38), which handles more than 200 properties. **WIMCO** (☎ 800/932–3222) is the agency's representative in the United States. Rents range from $1,000 to $2,000 per week for one-bedroom villas, $1,600 to $7,000 for two- and three-bedroom villas.

Nightlife

St. Barts is a mostly in-bed-by-midnight island—there are no casinos, no movie theaters, and only a few discos. There are many special places to go for the cocktail hour, and some of the hotels and restaurants provide late-night fun. Cocktail hour finds a crowd at **Le Repaire** (Gustavia, ☎ 590/27–72–48). The barefoot boating set gathers in the boisterous garden of Gustavia's **Le Select** (☎ 590/27–86–87). Those in search of quiet conversation and some gentle piano at the day's end head up the hill to the **Carl Gustaf** (☎ 590/27–82–83), which is Gustavia's best sunset-watching spot. Both the **Manapany** (☎ 590/27–66–55) and the **Guanahani** (☎ 590/27–66–60) also have piano bars. After dinner, the locals head to **Le Pélican** (St. Jean, ☎ 590/27–64–64) for live music. The retro-hip (there's a 1968 Cadillac Eldorado outside and lots of neon inside) **American Bar** (☎ 590/27–86–07) at L'Escale restaurant is another after-dinner hangout. There's a popular après-dîner cabaret show nightly at **Club La Banane** (☎ 590/27–68–25). For real late-night activity, head to Gustavia's **Le Petit Club** (☎ 590/27–66–33) and **Bar de l'Oubli** (☎ 590/27–70–06). On Friday and Saturday you can also check out the **Why Not?** (☎ 590/27–68–61) disco, near Gustavia.

20 St. Eustatius

THE FLIGHT APPROACH to the tiny Dutch island of St. Eustatius, commonly known as Statia (pronounced *Stay*-sha) in the Netherlands Antilles, is almost worth

Updated by
Marcy
Pritchard

the visit itself. The plane circles the Quill, a 1,968-foot-high extinct volcano that encloses a stunning primeval rain forest within its crater. Here you'll see giant elephant ears, ferns, flowers, wild orchids, fruit trees, wildlife, and birds hiding in the trees. The entire island is alive with untended greenery and abloom with flowers—bougainvillea, oleander, and hibiscus.

Little 12-square-mile Statia, past which Columbus sailed in 1493, prospered almost from the day the Dutch Zeelanders colonized it in 1636. In the 1700s, a double row of warehouses crammed with goods stretched for a mile along the bay, and there were sometimes as many as 200 ships tied up at the duty-free port. The island was called the "Emporium of the Western World" and "Golden Rock." There were almost 8,000 Statians on the island in the 1790s (today, there are about 1,700). Holland, England, and France fought one another for possession of the island, which changed hands 22 times. In 1816, it became a Dutch possession and has remained so to this day.

During the American War of Independence, when the British blockaded the North American coast, food, arms, and other supplies for the American revolutionaries were diverted through the West Indies, notably through neutral Statia. (Benjamin Franklin had his mail routed through Statia to ensure its safe arrival in Europe.) On November 16, 1776, the brig-of-war *Andrew Doria*, commanded by Captain Isaiah Robinson of the Continental Navy, sailed into Statia's port flying the Stars and Stripes and fired a 13-gun salute to the Royal Netherlands standard. Governor Johannes de Graaff ordered the cannons of Fort Oranje to return the salute, and that first official acknowledgment of the new American flag by a foreign power earned Statia the nickname America's Childhood Friend. In retaliation, British admiral George Rodney attacked and destroyed the island in 1781. Statia has yet to recover its prosperity, which, ironically, ended partly because of the success of the American Revolution: The island was no longer needed as a transshipment port, and its bustling economy gradually came to a stop.

Statia is in the Dutch Windward Triangle, 178 miles east of Puerto Rico and 35 miles south of St. Maarten. Oranjestad, the capital and only "city" (note quotes), is on the western side facing the Caribbean. The island is anchored at the north and the south by extinct volcanoes, like the Quill, that are separated by a central plain.

Statia is a wonderful playground for hikers and divers. Myriad ancient ships rest on the ocean floor alongside 18th-century warehouses that were slowly buried in the sea by storms. Much of the aboveground activity has to do with archaeology and restoration; students from William and Mary's College of Archaeology converge on the island each summer, the University of Leiden in the Netherlands has a pre-Columbian program, and the island's Historical Foundation is actively engaged in restoring Statian landmarks.

Most visitors will be content with a day visit from nearby St. Maarten, exploring some of the historical sights and enjoying a relaxed meal at the Old Gin House Terrace. Those who stay longer tend to be collectors of unspoiled islands with a need to relax and a taste for history. Perhaps the locals are the best reason to visit this island. Statians are warm, welcoming, and happy to stop and chat. People still say hello to strangers here—when passing drivers beep or wave, return the gesture. This is one of the very few remaining islands where tourists will not feel that locals resent their perceived wealth and luxurious lifestyle. But Statia is mindful of the potential gold mine of tourism and is making the necessary investments to restore the many historical buildings and forts, expand pier facilities, and improve the tourism infrastructure.

Before You Go

Tourist Information

Contact the **Caribbean Tourism Organization** (20 E. 46th St., New York, NY 10017–2452, ☎ 212/682–0435). You may also contact the **tourist board** on the island (Oranjestad, St. Eustatius, Netherlands Antilles, ☎ 599/38–2433), which is very willing to advise you on any aspect of planning a trip to Statia. Although telephone communications are good, it can take several weeks for mail to get through.

Arriving and Departing

BY PLANE

Windward Islands Airways (Winair, ☎ 599/5–54230 or 599/5–54210) makes the 20-minute flight from St. Maarten five times a day, the 10-minute flight from Saba daily, and the 15-minute flight from St. Kitts twice a week. Be sure to confirm your flight a day or two in advance, as schedules can change abruptly.

FROM THE AIRPORT

Planes put down at the **Franklin Delano Roosevelt Airport,** where taxis meet all flights and charge about $3.50 for the drive into town. There's an Avis outlet at the airport, should you decide to rent a car (*see* Getting Around, *below*).

Passports and Visas

All visitors must have proof of citizenship. A passport is preferred, but a birth certificate or voter registration card will do. (A driver's license will *not* do.) British citizens need a valid passport. All visitors need a return or ongoing ticket.

Language

Statia's official language is Dutch (it's used on government documents), but everyone speaks English. Dutch is taught as the primary language in the schools, and street signs are in both Dutch and English.

Staying in St. Eustatius

Important Addresses

Tourist Office: The **St. Eustatius Tourist Office** is at the entrance to Fort Oranje (3 Fort Oranjestraat, ☎ 599/38–2433). Office hours are weekdays 8–noon and 1–5.

EMERGENCIES

Police: ☎ 599/38–2333. **Hospital: Queen Beatrix Medical Center** (25 Prinsesweg, ☎ 599/38–2211 and 599/38–2371) has a full-time licensed physician on duty.

Currency

U.S. dollars are accepted everywhere, but legal tender is the Netherlands Antilles florin (NAf). Florins are also referred to as guilders, and you shouldn't be surprised to receive change in them. The exchange rate fluctuates but is about NAf1.75 to U.S.$1. Prices quoted here are in U.S. dollars unless noted otherwise.

Taxes and Service Charges

Hotels collect a 7% government tax and a 10%–15% service charge. The departure tax is $5 for flights to other islands of the Netherlands Antilles and $10 to foreign destinations. In addition, you'll probably be asked to contribute your leftover guilders to the latest cause.

Most restaurants add a 10%–15% service charge.

Guided Tours

All 10 of Statia's taxis are available for island tours. A full day's outing costs $35 per vehicle, usually including airport transfer.

Getting Around

To explore the island (and there isn't very much), car rentals are available through the **Avis** outlet at the airport (☎ 599/38–2421 and 800/331–1084) at a cost of $40 per day. **Rainbow Car Rental** (☎ 599/38–2811) has several Hyundais for rent. **Brown's** (☎ 599/38–2266) and **Lady Ama's Services** (☎ 599/38–2451) rent cars and Jeeps. Statia's roads are pocked with potholes and the going is slow and bumpy. Goats and cattle have the right of way.

Telephones and Mail

Statia has microwave telephone service to all parts of the world. To call Statia from the United States, dial 011–599/38 + the local number. When calling interisland, dial only the four-digit number. Direct dial is available. There are two pay phones on the island, one near the airport and one in Landsradio. Airmail letters to the United States are NAf1.30; postcards, NAf.60.

Opening and Closing Times

Most offices are open weekdays 8–noon and 1–4 or 5. **Barclays Bank** is open weekdays 8–2; **Windward Islands Bank** is open Monday–Thursday 8:30–noon and 1–3:30, Friday 8:30–noon and 2–4:30. Both are in Upper Town.

Exploring St. Eustatius

Numbers in the margin correspond to points of interest on the St. Eustatius map.

Oranjestad

① Statia's capital and only town, **Oranjestad** sits on the western coast facing the Caribbean. It's a split-level town: Upper Town and Lower Town. History buffs will enjoy poking around the ancient Dutch Colonial buildings, which are being restored by the historical foundation, while hikers will want to head for the hills of the Quill. Both Upper Town and Lower Town are easily explored on foot.

The first stop is the **tourist office,** which is right at the entrance to Fort Oranje. You can pick up maps, brochures, and friendly advice, as well as a listing of 12 marked hiking trails. You can also arrange for guides and guided tours.

② When you leave the tourist office, you will be at the entrance to **Fort Oranje.** With its three bastions, the fort has clutched these cliffs since 1636. In 1976, Statia participated in the U.S. bicentennial celebration by restoring the old fort, and now the black cannons point out over the ramparts. In the parade grounds a plaque, presented in 1939 by Franklin D. Roosevelt, reads, "Here the sovereignty of the United States of America was first formally acknowledged to a national vessel by a foreign official." The post office used to be located in the fort but burned in 1991. There are plans under way to rebuild the structure to house boutiques and restaurants.

From the fort, cross over to Wilhelminaweg (Wilhelmina Way) in the center of Upper Town. The award-winning **St. Eustatius Historical Foundation Museum** is in the Doncker house, a lovely building with slim columns and a high gallery. British admiral Rodney set up his headquarters here during the American Revolution, while he was stealing everything from gunpowder to port in retaliation for Statia's gallant support of the fledgling country. The house, acquired by the foundation in 1983 and completely restored, is Statia's most important intact 18th-century dwelling. Exhibits trace the island's history from the 6th century to the present. The basement exhibit details Statia's pre-Columbian history with the results of archaeological digs on the island. Statia is the only island thus far where ruins and artifacts of the Saladoid, a newly discovered tribe, have been excavated. *12 Van Tonningenweg,* ☎ *599/38–2288.* ☛ *$2 adults, $1 children.* ⊙ *Weekdays 9–5, weekends 9–noon.*

The museum also sells a sightseeing package, which includes a guided walking tour, a booklet detailing the sites on the tour, and museum admission. The tour begins in Lower Town at the Marina and ends at the museum. You can take the tour on your own with the book (there are corresponding numbered blue signs on most of the sites), but a guide may prove more illuminating.

Return to Fort Oranjestraat (Fort Orange St.) and turn left. Continue to Kerkweg (Church Way) and turn right. A little farther on the right you'll find the **Dutch Reformed church,** built in 1775. It has been partially restored and has lovely stone arches facing the sea. Ancient tales can be read on the gravestones in the 18th-century cemetery adjacent to the church.

Continue on Kerkweg and take the next two left turns onto Synagogepad (Synagogue Path) to **Honen Dalim** ("She Who Is Charitable to the Poor"), one of the Caribbean's oldest synagogues. Dating from 1738, it is now in ruins but is slated for restoration by groups from the United States and Holland.

TIME OUT The **Cool Corner** (☎ 599/38–2523; open Mon.–Sat. 7AM–2AM), just up from the tourist office, is a cool spot to have a beer and shoot the breeze if you want to catch up on island gossip. Inexpensive Chinese food is also available. For sandwiches, pizzas, or pastries, wander over to the **Sandbox Tree Bakery** (☎ 599/38–2469; open weekdays 5:30 AM–7 PM, Sat. 5:30 AM–1 PM) just behind the synagogue on Kerkweg.

Follow Prinsesweg back to the main square and zigzag down the cobblestone Fort Road to Lower Town. Warehouses and shops that in the 18th century were piled high with European imports are now either abandoned or simply used to store local fishermen's equipment, but the restoration of the 18th-century cotton mill, on the land side of Bay Road, now the **Old Gin House,** is impressive. The palms, flowering shrubs, and park benches along the water's edge are the work of the historical foundation members. All along the beach are the crumbling ruins of 18th-century buildings, dating from Statia's period of prosperity. The sea, which has slowly advanced since then, now surrounds many of the ruins, making for fascinating snorkeling.

❸ The Quill, the volcanic cone rising in the southern sector of the island, is 3 miles south of Oranjestad on the main road (*see* Hiking, *below*).

4 You'll need either a taxi or a car to visit this next site, and it's well worth the trouble. The **Lynch Plantation Museum,** also known as the Berkel Family Plantation, located out in Lynch Bay, is the only domestic museum in the Dutch Caribbean. It consists of two one-room buildings, set up as they were almost 100 years ago. There's a remarkable collection preserving this family's history—family pictures, Bibles, spectacles, a sewing machine, original furniture, and some farming and fishing implements give a detailed perspective of life in Statia. Ismael Berkel guides tours of the houses, and if you ask, he may proudly show you his two medals of honor from the Dutch royal families for his conservation efforts. Be sure to sign the guest register. *Lynch Bay, tours by appointment (call the tourist office at 599/38–2209 to arrange).* ☛ *Free; donations accepted.*

Off the Beaten Path

Local boys go up to the Quill by torchlight to catch delectable sand crabs. You can join them and ask your hotel to prepare your catch for dinner. The tourist board will make arrangements.

Beaches

Beachcombing is a sport for the intrepid: The beaches are pristine but tiny, unmaintained, and occasionally rocky. Sand is mainly volcanic black (actually varying shades of gray). The nicest strands are on the Atlantic side, but the surf is generally too rough for swimming. It is possible to hike around the coast at low tide, though a car is recommended to reach the more remote Atlantic stretches.

Smoke Alley Beach (also called **Oranje Beach**) is the nicest and most accessible. The beige-and-black-sand beach is on the Caribbean, off Lower Town, and is relatively deserted until late afternoon, when the locals arrive.

A 30-minute hike down an easy marked trail behind the Mountain Road will bring you to **Corre Corre Bay** and its gold-sand cove. Two bends north, **Lynch Bay** is somewhat protected from the wild swells. On the Atlantic side, especially around Concordia Bay, the surf is rough and there is sometimes a dangerous undertow, making beaches in this area better for sunning than swimming.

Zeelandia Beach is a 2-mile strip of black sand on the Atlantic side. A dangerous undertow runs here, but a small section is considered okay for swimming. Plans are being made to construct a breakwater to make the area safer for swimming. As is, it's a lovely and deserted stretch for sunning, walking, and wading.

A big deal on the beaches here is searching for Statia's famed blue glass beads. Manufactured in the 17th century by the Dutch West Indies Company, the blue glass beads were traded for rum, slaves, cotton, and tobacco. They were also awarded to faithful slaves or included as a part of the groom's settlement by the bride's father. Although they are found only on Statia, some researchers believe that it was beads like these that were traded for Manhattan. They're best unearthed after a heavy rain, but as the locals chuckle, "If you find one, it's a miracle, man."

Sports and the Outdoors

Fishing
Dive Statia (☎ 599/38–2435, 🖷 599/38–2539) has a 31-foot Chris-Craft available for deep-sea fishing. It also rents fishing gear.

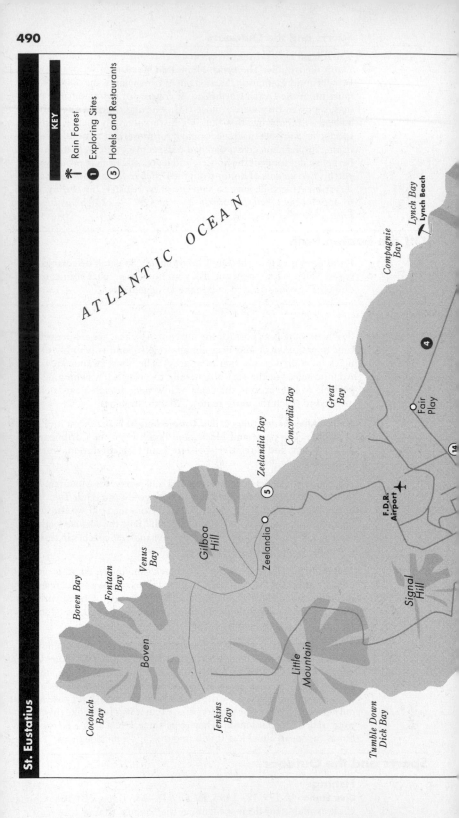

St. Eustatius

KEY

✳ Rain Forest

① Exploring Sites

⑤ Hotels and Restaurants

ATLANTIC OCEAN

Cocoluch Bay

Boven Bay

Fontaan Bay

Venus Bay

Boven

Gilboa Hill

Jenkins Bay

Little Mountain

Tumble Down Dick Bay

Zeelandia Bay

Zeelandia ⑤

Zeelandia

Concordia Bay

Great Bay

Signal Hill

F.D.R. Airport ✈

Compagnie Bay

Lynch Bay
Lynch Beach

Fair Play

④

⑭

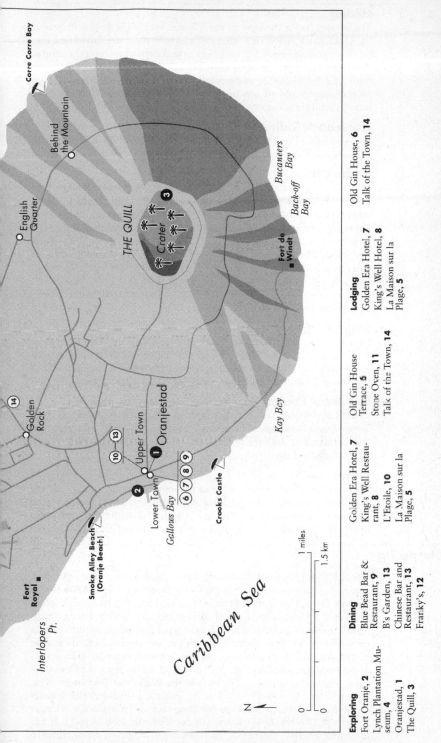

Exploring
Fort Oranje, **2**
Lynch Plantation Museum, **4**
Oranjestad, **1**
The Quill, **3**

Dining
Blue Bead Bar & Restaurant, **9**
B's Garden, **13**
Chinese Bar and Restaurant, **13**
Franky's, **12**
Golden Era Hotel, **7**
King's Well Restaurant, **8**
L'Etoile, **10**
La Maison sur la Plage, **5**
Old Gin House Terrace, **5**
Stone Oven, **11**
Talk of the Town, **14**

Lodging
Golden Era Hotel, **7**
King's Well Hotel, **8**
La Maison sur la Plage, **5**
Old Gin House, **6**
Talk of the Town, **14**

Corre Corre Bay

Behind the Mountain

English Quarter

THE QUILL

Crater

Bucaneers Bay

Back-off Bay

Fort de Windt

Golden Rock

Upper Town

Oranjestad

Lower Town

Gallows Bay

Kay Bay

Crooks Castle

Smoke Alley Beach (Oranje Beach)

Fort Royal

Interlopers Pt.

Caribbean Sea

N

0   1 miles

0   1.5 km

Hiking

Trails range from the easy to the "Watch out!" The big thrill here is the Quill, the 1,968-foot extinct volcano with its crater full of rain forest. Give yourself two to three hours to make the climb and the return. The tourist office has a list of 12 marked trails and can put you in touch with a guide (whose fee will be about $20). Wear layers: It can be cool on the summit and steamy in the interior. It is rumored that monkeys have taken up residence in the rain forest.

Horseback Riding

Eric and Sabra Pressman (☎ 599/38–2760) run a stable and offer trail rides, beach rides, and lessons.

Scuba Diving

Statia has more than 30 dive sites, including **Barracuda Reef,** where barracudas swim around colorful coral walls, and **Double Wreck,** where coral has taken on the shape of the two disintegrated ships. **Dive Statia** (☎ 599/38–2435, FAX 599/38–2539), a fully equipped and PADI-certified dive shop offering certification courses, is operated by Rudy and Rinda Hees out of a warehouse just down the road from the Old Gin House. Several hotels offer dive packages with Dive Statia, including the Golden Era, the Old Gin House, Kings Well, and Talk of the Town. Courses are also available in underwater photography, night diving, and multilevel diving.

Snorkeling

Crooks Castle has several stands of pillar coral, giant yellow sea fans, and sea whips. Jenkins Bay and Venus Bay are other favorites with snorkelers. For equipment rental, contact **Dive Statia** (*see* Scuba Diving, *above*). Equipment rentals are $5–$10; trips are about $20.

Spectator Sports

Cricket and soccer matches are played at the sports complex in Upper Town. Statia hosts teams from other Caribbean islands on weekends; admission is free. Call the office of the sports coordinator (☎ 599/38–2209) for schedules.

Tennis

There's a lone tennis court at the **community center** (☎ 599/38–2249) that's lighted at night. It has changing rooms, but you'll have to bring your own rackets and balls. The cost is $2 (check with the tourist office for more information). Volleyball and basketball are also played here.

Shopping

Though shopping on Statia is duty-free, it is also somewhat limited. A handful of shops do offer unusual items, however. The **Old Gin House** (Lower Town, Oranjestad, ☎ 599/38–2319) features handicrafts from around the Caribbean, as well as cottons silk-screened with traditional Statian motifs, sold both by the yard and made up into attractive resort wear. Barbara Lane shows her own sophisticated ceramic pieces, together with paintings and woven sculptures by local artists at the **Park Place Gallery** (☎ 599/38–2452) across from the Cool Corner in the center of town. The **Hole in the Wall** (Van Tonningen Weg, Upper Town, ☎ 599/38–2265) sells T-shirts, souvenirs, and jewelry on weekday mornings. **Mazinga Gift Shop** on Fort Oranjestraat in Upper Town (☎ 599/38–2245) is a small department store of sorts. It has duty-free jewelry, cosmetics, and liquor, in addition to beachwear, sports gear, stationery, film, books, and magazines. The **Paper Store** (Van Tonningen Weg, Upper Town, ☎ 599/38–2208) sells magazines, a few books, and stationery supplies. Check out the **Fun Shop** (Van Tonningen Weg, Upper Town, ☎ 599/38–82253) for toys and souvenirs.

Dining

The variety of cuisines here is surprising, given the size of the island. Besides the traditional West Indian fare, you can find French and Chinese cuisine. All restaurants are very casual, but do cover up your beachwear.

CATEGORY	COST*
$$$	over $25
$$	$15–$25
$	under $15

per person, excluding drinks and service

$$–$$$ **King's Well Restaurant.** "Good food, cold drinks and easy prices" reads the hand-painted sign at this breezy terrace eatery overlooking the sea, run by a fun-loving expatriate couple. Steaks are from Colorado, the lobster is fresh, and the *rostbraten* (roast beef) and schnitzels are authentic—one of the owners is German. ✕ *Bay Rd., Lower Town, Oranjestad,* ☎ *599/38–2538. Reservations advised. MC, V.*

$$ **B's Garden.** This patio spot in the courtyard next to the tourist office serves sandwiches and burgers—good enough to satisfy any homesick American—at lunch, and local cuisine, such as baked snapper with shrimp sauce and tenderloin steak with green peppercorn sauce, at dinner. The courtyard is surrounded by the beautiful old stone fort and government buildings. ✕ *Oranjestraat, Upper Town,* ☎ *599/38–2733. No credit cards. Dinner Tues. and Sat. only.*

$$ **Golden Era Hotel.** The restaurant and bar of this establishment are somewhat stark, but the Creole food is excellent and the large dining room is right on the water. Sunday-night buffets, a steal at $14, are popular, served outside by the pool and ocean, with a local band providing entertainment. ✕ *Golden Era Hotel, Bay Rd., Lower Town, Oranjestad,* ☎ *599/38–2345. AE, D, MC, V.*

$$ **La Maison sur la Plage.** The view here is of the Atlantic, and the fare is French. The two chefs (one is the owner; the other is well known in St. Barts restaurant circles) prepare some of the finest cuisine on the island. For dinner, start with the escargots and move on to the veal terrine with mushrooms and an herb sauce, served with a pastry top, or try the lamb medallions broiled with Roquefort cheese. Renovations under way in the restaurant will add a waterfall and a dark blue ceiling with lights simulating a starry night. ✕ *La Maison sur la Plage hotel, Zeelandia,* ☎ *599/38–2256. Reservations advised. MC, V.*

$$ **Old Gin House Terrace.** Dining is delightful on the oceanside terrace
★ across from the hotel. The menu may include lightly breaded stuffed crab, chicken salad, linguine Alfredo, New York strip steak, grouper fillet in lemon-dill sauce, and sandwiches. Lunch is more casual and offers lighter fare; dinner is by candlelight. Hearty breakfasts are also available. If renovations go as planned, dinner will soon be served in the old mansion in an elegant, candlelit, brick dining room full of antiques—call ahead to check. ✕ *Old Gin House, Bay Rd., Lower Town, Oranjestad,* ☎ *599/38–2319. Reservations advised. AE, D, MC, V.*

$$ **Talk of the Town.** Breakfast, lunch, and dinner are served at this pleasant restaurant midway between the airport and town. Pink tablecloths, an abundance of hanging plants, and softly seductive calypso music in the background weave a romantic spell. Local, Continental, and American dishes are offered, with seafood (predictably) the standout. Try the curried shrimp or the filet mignon. ✕ *L. E. Sadlerweg, near Upper Town,* ☎ *599/38–2236. AE, D, MC, V.*

$–$$ **Blue Bead Bar & Restaurant.** A friendly Dutch expatriate couple runs
★ this new restaurant with spectacular water views—don't miss a sunset cocktail here. Meals are served on a cheery bright blue- and yellow-trimmed veranda amid potted plants; the fare runs the gamut of influences: West Indian, Indonesian, Dutch, and American. The daily specials are recommended, as is anything made with owner and chef Phil's own saté sauce—a spicy, peanutty heaven. A steel band plays here on Saturday nights; the bar swings long after the kitchen closes. ✕ *Bay Rd., Lower Town,* ☎ *599/38–2873. No credit cards.*

$ **Chinese Bar and Restaurant.** Owner Kim Cheng serves up tasty Asian and Caribbean dishes—*Bamigoreng* (Indonesian chow mein), pork chops Creole—in hearty portions at his unpretentious establishment. Dining indoors can be slightly claustrophobic, but just ask your waitress if you may tote your Formica-top table out onto the terrace. She'll probably be happy to lend a hand and then serve you under the stars. ✕ *Prinsesweg, Upper Town, Oranjestad,* ☎ *599/38–2389. No credit cards.*

$ **Franky's.** Come here for good local barbecue: ribs, chicken, lobster,
★ and fish served later than at most other places on Statia. Try the bull-foot soup and goat-water stew. The less adventurous can get pizza on the weekend, when there is live music. ✕ *Ruyterweg, Upper Town, Oranjestad,* ☎ *599/38–2575. No credit cards.*

$ **L'Etoile.** West Indian dishes, such as spicy stuffed land crab and goat meat, are served at this simple snack bar–restaurant. You can also order hot dogs, hamburgers, and spareribs. ✕ *Heiligerweg, Upper Town, Oranjestad,* ☎ *599/38–2299. No credit cards.*

$ **Stone Oven.** A Spanish couple runs this cozy little eatery, offering such West Indian specialties as goat-water stew. You can eat either indoors in the little house or outside on the palm-fringed patio. ✕ *16A Feaschweg, Upper Town, Oranjestad,* ☎ *599/38–2543. No credit cards.*

Lodging

There are no luxury accommodations on Statia; as a rule, cheerful is the best you can expect. Many of the properties include breakfast, making most of them quite affordable.

CATEGORY	COST*
$$$$	over $125
$$$	$100–$125
$$	$75–$100
$	under $75

All prices are for a standard double room for two, excluding 7% tax and 10%–15% service charge.

Hotels

$$ **Golden Era Hotel.** This is a harborfront hotel whose rooms are neat, air-conditioned, and motel-modern, with minifridges, TVs, and phones, and simple (sometimes old) furniture. All have little terraces, but only half have a full or partial view of the sea; the rest look out over concrete or down onto the roof of the restaurant. There is little that is aesthetically attractive about this hotel, but at least it is central, by the water, and enjoys a cheerful clientele and an accommodating and friendly staff. 🏨 *Bay Rd., Box 109, Lower Town, Oranjestad,* ☎ *599/38–2345 or 800/223–9815,* ℻ *599/38–2445. 19 rooms, 1 suite. Restaurant, bar, saltwater pool. AE, D, MC, V. EP.*

$$ **La Maison sur la Plage.** The main attraction of this isolated area is the Atlantic, whose wild waters slap the 2-mile crescent of gray sand. The undertow for much of the strip here can be dangerous, but there is a safer area a few minutes' walk down the beach. The hotel's cozy lobby has rattan furnishings, a checkerboard on the coffee table, and shelves filled with books. There's a stone-and-wood bar, and a *très* French dining room bordered by a trellis and greenery. Owners Therese and Michel Viali are repainting, adding new roofs and louvered windows, renovating the French gourmet restaurant, and redecorating each of the five spartan cottages with pastel print spreads and drapes, natural wood furnishings, and ceiling fans. Rooms do not have TVs or phones. Continental breakfast is served on the porch of the main building, overlooking the water. ⊠ *Zeelandia Rd., Box 157, Zeelandia,* ☎ *599/38–2256,* FAX *599/38–2831. 10 rooms with bath. Restaurant, bar, lounge, saltwater pool, volleyball on beach, putting green. MC, V. CP.*

$$ **Old Gin House.** This property, fashioned by American expatriate John May out of the ruins of an 18th-century cotton-gin factory and warehouse, was once known as one of the finest inns in the Caribbean. With brand-new ownership (a resort interest from St. Kitts), hopes are high of major restoration and renewed luster. The main building is two stories high and has bougainvillea-swathed double balconies that overlook a secluded pool and courtyard. At press time, renovations of the elegant indoor dining room here were slated for completion by late 1995. Across the street, overlooking the sea, are the highly acclaimed Old Gin House Terrace restaurant and another building containing an additional six rooms. All the rooms, individually decorated with lovely antiques and artwork from the former owner's collection, have balconies. There are no phones, TV, or air conditioners—ceiling fans and ocean breezes cool the rooms. ⊠ *Box 172, Oranjestad,* ☎ *599/38–2319. 20 rooms. 2 restaurants, bar, lounge, pool, library. AE, D, DC, MC, V. EP.*

$–$$ **Kings Well Hotel.** Perched on the cliffs between Upper Town and Lower Town, this small hotel offers four rooms, each with water views, a balcony, minifridge, TV, and bath with shower only. The rooms are pleasant but sparsely furnished and don't have phones. The two back rooms are more spacious, offer the best views, have ceiling fans, and feature queen-size waterbeds—well worth the extra $20. The hotel is in the first stages of renovation; a new dining area and a combination pool-Jacuzzi were under construction at press time. The owners, an expatriate couple, hope to attract a sailing clientele; they will lease their yacht charter license to interested parties and also arrange sailing lessons. The restaurant serves a complimentary Continental breakfast, as well as lunch and dinner (*see* Dining, *above*). ⊠ *Bay Rd., Lower Town, Oranjestad,* ☎ *and fax 599/38–2538. 4 rooms. Restaurant, bar. MC, V. CP.*

$–$$ **Talk of the Town.** These simple but bright rooms are decorated with
★ locally handcrafted furnishings, dark carpeting, beamed ceilings, floral spreads, and local art. Four tidy cottages (nine rooms total) with red roofs and coral trim surround the pool. All rooms have air-conditioning, gleaming white baths with shower only, cable TV, and direct-dial phone. There is a swimming pool, a deck with lounge chairs, and a restaurant downstairs. The hotel is on the road between the airport and town, an excellent choice for those who don't need a water view. Breakfast is included. Children under 12 stay free. ⊠ *L. E. Saddlerweg,* ☎ *599/38–2236,* FAX *599/38–2640. 18 rooms, 2 with kitchenettes. Restaurant, bar, pool. MC, V. CP.*

Apartment Rentals

Statia has only a handful of apartments, though a spate of small developments and guest houses have gone up recently to meet demand.

As a general rule, figure $50 and under per night and don't expect much beyond a bathroom and kitchenette.

Check with the tourist office for information about other apartment rentals on the island.

Nightlife

Statia's five local bands stay busy on weekends. **Talk of the Town** (*see* Lodging, *above*) is the place to be for live music on Friday night. Saturday nights **Cool Corner** (*see* Dining, *above*) and the **Exit Disco** at the Stone Oven restaurant (*see* Dining, *above*) have dancing and occasionally host live bands. Sometimes the **community center** (☏ 599/38–2249) has a dance. Sunday nights find everyone at the **Golden Era Hotel** (*see* Lodging, *above*) for live music. Crowds are found all weekend at **Franky's** (*see* Dining, *above*) and the **Lago Heights Club and Disco** (at the shopping center in Chapelpiece, no phone), known to all as Gerald's, which has dancing and a late-night barbecue.

21 St. Kitts and Nevis

Updated by
Jordan Simon

FOR YEARS, VISITORS TO ST. KITTS AND NEVIS have tended to be self-sufficient types who know how to amuse themselves and appreciate the warmth and character of country inns. The Frigate Bay area of St. Kitts is the only area with a few larger hotels and condominium developments. However, big hotels are heading this way, and these islands will soon be attracting a broader clientele. The Four Seasons opened a resort in 1991 on tiny Nevis. Now several brand-name hotels are in the early stages of development on St. Kitts's South East Peninsula.

Tiny though it is, mountainous St. Kitts, the first English settlement in the Leeward Islands, crams some stunning scenery into its 65 square miles. Vast, brilliant green fields of sugarcane sweep down to the sea. The island is fertile and lush with tropical flora and has some fascinating natural and historical attractions: a rain forest, replete with waterfalls, thick vines, and secret trails; a central mountain range, dominated by the 3,792-foot Mt. Liamuiga, whose crater has been long dormant; and Brimstone Hill, the Caribbean's most impressive fortress, which was known in the 17th century as the Gibraltar of the West Indies.

The island is home to 35,000 people and hosts some 60,000 visitors annually. The shape of St. Kitts has been variously compared to a whale, a cricket bat, and a guitar. It's roughly oval, 19 miles long and 6 miles wide, with a narrow peninsula trailing off toward Nevis, 2 miles southeast across the strait.

The island is known as the mother colony of the West Indies because it was from here that the English settlers sailed to Antigua, Barbuda, Tortola, and Montserrat and the French dispatched colonizing parties to Martinique, Guadeloupe, St. Martin, St. Barts, La Désirade, and Les Saintes. The French, who inexplicably brought a bunch of monkeys with themas pets, arrived on St. Kitts a few years after the British.

In 1493, when Columbus spied a cloud-crowned volcanic isle during his second voyage to the New World, he named it *Nieves,* the Spanish word for "snows." It reminded him of the snowcapped peaks of the Pyrenees. Nevis (pronounced *Nee*-vis) rises out of the water in an almost perfect cone, the tip of its 3,232-foot central mountain smothered in clouds. It's less developed than its sister island, St. Kitts.

Nevis is known for its natural beauty—long beaches with white and black sand, lush greenery—for a half dozen mineral spa baths, and for the restored sugar plantations that now house small, charming inns. In 1628, settlers from St. Kitts sailed across the 2-mile channel that separates the two islands. At first they grew tobacco, cotton, ginger, and indigo, but with the introduction of sugarcane in 1640, Nevis became the island equivalent of a boomtown. As the mineral baths were drawing crowds, the island was producing an abundance of sugar. Slaves were brought from Africa to work on the magnificent estates, many of them nestled high in the mountains amid lavish tropical gardens.

The restored plantation homes that now operate as inns are the island's most sybaritic lures for the leisurely life. There is plenty of activity for the energetic—mountain climbing, swimming, tennis, horseback riding, snorkeling. But the going is easy here, with hammocks for snoozing, lobster bakes on palm-lined beaches, and candlelit dinners in stately dining rooms and on romantic verandas.

As rich in history as it is fertile and lush with tropical flora, St. Kitts is just beginning to develop its tourism industry, and this quiet member of the Leeward group has that rare combination of natural and historic attractions and fine sailing, island hopping, and water-sports options offshore.

Nevis is linked with St. Kitts politically. The two islands, together with Anguilla, achieved self-government as an Associated State of Great Britain in 1967. In 1983, St. Kitts and Nevis became a fully independent nation. Nevis papers sometimes run fiery articles advocating independence from St. Kitts, and the sister islands may separate someday. However, it's not likely that a shot will be fired, let alone one that will be heard around the world.

Before You Go

Tourist Information

Contact the **St. Kitts & Nevis Tourist Board** (414 E. 75th St., New York, NY 10021, ☎ 212/535–1234 or 800/582–6208, FAX 212/734–6511), **St. Kitts & Nevis Tourist Office** (11 Yorkville Ave., Suite 508, Toronto, Ontario M4W 1L3, ☎ 416/921–7717, FAX 416/921–7997), **St. Kitts & Nevis Tourist Office** (10 Kensington Ct., London W8 5DL, ☎ 0171/376–0881, FAX 0171/937–3611), and **St. Kitts & Nevis Tourist Office** (President's Plaza II, 8700 Bryn Mawr, Suite 800 S, Chicago, IL 60631, ☎ 312/714–5015, FAX 312/714–4910).

Arriving and Departing

BY PLANE

American (☎ 800/433–7300) and **Delta** (☎ 800/221–1212) fly from the United States to Antigua, St. Croix, St. Thomas, St. Maarten, and San Juan, Puerto Rico, where connections to St. Kitts (and to a lesser extent, to Nevis) can be made on regional carriers such as **American Eagle,** part of the **American Airlines** system (☎ 800/433–7300); **LIAT** (☎ 809/465–2511); and **Windward Island Airways** (☎ 809/465–0810). LIAT has two flights daily between St. Kitts and Nevis. **British Airways** (☎ 800/247–9297) flies from London to Antigua, and **Air Canada** (☎ 800/422–6232) flies from Toronto to Antigua. **Air St. Kitts–Nevis** (☎ 809/465–8571), **Nevis Express** (☎ 809/469–9755), and **Carib Aviation** (in St. Kitts, ☎ 809/465–3055; in Nevis, 809/469–9295; fax 809/469–9185) are reliable air-charter operations providing service between St. Kitts and Nevis and other islands.

FROM THE AIRPORT

Taxis meet every flight at the airports on both islands. The taxis are unmetered, but fixed rates, in E.C. dollars, are posted at the airport and at the jetty. On St. Kitts the fare from the airport to the closest hotel in Basseterre is E.C.$16; to the farthest point, E.C.$56. On Nevis some sample fares are from the ferry slip to Nisbet Plantation, E.C.$17, and to Golden Rock, E.C.$40. (The current exchange rate is E.C.$2.60 for U.S.$1.) Be sure to clarify whether the rate quoted is in E.C. or U.S. dollars. There is a 50% surcharge for trips made between 10 PM and 6 AM.

BY BOAT

The 150-passenger government-operated ferry MV *Caribe Queen* makes the 45-minute crossing from Nevis to St. Kitts daily except Thursday and Sunday. The schedule is a bit erratic, so confirm departure times with the tourist office. Round-trip fare is U.S.$8. A new, air-conditioned, 110-passenger ferry, MV *Spirit of Mount Nevis,* makes the run twice daily except Monday and Wednesday. The fare is U.S.$12 round-trip. Call **Nevis Cruise Lines** (☎ 809/469–9373) for information and reser-

500 St. Kitts and Nevis

vations. Sea-taxi service between the two islands is operated by dive master Kenneth Samuel (☎ 809/465–2670) and by Auston MacLeod of Pro-Divers (☎ 809/465–3223) for U.S.$20 (summer), $25 (winter).

Passports and Visas
Although it is always wiser to travel in the Caribbean with a valid passport, U.S. and Canadian citizens need only produce proof of citizenship in the form of a voter registration card or birth certificate (a driver's license will not suffice). British citizens must have a passport; visas are not required. All visitors must have a return or ongoing ticket.

Language
English with a strong West Indian lilt is spoken here.

Precautions
Visitors, especially women, are warned not to go jogging on long, lonely roads.

ST. KITTS

Staying in St. Kitts

Important Addresses
Tourist Information: St. Kitts/Nevis Department of Tourism (Pelican Mall, Bay Rd., Box 132, Basseterre, ☎ 809/465–2620 or 809/465–4040, FAX 809/465–8794) and the **St. Kitts–Nevis Hotel Association** (Box 438, Basseterre, ☎ 809/465–5304, FAX 809/465–7746).

EMERGENCIES
Police: Call 911. **Hospital:** There is a 24-hour emergency room at the **Joseph N. France General Hospital** (Basseterre, ☎ 809/465–2551). **Pharmacies:** In Basseterre, **Skerritt's Drug Store** (Fort St., ☎ 809/465–2008) is open Monday–Wednesday 8–5, Thursday 8–1, Friday 8–5:30, and Saturday 8–6; **City Drug** (Fort St., Basseterre, ☎ 809/465–2156) is open Monday–Wednesday and Friday–Saturday 8–7; Thursday 8–5, Sunday 8–10 AM; and **City Drug** (Sun 'n' Sand, Frigate Bay, ☎ 809/465–1803) is open Monday–Saturday 8:30–8, Sunday 8:30–10:30 AM and 4–6 PM.

Currency
Legal tender is the Eastern Caribbean (E.C.) dollar. At press time, the rate of exchange was E.C.$2.60 to U.S.$1. U.S. dollars are accepted practically everywhere, but you'll almost always get change in E.C. dollars. Prices quoted here are in U.S. dollars unless noted otherwise. Most large hotels, restaurants, and shops accept major credit cards, but small inns and shops usually do not. It's always a good idea to check current credit-card policies before you turn up with only plastic in your pocket.

Taxes and Service Charges
Hotels collect a 7% government tax and add a 10% service charge to your bill. In restaurants, a tip of 10%–15% is appropriate. The departure tax is $10. There is no departure tax from St. Kitts to Nevis, or vice versa.

Guided Tours
Tropical Tours (☎ 809/465–4167) can run you around the island and take you to the rain forest. **Kriss Tours** (☎ 809/465–4042) and **Greg's Safari** (☎ 809/465–4121) specialize in rain-forest and volcano tours.

Getting Around

TAXIS

Taxis rates are government regulated, and the rates are posted at the airport and the dock and in the free **Traveller** tourist guide. There are fixed rates to and from all the hotels and to and from major points of interest. Taxi drivers are also happy to give tours. Stop by the **St. Kitts/Nevis Department of Tourism** in Basseterre or the front desk of your hotel to arrange for a tour. You can also call the **St. Kitts Taxi Association** (☎ 809/465–4253; after hours, ☎ 809/465–7818). Expect to pay approximately $50 for a 3½-hour island taxi tour.

BUSES

A privately owned minibus circles the island. Check with the tourist office about schedules.

RENTAL CARS AND SCOOTERS

You'll need a local driver's license, which you can get by presenting yourself, your valid driver's license, and E.C.$30 (U.S.$12) at the police station on Cayon Street in Basseterre. Rentals are available at **Avis** (☎ 809/465–6507), **Holiday** (☎ 809/465–6507), and **Caines** (☎ 809/465–2366). **Economy Car** (☎ 809/465–8449) also rents scooter bikes. **TDC Rentals** (☎ 809/465–2991) has a wide selection of vehicles and the best service. Car rentals run about U.S.$35 per day. At press time, the price of gas was U.S.$2 per gallon. Remember to drive on the left!

Telephones and Mail

To call St. Kitts from the United States, dial area code 809, then access code 465 or 469 and the local four-digit number. Caribbean Phone Cards, which can be purchased in denominations of $5, $10, and $20, are handy for making local phone calls, calling other islands, and accessing USADirect lines. To make an intraisland call, simply dial the seven-digit number.

Airmail letters to the United States and Canada cost E.C.80¢ per half ounce; postcards require E.C.50¢. Mail takes at least 7–10 days to reach the United States. St. Kitts and Nevis issue separate stamps, but each also honors the other's. The beautiful stamps are collector's items, and you may have a hard time pasting them on postcards.

Opening and Closing Times

Although shops used to close for lunch from noon to 1, more and more establishments are remaining open Monday–Saturday 8–4. Some shops close earlier on Thursday. Hours vary somewhat from bank to bank but are typically Monday–Thursday 8–3 and Friday 8–5. St. Kitts & Nevis National Bank is also open Saturday 8:30–11.

Exploring St. Kitts

Numbers in the margin correspond to points of interest on the St. Kitts map.

Basseterre

➊ The capital city of **Basseterre,** set in the southern part of the island, is an easily walkable town. It is graced with tall palms, and although many of the buildings appear run-down and in need of paint, you will find interesting shopping areas, excellent art galleries, and some beautifully maintained houses. You can see the main sights of the capital city in a half hour or so; allow three to four hours for an island tour.

If you don't have a map, pick one up at the **St. Kitts tourist office** (Tourism Complex, Bay Rd.). Turn left when you leave there and walk past the handsome Treasury Building. It faces the octagonal **Circus,** which is built

502

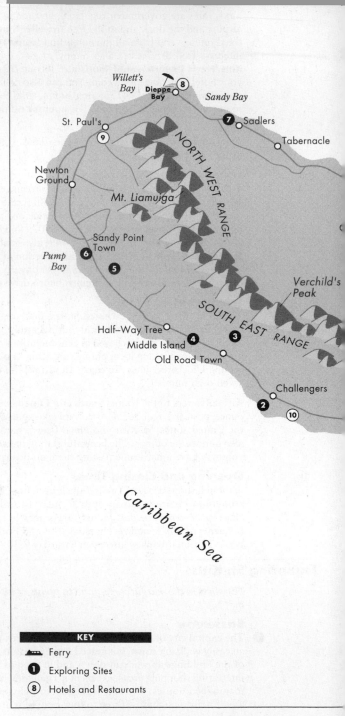

KEY

🚢 Ferry

1 Exploring Sites

8 Hotels and Restaurants

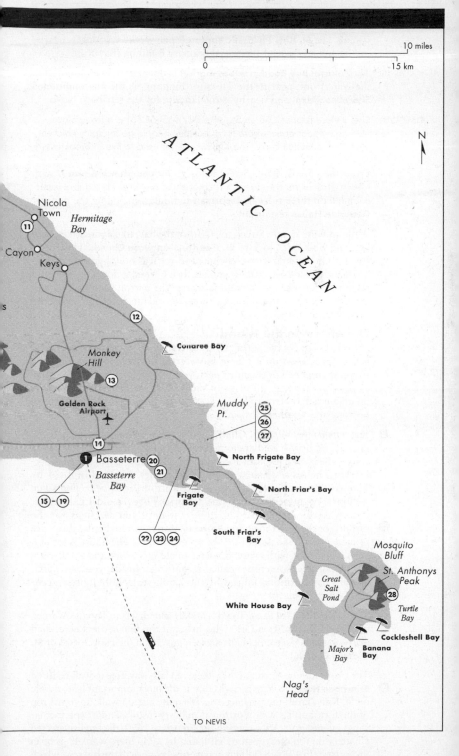

0   10 miles
0   15 km

N

ATLANTIC OCEAN

Nicola
Town
⑪
*Hermitage
Bay*
Cayon
Keys

⑫

🏖 **Conaree Bay**

*Monkey
Hill*
⑬

**Golden Rock
Airport**

*Muddy
Pt.*   ㉕
               ㉖
               ㉗

⑭

❶ **Basseterre** ⑳
⑪   ㉑
*Basseterre
Bay*

⑮ – ⑲

🏖 **North Frigate Bay**

🏖 **North Friar's Bay**

**Frigate
Bay**

㉒ ㉓ ㉔

🏖 **South Friar's
Bay**

*Mosquito
Bluff*
*St. Anthonys
Peak*
㉘

*Great
Salt
Pond*   *Turtle
Bay*

🏖 **White House Bay**

🏖 **Cockleshell Bay**

*Major's
Bay*   **Banana
Bay**

🛥

*Nag's
Head*

TO NEVIS

in the style of London's famous Piccadilly Circus. Duty-free shops can be found along the streets and courtyards leading off from around the Circus. The **St. Kitts Philatelic Bureau** (open weekdays 8–4) is nearby on the second floor of the Social Security Building (Bay Rd.).

The colorful **Bay Road produce market** is open on weekends only. On the waterfront, next to the Treasury Building, is the air-conditioned **Shoreline Plaza,** and nearby is the landing for the ferries to Nevis.

TIME OUT   **Chef's Place** (Upper Church St., ☎ 809/465–6176) is a lively place with an outdoor patio where local businesspeople go for spicy chicken platters and mutton curry. The Kittitian owner used to live in Brooklyn.

From the Circus, Bank Street leads to **Independence Square,** with lovely gardens on the site of a former slave market. The square is surrounded on three sides by Georgian buildings, including the popular **Georgian House** restaurant.

Walk up West Square Street, away from the bay, to Cayon Street, turn left, and walk one block to **St. George's Anglican Church.** This handsome stone building with crenellated tower was built by the French in 1670 and called Nôtre Dame. The British burned it down in 1706 and rebuilt it four years later, naming it after the patron saint of England. Since then, it has suffered fire, earthquake, and hurricanes and was once again rebuilt in 1859.

Elsewhere on the Island

Main Road traces the perimeter of the large, northwestern part of the island. Head west on it out of Basseterre, and be prepared for some stunning scenery. For the most part, you'll always have the sea in view as you drive through the acres of sugar fields that encircle the island's mountain range. Here and there you'll see tiny villages with tiny houses of stone and weathered wood.

2 Just outside the village of Challengers is **Bloody Point,** where, in 1629, French and British soldiers joined forces to repel a mass attack by the Caribs. Be on the lookout for signs for **Old Road Town,** the first permanent English settlement in the West Indies, founded in 1624 by Thomas Warner. Take the side road toward the interior to find some well-preserved Carib petroglyphs, testimony of even older habitation. Return to the main road and follow it until you see signs for the **3** turnoff for the rain forest and **Romney Manor,** where batik fabrics are printed at **Caribelle Batik** (*see* Shopping, *below*). The house is set in 6 acres of gardens, with exotic flowers, an old bell tower, and a 350-year-old saman tree (sometimes called a rain tree). Inside, you can watch artisans hand-printing fabrics by the 2,500-year-old Indonesian process known as *batik.*

4 The village after Old Road Town is **Middle Island,** where Thomas Warner, the "gentleman of London" who brought the first settlers here, died in 1648 and is buried beneath a green gazebo in the churchyard of **St. Thomas Church.**

The road continues through the village of Half-Way Tree to well-restored **5** **Brimstone Hill,** a 38-acre fortress that is the most important historic site on St. Kitts. From the parking area it's quite a steep walk up to the top of the fort, but it's well worth it if military history and/or spectacular views interest you. After routing the French in 1690, the English erected a battery on top of Brimstone Hill, and by 1736 there were 49 guns in the fortress. In 1782, 8,000 French troops lay siege to the fortress, which was defended by 350 militia and 600 regular troops of the Royal Scots and East Yorkshires. A plaque in the old stone wall marks the place where the fort was breached. When the English finally surrendered, the French allowed them to march from the fort in full formation out of respect for their bravery. (The English afforded the French the same honor when they surrendered the fort a mere year later.) A hurricane did extensive damage to the fortress in 1834, and in 1852 it was evacuated and dismantled. The beautiful stones were carted away to build houses.

The citadel has been partially reconstructed and its guns remounted. A seven-minute orientation film recounts the fort's history and restoration. You can see what remains of the officers' quarters, the redoubts, barracks, the ordnance store, and the cemetery. Its museums display, among other things, pre-Columbian artifacts, a new collection of objects pertaining to the African heritage of the island's slaves (masks, ceremonial tools, etc.), weaponry, uniforms, photographs, and old newspapers. In 1985, Queen Elizabeth visited Brimstone Hill and officially opened it as part of a national park. There's a splendid view from here that includes Montserrat and Nevis to the southeast, Saba and Statia to the northwest, and St. Barts and St. Maarten to the north. Nature trails snake through the tangle of surrounding hardwood forest and savannah (a fine spot to catch the green vervet monkeys skittering about). *Main Rd., Brimstone Hill.* ☞ *$5 adults, $2.50, children.* ☉ *Daily 9:30–5:30.*

TIME OUT **J's Place** (☎ 809/465–6264), across from the entrance to the fort, is ideal for a drink, a sandwich, or a full West Indian meal, including a sensational lobster salad.

6 Continuing on through seas of sugarcane, past breadfruit trees and old stone walls, you'll come to **Sandy Point Town.** The houses here are West Indian–style raised cottages. The **Roman Catholic church** has lovely stained-glass windows.

Farther along, just outside the village of **Newton Ground,** are the remains of an old sugar mill and some ancient coconut palms. Outside the village of **St. Paul's** is a road that leads to **Rawlins Plantation,** a restored sugar plantation that's popular for dining and lodging. The fishing town of **Dieppe Bay** is at the northernmost point of the island. Its tiny black-sand beach is backed by the **Golden Lemon,** one of the **7** Caribbean's most famous inns (*see* Lodging, *below*). **Black Rocks** on the Atlantic coast just outside the town of Sadlers, in Sandy Bay, are lava deposits, spat into the sea ages ago when the island's volcano erupted. They have since been molded into fanciful shapes by centuries of pounding surf. The drive back to Basseterre around the other side of the island is a pleasant one, through small, neat villages with centuries-old stone churches and pastel-colored cottages.

But perhaps the most spectacular drive is yet ahead of you. Go south through the **Frigate Bay** area (home to many hotels) and take the splendid $12 million Dr. Kennedy Simmonds Highway to the tip of the **South East Peninsula.** Reminiscent of California's famed Highway 1, this ultrasleek modern road twists and turns through the grassy hills (as yet virtually undeveloped) that rise between the calm Caribbean sea and the windswept Atlantic. At the far end, once you're back to sea level, follow the signs to Turtle Bay Beach for great views of Nevis and the OTI Turtle Beach Bar and Grill (*see* Dining, *below*).

Beaches

All beaches on the island are free and open to the public, even those occupied by hotels. The powdery white-sand beaches are all in the Frigate Bay area of the island or on the lower peninsula.

Two of the island's best beaches are the twin beaches of **Banana Bay** and **Cockleshell Bay,** which together cover more than 2 miles at the southeastern tip of the island. Several large hotels, including the Banana Bay and Casablanca, were abandoned in the early stages of development, their skeletal structures marring an otherwise idyllic scene.

Locals consider the Caribbean side of **Friar's Bay** the island's finest beach. You can haggle with fishermen here to take you out snorkeling off the eastern point. The waters on the Atlantic side are rougher, but the beach itself has a wild, desolate beauty. **White House Bay** is rocky, but the snorkeling, taking in several reefs surrounding a sunken tugboat, is superb. A tiny dirt road, virtually impassable after heavy rains, leads to **Sandbank Beach** on the Atlantic side. The shallow coves are protected here, making it ideal for families, and it's usually deserted.

North of these beaches is talcum-powder-fine **Frigate Bay,** on the Caribbean. On the Atlantic, **North Frigate Bay** is 4 miles wide and a favorite with horseback riders (*see* Sports and the Outdoors, *below*).

Beaches elsewhere on the island are of gray-black volcanic sand. **Conaree Bay** on the Atlantic side is a narrow strip of gray-black sand where the water is good for body surfing (no facilities). Snorkeling and windsurfing are good at **Dieppe Bay,** a black-sand beach on the north coast, where the Golden Lemon hotel is located.

Sports and the Outdoors

Boating
Sunfish and Hobie Cats can be rented at **Tropical Surf** (Turtle Bay, ☎ 809/469–9086) and **Mr. X Watersports** (Frigate Bay, ☎ 809/465–4995).

Deep-Sea Fishing
Angle for yellowtail snapper, wahoo, mackerel, tuna, dolphin, shark, and barracuda with **Tropical Tours** (☎ 809/465–4167) and **Captain Redbeard Boat Charters** (☎ 809/465–0482).

Golf
The **Royal St. Kitts Golf Club** (☎ 809/465–8339) is an 18-hole championship course in the Frigate Bay area.

Hiking
Trails in the central mountains vary from easy to don't-try-it-by-yourself. Monkey Hill and Verchild's Peak are not difficult, although the Verchild's climb will take the better part of a day. Don't attempt Mt. Liamuiga without a guide. You'll start at Belmont Estates on horseback, then proceed on foot to the lip of the crater at 2,600 feet. You can go down into the crater, clinging to vines and roots. **Greg Pereira** (☎ 809/465–4121) takes groups on half-day trips into the rain forest and on full-day hikes up the volcano. **Kriss Tours** (☎ 809/465–4042) takes small groups into the crater and to Dos d'Anse Pond on Verchild's Mountain. Oliver Spencer takes hikers **Off the Beaten Track** (☎ 809/465–6314) to the ruins of a fragrant, abandoned coffee plantation taken over by sprawling banyan trees.

Horseback Riding

Frigate Bay and Conaree Beach are great for riding. Guides from **Trinity Stable** (☎ 809/465–3226) will lead you into the hills at a leisurely gait. **Royal Stables** (☎ 809/465–2222) offers sunset beach rides and tours into the rain forest on horseback.

Scuba Diving and Snorkeling

Kenneth Samuel of **Kenneth's Dive Centre** (☎ 809/465–7043 or 809/465–2670) is a PADI-certified dive master who takes small groups of divers with C cards to nearby reefs. Auston MacLeod, a PADI-certified dive master–instructor and owner of **Pro-Divers** (☎ 809/465–3223), offers resort and certification courses. He also has Nikonos camera equipment for rent.

There are more than a dozen excellent dive sites on St. Kitts, all with a variety of sea life and color. **Coconut Tree Reef,** one of the largest in the area, includes sea fans, sponges, and anemones. **Black Coral Reef** features the rare black coral tree. **Brassball Wreck** is a shallow-water wreck, good for snorkeling and photography. **Redonda Bank** is an extensive area of reef that's just beginning to be explored. The shallow **Tug Boat** is a good spot for snorkelers.

Sea Excursions

Leeward Island Charters (☎ 809/465–7474) offers day and overnight charters on two catamarans—the 47-foot *Caona* and the 70-foot *Spirit of St. Kitts*. Day sails are from 9:30 to 4:30 and include barbecue, open bar, and snorkeling equipment. **Tropical Tours** (☎ 809/465–4167) offers moonlight cruises on the 52-foot catamaran *Cileca III* and glass-bottom boat tours. *Juzzle II* (☎ 809/465–3529) is another glass-bottom boat that cruises the southeastern coast, with free snorkeling equipment. *Tropical Dreamer* (☎ 809/465–8224) is another catamaran available for day and sunset cruises. For the ultimate underwater trip, call **Blue Frontier Ltd.** (☎ 809/465–4945); owner Lindsey Beck will take you for a half-hour ride off Frigate Bay in his two-man submarine.

Tennis

There are four lighted courts at **Jack Tar Village Beach Resorts** (☎ 809/465–8651), two lighted courts at **Sun 'n' Sand Beach Village** (☎ 809/465–6221), as well as one court each at **Bird Rock Beach Hotel** (☎ 809/465 8914), the **Golden Lemon** (☎ 809/465–7260), and **Rawlins Plantation** (☎ 809/465–6221).

Waterskiing and Windsurfing

Tropical Surf (☎ 809/469–9086) at Turtle Bay rents Windsurfers, surfboards, and boogie boards. **Fantasy Parasailing** (Frigate Bay, ☎ 809/465–8930) will have you flying as high as 600 feet above the turquoise waters.

Spectator Sports

Cricket matches are played in Warner Park from January to July, **soccer** from July to December, **softball** from January to August. Contact the tourist board (☎ 809/465–4040) for schedules.

Shopping

St. Kitts has limited shopping, but there are a few duty-free shops where you can find some good buys in jewelry, watches, perfume, china, and crystal. Excellent paintings and sculptures can be found at several galleries around the island. Among the island crafts, the best-known are the batik fabrics, scarves, caftans, and wall hangings of Caribelle Batik. There are also locally produced jams, jellies, herb teas, and handcrafts of local shell, straw, and coconut. And CSR (Cane Spirit Rothschild) is a "new cane spirit drink" that's distilled from fresh sugarcane right on St. Kitts.

Shopping Districts

Most shopping plazas are in downtown Basseterre near the Circus. Some shops have tiny branches in other areas, particularly in Dieppe Bay. The **Pelican Mall** has 26 stores, a restaurant, tourism offices, and a bandstand. This shopping arcade is designed to look like a traditional Caribbean street. **TDC Mall** is just off the Circus in downtown Basseterre. **Shoreline Plaza** is next to the Treasury Building, right on the waterfront in Basseterre. **Palms Arcade** is on Fort Street, also near the Circus.

Good Buys

TDC (TDC Plaza, on Bank St., ☎ 809/465–2511) carries fine china and crystal, along with cameras and other imports.

Slice of the Lemon (Palms Arcade, ☎ 809/465–2889) carries fine perfumes but is better known for its elegant jewelry. **Lemonaid** (Dieppe Bay, ☎ 809/465–7359) has select Caribbean handicrafts, antiques, and clothing by John Warden.

Island Crafts and Gifts

Caribelle Batik (Romney Manor, ☎ 809/465–6253) sells batik wraps, T-shirts, dresses, wall hangings, and the like. **Island Hopper** (The Circus, ☎ 809/465–2905) is a good place for island crafts, especially wood carvings. **Palm Crafts** (Palms Arcade, ☎ 809/465–2599) sells a variety of goodies, including savory Caribbean jams and jellies. **Spencer Cameron Art Gallery** (N. Independence Sq., ☎ 809/465–1617) has historical reproductions of Caribbean island charts and prints, in addition to owner Rosey Cameron's popular Carnevale clown prints and a wide selection of exceptional artwork by Caribbean artists. They will mail anywhere, so you don't have to lug home something that catches your eye. The **Plantation Picture House** (Fort St., ☎ 809/465–7740) showcases the enchanting silk pareus, jewelry, prints, and papiermâché works of Kate Spencer (who also has a studio at the Rawlins Plantation). **Rosemary Lane Antiques** (7 Rosemary La., ☎ 809/465–5450) occupies a beautifully retored 18th-century town house and is crammed with superlative, affordable antiques and objets d'art from throughout the Caribbean. They will gladly ship any purchases. **Splash** (TDC Plaza, Bank St., ☎ 809/465–9279) carries colorful beachwear by local designers. **Music World** (The Circus, ☎ 809/465–1998) offers a vast selection of island rhythms—lilting soca and zouk, pulsating salsa and merengue, wicked hiphop, and mellow reggae and calypso.

Dining

St. Kitts restaurants range from funky little beachfront bistros to small, elegant plantation dining rooms; there is an interesting variety of cuisine to sample, most tinged, one way or another, with the flavors of the Caribbean. Many restaurants offer a variety of West Indian specialties that are popular on St. Kitts, such as curried mutton, Arawak chicken (seasoned chicken, rice, and almonds served on breadfruit leaf), pepper pot, and honey-glazed garlic spare ribs.

What to Wear

Dress is casual at lunch (but no bathing suits!) throughout the island. Dinner, while not necessarily formal, definitely calls for long pants and sundresses.

CATEGORY	COST*
$$$$	over $40
$$$	$30–$40
$$	$20–$30
$	under $20

per person, excluding drinks and service. There is no sales tax on St. Kitts.

$$$$ **Patio Restaurant.** Owner Peter Mallalieu and his daughter Helen, a graduate of the Culinary Institute of America, prepare a full à la carte menu with complimentary wine and liqueur, by reservation only, in his flower-filled home. Try the flame-broiled mahimahi with shrimp, or treat yourself to a sampling of traditional local dishes, including *conki* (a coconut side dish) and pepper pot. Piña colada gâteau and tropical fruit mousses are tempting desserts. ✗ *Frigate Bay Beach,* ☎ 809/465–8666. *Reservations required. MC, V.*

$$$$ **Rawlins Plantation.** Elegant dinners are served in a lovely room with
★ fieldstone walls and high vaulted ceilings. The fixed-price, four-course dinner (U.S.$40 per person) changes nightly but always emphasizes local ingredients: Dishes may include christophine or pumpkin-and-coconut soup, smoked snapper and watercress salad, shrimp seviche with coriander and sour oranges, lobster in puff pastry with tarragon sauce, or shrimp with papaya and chili. The guava and lime parfaits and chocolate terrine with passion-fruit sauce are delicious. The bountiful lunch buffet (U.S.$24) offers such items as breadfruit salad, flying fish fritters, and *bobote* (ground beef, eggplant, spices, curry, and homemade chutney). ✗ *Mt. Pleasant,* ☎ 809/465–6221. *Reservations required by noon. AE, MC, V. No dinner Sun.*

$$$$ **The White House.** Lunch is served on the garden terrace. Romantic dinners, complete with candlelight and crystal, are served either in the elegant, antiques-filled dining room or outside under a marquee tent. The chef prepares a four-course dinner each night, which may include pumpkin or crab soup, Cornish game hen with banana stuffing, or fresh broiled local seafood. Many of the ultrafresh ingredients are cultivated in owner Janice Barber's gardens. Afternoon tea is also served here. ✗ *St. Peter's,* ☎ 809/465–8162. *Reservations required. AE, MC, V.*

$$$$ **The Golden Lemon.** Owner Arthur Leaman creates the recipes himself
★ for the West Indian, Continental, and American dishes served in his hotel, and he never repeats them more than once in a two-week period. The evening begins with cocktails and hors d'oeuvres on the patio. The three-course dinner, with its fixed menu, is served in a tastefully decorated room, with crystal chandeliers, white rattan furnishings, and antiques. Graceful arched doorways welcome the island breezes. The long-time Kittitian chef, Trevor Browne, makes delicious pumpkin soup, chicken with peanut sauce, and lobster medallions Creole. The patio, lush with bougainvillea and ferns, is a popular spot for Sunday brunch, which can include banana pancakes, rum beef stew, and curried conch fritters. ✗ *Dieppe Bay,* ☎ 809/465–7260. *Reservations required. AE, MC, V.*

$$$$ **The Royal Palm.** Set beside the pool at Ottley's Plantation, this is a restau-
★ rant to experience at night, under the latticed roof, gazing across manicured lawns to the lights of the elegantly restored great house. Pamela Yahn, a graduate of the prestigious Culinary Institute of America, is the island's most creative and assured chef. Her menu is an eclectic mix of California-Caribbean dishes, with some classic Italian, French, and Chinese items. Start with baked brie or Creole pumpkin soup, then have grilled sea scallops with Kittitian salsa, lobster *bambaya* (sautéed with ginger, tamarind, key lime juice, shallots, garlic, and sun-dried tomatoes), or South American vegetable soup atop pan-seared snapper with

feta and cilantro. For dessert, try banana fritters l'antillaise or mango mousse with raspberry sauce. This is the island's merriest dining spot, in no small part due to co-owners Art and Ruth Keusch. Art serenades diners with a twinkle in his eye, while Ruth comically rolls her eyes. The combination of superb food and warm bonhomie they offer is unbeatable. ✕ *Ottley's Plantation Inn,* ☎ *809/465–7234. Reservations required. AE, D, MC, V.*

$$$ **Ocean Terrace Inn.** The local elite frequent this spot. Dinner is by candlelight, in the inn's dining room or on a small balcony or terrace overlooking the bay. Lobster is the specialty—grilled, broiled, and thermidor. At the Friday-night buffet, a lobster and steak barbecue alternates with West Indian specialties. Dinner is followed by entertainment and dancing. ✕ *Fortlands, Basseterre,* ☎ *809/465–2754. Reservations advised. AE, MC, V.*

$$–$$$ **Fisherman's Wharf.** Part of the Ocean Terrace Inn (head straight rather than up the hill to the hotel's main building), this extremely casual waterfront eatery is decorated in swaggering nautical style, with rustic wood beams, rusty anchors, cannons, and buoys. Try the excellent conch chowder, followed by fresh grilled lobster or other seafood, and finish off your meal with a slice of the memorable banana cheesecake. The tables are long, wooden affairs and it's generally lively, especially on weekend nights. ✕ *Fortlands, Basseterre,* ☎ *809/465–2754. AE, MC, V. No lunch.*

$$–$$$ **Olivee's.** Robert Cramer and Ian Smith have converted their traditional
★ West Indian home, filled with antiques acquired on their extensive travels, into the island's most charming, convivial eatery. Drinks are served on the hillside terrace, set amid fragrant tropical gardens with smashing views of Basseterre and the Caribbean. Robert is the maître d'; Ian, the chef. The prix fixe menu, $20–$40 depending on your entrée, includes delectable homemade sourdough bread, soup or salad, appetizer, entrée, vegetables, dessert, and tea or coffee. Among Ian's savory Continental selections, delicately spiced with island flair, are saltfish fritters with red pepper coulis, sweet potato pâté, herb-stuffed chicken breast in kumquat glaze, and grilled lime-marinated swordfish with guava and red onion relish. Most of the fruits and vegetables are organically grown on the property. The bittersweet chocolate torte with gooseberry sauce is sublime. You can choose from their well-considered wine list. Sunday brunch is also served. Olivee's also functions as a B&B, with two rooms, priced at $75 and $90 a night, beautifully furnished with antiques, local crafts, and beds swaddled in mosquito netting. ✕ *Upper Buckley's, Basseterre,* ☎ *809/465–3662. Reservations advised. AE, MC, V. Restaurant closed May 15–Nov. 15.*

$$ **Arlecchino.** The shaded courtyard of this breezy trattoria is a pleasant place to while away the afternoon or evening. Enjoy a sublime minestrone, fresh pastas, creative pizzas, and excellent veal Parmigiana, then top off the meal with the best cappuccino and tiramisù on St. Kitts. ✕ *Cayon St., Basseterre,* ☎ *809/465–9927. AE, MC, V. Closed Sun.*

$$ **Blue Horizon.** On the cliffs of Bird Rock, this unassuming restaurant affords a panoramic, waterfront view of Basseterre and of spectacular sunsets. The charming menu is written in five different languages (including English) on dinner plates, and the tables, with red-and-white-checked tablecloths, are set to catch the breezes. The chef is Austrian, so specials such as Wiener schnitzel are often found alongside local fish dishes. The lobster bisque is outstanding. ✕ *Bird Rock (just outside Basseterre),* ☎ *809/465–5863. Reservations advised. AE, MC, V.*

$–$$ **OTI Turtle Beach Bar and Grill.** Simple but scrumptious cuisine has made this informal restaurant a popular daytime watering hole. Taste treats include honey-mustard ribs, calypso chicken, coconut-shrimp salad, and grilled, stuffed lobster. The glorified shack is on an isolated beach at the south end of the South East Peninsula Road: Just look for the signs. Business cards from around the world plaster the bar, and the room is brightly decorated with a small sailboat, colorful crusted bottles dredged from the deep, and painted wooden fish, turtles, and toucans. You can rent a kayak, Windsurfer, or mountain bike here to help you work off your meal, or schedule a deep-sea fishing trip. ✗ *Turtle Beach,* ☎ *809/469–9086. Dinner Fri. and Sat. only. AE, MC, V.*

$ **Ballahoo.** This second-floor terrace restaurant is in the heart of downtown, overlooking the Circus. It draws a crowd of locals and tourists for breakfast, lunch, and dinner. Lilting calypso and reggae on the sound system, whirring ceiling fans, potted palms, and colorful island prints create a tropical ambience. Specialties include conch simmered in garlic butter, madras beef curry, lobster and shrimp in a light creamy sauce, and (it's true) a rum and banana toasted sandwich. ✗ *Fort St., Basseterre,* ☎ *809/465–4197. AE, MC, V. Closed Sun.*

$ **Chef's Place.** Inexpensive West Indian meals are the draw here. Try the local version of jerk chicken (more moist than the original) or the goat stew. The best seats are outside on the wide white veranda. ✗ *Upper Church St., Basseterre,* ☎ *809/465–6176. No credit cards. Closed Sun.*

$ **PJ's Pizza.** "Garbage pizza" may not sound too appetizing, but this pie, topped with everything but the kitchen sink, is a favorite here. You can also choose from 10 other varieties of pizza or create your own. Sandwiches and other Italian standards are available (lasagna is a house specialty). Finish your meal with delicious, moist rum cake. This casual spot borders the golf course and is open to cooling breezes. The atmosphere is always boisterous. ✗ *Frigate Bay,* ☎ *809/465–8373. AE, MC, V. Closed Mon. and Sept.*

Lodging

St. Kitts has an appealing variety of places to stay—beautifully restored plantation inns, full-service hotels, condominium complexes, simple beachfront cottage colonies, and an all-inclusive hotel. There are also a number of guest houses and self-catering condominiums available to visitors. For information, contact the St. Kitts/Nevis Department of Tourism (Box 132, Basseterre, St. Kitts, ☎ 809/465–2620).

CATEGORY	COST*
$$$$	over $275
$$$	$200–$275
$$	$125–$200
$	under $125

All prices are for a standard double room for two, excluding 7% tax and 10% service charge.

$$$$ **The Golden Lemon.** Arthur Leaman, a former decorating editor of
★   *House and Garden,* created and runs this internationally famous, quiet retreat at the isolated north end of the island. There are nine rooms in the restored 17th-century great house, each one differently, and impeccably, decorated. There are canopied, wrought-iron, and four-poster beds, armoires, chaise longues, rocking chairs, and a variety of stunning fabrics. You can also stay in a one- or two-bedroom town house with a wraparound terrace and kitchenette (some have a private pool). These are decorated with an eclectic yet harmonious blend of West Indian crafts, antiques, and artworks culled from Arthur's world travels. The cool, dark, well-appointed bar and lounge offer a peaceful respite from the bright sun, and the restaurant is one of the best on the island. A gray-sand beach, guarded by rusty cannonballs and

shaded by spindly, elegant palms, offers views of St. Martin shimmering in the distance. The hotel allows no children under 18. ☎ *Box 17, Dieppe Bay,* ☎ *809/465–7260 or 800/633–7411,* FAX *809/465–4019. 34 rooms and suites. Restaurant, pool, duty-free shop, 1 tennis court. AE, MC, V. MAP (including afternoon tea).*

$$$$ **Ottley's Plantation Inn.** This former sugar plantation has been trans-
★ formed into a spectacularly elegant inn. It's nestled at the foot of Mt. Liamuiga, on 35 manicured acres that border a rain forest, and has views that sweep out to the wild Atlantic. The beautifully restored, 18th-century, English colonial–style great house and cut-stone cottages hold 15 guest rooms. All rooms are spacious, many with high ceilings and white wood floors, and they are decorated with an eclectic mix of white wicker, antiques, and floral print fabrics. The cottages, with exquisite old tile and stonework and English country house decor, are honeymoon heaven. All units are air-conditioned. The 65-foot, spring-fed pool stretches out from the remaining walls of the sugar factory, with an open-air bar at one end and the alfresco Royal Palm restaurant along one side. Take a stroll on the property's rain-forest trail. Engaging owners Art and Ruth Keusch will give you a personal orientation to the property and the island during your first breakfast; they're always available to dispense advice and good cheer. ☎ *Box 345, Ottley's,* ☎ *809/465–7234 or 800/772–3039,* FAX *809/465–4760. 15 rooms. Restaurant, bar, pool, shuttle to beach/town. AE, MC, V. MAP.*

$$$$ **Rawlins Plantation.** Another former sugar plantation, this lovely inn
★ is fairly isolated, on 12 acres on the northern end of the island. The views are spectacular: On one side of the inn, lush greenery climbs to the peak of Mt. Liamuiga; on the other side, the Caribbean sea stretches out to the island of Statia. Hammocks are slung among the pear and almond trees, and the plantation's original copper syrup vats crop up everywhere you look. Ten rooms, each with bath, are scattered across the grounds in various restored buildings of the old estate, including the original sugar mill, and each is unique. You'll find mahogany four-poster beds, wicker chairs, hardwood floors, and fabrics in soft pastel prints. Some might consider the furnishings a bit spare. There is no air-conditioning, but all units have ceiling fans and good cross-ventilation. The restaurant, well known on the island for its Continental-Caribbean cuisine, is decorated with antiques. Affable owners Paul and Claire Rawson provide attentive personal service. This is a great place to get away from it all. ☎ *Box 340, Mt. Pleasant,* ☎ *809/465–6221 or 800/621–1270,* FAX *809/465–4954. 10 rooms. Restaurant, pool, tennis court, croquet, and complimentary laundry service. AE, MC, V. MAP (including afternoon tea).*

$$$$ **The White House.** Three radiant acres of flowering gardens and manicured lawns surround this small, secluded property in the foothills above Basseterre. There are views of the Caribbean in the distance, but you'll have to take a ten-minute ride (there's a hotel shuttle) to get to the beach. The 18th-century plantation great house has been beautifully restored and the stable and carriage house rebuilt. You'll be greeted by the fierce posturing of the house English bulldogs (they're actually lambs), then by the gracious owners, Janice and Malcolm Barber. The tasteful, uncluttered bedrooms have hardwood floors and are individually decorated with 19th-century antiques, mahogany beds (many are four-poster), and Laura Ashley fabrics. There is no air-conditioning, but all rooms have ceiling fans and good cross-ventilation. The restaurant is among the best on the island (*see* Dining, *above*). ☎ *Box 436, St. Peter's,* ☎ *809/465–8162 or 800/223–1108,* FAX *809/465–8275. 10 rooms. Restaurant, bar, pool, lawn tennis court, croquet, laundry service, shuttle to beach/town. AE, MC, V. MAP (including afternoon tea).*

$$–$$$ **Jack Tar Village Beach Resorts and Casino.** A lively atmosphere pervades this appealing all-inclusive resort. A slew of sports are available, each day has a schedule of recreational activities and contests, and there are supervised programs for children. Two pools are a nice touch: One is for the vollcyball and water aerobics crowd, the other for those who want a quiet, relaxing dip. Nightly live entertainment, a disco, and the island's only casino keep the action going late into the night. Guest rooms are freshly decorated with floral linens, boating prints, and jade carpets. All have a small terrace or balcony, cable TV, safe, and phone. The restaurants are noted for their theme buffets, as well as for solid Continental and Creole fare. ⊞ *Box 406, Frigate Bay,* ☎ *809/465–8651 or 800/999–9182,* FAX *809/465–8651. 240 rooms, 2 suites. 2 restaurants, bars and lounges, casino, 2 pools, 4 lighted tennis courts, shuffleboard, Ping-Pong, basketball, scuba lessons, minigym, spa, massage, child care, exercise and aerobics classes, water-sports center, access to golf course. AE, MC, V. All-inclusive.*

$$ **Bird Rock Beach Resort.** Perched on a bluff overlooking its own beach, a few miles from the airport and downtown, this rather plain-looking resort has been expanding every year, with a new dive shop and casual beach grill slated to open by press time (fall 1995). Two-story buildings contain air-conditioned rooms and suites with direct-dial telephone, cable TV, and balcony with ocean view. Suites also have kitchenettes. The tile-floored rooms are simply furnished with rattan and wicker furniture and floral fabrics. An informal dining room is next to the pool, and there is shuttle service to the gourmet Lighthouse Restaurant, which is owned by the hotel. There is particularly excellent snorkeling and diving in the waters just off the resort's golden-sand beach. Golf and the larger Frigate Bay beaches are just five minutes away. ⊞ *Box 227, Basseterre,* ☎ *809/465–8914 or 800/621–1270,* FAX *809/465–1675. 38 units. 2 restaurants, 3 bars, 2 pools (one with swim-up bar), gift shop, tennis court, shuttle service to golf. AE, DC, MC, V. EP, MAP.*

$$ **Colony's Timothy Beach Resort.** If you don't mind trading some atmosphere for modern comfort at a good price, this could well be the ideal spot for a beach-oriented vacation. Set at the end of Frigate Bay beach, this casual hotel overlooks the Caribbean. Simple beige stucco buildings hold comfortable, adequately furnished rooms and suites. Larger units have kitchens and multiple bedrooms, and every room has air-conditioning, phone, and minifridge. Opt to stay in one of the original buildings, which sit right on the beach; they have better views than the recent additions and are larger and airier. You can choose from a wide variety of sports activities. Greens fees for the nearby golf course are included in the room rate. The hotel's Coconut Cafe is a local favorite. However, rates are based on EP, so you can sample the cuisine around St. Kitts. The management is attentive and friendly. ⊞ *Box 81, Frigate Bay,* ☎ *809/465–8597 or 800/838–5375,* FAX *809/465–7723; Colony Reservations Worldwide, 800/777–1700. 60 rooms. Restaurant, pool, water-sports center. AE, MC, V. EP.*

$$ **Inter Grande Frigate Bay Beach Hotel.** The third fairway of the island's golf course adjoins this property (guest here get discounts on greens fees), and the two nearby beaches—Caribbean and Atlantic—are reached by complimentary shuttle buses (the Caribbean beach is also easily reached by following the path from the far end of the pool, along the edge of the golf course). The whitewashed, air-conditioned buildings contain standard rooms as well as condominium units with fully equipped kitchens. There are hillside and poolside units; the latter are preferable. Rooms and condos have navy tile floors and are decorated with floral linens and sailing prints. All have cable TV, phone, ceiling fans, and sliding glass doors leading to a terrace or balcony. There's an Olympic-size pool with swim-up bar and a terraced restaurant overlooking the pool. Packages of all sorts are available. ✆ *Box 137, Basseterre,* ☎ *809/465–8935 or 800/266–2185,* FAX *809/465–7050. 64 rooms. Restaurant, bar, pool. AE, D, MC, V. EP, MAP.*

$$ **Ocean Terrace Inn.** Referred to locally as OTI, this is a rarity: a stylish,
★   intimate business hotel. The main building, which houses the fancier restaurant, reception, a pool with a swim-up bar, and many of the rooms, is set high on a hill overlooking the ocean, amid lovingly tended gardens dotted with gazebos. Condominium units are farther down the hill but also have water views. Accommodations range in size from smallish standard rooms to one- and two-bedroom condos with full kitchens. All are air-conditioned, have cable TV, phone, and minibar, and are handsomely decorated in rattan and bright fabrics. Fisherman's Wharf, on the waterfront at the bottom of the hill, is a casual seafood restaurant. The hotel's Pelican Cove Marina has its own fleet of boats that you can take out or charter. There is a daily shuttle to the hotel's beach at pretty Turtle Bay (a good 20 minutes away), where you'll find all the water sports and a restaurant-bar that's also owned by OTI. ✆ *Box 65, Basseterre,* ☎ *809/465–2754, 800/223–5695, or 800/524–0512,* FAX *809/465–1057. 54 units. 3 restaurants, 3 bars, beach (20 minutes away), 2 pools, outdoor Jacuzzi, fleet of boats, water-sports center. AE, MC, V. EP, MAP.*

$$ **Sun 'n' Sand Beach Village.** This simple complex is on the beach at North Frigate Bay, on the Atlantic side of the island. Studios in two-story buildings and two-bedroom, self-catering units in pretty, Antillean-style wood-and-stucco cottages stretch back from the beach. Decor is simple and tropical, with rattan furnishings, island prints and batiks, and tile floors. Studios are air-conditioned; each has twin or queen-size beds, cable TV, phone, bath with shower, and a private terrace. The cottages have a convertible sofa in the living room and a fully equipped kitchen; there's a window air conditioner in the bedroom and a ceiling fan in the living room. ✆ *Box 341, Frigate Bay,* ☎ *809/465–8037 or 800/223–6510,* FAX *809/465–6745. 32 studios, 18 2-bedroom cottages. Restaurant, beach, pool, children's pool, 2 lighted tennis courts, grocery store, gift shop. AE, D, MC, V. CP, MAP.*

$–$$ **Fairview Inn.** The main building of this old, quiet, and rather simple inn is an 18th-century great house, with graceful white verandas and Oriental rugs on hardwood floors. The rooms are in little cottages sprinkled around the backyard, in the shadow of a looming mountain. They're tiny and have functional furnishings (they look rather like rooms in an American motel in the middle of nowhere), with either twin or double beds, private patios, and radios. All have private baths with showers or bathtubs. Some have air-conditioning, some fans, some neither. Those in the converted stables have the most character, with exposed stone walls. Banks of yellow allemanda climb the trellises surrounding the pool, which has an ocean view. The restaurant serves West Indian cuisine. ✆ *Box 212, Basseterre,* ☎ *809/465–2472 or 800/223–9815,* FAX *809/465–1056. 30 rooms. Restaurant, 2 bars, pool. AE, D, MC, V. EP, MAP.*

$–$$ **Fort Thomas Hotel.** The new Canadian owners of this hotel, which has long been popular with business travelers and tour groups, have sunk a great deal of money into much-needed renovations. It's built on the site of an old fort, on a hillside overlooking Basseterre and the harbor. Unfortunately, the cannons anchoring the driveway and a few ramparts scattered about the grounds near the pool are the only reminders of its storied past. The building resembles an antiseptic Stateside motel, but the rooms are spacious, with seashell colors and wicker furnishings. All have two double beds, telephone, private bath, air-conditioning, and radio; most have cable TV. The second-floor rooms have far better views and are worth the minimal surcharge. There's a free shuttle bus to the Frigate Bay beaches, and you can walk to town and to the stores at Pelican Mall. The pool has great views of Basseterre and the ocean. ⌂ *Box 407, Basseterre,* ☎ *809/465–2695,* FAX *809/465–7518. 64 rooms. Restaurant, bar, pool, game room. AE, D, MC, V. EP, MAP.*

$–$$ **Morgan Heights Condominiums.** A laid-back atmosphere and reasonable prices are found at this complex along the Atlantic (although not on the beach), 10 minutes from Basseterre. The rooms are clean and comfortable, with simple contemporary white wicker furniture and ceramic tile floors. All are air-conditioned and have direct-dial phone, fully equipped kitchen, cable TV, and private bath. Covered patios overlook the water. The buildings are along a main highway and can be rather noisy during the day. The Atlantic Club serves excellent local cuisine and piña coladas with a punch. ⌂ *Box 536, Basseterre,* ☎ *809/465–8633,* FAX *809/465–9272. 5 2-bedroom units that can be rented as 1-bedroom units and individual hotel rooms. Restaurant, freshwater pool, beach shuttle. AE, D, MC, V. EP.*

Nightlife

Most of the Kittitian nightlife revolves around the hotels, which host folkloric shows and calypso and steel bands.

Casinos

The only game in town is at the **Jack Tar Village Casino** (*see* Lodging, *above*), where you'll find blackjack tables, roulette wheels, craps tables, and one-armed bandits. Dress is casual, and play continues till the last player leaves. *Note:* You do not need to purchase Jack Tar passes to play, even though the casino entrance is in the hotel lobby.

Discos

On Saturday night head for the **Turtle Beach Bar and Grill** (Turtle Bay, ☎ 809/469–9086), where there is a beach dance-disco. Play volleyball into the evening, then dance under the stars into the night. At **J's Place** (across from Brimstone Hill, ☎ 809/465–6264), you dance the night away with locals on Friday and Saturday. **Reflections Night Club** (☎ 809/465–6000), upstairs at Flex Fitness Center, is a hot Kittitian nightspot. It's open Tuesday through Sunday from 9 until well past midnight. Cover charge is E.C.$10 Thursday, Friday, and Saturday nights. Another disco popular with locals is the **Cotton House Club** (Canada Estate, no ☎), open weekends from 10 PM. Weekends, **Kool Runnins** (Morris Paul Dr., Pond Industrial Site, ☎ 809/466–5665) serves up jerk chicken, roti, and goat water stew, to the accompaniment of live local bands in an open-air gazebo. The hot spot for happy hour (free eats and occasional live music) is the tropical bar **Stonewalls** (Princes St., Basseterre, ☎ 809/465–5248).

NEVIS

Staying in Nevis

Important Addresses

Tourist Information: The **tourism office** (☎ 809/469–5521) is on Main Street in Charlestown. The office is open Monday and Tuesday 8–4:30 and Wednesday–Friday 8–4.

Police: Call 911. **Hospital:** There is a 24-hour emergency room at **Alexandra Hospital** (Charlestown, ☎ 809/469–5473). **Pharmacies: Evelyn's Drugstore** (Charlestown, ☎ 809/469–5278) is open weekdays 8–5, Saturday 8–7:30, and Sunday 7 AM–8 PM; the **Claxton Medical Centre** (Charlestown, ☎ 809/469–5357) is open Monday–Wednesday and Friday 8–6, Thursday 8–4, Saturday 7:30–7, and Sunday 6–8 PM.

Currency

Legal tender is the Eastern Caribbean (E.C.) dollar. The rate of exchange fluctuates but hovers around E.C.$2.60 to U.S.$1. The U.S. dollar is accepted everywhere, but you'll almost always get change in E.C.s. Prices quoted here are in U.S. dollars unless noted otherwise.

Taxes and Service Charges

Hotels collect a 7% government tax, and most add a 10% service charge to your bill. In restaurants, a 15% tip for good service is the norm. The departure tax is $10. Taxi drivers typically receive a 10% tip.

Guided Tours

The **taxi driver** who picks you up will probably offer to act as your guide to the island. Each driver is knowledgeable and does a three-hour tour for $50. He can also make a lunch reservation at one of the plantation restaurants, and you can incorporate this into your tour. **Fitzroy "Teach" Williams** (☎ 809/469–1140) is particularly recommended.

All Seasons Streamline Tours (☎ 809/469–5705 or 809/469–1138, FAX 809/469–1139) has a fleet of air-conditioned, 14-seat vans and uniformed drivers to take you around the island at a cost of $75 for three hours.

Another tour option is **Jan's Travel Agency** (Arcade, Charlestown, ☎ 809/469–5578), which arranges half- and full-day tours of the island.

Getting Around

Arrive in Nevis with a valid driver's license, and your car-rental agency will help you obtain a local license at the police station. The cost is E.C.$30 (U.S.$12), and it is valid for one year.

You may not want to drive here. The island's roads are pocked with crater-size potholes; driving is on the left, and, to make it more difficult, you may be given a right-drive vehicle. Pigs, goats, and cattle crop up out of nowhere to amble along the road, and if you deviate from Main Street, you're likely to have trouble finding your way around.

TDC Rentals, Ltd. (Charlestown, ☎ 809/469–5690), known for its exceptional service, rents a wide range of vehicles, has offices on St. Kitts, and offers a three-day rental that includes a car on both islands. **Avis** (Stoney Grove, ☎ 809/469–1240) provides Suzuki Jeeps and Nissan cars. **Striker's Car Rental** (Hermitage, ☎ 809/469–2654) has minimokes (simple open-air vehicles) and compacts. **Nisbett Rentals Ltd.** (Charlestown, ☎ 809/469–1913 or 809/469–6211) rents cars, minimokes, and Jeeps. None of these companies charge for mileage, and all of them accept major credit cards.

Taxi service (☎ 809/469–5621; after dark, 809/469–5515) is available at the airport and by the dock in Charlestown. You can also arrange for a taxi through your hotel.

Telephones and Mail

To call Nevis from the United States, dial area code 809, followed by 469 and the local four-digit number. Communications are excellent, both on the island and with the United States, and direct-dial long distance is in effect.

Airmail letters to the United States and Canada require E.C.80¢ per half ounce; postcards, E.C.50¢. It will take at least a week to 10 days for mail to reach home. Nevis and St. Kitts have separate stamp-issuing policies, but each honors the other's stamps, and stamps from both islands are beautiful.

Opening and Closing Times

Shops are open Monday–Friday 8–noon and 1–4; some are open on Saturday. Banking hours vary but are generally Monday–Thursday 8–2 and Friday 8–5. **St. Kitts–Nevis–Anguilla National Bank** and the **Bank of Nevis** are open Saturday 8:30–11 AM.

Exploring Nevis

Numbers in the margin correspond to points of interest on the Nevis map.

Charlestown

❶ About 1,200 of the island's 9,300 inhabitants live in **Charlestown,** the capital of Nevis. It faces the Caribbean, about 12½ miles south of Basseterre in St. Kitts. If you arrive by ferry, as most people do, you'll walk smack onto Main Street from the pier. You can tour the capital city in a half hour or so, but you'll need three to four hours to explore the entire island.

Turn right on Main Street and look for the **Nevis Tourist Office** (on your right as you enter the main square). Pick up a copy of the Nevis Historical Society's self-guided tour of the island and stroll back onto Main Street.

While it is true that tiny Charlestown has seen better days—it was founded in 1660—it's easy to imagine how it must have looked in its heyday. The buildings may be weathered and a bit worse for wear now, but there is still evidence of past glory in their fanciful galleries, elaborate gingerbread, wood shutters, and colorful hanging plants.

The stonework building with the clock tower at the corner of Main and Prince William streets houses the **courthouse** and **library.** A fire in 1873 severely damaged the building and destroyed valuable reccords; the current building dates from the turn of the century. You're welcome to poke around the second-floor library (open Mon.–Sat. 9–6), which is one of the coolest places on the island.

If you intend to rent a car, the **police station** across from the courthouse is the place to go to for your local driver's license.

The little park opposite the courthouse is **Memorial Square,** dedicated to the fallen of World Wars I and II.

TIME OUT Drop into the **Courtyard Cafe** (across the street from the tourist office, ☎ 809/469–5685), Caribbean Confections's lush, foliage-filled outdoor restaurant, for coffee and homemade pastries. There are also sandwiches, peanut-butter cookies, and popcorn.

When you return to Main Street from Prince William Street, turn right and go past the pier. Main Street curves and becomes Craddock Road, but keep going straight and you'll be on Low Street. The **Alexander Hamilton Birthplace,** which contains the **Museum of Nevis History,** is on the waterfront, covered in bougainvillea and hibiscus. This Georgian-style house is a reconstruction of the statesman's original home,

Nevis

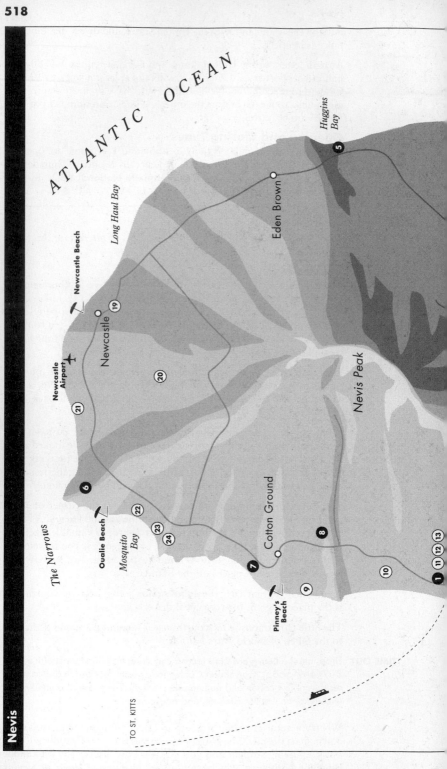

ATLANTIC OCEAN

Huggins Bay

5

Eden Brown

Long Haul Bay

Newcastle Beach

19
Newcastle

Newcastle Airport

20

21

Nevis Peak

6

22
Oualie Beach
23
Mosquito Bay
24

The Narrows

Cotton Ground

7

8

9
Pinney's Beach

10

1 11 12 13

TO ST. KITTS

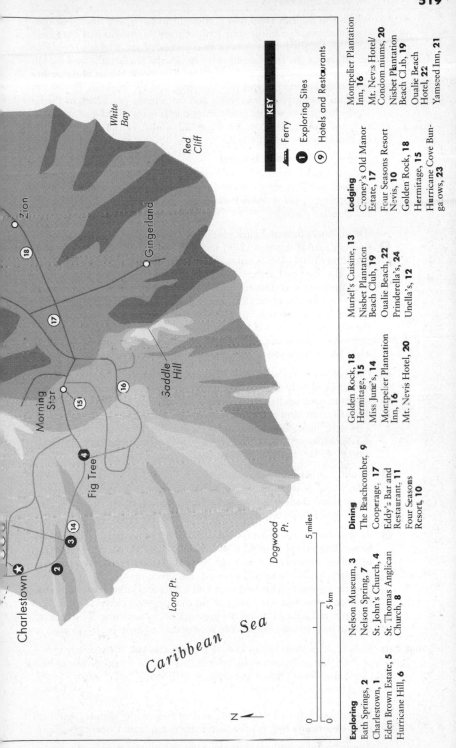

White
Bay

Red
Cliff

Zion

Gingerland

Morning
Star

Saddle
Hill

Fig Tree

Dogwood
Pt.

Long Pt.

Charlestown

Caribbean Sea

N

KEY

⚓ Ferry

1 Exploring Sites

9 Hotels and Restaurants

5 miles

5 km

0

Exploring
Bath Springs, **2**
Charlestown, **1**
Eden Brown Estate, **5**
Hurricane Hill, **6**

Nelson Museum, **3**
Nelson Spring, **7**
St. John's Church, **4**
St. Thomas Anglican
Church, **8**

Dining
The Beachcomber, **9**
Cooperage, **17**
Eddy's Bar and
Restaurant, **11**
Four Seasons
Resort, **10**

Golden Rock, **18**
Hermitage, **15**
Miss June's, **14**
Montpelier Plantation
Inn, **16**
Mt. Nevis Hotel, **20**

Muriel's Cuisine, **13**
Nisbet Plantation
Beach Club, **19**
Oualie Beach, **22**
Prinderella's, **24**
Unella's, **12**

Lodging
Croney's Old Manor
Estate, **17**
Four Seasons Resort
Nevis, **10**
Golden Rock, **18**
Hermitage, **15**
Hurricane Cove Bun-
galows, **23**

Montpelier Plantation
Inn, **16**
Mt. Nevis Hotel/
Condominiums, **20**
Nisbet Plantation
Beach Club, **19**
Oualie Beach
Hotel, **22**
Yamseed Inn, **21**

which was built in 1680 and is thought to have been destroyed during an earthquake in the mid-19th century. Hamilton was born here in 1755. He left for the American colonies 17 years later to continue his education; he became secretary to George Washington and died in a duel with political rival Aaron Burr. The **Nevis House of Assembly** sits on the second floor of this building, and the museum downstairs contains Hamilton memorabilia and documents pertaining to the island's history, as well as fascinating displays on island geology, politics, and cuisine. *Low St., no ☎. ☛ $2 adults, $1 children under 18. ⊙ Weekdays 8–4, Sat. 10–1.*

Elsewhere on the Island

The main road makes a 20-mile circuit, with various offshoots bumping and winding into the mountains. Take the road south out of Charlestown, passing **Grove Park** along the way, where soccer and cricket matches are played.

② About ¼ mile from the park you'll come to the ruins of the **Bath Hotel** (built by John Huggins in 1778) and **Bath Springs.** The springs, with temperatures of 104–108°F, emanate from the hillside. Huggins's 50-room hotel, the first hotel in the Caribbean, was adjacent to the waters. Eighteenth-century accounts reported that a few days of imbibing in these waters resulted in miraculous cures. It would take a minor miracle to restore the decayed hotel to anything like grandeur—it closed down in the late 19th century—but the spring house has been partially restored, and some of the springs are still as hot and restorative as ever. *Bathing costs $2. ⊙ Weekdays 8–noon and 1–3:30, Sat. 8–noon.*

③ On Bath Road is the **Nelson Museum,** worth a visit for the memorabilia of Lord Nelson, including letters, documents, paintings, and even furniture from his flagship. Nelson was based in Antigua but returned often to court, and eventually to marry, Frances Nisbet, who lived on a 64-acre plantation here. *Bath Rd., ☎ 809/469–0408. ☛ $2 adults ($1 if admission paid to Nevis History Museum), $1 children. ⊙ Weekdays 9–4, Sat. 10–1.*

④ About 2 miles from Charlestown, in the village of Fig Tree, is **St. John's Church,** which dates from 1680. Among its records is a tattered, prominently displayed marriage certificate that reads: "Horatio Nelson, Esquire, to Frances Nisbet, Widow, on March 11, 1787."

⑤ At the island's east coast, you'll come to the government-owned **Eden Brown Estate,** built around 1740 and known as Nevis's haunted house, or, rather, haunted ruins. In 1822, apparently, a Miss Julia Huggins was to marry a fellow named Maynard. However, on the day of the wedding the groom and his best man had a duel and killed each other. The bride-to-be became a recluse, and the mansion was closed down. Local residents claim they can feel the presence of . . . someone . . . whenever they go near the old house. You're welcome to drop by. It's free.

TIME OUT   For real, local West Indian fare, stop at **Cla-Cha-Del.** The specialty is seafood, but on Saturdays be adventurous and try the goat-water or bullhead stew. *Shaw's Rd., Newcastle, ☎ 809/469-9640. ⊙ Tues.–Sat. 9 am–11 pm, Sun. 6–11 pm.*

⑥ Rounding the top of the island, west of Newcastle Airport, you'll arrive at **Hurricane Hill,** from which there is a splendid view of St. Kitts.

About 1½ miles farther along the Main Road, **Fort Ashby,** overgrown with tropical vegetation, overlooks the place where the settlement of

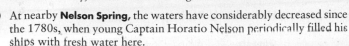

Jamestown fell into the sea after a tidal wave hit the coast in 1680. Needless to say, this is a favored target of scuba divers.

❼ At nearby **Nelson Spring,** the waters have considerably decreased since the 1780s, when young Captain Horatio Nelson periodically filled his ships with fresh water here.

Before driving back into Charlestown, a little over a mile down the road, **❽** stop to see the island's oldest church, **St. Thomas Anglican Church.** The church was built in 1643 and has been altered many times over the years. The gravestones in the old churchyard have stories to tell, and the church itself contains memorials to the early settlers of Nevis.

Beaches

All the beaches on the island are free to the public. There are no changing facilities, so you'll have to wear a swimsuit under your clothes. If you're doing a cab tour, you may arrange with your driver to drop you off at the beach and pick you up later.

Pinney's Beach is the island's showpiece beach. It's almost 4 miles of soft, golden sand lined with a magnificent grove of palm trees, and it's on the calm Caribbean Sea. The palm-shaded lagoon is a scene right out of *South Pacific*. The Four Seasons Resort is now here, and several of the mountain inns have private cabanas and pavilions on the beach, but it is, nevertheless, a public beach.

Oualie Beach, at Mosquito Bay, just north of Pinney's, is a black-sand beach where Oualie Beach Club (☎ 809/469–9518) can mix you a drink and fix you up with water-sports equipment.

Newcastle Beach is the location of Nisbet Plantation. Popular among snorkelers, it's a broad beach of soft, white sand shaded by coconut palms on the northernmost tip of the island, on the channel between St. Kitts and Nevis.

Sports and the Outdoors

Boating
Hobie Cats and Sunfish can be rented from **Oualie Beach Club** (☎ 809/469–9518). **Newcastle Bay Marina** (Newcastle, ☎ 809/469–9395) has Phantom sailboats, a 23-foot KenCraft powerboat, and several inflatables with outboards available for rent. **Frank Morse** (Oualie Beach, ☎ 809/469–9735) has a 65-foot aluminum sloop, *Never Say Never,* on which he takes guests for day sails.

Deep-Sea Fishing
The game here is kingfish, wahoo, grouper, tuna, and yellowtail snapper. If you want local expertise, call **Captain Valentine Glasgow** (☎ 809/469–1989), who has a 31-foot Ocean Master, *Lady James,* to take you in search of the big ones. **Jans Travel Agency** (☎ 809/469–5578) arranges deep-sea fishing trips.

Hiking
The center of the island is Nevis Peak, which soars up to 3,232 feet, flanked by Hurricane Hill on the north and Saddle Hill on the south. If you plan to scale Nevis Peak, a daylong affair, it is highly recommended that you go with a guide. Your hotel can arrange it for you; you can also ask the hotel to pack a picnic lunch. Both the **Nevis Academy** (☎ 809/469–2091, FAX 809/469–2113), headed by David Rollinson, and **Top to Bottom** (☎ 809/469–5371) offer ecorambles (slower tours)

and hikes. Three-hour rambles or hikes are $20 per person, $30 for the more strenuous climb up Mt. Nevis.

Horseback Riding
You can arrange for mountain-trail and beach rides through **Cane Gardens** (☎ 809/469–5648).

Scuba Diving and Snorkeling
The village of **Jamestown** was washed into the sea around Fort Ashby; the area is a popular spot for snorkeling and diving. Reef-protected **Pinney's Beach** offers especially good snorkeling. Try **SCUBA Safaris** (at Oualie Beach Club, ☎ 809/468–9518) for everything from a resort course to full certification.

Tennis
There are 10 tennis courts at the **Four Seasons Resort Nevis** (☎ 809/469–1111), 2 at **Pinney's Beach Hotel** (☎ 809/469–5207), and 1 court each at **Nisbet** (☎ 809/469–9325), **Montpelier Plantation** (☎ 809/469–3462), and **Golden Rock** (☎ 809/469–3346).

Water Sports
Montpelier Plantation (☎ 809/469–3462) has a 17-foot Boston whaler for scuba, snorkeling, and waterskiing trips. Snorkeling and waterskiing trips can also be arranged through **Oualie Beach Club** (☎ 809/469–9518) and **Newcastle Bay Marina** (☎ 809/469–9395). Windsurfers can also be rented at both places.

Windsurfing
For windsurfing, **Winston Crooke** (☎ 809/469–9615) rents equipment and teaches classes. A two-hour beginner's class is $40 per person. If you rent equipment only, it's $12 an hour per person.

Spectator Sports
Grove Park is the venue for **cricket** (Jan.–July) and **soccer** (July–Dec.). Your hotel or the tourist board can fill you in on dates, times, and grudge matches of particular interest between Kittitians and Nevisians.

One of the Caribbean's most endearing, unusual events is the occasional "Day at the Races" sponsored by the **Nevis Turf and Jockey Club** (☎ 809/469–3477). The races, which attract a "pan-Caribbean field" (as the club likes to boast), are held on a wild, windswept course overlooking the "white horses" of the Atlantic. Last-minute changes and scratches are common, and a party atmosphere prevails.

Shopping

Nevis is certainly not the place for a shopping spree, but there are unique and wonderful surprises here, notably the island's stamps, batik and hand-embroidered clothing, and the artwork of Dame Eva Wilkins, who died in 1989.

For more than 50 years Wilkins painted island people, flowers, and landscapes. An Eva Wilkins mural hangs over the bar at the Golden Rock (*see* Dining, *below*). Her originals sell for $100 and up, and prints are available in some of the local shops.

For dolls and baskets handcrafted in Nevis, visit the **Sandbox Tree** (☎ 809/469–5662) in Evelyn's Villa, Charlestown. Among other items available here are hand-painted chests. This is an appealing shop even if you are only browsing. The **Nevis Handicraft Co-op Society** (☎ 809/469–5509), next door to the tourist office, offers work by local artisans, including clothing, woven goods, and homemade jellies. Heading out of town, just past Alexander Hamilton's birthplace, you'll see the

Nevis Crafts Studio Cooperative (no ☎). Here Alvin Grante, a multi-talented Nevisian artisan, displays his works and those of Ashley Phillips: hand-blocked prints, watercolors of the local landscape and architecture, hand-painted T-shirts, and baskets.

Stamp collectors should head for the **Philatelic Bureau,** just off Main Street opposite the tourist office. St. Kitts and Nevis are famous for their decorative, and sometimes lucrative, stamps. An early Kittitian stamp recently brought in $7,000.

Other local items of note are the batik caftans, scarves, and fabrics found in the Nevis branch of **Caribelle Batik** (in the Arcade of downtown Charlestown, ☎ 809/469–1491). Kate Spencer's lovely island paintings and silk scarves and pareus are on sale at the **Plantation Picture House** (Main St., Charlestown, ☎ 809/469–5694). **Amanda's Fashions** (Prince William St., Charlestown, ☎ 809/469–5774) will custom-make hand-painted sarongs and T-shirts. **Knick Knacks** (The Courtyard, off Main St., Charlestown, ☎ 809/469–5784) showcases top local artisans, including Marvin Chapman (stone and wood carvings) and Jeannie Digby (exquisite dolls). They also sell whimsical hats, silk and cotton beach wraps, and glazed pottery. Nevis is known for the quality of its joiners, including **Paintfield Hill and Snos** (Morning Hill, ☎ 809/469–2499), whose superlative hardwood furniture can be shipped.

Dining

Dinner options on Nevis include the elegance of the dining room at the Four Seasons Resort, intimate dinners at plantation guest houses (where the menu is often set), and a variety of more casual eateries. Seafood is ubiquitous, and there are many places in which to sample excellent West Indian fare.

What to Wear

As in St. Kitts, dress is casual at lunch, although beach attire is unacceptable. Dress pants or a sundress is apropos for dinner; men may even want to don a jacket in season at some of the inns and at the Four Seasons Resort.

CATEGORY	COST*
$$$$	over $40
$$$	$30–$40
$$	$20–$30
$	under $20

per person, excluding drinks and service

$$$$ **Four Seasons Resort.** This elegant dining room, paneled in imported South American hardwood, has tables set with glistening silver and china, and graceful, 12-foot-high doors that open to the breezes and sweeping views of Pinney's Beach and the sea beyond. Cuisine is nouvelle with a Caribbean flair—Antiguan wahoo baked in a banana leaf with coconut milk; curry and scotch bonnet broth; and pan-seared local red snapper with mango salsa and bitter orange sauce. There is a weekly Caribbean buffet with a full steel band. ✕ *Pinney's Beach, ☎ 809/469–1111. Reservations required. AE, D, MC, V.*

$$$$ **Miss June's.** Dinner with Miss June Mestier, a lady from Trinidad, could never be called ordinary. While she prepares the fare, her son serves beverages to the guests (limited to 20) on the veranda. Promptly at 8:30 everyone heads to the dining room, where several tables are set with fine china and crystal. The first course is a soup of Miss June's creation, usually something spicy. Then guests turn to the buffet table laden with at least 18 dishes. Selections change nightly but always include curries; local vegetable dishes, such as christophine in red wine and orange sauce and sweet potatoes in rum punch; and seafood, such as conch simmered with garlic—all adapted by Miss June from Trinidadian recipes. At the meal's end, Miss June will join you for coffee and brandy. ✗ *Stoney Grove Plantation Ruins,* ☎ *809/469–5330. Reservations required. MC, V.*

$$$$ **Nisbet Plantation Beach Club.** The antiques-filled dining room in the great house at Nisbet has long been a popular place for lunch and dinner. There are also tables on the screened-in veranda, where there's a view down the palm-tree-lined fairway to the sea. The five-course menu is unusually varied for Nevis. A combination of Continental and Caribbean cuisines is prepared with many local ingredients. Sumptuous choices include sautéed scallops on angel hair pasta in cinnamon sauce, chilled avocado and apricot soup, roast quail stuffed with herb duxelles in raspberry sauce, grilled red grouper in lemongrass sauce, and banana and Tia Maria mousse in a chocolate shell. Lighter fare (sandwiches, salads, hamburgers) is served at lunch at the beach restaurant, Coconuts. ✗ *Nisbet Plantation,* ☎ *809/469–9325. Reservations required. AE, MC, V.*

$$$ **Golden Rock.** Tables are draped in pink and arranged in a romantic, dimly lit room whose fieldstone walls date back to when this was a plantation house. Local Nevisian cuisine is the specialty here; chicken in a raisin curry, grilled local snapper with tania (a type of tuber) fritters, and green papaya pie are house favorites. ✗ *Golden Rock,* ☎ *809/469–3346. Reservations required. AE, MC, V. Closed Sun.*

$$$ **Hermitage.** Dinner is served at one long table on the outside veranda, after cocktails in the antiques-filled parlor. The four-course preset menu might include carrot and tarragon soup, red snapper in ginger sauce, fried conch steak, and a rum soufflé. The conversation is always lively, thanks to witty, gregarious owners Maureen and Richard "Loopy" Lupinacci. ✗ *Hermitage Plantation,* ☎ *809/469–3477. Reservations required. AE, MC, V. Personal checks accepted.*

$$$ **Montpelier Plantation Inn.** Genial owners James and Celia Gaskell
★ preside over an elegant evening. Cocktails and hors d'oeuvres are served amid the antiques in the parlor of the great house. Dinner is by candlelight on the white terrace. Cream of avocado and coconut soup, lobster, red snapper, chicken calypso, sirloin steak Bordelaise, and roast beef and Yorkshire pudding are some of the choices on the sterling menu. Many of the fresh ingredients are homegrown in the extensive gardens. ✗ *Montpelier Plantation,* ☎ *809/469–3462. Reservations required. AE, MC, V. Closed late Aug.–early Oct.*

$$$ **Mt. Nevis Hotel.** The airy 60-seat dining room, where white wicker tables are draped with coral napery and set with fine china and silver, opens onto the terrace and pool. During the day, there is a splendid view of St. Kitts in the distance. The menu is one of the island's most creative, thanks to head chef James de Barbieri. Starters include grilled portobello mushrooms—with goat cheese and black olives in sherry vinaigrette—and lobster bisque. Entrées may include yellowtail fragrant with coriander, mango and ginger; penne with smoked chicken, shiitakes, and roast peppers; or veal chop stuffed with spiced walnuts in caper sauce. ✗ *Mt. Nevis Hotel/Condominiums, Newcastle,* ☎ *809/469–9373. Reservations advised. AE, D, MC, V.*

$$–$$$ **Cooperage.** An old stone dining room provides an elegantly rustic setting. This is classic Caribbean hotel dining, old-fashioned and drowned in butter but very good. Among the specialties are green-pepper soup, curried chicken breasts, coconut shrimp, veal in champagne morel sauce, and sorbets. An à la carte menu has been added; lobster for $19.50

is the most expensive item. ✕ *Croney's Old Manor Estate,* ☎ *809/469–3445. Reservations required. AE, D, MC, V.*

$–$$ The Beachcomber. This laid-back seaside eatery is a popular place to lime and watch the sun drift across the sky. Reggae blasts on the sound system, locals commandeer the pool table, and live bands entertain on Tuesday, Thursday, and Friday, all of which makes food seem extraneous. It's very good, nonetheless, with standouts including mozzarella in carrozza, flying fish and chips, and snapper en papillote. The staff is ultrafriendly. ✕ *Pinney's Beach,* ☎ *809/469–1192. MC, V. Closed Mon.*

$–$$ Prinderella's. This casual open-air restaurant enjoys a stunning setting on Tamarind Bay, with views across the channel to St. Kitts. A lovely mural behind the bamboo bar suffices for decor. Seafood is the obvious specialty, although the English owners, Ian and Charlie Mintrim, do a proper shepherd's pie and roast beef with Yorkshire pudding. Yachties (it has a great anchorage) buzz around the bar, there's wonderful snorkeling right around the point, and Friday brings a boisterous happy hour, with free finger food like salmon mousse, hummus, and chicken wings. The ambience is the furthest thing from stuffy. Ask Charlie to tell you the story behind the restaurant's name; it features Prinderella, a cince, and a gairy frogmother. You'll want a bouble dourbon when she's finished. ✕ *Jones Bridge,* ☎ *809/469–1291. AE, MC, V. Closed Mon. June–Sept (Mon.–Wed. in Oct., Nov., and Apr. 15–May 31).*

$ Eddy's Bar and Restaurant. Colorful flags flutter from the veranda of
★ this second-story restaurant, overlooking Memorial Square in the center of Charlestown. A local artist designed the tablecloths and bright, boldly colored wall hangings. You'll find fine stir-fries and local West Indian specialties, such as cream of cauliflower soup and tender, crispy conch fritters with just the right amount of sass in the sauce. Eddy's mom, Eulalie Williams, makes the terrific hot sauce, which you can buy at the Main Street Supermarket down the street. His wife, Sheila, is an amiable hostess. Stop by between 5 and 8 on Wednesday for happy hour; drinks are half price, snacks are free. ✕ *Main St., Charlestown,* ☎ *809/469–5958. Reservations advised. AE, MC, V. Closed Thurs., Sun., and Sept.*

$ Muriel's Cuisine. Hanging plants, local still lifes, and scarlet carnations
★ on the tables dress up this simple eatery. Three meals are served daily, except Sunday. Bountiful entrées come with mounds of rice and peas and fresh vegetables, a side salad, and garlic bread. The subtly spiced jerk chicken would pass muster in many a Jamaican kitchen, and the goat water and beef stew are fabulous: full-bodied and fragrant with garlic and coriander. Muriel St. Jean is the gracious hostess. Her restaurant attracts a very local clientele—women in hair curlers and young men who come to flirt shyly with the waitresses. ✕ *Upper Happy Hill Dr., Charlestown,* ☎ *809/469–5920. AE, D, MC, V. Closed Sun.*

$ Unella's. The atmosphere is nothing fancy, just simple tables set on a second-floor porch overlooking the waterfront in Charlestown, but the fare is good West Indian. Stop here for exceptional lobster (more expensive than the rest of the menu), curried lamb, island-style spare ribs, and steamed conch, all served with local vegetables, rice, and peas. Unella opens shop around 9 in the morning, when locals and boaters appear waiting for their breakfast; she stays open all day. ✕ *Waterfront, Charlestown,* ☎ *809/469–5574. No credit cards.*

$ Oualie Beach. This low-key, casual bar and restaurant on Oualie Bay is the perfect stop for authentic Nevisian fare after a long day on the beach. Try the delicious homemade soups, including ground-nut or breadfruit vichyssoise. Then move on to Creole conch stew, lobster crepes, or chicken breasts stuffed with spinach. The atmosphere is rollicking on weekends, with live music and local crowds. ✕ *Oualie Beach,* ☎ *809/469–9735. AE, D, MC, V.*

Lodging

With the exception of the Four Seasons Resort, most hotels on Nevis are beautifully restored manor or plantation houses. Typically, the owners of the inn live there with their families. Visitors are received warmly and graciously, almost like friends, and it is easy to begin thinking you have been personally invited down for a visit. In the evening, before dinner, it is common for the family, inn guests, and those visitors who have come to eat at the restaurant to gather in a drawing room or on a terrace for cocktails and to exchange stories of the day. Most of the inns operate on the Modified American Plan (MAP) and offer a free shuttle to their private stretch on Pinney's Beach.

CATEGORY	COST*
$$$$	over $300
$$$	$225–$300
$$	$150–$225
$	under $150

*All prices are for a standard double room for two, MAP, excluding 7% tax and 10% service charge.

$$$$ **Nisbet Plantation Beach Club.** From the manor house of this 18th-cen-
★ tury plantation you can see the beach at the end of a long avenue of coconut palms, and from the bar you look out over an old sugar mill covered with hibiscus, cassia, frangipani, and flamboyants. Well-maintained Nisbet offers a range of accommodations, from plantation-style cottages to lanai suites, all simply but tastefully appointed in whitewashed wicker and rattan and tropical prints and situated along an avenue of palms that leads to a blinding white-sand beach and the ocean. ⌂ *Newcastle Beach,* ☎ *809/469–9325; in the U.S., 800/344–2049; fax 809/469–9864. 38 rooms. 2 restaurants, 2 bars, beach, pool, tennis court, croquet, free laundry, boutique, free snorkeling gear. AE, MC, V. EP, MAP.*

$$$$ **Four Seasons Resort Nevis.** This prestigious Canadian company's first
★ foray into the Caribbean is a real winner. The 196-room property manages to combine world-class elegance with West Indian ambience and hospitality. On a stunning stretch of Pinney's Beach, with a spectacular view of St. Kitts in the distance, the hotel offers a complete range of water activities, along with clay and all-weather tennis courts, a free-form pool, a challenging 18-hole golf course designed by Robert Trent Jones II, and a full-service health club. Spacious guest rooms are richly furnished with mahogany armoires and headboards and cushioned rattan sofas and chairs, and have large indoor and veranda seating areas, which can be used for private dining. Contemporary bathrooms have marble double sinks, a stall shower, and a soaking tub. Rooms have both ceiling fans and air-conditioning, ice maker, fully stocked refrigerated bar, and a cable TV/VCR. There are two outstanding restaurants, one of which is fairly formal (although jacket and tie are not required). Special activities for children are scheduled regularly. There are usually good-value sports and romantic packages, even during the high season. ⌂ *Box 565, Charlestown,* ☎ *809/469–1111; in the U.S., 800/332–3442; in Canada, 800/268–6288; fax 809/469–1112. 196 rooms. 2 dining rooms, pub, casual outdoor dining, pool, beach, water sports, catamaran rentals, fitness center, free daily aerobics, 10 tennis courts, 18-hole golf*

course, children's program, baby-sitting, laundry service and free washer/dryers, 2 boutiques. AE, D, MC, V. EP, MAP, FAP.

$$$ **Hermitage.** A 250-year-old great house, said to be the oldest wooden
★ house on the island, houses the restaurant and forms the core of this appealing inn set in the hills. The duplex guest cottages are some of the prettiest accommodations on the island. Rooms are furnished with antiques, including four-poster canopy beds (mostly king-size), and have patios or balconies, ceiling fans, phones, and minifridges; some also have lovely views of the distant ocean, and some have full kitchens. Also available is a two-bedroom replica of a manor house, with its own pool. The beach is 15 minutes away, and if you haven't got a car, transportation will be arranged. Many guests simply relax in a hammock or spend the day by the pool at this peaceful retreat. What really makes the Hermitage special is vivacious owners Marueen and Richard Lupinacci, who will quickly introduce you to Nevisian society. ✆ *St. Johns, Fig Tree Parish,* ☎ *809/469–3477,* FAX *809/469–2481. 12 suites. Restaurant, bar, pool, free beach shuttle, tennis court, stables. AE, MC, V. EP, MAP.*

$$$ **Montpelier Plantation Inn.** Iron gates provide a majestic entrance to this intimate and charming inn set on 100 beautifully landscaped hillside acres. Reception, evening cocktails, and dinner take place in and around the great house, an imposing fieldstone structure furnished with antiques. Accommodations are in simple cottages scattered along the hillside. Each cottage contains one or two rooms, has two patios, and is adequately but sparely furnished. Rooms have Italian ceramic tile floors and large bathrooms with bathtub, shower, and full-length mirror. The pool is large and pretty (a gorgeous mural decorates one of the pool area's walls), but beach lovers can head (via complimentary transportation) to Pinney's Beach, where the estate has a 3-acre private section of beach and a pavilion. The estate also has a 17-foot Boston whaler for waterskiing, snorkeling, and fishing. Guests come not for the amenities so much as the incomparable air of quiet elegance. Owners James and Celia Gaskell downplay their royal connections (Princess Di stays here); James prefers to talk about his extensive organic gardens. Montpelier is the most proper hostelry on Nevis; guests seeking a hopping ambience will be happier elsewhere. ✆ *Box 474, Charlestown,* ☎ *809/469–3462 or 800/243–9420,* FAX *809/469–2932. 17 rooms. Restaurant, bar, pool, beach (away from hotel), tennis court. AE, MC, V. Closed late Aug.–early Oct. BP, MAP.*

$$ **Croney's Old Manor Estate.** Vast tropical gardens surround this restored sugar plantation in the shadow of Mt. Nevis. Many of the enormous guest rooms have high ceilings, gorgeous stone or tile floors, marble vanities, exposed wood beams, king-size four-poster beds, and colonial reproductions, but some units are a bit gloomy and dark, with old-fashioned dowdy madras settees and soiled carpets. The air throughout is one of faded, slightly shabby elegance. The outbuildings, such as the smokehouse and jail, have been imaginatively restored, and the old cistern is now the pool. This is the home of the Cooperage, a well-respected restaurant (*see* Dining, *above*). There's transportation to and from the beach. The hotel is not recommended for children under 12. ✆ *Box 70, Charlestown,* ☎ *809/469–3445; in the U.S., 800/223–9815 or 800/892–7093; fax 809/469–3388. 14 rooms. 2 restaurants, 2 bars, pool. AE, MC, V. EP, MAP.*

$$ **Golden Rock.** Co-owner Pam Barry runs this inn, which was built by her great, great, great grandfather over 200 years ago. She has decorated the 16 units with four-poster beds of mahogany or bamboo, native grass rugs, rocking chairs, and island-made floral-print fabrics. All rooms have a private bath and a patio. The restored sugar mill is a two-level suite (with a glorious wood-and-bamboo staircase), and the old cistern is now a spring-fed swimming pool. Although charming, many of the rooms are somewhat worn. The estate covers 150 mountainous acres and is surrounded by 25 acres of lavish tropical gardens, including a sunken garden. Enjoy the Atlantic view and cooling breeze from the bar. The Saturday night West Indian buffet is very popular, December through June. Barry also organizes historical and nature hikes. ☎ *Box 493, Gingerland,* ☎ *809/469–3346 or 800/223–9815,* FAX *809/469–2113. 16 rooms, 1 suite. Restaurant, bar, pool, tennis court, educational activities. AE, MC, V. EP, MAP.*

$$ **Mt. Nevis Hotel/Condominiums.** Air-conditioned standard rooms and suites at this hotel are done up with handsome white wicker furnishings, southwestern pastel fabrics, glass-top tables, and colorful island prints. Suites have full, modern kitchens and dining areas; all units have a balcony, direct-dial phone, minifridge, cable TV, and VCR. The main building houses the casual restaurant and bar, which open onto a terrace that overlooks the pool and provides a view of St. Kitts in the distance. Shuttle service is provided to the water-sports center at Newcastle Beach, replete with a boutique and outdoor restaurant-bar. The hotel also has its own ferry, which is used for moonlight cruises when it's not taking passengers to and from St. Kitts. ☎ *Box 494, Newcastle,* ☎ *809/469–9373 (collect),* FAX *809/469–9375. 32 rooms. Restaurant, bar, pool, water sports, beach club, boutique. AE, D, MC, V. EP, MAP.*

$ **Hurricane Cove Bungalows.** Don't be deceived by the ramshackle exterior of these cottages clinging precariously to a hill overlooking lovely Tamarind Bay. The interiors are charmingly rustic, with hand-carved wood furnishings and gleaming tile floors. All have full kitchens and an enclosed patio with breathtaking ocean views (save for one way in back). Several have private pools. The postage-stamp-size hotel pool is in the foundation of a 250-year-old fort. It's a three-minute walk to the beach. ☎ *Tamarind Bay,* ☎ *and fax 809/469–9462. 10 1-, 2- and 3-bedroom bungalows. Pool. MC, V.*

$ **Oualie Beach Hotel.** Every few years this beachside spot builds a few more charming West Indian–style cottages, and there are now 22 rooms, including air-conditioned deluxe rooms with mahogany four-poster canopy beds and marble vanities. All rooms look across the water to stunning views of neighboring St. Kitts. The rooms are bright, airy, and simply furnished, and all have refrigerator, cable TV, phone, and safe. Studio units have a full kitchen. There is a full dive shop here offering NAUI-certified instruction, and dive packages are available. Sunfish and Windsurfers may be rented, and the hotel has introduced Skimmer waterborne rowing machines. Breakfast, lunch, and dinner are served at an informal restaurant and bar. ☎ *Oualie Beach,* ☎ *809/469–9735,* FAX *809/469–9176. 22 rooms. Restaurant, bar, watersports and dive center. AE, D, MC, V. EP, MAP.*

$ **Yamseed Inn.** A very rough access road leads to this pale yellow bed-and-breakfast overlooking St. Kitts, tucked away from resort and plantation hotels on its own private patch of glittering white sand. Friendly innkeeper Sybil Siegfried offers four rooms in her house right by the sea, nestled amid beautiful grounds (Sybil's an avid gardener). Chirping hummingbirds welcome you into the stylish reception area. Each room has a private bath and is handsomely appointed with a mahogany bed, wood-panel ceiling, throw rugs, white-tile floors, and antiques. Breakfast includes delicious homemade muffins and grated coconut muesli. Sybil is a gracious hostess, having lost neither her southern accent nor her charm. The only flaw in paradise is Yamseed's location near the airport, which puts it in the flight path (fortunately, air traffic isn't busy). ⊡ *On the beach, Newcastle,* ☎ *809/469–9361. 4 rooms. 3-night minimum. No credit cards. BP.*

Nightlife

In season, it is usually easy to find a local calypso singer or a steel or string band performing at one of the hotels on weekends. You can count on entertainment at the **Four Seasons Resort** (☎ 809/469–1111) on both Friday and Saturday nights. On Friday night the Shell All-Stars steel band entertains in the gardens at **Croney's Old Manor** (☎ 809/469–3445). The **Golden Rock** (☎ 809/469–3346) brings in David Freeman's Honeybees String Band to jazz things up for the Saturday-night buffet. You can have dinner and a dance on Wednesday night at **Pinney's Beach Hotel** (☎ 809/469–5207). **Oualie Beach Hotel** (☎ 809/469–9735) throws a popular Saturday-night buffet with live string band and masquerade troupe. **Eddy's Bar and Restaurant** (*see* Dining, *above*) holds raucous West Indian nights with theme buffet and live string band Friday and Saturday.

Apart from the hotel scene, there are a few places where young locals go for late-night calypso, reggae, and other island music. **Club Trenim** (no ☎), on Government Road in Charlestown, has disco dancing starting at 8:30 every night except Tuesday. **Dick's Bar** (no ☎) in Brickiln has live music or a DJ on Friday and Saturday evenings.

22 St. Lucia

Updated by
Kate Sekules

CONTRARY TO POPULAR FOLKLORE, Columbus never set foot on St. Lucia; until recently, neither did most Americans. A boom in all-inclusive resort construction has been drawing increasing droves of Yankees—a bit to the dismay of Brits and Europeans who've cherished this lush, oval island for decades. St. Lucia, a 238-square-mile island toward the southern end of the Windwards, has honey-colored sand beaches and fancy hotels in the north. In the south, striking natural attractions dominate: The island's twin peaks, the Pitons (Petit and Gros), rise straight out of the sea to more than 2,400 feet; a dense rain forest permeates much of the topography; and bubbling sulfur springs gurgle at the mouth of a low-lying volcano that erupted thousands of years ago and now produces highly acclaimed curative waters.

Thanks to this pulchritude, St. Lucia is often referred to as "the Helen of the West Indies," and her coastline is familiar to sailors and divers alike—the reefs near the Pitons at Anse Chastanet being especially sought-after scuba sites. In between the populous north and the gorgeous south runs a sometimes tortuously winding road passing lush valleys, rain forest, banana plantations, secluded bays, and small villages. Marigot Bay, whose claim to fame is having been the filming location for *Doctor Doolittle,* is one of the Caribbean's prettiest, while the southern village of Choiseul is an important arts center, maintaining Carib traditions and nurturing local talent. Damage wrought by Tropical Storm Debbie, which did its best to wash St. Lucia away in 1994, is now visible only at poor Anse La Raye, a picturesque village on the west coast, which was the hardest hit. In its less secluded regions, St. Lucia is noticeably sophisticated, hosting not only the usual carnival but also its world-renowned Jazz Festival in late spring.

Another St. Lucian festival celebrates December 13, 1502, and is still known as Discovery Day, even though historians now think the island was sighted in 1499 by Juan de la Cosa, Columbus's navigator. In any case, the island's true first inhabitants, the Arawaks, paddled up from South America sometime before AD 200. The warlike Caribs followed and conquered around AD 800 and were still here when the first Europeans attempted to set up camp.

In 1605, 67 English settlers bound for Guiana blew off course and landed near Vieux Fort. Within a few weeks the Caribs had killed all but 19, who escaped in a canoe. Another group of English settlers dropped by 30 years later but were met with a similar lack of hospitality. Finally, the French signed a treaty with the Caribs in 1660 and took control of the island.

Thus began a 150-year period of battles between the French and the English that saw a dizzying 14 changes in power before the British took permanent possession in 1814. During those battle-filled years, Europeans colonized the island. They developed sugar plantations, using slaves from West Africa to work the fields. By 1838, when slaves were emancipated, more than 90% of the island consisted of African descendants, and this is still largely true of today's 140,000 St. Lucians. The coal industry was begun on the island in 1883, and until about 1920, Castries, the capital, was a leading coal port in the West Indies. Sugarcane became the next major money crop, followed by bananas during the 1960s.

On February 22, 1979, St. Lucia became an independent state within the British Commonwealth of Nations, with a resident governor-general appointed by the Queen. Still, there are many relics of French occupation, notably in the island patois—which you will hear spoken everywhere—the Creole cuisine, and the names of the places and the people.

Nowadays, bananas and tourism are neck-and-neck as top revenue earners, with tourism coming out on top for the first time in 1993. This pleases the savvy St. Lucians, who are working hard to avoid ruining their island with opportunistic overbuilding—as has happened on many other islands—while diversifying their agriculture in order to reduce the need to import, and strengthening their economy further. Consequently, there is a tangible solidity to St. Lucia, an optimism reflected in general friendliness as well as in the startling number of shiny new hotels and resorts.

Before You Go

Tourist Information

Contact the **St. Lucia Tourist Board.** In the United States: 820 2nd Ave., 9th Floor, New York, NY 10017, ☎ 212/867–2950 or 800/456–3984, FAX 212/370–7867). In Canada: 4975 Dundas St. W, Suite 457, Etobicoke D, Islington, Ontario M9A 4X4, ☎ 416/236–0936 or 800/456–3984, FAX 416/236–0937. In the United Kingdom: 421A Finchley Rd., London NW3 6HJ, ☎ 0171/431–4045, FAX 0171/437–7920.

Arriving and Departing

BY PLANE

There are two airports on the island. Wide-body planes use Hewanorra International Airport, on the southern tip of the island. Vigie Airport, near Castries, handles interisland and charter flights. **BWIA** (☎ 800/327–7401) has direct service from Miami and, on Sunday, New York. **American** (☎ 800/433–7300) has a nonstop service to St. Lucia from New York on Saturday and Sunday, plus daily service from most major U.S. cities, with a transfer in San Juan. (**American Eagle** flights from San Juan land at Vigie Airport.) **Air Canada** (☎ 800/776–3000; in Canada, 800/268–7240) has direct weekend service from Toronto. **British Airways** (☎ 0181/897–4000) has service from London to St. Lucia with a stop in Antigua on Thursdays, Saturdays, and Sundays. **LIAT**'s (☎ 809/462–0701) small island-hoppers fly into Vigie Airport, linking St. Lucia with Barbados, Trinidad, Antigua, Martinique, Dominica, Guadeloupe, and other islands.

FROM THE AIRPORT

Taxis are unmetered, and the government's list of suggested fares is not binding. Negotiate with the driver *before* you get in, and be sure that you both understand whether you've agreed upon E.C. or U.S. dollars. The drive from Hewanorra to Castries takes about 75 minutes and costs about $50.

Many guests to northern St. Lucia opt for the expensive but quick means of helicopter transportation. The cost from Castries is $90 per person, including luggage, and the flight takes 10–15 minutes. Aside from Vigie Airport, there are helipads at Pointe Seraphine, Windjammer Landing, Jalousie Plantation, and several other locations. Contact **Eastern Caribbean Helicopters** (☎ 809/453–6952) or **St. Lucia Helicopters** (☎ 809/453–6950). Both of these companies arrange sightseeing tours, too.

Passports and Visas

U.S., Canadian, and British citizens must produce a driver's license or passport and a return or ongoing ticket.

Language
The official language is English, but you'll also hear the local French Creole patois.

Precautions
The water supply was slightly contaminated by Tropical Storm Debbie, so ask before you drink from the faucet. Bring along insect repellent to ward off mosquitoes and sand flies. Be aware that sea urchins live among the rocks on the coastline; should one's long black spines lodge under your skin, don't try to pull them out. Apply an ammonia-based liquid and the spine will retreat, allowing you to ease it out. Manchineel trees have poisonous fruit and leaves that can cause skin blisters on contact. Even raindrops falling off the trees can cause blisters; these trees are usually marked when on hotel property. Do not swim on the rough ocean side of the island.

Staying in St. Lucia

Important Addresses
Tourist Information: St. Lucia Tourist Board is based at the Pointe Seraphine duty-free complex on Castries Harbor (☏ 809/452–4094 or 809/452–5968). The office is open weekdays 8–4:30. There are also offices in downtown Castries (Jeremie St., ☏ 809/452–2479), Soufrière (Bay St., ☏ 809/459–7200), at Vigie Airport (☏ 809/452–2595), and at Hewanorra International Airport (☏ 809/454–6644).

EMERGENCIES
Police: Call 999. **Hospitals:** Hospitals with 24-hour emergency rooms are **Victoria Hospital** (Hospital Rd., Castries, ☏ 809/452–2421) and **St. Jude's Hospital** (Vieux Fort, ☏ 809/454–6041), a privately endowed hospital run by nuns, which is said to have the better equipment. **Pharmacies:** Try **Williams Pharmacy** (Williams Bldg., Bridge St., Castries, ☏ 809/452–2797) or **M&C's Drugstore** (Gablewoods Mall, Gros Islet Hwy., north of Castries, ☏ 809/451–7808).

Currency
The official currency is the Eastern Caribbean dollar (E.C.$). Figure about E.C.$2.60 to U.S.$1. U.S. dollars are readily accepted, but you'll usually get change in E.C. dollars. Major credit cards are widely accepted, as are traveler's checks. Prices quoted here are in U.S. dollars unless indicated otherwise.

Taxes and Service Charges
Hotels collect an 8% government tax. Hotels and most restaurants add a 10% service charge. Taxi drivers appreciate a 10% tip. The departure tax is $11 or E.C.$27.

Guided Tours
Taxi drivers generally know the island and can give you a full tour—and often an excellent one, since government-sponsored training programs were introduced in 1994. Expect to pay $120 for up to four people (add $20 for a fifth) not including tip. It will take about six hours. The cost of hiring a taxi by the hour is $20.

The **Carib Touring Company** (☏ 809/452–6791) and **Sunlink International** (☏ 809/452–8232) offer a variety of half- and full-day tours. **Barnards Travel** (Micoud St., Castries, ☏ 809/452–2214) also offers a full range of half- and full-day island tours, as well as excursions to Dominica, Martinique, St. Vincent, and the Grenadines. **St. Lucia Representative Services Ltd.** (☏ 809/452–3762) offers a full range of half-

and full-day island tours, as well as excursions to a number of neighboring islands.

Eastern Caribbean Helicopters (☎ 809/453–6952) and **St. Lucia Helicopters** (☎ 809/453–6950) give sightseeing tours of the island.

Getting Around

BUSES
This is a cheap, though not always dependable, means of transportation. Minivans cruise the island and, like taxis, will stop when hailed. You can also catch a minivan in Castries at the corner of Micoud and Bridge streets.

TAXIS
Taxis are always available at the airport, the harbor, and in front of the major hotels, but they are expensive and do not have meters. Most hotels post the names and phone numbers of drivers and a table of fares suggested by the taxi commission. Determine the fare before you get in. The cost from Vigie Airport to most resorts in the north is $7–$15.

RENTAL CARS
To rent a car, you have to be 25 years or older and hold a valid driver's license and a credit card. You must buy a temporary St. Lucian license at the airports or police headquarters (Bridge St., Castries); however, most resorts have their own branches of major rental agencies, which will obtain the temporary license for you—it costs $12. Rates begin at about $45 per day or $270 per week. Rental agencies include **Avis** (☎ 809/452–2700 or 800/331–1212), **Budget** (☎ 809/452–0233 or 800/527–0700), **National** (☎ 809/450–8721 or 800/328–4567), and **Dollar** (☎ 809/452–0994 or 800/800–4000). Driving in St. Lucia is on the left, and the roads are often deeply pitted, to say the least, with not quite two-thirds of the 500 miles of road paved at all. Furthermore, drivers tend to improvise on the good bits; you may wish to think twice about driving.

BY FERRY
The **Rodney Bay Ferry** (☎ 809/452–1267) has ferry service three times daily from Rodney Bay (right by the Lime restaurant) to Pigeon Island. The fare is $10 per person round-trip, including the entrance fee to Pigeon Island. Service from Pointe Seraphine to Castries (when cruise ships are in port) was added in 1994.

Telephones, Electricity, and Mail
To call St. Lucia from the United States, dial area code 809, access code 45, and the local five-digit number. You can make direct-dial long-distance calls from the island, and the connections are excellent. To place interisland calls, dial the local five-digit number.

Electric voltage is 220/240 AC, 50 cycles. American appliances require an adapter and/or transformer.

Postage for airmail letters to the United States, Canada, and Great Britain is E.C.95¢ for up to 1 ounce. Postcards are E.C.75¢ to the United States and Canada, E.C.85¢ to Great Britain.

Opening and Closing Times
Shops are open weekdays 8–4, Saturday 8–noon. Banks are open Monday–Thursday 8–3, Friday 8–5, and, at a few branches in Rodney Bay, Saturdays 9–noon.

Exploring St. Lucia

Numbers in the margin correspond to points of interest on the St. Lucia map.

Castries

❶ **Castries,** on the northwest coast, is a busy commercial city of about 60,000 on the shore of a sheltered bay surrounded dramatically by green Morne Fortune. The city's charm lies entirely in its liveliness, since practically all the colorful old colonial buildings were razed by four great fires between 1796 and 1948. Ships carrying bananas, coconut, cocoa, mace, nutmeg, and citrus fruits for export leave from **Castries Harbour,** one of the busiest ports in the Caribbean.

Cruise ships dock across the harbor at **Pointe Seraphine,** about a 20-minute walk or short cab ride from the city center—or you can take the shuttle boat, available when ships are in port. Spanish-style Pointe Seraphine has 23 mostly upscale duty-free shops, a tourist information center where you can get island maps, and a taxi stand. This is the starting point for many of the island tours.

Morne Fortune (the Hill of Good Luck) has had more than its share of bad luck over the years, including devastating hurricanes and those four fires. Head first to **Derek Walcott Square,** a green oasis ringed by Brazil, Laborie, Micoud, and Bourbon streets. Formerly Columbus Square, it was renamed in 1993 after Nobel poet and St. Lucian son Derek Walcott—one of two Nobel laureates from the island, the other being the late economist Sir Arthur Lewis. At the corner of Laborie and Micoud streets there is a 400-year-old saman tree. A favorite local story is of the English botanist who came to St. Lucia many years ago to catalogue the flora. Awestruck by this huge old tree, she asked a passerby what it was. "Massav," he replied, and she gratefully jotted that down in her notebook, unaware that "massav" is patois for "I don't know." Directly across the street is the Roman Catholic **Cathedral of the Immaculate Conception,** which was built in 1897. Some of the 19th-century buildings that managed to survive fire, winds, and rains can be seen on Brazil Street, the southern border of the square.

TIME OUT In the courtyard of the Victorian building that houses Rain restaurant (*see* Dining, *below*), the **Pizza Park** (Derek Walcott Sq., ☎ 809/452–3022) sells takeout or eat-in pizza all day.

Head north on Laborie Street and walk past the government buildings on your right. On the left, William Peter Boulevard is one of Castries's shopping areas. "The Boulevard" connects Laborie Street with Bridge Street, which is another shopping street. The shopping here is of mostly local appeal, however; die-hard shoppers will be happier at Pointe Seraphine.

Continue north for one more block on Laborie Street and you'll come to Jeremie Street. Turn right, and head a few blocks to the **market** on the corner of Jeremie and Peynier streets. The hot, smelly, and crowded old indoor market is undergoing renovations, and there's now a new redbrick semi-open-air produce market with all the color and bustle still intact. The market is most crowded on Saturday mornings, when farmers bring their produce to town.

Elsewhere on the Island

MORNE FORTUNE

To reach **Morne Fortune,** head due south on Bridge Street, turning right onto Government House Road. The drive will take you past the **Government House,** the official residence of the governor-general of St. Lucia and one of the island's few remaining examples of Victorian architecture. Also on the road and worth a stop is **Bagshaw Studios,** producing its instantly recognizable screen-printed clothing and linens in wildly tropical colors and intricate designs—the most distinctive St. Lucian gifts, since Bagshaw's products are not exported. From the top of ❷ the hill, at **Fort Charlotte,** you'll see Martinique to the north and the twin peaks of the Pitons to the south.

Fort Charlotte was begun in 1764 by the French as the *Citadelle du Morne Fortune.* It was completed after 20 years of battling and changing hands. Its old barracks and batteries have now been converted to government buildings and local educational facilities, but you can drive around and look at the remains, including redoubts, a guardroom, stables, and cells. At the end of the road you can also walk up to the Inniskilling Monument, a tribute to one of the most famous battles, fought in 1796, when the 27th Foot Royal Inniskilling Fusiliers wrested the Hill of Good Fortune from the French. Stop also in the Military Cemetery, which was first used in 1782; faint inscriptions on the tombstones tell the tales of the French and English soldiers who died here. Six former governors of the island are buried here as well.

SOUTH OF CASTRIES

The road from Castries to Soufrière travels through beautiful country. The entire west-coast road has been undergoing a widening face-lift since 1992, which, at press time was still under way, having suffered slightly from 1994's Tropical Storm Debbie. Originally planned for completion as far as Soufrière in 1995, it is anyone's guess how far the road has got by now, and you should check its status before you set out for anywhere on the west coast. As it stands, it takes about three hours to drive the whole loop from Castries down the west coast, back up the east coast, and across the Barre de L'Isle Ridge—and that's with ideal conditions and no stops.

❸ A few miles south of Castries, stop by **Marigot Bay,** one of the most beautiful natural harbors in the Caribbean. In 1778, British admiral Samuel Barrington took his ships into this secluded bay within a bay and covered them with palm fronds to hide them from the French. The resort community today is a great favorite of yachtspeople. Parts of *Doctor Doolittle* were filmed here 30 years ago. You can arrange to charter a yacht, swim, snorkel, or lime with the yachting crowd at one of the bars. A 24-hour water taxi connects the various points on the bay.

TIME OUT Stop for rum punch, lunch, and atmosphere at the **Rusty Anchor** (Hurricane Hotel, ☎ 809/453–4230), a happy haunt of boaters.

If you continue south, you'll be in the vicinity of one of the island's two rum distilleries. Major production of sugar ceased here in around 1960, and distilleries now make rum with imported molasses. You're still in banana country, with acres of banana trees covering the hills and valleys. More than 127 different varieties of bananas (often called "figs") are grown on the island.

In the mountainous region ahead you'll see **Mt. Parasol,** and if you look hard enough through the mists, you may be able to make out **Mt. Gimie** (pronounced "Jimmy"), St. Lucia's highest peak, rising to 3,117 feet.

❹ The next village you'll come to is **Anse-la-Raye.** The beach here is a colorful sight, with fishing nets hanging on poles to dry and brightly painted fishing boats bobbing in the water. The fishermen of Anse-la-Raye still make canoes by the old-fashioned method of burning out the center of a log. This was where Tropical Storm Debbie hit hardest; you can still see the gulf where the floodwaters swept through.

SOUFRIÈRE

❺ As you approach **Soufrière,** you'll be in the island's breadbasket, where most of the mangoes, breadfruit, tomatoes, limes, and oranges are grown.

Soufrière, which dates from the mid-18th century, was named after the nearby volcano and has a population of about 9,000 people. The harbor is the deepest on the island, accommodating smaller cruise ships that nose right up to the wharf. A nearby jetty contains an excellent small-crafts center. The **Soufrière Tourist Information Centre** (Bay St., ☎ 809/459–7200) provides information about area attractions, which, in addition to the Pitons, include La Soufrière (billed as the world's only drive-in volcano), sulfur springs, the Diamond Mineral Baths, and the rain forest. You can also ask at the Tourist Centre about Soufrière Estate, on the east side of town, replete with botanical gardens and a minizoo.

❻ Adjoining Soufrière Estate are the **Diamond Falls and Mineral Baths,** which are fed by an underground flow of water from the sulfur springs. Louis XVI provided funds for the construction of these baths for his troops to "fortify them against the St. Lucian climate." During the Brigand's War, just after the French Revolution, the baths were destroyed. They were restored in 1966, and you can see the waterfalls and the beautifully kept botanical gardens before slipping into your swimsuit for a dip in the steaming curative waters. *Soufrière.* ☞ *E.C.$5.* ⊙ *Daily 10–5.*

❼ The island's dense tropical **rain forest** is most easily accessible from the east of Soufrière on the road to Fond St. Jacques. It actually covers about 10% of the island. A trek through the lush landscape can take from three hours to a full day, and you'll need a guide (contact the Forestry Division, ☎ 809/452–3231) and plenty of stamina. Mt. Gimie, Piton Canaries, Mt. Houlom, and Piton Tromasse are all part of this immense forest reserve. The views of the mountains and valleys are spectacular.

❽ For the best land view of the **Pitons,** take the road south out of Soufrière. The road is awful and leads up a steep hill; if you persevere, you'll be rewarded by a magnificent look at the twin peaks, which rise precipitously out of the azure Caribbean. The perfectly shaped pyramidal cones, covered with tropical greenery, were formed of lava from a volcanic eruption 30 million to 40 million years ago. They are not identical twins, since—confusingly—Petit Piton, at 2,619 feet, is rather taller than Gros Piton (2,461 feet), though "Gros" is, indeed fatter, or squatter. Since the mud slides triggered by Tropical Storm Debbie, Gros Piton has also been the only one it is legal to climb, though the way up even the shorter Piton is one very tough trek and requires the permission of the Forestry Division (☎ 809/452–3231) and a knowledgeable guide.

❾ To the south of Soufrière, your nose will note the left turn that takes you to **La Soufrière,** the drive-in volcano, and its **sulfur springs.** Here are more than 20 pools of black, belching, smelly sulfurous waters and multicolored sulfur and assorted other mineral deposits baking and steaming. Despite its intriguing title, the sulfur springs are neither strictly drive-in nor an actual volcano. Instead, you walk—behind your guide, whose service is included in admission—around a fault in

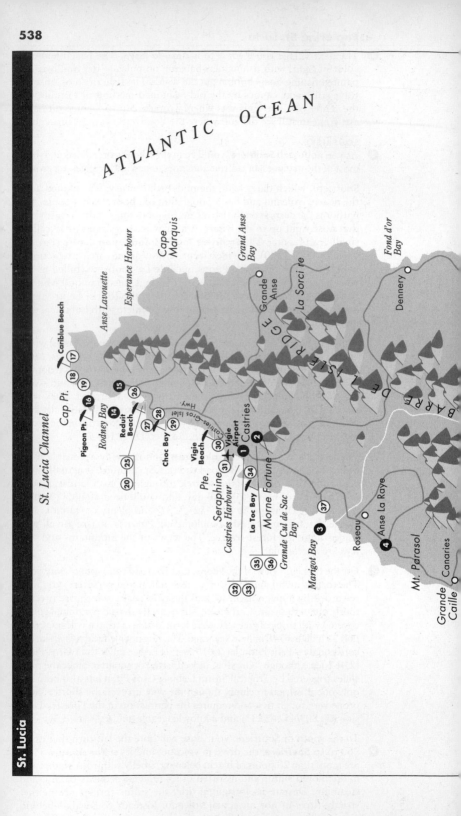

ATLANTIC OCEAN

St. Lucia Channel

Cap Pt.

Cariblue Beach

Pigeon Pt.

Rodney Bay

Reduit Beach

Choc Bay

Vigie Beach

Pte.

Castries Harbour

Seraphine

La Toc Bay

Morne Fortune

Grande Cul de Sac Bay

Marigot Bay

Anse Lavouette

Esperance Harbour

Cape Marquis

Grand Anse Bay

Grande Anse

La Sorcière

BARRE DE L'ISLE RIDGE

Fond d'or Bay

Dennery

Vigie Airport

Castries

Anse La Raye

Roseau

Mt. Parasol

Grande Caille

Canaries

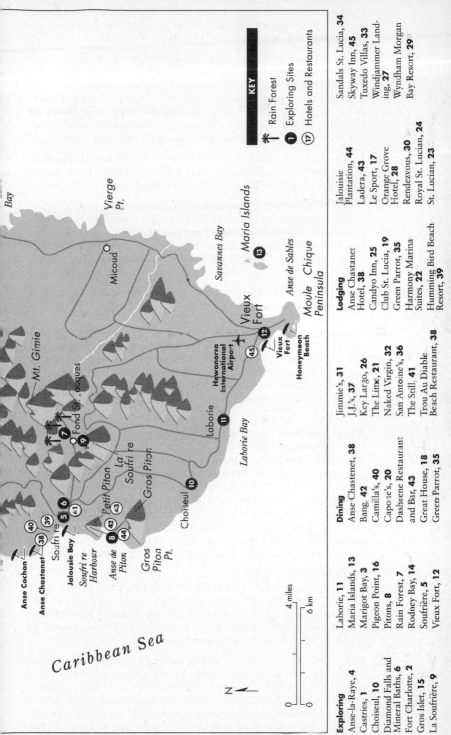

KEY

🌴 Rain Forest

① Exploring Sites

⑰ Hotels and Restaurants

Sandals St. Lucia, **34**
Skyway Inn, **45**
Tuxedo Villas, **33**
Windjammer Landing, **27**
Wyndham Morgan
Bay Resort, **29**

Jalousie
Plantation, **44**
Ladera, **43**
Le Sport, **17**
Orange Grove
Hotel, **28**
Rendezvous, **30**
Royal St. Lucian, **24**
St. Lucian, **23**

Lodging
Anse Chastanet
Hotel, **38**
Candyo Inn, **25**
Club St. Lucia, **19**
Green Parrot, **35**
Harmony Marina
Suites, **22**
Humming Bird Beach
Resort, **39**

Jimmie's, **31**
J.J.'s, **37**
Key Largo, **26**
The Lime, **21**
Naked Virgin, **32**
San Antoine's, **36**
The Still, **41**
Trou Au Diable
Beach Restaurant, **38**

Dining
Anse Chastenet, **38**
Bang, **42**
Camilla's, **40**
Capone's, **20**
Dasheene Restaurant
and Bar, **43**
Great House, **18**
Green Parrot, **35**

Laborie, **11**
Maria Islands, **13**
Marigot Bay, **3**
Pigeon Point, **16**
Pitons, **8**
Rain Forest, **7**
Rodney Bay, **14**
Soufrière, **5**
Vieux Fort, **12**

Exploring
Anse-la-Raye, **4**
Castries, **1**
Choiseul, **10**
Diamond Falls and
Mineral Baths, **6**
Fort Charlotte, **2**
Gros Islet, **15**
La Soufrière, **9**

the substratum rock, which makes for a fascinating 20-minute experience, but an experience that can be stinking and sweaty as hell (maybe literally) on a hot day. *La Soufrière.* ☞ *E.C.$3.* ⊙ *Daily 9–5.*

Follow the road farther south and you'll come next to the coastal town of **Choiseul,** home to wood-carving and pottery shops. At the turn of the road past the Anglican Church, built in 1846, a bridge crosses the River Dorée, so named because the riverbed is blanketed with fool's gold. In La Fargue, just to the south, the **Choiseul Art & Craft Centre** (☎ 809/459–3226) sells superb traditional Carib handicrafts, including pottery, wickerwork, and braided khuskhus grass mats and baskets.

The next stop is **Laborie,** the prototypical St. Lucian fishing village, little changed over the centuries. There's not much to see here, but you can stop to buy some local bread and fresh fish.

Now drive along the southern coast of the island to **Vieux Fort,** St. Lucia's second-largest city and home of the Hewanorra International Airport. Drive out on the **Moule à Chique Peninsula,** the southernmost tip of the island. From here you can see all of St. Lucia to the north and St. Vincent 21 miles south. Looking straight down, you can see where the clear waters of the Caribbean blend with the bluer Atlantic waters.

TIME OUT   **Chak Chak** (Beanfield Rd., Vieux Fort, ☎ 809/454–6260) is a casual, airy restaurant that serves Creole dishes.

The **Maria Islands Nature Reserve,** which has its own interpretive center, consists of two tiny islands in the Atlantic off the southeast coast. The 25-acre Maria Major and its little sister, 4-acre Maria Minor, are inhabited by rare species of lizards and snakes that share their home with frigate birds, terns, doves, and other wildlife. *Moule à Chique,* ☎ 809/454–5014. ☞ *Wed.–Sat. E.C.$3, Sun. E.C.$.50.* ⊙ *Wed.–Sun. 9:30–5.*

A road leads from Vieux Fort through the towns on the Atlantic coast. Don't be fooled by its smooth start; it gets bumpier and bumpier as you progress. It takes you past **Honeymoon Beach,** a wide, grassy, flat Anse l'Islet peninsula jutting into the ocean. Drive through Micoud and, a few miles farther north, Dennery, both of which are residential towns overlooking the Atlantic. At Dennery the road turns west and climbs across the Barre de l'Isle Ridge, through the northern tip of St. Lucia's rain forest with its dense vegetation. There are trails along the way that lead to lookout points where you can get a view of the entire National Forest Preserve, to the south. The road eventually winds back to Castries.

THE NORTH END AND GROS ISLET

The west coast north of Castries is the most developed part of the island and is easy and safe to navigate. Take the John Compton Highway north toward the Vigie Airport. This whole stretch is of far more interest to the hedonist than to the historian, but it features some of the island's best beaches and resort hotels.

About 15 minutes north of Castries, **Rodney Bay,** named after Admiral Rodney, is an 80-acre man-made lagoon surrounded by hotels and restaurants. The St. Lucian Hotel and Royal St. Lucian are in this area, as are Capone's, Lime, and several other popular eateries. North of the lagoon, **Gros Islet** (pronounce it "grow zeelay") is a quiet little fishing village not unlike Anse-la-Raye to the south. But on Friday nights, Gros Islet springs to life with a wild and raucous street festival to which everyone is invited (*see* Nightlife, *below*).

PIGEON POINT

⑯ **Pigeon Point,** jutting out on the northwest coast, was Pigeon Island until a causeway was built several years back, connecting it to the mainland. Tales are told of the pirate Jambe de Bois (Wooden Leg), who used to hide out here. This 40-acre hilltop island, a strategic point during the struggles for control of the island, is now a national park, with long sandy beaches, calm waters for swimming, and areas for picnicking. On the grounds you'll see ruins of barracks, batteries, and garrisons dating from the French and English battles. *Pigeon Point, no* ☎. ☞ *E.C.$3. Guided tours cost E.C.$10.* ◎ *Mon.–Sat. 9–4.*

Off the Beaten Track

If you want a close-up of a working banana plantation and are willing to get a little wet and muddy in the process, you can tour the island's largest—the **Marquis Plantation. St. Lucia Representative Services Ltd.** (*see* Guided Tours, *above*) will pick you up at your hotel in an air-conditioned bus. Wear your most casual clothes, and be prepared to rough it.

Beaches

Beaches are all public, and many are flanked by hotels, where you can rent water-sports equipment and have a rum punch. On the other hand, some are difficult to reach because they abut resort property. There are also secluded beaches, accessible only by water, to which hotels can arrange boat trips. Don't swim along the windward (east) coast; the Atlantic waters are rough and sometimes dangerous.

Pigeon Point, part of the Pigeon Island National Historic Park (☞ E.C.$3), has a long white-sand beach and a small restaurant; it's great for picnicking and swimming.

Reduit Beach is a long stretch of beige sand facing Rodney Bay and is home to the St. Lucian and Royal St. Lucian hotels, which offer numerous water sports.

Anse Cochon, an uncrowded cove south of Anse-la-Raye, is a black-sand beach most easily reached by boat. The waters are superb for swimming and snorkeling.

Anse Chastanet is a gray-sand beach just north of Soufrière with a backdrop of green hills and the island's best reefs for snorkeling and diving. The wooden gazebos of the Anse Chastanet Hotel are nestled among the palms, with a dive shop, restaurant, and bar on the beach (*see* Dining and Lodging, *below*).

Black-sand **Anse des Pitons,** south of Soufrière in Jalousie Bay, sits directly between the Pitons and is accessible through Jalousie Plantation (*see* Lodging, *below*) or by boat; it offers great snorkeling and diving.

Vieux Fort, at the southernmost tip of St. Lucia, has a long secluded stretch of white sand and waters protected by reefs. **Honeymoon Beach,** just west of Vieux Fort, is another sandy escape.

Sports and the Outdoors

Most hotels offer Sunfish, water skis, fins, masks, and other water-sports equipment free to guests and for a fee to nonguests.

Boating

Cat Inc. (Castries, ☎ 809/450–8651) takes revelers on a journey along the Caribbean coast aboard the 56-foot-long catamarans *Endless Sum-*

mer I and *II*. Bareboat or skippered yacht charters are available through **Sunsail Stevens** (Castries, ☎ 809/452–8648), which has a fleet of 39- to 56-foot sailing yachts; **Trade Wind Yacht Charters** (Rodney Bay, ☎ 809/452–8424); and the **Moorings Yacht Charter** (Marigot Bay, ☎ 809/451–4256 or 800/535–7289).

Deep-Sea Fishing

Among the sea creatures in these waters are dolphin, Spanish mackerel, barracuda, and white marlin. Contact **Captain Mike's** (☎ 809/452–0216) or **Mako Watersports** (☎ 809/452–0412) to steer you in the right direction.

Fitness Centers

If your resort lacks the kind of equipment you'd expect for what you're paying—and many do—try the **St. Lucia Racquet Club** (Cap Estate, ☎ 809/450–0551), which has Nautilus equipment, exercise machines, and aerobics and step aerobics classes. It's the best gym on the island. Day passes are also available to **Jalousie Plantation** (Soufrière, ☎ 809/459–7666) and **Le Sport** (Cap Estate, ☎ 809/452–8551), which have excellent facilities.

Golf

There are 9-hole courses at **Sandals St. Lucia** (☎ 809/452–3081) and **Cap Estate Golf Club** (☎ 809/452–8523). A caddy is required at the former; greens fees are $15–$20 at either for 18 holes. Club rentals are another $10. These courses are scenic and good fun, but they're not of professional caliber.

Hiking

The island is laced with trails, but you should not attempt the challenging peaks on your own. Your hotel, the tourist board, or the **Forestry Division** (☎ 809/452–3231) can provide you with a guide. **The St. Lucia National Trust** (☎ 809/452–5005), established to preserve the island's natural and cultural heritage, tours several sites, including Pigeon Island, the Maria Islands, and Fregate Island.

Horseback Riding

For trail rides on the beach, contact **Trim's Riding School** (Gros Islet, ☎ 809/452–8273), **North Point Riding Stables** (☎ 809/450–8853), or **Jalousie Plantation** (☎ 809/459–7666).

Jogging

You can jog on the beach by yourself or team up with the **Roadbusters** (☎ Jimmy at 809/452–5142 or evenings at 809/452–4790).

Parasailing

Contact the **St. Lucian** hotel (☎ 809/452–8351).

Scuba Diving

Scuba St. Lucia (☎ 809/459–7355) is a PADI five-star training facility, with dive shops at Anse Chastanet (which is, among aficionados, one of the most highly regarded dive sites anywhere) and the St. Lucian hotel, that offers daily beach and boat dives, resort courses, underwater photography, and day trips. Trips are also arranged through **Buddies Scuba** (☎ 809/452–5288), **Dive Jalousie** (☎ 809/459–7666), the **Moorings Scuba Centre** (☎ 809/451–4357), and **Windjammer Diving** (☎ 809/452–0913).

Sea and Snorkeling Excursions

The 140-foot square-rigger *Brig Unicorn* (☎ 809/452–6811) sails to Soufrière, with steel bands, a swim stop, rum punch, and soda. **Captain Mike's** (☎ 809/452–0216) does swimming and snorkeling cruises.

Sea and snorkeling excursions can also be arranged through **Mako Watersports** (☎ 809/452–0412) and the **Surf Queen** (☎ 809/452–8351, ext. 515) or through your hotel.

Squash

The **St. Lucia Racquet Club** (adjacent Club St. Lucia, ☎ 809/450–0551) has one court and its own pro, who gives lessons and clinics. It is not air-conditioned, however. **Jalousie Plantation** (☎ 809/459–7666) also has a squash court open to nonguests.

Tennis

All the major hotels have their own tennis courts, but many restrict use to their own guests. The **St. Lucia Racquet Club** (adjacent to Club St. Lucia, ☎ 809/450–0551) opened in 1991 and is one of the top tennis facilities in the Caribbean—probably the best in the Lesser Antilles. Apart from hosting many tour events, its seven floodlit courts are in perfect shape, the pro shop is extensive, and the staff knowledgeable. **Jalousie Plantation** (☎ 809/459–7666) has four lighted courts open to nonguests.

Waterskiing

Contact **Mako Watersports** (☎ 809/452–0412). Rentals are also available at most of the hotels.

Windsurfing

The **St. Lucian** hotel is the local agent for Mistral Windsurfers (☎ 809/452–8351). Also contact **Marigot Bay Resort** (☎ 809/453–4357) and **Mako Watersports** (☎ 809/452–0412). Most hotels rent Windsurfers to nonguests.

Spectator Sports

Cricket and **soccer,** the two national pastimes, are played at **Mindoo Philip Park** in Marchand, 2 miles east of Castries. The **St. Lucia Racquet Club** (☎ 809/450–0551), which hosted the Davis Cup in 1994, is frequently the site of major and regional **tennis** events, the most important being the **St. Lucian Open** in early December.

Contact the tourist board (☎ 809/452–4094) for specific information regarding schedules.

Shopping

Shopping on St. Lucia has been traditionally low-key, but as tourism is increasing, so are the options for shopping. The island's best-known products are the unique hand-silk-screened and hand-printed designs of Bagshaw Studios, which are designed, printed, and sold only on St. Lucia. The island is also home to Windjammer Clothing, which is sold on virtually every Caribbean island. Apart from those indigenous products, there are native-made wood carvings, pottery, and straw hats and baskets.

Shopping Areas

For a duty-free spree, visit **Pointe Seraphine,** a Spanish-style complex by the harbor, where 23 shops sell designer perfumes, china and crystal, jewelry, watches, leather goods, liquor, and cigarettes. Native crafts are also sold in the shopping center. Though Castries has a number of shops, mostly on **Bridge Street** and **William Peter Boulevard,** selling locally made souvenirs, you can find the same items at the crafts stands and shopping arcades at virtually every resort; the **St. Lucian** hotel has one of the best selections. **Gablewoods Mall** (Gros Islet Hwy., north of Castries), which opened in 1993, has about 25 shops selling groceries, spirits and wines, jewelry, clothing, local crafts, foreign news-papers, books, music, and household goods.

Good Buys

DUTY-FREE

In Pointe Seraphine, look for designer perfumes at **Images** (☎ 809/452–6883). **Little Switzerland** (☎ 809/452–7587) carries fine china and crys-tal. **A Touch of Class** (☎ 809/452–7443) is the place for Caribbean literature and local souvenirs. Leather handbags, jewelry, crystal, and perfumes can be found at **Meli's Boutique** (☎ 809/452–7587). Be sure to bring your passport and airline ticket to get duty-free prices.

FABRICS AND CLOTHING

Bagshaw's (La Toc Rd., La Toc Bay, ☎ 809/452–7570; Vigie Airport, Pointe Seraphine, no ☎) sells silk-screened fabrics and clothing. **Wind-jammer Clothing Company** (☎ 809/452–1041) has its main store at Vigie Cove and an outlet at Pointe Seraphine. **Caribelle Batik** (Old Vic-toria Rd., the Morne, Castries, ☎ 809/452–3785) creates batik cloth-ing and wall hangings. Visitors are welcome to watch the craftspeople at work. The **Batik Studio** at Humming Bird Beach Resort (Soufrière, ☎ 809/459–7232) offers superb sarongs, scarves, and wall panels.

LOCAL MUSIC

Take home a cassette recording of the band you've been jumping-up with every night from **Jeremie's Records** (83 Brazil St., Castries, ☎ 809/452–5079), a tiny store selling customized and prerecorded tapes.

NATIVE CRAFTS

Trays, masks, and figures are carved from mahogany, red cedar, and eucalyptus trees in the studio adjacent to **Eudovic Art Studio** (Morne Fortune, ☎ 809/452–2747). Hammocks, straw mats, baskets and hats, and carvings, as well as books and maps of St. Lucia, are at **Noah's Arkade** (Jeremie St., Castries, and Pointe Seraphine, ☎ 809/452–2523). **Artsibit** (corner Brazil and Mongiraud Sts., ☎ 809/452–7865) features works by top St. Lucian artists. The **Choiseul Art & Craft Cen-tre** (Lafargue, ☎ 809/454–3226) has a huge selection of handmade basketware, ceramics, from pots to sculpture, bas-reliefs from local woods, and many small and portable pieces, too.

Dining

If you stop by the Castries market (*see* Exploring St. Lucia, *above*) on a Saturday, you'll see the riches produced in this fertile volcanic soil. Mangoes, plantains, breadfruits, limes, pumpkins, cucumbers, pawpaws (pronounced *poh-poh* here, known as papaya elsewhere), yams, christophines (a green, squashlike vegetable), and coconuts are among the fruits and vegetables that appear on menus throughout the island. Every menu lists the catch of the day (usually flying fish, kingfish, and dolphin fish) along with the ever-popular lobster, and you may see the national dish, saltfish and green fig—a concoction of dried, salted white fish and the bananalike plantain—which is definitely an ac-quired taste. More usual Eastern Caribbean standards you'll see include callaloo, stuffed crab back, and *lambi* (conch). Chicken, pork, and bar-becues are also big-time here. Most of the meats are imported—beef from Argentina and Iowa, lamb from New Zealand. The French in-fluence is strong in St. Lucian restaurants, and most chefs cook with a Creole flair, pre–nouvelle cuisine.

What to Wear

Dress on St. Lucia is casual but conservative. Nice shorts are usually fine during the day, but locals frown on bathing suits. In the evening, things are a little more elegant, but even the most formal places expect only a jacket for men and a sundress for women.

CATEGORY	COST*
$$$$	over $40
$$$	$25–$40
$$	$15–$25
$	under $15

per person, excluding drinks and service

Soufrière

$$$$ **Dasheene Restaurant and Bar.** Part of the fanciful Ladera resort (*see*
★ Lodging, *below*), Dasheene is a small, casual mountaintop retreat with breathtaking views of the Pitons and the clear Caribbean sea between them. This is some of the best food in St. Lucia—Caribbean specialties with new American and Continental accents. Appetizers on a frequently changing menu may include smoked kingfish crepes and spicy seafood gazpacho. Typical entrées are tuna steak with coconut-avocado cream sauce and chicken breast with a mango or a pecan-and-peanut sauce. For dessert, the chocolate crème brûlée flambé takes about five minutes to cool down but is well worth the wait. There's live entertainment many nights and soft, jazzy tunes playing otherwise. This is the stuff of wedding anniversaries and very special occasions. ✗ *Soufrière, ☎ 809/454–7323. Reservations advised. AE, MC, V.*

$$$ **Anse Chastenet.** Too many cooks spoil the broth? Not here on two ter-
★ races—one magically suspended among the trees, the other a spacious rooftop—at the wonderful mountainside resort (*see* Lodging, *below*), where the new French executive chef, Jacky Rioux, works with a St. Lucian maestro to invent sublime variations on local dishes. The menus hadn't been set on our visit, but preview samplings included a creamed conch soup *en croute* (with a latticed puff-pastry lid), roast grouper stuffed with lobster mousse, dolphin poached in coconut milk with a lime sauce, and—the best local food joke you'll ever taste—"St. Lucian apple pie," made not with (nonexistent) apples but with candied, spiced christophines and served with passion-fruit ice cream. Between them, these chefs cater to every culinary fantasy, competing easily with their big-city cousins. ✗ *North of Soufrière, ☎ 809/459–7354. Reservations advised. AE, DC, MC, V.*

$$ **The Still.** For visitors to Diamond Falls, lunching at the Still is not so much an option as it is an inevitability. This mammoth hall seats up to 400 and is popular with tour groups and cruise passengers. The emphasis is on local foods—christophines, breadfruits, yams, callaloo, and seafood, but there are also pork chops and beef dishes. ✗ *Soufrière, ☎ 809/454–7224. Reservations advised. MC, V. No dinner.*

$$ **Trou Au Diable Beach Restaurant.** This beachside open-air lunch spot
★ at the Anse Chastanet resort (*see* Lodging, *below*) is the perfect place to break from a day of diving or sunbathing. The West Indian cuisine is delicious, and many specialties are prepared right before your eyes on a barbecue grill. The *rotis* (Caribbean-style burritos) here are the best on the island, served with homemade mango chutney you could eat by the jar. Try also the island pepper pot—pork, beef, or lamb simmered for many hours with local veggies and spices; or a good old tuna melt in case you're homesick. Dessert always features an unusual flavor of ice cream, maybe soursop or anise seed; try it! There's always a young and lively crowd here, and although the restaurant caters mostly to the resort's guests, everyone is quite welcome. ✗ *Anse Chastanet, Soufrière, ☎ 809/459–7000. AE, DC, MC, V. No dinner.*

$–$$ **Bang.** The eccentric Brit Colin Tennant (a.k.a. Lord Glenconner), founder of the glamorous hideaway island of Mustique, came to St. Lucia to open his dream resort between the Pitons, over which he lost control (it's a long story). The resort became Jalousie Plantation, but Tennant stayed on to open this wickedly cute spoof on a Jamaican jerk joint, with ice-cream-colored paintwork, assorted ramshackle wooden chairs and cushion-strewn booths, a cerise velvet-draped stage for music, and a buzz like the early days of Mustique, when Jagger was young. Drink rum, eat barbecue from "Ye Olde Jerk Pit," but beware—this place closes at whim. ✗ *Next to Jalousie, north of Soufrière,* ☎ *809/459–7864. Reservations advised. No credit cards.*

$ **Camilla's.** About the only decent restaurant actually in the town of Soufrière, the tiny, second-floor Camilla's is pretty in pink, somewhat underventilated on a hot night (apart from the two balcony tables), but friendly as anything. The menu is admirably simple and all local—you can have today's catch curried, Creole-style, or grilled with lemon sauce, or there's barbecue chicken with garlic sauce and fries, or lobster salad. There's also a list of tropical cocktails bigger than the entire restaurant. ✗ *7 Bridge St., Soufrière,* ☎ *809/459–5379. Reservations advised. AE.*

Castries

$$$ **Green Parrot.** The Green Parrot comes complete with sommelier and crisp napery. The menu of local and international dishes always includes a lot of seafood. There's lively entertainment—a belly dancer on Wednesday night and limbo night on Saturday—but the real reason to dine here is the view over Castries and the harbor. This is a hot spot for locals and tourists. ✗ *Tape La., Morne Fortune,* ☎ *809/452–3399. Reservations required. Jacket required. AE, MC, V.*

$$–$$$ **Jimmie's.** This popular, open-air, mom-and-pop-cozy restaurant and bar perched above the bay makes a relaxing daytime stop and becomes a romantic dinner spot when the harbor lights twinkle below. Appetizers on the seafood-dominated menu include a great Creole stuffed crab, while a wise choice of entrée is the special seafood platter with samplings from every part of today's catch; all entrées come with several local vegetables—pumpkin, black beans, christophines, greens—plus garlic bread. Dessert lovers had better be in a banana mood, since the menu lists about 10 options—every single one, from fritters to ice cream, made with St. Lucian "figs." ✗ *Vigie Cove, Castries,* ☎ *809/452–5142. No reservations. AE, MC, V.*

$$–$$$ **Naked Virgin.** Tucked away in the quiet Castries suburb of Marchand (just opposite the local post office—keep asking), this pleasant hangout offers terrific Creole cuisine, and every guest leaves with a free T-shirt. The owner, Paul John, has worked in many of the island's major hotels, and his rum concoction, the Naked Virgin, could be the best punch you've ever tasted. Shrimp Creole and fried flying fish are highly recommended. ✗ *Marchand Rd., Castries,* ☎ *809/452–5594. Reservations advised. AE, MC, V.*

$ **J. J.'s.** Not only are the prices right here, but the food is some of the best on the island. Superbly grilled fish with fresh vegetables is tops. Tables are on a terrace above the road, and the welcome is friendly and casual. On Friday nights the music blares, and the locals come for liming (hanging out) and dancing in the street. ✗ *Marigot Bay Rd. (3 mi before the bay), Marigot,* ☎ *809/451–4076. No reservations. No credit cards.*

$ **San Antoine's.** High on the Morne, with splendid views of Castries below and Martinique in the distance, this historic building was originally the great house of the San Antoine Hotel, built in the late 1800s, destroyed by fire in 1970, and restored soon after. This is one of the most elegantly appointed restaurants on the island. Try the superbly grilled fish with fresh vegetables. Tables are on a terrace above the road, and the welcome is friendly and casual. On Friday nights the music blares, and the locals come for liming and dancing in the street. ✕ *Marigot Bay Rd. (3 mi before the bay), Marigot,* ☎ *809/453–4076. No reservations. No credit cards.*

Rodney Bay

$$$$ **Great House.** From this romantic spot, perched on a hill overlooking Anse Becune Bay, you can enjoy views of the water and of Martinique in the distance. The restaurant is run by the owners of Club St. Lucia and is thus very popular with guests of that resort. Traditional French dishes are given Creole overtones, as in the appetizer of pumpkin soup with glazed leeks, and entrées like baked red snapper in a chive sauce, Antillean shrimp sautéed in a garlic-and-parsley butter, or curried goat. The food is good, but you really come here to enjoy the view and elegant setting. ✕ *Cap Estate,* ☎ *809/450–0450 or 809/450–0211. Reservations advised. Jacket advised. AE, DC, MC, V. No lunch.*

$$–$$$ **Capone's.** The tropics meet the Jazz Age in this restaurant. In a setting
★ of black-and-white tile floors, a polished wood bar, and a player piano, waiters and waitresses dressed like gangsters serve rum drinks called Valentine's Day Massacre and Mafia Mai Tai. Your check is delivered in a violin case. The pasta is fresh, and the meat dishes include *osso buco alla Milanese* (veal knuckle) and chicken rotisserie. The **Pizza Parlour** (open 11 AM–midnight) turns out burgers and sandwiches, as well as pizza. The management also runs **Sweet Dreams** across the street, with more than 150 tempting dessert options. ✕ *Rodney Bay, across from the St. Lucian hotel,* ☎ *809/452–0284. Reservations advised. AE, MC, V. Closed Mon. No lunch.*

$$ **The Lime.** Across the street from Capone's, the Lime is a favorite site
★ for "liming" (hanging out). A casual place with lime-colored gingham curtains, straw hats decorating the ceiling, and hanging plants, it offers a businessman's three-course lunch and a buffet of local dishes, like callaloo and lambi. Starters may include homemade pâté or stuffed crab back. Entrée choices may be medallions of pork fillet with the chef's special orange-and-ginger sauce, stewed lamb, or fish fillet poached in white wine and mushroom sauce. The prices are more reasonable than at neighboring Capone's, which is perhaps why the expatriates and locals gather here in the evenings. Next door is Late Limes, where they gather when the evening starts turning into morning. ✕ *Rodney Bay,* ☎ *809/452–0761. Reservations advised for dinner. MC, V. Closed Tues.*

$–$$ **Key Largo.** Brick-oven gourmet pizzas are the specialty at this casual eatery across the lagoon from Rodney Bay's many hotels. You're welcome simply to stop in for an espresso or cappuccino, but the popular Pizza Key Largo—topped with shrimp, artichokes, and what seems like a few pounds of mozzarella—is tough to pass up. ✕ *Rodney Bay,* ☎ *809/452–0282. MC, V.*

Lodging

St. Lucia is beginning to rival Jamaica in the number of all-inclusives and large resorts dotting the island. Sandals opened two couples-only compounds here in 1993 and 1994, respectively. Wyndham's all-inclusive debuted in 1992, Anse Chastanet plans to add a small resort to its 25-year-old property in 1996, and Jalousie Plantation and Ladera opened between the Pitons in 1992. Additionally, a few small and inexpensive lodgings have popped up around Rodney Bay, offering bright, clean modern suites at bargain prices. Virtually all the development is along the calm Caribbean coast, either around Soufrière to the south or, more commonly, from Castries to Cap Estate in the north.

Fortunately, there is not a glut of resorts or hotels in any one price range or catering to any one type of tourist. You'll find some that draw principally Europeans, others Americans. Some are lavish, others laid-back and less costly. Some have all-inclusive meal plans; just as many are MAP or EP. And many cater to honeymooners: St. Lucian law requires residence for only three days for couples to acquire a marriage license.

Just about every resort has friendly, accommodating service and is located in a fairly secluded cove or along an unspoiled beach. Keep in mind that the all-inclusives in this section will save each guest from $50 to $100 daily on meals and drinks, meaning, for example, that a one-week stay at Le Sport—listed below as in the *$$$$* category—may actually cost you less than a week at the Royal St. Lucian or at Windjammer Landing, which are priced in lower categories because they don't cover meals. Also, consider spending the final night or two of your stay at one of the lodgings in Soufrière, about 35 minutes from Hewanorra International Airport, or at the new Skyway Inn, just across the street from the airport. The foremost complaint of visitors to St. Lucia is the 60- to 90-minute topsy-turvy sickness-inducing drive from their hotel to Hewanorra; it pays to break up the long drive in any way possible. For winter, reserve at least four months in advance.

For private-home rentals, contact **Happy Homes** (Box 12, Castries, St. Lucia) or **Tropical Villas** (Box 189, Castries, ☎ 809/452–8240).

CATEGORY	COST*
$$$$	over $350
$$$	$200–$350
$$	$125–$200
$	under $125

All prices are for a standard double room for two, excluding 8% tax and 10% service charge.

$$$$ **Jalousie Plantation.** This fancy all-inclusive resort opened in late 1992 and has suffered some under the harsh glare of controversy. Some of the early criticism about disorganization was probably fair, but a new general manager took over in 1993, and the staff now seems professional, friendly, and quite together. Building a resort in this dramatic setting, between the Pitons, angered many locals and St. Lucia lovers who felt this land should never have been developed—but you can't not love this location. Brown wood cottages tumble down the steep hillside to a small bay, and tropical gardens lead down from the main buildings, with restaurants and lounges, to the oval pool, water-sports facilities, and gray-sand beach. People movers shuttle guests around the resort. Public areas are designed and decorated with the formality of a palazzo—some would call it the flair of a suburban planning committee—the cottages crowd together a bit, and the smaller of the two types of plunge pools is lilliputian. But otherwise, this is everything you would expect from a luxury resort: Larger cottages have an extra shower and a large sitting area; all rooms have a stocked refrigerator, air-conditioning, cable TV, elegant dark-wood furniture, and plenty of closet space. The sports and beauty facilities are excellent, and the wealth of space and amenities ensures that you'll seldom have to battle crowds, whether at dinner or when reserving a tennis court. ☎ *Box 251, Soufrière,* ☎ *809/459–7666 or 800/877–3643,* FAX *809/459–7667. 103 cottages, 12 suites. 4 restaurants, 3 bar-lounges, tennis, squash, water sports and scuba diving (offshore scuba diving*

is extra), horseback riding (extra), massage, spa and beauty treat-
ments, deep-sea-fishing charters, boat shuttle to Soufrière and Castries
(extra). AE, DC, MC, V. All-inclusive.

$$$$ **Le Sport.** Boredom will never strike at this unique and beautiful resort,
★ which is not easy to pigeonhole. Though crowned by the Oasis—a $3.5
million temple to well-being that looks like a sun-bleached Moorish
palace—it is not a spa, and, despite its name, it's no jock's hotel.
Health nuts will be very happy here, but it is also possible to eat enormous quantities of the excellent kitchen's cuisine and accomplish nothing but the acquisition of a dangerous suntan on the perfect U-shaped
beach. Most guests laze around in white robes awaiting thalassotherapy—seawater beauty treatments, which Le Sport (and its Grenadian
sister, Le Source) pioneered—before throwing themselves into one of
the 30-something things-to-do coordinated by the charming Charles
Simon and his team of "Body Guards" (archery, tai chi, fencing, waterskiing, scuba, tennis, volleyball etc., etc.). You may not see much of
your room, but these have central air, queen-size beds, marble baths,
phones, fridges, and small balconies with ocean views; costlier versions
have cool marble floors and four-poster beds. There are 30 brand-new
oceanfront rooms scheduled for completion by press time, with—a welcome improvement—bigger balconies. The evening entertainment and
popular late-night piano bar are classier than what's found at the average all-inclusive. The only disappointment is the small and low-tech
gym. ⊠ *Box 437, Cariblue Beach,* ☎ *809/450–8551 or 800/544–2883,*
℻ *809/452–0368. 130 rooms, 2 suites, 1 plantation house. Restau-*
rant, 2 bars, 2 pools, aerobics, meditation, tai chi, yoga, dance, fenc-
ing classes, bicycles, lighted tennis court, archery, water-sports center,
thalassotherapy, laundry, beauty salon, beauty and rejuvenation treat-
ments, Jacuzzi, Turkish baths, exercise rooms, health shop, boutique,
bank, medical facilities. AE, DC, MC, V. All-inclusive.

$$$$ **Wyndham Morgan Bay Resort.** The expanding Wyndham Hotel group
took over this property from the French-owned Hotel Pullman in
1992. Early glitches (like insufficient AC/DC adapters) have been
ironed out, and the landscaping is growing up, beautifying the eight
three-story blocks that fan out from the central pool-restaurant-bar area.
Nothing's going to change the mostly partial sea views from the rooms,
though. Their balconies are tiny, and decor the usual Caribbean pale
florals and peach wicker, but beds are king-size and especially firm and
comfortable, and there's an ingenious angle on the mirrors that shows
you your entire self from the back (always useful where bikinis are worn).
Except for minibars, amenities are present and correct—air-conditioning, cable TV, clock radio, phone, hair dryer. There's everything
for the party animal and sportif type, too, with drinks and entertainment freely flowing—from early morning aerobics to midnight pizza
at the beachside Palm Grill—to the delight of a largely European
crowd. Americans are just discovering Wyndham, although the hundred new rooms being added this year will probably speed the process. The narrow, gray-sand beach with cloudy water is the biggest
disappointment. ⊠ *Box 2216, Gros Islet,* ☎ *809/450–2511,* ℻
809/450–1050. 340 rooms. 2 restaurants, 2 bars, beach grill, boutique,
4 tennis courts, pool, game room, Jacuzzi, exercise room, sauna, water-
sports center, archery, aerobics. AE, D, MC, V. All-inclusive.

$$$–$$$$ **Anse Chastanet Hotel.** If you invest in one of the Hillside Premium or
★ Deluxe rooms (Numbers 7 and 14) here, you are in for a slice of
heaven. Nick Troubetskoy, the Canadian owner-architect, designed each
to meld into the tropical mountainside, with louvered wooden walls
open to stunning Piton and Caribbean vistas or to the deep shady green
of the forest. Each has a terra-cotta-tiled floor, fun madras cotton fab-

rics, chunky wood furniture, great circles of upside-down baskets acting as lamp shades (small yellow birds like to rest on these), and truly covetable burlap and carved wood artworks. Most rooms have an irresistible quirk. Number 14B has a tree growing in the bathroom; Number 7F has a vast bathroom, its shower completely open to the panorama of the Pitons. Lesser rooms (the "Superior" Numbers 5S and 6S) are mostly octagonal gazebos, with the same decor but far less space, less privacy in many cases, and fewer of the special touches. This is a magical setting, though, as long as you're fit to climb the hundreds of steps from the gray-sand beach (one of the island's best) to the bar-restaurant and the rooms, and as long as you're not a TV and telephone addict. Good food and great scuba would be fine habits here, though, since divers come from the earth's four corners to peep at these reefs, and a new executive chef has raised the hotel's already high standards of cuisine. ⌖ *Box 7000, Soufrière,* ☎ *809/459–7000,* ℻ *809/454–7067. 36 rooms and 12 suites. 2 restaurants, 2 bars, tennis court, dive shop, water-sports center. AE, DC, MC, V. EP, MAP.*

$$$–$$$$ **Club St. Lucia.** Refurbished bit by bit over the past 12 years, this bustling, friendly resort is the island's largest. Of the all-inclusives, this is the least expensive; it's not particularly luxurious. It caters mostly to Brits, but tennis enthusiasts come here to be close to the adjacent St. Lucia Racquet Club (*see* Sports, *above*), which is available to guests for a nominal fee. Others come here to get hitched; expect to see three to five weddings per day. The resort sits on 50 acres, with rooms and suites in bungalows scattered over the hillside, and has two beaches. Accommodations are spacious, with king-size beds (twins on request), tile floors, patios, baths with tubs and showers, and air-conditioning in all but the standard rooms, which have ceiling fans. There are clock radios in all the rooms, but no ☎s. Live entertainment is scheduled nightly. Though the food is adequate at best, guests receive a discount and free transportation to the Great House Restaurant (*see* Dining, *above*). A pizza parlor and 40 rooms were added in 1994. ⌖ *Box 915, Smugglers Village, Castries,* ☎ *809/452–0551 or 800/223–9815,* ℻ *809/452–0281. 352 rooms and suites. Restaurant, pizza parlor, 2 bars, pool, tennis, disco, minimart, several shops, Jacuzzi, water-sports center, transport to stables, laundry. AE, DC, MC, V. All-inclusive.*

$$$–$$$$ **Ladera.** This quiet, luxurious hideaway is nestled amid lush botanical ★ gardens overlooking the Pitons, the Caribbean sea, and Jalousie Plantation. It opened in 1992 and has immediately become one of the most exclusive and unusual small resorts in the Caribbean—a home away from home for rock stars, corporate VIPs, and honeymooners. Most guests are American, and many stay here for the last night or two at the end of a longer vacation spent at a larger resort. The two-story suites and three-bedroom villas, furnished with a harmonious blend of French colonial antiques and local crafts, have a completely open western wall affording dazzling unobstructed views. Many units have sizable plunge pools, and some have a Jacuzzi. You may have a banana tree in your living room, salamanders scurrying across your kitchen counter, or even the odd bat (remember, they eat the mosquitoes!) fluttering under your rafters—so expect the unexpected. Staying here is for many a once-in-a-lifetime treat. Reserve your room at least six months in advance. ⌖ *Box 255, Soufrière,* ☎ *809/454–7323. 7 villas, 12 suites. Restaurant, bar, pool, gift shop. AE, MC, V. MAP.*

$$$–$$$$ **Rendezvous.** Formerly Couples, this all-inclusive resort on Malabar Beach, now under the same ownership as Le Sport, is still for couples only. Things tend to be quite active, with volleyball in the pool and on the beach, and aerobics and water exercise classes. The activities desk can arrange anything, including a wedding. Accommodations have pink marble

floors, king-size four-poster beds, a balcony or terrace, and air-conditioning—but no TVs. There is nightly live music for dancing and a piano bar that's open until the last couple leaves. ⌧ *Box 190, Malabar Beach,* ☎ *809/452–4211 or 800/221–1831,* 𝔽𝔸𝕏 *809/452–7419. 84 rooms, 8 suites, 8 cottages. 2 restaurants, 3 bars, 2 pools, lighted tennis court, sauna, Jacuzzi, exercise room, bicycles, horseback riding, water-sports center, dive shop, catamaran. AE, MC, V. All-inclusive.*

$$$–$$$$ **Royal St. Lucian.** This property caters to your every whim. The colonnaded reception area is stunning—an Italian palazzo with cool marble, a gurgling fountain, and a sweeping grand staircase. However, the russet-roofed white buildings form an uninspired "U" in the pristine landscaped grounds. The large, rambling pool is laced with Japanese bridges and has a natural rock waterfall. The split-level ocean-view suites are sumptuous (some people reckon they're the best on the island), with a soothing pastel color scheme, cable TV, air-conditioning, three phones, a minibar, and a jet shower. Guests, who tend to be European, may use the tennis and water-sports facilities at the adjacent sister property, the St. Lucian. Not the most authentic Caribbean experience in St. Lucia, the food, service, and decorating are nevertheless stellar. ⌧ *Box 977, Castries,* ☎ *809/452–0999 or 800/225–5859,* 𝔽𝔸𝕏 *809/452–9639. 98 suites. 2 restaurants, 2 bars, pool. AE, DC, MC, V. EP, MAP.*

$$$–$$$$ **Sandals St. Lucia.** Sandals, the all-inclusive, couples-only chain of resorts, debuted here in April 1993 and has been a smashing success. This secluded 155-acre property is within a 10-minute drive of Castries. The list of perks here goes on and on: private plunge pools, a ¼-acre swimming pool, a lovely beach, a nine-hole golf course, four floodlit tennis courts, an outstanding fitness center, etc. There's no shortage of restaurants either; take your choice of Asian, Continental, French, southwestern, or Caribbean cuisine. Guest rooms and suites, done in mahogany furnishings with king-size four-poster beds, all have air-conditioning, hair dryers, direct-dial telephones, and cable TV. Suites have concierge service. Most important, guests, who are mostly American, seem to have a blast—thanks in part to a young, raucous, and fun-loving staff. There's a second St. Lucian Sandals at Choc Bay (☎ 809/453–0222) if this one's booked up. The Choc Bay version is on a beach with calmer waters and offers a greater array of water sports. ⌧ *La Toc Rd., Castries,* ☎ *809/452–3081,* 𝔽𝔸𝕏 *809/453–7089. 213 rooms, 60 suites. 5 restaurants, 5 bars, 5 tennis courts, 9-hole golf course, water-sports center, fitness center. AE, DC, MC, V. All-inclusive.*

$$$ **Windjammer Landing.** This sun-kissed resort, with sweeping prospects
★ of one of St. Lucia's prettiest bays, fulfills anyone's beachcombing fantasies. White stucco villas crowned with tile alternate with a porticoed reception area and thatch-hut public rooms. Villas are huge and tastefully decorated in the ubiquitous island pastels and rattan furnishings. All have air-conditioning, a VCR and cable TV, a stereo, microwave, coffeemaker, and blender; and you can arrange to have dinner prepared in your kitchen and served on your terrace. The ambience is rustic simplicity with painted natural wood timbers, tile floors, wicker chairs, and straw mats. Guests tend toward young, and most are American and love the energetic staff. A people mover transports guests to their villas, up the steep hill from the main building and the shops. This is truly an idyllic spot. Though expensive for one couple, the Windjammer is a steal for six guests in a three-bedroom villa. ⌧ *Box 1504, Labrelotte Bay, Castries,* ☎ *809/452–0913,* 𝔽𝔸𝕏 *809/452–9454. 114 1-, 2-, and 3-bedroom villas. 3 restaurants, 2 bars, picnic meals, tennis, 3 pools, minimarket, 3 boutiques, water sports, laundry. AE, MC, V. EP, MAP.*

$$$ Green Parrot. The hillside setting is the draw at this hotel, set high up in Morne Fortune above Castries. The motel-like rooms have a patio, phone, air-conditioning, and bath with tub/shower and vanity. In addition to the Green Parrot restaurant, which is open to the public, hotel guests have access to a separate dining room with a sunken bar. The hotel arranges boat trips to Jambette Beach for barbecue and snorkeling, and a free bus scoots you to town and the beach. ☎ *Box 648, Castries,* ☎ *809/452–3399,* FAX *809/453–2272. 60 rooms. 2 restaurants, bar, game room, pool, nightclub. AE, MC, V. EP, MAP.*

$$–$$$ Harmony Marina Suites. Your suite may have a view of the pool or Rodney Bay Marina, but don't fear, Reduit Beach is only 200 yards away. This two-story all-suite hotel was completely overhauled in 1993. The 22 suites have air-conditioning, a red-tile balcony or terrace, wet bar, direct-dial phones, refrigerator, cable TV, and coffeemaker; four also have kitchenettes. The eight VIP suites have additional 10-foot sundecks, a whirlpool bath, a four-poster bed, Australian sheepskin throw rugs, but no kitchen. A rarity: The terrace furniture is not the plastic junk the Caribbean is notorious for, consisting instead of comfortable, cushioned chaise longues. This is a nice alternative to the megaresort scene, and the adjacent minimarket—one of the best-stocked on the island—makes the kitchenette suites ideal for long-term stays. The Mortar and Pestle restaurant is right on the bay and serves excellent food, including Malaysian, Indian, and Chinese specialties. ☎ *Box 155, Castries,* ☎ *809/452–8756 or 800/223–6510,* FAX *809/452–8677. 30 units. Restaurant, bar, minimarket, pool, water sports, laundry. MC, V. EP, MAP.*

$$ St. Lucian. From the lobby—broad, white, and informal, with potted plants and upholstered sofas—a corridor leads to the gardens, pool area, and beach. This was once two hotels, and the rooms are spread out over considerable acreage, some on Reduit Beach, some in gardens. All have double or king-size beds, clock radios, direct-dial phones, and patios or terraces. Most have air-conditioning and tubs; 36 have ceiling fans and showers. Discounted package tours from Britain have taken their toll on this resort and the furnishings have a well-worn, drab look, but there is lots of action to distract you. This is the home of Splash, one of the island's hottest discos, and the local agent for Mistral Windsurfers. Many of the water sports are free to hotel guests. ☎ *Box 512, Reduit Beach, Castries,* ☎ *809/452–8351,* FAX *809/452–8331. 260 rooms. 2 restaurants, 3 bars, disco, pool, laundry/dry cleaning, lighted tennis court, dive shop, boutiques, ice-cream parlor, beauty salon, minimarket, water-sports center. AE, DC, MC, V. EP, MAP.*

$$ Tuxedo Villas. This pristine-white apartment complex set around a tiny swimming pool in a peaceful corner close to Reduit Beach is a good value, as long as you insist on one of the newly decorated apartments (the three elderly first-floor ones have dingy '70s decor with louvered closets and sloping pine ceilings). There's individually controlled air-conditioning in all the bedrooms, which are tiny but comfortable, each with its own en suite tubless bathroom. Kitchens are well equipped, with full-size fridge-freezers, plus glass-topped bamboo tables, and breakfast bars, while compact lounges have rattan couches, cable TV, phones, and cool white tile floors. There's nothing exciting here, but everything works, everything's spotless, and the staff is friendly. ☎ *Box 419, Castries,* ☎ *809/452–8553,* FAX *809/452–8577. 10 apartments. Pool, restaurant, bar. AE, MC, V. EP.*

$ Candyo Inn. This small pink hotel, which opened in 1992 in the heart
★ of Rodney Bay, is one of the best buys in the Caribbean. It's a five-minute walk from beaches and several good restaurants, and it has a small pool and a lanai decked with the usual plastic lawn furniture and potted palms.

An outdoor bar near the pool serves drinks and snacks. The two-story building and its lush green grounds are carefully looked after and spotless. All 12 rooms have air-conditioning, cable TV, clock radio, direct-dial phone, veranda, white-tile floors, and white contemporary furniture with floral upholstery. The eight suites have kitchenettes, larger sitting areas, and tubs; they're worth the extra $15 a night. A small atrium lobby has a small convenience shop. The staff is delightful. ☎ *Box 386, Rodney Bay, ☎ 809/452–0712, FAX 809/452–0774. 4 rooms, 8 suites. Drink/snack bar, minimarket, pool. AE, MC, V. EP.*

$ Humming Bird Beach Resort. This charming little spot is at the edge of Soufrière. Rooms are a bit dark and would fare better without the dingy carpeting, but four-poster beds and African sculpture are nice touches. The restaurant is a favorite hangout of locals and expatriates. Joyce Alexander, the owner, is a marvelous, dynamic hostess who, when not making improvements to her small hotel, designs batiks for the adjoining boutique. ☎ *Box 280, Soufrière, ☎ 809/454–7232. 10 units. Restaurant, bar, pool. D, MC, V. EP, MAP.*

$ Orange Grove Hotel. Up a long hill off the road to Windjammer Landing you'll come upon this hilltop motel with a nondescript exterior. It looks like a budget accommodation and it is one. Surprisingly, the rooms—which are large, light, and clean—are packed with all the conveniences you'd expect at a large resort: two phones, two cable TVs, air-conditioning, full bath, white-tile floors, and new but typical Caribbean-style furniture. All have separate sitting areas and balconies or patios overlooking the hillside. And although you're away from the beach, you are welcome to use the beach facilities at Club St. Lucia 15 minutes away; free transportation is available. The hotel tripled in size in 1994 and is getting to be better known among Americans, as well it might when a suite costs less than $80, off-season. The restaurant serves West Indian cuisine for similarly low prices. ☎ *Box 98, Castries, ☎ 809/452–8213. 51 rooms, 11 suites. Restaurant, bar, pool. AE, MC, V. EP, MAP.*

$ Skyway Inn. If you're staying in the north but have an early flight to catch from Hewanorra in the morning, this is the ideal place to stay, just 100 yards from the airport and minutes from Vieux Fort and its beaches. The inn is clean and comfortable, with air-conditioned rooms, cable TV, meeting facilities, and a free shuttle to the beach. There's an open-air restaurant and bar on the roof and a pool down below. You don't want to spend a week here, but as far as airport hotels go, it's quite impressive. ☎ *Box 353, Vieux Fort, ☎ 809/454–7111, FAX 809/454–7116. 32 rooms, 1 suite. Restaurant, bar, gift shop. AE, MC, V.*

Nightlife

Most of the action is in the hotels, which feature entertainment of the island variety—limbo dancers, fire-eaters, calypso singers, and steel-band jump-ups. Many offer entertainment packages, including dinner, to nonguests.

The **Splash Disco** (St. Lucian hotel, ☎ 809/452–8351) has a good dance floor and splashy lighting effects. It's open Monday–Saturday from 9 PM.

On weekends, locals usually hang out at the **Lime** (Rodney Bay, ☎ 809/452–0761); **Capone's** (Rodney Bay, ☎ 809/452–0284), an art deco place right out of the Roaring '20s, with a player piano and rum drinks; or **A-Pub** (☎ 809/452–8725), a lounge in an A-frame building overlooking Rodney Bay. The **Charthouse** (Rodney Bay, ☎ 809/452–8115) has a popular bar, jazz on stereo, and live music on Saturday.

Young boaters tie up at the **Bistro** (Rodney Bay, ☎ 809/452–9494) for drinks, chess, darts, and backgammon. The **Green Parrot** (the Morne, ☎ 809/452–3399) is in a class all by itself. Chef Harry Edwards hosts the floor show, which features limbo dancers. Harry has been known to shimmy under the pole himself. There are also belly dancers. Dress semiformally for this great fun.

On Friday nights, sleepy Gros Islet becomes sin city, like Bourbon Street during Mardi Gras, as the entire village is transformed into a street fair. At the far end of the street, mammoth stereos loudly beat out sounds as locals and strangers let their hair down. **Club Society** (Grande Rivière, Gros Islet, ☎ 809/453–0312) and the **Golden Apple** (Grande Rivière, ☎ 809/450–0634) are probably the best spots for meeting locals. The **Banana Split** (St. Georges St., Gros Islet, ☎ 809/450–8125) offers entertainment and special theme nights, with a perpetual "spring break" atmosphere. It can get rowdy, so it's best to travel in a group and keep your wits about you. But then Friday night is *the* night to hang, party, lime. Worried about crashing the party? Just roll down your window and ask: You'll know if you're invited. Another Friday-night street scene and a popular alternate venue for liming can be found just before you enter Marigot Bay. The music is supplied by **J. J.'s** restaurant (☎ 809/451–4076), and the popular fare is curried goat. More and more locals are choosing to come here instead of the more touristy Gros Islet happening.

23 St. Martin/ St. Maarten

Updated by
Marcy
Pritchard

THERE ARE FREQUENT NONSTOP FLIGHTS from the United States to St. Martin/St. Maarten, so you don't have to spend half your vacation getting here—a critical advantage if you have only a few days to enjoy the sun. The 37-square-mile island is home to two sovereign nations, St. Maarten (Dutch) and St. Martin (French), so you can experience two cultures for the price of one. However, the Dutch side has lost much of its European flavor.

The island, particularly the Dutch side, is ideal for people who like to have lots of things to do. Whatever can be done in or on the water—snorkeling, windsurfing, waterskiing—is available here; there is golf and tennis as well. Especially on the French side, there are enough good-quality restaurants for serious diners to try a different one each night, even on a two-week stay. The duty-free shopping is as good as anywhere else in the Caribbean, except perhaps in the U.S. Virgin Islands. There's an active nightlife, with discos and casinos. Water-sports enthusiasts will love Simpson Bay Lagoon, the largest inland body of water in the Caribbean. Day trips can be taken by ship or plane to the nearby islands of Anguilla, Saba, St. Eustatius, and St. Barthélemy. There are hotels for every taste and budget—from motel-type units for the package tour trade to some of the most exclusive resorts in the Caribbean. The standard of living is one of the highest in the Caribbean, so the islanders can afford to be honest and to treat visitors as welcome guests. If you wander even slightly off the beaten track, you'll find friendly and opinionated locals willing and eager to share their insider knowledge. Corruption and crime, which had been on the rise, have decreased dramatically in the '90s, thanks to an exemplary cooperative effort between the two governments.

On the negative side, St. Martin/St. Maarten has been thoroughly discovered and exploited; unless you stay in an exclusive resort, you are likely to find yourself sharing beachfronts with tour groups or conventioneers. Yes, there is gambling, but the table limits are so low that hard-core gamblers will have a better time gamboling on the beach. It can be fun to shop, and there's an occasional bargain, but many goods, particularly electronics, are cheaper in the United States. As is often the case in the Caribbean, the island infrastructure has not kept pace with development. While there are plans to expand marina, airport, and road services, you will probably run into congestion at the airport and seemingly endless traffic on the roads.

Before You Go

Tourist Information

For information about the Dutch side, contact the **tourist office** on the island directly (☎ 599/5–22337), or, in Canada, contact **St. Maarten Tourist Information** (243 Ellerslie Ave., Willowdale, Toronto, Ontario M2N 1Y5, ☎ 416/223–3501). Information about French St. Martin can be obtained by writing the **French West Indies Tourist Board** (610 5th Ave., New York, NY 10020) or by calling France-on-Call at 900/990–0040 (50¢ per minute). You can also write to or visit the **French Government Tourist Office** (444 Madison Ave., 16th Floor, New York, NY 10022; 9454 Wilshire Blvd., Suite 303, Beverly Hills, CA 90212; 645 N. Michigan Ave., Suite 3360, Chicago, IL 60611; 1981 McGill College Ave., Suite 490, Montreal, Québec H3A 2W9, ☎ 514/288–4264; 30 St. Patrick St., Suite 700, Toronto, Ontario M5T 3A3, ☎ 416/593–4723; and 178 Piccadilly, London W1V OAL, ☎ 0171/629–9376).

Arriving and Departing

BY PLANE

There are two airports on the island. **L'Espérance** (☎ 590/87–53–03) on the French side is small and handles only island-hoppers. Bigger planes fly into **Princess Juliana International Airport** (☎ 599/5–4211) on the Dutch side. The most convenient carrier from the United States is **American Airlines** (☎ 800/433–7300), with daily nonstop flights from New York and Miami, as well as connections from more than 100 U.S. cities via its San Juan hub. **Continental Airlines** (☎ 800/231–0856) has daily flights from Newark. **LIAT** (☎ 809/462–0701) has daily service from San Juan and several Caribbean islands including St. Thomas and St. Kitts; **ALM** (☎ 800/327–7230) from Aruba, Bonaire, Curaçao, the Dominican Republic, and from Atlanta and Miami via Curaçao. ALM also offers a Visit Caribbean Air Pass, which offers savings for traveling to several Caribbean islands. **BWIA** (☎ 800/327–7401) offers twice-weekly service from Miami. **Air Martinique** (☎ 596/51–08–09 or 599/5–4212) connects the island with Martinique twice a week. **Windward Islands Airways** (Winair, ☎ 599/5–4230), which is based on St. Maarten, has daily scheduled service to Anguilla, Saba, St. Barts, St. Eustatius, Barts, St. Kitts/Nevis, and St. Thomas. **Air Guadeloupe** (☎ 599/5–4212 or 590/87–53–74) has several flights daily to St. Barts and Guadeloupe from both sides of the island. **Air St. Barthélemy** (☎ 590/87–73–46 or 599/5–3150) has frequent service between Juliana or Espérance and St. Barts. Tour and charter services are available from Winair and **St. Martin Helicopters** (Dutch side, ☎ 599/5–4287).

BY BOAT

Motorboats zip several times a day from Anguilla to the French side at Marigot, three times a week from St. Barts. Catamaran service is available daily from the Dutch side to St. Barts on the *White Octopus* (☎ 599/5–24096 or 599/5–23170). The high-speed ferry *Edge* (☎ 599/5–22167) slaps across from Saba three times a week.

Passports and Visas

U.S. citizens need proof of citizenship. A passport (valid or not expired more than five years) is preferred. An original birth certificate with raised seal (or a photocopy with notary seal) or a voter registration card is also acceptable. All visitors must have a confirmed room reservation and an ongoing or return ticket. British and Canadian citizens need valid passports.

Language

Dutch is the official language of St. Maarten, and French is the official language of St. Martin, but almost everyone speaks English. If you hear a language you can't quite place, it's Papiamento, a Spanish-based Creole of the Netherlands Antilles.

Staying in St. Martin/St. Maarten

Important Addresses

Tourist Information: On the Dutch side, the **tourist information bureau** is on Cyrus Wathey (pronounced *watty*) Square in the heart of Philipsburg, at the pier where the cruise ships send their tenders. The administrative office is on Walter Nisbeth Road 23 (Imperial Building) on the third floor. ☎ 599/5–22337. ☉ *Weekdays 8–noon and 1–5, except holidays.*

On the French side, there is the very helpful **tourist information office** on the Marigot pier. ☎ 590/87–57–21, FAX 590/87–56–43. ☉ *Week-*

days 8:30–1 and 2:30–5:30, Sat. 8–noon. Closed holidays and the afternoon preceding a holiday.

EMERGENCIES
Police: Dutch side (☎ 599/5–22222), French side (☎ 590/87–50–10). **Ambulance:** Dutch side (☎ 599/5–22111), French side (☎ 590/87–50–06). **Hospital: St. Maarten Medical Center** (Cay Hill, ☎ 599/5–31111) is a fully equipped hospital. **Pharmacies,** which are open Monday–Saturday 7–5, include the **Central Drug Store** (Philipsburg, ☎ 599/5–22321), **Mullet Bay Drug Store** (Mullet Bay Resort, ☎ 599/5–52801, ext. 342), and **Pharmacie du Port** (Marigot, ☎ 590/87–50–79).

Currency
Legal tender on the Dutch side is the Netherlands Antilles florin (guilder), written NAf; on the French side, the French franc (F). The exchange rate fluctuates, but in general it is about NAf 1.78 to U.S.$1 and 5F to U.S.$1. On the Dutch side, prices are usually given in both NAf and U.S. dollars, which are accepted all over the island, as are credit cards. Note: Prices quoted here are in U.S. dollars unless otherwise noted.

Taxes and Service Charges
On the Dutch side, a 5% government tax is added to hotel bills. On the French side, a *taxe de séjour* (visitor's tax) is tacked on to hotel bills (the amount differs from hotel to hotel, but the maximum is $3 per day, per person). Departure tax from Juliana airport is $5 to destinations within the Netherlands Antilles and $10 to all other destinations. It will cost you 15 French francs to depart by plane from l'Espérance Airport or by ferry to Anguilla from Marigot's pier.

In lieu of tipping, service charges are added to hotel bills all over the island and, by law, are included in all menu prices on the French side. On the Dutch side, most restaurants add 10%–15% to the bill.

Hotels on the Dutch side add a 15% service/energy charge to the bill. Hotels on the French side add 10%–15% for service.

Taxi drivers expect a 10% tip.

Guided Tours
A 2½-hour taxi tour of the island costs $35 for one or two people, $10 for each additional person. Your hotel or the tourist office can arrange it for you. Best bets are **St. Maarten Sightseeing Tours** (Philipsburg, ☎ 599/5–22753) and **Calypso Tours** (Philipsburg, ☎ 599/5–42858), which offer, among other options, a 2½-hour island tour for $15 per person. You can tour in deluxe comfort with **St. Maarten Limousine Service** (☎ 599/5–24698) for $40–$50 per hour; there's a three-hour minimum. Fully equipped Lincoln Continentals accommodate up to six people and are furnished with stereo, fully stocked bar, and air-conditioning. The limo service also offers transportation to and from Juliana airport at rates ranging from $30 to $65 one-way. (This includes one hour of waiting time free of charge for late arrivals.) On the French side, both **R&J Tours** (Colombier, ☎ 590/87–56–20) and **Hanna Tours** (Marigot, 590/29–29–29) will show you the island; prices vary with the number of people and the itinerary.

Getting Around
Although there are other means of transportation, we recommend renting a car. You'll find it's needed to explore the island fully and visit a variety of beaches and restaurants.

TAXIS

Taxi rates are government regulated, and authorized taxis display stickers of the St. Maarten Taxi Association. There is a taxi service at the Marigot port near the Tourist Information Bureau. Fixed fares apply from Juliana International Airport and the Marigot ferry to the various hotels and around the island. Fares are 25% higher between 10 PM and midnight, 50% higher between midnight and 6 AM.

BUSES

One of the island's best bargains at 80¢ to $2, depending on your destination, buses operate frequently between 7 AM and 7 PM (less often 7–10 PM) and run from Philipsburg through Cole Bay to Marigot. There are no official stops: You just stand by the side of the road and flag the bus down. Exact change is preferred though not required, and drivers don't accept bills over $5.

RENTAL CARS

You can book a car at Juliana International Airport, where all major rental companies have booths, but to give taxi drivers work, you must collect the car at the rental offices located off the airport complex. (The Hertz office is closest to the airport, just a quarter of a mile away.) There are also rentals at every hotel area. Rental cars are inexpensive—approximately $35–$45 a day for a subcompact car. All foreign driver's licenses are honored, and major credit cards are accepted. **Avis** (☎ 800/331–1212), **Budget** (☎ 800/527–0700), **Dollar** (☎ 800/421–6868), **Hertz** (☎ 800/654–3131), and **National** (☎ 800/328–4567) all have offices on the island. Scooters rent for $18–$35 a day at **Honda** (Pondfill, Philipsburg, ☎ 599/5–25712) and **Rent 2 Wheels** (Nettlé Bay, ☎ 590/87–20–59).

Telephones and Mail

To call the Dutch side from the United States, dial 011–599 + local number; for the French side, 011–590 + local number. To phone from the Dutch side to the French, dial 06 + local number; from the French side to the Dutch, 011–5995 + local number. Keep in mind that a call from one side to the other is an overseas call, not a local call.

At the Landsradio in Philipsburg, there are facilities for overseas calls and an AT&T USADirect telephone, where you are directly in touch with an AT&T operator who will accept collect or credit-card calls.

On the French side, it is not possible to make collect calls to the United States, and there are no coin phones. If you need to use public phones, go to the special desk at Marigot's post office and buy a Telecarte (it looks like a credit card), which gives you 40 units (it takes 120 units to cover a five-minute call to the United States) for around 31F or 120 units for 93F. There is a public phone on the side of the tourist office in Marigot where you can make credit card calls: The operator takes your credit card number (any major card) and assigns you a PIN (Personal Identification Number), which you can then use to charge calls to your card.

Calls from anywhere on the island to the United States cost $4 per minute.

Letters from the Dutch side to the United States and Canada cost NAf1.30; postcards, NAf.60. From the French side, letters up to 20 grams, 4.10F; postcards, 3.50F.

Opening and Closing Times

Shops on the Dutch side are open Monday–Saturday 8–noon and 2–6; on the French side, Monday–Saturday 9–noon or 12:30, and 2–6. Some of the larger shops on both sides of the island open Sunday and holidays when the cruise ships are in port. Some of the small Dutch and French shops set their own capricious hours.

Banks on the Dutch side are open Monday–Thursday 8:30–3:30 and Friday 8:30–4:40. French banks are open weekdays 8:30–1:30 and 2–3 and close afternoons preceding holidays.

Exploring St. Martin/St. Maarten

Numbers in the margin correspond to points of interest on the St. Martin/St. Maarten map.

Philipsburg

❶ The Dutch capital of **Philipsburg,** which stretches about a mile along an isthmus between Great Bay and the Salt Pond, has three more or less parallel streets: Front Street, Back Street, and Pondfill. Front Street has been recobbled, cars are discouraged from using it, and the pedestrian area has been widened. Shops, restaurants, and casinos vie for the hordes coming off the cruise boats. Head for **Wathey Square** and stroll out on the pier. **Great Bay** is rolled out before you, and the beach stretches alongside it for about a mile. The square bustles with vendors, souvenir shops, and tourists. There's a taxi stand, where you can arrange for a driver to take you around if you'd rather not rent a car. Philipsburg should be explored on foot, but you'll need wheels to get around the island.

Directly across the street from Wathey Square, you'll see a striking white building with a cupola. It was built in 1793 and has since served as the commander's home, a fire station, and a jail. It now serves as the town hall, courthouse, and the post office.

The square is in the middle of the isthmus on which Philipsburg sits. To your right and left the streets are lined with hotels, duty-free shops, fine restaurants, and cafés, most of them in pastel-colored West Indian cottages gussied up with gingerbread trim. Narrow alleyways lead to arcades and flower-filled courtyards where there are yet more boutiques and eateries.

The **Simart'n Museum** has just moved to a new building on Front Street. It hosts rotating cultural exhibits and a permanent historical display entitled "Forts of St. Maarten/St. Martin," featuring artifacts ranging from Arawak pottery shards to articles salvaged from the wreck of HMS *Proselyte. 9 Front St., Philipsburg, no ☏. ☛ $1. ☉ Weekdays 9–4, Saturday 9–noon.*

Little lanes called *steegjes* connect Front Street with Back Street, which is considerably less congested because it has fewer shops.

Our drive begins at the western end of Front Street, right before it becomes Sucker Garden Road. Follow the road north along Salt Pond; it begins to climb and curve just outside of town. Take the first right ❷ to **Guana Bay Point,** from which there is a splendid view of the island's east coast, tiny deserted islands, and small St. Barts, which is anything but deserted.

Sucker Garden Road continues north through spectacular scenery. Continue along a paved roller-coaster road down to **Dawn Beach,** one of the island's best snorkeling beaches.

❸ **Oyster Pond,** just north of Dawn Beach on the same road, is the legendary point where two early settlers, a Frenchman and a Dutchman, allegedly began to pace in opposite directions around the island to divide it between their respective countries. Local legend maintains that the obese sweaty Hollander stopped frequently to refresh himself with gin—the reason that the French side is nearly twice the size of the Dutch. (The official boundary marker is on the other side of the island.)

Elsewhere on the Island

4 From Oyster Pond, follow the road along the bay and around Étang aux Poissons (Fish Lake), all the way to **Orléans.** This settlement, which is also known as the French Quarter, is the oldest on the island. Noted local artist Roland Richardson makes his home here. He opens his studio to the public on Thursday from 10 to 6, or by appointment (☎ 590/87–32–24). He's a proud islander ready to share his wealth of knowledge about the island's cultural history.

A rough dirt road leads northeast to **Orient Beach,** the island's best-known nudist beach. There's even a pricey rustic resort catering to "naturists." Offshore, little **Ilet Pinel** is an uninhabited island that's fine for picnicking, sunning, and swimming.

5 Farther north you'll come to **French Cul de Sac,** where you'll see the French colonial mansion of St. Martin's mayor nestled in the hills. Little red-roof houses look like open umbrellas tumbling down the green hillside. The scenery here is glorious, and the area is great for hiking. There is a lot of construction, however, as the surroundings are slowly being developed. From the beach here, shuttle boats make the five-minute trip to Ilet Pinel.

The road swirls south through green hills and pastures, past flower-**6** entwined stone fences. Past L'Espérance Airport is the town of **Grand Case.** Though it has only one mile-long main street, it's known as the "Restaurant Capital of the Caribbean": More than 20 restaurants serve French, Italian, Indonesian, and Vietnamese fare, as well as fresh seafood. The budget-minded will appreciate the "loloo" stands along the waterfront selling savory barbecue. **Grand Case Beach Club** (*see* Lodging, *below*) is at the end of this road and has two beaches where you can take a short dip. Better yet, travel down the road about 5 miles toward Marigot, and on the right is a turnoff to **Friar's Beach,** a small, picturesque cove that attracts a casual crowd of locals. A small snack bar, **Kali's,** owned by a welcoming gentleman wearing dreadlocks, serves refreshments. From here, you can turn inland and follow a bumpy tree-canopied road to Pic du Paradis, at 1,278 feet the highest point on the island, affording breathtaking vistas of the Caribbean.

7 Just before entering the French capital of **Marigot,** you will notice a shopping complex on the left. At the back of it is **Match** (☎ 590/87–92–36), the largest supermarket on the French side, carrying a broad selection of tempting picnic makings—from country pâté to foie gras—and a vast selection of wines.

If you are a shopper, a gourmet, or just a Francophile, you'll want to tarry awhile in Marigot. Marina Port La Royale is the shopping complex at the port, but rue de la République and Rue de la Liberté, which border the bay, are also filled with duty-free shops, boutiques, and bistros. The harbor area has a jumble of stalls selling everything from handmade crafts to fish so fresh they're still mad. Across from these stalls, on the pier road leading to the ferries for Anguilla, is the helpful **French tourist office,** where you can pick up the usual assortment of free maps and brochures.

TIME OUT With a roguish glint in his eye, owner Roger Drovin proclaims the melt-in-your-mouth croissants at **Cafe Terrasse Mastedana** (rue de la Liberté, no ☎) to be "zee best." This humble little establishment along the main

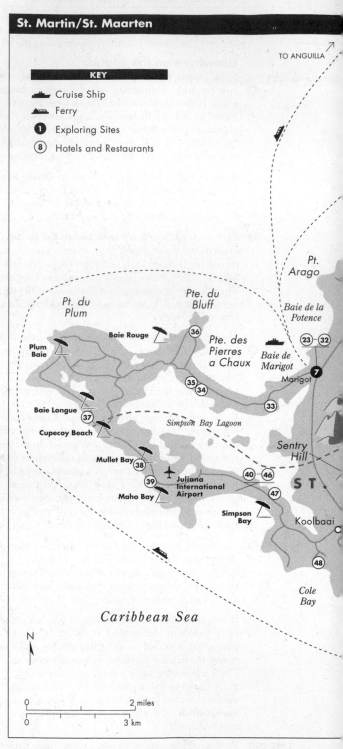

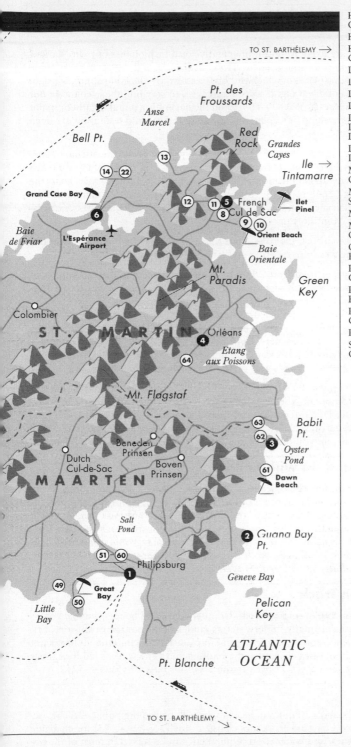

road by Port La Royale, bedecked with pennants from around the world, is perfect for a light breakfast or snack.

You are likely to find more creative and fashionable buys in Marigot than in Philipsburg. There is less bustle here, and the open-air cafés are tempting places in which to stop for a rest. Unlike Philipsburg, Marigot does not die at night, so you may wish to stay into the evening. **Le Bar de la Mer** (☎ 590/87–81–79) on the harbor is a popular gathering spot in the evening (it's open 'til 2), though the bar and restaurant are open all day.

The road due south of Marigot to Philipsburg passes the official boundary, where a simple border marker, erected by the Dutch and French citizenry to commemorate 300 years of peaceful coexistence, bears the dates "1648 to 1948." Straddling the border are the mammoth Port de Plaisance condominium hotel complex and the adjacent extravagant Mont Fortune casino.

At the airport, the road from Marigot to the north and Simpson Bay to the west join together and lead to Philipsburg.

The other road from Marigot leads west, hugging the coastline, and crosses a small bridge to Sandy Ground. It continues along Baie Nettlé, with its many reasonably priced hotels. Soon thereafter, on the right, you'll come to the Mediterranean-style village resort of **La Belle Creole,** commanding Pointe du Bluff. Then you'll begin to see some of the island's best beaches—**Baie Rouge, Plum Baie,** and **Baie Longue**— clinging to its westernmost point. They are all accessible down bumpy but short dirt roads and perfect for swimming and picnicking.

At the end of Baie Longue and running eastward along the south coast is **La Samanna,** the fashionable jet-set resort. Just after this hotel you'll reenter Dutch territory at **Cupecoy Beach.** You'll have to endure the huge, garish vacation condo-hotel complexes of Mullet Bay and Maho Bay before you reach Juliana International Airport and Philipsburg.

What to See and Do with Children

St. Maarten Zoological and Botanical Garden. This ambitious development, the labor of love of a local policeman, features plants and animals indigenous to the Caribbean basin and South America, including coatimundis, ocelots, peccaries, and boa constrictors. The two large walk-through aviaries, petting zoo, and playground should delight children of all ages. *Arch Rd., Madame Estate,* ☎ *599/5–32030.* ☞ *$4 adults, $2 children.* ⊘ *Weekdays 9–5, weekends 10–6.*

Off the Beaten Track

Ocean Explorers Sea Walk. Uniquely designed helmets enable you to breathe normally underwater as guides point out the profusion of riotously colored marine life in Simpson Bay. Swimming ability is not required, just curiosity and a bathing suit. The walk is led four times daily and costs $35 per person. *Simpson Bay,* ☎ *599/5–45252.*

Beaches

The island's 10 miles of beaches are all open to the public. Beaches occupied by resort properties charge a small fee (about $3) for changing facilities, and water-sports equipment can be rented in most of the hotels. You cannot, however, enter the beach via the hotel unless you are a paying guest or will be renting equipment there. Some of the 37 beaches are secluded, and some are located in the thick of things. Topless bathing is virtually de rigueur on the French side, where the beaches are generally better than on the Dutch side. If you take a cab to a remote beach, be sure to arrange a specific, clearly understood time for your driver to return to pick you up, and don't leave valuables unattended on the beach.

Hands down, **Baie Longue** is the best beach on the island. It's a beautiful, mile-long curve of white sand on the westernmost tip of the island. This is a good place for snorkeling and swimming, but beware of a strong undertow when the waters are rough. You can sunbathe in the buff, though only a few do. There are no facilities.

Beyond Baie Longue is **Plum Baie,** where the beach arcs between two headlands and the occasional sunbather discloses all.

Baie Rouge is one of the most secluded beaches on the island. This little patch of sand is at the base of high cliffs and is backed by private homes rather than by hotels. Some rate it the prettiest beach on the island. The waves here can be rough. There's a small snack and soda stand at the beach's entrance.

Orient Beach is the island's best-known "clothes-optional" beach—it's on the agenda for voyeurs from visiting cruise ships. You can enter from the parking area or through the **Club Orient Hotel** (☎ 590/87–33–85), where you can rent water-sports equipment.

You have to approach the **Dawn Beach–Oyster Pond** area through the grounds of the Dawn Beach Hotel. The long white-sand beach is partly protected by reefs (good for snorkeling), but the water is not always calm. When the waves come rolling in, this is the best spot on the island for bodysurfing.

Ilet Pinel is a little speck off the northeast coast with about 500 yards of beach where you can have picnics and privacy. There are no facilities. Putt putts (small boats) are available to take you from French Cul de Sac and Orient Beach.

Simpson Bay is a long half-moon of white sand near Simpson Bay Village, one of the last undiscovered hamlets on the island. In this small fishing village you'll find refreshments, **Ocean Explorers Dive Shop** (*see* Sports and the Outdoors, *below*) for water-sports equipment rentals, and neat little ultra-Caribbean town homes.

Ecru-color sand, palm and sea-grape trees, calm waters, and the roar of jets lowering to nearby Juliana International Airport distinguish the beach at **Maho Bay.** Concession stand, beach chairs, and facilities are available.

At **Mullet Bay,** the powdery white-sand beach is crowded with guests of the Mullet Bay Resort.

Cupecoy Beach is a small shifting arc of white sand fringed with eroded limestone cliffs, just south of Baie Longue on the western side of the island, near the Dutch-French border. On the first part of the beach swimwear is worn, but farther up, sun worshipers start shedding their attire. There are no facilities, but a truck is often parked at the entrance, with a vendor who sells cold sodas and beers.

Sports and the Outdoors

All the resort hotels have activities desks that can arrange virtually any type of water sport.

Boating

Motorboats, speedboats, Dolphins, pedal boats, sailboats, and canoes can be rented at **Lagoon Cruises & Watersports** (Mullet Bay Resort, ☎ 599/5–52898), **Caribbean Watersports** (Nettlé Bay, ☎ 590/87–58–66), and **Caraibes Sport Boats** (Marina Port la Royale, ☎ 590/87–89–38).

Sun Yacht-Charters (☎ 800/772–3500), based in Oyster Pond, has a fleet of 50 Centurion sailboats for hire. The cost of a week's bareboat charter for a 36-foot Centurion with six berths is $2,850 in peak winter season. Also in Oyster Pond, the **Moorings** (☎ 800/535–7289 or 590/87–32–55) has a fleet of Beneteau yachts, and bareboat and crewed catamarans. **Dynasty** (☎ 590/87–85–21), in Marigot's Port la Royale Marina, offers an excellent fleet of Dynamique yachts, ranging in size from 47 to 80 feet.

Deep-Sea Fishing

Angle for yellowtail, snapper, grouper, marlin, tuna, and wahoo on half- or full-day deep-sea excursions. Prices usually include bait and tackle, instruction for novices, and an open bar. Contact **Wampum** (Bobby's Marina, Philipsburg, ☎ 599/5–22366) or **Sailfish Caraibes** (Port Lonvilliers, ☎ 590/87–31–94).

Fitness

Le Privilège (☎ 590/87–37–37), a sports complex at Anse Marcel above Meridien L'Habitation, has a full range of exercise equipment. **Fitness Caraibes** (☎ 590/87–97–04) is a toning center at Nettlé Bay. **Club Crazy** (Marigot, ☎ 590/87–05–94) offers weight training and aerobics classes. On the Dutch side, **L'Aqualigne** at the Pelican Resort (☎ 599/5–42426) is a health spa with gym, sauna, and beauty treatments, including manicures, facials, and massages.

Golf

Mullet Bay Resort (☎ 599/5–52801) has an 18-hole championship course. Surprisingly, this is the only course on the island. Greens fees are $95 in high season, $65 in low.

Horseback Riding

You can arrange rides through your hotel, or you can contact **Crazy Acres Riding Center** (Wathey Estate, Cole Bay, ☎ 599/5–42793), **Bayside Riding Club** (Orient Bay, 590/87–36–64), **O.K. Corral** (Oyster Pond, ☎ 590/87–40–72), or **Caid & Isa** (Anse Marcel, ☎ 590/87–45–70). All the outfits offer beach rides and can accommodate different skill levels.

Jetskiing and Waterskiing

On the Dutch side, rent equipment through the **Divi Little Bay Resort**'s watersports activity center (☎ 599/5–22333). On the French side, try **Orient Bay Watersports** (☎ 590/87–33–85) or **Laguna Watersports** (☎ 590/87–91–75) at Nettlé Bay.

Parasailing

A great high can be arranged through **Lagoon Cruises & Watersports** (☎ 599/5–52898).

Running

The **Road Runners Club** meets Wednesday in the parking lot of the Raoul Illidge Sportscomplex for a 5 PM Fun Run and Sunday at 6:45 AM in the parking lot of the Pelican Resort for a 2–15K run. For more information, contact Dr. Frits Bus at 599/5–22467 or Ron van Sittert at 599/5–22842.

Scuba Diving

The water temperature here is rarely below 70°F, and there's usually excellent visibility. There are many diving attractions, both right around the island and around numerous offshore islands. On the Dutch side is Proselyte Reef, named for the British frigate HMS *Proselyte,* which sank south of Great Bay in 1801. In addition to wreck dives, reef, night, and cave dives are popular. Off the northeast coast of the French side, dive sites include Ilet Pinel, for good shallow diving; Green Key, with its vibrant barrier reef; and Tintamarre, for sheltered coves and underwater geologic faults.

On the Dutch side, SSI- (Scuba Schools International) and PADI-certified dive centers include **Trade Winds Dive Center** (Bobby's Marina, ☎ 599/5–75176), **St. Maarten Divers** (Philipsburg, ☎ 599/5–22446), **Leeward Island Divers** (Simpson Bay, ☎ 599/5–42268), and **Ocean Explorers Dive Shop** (Simpson Bay, 599/5–45252). On the French side, **Lou Scuba** (Marine Hotel Simson Beach, Nettlé Bay, ☎ 590/87–22–58) and **Pelican Dive Adventures** (Pelican Resort Marina, ☎ 599/5–42503, ext. 1553) are PADI-certified dive centers. **Blue Ocean** (Marigot, ☎ 590/87–89–73) is PADI and CMAS certified. **Octoplus** (Grand Case Blvd., ☎ 590/87–20–62) is a complete dive center.

Sea Excursions

You can take a daylong picnic sail to nearby islands or secluded coves aboard the 45-foot ketch *Gabrielle* (☎ 599/5–23170), the sleek, new 76-foot catamaran *Golden Eagle* (☎ 599/5–22167), or the 70-foot schooner *Gandalf* (☎ 599/5–45427). The 50-foot catamaran *Bluebeard II* (☎ 599/5–52898), moored in Simpson Bay, sails around Anguilla's south and northwest coasts to Prickly Pear, where there are excellent coral reefs for snorkeling and powdery white sands for sunning. The *Lady Mary* (☎ 599/5–53892) sails around the island each evening from La Palapa Center on Simpson Bay; $60 per person includes dinner, open bar, and live calypso music. It's tremendous fun. The *Laura Rose* (☎ 599/5–70710) offers a variety of half- and full-day sails. The *Karib One* glass-bottom boat (☎ 590/87–89–73) makes three cruises daily, including dinner-and-disco trips.

The luxurious 75-foot motor catamaran *White Octopus* (☎ 599/5–24096 or 599/5–23170) makes the run to St. Barts, departing at 9 AM from Bobby's Marina or Captain Oliver's Marina and returning at 5 PM.

In St. Martin, sailing, snorkeling, and picnic excursions to nearby islands can be arranged through **Orient Bay Watersports** (Club Orient, ☎ 590/87–33–85), **Le Meridien L'Habitation** (☎ 590/87–33–33), **La Belle Creole** (☎ 590/87–66–00), and **La Samanna** (☎ 590/87–51–22).

Snorkeling

Coral reefs teem with marine life, and clear water allows visibility of up to 200 feet. Some of the best snorkeling on the Dutch side can be had around the rocks below Fort Amsterdam off Little Bay Beach, in the west end of Maho Bay, off Pelican Key, and the around the reefs off Dawn Beach and Oyster Pond. On the French side, the area around Orient Bay, Green Key, Ilet Pinel, and Flat Island (or Tintamarre) is especially lovely for snorkeling and should soon be officially classified a regional underwater nature reserve. Arrange rentals and trips through **Ocean Explorers** (☎ 599/5–45252) and **Orient Bay Watersports** (☎ 590/87–33–85).

Tennis

If you want to play tennis at a hotel at which you are not a guest, be sure to call ahead to find out whether they allow visitors. You'll probably need to make reservations, and there's usually an hourly fee.

There are 2 lighted courts at the **Dawn Beach Hotel** (☎ 599/5–22929); 6 lighted courts at the **Pelican Resort** (☎ 599/5–42503); 3 lighted courts at the **Divi Little Bay Beach Resort** (☎ 599/5–22333); 4 lighted courts at the **Maho Beach Hotel** (☎ 599/5–52115); 6 lighted courts at **Le Privilège** (Anse Marcel, ☎ 590/87–38–38), which also has 4 squash and 2 racquetball courts; 14 courts (7 lighted) at **Port de Plaisance** (☎ 599/5–45222); four lighted courts at **La Belle Creole** (☎ 590/87–66–00); 2 lighted courts at the **Mont Vernon Hotel** (☎ 590/87–62–00); 1 lighted court at the **Marine Hotel Simson Beach** (☎ 590/87–54–54); 14 courts at **Mullet Bay Resort** (☎ 599/5–52801); 2 courts at the **Oyster Pond Beach Hotel** (☎ 599/5–22206); and 1 lighted court each at the **Grand Case Beach Club** (☎ 590/87–51–87) and the **Coralita Beach Hotel** (☎ 590/87–31–81).

Windsurfing

Rental and instruction are available at **Divi Little Bay Beach Resort** (☎ 599/5–22333, ext. 186) and **Orient Watersports** (590/87–33–85). The new **Nathalie Simon Windsurfing Club** (☎ 590/87–48–16) offers rentals and lessons in Orient Bay.

Shopping

About 180 cruise ships call at St. Maarten each year, and they do so for about 500 reasons. That's roughly the number of duty-free shops on the island.

Prices can be 25%–50% below those in the United States and Canada on French perfumes, liquor, cognac and fine liqueurs, cigarettes and cigars, Swedish crystal and Finnish stoneware, Irish linen, Italian leather, German cameras, European designer fashions, plus thousands of other things you never knew you wanted. But check prices before you leave home, especially if you live in the New York City area—Manhattan's prices for cameras and electronic equipment are hard to beat anywhere. If you're shopping for electronics in Philipsburg, try negotiating for a lower price. Competition is fierce, and some stores will bargain if you pay cash. In general, you will find more fashion on the French side in Marigot, although stalwarts like Polo Ralph Lauren and Benetton have Philipsburg outlets.

St. Maarten's best-known "craft" is its guavaberry liqueur, made from rum and the wild local berries (not to be confused with guavas) that grow only on this island's central mountains.

Prices are quoted in florins, francs, and dollars; shops take credit cards and traveler's checks. Most shopkeepers, especially on the Dutch side, speak English. (If more than one cruise ship is in port, avoid Front Street. It's so crowded you won't be able to move.) Although most merchants are reputable, there are occasional reports of inferior or fake merchandise passed off as the real thing. As a rule of thumb, if you can bargain excessively, it's probably not worth it.

Shopping Areas

In St. Maarten: **Front Street,** Philipsburg, is one long strip lined with sleek boutiques and colorful shops. **Old Street,** near the end of Front Street, has 22 stores, boutiques, and open-air cafés. There is a slew of boutiques in the **Mullet** and **Maho** shopping plazas, as well as at the **Plaza del Lago,** at the Simpson Bay Yacht Club complex.

In St. Martin: Wrought-iron balconies, colorful awnings, and gingerbread trim decorate Marigot's smart shops, tiny boutiques, and bistros in the **Marina Port La Royale** complex and on the main streets, **rue de la Liberté** and **rue de la République**.

Good Buys
Little Switzerland (Marigot, ☎ 590/87–50–03, and Philipsburg, ☎ 599/5–23530) handles fine crystal, china, perfume, and jewelry. **Spritzer and Fuhrmann** (Marigot, ☎ 590/87–59–62, and Philipsburg, ☎ 599/5–44381) also sells lovely settings of crystal and china.

Jewelry and watches can be found at **Oro de Sol** (Marigot, ☎ 590/87–56–51); you can also find perfume, cosmetics, and Cuban cigars here. Look for china and jewelry at **Carat** (Marigot, ☎ 590/87–73–40, and Philipsburg, ☎ 599/5–22180). **Little Europe** (Philipsburg, ☎ 599/5–24371) sells fine jewelry, along with crystal and china. **H. Stern** (Philipsburg, ☎ 599/5–23328) specializes in colorful jewelry and elegant watches.

Pick up a bottle of wine for your picnic at **La Cave du Savour Club** (Marigot, ☎ 590/87–58–51).

Lipstick (Marina Port la Royale, ☎ 590/87–73–24; Marigot, 590/87–53–92; Philipsburg, ☎ 599/5–26051) carries an enormous selection of perfume and cosmetics (including sunscreen). The **Yellow House** (Philipsburg, ☎ 599/5–23438) carries perfumes, cosmetics, and gifts.

For designer fashions head to **La Romana** (2 locations on Front St., ☎ 599/5–22181). On the French side try **Havane** (Marigot, ☎ 590/87 70–39).

The **New Amsterdam Store** (Philipsburg, ☎ 599/5–22787) handles designer fashions, fine linens, and porcelain.

The **Lil' Shoppe** (Philipsburg, ☎ 599/5–22177) carries eel-skin wallets, handbags, perfumes, and a large selection of swimwear.

Island Specialties
Caribelle batik, hammocks, handmade jewelry, the local guavaberry liqueur, and herbs and spices are stashed at the **Shipwreck Shop** (Philipsburg, ☎ 599/5–22962, and Port La Royale, ☎ 590/87–27–37). T-shirts, beach towels, native dolls, Indian glass bangles, and hand-painted delft souvenirs can all be found at **Sasha's** (Philipsburg, ☎ 599/5–24331). The restaurant **Le Poisson D'Or** (Marigot, ☎ 590/87–72–45) houses a gallery featuring the work of local artists. **ABC Art Gallery** (Marigot, ☎ 590/87–96–00) also exhibits the work of local artists. The **Gingerbread Galerie** (Port La Royale, ☎ 590/87–73–21) specializes in Haitian art. **Galerie Lynn** (83 blvd. de Grand Case, ☎ 590/87–77–24) sells stunning paintings and sculptures. **Minguet** (Rambaud Hill, 590/87–76–06) carries pictures by the artist Minguet depicting island life. **Greenwith Galleries** (Philipsburg, ☎ 599/5–23842) specializes in Caribbean art. **Calabash** (Philipsburg, ☎ 599/5–25221) gallery showcases the work of local artists.

Dining

It may seem that this island has no monuments. Au contraire, there are many of them, all dedicated to gastronomy. You'll scarcely find a touch of Dutch; the major influences are French and Italian. This season's "in" eatery may be next season's remembrance of things past, as things do have a way of changing rapidly. The generally steep prices reflect both the island's high culinary reputation and the difficulty of obtaining fresh ingredients. Not surprisingly, the hotel restaurants on the French side are usually more sophisticated, but at prices that would make almost anyone but a Rockefeller go Dutch. In high season, *be sure to make reservations,* and call to cancel if you can't make it. Many restaurants close completely or just for lunch during August, September, and into October. We've tried to note all seasonal closings, but since not all restaurants have offical policies, it's a good idea to call ahead during the off-season.

What to Wear

There's a big range of appropriate dining attire on this island, ranging from swimsuits to sport jackets. You can often tell by the price category—the more expensive a restaurant is, the more dressed up you should get. For men, a jacket and khakis will take you anywhere; for women, dressy pants, a skirt, or even fancy shorts will be acceptable almost everywhere. Jeans are de rigueur in the less formal eateries. In the listings below, dress is casual (and chic, of course) unless otherwise noted, but ask when making reservations if you're unsure.

CATEGORY	COST*
$$$$	over $50
$$$	$35–$50
$$	$25–$35
$	under $25

per person, excluding drinks and service

DUTCH SIDE

$$$$ **Felix.** This classy yet casual little beachside eatery serves dinner by candlelight. At lunchtime, take a dip at Simpson Bay Beach (you can come here in your swimsuit as long as you're not wet) before feasting on salad Felix (an imaginative concoction of bananas, sweet potatoes, and avocado), rack of lamb Provençale, or steak au poivre. The restaurant is on the road to Pelican Resort. ✕ *Pelican Key,* ☎ *599/5–42797. Reservations advised. AE, D, DC, MC, V. No dinner Wed.*

$$$ **Le Bec Fin.** To reach the well-known upstairs restaurant, you stroll through a flowery courtyard. The rotation of chefs here has unfortunately lead to inconsistency in the quality of the classical French cuisine. Starters include vol-au-vent (pastry) bursting with escargots in fennel cream sauce and tagliatelle with shrimp in ginger. Fish, such as red snapper fillet in rum butter sauce, is your best bet for a main course. The meringue swan with mint ice cream is delightful to the eye and the palate. The breezy downstairs café annex serves breakfast and lunch with great crepes (try the seafood) and salads. ✕ *119 Front St., Philipsburg,* ☎ *599/5–22976. Reservations advised.*

$$$ **Le Perroquet.** A cool green-and-white West Indian–style house overlooking a lagoon is the peaceful setting for this restaurant. Chef Pierre Castagna prepares exotic specialties, such as grilled breast of ostrich in a Bordelaise sauce. ✕ *Airport Rd., Simpson Bay,* ☎ *599/5–44339. Reservations advised. AE, MC, V. Closed Mon.*

$$$ **Oyster Pond Beach Hotel.** A more genteel evening on St. Maarten is
★ hard to find. A delightful terrace with wonderful sea views is decked with fine linens and china and fresh flowers. Lobster medallions dancing in a truffle, tomato, and basil sauce; fillet of red snapper in sauce piquante; and sweet, billowy dessert soufflés are specialties. The hotel's guests have priority in this romantic dining room, so you should reserve well in advance. ✕ *Oyster Pond,* ☎ *599/5–22206 or 599/5–23206. Reservations required. AE, MC, V.*

$$$ **Saratoga.** The handsome mahogany-outfitted dining room in the Yacht
★ Club's stucco and red tile building has views of the Simpson Bay Marina. The menu changes daily, according to the whim of owner and chef

John Jackson, who trained at the Culinary Institute of America; everything is flown in fresh. He dubs his cuisine "freestyle creative contemporary," merrily borrowing from various influences, from Asian to southwestern. You might start with Malpeque oysters with balsamic-horseradish sauce or seven-seaweed salad with sea beans, daikon, and sesame, then segue into crispy fried roundhead snapper in fermented black bean sauce or grilled chicken breast in a cumin-Gouda crust. The wine list is admirably balanced and reasonably priced, with 10–12 wines offered by the glass. ✕ *Simpson Bay Yacht Club, Airport Rd.,* ☎ *599/5–42421. Reservations required in season. AE, MC, V. Closed Sun. No lunch.*

$$$ Spartaco. Every element of the northern Italian cuisine served in this 200-year-old stone plantation house is either homemade or imported from Italy. Some of the specialties are black angel-hair pasta with shrimp and garlic; swordfish baked with pink peppercorns and rosemary, served over linguine; and veal Vesuviana, with mozzarella, oregano, and tomato sauce. ✕ *Almond Grove, Cole Bay,* ☎ *599/5–45379. Reservations advised. AE, MC, V. Closed Mon.*

$$–$$$ Antoine. Pay a visit to this elegant, airy terrace overlooking Great Bay for a romantic evening. Candles glow on tables set with crisp blue and white napery and gleaming silver, and the sound of the surf drifts up from the beach. You might start your meal with French onion soup or lobster bisque, then move on to steak au poivre, duck in brandy sauce with cherries, or lobster thermidor. Pastas and Creole specials are also available. For dessert, try the sublime Grand Marnier soufflé. ✕ *Front St., Philipsburg,* ☎ *599/5–22964. Reservations required in high season. AE, MC, V. Closed Sun.*

$$ L'Escargot. A lovely 19th-century house wrapped in verandas is home to one of St. Maarten's oldest classic French restaurants. Starters include frogs' legs in garlic sauce and crepes filled with caviar and sour cream. There is also, of course, a variety of snail dishes. For an entrée, try grilled red snapper with red wine and shallot sauce or *canard de l'escargot* (crisp duck in pineapple and banana sauce). There's a fun cabaret Wednesday night; you don't have to pay the cover charge if you come for dinner. ✕ *84 Front St., Philipsburg,* ☎ *599/5–22483. Reservations advised. AE, MC, V.*

$–$$ Wajang Doll. Indonesian dishes are served in the garden of this West Indian–style house. *Nasi goreng* (fried rice) and red snapper in a sweet soy glaze are standouts, but the specialty is rijsttafel, a traditional Indonesian meal of rice accompanied by 15 to 20 different dishes. ✕ *137 Front St., Philipsburg,* ☎ *599/5–22687. AE, MC, V. Closed Sun. No lunch.*

$ Chesterfield's. Casual lunches of burgers and salads and more elaborate Continental dinners are served at this informal, nautically themed restaurant at the marina. The dinner menu includes French onion soup, roast duckling with fresh pineapple and banana sauce, and several different preparations of shrimp. The Mermaid Bar is a popular spot with yachtsmen. ✕ *Great Bay Marina, Philipsburg,* ☎ *599/5–23484. No credit cards.*

$ Harbour Lights. This modest family-run spot is in a historic building built in 1870. The decor is warm, with peach and coral walls and seafoam-green tablecloths. Choose among excellent rotis and pilafs and even better stewed or curried chicken, meats, and seafood. Try one of the knockout cocktails made with the local guavaberry liqueur. Tables on the second-floor balcony overlook Back Street and make for pleasant alfresco dining. ✕ *30 Back St., Philipsburg,* ☎ *599/5–23504. AE, MC, V.*

$ Shiv Sagar. Authentic East Indian cuisine, emphasizing Kashmiri and ★ Mogul specialties, is served in this small mirrored room fragrant with cumin and coriander. Marvelous tandooris and curries are offered, but try one of the less-familiar preparations like *madrasi machi* (red snapper cooked in a blend of hot spices). A large selection of vegetarian dishes is also offered. There's a friendly open-air bar out front. ✕ *3 Front St., Philipsburg,* ☎ *599/5–22299. AE, D, DC, MC, V. Closed Sun.*

$ **Turtle Pier Bar & Restaurant.** Chattering monkeys and squawking par-
★   rots greet you at the entrance to this classic Caribbean hangout, teetering over the lagoon and festooned with creeping vines. There are 200 animals in this informal zoo, but that's nothing compared to the menagerie hanging out at the bar during happy hour. The genial owner, Sid Wathey, whose family is one of the island's oldest, and his American wife, Lorraine, have fashioned one of the funkiest, most endearing places in the Caribbean, with cheap beer on draft, huge American breakfasts, all-you-can-eat ribs dinners for $9.95, and live music several nights a week. ✕ *Airport Rd.,* ☎ *599/5–52230. No credit cards.*

French Side

$$$$ **Chez Martine.** A charming, globe-trotting French couple, Eliane and
★   Jean-Pierre, have made this small hotel into a personable hostelry with an excellent French restaurant. Dine by the water's edge in an intimate room with polished silverware, blue glassware, and white napery. The chef, Thierry de Launay, studied under Joël Robuchon. You might begin with superb velvety seafood consommé, then segue into roast lamb on a bed of eggplant and spinach in corn sauce or lobster in puff pastry; the homemade duck-liver pâté also claims a loyal following. There are two new prix fixe menus: one without wine at $60, and one with selected wines for each course at $89. The wine list has several very drinkable wines for under $20. ✕ *140 blvd. Grand Case, Grand Case 97150,* ☎ *590/87–51–59. Reservations advised. DC, MC, V. No lunch off-season.*

$$$$ **La Samanna.** This restaurant has an exquisite setting in the celebrated hotel; you'll dine by candlelight on a tented terrace surrounded by bougainvillea. The clientele is chic, international, and often famous. Innovative chef Mark Ehrler (from Maxim's in Paris and New York) might seduce the palate with seafood risotto, sautéed snapper over Creole black sausage, or roasted lamb chops with seasonal salad and chick peas sprinkled with fruity cold-press olive oil. Three kinds of caviar are served with blinis and chilled Absolut. Dinner for two (with wine) can easily set you back $175. The superb wine cellar holds more than 25,000 bottles. ✕ *Baie Longue,* ☎ *590/87–51–22. Reservations required. Jacket required. Reservations required. AE, DC, MC, V.*

$$$$ **Le Santal.** The approach to this dazzler, through a working-class sub-
★   urb of Marigot, is forbidding. The exterior appears ramshackle, but the interior is transformed by soft lighting, china, and crystal. Specialties of the house include lobster soufflé on a bed of spinach and eggplant, foie gras sautéed in cassis, and lacquered duck. The owners also run the excellent Jean Dupont and Asia, but this is their showplace. Reservations are not required, but they're highly recommended if you want to eat at one of the five tables by the water. ✕ *Sandy Ground,* ☎ *590/87–53–48. Reservations advised. AE, MC, V. No lunch.*

$$$–$$$$ **Le Poisson d'Or.** Feast in this posh popular place on a constantly
★   changing menu of dishes such as sautéed foie gras with pear and walnut cream sauce or smoked lobster in champagne sauce. The setting is a restored stone house, with a huge veranda holding 20 tables. The space doubles as a gallery exhibiting works of top-notch Caribbean artists. ✕ *Rue d'Anguille, Marigot,* ☎ *590/87–72–45. Reservations advised. AE, MC, V. No lunch.*

$$$–$$$$ **Rainbow.** In a town of splendid seaside boîtes, this is one of the best.
★   The cobalt blue and white decor of the split-level dining room is strik-

ingly simple, and the atmosphere, created by lapping waves and murmuring guests, is highly romantic. Fleur and David are the stylish, energetic hosts, and chef Mario Tardif is from one of the world's gastronomic capitals, Québec City. Try his shrimp and scallop fricassee with Caribbean chutney, duck *magret* (breast meat served with its skin), grilled swordfish, or sautéed veal scaloppine with capers, garlic, and chives. Dishes are dressed with fanciful touches like red cabbage crisps. Finish the meal off with sublime orange, honey, and ginger soufflé. ✗ *Grand Case,* ☎ *590/87–55–80. Reservations advised. AE, MC, V. Closed Sun. No lunch.*

$$$–$$$$ **La Vie En Rose.** This bustling restaurant is right off the pier, about a 30-second stroll from the tourist information office. The menu is classic French with an occasional Caribbean twist—fillet of swordfish sautéed in a passion-fruit butter sauce, freshwater crayfish in puff pastry. Appetizers include a delightful warm smoked salmon with potatoes and chives and lobster salad spiced with a touch of ginger. Save room for chocolate mousse cake topped with vanilla sauce. The ground-floor tearoom and pastry shop serve an excellent luncheon with wine for $20. In season, you may make dinner reservations up to one month in advance. ✗ *Rue de la République, Marigot,* ☎ *590/87–54–42. Reservations required in season. AE, D, DC, MC, V. No credit cards at lunch. No lunch Sun.*

$$$ **Alizéa.** Many claim that this elegant terrace restaurant offers the best
★ cuisine on the island. French chef Laurent Guyon trained with Roger Verge from the famous Moulin de Mougins. The prix fixe menu is an excellent value at $40. Sample the homemade foie gras with red wine jelly or roasted sea scallop appetizers. Entrées include mahimahi with fennel and sweet potatoes, and beef tenderloin with stewed shallots in red wine sauce. There are several vegetarian selections. Try crème brûlée with honey and vanilla for dessert ✗ *Hotel Alizéa, Mont Vernon,* ☎ *590/87–41–20. Reservations advised. AE, DC, MC, V.*

$$$ **Le Tastevin.** A chic pavilion, with tropical plants, ceiling fans, and water views, provides an elegant dining setting. Owner Daniel Passeri, a native of Burgundy, also founded the homey Auberge Gourmande across the street. The menu here is more ambitious, including foie gras in Armagnac sauce, duck breast in banana-lime sauce, and red snapper fillet with curry and wild-mushroom sauce. ✗ *Grand Case,* ☎ *590/87–55–15. Reservations required in season. AE, DC, MC, V. No credit cards at lunch.*

$$–$$$ **Maison sur le Port.** Watching the sunset from the palm-fringed terrace is not the least of the pleasures in this old West Indian house surrounded by romantically lit garden fountains. Try the sautéed duck fillet in passion-fruit sauce or red snapper with beurre blanc. There are also three-course fixed-price menus at $21.50 and $29. Chef Jean-Paul Fahrner's imaginative salads are lunchtime treats. There is a children's menu with burgers and chicken sandwiches. ✗ *On the port, Marigot,* ☎ *590/87–56–38. AE, D, MC, V. Closed Sun.*

$$–$$$ **Mark's Place.** Sunday dinner at this barnlike roadside restaurant is an island institution. You may start with pumpkin soup or stuffed crab, then follow with linguine Bolognese or curried goat. Scrumptious daily specials, including homemade pies and pastries, are posted on a blackboard. Groups of 6–12 can eat a five-course meal in the snug wine cellar with their own chef and staff for $50 per person. All Mark needs to whip up a gourmet repast just for you is 24 hours' notice. ✗ *French Cul de Sac,* ☎ *590/87–34–50. AE, MC, V. Closed Mon.*

$$ **Cha Cha Cha Caribbean Café.** A gaudy decor, with Japanese gardens and
★ loud colors, and an even gaudier clientele haven't stopped Pascal and Christina Chevillot's restaurant from becoming an island hot spot. Of

course, the mouthwatering haute Caraibes cuisine and reasonable prices don't hurt. Try the roasted pork tenderloin with ginger sauce or the grilled snapper with pesto, and wash it down with a Grand Case Sunset—a rum concoction made with fresh orange, grapefruit, and mango juices. ✗ *Grand Case,* ☎ *590/87–53–63. MC, V. Closed Sun. No lunch.*

$$ Le Marocain. This exotic oasis in the middle of Marigot resembles a pasha's posh digs, with lush potted plants, intricate mosaics, hand-painted tiles, and wood carvings. The food is as colorful and enticing as the decor, with wonderfully perfumed *tajines* (casseroles of chicken or meat) and *pastillas* (fragrant pastries filled with spices, raisins, and meat or chicken) among the standouts. ✗ *Rue de Hollande, Marigot,* ☎ *590/87–83–11. AE, MC, V.*

$$ Mini Club. This popular eatery, on an upstairs terrace nestled amid coconut palms, has the feel of a treehouse. Dining here is always pleasant, but on Wednesday and Saturday night there's a sumptuous buffet of more than 30 dishes—salads, roast pork, suckling pig, beef, fish, lobster—all for $40 per person, with wine. There is also a $25 prix fixe menu at lunch and dinner. Standard menu selections include poached fish in Creole sauce and steak Béarnaise. ✗ *Rue d'Anguille, Marigot,* ☎ *590/87–50–69. AE, MC, V.*

$–$$ Bistrot Nu. For simple, unadorned fare at a reasonable price, this may be the best spot on the islands. Traditional brasserie-style food—coq au vin, fish soup, snails, pizza, and seafood—is served in a friendly atmosphere. The place is enormously popular; its tables are packed until it closes at 2 AM. ✗ *Rue de Hollande, Marigot,* ☎ *590/87–97–09. MC, V. Closed Sun.*

$–$$ Don Camillo da Enzo. Country-style decor and excellent service distinguish this small eatery. Both northern and southern Italian dishes are served. Some favorites are the carpaccio, green gnocchi in Gorgonzola cream sauce, and veal medallions in marsala sauce. ✗ *Port La Royale, Marigot,* ☎ *590/87–52–88. AE, MC, V.*

$–$$ La Plaisance. The cool strains of jazz waft through this lively open-air brasserie as you sample terrific salads (try the Niçoise or *landaine*—duck, smoked ham, croutons, and fried egg), pizzas (wonderful lobster), pastas (garlic and basil pistou), and fresh grilled seafood at unbeatable prices. This is one of several fine ultracasual eateries at Port La Royale, all offering simple, appetizing food, fixed-price menus, and happy hours. ✗ *Port La Royale, Marigot,* ☎ *590/87–85–00. AE, MC, V.*

$ Yvette's. ★ The attempts at romance couldn't be more endearing: Classical music plays softly, and the tiny, eight-table room is a symphony in Valentine red, from the curtains, tablecloths, and roses to the hot pepper sauce. Yvette herself couldn't be more down-home, nor her food more delicious. Plates are piled high with lip-smacking Creole specialties, such as *accras* (spicy fish fritters), stewed chicken with rice and beans, and conch and dumplings. This is the kind of place that is so good you're surprised to see other tourists—but word gets around. ✗ *Orleans,* ☎ *590/87–32–03. AE (5% surcharge).*

Lodging

Until recently, the Dutch side commanded all the big, splashy resorts. The casinos are still to be found exclusively on the Dutch side—gambling is illegal on the French side. However, St. Martin is having something of a building boom, especially in the area around Nettlé and Orient bays. All the hotels on the French side have an English-speaking staff. There are also small inns and Mediterranean-style facilities on both sides of the island. Many of the hotels offer enticing packages that are worth investigating. You'll save substantially if you travel off-season;

the downside of this is that many hotels and restaurants are closed for refurbishing or just plain recovering from the winter onslaught. In general, the French resorts are more intimate and romantic, but what the Dutch properties lack in ambience, they compensate for in clean, functional, comfortable rooms with all the "extras." Most of the larger Dutch resorts feature time-share annexes; the units are often available for rental for those who prefer the condo lifestyle at comparable rates.

Worth noting on the French side is a coalition of seven small inns called Les Hotels de Charme. They are dedicated to providing "warmth, individual attention, and homey feeling," with rates that range from inexpensive ($) to moderate ($$); some include breakfast. The participating hotels are Alizéa, Panoramic Privilege, L'Hoste, Blue Beach, Hotel du Golf, Chez Martine, and the Sunrise Hotel. For information on any of these inns, call 800/468–6796 in the United States or 590/87–33–44 in St. Martin.

As a rule, rooms on the beach or with a sea view command the highest prices. Most properties are EP or CP (the latter usually only in season), though meal plans are sometimes available.

Both sides of the island offer a wide variety of homes, villas, condominiums, and housekeeping apartments. Information in the United States can be obtained through **WIMCO** (Box 1461, Newport, RI 02840, ☎ 800/932–2222), **Caribbean Home Rentals** (Box 710, Palm Beach, FL 33480, ☎ 407/833–4454), **Jane Condon Corp.** (211 E. 43rd St., New York, NY 10017, ☎ 212/986–4373), and **St. Maarten Villas** (707 Broad Hollow Rd., Farmingdale, NY 11735, ☎ 516/249–4940). On the island, contact **Carimo** (☎ 590/87–57–58) or **St. Martin Rentals** (☎ 599/5–54330, or, in the U.S., ☎ 800/872–8356).

CATEGORY	COST*
$$$$	over $300
$$$	$225–$300
$$	$150–$225
$	under $150

All prices are for a standard double room for two in high season, excluding 5% tax (Dutch side), a taxe de séjour (set by individual hotels on the French side), and a 10%–15% service charge.

Dutch Side

$$$$ **Port de Plaisance.** The drawback at this 200-acre Sheraton resort on Simpson Bay Lagoon is its lack of a beach or even a beach shuttle. No detail was overlooked in planning the 88 luxurious studios and one- and two-bedroom apartments, however. All units are air-conditioned and have a fully equipped kitchen (including dishwasher and microwave), TV with VCR, two phones, and even a trouser press. Interiors are done in soothing pink and beige. Views are of either the lagoon or the resort's own marina. One of the two pools is carved out of rock and has a majestic waterfall. The spa offers every imaginable beauty treatment, from seaweed wraps to aromatherapy, and the extensive sports facilities include 14 tennis courts (7 lighted). The polished marble entrance to the gleaming casino is dominated by a stunning 25-foot bronze statue of a mermaid astride four dolphins. ▣ *Box 2089, Cole Bay,* ☎ *599/5–45222 or 800/732–9479,* FAX *599/5–42428. 88 apartments. 2 restaurants, 5 bars, casino, spa and fitness center, 2 pools, marina, 14 tennis courts (7 lighted), Jacuzzi, 2 boats, 2 shopping arcades, 2 boats, car rental, nightclub. AE, D, DC, MC, V. EP.*

$$$ **Dawn Beach Hotel.** The 16 acres of this hotel are a bit out of the way, but there's a beach and a restaurant, and if you need more than that, there's a bus that runs to town twice a day (not complimentary). Air-conditioned rooms are in villas on the hillside or the beach. All are spacious, with handsome rattan furnishings, combination living room/bedroom with king-size bed, kitchenette, TV, and private patio with ocean view. (If you prefer tubs to showers, opt for the hillside villa.) The pool has a waterfall, and the white-sand beach is one of the island's best for snorkeling, but the breeze is often strong and can whip up the waves. This property is considering becoming all-inclusive in the off-season; ask when you make reservations. ☒ *Box 389, Philipsburg,* ☎ *599/5–22929 or 800/223–9815,* ℻ *599/5–24421. 155 rooms. Restaurant, snorkeling, kayaks, windsurfing, pool, 2 lighted tennis courts, car-rental desk. AE, MC, V. EP, MAP.*

$$$ Maho Beach Hotel & Casino. This pink-and-white colossus is a self-contained megaresort. The rooms, which have either sea or garden views, are airy and spacious, with cathedral ceilings and light pastel and deep ocean-colored decors. All rooms have a private balcony and either two double beds or a king-size bed. The trick is to get a room far enough away from the airport's landing strip (those behind the main lobby are the quietest): The roaring plane engines drown out the surf at the otherwise lovely beach. Restaurants include excellent Italian dining at Tiberio, burgers and live music at Cheri's Café, and beachside Middle Eastern food at Orient Express. The hotel complex is home to 75 shops and both the island's largest casino and its largest pool. There's a lively night scene at the open-air La Luna disco. Unfortunately the service can't keep up with the sprawl, and you may be neglected as the staff struggles to meet guest needs. ☒ *Maho Bay,* ☎ *599/5–52115 or 800/223–0757,* ℻ *599/5–53180. 688 rooms. 10 restaurants, 3 bars, casino, disco, 2 pools, boutiques, 4 tennis courts (2 lighted), 75 shops, all water sports. AE, D, MC, V. EP, MAP.*

$$$ Mullet Bay Resort and Casino. Of the self-contained megaresorts, Mullet Bay offers the most privacy, because it's spread out over 172 acres (easily negotiable by the ubiquitous golf carts) rather than condensed in high-rises. There are an excellent championship 18-hole golf course (the only one on the island), a gleaming crescent of sand, water sports galore, and comfortable, well-maintained accommodations, with standard but pleasing pastel decor and rattan furnishings. Restaurant choices include Chinese, Italian, seafood, and a steak house. The disco, Studio 7, is popular with both guests and locals. For those who like constant activity and variety, Mullet Bay is the place. ☒ *Box 309, Mullet Bay,* ☎ *599/5–52801,* ℻ *599/5–54281. 611 rooms. 6 restaurants, 2 bars, 2 pools, 14 lighted tennis courts, golf course, water-sports center, disco, shopping arcade, medical center, bank, food mart. AE, D, DC, MC, V. EP, MAP.*

$$$ Pelican Resort & Casino. Walk into the reception area and one-armed bandits and gaming tables greet you. On the lower level is a sales office enticing you to buy into this hotel-condo complex. An assortment of white stucco buildings house the resort's air-conditioned apartments, suites, and deluxe studios, all of which have a sweeping view of the Caribbean. Each has a fully equipped kitchen (including microwave), satellite TV, and rattan furniture; some have king-size beds. The resort has 1,400 feet of beach (though it's not great for swimming because of the seaweed) and its own 60-foot catamaran, *El Tigre,* which is available for charters. ☒ *Simpson Bay,* ☎ *599/5–42503 or 800/626–9637,* ℻ *599/5–42133. 660 suites and studios. 2 restaurants, 4 bars, casino, 8 pools, health spa, 6 lighted tennis courts, car rental, medical center, children's playground with pool, grocery store, water-sports center. AE, D, DC, MC, V. EP.*

$$–$$$ **Horny Toad Guesthouse.** This is one of the most charming properties
★ on the island, thanks to the caring touch of owners Bette and Earle
Vaughn, who keep things as immaculate as if it were their own home
(which it is most of the year). Each of the eight apartments on the beach
is individually decorated; some have air-conditioning, and some have
ceiling fans. Many repeat guests request the same apartment. The blue-
and-white sun terrace duplicates the patterns of delft china; chirping
birds and fresh flowers greet you every morning; and Bette and Earle
always treat you like family. There is a barbecue area for guests to use,
but no restaurant. ☎ *Box 397, Simpson Bay,* ☎ *599/5–54323, or
800/223–9815,* FAX *599/5–53316. 2 studios, 6 1-bedroom apartments.
Library, barbecue. No credit cards. EP.*

$$–$$$ **Oyster Pond Beach Hotel.** The refined elegance of this hotel is quite
★ out of character with the rest of St. Maarten. The original buildings
surround a courtyard furnished with tables and chairs. Two towers with
Moorish arches and stone walls hold split-level suites and standard rooms
(there are also rooms along the corridors that connect the towers), all
with terra-cotta floors, white wicker furnishings, ceiling fans, and pastel French cottons. All rooms have a secluded balcony or terrace and
a view of the ocean, the courtyard, or the yacht basin. A newer building offers larger rooms with the same white-wicker furnishings and balconies facing the sea. Rooms in all of the buildings are air-conditioned
and have a phone and cable TV. The hotel is a one-minute walk from
Dawn Beach, which is excellent for snorkeling, though not for sunbathing
or swimming. The dining room (*see* Dining, *above*) opens onto the Atlantic Ocean, and the pool is perched right at the water's edge. A PADI-
certified dive shop is on the premises. Breakfast is included. ☎ *Oyster
Pond, Box 239, Philipsburg,* ☎ *599/5–22206, 599/5–23206, or
800/374–1323;* FAX *599/5–25695. 40 rooms. Restaurant, bar, saltwater pool, water-sports center. AE, D, MC, V. BP.*

$$ **Great Bay Beach Hotel & Casino.** One of the island's few properties
offering an all-inclusive rate, this resort, a 10-minute walk from the
center of Philipsburg, has its own stretch of beach and terrific views
of the bay. The bustling open-air lobby, with striped awnings overlooking
the sea, is more striking than the rooms, which are furnished in typi-
cal muted pastels and have the usual amenities, including a TV and
phone, but lack any attempt at charm or interest. You do get a private
balcony or terrace with an ocean or mountain view. A list of activities
is posted each morning, and the hotel staff can arrange virtually any
type of island excursion or sport. The clientele is generally friendly, fun
seeking, and active. ☎ *Box 910, Philipsburg,* ☎ *599/5–22446,* FAX
*599/5–23859. 285 rooms, 10 1-bedroom suites. 2 restaurants, 3 bars,
2 pools, casino, nightclub, water-sports center, 1 lighted tennis court,
gift shop, car rental. AE, DC, MC, V. EP, All-inclusive.*

$$ **La Vista.** On this intimate property, quaint Antillean buildings are
connected by brick walkways lined with riotous hibiscus and bougainvil-
lea. All accommodations are air-conditioned suites with cable TV,
phone, and balcony. Most have king-size beds; some have a queen or
two twins. Guests have the use of the facilities at the adjacent Pelican
Resort. ☎ *Box 40, Pelican Key,* ☎ *599/5–43005 or 800/365–8484,*
FAX *599/5–43010. 24 suites. Restaurant, horseback riding, pool, tennis. AE, MC, V. EP.*

$–$$ **Divi Little Bay Beach Resort.** Quaint red-tile and whitewashed build-
ings are nestled on an emerald hill overlooking the bay and ecru-sand
beach. All the spacious rooms have dazzling ocean views, terrace or
balcony, cable TV, air-conditioning, and minifridge; the newer deluxe
oceanfront rooms also have a hot tub. The decor is pleasing, with aquamarine or terra-cotta tile floors and fresh-looking floral upholstery. ☎

Box 61, Philipsburg, ☎ *599/5–22333 or 800/367–3484,* FAX *599/5–23911. 163 rooms. 3 restaurants, 3 bars, 2 pools, car-rental desk, water-sports center, 3 lighted tennis courts, shops, casino. AE, DC, MC, V. EP, FAP, MAP.*

$–$$ **Holland House Beach Hotel.** This is a centrally situated hotel, with the shops of Front Street at its doorstep and a mile-long backyard called Great Bay Beach. Each room has white rattan furnishings with muted-pastel spreads and drapes, balcony, phone, cable TV, and air-conditioning; most have kitchenettes. The huge suites are two large rooms: living room with dining table, sofa, coffee table, chairs, and TV area, and bedroom with king-size bed, a second TV, and phone. Ask for a beach view. The delightful open-air restaurant overlooking the water serves reasonably priced dinners, and the indoor-outdoor patio lounge is a popular and friendly spot to watch the sunset. ☎ *35 Front St., Box 393, Philipsburg,* ☎ *599/5–22572 or 800/223–9815,* FAX *599/5–24673. 54 rooms, 6 suites. Restaurant, lounge, meeting room, gift shop, activities desk. AE, D, DC, MC, V. EP.*

$ **Golden Tulip St. Martin.** This new resort, in the somewhat isolated Cul de Sac area, opened in early 1994. It offers a luxury feel for a budget price. Clusters of blue bungalows with white gingerbread trim, each housing a suite, are spread out along the water. Garden suites are set farther up from the sea; ocean suites are closer to the beach. Each unit has a kitchenette, TV, phone, minibar, and a porch facing the sea. The interiors are spacious, with white tile floors, a seating area, and elegant woven-rattan furniture. Pretty floral fabrics are used for the bedspreads, drapes, and upholstery. ☎ *BP 5240, Cul de Sac 97072,* ☎ *590/87–89–98 or 800/344–1212,* FAX *590/87–35–14. 94 units. Restaurant, bar, poolside snack bar, water sports, horseback riding, 5 pools, boutique, baby-sitting. AE, DC, MC, V. EP.*

$ **Passangrahan Royal Guest House.** It's entirely appropriate that the bar
★ here is named Sidney Greenstreet. This is the island's oldest inn, and it looks like a set for an old Bogie-Greenstreet film. The green-and-white building was once Queen Wilhelmina's residence and the government guest house. Wicker peacock chairs, slowly revolving ceiling fans, balconies shaded by tropical greenery, king-size mahogany headboards, and a broad tile veranda are some of the hallmarks of this guest house. A complimentary afternoon tea is served. There are no TVs or phones in the rooms, and you're offered just a sliver of Great Bay Beach. ☎ *15 Front St., Box 151, Philipsburg,* ☎ *599/5–23588,* FAX *599/5–22885. 30 rooms, 1 suite. Bar, restaurant. AE, MC, V. EP.*

$ **Seaview Hotel & Casino.** This is another good buy on Front Street and Great Bay Beach. The air-conditioned, twin-bed rooms are very modest, cheerful, and clean. All have baths (some with showers only), TV, and phone. Ten of the rooms look out on the courtyard, where breakfast is sometimes served; four rooms face the sea. Children under 12 stay free. ☎ *59 Front St., Box 65, Philipsburg,* ☎ *599/5–22323 or 800/223–9815; in NY, 212/545–8469; in Canada, 800/468–0023;* FAX *599/5–24356. 45 rooms. Breakfast room, casino. AE, D, MC, V. EP.*

French Side

$$$$ **La Belle Creole.** This 25-acre re-creation of an old Mediterranean vil-
★ lage fans out from a central stone plaza. Enormous rooms and suites are in one- to three-story villas linked by stone-paved streets and graceful courtyards. Most rooms have private balconies, and you can select a view of the island, Marigot Bay, or the ocean. Each unit has a king-size or two double beds, air-conditioning, direct-dial phone, cable TV, marble and tile bathroom, and minibar. Grand as it is, La Belle Creole has a casual, relaxed atmosphere even when it's crowded. A water-

sports complex has been added, and the tennis program is the island's finest. Though on its own estate, the hotel has the advantage of quick and easy access to Marigot and the island's best beaches. La Provence is a fine gourmet restaurant, with especially popular weekly seafood and barbecue buffets. Mindful of the exorbitant cost of eating out, the management added a casual patio bistro. ☎ *Box 118, Marigot 97150,* ☎ *590/87–66–00,* FAX *590/87–56–66. 162 rooms. Activities desk, gift shop, pool, 4 lighted tennis courts, fitness/beauty center, 2 restaurants, 3 bars, water-sports center. AE, DC, MC, V. CP.*

$$$$ **La Samanna.** This luxurious, secluded hotel looks as if it were trans-
★ ported to St. Martin from Morocco. It's set in a tropical garden on a slope overlooking the ravishing Baie Longue beach. Red hibiscus is everywhere. Studios and one- and two-bedroom villas all have private patio, minibar, full bath, and such thoughtful touches as potpourri and fresh flowers. The decor is stunning: cool mint, apricot, and teal fabrics; unusual ceramic work; painted tiles; and clever variations on traditional Caribbean wicker and rattan. The restaurant is one of the island's finest (*see* Dining, *above*). ☎ *Box 159, Marigot 97150,* ☎ *590/87–51–22 or 800/854–2252,* FAX *590/87–87–86. 25 rooms, 30 1-bedroom suites and 30 2-bedroom suites. Restaurant, lounge, pool, fitness center, 3 tennis courts, library, TV room, boutique, water-sports center. AE. CP.*

$$$$ **Le Meridien L'Habitation Le Domaine.** There are better bargains on the island, yet this bustling resort remains wildly popular with tour groups and families. There are 1,600 feet of white-sand beach and a slew of sports facilities, but no matter where you stay on the compound, few units boast an ocean view, the ambience is lacking, the service is polite but impersonal, and French Muzak is annoyingly omnipresent. The setting is pleasant enough—at the end of a white-knuckle road, amid beautifully landscaped gardens on enchanting Marcel Cove. The two-story main building that houses the lobby is a white-column structure with red-tile roof and graceful galleries. All the air-conditioned rooms, suites, and apartments have spacious baths, balconies, TVs, phones, and refrigerators. One-bedroom apartments on the marina have fully equipped kitchens and private patios. A couple of two-story buildings dubbed Le Domaine contain rooms and suites that are smaller and pricier but brighter and more tropical. Guests have free access to the facilities of Le Privilège, a sports and entertainment complex on the hill (a minibus makes frequent trips to it). La Belle France is a typically solid and *très cher* gourmet restaurant. ☎ *Box 581, Anse Marcel 97150,* ☎ *590/87–33–33 or 590/87–78–80; in the U.S., 800/543–4300;* FAX *590/87–30–38. 400 rooms, 82 suites. 4 restaurants, 4 bars, beach, boutiques, aerobics, car rental, disco, 6 lighted tennis courts, minigolf, 2 pools, 4 squash courts, 2 racquetball court, 100-slip marina, water-sports center. AE, DC, MC, V. EP.*

$$$–$$$$ **Esmeralda Resort.** It looks like a housing development in the Sun Belt, but the interiors of these deluxe villas are tastefully decorated. The 51 rooms and suites in 15 villas can be combined any way you like, from studio to five-bedroom palatial digs. Each villa has a private pool, and all the rooms have TV, fully equipped kitchenette, phone, and private terrace. L'Astrolabe has a reputation for excellent French cuisine. ☎ *Box 541, Orient Bay,* ☎ *590/87–36–36 or 800/622–7836,* FAX *590/87–35–18. 15 villas. 5 beach restaurants, 1 indoor restaurant, water-sports center, 2 lighted tennis courts, gift shop. AE, D, MC, V. CP.*

$$$ **Grand Case Beach Club.** This informal condo complex is situated on Grand Case's crescent-shape beach, with another "secret" strand of sand a two-minute walk away. Air-conditioned studios and one- and two-bedroom apartments all have balconies or patios and kitchenettes.

The 62 oceanfront units are much in demand, despite their undistinctive pastel decor. There are lots of repeat guests, so reserve well in advance. Attractive packages are offered. The kitchen at the aptly named Café Panoramique restaurant has been upgraded since it spirited chef Alain Billard away from Le Bec Fin. *Box 339, Grand Case 97150, 590/87–51–87 or 800/223–1588, FAX 590/87–59–93. 40 studios and 33 1- and 2-bedroom apartments. Restaurant, lounge, 1 lighted tennis court, billiards, car rental, catamaran. AE, MC, V. CP.*

$$–$$$ Captain Oliver's. These bungalows are a good bargain and a good way
★ to avoid the hustle and bustle of St. Maarten. The small hotel faces a beautiful horseshoe-shape bay; bungalows have a view of the bay or garden. The exceptionally clean, fresh, air-conditioned rooms have patio deck, satellite TV, minibar, direct-dial phone, and kitchenette. The property straddles the border: Stay in France, and dine in the Netherlands (in the engaging open-air marina bistro). Sail-and-stay packages can be arranged by the friendly helpful staff. *Oyster Pond, 97150, 590/87–40–26 or 800/223–9862, FAX 590/87–40–84. 50 rooms. Restaurant, snack bar. AE, DC, MC, V. CP.*

$$–$$$ Pavillon Beach Hotel. Every room and suite at this small hotel faces the sea and has a private balcony. The spacious studios and one-bedroom suites are decorated in warm pastel colors and have tile floors and elegant rattan furniture. On the balcony is a small kitchenette. Bathrooms come with a hair dryer and shower but no tub. From the ground-level rooms, you can walk right onto the beach through sliding wooden shutters. You may prefer the upper-story rooms, where you can leave the shutters open without as much exposure. The managers, Paul and Marie-Florence, are wonderfully warm-hearted and helpful. *Plage de Grand Case, RN 7, Grand Case 97150, 590/87–96–46 or 800/223–9815, FAX 590/87–71–04. 17 rooms. MC, V. EP.*

$–$$$ Mont Vernon. Delicate lacelike gingerbread work decorates this rambling hotel, which sits on a bluff overlooking Orient Bay. The light, airy quality of the exterior is maintained as you enter the huge, open reception area filled with rattan furniture. Each room has either a king-size bed or twin beds and a private balcony. The bathrooms are equipped with hair dryers, the sitting area with satellite TV. The rooms in the buildings on the crest facing the ocean have the best views and are slightly larger than the others. The other choice rooms are in the buildings by the pools and beach. This is a big resort that lures package-tour groups as well as business seminars. *Baie Orientale, BP 1174, 97062, 590/87–62–00 or 800/223–0888, FAX 590/87–37–27. 394 suites. 2 restaurants, 2 bars, pool, 2 lighted tennis courts, snorkeling, windsurfing, fitness center, shops, car rentals. AE, DC, MC, V. CP, MAP.*

$$ Alizéa. The view of Orient Bay from this Mont Vernon hill setting is stunning. There is a path to the beach (a 10-minute walk). An open-air feeling pervades the hotel from its terrace restaurant, where the food is superb, to the 26 guest apartments done up with contemporary light-wood furnishings and pastel floral-print fabrics. Rooms vary in style and design, but all are tasteful and each has a kitchenette and a large private patio balcony. Each also has TV, phone, and large bathroom. A fitness room was slated for completion by press time. *Mont Vernon 25, 97150, 590/87–33–42, FAX 590/87–41–15. 8 1-bedroom bungalows, 18 studios. Restaurant, bar, gym, pool. AE, D, MC, V. CP.*

$$ Anse Margot. This quiet, thoroughly French property is one of the many hotels that line the stretch of land between the sea and Simpson's Bay, known as Baie Nettlé. The rooms here are in eight three-story townhouse buildings. Standard rooms offer either two twins or a king-size bed, a seating area, and a writing desk; suites are duplexes with two baths, a seating area, and two desks. All units have TV, phone, bathtub with hand-held shower, and private balcony with either garden or beach view. Upholstery, drapes, and spreads are a brown-and-coral geometric print. There are two pools and a stretch of beach along Simpson Bay that's good for sunbathing but not swimming. You may prefer the Nettlé beach across the street. A complimentary breakfast buffet is served in the open-air Entre Deux Mers, one of the better hotel restaurants. It's about a five-minute drive to Marigot. ☎ *Box 979, Baie Nettlé 97150, ☎ 590/87–92–01 or 800/742–4276, ⅀ 590/87–92–13. 96 rooms, 35 1-bedroom suites. Restaurant, bar, 2 pools, hot tub, meeting room, water-sports center, gift shop. AE, D, DC, MC, V. BP.*

$–$$ **Hôtel l'Atlantide.** This small hotel has four sun-drenched units, ranging in size from a studio to a two-bedroom suite. Private balconies overlook Grand Case Bay and the beach. Each unit has a TV and phone; suites have large living areas and fully equipped kitchens. The decor is airy, with gleaming white tile floors, elegant rattan furniture, and crisp pastel-striped or floral upholstery. There's no restaurant or bar, but the village of Grand Case is known for its lively restaurant scene. *BP 5140, Grand Case 97150, ☎ 590/87–09–80, ⅀ 590/87–30–09. Four units. No credit cards. EP.*

$–$$ **Hôtel L'Esplanade Caraibes.** Opened in 1992, this complex still sparkles
★ as if brand-new. It's built on a hillside overlooking Grand Case Bay, a three-minute walk from the beach. Two curved stone staircases with inlaid tile and brick lead up from the bougainvillea beds to the open-air reception area. The standard suites are large, with complete kitchens, large private balconies with table and chairs, elegant rattan furniture, king-size beds, gleaming wood ceilings, and ceiling fans; some have an office alcove with a desk. All have phone, TV, and air-conditioning. Duplexes have elegant cathedral ceilings and mahogany staircases, as well as an extra half bath, an upstairs loft bedroom, and a sleeper sofa in the living room. Upholstery throughout is striped with muted pinks and corals; drapes have crisp tropical prints. There is no restaurant at the hotel, but Grand Case's roster of gourmet spots is just a short walk away. ☎ *Box 5007, Grand Case 97150, ☎ 590/87–06–55, ⅀ 590/87–29–15. 24 units. Pool, deep-sea-fishing boat for rental. AE, D, MC, V. EP.*

$–$$ **Marine Hotel Simson Beach.** This sprawling complex may be the best
★ buy on the hotel strip known as Nettlé Bay. Rooms and duplex suites are cheerfully decorated. Most have a view of the water; all have kitchenette, balcony, TV, and phone. The youthful, fun-loving clientele makes sure there's never a dull moment. Budget-conscious Europeans love this place because of the many extras, like a huge breakfast buffet and nightly local entertainment. There are shuttles to Marigot, Philipsburg, and beaches (not complimentary). ☎ *Box 172, Nettlé Bay, ☎ 590/87–54–54, ⅀ 590/87–92–11. 120 studios, 45 1-bedroom duplexes. Restaurant, lighted tennis court, bar, beach, pool, water-sports center, activity center, car and bike rental, minimart, gift shop, laundromat, dive shop. AE, DC, MC, V. CP.*

$ **Hevea.** This small white guest house with smart striped awnings is across
★ the street from the beach in the heart of Grand Case. The rooms are dollhouse small but will appeal to romantics. There are beam ceilings, washstands, and carved-wood beds with lovely white coverlets and mosquito nets. The five air-conditioned rooms, studios, and apartment are on the terrace level; three fan-cooled studios and apartments are on the garden level. Hotel guests can get a special "house" dinner at the delightful gourmet restaurant for $30. ☎ *163 blvd. de Grand Case, Grand Case 97150, ☎ 590/87–56–85 or 800/423–4433, ⅀ 590/87–83–88. 8 units. Restaurant. MC, V. EP.*

$ **La Residence.** The downtown location and soundproof rooms of this
★ Marigot hotel make it a popular place for business travelers. All the
accommodations have bath (with shower only), king-size bed, balcony,
dark rattan furniture, tile floors, phone, TV, and minibar. You've a
choice among single or double rooms, some with mezzanine loft beds.
The intimate restaurant offers a good $28 three-course menu. You'll
have to take a cab to get to the beach. ☎ *Rue du Général de Gaulle,
Marigot 97150,* ☎ *590/87–70–37 or 800/223–9815,* FAX *590/87–90–
44. 21 rooms. Restaurant, lounge, sundry shop. AE, D, MC, V. MAP,
CP.*

$ **Le Royale Louisiana.** Located in downtown Marigot in the boutique
shopping area, this upstairs hotel is pleasant and pretty. White and pale
green galleries overlook the flower-filled courtyard. There's a selection
of twin, double, and triple air-conditioned duplexes, all with private
bath (tub and shower), TV, and phone. You can reach the nearest beach
by a 20-minute walk or by taxi. ☎ *Rue du Général de Gaulle, Box
476, Marigot 97055,* ☎ *590/87–86–51,* FAX *590/87–96–49. 68 rooms.
Restaurant, snack bar, beauty salon. AE, MC, V. CP.*

Nightlife

To find out what's doing on the island, pick up any of the following
publications: *St. Maarten Nights, What to Do in St. Maarten, St.
Maarten Events,* or *St. Maarten Holiday*—all distributed free in the
tourist office and hotels. *Discover St. Martin/St. Maarten,* also free, is
a glossy magazine that includes articles about the island's history and
the latest on shops, discos, restaurants, and even archaeological digs.

Each of the resort hotels has a Caribbean spectacular one night a
week, replete with limbo and fire dancers and steel bands.

Casinos are the main focus on the Dutch side, but there are discos that
usually start late and keep on till the fat lady sings.

Bars and Nightclubs

Cheri's Cafe (across from the Maho Beach Hotel, ☎ 599/5–53361) is
a local institution, with cheap food and great live bands. **Turtle Pier
Bar & Restaurant** (Airport Rd., ☎ 599/5–52230) always hops with a
lively crowd. **Coconuts Comedy Club** (Maho Plaza, ☎ 599/5–52115)
headlines top comedy acts Sunday–Friday. **David's** (Rue de la Liberté,
Marigot, ☎ 590/87–51–58) is run by an expatriate Brit; its raucous
Tuesday and Friday trivia nights are legendary. **Bamboo Cocktail Bar**
(Rue de la Liberté, Marigot, ☎ 590/29–01–00) is the place for karaoke
fans. On Grand Case Boulevard, happy hours rock at the American-
owned **Surf Club South** (no ☎), and **Jimbo Lolo** (no ☎) stays open until
midnight for French punks and American wanna-bes who then head
over for a nightcap at **Cha Cha Cha Caribbean Café** (☎ 590/87–53–
63). The friendly **News Music Cafe** (Airport Rd., Simpson Bay, ☎
599/5–42236) serves food into the wee hours.

Casinos

All the casinos have craps, blackjack, roulette, and slot machines. You
must be 18 years old or older to gamble. The casinos are located at
the **Great Bay Beach Hotel, Divi Little Bay Beach Resort, Pelican Resort, Mullet Bay Resort, Seaview Hotel** and the **Coliseum** in Philipsburg;
Port de Plaisance; and **Casino Royal at Maho Beach.**

Discos

Last Stop (A. T. Illidge Road, no ☎) and the **Tropics** (by Madame Estate in the Royal Inn Motel, no ☎) are hot, somewhat rowdy discos
frequented by locals. There have been reports of drug activity at the

latter. **Studio 7** (Mullet Bay, ☎ 599/5–42115) attracts a young crowd of locals and visitors Tuesday through Saturday. **Casino Royale,** across from the Maho Beach Hotel, produces the splashy "Paris Revue Show," and **La Luna** is Maho's disco, popular with young people. French nationals and locals flock to the **Copacabana** disco (☎ 87–42–52) in Marina Royale in Marigot for salsa and soca. **Night Fever** (Colombier, outside Marigot, no ☎) attracts a young crowd of locals who gyrate to the latest Eurodisco beat.

24 St. Vincent and the Grenadines

Updated by
Kate Sekules

ST. VINCENT AND THE GRENADINES is a nation comprising 32 lush, mountainous islands and cays—the southernmost of the Windwards, except for Grenada, Trinidad, and Tobago. St. Vincent, only 18 miles long and 9 miles wide, sits just over 13° north of the equator, with the Grenadines lined up like a tadpole tail for 45 miles to the southwest. They are, each in a different way, islands for the demanding escapist, devoid of all-inclusive resorts, glitzy disco clubs, and duty-free shopping malls, but rich in natural beauty.

St. Vincent itself produces most of the world's arrowroot, though its major export is bananas, and these plants, along with coconut palms and breadfruit trees, crowd more of the island than the 99,000-person population does. This has obvious charm for the nature lover, who can spend weeks hiking St. Vincent's not always well-paved trails, perhaps sighting the rare St. Vincent parrot in the Vermont Valley, or climbing the Caribbean's most active volcano, La Soufrière, which last erupted in 1979. Below sea level, snorkeling and scuba landscapes are similarly exciting, both off St. Vincent and around the Grenadines.

Despite its unspoilt beauty, most people don't linger long in St. Vincent, using it as a stop-off en route to their preferred Grenadine. That has a lot to do with the beaches, which are narrow and mostly black—in contrast to the Grenadines' picture-postcard expanses of powdery white sand—and with the fact that St. Vincent is not really set up for tourists.

While the islands have their share of the poor and unemployed, the superfertile soil allows everyone to grow enough food to eat and trade for necessities. Since the locals haven't come to regard tourists as meal tickets, beggars are few. Recent progress (improved roads, Bequia's new airport), however, has its price: It is no longer entirely safe to hike alone along forest trails, and petty theft has become a reality.

Historians believe that in 4300 BC, long before King Tut ruled Egypt, the Ciboney Indians first inhabited St. Vincent. Unhampered by passports and political unrest, the Ciboney made their way to Cuba and Haiti, leaving St. Vincent to the Arawaks. Columbus sailed by in 1492, while the Arawaks were involved in intermittent skirmishes with the bellicose Caribs; though Columbus never actually stopped on St. Vincent, Discovery Day (or St. Vincent and the Grenadines' Day) is still commemorated on January 22.

Declared a neutral island by French and British agreement in 1748, St. Vincent became something of a political football in the years that followed. Ceded to the British in 1763, it was captured by the French in 1779 and restored to the British by the Treaty of Versailles in 1783. By the 19th century, St. Vincent was quite sure it was more British than French, and on October 27, 1979, it gained independence from Great Britain.

In contrast to their colorful history, the Grenadines seem timeless, as free from politics as the beaches are free from debris and crowds. Nine miles south of St. Vincent is Bequia, the second-largest Grenadine. Admiralty Bay is one of the finest anchorages in the Caribbean. With superb views, snorkeling, hiking, and swimming, the island has much to offer the international mix of backpackers and luxury-yacht owners who frequent its shores.

A two-hour sail (or 10-minute flight) south is the private island of Mustique. More arid than Bequia, Mustique does not need to tout itself for tourists, least of all those hoping for a glimpse of the rich and fa-mous (Princess Margaret, Mick Jagger, David Bowie) who own houses here. The appeal of Mustique is seclusion and privacy.

Just over 3 square miles, Canouan is an unspoiled island that offers travelers an opportunity to relax, snorkel, and hike.

Numerous yachts and catamarans can be chartered for day sails from any of the Grenadines to the tiny uninhabited Tobago Cays. Avid snorkelers claim that the cays have some of the best hard and soft coral formations found outside the Pacific Ocean. The beaches here are per-fect for secluded picnics.

The tiny island of Mayreau has 182 residents, no ☎s, and one of the area's most beautiful beaches. The Caribbean is often mirror-calm, yet just yards away on the southern end of this narrow island is the rolling Atlantic surf.

John Caldwell has spent 20 years turning Palm Island from a mosquito-infested mangrove swamp into a small island paradise. The Caldwell family also hosts day-tripping cruise passengers who come to lounge on the wide white beaches, which are dotted and fringed with palm trees.

Union Island isn't really a place for landlubbers: The island caters al-most completely to French sailors, who keep very much to themselves. Surface transport is limited, and to see the island you need a boat. You won't find the laid-back friendliness of the other Grenadines here.

Petit St. Vincent is another private luxury-resort island, reclaimed from the jungle by manager Haze Richardson. It's actually possible to spend your entire vacation in one of the resort's widely spaced stone houses without ever seeing another human being.

Before You Go

Tourist Information
Contact the **St. Vincent and the Grenadines Tourist Office** (801 2nd Ave., 21st Floor, New York, NY 10017, ☎ 212/687–4981 or 800/729–1726, FAX 212/949–5946, or 6505 Cove Creek Pl., Dallas, TX 75240, ☎ 214/239–6451, FAX 214/239–1002. In Canada: 100 University Ave., Suite 504, Toronto, Ontario M5J 1V6, ☎ 416/971–9666, FAX 416/971–9667. In the United Kingdom: 10 Kensington Court, London W8 5DL, ☎ 0171/937–6570, FAX 0171/937–3611). Ask for their visitor's guide, which is filled with useful, up-to-date information.

Arriving and Departing
BY PLANE
Most U.S. visitors fly via **American** (☎ 800/433–7300) into Barbados or St. Lucia, then take a small plane to St. Vincent's E.T. Joshua Air-port or to Bequia, Mustique, Canouan, or Union. (Other destinations require a boat ride on either a scheduled ferry, a chartered boat, or your hotel's launch.) Other airlines that connect with interisland flights are **BWIA** (☎ 800/JET–BWIA), **British Airways** (☎ 800/247–9297), **Air Canada** (☎ 800/776–3000), and **Air France** (☎ 800/237–2747).

LIAT (Leeward Islands Air Transport, ☎ 809/462–0700; in NY, 212/251–1717; elsewhere in the U.S., 800/253–5011), **Air Martinique** (☎ 809/458–4528), and **SVGAIR** (☎ 809/456–5610, FAX 809/458–4697) fly interisland. Delays are common but usually not outrageous. A surer way to go is with **Mustique Airways** (☎ 809/458–4380). In the U.S., contact **Stratton Travel** (795 Franklin Ave., Franklin Lakes, NJ

07417, ☎ 201/891–0111 or 800/526–4789). Its six- or eight-seat charter flights meet your major carrier's arrival and wait if it's delayed.

FROM THE AIRPORT
Taxis and buses are readily available at E.T. Joshua Airport and are available, but rarer, on those Grenadine islands with airstrips. A taxi from the airport to Kingstown will cost about $6 (E.C.$15); bus fare is less than 50¢. If you have a lot of luggage, it might be best to take a taxi—buses (actually minivans) are very short on space.

Passports and Visas
U.S., U.K., and Canadian citizens must have a passport; all visitors must hold return or ongoing tickets. Visas are not required.

Language
English is spoken everywhere in the Grenadines, often with a Vincentian patois or dialect.

Precautions
Insects are a minor problem on the beach during the day, but when hiking and sitting outdoors in the evening, you'll be glad you brought industrial-strength mosquito repellent.

Beware of the manchineel tree, whose little green apples look tempting but are toxic. Even touching the sap of the leaves will cause an uncomfortable rash, and you should not shelter beneath them during rainstorms. Most trees on hotel grounds are marked with signs; on more remote islands, the bark may be painted red. Hikers should watch for brazilwood trees/bushes, which look and act similar to poison ivy.

When taking photos of market vendors, private citizens, or homes, be sure to ask permission first, and expect to give a gratuity for the favor.

There's relatively little crime here, but don't tempt fate by leaving your valuables lying around or your room or car unlocked.

Staying in St. Vincent and the Grenadines

Important Addresses
Tourist Information: The **St. Vincent Board of Tourism** (☎ 809/457–1502) is in the new financial complex, close to the port on Upper Bay Street.

EMERGENCIES
Police: ☎ 809/457–1211. **Hospital: Kingston General Hospital** (☎ 809/456–1185). **Pharmacies: Deane's** (☎ 809/456–2877) and **Reliance** (☎ 809/456–1734), both in Kingstown; on Bequia, **Bequia Pharmacy** (☎ 809/458–3296).

Currency
Although U.S. and Canadian dollars are taken at all but the smallest shops, Eastern Caribbean currency (E.C.$) is accepted and preferred everywhere. At press time, the exchange rate was fixed at E.C.$2.67 to U.S.$1; hotels and shops generally give a rate of E.C.$2.5–2.6 to U.S.$1.

Price quotes are normally given in E.C. dollars; however, when you negotiate taxi fares and such, be sure you know which type of dollar you're agreeing on. Note: Prices quoted here are in U.S. dollars unless indicated otherwise.

Taxes and Service Charges
The departure tax from St. Vincent and the Grenadines is $7.50 (E.C.$20). Restaurants and hotels charge a 5% government tax, and if a 10% service charge is included in your bill, no additional tip is necessary.

Guided Tours

Tours can be informally arranged through taxi drivers who double as knowledgeable guides. Your hotel or the tourism board will recommend a driver, or call Kelvin Harry (☎ 809/457–1316), president of the Taxi Driver's Association, who will send one of the Association's members, identifiable by a round yellow-and-blue decal on the windshield. Always settle the fare first, in either U.S. or E.C. dollars. The average cost is E.C.$35 per hour.

Father and son, Austin and Chris Patterson, of **Dolphins** (Villa, ☎ 809/457–4337), have four-wheel-drive Jeeps, a ketch, a speedboat, and ins all over the island. Tours include navigation of the Mesopotamia Valley underwater river, or a day sail to their secret deserted island, plus the usual volcano and falls, and come complete with locally cooked lunches—plus lots of insider knowledge. **Grenadine Tours** (St. Vincent, ☎ 809/458–4818) arranges air, sea, and land excursions throughout the islands.

Getting Around

BUSES

Public buses come in the form of brightly painted minivans with names like "Easy Na," "Irie," and "Who to Blame." Bus fares run E.C.$1–$6 in St. Vincent, with the route direction indicated on a sign in the windshield. Just wave from the road, and the driver will stop for you, then pay the man by the door on the way out, with the correct change in EC$ coins, if at all possible. In Kingstown, buses leave from the Terminus in Market Square.

Smaller islands also have taxi-vans and pickup trucks with benches in the back and canvas covers for when it rains.

RENTAL CARS

Rental cars cost an average of $45–$50 per day; driving is on the left. Although major improvements are being made, many roads are not well marked or maintained. You may want to take a taxi instead of renting a car.

If you decide to rent a car, you'll need a temporary Vincentian license (unless you already have an international driver's license), which costs E.C.$40, from the airport or the police station on Bay Street. Among the rental firms are **Avis** (Kingston, ☎ 809/556–5610), **Kim's** (Kingston, ☎ 809/456–1884), and Sunshine Rentals (Arnos Vale, ☎ 809/456–5380).

Telephones and Mail

The area code for St. Vincent and the Grenadines is 809. If you use Sprint or MCI in the United States, you may need to access an AT&T line to dial direct to St. Vincent and the Grenadines. From St. Vincent and most Grenadines, you can direct dial to other countries; ask the hotel operator for the proper country code and the probable charge, surcharge, and government tax on the call. Local information is 118; international is 115.

When you dial a local number from your hotel in the Grenadines, you can drop the 45 prefix. Pay phones are best operated by the prepaid card available from stores and usable in several Caribbean islands.

Mail between St. Vincent and the United States takes two to three weeks. Airmail postcards cost 45¢; airmail letters cost 65¢ an ounce.

Federal Express is located on Bay Street in Kingstown (☎ 809/456–1649) and at Solana's Boutique in Bequia (☎ 809/458–3554).

Opening and Closing Times

Stores and shops in Kingstown are open weekdays 8–4. Many close for lunch from noon to 1 or so. Saturday hours are 8–noon. Banks are open weekdays 8–1, 2, or 3, Friday from 3 to 5. The branch of National Commercial Bank of St. Vincent at the airport is also open Saturday 7–5.

ST. VINCENT

Exploring St. Vincent

Numbers in the margin correspond to points of interest on the St. Vincent map.

Kingstown's shopping and business district, cathedrals, and sights can easily be seen in a half-day tour, with a further half day for the Botanical Gardens. Outlying areas and the Falls of Baleine will each require a full day of touring, while trips to La Soufrière and the Vermont Trail are major undertakings, requiring a very early start and a full day's strenuous hiking. City maps are in the "Discover SVG" booklet, available everywhere.

Kingstown

❶ The capital and port of St. Vincent, **Kingstown** is at the southeastern end of the island. It is very much a working city with no concessions made to tourists, or to cruise-line day-trippers. The **harbor** is far more likely to be hosting a freight liner than a passenger ship anyway, but what few gift boutiques there are can be found nearby, on and around Bay Street. Here you will also find the three-year-old **financial complex,** a cool and tall structure, of which the island is inordinately proud. Among its official duties, it houses the tourist office.

The most exciting thing to do in Kingstown is browse among the 2,000 varieties of breadfruitlike root vegetables and soursoplike fruits (only kidding) in **Kingstown Market.** There are outdoor and indoor sections, the latter featuring many homemade-lunch stalls around the periphery, and though the bustle is greatest on Saturdays before 11 AM, there is usually a seething and frenetic crowd. Take a look at the indoor **fish market,** too. This was a gift from the Japanese people, who also donated ecological deep-sea-fishing lessons, plus a sister market (under construction at press time) on Union Island.

Since there isn't much actually to buy, try the **Philatelic Bureau** on Lower Bay Street, or the **post office** on Granby Street east of Egmont. St. Vincent is known worldwide for its particularly beautiful and colorful issues, which commemorate flowers, undersea creatures, and architecture.

Follow Granby Street west past the Methodist Church to **St. George's Cathedral,** a yellow Anglican church built in the early 19th century. The dignified Georgian architecture includes simple wood pews, an ornate hanging candelabra, and stained-glass windows. The gravestones tell the history of the island.

Across the street is **St. Mary's Roman Catholic Cathedral,** built in 1823 and renovated in the 1930s. The renovations resulted in a strangely appealing blend of Moorish, Georgian, and Romanesque styles in black brick.

A few minutes away by taxi or bus is St. Vincent's famous **Botanical Gardens.** Founded in 1765, it is the oldest botanical garden in the Western Hemisphere. Captain Bligh—yes, that is the captain of the *Bounty*—

brought the first breadfruit tree to this island, a direct descendant of which you can see today in the gardens. St. Vincent parrots and green monkeys are housed in cages, and unusual trees and bushes cover the well-kept grounds. Local guides offer their services for $2–$4 an hour. *Information: c/o Minister of Agriculture, Kingstown,* ☎ *809/457–1003.* ⊙ *Weekdays 7–4, Sat. 7–11 AM, Sun. 7–6.*

The tiny **National Museum** just inside the entrance to the gardens houses a series of maps tracing the migrations of the Ciboney, the very first Vincentians, who arrived around 4000 BC, plus pre-Columbian Indian clay pottery found by Dr. Earle Kirby, St. Vincent's resident archaeologist and the museum's director. Dr. Kirby's historical knowledge is as entertaining as it is extensive, and a visit here is much enhanced by his annotations, since the labels in the museum offer little information. ☎ *809/456–1787.* ⊙ *Wed. 9:45–noon, Sat. 4–6.*

2 Flag a taxi for the 10-minute ride to **Fort Charlotte,** built in 1806 to keep Napoleon at bay. The fort sits 636 feet above sea level, with cannons and battlements perched on a dramatic promontory overlooking the city and the Grenadines to the south, Lowman's Beach and the calm east coast to the north. The fort saw little military action. Nowadays it is the island's women's prison. Next to it, and visible from the water, is the old leper's colony.

Outside Kingstown

The coastal roads of St. Vincent offer panoramic views and insights into the island way of life. Life in the tiny villages has changed little in centuries. This full-day driving tour includes Layou, Montreal Gardens, Mesopotamia Valley, and the windward coast. Be sure to drive on the left, and honk your horn before you enter the blind curves.

3 Beginning in Kingstown, take the Leeward Highway about 45 minutes north through hills and valleys to **Layou,** a small fishing village. Just north of the village are **petroglyphs** (rock carvings) left by the Caribs 13 centuries ago. If you're seriously interested in archaeological mysteries, you'll want to stop here. Phone the tourism board to arrange a visit with Victor Hendrickson, who owns the land. For E.C.$5, Hendrickson or his wife will meet you and escort you to the site.

4 Half an hour farther north is **Barrouallie** (pronounced *bar*-relly), a one-time whaling village whose inhabitants now trawl for blackfish.

TIME OUT Ten minutes north of Barrouallie is **Wallilabou** (wally-la-*boo*), a bay where you can stop for a picnic or simple lunch at the new yacht services building, sunbathe, and swim (there are no showers, but a small waterfall is a short, lovely stroll away).

5 Backtrack to Kingstown and continue toward Mesopotamia to the **Montreal Gardens,** another extensive collection of exotic flowers, trees, and spice plants. It's not as well maintained as the Botanical Gardens, but the aroma of cocoa powder and nutmeg wafting on the cool breeze is enticing. Spend an hour with well-informed guides or wander on your own along the narrow paths. Vincentian newlyweds often spend their honeymoon in the garden's tiny cottage, appropriately named Romance. ☎ *809/458–5452.* ☞ *Free.* ⊙ *Daily.*

6 Now drive southeast (roads and signs aren't the best, so ask directions at Montreal Gardens) to the **Mesopotamia region.** The rugged, ocean-lashed scenery along St. Vincent's windward coast is the perfect counterpoint to the lush, calm west coast. Mesopotamia is full of dense forests, streams, and bananas. The blue plastic bags on the trees protect the fruit from damage in high winds. Coconut, breadfruit, sweet corn, peanuts, and arrowroot grow in the rich soil here.

❼ Turn north on the Windward Highway up the jagged coast road toward Georgetown, St. Vincent's second largest city. You'll pass many small villages and the town of **Colonarie.** In the hills behind the town are hiking trails. Locals are helpful with directions, because signs are limited.

❽ Continue north to **Georgetown,** amid coconut groves and the long-defunct Mount Bentinck sugar factory. A few miles north is the **Rabacca Dry River,** a rocky gulch carved out by the lava flow from the 1902 eruption of La Soufrière. Here hikers begin the two-hour ascent to the volcano. Return south to Kingstown via the Windward Highway.

Fort Duvernette and the Falls of Baleine

❾ Drive back to Villa Beach, south of Kingstown, in time to catch the sunset at **Fort Duvernette,** the tiny island that juts up like a loaf of pumpernickel bread behind Young Island Resort. Take the *African Queen*–style ferry for a few dollars from the dock at Villa Beach near Kingstown (call the boatman from the phone on the dock), and set a time for your return (60–90 minutes is plenty for exploring). When you arrive at the island, climb the 100 or more steps carved into the mountain. Views from the 195-foot summit are terrific, but enter the little overgrown house at your peril—you may encounter (harmless) bats. Rusting cannons from the early 1800s are still here, aimed not at seagoing invaders but at the marauding Caribs.

❿ Impossible to get to by car, the **Falls of Baleine** are an absolute must to see on an escorted all-day boat trip or by chartered boat from Villa Beach or the Lagoon Marina (*see* Sports and the Outdoors, *below*). The ride offers scenic island views. When you arrive, be prepared to climb from the boat into shallow water to get to the beach. Local guides help visitors make the easy five-minute sneakers-and-swimsuit trek to the falls. Swim in the freshwater pool, climb under the 63-foot falls (they're chilly), and relax in this bit of utterly untouched Eden.

Beaches

Most of the hotels and white-sand beaches are near Kingstown; black-sand beaches ring the rest of the island. The placid west coast includes the island's main beach (although it's hardly big enough to merit such a title), the white sand **Villa,** with the adjacent, slightly rocky **Indian Bay.** Farther up the westward (leeward) coast are the black-sand **Questelle's** (pronounced keet-*ells*) **Bay,** next to the Camden Park Industrial Site, and tiny **Buccament Bay,** which is good for swimming. The beaches at Villa and the CSY Yacht Club are small but safe, with dive shops nearby. The exposed Atlantic coast is dramatic, but the water is rough and unpredictable. No beach has lifeguards, so even experienced swimmers are taking a risk. The windward side of the island has no beachfront facilities.

Sports and the Outdoors

Hiking

Dorsetshire Hill, about 3 miles from Kingstown, rewards you with a sweeping view of city and harbor; picturesque Queen's Drive is nearby. Mount St. Andrew, on the outskirts of the city, is a pleasant climb through a rain forest on a well-marked trail. Buccament Valley contains two well-marked trails, including the Vermont Trail, where you may be lucky enough to see the rare St. Vincent parrot, *Amazona guidingii*, for which a 5 AM start is recommended.

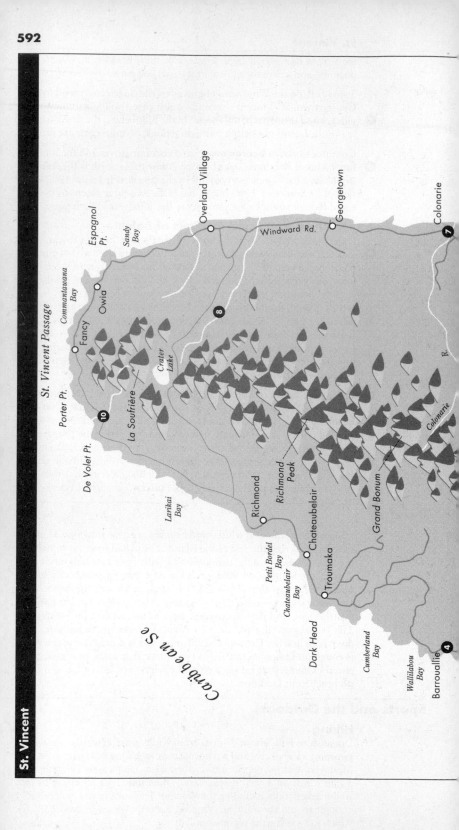

St. Vincent Passage

Caribbean Sea

Porter Pt.
Commantawana Bay
Espagnol Pt.
Sandy Bay
Overland Village
Windward Rd.
Georgetown
Colonarie

Fancy
Owia

De Volet Pt.

La Soufrière
Crater Lake

Larikai Bay

Richmond
Richmond Peak

Petit Bordel Bay
Chateaubelair Bay

Chateaubelair
Troumaka

Dark Head

Grand Bonum

Colonarie

Cumberland Bay

Wallilabou Bay
Barrouallie

7
8
10
4

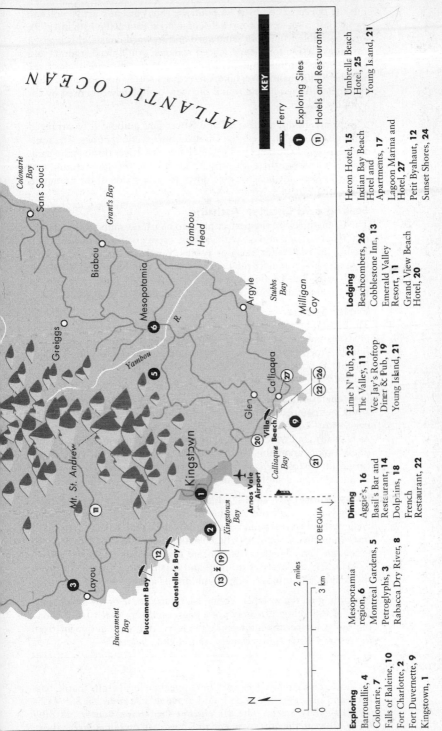

But the queen of climbs is La Soufrière, St. Vincent's active volcano (which last erupted, appropriately enough, on Friday the 13th in 1979). Approachable from both windward and leeward coasts, this is *not* a casual excursion for inexperienced walkers; you'll need stamina and sturdy shoes for this climb of just over 4,000 feet. Be sure to check the weather before you leave; hikers have been sorely disappointed when they reached the top and found the view completely obscured by enveloping clouds.

Climbs are all-day affairs; a Land Rover and guide can be arranged through your hotel, or *see* the Guided Tours section, *above*. The four-wheel-drive vehicle takes you past Rabacca Dry River through the Bamboo Forest. From there it's a two-hour hike to the summit, and you can arrange in advance to come down the other side of the mountain to the Chateaubelair area.

Sailing and Charter Yachting

The Grenadines are the perfect place to charter a sailboat or catamaran (bareboat or complete with captain, crew, and cook) to weave you around the islands for a day or a week. Boats of all sizes and degrees of luxury are available; the Lagoon Marina and Hotel (☎ 809/458–4308) in the Blue Lagoon area of St. Vincent has 44-foot crewed sloops from $200 per day. Hotels can also recommend charter yachts.

Water Sports

The constant trade winds are perfect for windsurfing, and 80-foot visibility on numerous reefs means superior diving. Many experienced divers find St. Vincent and Bequia far less crowded and nearly as rich in marine life as Bonaire and the Caymans; snorkeling in the Tobago Cays is among the world's best.

Dive operations are small and often less luxurious than on other islands, but competent and professional. Many offer three-hour beginner "resort" courses, full certification courses and excursions to nearby reefs, walls, and wrecks. Dive shops are on St. Vincent, Bequia, Mustique, Union, and Palm islands; individual island listings have full information. Most dive shops and larger hotels also rent Sunfish, Windsurfers, and snorkel gear.

Dive St. Vincent (☎ 809/457–4714), on Villa Beach, just across from Young Island, is where NAUI instructor Bill Tewes and his staff offer beginner and certification courses and trips to the Falls of Baleine. A single-tank dive is about $50. Based at the Lagoon Marina Hotel, NAUI instructor Perry Hughes's **St. Vincent Dive Experience** (☎ 809/456–9741) offers all levels of training and certification, plus night dives, snorkeling, and tours. A single-tank dive is about $40.

Depending on the weather, Young Island has some of the area's most colorful snorkeling. If you're not a guest on this private island, phone the resort for permission to take the ferry and rent equipment from the resort's water-sports center (*see* Lodging, *below*).

Shopping

St. Vincent isn't a duty-free port, but appealing local crafts (batik, baskets) and resort wear can be found at **Noah's Arkade** (☎ 809/457–1513) on Bay Street. The **St. Vincent Craftsmen Center** (☎ 809/457–1288), in the northwest end of Kingstown on James Street above Granby Street, sells grass floor mats and other woven items. Swiss watches, crystal, china, and jewelry can be found at **Stecher's** (☎ 809/

457–1142) on Bay Street in the Cobblestone Arcade (a branch is at the airport).

Dining

West Indian food is the way to go in St. Vincent. You'll enjoy interesting local fare that is reasonably priced at all but the expensive hotels. Dishes include callaloo soup, made from the spinachlike vegetable, dasheen; goat stew; *rotis* (burritos filled with curried potatoes and meat or conch); seasonal seafood, including lobster, kingfish, snapper, and dolphin ("not Flipper," as everyone assures you, but dolphin*fish*); local vegetables such as christophines, breadfruit, and eddoes; and exotic fruit ranging from sugar apples and soursop to pineapple and papaya. Fried chicken and burgers are available everywhere, but look for the "imported beef" note on the menu; local beef is not aged, so it tends to be extremely chewy. The local lager, Hairoun, is brewed at Camden Park on the leeward coast, according to a German recipe.

What to Wear

Restaurants on St. Vincent are, for the most part, very casual. In Kingston, the closest thing on the island to a big city, you may want to dress a little more formally—maybe put on a pair of khakis—but none of the places listed below require a jacket or tie. On the Grenadines ultracasual is fine everywhere.

CATEGORY	COST*
$$$	over $20
$$	$10–$20
$	under $10

per person, excluding drinks and 5% sales tax

$$$ **Basil's Bar and Restaurant.** This air conditioned restaurant, downstairs in the Cobblestone Inn, is owned by the infamous Basil of Mustique but has little else in common with that laid-back Grenadine glitterati hangout. This is the Kingstown power-lunch venue, serving a daily buffet of local fish dishes, plus the likes of seafood pasta and chicken in fresh ginger and coconut milk, to local businessmen and yachties for about $12 an entrée. The bar can get lively in the evenings, when dinner tables are candlelit; and there's a Chinese buffet on Fridays. ✕ *Bay St., Kingstown,* ☎ *809/457–2713. Reservations advised. AE, MC, V.*

$$$ **French Restaurant.** Referred to as "the French," this Caribbean insti-
★ tution on Villa Beach is where everyone goes when they're feeling posh, especially when in a lobster mood, since there is a state-of-the-art lobster pool on the terrace facing Young Island, from which you can observe the staff of somewhat unfriendly local girls fish for your supper. As befits a place run by a couple from Orléans, most dishes are the gallic version of local cuisine. Stuffed crab back, for instance, comes in a shell of pastry, not crab; steak—*au poivre,* with garlic butter, or béarnaise—is imported; onion soup and lemon tart are *comme il faut;* and bread is warm, fresh, real baguette. The inside bar, complete with eccentric, giggling barman, serves frothy cocktails and Martinique-style tea punch to yacht people who hang out here in the winter season. ✕ *Villa Beach,* ☎ *809/458–4972. Dinner reservations advised. AE, V.*

$$$ **The Valley.** It's a long drive to dinner, but this pretty, green-floored terrace hung with fishing nets is part of the Emerald Valley Resort, which includes the only casino in the Grenadines, and if it's Saturday (also some Fridays), a local band serenades diners, too. The pride of the kitchen is river lobster, retrieved from the Vermont River, which runs through here; other dishes are a local–international mix: tomato, mozzarella, and basil salad; baked red snapper with coconut stuffing; broiled

poussin (young chicken) with local herbs. Get directions if you're driving, and call first—the restaurant has an unpredictable tendency to be closed. ✗ *Penniston Valley,* ☎ *809/456–7140. Reservations advised. AE, MC, V.*

$$$ Young Island. Five course chef's-choice dinners of seafood, roast pig, beef, and chicken tend to be heavy and old-fashioned, but fare is lighter at the Lucullan Tuesday buffets and at the Saturday barbecues, when a steel band plays. Lunch is served buffet- or barbecue-style on the beach daily and features fish and seafood, fresh fruits, salads, and cold cuts, with an assortment of fresh breads. Pink-clothed tables are secreted individually in palm-thatched huts dotted around the beach, with more in the stone-floored terrace dining room; they're romantically candlelit at night. You must make reservations, unless you are a hotel guest. ✗ *Young Island,* ☎ *809/458–4826. Reservations required. AE, MC, V.*

$–$$ Dolphins. Sandwiched between the Lime N' Pub and the French, and
★ fast becoming the island's gossip center, is this welcome addition to the Villa scene. The well-traveled, Scottish-born father-and-son owners insist on fresh local ingredients for everything on the Dolphins menu, and from the kingfish, snapper, lobster, conch, and shrimp to the dressing on the chef's salad, nothing is bottled, canned, or artificial. Sit on the large covered terrace or take up residence in the bar, with its separate menu, old-fashioned Naugahyde booths, and barkeep who mixes a mean punch. Local musicians play (Friday and Saturday), and the work of local artists, including former classical violinist owner Austin Patterson, decks the walls. Dolphins is also the pioneer of St. Vincent home delivery, so note the number if you're staying nearby. ✗ *Villa Beach,* ☎ *809/457–4337. MC, V.*

$–$$ Lime N' Pub. Although this sprawling, waterfront, indoor-outdoor restaurant and bar is named after the *pursuit* of liming, its decor happens to feature a great deal of virulent green, which could prove painful after several cocktails. An eclectic menu caters to burger and pizza eaters as well as seafood fans and even provides for hybrid diners if they're brave enough to order the smoked sailfish pizza. Good rotis and coconut shrimp go down well with Hairoun. Shop before dinner at the swimwear-and-batik boutique, or stay late and dance on weekends, when the place resembles a singles bar. ✗ *Opposite Young Island,* ☎ *809/458–4227. AE.*

$–$$ Vee Jay's Rooftop Diner & Pub. This local dive above Roger's Photo Studios (have your pix developed while you eat), nearly opposite the Cobblestone Hotel, offers downtown Kingstown's best port view from beneath its green corrugated plastic roof. Among "authentic Vincie cuisine" specials chalked on the blackboard are mutton or fish stew; chicken, vegetable, or liver rotis; or not remotely Vincie sandwiches and burgers, which can be authentically washed down with mauby (a bittersweet drink made from tree bark—an acquired taste), linseed, peanut punch, sorrel cordials, or a cocktail. Lunch is buffet-style. ✗ *Upper Bay St., Kingstown,* ☎ *809/457–2845. Reservations required for dinner. AE, MC, V. Closed Sun.*

$ Aggie's. Up on the second floor opposite the Sardine Bakery on Grenville, the Kingstown shopping street, is this casual bar and restaurant, with a swimming-pool-blue ceiling and trellised arches. It serves local seafood dishes, like conch souse and kingfish steak, various soups, including callaloo and pumpkin, rotis, and salads, right up to midnight. There's a Friday happy hour from 4 to 6. ✗ *Grenville St., Kingstown,* ☎ *809/456–2110. No credit cards.*

Lodging

Luxury resorts require booking about six months in advance, but most St. Vincent hotels can squeeze you in with far less notice. There's a bit of a lull in January, between Christmas week and the February rush, when rooms are sometimes available on a day's notice. Many hotels offer MAP (Modified American Plan, with breakfast and dinner included).

CATEGORY	COST*
$$$$	over $200
$$$	$130–$200
$$	$80–$130
$	under $80

All prices are for a standard double room for two, excluding 5% tax and 10% service charge.

Young Island

$$$$ **Young Island.** A mere 200 yards from Villa beach lies a 25-acre island
★ populated by prosperous couples who dream of being shipwrecked on a tropical island but don't want to get their feet wet. You arrive by ferry, are handed a rum punch crowned with a hibiscus blossom, and are conducted to one of 29 houselets. Each has its own patio; fridge; king-size bed; rattan, palm-weave, and cane decor; and a bathroom that opens into an open-air, but private, shower; as well as a new plunge pool, if you're in number 6 or 10. Keys are optional, but you have a wall safe; phones are nonexistent, but messages are brought promptly; and there's dual voltage. "Superior" accommodations are lower down, among the tumbling masses of flamboyant, nutmeg, almond, mango, ferns, coffee, breadfruit, etc., etc., while the more expensive deluxe and luxury cottages, with sitting area, are high over the sea; all are exactly halfway between the Swiss Family Robinson's tree house and the Ritz. The landscape conceals a lagoon pool, shaded hammocks, beach (it's tiny, but white-sand) loungers, tennis court, bar, swim-up Coconut Bar, restaurant, plus various bird families. Watch hummingbirds over a Creole French toast breakfast (made with banana bread) on your terrace, and you may feel like you've taken a five-minute boat to heaven. ☎ *Box 211, Young Island,* ☎ *809/458–4826,* FAX *809/457–4567. U.S. agent: Ralph Locke Islands, Box 800, Waccabuc, NY 10597,* ☎ *914/763–5526 or 800/223–1108. 29 rooms. Scuba diving, saltwater pool, water-sports center, lighted tennis court, yacht charters. AE, D, MC, V. MAP, AP.*

Emerald Valley

$ **Emerald Valley Resort.** The rural, rain-forested Penniston Valley, half an hour by road from Kingstown, is the unlikely setting for the Grenadines' only casino, which is, equally improbably, attached to this newly renovated family-friendly 5-acre resort. Two pairs of Brits toiled for two years to bring a run-down property up to very high standards, installing air-conditioning, fans, satellite TV, VCRs and phones, locally made wood-frame king-size or twin beds, stone-floored terraces, and (stoveless) kitchenettes in the 12 chalets. In the garden grounds are an outdoor bar, a two-level pool bisected by a wooden bridge and diving platform, a stage for local bands on weekends, a tennis court (pro lessons available), a nine-hole golf course (make sure this is finished before you book), and the pretty Valley restaurant (*see* Dining, *above*). What you don't get, of course, is a beach, and the nearest groceries are in Kingstown, but the Vermont Nature Trail is 2½ miles away, and you can gamble till the small hours if bored. ☎ *Penniston Valley, Box 1081, St. Vincent,* ☎ *809/456–7140,* FAX *809/456–7145. 12 chalets. Restau-*

rant, casino with bar, 2 bars, 2 tennis courts, grass volleyball court, croquet, pool. AE, MC, V. EP.

Villa Beach

$$$ **Grand View Beach Hotel.** The Sardine family's turn-of-the-century cot-
★ ton plantation great house is now Tony and Heather Sardine's beau-
tiful hotel, perched on a lookout point just east of Indian Bay. It
manages to have both great facilities and down-home charm. Eight acres
of landscaped grounds include not only the expected swimming pool
(with swim-up bar) but also a fitness center and sauna, a tennis court,
plus one of the island's few squash courts. Most of the simple white-
walled rooms with hardwood floors enjoy the sweeping vista toward
the Grenadines, and all have air-conditioning or fan, direct-dial phones,
and satellite TV. A "Luxury Level" was added recently, with big ocean-
facing terraces and a pair of honeymoon suites with king-size beds and
whirlpool tubs. ✉ *Box 173, Villa Point, St. Vincent,* ☎ *809/458–4811,*
FAX *809/457–4174. U.S. agent: Charms Caribbean Vacations,* ☎ *800/
223–6510. 17 rooms. Restaurant, tennis and squash courts, fitness cen-
ter, sauna, massage, pool, reading room, water-sports center nearby.
AE, MC, V. CP, MAP.*

$$–$$$ **Sunset Shores.** This U-shape, lemon-colored low rise is the nearest thing
on St. Vincent to a corporate hotel, which is not very near at all.
There's a Caribbean news update board in the lobby, conference fa-
cilities for 100, and the Lions—the local Rotary Club—tend to hold
their roisterous meetings here, attended by half the island and its fam-
ily, but other than that, you won't be bothered by men in suits. All rooms
overlook the large-enough pool in the center of the U, which faces the
sea at Indian Bay. Basic rooms have air-conditioning and phones; su-
perior ones have patios, carpets, and TVs, too, and really are superior
to the rest. The poolside Sunrunner Bar is nicely placed opposite the
sunset. ✉ *Box 849, Villa Beach, St. Vincent,* ☎ *809/458–4411,* FAX
*809/457–4800. 31 air-conditioned rooms. Restaurant, 2 bars, conference
facilities, table tennis, pool, water-sports center nearby. AE, D, MC,
V. EP, MAP.*

$ **Beachcombers.** At Villa, next to Sunset Shores, Flora and Richard
★ Gunn have built a tiny and darling village on their sloping lawns, with
a pair of chalet buildings containing the guest rooms, an open-terraced
bar-restaurant, and the reception area, which includes a shop and a li-
brary. You could eat breakfast (included) off the floor of any bedroom
here, such is the standard of housekeeping, though some rooms are pret-
tier than others. Numbers 1–3 are prime, since they face the sea, and
1, in top-to-toe dark-wood paneling, has a baby kitchen, too, for $5
extra; 4–6 are in back of these, with no view to speak of. The other
building, containing rooms 7–12, faces the "Bridal Bridge" (they do
weddings) and the garden's frenzy of flowers and has a communal red-
tile terrace in front. There's air-conditioning in Numbers 2, 5, and 7,
ceiling fans elsewhere. Bathrooms lack tubs, and rooms lack phones
or soft lighting, but these are insignificant privations when the welcome
is this warm and the rates this low. Room 11 is not usually bookable,
because Flora uses it for her other career—as beauty and massage ther-
apist. Yes, this is the only Vincentian B&B featuring top-class aro-
matherapy, reflexology, and facials. ✉ *Box 126, Villa Beach, St Vincent,*
☎ *809/458–4283. 12 rooms. Restaurant, bar, beauty treatments,
shop. AE, MC, V. BP.*

$ **Indian Bay Beach Hotel and Apartments.** This pretty, whitewashed, two-
story building sits on Indian Bay, with its small, sheltered, somewhat
rocky white-sand beach, which is good for snorkelers. The simple
apartments have either one or two bedrooms, air-conditioning, and kitch-

enettes; the best overlook the bay, with use of a large terrace on top of the restaurant, A La Mer—an airy space with white-trellised arches and a sapphire-blue awning. Both baby-sitting and lower weekly rates are available, making this spot useful for families. ⚄ *Box 538, Kingstown, St. Vincent,* ☎ *809/458–4001,* FAX *809/457–4777. 12 apartments. Restaurant, bar, beach, water sports nearby. AE, MC, V. EP, CP, MAP.*

$ **Umbrella Beach Hotel.** If you're prepared to sacrifice gorgeous bedroom decor for the sake of your pocketbook but still want to be well located, this very simple cluster of small apartment rooms may fit the bill. All are clean and equipped with ceiling fan, phone, kitchenette with fridge and Calor gas stove, and shower-only bathroom, but, make no mistake, they're dark and plain, with white walls, red marble-chip floors with a rush mat, and plastic chairs at a small Formica table. Steps away are Villa Beach, across from Young Island (ask permission to take the ferry over), the Lime N' Pub, and the French, where you could spend the cash you saved on the room. ⚄ *Villa Beach, St. Vincent,* ☎ *809/ 458–4651,* FAX *809/457–4930. 9 rooms. Beach and water sports nearby. MC, V. EP.*

Petit Byahaut

$$$ **Petit Byahaut.** Sort of a Young Island for those with Swiss Family Robinson fantasies who *do* want to get their feet wet, this 50-acre valley resort accommodates its guests in tents, albeit permanent, wood-floored, 10-by-13-foot tents, complete with private deck, queen-size beds, and solar-heated showers. This adults' camp is accessible only by boat, which collects you from Kingstown (rates include this, as well as all meals), and there is a selection of other boats to play with once you're settled in, along with scuba and snorkeling equipment. In the grounds are a big, black-sand beach, hammocks, and some interesting Carib Indian finds. There's a boutique, excursions are easily arranged, and that's about the extent of the facilities, but then, you don't stay here unless you're reasonably adventuresome and interested in seclusion. ⚄ *Petit Byahaut Bay, St. Vincent,* ☎ *and fax 809/457–7008. 6 tents. Restaurant, bar, beach, gardens, solar-heated showers, water sports, ferry service. MC, V. FAP.*

Blue Lagoon

$$ **Lagoon Marina and Hotel.** The only hotel overlooking sheltered Blue
★ Lagoon Bay may well be the friendliest hotel on the island. Thanks to its full-service yacht marina, complete with the best-equipped marine shop in St. Vincent, there are usually seafaring types liming in the terrace bar, and plenty of yacht traffic to watch from your big, comfortable balcony with its two couches. Sliding patio doors lead onto these from the high wood-ceilinged, carpeted rooms; you can practically dive into the sea from numbers 1–9, which hang over the wooden quay and face the sunset; 10–20 overlook the narrow, curved black-sand beach. Basic wooden furniture, twin beds, rather dim lighting, phones, tiled bathrooms, and ceiling fans provide an adequate level of comfort; about half the rooms have air-conditioning (for a few dollars extra), but don't expect luxury. Sloping garden grounds contain a secluded two-level pool and the St. Vincent Dive Experience Headquarters, and there's a pretty, candlelit terrace restaurant. ⚄ *Box 133, Blue Lagoon, St. Vincent,* ☎ *809/458–4308,* FAX *809/457–4716. U.S. agent: Charms Caribbean Vacations,* ☎ *800/742–4276. 19 rooms. Restaurant, bar, yacht marina, yacht charter, beach, pool, conference room, scuba, and water sports. AE, V. EP.*

Kingstown

$ **Cobblestone Inn.** Downtown in the city, as Vincentians call Kingstown, this 1814 stone-built onetime sugar warehouse has a delightful, sunny interior courtyard and arched passageways, which most rooms lead from, and a popular rooftop bar-restaurant for breakfast and soup-salad-burger lunches (come dinnertime, Basil's is downstairs). All the rooms have air-conditioning, phones, small, sparkling bathrooms, exposed stone walls painted white, and rattan furniture. Number 5 at the front is lighter and bigger than most of the other rooms but noisier, too, and many are rather dark, with a faint, not unpleasant, smell of dungeon emanating from the stones. Next to Basil's downstairs is an array of shops selling local craftwork and fashions. The staff is lackadaisical but efficient enough. ⌧ *Box 867, Kingstown, St. Vincent,* ☎ *809/456–1937. 19 rooms. Restaurant, bar. AE, D, MC, V. CP.*

$ **Heron Hotel.** Steps away from the Grenadines wharf, on the second floor above a Georgian plantation warehouse that now contains shops but once provided lodgings for the plantation bosses, the Heron now caters mostly to stopover island-hoppers. It has managed to retain an old-fashioned atmosphere, maybe due to the grouchy manager, or the radio tuned faintly to a religious station, or the rooms themselves, which are straight out of a '50s boardinghouse, with thin, wine red or navy carpets; billowing faded floral drapes; single beds; bentwood chairs; and tiny cream-color bathrooms. Rooms have air-conditioning and phones and fan out from a palm-filled central courtyard, with tables set on a veranda for breakfast (light lunches, drinks, and West Indian dinners are also available). There's also a corner TV lounge with rows of wooden armchairs, black floorboards, and two giant ficus plants. ⌧ *Box 226, Kingstown, St. Vincent,* ☎ *809/457–1631,* ⨳ *809/457–1189. 12 rooms. Dining room, courtyard, lounge. MC, V. CP.*

Nightlife

Don't look for fire-eaters and limbo demonstrations on St. Vincent. Nightlife here consists mostly of hotel barbecue buffets and jump-ups, so called because the lively steel-band music makes listeners jump up and dance.

The Attic (1 Melville St., above Kentucky Fried Chicken, ☎ 809/457–2558), a jazz club with modern decor, features international artists and steel bands. There is a small cover charge; call ahead for hours and performers.

Young Island (☎ 809/458–4826) hosts sunset cocktail parties with hors d'oeuvres once a week on Fort Duvernette, the tiny island behind the resort. On that night, 100 steps up the hill are lit by flaming torches, and a string band plays. Reservations are necessary for nonguests.

The **Emerald Valley Casino** (☎ 809/456–7140) has the homey atmosphere of an English pub but offers bar, food, and all the gaming of Vegas—three roulette tables (the only single-zero ones in the Caribbean), three blackjack, one Caribbean stud poker, one craps, five video slots, three slots—and is open daily except Tuesday 9 PM–3 AM, until 4 AM on Saturday.

THE GRENADINES

The Grenadines are wonderful islands to visit for fine diving and snorkeling opportunities, good beaches, and unlimited chances to laze on the beach with a picnic, waiting for the sun to set so you can go to dinner. Travelers seeking privacy, peace and quiet, or active water sports and informal socializing will be happy on a Grenadine, though which one may take some trial and error—these islands are by no means interchangeable.

Bequia

Arriving and Departing

BY PLANE

Mustique Airways (☎ 809/458–4380 or 809/458–4818) flies into Bequia's airport daily from Barbados. **LIAT** (☎ 809/458–4841 or 800/ 253–5011) usually offers day-trip airfare to any three Grenadines and back to St. Vincent for around $170.

BY FERRY

The MV *Admiral I* and the MV *Admiral II* motor ferries leave Kingstown for Bequia Monday through Friday at 9 AM, 10:30 AM, 4:30 PM, and, depending on availability, 7 PM. Saturday departures are at 12:30 PM and 7 PM; Sunday, 9 AM and 7 PM. Schedules are subject to change, so be sure to check times upon your arrival. All scheduled ferries leave from the main dock in Kingstown. The trip takes 60 minutes and costs $4.

The MV *Snapper* mail boat travels south on Saturdays, Mondays, and Thursdays at about 10:30 AM, stopping at Bequia, Canouan, Mayreau, and Union, and returns north on Tuesdays and Fridays, departing Bequia at 11 AM. The cost is about $4.

Weekday service between St. Vincent and Bequia is also available on the island schooner *Friendship Rose,* which leaves St. Vincent at about 12:30 PM. The *Discover St. Vincent and the Grenadines* booklet, available in hotels and at the airport, has complete interisland schedules.

Important Addresses

Tourist Information: The **Bequia Tourism Board** (☎ 809/458–3286) is located on the main dock.

EMERGENCIES

Police: ☎ 809/456–1955. **Medical emergencies:** ☎ 999. **Hospital: Bequia Hospital** (☎ 809/458–3294).

Guided Tours

To see the views, villages, and boat-building around the island, hire a taxi (Gideon, ☎ 809/458–3760, is recommended) and negotiate the fare in advance. Water taxis, available from any dock, will also take you by Moonhole, a private community of stone homes with glassless windows, some decorated with bleached whale bones. The fare is about $11.

For those who prefer sailboats to motorboats, Arne Hansen and his catamaran *Toien* can be booked through the **Frangipani Hotel** (☎ 809/ 458–3255). Day sails to Mustique run $35–$40 per person, including drinks. An overnight snorkel-sail trip to the Tobago Cays costs about $150 for two people, including breakfast and drinks.

Beaches

A half-hour walk from the Plantation House Hotel will lead you over rocky bluffs to **Princess Margaret Beach,** which is quiet and wide, with a natural stone arch at one end. Though it has no facilities, this is a popular spot for swimming, snorkeling, or simply relaxing under palms and sea-grape trees. Snorkeling and swimming are also excellent at **Lower Bay,** a wide, palm-fringed beach that can be reached by taxi or by hiking beyond Princess Margaret Beach; wear sneakers, not flip-flops. Facilities for windsurfing and snorkeling are here, as well as the **De Reef** restaurant.

Friendship Bay can be reached by land taxi and is well equipped with windsurfing and snorkeling rentals and an outdoor bar.

Hope Beach, on the rougher Atlantic side, is accessible by a long taxi ride (about E.C.$20—every driver knows how to get there) and a mile-long walk downhill on a semipaved path. Your reward is a magnificent beach and total seclusion, and—if you prefer—nude bathing. Be sure to ask your taxi driver to return at a prearranged time. Bring your own lunch and drinks; there are no facilities. Swimming can be dangerous.

Industry Bay boasts towering palm groves, a nearly secluded beach, and a memorable view of several uninhabited islands. The tiny, three-room Crescent Bay Lodge is here; its huge bar offers drinks and late lunches (☎ 809/458–3400).

Sports and the Outdoors

WATER SPORTS
Of Bequia's two dozen dive sites, the best are Devil's Table, a shallow dive rich in fish and coral; a sailboat wreck nearby at 90 feet; the 90-foot drop at the Wall, off West Cay; the Bullet, off Bequia's north point for rays, barracuda, and the occasional nurse shark; the Boulders for soft corals, tunnel-forming rocks, thousands of fish; and Moonhole, shallow enough in places for snorkelers to enjoy.

Dive Bequia (☎ 809/458–3504, 🖷 809/458–3886) and **Sunsports** (☎ 809/458–3577, 🖷 809/457–3031) offer one- and two-tank dives, night dives, and certified instruction, plus snorkel excursions and equipment rental.

For snorkeling on your own, take a water taxi to the bay at Moonhole and arrange a pickup time.

Shopping
All Bequia's shops are along the beach and are open weekdays 10:30–5 or 6, Saturdays 10:30–noon.

BEST BUYS
Handmade model boats (you can special-order a replica of your own yacht) are at **Mauvin's** (¼ mile down the road to the left of the main dock, no ☎). Along Admiralty Bay, hand-printed and batik fabric, clothing, and household items are sold at the **Crab Hole** (☎ 809/458–3290). You can watch the fabrics being made in the workshop out back. **Solana's** (☎ 809/458–3554) offers attractive beachwear, saronglike pareus, and handy plastic beach shoes. The **Bequia Bookshop** (☎ 809/458–3905) has an exhaustive selection of Caribbean literature, plus cruising guides and charts, beach novels, souvenir maps, and exquisite hand-carved and -etched whalebone penknives. **Local Color** (☎ 809/458–3202), above the Porthole restaurant in town, has an excellent and unusual selection of handmade jewelry, wood carvings, and resort clothing. Next door is **Melinda's By Hand** (☎ 809/458–3409), with hand-painted cotton and silk clothing and accessories.

Dining
Dining on Bequia ranges from West Indian to gourmet cuisine, and it's consistently good. Barbecues at Bequia's hotels mean spicy West Indian seafood, chicken, or beef (although it is usually tougher than Hulk Hogan), plus a buffet of spicy side dishes and sweet desserts. Restaurants are occasionally closed on Sundays; phone to check.

For price information on restaurants and hotels, *see* the price charts in the Dining and Lodging sections of St. Vincent, *above.*

$$$ **Le Petit Jardin.** The chef at this chalet-style restaurant prepares gourmet
★   lobster and fish with West Indian ingredients, and according to French recipes. If you're missing your prime rib, the house specialty is steak imported from the United States, which you can wash down with a bottle from the longer-than-average wine list. ✕ *Port Elizabeth,* ☎ *809/ 458–3318. Reservations required. No credit cards.*

$$$ **The Old Fort.** Otmar and Sonja Schaedle restored this mid-1700s building overlooking the Atlantic to its bougainvillea-shaded, stone-arched, candlelit beauty and continue to serve food good enough to attract non-hotel guests up the newly paved road. Try a tuna steak, trendily *au point,* accompanied by fresh, homemade bread and a curry of pigeon peas, or char-grilled whole snapper. ✕ *Old Fort Hotel, Mt. Pleasant,* ☎ *809/458–3440. Reservations required MC, V.*

$$$ **Plantation House.** He arrived too late for this year's reviewer, but this refurbished fancy hotel now has a fancy chef to match, who earned the ultimate French accolade of a Michelin star in a previous job. No menu details were available at press time, but this looks well worth your attention. ✕ *Plantation House Hotel, Admirality Bay,* ☎ *809/458– 3425. Reservations advised. AE, MC, V.*

$–$$$ **De Reef.** This duo of a restaurant and a café on Lower Bay is the essential feeding station for long, lazy beach days, with the restaurant taking over when the café closes at dusk, as long as you've made reservations. For lunch or dinner, conch, lobster, whelks, and shrimp are treated the West Indian way, and the mutton curry is famous. For breakfast (from 7 AM), or light lunch, the café bakes its own breads, croissants, coconut cake, and cookies and blends fresh juices to accompany them. ✕ *Lower Bay,* ☎ *809/458–3484. Reservations required for dinner. No credit cards.*

$$ **La Mezzaluna.** This is an incongruously traditional Italian trattoria, owned by its Roman chef and useful for city dwellers with pasta withdrawal symptoms. Here, ravioli is more likely to be stuffed with local lobster than spinach and ricotta, but eggplant parmigiana, beef carpaccio, and grissini they have got. ✕ *Above Port Elizabeth,* ☎ *809/457– 3080. Reservations advised. No credit cards. Closed Tues.*

$–$$ **Dawn's Creole Garden.** The walk up the hill is worth it for the delicious West Indian lunches and dinners, especially the Saturday-night barbecue buffet and the major five-course, two-entrée dinners, including the fresh christophine and breadfruit accompaniments that Dawn's is known for. There's a wonderful view and live guitar entertainment most Saturday nights. ✕ *At the far end of Lower Bay beach,* ☎ *809/458–3154. Dinner reservations required. No credit cards.*

$–$$ **Mac's Pizzeria.** The island's best lunches and casual dinners are enjoyed
★   amid fuchsia bougainvillea on the covered outdoor terrace overlooking the harbor. Choose from mouthwatering lobster pizza, quiche, pita sandwiches, lasagna, home-baked cookies, and muffins. ✕ *On the beach, Port Elizabeth,* ☎ *809/458–3474. Dinner reservations required. No credit cards.*

$–$$ **Theresa's Restaurant.** On Monday nights, Theresa and John Bennett
★   offer a rotating selection of enormous and tasty Greek, Indian, Mexican, or Italian buffets. West Indian dishes are served at lunch and dinner the rest of the week. ✕ *At the far end of Lower Bay beach,* ☎ *809/ 458–3802. Dinner reservations required. No credit cards.*

Lodging

$$$$ **Plantation House Hotel.** You can't help but pass by the pale peach Plan-
★ tation House when strolling to Princess Margaret or Lower Bay. Set
in 10 grassy acres of manicured gardens, dotted with palms, hammocks,
loungers, and a raised pool, the five-room main house is appended by
17 cabanas, plus a brand-new hillside house with 10 further rooms.
Since the current Dutch/Austrian husband-and-wife managers took over
in 1994, just about everything has been redone and made gorgeous,
with a new Carib-luxe, rattan and wicker decor, air-conditioning,
phones, minibars, and TVs in all rooms and also in the cabanas (which
had been needing an overhaul). The bar, also refashioned, promises to
be *the* Bequia social center now, prompted by the new chef's presence
(*see* Dining, *above*). ⊠ *Box 16, Admiralty Bay, Bequia, St. Vincent,*
☎ *809/458–3425,* ℻ *809/458–3612. U.S. agent: E & M Assoc., 211
E. 43 St., NY 10017,* ☎ *800/223–9832. 15 rooms, 18 cottages. Restaurant, bar, water sports, scuba diving, tennis, boutique, pool. AE, MC,
V. MAP.*

$$$ **Spring on Bequia.** Spring is nestled in green hills overlooking groves
of tall palms and grazing goats. It's about a mile above town (a pretty
walk, though you may want to take a taxi back uphill), and the near-
est beach, lovely but too shallow and occasionally seaweedy for seri-
ous swimming, is a 10-minute stroll away. The large wood-and-stone
rooms attract upscale travelers who want serenity and seclusion. The
airy veranda bar is the site of manager Candy Leslie's deservedly fa-
mous Sunday curry lunch (reservations necessary). ⊠ *Bequia, St. Vin-
cent,* ☎ *809/458–3414. U.S. agent: Spring on Bequia, Box 19251,
Minneapolis, MN 55419,* ☎ *612/823–1202. 10 rooms. Restaurant,
bar, pool, tennis. AE, D, MC, V. EP.*

$$–$$$ **Friendship Bay Hotel.** This sprawling white house on a hill with large
terraces and sweeping views overlooks another group of pretty, coral
stone accommodations close to the beach. Friendship offers a beauti-
ful curve of white-sand beach and tropical plant-filled grounds and,
on Saturday nights around the Mau Mau Beach Bar, one of the liveli-
est barbecue and jump-ups in the Caribbean. This is distinguished
from the hundreds of beach bars you have known by its swing seats,
cleverly built to keep you upright even after potent rum punches. ⊠
Box 9, Bequia, St. Vincent, ☎ *809/458–3222,* ℻ *809/458–3840. 27
rooms. Restaurant, 2 bars, water-sports center, tennis, boutique. AE,
MC, V. CP.*

$$–$$$ **Old Fort Hotel.** A stunning setting on a cliff above the Atlantic, in a
stone estate house built by the French 200 years ago, marks this prop-
erty out from the others and endows its rooms with some of the most
panoramic Grenadine vistas around, plus the most cooling of trade-wind
breezes, obviating any need for air-conditioning. There are only six rooms
here, all done out like Captain Bligh's cabin crossed with a Provençal
farmhouse, featuring chunky hardwoods and exposed stone. This mod-
est scale, and the fact that the nearest beach, Ravine, is nearly 500 feet
below, and a bit too rough for swimming, makes the Old Fort a get-
away destination rather than a lazy vacation base. Luckily, the restau-
rant (*see* Dining, *above*) is excellent, because it's a trek into town. ⊠
Mt. Pleasant, Bequia, St. Vincent, ☎ *809/458–3440,* ℻ *809/458–
3824. 6 rooms. Restaurant, bar, hiking. MC, V. EP, MAP.*

$–$$ **Frangipani Hotel.** The Frangipani, which has gained the status of ven-
★ erable institution partly because its owner is St. Vincent's prime minis-
ter, James Mitchell, who lives here on Bequia, is a local gossip center
for international yachties and tourists. (The PM's wife, Pat, by the way,
owns the nearby Gingerbread. Why don't they live together? Listen to
the local Calypso for the whole story.) Surrounded by flowering bushes,

the garden units are built of stone, with private verandas and baths. Four simple, less-expensive rooms are in the main house, only one with a private bath. A two-bedroom house with a patio and another apartment with a large bedroom and kitchen are nearby. String bands appear on Mondays, with folksingers on Friday nights during tourist season. The Thursday-night steel-band jump-up at the beachfront bar is a must; the bar, with its huge, white-painted wooden armchairs facing the sunset, is probably the nicest around. ✉ *Box 1, Bequia, St. Vincent,* ☎ *809/458–3255,* FAX *809/458–3824. 13 rooms. Restaurant, bar, tennis, water-sports center, yacht excursions, boutique. MC, V. EP.*

$ **Isola and Julie's Guest House.** Right on the water in Port Elizabeth, these two separate buildings share a small restaurant and bar. Furnishings (which are few) run to early Salvation Army, but the food is great and the rooms are airy and light, with private baths; some have hot water. ✉ *Box 12, Bequia, St. Vincent,* ☎ *809/458–3304, 809/458–3323 or 809/458–3220. 25 rooms. Restaurant, bar. No credit cards. MAP.*

$ **Keegan's Guest House.** If you want budget beach accommodations with a quiet, friendly atmosphere, look no further. Located on Lower Bay, this *very* simple place offers family-style West Indian breakfasts and dinners for its guests. Rooms 3, 4, and 5 have a shared bath and are cheaper, although there is no hot water to be found (you really do get used to it). ✉ *Bequia, St. Vincent,* ☎ *809/458–3254 or 809/458–3530. 11 rooms. Dining room. No credit cards. MAP.*

Nightlife

As well as the various jump-ups at hotels, the newish **Harpoon Saloon,** clearly visible above the bay to port side as you sail into Bequia, regularly hosts local bands and is the nearest thing to a nightclub for miles.

Canouan

Goat-herding is still a career option here, and organized activities are nil. Walk, loaf, swim, or snorkel; those are your options on Canouan, where a brand-new hotel—the fourth!—is doing not a lot to bring the island into this century.

Dining and Lodging

$$$$ **Canouan Beach Hotel.** This hotel, perched on a tongue of beach poking out from the southwest end of the island, is biased toward French people, who dominate at any time of year. Simple white cottages, all renovated late in 1994, have air-conditioning, patios, and bathrooms with shower. Tennis, a golf driving range, catamaran day sails weekdays, and live music twice a week are what's offered here. ✉ *Canouan, St. Vincent,* ☎ *809/458–8888,* FAX *809/458–8875. 43 rooms. Restaurant, bar, marina, windsurfing, snorkeling, scuba, tennis, driving range. AE, MC, V. MAP, All-inclusive.*

$$$ **Tamarind Beach Hotel.** This is Canouan's sparkling new hostelry, which, unfortunately, did not open in time for our inspection this year. All we can say for sure is that rooms have ceiling fans and minibars, and water sports, day sails, two restaurants, and two bars are available. Don't fail to call ahead to check on its status. ✉ *Charlestown, Canouan, St. Vincent,* ☎ *809/458–8753 or 800/961–5006,* FAX *809/458–8851. 48 rooms. 2 restaurants, bar, beach bar, shop, day sails, windsurfing, scuba. No credit cards.*

$$–$$$ **Crystal Sands Beach Hotel.** A local family runs this extremely simple place on Charleston Bay. Cottages share a connecting door for larger groups and have private baths and patios. There's a fine beach and a veranda bar and dining area. If you take the mail boat from Kingstown (*see* Arriving and Departing in Bequia, *above*), pack light and be pre-

The Grenadines

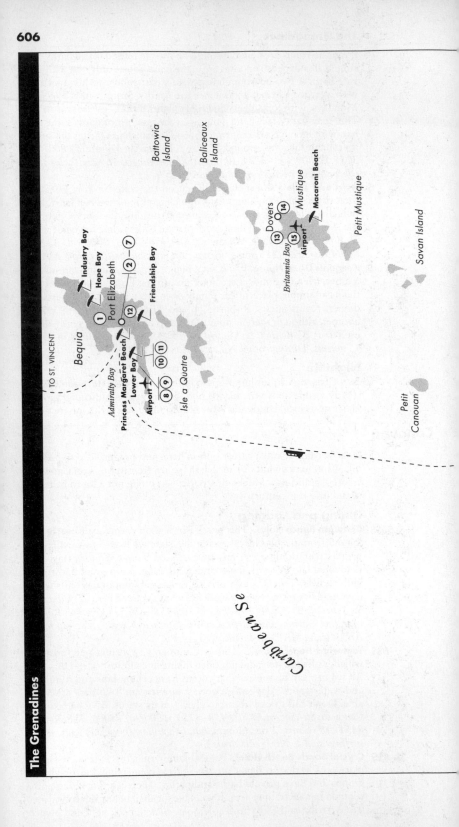

TO ST. VINCENT

Bequia

Industry Bay

Hope Bay

Port Elizabeth

①

② — ⑦

Friendship Bay

⑫

Admiralty Bay

Princess Margaret Beach

Lower Bay

Airport

⑩ ⑪

⑧ ⑨

Isle a Quatre

Battowia Island

Baliceaux Island

Mustique

Macaroni Beach

Dovers

⑬ ⑭

Britannia Bay

⑮

Airport

Petit Mustique

Savan Island

Petit Canouan

Caribbean Sea

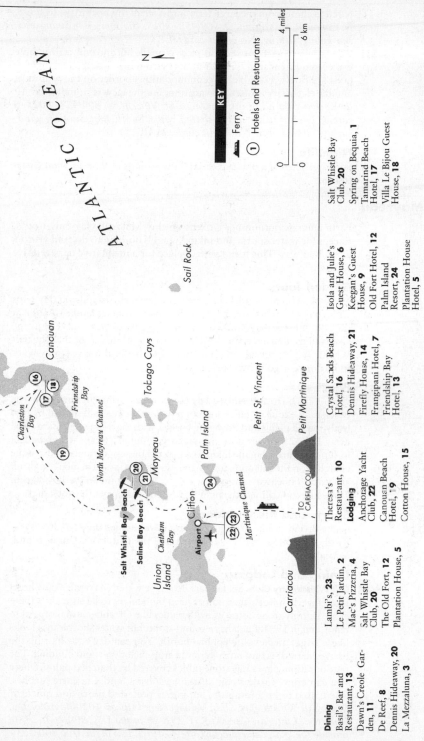

ATLANTIC OCEAN

KEY

⚓ Ferry

① Hotels and Restaurants

4 miles
6 km

N

Cancuan

Sail Rock

Charleston Bay

Friendship Bay

⑯ ⑱
⑰

⑲

North Mayreau Channel

Totago Cays

⑳
㉑ Mayreau

Salt Whistle Bay Beach

Saline Bay Beach

Union Island

Chatham Bay

Clifton

Airport

⑳ ㉑

Palm Island

Petit St. Vincent

Petit Martinique

Martinique Channel

TO CARRIACOU

Carriacou

Dining
Basil's Bar and Restaurant, **13**
Dawn's Creole Garden, **11**
De Reef, **8**
Dennis Hideaway, **20**
La Mezzaluna, **3**

Lambi's, **23**
Le Petit Jardin, **2**
Mac's Pizzeria, **4**
Salt Whistle Bay Club, **20**
The Old Fort, **12**
Plantation House, **5**

Theresa's Restaurant, **10**
Lodging
Anchorage Yacht Club, **22**
Canouan Beach Hotel, **19**
Cotton House, **15**

Crystal Sands Beach Hotel, **16**
Dennis Hideaway, **21**
Firefly House, **14**
Frangipani Hotel, **7**
Friendship Bay Hotel, **13**

Isola and Julie's Guest House, **6**
Keegan's Guest House, **9**
Old Fort Hotel, **12**
Palm Island Resort, **24**
Plantation House Hotel, **5**

Salt Whistle Bay Club, **20**
Spring on Bequia, **1**
Tamarind Beach Hotel, **17**
Villa Le Bijou Guest House, **18**

pared to climb from the large ferry into a small rowboat to get to shore. ☎ *Canouan, St. Vincent, ☎ 809/458–8015. 10 rooms. Bar, dining area, snorkeling, fishing. No credit cards. EP.*

$$–$$$ **Villa Le Bijou Guest House.** This place is up the hill and only a 10-minute walk from Friendship Bay (15 minutes from the airstrip; pack light—taxis are rarely available). Accommodations border on the primitive, and the electricity is often on vacation, but the view is stunning. ☎ *M. de Roche, Villa La Bijou, Canouan, St. Vincent, ☎ 809/458–8025. 6 rooms. No hot water in the shared baths. Snorkeling, Sunfish, windsurfing, dining area. No credit cards. MAP.*

Nightlife
Surprise: There's a bar and disco on weekends at **Villa Le Bijou Guest House.**

Mayreau

Farm animals outnumber citizens on tiny Mayreau (say "my-*row*"). Except for water sports and hiking, there's nothing to do, and visitors like it that way. This is the perfect place for a meditative or vegetative vacation.

Guided Tours
You can swim and snorkel in the cays or nearby islands on day trips with charter yachts arranged by the hotel. Contact **Undine Potter** at the Salt Whistle Bay Club (from the U.S., ☎ 800/263–2780; in the Grenadines, marine radio VHF channel 16 or 68). Note that the Salt Whistle Bay's snorkel equipment has seen better days; you may want to buy or rent your own before you arrive.

Beaches
Top honors go to **Salt Whistle Bay Beach**—the Caribbean's prettiest. The beach is an exquisite half-moon of powdery white sand, shaded by perfectly spaced palms and flowering bushes, with the rolling Atlantic a stroll away. Hike 25 minutes over Mayreau's mountain (wear shoes; bare feet or flip-flops are a big mistake) to a good photo opportunity at the stone church atop the hill and stunning views of the Cays. Then have a drink at Dennis Hideaway and enjoy a swim at beautiful **Saline Bay Beach.** There are no facilities; the mail boat's tender stops at the dock here.

Sports and the Outdoors
Scuba diving can be arranged through **Grenadines Dive** (☎ 809/458–8138 or 809/458–8122; *see* Sports and the Outdoors, Union Island, *below).*

Dining and Lodging
$$$$ **Salt Whistle Bay Club.** Set far back from the water, Mayreau's only hotel is so cleverly hidden that sailors need binoculars to be sure a it's there at all. Roomy stone cottages, with names like Oleander and Ivora, were renovated in 1994. Each has a round-stone, hot-water shower that looks like a large, medieval telephone booth. You can dry your hair on the breezy, shared second-story veranda atop each two-room building. The outdoor dining area has stone tables covered by thatched palms where you can enjoy turtle steak, duckling, lobster, and à la carte lunches. There used to be a jump-up, but guests preferred peace and quiet. ☎ *Write Salt Whistle Bay Club, Management Offices, 1020 Bayridge Dr., Kingston, Ontario, Canada K7P 2S2. ☎ in the U.S. 800/263–2780; outside the U.S., call collect 613/634–1963. Fax in the U.S. 800/263–2780; outside the U.S., 613/384–6300. In the Caribbean, marine radio VHF channel 68; boat phone 493–9609. 10 cottages, 4 suites.*

Restaurant, bar, windsurfing, snorkeling, catamaran charter. No credit cards. FAP.

$–$$ **Dennis Hideaway.** It's practically the only place on the island, but that's no great hardship, since Dennis (who plays the guitar two nights a week) is a charmer, the food is great, the drinks are strong, and the view is heaven. The rooms are clean but very simple: a bed, nightstand, chair, and a place to hang some clothes. ⌂ *Saline Bay,* ☎ *809/458–8594. 3 rooms. Restaurant ($$–$$$). Reservations advised. No credit cards. EP.*

Mustique

Princess Margaret put this 3- by 1½-mile former copra, cotton, and sugarcane estate on the map, once her compatriot, Colin Tennant (now Lord Glenconner), bought it. The company he formed in 1968 to develop Mustique into the glamorous hideaway island it remains now has 37 shareholders and a House Rentals Department you'd need to contact about a year in advance if you wanted to rent the royal holiday home, Balliceaux, or another of the 40-odd luxury villas that pepper the northern half of the island. Some house owners keep their villas empty in their absence, including Mustique's two most glittering habitués, Mick Jagger and David Bowie. Their villas are concealed behind Brobdingnagian fences, but anyone who insists on star-gawking will get to see whoever's "on island" at Basil's Bar, the unofficial social center, sooner or later.

Next to his bar, in a cluster of candy-colored houses that don't quite qualify as a town, Basil also runs a boutique crammed with clothes and accessories imported and specially commissioned from all over the world, a cornucopian delicatessen to feed residents fresh Brie and Moët, and an antiques shop stocked with fabulous pieces for those fabulous houses. There's also a fish market, a grocery warehouse, a gas station—and a police station with nothing much to do. To some, that adds up to paradise; others *hate* it, but you pays yer money, you takes yer choice.

Beaches

Macaroni Beach is Mustique's most famous stretch of sand, offering surfy swimming (no lifeguards, so be careful), powdery white sand, a few palm huts for shade, and picnic tables on a grassy garden behind. From the northern coast, working west, L'Ansecoy, Endeavour, and Britannia Bays are also fine, and much calmer, the last being the best for day-trippers, with Basil's Bar adjacent for lunch. Farther south, Gelliceaux Bay, by the Cotton House, provides the best snorkeling beach.

Sports and the Outdoors

Water-sports facilities are available at the Cotton House, and most villas have equipment of various sorts. Scuba is best arranged through **Dive Mustique** (☎ 809/458–4621). There's a communal tennis court for those whose villa lacks its own, a cricket ground for the Brits, and motorbikes for trail-riding around the bumpy roads for rent at $45 per day. The best sport to indulge in on Mustique, however, is horseback riding, since this is one of the few islands where you can rent a decent animal. Rides leave Monday–Saturday at 8 and 9 AM, 3 and 4 PM from the **Equestrian Centre** (☎ 809/458–4316), and rates are $40 per hour.

Dining

$–$$$ **Basil's Bar and Restaurant.** Basil's is the only place to be seen on Mustique, and only partly because it *is* the only place on Mustique, apart
★ from the more formal, quieter Cotton House. Resembling many a beachside terrace restaurant, with its wooden deck built over the

waves, palm-roofed at the edges with a central bar and dance floor open to the stars, there's something about the atmosphere that hints at happenings. Well, you never know who you may run into. . . . The food is simple and good—mostly fish hauled out of the water a hundred yards away, homemade ice cream, burgers and salads, great French toast, the usual cocktails, many unusual wines—though it takes far too long to reach your starving mouths. The Wednesday barbecue is the regular party night, and there's live music Mondays. ✕ ☎ *809/458–4621. Reservations advised. AE, MC, V.*

Lodging

$$$$ **Cotton House.** The island's only hotel centers on the stone-and-coral
★ former estate warehouse, originally converted by the late Oliver Messel (the great British theater designer-decorator-architect, who was to Mustique as Haussmann was to Paris). The whole place has undergone a complete overhaul under the aegis of utterly charming supermanager Warren Francis and his wonderful wife Gilly, transforming what had sunk into an expensively underwhelming hostelry back to an hotel in the world's top rank. The 18th-century plantation house was used to store cotton, sugar, and rum and, along with the stone mill which is now the hotel boutique, is the oldest structure on Mustique. The wraparound wooden veranda functions as lounge, bar, tea terrace, restaurant, and island social center. Breakfast is taken around the hilltop pool, in Messel's outrageous ruined Scottish castle folly. Off the pool path are baby cottages containing junior suites (numbers 9–11), which, with their breezy walk-through layouts, are the cutest of the three room types. The deluxe suites (12–16) are mere steps away from the main house but have nothing but this and their size—they were eight rooms before the renovations—to recommend them over the fantastic quartet of deluxe rooms in high-up Battowia House. These have balconies perched over Mustique's northern coast, with a particularly gorgeous view from corner room number 6, and come in at around $200 a night less than a deluxe suite—as do the two beach rooms (numbers 21 and 22). Decor is faithful to Messel's vision of Caribbean simplicity and light, with white walls and ceiling fans, antiques, and rattan furniture. Bathrooms have marble fittings, and rooms have dressing areas, French windows, desks, minibars, phones—and perfect peace. In addition to the restaurant, there's a beach bar with a weekly barbecue. There are water sports, tennis, and a driver to chauffeur you to Basil's. ☎ *Box 349, Mustique, St. Vincent, ☎ and fax 809/456–4777. U.S. agent: Ralph Locke Islands, ☎ 800/223–1108. 10 rooms, 10 suites. Restaurant, bar, pool, library, boutique, water sports, tennis, horseback riding. AE, D, MC, V. FAP.*

$–$$ **Firefly House.** Tiny and charming with just five rooms, this is the island's only budget choice, but it's still well located, above Britannia Bay, and the rooms have private baths, fridges, and picnic equipment, plus, for $5 extra, air-conditioning. "You don't have to be rich and famous to enjoy Mustique" says the Firefly flier, but the sensitive and/or paranoid may suffer a poor relations complex staying here. ☎ *Mustique, Box 349, ☎ 809/456–3414. 5 rooms. Bar, water sports. No credit cards. CP.*

Villa Rentals

Renting one of Mustique's privately owned villas is not as expensive as it seems at first glance, since rates include a full staff, with cook but no groceries, laundry service, and a vehicle or two; rates are per house, not per person. Houses range from simple rusticity—if you can call ensuite bathrooms for every bedroom, at least one phone line, probably a pool, cable TV, VCR, CD, and even fax, rustic—to extravagant, expansive, faux-Palladian follies with resident butler; but all are de-signer-elegant and immaculately maintained. Rates start at $2,800 a week for the two-bed Pelican Beach off-season and go way up to $13,000 a week for the palatial five-bed, five-person staff, two Jeep, one-Jacuzzi Blackstone, during winter. Princess Margaret's three-bed place is surprisingly modest, at a mere $3,200 a week in summer. ☎ *House Rentals Dept., Mustique Co. Ltd., Box 349,* ☎ *809/458–4621,* ℻ *809/456–4565. 42 villas. AE, DC, MC, V. FAP.*

Palm Island

$$$$ Palm Island Resort. A seafarer was shipwrecked, stranded on a desert island, reunited with his new wife, had two sons, found a swamp-rid-den, mosquito-infested jungle called Prune Island, and toiled with his family for 25 years to turn it into a resort. What is this? A Judith Krantz novel? A Sly Stallone movie? No, it's how Palm Island came to be, and you can read all about it over tea, delivered at 4 PM to your ca-bana terrace. In the better, newer cabanas (numbers 11–18), you'll enjoy a private sunset view from your room-width patio doors, over the northwest facing Casuarina Beach. If you got an older room (numbers 1–6 and 19–22), you will lack both big windows and much in the way of privacy, and you may also tire of the pink-and-green color scheme that is overdue for retirement. Bathrooms aren't the greatest, with drib-bly but scenic outdoor showers in the newer cabanas, scant towels, and the same marble-chip floors as in the bedroom in all, but balanced against that is a collective and genuine warmth in the staff, which has people coming back year after year. The food is important when you're a cap-tive audience; the island buffets and full-service dinners here are just fine, and the new pastry chef promises great breakfast improvements, too. Adjacent to the hotel is a separate yacht club where you can go for the only change of scene apart from a jog on "Highway 90" (1.25 miles around), or a day sail to the Tobago Cays. You could view this as a cut-rate Petit St. Vincent. ☎ *Palm Island, St. Vincent,* ☎ *809/458–8224,* ℻ *809/458–8804. U.S. agent: Paradise Found,* ☎ *800/776–7256. 24 rooms, 15 self-catering villas. Open-air bar-restaurant, jogging trail, water sports (scuba at extra charge), game room, tennis, boutique, grocery, catered charter yacht sails, yacht provisioning. AE, MC, V. FAP.*

Petit St. Vincent

$$$$ Petit St. Vincent. This is a very special 113 acre private island, where you can indulge shipwreck fantasies without forgoing the frozen mango daiquiri at sunset, room service breakfast, the skills of a great chef, and so on. There are only 22 houses on PSV, with bedroom, sitting room, and one or two bathrooms in a U-shape around a big, partly covered wooden deck. Floors are tiled and grass matted, walls are of stone, and—on two sides—glass, with patio doors that slide away entirely, giving you trade winds for a lullaby. Despite their rustic appearance, with copra matting vanities and cobblestoned shower stalls, bathrooms conceal the Grenadines' best toiletries, robes, beach bags, and towels, and an iron, and they have American-style 110-volt, two-prong outlets, so you don't need transformers. No house is more than a five-minute walk from dinner, yet each is completely private, with a sweet system of flags and bamboo mailbox to convey whims to the staff (who outnumber guests two to one), since there are no ☎s. Hoist your red flag, and no-body *dreams* of approaching; hoist the yellow, and you can have lunch or dinner, tea or drinks, a ride to the jetty, or a picnic for a day on the "West End" promptly delivered. Some prefer the houses that fringe the windward beach (numbers 6–11), others like the distant trio high up on the bluff (numbers 1–3), and still others swear by the three perched above the Atlantic surf (numbers 20–22), with new stone steps to the beach. All benefit from the soft white strand that encircles the island, as well as from the hiking paths, water sports, tennis court, and fitness trail. Also available are day trips to neighboring Mopion—a.k.a. Petit St. Richardson, after visionary owner Haze Richardson. You'll probably meet him, along with a selection of his seven yellow Labradors—the happiest dogs in the world. *PSV, Box 12506, Cincinnati, OH 45212, ☏ 513/242–1333, 800/654–9326, or 809/458–8801. 22 houses. No credit cards. Closed Sept. and Oct. FAP.*

Union

Union's airstrip is right behind the Anchorage Yacht Club, which is the island's unofficial center for visitors. Gorgeous from a distance, Union doesn't offer the charm or friendliness of other Grenadines.

Beaches

The beach around Clifton Harbour is narrow, unattractive, rocky, and shadeless. Other beaches have no facilities and are virtually inaccessible without a boat; the desolate but lovely Chatham Bay offers good swimming.

Sports and the Outdoors

Grenadines Dive (☏ 809/458–8138 or 809/458–8122), run by NAUI instructor Glenroy Adams, is the local operation, including Tobago Cays trips and wreck dives at the *Purina,* a sunken World War I English gunship.

Dining

$$ **Lambi's.** On the main street in Clifton, Lambi's offers good conch Creole and walls made from their shells. ✕ ☏ *809/458–8549. No credit cards.*

Lodging

$$–$$$ **Anchorage Yacht Club.** Between the airstrip and what little beach there is are rooms and bungalows with concealed outdoor showers and terraces facing the water, all comfortably refurbished, with water sports and yacht chartering galore for entertainment. The full-service marina makes for a cosmopolitan buzz around the place, and in the enormous bar-café area in front, where all three meals are served. There's also a pizza and sandwich counter, and a jump-up on Mondays for all those sailors who got stranded here. ⊞ *Union, St. Vincent, ☏ 809/458–8221, FAX 809/458–8365. 10 rooms, 6 bungalows. Restaurant, bar, water-sports center, boutique, air-conditioning, yacht provisioning and charters. AE, MC, V. CP.*

25 Trinidad and Tobago

Updated by
Barbara Hults

OOD NEWS FROM THE MOST SOUTHERLY ISLANDS in the Caribbean: Trinidad has changed radically and Tobago has not. Trinidad, once an island on no one's list, has emerged from many of its problems with a fresher outlook, a cleaner capital, and, wonder of wonders, a newly renovated airport. The general spirit of the island is good, and many new entrepreneurial businesses in the capital, Port-of-Spain, seem to be doing well. Another bit of good news for the island is that major carrier BWIA has begun to take itself seriously as a tourist airline. Sparkling new planes and better-trained flight attendants are offering much-improved service to Trinidad. Since this is one of the few airlines with regular service to the island, its image is critical to Trinidad's revival.

Around 51,000 of Trinidad's 1.3 million residents—Africans, Indians, Americans, Europeans, and Asians, each with their own language and customs—live in the capital city of Port-of-Spain, one of the most active commercial cities in the West Indies. However, you have to leave the capital to find a good beach, and most visitors are still business travelers. Trinidad has known prosperity from oil (it's one of the biggest producers in the Western Hemisphere), a steel plant, natural gas, and a multiplicity of small businesses. The island is also home to a spectacular Carnival, the birthplace of steel-band music.

Tobago, an island almost unknown to American tourists, has begun to realize the advantages of unspoiled rain forests, a mostly undeveloped coastline, and a colorful population of birds that would keep the most avid bird-watcher happy for years. Buccoo and Speyside reefs are underwater wonderlands for scuba divers and snokelers. The island has delightful hotels and restaurants, and now direct air service from Miami and Barbados has made getting there easier, without the need to change planes in Trinidad. However, with all those wide-bodied planes delivering tourists, new hotels are being planned, and without careful control, the island could lose its Robinson Crusoe wilderness. Now is the time to savor an island that would charm Gauguin.

The islands together have more than 600 species of birds, more than 200 species of plants, and more than 100 species of mammals—within pristine rain forests, lowlands and savannahs, and fresh- and saltwater swamps. Birdsong, a disappearing music in the rest of the world, is easily heard, since restaurants often hang feeders outside their porches, as much to keep the birds away from your food as to provide a chance for observation.

Columbus reached these islands on his third voyage, in 1498. Three prominent peaks around the southern bay of Trinidad prompted him to name the land La Trinidad, after the Holy Trinity. Trinidad was captured by British forces in 1797, ending 300 years of Spanish rule. Tobago's history is more complicated. It was "discovered" by the British in 1508. The Spanish, Dutch, French, and British all fought for it until it was ceded to England under the Treaty of Paris in 1814. In 1962, both islands—T&T, as they're commonly called—gained their independence within the British Commonwealth, finally becoming a republic in 1976.

In 1986, the National Alliance for Reconstruction (NAR) won a landslide victory, toppling the People's National Movement (PNM), which had been in power for 30 years but had brought the country to the brink of economic ruin. Then, in the 1991 elections, power was returned to the PNM. The new government, especially because of the decline in oil prices, seems eager to create a new tourist economy without spoiling the great tourist advantages that lack of development has brought.

Before You Go

Tourist Information

Contact the very helpful and efficient **Trinidad and Tobago Tourism Development Authority.** In the United States: 25 W. 43rd St., Suite 1508, New York, NY 10036, ☎ 212/719–0540 or 800/232–0082, FAX 212/719–0988. In the United Kingdom: 8a Hammersmith Broadway, London W6 7AL, ☎ 0181/741–4466, FAX 0181/741–1013. In Canada: 40 Holly St., Suite 102, Toronto, Ontario M4S 3C3, ☎ 416/486–4470 or 800/268–8986, FAX 416/440–1899.

Arriving and Departing

BY PLANE

There are daily direct flights to Piarco Airport, about 30 minutes east of Port-of-Spain, from New York, Miami, Toronto, and London on **BWIA** (☎ 800/538–2942), Trinidad and Tobago's national airline. **American** (☎ 800/433–7300) offers direct flights from Miami to Trinidad. They also offer connecting service, through Miami or San Juan, from all of the cities they serve in the United States. **Air Canada** (☎ 800/422–6232) flies to Trinidad from Toronto, via Miami or San Juan. There are numerous interisland flights in the Caribbean on BWIA and **LIAT** (☎ 809/462–0701). All flights to Trinidad alight at Piarco Airport. BWIA and Air Caribe flights from Trinidad to Crown Point Airport in Tobago take about 15 minutes and depart 6 to 10 times a day. For those wishing to circumvent Trinidad entirely, LIAT has direct service from Barbados and Grenada to Tobago, and BWIA flies direct from Miami to Tobago. **Caledonia Airways** (0293/567–1000) also flies to Tobago from London.

Package tours aren't generally touted as heavily as they are for other Caribbean islands, but there are bargains to be had, especially around Carnival. One particularly good tour operator is **Pan Caribe Tours** (Box 3223, Austin, TX 78764, ☎ 512/266–7995 or 800/525–6896, FAX 512/266–7986). BWIA also has a variety of Caribbean tours.

BY BOAT

The Port Authority maintains daily ferry service between Trinidad and Tobago, although flying is preferable, because the sea can be very rough. The ferry leaves once a day, and the trip takes about five hours. Round-trip fare is TT$60, about U.S.$11. Cabin fare is $22 (one-way, double occupancy), with an extra charge for vehicles. Tickets are sold at offices in Port-of-Spain (☎ 809/625–3055) and at Scarborough, in Tobago (☎ 809/639–2417).

FROM THE AIRPORT

Taxis are readily available at Piarco Airport. The fare to Port-of-Spain is set at $20, to the Hilton at $24. By car, take Golden Grove Road north to Arouca, then follow Eastern Main Road west for about 10 miles to Port-of-Spain. In Tobago, the fare from Crown Point Airport to Scarborough is fixed at $8, to Speyside at $32.

Passports and Visas

Citizens of the United States, the United Kingdom, and Canada who expect to stay for less than six weeks may enter the country with a valid passport. A visa is required for longer stays.

Language

The official language is English, although there is no end of idiomatic expressions used by the loquacious Trinis. You will also hear smatterings of French, Spanish, Chinese, and Hindi. (Trinidad's population is about one-quarter Indian.)

Precautions

Insect repellent is a must during the rainy season (June–December) and is worth having around anytime. Trinidad is only 11 degrees north of the equator, and the sun here can be intense. Even if you tan well, it's a good idea to use a strong sunblock, at least for the first few days.

Staying in Trinidad and Tobago

Important Addresses

Tourist Information: Information is available from the **Trinidad & Tobago Tourism Development Authority** (134–138 Frederick St., Port-of-Spain, ☎ 809/623–1932, FAX 809/623–3848; Piarco Airport, ☎ 809/664–5196). For Tobago, contact the **Tobago Division of Tourism** (N.I.B. Mall, Scarborough, ☎ 809/639–2125, FAX 809/639–3566), or drop in at its information booth at Crown Point Airport (☎ 809/639–0509).

EMERGENCIES

Police: Call 999. **Fire and ambulance:** Call 990. **Hospitals: Port-of-Spain General Hospital** is at 169 Charlotte Street (☎ 809/623–2951); **Tobago County Hospital** is on Fort Street in Scarborough (☎ 809/639–2551). **Pharmacies: Oxford Pharmacy** (☎ 809/627–4657) is at Charlotte and Oxford streets near the Port-of-Spain General Hospital; **Ross Drugs** (☎ 809/639–2658) is in Scarborough. For a complete list of other pharmacies, check the T&T Yellow Pages.

Currency

The Trinidadian dollar (TT$) has been devalued twice in recent years. The current exchange rate is about TT$5.50 to U.S.$1. The major hotels in Port-of-Spain have exchange facilities whose rates are comparable to official bank rates. Trinidad's best rate is found at the Hilton. Most businesses on the island will accept U.S. currency if you're in a pinch. Note: Prices quoted here are in U.S. dollars unless indicated otherwise.

Taxes and Service Charges

Restaurants and hotels add a 15% value-added tax (VAT). Many also add a 10% service charge to your bill. If the service charge is not added, you should tip 10%–15% of the bill for a job well done. The airport departure tax is TT$75, or about U.S.$13.50.

Guided Tours

One of Trinidad's best tour operators is the **Travel Centre** (Box 1254, Port-of-Spain, ☎ 809/625–1636, FAX 809/623–5101). Their office is also American Express's cardmember service office, for check-cashing and other matters. For a personal guide in Trinidad who speaks German as well as English, contact **Maria Lopez** (3 Palm Ave. W, Petit Valley, ☎ 809/637–3642). On Tobago, **Helen Grant** (☎ 809/639–3581) gives tours in English. You can also ask the tourism office in Tobago for a list of guides. Almost any **taxi driver** in Port-of-Spain will be willing to take you around the town and to the beaches on the north coast. It costs around $70 for up to four people to go Maracas Bay beach, plus $20 per hour extra if you decide to go farther; you may be able to haggle for a cheaper rate. For a complete list of tour operators and sea cruises, contact the tourism office. For nature guides, *see* Sports and the Outdoors, *below.*

Getting Around

TAXIS

Taxis in Trinidad are easily identified by their license plates, which begin with the letter H. Passenger vans, called Maxi Taxis, pick up and drop off passengers as they travel and are color coded according to which of four areas they cover. They are easily hailed day or night along most of the main roads near Port-of-Spain. For longer trips you will need to hire a private taxi. There are set rates, though they are not always observed, particularly at Carnival. Pick up a rate sheet from the tourism office. On the whole, the drivers are honest, friendly, and informative, and the experience of riding in a Maxi Taxi with a souped-up sound system during Carnival is worth whatever fare you pay.

RENTAL CARS/SCOOTERS

If you are a first-time visitor to Port-of-Spain, where the streets are often jammed with traffic and drivers who routinely play "chicken" with one another, taxis are your best bet, though expensive if you plan to see everything on the island, and you may feel immobile. Nor is the city easy to negotiate on foot, though Maxi Taxis are plentiful and cheap. Car-rental services include **Auto Rentals** (☎ 809/675–7368, FAX 809/675–2258), with many locations, and **Kalloo's Auto Rental and Taxi Service** (☎ 809/622–9073). Mr. Kalloo goes out of his way to help, and his cars are reliable. As befits one of the world's largest exporters of asphalt, Trinidad's roads are generally good, although you may encounter roadwork in progress as major resurfacing is done. In the outback, roads are often narrow, twisting, and prone to washouts in the rainy season. Inquire about conditions before you take off, particularly if you're heading toward the north coast. Never drive into downtown Port-of-Spain during afternoon rush hour.

In Tobago you might be better off renting a Jeep than relying on taxi service, which is much more expensive. A four-wheel-drive vehicle is far better and safer than a car, because many roads, particularly in the interior, or on the far coast near Speyside and Charlotteville, are bumpy, pitted, winding, and/or steep (though the main highways are smooth and fast). Ask your hotel about rentals and taxis, or contact **Sweet Jeeps** (☎ 809/639 8391, FAX 809/639–8495) or **Singh's Auto Rentals** at Grafton Beach Resort (☎ 809/639–0191, ext. 53). Various tours are also offered by rental agencies on both islands, and rates are negotiable. All agencies require a credit-card deposit, and in season you must make reservations well in advance of your arrival. Figure on paying $40–$60 per day. Don't forget to drive on the left.

Telephones and Mail

The area code for both islands is 809. For telegraph, telefax, teletype, and telex, contact **Textel** (1 Edward St., Port-of-Spain, ☎ 809/625–4431). Faxes can be sent from major hotels.

To place an intraisland call, dial the local seven-digit number. To reach the United States, dial 1, the appropriate area code, and the local number.

Postage for first-class letters to the United States is TT$2.25; for postcards, TT$2.

Opening and Closing Times

Most shops open Monday–Thursday 8–4, Friday 8–6, and Saturday 8–noon. Banking hours are Monday–Thursday 8–2 and Friday 8–noon and 3–5.

618

Trinidad

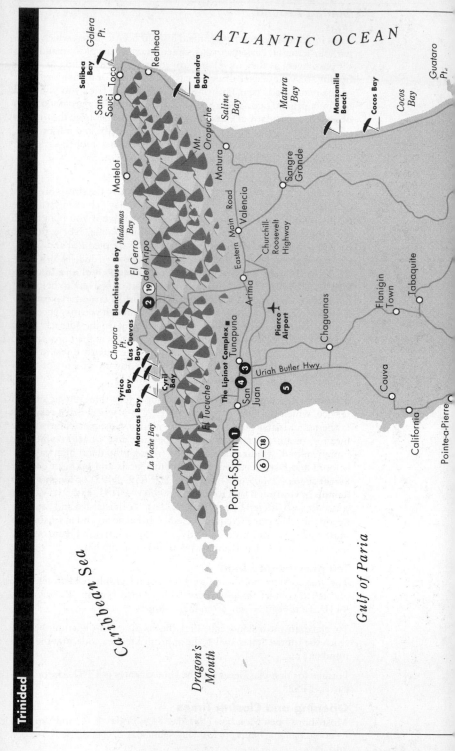

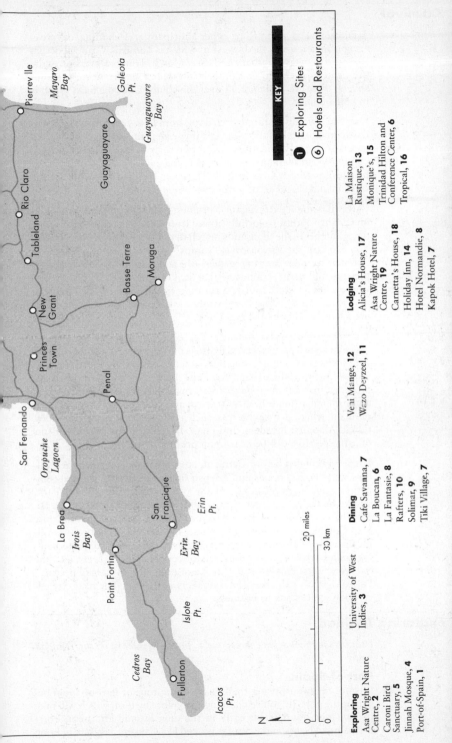

KEY

1 Exploring Sites

6 Hotels and Restaurants

Pierrev Ile

Mayaro Bay

Galeota Pt.

Guayaguayare

Guayaguayare Bay

Rio Claro

Tableland

New Grant

Basse Terre

Moruga

Princes Town

Penal

Sar Fernando

Oropuche Lagoon

La Brea

Trois Bay

San Franciqje

Erin Pt.

Point Fortin

Erin Bay

Islote Pt.

Cedros Bay

Fullarton

Icacos Pt.

N

0   20 miles

0   30 km

Exploring
Asa Wright Nature Centre, **2**
Caroni Bird Sanctuary, **5**
Jinnah Mosque, **4**
Port-of-Spain, **1**

University of West Indies, **3**

Dining
Café Savanna, **7**
La Boucan, **6**
La Fantasie, **8**
Rafters, **10**
Solimar, **9**
Tiki Village, **7**

Veai Mange, **12**
Wezo Dezyzel, **11**

Lodging
Alicia's House, **17**
Asa Wright Nature Centre, **19**
Carnetta's House, **18**
Holiday Inn, **14**
Hotel Normandie, **8**
Kapok Hotel, **7**

La Maison Rustique, **13**
Monique's, **15**
Trinidad Hilton and Conference Center, **6**
Tropical, **16**

Carnival

Trinidad always seems to be either anticipating, celebrating, or recovering from a festival, the biggest of which is **Carnival.** Carnival occurs each year between February and early March. Trinidad's version of the pre-Lenten bacchanal is reputedly the oldest in the Western Hemisphere; there are festivities all over the country, but the most lavish is in Port-of-Spain.

Carnival officially lasts only two days, from J'ouvert (sunrise) on Monday to midnight the following day. If you're planning to go, it's a good idea to arrive in Trinidad a week or two early to enjoy the events leading up to Carnival. Not as overwhelming as its rival in Rio or as debauched as Mardi Gras in New Orleans, Trinidad's festival has the warmth and character of a massive family reunion.

Carnival is about extravagant costumes: Individuals prance around in imaginative outfits. Colorfully attired troupes—called *mas*—that sometimes number in the thousands march to the beat set by the steel bands. You can visit the various mas "camps" around the city where these elaborate costumes are put together—the addresses are listed in the newspapers—and perhaps join one that strikes your fancy. Fees run anywhere from $35 to $100; you get to keep the costume. Children can also parade in a Kiddie Carnival that takes place on Saturday morning a few days before the real thing.

Throwing a party is not the only purpose of Carnival; it's also a showcase for calypso performers. Calypso is music that mixes dance rhythms with social commentary, sung by characters with such evocative names as Shadow, the Mighty Sparrow, and Black Stalin. As Carnival approaches, many of these singers perform nightly in calypso tents, which are scattered around the city. You can also visit the pan yards of Port-of-Spain, where steel orchestras, such as the Renegades, Desperadoes, Catelli All-Stars, Invaders, and Phase II, rehearse their arrangements of calypso. Most can be heard practically year-round.

For several nights before Carnival, costume makers display their talents, and the steel bands and calypso singers perform in spirited competitions in the grandstands of the old racetrack in Queen's Park, where the Calypso Monarch was crowned until 1993, when the Dimanche Gras festivities moved to the National Stadium in the Cruise Ship Complex at the Port. At sunrise, or J'ouvert, the city starts filling up with metal-frame carts carrying steel bands, flatbed trucks hauling sound systems, and thousands of revelers who squeeze into the narrow streets. Finally, at the stroke of midnight on "Mas Tuesday," Port-of-Spain's exhausted merrymakers go to bed. The next day everybody settles back to business.

Exploring Trinidad

Numbers in the margin correspond to points of interest on the Trinidad map.

Port-of-Spain

❶ It is not really surprising that a sightseeing tour of **Port-of-Spain** begins at the port. (If you're planning to explore by foot, which will take two to four hours, start early in the day; by mid-afternoon Port-of-Spain can be hot and is always packed like Calcutta.) Be sure to bring lots of film—the renewed charms of the city are worthy of photographing. Though it is no longer as frenetic as it was during the oil boom of the 1970s, **King's Wharf** entertains a steady parade of cruise and cargo ships, a reminder that the city started from this strategic harbor. Across Wrightson Road is **Independence Square,** which is not a square at all: It's a wide, dusty thoroughfare crammed with pedestrians, car traffic, taxi stands, and peddlers of everything from shoes to coconuts—not a pleasant walk for lone females. Flanked by government buildings and the familiar twin towers of the Financial Complex (familiar because it adorns one side of all T&T dollar bills), the square is gloriously chaotic, loud, and confusing.

Walk all the way west along the square to Wrightson Road, where stands the Gothic-style Cathedral of the Immaculate Conception. On the south side is the Cruise Ship Complex, full of duty-free shops, forming an enclave of international anonymity with the Holiday Inn. Alternatively, at the midpoint of Independence Square, head north up Frederick Street. This is the main shopping drag, a market street of scents—corn roasting and Indian spices—and crowded shops. At the corner of Prince Street, look across **Woodford Square** toward the magnificent **Red House,** a Renaissance-style building that takes up an entire city block. Trinidad's House of Parliament takes its name from a paint job done in anticipation of Queen Victoria's Diamond Jubilee in 1897. Woodford Square has served as the site of political meetings, speeches, public protests, and occasional violence. The original Red House, in fact, was burned to the ground in a 1903 riot. The present structure was built four years later. The chambers are open to the public.

The view of the south side of the square is framed by the Gothic spires of **Trinity,** the city's other cathedral, and, on the north, by the impressive **public library** building, the **Hall of Justice** and **City Hall.**

TIME OUT Two blocks south of Queen's Park, and one block west to Rust Street, stop for tea and pastries (or even an American breakfast) at **La Maison Rustique** (809/622-1512), a pretty white house set amid tropical gardens. It's also a pleasant bed-and-breakfast.

Continue north along Pembroke Street and note the odd mix of modern and colonial architecture, gingerbread and graceful estate houses, and stucco storefronts. After five blocks, Pembroke crosses Keate Street at **Memorial Park,** from which a short walk north leads to the greater green expanse of **Queen's Park,** more popularly called the **Savannah.**

The **National Museum and Art Gallery,** at the southeast corner of the Savannah, is worth a visit, if only to see the Carnival exhibits, the Amerind collection and historical re-creations, and the fine 19th-century paintings of Trinidadian artist Cazabon.

Buy a cool coconut water from any of the vendors operating out of flatbed trucks along the Savannah. For about 50¢, he'll lop the top off a green coconut with a deft swing of the machete and, when you've finished drinking, lop again, making a bowl and spoon of coconut shell for you to eat the young pulp—the texture of a boiled egg white. According to Trinis, "It'll cure anyt'ing dat ail ya, mon."

Proceeding west along the Savannah, you'll come to a garden of architectural delights: the elegant lantern-roof **George Brown House**; what remains of the **Old Queen's Park Hotel**; and a series of astonishing buildings constructed in a variety of 19th-century styles, known as the **Magnificent Seven.**

Notable among these buildings are **Killarney,** patterned (loosely) after Balmoral Castle in Scotland, with an Italian-marble gallery surrounding the ground floor; **Whitehall,** constructed in the style of a Venetian

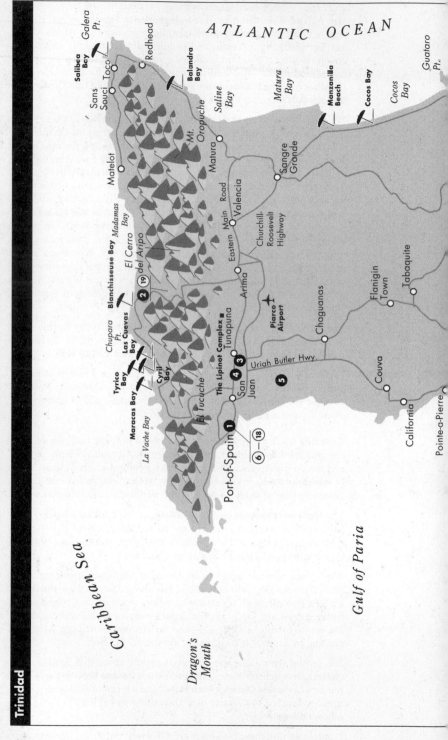

ATLANTIC OCEAN

Galera Pt.

Salibea Bay

Redhead

Sans Souci

Toco

Balandra Bay

Saline Bay

Matura Bay

Manzanilla Beach

Cocos Bay

Guataro Pt.

Matelot

Mt. Aripo

Oropuche

Matura

Cocos Bay

Sangre Grande

Madamas Bay

Blanchisseuse Bay

El Cerro del Aripo

Valencia

Eastern Main Road

Churchill-Roosevelt Highway

Chupara Pt.

Las Cuevas Bay

Cyril Bay

Tyrico Bay

Maracas Bay

Arima

Piarco Airport

Chaguanas

Flanagin Town

Tabaquite

La Vache Bay

El Tucuche

Tunapuna

The Lipinot Complex

San Juan

Uriah Butler Hwy.

Couva

California

Pointe-a-Pierre

Port-of-Spain

Caribbean Sea

Dragon's Mouth

Gulf of Paria

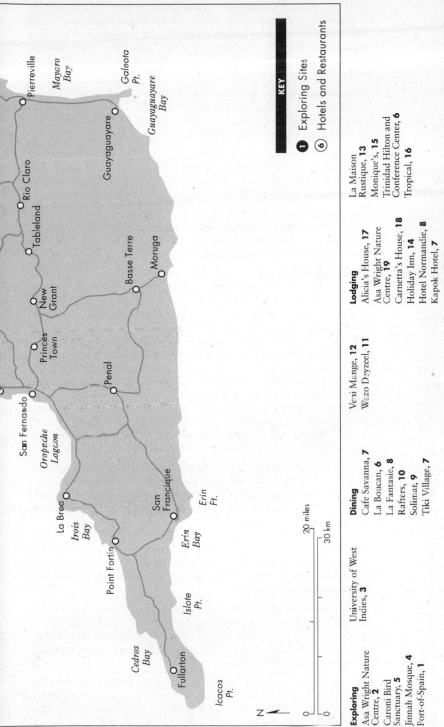

Mayaro Bay
Pierreville

Galeota Pt.

Guayaguayare

Guayaguayare Bay

Rio Claro

Tableland

Basse Terre

Moruga

New Grant

Princes Town

Penal

San Fernando

Oropuche Lagoon

San Francique

Erin Pt.

Erin Bay

La Brea

Irois Bay

Point Fortin

Islote Pt.

Cedros Bay

Fullarton

Icacos Pt.

N

0	20 miles
0	30 km

KEY

❶ Exploring Sites

⑥ Hotels and Restaurants

Exploring
Asa Wright Nature Centre, **2**
Caroni Bird Sanctuary, **5**
Jinnah Mosque, **4**
Port-of-Spain, **1**
University of West Indies, **3**

Dining
Cafe Savanna, **7**
La Boucan, **6**
La Fantasie, **8**
Rafters, **10**
Solimar, **9**
Tiki Village, **7**
Veni Mange, **12**
Wazo Deyzeel, **11**

Lodging
Alicia's House, **17**
Asa Wright Nature Centre, **19**
Carnetta's House, **18**
Holiday Inn, **14**
Hotel Normandie, **8**
Kapok Hotel, **7**
La Maison Rustique, **13**
Monique's, **15**
Trinidad Hilton and Conference Center, **6**
Tropical, **16**

palace by a cacao-plantation magnate and currently the office of the prime minister; **Roomor,** a flamboyantly baroque colonial-period house with a preponderance of towers, pinnacles, and wrought-iron trim that suggests an elaborate French pastry; and the **Queen's Royal College,** in German Renaissance style, with a prominent tower clock that chimes on the hour.

The **racetrack** at the southern end of the Savannah is no longer a venue for horse racing, but it is still the setting for music and costume competitions during Carnival and, when not jammed with calypso performers, tends toward quietude.

The northern end of the Savannah is devoted to plants. A rock garden, known as the **Hollow,** and a fish pond add to the rusticity. The **Botanic Gardens,** across the street, date from 1820. The official residences of the president and prime minister are on these grounds.

Way east on Picton Road in the scruffy, industrial district of Laventille, are **Fort Chacon** and **Fort Picton,** erected to ward off invaders by the Spanish and British regimes, respectively. The latter is a martello tower with a fine view of the gulf.

Out on the Island

The intensely urban atmosphere of Port-of-Spain belies the tropical beauty of the countryside surrounding it. It is truly stunning, but you will need a car, and three to eight (if you include the Caroni swamp) hours to find it. Begin by circling the Savannah—seemingly obligatory to get almost anywhere around here—to Saddle Road, in the residential district of **Maraval.** After a few miles the road begins to narrow and curve sharply as it climbs into the Northern Range. Here you'll find undulating hills of lush, junglelike foliage. Stop at the **Lookout**—and have Keith Davis sing you a hilarious calypso, complete with any biographical details you give him. (He's not allowed to ask, but a few T&T dollars are appreciated—and deserved.) Half an hour through this hilly terrain will lead you to **Maracas Bay,** the island's most popular beach, with smaller **Tyrico Bay** adjacent.

TIME OUT Try a shark-and-bake from one of the huts ranged along the road at Maracas. It's a deep-fried pita-type–bread shark sandwich, served with hot sauce and cilantro-garlic salsa. Patsy's is considered the best. Wash it down with a grenadillo (like a giant passion fruit) juice from the stand on Patsy's right, if it's available.

About four miles along is **Las Cuevas Beach.** Follow the same road through tiny La Fillete for several miles, crossing the bridge over the Yarra River. Here, washerwomen hang their laundry out, which is how **Blanchisseuse** got its name.

In this town the road narrows again, winding through canyons of moist, verdant foliage, towering palms and "big bamboo" (it's so gigantic they wrote a calypso song about it), and mossy grottoes. As you painstakingly execute the hairpin turns, you'll begin to think you've entered a tropical rain forest. You have.

Keep an eye out for vultures, parakeets, hummingbirds, toucans, and, if you're lucky, even red-bellied yellow-and-blue macaws. And, by the way, the mass of white cotton-candy substance on the rocks by the road hides tarantula nests.

About half an hour from Blanchisseuse, the road forks. Take the right, signposted to Arima, and another half hour on this road (and a *very* sharp right at the green hut) brings you to a bird-watcher's paradise,

❷ the **Asa Wright Nature Centre** (*see* Lodging, *below*). The grounds (almost 500 acres) are covered plants, trees, and multihued flowers, and the surrounding acreage is atwitter with more than 170 species of birds, from the gorgeous blue-green motmot to the rare nocturnal oilbird. The oilbirds' breeding grounds in Dunston Cave are included among the sights along the center's guided hiking trails. If you're feeling languid, relax on the veranda of the inn here and watch the diversity of birds that swoop about the porch feeders—an armchair bird-watcher's nirvana. This stunning plantation house looks out to the Arima valley, as lush and untouched as the earth offers. You can also have lunch or stay for the night in old-fashioned splendor. ☎ 809/667–4655. ☛ *$6 adults, $4 children.* ⊙ *Daily 9–5. Guided tours at 10:30 and 1:30; reservations necessary.*

The descent to **Arima,** about 7 miles, is equally pastoral. You may want to look out for the tiny Hindu shrine on the left side of the road as you descend. In late October it's lit with candles for Divali, a festival celebrated at the October full moon. The Eastern Main Road connecting Arima to Port-of-Spain is a busy, bumpy, and densely populated corridor full of roadside stands and businesses. Along the way you'll
❸ pass the **University of West Indies** campus in Curepe and the majestic
❹ turrets and arches of the **Jinnah Mosque** in St. Joseph.

Proceed west from Arima along the Churchill-Roosevelt Highway, a limited-access freeway that runs parallel to the Eastern Main Road a few miles to the south. Both avenues cross the Uriah Butler Highway just outside Port-of-Spain in San Juan; a few miles south on Butler High-
❺ way, take the turnoff for the **Caroni Bird Sanctuary.** Across from the sanctuary's parking lot is a sleepy canal with several boats and guides for hire; the smaller boats are best.

The Caroni is a large swamp with mazelike waterways bordered by mangrove trees, some plumed with huge termite nests. In the middle of the sanctuary are several islets that are home to Trinidad's national bird, the scarlet ibis. Just before sunset the ibis arrive by the thousands, their richly colored feathers brilliant in the gathering dusk, and, as more flocks alight, they turn their little tufts of land into bright Christmas trees. It's not something you see every day. Bring a sweater and insect repellent for your return trip. The boat fee is usually about $6–$15. Advance reservations can be made with boat operators Winston Nanan (☎ 809/645–1305) or David Ramsahai (☎ 809/663–4767). Mr. Nanan also arranges highly recommended bird-watching tours to nearby Guyana and Venezuela.

What to See and Do with Children

Emperor Valley Zoo and the **Botanical Gardens** are a cultivated expanse of parkland just north of the Savannah, the site of the president's official residence. A meticulous lattice of walkways and local flora, the parkland was first laid out in 1820 and is a model of what a tropical garden should be. In the midst of this serene wonderland is the zoo, leisurely apportioned on 8 acres and largely featuring birds and animals of the region—from the brilliantly plumed scarlet ibis to slithering anacondas and pythons; wild parrots breed in the area and can be seen (and heard) in the surrounding foliage. The zoo draws a quarter of a million visitors a year and more than half of them are children, so admission is priced accordingly—a mere TT$3, or TT$1.50 for under-12s. *Botanical Gardens, Port-of-Spain,* ☎ *809/622–3530.* ⊙ *Daily 9:30–6.*

The **Water Park** at the Valley Vue Hotel is open to nonguests and has the biggest, wettest slides in the West Indies—three 400-foot chutes leading to a shallow pool. *Ariapita Rd., St. Ann's, Port-of-Spain,* ☎ *809/624–0940.* ☛ *$4 adults, $3 children.* ☉ *Daily 10–6.*

Junior Carnival (*see* Carnival, *above*).

Off the Beaten Track

The **Lopinot Complex** is the restored estate house of a French count, Charles Joseph de Lopinot, who came to Trinidad in 1800 and chose this magnificent site to plant cocoa. His home has been turned into a museum where, it's said, his ghost prowls on stormy nights. (A guide is available from 10 to 6.) This is one of the main centers for Parang, a beautiful string-based folk music, which has become Trinidad's equivalent of Christmas carols. To get there, take the Eastern Main Road from Port-of-Spain to Arouca and look for the sign that points north.

Exploring Tobago

Numbers in the margin correspond to points of interest on the Tobago map.

A driving tour of Tobago, from Scarborough to Charlotteville and back, can be done in about four hours, but you'd never want to undertake this spectacular, and very hilly, ride in that time. Plan to spend at least one night at the Speyside end of the island and give yourself a chance to enjoy this largely untouched country and seaside at leisure. The Blue Waters Inn (*see* Lodging, *below*) is open for meals and for overnighting; it's about as close to the sea as you can get without swimming.

① **Scarborough,** near the airport, is nestled around **Rockley Bay,** and it gives the feeling that not much here has changed since the area was settled two centuries ago. Although it is not one of the pastel-colored, delightful cities of the Caribbean, it does have its charms.

TIME OUT Before starting out, be sure to stop for a meal or snack at the **Blue Crab** (*see* Dining, *below*), where wonderful island food and delicious Indian meals are provided on a delightful porch above the town that's shaded by mango trees in the garden. Note the red and yellow Methodist Church on the hillside above, one of Tobago's oldest churches.

② The road east from Scarborough soon narrows as it twists through **Mt. St. George,** a village that clings to a cliff high above the ocean. Fort King George is a lovely, tranquil spot commanding sweeping views of the bay, with a restored 18th-century English fort and barracks, a fine-arts center, and lush landscaped gardens.

The sea dips in and out of view as you pass through a series of small settlements and the town of Roxborough. About an hour's drive will **③** bring you to **King's Bay,** an attractive crescent-shape beach. Just before you reach the bay there is a bridge with an unmarked turnoff that leads to a gravel parking lot; beyond that, a landscaped path leads to a waterfall with a rocky pool where you can refresh yourself. You may meet enterprising locals who'll offer to guide you to the top of the falls, a climb that you may find not worth the effort.

After King's Bay the road rises dramatically; just before it dips again **④** there's a marked lookout with a vista of **Speyside,** a small fishing village, and several offshore islands.

TIME OUT **Jemma's Sea View Kitchen** (☎ 809/660–4066), along the main road in Speyside, offers tasty West Indian meals served in a house on stilts by the ocean. You'll find nothing fancy here, just delicious Tobagonian home cooking, including a wondrous baked chicken, and great views.

⑤ Past Speyside the road cuts across a ridge of mountains that separates the Atlantic side of Tobago from the Caribbean. On the far side is **Charlotteville,** a delightful fishing village set on a hill above Man O' War Bay. Fishermen here announce the day's catch (usually flying fish, redfish, or bonito) by sounding their conch shells. A view of Man O' War Bay with Pigeon Peak, Tobago's highest mountain, behind it at sunset is an exquisite treat for the eye.

⑥ The paved road ends a few miles outside Charlotteville, in Camberton. Returning to Speyside, take a right at the sign for **Flagstaff Hill.** Follow a well-traveled dirt road for about 1½ miles to a radio tower. It's one of the highest points in Tobago, surrounded by ocean on three sides and with a view of the hills, Charlotteville, and Bird of Paradise Island in the bay.

Beaches

Trinidad

Trinidad is not the beach destination that Tobago is, yet it has its share of fine shoreline, spread out along the North Coast Road within an hour's drive of Port-of-Spain.

Maracas Bay is a long stretch of sand with a cove and a fishing village at one end. It's a local favorite, so it can get crowded on weekends. Parking sites are ample, and there are snack bars and rest facilities. **Tyrico Bay,** just past Maracas, is a small beach lively with surfers who flock here to enjoy the excellent surfing. The strong undertow may be too much for some swimmers.

A few miles farther along the North Coast Road **Las Cuevas Bay,** a narrow, picturesque strip of sand named for the series of partially submerged and explorable caves that ring the beach. A food stand offers tasty snacks, and vendors hawk fresh fruit across the road. It's less crowded here, and seemingly serene, although, as at Maracas, the current can be treacherous. About 8 miles east, along the North Coast Road, is another narrow beach, palm-fringed **Blanchisseuse Bay.** Facilities are nonexistent, but the beach is ideal for a romantic picnic. You can haggle with local fishermen to take you out in their boats to explore the coast. Two miles or so farther along the North Coast Road, you come to **Marianne Beach,** the quietest and prettiest of all, with a natural freshwater lagoon at the east end. Pay Vincent James TT$3 to park on his land; you can also rent the three-room first floor of the house you see for about $13—it's very basic (☎ 809/674–7145 after 1 PM).

The drive to the northeast coast takes several hours. To get there you must take the detour road to Arima, but "goin' behind God's back," as the Trinis say, does reward the persistent traveler with gorgeous vistas and secluded beaches. **Balandra Bay,** sheltered by a rocky outcropping, is popular among bodysurfers. **Salibea Bay,** just past Galera Point, which juts toward Tobago, is a gentle beach with shallows and plenty of shade—perfect for swimming. Snack vendors abound in the vicinity. The road to **Manzanilla Beach** and **Cocos Bay** to the south, nicknamed the Cocal, is lined with stately palms whose fronds vault like the arches at Chartres. This is where many well-heeled Trinis have vacation homes. Manzanilla has picnic facilities and a postcard-pretty

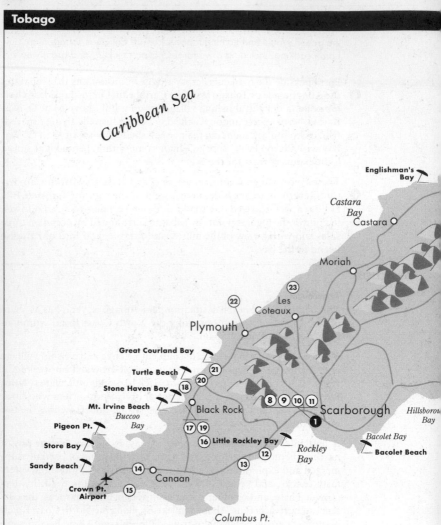

Exploring
Charlotteville, **5**
Flagstaff Hill, **6**
King's Bay, **3**
Mt. St. George, **2**
Scarborough, **1**
Speyside, **4**

Dining
Blue Crab, **9**
Cocrico Inn, **22**
Dillon's, **14**
Grafton's, **19**
Kariwak Village, **15**
Mount Marie, **8**
Old Donkey Cart House, **10**
Papillon, **18**
Rouselles, **11**

Lodging
Arnos Vale Hotel, **23**
Blue Horizon Resort, **16**
Blue Waters Inn, **7**
Grafton Beach Resort, **19**
Kariwak Village, **15**

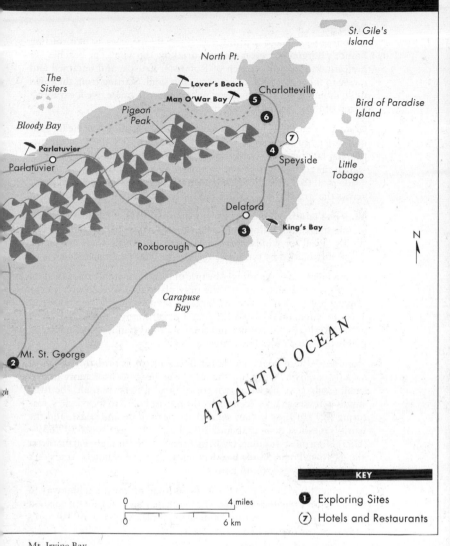

The Sisters

North Pt.

Lover's Beach

Man O'War Bay

Charlotteville

St. Gile's Island

Bird of Paradise Island

Pigeon Peak

Bloody Bay

5

6

⑦

4

Speyside

Little Tobago

Parlatuvier

Parlatuvier

Delaford

3

King's Bay

Roxborough

N

Carapuse Bay

Mt. St. George

2

zh

ATLANTIC OCEAN

0   4 miles

0   6 km

KEY

❶ Exploring Sites

⑦ Hotels and Restaurants

Mt. Irvine Bay
Hotel, **17**

Ocean Point, **13**

Palm Tree Village, **12**

Plantation Beach Villas, **21**

Turtle Beach
Hotel, **20**

view of the Atlantic, though its water is occasionally muddied by the Orinoco River, which flows in from South America.

Tobago

Traveling to Tobago without sampling the beaches is like touring France's Burgundy region without drinking the wine. The beaches are perfection to those in search of Robinson Crusoe, and untamed and messy to those in search of country-club sand. Starting from the town of Plymouth and slowly proceeding counterclockwise, we'll explore a dozen of the island's more memorable sand spots.

Great Courland Bay, near Fort Bennett, is a long stretch of clear, tranquil water, bordered on one end by **Turtle Beach,** so named for the turtles that lay their eggs here at night between April and May. (You can watch; the turtles don't seem to mind.) A short distance west, there's a side road that runs along **Stone Haven Bay,** a gorgeous beach that's across the street from Grafton Beach Resort, a luxury hotel complex.

Mt. Irvine Beach, across the street from the Mt. Irvine Beach Hotel, is an unremarkable setting, but it has great surfing in July and August. It's also ideal for windsurfing in January and April. There are picnic tables surrounded by painted concrete pagodas and a snack bar.

Pigeon Point is the stunningly beautiful locale inevitably displayed on Tobago travel brochures. It's the only privately owned beach on the island, part of what was once a large coconut estate, and you must pay a token admission (about $2) to enter the grounds. The beach is lined with towering royal palms, and there's a food stand, a gift shop, and paddleboats for rent. The waters are calm.

Store Bay, where boats depart for Buccoo Reef, is probably the most socially convivial setting in the area. The beach is little more than a small sandy cove between two rocky breakwaters, but, ah, the food stands here: six shacks licensed by the tourist board to local ladies, featuring *roti* (an East Indian sandwich), *pelau* (rice and peas), and the world's messiest dish, crab and dumplings. Miss Jean's (☏ 809/639–0563) is the most popular; try Miss Esmie's crab, though. Farther west along Crown Point, **Sandy Beach** is abutted by several hotels. You won't lack for amenities around here.

Just west of Scarborough, take Milford Road off the main highway to the shores of **Little Rockley Bay.** The beach is craggy and not much good for swimming, but it is quiet and offers a pleasing view of Tobago's capital across the water.

After driving through Scarborough, continue south on Bacolet Street 4 miles to **Bacolet Beach,** a dark-sand beach that was the setting for the films *Swiss Family Robinson* and *Heaven Knows, Mr. Allison.*

The road from Scarborough to Speyside has plenty of swimming sites, of which **King's Bay Beach,** surrounded by steep green hills, is the most visually satisfying—the bay hooks around so severely that you feel as if you're swimming in a lake. It's easy to find because it's marked by a sign about halfway between Roxborough and Speyside.

Man O' War Bay in Charlotteville is flanked by one of the prettiest fishing villages in the Caribbean. You can lounge on the sand and purchase the day's catch for your dinner. Farther west across the bay is **Lover's Beach,** so called because of its pink sand and because it is so secluded: You have to hire a local to take you there by boat.

Parlatuvier, on the north side of the island, is best approached via the road from Roxborough. The beach here is a classic Caribbean crescent, a scene peopled by villagers and local fishermen. The next beach over, **Englishman's Bay,** is equally seductive and completely deserted.

Sports and the Outdoors

Bird-Watching

Bird-watchers can fill up their books with notes on the variety of species to be found in Trinidad at the **Asa Wright Nature Centre,** the **Caroni Bird Sanctuary** (*see* Exploring Trinidad, *above*), and the **Pointe-à-Pierre Wild Fowl Trust,** which is located within the unlikely confines of a petrochemical complex (42 Sandown Rd., Pt. Cumana, ☎ 809/637–5145). In Tobago, naturalist **David Rooks** offers walks inland and trips to offshore bird colonies (☎ 809/639–4276).

Deep-Sea Fishing

The islands off the northwest coast of Trinidad offer excellent waters for deep-sea fishing; the ocean here was a favorite angling spot of Franklin D. Roosevelt. Members of the **Trinidad and Tobago Yacht Club** (Bayshore, ☎ 809/637–4260) may be willing to arrange a tour.

On Tobago, **Dillon's Fishing Charter** (Pigeon Point, ☎ 809/639–8765) is the best for whole- and half-day trips for kingfish, barracuda, wahoo, dolphinfish, blue marlin, etc. Trips start at $165 for four hours, including equipment.

Golf

There are nine golf courses in the country, the best of which are the **Mt. Irvine Golf Club** (☎ 809/639–8871) in Tobago and **St. Andrew's Golf Club** in Moka, Maraval (☎ 809/629–2314), just outside Port-of-Spain.

Horseback Riding

Palm Tree Village (Tobago, ☎ 809/639–4347) has (very) old race horses on which to amble along the beach at low tide.

Scuba Diving

Tobago draws scuba-diving aficionados from around the world. You can get information, supplies, and instruction at **Dive Tobago** (☎ 809/639–0202), **Man Friday Diving** (☎ 809/660–4676), **Tobago Dive Experience** (☎ 809/639–0191), and **Viking Dive and Sail/Yacht Chartering** (809/639–9209).

Snorkeling

The best spots for snorkeling are on Tobago. **Buccoo Reef** is easily the most popular—perhaps too popular. Over the years the reef has been damaged by the ceaseless boat traffic and by the thoughtless visitors who take pieces of coral for souvenirs. Even so, it's still a trip worth experiencing, particularly if you have children. Daily 2½-hour tours by flat, glass-bottom boats let you snorkel at the reef, swim in a shallow lagoon pool, and take a look at Coral Gardens, where fish and coral are yet untouched. The trip costs about $8, and masks, snorkeling equipment and reef shoes are provided. Departure is at 11 AM from Pigeon Point. Most of the scuba-diving companies also arrange scuba tours. There is also good snorkeling by the beach near the **Arnos Vale Hotel** and at **Blue Waters,** and the government is slowly developing reefs around Speyside that rival, if not surpass, Buccoo.

Tennis

The following private tennis courts allow nonmembers or nonresidents to play: in Trinidad, the **Trinidad Hilton** (☎ 809/624–3211), the **Trinidad Country Club** (☎ 809/622–3470), the **Tranquility Square Lawn Tennis Club** (Victoria Ave., Port-of-Spain, ☎ 809/625–4182); on Tobago,

Turtle Beach (☎ 809/639–2851), **Mt. Irvine** (☎ 809/639–8817), and the **Blue Waters Inn** (☎ 809/660–4341).

Shopping

Thanks in large part to Carnival costumery, there's no shortage of fabric shops on the islands. The best bargains for Asian and East Indian silks and cottons can be found in downtown Port-of-Spain, on **Frederick Street** and around **Independence Square.** Other good buys are such duty-free items as Angostura Bitters and Old Oak or Vat 19 rum, all widely available throughout the country.

Upscale boutiques at the **Trinidad Hilton** and in the **Long Circular Mall** (Long Circular Rd., St James, ☎ 809/622–4925) make for relaxed browsing. **Meiling** (Ellerslie Plaza, Cotton Hill, behind the Kapok Hotel, Port-of-Spain, ☎ 809/628–6205) is a fine designer whose shop features cottons in ecru or white and smart little girls' dresses with shirred tops. **Ellerslie Plaza,** where Meiling is located, is an attractive new mall well worth browsing in. You can drop by for a snack at the Patisserie or lunch at the stylish new Gourmet Club. Traditional luxury duty-free items are available at **Y. de Lima** (High St., Port-of-Spain; West Mall, Port-of-Spain). **Stecher's** (Trinidad Hilton, Lady Young Rd., Port-of-Spain; Long Circular Mall, Port-of-Spain) also sells typical duty-free items and will arrange for purchases to be delivered at the airport.

LOCAL CRAFTS

The tourism office can provide an extensive list of local artisans who specialize in everything from straw and cane work to miniature steel pans. A charming experience is to be had at Monica Monceaux's **Craft Boutique** (corner of Adam Smith Sq. S and Murray St. in the Woodbrook section of Port-of-Spain, ☎ 809/627–2736). Monica's house is a delight in gingerbread wood tracery. Almost every inch of the house is utilized by Monica and her craftspeople, who make carnival and folk dolls, Christmas ornaments (even those for the Hilton tree), crocheted picture frames, preserves, and dozens of other items in merry disarray. At the new Ellerslie Plaza behind the Kapok Hotel, stop at **Bonga!** (☎ 809/624–8819) for smart T-shirts, carryalls, shorts, and bathing suits. **Poui Boutique** (Ellerslie Plaza, ☎ 809/622–5597) has stylish hand-done wax batik wear and Ajoupa pottery, an attractive local terra-cotta pottery. The **Market** (Nook Ave. by the Hotel Normandie) is a mall with several shops that specialize in indigenous fashions, crafts, jewelry, basketwork, and ceramics. On Tobago, the **Cotton House** on lovely Bacolet Street in Scarborough (☎ 809/639–2727) is a good bet for jewelry and imaginative batik work. Paula Young runs her shop like an art school. You can visit the upstairs studio; if it's not too busy, you can even make a batik square at no charge. A good line (Forro brand) of homemade tamarind chutney, marmalade of lime or lemon, hot sauce, and guava or golden apple jelly can be found at **Forro's** (Wilson Rd., across from the Scarborough market, ☎ 809/639–2979) or at the airport in Tobago. Mrs. Eileen Forrester, wife of the Anglican priest at St. David's in Plymouth, supervises a kitchen full of good cooks who boil and bottle the condiments and pack them in little straw baskets. Most jars are small, easily carried, and very inexpensive. Straw baskets and other crafts are sold at the **Souvenir and Gift Shop** (Port Mall, Scarborough, ☎ 809/639–5632).

RECORDS

For the best selection of calypso and soca music, check out **Rhyner's Record Shop** (54 Prince St., ☎ 809/623–5673; Cruise Ship Complex, ☎ 809/627–8717).

Dining

Ask what Creole seasoning is and you'll hear a different answer from each person you ask. The herbs and spices used on the island range from fresh bay leaves (bright green, not dried) to nutmegs from the trees and a variety of peppers. The cooking also uses a lot of guava, plantain, and local fish and meat. Asian, Indian, African, French, and Spanish influences, among others, can be tasted, often in a single meal. Indian food is a favorite: Rotis are served as a fast food; a mélange of curried meat or fish and vegetables frequently makes an appearance; and a wide selection of *vindaloos* (spicy hot meat, vegetable, and seafood dishes) and poori can be had. Crab lovers will find large blue-backs curried, peppered, and served with tomatoes, and used in callaloo soup (a national treasure made of green dasheen leaves mixed with okra, coconut milk, and crabmeat). Shark-and-bake is the sandwich of choice, made of lightly seasoned, fried shark meat.

Macaroni pie and chicken is Tobago's Sunday dinner favorite, perhaps with fried plantain or potatoes. Oil Down tastes better than it sounds: It's a gently seasoned mixture of boiled breadfruit and salted beef or pork flavored with coconut milk. For dessert, mango ice cream or a sweetly sour tamarind ball is a tasty finish. You may want to take home some hot pepper sauce or chutney to a spice-loving friend or relative. Hotel restaurants, of course, cater to a less adventuresome market. Good Italian food and other European cuisines can now be had in Trinidad, as indicated below.

No Trinibagan dining experience can be complete, of course, without a rum punch with fresh fruit and the legendary Angostura Bitters, made by the same local company that produces the excellent Old Oak rum, but watch out for the fiendish sugar content. Light, refreshing Carib beer is the local lager; dark-beer aficionados can try Royal Extra Stout (R.E.), which is even sweeter than Guinness. Local chocolate, found in supermarkets, is made in squares and often flavored with bay leaf and nutmeg.

What to Wear

The restaurants of Trinidad and Tobego are informal: You won't find any jacket and tie requirements. Beachwear, however, is a little too casual for most places. A nice pair of shorts is apropos for lunch. For dinner, you'll probably feel most comfortable in a pair of slacks or a casual sundress. If in doubt, ask about appropriate attire when making your reservations.

CATEGORY	COST*
$$$	over $25
$$	$15–$25
$	under $15

per person, excluding drinks, service, and 15% tax

Trinidad

$$$ **La Boucan.** Trinidadian dancer Geoffrey Holder painted the large mural of a social idyll in the Savannah that dominates one wall of this room at the Hilton. Geoffrey dances better than he paints, but the food here has improved in leaps and bounds, thanks in part to a very fine food-and-beverage manager. Its old charm of silver service, uniformed waiters, candlelight, pink tablecloths, and the soft serenade of a grand piano remains. Most island food will be mild unless you assure them that you like it spicy. The menu, however, is international, with meat and fish cooked to order. Afternoon tea is a treat. The more casual pool-

side eatery is charming, a good place to enjoy island shrimp and other treats at lavish buffets. Breakfast is served here as well. ✕ *Trinidad Hilton, Lady Young Rd., Port-of-Spain, ☎ 809/624–3211. Reservations advised. Jacket required. AE, DC, MC, V.*

$$–$$$ **Solimar.** Dining here is oddly, but not unpleasantly, like dining under the Caribbean, thanks to the huge turquoise-lit fish tank, jungle of greenery, and candlelight. The chef offers a menu that tries to travel the world in one meal: You can eat shrimp tempura, Irish smoked salmon, Hawaiian barbecued mahimahi, Greek salad, linguine Alfredo, or Zwiebel schnitzel, all while listening to John Denver singing "I think I'd rather be a cowboy." Best bets are the day's specials—seafood mixed grill, perhaps (which is not, in fact, grilled, but fried, like everything else on Trinidad), then hot chocolate soufflé with chilled coconut cream. Solimar is popular with expat types and tends toward careful casualness. ✕ *6 Nook Ave., St. Ann's, Port-of-Spain, ☎ 809/624–1459. AE, DC, MC, V.*

$$ **Cafe Savanna.** Consistently tasty and distinctive Trinidadian fare is served
★   at this cozy den. Try Christmas Salad, a combination of turkey, pineapple, apple, and sorrel tossed in orange vinaigrette; cinnamon-dipped, baked fillets of red snapper, topped with pineapple and papaya (pawpaw) sauce; seafood lasagna with cream, cheddar, and fresh spices; and, for dessert, Doux-Doux, a fresh Caribbean fruit salad topped with coconut-mocha mousse, or Yuh Tink It Sof, a traditional black fruitcake served with fresh fruit salad. The callaloo soup here sets the standard for other island eateries. A three-course lunch menu gives you choices for TT$65–$85. The atmosphere is very casual—just bare wood walls and Sade on the sound system. ✕ *Kapok Hotel, 16–18 Cotton Hill, Port-of-Spain, ☎ 809/622–6441. Reservations advised. AE, DC, MC, V. Closed Sun.*

$$ **La Fantasie.** The Hotel Normandie's restaurant is pretty, pink, and glacially air-conditioned inside, with pink-clothed wrought-iron tables on the terrace out front. Despite the names, most of the dishes are familiar French-style arrays, and often they are a lighter alternative to local fare. (They pioneered *cuisine nouvelle créole.*) Seafood is the best bet; the day's catch best of all—grilled snapper stuffed with shrimp in tart tomato sauce, perhaps. The homemade ice cream gets rave reviews, but it's often unavailable. ✕ *Hotel Normandie, 10 Nook Ave., St. Ann's, Port-of-Spain, ☎ 809/624–1181. Reservations advised. AE, DC, MC, V.*

$$ **Tiki Village.** Cosmopolitan Port-of-Spainers are as passionate about their Asian food as New Yorkers and San Franciscans are. Everyone touts their favorite, but this eatery, a serious (nonkitsch) version of Trader Vic's, is the most reliable. It's high under the rafters atop the Kapok Hotel, air-conditioned, clean-lined, and sunlit. Fine Asian food is served, including the very popular dim sum, which you order by checking off your picks on a multiple-choice card. ✕ *Kapok Hotel, 16–18 Cotton Hill, Port-of-Spain, ☎ 809/622–6441. Reservations advised. AE, D, DC, MC, V.*

$$ **Veni Mange.** The best lunches in town are served inside this small stucco
★   house. Credit Allyson Hennessy, a Cordon Bleu–trained cook who has become a celebrity of sorts because of a TV talk show she hosts, and her sister-partner, Rosemary Hezekiah. The cuisine is Creole. ✕ *13 Lucknow St., St. James, Port-of-Spain, ☎ 809/622–7533. No credit cards. No dinner.*

$–$$ **Rafters.** Behind a stone facade with green rafters stands a pub that has become an urban institution. Once it was a rum shop; currently it's a bar and a restaurant. The pub is the center of activity, especially Friday night. In late afternoons the place begins to swell with Port-of-

Spainers ordering from the tasty selection of burgers, barbecues, and burritos and generally loosening up. The Seafood Medley platter (seasonal fin and shellfish, including shrimp and conch) is served with baked potato and tartar sauce for about $8 (TT$45). In the evening an unexpectedly romantic candlelit restaurant opens in another part of the delightful old building. ✕ *6A Warner St., Port-of-Spain,* ☏ *809/628–9258. AE, DC, MC, V.*

$ **Wazo Deyzeel.** Wazo ("oiseaux des isles"—get it?) is adored by all for its setting, high up in the hills of St. Ann, with Port-of-Spain spread out below; its live bands and dancing on weekends; its friendliness; and its prizewinning cocktails (the cucumber-lime-rum-syrup Wazo Combo is essential); as well as for its food. The Thursday night all-you-can-eat Caribbean buffet might include grouper, flying fish, red snapper, macaroni pie, cou-cou (cornmeal and coconut dumplings), *bhajia* (East Indian spinach fritters), and savory pumpkin pie, and at about $10 is probably the best bargain in the city. Other nights (except Monday–Wednesday) you could go for a seafood platter or a beef pot roast, all cooked by three Jamaican ladies. Candy-colored director's chairs, white walls, a big, open-air terrace for admiring the view, wining (a naughty dance style), and liming (hanging out) set the tone. ✕ *Carib Way, 23 Sydenham Ave., St. Ann's, Port-of-Spain,* ☏ *809/623–0115. MC, V. Closed Mon.–Wed.*

Tobago

$$–$$$ **Dillon's.** Stanley Dillon's other career as a fishing-charter operator ★ guarantees the freshest catch at his seafood restaurant by the airport. White walls hung with local art, red plaid tablecloths, and a silver service waitstaff create a soothing atmosphere halfway between homey and posh. The menu mixes traditional favorites, such as shrimp cocktail, French onion soup, lobster thermidor, and surf and turf, with callaloo, stuffed kingfish, chunky fish broth, and other Creole dishes. Get here early on weekends, before the line stretches to the runway. ✕ *Airport Rd. near Crown Pt.,* ☏ *809/639–8765. AE, MC, V.*

$$–$$$ **Grafton's.** The resort's main restaurant is a large open terrace overlooking the Caribbean, but with a clearer view of the hotel pool, bar, and evening's entertainment than of the waves. Attend one of the all-you-can-eat lunch buffets, which might include char-grilled chicken, steak and pork, a suckling pig, Creole dolphinfish, curried blue crab, any number of root vegetables, spaghetti, pelau, cauliflower with cheese, a salad bar, and an array of desserts; you'll wish you'd remembered to pack the Tums. ✕ *Grafton Beach Resort, Black Rock,* ☏ *809/639–0191. Reservations advised. AE, DC, MC, V.*

$$ **Cocrico Inn.** A café with a bar against one wall, the Cocrico offers delectable home cooking. The three rotating chefs use fresh fruits and vegetables grown in the neighborhood. They zealously guard their recipes, including a marvelous *cou-cou* (a dumpling of cornmeal and coconut) and lightly breaded, subtly spiced grouper. There is nothing fancy here, just warm and delicious food and cool air-conditioning. ✕ *Corner of North and Commissioner Sts., Plymouth,* ☏ *809/639–2661. AE, V.*

$$ **Kariwak Village.** Steel-band music (on tape) plays gently in the back-★ ground at this romantic candlelit spot. In a bamboo pavillion created by her architect-husband to resemble an Amerindian round hut, Christine Clovis orchestrates a very original four-course menu. Changing daily, the choices may include christophine soup, curried green fig, kingfish with shrimp sauce, and coconut cake. Whatever it is, it will be full of herbs and vegetables freshly picked from Christine's own organic garden, and everything will be bursting with flavor, including the

home-baked breads. It's a treat for vegetable lovers, because Kariwak knows how to honor the simple squash and green beans. The nonalcoholic drinks are wonderful, even the iced coffee, which is more like a frozen coconut cappuccino. Saturday buffets, with live jazz or calypso, are a Tobagonian highlight. ✗ *Kariwak Village, Crown Pt.,* ☎ *809/639–8442. AE, DC, MC, V.*

$$ Old Donkey Cart House. The name is something of a curiosity, since this restaurant is set in and around an attractive green-and-white colonial house (2 miles south of Scarborough). There's outdoor dining in a garden with twinkling lights. The cuisine is standard Caribbean, nothing special, but German side dishes and an extensive selection of Rhine and Moselle wines set it apart. ✗ *Bacolet St., Scarborough,* ☎ *809/639–3551. AE, V.*

$$ Papillon. Named after one of the proprietor's favorite books, this seafood restaurant is a homey room with an adjoining patio. Lobster Buccoo Bay is marinated in sherry and broiled with herbs and garlic-butter sauce. Seafood casserole au gratin means chunks of lobster, shrimp, fish, and cream, all seasoned in ginger wine. Baby shark is marinated in rum and lime. Or you can just enjoy some good broiled chicken or pork cutlets with pineapple. Papillon is one good reason for staying at the Old Grange Inn next door, owned by the same Trinidadian family. ✗ *Buccoo Bay Rd., Mt. Irvine,* ☎ *809/639–0275. AE, DC, MC, V.*

$$ Rouselle's. An enchanting terrace high above Scarborough Bay with a
★ big, congenial bar, Rouselles was just a liming spot until friends and regulars demanded proper food. Bet they didn't expect food that could compete with big-city cuisine, though. The small menu dons different accessories rather than changing completely, so you may find grouper, broiled and served with a fresh Creole sauce and several vegetables—garlicky green beans, carrots with ginger, a raw bok choy salad, and potato croquette with spices and celery—or dolphinfish with white wine sauce, or lobster, steamed just so, which is very hard to procure. Whatever there is, you can trust that it'll be delicious. A sizable *amuse-gueule* (appetizer), hot garlic bread, plus dessert (save room for pineapple pie or homemade ice cream) are included in the entrée price, and don't forgo the Rouselles punch. The recipe's a secret, but the lovely, welcoming co-owners, Bobbie and Charlene, will probably let you in on it. ✗ *Old Windward Rd., Bacolet,* ☎ *809/639–4738. Lunch by reservation only. AE, MC, V.*

$–$$ Blue Crab. Alison Sardinha is Tobago's most ebullient and kindly hostess, and her husband, Ken, one of its best chefs. He cooks "like our mothers cooked," serving the local food with heavy East Indian influence, a bit of Portuguese, and occasionally Asian, too. There might be rolled flying fish, *katchowrie* (spiced split pea patties, a little like falafel), curry chicken, or long-cooked suckling pig. There's always a callaloo, differently flavored on different days, fine rotis and cou-cou, and sometimes a "cookup"—pelau-type rice, with *everything* in it. The place is officially open only on Wednesday and Friday nights, but Miss Alison will open up on other evenings (and for weekend lunches, too) even for one table, if you call in the morning. The setting, on a wide, shady terrace overlooking the bay, is just about perfect, and there's a bar for cocktails. Two guest rooms (the front one's a beauty) in the Sardinhas' home are also available. If you want to see the joy of Caribbean cooking in one presentation, ask Alison how to make one of the dishes: Her expressions, gestures, and advice should be exported. They epitomize the joy of living. ✗ *Robinson St. at Main St., Scarborough,* ☎ *809/639–2737. No credit cards.*

$ Mount Marie. If you want to find a spotlessly clean, air-conditioned restaurant in Scarborough that serves good local and international fare, look no further. The menu changes according to what's available at the market but usually includes pasta and seafood dishes. The place is owned by the local police pension fund and managed by the very stylish and efficient Petunia Thomas. Best of all, the place is a real bargain. ✕ *Mt. Marie, near the Rockley Bay harbor just off Claude Noel Hwy.,* ☎ *809/639–2014. AC, MC, V.*

Lodging

On Trinidad most lodging establishments are within the vicinity of Port-of-Spain, far from any beach. On Tobago, it's the opposite; nearly every establishment listed here is either on or within walking distance of the ocean. Carnival week is one of two times in the year for which you should book reservations far in advance (the other is Christmas); expect to pay twice the price charged the rest of the year.

Most places do offer breakfast and dinner for an additional flat rate (MAP), but on the whole these offer less variety than you'll get if you strike out for meals on your own. If you're lodging on the east side of Tobago, however, MAP is almost essential because of the dearth of restaurants.

The number of private homes in Trinidad and Tobago offering bed-and-breakfast accommodations is growing each year. This is an excellent, inexpensive option and a wonderful way to meet the friendly locals. Contact the **Trinidad and Tobago Bed and Breakfast Association** (Box 323, Diego Martin, or Park Lane Court, Amethyst Dr., El Dorado, Tunapuna, ☎ 809/663–5265).

CATEGORY	COST*
$$$$	over $175
$$$	$100–$175
$$	$60–$100
$	under $60

*All prices are for a standard double room for two, excluding 15% tax and 10% service charge.

Trinidad

$$$–$$$$
★ **Trinidad Hilton and Conference Center.** Perched above the Gulf of Paria and Queen's Park Savannah, and set on landscaped gardens, the Hilton radiates comfort and tropical breezes. It stretches out horizontally, across the hilltop, and gently moves down the hillside: You take the elevator *down* to your room. Extreme efficiency is maintained, without the loss of tropical ambience. Each of the 394 rooms has a balcony, which either opens to a fine view of Queen's Park, the city, and the sea beyond or overlooks the inviting Olympic-size pool, shaded by trees harboring brightly crested cornbirds. Rooms are decorated in a mellow pastels. This is Port-of-Spain's most stylish hotel, and it has hired a recent Miss World, Trinidad's Giselle Laronde-West, as public relations manager, for her competency as well as her glamour. The executive floors have good working desks and a pleasant clubroom for breakfast or meetings. The only puzzlement: Where are the hair dryers? *Lady Young Rd., Box 442, Port-of-Spain,* ☎ *809/624–3211; in the U.S., 800/445–8667;* FAX *809/624–4485. 394 rooms. 2 restaurants, 3 bars, conference rooms, satellite TV, pool, 2 lighted tennis courts, drugstore, gift shops, car rental, taxi service. AE, DC, MC, V. EP.*

$$$ Holiday Inn. Proximity to the port and Independence Square results in a lovely pastel panorama of the old town and of ships idling in the Gulf of Paria. All there is within walking distance is the Cruise Ship Complex, where the National Stadium now hosts the pre-Carnival Dimanche Gras, and crazy, traffic-clogged Independence Square. The rooms are in standard international mode, complete with hair dryers, a rarity on Trinidad. The hotel's rooftop restaurant, La Ronde, is a revolving bistro that offers a striking view of the city at night. This is a more moderate alternative to the swankier, but similar, Hilton. ☎ *Wrightson Rd., Box 1017, Port-of-Spain, ☎ 809/625–3361; in the U.S., 800/465–4329; FAX 809/625–4166. 235 rooms. Satellite TV, pool, health spa, conference rooms, beauty salon, taxi service. AE, DC, MC, V. BP.*

$$–$$$ **Hotel Normandie.** Built by French Creoles in the 1930s on the ruins
★ of an old coconut plantation, the Normandie has touches of Spanish, English colonial, and even postmodern architecture. The standard rooms, set around a pretty pool courtyard, have beige textured-vinyl walls, wood floorboards and fittings, TV, phone, noisy but efficient air-conditioning, and very little light. The 13 loft rooms are far better: For $25 more, you get a towering duplex with simple wood furniture, exposed eaves, and a bigger bathroom. Number 236 is especially bright and beautiful, with a big window upstairs, and 231 has extra space. These are great for families, since two under-12s can share for free. The conference facilities ensure a steady flow of convention groups, who also like the quiet location, set back from residential St. Ann's Road in the center of an artsy mall of crafts and clothes shops and galleries. Service is friendly and efficient. La Fantasie (*see* Dining, *above*) provides room service until 11 PM. ☎ *10 Nook Ave., St. Ann's, Port-of-Spain, ☎ and fax 809/624–1181. 61 rooms. Restaurant and bar, pool, meeting rooms, gallery, café, shops, car rental, taxi service. AE, DC, MC, V. EP, MAP.*

$$–$$$ **Kapok Hotel.** Although now part of the Golden Tulip hotel chain, this
★ hotel has been run by the Chan family for years and gleams with cheerful efficiency. The rooms, done in pink and white, are spotless, spacious, and sunlit, with rattan furniture and Polynesian prints the colors of highlighting markers. Front ones are best for the view over the Savannah—the Kapok is next to it, but away from the hubbub—and even better are the studios, with kitchenette included for the same price as a room. Request a refrigerator when you book, and a hair dryer (they're built into about a quarter of the bathrooms); all rooms have quiet air-conditioning, satellite TVs, push-button phones with an extra fax-friendly jack, and full-length mirrors. Suites are vast, and fine for families, who will also like the Laundromat and the birds and monkeys who live by the pool. The two restaurants, Cafe Savanna and Tiki Village (*see* Dining, *above*), are popular with locals. With facilities and ambience this sophisticated, you'd think the Kapok would cost far more. ☎ *16–18 Cotton Hill, St. Clair, Port-of-Spain, ☎ 809/622–6441, FAX 809/622–9677. 65 rooms, 6 suites. 2 restaurants, shops, hair salon, satellite TV, pool, taxi service. AE, DC, MC, V. EP.*

$–$$ **La Maison Rustique.** This little bed-and-breakfast in a gingerbread house is a charmer, and it has a great location, near Queen's Park Savannah amid other wonderful Victorian homes. Rooms in the garden cottage are the nicest, but all rooms are cleans and serviceable. Some are air-conditioned, and a few have private baths. The proprietor, Maureen Chin-Asiong, is a hotel school graduate and lists the Wilton School of Cake Decorating in Chicago among her credits. She not only serves good breakfasts—popovers, croissants, quiche—but also whips up afternoon tea, snacks, and picnic baskets. There's a five-night Carnival package for U.S.$500. ☎ *16 Rust St., St. Clair, Port-of-Spain, ☎ and fax 809/622–1512. 7 rooms (3 with private bath). No credit cards. BP.*

$ Alicia's House. The Govias managed to keep the family atmosphere when
★ they converted their home for guests, so all here is welcoming and re-
assuring. The enormous, breezy lounge has squashy sofas, round tables,
cane chairs, a piano, and a tank of fish; it leads into the dining area,
where you may take breakfast, and other meals if you ask. Rooms vary
greatly. Admiral Rooney (a local flower) is a big one with mahogany
furniture, a cute garden-view desk, and a giant bathtub; the Back Room
is very small but also very bright, and it has a private spiral staircase
to the pool; Alicia's Room (she's the owners' daughter) is a petite apartment with twin cherry-red sofas, many windows, an acre of closets, a
pink bathroom with a huge bathtub, and mirror tiles over the bed. Extras—which you shouldn't expect for the low rates but get anyway—
include a hot tub and a water cooler by the pool, 14-channel U.S. cable
TV, air-conditioning, private bathrooms, and push-button phones in every
room. It's a 10-minute walk from the Savannah, very near the Normandie.
🖼 *7 Coblentz Gardens, St. Ann's, Port-of-Spain,* ☎ *809/623–2802;
toll-free from airport, 223;* FAX *809/622–8560. 16 rooms. Cable TV,
lounge, dining room, pool, hot tub. MC, V. EP, CP, MAP.*

$ Asa Wright Nature Centre. Bird-watchers and nature photographers
are frequently among the guests at this handsome lodge. Built in 1908,
it's set in a lush rain forest (about 90 minutes east of Port-of-Spain)
populated by nearly 200 species of birds. There are impressive views
of the verdant Arima Valley and the Northern Range from the veranda,
where tea is served each afternoon. Just inside is an elegant, comfortable lounge with black lacquered floorboards, bookcases, antiques, and
ornithological memorabilia. The two huge bedrooms that abut this share
its romantic atmosphere, with fans turning slowly on tall ceilings,
hardwood closets, and antique beds. All other rooms are in modern
lodges near the house, simply outfitted with marble floors, spartan wood
furniture, and private covered terraces. You'll feel you're miles from
anywhere, and, actually, you are, so you'll need the three meals a day
and evening rum punch that are included in the rates. A car is essential, unless bird-watching at the center and being alone are your sole
aims, in which case airport transfers cost $40. (For more information
about the center, *see* Exploring, *above.*) 🖼 *Box 4710, Arima, Trinidad,*
☎ *809/667–4655,* FAX *809/667–0493. 23 rooms. Dining room, veranda,
lounge, guided field trips. No credit cards.*

$ Carnetta's House. When Winston Borrell retired as director of tourism
for Trinidad and Tobago, he and his wife, Carnetta, opened up their
suburban two-story house to guests. One guest room is on the upper
floor, the same level as the lounge and terrace dining room. The other
four are on the ground floor, with the choice room, Le Flamboyant,
opening onto the garden's patio. All rooms have a private bathroom
with shower, telephone, radio, and TV. And, although there is air-conditioning, cool breezes usually do the trick. Unfortunately, the doors
need to be shuttered at night for security reasons. Winston is a keen
gardener, and his garden has a sampling of plants that are a fascinating introduction to tropical flowers and herbs. Carnetta uses the herbs
in her cooking, and she can prepare some of the best dinners that you
may find in Port-of-Spain. Equally important is the fund of information that both Carnetta and Winston can offer on what to see and do
in Trinidad and the necessary arrangements they can make to do it. 🖼
28 Scotland Terrace, Andalusia, Maraval, Port-of-Spain, ☎ *809/628–
2732,* FAX *809/628–7717. 5 rooms. Dining room, lounge, laundry facilities, car-rental arrangements, airport transfers. AE, DC, MC, V. EP,
BP, MAP.*

$ Monique's. Mike and Monique Charbonné really *like* having guests,
★   as they have been proving for more than 10 years. In fact, they like it
so much, they've built an annex close to their house, with a further 10
rooms. Rooms are sizable, spotless, and, mostly, light. Each has air-
conditioning, phone, and private bathroom; the newer rooms also
have TV and kitchenette. Numbers 25 and 26 are enormous and can
sleep up to six. They're darker than the other rooms, but each has a
little sunken red stone patio where you can soak up some sun. Breakfast is in the parlorlike dining room, where you can ask to have dinner, too. The airy, marble-floored lounge is a great place to hang
out—with the hosts often as not. Mike sometimes organizes a picnic
to the couple's 100-acre plantation near Blanchisseuse. ⌂ *114 Saddle
Rd., Maraval, Port-of-Spain,* ☎ *809/628–3334,* FAX *809/622–3232. 26
rooms. Dining room, common room with TV. AE, EP, MAP.*

$ Tropical. Crazy-paved steps take you into a pretty reception area with
a clicking ceiling fan, murmuring TV, pea-green Lloyd Loom chairs,
white arches, and white wrought-iron gates shielding a central, clois-
terlike courtyard. That's about it for the grounds, except for the small
pool. Rooms, too, are spartan, if psychedelic, with their fuchsia-and-
tomato drapes, bedcovers, and shower curtains. Most are big, and all
have air-conditioning and bathrooms. Big pluses are the excellent
restaurant-bar and club attached, serving local food, and the low rates.
⌂ *6 Rookery Nook, Maraval, Port-of-Spain,* ☎ *809/622–5815,* FAX
809/622–3174. 13 rooms. Restaurant, pool. AE, EP.

Tobago

$$$$ Arnos Vale Hotel. It's always been the most romantic spot on Tobago,
crossing Tobagonian horticulture with Mediterranean design. However, when we visited to inspect it this year, we found it under new ownership (reportedly the Milan soccer team!) and closed for repairs (slated
to reopen by fall 1995). It's always been under Italian ownership, and
some guests report that Italians are given priority as clients, but, Tobago being a democracy, things may change. We hope that the level of
service will remain high. Suites and rooms are in white stucco cottages
set on a hill that descends, through a series of winding paths, to a secluded beach, pool, and bar. The elegant hilltop restaurant, with iron-
lattice tables, a chandelier, and a hand-painted piano, leads to a
crescent-shape patio that offers a sweeping view of the sea. ⌂ *Arnos
Vale, Box 208, Scarborough,* ☎ *809/639–2881,* FAX *809/639-4629. 30
rooms. Restaurant, bar, pool, tennis, beach, snorkeling dive shop,
disco, gift shop. AE, DC, MC, V. EP.*

$$$$ Grafton Beach Resort. If any hotel has the action on Tobago, it's the
★   Grafton. It's full most of the year, and the guests seem to enjoy themselves quite a bit. Yet it's stretched out languidly along the shore under
the tall palms, and so it's possible, with seaview rooms, to feel away
from it all, but never alone. This sparkling complex has the most international ambience of any Tobago hotel, from the huge, lobby-bar-
restaurant-pool area—all within view of one another, and perched
over the sea—to the top-class in-room facilities. These include, as well
as the expected satellite TV, phone, balcony, full-length mirror, and so
on, a hair dryer, minibar, 24-hour room service, and inaudible air-conditioning. Solid teak furniture and terra-cotta-tiled floors, subtle lighting, and marble bathrooms make up the decor. The Neptune seafood
restaurant and the bar, where local folk shows and bands perform nightly,
are perched, cruise-liner-style, above and around the bigger-than-av-
erage pool, with Grafton's (*see* Dining, *above*) to one side. A walkway
leads directly to a fine beach, with its own bar, and there are showers
at the top where you can rinse off. You can dance in the disco, learn

to scuba, play squash, work out in the gym, go canoeing, sailing, windsurfing, or surfing—all inclusive in the rates. ⚏ *Black Rock, Tobago,* ☎ *809/639–0191,* FAX *809/639–0030. 99 rooms, 2 suites. 2 restaurants, bar, beach, pool and beach bar, water sports, scuba training, golf nearby, beauty shop, discotheque, live entertainment, satellite TV, shopping arcade, 2 air-conditioned squash courts, gym with sauna. AE, DC, MC, V. EP, MAP.*

$$$$ **Mt. Irvine Bay Hotel.** The advantage of this low-key, somewhat over-priced hotel is golf, on the 18-hole, par-72, 127-acre International Championship course, for which guests get special rates. The carpeted bedrooms aren't so special, although all amenities are on tap, from quiet air-conditioning, good-sized desks, full-length mirrors, and 24-hour room service to HBO, Cinemax, and CNN on TV. Bathrooms boast hair dryers and the only robes on Tobago. Unfortunately, the service at present is unprofessional; management needs to take a closer look at operations. Fifty-one cottages set in an arc around the main building cost double the room rate, for which you get a private patio and a mottled marble floor, but no kitchenette or lounge. A 17th-century mill is the focal point of the main restaurant, and there are two more restaurants besides—a dressy French one, Le Beau Rivage, and the Jacaranda, plus Cocrico Bar, serving a local-international menu, when it's open. You can swim up to the bar at the largest of the island's hotel pools, play tennis on two floodlit courts, take the private track across the road to the beach, where there's another bar—or just play golf all day. The grounds are indeed lovely, and those who seek an English golf club will be happy, if service is a secondary consideration. ⚏ *Mt. Irvine Bay, Box 222, Tobago,* ☎ *809/639–8871,* FAX *809/639–8800. 107 rooms, 5 suites, 51 cottages. 3 restaurants, 2 bars, golf course, pool, 2 lighted tennis courts, convention facilities, beach across the street, beauty parlor, shops, taxi service, sauna, health spa. AE, DC, MC, V. EP, CP, MAP.*

$$$$ **Plantation Beach Villas.** Nestled on a hillside above a palm-fringed beach, these pink and white villas are comfortably furnished in colonial style and decorated with West Indian fretwork. If you're traveling with a group or a large family, the price is not high for the lovely villas. Each has three bedrooms, each with its own bath. One bedroom is air-conditioned and the others have ceiling fans. Kitchens are fully equipped, with microwaves and dishwashers. Cleaning service and linens are included, and a cook can be provided on request. Each villa has a teak veranda with a view of the sea. Serenity and elegance is the mood. Birdsong emanates from the bird sanctuary next door. There is a beach bar and pool. The villas are on the west coast, 15 minutes from Crown Point Airport. ⚏ *Plantation Beach Villas, Stonehaven Bay, Blackrock,* ☎ *and fax 809/639–0455; or write to Box 1020, Port-of-Spain, Trinidad. 6 villas. MC, V.*

$$–$$$ **Turtle Beach Hotel.** If you're taking the kids, this may be your dream hotel: There's baby-sitting and many planned activities for children (on holidays they go all out to entertain the little ones, with hundreds of little lanterns for a Hindu festival and lights climbing way up the skyscraper palm trees at Christmas). There's no lack of space at this well-maintained 24-year-old beachfront property, with its sprawling lobby, lounge, bar, and restaurant open to the sea and filled with plants and birdsong. Rates drop way down in the summer season, meaning occupancy is high year-round, though winter guests miss out on the turtles who use this beach to lay their eggs from March to August. Another good deal is the triple room—not the usual fold-down in the corner, but a small extra bedroom for $21 more. Bedroom balconies all overlook the sea and, as with all the leeside hotels, offer great views of the fabulous sunset. Typical Tobagonian wooden ceilings, marble-

chip floors, and textured white plaster walls make for a functional feel, some air-conditioning units are noisy, and there's no in-room TV, but otherwise Turtle Beach's popularity is not hard to understand. Security guards in uniform are very present, to keep beach peddlers away, but they somehow make the problem seem more severe than it is. ⌑ *Great Courland Bay,* ☏ *809/639–2851; write to Box 201, Scarborough, Tobago;* FAX *809/639–1495. 125 rooms. Restaurant, 2 bars, beach, small pool, 2 tennis courts, water-sports center, bike rentals, gift shop. AE, DC, MC, V. EP, MAP.*

\$–\$\$\$ **Blue Waters Inn.** If your dream of the tropics is a simple place as close
★ to the waves as possible, set amid 46 acres of greenery, including massive gnarled beach plum trees that seem to hold up the house, this is for you. A good 90-minute drive from Scarborough and up a bumpy driveway bring you to this beach hotel and its villas on the northeast Atlantic coast, with Little Tobago and Bird of Paradise island across Bateaux Bay. From your bedroom balcony, you'll see a little beach fringed with mangos, palms, and hardy twisted sea grape trees. Rooms have little more than the basics, but you're guaranteed the sounds of waves all night and a chorus of bright birds to greet the dawn. The bungalows have one or two bedrooms, living room, and kitchen. The "self-catering" apartments, oddly enough, have no kitchens. Do your shopping in Scarborough before you set out, if possible: Local stores are small. But the freshest fish are to be had daily, and there is a good bar and restaurant. Bring along books and binoculars: This is more a place for bird-watchers and nature lovers (and lovers) than it is for those who want TV or nightlife. ⌑ *Bateaux Bay, Speyside, Tobago,* ☏ *809/660–4341,* FAX *809/660–5195. 23 rooms, 4 apartments, 3 suites. Restaurant, bar, tennis court, beach, dive instruction. AE, MC, V. EP, CP, MAP, FAP.*

\$\$ **Kariwak Village.** People fall helplessly in love with Allan and Chris-
★ tine Clovis's cabana village, which is to the average hotel as the scarlet ibis is to the city pigeon. You enter a bamboo, raw teak, and coral stone lobby and bar area. Outside, in a bamboo pavillion, is the highly respected restaurant (*see* Kariwak Village in Dining, *above*). Nine large, round palm-thatched cabanas, each containing two bedrooms, are in a semicircle around a pretty pool. Rooms are simple and air-conditioned, with loft-height dark-wood ceilings, carpeted floors, and wicker armchairs; each has a separate bathroom and dressing area and a little terrace outside the patio doors. Lush flora makes a fairly small site seem more spacious, and an herb-and-vegetable garden out back, which furnishes Christine's kitchen with ingredients, provides a place for an extra stroll. The best breakfast around—fresh cocoa made with local chocolate, homemade yogurt, granola, whole-wheat bread, and spice tea—plus the best rum punches and local bands playing on weekends make this a favored liming spot as well as a lively holiday base. It's very near the airport (where the main activity is the hourly small plane from Trinidad), Store Bay, and Pigeon Point. ⌑ *Crown Pt., Tobago,* ☏ *809/639–8442; write to Box 27, Scarborough, Tobago;* FAX *809/639–8441. 18 rooms. Restaurant, bar, shuttle service to beach, pool. AE, DC, MC, V. EP, MAP.*

\$\$ **Palm Tree Village.** Across the rural old coast road from Little Rockley Bay, a five-minute drive from Scarborough, this place offers peace and quiet with a useful array of facilities. Choose either a "superior room," facing the beach, with a hardwood floor and furniture, or a two- or four-bedroom villa set back from the Atlantic in the manicured, but barely landscaped, grounds. "Standard rooms," in cottages close to the main building, have small lounge areas and plenty of windows, but these—in a confusing lineup of packages and plans—are usually only available at TT$ rates to locals. Try negotiating for one, though. There can be a forlorn feeling here, perhaps due to the lack of trees on site, the narrowness of the 2-mile-long beach (except at low tide), or the tininess of the pool; but Phillies, the new German-run pub in a converted barn, could liven things up. ☒ *Box 327, Little Rockley Bay, Scarborough,* ☎ *809/639–4347,* ⨪ *809/639–4180. 18 villas, 20 "superior rooms," 36 "standard rooms." Pub, bar, beach, pool, disco, piano room, conference center, tennis court, horseback riding, water sports. AE, DC, MC, V. EP, MAP.*

$–$$ **Blue Horizon Resort.** "Resort" is a misnomer for this compact red-roofed apartment complex set above the Mt. Irvine golf course, since all it offers in the way of facilities are a small pool, which the apartments overlook, a barbecue pit, and an understocked minimart. However, it does offer peace and quiet and sunset views from the deluxe apartments, which are a far better deal than the first-floor, viewless standards. Another advantage is the spaciousness of the rooms, and parents can observe little ones in the pool from each unit. Decor is basic—small, straight-backed plaid sofas and chairs around the satellite TV are the only lounge furniture—with pine-fitted kitchens and utility-tiled bathrooms. Deluxe apartments have spiral staircases leading to galleried lofts that children will adore—though little ones could easily fall from them. Balconies overlook each other, except for that of the single "luxurious" apartment; its "luxury" comprising an extra bedroom and tons of space. Free airport transfers are provided, and there's no charge for children under 12, making this a good budget family pick. ☒ *Jacamar Drive, Mt. Irvine, Tobago,* ☎ *809/639–0433,* ⨪ *305/592–4935. 13 apartments. Pool, minimart. AE, MC, V. EP.*

$–$$ **Ocean Point.** A resort in miniature, this friendly "condo hotel," as owner-manager Dewan Kalliecharan dubs it, is complete with tiny kitsch fountain, a quartet of parakeets and Raj the macaw, a barbecue pit, and a palm-thatched bar-restaurant (East Indian food is the specialty) at one end of a child-size, kidney-shape pool. Five studios with five split-level loft apartments above them constitute the living quarters, all sparkly white with pine fittings and terra-cotta floors, big showers in the bathrooms, plus an inviting hammock on the balcony (upstairs) or porch (downstairs). All apartments have kitchenette, TV, and air-conditioning (though signs reading "Ocean Breeze! Pure and Natural. It's Healthier!!" seem to discourage its use). Lofts have views of the sunrise over the ocean. The studios face the pool, and the noise can be annoying during the day. (Little Rockley beach is a minute's walk away, but it's narrow and rocky—not the best for sunbathing.) A 10-minute drive takes you to Store Bay. A free shuttle to the airport, supermarket, and golf course is provided. ☒ *Milford Rd., Lowlands, Tobago,* ☎ *and fax 809/639–0973. 5 studios, 5 apartments. Restaurant/bar, airport/supermarket shuttle, pool. No credit cards. EP.*

The Arts and Nightlife

Trinidad

Trinidadian culture doesn't end with music, but it definitely begins with it. While both calypso and steel bands are best displayed during Carnival, the steel bands play at clubs, dances, and fêtes throughout the year. There's no lack of nightlife in Port-of-Spain. A type of music that's popular right now is "sweet Parang," a mixture of Spanish patois and calypso sung to tunes played on a string instrument much like a mandolin.

The Blue Iguana (no ☎) is the place to go. It's about 20 minutes west of town in Chaguanas, so get a party together from your hotel and hire a cab. It opens at 10 PM, Wednesday through Sunday. **Mas Camp Pub** (corner of Ariapata and French Sts., Woodbrook, ☎ 809/627–8449) is Port-of-Spain's most comfortable and dependable nightspot. There are tables, a bar, an ample stage in one room, and an open-air patio with more tables and a bar with a TV. There's a kitchen if you're hungry, and **Hush**, which makes delicious fruit-flavored ice cream, is right next door. **Cricket Wicket** (149 Tragarete Rd., ☎ 809/622–1808), a popular watering hole with a cupola-shape bar in the center, is a fine place to hear top bands, dance, or just sit and enjoy the nocturnal scenery. **Wazo Deyzeel** (23 Sydenham Ave., St. Ann's, ☎ 809/623–0115; closed Mon.–Wed.) is the current fave with a mixed age group for its music, dancing, drinking, views, and great food cooked by three Jamaican ladies. The **Pelican** (2–4 Coblentz Ave., St. Ann's, ☎ 809/627–6271), an English-style pub, gets increasingly frenetic as the week closes, with a singles bar atmosphere. Collect gossip over a beer at **Smokey & Bunty** (Western Main Rd. and Dengue St., St James, no ☎), which calls itself a sports bar but is really just the essential liming corner. Finally, **Moon Over Bourbon Street** (Southern Landing, Westmall, Westmoorings, ☎ 809/637–3448) has comedy or music most nights, plus long, long happy hours.

There are several excellent theaters in Port-of-Spain. Consult local newspapers for listings.

Tobago

People will tell you there's no nightlife on Tobago. Don't believe them. Some kind of organized cabaret-style event happens every night at the **Grafton Beach Resort** (☎ 809/639–0191). Even if you hate that touristy stuff, check out Les Couteaux Cultural Group, who do a high-octane dance version of Tobagonian history. Performances are held at the **Grafton** and at the **Turtle Beach Hotel** (☎ 809/639–2851), where similar shows are staged Wednesday and Sunday. Hip hotel entertainment, frequented as much by locals as tourists, is found at the **Kariwak Village** (☎ 809/639–8441) Friday and Saturday night—almost always one of the better local jazz/calypso bands. But the most authentic nightlife of all is anywhere in downtown Scarborough, any weekend. The entire town throbs with competing sound systems and impromptu or prearranged parties, any of which will welcome extra guests.

Between the two extremes, the **Starting Gate** (Shirvan Rd., ☎ 809/639–0225), an indoor-outdoor pub, is the venue for frequent party-discos, while Sunday night at Buccoo there is an informal hop, affectionately dubbed Sunday School, at **Henderson's disco** (no ☎). It's great fun. "Blockos" (spontaneous block parties) spring up all over the island; look for the hand-painted signs. Tobago also has Harvest parties on Sunday, when a particular village opens its doors to visitors for hospitality. These occur throughout the year and are a great way to meet the locals.

26 Turks and Caicos Islands

Updated by
Anna
Moschovakis

THE TURKS AND CAICOS ISLANDS are relatively unknown except to scuba divers and aficionados of
beautiful beaches, who religiously return to these wa-
ters year after year. The people of these islands have officially adopted
the designation "Beautiful by Nature" to reflect the islands' tranquillity and natural wonders.

It is claimed that Columbus's first landfall was on Grand Turk. First settled by the English more than 200 years ago, the British Crown Colony
of Turks and Caicos is renowned in two respects: Its booming banking
and insurance institutions lure investors from the United States and elsewhere, and its offshore reef formation entices divers to the world of colorful marine life surrounding its more than 40 islands and small cays,
only 8 of which are inhabited. The total landmass is 193 square miles;
the population of the eight inhabited islands and cays is some 12,350.

The Turks and Caicos are two groups of islands in an archipelago lying
575 miles southeast of Miami and about 90 miles north of Haiti. The
Turks Islands include Grand Turk, which is the capital and seat of government, and Salt Cay, with a population of about 200. According to
local legend, these islands were named by early settlers who thought
the scarlet blossoms on the local cactus resembled the Turkish fez.

Approximately 22 miles west of Grand Turk, across the 7,000-foot-deep
Christopher Columbus Passage, is the Caicos group, which includes South,
East, West, Middle, and North Caicos and Providenciales. South Caicos,
Middle Caicos, North Caicos, and Providenciales (nicknamed Provo)
are the only inhabited islands in this group; Pine Cay and Parrot Cay
are the only inhabited cays. "Caicos" is derived from *cayos*, the Spanish word for cay, and is believed to mean "string of islands."

In the years following Ponce de León's landing in 1515, a band of pirates also established communities in the archipelago. Around 1678,
Bermudians, lured by the wealth of salt in these islands, began raking
salt from the flats and returning to Bermuda to sell their crop. Despite
French and Spanish attacks and pirate raids, the Bermudians persisted
and established a trade that became the bedrock of the Bermudian economy. In 1766, Andrew Symmers settled here to hold the islands for England. Later, Loyalists from Georgia obtained land grants in the Caicos
Islands, imported slaves, and continued the lifestyle of the pre–Civil
War American South.

Today, with an eye toward tourism dollars to create jobs and increase
the standard of living, the government has devised a long-term development plan to improve the visibility of the Turks and Caicos in the
Caribbean tourism market. Providenciales, in particular, is slated not
only for tourism development but also for the development of banking, registration of business companies, and offshore insurance. Mass
tourism on the scale of some other island destinations, however, is not
in the cards; government guidelines promote a "quality, not quantity,"
policy toward visitors, including conservation awareness and firm restrictions on building heights and casino construction.

Before You Go

Tourist Information
Contact the **Turks and Caicos Islands Tourist Board** (☎ 800/241–
0824). The **Caribbean Tourism Organization** (20 E. 46th St., New
York, NY 10017, ☎ 212/682–0435) is another source of information.

In the United Kingdom, contact **Morris-Kevan International Ltd.** (International House, 47 Chase Side, Enfield Middlesex EN2 6NB, ☎ 0181/367–5175).

Arriving and Departing

BY PLANE

American Airlines (☎ 800/433–7300) flies daily between Miami and Provo. **Turks & Caicos Islands Airlines** (☎ 800/845–2161 or 809/94–64255) flies nonstop several days a week from Miami to both Provo and Grand Turk. It also serves Provo from Nassau four days a week. Both **Turks & Caicos Islands Airlines** and **InterIsland Airways** (☎ 809/94–15481) provide regularly scheduled service between Provo and Grand Turk.

FROM THE AIRPORT

Taxis are available at the airports; expect to share a ride. Rates are fixed. A trip between Provo's airport and most major hotels runs about $15. On Grand Turk, a trip from the airport to town is about $5; from the airport to hotels outside town, $6–$11.

BY BOAT

Because of the superb diving, three live-aboard dive boats call regularly. Contact the **Aquanaut** (c/o See & Sea, ☎ 800/348–9778), the **Sea Dancer** (c/o Peter Hughes Diving, ☎ 800/932–6237), or the **Turks and Caicos Aggressor** (c/o Aggressor Fleet, ☎ 504/385–2628 or 800/348–2628, FAX 504/384–0817).

Passports and Visas

U.S. citizens need some proof of citizenship, such as a birth certificate (original or certified copy), plus a photo I.D. or a current passport. British subjects must have a current passport. All visitors must have an ongoing or return ticket.

Language

The official language of the Turks and Caicos is English.

Precautions

Petty crime does occur here, and you're advised to leave your valuables in the hotel safe-deposit box. During the rainy season bring along a can of insect repellent: The mosquitoes can be vicious.

If you plan to explore the uninhabited island of West Caicos, be advised that the interior is overgrown with dense shrubs that include manchineel, which has a milky, poisonous sap that can cause painful, scarring blisters.

In some hotels on Grand Turk, Salt Cay, and South Caicos, there are signs that read, "Please help us conserve our precious water." These islands have no freshwater supply other than rainwater collected in cisterns, and rainfall is scant. Drink only from the decanter of fresh water your hotel provides; tap water is safe for brushing your teeth or other hygiene uses.

Staying in the Turks and Caicos Islands

Important Addresses

Tourist Information: The **Government Tourist Office** (Front St., Cockburn Town, Grand Turk, ☎ 809/94–62321, and Turtle Cove Landing, Provo, ☎ 809/94–64970) is open Monday–Thursday 8–4:30 and Friday 8–5.

EMERGENCIES

Police: Grand Turk, ☎ 809/94–62299; Providenciales, ☎ 809/94–64259; North Caicos, ☎ 809/94–67116; South Caicos, ☎ 809/94–63299. **Hospitals:** There is a 24-hour emergency room at **Grand Turk Hospital** (Hospital Rd., ☎ 809/94–62333) and at **Providenciales Health-Medical Center** (Leeward Hwy. and Airport Rd., ☎ 809/94–64201). **Pharmacies:** Prescriptions can be filled at the **Government Clinic** (Grand Turk Hospital, ☎ 809/94–62040) and at the **Providenciales Health-Medical Center** in Provo (Leeward Hwy. and Airport Rd., ☎ 809/94–64201).

Currency

The unit of currency is U.S. dollars.

Taxes and Service Charges

Most hotels collect a 7%–8% government tax; all add a 10%–15% service charge to your bill. Restaurants collect a 7% government tax and add a 10% service charge to your bill. Taxi drivers expect a token tip. The departure tax is $15.

Guided Tours

A **taxi** tour of the islands costs between $25 and $30 for the first hour and $25 for each additional hour. On Provo, contact **Paradise Taxi Company** (☎ 809/94–13555). **Executive Tours** (☎ 809/94–64524) offers a guided tour in an air-conditioned bus for $10 per person, for a minimum of 8 people and a maximum of 22. **Turtle Tours** (☎ 809/94–65585) offers a variety of bus and small-plane tours. A bus tour takes in all of Provo, including the conch farm, and stops for drinks at Hey Jose. You can also fly to Middle Caicos, the largest of the islands, for a visit to its mysterious caves or to North Caicos to see the ruins of a former slave plantation. If you want to island-hop on your own schedule, air charters are available through **Blue Hills Aviation** (☎ 809/94–65226) and **Flamingo Air Services** (☎ 809/94–62109 or 809/94–64933).

Getting Around

BY BUS

On Provo, shuttle buses operated by **Executive Tours** (☎ 809/94–64524) run from the hotels into town every hour, Monday through Saturday 9 AM–6 PM. Fares are $2 each way. A new public bus system on Grand Turk charges 50¢ one-way to any scheduled stop.

TAXIS

Taxis are unmetered, and rates, posted in the taxis, are regulated by the government.

FERRIES

Caicos Express (☎ 809/94–67111) offers two scheduled interisland ferries between Provo, Pine Cay, Middle Caicos, Parrot Cay, and North Caicos daily except Sunday. Tickets cost $15 each way.

RENTAL CARS

Local rental agencies on Provo are **Turks & Caicos National** (☎ 809/94–64701), **Provo Rent-A-Car** (☎ 809/94–64404), **Rent A Buggy** (☎ 809/94–64158), and **Turquoise Jeep Rentals** (☎ 809/94–64910); on Grand Turk, **Dutchie's Car Rental** (☎ 809/94–62244). Rates average $40 to $65 per day, plus a $10-per-rental-agreement government tax. To rent cars on South Caicos, check with your hotel manager for rates and information.

SCOOTERS

You can scoot around Provo by contacting **Scooter Rentals** (☎ 809/94–64684) or the **Honda Shop** (☎ 809/94–64397). On Grand Turk, contact **Kittina Scooter Rental** (☎ 809/94–62232). Rates generally start at $25 per day for a one-seater and $40 a day for a two-seater, plus a one-time $5 government tax, plus gas.

Telephones and Mail

You can call the islands direct from the United States by dialing 809 and the number. To call home from Turks and Caicos, dial direct from most hotels, from some pay phones, and from **Cable and Wireless,** which has offices in Provo (☎ 809/94–64499) and Grand Turk (☎ 809/94–62200), open Monday–Thursday 8–4:30 and Friday 8–4. You must dial 0, followed by the country code (1 for U.S. and Canada; 44 for U.K.), area code, and local number.

Postal rates for letters to the United States, Bahamas, and Caribbean are 50¢ per half ounce; postcards, 35¢. Letters to the United Kingdom and Europe, 65¢ per half ounce; postcards, 45¢. Letters to Canada, Puerto Rico, and South America, 65¢; postcards, 45¢.

Opening and Closing Times

Most offices are open weekdays from 8 or 8:30 till 4 or 4:30. Banks are open Monday–Thursday 8:30–2:30, Friday 8:30–12:30 and 2:30–4:30.

Exploring the Turks and Caicos Islands

Numbers in the margin correspond to points of interest on the Turks and Caicos Islands map.

Grand Turk

Horses and cattle wander around as if they owned the place, and the occasional donkey cart clatters by, carrying a load of water or freight. Front Street, the main drag, lazes along the western side of the island and eases through **Cockburn Town,** the colony's capital and seat of government. Buildings in the capital reflect the 19th-century Bermudian style of architecture, and the narrow streets are lined with low stone walls and old street lamps, now powered by electricity.

The **Turks & Caicos National Museum** opened in 1993 in the restored Guinep House. One of the oldest native stone buildings in the islands, the museum now houses the Molasses Reef wreck of 1513, the earliest shipwreck discovered in the Americas, and natural history exhibits that include artifacts left by African, North American, Bermudian, French, Hispanic, and Taino settlers. An impressive new addition to the museum is the coral reef and sea life exhibit, faithfully modeled on a popular dive site just off the island. ☎ *809/94–62160.* ☞ *$5.* ☺ *Mon.–Tues. and Thurs.–Fri. 9–4, Wed. 9–6, Sat. 10–1.*

TIME OUT   The **Pepper Pot** (no ☎) is a little blue shack at the end of Front Street where Peanuts Butterfield makes his famous conch fritters.

Fewer than 4,000 people live on this 7½-square-mile island. Diving is definitely the big deal here. Grand Turk's Wall, with a sheer drop to 7,000 feet, is well known to divers.

Salt Cay

Only 200 people live on this tiny 2½-square-mile dot of land. There's not much in the way of development—just the Windmills Plantation hotel and a few stores in **Balfour Town**—but there are splendid beaches on the north coast. Old windmills, salt sheds, and salt ponds are silent reminders of the days when the island was a leading producer of salt.

Turks and Caicos Islands

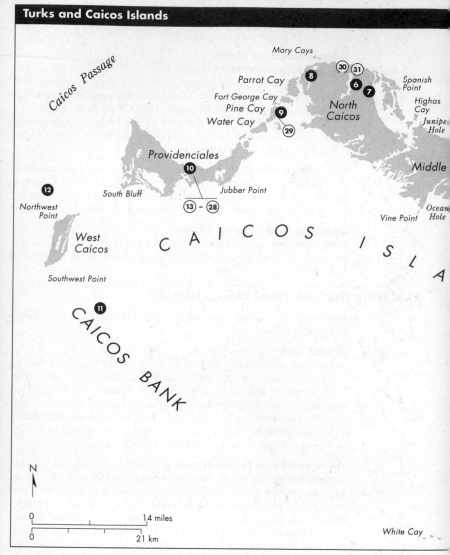

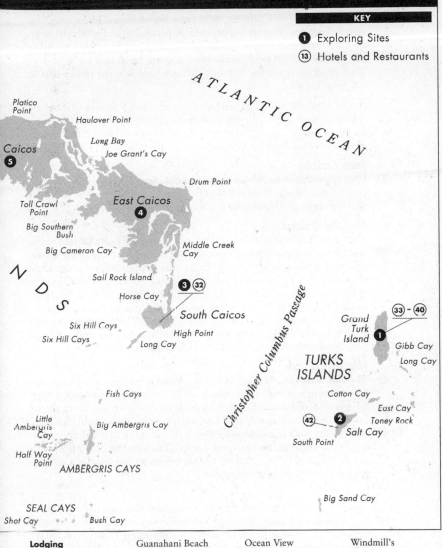

KEY

1 Exploring Sites

(13) Hotels and Restaurants

ATLANTIC OCEAN

Platico Point

Haulover Point

Caicos
5

Long Bay

Joe Grant's Cay

Drum Point

Toll Crawl Point

East Caicos
4

Big Southern Bush

Big Cameron Cay

Middle Creek Cay

N D S

Sail Rock Island

Horse Cay

3 (32)

South Caicos

Christopher Columbus Passage

Six Hill Cays

Six Hill Cays

High Point

Long Cay

Grand Turk Island
1

(33) – (40)

Gibb Cay

Long Cay

TURKS ISLANDS

Fish Cays

Cotton Cay

East Cay

Little Ambergris Cay

Big Ambergris Cay

(42) 2

Toney Rock

Salt Cay

South Point

AMBERGRIS CAYS

Half Way Point

Big Sand Cay

SEAL CAYS

Shot Cay   Bush Cay

Lodging

Club Carib Harbour Hotel, **32**

Club Med Turkoise, **22**

Club Vacanze Prospect of Whitby Hotel, **31**

Coral Reef Resort, **33**

Erebus Inn Resort, **15**

Grace Bay Club, **23**

Guanahani Beach Hotel, **39**

Hotel Kittina, **35**

Island Princess, **19**

Le Deck Hotel & Beach Club, **20**

Meridian Club, **29**

Ocean Beach Hotel Condominiums, **30**

Ocean Club, **27**

Ocean View Hotel, **40**

Ramada Turquoise Reef Resort & Casino, **21**

Salt Raker Inn, **34**

Treasure Beach Villas, **24**

Turk's Head Inn, **37**

Turtle Cove Inn, **25**

Windmill's Plantation, **41**

South Caicos

 Cockburn Harbour, the best natural harbor in the Caicos chain, is home to the South Caicos Regatta, held each year in May. The 8½-square-mile island was once an important salt producer; today it's the heart of the fishing industry. Spiny lobster and queen conch are found in the shallow Caicos bank to the west and are harvested for export by local processing plants. The bonefishing here is some of the best in the West Indies.

At the northern end of the island there are fine, white-sand beaches; the south coast is great for scuba diving along the drop-off; and there's excellent snorkeling off the windward (east) coast, where large stands of elkhorn and staghorn coral shelter a variety of small tropical fish.

East Caicos

4 Uninhabited and accessible only by boat, **East Caicos** has a magnificent 17-mile beach stretching along its north coast. The island was once a cattle range and the site of a major sisal-growing industry.

Middle Caicos

5 The largest (48 square miles) and least developed of the inhabited Turks and Caicos Islands, Middle Caicos is home to limestone **Conch Bar Caves,** with eerie underground lakes and milky-white stalactites and stalagmites. Archaeologists have discovered Arawak and Lucayan Indian artifacts in the caves and the surrounding area. Since telephones are a rare commodity here, the boats that dock here and the planes that land on the little airstrip provide the island's 270 residents with their main connection to the outside world. **Executive Tours** can fly you over and take you through the mysterious caves (*see* Guided Tours, *above*).

North Caicos

6 The **Club Vacanze Prospect of Whitby Hotel** is on the north end of this 41-square-mile island. To the south of Whitby is **Flamingo Pond,** a nesting place for the beautiful pink birds. If you take a taxi tour of the island, you'll see the ruins of the old plantations and, in the little

7 8 settlements of **Kew** and **Sandy Point,** a profusion of tropical trees bearing limes, papayas, and custard apples. The beaches here are superb for shelling and lolling, and the waters offshore offer excellent snorkeling, scuba diving, and fishing.

Pine Cay

One of a chain of small cays connecting North Caicos and Provo, 800-

9 acre **Pine Cay** is privately owned and under development as a planned community. It's home to the exclusive **Meridian Club** resort, playground of jet-setters, and its 2½-mile beach is the most beautiful in the archipelago. The island has a 3,800-foot airstrip and electric carts for getting around.

Providenciales

In the mid-18th century, so the story goes, a French ship was wrecked near here and the survivors were washed ashore on an island they gratefully christened La Providentielle. Under the Spanish, the name was

10 changed to **Providenciales.**

Provo's 44 square miles are by far the most developed in the Turks and Caicos. With its rolling ridges and 12-mile beach, the island is a prime target for developers. More than two decades ago a group of U.S. investors, including the DuPonts, Ludingtons, and Roosevelts, opened up this island for visitors and those seeking homesites in the Caribbean. In 1990 the island's first luxury resort, the **Ramada Turquoise Reef Resort & Casino,** opened, and with it, the island's first gourmet Italian restaurant. The luxurious **Ocean Club,** a condominium resort at Grace Bay, was also completed in 1990 and was followed by the upscale **Grace Bay Club** resort in 1992. The competition created by the new resorts spurred many of the older hotels to undertake much-needed renovations.

Downtown Provo, near Providenciales International Airport, is a cluster of stone and stucco buildings that house car-rental agencies, law offices, boutiques, banks, and other businesses.

TIME OUT Stop in at **Fast Eddie's** (Airport Rd., ☎ 809/94–64075), a casual eatery, for a relaxing drink and a platter of seafood.

Provo is home to the **Island Sea Center** (on the northeast coast, ☎ 809/94–65330), where you can learn about the sea and its inhabitants. Here you'll find the **Caicos Conch Farm** (☎ 809/94–65849), a major mariculture operation where the mollusks are farmed commercially. The farm's tourist facilities include a video show, boutique, and a "hands-on" tank. A geodesic dome, housing natural history exhibits, was severely damaged in a 1993 fire but was slated to reopen by the end of 1995. Established by the PRIDE Foundation (Protection of Reefs and Islands from Degradation and Exploitation), the **JoJo Dolphin Project,** named after a 7-foot-long male bottle-nosed dolphin who cruises these waters and enjoys playing with local divers, is also here. You can watch a video on JoJo and learn how to interact with him safely if you see him on one of your dives.

About 6,000 people live on Provo, a considerable number of whom are expatriate U.S. and Canadian businesspeople and retirees.

West Caicos
Over the past few centuries numerous wrecks have occurred in the area between West Caicos and Provo, and author Peter Benchley is among the treasure-seekers who have been lured to this island. **Molasses Reef** is rumored to be the final resting place of the *Pinta*, which is thought to have been wrecked here in the early 1500s.

Accessible only by boat, this island is uninhabited and untamed, and there are no facilities whatsoever. A glorious white beach stretches for a mile along the northwest point, and offshore diving is among the most exotic in the islands. A wall inhabited by countless species of large marine life begins ¼ mile offshore, and the **Northwest Reef** offers great stands of elkhorn coral and acres of staghorn brambles. But this area is only for experienced divers. The wall starts deep, the currents are strong—and there are sharks in the waters.

If you do tour West Caicos, take along several vats of insect repellent. It won't help much with the sharks, but it should fend off the mosquitoes and sand flies. Be advised, too, that the interior is overgrown with dense shrubs, including manchineel.

Beaches

There are more than 230 miles of beaches in the Turks and Caicos Islands, ranging from secluded coves to miles-long stretches. Most beaches are soft coralline sand. Tiny uninhabited cays offer complete isolation for nude sunbathing and skinny-dipping. Many are accessible only by boat.

Big Ambergris Cay, an uninhabited cay about 14 miles beyond the Fish Cays, has a magnificent beach at **Long Bay.**

East Caicos, an uninhabited island accessible only by boat, has a beautiful 17-mile beach along its north coast.

Governor's Beach, a long white strip on the west coast of **Grand Turk,** is one of the nicest beaches on this island.

The north and east coasts of **North Caicos** are bordered by great beaches for swimming, scuba diving, snorkeling, and fishing.

Pine Cay, a private upscale retreat, has a 2½-mile strip of beach—the most beautiful in the archipelago.

A fine white-sand beach stretches 12 miles along the northeast coast of **Providenciales.** Other good beaches are at **Sapodilla Bay** and rounding the tip of the northwest point of the island.

There are superb beaches on the north coast of **Salt Cay,** as well as at **Big Sand Cay,** 7 miles to the south.

Only in South Caicos are the beaches small and unremarkable, but the vibrant reef makes it a popular destination for divers.

Sports and the Outdoors

Bicycling

Provo has a few steep grades to conquer, but very little traffic. Bikes can be rented at the **Island Princess** hotel at the Bight (☎ 809/94–64260) for $10 a day, through **Turtle Inn Divers** (Turtle Cove Inn, ☎ 809/94–15389) for $12 a day and $60 a week, or at the **Ramada Turquoise Reef Resort & Casino** (Grace Bay, ☎ 809/94–65555) for $14 a day. In Grand Turk on Duke Street, both the **Salt Raker Inn** (☎ 809/94–62260) and the **Hotel Kittina** (☎ 809/94–62232) rent bikes for $10 per day, $40 per week.

Boat Rentals

You can rent a boat with private pilot for a half or full day of sportfishing through **Black Diamond Tours** (Provo, ☎ 809/94–64451) or **Porpoise** (Salt Cay, ☎ 809/94–66927) for about $300 a day. **Dive Provo** (Ramada Turquoise Reef Resort, Provo, ☎ 809/94–65040 or 800/234–7768) rents small sailboats for $20 per hour and provides beginning instruction for $40 for up to two hours. Sailing not your bent? Try open-cockpit ocean kayaking, available at Dive Provo for $10 per hour for one and $15 per hour for two.

Fishing

Black Diamond Tours (Provo, ☎ 809/94–64451) will take a maximum of three people out for half- or full-day bonefish or bottom fishing expeditions, bait and tackle included, for $150 per half day. The same outfit will arrange half- or full-day deep-sea fishing trips in search of shark, marlin, kingfish, sawfish, wahoo, and tuna, with all equipment furnished. Deep-sea, bonefishing, and bottom fishing are also available aboard the *Sakitumi* (☎ 809/94–64203 or 809/94–64393).

Golf

A 6,529-yard golf course opened on Providenciales in late 1991. **Provo Golf Club** (☎ 809/94–65991) is an 18-hole par-72 championship course, designed by Karl Litten, that is sustained by a desalination plant producing 250,000 gallons of water a day. The turf is sprinkled in green islands over 12 acres of natural limestone outcroppings, creating a desert-style design of narrow "target areas" and sandy waste areas—a formidable challenge to anyone playing from the championship tees. Fees are $65 plus $15 for a mandatory electric cart. A pro shop, driving ranges, and a restaurant and bar round out the club's facilities.

Horseback Riding

Horses roam lazily around the main roads on Grand Turk. While there is no organized riding program, most hotels will make arrangements for their guests, and rates can be negotiated with individual owners.

Parasailing

A 15-minute flight is available for $45 at either **Dive Provo** (Ramada Turquoise Reef Resort, Provo, ☎ 809/94–65040 or 800/234–7768) or **Turtle Inn Divers** (Turtle Cove Inn, ☎ 809/94–15389).

Scuba Diving

Diving is the top attraction here. (All divers must carry and present a valid certificate card before they'll be allowed to dive.) These islands are surrounded by a reef system of more than 200 square miles—much of it unexplored. Grand Turk's famed wall drops more than 7,000 feet and is one side of a 22-mile-wide channel called the Christopher Columbus Passage. From January through March, an estimated 6,000 eastern Atlantic humpback whales swim through this passage en route to their winter breeding grounds. There are undersea cathedrals, coral gardens, and countless tunnels. Among the operations that provide instruction, equipment rentals, underwater video equipment, and trips are **Sea Eye Divers** (Grand Turk, ☎ 809/94–61407), **Blue Water Divers** (Salt Raker Inn, Grand Turk, ☎ 809/94–62432), **Off the Wall Divers** (Grand Turk, ☎ 809/94–62159), **Dive Provo** (Ramada Turquoise Reef Resort, Provo, ☎ 809/94–65040 or 800/234–7768), **Flamingo Divers** (Provo, ☎ 809/94–64193), **Provo Turtle Divers** (Provo, ☎ 809/94–64232), **Porpoise Divers** (Salt Cay, ☎ 809/94–66927), and **Tradewinds Divers** (Club Vacanze Prospect of Whitby Hotel, North Caicos, ☎ 809/94–67377).

Note: A modern hyperbaric/recompression chamber is located on Provo (☎ 809/94–64242) in the **Menzies Medical Centre** on Leeward Highway. Divers in need on Grand Turk are airlifted to Provo—a 30 minute flight.

Sea Excursions

The *Ocean Outback* (☎ 809/94–64080), a 70-foot motor cruiser, does barbecue-and-snorkel cruises to uninhabited islands. Both the 37-foot catamaran *Beluga* (☎ 809/94–15196, $39 per half day) and the 56-foot trimaran *Tao* (☎ 809/94–65040) run sunset cruises, as well as sailing and snorkeling outings. A full-day outing on the *Tao* is $59 per person, including snorkel rental and lunch. For $20 per person, **Dive Provo** (Ramada Turquoise Reef Resort, ☎ 809/94–65040 or 800/234–7768) gives two-hour glass-bottom-boat tours of the spectacular reefs. **Turtle Inn Divers** (Turtle Cove Inn, ☎ 809/94–15389) offers full-day Sunday excursions for divers for $64.50 per person ($25 per person for nondivers and snorkelers). The *Turks and Caicos Aggressor* (☎ 504/385–2628 or 800/348–2628, FAX 504/384–0817) offers luxury six-day dive cruises with full accommodations.

Snorkeling

Dive Provo (Provo, ☎ 809/94–65040 or 800/234–7768), **Blue Water Divers** (Salt Raker Inn, Grand Turk, ☎ 809/94–62432), and **Provo Turtle Divers** (Provo, ☎ 809/94–64232) all provide rentals for about $10 and trips for $20. **Sea Eye Diving** (Grand Turk, ☎ 809/94–61407) offers equipment and trips, as well as diving packages and instruction.

Tennis

On Provo, there are two lighted courts at **Turtle Cove Inn** (☎ 809/94–64203), eight courts (four lighted) at **Club Med Turkoise** (☎ 809/94–65500), two courts at the **Ramada Turquoise Reef Resort** (☎

809/94–65555), two lighted courts at the **Erebus Inn** (☎ 809/94–64240), one court at **Treasure Beach Villas** (☎ 809/94–64211), and two lighted courts at **Grace Bay Club** (☎ 809/94–65050). On Grand Turk, the **Coral Reef Resort** (☎ 809/94–62055) has one lighted court. There is also one court at the **Meridian Club** (Pine Cay, ☎ 800/225–4255) and one court at the **Club Vacanze Prospect of Whitby Hotel** (North Caicos, ☎ 809/94–67119).

Waterskiing

Waterskiers will find the calm turquoise water ideal for long-distance runs. **Dive Provo** (Ramada Turquoise Reef Resort, Provo, ☎ 809/94–65040 or 800/234–7768) charges $35 for a 15-minute run.

Windsurfing

Rental and instruction are available at the **Club Vacanze Prospect of Whitby Hotel** (North Caicos, ☎ 809/94–67119) and **Dive Provo** (Ramada Turquoise Reef Resort, Provo, ☎ 809/94–65040 or 800/234–7768).

Spectator Sports

Cricket is the most popular game in town. The season runs from July through August. Tennis, basketball, softball, and darts are other local favorites. You're welcome to join in. Inquire at the tourist board (☎ 800/241–0824) for a list of events.

Shopping

Shopping is limited to hotel gift shops, airports, and occasional street vendors, except on Provo, where new shops and franchises open every month. Most of these stores can be found in four main shopping complexes: Market Place, Central Square, and Caribbean Place, all on Leeward Highway, and Turtle Cove Landing, in Turtle Cove. Delicate baskets woven from the local top grasses are the only craft native to the Turks and Caicos, and they are sold in many of the shops.

The **Bamboo Gallery** (Market Place, Provo, ☎ 809/94–064748) sells all types of Caribbean art, from vivid Haitian paintings to wood carvings. **Greensleeves** (Central Square, Provo, ☎ 809/94–64147) is the place to go for paintings by local artists, island-made rag rugs, baskets, jewelry, and sisal mats and bags. **Local Color** (Governor's Rd., Grace Bay, Provo, no ☎) sells art and sculpture made by local artists as well as native basketry, hand-painted tropical clothing, tie-dyed pareos, and silk-screened T-shirts. On the ground floor of **Pelican's Pouch/Designer I** (Turtle Cove Landing, Provo, ☎ 809/94–64343), you'll find resort wear, sandals, Provo T-shirts, perfumes, and gold jewelry; head upstairs for basketry, sculpture, and watercolors. **Paradise Gifts/Arts** (Central Square, Provo, ☎ 809/94–64637) has a ceramics studio on the premises; in addition to ceramics, jewelry, T-shirts, and paintings by local artists are sold here. **Royal Jewels** (Leeward Highway, Provo, ☎ 809/94–64885; Ramada Turquoise Reef Resort, Provo, ☎ 809/94–65311; Airport, Provo, ☎ 809/94–65311) sells gold and jewelry, designer watches, and perfumes, all at significant savings.

Dining

Like everything else on these islands, dining out is a very laid-back affair, which is not to say that it is cheap. Because of the high cost of importing all edibles, the cost of a meal is usually higher than that of a comparable meal in the United States, and all the menus are à la carte.

A 7% government tax and a 10% service charge are added to your check. Reservations are not required. Dress is casual throughout the island.

CATEGORY	COST*
$$$	over $25
$$	$15–$25
$	under $15

per person, excluding drinks, service, and 7% sales tax

Grand Turk

$$ Salt Raker Inn. Starters at this rustic, informal patio restaurant include tomato and mozzarella salad and melon with ginger. Lobster in cream and sherry sauce, barbecued steak, and seafood curry are oft-ordered entrées. For dessert, try the tasty apple pie. The Sunday dinner and sing-along is popular. ✕ *Salt Raker Inn,* ☎ *809/94–62260. AE, D, MC, V.*

$$ Sandpiper. Candles flicker on the Sandpiper's terrace beside a flower-filled courtyard. A peaceful, leisurely atmosphere pervades this restaurant. Blackboard specialties may include pork chops with applesauce, lobster, filet mignon, or seafood platter. ✕ *Hotel Kittina,* ☎ *809/94–62232. AE, D, MC, V.*

$–$$ Turk's Head Inn. The menu changes daily at this lively restaurant, touted by many residents as the best on the island. Some staples include escargots, pâté, and a handful of other delectables, including local grouper fingers perfectly fried for fish-and-chips. Look for lobster, quiche, steaks, and homemade soups on the blackboard menu. You may not want to leave after your meal—come nightfall, the inn's bar is abuzz with local gossip and mirthful chatter. ✕ *Turk's Head Inn, Duke St.,* ☎ *809/94–62466. AE, MC, V.*

$ Regal Begal. Drop by this popular local catery for native specialties such as cracked conch, minced lobster, and fish-and-chips. The atmosphere is casual and the decor unmemorable, but the portions are large and the prices easy on your wallet. ✕ *Hospital Rd.,* ☎ *809/94–62274. No credit cards.*

$ The Water's Edge. Relaxed waterfront dining awaits you at this pleasantly rustic eatery. The limited menu covers the basics with a twist—from barbecued grouper to a fresh seafood crepe. A kids' menu is also available. The food is authentic and filling, and the view at sunset breathtaking, but the irresistible homemade pies are enough to justify a visit. ✕ *Duke St.,* ☎ *809/94–61680. MC, V. Closed Mon.*

Providenciales

$$–$$$ Alfred's Place. Austrian owner Alfred Holzfeind caters to an American palate with an extensive menu featuring everything from prime rib to chicken salad. The alfresco lounge is a popular watering hole for locals and tourists alike. ✕ *Turtle Cove,* ☎ *809/94–64679. AE, D, MC, V. Closed Mon. July–Oct.*

★

$$–$$$ Anacaona. This exquisitely designed restaurant offers a true gourmet dining experience minus the tie, the air-conditioning, and the attitude. Located at the equally impressive Grace Bay Club, this is Caribbean-Continental open-air dining at its best. Start with a bottle of fine wine from the extensive cellar, then enjoy a three- or four-course meal of the chef's light but flavorful cooking, which combines traditional French recipes with fresh seafood and Caribbean fruits, vegetables, and spices. Oil lamps on the tables, gently circulating ceiling fans, and a natural soundtrack of the breeze, the ocean, birds, and even a few neighboring frogs all add to the Eden-like environment. ✕ *Grace Bay Club,* ☎ *809/94–65757. AE, MC, V.*

★

$–$$ Dora's. This popular local eatery serves up island fare—turtle, shredded lobster, spicy conch chowder—seven days a week, from 7 AM until the last person leaves the bar. Plastic print and lace tablecloths, hanging plants, and Haitian art add to the island ambience. Soups ($4) come with homemade bread, and entrées such as fish-and-chips, conch Creole, and grilled pork chops come with a choice of vegetable. Be sure to come early for the packed Monday- and Thursday-night all-you-can-eat $20 seafood buffet. The price includes round-trip transportation to your hotel. ✗ *Leeward Hwy.,* ☎ *809/94–64558. No credit cards.*

$–$$ Fast Eddie's. Plants festoon this cheerful restaurant, which is across from the airport. Broiled turtle steak, fried grouper fingers, and other island specialties are joined on the menu by old American standbys such as cheeseburgers and cherry pie. Wednesday evening there's a $20 ($10 for children) all-you-can-eat seafood buffet. Friday is prime rib and live music night. Free transportation to and from your hotel is provided. ✗ *Airport Rd.,* ☎ *809/94–64075. MC, V.*

$–$$ Hong Kong Restaurant. A no-frills place with plain wood tables and chairs, the Hong Kong offers dine-in, delivery, or takeout. The menu includes lobster with ginger and green onions, chicken with black-bean sauce, sliced duck with salted mustard greens, and sweet-and-sour chicken. The Peking duck is a house specialty. ✗ *Leeward Hwy.,* ☎ *809/94–65678. AE, MC, V. No lunch Sun.*

$ Banana Boat. Buoys and other sea relics deck the walls, and white plastic chairs surround colorful, well-spaced tables, but what this restaurant lacks in elegance it makes up for in hospitality. You could stay here all night, munching on pizza, burgers, and various finger food, then washing down your meal with those famous, tropical, rum-filled cocktails. ✗ *Turtle Cove,* ☎ *809/94–15706. AE, MC, V.*

$ Caicos Cafe. Elegant street lanterns line the walkway to this popular restaurant, and there's a pervasive air of celebration in the uncovered outdoor dining area. Choose from a selection of local and American cuisine, including lobster sandwiches, hamburgers, and a variety of excellent salads. ✗ *Across from the Ramada,* ☎ *809/94–65278. No credit cards.*

$ Hey, José. This restaurant claims to serve the island's best margaritas.
★ Customers also return for the tasty Tex-Mex treats: tacos, tostados, nachos, burritos, fajitas, and José's special-recipe hot chicken wings. Creative types can build their own pizzas. ✗ *Central Square,* ☎ *809/94–64812. AE, MC, V. Closed Sun.*

$ Pub on the Bay. If beachfront dining is what you're after, it doesn't get much better than this. Located in the Blue Hill residential district, a five-minute drive from downtown Provo, this restaurant serves fried or steamed fish, chicken and pork, various sandwiches, calamari, fried zucchini, and even turtle steak. There is no air-conditioning inside the restaurant, so you may as well cross the street to one of three thatched roof "huts," which stand quite literally on the beach. ✗ *Blue Hill Rd.,* ☎ *809/94–14309. AE, MC, V.*

$ Top O' the Cove Gourmet Delicatessen. You can easily walk to this tiny café on Leeward Highway from the Turtle Cove and Erebus Inns. Don't be put off by the location in the Napa Auto Parts plaza—the restaurant's interior is not at all garagelike! You can order breakfast, deli subs, sandwiches, or salads to go or have a seat at a bistro table topped with a colorful tropical cloth. This is one of the few places on the island that serve a potable cup of coffee, as well as genuine espresso and frothy cappuccino—and it's open every day but Christmas and New Year's from 7 AM to 3:30 PM. ✗ *Leeward Hwy.,* ☎ *809/94–64694. No credit cards.*

Lodging

Hotel accommodations are available on Grand Turk, North Caicos, South Caicos, Pine Cay, and Provo. There are also some small, non-air-conditioned guest houses on Salt Cay and Middle Caicos. Accommodations range from small island inns to the splashy Club Med Turkoise to the new luxury Grace Bay Club in Providenciales. Because of the popularity of scuba diving here, virtually all the hotels have dive shops and offer dive packages. Dive packagers offering air-hotel-dive packages include **Dive Provo** (☎ 800/234–7768) and **Undersea Adventures** (☎ 800/234–7768). Most of the medium and large hotels offer a choice of EP and MAP. People who don't rent a car or scooter tend to eat at their hotels, so MAP may be the better option. Another option favored by many visitors, particularly families, is renting a self-contained villa or private home; contact the Ministry of Tourism (☎ 809/94–62321) three to six months in advance for more information. Please note that the government hotel tax does not apply to guest houses with fewer than four rooms.

CATEGORY	COST*
$$$$	over $250
$$$	$170–$250
$$	$110–$170
$	under $110

All prices are for a standard double room for two in winter season, excluding 7% tax and 10%–15% service charge. Please note that some hotels are now charging 8% tax.

Grand Turk

$$–$$$ **Guanahani Beach Hotel.** One of the finest stretches of beach on the island belongs to this hotel; the palm-tree lined property is popular with honeymooners. Fully renovated by new owners in 1994, the rooms now have pale ceramic tile floors and bright, primary-color Caribbean print bedspreads and curtains. Every room has an ocean view, two double beds, and a full bathroom, traits that set this hotel apart from others. A crewed yacht is available to rent for day trips or romantic moonlight rides. ✕ *Box 178,* ☎ *809/94–62135,* ☞ *809/94–61460. 16 rooms. Restaurant, 2 bars, pool, 35-foot yacht, gift shop, dive packages with Blue Water Diving. MC, V.*

$$ **Hotel Kittina.** This family-owned hostelry, the largest hotel on Grand
★ Turk, is split in two by the town's main drag. On one side, comfortable, lodge-style rooms and sleek balconied suites with kitchens sit on a gleaming white-sand beach. Across the street, the older main house holds a lively dining room and rooms that ooze island atmosphere. Behind the house are the pool and garden. Tile floors and air-conditioning were added to all of the rooms and suites in 1994. Be sure to catch the occasional Friday-night poolside barbecue. ✕ *Duke St., Box 42,* ☎ *809/94–62232 or 800/548–8462,* ☞ *809/94–62877. 43 rooms and 2 suites. 2 restaurants, 2 bars, pool, boutique, Omega Dive Shop, T&C Travel Agency, scooter and bicycle rentals, windsurfing, baby-sitting, room service, boat rentals. AE, MC, V. EP, MAP.*

$ **Coral Reef Resort.** One- and two-bedroom units here have complete kitchens, air-conditioning, and contemporary furnishings. The resort is a short drive from town, and the beach is a few steps from your door. ✕ *Box 10,* ☎ *809/94–62055,* ☞ *809/94–62911. 18 units. ✕ Restaurant, bar, lighted tennis court, pool, boutique, mini–fitness center, water sports arranged with dive operations. AE, MC, V. EP, MAP.*

$ **Ocean View Hotel.** A white picket fence, slightly worn wood and rattan furniture, and hand-stenciled walls and doors give this popular hotel a home-sweet-home atmosphere. Guest rooms are individually decorated and have cool tile floors and clean white walls. Hearty home-made meals are served in the breezy dining area, and the lively bars stay open until midnight or until the last person goes home (whichever comes later). The beach is right across the street. ☎ *Box 97,* ☎ *809/94–62517. 14 rooms and 3 suites. Restaurant, 2 bars, bicycle rentals, horseback riding, dive packages with Sea Eye Diving and Omega Diving. AE, D, MC, V. MAP.*

$ **Salt Raker Inn.** Across the street from the beach, this galleried house was the home of a Bermudian shipwright 180 years ago. The rooms and suites are not elegant but are individually decorated and have a homey atmosphere, and each has a minifridge. The three garden rooms are desirable for their screened porches and ocean views. ☎ *Duke St., Box 1,* ☎ *809/94–62260,* FAX *809/94–62817. U.K. reservations, 44 Birchington Rd., London NW6 4LJ,* ☎ *0171/328–6474. 10 rooms and 2 suites. Restaurant, bar, dive packages with Blue Water Diving, bicycle rentals. AE, D, MC, V. EP.*

$ **Turk's Head Inn.** Built in 1850 by a prosperous salt miner, this classic Bermudian building has had incarnations as the American Consulate and as the governor's guest house (the queen reportedly took a room here on her last visit to the island). Now run by a Frenchman known as Mr. X, the inn has acquired a strong European flavor. A plethora of Brits and other expat Europeans make it their stomping ground. The seven distinctive rooms are lovingly furnished with antiques and island artifacts, and the owner's own drawings and detailed maps adorn many of the walls. In the front courtyard, an oversize hammock provides the perfect vantage point from which to admire the well-tended garden. The beach is only a few strides away. The bar and restaurant area bustle at night. ☎ *Duke St., Box 58,* ☎ *809/94–62466,* FAX *809/94–62825. 7 rooms and 1 self-contained apartment. Showers only. Restaurant, bar, dive packages with Sea Eye Diving. AE, MC, V.*

North Caicos

$$ **Club Vacanze Prospect of Whitby Hotel.** Italian resort chain Club Vacanze took over this secluded retreat in 1994. Seven miles of beach are
★ yours for sunbathing, windsurfing, or snorkeling. Spacious guest rooms have a simple but elegant Mediterranean theme; in true getaway fashion, they lack both TVs and radios. Both the service and the restaurant here are superb. ☎ *Kew Post Office, North Caicos,* ☎ *809/ 94–67119,* FAX *809/94–67114. 28 rooms and 4 suites. Restaurant, bar, pool, tennis court, windsurfing, dive shop, baby-sitting, tour desk. AE, MC, V. EP, MAP.*

$$ **Ocean Beach Hotel Condominiums.** This unpretentious place provides family-style accommodations on an impressive 10-mile stretch of sheltered beach. The spacious units, each with kitchenette, are in a U-shape stone and cedar building; all face the ocean. Cool and constant trade winds, invited in through large sliding glass doors, replace the need for air-conditioning. A decor of warm earth tones and colorful artwork creates a homey feel. The hotel offers an intimate, catered lifestyle away from the fray: Home-baked bread, on-site groceries, and frequent reel-to-restaurant fresh seafood specials are some of the special touches that keep guests coming back year after year. ☎ *Whitby, North Caicos,* ☎ *809/94–67113 or 800/710–5204; in Canada, 905/336–2876;* FAX *809/94–67386. 10 units. Restaurant, bar-lounge, bicycle and car rental, fishing trips. MC, V. MAP.*

Pine Cay

$$$$ **Meridian Club.** High rollers vacation in high style on this privately
★ owned 800-acre island. Club guests enjoy an unspoiled cay with 2½ miles
of soft white sand and a 500-acre nature reserve with tropical landscaping,
freshwater ponds, and nature trails that lure bird-watchers and botanists.
A stay here is truly getting away from it all, as there are no air conditioners, telephones, or TVs. The accommodations range from spacious
rooms with king-size beds (or twin beds on request) and patios to one-
to four-bedroom cottage-homes that range in decor and amenities from
rustic to well appointed. There's also a "round room" cottage and two
ocean-view atrium units that are separated by a lovely interior garden.
Rooms in the main complex run over $485 a night for two in winter
and include all meals. Cottage homes start at $3,000 a week EP. ☎ *Pine
Cay,* ☎ *800/225–4255; in NY, 800/331–9154;* FAX *809/94–65128. 12
rooms and 13 cottage-homes. Restaurant, bar, pool, tennis court, bicycles, windsurfing, sailing. No credit cards. EP, FAP.*

Providenciales

$$$ **Club Med Turkoise.** This lavish $23 million resort is one of the most
sumptuous of all Club Med's villages. One-, two-, and three-story
bungalows line a mile-long beach, and all the usual sybaritic pleasures
are here. This club is especially geared toward couples, singles aged
28 and over, and divers. The one-price-covers-all-except-drinks pack-
age includes all the diving, water sports, and daytime activities you can
handle. ☎ *Providenciales,* ☎ *809/94–65500 or 800/258–2633; in NY,
212/750–1684 or 212/750–1687,* FAX *809/94–65501. 298 rooms. 3
restaurants, snack bar, bar, disco, boutique, 8 tennis courts (4 lighted),
bicycles, TV/video room, library, beach, pool, dive center, deep-sea-fish-
ing excursions, water-sports center, fitness center, nightly entertainment.
AE, MC, V. All-inclusive (except for drinks).*

$$$ **Grace Bay Club.** Staying at this Swiss-owned, Mediterranean-style re-
★ sort is a little like being the guest of honor of a very gracious host with
unbeatable taste. The suites, which all feature a breathtaking view of
Grace Bay's stunning turquoise waters, are tastefully furnished with
rattan and pickled wood. Mexican-tile floors are elegantly appointed
with throw rugs from Turkey and India. If you choose to take advantage of the myriad activities (from diving to golf to individually planned
and catered picnics on surrounding islands), you will be expertly provided for; but the main attraction here is natural beauty. Relax and
enjoy a getaway that is peaceful, invigorating, and wonderfully pampering. ☎ *Box 128, Providenciales,* ☎ *809/94–65050 or 800/677–
9192,* FAX *809/94–65758. 22 suites. Restaurant, bar, pool, beach,
Jacuzzi, water sports, fitness classes, 2 lighted tennis courts, video/book
library. AE, MC, V. EP, MAP.*

$$$ **Ramada Turquoise Reef Resort & Casino.** Since it opened in 1990, this
★ beachfront hotel has been the island's leading full-service luxury re-
sort. Oversize oceanfront rooms have rattan furniture and a rich
Caribbean color scheme. Furnished with a king or two double beds,
all rooms are air-conditioned and have a color TV and ceiling fan, and
either a terrace or a patio. The island's only casino is here. Guests enjoy
a free daily-activities program that includes pool volleyball and chil-
dren's treasure hunts. ☎ *Box 205, Provo,* ☎ *809/94–65555, 800/228–
9898, or 800/854–7854;* FAX *809/94–65522. 228 rooms. 3 restau-
rants, 3 bars, beach, pool, Jacuzzi, water-sports facility, 2 tennis courts,
dive shop, boutiques, duty-free shop, exercise/fitness room, room ser-
vice, live nightly entertainment/disco, casino, tour desk, baby-sitting,
daily activities program. AE, MC, V. EP, MAP.*

$$ Island Princess. Wood walkways at this hotel lead up to and around the rooms, which are situated in two wings. All rooms have cable TV and a private balcony. This is a great little hotel for families. It's on the beach, the restaurant serves excellent Italian and Caribbean food, and there's nightly entertainment. ☎ *The Bight,* ☎ *809/94–64260,* FAX *809/946–4666. 80 rooms. Restaurant, bar, 2 pools, game room, playground, boat rentals, water-sports center. AE, D, MC, V. MAP.*

$$ Le Deck Hotel & Beach Club. This 27-room pink hostelry was built in
★ classic Bermudian style around a tropical courtyard that opens onto a tiki-hut-and-palm-tree-dotted beach on Grace Bay. Completely refurbished in December 1994, it offers clean rooms with a tile floor, color TV, phone, and air-conditioning. Le Deck is especially popular with divers, and its atmosphere is informal and lively with a mostly thirty-something-and-over crowd. ☎ *Box 144, Grace Bay, Provo,* ☎ *809/94– 65547 or 800/282–4753,* FAX *809/94–65770. 27 rooms, including 2 suites. Restaurant, bar, pool, boutique, water sports, beach. AE, D, MC, V. EP, BP, MAP, FAP.*

$$ Ocean Club. "Escape the Stress of Success" is the slogan for this luxury beachfront suite resort, which was undergoing major renovations at press time. It's situated on Grace Bay's 12-mile stretch of pristine beach, a short walk away from Provo's only golf course. The all-suite accommodations range from efficiency studios to deluxe versions with ocean view, full screened balcony, kitchen, dining room, and living room. The decor is basic and refreshing; pale pink tile floors and a pastel color scheme are set off by glass-top dining tables and pickled-wood furnishings. Third-floor rooms have striking slanted ceilings, and all but efficiency accommodations include washer and dryer. Efficiency suites fall into our inexpensive category (*$*); other rooms are moderate (*$$*). ☎ *Box 240, Providenciales,* ☎ *809/94–65880 or 800/742–4276,* FAX *809/94–65845. Restaurant, bar, pool, lighted tennis court, dive shop, duty-free shop, golf, health club, playground. AE, MC, V.*

$$ Treasure Beach Villas. These one- and two-bedroom modern, self-catering apartments have fully equipped kitchens and ceiling fans. You may want a car or bike (Treasure Beach has rentals) to reach the grocery store or restaurants; bus service is limited. Provo's 12 miles of white sandy beach is just outside your door, and the hotel can set up fishing, snorkeling, and scuba expeditions. ☎ *The Bight,* ☎ *809/94–64211,* FAX *809/94–64108; in the U.S., Box 8409, Hialeah, FL 33012. 8 single, 10 double rooms. Pool, tennis court. AE, D, MC, V. EP.*

$$ Turtle Cove Inn. A marina, a free-form pool, a dive shop with equipment rentals and instruction, and lighted tennis courts attract the sporting crowd to Turtle Cove. There's a free boat shuttle to the nearby beach and snorkeling reef. All rooms have a TV, phone, and air-conditioning, and eight also have minifridges. A handful of good restaurants are within walking distance. ☎ *Providenciales,* ☎ *809/94–64203 or 800/887–0477,* FAX *809/94–64141. 30 rooms, 1 suite. 2 restaurants, 2 bars, 2 lighted tennis courts, pool, marina, dive shop, bicycle rentals. AE, MC, V. EP.*

$–$$ Erebus Inn Resort. All units in this modest resort have two double beds,
★ modern wicker furnishings, and original island artwork, including some lovely and unique Haitian wall hangings. Rooms in the older chalet cost under $110 a night double occupancy in the winter. For those preferring creature comforts, we recommend the units in the newer section (*$$*); each has air-conditioning, cable TV, and phone. The hotel sits on a cliff overlooking Turtle Cove and has wonderful views of the marina and the Caribbean beyond. Frequent bus shuttles take guests to a nearby beach. The restaurant and bar, always one of Provo's liveliest spots, has a menu of French and Caribbean cuisine. Five af-

fordable restaurants are within walking distance, as are a shopping center and several dive operations. ⌂ *Turtle Cove, Box 238, Providenciales,* ☎ *809/94–64240,* FAX *809/94–64704. 30 rooms. restaurant, bar, 2 pools (1 saltwater), fitness center, aqua-aerobics, 2 lighted tennis courts, baby-sitting. AE, MC, V. EP, MAP.*

Salt Cay

$$$$ **Windmills Plantation.** The attraction here is the lack of distraction: no
★   nightlife, no cruise ships, no crowds, and no shopping. Owner-manager-architect Guy Lovelace and his interior designer wife, Patricia, built the hotel as their version of a colonial-era plantation. The great house has four suites, each with a sitting area, four-poster bed, ceiling fans, and a veranda or balcony with a view of the sea. All are furnished in a mix of antique English and wicker furniture. Four other rooms are housed in two adjacent buildings. Room rates, which during the height of winter run from $415 a night and up for two people, include snorkeling equipment, three meals, and unlimited bar drinks, wine, and beer. ⌂ *Salt Cay,* ☎ *809/94–66962 or 800/822–7715,* FAX *809/94–66930. 4 rooms, 4 suites. Restaurant, bar, pool, library, 2½-mile nature trail, fishing, horseback riding, snorkeling, beach. AE, MC, V. FAP.*

South Caicos

$–$$ **Club Caribe Beach & Harbour Hotel.** Cockburn Harbour, the only natural harbor in the Turks and Caicos Islands, is the perfect setting for this hotel. The 17 beachfront villas, which can be rented as studios or as one-, two-, or three-bedroom apartments, have cool tile floors and kitchenettes equipped with minifridge and microwave. Half of the rooms don't have air-conditioning, but they get a nice breeze around the clock. The 24 harbor rooms are smaller than the others but have air-conditioning and wall-to-wall carpeting. There's a dive shop with a full-time instructor. ⌂ *Box 1, South Caicos,* ☎ *809/94–63444 or 800/722–2582,* FAX *809/94–63446. 40 rooms. Restaurant, bar, bicycle rentals, Windsurfers, dive shop. AE, D, MC, V. EP, MAP.*

Nightlife

On Provo, a full band plays native, reggae, and contemporary music on Thursday night at the **Erebus Inn** (☎ 809/94–64240). **Le Deck** (☎ 809/94–65547) offers one-armed bandits every night. A lively lounge can be found at the **Ramada Turquoise Reef Resort** (☎ 809/94–65555), where a musician plays to the mostly tourist crowd. The Ramada is also the location of **Port Royale** (☎ 809/94–65508), the island's only gambling casino. **Bacchus** (opposite the Ramada Turquoise Reef Resort, ☎ 809/94–65214) is open Thursday, Friday, and Saturday night for drinks and dancing. **Disco Elite** (Airport Rd., ☎ 809/94–64592) has strobe lights and an elevated dance floor. The newest hot spot here is **Casablanca** (next to Club Med, ☎ 809/94–65449), a Monte Carlo–style nightclub complete with mirrors and a decked-out crowd. On Grand Turk, Xavier Tonneau (a.k.a. Mr. X) leads sing-alongs in his bar at the **Turk's Head Inn** almost every night (☎ 809/94–62466), and there's music at the **Salt Raker Inn** (☎ 809/94–62260) on Wednesday and Sunday nights. For a lively bar filled with local color, try **Smokey's on the Beach** (near Le Deck hotel, ☎ 809/94–13466). Night owls can head over to the **Lady** for dancing (at the former naval base, no ☎) or to the **Rack Room** (Back Salina, ☎ 809/94–61802) for music and gaming.

27 The U.S. Virgin Islands

St. Thomas, St. Croix, St. John

IT IS THE COMBINATION of the familiar and the exotic in the U.S. Virgin Islands that defines this "American Paradise" and explains much of its appeal. The effort to be all things to all people—while remaining true to the best of itself—has created a sometimes paradoxical blend of island serenity and American practicality in this U.S. territory 1,000 miles from the southern tip of the U.S. mainland.

Updated by Pamela Acheson and Gail Gillen de Haas

The postcard images you'd expect from a tropical paradise are here: Stretches of beach arc into the distance, and white sails skim across water so blue and clear it stuns the senses; red-roof houses add their spot of color to the green hillsides' mosaic, along with the orange of the flamboyant tree, the red of the hibiscus, the magenta of the bougainvillea, and the blue stone ruins of old sugar mills; and towns of pastel-tone European-style villas, decorated by filigree wrought-iron terraces, line narrow streets climbing up from a harbor.

The other part of the equation are all those things that make it so easy and appealing for Americans to visit this cluster of islands. The official language is English, the money is the dollar, and the U.S. government runs things. There's cable TV, Pizza Hut, and McDonald's. There's unfettered immigration to and from the mainland, and investments are protected by the U.S. flag. Visitors to the U.S.V.I. have the opportunity to delve into a "foreign" culture while anchored by familiar language and landmarks.

Your destination here will be St. Thomas (13 miles long); its neighbor St. John (9 miles long); or, 40 miles to the south, St. Croix (23 miles long). A pro/con thumbnail sketch of these three might have it that St. Thomas is bustling (hustling), the place for shopping and discos (commercial glitz and overdevelopment); St. Croix is more Danish, picturesque, and rural (more provincial and duller, particularly after dark); and St. John is matchless in the beauty of its National Park Service–protected land and beaches (a one-village island mostly for the rich or for campers). Surely not everything will suit your fancy, but chances are that among the three islands you'll find your own idea of paradise.

Before You Go

Tourist Information

Information about the U.S. Virgin Islands is available through the following organizations. **U.S.V.I. government tourist offices:** 225 Peachtree St., Suite 760, Atlanta, GA 30303, ☎ 404/688–0906, FAX 404/525–1102; 122 S. Michigan Ave., Suite 1270, Chicago, IL 60603, ☎ 312/461–0180, FAX 312/461–0765; 3460 Wilshire Blvd., Suite 412, Los Angeles, CA 90010, ☎ 213/739–0138, FAX 213/739–2005; 2655 Le Jeune Rd., Suite 907, Coral Gables, FL 33134, ☎ 305/442–7200, FAX 305/445–9044; 1270 6th Ave., New York, NY 10020, ☎ 212/582–4520, FAX 212/581–3405; 900 17th Ave. NW, Suite 500, Washington, DC 20006, ☎ 202/293–3707, FAX 202/785–2542; 1300 Ashford Ave., Condado, Santurce, Puerto Rico 00907, ☎ 809/724–3816, FAX 809/724–7223; and 2 Cinnamon Row, Plantation Wharf, York Pl., London, England SW11 3TW, ☎ 0171/978–5262, telex 27231, FAX 0171/924–3171.

You can also call the Division of Tourism's toll-free number (☎ 800/878-4463).

Arriving and Departing

BY PLANE

One advantage of visiting the U.S.V.I. is the abundance of nonstop flights that can have you at the beach in a relatively short time (three to four hours from most East Coast departures). You may fly into the U.S.V.I. direct via **Continental** (☎ 800/231–0856), **Delta** (☎ 800/221–1212), **USAir** (☎ 800/428–4322), or **American** (☎ 800/433–7300), or you may fly via San Juan on all the above plus **American Eagle** (☎ 800/474–4884).

BY BOAT

Some 20 cruise lines, ranging from floating budget hotels to small luxury yachts taking only 100 passengers, stop at St. Thomas or St. Croix.

Among those that stop over at St. Thomas are **Holland American Line** (300 Elliott Ave. W, Seattle, WA 98119, ☎ 206/281–3535), **Princess Cruises** (10100 Santa Monica Blvd., Los Angeles, CA 90067, ☎ 310/553–1770 or 800/421–0522), **Royal Caribbean Cruises** (1050 Caribbean Way, Miami, FL 33132, ☎ 800/327–6700; in Canada, 800/245–7225), **Royal Viking Line** (95 Merrick Way, Coral Gables, FL 33134, ☎ 800/422–8000), **Cunard Line** (555 5th Ave., New York, NY 10017, ☎ 800/528–6273 or 800/458–9000), and **Renaissance Cruises** (1800 Eller Dr., Suite 300, Box 350307, Fort Lauderdale, FL 33335, ☎ 800/525–2450). For a smaller luxury cruise on which caviar-and-champagne service is the norm 24 hours a day, contact **Seabourne Cruise Line** (55 Francisco St., San Francisco, CA 94133, ☎ 800/929–9595).

Increasingly popular are cruises aboard oversize sailboats. Although the sails on these rather odd-looking ships are more often cosmetic than functional, the ships usually offer a more relaxed itinerary and stop at less-traveled anchorages. You can experience a **Club Med** (☎ 800/258–2633) all-inclusive vacation on the sea aboard *Club Med I,* a 617-foot ship with seven computerized sails that Club Med bills as the largest sailing ship in the world. The ship sails out of Guadeloupe on seven-day winter cruises (it's in St. Thomas for one day) and spends summers in the Mediterranean. **Windjammer Barefoot Cruises** (Box 120, Miami Beach, FL 33119-0120, ☎ 800/327–2601) sails from the U.S.V.I. to neighboring islands on cruises of 6- to 13-day durations. **Star Clippers** (4101 Salzedo Ave. Coral Gables, FL 33146, ☎ 800/442–0551) offers seven-day cruises.

Passports and Visas

Upon entering the U.S.V.I., U.S. and Canadian citizens are required to present some proof of citizenship—if not a passport, then a birth certificate or voter-registration card with a driver's license or photo ID. If you are arriving from the U.S. mainland or Puerto Rico, you need no inoculation or health certificate.

Britons need a valid 10-year passport to enter the U.S.V.I. (cost: £15 for a standard 32-page passport, £30 for a 94-page passport). You do not need a visa for the U.S.V.I. if you are visiting either on business or pleasure, are staying fewer than 90 days, have a return ticket or on-going ticket, are traveling with a major airline (in effect, any airline that flies from the United Kingdom to the United States), and complete visa waiver I-94W, which is supplied either at the airport of departure or on the plane.

Language

English, often with a Creole or West Indian lilt, is what's spoken on these islands.

Precautions

Crime exists here, but not to the same degree that it does in larger cities on the U.S. mainland. Still, it's best to stick to well-lit streets at night and use the same kind of street sense (don't wander the back alleys of Charlotte Amalie after five rum punches, for example) that you would in any unfamiliar territory. If you plan on carrying things around, rent a car, not a Jeep, and lock possessions in the trunk. Keep your rental car locked wherever you park. Don't leave cameras, purses, and other valuables lying on the beach while you're off on an hour-long snorkel, whether at the deserted beaches of St. John or the more crowded Magens and Coki beaches on St. Thomas.

Staying in the U.S. Virgin Islands

Important Addresses

Tourist Information: The **U.S. Virgin Islands Division of Tourism** has offices in St. Thomas (Box 6400, Charlotte Amalie, U.S.V.I. 00804, ☎ 809/774–8784, FAX 809/774–4390), St. Croix (Box 4538, Christiansted, U.S.V.I. 00822, ☎ 809/773–0495, and on the pier, Strand St., Frederiksted, U.S.V.I. 00840, ☎ 809/772–0357), and St. John (Box 200, Cruz Bay, U.S.V.I. 00830, ☎ 809/776–6450).

There are two **visitor centers** in Charlotte Amalie: one across from Emancipation Square and one at Havensight Mall. The center on St. John is next to the post office in Cruz Bay. On St. Croix, go to the Old Scale House at the waterfront in Christiansted, across from Fort Christiansvaern. The **National Park Service** also has visitor centers at the ferry areas on St. Thomas (Red Hook) and St. John (Cruz Bay).

EMERGENCIES
Police: Dial 915 or 911.

Hospitals: The emergency room of **St. Thomas Hospital** (☎ 809/776–8311) in Sugar Estate, Charlotte Amalie, is open 24 hours a day. In Christiansted there is the **St. Croix Hospital and Community Health Center** (6 Diamond Bay, north of Sunny Isle Shopping Center, on Rte. 79, ☎ 809/778–6311), and in Frederiksted, the **Frederiksted Health Center** (☎ 809/772–1992). On St. John contact the **Morris F. DeCastro Clinic** (Cruz Bay, ☎ 809/776–6400) or call an **emergency medical technician** directly (☎ 809/776–6222).

Air Ambulances: Bohlke International Airways (☎ 809/778–9177) operates out of the airport in St. Croix. **Air Medical Services** (☎ 800/443–0013) and **Air Ambulance Network** (☎ 800/327–1966) also serve the area from Florida.

Coast Guard: For emergencies on St. Thomas or St. John, call the **Marine Safety Detachment** (☎ 809/776–3497) from 7 to 3:30 weekdays; on St. Croix, call 809/778–2692. If there is no answer, call the **Rescue Coordination Center** (☎ 809/729–6770 or 809/729–6800, ext. 140–145) in San Juan, open 24 hours a day.

Pharmacies: On St. Thomas, **Sunrise Pharmacy** has branches in Red Hook (☎ 809/775–6600) and in the Wheatley Center (☎ 809/774–5333); **Drug Farm Pharmacy**'s main store (☎ 809/776–7098) is across from the General Post Office, with another branch (☎ 809/776–1880) next to St. Thomas Hospital. On St. Croix, try **People's Drug Store, Inc.** in Christiansted (☎ 809/778–7355) and Sunny Isle Shopping Center (☎ 809/778–5537) or **D & D Apothecary Hall** (☎ 809/772–1890) in Frederiksted. On St. John, the **St. John Drug Center** (☎ 809/776–6353) is in Cruz Bay.

Currency

The U.S. dollar is the medium of exchange here.

Taxes and Service Charges

An 8% tax is added to hotel rates. Departure tax for the U.S.V.I. is included in the cost of your airplane ticket. Some hotels and restaurants add a 10% or 15% service charge to your bill, generally only if you are part of a group of 15 or more. There is no sales tax in the U.S.V.I.

Guided Tours

On St. Thomas, the **V.I. Taxi Association City-Island Tour** (☎ 809/774–4550) gives a two-hour tour aimed at cruise-ship passengers that includes stops at Drake's Seat and Mountain Top. **Tropic Tours** (☎ 809/774–1855 and 800/524–4334) offers half-day shopping and sightseeing tours of St. Thomas by bus six days a week for $20 per person, and full-day snorkeling tours to St. John every day for $50 per person (including lunch). It picks up at all the major hotels. Bird-watching, whale-watching, and a chance to wait hidden on a beach while the magnificent hawksbill turtles come ashore to lay their eggs are all open to visitors. Write the **St. Croix Environmental Association** (Box 3839, St. Croix 00822, ☎ 809/773–1989) for more information on hikes and special programs, or check the community calendar in the *Daily News* for up-to-date information.

Van tours of St. Croix are offered by **St. Croix Safari Tours** (☎ 809/773–6700) and **St. Croix Transit** (☎ 809/772–3333). The tours, which depart from Christiansted and last about three hours, start at $20 per person. One of the best ways to see the rain forest and hills of the west end may be a tour by horseback with **Paul and Jill's Equestrian Stable** (☎ 809/772–2880 or 809/772–2627).

On St. John, contact the **St. John Taxi Association** (☎ 809/776–6060) for tours of the island. The park service also gives a variety of guided tours on- and off-shore. For more information, or to arrange a tour, contact the **St. John National Park Visitor Center** (Cruz Bay, ☎ 809/776–6201).

Getting Around

BY CAR

Any U.S. driver's license is good for 90 days here; the minimum age for drivers is 18, although many agencies won't rent to anyone under the age of 25. Driving is on the left side of the road (although your steering wheel will be on the left side of the car). Many of the roads are narrow and the islands are dotted with hills, so there is ample reason to drive carefully. Jeeps are particularly recommended on St. John, which has well-paved main roads but many dirt side roads.

On St. Thomas, you can rent a car from **ABC Rentals** (☎ 809/776–1222 or 800/524–2080), **Anchorage E-Z Car** (☎ 809/775–6255 or 800/524–2027), **Avis** (☎ 809/774–1468), **Budget** (☎ 809/776–5774), **Cowpet Car Rental** (☎ 809/775–7376 or 800/524–2072), **Dependable** (☎ 809/774–2253 or 800/522–3076), **Discount** (☎ 809/776–4858), **Hertz** (☎ 809/774–1879), **Sea Breeze** (☎ 809/774–7200), **Sun Island** (☎ 809/774–3333 or 800/233–7941), or **Thrifty** (☎ 809/776–7282).

On St. Croix, call **Atlas** (☎ 809/773–2886 or 800/426–6009), **Avis** (☎ 809/778–9355), **Budget** (☎ 809/778–9636), **Caribbean Jeep & Car** (☎ 809/773–4399), **Hertz** (☎ 809/778–1402), **Olympic** (☎ 809/773–2208 or 800/344–5776), and **Thrifty** (☎ 809/773–7200).

On St. John, call **Avis** (☎ 809/776–6374), **Budget** (☎ 809/776–7575), **Cool Breeze** (☎ 809/776–6588), **Hertz** (☎ 809/776–6695), **O'Connor**

Jeep (☎ 809/776–6343), **St. John Car Rental** (☎ 809/776–6103), or **Spencer's Jeep** (☎ 809/776–7784).

TAXIS

Taxis of all shapes and sizes are available at various ferry, shopping, resort, and airport areas on St. Thomas and respond quickly to a call.

In Charlotte Amalie, taxi stands are across from **Emancipation Gardens** (in front of Little Switzerland behind the post office) and along the waterfront. Away from Charlotte Amalie, you'll find taxis available at all major hotels and at such public beaches as Magens Bay and Coki Point, as well as at the Red Hook ferry dock. Calling taxis will work, too, but allow plenty of time.

Taxis on St. Croix, generally station wagons or minivans, are a phone call away from most hotels and are available in downtown Christiansted, at the Alexander Hamilton Airport, and at the Frederiksted pier during cruise-ship arrivals. Rates, set by law, are prominently displayed at the airport, and drivers are required to show a rate sheet if passengers request it. Try the **St. Croix Taxi Association** (☎ 809/778–1088) at the airport and **Antilles Taxi Service** (☎ 809/773–5020) or **Cruzan Taxi and Tours** (☎ 809/773–6388) in Christiansted.

On St. John buses and taxis are the same thing: open-air safari buses. Technically the safari buses are private taxis, but everyone uses them as an informal bus system. They congregate at the Cruz Bay Dock, ready to take you to any of the beaches or other island destinations; you can also pick them up anywhere on the road by signaling.

BUSES

Public buses are not the quickest way to get around on the islands, because service is minimal, but the deluxe mainland-size buses on St. Thomas and St. Croix make public transportation a very reasonable and comfortable way to get from east and west to town and back (on St. Thomas there is no service north). Fares are $1 between outlying areas and town and 75¢ in town. St. John has no public bus system, and residents rely on the kindness of taxi vans and safari buses for mass transportation.

FERRIES

Ferries ply two routes between St. Thomas and St. John—either between the Charlotte Amalie waterfront and Cruz Bay or between Red Hook and Cruz Bay. The schedules for daily service between Red Hook, St. Thomas, and Cruz Bay, St. John: Ferries leave Red Hook weekdays 6:30 and 7:30 AM, and all week long hourly 8 AM to midnight. They leave Cruz Bay for Red Hook hourly 6 AM to 10 PM and at 11:20 PM. The 15- to 20-minute ferry ride is $3 one way for adults, $1.50 for children under 12.

Telephones and Mail

The area code for all the U.S.V.I. is 809, and there is direct dial to the mainland. Local calls from a public phone cost 25¢ for each five minutes. On St. John the place to go for any telephone or message needs is **Connections** (☎ 809/776–6922). On St. Thomas, it's **Islander Services** (☎ 809/774–5302), behind the Greenhouse Restaurant in Charlotte Amalie, or **East End Secretarial Services** (☎ 809/775–5262, FAX 809/775–3590), upstairs at the Red Hook Plaza. On St. Croix, visit **AnswerPLUS** (5005B Chandlers Wharf, Gallows Bay, ☎ 809/773–4444) or **Worldwide Calling** (head of the pier in Frederiksted, ☎ 809/772–2490).

The U.S. Virgin Islands

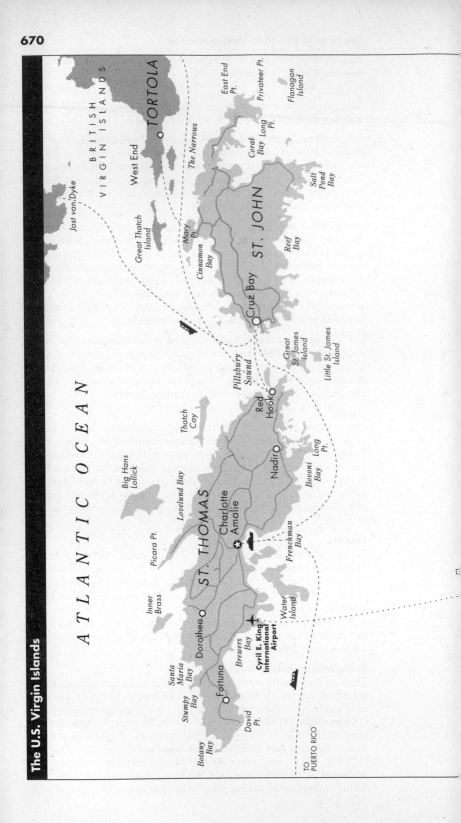

ATLANTIC OCEAN

BRITISH VIRGIN ISLANDS

TORTOLA

West End

East End Pt.

Privateer Pt.

Long Pt.

Flanagan Island

The Narrows

Coral Bay

Jost van Dyke

Great Thatch Island

Mary Pt.

Cinnamon Bay

ST. JOHN

Salt Pond Bay

Cruz Bay

Reef Bay

Pillsbury Sound

Great St. James Island

Little St. James Island

Thatch Cay

Red Hook

Big Hans Lollick

Loveland Bay

Nadir

Bovoni

Long Pt.

Picara Pt.

Charlotte Amalie

ST. THOMAS

Inner Brass

Frenchman Bay

Dorothea

Water Island

Santa Maria Bay

Brewers Bay

Cyril E. King International Airport

Fortuna

Stumpy Bay

David Pt.

Botany Bay

TO PUERTO RICO

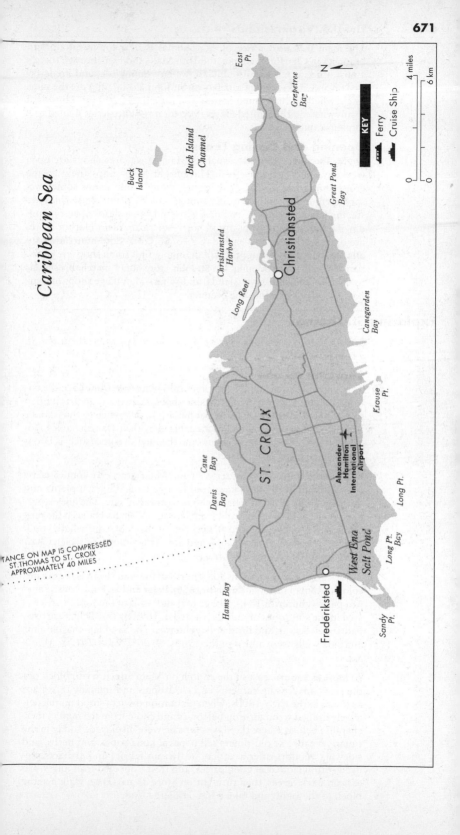

Caribbean Sea

KEY
Ferry
Cruise Ship

N

4 miles
6 km

East Pt.

Grapetree Bay

Buck Island

Buck Island Channel

Great Pond Bay

Christiansted

Christiansted Harbor

Long Reef

Canegarden Bay

Krause Pt.

ST. CROIX

Alexander Hamilton International Airport

Cane Bay

Davis Bay

Long Pt.

Long Pt. Bay

TANCE ON MAP IS COMPRESSED
ST.THOMAS TO ST. CROIX
APPROXIMATELY 40 MILES

Hams Bay

Frederiksted

West End Salt Pond

Sandy Pt.

The main **U.S. post office** on St. Thomas is near the hospital, with branches in Charlotte Amalie, the Tutu Mall, and Frenchtown; there's a post office at Christiansted, Gallows Bay, Sunny Isle, and Frederiksted on St. Croix, and at Cruz Bay on St. John. Postal rates are the same as elsewhere in the United States: 32¢ for a letter, 20¢ for a postcard to anywhere in the United States, 50¢ for a ½-ounce letter mailed to a foreign country.

Opening and Closing Times

On **St. Thomas,** Charlotte Amalie's Main Street–area shops are open weekdays and Saturday 9–5. Havensight Mall shops (next to the cruise-ship dock) hours are the same, though some shops sometimes stay open until 9 on Friday, depending on how many cruise ships are staying late at the dock. You may also find some shops open on Sunday if a lot of cruise ships are in port. American Yacht Harbor stores are open weekdays and Saturday 9–6. **St. Croix** store hours are usually weekdays 9–5, but you will definitely find some shops in Christiansted open in the evening. On **St. John,** store hours are reliably similar to those on the other two islands, and Wharfside Village shops in Cruz Bay are often open into the evening.

Exploring St. Thomas

Numbers in the margin correspond to points of interest on the St. Thomas map.

Charlotte Amalie

 This tour of historic (and sometimes hilly) **Charlotte Amalie** and environs is on foot, so wear comfortable shoes, start early, and stop often to refresh. A note about the street names: In deference to the island's heritage, the streets downtown are labeled by their Danish names. Locals will use both the Danish name and the English name (such as Dronnigen's Gade and Main Street).

Begin at the waterfront. Waterfront and Main streets are connected by cobblestone-paved alleys kept cool by overhanging green plants and the thick stone walls of the warehouses on either side. The alleys (particularly Royal Dane Mall and Palm Passage, Main St. between the post office and Market Sq., and Bakery Sq. on Back St.) are where you'll find the unique and glamorous—and duty-free—shops for which Charlotte Amalie is famous (*see* Shopping, *below*).

At the end of Kronprindsens Alley north of the waterfront is the cream-colored Roman Catholic **Cathedral of St. Peter and St. Paul,** consecrated as a parish church in 1848. The ceiling and walls of the church are covered in the soft tones of murals painted in 1899 by two Belgian artists, Father Leo Servais and Brother Ildephonsus. The San Juan–marble altar and side walls were added in the 1960s. ☎ *809/774–0201.* ☼ *Mon.–Sat. 8–5.*

At **Market Square,** east of the church on Main Street, try to block out the signs advertising cameras and electronics and imagine this place as it was in the early 1800s, when plantation owners stood on the delicately draped wrought-iron balconies and chose from the human merchandise below, where the slaves for sale were displayed. Today in the square, a cadre of old-timers sell papaya, tania roots, and herbs, and sidewalk vendors offer a variety of African fabrics and artifacts, tie-dyed cotton clothes at good prices, and fresh-squeezed fruit juices. Go east on Back Street, then turn left on Store Tvaer Gade; walk a short block to the right, and take a left on Bjerge Gade.

As you walk up Bjerge Gade you'll end up facing a weather-beaten but imposing two-story red house known as the **Crystal Palace,** so named because it was the first building on the island to have glass windows. The Crystal Palace anchors the corner of Bjerge and Crystal Gade. Here the street becomes stairs, which you can climb to Denmark Hill and the old Greek Revival **Danish Consulate building** (1830)—look for the red-and-white flag.

Descend to Crystal Gade and go east. At Number 15 you'll come to the **Synagogue of Beracha Veshalom Vegmiluth Hasidim.** Its Hebrew name translates as the Congregation of Blessing, Peace, and Loving Deeds. Since the synagogue first opened its doors in 1833, it has held a weekly Sabbath service, making it the oldest synagogue building in continuous use under the American flag, and the second-oldest (after the one on Curaçao) in the Western Hemisphere. *15 Crystal Gade,* ☎ *809/774–4312.* ⊙ *Weekdays 9–4.*

One block east, down the hill, you'll come to the corner of Nye Gade. On the right corner is the St. Thomas **Dutch Reformed Church,** founded in 1744, burned in 1804, and rebuilt to its austere loveliness in 1844. The unembellished cream-color hall exudes peace—albeit monochromatically. The only touches of another color are the forest-green shutters and carpet. ☎ *809/776–8255.* ⊙ *Weekdays 9–5. Call ahead of time, as the doors are sometimes locked.*

Continue on Crystal Gade one block east and turn left (north) on Garden Street. The **All Saints Anglican Church** was built in 1848 from stone quarried on the island. Its thick, arched window frames are lined with the yellow brick that came to the islands as ballast aboard merchant ships. The church was built in celebration of the end of slavery in the Virgin Islands in 1848. ☎ *809/774–0217.* ⊙ *Mon.–Sat.* 6 AM–3 PM.

Return down Garden Street and go east on Kongen's Gade. Keep walking up the hill to the east and you'll find yourself at the foot of the **99 Steps,** a staircase "street" built by the Danes in the 1700s. (If you count the stairs as you go up, you'll discover, like thousands before you, that there are more than 99.)

Up the steps you'll find the neighborhood of **Queen's Street.** The homes are privately owned except for two inns—the Mark St. Thomas and Blackbeard's Castle. The tower of **Blackbeard's Castle** was built in 1679 and is believed to have been used by the notorious pirate Edward Teach. The castle is now a National Historic Landmark and a charming inn and restaurant.

TIME OUT You might want to stop at **Blackbeard's Castle** for some of the island's best food and a swim—the pool is open to daytime customers. As you lunch on the terrace, you can take in the view of Charlotte Amalie and the harbor.

Go back down the steps and continue east to **Government House.** This elegant home, built in 1867, is the official residence of the governor of the U.S.V.I., and the first floor is open to the public. The staircases are carved from native mahogany, as are the plaques hand-lettered in gold with the names of the governors appointed and, since 1970, elected. The three murals at the back of the lobby were painted by Pepino Mangravatti in the 1930s as part of the U.S. government's Works Projects Administration (WPA). The murals depict Columbus's landing on St. Croix during his second voyage in 1493, the transfer of the islands from Denmark to the United States in 1917, and a sugar plantation on St. John.

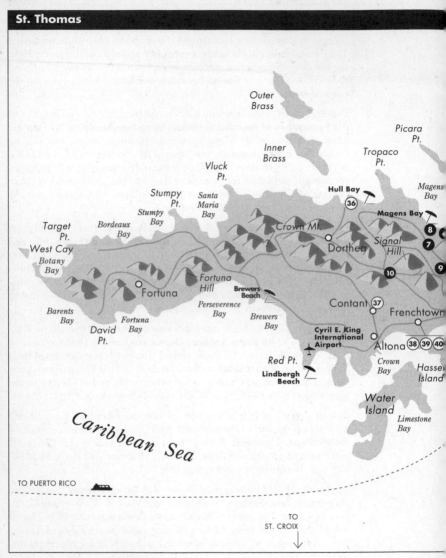

Exploring
Charlotte Amalie, **1**
Coral World, **4**
Drake's Seat, **6**
Estate St. Peter
Greathouse Botanical
Gardens, **7**
Fairchild Park, **9**
Four Corners, **10**
Havensight Mall, **2**
Mountain Top, **8**
Red Hook, **3**
Tillet's Gardens, **5**

Dining
Alexander's Cafe, **38**
Blackbeard's
Castle, **16**
Bryan's Bar and
Restaurant, **36**
Chart House, **39**
Entre Nous, **14**
Eunice's Terrace, **33**
For the Birds, **23**
Hard Rock Café, **19**
Hotel 1829, **12**
Il Cappuccini, **20**

Little Bopeep, **15**
Piccola Marina
Cafe, **25**
Romanos, **34**
Tickle's Dockside
Pub, **27**
Virgilio's, **13**
Zorba's Cafe, **17**

Lodging
Admiral's Inn, **40**
Blackbeard's
Castle, **16**
Bolongo Elysian
Beach Resort, **24**
Bolongo Club Every-
thing, **22**
Grand Palazzo, **26**
Hotel 1829, **12**
Island View Guest-
house, **37**

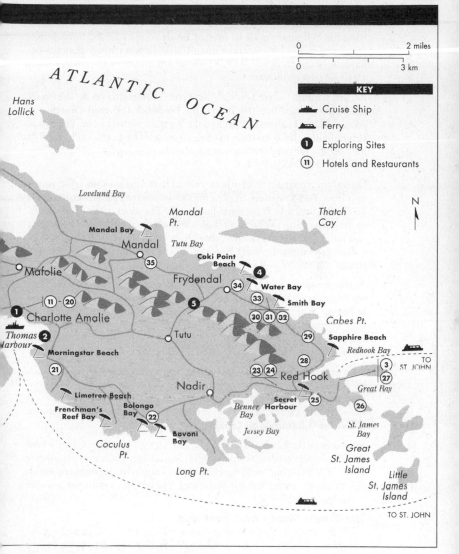

ATLANTIC OCEAN

Hans
Lollick

Lovelund Bay

Mandal
Pt.

Thatch
Cay

Mandal Bay

Mandal

Tutu Bay

Mafolie

Coki Point
Beach

4

Frydendal

34

Water Bay

33

Smith Bay

5

20 **31** **32**

11 – **20**

Charlotte Amalie

Tutu

29

Cabes Pt.

Sapphire Beach

Thomas
Harbour

2

Redhook Bay

3

TO
ST. JOHN

Morningstar Beach

21

28

Nadir

23 **24**

Red Hook

27

Great Bay

Limetree Beach

Frenchman's
Reef Bay

Bolongo
Bay

22

Benner
Bay

Secret
Harbour

25

26

Coculus
Pt.

Bovoni
Bay

Jersey Bay

St. James
Bay

Great
St. James
Island

Little
St. James
Island

Long Pt.

TO ST. JOHN

35

N

KEY

- Cruise Ship
- Ferry
- **1** Exploring Sites
- **11** Hotels and Restaurants

0   2 miles
0   3 km

Marriott's French-
man's Reef
and Morning Star
Beach Resorts, **21**

Pavilions & Pools, **28**

Point Pleasant
Resort, **31**

Sapphire
Beach Resort and
Marina, **29**

Sign of the Griffin, **35**

Stouffer Renaissance
Grand Beach
Resort, **32**

Sugar Bay   Planta-
tion, **30**

Villa Blanca Hotel, **18**

Villa Santana, **11**

Head to your left and look for the **Seven Arches Museum.** This restored West Indian home was built around 1800 and is still a private residence. Ring the bell, and you'll be invited inside to see historic furnishings, cannonballs, gas lamps, and a quaint West Indian cottage that sits behind the house. ☎ 809/774–9295. *Suggested donation $5.* ☉ *Tues.–Sun. 10–3 or by appointment.*

Return west on Norre Gade (Main Street) toward town. In the block before the post office you'll pass the **Frederick Lutheran Church,** the second-oldest Lutheran church in the Western Hemisphere. The inside is highlighted by a massive mahogany altar. The pews, each with its own door, were once rented to families of the congregation. ☎ 809/776–1315. ☉ *Mon.–Sat. 9–4.*

Directly across from the Lutheran Church, through a small side street, you'll see **Fort Christian,** St. Thomas's oldest standing structure, built 1672–87, and a U.S. national landmark. The clock tower was added in the 19th century. This remarkable redoubt has, over time, been used as a jail, governor's residence, town hall, courthouse, and church. The building is currently being restored, so the interior is not open to the public. ☎ 809/776–4566.

Across from the fort is **Emancipation Garden,** which honors the freeing of slaves in 1848. On the other side of the garden is the **legislature building,** its pastoral-looking lime-green exterior concealing the vociferous political wrangling going on inside. Built originally by the Danish as a police barracks, the building was later used to billet U.S. Marines, and much later it housed a public school.

Stop in the **post office** to contemplate the murals of waterfront scenes by *Saturday Evening Post* artist Stephen Dohanos. His art was commissioned as part of the WPA in the 1930s. Behind the post office, on the waterfront side of Little Switzerland, are the hospitality lounge and **V.I. Visitor's Information Center.**

As you head back toward Market Square along Main Street, you'll pass the Tropicana Perfume Shop, between Store Tvaer Gade and Trompeter Gade. The building the shop is in is also known as the **Pissarro Building** because it was the birthplace of French Impressionist painter Camille Pissarro.

The South Shore and East End

Leaving Charlotte Amalie, take Veterans Drive (Rte. 30) east along the waterfront. Once you bear to the right at **Nelson Mandela Circle** (Yacht Haven is on your right), you'll make quicker progress. You may want to stop at **Havensight Mall,** across from the dock. This shopping center is a less crowded (and less charming) version of the duty-free shopping district along Main Street in town. Or turn left across the street from Havensight Mall and ride the new **Paradise Point Gondola** ($10 adults, $5 children 3–12 round-trip), a cable car that will fly you straight up the hill to Paradise Point. This scenic overlook has breathtaking views of Charlotte Amalie and the harbor, and a bar, restaurant, and several shops.

Route 30 is narrow and winds up and down. It also changes names several times along the way; it is called Frenchman's Bay Road just outside town (take a sharp left turn just before the entrance to Marriott's Frenchman's Reef Hotel and its luxurious companion, Morning Star Beach Resort). It then becomes Bovoni Road around Bolongo Bay. Whatever it is called, on it you will be treated to some southerly vistas of the Caribbean Sea (and, on clear days, St. Croix, 40 miles away).

Eventually, Route 30 forks into Route 322 on the right, which heads out to several hotels and the **Virgin Island National Park Headquarters,** and Route 32 on the left, which heads into **Red Hook,** where you can catch the ferry to St. John (parking available for $5 a day). Red Hook has grown from a sleepy little town connected to the rest of the island only by dirt roads (or by boat) to an increasingly self-sustaining village. Here you will find **American Yacht Harbor,** a new waterfront arcade with branches of many Charlotte Amalie shops, a deli, and a few restaurants. You can walk along the docks and visit with sailors and fishermen and stop for a beer at Piccola Marina Cafe or the Warehouse bar.

Above Red Hook the main road swings toward the north shore and becomes Route 38, or Smith Bay Road, taking you past Sapphire Beach, a resort and restaurant with water-sports rentals and a popular snorkeling and windsurfing spot, Sugar Bay Resort, Pavilions & Pools, Point Pleasant Resort, and Stouffer Grand Beach Resort. Look for the turnoff to the right for Coki Point Beach and **Coral World,** with its three-level underwater observatory, the world's largest reef tank, and an aquarium with more than 20 TV-size tanks providing capsulized views of sea life. A semisubmarine (a craft that has glass sides below deck for underwater viewing) offers 20-minute undersea tours for $12 per person. Coral World's staff will answer your questions about the turtles, iguanas, parrots, and flamingos that inhabit the park. The facility also has a restaurant, a souvenir shop, and the world's only underwater mailbox, from which you can send postcards home. ☎ 809/ 775–1555. ☛ *$16 adults, $10 children.* ☾ *Daily 9–6.*

Continue west on Route 38 and you'll come to **Tillet's Gardens,** where local artisans craft stained glass, pottery, and ceramics and where well-known artist Jim Tillet's paintings and silk-screened fabrics are on display and for sale.

North Shore, Center Islands, and West
The north shore is home to many inviting attractions, not to mention much lusher vegetation than is found on the rest of the island. The most direct route from Charlotte Amalie is Mafolie Road (Rte. 35), which can be picked up east of Government Hill.

In the heights above Charlotte Amalie is **Drake's Seat,** the mountain lookout from which Sir Francis Drake was supposed to have kept watch over his fleet, looking for enemy ships of the Spanish fleet. Magens Bay and Mahogany Run are to the north, with the British Virgin Islands and Drake's Passage to the east. Off to the left, or west, are Fairchild Park, Mountain Top, Hull Bay, and such smaller islands as the Inner and Outer Brass islands. The panoramic vista is especially striking (and romantic) at dusk, and if you arrive late in the day you'll miss the hordes of day-trippers on taxi tours who stop at Drake's Seat to take a picture and buy a T-shirt from one of the vendors there. The vendors are gone by the afternoon.

West of Drake's is the island's newest attraction, the **Estate St. Peter Greathouse Botanical Gardens.** On a mountainside 1,000 feet above sea level, with views of more than 20 other islands and islets, the estate has a gallery displaying local art and a nature trail that winds through nearly 200 varieties of tropical trees and plants, including an orchid jungle. ☎ 809/774–4999. ☛ *$8 adults, $4 children 12 and under.* ☾ *Mon.–Sat. 9–4:30.*

8 Also nearby, but higher above sea level (1,500 ft), is **Mountain Top,** which has an interesting collection of shops, a bar that claims to have invented the banana daiquiri, and some spectacular views.

9 Below Mountain Top is **Fairchild Park,** a gift to the people of the U.S.V.I. from the philanthropist Arthur Fairchild.

10 If you head west from Mountain Top, on Crown Mountain Road (Rte. 33) you'll come to **Four Corners.** Take the extreme right turn and drive along the northwestern ridge of the mountain through **Caret Bay, Sorgenfri,** and **Pearl.** There's not much here except peace and quiet, junglelike foliage, and spectacular vistas.

Turn onto Route 301 to Route 30 and head south to Brewer's Bay, then follow Route 30 east back to Frenchtown and Charlotte Amalie.

TIME OUT Pull into Frenchtown and reward yourself for a long day's travels with a stop at **Epernay,** a wine bar tucked behind Alexander's Cafe. You'll find wines and champagnes by the glass and hors d'oeuvres and light snacks to linger over while you contemplate life on the islands. ☎ 809/774–5348. ☉ Mon.–Sat. 4:30 pm–1 am (often until later Fri. and Sat.). Food served 5 pm–midnight. AE, MC, V.

Exploring St. Croix

Numbers in the margin correspond to points of interest on the St. Croix map.

1 This tour starts in the historic, Danish-style town of **Christiansted,** St. Croix's commercial center. Many of the structures, which are built from the harbor up into the gentle hillsides, date from the 18th century. An easy-to-follow walking tour begins at the **visitors' bureau,** at the harbor. The building was constructed in 1856 and once served as a scale house, where goods passing through the port were weighed and inspected. Directly across the parking lot, at the edge of D. Hamilton Jackson Park (the park is named for a famed labor leader, journalist, and judge), is the **Old Customs House.** Completed in 1829, this building now houses the island's national park offices. To the east stands yellow **Fort Christiansvaern.** Built by the Danish from 1738 to 1749 to protect the harbor against attacks on commercial shipping, the fort was repeatedly damaged by hurricane-force winds and was partially rebuilt in 1772. It is now part of the National Historic Site and the best-preserved of the remaining Danish-built forts in the Virgin Islands. Five rooms, including military barracks and a dungeon, have been restored to demonstrate how the fort looked in the 1840s, when it was at its height as a military establishment. There is also an exhibit that documents the Danish military's 150-year presence in Christiansted. *Box 160, Christiansted 00822,* ☎ *809/773–1460.* ☛ *$2 (includes ☛ to Steeple Bldg.); free to children under 16 and senior citizens.* ☉ *Weekdays 8–5, weekends and holidays 9–5. Closed Dec. 25, Easter, and Thanksgiving.*

Cross Hospital Street from the customs house to reach the **post office building.** This 1749 structure once housed the Danish West India & Guinea Company warehouse. To the south of the post office, across Company Street, stands the maroon-and-white **Steeple Building.** Built by the Danes in 1754, the building was the first Danish Lutheran church on St. Croix. It is now a national-park museum and contains exhibits documenting the island's habitation by its native population through an extensive array of archaeological artifacts. There are also displays on the architectural development of Christiansted and the African-American experience in the town during the Danish Colonial rule. *Box 160, Christiansted 00822,* ☎ *809/773–1460.* ☞ *$2 (includes* ☞ *to fort).* ⊙ *Tues.–Thurs. and weekends 9–4.*

One of the town's most elegant buildings is **Government House,** on King Street. It was built in 1747 as a home for a Danish merchant, and today the building houses U.S.V.I. government offices and the U.S. District Court. Slip into the peaceful inner courtyard to admire the still pools and gardens. A sweeping staircase leads visitors to a second-story ballroom, still the site of official government functions.

To leave Christiansted, drive up Hospital Street from the tourist office and turn right onto Company Street. Follow Company Street for several blocks and turn right with the flow of traffic past the police station. Make a quick left onto King Street, and follow it out of town. At the second traffic light, make a right onto Route 75, Northside Road. A few miles up the road, you can make a side trip by turning right, just past the St. Croix Avis building, onto Route 751, which leads you ➋ past the St. Croix by the Sea hotel to **Judith's Fancy,** the ruins of an old great house and the tower left from a 17th-century château that was once home to the governor of the Knights of Malta. The "Judith" comes from the first name of a woman buried on the property. From the guardhouse at the entrance to the neighborhood, follow Hamilton Drive to its end for a view of Salt River Bay, where Christopher Columbus anchored in 1493. The area surrounding Salt River Landing was made a National Historic Park and Ecological Preserve in 1993. It holds sites of cultural significance, such as a prehistoric ceremonial ball court and burial site; and it includes a biologically diverse coastal estuary that's home to several endangered species and the largest remaining mangrove forest in the U.S.V.I. Plans are being developed for a museum, interpretive walking trails, and a replica of a Carib village.

After driving back to Route 75, continue west for 2 miles and turn right at Tradewinds Road onto Route 80, which quickly returns to the grassy ➌ coastline and **Cane Bay.** This is one of St. Croix's best beaches for scuba diving, and near the small stone jetty you may see a few wet-suited, tank-backed figures making their way out to the drop-off (a bit farther out there is a steeper drop-off to 12,000 feet). Rising behind you is St. Croix's highest peak, 1,165-foot Mt. Eagle. Leaving Cane Bay and passing North Star beach, follow the beautiful coastal road as it dips briefly into the forest, then turn left. There is no street sign, but you'll know the turn: The pavement is marked with the words "The Beast" and a set of giant paw prints—the hill you are about to climb is the infamous Beast of the America's Paradise Triathlon, an annual St. Croix event in which participants must bike up this intimidating slope.

Follow this road, Route 69, as it twists and climbs up the hill and south across the island. The golf course you pass on the right is a Robert Trent Jones course, part of the Carambola resort complex. You will eventu-➍ ally bear right to join Route 76, **Mahogany Road.** Follow Mahogany Road through the heart of the rain forest until you reach the end of the road at Ham's Bluff Road (Rte. 63), running along the west coast of the island. Turn right and, after a few miles, look to the right side ➎ of the road for the **Estate Mount Washington Plantation** (☎ 809/772–1026). Several years ago, while surveying the property, the owners discovered the ruins of a historic sugar plantation buried beneath the rain-forest brush. The grounds have since been cleared and opened to the public. A free, self-guided walking tour of the animal-powered mill, rum factory, and other ruins is available daily, and the antiques shop located in the old stables is open on Saturdays.

St. Croix

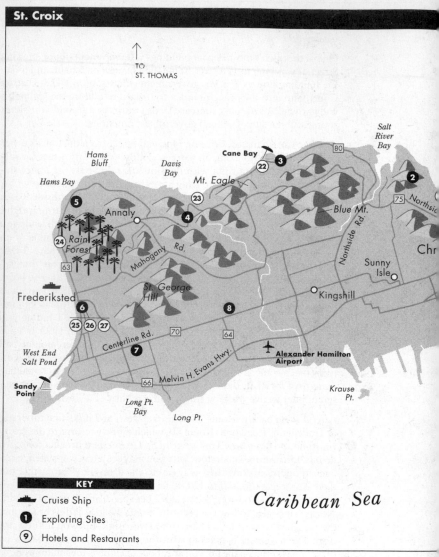

KEY

🚢 Cruise Ship

1 Exploring Sites

9 Hotels and Restaurants

Caribbean Sea

Exploring

Cane Bay, **3**

Christiansted, **1**

Estate Mount
Washington
Plantation, **5**

Estate Whim
Plantation
Museum, **7**

Frederiksted, **6**

Judith's Fancy, **2**

Mahogany Road, **4**

St. George Village
Botanical Gardens, **8**

Dining

Blue Moon, **25**

Cafe Madeleine, **18**

Camille's, **11**

Dino's, **10**

Harvey's, **15**

Kendricks, **14**

Le St. Tropez, **27**

Pangaea, **16**

Top Hat, **12**

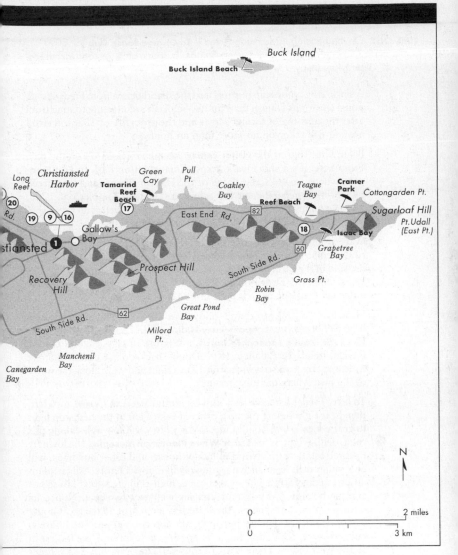

Lodging

The Buccaneer, **17**
Carambola Beach
Resort, **23**
Club St. Croix, **19**
Cormorant Beach
Club and Villas, **20**
The Frederiksted, **26**

Hibiscus Beach
Hotel, **21**
Hotel Caravelle, **9**
Pink Fancy, **13**
Sprat Hall, **24**
Villa Madeleine, **18**
Waves at Cane
Bay, **22**

6   Double back along Ham's Bluff Road to reach the historic coastal town of **Frederiksted,** which was founded in 1751.

TIME OUT   On the beach outside Frederiksted is **La Grange Beach Club** (☎ 809/772-5566). Stop in for yummy salads, burgers, chili, or sandwiches, and then enjoy a swim at their beach.

A single long cruise-ship pier juts into the sparkling sea from Frederiksted, noted less for its Danish than for its Victorian architecture (dating from after the uprising of former slaves and the great fire of 1878). A stroll around will take you no more than an hour.

Begin your tour at the **visitor center** (☎ 809/772–0357) on the pier. From here, it's a short walk across Emancipation Park to **Fort Frederik,** where, in 1848, the slaves of the Danish West Indies were freed by Governor-general Peter van Scholten. The fort, completed in 1760, houses a number of interesting historical exhibits as well as an art gallery. ☎ 809/772–2021. ☛ Free. ☉ Weekdays 8:30–4:30.

Walk along King Street to Market Street and turn left. At the corner of Queen Street is the **Market Place,** where fresh fruits and vegetables are sold in the early morning, just as they have been for more than 200 years. One block farther on the left is the coral-stone **St. Patrick's Church,** a Roman Catholic church built in 1842.

Head back to King Street and follow it to King Cross Street. A left turn here will bring you to **Apothecary Hall,** built in 1839, and on the next block, **St. Paul's Episcopal Church,** a mixture of classical and Gothic Revival architecture, built in 1812. Double back along King Cross Street to Strand Street and the waterfront. Turn right and walk along the water to the pier, where the tour began.

7   To leave Frederiksted, drive south on Strand Street to its end, turn left, then bear right before the post office. Make a left at the first stop light to get on Centerline Road (Queen Mary Hwy.). A few miles along this road, on the right, is the **Estate Whim Plantation Museum.** The lovingly restored estate, with a windmill, cookhouse, and other buildings, will give you a true sense of what life was like on St. Croix's sugar plantations in the 1800s. The oval-shaped, high-ceilinged great house has antique furniture, decor, and utensils well worth seeing. Notice its fresh and airy atmosphere—the waterless moat around the great house was used not for defense but for gathering cooling air. The house is built of stone, coral, and lime. Its apothecary exhibit is the largest in all the West Indies. There is also a museum gift shop. *Box 2855, Frederiksted 00841,* ☎ *809/772–0598.* ☛ *$5 adults, $1 children.* ☉ *Mon.–Sat. 10–4.*

8   Continue along Centerline Road to the St. George Estate. Turn left here to reach the **St. George Village Botanical Gardens,** 17 acres of lush and fragrant flora amid the ruins of a 19th-century sugarcane plantation village. The gardens include miniature versions of each ecosystem on St. Croix, from a semiarid cactus grove to a verdant rain forest. *Box 3011, Kingshill 00851–3011,* ☎ *809/772–3874.* ☛ *$5 adults, $1 children.* ☉ *Daily 9–4. Closed federal holidays.*

Continue east along Centerline Road all the way back to Christiansted.

Exploring St. John

Numbers in the margin correspond to points of interest on the St. John map.

St. John may be small, but the roads are narrow and wind up and down steep hills, so don't expect to get anywhere in a hurry. Bring along your swimsuit for stops at some of the most beautiful beaches in the world.

❶ Cruz Bay town dock is the starting point for just about everything on St. John. Take a leisurely stroll through the streets of this colorful, compact town: There are plenty of shops through which to browse, along with a number of watering holes where you can stop to take a breather.

Follow the waterfront out of town (about 100 yards) to another dock at the edge of a parking lot. At the far side of the lagoon here is the **St. John National Park Service Visitors Center** (☎ 809/776–6201), where you can pick up a handy guide to St. John's hiking trails or see various large maps of the island. If you see an island map featuring Max the Mongoose, grab it; it's full of information.

Begin your tour traveling north out of Cruz Bay. You'll pass **Mongoose Junction,** one of the prettiest shopping areas in the Caribbean. At the ½-mile mark you'll come to the well-groomed gardens and beaches of **Caneel Bay,** purchased from the Danish West India Company and developed by Laurance Rockefeller in the 1950s, who then turned over much of the island to the U.S. government as parkland. Caneel Bay Beach (home of two friendly stingrays that have been fed by snorkelers) is reached by parking in the Caneel parking lot and walking through the grounds (ask for directions). Visitors are welcome at the three restaurants and other designated areas.

Continue east on North Shore Road and you'll see, one after another, four of the most beautiful beaches in all of the Caribbean. The road is narrow and hilly with switchbacks and steep curves that make driving a challenge. **Hawksnest,** the first beach you will come to, is quite narrow but has a fine reef close to shore. This is where Alan Alda shot scenes for his film *Four Seasons.* Just past Hawksnest Hill swing left **❷** to Peace Hill, sometimes called Sugarloaf Hill, to the **Christ of the Caribbean statue** and an old sugar-mill tower. Park in the small unmarked parking lot and walk about 100 yards up a rocky path. The area is grassy, and views of the ocean do not get much better than this. *Christ of the Caribbean* was erected in 1953 by Colonel Julius Wadsworth and donated, along with 9 acres of land, to the national park in 1975.

Your next stop, and that of quite a few tourist-filled safari buses, is **Trunk Bay,** a beautiful beach with an underwater trail that's good for beginner snorkelers.

Continuing on the beach hunt, you'll come to wide **Cinnamon Bay.** The snorkeling around the point to the right is good unless the waves are up—look for the big angelfish and the swarms of purple triggerfish that live here. The national-park campground is at Cinnamon Bay and includes a snack bar, bathhouse, boutique, restaurant, general store, water-sports equipment rental, and a self-guided museum. Across the road from the beach parking lot is the beginning of the two Cinnamon Bay hiking trails: Look for the ruins of a sugar mill to mark the trailhead. The nature trail here takes you on a flat circle through the woods, following signs that identify the flora. The other trail heads all the way up to Centerline Road.

As you leave Cinnamon, the road flattens out and you'll find yourself on a shaded lane running under flowering trees. **Maho Bay** comes almost to the road here, and you may want to stop and take a dip. The Maho Bay Campground is here, too—a wonderful mélange of open-air cottages nestled in the hillside above. The team that built and developed the campground is also responsible for the adjacent Harmony, a hotel where you can be "green" without actually roughing it.

❸ The partially restored **Annaberg Plantation** at Leinster Bay, built in the 1780s and once an important sugar mill, is just ahead on North Shore Road. As you stroll around, look up at the steep hillsides and imagine cutting sugarcane against that grade in the hot sun. Slaves, Danes, and Dutchmen toiled here to harvest the sugarcane that produced sugar, molasses, and rum for export. There are no official visiting hours, no charge for entry, and no official tours, although some well-informed taxi drivers will show you around. Each day from 9 to noon, artisans provide free demonstrations of various island crafts, while local ladies bake luscious johnnycakes (the Caribbean Egg McMuffin). *For more information on talks and cultural demonstrations, contact the St. John National Park Service Visitors Center,* ☎ *809/776–6201.*

❹ From Annaberg keep to the left and go south, then head uphill and bear left at the junction to Route 10, to **Coral Bay,** named for its shape rather than for its underwater life. (The word *coral* comes from *krawl,* Danish for *corral.*) The community at the dry, eastern end of the island is the ultimate in laid-back style. It's quiet, neighborhoody, local, and independent. The small wood-and-stucco West Indian homes here house everyone from families born here to newer residents who offer palm readings and massage. This is a place to get away from it all.

❺ The road forms a loop around Coral Bay. Head northeast along Route 10 to Hurricane Hole at the remote and pristine **East End,** only a 15- to 20-minute ride from Coral Bay, where Arawak Indians are believed to have first settled on the island 2,000 years ago. At **Haulover Bay,** only a couple hundred yards separate the Atlantic Ocean from the Caribbean.

❻ Route 107 takes you south to the peninsula of **Salt Pond,** which is only about 1 foot above sea level. If you'd like a break from driving, you should hike the trail south to the spectacular cliffs of **Ram Head.** In any case you or your rented car can't proceed much farther on 107 without venturing onto a truly rocky road that heads west. Be sure at least to get a view of **Lameshur Bay,** one of the best snorkeling places on St. John and an area used for underwater training by the U.S. Navy.

❼ Once you've run out of road on Route 107, retrace your steps to Coral Bay and go west (left) on Route 10 again, which takes you over the heights of the island toward Cruz Bay. On your left is the turnoff for **Bordeaux Mountain,** at 1,277 feet St. John's highest peak. Stop for a moment hereabouts and you'll find bay trees. Crackle a leaf from one, and you'll get a whiff of the spicy aroma that you may recognize from the bay rum for which St. John is famous. To appreciate the Bordeaux Mountain region fully, save some time during your stay to hike the **Reef Bay Trail.** Join a hike led by a National Park Service ranger, who can identify the trees and plants on the hike down, fill you in on the history of the Reef Bay Plantation, and tell you about the carvings you'll find in the rocks at the bottom of the trail. The National Park Service provides a boat ($10) to take you back to Cruz Bay, saving you the uphill return climb (*see* Guided Tours, *above*).

Beaches

All beaches on these islands are open to the public, but often you will have to walk through a resort to reach them. Once there, you'll find that resort guests may have access to lounge chairs and beach bars that are off limits to you; for this reason, you may feel more comfortable at one of the beaches not associated with a resort. Whichever one you choose, remember to remove your valuables from the car.

St. Thomas

Coki Point Beach, next to Coral World, is a popular snorkeling spot for cruise-ship passengers; it's common to find a group of them among the reefs on the east and west ends of the beach. If you are visiting Coral World, you can use its lockers and changing rooms. **Magens Bay** is usually lively because of its spectacular arc of white sand, more than a half-mile long, and its calm waters—two peninsulas protect it. The bottom is flat and sandy, so this is a place for sunning and swimming rather than snorkeling. The condo resort at **Secret Harbour** doesn't at all detract from the attractiveness of this covelike East End beach. Not only is it pretty, it is also superb for snorkeling—go out to the left, near the rocks. At **Morningstar Beach,** close to Charlotte Amalie, many young residents show up for body surfing or volleyball. This pretty curve of beach fronts the Morning Star section of the Marriott's Frenchman's Reef Hotel. Snorkeling is good here near the rocks. From **Sapphire Beach** there is a fine view of St. John and other islands. Snorkeling is excellent at the reef to the right or east, near Pettyklip Point. All kinds of water-sports gear are for rent. **Hull Bay,** on the north shore, faces Inner and Outer Brass cays and attracts fishermen and beachcombers. It is open to rough Atlantic waves and is the only place to surf on the island.

St. Croix

Buck Island and its reef, which is under environmental protection, can be reached only by boat; nonetheless, a visit here is a must on any trip to St. Croix. Its beach is beautiful, but its finest treasures are those you can see when you plop off the boat and adjust your face mask, snorkel, and flippers. The waters are not always gentle at **Cane Bay,** a breezy north-shore beach, but the scuba diving and snorkeling are wondrous, and there are never many people around. Just swim straight out to see elkhorn and brain corals. Less than 200 yards out is the drop-off or so-called Cane Bay Wall. **Tamarind Reef Beach** is a small but attractive beach east of Christiansted. Both Green Cay and Buck Island seem smack in front of you and make the view arresting. Snorkeling is good. There are several popular West End beaches along the coast north of Frederiksted. **Rainbow Beach,** the beach at the West End Beach Club, has a bar, water sports, and volleyball. South of Frederiksted, try the beach at the **On the Beach Resort;** palm trees can provide plenty of shade for those who need it, and there is a fine beachside restaurant for a casual lunch on weekends.

St. John

Caneel Bay is actually seven white-sand beaches on the north shore, six of which can be reached only by water if you are not a hotel guest. The main beach (ask for directions) provides easy access to the public. **Hawksnest Beach** is becoming more popular every day; it's narrow and lined with sea-grape trees. There are rest rooms, cooking grills, and a covered shed for picnicking. It's popular for group outings and is the closest beach to town, so it is often fairly crowded. **Trunk Bay** is probably St. John's most-photographed beach and the most popular spot for beginning snorkelers because of its underwater trail. It's the St. John stop for cruise-ship passengers who choose a snorkeling tour for the day, so if you're looking for seclusion, check cruise-ship listings in *St. Thomas This Week* to find out what days the lowest number are in port. There are changing rooms, a snack bar, picnic tables, a gift shop, telephones, small lockers, and snorkeling equipment for rent. **Cinnamon**

St. John

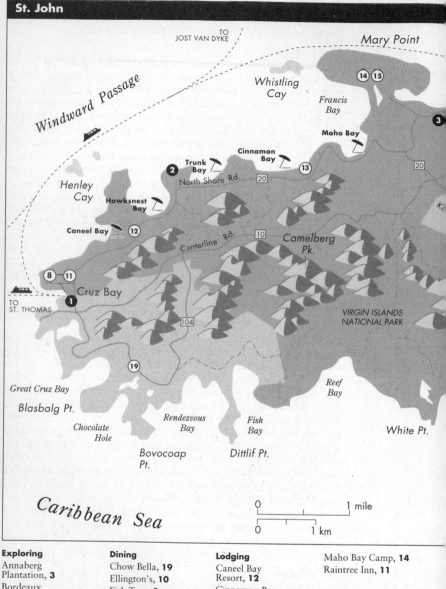

TO JOST VAN DYKE

Mary Point

Windward Passage

Whistling Cay

Francis Bay

14 15

Maho Bay

3

Cinnamon Bay

20

Trunk Bay

2

North Shore Rd.

20

13

Henley Cay

Hawksnest Bay

Caneel Bay

12

Centerline Rd.

10

Camelberg Pk.

8 — 11

Cruz Bay

1

TO ST. THOMAS

104

VIRGIN ISLANDS NATIONAL PARK

19

Great Cruz Bay

Blasbalg Pt.

Chocolate Hole

Rendezvous Bay

Fish Bay

Reef Bay

Bovocoap Pt.

Dittlif Pt.

White Pt.

Caribbean Sea

0   1 mile

0   1 km

Exploring
Annaberg Plantation, **3**
Bordeaux Mountain, **7**
Christ of the Caribbean Statue, **2**
Coral Bay, **4**
Cruz Bay, **1**
East End, **5**
Salt Pond, **6**

Dining
Chow Bella, **19**
Ellington's, **10**
Fish Trap, **8**
Le Chateau de Bordeaux, **16**
Paradiso, **9**
Shipwreck Landing, **18**

Lodging
Caneel Bay Resort, **12**
Cinnamon Bay Campground, **13**
Estate Concordia, **17**
Gallows Point Suite Resort, **10**
Harmony, **15**
Hyatt Regency St. John, **19**

Maho Bay Camp, **14**
Raintree Inn, **11**

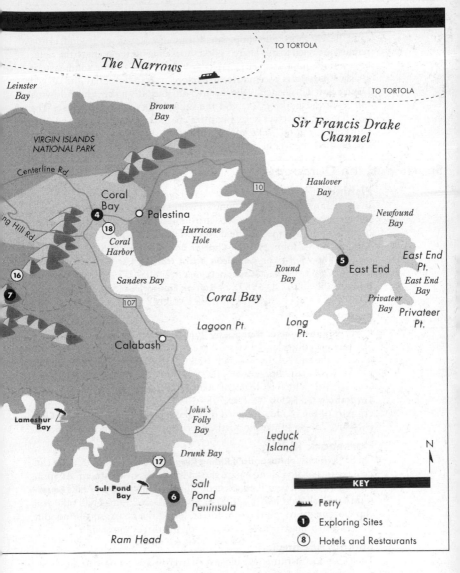

TO TORTOLA

The Narrows

TO TORTOLA

Leinster Bay

Brown Bay

Sir Francis Drake Channel

VIRGIN ISLANDS NATIONAL PARK

Centerline Rd

Coral Bay

Haulover Bay

10

○ Palestina

Newfound Bay

④

⑱

Coral Harbor

Hurricane Hole

ng Hill Rd.

East End Pt.

⑯

Sanders Bay

Round Bay

⑤ East End

East End Bay

⑦

107

Coral Bay

Privateer Bay

Privateer Pt.

Lagoon Pt.

Long Pt.

Calabash ○

John's Folly Bay

Leduck Island

Lameshur Bay

Drunk Bay

N ↑

⑰

KEY

Salt Pond Bay

⑥

Salt Pond Peninsula

⚓ Ferry

❶ Exploring Sites

❽ Hotels and Restaurants

Ram Head

Bay, a long, sandy beach facing beautiful cays, serves the adjoining na-tional-park campground. Facilities (showers, toilets, commissary, restau-rant, beach shop, gift shop, small museum, kayak and windsurfing rentals) are open to all. There's good snorkeling off the point to the right, and rental equipment is available. **Salt Pond Bay,** on the southeastern coast of St. John, is a scenic area to explore, next to Coral Bay and rugged Drunk Bay. This beach is for the adventurous. It's a short hike down a hill from the parking lot, and the only facility is an outhouse. The beach is a little rockier here, but there are interesting tide pools and the snorkeling is good. Take special care to leave nothing valuable in the car, because reports of thefts are numerous here.

Sports and the Outdoors

Fishing

In the past quarter-century, some 20 world records, many for blue mar-lin, have been set in the waters surrounding the Virgin Islands, most notably at St. Thomas's famed North Drop. To book a boat from St. Thomas or St. John, call the **Charter Boat Center** (☎ 809/775–7990 or 800/866–5714) or **American Yacht Harbor** (☎ 809/775–0685). On St. Croix, contact **Cruzan Divers** (☎ 809/772–3701), **Captain Bunny's** (☎ 809/778–6987), or **Ruffian Enterprises** (St. Croix Marina, ☎ 809/773–6011 day, 809/773–0917 night).

Golf

On St. Thomas, scenic **Mahogany Run** (☎ 809/775–5000), with a par-70, 18-hole course and a view of the B.V.I., lies to the north of Char-lotte Amalie and has the especially tricky "Devil's Triangle" trio of holes. On St. Croix, the **Buccaneer**'s (☎ 809/773–2100) 18-hole course is conveniently close to (east of) Christiansted. More spectacular is **Carambola Golf Club** (☎ 809/778–5638), in the valleyed northwest-ern part of the island, designed by Robert Trent Jones. The **Reef Club** (☎ 809/773–8844), at the northeastern part of the island, has 9 holes.

Horseback Riding

On St. Thomas, at **Rosendahl Riding Ring** (☎ 809/777–3655), you can take lessons or ride along a path through the hills of Wintberg. At Sprat Hall on St. Croix, near Frederiksted, Jill Hurd runs **Paul and Jill's Eques-trian Stables** (☎ 809/772–2880 or 809/772–2627) and will take you clip-clopping through the rain forest, along the coast, or on moonlit rides. Costs range from $50 to $75 for the three-hour rides.

Sailing/Boating

The U.S.V.I. constitutes the biggest charter-boat fleet base in the West-ern Hemisphere. You can go through a broker to book a private sail-ing vessel with crew or contact a charter-boat company directly. Among brokers for the U.S.V.I., **Blue Water Cruises** (Box 1345 Camden, ME 04843, ☎ 800/524–2020) has an excellent worldwide reputation. Charter-boat companies on St. Thomas include **Avery's Marine, Inc.** (Box 5248, St. Thomas 00803, ☎ 809/776–0113), at Charlotte Amalie, and **Island Yachts** (6100 Red Hook Plaza, Suite 4, 00802, ☎ 809/775–6666 or 800/524–2019), in Red Hook. On St. Croix, the **Annapolis Sailing School** (Box 3334, 601 6th St., Annapolis, MD 21403, ☎ 410/267–7205 or 800/638–9192) offers one-week live-aboard cruises leaving from Christiansted. On St. John, **Hinckley Charters Caribbean** (Box 70, Cruz Bay 00830, ☎ 809/776–6256) is a small operation based out of Caneel Bay.

This is an interesting—and surprisingly affordable—way to see the islands. **Club Nautico** (American Yacht Harbor, St. Thomas, 00802, ☎ 809/779–2555) and **Nauti Nymph** (American Yacht Harbor, St. Thomas, 00802, ☎ 809/775 5066) both have a variety of 21- to 27-foot boats.

The following businesses can effortlessly book you on a submarine ride, a parasail boat, a kayak trip, a Jet Ski ride, a Hobie Cat sail, or a half-day inshore light-tackle fishing excursion. They get customer feedback on a daily basis and know exactly what type of boats and crew they are booking. They will be happy to answer any questions.

On St. Thomas, call the **Red Hook Charter office** (Box 57, 00802, ☎ 809/775–9333). **Coconut Charters** (Suite 202, Red Hook Plaza, 00802, ☎ 809/775–5959) usually has a number of multihull vessels doing day sails.

On St. Croix, try **Mile-Mark Charters** (Box 3045, 59 King's Wharf, Christiansted 00822, ☎ 809/773–2628 or 800/524–2012, FAX 809/773–9411). **Big Beard's Adventure Tours** (Box 4534, Pan Am Pavilion, Christiansted 00822, ☎ 809/773–4482) runs trips to Buck Island and beach barbecues using two catamarans, one with a glass bottom. **Buck Island Charters** (Box 2881, Christiansted, ☎ 809/773–3161) with Captain Heinz's trimaran, the *Teroro II,* departs for full- or half-day Buck Island trips from Green Cay Marina.

On St. John, **Connections** (Box 37, 00831, ☎ 809/776–6922) represents a dozen of the finest local boats; many of its employees have actually worked on the boats they book.

Scuba Diving/Snorkeling
There are numerous dive operators on the three islands, and some of the hotels offer dive packages. Many of the operators listed below also offer snorkeling trips; call individual operators for details.

Aqua Action Watersports (6501 Red Hook Plaza, Suite 15, 00802, ☎ 809/775–6285) is a full-service, PADI five-star shop with all levels of instruction. They also rent sea kayaks and Windsurfers.
Chris Sawyer Diving Center (6300 Estate Frydenhoj 00802-1411, Suite 29, ☎ 809/775–7320 or 800/882–2965; locations at Compass Point, American Yacht Harbor, and the Stouffer Renaissance Grand Beach Resort) is a five-star PADI facility as well as a NAUI certification center offering instruction up to dive master. It specializes in dives to the 310-foot RMS *Rhone.*
Seahorse Dive Boats (Crown Bay Marina 00802, Suite 505, ☎ 809/774–2001) now has two locations and an expanding teaching facility at Emerald Beach. It is a PADI five-star operation and does both day and night dives on local wrecks and reefs.
Underwater Safaris (Box 8469, 00801, ☎ 809/774–1350) is conveniently located in Long Bay at the Ramada Yacht Haven Marina—which is also home to the U.S.V.I. charter-boat fleet. It is a PADI five-star dive operation that specializes in Buck Island dives to the wreck of the World War I cargo ship *Cartenser Sr.*

Anchor Dive (Box 5588, Salt River Marina, Sunny Isle 00823, ☎ 809/778–1522) has wall and boat dives.
Dive Experience, Inc. (Box 4254, Strand St., Christiansted 00822–4254, ☎ 809/773–3307 or 800/235–9047) is a PADI five-star training facility providing the range from certification to introductory dives.

Dive St. Croix (59 King's Wharf, Box 3045, Christiansted 00820, ☎ 809/773–3434 or 800/523–3483, FAX 809/773–9411), takes divers to walls and wrecks—more than 50 sites—and offers introductory, certification, and PADI, NAUI, and SSI C-card completion courses. It has custom packages with five hotels. Dive St. Croix is the only dive operation on the island allowed to run dives to Buck Island.

V.I. Divers, Ltd. (Pan Am Pavilion, Christiansted 00820, ☎ 809/773–6045 or 800/544–5911) is a PADI five-star training facility with a 35-foot dive boat and hotel packages.

ST. JOHN

Cruz Bay Watersports Co., Inc. (Box 252, 00830, ☎ 809/776–6234 or 800/835–7730, FAX 809/693–8720) is a PADI five-star diving center with two locations in Cruz Bay. Owner-operators Patty and Marcus Johnston offer regular reef, wreck, and night dives aboard three custom dive vessels.

Low Key Water Sports (Box 716, 00830, ☎ and fax 809/693–8999), at the Wharfside Village, offers PADI certification and resort courses, one- and two-tank dives, wreck dives, and specialty courses.

St. John Watersports (Box 70, 00830, ☎ 809/776–6256) is a five-star PADI center in the Mongoose Junction shopping mall.

Tennis

ST. THOMAS

Most hotels rent time to nonguests. For reservations call **Bluebeard's Castle Hotel** (☎ 809/774–1600, ext. 196), **Marriott's Frenchman's Reef Tennis Courts** (☎ 809/776–8500, ext. 486), **Limetree Center** (☎ 809/774–8990), **Mahogany Run Tennis Club** (☎ 809/775–5000), **Sapphire Beach Resort** (☎ 809/775–6100, ext. 2131), **Stouffer Renaissance Grand Beach Resort** (☎ 809/775–1510), and **Sugar Bay Plantation Resort** (☎ 809/777–7100). All the above courts have lights and are open into the evening. **Bolongo Club Everything** (☎ 809/775–1800, ext. 6421) has courts for the use of guests only. There are two public courts at **Sub Base** (next to the Water and Power Authority), open on a first-come, first-served basis.

ST. CROIX

There are courts at the **Buccaneer** (Gallows Bay, ☎ 809/773–2100), **Carambola Beach Resort** (Kingshill, ☎ 809/778–3800), **Chenay Bay Beach Resort** (Christiansted, ☎ 809/773–2918), **St. Croix by the Sea** (North Shore, ☎ 809/778–8600), **Cormorant Beach Club** (North Shore, ☎ 809/778–8920), **Villa Madeleine** (East End, ☎ 809/778–7377), and **Club St. Croix** (Christiansted, ☎ 809/773–7077) hotels. The **Reef Club** (East End., ☎ 809/773–8844) also has courts. Public courts can be found at Conegata Park (two) and Fort Frederik (two), though they may not be in the best condition.

ST. JOHN

Caneel Bay Resort (☎ 809/776–6111) has 11 courts (none lighted) and a pro shop. The **Hyatt Regency** (☎ 809/776–7171) has 6 lighted courts and a pro shop. The public courts near the fire station are lighted until 10 PM and are available on a first-come, first-served basis.

Shopping

St. Thomas

Most people would agree that St. Thomas lives up to its self-described billing as a shopper's paradise. Even if shopping isn't your idea of paradise, you still may want to slip in on a quiet day (check the cruise-ship listings—Monday and Saturday are usually the least crowded) to check out the prices. Among the best buys are liquor, linens, imported china, crystal (most stores ship), and jewelry. The sheer volume of jewelry available makes this one of the few items for which comparison shopping is worth the effort.

Most stores take major credit cards. There is no sales tax in the U.S.V.I., and shoppers can take advantage of the $1,200 duty-free allowance per family member and the additional 10% discount on the next $1,000 worth of goods (you only pay a flat rate of 5% as compared to 15% when returning from most foreign countries), but remember to save your receipts.

SHOPPING DISTRICTS
The prime shopping area in **Charlotte Amalie** is between Post Office and Market squares and consists of three parallel streets running east to west (Waterfront, Main Street, and Back Street) and the alleyways connecting them. **Vendors Plaza,** on the waterfront at Emancipation Gardens, is a centralized location for all the vendors who used to clog the sidewalks with their merchandise.

Havensight Mall, next to the cruise-ship dock, has parking and many of the same stores as Charlotte Amalie, though it's not as charming. West of town, the pink-stucco **Nisky Center** is more of a hometown shopping center than a tourist area, but there's a bookstore (next to a bakery and yogurt shop), as well as a bank, gift shops, and clothing stores.

Out east, at Red Hook, **American Yacht Harbor** is a waterfront shopping arcade with branches of some of the Charlotte Amalie stores as well as a deli, a candy store, and a few restaurants.

ART GALLERIES
A.H. Riise Caribbean Print Gallery (Riise's Alley off Main St., ☎ 809/776-2303) displays and sells Haitian and Virgin Islands art, along with art books and the exquisite botanical prints and note cards from Mapes de Monde.

The Gallery (Veteran's Dr., ☎ 809/776-4641) carries Haitian art, along with works by a number of Virgin Islands artists.

BOOKS AND MAGAZINES
Dockside Bookshop (Havensight Mall, Bldg. IV, ☎ 809/774-4937) has a wide selection of books, including those written in and about the Caribbean and the Virgin Islands, from literature to chartering guides to books on seashells and tropical flowers.

CAMERAS AND ELECTRONICS
Boolchand's (31 Main St., ☎ 809/776-0794, and Havensight Mall, ☎ 809/776-0302) sells a variety of brand-name cameras as well as audio and video equipment.

Royal Caribbean (two locations on Main St., ☎ 809/776-4110, and Havensight Mall, ☎ 809/776-8890) has attractive prices on some cameras and accessories; portable cassette players are usually good buys here.

CHINA AND CRYSTAL
A.H. Riise Gift Shops (Riise's Alley off Main St.; Havensight Mall; ☎ 809/776-2303) carry Waterford, Wedgwood, Royal Crown, and Royal Doulton at good prices.

The English Shop (waterfront, ☎ 809/776-5399, and Havensight Mall, ☎ 809/776-3776) sells china and crystal from major European and Japanese manufacturers.

Little Switzerland (locations at Main St., Emancipation Park, Havensight Mall, and American Yacht Harbor, ☎ 809/776–2010) carries crystal from Lalique, Baccarat, Waterford, Riedel, and Orrefors, and china from Villeroy & Boch and Wedgwood, among others.

CLOTHING

G'Day (waterfront at Royal Dane Mall, ☎ 809/774–8855) is a tiny shop drenched in the bright colors of Australian artist Ken Done and Scandinavian artist Sigrid Olsen; swimwear, resort wear, accessories, and umbrellas are sold here.

Janine's Boutique (A-2 Palm Passage, ☎ 809/774–8243) has women's and men's dressy and casual apparel from European designers and manufacturers, including the Louis Feraud collection, and select finds from Valentino, Christian Dior, YSL, and Pierre Cardin.

Java Wraps (American Yacht Harbor, Red Hook, ☎ 809/777–3450) specializes in Indonesian batik creations and offers a complete line of beach cover-ups, swimwear, and leisure wear for women, men, and children.

Local Color (Garden St., ☎ 809/774–3727) sells cool cotton T-shirts and other casual clothing with the designs of St. Thomas artist Kerry Topper. Brightly printed sundresses, shorts, and shirts by Jams; big-brim straw hats dipped in fuchsia, turquoise, and other tropical colors; and unique jewelry are also for sale here.

Polo/Ralph Lauren Factory Store (Garden Street, ☎ 809/774–3806) changes its selection frequently, and it's worthwhile to check often for amazing markdowns on a range of men's and women's clothing.

Thriving Tots Boutique (Garden St., ☎ 809/776–0009) has Caribbean clothing for children (infants to size 16), including locally made shorts sets and sundresses.

CRAFTS AND GIFTS

The **Caribbean Marketplace** (Havensight Mall, Bldg. III, ☎ 809/776–5400) is the place to look for Caribbean handicrafts, including Caribelle batiks from St. Lucia; bikinis from the Cayman Islands; and Sunny Caribee spices, soaps, teas, and coffees from Tortola.

The **Cloth Horse** (Fort Mylner Shopping Center, ☎ 809/779–2222) has signed pottery from the Dominican Republic; wicker furniture and household goods from the island of Hispaniola; and pottery, rugs, and bedspreads from all over the world.

Down Island Traders (Bakery Sq., Veteran's Dr., and Frenchman's Reef, ☎ 809/776–4641) deals in hand-painted calabash bowls ($10); finely printed Caribbean note cards; jams, jellies, spices, and herbs; herbal teas made of rum, passion fruit, and mango; high-mountain coffee from Jamaica; and a variety of handicrafts from throughout the Caribbean.

Shanghai Silk and Handicrafts (Royal Dane Mall, ☎ 809/776–8118) has frames, figurines, and other Asian crafts on sale. It also carries silk fabric and silk clothing; scarves that cost less than $15 each make distinct, packable gifts.

FOOD

Gourmet Gallery (Yacht Haven, ☎ 809/774–5555, Sub Base, ☎ 809/776–8555) has an excellent and reasonably priced wine selection, as well as condiments, cheeses, and specialty ingredients for everything from tacos to curries to chow mein. For fruits and vegetables, go to the **Fruit Bowl** (Wheatley Center, ☎ 809/774–8586). **Marina Market**

(across from Red Hook ferry, ☎ 809/779–2411) offers the islands' freshest meats and seafoods as well as various sundries.

JEWELRY

A.H. Riise Gift Shop (Riise's Alley off Main St.; Havensight Mall; ☎ 809/776–2303) is St. Thomas's oldest and largest shop for luxury items, with jewelry, pearls, ceramics, china, crystal, flatware, perfumes, and watches.

Amsterdam Sauer (14 Main St., ☎ 809/774–2222) displays many fine one-of-a-kind designs.

Cardow's (3 stores on Main St., ☎ 809/776–1140, 2 on the waterfront, 1 at Marriott's Frenchman's Reef Hotel, 2 at Havensight, ☎ 809/774–0530) offers a "chain bar" more than 100 feet long, where you're guaranteed 30%–50% savings off U.S. retail prices or your money will be refunded (within 30 days of purchase).

Cartier (30 Trompeter Gade, ☎ 809/774–1590) has fantastically beautiful and fantastically priced items as well as a surprising number of affordable ones.

Colombian Emeralds (2 on Main St., 1 on the waterfront, and 1 at Havensight Mall, ☎ 809/774–3400) offers set and unset gems of every description, including high-quality emeralds.

H. Stern (3 stores on Main St., ☎ 809/776–1939; 1 at Havensight Mall, ☎ 809/776–1223; 1 at Frenchman's Reef, ☎ 809/774–7658) is one of the most respected names in gems.

Irmela's Jewel Studio (Tolbod Gade, ☎ 809/774–5875) has long offered some of the Caribbean's most exquisite gems.

Little Switzerland (Main St., Emancipation Gardens, Havensight Mall, all ☎ 809/776–2010; American Yacht Harbor, ☎ 809/777–3100) is the sole U.S.V.I. distributor for Rolex watches. The store also does a booming mail-order business.

Opals of Australia (Drake's Passage, ☎ 809/774–8244) offers a wide variety of these iridescent wonders.

LEATHER GOODS

Gucci (Riise's Alley off Main St., ☎ 809/774–7841, and Havensight Mall, ☎ 809/774–4090) sells the traditional insignia-designed items for men and women.

In the Bag (Riise's Alley off Main St., ☎ 809/774–6078) is a small shop housed within 18th-century brick walls that offers Coach, Carlos Falchi, Tumi, and Kenneth Cole, as well as Liz Claiborne and a large variety of Italian leathers.

The **Leather Shop** (Main St., ☎ 809/776–3995, and Havensight Mall, Bldg. II, ☎ 809/776–0040) has big names at big prices: Fendi and Bottega Veneta are prevalent. However, there are also reasonably priced purses, wallets, and briefcases.

Traveler's Haven (Havensight Mall, ☎ 809/775–1798) sells leather bags, backpacks, vests, and money belts.

Zora's (Norre Gade across from Roosevelt Park, ☎ 809/774–2559) specializes in fine leather sandals made to order; they're sold alongside made-only-in-the-Virgin-Islands backpacks, briefcases, and "fish" purses in durable, brightly colored canvas.

Shanghai Linen (Waterfront, ☎ 809/776–2828) does a brisk trade in linen.

Mr. Tablecloth (Main St., ☎ 809/774–4343) has a friendly staff who will help you choose from a floor-to-ceiling array of linens.

LIQUOR AND WINE
A.H. Riise Liquors (Riise's Alley off Main St.; Havensight Mall; ☎ 809/776–2303) offers a large selection of liquors, cordials, wines, and tobacco, including rare vintage cognacs, Armagnacs, ports, and Madeiras. They also stock imported cigars, fruits in brandy, and barware from England.

Al Cohen's Discount Liquor (across from Havensight Mall, Long Bay Rd., ☎ 809/774–3690) is a warehouse-style store with a large wine department.

MUSIC
Parrot Fish Records and Tapes (Back St., ☎ 809/776–4514) stocks standard Stateside tapes and compact discs, along with a good selection of music by Caribbean artists, including local groups. For a catalogue of calypso, soca, steel band, and reggae music, write to Parrot Fish, Box 9206, St. Thomas 00801.

Modern Music (across from Havensight Mall, ☎ 809/774–3100; Nisky Center, ☎ 809/777–8787; Four Winds Plaza, ☎ 809/775–3310) has the latest Stateside and Caribbean CD and cassette releases, plus oldies, classical, and new-age music.

PERFUMES
Sparky's (Main St., ☎ 809/776–7510) is staffed by impeccably turned-out salesclerks who can give you a facial and makeup lesson.

Tropicana Perfume Shoppes (2 Main St., ☎ 809/774–0010, and 14 Main St., ☎ 809/774–1834) has the largest selection of fragrances for men and women in all of the Virgin Islands; both locations give small free samples to customers.

SUNGLASSES
Fashion Eyewear (Garden St., ☎ 809/776–9075), tucked into a tiny building, is a tiny shop that sells sunglasses priced from $40 to $450. They'll also copy the prescription from your current glasses and make new clear-lensed glasses or sunglasses in a few hours.

TOYS
Animal Crackers Fun Factory (Inside Sparky's, off Royal Dane Mall, ☎ 809/774–4939) is a must-visit, whether children are with you or back home anticipating their gifts. It's a playland jungle aswarm with parrots and pirates, teddy bears, and penguins.

Land of Oz (Royal Dane Mall, ☎ 809/776–7888) has a huge selection of toys fashioned by European craftsmen that include Royal Doulton collector dolls, Brio wood trains, German nutcrackers, and English wood sailboats.

St. Croix

Although St. Croix doesn't offer as many shopping opportunities as St. Thomas, the island does have an array of smaller stores with unique merchandise. In Christiansted, the best shopping areas are the Pan Am Pavilion and Caravelle Arcade off Strand Street and along King and Company streets.

BOOKS

The Bookie (1111 Strand St., Christiansted, ☎ 809/773–2592) carries paperback novels, stationery, newspapers, and greeting cards. Stop in for the latest local gossip and events.

CHINA AND CRYSTAL

Little Switzerland (Hamilton House, 56 King St., Christiansted, ☎ 809/773–1976), the St. Croix branch of a Virgin Islands institution, features a variety of Rosenthal flatware, Lladro figurines, Waterford and Baccarat crystal, Lalique figurines, and Wedgwood and Royal Doulton china.

At the **Royal English Shop** (5 Strand St., Frederiksted, ☎ 809/772–4886) Natchman and Beyer crystal cost significantly less than on the mainland. Store hours vary, depending on the cruise-ship schedule, so call ahead.

CLOTHING

Caribbean Clothing Company (55 Company St., Christiansted, ☎ 809/773–5012) features contemporary sportswear by top American designers.

From the Gecko (1233 Queen Cross St., ☎ 809/778–9433) offers the hippest buys on St. Croix, from superb batik sarongs to hand-painted scarves.

Java Wraps (Company St., Christiansted, and Pan Am Pavilion, ☎ 809/773–3770) sells Indonesian batik cover-ups and resort wear for men, women, and children.

Tribal Threadz (52 C Company St., Christiansted, ☎ 809/773–2883) stocks urban island wear by Karl Kani, No Fear, and many more popular lines—for contemporary guys and gals.

Wayne James Boutique (42 Queen Cross St., ☎ 809/773–8585) is the venue of an engaging Crucian who has designed vestments for the pope and evening wear for the queen of Denmark. His bright, savvy clothes are inspired by island traditions and colors.

CRAFTS AND GIFTS

American West India Company (1 Strand St., Christiansted, ☎ 809/773–7325) offers a range of goods from around the Caribbean, including Jamaican allspice and Haitian metalwork.

Green Papaya (Caravelle Arcade No. 15, Christiansted, ☎ 809/773–8848) sells handcrafted furniture and accessories for the home with attention to the unusual. Asian baskets and lovely wrought-iron lamps and hurricanes with handblown teardrop lanterns are among its selection of goods from all over the world.

Folk Art Traders (1B Queen Cross St. at Strand St., Christiansted, ☎ 809/773–1900) has energetic owners who travel to Haiti, Jamaica, Guayama, and elsewhere in the Caribbean to find the treasures sold in their shop, including baskets, masks, pottery, and ceramics.

JEWELRY

Colombian Emeralds (43 Queen Cross St., Christiansted, ☎ 809/773–1928 or 809/773–9189) specializes—of course—in emeralds, including some that are under $100, and also carries diamonds, rubies, sapphires, and gold.

Crucian Gold (57A Company St., Christiansted, ☎ 809/773–5241), located in a small courtyard in a West Indian–style cottage, carries the unique gold creations of St. Croix native Brian Bishop.

Sonya's (1 Company St., Christiansted, ☎ 809/778–8605) is the home of the island's signature hook bracelet, which was designed by owner Sonya Hough.

LIQUOR

Grog and Spirits (Chandlers Wharf, Gallows Bay, ☎ 809/773–8485) is a conveniently located shop with a good selection of liquor.

Woolworth's (Sunny Isle Shopping Center, Centerline Rd., ☎ 809/778–5466) carries a huge line of discount, duty-free liquor.

PERFUMES

Frontier Duty Free (53AB Company St., Christiansted ☎ 809/773–3663 or 800/408–3337) has a full line of perfumes, along with cosmetics, leather goods, and liquors at duty-free prices.

St. Croix Perfume Center (1114 King St., Christiansted, ☎ 809/773–7604) offers an extensive array of fragrances, including all the major brands.

St. John

Because of the island's many natural wonders, travel literature about St. John often all but overlooks the pleasures of shopping there. But the blend of luxury items and handicrafts found in the shops on St. John makes for potentially excellent shopping opportunities. With several levels of cool, stone-wall shops, set off by colorfully planted terraces and courtyards, **Mongoose Junction** is one of the prettiest malls in the Caribbean. **Wharfside Village,** on the other side of Cruz Bay, is a painted-clapboard village with shops and restaurants.

Dining

Just about every kind of cuisine you can imagine is available in the U.S.V.I. The beauty and freedom of the islands have attracted a cadre of professionally trained chefs who know their way around fresh fish and local fruits. If you are staying in a large hotel, you will pay prices similar to those in New York City or Paris—in other words, dining out is usually expensive.

St. Thomas is the most cosmopolitan of the islands and has the most visitors, so it is not surprising that the island also has the largest number and greatest variety of restaurants. St. Croix restaurants are both more relaxed and, in some ways, more elegant. Dining on St. John is, in general, more casual; the emphasis is on simple food prepared to order and served in an informal setting at reasonable prices.

What to Wear

Restaurants in the U.S.V.I. are relaxed and informal. During the day, many people eat in their beach attire. In the evening, however, shorts and T-shirts are inappropriate for the nicer restaurants and luxury resorts. Pants and collared shirts, for men and women, are usually appropriate at such establishments.

CATEGORY	COST*
$$$$	over $35
$$$	$25–$35
$$	$15–$25
$	under $15

*average cost of a three-course dinner, per person, excluding drinks and service

St. Thomas

$$$$ **Blackbeard's Castle.** This romantic hillside restaurant is one of St.
★ Thomas's best. Diners here have a spectacular view of Charlotte Amalie
and the harbor as they dine alfresco on such gourmet delights as
tournedos of beef with fried green tomatoes; lavender cheese with
pepper relish; or macadamia-nut-crusted mahimahi with pineapple
salsa and plantain chips. Lunch offerings include excellent soups, sandwiches, and several pasta dishes. The à la carte Sunday brunch is immensely popular. ✗ *Blackbeard's Castle, Charlotte Amalie,* ☎ *809/*
776–1234. Reservations advised. AE, D, DC, MC, V.

$$$$ **Entre Nous.** The view here, from high over Charlotte Amalie's harbor,
is as exhilarating as the dining is elegant. In the evening, you can
watch the light-bedecked cruise ships pull slowly out of the harbor while
deciding among such main courses as rack of lamb, Caribbean lobster,
veal, and Chateaubriand. ✗ *Bluebeard's Castle, Charlotte Amalie,* ☎
809/774–4050. Reservations advised. AE, MC, V. No lunch.

$$$$ **Hotel 1829.** You'll dine by candlelight flickering over stone walls and
pink table linens at this restaurant on the terrace of the hotel. The menu
and wine list are extensive, from Caribbean rock lobster to rack of lamb.
Many items, including a warm spinach salad, are prepared tableside,
and the restaurant is justly famous for its dessert soufflés, made of chocolate, Grand Marnier, raspberry, or coconut, to name a few. ✗ *Gov-*
ernment Hill, near Main St., Charlotte Amalie, ☎ *809/776–1829.*
Reservations required. No lunch. AE, D, MC, V.

$$$$ **Romanos.** The inside of this huge old stucco house in Smith Bay is a
★ delightful spare, elegant setting in which to eat superb northern Italian cuisine. Owner Tony hasn't advertised since the restaurant opened
in 1988, but it's always packed. Try the pastas, either with a classic
sauce or one of the unique combinations created by Tony, such as a
cream sauce with mushrooms, prosciutto, pine nuts, and Parmesan.
✗ *97 Smith Bay,* ☎ *809/775–0045. Reservations advised. Closed*
Sun. No lunch.

$$$$ **Virgilio's.** This intimate, elegant hideaway serves the best northern Ital-
★ ian cuisine on the island. Eclectic groupings of paintings and prints cover
the two-story-high brick walls. Come here for superb minestrone; perfectly cooked capellini with fresh tomatoes and garlic; spaghetti peas-
ant style (a rich tomato sauce with mushrooms and prosciutto); exquisite
fresh fish, veal, and chicken dishes; and a host of daily specials. Maître
d' Regis is on hand day and night, welcoming customers and helping
the very gracious staff. Don't leave without having a Virgilio's cappuccino, a chocolate-and-coffee drink so rich it's dessert. ✗ *Main St.,*
Charlotte Amalie, ☎ *809/776–4920. Reservations advised. AE, MC,*
V. Closed Sun.

$$$ **Piccola Marina Cafe.** Dockside dining at its friendliest is the trademark
of this open-air restaurant close to the St. John ferry dock at Red Hook.
The clientele is a mix of sailors and fishers, who work on the docks
your table overlooks. The food is so-so, but the atmosphere is delightful.
Try one of their crispy pizzas, baked in a wood-burning oven. ✗ *Red*
Hook, ☎ *809/775–6350. Reservations advised. AE, MC, V.*

$$–$$$ **Alexander's Cafe.** This charming restaurant is a favorite with the peo-
ple in the restaurant business on St. Thomas—always a sign of quality.
Local media types and wine aficionados (the always-changing wine list
offers the best value on the island) are often among the crowd that packs
this place. Alexander is Austrian, and the schnitzels are delicious and
reasonably priced; the baked-brie-and-fruit plate and pasta specials are
fresh and tasty. Save room for strudel. ✗ *24A Honduras, Frenchtown,*
☎ *809/776–4211. Reservations advised. AE, D, MC, V. Closed Sun.*

$$–$$$ **Chart House.** In an old great house on the tip of the Frenchtown penin-
sula, this restaurant has a superb view. The menu includes fresh fish
and teriyaki dishes, lobster, and Hawaiian chicken; there's also a large
salad bar. ✕ *Villa Olga, Frenchtown,* ☎ *809/774–4262. Reservations
accepted for 10 or more. AE, D, DC, MC, V.*

$$–$$$ **For the Birds.** The beer is served in mason jars, and margaritas are avail-
able in 46-ounce servings at this beach restaurant with a disco floor.
You can have sizzling fajitas, barbecued baby-back ribs, seafood, or
steak. For children there are coloring place mats and crayons. Sunday
is ladies' night. ✕ *Scott Beach, near Compass Point, East End,* ☎ *809/
775–6431. Reservations required for 6 or more. AE, MC, V.*

$$ **Little Bopeep.** Inside this unpretentious restaurant is some of the best
West Indian food on the island. Try the curried chicken, conch in Cre-
ole sauce, sweet-potato stuffing, and fried plantains. Bring a group of
six and one person gets a meal for only 10¢. ✕ *Barbel Plaza, Char-
lotte Amalie,* ☎ *809/774–1959. AE, MC, V.*

$$ **Tickles Dockside Pub.** The Crown Bay location has been a choice spot
★ of locals for five years, but this branch of the casual alfresco restau-
rant, just off the docks, is new to East End. Enjoy sandwiches, ribs,
and chicken (served with generous portions of spicy fries) while you
watch the iguanas beg for table scraps—bring your camera! ✕ *American Yacht Harbor, Bldg. D,* ☎ *809/775–9425. Reservations accepted.
AE, MC, V.*

$$ **Zorba's Cafe.** Tired of shopping? Summon up one last ounce of en-
ergy and head up Government Hill to Zorba's. Sit and have a cold beer
or bracing iced tea in the 19th-century stone-paved courtyard surrounded
by banana trees to replenish. Greek salads and appetizers, moussaka,
and an excellent vegetarian plate top the menu. ✕ *Government Hill,
Charlotte Amalie,* ☎ *809/776–0444. AE, MC, V. No lunch Sun.*

$–$$ **Bryan's Bar and Restaurant.** Located high on the cool north side of
the island, overlooking Hull Bay, this surfer's bar dishes out gargan-
tuan portions of grilled fish, steaks, and a great teriyaki-chicken sandwich. A local hangout complete with pool table, it's casual and cheap.
✕ *Hull Bay,* ☎ *809/774–3522. No credit cards. No lunch.*

$–$$ **Eunice's Terrace.** Eunice is deservedly famous for her excellent West
Indian cooking. Her roomy two-story restaurant has a spacious bar
and a menu of native dishes, including callaloo (a West Indian soup),
conch fritters, fried fish, local sweet potato, fungi, and green banana.
✕ *Rte. 38, near Stouffer Grand Beach Resort and Coral World, Smith
Bay,* ☎ *809/775–3975. AE, MC, V.*

$–$$ **Hard Rock Cafe.** A hot spot from the day it opened, this waterfront restau-
rant is pretty much like its namesakes around the world. Rock-and-roll
memorabilia dominate the decor, and the menu is full of hamburgers,
sandwiches, salads, and great desserts. Doors open at 11 AM and stay
open until 2 AM, and there's always a wait during prime meal times. ✕
International Plaza on the Waterfront, ☎ *809/777–5555. AE, MC, V.*

$–$$ **Il Cappuccini.** In the lower courtyard of the Taste of Italy shopping area
is this quiet indoor-outdoor café that serves a variety of sandwiches (including an excellent Italian ham sandwich) and pasta dishes. ✕ *A Taste
of Italy, 4–5 Back St.,* ☎ *809/775–1090. AE, MC, V. No dinner.*

St. Croix

$$$$ **Cafe Madeleine.** This elegant restaurant, part of the Villa Madeleine
resort nestled in the hills on St. Croix's East End, features such diverse
cuisine as chicken alla Bolognese, swordfish medallions sautéed with
green tomato and asparagus, and a number of fine beef dishes. The
wine list is extensive. ✕ *Teague Bay (take Rte. 82 out of Christiansted*

and turn right at the Reef Condominiums), ☎ 809/778–7377. *Reservations advised. AE, D, DC, MC, V. Closed Mon. and Tues.*

$$$$ **Kendricks.** This restaurant is a tranquil oasis of civility in the heart of
★ Christiansted. Waiters dote on diners seated at tables laid with crisp linens and fine china, serving such dishes as coconut shrimp with jalapeño and chive aioli or roasted-pecan-crusted pork loin with ginger mayonnaise. The owners' informal eatery across the street, Simply Lobster, serves daily lunches of reasonably priced lobster dishes, including their signature lobster spring rolls. ✕ *Queen Cross St., Christiansted,* ☎ 809/773–9199. *Reservations advised. AE, V, MC. Closed Sun. and Tues. No lunch.*

$$$ **Dino's.** Homemade Italian food, often with a West Indian twist, is served
★ at this cozy restaurant, one of the island's best. Creative, boldly flavored pastas (try the eggplant or sweet-potato ravioli) are made fresh daily by chef-owner Dino Natale. The hot antipasto appetizer features bacon-wrapped and grilled shrimp; broiled tomato with a veil of fresh pesto; and grilled, succulent scallops. ✕ *4-C Hospital St., Christiansted,* ☎ 809/778–8005. *Reservations advised. AE. Closed all of Sept.; Sun. and Wed. during summer.*

$$$ **Pangaea.** The restaurant's name—meaning all-earth—is certainly re-
★ flected in the ambitious, eclectic menu, which synthesizes African, Caribbean, and Middle Eastern influences and ingredients with aplomb. Specials might include mahimahi in two salsas (mango and tomato cilantro) and slow-roasted duck breast in honey-raspberry glaze. The ambience is best described as Peace Corps–Bohemian, with incense, wind chimes, and travel souvenirs such as Hawaiian coconut masks and Japanese watercolors. The waitstaff is hip and very friendly; the house's cat, Shadow, even more so. ✕ *2203 Queen Cross St.,* ☎ 809/773–7743. *No credit cards. Closed Tues. and Wed. No lunch.*

$$$ **Top Hat.** This restaurant, owned by a delightful Danish couple, has been in business for more than 20 years, serving international cuisine with an emphasis on Danish specialties—roast duck stuffed with apples and prunes, fried Camembert with lingonberries, and smoked eel. The old West Indian structure, complete with gingerbread trim, is nicely accented in gray, white, and pink. The photographs on the walls are the work of owner and European-trained chef Hans Rasmussen. ✕ *52 Company St., Christiansted,* ☎ 809/773–2346. *Reservations advised. AE, D, MC, V. Closed Sun. and May–Oct. No lunch.*

$$ **Blue Moon.** This terrific little bistro, popular for its live jazz on Friday nights, has an eclectic, often-changing menu that draws heavily on Asian, Cajun, and French influences. Try the seafood chowder as an appetizer and leave room for the bittersweet chocolate torte for dessert. ✕ *17 Strand St., Frederiksted,* ☎ 809/772–2222. *AE. Closed Mon. and July–Sept. No lunch.*

$$ **Le St. Tropez.** A dark-wood bar and soft lighting add to the Mediterranean atmosphere at this pleasant bistro, tucked into a courtyard off Frederiksted's main thoroughfare. Diners, seated either inside or on the adjoining patio, order from a menu of light French fare, such as quiches, salads, brochettes, and crepes. Daily specials often take advantage of fresh local seafood. ✕ *67 King St., Frederiksted,* ☎ 809/772–3000. *Reservations accepted. AE, MC, V. Closed Sun.*

$ **Camille's.** This tiny, lively spot is perfect for lunch or a light supper. Sandwiches and burgers are the big draw here, though the daily seafood special, often wahoo or mahimahi, is also popular. A limited children's menu is available. ✕ *Queen Cross St., Christiansted,* ☎ 809/773–2985. *No credit cards. Closed Sun.*

$ **Harvey's.** The plain, even dowdy room contains just 12 tables, whose plastic flowered tablecloths qualify as the sole attempt at decor; but the delicious local food ranks among the island's best. Daily specials such as mouthwatering goat stew and melting whelks in butter, sided with heaping helpings of rice, fungi, and vegetables, are listed on the blackboard. Genial owner Sarah Harvey takes great pride in her kitchen, bustling out from behind the stove to chat and urge you to eat up. ✕ *11 Company St., ☎ 809/773–3343. No credit cards. Closed Sun. No lunch. Call for hours during high season.*

St. John

$$$–$$$$ **Chow Bella.** In this classy restaurant (i.e., no shorts or collarless shirts), column A and column B give you transcultural choices: Chinese and Italian. Order from one side of the menu for such delights as Szechuan sesame noodles or wok-roasted duck. From the other side, you can have delicious pasta, calamari, or veal saltimbocca, and amaretto cheesecake. And, of course, you can certainly mix your dishes. ✕ *Hyatt Regency, ☎ 809/776–7171. Reservations advised. AE, MC, V. Closed Mon. No lunch.*

$$$ **Ellington's.** Extending onto the second-story veranda of the Gallows Point Suite Resort's central building, Ellington's is a peaceful, appealing spot. The outside tables are particularly quiet and romantic. The menu is Continental, with chicken, fish, and steak dishes. You might start with the jumbo shrimp cooked in sweet coconut and served with a mango sauce, or the seafood chowder. Entrées include sea scallops and pesto, swordfish scampi, filet mignon, and fresh lobster. Save room for dessert, perhaps the banana chocolate chip cake or the white chocolate brownie. ✕ *Gallows Point Suite Resort, ☎ 809/693–8490. Reservations accepted. AE, MC, V.*

$$$ **Le Chateau de Bordeaux.** The best view you're going to find to dine
★   by is on the terrace here or in the air-conditioned dining room (go at sunset). The rustic cabin is magically transformed into an elegant, ultraromantic aerie by wrought-iron chandeliers, lace tablecloths, and antiques. The innovative preparations appeal equally to the eye and the palate. You might start with velvety carrot soup, perfectly contrasted with roasted chilies. Segue into the rosemary-perfumed rack of lamb with a honey-dijon-nut crust in a shallot-and-port-wine sauce, or the macadamia-coated salmon with crème fraîche dill glaze. Don't miss the whelks, which are done to perfection. ✕ *Rte. 10, just east of Centerline Rd., ☎ 809/776–6611. AE, MC, V.*

$$$ **Paradiso.** Come here for good Italian food. This popular place, on the
★   upper level of Mongoose Junction, is open to the breezes and also has an outdoor terrace lined with tables. There are nightly pasta and fish specials as well as classic veal and chicken dishes. ✕ *Mongoose Junction, ☎ 809/693–8899. Reservations accepted. No lunch. AE, MC, V.*

$$ **Fish Trap.** There are several rooms here, all open to the breezes, and all
★   busy with happy diners. This local favorite serves up six kinds of fresh fish nightly, along with tasty appetizers, such as conch fritters and Fish Trap chowder. The menu also includes steak, pasta, chicken, and hamburgers. ✕ *Downtown, Cruz Bay, ☎ 809/693–9994. AE, D, MC, V. Closed Mon. No lunch.*

$ **Shipwreck Landing.** Start with a house drink, perhaps a fresh-squeezed concoction of lime, coconut, and rum, then move on to hearty taco salads, fried shrimp, teriyaki chicken, and conch fritters. The birds keep up a lively chatter in the bougainvillea that surrounds the open-air restaurant, and there's live music on Sunday nights in season. ✕ *Coral Bay, ☎ 809/693–5640. MC, V.*

Lodging

The U.S.V.I. has lodging options to suit any style, from luxury five-star resorts to casual condominiums and national-park campgrounds.

On St. Thomas, guest houses and smaller hotels are not typically on the beach, but they offer pools and shuttle service to nearby beaches (St. Thomas is not a walking island), and the several historic inns above town have a pleasing island ambience. In keeping with its small-town atmosphere and more relaxed pace, St. Croix offers a good variety of more moderately priced small hotels and guest houses, which are either on the beach or in a rural setting where a walk to the beach is easy. Accommodations on St. John defy easy categorization. The national-park campground sites start bare and progress through standing tents, tent cabins, and small cottages. At the other end of the spectrum are luxury retreats of understated elegance that offer rest and relaxation of a high—and pricey—order.

The prices below reflect rates during high season, which generally runs from December 15 to April 15. Rates are 25% to 50% lower the rest of the year.

CATEGORY	COST*
$$$$	over $200
$$$	$150–$200
$$	$100–$150
$	under $100

All prices are for a standard double room, excluding 8% accommodations tax.

St. Thomas

$$$$ **Bolongo Elysian Beach Resort.** At this East End property, coral-color villas are stepped down the hillside to the edge of Cowpet Bay. Rooms, decorated in muted tropical floral prints, all have air-conditioning, terraces, ceiling fans, cable TV, telephone, and honor bar, and some have full kitchens. Activity centers on a kidney-shape pool complete with waterfall and thatched-roof pool bar. The Palm Court restaurant has gained a strong local following, a sure sign of success. There is shuttle service to Bolongo Club Everything. ☎ *Box 51, Red Hook, 00802,* ☎ *809/775–2700 or 800/753–2554,* 𝖥𝖠𝖷 *809/779–2400. 175 rooms. 2 restaurants, 2 bars, freshwater pool, lighted tennis court. AE, MC, V. CP.*

$$$$ **Grand Palazzo.** The main building of this luxury resort resembles a
★ Venetian villa; through the French doors in its lobby views are stunning. Guest rooms are in six buildings that fan out from the main villa. They're spacious and luxuriously furnished with European fabrics—they just might tempt you to stay inside. When you do venture out, you'll find elegance everywhere, from the beautiful pool to the gourmet restaurant and the casual alfresco lunch area. A multilingual staff, classical music, and 24-hour room service enhance the sophisticated atmosphere. Although a tone of European reserve and elegance abides in this resort, the accompanying service is still developing. ☎ *Great Bay Estate, 00802,* ☎ *809/775–3333 or 800/545–0509,* 𝖥𝖠𝖷 *809/775–4444. 152 rooms. 2 restaurants, 3 bars, health club, pool, beach, 4 tennis courts, water sports. AE, D, DC, MC, V.*

$$$$ **Marriott's Frenchman's Reef Hotel and Morning Star Beach Resorts.**
★ Sprawling, luxurious, and situated on a prime harbor promontory east of Charlotte Amalie like a permanently anchored cruise ship, these two resorts are St. Thomas's full-service American superhotels. All rooms are spacious and furnished with contemporary furniture and soft pastels. Many Frenchman's Reef rooms have glorious ocean and

harbor views (but a few look out over the parking lot). Morning Star rooms are more luxurious and are in buildings tucked among the foliage that stretches along the fine white sand of Morningstar Beach; the sound of the surf can lull you to sleep. In addition to various snack and sandwich stops and a raw bar, there are alfresco American and gourmet Caribbean restaurants and a Japanese steak house; there's also a lavish buffet served overlooking the sparkling lights of Charlotte Amalie and the harbor. Dinner theater, live entertainment and disco, scheduled activities for all ages, branches of several duty-free shops, and a shuttle boat to town make it hard not to have fun. This is a property you don't have to leave. ☎ *Box 7100, 00801,* ☎ *809/776–8500 or 800/524–2000,* FAX *809/776–3054. 503 rooms, 18 suites. 7 restaurants, two snack bars, 6 bars, 2 pools, 4 tennis courts, beach, water sports, helicopter tours. AE, D, DC, MC, V. EP, MAP.*

$$$$ Pavilions & Pools. Simple, tropical-cool decor and privacy set the mood here, where each island-style room has its own very private 22- by 14-foot or 18- by 16-foot pool and a small sundeck. The unpretentious accommodations include air-conditioning, telephones, full kitchens, and VCRs. Water sports are available at Sapphire Beach on the adjacent property. ☎ *6400 Estate Smith Bay 00802,* ☎ *809/775–6110 or 800/524–2001,* FAX *809/775–6110. 25 rooms. Restaurant. AE, MC, V. CP.*

$$$$ Point Pleasant Resort. This is almost an "eco" resort, with its lovingly
★   preserved natural vegetation and wonderful nature trail. Stretching up a steep, tree-filled hill from Smith Bay, affording a great view of St. John and Drake's Passage to the east and north, this resort offers a range of accommodations, from simple bedrooms to multiroom suites. Units are in a number of buildings hidden among the trees, and all have striking views. The air-conditioned rooms have balconies, and all rooms have kitchens. Three appealing, nice-size pools surrounded by decks are placed at different levels on the hillside. Although there are water sports here, the beach is almost nonexistent; guests are granted beach privileges next door at Stouffer Grand resort, a one-minute walk away. Every guest gets four hours' use of a car daily. (They need only pay the $9.50 per day insurance cost.) ☎ *6600 Estate Smith Bay #4, 00802,* ☎ *809/775–7200 or 800/524–2300,* FAX *809/776–5694. 134 rooms. 2 restaurants, bar, tiny beach, 3 pools, lighted tennis court, exercise room, water sports. AE, D, MC, V. EP, MAP.*

$$$$ Sapphire Beach Resort and Marina. This resort sits right on Sapphire
★   Beach, one of St. Thomas's prettiest, where on a clear day the lush green mountains of the neighboring B.V.I. seem close enough to touch. There's excellent snorkeling on the reefs to each side of the beach. This is usually a quiet retreat where you can nap while swinging in one of the hammocks strung between the palm trees in your front yard, but on Sunday the place rocks with a beach party. All units have fully equipped kitchens, air-conditioning, telephones, and cable TV. Children are welcome and may join the Little Gems Kids Klub. Children under age 12 sleep in their parents' accommodations at no extra charge and eat free at the Sea Grape restaurant when dining with their parents. ☎ *Box 8088, 00801,* ☎ *809/775–6100 or 800/524–2090,* FAX *809/775–4024. 171 rooms. 3 restaurants, 3 bars, beach, marina, 4 tennis courts, water sports. AE, MC, V. EP, MAP.*

$$$$ Stouffer Renaissance Grand Beach Resort. This resort's zigzag architectural angles spell luxury, from the marble atrium lobby to the one-bedroom suites with private whirlpool baths. The beach is excellent, as is the fitness center. The lobby is often populated by those lucky business types whose companies favor the resort as a convention and conference center. This tends to be a very busy hotel in general, with lots of people in the restaurants and on the beach. Daily organized activities for children include iguana hunts, T-shirt painting, and sand-castle building. ☎ *Smith Bay Rd., Box 8267, 00801,* ☎ *809/775–1510 or 800/322–2976,* FAX *809/775–3757. 297 rooms. 2 restaurants, snack bar, beach, 6 lighted tennis courts, 2 pools, water sports, fitness center. AE, D, DC, MC, V. EP.*

$$$$ **Sugar Bay Plantation Resort.** From afar, this large cluster of bulky white buildings looks rather overwhelming. Built as a Holiday Inn Crowne Plaza, the resort is now a Wyndham Resort managed by Carnival (the cruise-ship company). Most rooms have water views and some have great views of the British Virgin Islands. All units have balconies and are spacious and comfortable with contemporary furnishings and such amenities as hair dryers and coffeemakers. The beach is small for a property of this size, but there is a giant pool with waterfalls, all manner of water sports, tennis courts and a tennis stadium, and plenty of other diversions for people of all ages. Children under 19 stay free in same room with parents. ☎ *6500 Estate Smith Bay, 00802,* ☎ *809/777– 7100 or 800/927–7100,* FAX *809/777–7200. 300 rooms. 2 restaurants, 4 bars, 3 pools, health club, beach, 7 tennis courts, snorkeling equipment. AE, D, DC, MC, V. BP, MAP.*

$$$–$$$$ **Bolongo Club Everything.** Onetime sister resorts Bolongo Bay Beach and Tennis Club and Limetree Beach Resort (whose beaches sat next to each other) have combined into one megaresort. Oceanfront and garden-view rooms and villas all have air-conditioning, cable TV, VCR, phone, and safes. All villas have full kitchens, and many rooms have kitchenettes. Guests are part of Club Everything, which means the room rates include full breakfast, airport transfers, shuttle to town, use of tennis courts, snorkel gear, canoes, Sunfish sailboats, Windsurfers, paddleboats, a scuba lesson, and vouchers for an all-day sail, a cocktail cruise, and a half-day snorkel tour on one of the resort's yachts. The All-Inclusive-Club-Everything rate (three-night minimum) includes the above plus lunch, dinner, and some drinks. Kids Corner offers daytime child-care. ☎ *50 Estate Bolongo, 00802,* ☎ *809/775–1800 or 800/524–4746,* FAX *809/775–4465. 225 units, from hotel rooms to 1- to 3-bedroom villas. 5 restaurants, 2 nightclubs, 3 pools, 2 beaches, 6 tennis courts, extensive health club, water sports, volleyball, shuffleboard. AE, D, DC, MC, V. BP, All-inclusive.*

$ $$$$ **Hotel 1829.** This historic Spanish-style inn is popular with visiting gov-
★ ernment officials and people with business at Government House down the street. It's on Government Hill, just at the edge of Charlotte Amalie's shopping area. Rooms on several levels (stairs only) range from elegant and roomy to quite small but are priced accordingly, so there is one for every budget. All rooms have refrigerators, TV, and air-conditioning. Author Graham Greene is said to have stayed here, and it is easy to imagine him musing over a drink in the small, dark bar. You might enjoy the gourmet terrace restaurant more (*see* Dining, *above*), a romantic spot for dinner. There's a tiny, tiny pool for cooling off. ☎ *Box 1567, Charlotte Amalie, 00801,* ☎ *809/776–1829 or 800/524– 2002,* FAX *809/776–4343. 15 rooms. Restaurant, pool. AE, D, DC, MC, V. EP.*

$$$ **Blackbeard's Castle.** This small and very popular hillside inn is laid
★ out around a tower from which, it's said, Blackbeard watched for invaders on the horizon. It's an elegantly informal kind of place, where guests while away Sunday mornings with the *New York Times.* Stunning views (especially at sunset) of the harbor and Charlotte Amalie can be had from the gourmet restaurant (*see* Dining, *above*), the large freshwater pool, and the outdoor terrace, where locals come for sunset cocktails. Charlotte Amalie is a short walk down the hill, and

beaches are a short taxi ride away. Rates include a Continental breakfast. ☎ *Box 6041, Charlotte Amalie 00804,* ☎ *809/776–1234 or 800/344–5771,* ℻ *809/776–4321. 20 rooms. Restaurant, bar, freshwater pool. AE, D, DC, MC, V. CP.*

$$ Sign of the Griffin. If it's a house party you have in mind, you might want to consider these privately owned, furnished, one- and two-bedroom homes with great views on a hillside 500 feet above Tutu Bay. Each house has a fully equipped kitchen, telephone, private garden, and covered terrace. You'll need a car to get around from here. Maid service is provided on weekdays, and for stays of three weeks or more you'll receive a 10% discount. ☎ *Box 11668, 00801,* ☎ *809/775–1715. 5 houses. No credit cards.*

$$ Villa Blanca Hotel. Above Charlotte Amalie and surrounded by an attractive garden on Raphune Hill is this secluded hotel. Here, modern, balconied rooms have rattan furniture, kitchenettes, cable TVs, and ceiling fans (six have air-conditioning). All of the rooms have eastern views of Charlotte Amalie Harbor and partial westerly views of Drake's Channel and the B.V.I. ☎ *Box 7505, Charlotte Amalie, 00801,* ☎ *809/776–0749 or 800/237–0034,* ℻ *809/779–2661. 12 rooms. Pool, honor bar. AE, D, DC, MC, V. EP.*

$$ Villa Santana. Built by General Santa Anna of Mexico, circa 1857, this
★ villa still provides a panoramic view of Charlotte Amalie harbor along with plenty of age-old West Indian charm. Guests at this St. Thomas landmark, which is a five-minute walk from town, have a choice of five different villa-style rooms. Dark wicker furniture, white plaster and stone walls, shuttered windows, cathedral ceilings, and interesting nooks contribute to the feeling of romance and history. Villas La Torre and La Mansion are split level with spiral staircases, and all units have full kitchens and either four-poster or cradle beds. Rooms are kept cool by ceiling fans and natural trade winds and do not have telephones. ☎ *Denmark Hill, Charlotte Amalie, 00802,* ☎ *and fax 809/776–1311. 5 villa-style rooms, 2 with spiral staircases. Pool, croquet field. AE.*

$ Admiral's Inn. This charming inn stretches down a hillside on the point of land known as Frenchtown, just west of Charlotte Amalie. All rooms have wonderful views of either the town and the harbor or the ocean; the four ocean view rooms have private balconies and refrigerators. The units have rattan furniture; cream or teal vertical blinds; coral, cream, or teal bedspreads; carpeting; and large tiled vanity areas. The shore is rocky here, but there's a small sandy area and a swimmable saltwater pool that was formed naturally by coral; the inn's man-made pool is surrounded by a large wooden deck. There's bar service and Continental breakfast included. ☎ *Villa Olga, 00802,* ☎ *809/774–1376 or 800/544–0493,* ℻ *809/774–8010. 16 rooms. Pool, bar, tiny beach, restaurant on property. AE, D, MC, V.*

$ Island View Guest House. This clean, simply furnished guest house rests amid tropical foliage on the south face of 1,500-foot Crown Mountain, the highest point on St. Thomas. As a result, it has one of the most sweeping views of Charlotte Amalie harbor from its pool and shaded terrace, where complimentary breakfast as well as a dinner (only four or five nights a week) is served. All rooms also have some view, but on the balconies of the six newer rooms (all with air-conditioning and a ceiling fan) perched on the very edge of the hill, you feel suspended in midair. ☎ *Box 1903, 00801,* ☎ *809/774–4270 or 800/524–2023,* ℻ *809/774–6167. 14 rooms, 12 with private bath; 2 with shared bath; 3 have kitchenettes. Pool. AE, MC, V. CP.*

St. Croix

$$$$ **The Buccaneer.** If you want a self-contained tropical beach resort with
★ golf, all water sports, tennis, nature/jogging trail, shopping arcade, health
spa, and several restaurants, this 300-acre property is the place for you.
A palm tree–lined main drive leads to the large pink hotel at the top
of a hill; a number of smaller guest cottages, shops, and restaurants
are scattered throughout the property's rolling, manicured lawns.
Stroll through the elegant lobby, with its green-and-white marble
checkerboard floor, into the open-air terrace, where guests can relax
and take in the view. Most of the guest rooms in this former sugar plantation have been renovated to incorporate eye-catching marble or colorful tile floors, four-poster beds and massive wardrobes of pale wood,
pastel fabrics, and locally produced artwork, along with such modern
conveniences as refrigerators and cable TVs. Spacious bathrooms are
noteworthy for their marble bench showers and double sinks. ⊞
25200 Gallows Bay 00824, ☎ *809/773–2100 or 800/225–3881,* FAX
*809/778–8215. 150 rooms. 4 restaurants, 3 beaches, golf, health spa,
2 pools, 8 tennis courts (2 lighted), jogging trail, water sports, shopping arcade, in-room safes, full complimentary breakfast, holiday activities for children. AE, D, DC, MC, V. EP.*

$$$$ **Carambola Beach Resort.** The 25 quaint two-story red-roofed villas con-
★ nected by lovely arcades seem hacked from the luxuriant undergrowth.
All rooms are identical; the only difference is the view—ocean or garden. Decor is Laura Ashley–style English country house, with rocking
chairs and sofas upholstered in soothing floral patterns, terra-cotta floors,
rough-textured ceramic lamps, and mahogany ceilings and furnishings.
All have private patio and huge bathroom (showers only). The two-
bedroom suite, with its 3-foot-thick plantation walls and large patio,
is the perfect family dwelling. On the property are two fine restaurants
(the Sunday buffet brunch—available in both—is already legendary for
its munificent table), an exquisite ecru beach, and lots of quiet nooks
perfect for a secluded drink. ⊞ *Box 3031, Kingshill,* ☎ *809/778–3800
or 800/333–3333,* FAX *809/778–1682. 151 rooms, 1 2-bedroom suite.
2 restaurants, deli, lounge, pool, water-sports center, 4 tennis courts
(2 lighted), library, gift shop. AE, D, DC, MC, V.*

$$$$ **Cormorant Beach Club and Villas.** Breeze-bent palm trees, hammocks,
★ the thrum of north-shore waves, and a blissful sense of respected privacy rule here. The open-air public spaces are filled with tropical
plants and comfy wicker furniture in cool peach and mint green shades.
Ceiling fans and tile floors add to the atmosphere at this top-shelf resort, which resembles a series of connected Moorish villas. The beachfront rooms are lovely, with dark wicker furniture, pale peach walls,
white-tile floors, and floral-print spreads and curtains; all rooms have
a patio or balcony and telephone, cable TV, and electronic safes. Bathrooms stand out for their coral-rock-wall showers, marble-top double
sinks, and brass fixtures. Morning coffee and afternoon tea are set out
daily in the building breezeways, and you'll receive a "CBC" terry robe
to wear when you walk to the beautifully ledged polygonal pool. The
airy, high-ceilinged restaurant is one of St. Croix's best. ⊞ *4126 La
Grande Princesse, Christiansted 00820,* ☎ *809/778–8920 or 800/548–
4460,* FAX *809/778–9218. 34 rooms, 4 suites, 14 2- and 3-bedroom villas. Restaurant, bar, beach, pool, snorkeling, 2 tennis courts, library
with TV and VCR, croquet lawns. AE, DC, MC, V. EP, FAP.*

$$$$ **Villa Madeleine.** Since this exquisite hotel opened in 1990 it has quickly
★ earned a reputation as one of St. Croix's best. The main building was
patterned after a turn-of-the-century West Indian plantation great house.
Richly upholstered furniture, Oriental rugs, teal walls, and whimsically
painted driftwood set the mood in the billiards room, in the austere li-

brary-and-sitting room, and at Cafe Madeleine, the resort's highly praised Continental restaurant (*see* Dining, *above*). The great house sits atop a hill, on which private guest villas are scattered in both directions, affording views of the north and south shores. The villas' decor is modern tropical, with rattan and plush cushions, and many bedrooms have bamboo four-poster beds. Each villa has a full kitchen and a private swimming pool. Special touches in the rooms include pink-marble showers and, in many cottages, hand-painted floral borders along the walls, done in splashy tropical colors. ☎ *Box 3109, Christiansted 00822,* ☎ *809/778–7377 or 800/548–4461,* ℻ *809/773–7518. 43 villas. Restaurant, bar, private pools, billiards room, library, tennis court, concierge, nearby golf course. AE, D, DC, MC, V. EP.*

\$\$–\$\$\$ **Sprat Hall.** This 20-acre seaside Frederiksted property is a restored 1670 plantation estate, the oldest in the U.S.V.I. The homey, antiques-filled great house (no smoking, please) has guest rooms that hark back to more genteel days, with high-standing four-poster beds, antique furniture, bowls of fresh-cut bougainvillea and ginger thomas, and no air-conditioning. There are also family cottages on the grounds, but these in general are rather dingy (although Number 22 and Number 23 are newly refurbished) and not in the same class as the great-house rooms. The Hurd family also operates extensive horseback riding facilities here as well as serving complimentary Continental breakfast daily, and fine dinners upon request for guests only. ☎ *Box 695, Frederiksted 00841,* ☎ *809/772–0305. 8 rooms, 6 suites, 1 1-bedroom cottage. Restaurant, beach, horseback riding, water sports. AE. EP.*

\$\$–\$\$\$ **Waves at Cane Bay.** Owners Kevin and Suzanne Ryan have done won-
★   ders with this 25-year-old property since purchasing it in 1989. The two peach-and-mint-green buildings house enormous, balconied guest rooms done in cream and soft pastel prints, all with kitchens or kitchenettes. The small inn caters to couples and to divers, who take advantage of the fine reef just offshore. The hotel is rather isolated and its beachfront is rocky, but Cane Bay Beach is right next door, and there is a small patch of sand at poolside for sunbathing. The pool itself is unusual, having been carved from the coral along the shore: The floor and one wall are concrete, but the seaside wall is made of natural coral, and the pool water is circulated as the waves crash dramatically over the side, creating a foamy Jacuzzi on blustery days. ☎ *Box 1749, Kings Hill, 00851,* ☎ *809/778–1805 or 800/545–0603. 12 rooms, 1 suite (8 with air-conditioning). Bar, pool, complimentary snorkeling gear, dinner Tues. and Fri., in-room safes. AE, MC, V. EP.*

\$\$ **Club St. Croix.** Popular with honeymooners, this condominium resort's studio, one-, and two-bedroom apartments are spacious and bright. Indian-print throw rugs and cushions complement the bamboo furniture and rough, white-tile floors; the modern decor is further highlighted by glass-top tables and mirrored closet doors. Penthouses have loft bedrooms reached by spiral staircases, and studios enlist Murphy beds in the sitting rooms. Every room has a full kitchen and a sundeck, with waterfront views of Christiansted and Buck Island. On the beach you'll find a poolside restaurant and bar and a dock. Guests can take a sunset sail or go snorkeling with the hotel's 42-foot catamaran. Although the rooms are well kept, more thorough attention is needed on the grounds. ☎ *Estate Golden Rock, Christiansted 00820,* ☎ *809/773–7077 or 800/635–1533,* ℻ *809/773–4805. 54 suites. Restaurant, bar, 3 tennis courts, conference room, dock, pool, whirlpool, laundry room, water sports. AE, D, MC, V. EP.*

\$\$ **Hibiscus Beach Hotel.** This appealing, affordable property is set on the same stretch of palm tree–lined beach as its sister hotel, the Cormorant. Guest rooms at the Hibiscus Beach are divided among five two-story pink buildings, each named for a tropical flower. All have views of the oceanfront, thanks to the staggered placement of the buildings, but request a room in the Hibiscus building—it's closest to the water. Rooms have welcome amenities like cable TV, safe, and minibar and are tastefully furnished. White-tile floors and white walls are brightened with pink-striped curtains; bright, flowered bedspreads; and fresh-cut hibiscus blossoms. Bathrooms are nondescript but clean—both the shower stalls and the vanity mirrors are on the small side. Every unit has a roomy balcony facing the sea. The staff is friendly and helpful, and the manager's party in the open-air bar-and-restaurant is a pleasant gathering. ⌸ *Box 4131, La Grande Princesse 00820–4441,* ☎ *809/ 773–4042,* ℻ *809/773–7668. 37 rooms with bath. Bar, restaurant, 1 kitchenette-equipped room, pool, complimentary snorkel equipment, minibar, room safes. AE, D, MC, V. EP.*

$$ Hotel Caravelle. The charming three-story Caravelle is an excellent choice for moderately priced lodging in Christiansted. All rooms have refrigerators and are painted in tasteful dusky blues and whites, with floral-print bedspreads and curtains and vaulted ceilings. Baths are clean and new, though the unique tile in the showers is a holdover from when the hotel was built in the '60s. Superior rooms overlook the harbor, but most rooms do have some sort of ocean view. Owners Sid and Amy Kalmans are friendly and helpful. The Banana Bay Club, a casual terrace eatery serving seafood and Continental cuisine, is also on the premises. ⌸ *44A Queen Cross St., Christiansted, 00820,* ☎ *809/773– 0687 or 800/524–0410,* ℻ *809/778–7004. 43 rooms, 1 2-bedroom suite. Restaurant, bar, pool, water sports, conference room, gift shops, guest parking. AE, D, DC, MC, V. EP.*

$ The Frederiksted. Don't be put off by the neat but unprepossessing exterior: This modern four-story inn is your best bet for lodging in Frederiksted. In an inviting, outdoor tiled courtyard, the glass tables and yellow chairs of the hotel's bar and restaurant crowd around a small freshwater swimming pool where live music can be enjoyed on occasional Friday and Saturday nights. Yellow-stripe awnings and tropical greenery create a sunny, welcoming atmosphere. Steps at one side of the courtyard lead to the second floor's main desk and sundeck. The bright, pleasant guest rooms are outfitted with bars, refrigerators, and microwaves and are decorated with light-color rattan furniture and print bedspreads. Bathrooms are on the small side but are bright and clean. The nicest rooms are those with an ocean view; these are also the only rooms that have a bathtub in addition to a shower. ⌸ *20 Strand St., Frederiksted, 00840,* ☎ *809/772–0500 or 800/524–2025,* ℻ *809/778– 4009. 40 rooms. Restaurant, bar, outdoor pool, sundeck, live entertainment. AE, DC, MC, V. EP.*

$ Pink Fancy.
★ This homey, restful place is a few blocks west of the center of town in a much less touristy neighborhood. The oldest of the four buildings here is a 1780 Danish town house, and old stone walls and foundations enhance the setting. The inn's efficiency rooms are basic but clean and well tended; all have hardwood floors, tropical print fabrics, and wicker furniture. The hotel is laid out around the pool, where pink-and-white awnings throw shade over the patio, hammock, and small bar. Complimentary breakfast and cocktails are included in room rates. ⌸ *27 Prince St., Christiansted, 00820,* ☎ *809/773–8460 or 800/524–2045,* ℻ *809/773–6448. 12 rooms. Bar, pool. AE, MC, V. CP.*

St. John

$$$$ Caneel Bay Resort.
★ This 170-acre peninsula resort was a Rockresort for many years, and it has maintained its atmosphere of quiet, unas-

suming elegance. There are no crowds, no loud groups at the bar (in fact, there are no bars, just lounges where you may sit at tables and order beverages), and no glitz. Visitors return year after year—some weeks in February are booked a year in advance. Attention is paid to every detail, and the grounds are immaculately maintained. The flamboyant trees here even seem to shed their blossoms neatly. The property has seven beaches and three restaurants, one in a restored 18th-century sugar mill. The spacious rooms have simple interiors and no telephone or TV. Jackets are requested for men (during winter season) in restaurants after 6 PM. Rates formerly included all meals, but now there is also a room rate without meals. ☎ *Box 720, Cruz Bay, 00830,* ☎ *809/776–6111 or 800/223–7637,* ℻ *809/776–2030. 171 rooms. 3 restaurants, 7 beaches, 11 tennis courts, water sports. AE, MC, V. EP, MAP.*

$$$$ **Hyatt Regency St. John.** This 34-acre property at Great Cruz Bay shuns the weathered, old-money elegance of Caneel and lays on the gloss and glitz to the point that even the landscaping looks freshly polished. It's a beautiful place: The grounds are positively iridescent, and the pool area is a sybarite's delight, with waterfalls and islands and a poolside bar. Spacious, well-appointed guest rooms line the beach and encircle the pool, while some suites and luxurious town houses are set back slightly from the water. Try the on-site Chow Bella restaurant or the fabulous Sunday buffet down by the beach. There are morning, afternoon, and evening children's programs that include beach games, stargazing, island tours, and arts and crafts. ☎ *Box 8310, Great Cruz Bay, 00830,* ☎ *809/776–7171 or 800/323–7249,* ℻ *809/779–4985. 285 rooms. 3 restaurants, beach, marina, pool, water sports, fitness room, 6 tennis courts. AE, DC, MC, V. EP, MAP.*

$$$ **Gallows Point Suite Resort.** These soft-gray buildings with peaked roofs and shuttered windows are clustered on the peninsula south of the Cruz Bay ferry dock. The garden apartments have sky-lighted, plant-filled showers big enough to frolic in. The upper-level apartments have loft bedrooms and better views. There's no air-conditioning; harborside villas get better trade winds but are noisier. Daily maid service is included in the rates. Ellington's restaurant bridges the entranceway. ☎ *Box 58, Cruz Bay 00831,* ☎ *809/776–6434 or 800/323–7229,* ℻ *809/776–6520. 60 rooms. Tiny beach, pool, snorkeling. AE, DC, MC, V. EP.*

$$–$$$ **Estate Concordia.** The newest brainchild of Stanley Selengut, the developer of Maho Bay Campgrounds, these environmentally correct studios and duplexes are located on 51 oceanfront acres on remote Salt Pond Bay. The spacious units are constructed from recycled materials. Energy is wind- and solar-generated (even the ice maker is solar-powered). ☎ *Salt Pond Bay, 00830,* ☎ *809/693–5855. 9 units. Pool, laundry room, convenience store, short downhill hike to beach. No credit cards.*

$$ **Harmony.** Nestled in the tree-covered hills adjacent to the Maho Bay Campground is another Selengut ecotourism resort. The spacious, two-story units here have your Caribbean basics—decks, sliding glass doors, living-dining areas, and great views—but staying here is definitely a learning experience. As at the Estate Concordia, buildings are constructed from recycled materials and energy comes entirely from wind and sun. You can use your unit's laptop computer to read about how to be good to the environment at the beach and how to monitor your electricity consumption, sure to be lowered by the energy-saving appliances. Tile floors, undyed organic cotton linens, and South American handicrafts create a look to match the ideals. ☎ *Maho Bay, 00830,* ☎ *809/776–6240. 8 units (32 eventually). Self-service restaurant, beach down the hill. No credit cards.*

$$ Maho Bay Camp. Eight miles from Cruz Bay, this private campground is a lush hillside community of tent cottages (canvas and screens) linked by boardwalks, stairs, and ramps that also lead down to the beach. The 16- by 16-foot shelters have beds, dining table and chairs, electric lamps (and outlets), propane stove, ice cooler, kitchenware, and cutlery. The camp has the chummy feel of a retreat and is very popular, so book well in advance. ✉ *Cruz Bay, 00830,* ☎ *212/472–9453 or 800/392–9004. 113 tent cottages. Restaurant, commissary, barbecue areas, beach, bathhouses (showers, sinks, and toilets), water sports. No credit cards.*

$–$$ Cinnamon Bay Campground. Tents, cottages with four one-room units in each cottage, and bare sites are available at this National Park Service location surrounded by jungle and set at the edge of big, beautiful Cinnamon Bay Beach. The tents are 10 by 14 feet, with flooring, and come with living, eating, and sleeping furnishings and necessities; the 15- by 15-foot cottages have twin beds. Bare sites, which come with a picnic table and a charcoal grill, can be reserved up to eight months in advance. You can reserve by phone with a credit card. The bare sites are cheap—at press time they were $15 a site—but, if you're thinking of this option for budgetary reasons alone, be warned: The tent sites and cottages range from around $86 to $95 in season for two people per night. Security is minimal so be careful with your belongings. ✉ *Cruz Bay, 00830–0720,* ☎ *809/776–6330 or 800/223–7637. 44 tents, 40 cottages, 26 bare sites. Cafeteria, beach, commissary, bathhouses (showers and toilets), water sports. AE, MC, V.*

$–$$ Raintree Inn. If you want to be right in the center of the action in town and bunk at an affordable island-style place, go no farther. The darkwood rooms, some with air-conditioning, have a simple, tropical-cabin decor. Lower-floor rooms are very small. Three efficiencies have kitchens and a comfortable sleeping loft—which you have to climb an indoor ladder to reach. The Fish Trap restaurant is next door. This is a no-smoking property. *Box 566, Cruz Bay, 00831,* ☎ *and fax 809/693–8590 or 800/666–7449. 11 rooms. AE, D, MC, V. EP.*

Nightlife

Nightlife in the U.S.V.I. is a spontaneous affair. Although there are many tourist-oriented cultural shows that can make for a fun night out—including Calypso Carnival at Marriott's Frenchman's Reef and some broken-bottle dancing at various hotels—socializing is what the evenings are about. Most of the music scene is in small clubs with dance floors.

St. Thomas

NIGHTSPOTS

Barnacle Bill's (☎ 809/774–7444), Bill Grogan's Crown Bay landmark with the bright red lobster on its roof, is a musicians' home away from home.

Castaways (☎ 809/774–8446) is the watering hole and dance floor for the crews, owners, and those chartering the boats anchored at Yacht Haven.

Club Z (☎ 809/776–4655), still one of the hottest spots on the island, is a disco-style club located on Contant Hill, with a spectacular view of glittering harbor lights to enjoy on the terrace between dances.

Sugar's Nightclub at the Old Mill (☎ 809/776–3004), located in—you guessed it—an old mill, is a rock-till-you-drop late nightspot. Whatever the tunes, the place is lively, and there's a small dance floor as well as a good sound system.

Top of the Reef, at Marriott's Frenchman's Reef (☎ 809/776–8500), is where you can enjoy Pistarckle Theater's dinner theater performances Thursday through Sunday year-round. Call ahead for reservations.

JAZZ AND PIANO BARS

The **Shark Room** (☎ 809/775–1919), an East End hot spot, has at least one live jazz act per evening, from 9:30 PM to 1:30 AM, seven nights a week. The admission of $3 per person could buy you any array of artists, including Stateside cabaret, blues, and local bands. Sit at the bar or around small cocktail tables in this dark and lively lounge and enjoy a drink with the tunes.

You'll find piano bars at the **Grand Palazzo** (☎ 809/775–3333) and **Provence** (☎ 809/777–5600) in Frenchtown. The player at Provence has been entertaining with his show "Gray, Gray, Gray" for many years and shouldn't be missed.

St. Croix

Christiansted has a lively and eminently casual club scene near the waterfront. At **Mango Grove** (53 King St., ☎ 809/773–0200) you'll hear live guitar and vocals in an open-air courtyard with a bar and Cinzano umbrella-covered tables. The upstairs **Moonraker Lounge** (43A Queen Cross St., ☎ 809/773–8492) presents a constant calendar of live music, usually a singer with an acoustic guitar playing all your favorites, from Jimmy Buffet to Bob Dylan. Easy jazz music can be heard in the courtyard bar at **Indies** Saturday evenings (55-56 Company St., ☎ 809/692–9440). To party under the stars, head to the **Wreck Bar** (☎ 809/773–6092), on Christiansted's Hospital Street, for crab races as well as rock and roll. At **Calabash** (Strand St., ☎ 809/778–0001) you'll find steel-band music from Wednesday through Saturday, and on Friday there's a broken-bottle dancer. **Hotel on the Cay** (Protestant Cay, ☎ 809/773–2035) has a West Indian Buffet on Tuesday nights that features a broken-bottle dancer and Mocko Jumbie. On Thursday nights, the **Cormorant** (La Grande Princess, ☎ 809/778–8920) throws a similar event. The **2 Plus 2 Disco** (17 La Grande Princesse, ☎ 809/773–3710) spins a great mix of calypso, soul, disco, and reggae, with live acts on weekends.

Although less hopping than Christiansted, Frederiksted restaurants and clubs have a variety of weekend entertainment. **Blue Moon** (17 Strand St., ☎ 809/772–2222), a waterfront restaurant, is the place to be for live jazz on Friday 9 PM–1 AM. The island's premier calypso band, Blinky and the Roadmasters, performs every Sunday night at **Stars of the West** (14 Strand St., ☎ 809/772–9039). The **Lost Dog Pub** (King St., ☎ 809/772–3526) is a favorite spot for a casual drink, a game of darts, and occasional live rock and roll on Sunday nights. Head north of town to the **Sand Bar** (Estate La Grange, no ☎) on Sunday night to hear Green Flash play rock and roll. Up Mahogany Road at the **Mt. Pellier Hut Domino Club** (50 Mt. Pellier, ☎ 809/772–9914), a variety of local bands play Friday through Sunday.

St. John

Some friendly hubbub can be found at the rough-and-ready **Backyard** (☎ 809/693–8886), *the* place for sports watching as well as grooving to Bonnie Raitt et al. There's calypso and reggae on Wednesday and Friday at **Fred's** (☎ 809/776–6363). The **Etta's** at the Inn at Tamarind Court (☎ 809/776–6378) serves up a blend of jazz and rock on Friday.

Notices on the bulletin board across from the **U.S. post office** and at **Connections** (and on telephone poles) will keep you posted on special events: comedy nights, movies, and the like.

INDEX

X = restaurant, ⊞ = hotel

Fodor's Travel Publications

Available at bookstores everywhere, or call 1–800–533–6478, 24 hours a day.

Gold Guides

U.S.

Alaska

Arizona

Boston

California

Cape Cod, Martha's Vineyard, Nantucket

The Carolinas & the Georgia Coast

Chicago

Colorado

Florida

Hawaii

Las Vegas, Reno, Tahoe

Los Angeles

Maine, Vermont, New Hampshire

Maui

Miami & the Keys

New England

New Orleans

New York City

Pacific North Coast

Philadelphia & the Pennsylvania Dutch Country

The Rockies

San Diego

San Francisco

Santa Fe, Taos, Albuquerque

Seattle & Vancouver

The South

U.S. & British Virgin Islands

USA

Virginia & Maryland

Waikiki

Washington, D.C.

Foreign

Australia & New Zealand

Austria

The Bahamas

Bermuda

Budapest

Canada

Cancún, Cozumel, Yucatán Peninsula

Caribbean

China

Costa Rica, Belize, Guatemala

Cuba

The Czech Republic & Slovakia

Eastern Europe

Egypt

Europe

Florence, Tuscany & Umbria

France

Germany

Great Britain

Greece

Hong Kong

India

Ireland

Israel

Italy

Japan

Kenya & Tanzania

Korea

London

Madrid & Barcelona

Mexico

Montréal & Québec City

Moscow, St. Petersburg, Kiev

The Netherlands, Belgium & Luxembourg

New Zealand

Norway

Nova Scotia, New Brunswick, Prince Edward Island

Paris

Portugal

Provence & the Riviera

Scandinavia

Scotland

Singapore

South Africa

South America

Southeast Asia

Spain

Sweden

Switzerland

Thailand

Tokyo

Toronto

Turkey

Vienna & the Danube

Fodor's Special-Interest Guides

Branson

Caribbean Ports of Call

The Complete Guide to America's National Parks

Condé Nast Traveler Caribbean Resort and Cruise Ship Finder

Cruises and Ports of Call

Fodor's London Companion

Gay USA

France by Train

Halliday's New England Food Explorer

Healthy Escapes

Italy by Train

Kodak Guide to Shooting Great Travel Pictures

Shadow Traffic's New York Shortcuts and Traffic Tips

Sunday in New York

Sunday in San Francisco

Walt Disney World, Universal Studios and Orlando

Walt Disney World for Adults

Where Should We Take the Kids? California

Where Should We Take the Kids? Family Adventures

Where Should We Take the Kids? Northeast

Special Series

Affordables
Caribbean
Europe
Florida
France
Germany
Great Britain
Italy
London
Paris

Fodor's Bed & Breakfasts and Country Inns
America's Best B&Bs
California's Best B&Bs
Canada's Great Country Inns
Cottages, B&Bs and Country Inns of England and Wales
The Mid-Atlantic's Best B&Bs
New England's Best B&Bs
The Pacific Northwest's Best B&Bs
The South's Best B&Bs
The Southwest's Best B&Bs
The Upper Great Lakes' Best B&Bs

The Berkeley Guides
California
Central America
Eastern Europe
Europe
France
Germany & Austria
Great Britain & Ireland
Italy
London
Mexico
Pacific Northwest & Alaska
Paris
San Francisco

Compass American Guides
Arizona
Chicago
Colorado
Hawaii
Idaho
Hollywood
Las Vegas
Maine
Manhattan
Montana
New Mexico
New Orleans
Oregon
San Francisco
Santa Fe
South Carolina
South Dakota
Southwest
Texas
Utah
Virginia
Washington
Wine Country
Wisconsin
Wyoming

Fodor's Citypacks
Atlanta
Hong Kong
London
New York City
Paris
Rome
San Francisco
Washington, D.C.

Fodor's Español
California
Caribe Occidental
Caribe Oriental
Gran Bretaña
Londres
Mexico

Nueva York
Paris

Fodor's Exploring Guides
Australia
Boston & New England
Britain
California
Caribbean
China
Egypt
Florence & Tuscany
Florida
France
Germany
Ireland
Israel
Italy
Japan
London
Mexico
Moscow & St. Petersburg
New York City
Paris
Prague
Provence
Rome
San Francisco
Scotland
Singapore & Malaysia
Spain
Thailand
Turkey
Venice

Fodor's Flashmaps
Boston
New York
San Francisco
Washington, D.C.

Fodor's Pocket Guides
Acapulco
Atlanta
Barbados

Jamaica
London
New York City
Paris
Prague
Puerto Rico
Rome
San Francisco
Washington, D.C.

Rivages Guides
Bed and Breakfasts of Character and Charm in France
Hotels and Country Inns of Character and Charm in France
Hotels and Country Inns of Character and Charm in Italy

Short Escapes
Country Getaways in Britain
Country Getaways in France
Country Getaways in New England
Country Getaways Near New York City

Fodor's Sports
Golf Digest's Best Places to Play
Skiing USA
USA Today The Complete Four Sport Stadium Guide

Fodor's Vacation Planners
Great American Learning Vacations
Great American Sports & Adventure Vacations
Great American Vacations
National Parks and Seashores of the East
National Parks of the West

Before Catching Your Flight, Catch Up With Your World.

Fueled by the global resources of CNN and available in major airports across America, CNN Airport Network provides a live source  of current domestic and international news,  sports, business, weather and lifestyle programming. Plus two daily Fodor's features for the facts you need: "Travel Fact," a useful and creative mix of travel trivia; and "What's Happening," a comprehensive round-up of upcoming events in major cities around the world.

With CNN Airport Network, you'll never be out of the loop.

HERE'S YOUR OWN PERSONAL VIEW OF THE WORLD.

Here's the easiest way to get up-to-the-minute, objective, personalized information about what's going on in the city you'll be visiting—before you leave on your trip! Unique information you could get only if you knew someone personally in each of 160 destinations around the world.

Everything from special places to dine to local events only a local would know about.

It's all yours—in your Travel Update from Worldview, the leading provider of time-sensitive destination information.

Review the following order form and fill it out by indicating your destination(s)

and travel dates and by checking off up to eight interest categories. Then mail or fax your order form to us, or call your order in. (We're here to help you 24 hours a day.)

Within 48 hours of receiving your order, we'll mail your convenient, pocket-sized custom guide to you, packed with information to make your travel more fun and interesting. And if you're in a hurry, we can even fax it.

Have a great trip with your Fodor's Worldview Travel Update!

Fodor's WORLDVIEW
TRAVEL UPDATE

Insider perspective

Time-sensitive

Customized to your interests and dates of travel

DESTINATIONS

Worldview covers more than 160 destinations worldwide. Choose the destination(s) that match your itinerary from the list below:

Europe
Amsterdam
Athens
Barcelona
Berlin
Brussels
Budapest
Copenhagen
Dublin
Edinburgh
Florence
Frankfurt
French Riviera
Geneva
Glasgow
Lausanne
Lisbon
London
Madrid
Milan
Moscow
Munich
Oslo
Paris
Prague
Provence
Rome
Salzburg
Seville
St. Petersburg
Stockholm
Venice
Vienna
Zurich

**United States
(Mainland)**
Albuquerque
Atlanta
Atlantic City
Baltimore
Boston
Branson, MO
Charleston, SC
Chicago
Cincinnati
Cleveland
Dallas/Ft. Worth
Denver
Detroit
Houston
Indianapolis
Kansas City
Las Vegas
Los Angeles
Memphis
Miami
Milwaukee
Minneapolis/St. Paul
Nashville
New Orleans
New York City
Orlando
Palm Springs
Philadelphia
Phoenix
Pittsburgh

Portland
Reno/Lake Tahoe
St. Louis
Salt Lake City
San Antonio
San Diego
San Francisco
Santa Fe
Seattle
Tampa
Washington, DC

Alaska
Alaskan Destinations

Hawaii
Honolulu
Island of Hawaii
Kauai
Maui

Canada
Quebec City
Montreal
Ottawa
Toronto
Vancouver

Bahamas
Abaco
Eleuthera/
 Harbour Island
Exuma
Freeport
Nassau &
 Paradise Island

Bermuda
Bermuda Countryside
Hamilton

**British Leeward
Islands**
Anguilla
Antigua & Barbuda
St. Kitts & Nevis

British Virgin Islands
Tortola & Virgin
 Gorda

**British Windward
Islands**
Barbados
Dominica
Grenada
St. Lucia
St. Vincent
Trinidad & Tobago

Cayman Islands
The Caymans

Dominican Republic
Santo Domingo

Dutch Leeward Islands
Aruba
Bonaire
Curacao

**Dutch Windward
Island**
St. Maarten/St. Martin

French West Indies
Guadeloupe
Martinique
St. Barthelemy

Jamaica
Kingston
Montego Bay
Negril
Ocho Rios

Puerto Rico
Ponce
San Juan

Turks & Caicos
Grand Turk/
 Providenciales

U.S. Virgin Islands
St. Croix
St. John
St. Thomas

Mexico
Acapulco
Cancun & Isla Mujeres
Cozumel
Guadalajara
Ixtapa & Zihuatanejo
Los Cabos
Mazatlan
Mexico City
Monterrey
Oaxaca
Puerto Vallarta

South/Central America
Buenos Aires
Caracas
Rio de Janeiro
San Jose, Costa Rica
Sao Paulo

Middle East
Istanbul
Jerusalem

**Australia & New
Zealand**
Auckland
Melbourne
South Island
Sydney

China
Beijing
Guangzhou
Shanghai

Japan
Kyoto
Nagoya
Osaka
Tokyo
Yokohama

Pacific Rim/Other
Bali
Bangkok
Hong Kong & Macau
Manila
Seoul
Singapore
Taipei

INTERESTS

For your personalized Travel Update, choose the eight (8) categories you're most interested in from the following list:

1. Business Services	Fax & Overnight Mail, Computer Rentals, Protocol, Secretarial, Messenger, Translation Services

Dining

2. All-Day Dining	Breakfast & Brunch, Cafes & Tea Rooms, Late-Night Dining
3. Local Cuisine	Every Price Range — from Budget Restaurants to the Special Splurge
4. European Cuisine	Continental, French, Italian
5. Asian Cuisine	Chinese, Far Eastern, Japanese, Other
6. Americas Cuisine	American, Mexican & Latin
7. Nightlife	Bars, Dance Clubs, Casinos, Comedy Clubs, Ethnic, Pubs & Beer Halls
8. Entertainment	Theater — Comedy, Drama, Musicals, Dance, Ticket Agencies
9. Music	Classical, Opera, Traditional & Ethnic, Jazz & Blues, Pop, Rock
10. Children's Activites	Events, Attractions
11. Tours	Local Tours, Day Trips, Overnight Excursions
12. Exhibitions, Festivals & Shows	Antiques & Flower, History & Cultural, Art Exhibitions, Fairs & Craft Shows, Music & Art Festivals
13. Shopping	Districts & Malls, Markets, Regional Specialties
14. Fitness	Bicycling, Health Clubs, Hiking, Jogging
15. Recreational Sports	Boating/Sailing, Fishing, Golf, Skiing, Snorkeling/Scuba, Tennis/Racket
16. Spectator Sports	Auto Racing, Baseball, Basketball, Golf, Football, Horse Racing, Ice Hockey, Soccer
17. Event Highlights	The best of what's happening during the dates of your trip.
18. Sightseeing	Sights, Buildings, Monuments
19. Museums	Art, Cultural
20. Transportation	Taxis, Car Rentals, Airports, Public Transportation
21. General Info	Overview, Holidays, Currency, Tourist Info

Please note that content will vary by season, destination, and length of stay.

Name _____

Address _____

City _____ **State** ____ **Country** _____ **ZIP** _____

Tel # ( ) - **Fax #** ( ) -

Title of this Fodor's guide: _____

Store and location where guide was purchased: _____

INDICATE YOUR DESTINATIONS/DATES: You can order up to three (3) destinations from the previous page. Fill in your arrival and departure dates for each destination. **Your Travel Update itinerary (all destinations selected) cannot exceed 30 days from beginning to end.**

		Month	Day		Month	Day
(Sample) **LONDON**	From:	**6** /	**21**	To:	**6** /	**30**
1	From:	/		To:	/	
2	From:	/		To:	/	
3	From:	/		To:	/	

CHOOSE YOUR INTERESTS: Select up to eight (8) categories from the list of interest categories shown on the previous page and circle the numbers below:

1 2 3 4 5 6 7 8 9 10 11 12 13 14 15 16 17 18 19 20 21

CHOOSE WHEN YOU WANT YOUR TRAVEL UPDATE DELIVERED (Check one):
❏ Please send my Travel Update immediately.
❏ Please hold my order until a few weeks before my trip to include the most up-to-date information.
Completed orders will be sent within 48 hours. Allow 7–10 days for U.S. mail delivery.

ADD UP YOUR ORDER HERE. SPECIAL OFFER FOR FODOR'S PURCHASERS ONLY!

	Suggested Retail Price	Your Price	This Order
First destination ordered	$ 9.95	$ 7.95	$ 7.95
Second destination (if applicable)	$ 6.95	$ 4.95	+
Third destination (if applicable)	$ 6.95	$ 4.95	+

DELIVERY CHARGE (Check one and enter amount below)

	Within U.S. & Canada	Outside U.S. & Canada
First Class Mail	❏ $2.50	❏ $5.00
FAX	❏ $5.00	❏ $10.00
Priority Delivery	❏ $15.00	❏ $27.00

ENTER DELIVERY CHARGE FROM ABOVE: + _____

TOTAL: $ _____

METHOD OF PAYMENT IN U.S. FUNDS ONLY (Check one):
❏ AmEx ❏ MC ❏ Visa ❏ Discover ❏ Personal Check (U. S. & Canada only)
❏ Money Order/International Money Order

Make check or money order payable to: Fodor's Worldview Travel Update

Credit Card _/_/_/_/_/_/_/_/_/_/_/_/_/_/_/_/ **Expiration Date:**_/_

Authorized Signature _____

SEND THIS COMPLETED FORM WITH PAYMENT TO:
Fodor's Worldview Travel Update, 114 Sansome Street, Suite 700, San Francisco, CA 94104

OR CALL OR FAX US 24-HOURS A DAY
Telephone **1-800-799-9609** • Fax **1-800-799-9619** (From within the U.S. & Canada)
(Outside the U.S. & Canada: Telephone 415-616-9988 • Fax 415-616-9989)

(Please have this guide in front of you when you call so we can verify purchase.)
Code: FTG   Offer valid until 12/31/97